Management

Management
Eleventh Edition

ROBERT KREITNER
Arizona State University

SOUTH-WESTERN
CENGAGE Learning

Australia • Brazil • Japan • Korea • Mexico • Singapore • Spain • United Kingdom • United States

SOUTH-WESTERN
CENGAGE Learning™

Management, Eleventh Edition
Robert Kreitner

VP/Editorial Director: Jack W. Calhoun

Editors-in-Chief: Melissa Acuna, George Hoffman

Executive Editors: Joe Sabatino, Kathleen McMahon, Lisé Johnson

Executive Marketing Manager: Kimberly Kanakes

Marketing Managers: Clint Kernen, Nicole Hamm

Senior Marketing Coordinator: Sarah Rose

Senior Marketing Communications Manager: Jim Overly

Senior Development Editor: Julia Chase

Senior Project Editor: Shelley Dickerson

Senior Content Manager: Rachel Wimberly

Art Director: Jill Haber

Cover Designer: Anne S. Katzeff

Senior Photo Editor: Jennifer Meyer Dare

Cover Image: © age footstock/Aaron Graubart

Senior First Print Buyer: Doug Wilke

Library of Congress Control Number: 2008934714

U.S. Student Edition:
ISBN-13: 978-0-547-14848-9
ISBN-10: 0-547-14848-8

South-Western Cengage Learning
5191 Natorp Boulevard
Mason, OH 45040
USA

Cengage Learning products are represented in Canada by Nelson Education Ltd.

For your course and learning solutions, visit **www.cengage.com**

Purchase any of our products at your local college store or at our preferred online store **www.ichapters.com**.

With love to my wife, college sweetheart, best friend, and hiking and Alaska fishing buddy, Margaret—Bob

Printed in China by China Translation & Printing Services Limited
2 3 4 5 6 7 12 11 10 09

BRIEF CONTENTS

CONTENTS

PART TWO   Planning and Decision Making   143

PART THREE   Organizing, Managing Human Resources, and Communicating   235

PART FOUR   Motivating and Leading   331

PREFACE

T oday's managers face a complex web of difficult and exciting challenges. A global economy in which world-class quality is the ticket to ride, increased diversity in the work force, new technologies and e-business, and demands for more ethical conduct promise to keep things interesting. As trustees of society's precious human, material, financial, and informational resources, today's and tomorrow's managers hold the key to a better world. A solid grounding in management is essential to successfully guiding large or small, profit or non-profit organizations in the twenty-first century. *Management,* Eleventh Edition, represents an important step toward managerial and personal success in an era of rapid change. It is a comprehensive, up-to-date, and highly readable introduction to management theory, research, and practice. This eleventh edition is the culmination of my thirty-six years in management classrooms and management development seminars around the world. Its style and content have been shaped by interaction with thousands of students along with many instructors, reviewers, editors, and managers. All have taught me valuable lessons about organizational life, management, and people in general. Organized along a time-tested functional/process framework, *Management,* Eleventh Edition, integrates classical and modern concepts with a rich array of contemporary real-world examples, cases, captioned photos, and Interactive Annotations.

NEW TOPICS AND A NEW LOOK

Many changes have been made in response to feedback from students, colleagues, and managers who read the previous edition and in reflection of the latest trends in management thinking. **There are 926 source material references throughout this new edition dated 2007.**

Significant Changes and Improvements

These significant improvements can be found in the eleventh edition of *Management:*

- The book has been **shortened** from 17 **to 16 chapters.**
- **Organizational theory, design, effectiveness, and cultures are now covered in one chapter** (Chapters 9 and 10 in the prior edition are now covered in Chapter 9).
- **Chapter 9** is now titled Organizations: Effectiveness, Design, and Cultures.
- Chapters 11–17 in the prior edition have been **renumbered to 10–16.**
- A **new two-column text format** and fresh interior design make this new edition very readable, accessible, and user-friendly.
- More extensive **ethics** coverage includes a **new in-text boxed feature in every chapter** titled **Ethics: Character, Courage, and Values** (each box includes a **discussion question**).
- **Fifteen** of the 17 **Ethics boxes are new** to this edition.
- All 16 **chapter-opening cases are new** to this edition (answers to all of the discussion questions are in the *Instructor's Resource Manual*).

- **Ninety-one** of the 133 (68%) **Interactive Annotations** in the margins are **new** (responses to every one of them are in the *Instructor's Resource Manual*).
- The in-text **boxed features** have been **renamed** Valuing Diversity, Window on the World, Best Practices, and Ethics: Character, Courage, and Values.
- **Three** of the seven **Valuing Diversity** boxed features throughout the text are **new.**
- **All** five of the **Window on the World** boxed features throughout the text are **new.**
- **Three** of the five **Best Practices** boxed features throughout the text are **new.**
- **End-of-chapter activities** have been renamed **Manager's Toolkit** (two are new) and **Action Learning Exercise** (one is new).
- **Seven** of the 16 **chapter-closing cases** are **new** (answers to all of the discussion questions are in the Instructor's Resource Manual).
- There are eight new **cartoons.**
- All **vital statistics** have been **updated** (e.g., demographics, global economy, job outlook, female executives, small businesses).
- **New and/or improved coverage** includes Internet transactions, glass ceiling data, nine cultural competencies, business ecosystem in action, e-Business, and tips for managing a virtual team.

COMPLETE HARMONY WITH AACSB INTERNATIONAL'S REVISED ACCREDITATION STANDARDS

AACSB International (The Association to Advance Collegiate Schools of Business), the leading accrediting organization for business, management, and accounting programs, revised its Standards for Business Accreditation in 2003. Rather than specifying what courses need to be taught, AACSB now emphasizes mastery of knowledge and skill areas. These "learning outcomes" (cross-referenced to key chapters in *Management*, Eleventh Edition) include:

- Communication abilities (chapters 11, 12, 13, 14, and 15)
- Ethical understanding and reasoning abilities (chapters 1, 3, and 5)
- Analytic skills (all chapters especially chapter 6 and Action Learning Exercises following every chapter)
- Use of information technology (chapters 1, 7, and 11)
- Multicultural and diversity understanding (chapters 3, 4, and 10)
- Reflective thinking skills (all chapters, especially chapter 8)

Source for list: http://www.aacsb.edu/accreditation/process/documents/AACSB_STANDARDS_Revised_Jan08.pdf (p. 15)

Learning objectives at the beginning of each chapter and answered in the chapter summary make this entire textbook **"outcome-focused."**

Moreover, topical coverage in *Management*, Eleventh Edition, aligns very closely with AACSB International's list of "management-specific knowledge and skills." Among them are: "Ethical and legal responsibilities in organizations and society; Creation of value through the integrated production and distribution of goods, services, and information; Group and individual dynamics in organizations; Information technologies as they influence the structure and processes of organizations and economies, and as they influence the roles and techniques of management; Domestic and global economic environments of organizations." (*Source:* Ibid., pp. 15–16.)

MAJOR THEMES

The study of management takes in a great deal of territory, both conceptually and geographically. Therefore, it is important for those being introduced to the field to have reliable guideposts to help them make sense of it all. Four major themes guiding our progress through the fascinating world of management are change, skill development, diversity, and ethics and green practices.

An Overriding Focus on Change

It may be a cliché to say "the only certainty today is change," but it is nonetheless true. The challenge for today's and especially tomorrow's managers is to be aware of *specific* changes, along with the factors contributing to them and their likely impact on the practice of management. Change has been woven into the fabric of this new edition in the following ways:

- Under the heading of "The Changing Workplace," each chapter-opening case introduces students to real-world managers and changes at large and small, domestic and foreign organizations (all 16 opening cases are new to this edition).
- Chapter 1 profiles twenty-first-century managers and ten major changes in the practice of management.
- Chapter 2 provides an overview of the Internet and e-business revolution.
- Chapter 3 is entirely devoted to the changing social, political/legal, economic, and technological environment that management faces. Workplace demographics document the changing face of the work force. The innovation process is explained.
- Chapter 4 discusses the growth of global and transnational corporations and how to adapt to cross-cultural situations.
- Chapter 6 covers project planning/management, underscoring the ad hoc nature of today's workplaces.
- Chapter 7 has an updated section titled "E-business Strategies for the Internet," including seven basic Internet business models.
- Chapter 8 discusses knowledge management as a strategic tool for better decision making.
- Chapter 9 describes the new virtual organizations.
- Chapter 10 covers the concept of "human capital" and features Pfeffer's seven people-centered practices.
- Chapter 11 covers blogs, social networking, e-mail, text messaging, cell phone etiquette, videoconferencing, and telecommuting.
- Chapter 13 covers virtual teams and how to build them.
- Chapter 14 covers emotional intelligence, a vital trait for adaptable managers and leaders.
- Chapter 15 offers comprehensive treatment of change, resistance to change, and how to bring about unofficial grassroots change.
- Chapter 16 covers the timely topic of crisis management.

Emphasis on Skill Development

Managers tell us they want job applicants who know more than just management theory. They value people who can communicate well, solve problems, see the big picture, and work cooperatively in teams. Consequently, this edition has a very strong skills orientation.

- *Manager's Toolkit* sections at the end of each chapter teach students how to manage their career, stay current with management literature, help women break the glass ceiling, take a foreign business trip, behave ethically around the world, write a new business plan, reengineer the organization, construct a fishbone diagram (for problem finding), demonstrate initiative, successfully handle a job interview, give feedback, manage stress,

use cooperative conflict to avoid groupthink, empower employees, constructively express anger, and avoid public-relations problems in a crisis.
- *How-to-do-it instructions* are integrated into the text for the following skills and tasks: preparing employees for foreign assignments, examining the ethics of a business decision, using management by objectives (MBO), constructing flow charts and Gantt charts, building a PERT network, performing a break-even analysis, writing planning scenarios, making decisions, avoiding decision-making traps, managing creative people, avoiding layoffs, delegating, cellphone etiquette, interviewing, discouraging sexual harassment, communicating via e-mail, participating in a videoconference, listening, writing effectively, running a meeting, using rewards, making employee participation programs work, curbing organizational politics, preventing groupthink, building trust, modifying behavior, managing change, overcoming resistance to change, managing conflict, negotiating, using Deming's Plan-Do-Check-Act cycle, and improving product and service quality.
- *Best Practices boxes* distributed throughout the text (3 of the 5 are new) describe how real managers are dealing with real problems.
- *Managers-in-Action Videos,* following each major part of the text, emphasize the development of essential management skills and focus on topics such as managing customer service, being an entrepreneur, shaping organizational culture, motivating, leading, and managing quality.

Emphasis on Diversity

Labor forces and customers around the globe, particularly in the United States, are becoming more diverse in terms of national origin, race, religion, gender, predominant age categories, and personal preferences. Managers are challenged to manage diversity effectively to tap the *full* potential of *every* individual's unique combination of abilities and traits. The following diversity coverage and themes can be found in this edition:

- Seven boxed features (three new) throughout the text, titled **Valuing Diversity,** focus needed attention on women as top executives, dealing with religion in the workplace, bias in decision making, global diversity, Native American empowerment, and how to change the organization's culture by being a "tempered radical."
- Women play important managerial roles in the chapter-opening cases for Chapters 2, 7, 9, 10, 12, 15, and 16 and the chapter-closing cases for Chapters 1, 3, 10, 12, and 13.
- A diverse selection of individuals is featured in cases, boxes, examples, and photos.
- Chapter 1 describes the demand for multilingual and multicultural managers.
- Chapter 3 includes a section on managing diversity.
- Chapter 4 discusses managing across cultures and emphasizes the importance of learning foreign languages. Chapter 4 also describes the work goals and leadership styles in different cultures.
- Chapter 5 discusses different value systems.
- Chapter 8 describes different information-processing styles and how to manage creative individuals.
- Chapter 10 discusses moving from tolerance to appreciation when managing diversity. It also covers equal employment opportunity, affirmative action, the Americans with Disabilities Act (ADA), and how to develop policies for sexual harassment and substance abuse.
- Chapter 12 discusses how to motivate a diverse work force and provides coverage of the U.S. Family and Medical Leave Act (FMLA).
- Chapter 13 includes major coverage of teamwork.
- Chapter 14 discusses women and the use of power as well as different leadership styles.
- Chapter 15 discusses *cooperative* conflict and describes different conflict resolution styles.

Emphasis on Ethics and Green Practices

Simply put, society wants managers to behave better. Ethical concerns are integrated throughout this edition, as well as featured in Chapter 5. Ethical coverage is evidenced by:

- Seventeen (15 new) **Ethics: Character, Courage, and Values** boxes throughout the text (each box contains a **discussion question**)
- Offshoring of jobs controversy (Chapter 1)
- Discussion of management's ethical reawakening (Chapter 1)
- Chapter 5, in Part One, entirely devoted to management's social and ethical responsibilities, provides an ethical context for the entire book
- Carroll's global corporate social responsibility pyramid (Chapter 5)
- Research: how people rationalize unethical conduct (Chapter 5)
- Ethical aspects of e-commerce (Chapter 7)
- Value judgments in decision making (Chapter 8)
- Is Wal-Mart an ethical organization? (Chapter 9)
- Ethical implications of blogs and social networking (Chapter 11)
- Ethical implications of group norms and avoiding groupthink (Chapter 13)
- Greenleaf's ethical "servant leader" (Chapter 14)
- Covey's ethical win-win negotiating style (Chapter 15)
- **Environmentalism**, efficient use of resources, sustainability, and recycling are an "ethical green thread" running throughout *Management*, Eleventh Edition, including dozens of **green practices** covered in examples, cases, boxes, and exercises

AN INTERACTIVE TEXTBOOK

Active rather than passive learning is the preferred way to go these days. As well it should be, because active learning is interesting and fun. This textbook employs two interactive-learning strategies: Web-linked interactive annotations and action learning exercises.

Interactive Annotations

This feature, unique to *Management,* was introduced in the seventh edition. The idea was to link the textbook and the Internet to create a dynamic, instructive, and interesting learning tool. In short, we wanted to make the textbook come alive. This pedagogical experiment has been a great success. (In fact, students say they read the annotations first when turning to a new page.) Consequently, there are **133 interactive annotations** in this eleventh edition (91 are new and some have been updated) that integrate timely facts, provocative ideas, discussion questions, and back-to-the-opening-case questions into the flow of the book.

Answers and interpretations for the annotations are provided in the *Instructor's Resource Manual* and on the Instructor Web site.

At the instructor's discretion, many of the annotations provide stimulating opportunities for cooperative learning. Valuable new insights are gained and interpersonal skills are developed when students work together in groups and teams.

Action Learning Exercises

There is one Action Learning Exercise at the end of each chapter. These exercises strive to heighten self-awareness and build essential managerial skills. The exercises can be completed alone or in cooperative-learning teams. Each exercise is followed by a set of questions for personal consideration and/or class discussion. The 16 Action Learning Exercises include: an entrepreneur's quiz, open-system thinking and recycling, rating the probability of futuristic predictions, a cultural-awareness survey, a personal values survey, how to write good objectives and plans, doing a strategic SWOT analysis, a creativity test, an organizational culture assessment, a field study on organization structure and design, writing behavioral interview questions, communicating in an awkward situation, a quality-of-worklife survey, a management teamwork survey, an emotional intelligence (EQ) test, managing a conflict, and measuring service quality.

SUCCESSFUL PEDAGOGICAL STRUCTURE FOR STUDENTS

As with the previous edition, pedagogical features of the text, along with student ancillaries, make *Management,* Eleventh Edition, a complete and valuable learning tool—one that will satisfy the needs of both students and professors. This is demonstrated by the following:

- Chapter learning objectives at the beginning of each chapter focus the reader's attention on key concepts.
- Key terms are emphasized in bold where first defined, repeated in marginal notes, and listed at the close of each chapter (with page numbers) to reinforce important terminology and concepts.
- A stimulating photo/art program and an inviting, user-friendly layout make the material in this edition visually appealing, accessible, and interesting. Captioned color photographs of managers in action and organizational life enliven the text discussion.
- In-text examples and boxes with four different themes—ethics, global management, diversity, and best practices—provide students with extensive, interesting real-world illustrations to demonstrate the application and relevance of topics important to today's managers.
- Clear, comprehensive chapter summaries refresh the reader's memory of important material.
- Cases at the beginning and end of each chapter provide a real-world context for handling management problems. Twenty-three (72 percent) of the cases in this edition are new.
- A Manager's Toolkit section follows each chapter to give today's and tomorrow's managers practical tools for the twenty-first-century workplace.
- An Action Learning Exercise follows each chapter to provide interactive and experiential learning.
- A "Test Prepper" at the end of each chapter provides a handy self-quiz with 10 true-false and 10 multiple-choice items. An answer key is provided at the end of the book.
- Managers-in-Action Videos at the end of each part foster experiential learning by providing real-world exposure to key managerial skills.

ACKNOWLEDGMENTS

Countless people, including colleagues, students, and relatives, have contributed in many ways to the many editions of this book. For me, this project has been a dream come true; it is amazing where life's journey leads when you have a clear goal, the support of many good people, and a bone-deep belief in the concept of continuous improvement. Whether critical or reinforcing, everyone's suggestions and recommendations have been helpful and greatly appreciated.

While it is impossible to acknowledge every contributor here, some key people need to be identified and sincerely thanked. I particularly appreciate the help and thoughtful comments of my colleague, co-author, and good friend, Professor Angelo Kinicki. I am grateful for the cornerstone reviews of earlier editions by Professors Jack L. Mendleson and Angelo Kinicki. A hearty thank you to Professor Amit Shah, Frostburg State University, for a top-quality job on the *Test Bank*. Sincere thanks also to Maria Muto-Porter for her usual outstanding and creative work on the *Instructor's Resource Manual*.

Warmest thanks are also extended to the following colleagues who have provided valuable input for this and prior editions by serving as content advisers or manuscript reviewers:

Teshome Abebe
University of Southern Colorado

Benjamin Abramowitz
University of Central Florida

Raymond E. Alie
Western Michigan University

Stephen L. Allen
Northwest Missouri State University

Douglas R. Anderson
Ashland University

Mark Anderson
Point Loma Nazarene College

Eva Beer Aronson
Interboro Institute

Debra A. Arvanites
Villanova University

Robert Ash
Rancho Santiago College

Seymour Barcun
St. Frances College

R. B. Barton Jr.
Murray State University

Andrew J. Batchelor
Ohio University— Chillicothe

Dorman C. Batson
Glenville State College

Walter H. Beck Sr.
Kennesaw State University and *Reinhardt College*

Roger Best
Louisiana College

Gerald D. Biby
Sioux Falls College

Glenn M. Blair
Baldwin-Wallace College

Bruce Bloom
DeVry University

Bob Bowles
Cecils College

Barbara Boyington
Brookdale Community College

Steve Bradley
Austin Community College

Margaret Britt
Mount Vernon Nazarene University

Molly Burke
Rosary College

Marie Burkhead
University of Southwestern Louisiana

John Cantrell
Cleveland State Community College

Thomas Carey
Western Michigan University

Elaine Adams Casmus
Chowan College

Julia M. Chambers
Bloomfield College

David Chown
Minnesota State University, Mankato

Anthony A. Cioffi
Lorain County Community College

Richard Coe
Richard Stockton College of New Jersey

George M. Coggins
High Point College

Naomi Berger Davidson
California State University—Northridge

Pamela Davis
Eastern Kentucky University

Richard A. Davis
Rosary College

Thomas Daymont
Temple University— Philadelphia

Tim Donahue
Sioux Falls College

Thomas Duda
S.U.N.Y. Canton Tech College

Deborah J. Dwyer
University of Toledo

Sally Martin Egge
Cardinal Stritch University

Gary Ernst
North Central College

Janice Feldbauer
Macomb Community College

Jacque Foust
University of Wisconsin— River Falls

Ellen Frank
Southern Connecticut State University

Edward Fritz
Nassau Community College

Phyllis Goodman
College of DuPage

Sue Granger
Jacksonville State University

Judith Grenkowicz
Kirtland Community College

John Hall
University of Florida

Susan C. Hanlon
University of Akron

Kimberly Harris
Durham Technical Community College

Nell Hartley
Robert Morris College

Lindle Hatton
University of Wisconsin—Oshkosh

Samuel Hazen
Tarleton State University

Rick Hebert
East Carolina University

Brian R. Hinrichs
Illinois Wesleyan University

Larry W. Howard
Middle Tennessee State University

Jerome Hufnagel
Horry Georgetown Tech

Cathy Jensen
University of Nebraska—Lincoln

Kathleen Jones
University of North Dakota

Marvin Karlins
University of South Florida

Velta Kelly
University of Cincinnati

Sylvia Keyes
Bridgewater State College

Mary Khalili
Oklahoma City University

John Lea
Arizona State University

Charles Lee
Baldwin-Wallace College

Roger D. Lee
Salt Lake Community College

James LoPresti
University of Colorado, Boulder

Bob Lower
Minot State University

James L. Mann
Ashland Community College

Randall Martin
Florida International University

Irvin Mason
Herkimer County Community College

Fredric L. Mayerson
CUNY—Kingsboro Community College

Daniel McAlister
University of Nevada, Las Vegas

Ann McClure
Ft. Hays State University

Barbara McIntosh
University of Vermont

Debra Miller
Ashland Community College

Mark S. Miller
Carthage College

Peggy M. Miller
Ohio University—Athens

Ray Moroye
University of Denver & Metropolitan State College

John Nagy
Cleary College

James Nead
Vincennes University

Joan Nichols
Emporia State University

Alice E. Nuttall
Kent State University

Darlene Orlov
New York University

Robert Ottemann
University of Nebraska—Omaha

Clyde A. Painter
Ohio Northern University

Herbert S. Parker
Kean College of New Jersey

Gus Petrides
Borough of Manhattan Community College

J. Stephen Phillips
Ohio University—Chillicothe

Allen H. Pike
Ferrum College

Khush Pittenger
Ashland University

Jyoti N. Prasad
Eastern Illinois University

Abe Qastin
Lakeland College

Lynn J. Richardson
Fort Lewis College

Robert W. Risteen
Ohio University—Chillicothe

Ralph Roberts
University of West Florida

Jake Robertson
Oklahoma State University

Robert Rowe
New Mexico State University—Alamogordo and *Park College, Holloman Air Force Base*

Daniel James Rowley
University of Northern Colorado

Wendell J. Roye
Franklin Pierce College

Doug Rymph
Emporia State University

Nestor St. Charles
Dutchess County Community College

John Sagi
Anne Arundel Community College

John T. Samaras
Central State University

Roger C. Schoenfeldt
Murray State University

Gregory J. Schulz
Carroll College

C. L. Scott III
Indiana University NW—Gary

Kathryn Severance
Viterbo College

Jane Shuping
Western Piedmont Community College

Marc Siegall
California State University—Chico

Peter Sietins
Bridgewater State College

G. David Sivak
Westmoreland County Community College

Mick Stahler
Stautzenberger College

Jacqueline Stowe *McMurray University*	Joe F. Walenciak *John Brown University*	Ty Westergaard *Lincoln University*
Sharon Tarnutzer *Utah State University*	Dorothy Wallace *Chowan College*	Timothy Wiedman *Ohio University—Lancaster*
Margo Underwood *Brunswick College*	Stanley Welaish *Kean College of New Jersey*	Mary Williams *College of South Nevada*
John Valentine *Kean College of New Jersey*	Richard A. Wells *Aiken Technical College*	James Wittman *Rock Valley College*

My partnership with South-Western Cengage Learning has been productive and enjoyable. Many Cengage Learning people have contributed enormously to this project. I would like to offer a hearty thank you to everyone by acknowledging the following key contributors: George Hoffman, Lisé Johnson, Kathleen McMahon, Julia Chase, Nicole Hamm, and Shelley Dickerson. Thanks to our great new team at Cengage—Joe Sabatino, Kimberly Kanakes, and Clint Kernen.

The discussion of mentoring in Chapter 14 is dedicated once again to Professor Fred Luthans, University of Nebraska–Lincoln, for getting me into the textbook business. His love for our field of study and incredible work ethic continue to inspire me. To Margaret—my wife, best friend, and hiking buddy—thanks for being my center of gravity and for keeping the spirit of the dancing bears alive. Our long marriage is a cherished treasure. Our cats Yahoo and Sweetie Pie did a great job of "managing" my home office.

Finally, I would like to thank the thousands of introductory management students I have had the pleasure of working with through the years for teaching me a great deal about tomorrow's managers. Best wishes for a rewarding career in management.

Bob Kreitner

PART 1

The Management Challenge

1

Managers
and
Entrepreneurs

Management is a practice that has to combine a good deal of craft, namely experience, with a certain amount of art, as vision and insight, and some science, particularly in the form of analysis and technique.[1]

—HENRY MINTZBERG

OBJECTIVES

- **Define** the term *management,* and **explain** the managerial significance of the terms *effectiveness* and *efficiency*.

- **Identify** and **summarize** five major sources of change for today's managers.

- **Distinguish** between managerial functions and skills, and **identify** the eight basic managerial functions.

- **Demonstrate** your knowledge of Wilson's three managerial skill categories, and **explain** the practical significance of his research findings.

- **Explain** how managers learn to manage.

- **Challenge** two myths about small businesses, and **describe** entrepreneurs.

THE CHANGING WORKPLACE

It Was the School of Hard Knocks for the CEO of Switzerland's Novartis

During the past 50 years, leadership scholars have conducted more than 1,000 studies in an attempt to determine the definitive styles, characteristics, or personality traits of great leaders. None of these studies has produced a clear profile of the ideal leader. Thank goodness. If scholars had produced a cookie-cutter leadership style, individuals would be forever trying to imitate it. They would make themselves into personae, not people, and others would see through them immediately.

No one can be authentic by trying to imitate someone else. You can learn from others' experiences, but there is no way you can be successful when you are trying to be like them. People trust you when you are genuine and authentic, not a replica of someone else. . . .

Let's focus now on one leader in particular, Novartis chairman and CEO Daniel Vasella, whose life story was one of the most difficult of all the people we interviewed. He emerged from extreme challenges in his youth to reach the pinnacle of the global pharmaceutical industry, a trajectory that illustrates the trials many leaders have to go through on their journeys to authentic leadership.

Vasella was born in 1953 to a modest family in Fribourg, Switzerland. His early years were filled with medical problems that stoked his passion to become a physician. His first recollections were of a hospital where he was admitted at age four when he suffered from food poisoning. Falling ill with asthma at age five, he was sent alone to the mountains of eastern Switzerland for two summers. He found the four-month separations from his parents especially difficult because his caretaker had an alcohol problem and was unresponsive to his needs.

At age eight, Vasella had tuberculosis, followed by meningitis, and was sent to a sanatorium for a year. Lonely and homesick, he suffered a great deal that year, as his parents rarely visited him. He still remembers the pain and fear when the nurses held him down during the lumbar punctures so that he would not move. One day, a new physician arrived and took time to explain each step of the procedure. Vasella asked the doctor if he could hold a nurse's hand rather than being held down. "The amazing thing is that this time the procedure didn't hurt," Vasella recalls. "Afterward, the doctor asked me, 'How was that?' I reached up and gave him a big hug. These human gestures of forgiveness, caring, and compassion made a deep impression on me and on the kind of person I wanted to become."

Throughout his early years, Vasella's life continued to be unsettled. When he was ten, his 18-year-old sister passed away after suffering from cancer for two years. Three years later, his father died in surgery. To support the family, his mother went to work in a distant town and came home only once every three weeks. Left to himself, he and his friends held beer parties and got into frequent fights. This lasted for three years until he met his first girlfriend, whose affection changed his life.

At 20, Vasella entered medical school, later graduating with honors. During medical school, he sought out psychotherapy so he could come to terms with his early experiences and not feel like a victim. Through analysis, he reframed his life story and realized that he wanted to help a wider range of people than he could as an individual practitioner. Upon completion of his residency, he applied to become chief physician at the University of Zurich; however, the search committee considered him too young for the position.

Disappointed but not surprised, Vasella decided to use his abilities to increase his impact on medicine. At that time, he had a growing fascination with finance and business. He talked with the head of the pharmaceutical division of Sandoz, who offered him the opportunity to join the company's U.S. affiliate. In his five years in the United States, Vasella flourished in the stimulating environment, first as a sales representative and later as a product manager, and advanced rapidly through the Sandoz marketing organization.

When Sandoz merged with Ciba-Geigy in 1996, Vasella was named CEO of the combined companies, now called Novartis, despite his young age and limited experience. Once in the CEO's role, Vasella blossomed as a leader. He envisioned the opportunity to build a great global health care company that could help people through lifesaving new drugs, such as Gleevec, which has proved to be highly effective for patients with chronic myeloid leukemia. Drawing on the physician role models of his youth, he built an entirely new Novartis culture centered on compassion, competence, and competition. These moves established Novartis as a giant in the industry and Vasella as a compassionate leader.

Source: Excerpted from Bill George, Peter Sims, Andrew N. McLean, and Diana Mayer, "Discovering Your Authentic Leadership," *Harvard Business Review,* 85 (February 2007): 129–138. Reprinted by permission of HBS Publishing.

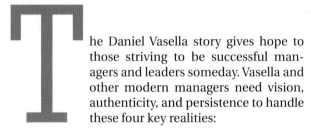he Daniel Vasella story gives hope to those striving to be successful managers and leaders someday. Vasella and other modern managers need vision, authenticity, and persistence to handle these four key realities:

1. The only certainty today is *change*. Challenging *goals* motivate people to strive for improvement and overcome obstacles and resistance to change.
2. *Speed, teamwork,* and *flexibility* are the orders of the day, from both strategic and operational standpoints.
3. Managers at all levels need to stay close to the *customer*. Product/service *quality* is the driving force in the battle to stay competitive.
4. Without *continuous improvement* and *lifelong learning,* there can be no true economic progress for individuals and organizations alike.

Keep these managerial realities in mind as you explore the world of management in this book.

Every one of us—whether as an employee, a customer, a stockholder, or a member of the surrounding community—has a direct stake in the quality of management. Joan Magretta, a management consultant who went on to become an editor at *Harvard Business Review,* offers this perspective:

> *Management's business is building organizations that work. Underneath all the theory and the tools, underneath all the specialized knowledge, lies a commitment to performance that has powerfully altered our economy and our lives. That, ultimately, is why management is everyone's business.*[2]

Accordingly, bad management is a serious threat to our quality of life. Terry Bragg, president of a management training company in Utah, recently put it this way: "For most employees, the immediate boss is the prime representative of the organization. . . . If they don't like their immediate boss, they don't like the company."[3]

Effective management is the key to a better world, but mismanagement squanders our resources and jeopardizes our well-being. Every manager, regardless of level or scope of responsibility, is either part of the solution or part of the problem. Management or mismanagement—the choice is yours. A basic knowledge of management theory, research, and practice will help prepare you for productive and gainful employment in a highly organized world in which virtually everything is managed.

MANAGEMENT DEFINED

We now need to define management, in order to highlight the importance, relevance, and necessity of studying it. **Management** is the process of working with and through others to achieve organizational objectives in a changing environment. Central to this process is the effective and efficient use of limited resources. (*Note:* The term *management,* when used to describe workers with supervisory duties, is a legal designation in the United States wrapped in controversy over issues such as who can join a union and who qualifies for overtime pay.)[4]

> **management:** the process of working with and through others to achieve organizational objectives in a changing environment

Five components of this definition require closer examination: (1) working with and through others, (2) achieving organizational objectives, (3) balancing effectiveness and efficiency, (4) making the most of limited resources, and (5) coping with a changing environment (see Figure 1.1).

Working with and Through Others

Management is, above all else, a social process. Many collective purposes bring individuals together—building cars, providing emergency health care,

FIGURE **1.1** Key Aspects of the Management Process

publishing books, and on and on. But in all cases, managers are responsible for getting things done by working with and through others.

Aspiring managers who do not interact well with others hamper their careers. This was the conclusion two experts reached following interviews with 62 executives from the United States, the United Kingdom, Belgium, Spain, France, Germany, and Italy. Each of the executives was asked to describe two managers whose careers had been *derailed*. Derailed managers were those who had not lived up to their peers' and superiors' high expectations. The derailed managers reportedly had these shortcomings:

- Problems with interpersonal relationships
- Failure to meet business objectives
- Failure to build and lead a team
- Inability to change and adapt during a transition[5]

Significantly, the first and third shortcomings involve failure to work effectively with and through others. Derailed managers experienced a number of interpersonal problems; among other things, they were perceived as manipulative, abusive, untrustworthy, demeaning, overly critical, not team players, and poor communicators. The former CEO of PeopleSoft tripped over this particular hurdle when he was fired by the board of directors in 2004 for a number of reasons, including "managing abrasively."[6]

Achieving Organizational Objectives

An objective is a target to be strived for and, one hopes, attained. Like individuals, organizations are usually more successful when their activities are guided by challenging, yet achievable, objectives. From an individual perspective, scheduling a course load becomes more systematic and efficient when a student sets an objective, such as graduating with a specific degree by a given date.

Although personal objectives are typically within the reach of individual effort, organizational objectives or goals always require collective action. For example, "Nokia's goal is to boost the total number of mobile-phone users worldwide to 5 billion by 2015, up from an estimated 3 billion by the end of 2007, largely on the back of developing markets."[7] This ambitious target will require a unique mix of product design and marketing skills for Nokia's 68,483 employees as they

Let the celebration begin! Microsoft employees celebrate the incredible collective effort it took to create and launch its new Vista operating system for computers. We need organizations to do what we cannot accomplish alone.

strive to increase their dominant 38 percent market share among diverse customers around the world.[8]

Organizational objectives also serve later as measuring sticks for performance. Without organizational objectives, the management process, like a trip without a specific destination, would be aimless and wasteful.

Balancing Effectiveness and Efficiency

Distinguishing between effectiveness and efficiency is much more than an exercise in semantics. The relationship between these two terms is important, and it presents managers with a never-ending challenge. **Effectiveness** entails promptly achieving a stated objective. For instance, Wal-Mart needs to meet its quarterly profit objective. But given the reality of limited resources, effectiveness alone is not enough. **Efficiency** enters the picture when the resources required to achieve an objective are weighed against what was actually accomplished. The more favorable the ratio of benefits to costs, the greater the efficiency. For giant companies such as Wal-Mart, seemingly small efficiencies can yield huge payoffs. "Wal-Mart wants to reduce packaging by 5%, which it estimates will save the company and its suppliers about $11 billion. About 30% of municipal waste comes from packaging, the EPA says."[9]

Managers are responsible for balancing effectiveness and efficiency (see Figure 1.2). Too much emphasis in either direction leads to mismanagement. On the one hand, managers must be effective by getting the job done. On the other hand, managers need to be efficient by reducing costs and not wasting resources. Of course, managers who are too stingy with resources may fail to get the job done.

effectiveness: a central element in the process of management that entails achieving a stated organizational objective

efficiency: a central element in the process of management that balances the amount of resources used to achieve an objective against what was actually accomplished

At the heart of the quest for *productivity improvement* (a favorable ratio between inputs and output) is the constant struggle to balance effectiveness and efficiency.[10] A good case in point is the adoption of new intensive-care unit (ICU) technology at Sentara Healthcare, a seven-hospital nonprofit organization in Norfolk, Virginia:

Sentara became the first client for the electronic ICU (eICU)—a technology that combines software,

video feeds, and real-time patient information to let intensive-care specialists . . . cover 11 ICUs at six hospitals, spread 60 miles apart, around the clock. Today, the eICU is providing some of the most solid evidence that telemedicine, full of promise for years, is finally becoming real.

The eICU technology, sold by Baltimore's Visicu Inc., lets hospitals leverage the scarce resources of specially trained intensive-care doctors and nurses. A single physician and nurse can support bedside caregivers for more than 100 patients at once. . . . [Says one industry observer:] "How do you do better with less, and how do you improve care when intensive-care specialists and nurses are scarce?"[11]

Productivity improvement that saves lives—now *that's* good management!

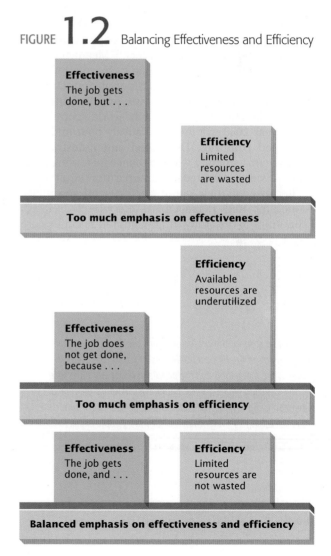

FIGURE **1.2** Balancing Effectiveness and Efficiency

Effectiveness
The job gets done, but . . .

Efficiency
Limited resources are wasted

Too much emphasis on effectiveness

Efficiency
Available resources are underutilized

Effectiveness
The job does not get done, because . . .

Too much emphasis on efficiency

Effectiveness
The job gets done, and . . .

Efficiency
Limited resources are not wasted

Balanced emphasis on effectiveness and efficiency

Making the Most of Limited Resources

We live in a world of scarcity. Those who are concerned with such matters worry not only about running out of nonrenewable energy and material resources but also about the lopsided use of those resources. The United States, for example, with about 5 percent of the world's population, is currently consuming about 25 percent of the world's annual oil production and generating 25 percent of the world's CO_2, a greenhouse gas linked to global warming.[12]

Although experts and nonexperts alike may quibble over exactly how long it will take to exhaust our nonrenewable resources or come up with exotic new technological alternatives,[13] one bold fact remains: our planet is becoming increasingly crowded.

Demographers who collect and study population statistics tell us that Earth's human population is growing by 2 1/3 people every *second,* by 203,024 every *day,* and by 6.2 million every *month.*[14] The present world population of over 6.7 billion people is projected to reach 9 billion within 70 years.[15] Meanwhile, our planet's carrying capacity is open to speculation. (For up-to-the-minute global and U.S. population statistics, go to: **www.census.gov/main/www/popclock.html.**)

Approximately 83 percent of the world's population in the year 2020 will live in relatively poor and less-developed countries. Developed and industrialized nations, consequently, will experience increasing pressure to divide the limited resource pie more equitably.[16]

Because of their common focus on resources, economics and management are closely related. Economics is the study of how limited resources are distributed among alternative uses. In productive organizations, managers are the trustees of limited resources, and it is their job to see that the basic factors of production—land, labor, and capital—are used efficiently as well as effectively. Management could be called "applied economics."

Coping with a Changing Environment

Successful managers are the ones who anticipate and adjust to changing circumstances rather than being passively swept along or caught unprepared. Employers today are hiring managers who can take unfamiliar situations in stride. *Business Week* served up this amusing but challenging profile of tomorrow's managers: "The next generation of corporate leaders will need the charm of a debutante, the flexibility of a gymnast, and the quickness of a panther. A few foreign languages and a keen understanding of technology won't hurt either."[17] Also in the mix are a sense of humor, passion, and the ability to make decisions rapidly.

Chapter 3 provides detailed coverage of important changes and trends in management's social, political-legal, economic, and technological environments. At this point, it is instructive to preview major changes for managers doing business in the twenty-first century[18] (see Table 1.1). This particular collection of changes is the product of five overarching sources of change: globalization, the evolution of product quality, environmentalism, an ethical reawakening, and the Internet revolution. Together, these factors are significantly reshaping the practice of management.

GLOBALIZATION.   Figuratively speaking, the globe is shrinking in almost every conceivable way. Networks of transportation, communication, computers, music, and economics have tied the people of the world together as never before. Companies are having to become global players just to survive, let alone prosper. For example, McDonald's has "more than 30,000 local restaurants serving 52 million people in more than 100 countries each day"[19] and "Intel, Altria and ExxonMobil get more than 70% of their revenue abroad."[20] Import figures are equally stunning. For instance, the United States currently imports about 60 percent of its oil, with 68 percent the figure forecasted for the year 2025.[21] An even higher proportion (81 percent) of the seafood consumed in the United States is foreign-sourced.[22]

A controversial aspect of globalization is the practice of **offshoring,** the outsourcing of jobs from

offshoring: controversial practice of sending jobs to low-wage countries

---

1b   Drink Up

. . . in Fiji, a state-of-the-art factory spins out more than a million bottles a day of the hippest bottled water on the U.S. market today, while more than half the people in Fiji do not have safe, reliable drinking water. Which means it is easier for the typical American in Beverly Hills or Baltimore to get a drink of safe, pure, refreshing Fiji water than it is for most people in Fiji.

Source: Charles Fishman, "Message in a Bottle," Fast Company, no. 117 (July–August 2007): 113.

QUESTIONS:
Does this situation trouble you in any way? If so, what constructive steps would you recommend? If not, why not?

TABLE **1.1** The Twenty-First-Century Manager: Ten Major Changes

	MOVING AWAY FROM	MOVING TOWARD
Administrative role	Boss/superior/leader	Team member/facilitator/teacher/sponsor/advocate/coach
Cultural orientation	Monocultural/monolingual	Multicultural/multilingual
Quality/ethics/environmental impacts	Afterthought (or no thought)	Forethought (unifying themes)
Power bases	Formal authority; rewards and punishments	Knowledge; relationships; rewards
Primary organizational unit	Individual	Team
Interpersonal dealings	Competition; win-lose	Cooperation; win-win
Learning	Periodic (preparatory; curriculum-driven)	Continuous (lifelong; learner-driven)
Problems	Threats to be avoided	Opportunities for learning and continuous improvement
Change and conflict	Resist/react/avoid	Anticipate/seek/channel
Information	Restrict access/hoard	Increase access/share

developed countries to lower-wage countries.[23] This is a long-standing practice that has been going on for decades. Tens of thousands of jobs in the textile, steel, and consumer electronics industries are long gone from the United States. Thanks to the broadband Internet, skilled jobs in areas such as hardware and software engineering, architecture, tax return preparation, and medical diagnosis are being outsourced to well-educated workers in India, China, the Philippines, and Russia.[24] A recent study puts the situation in perspective:

> Meta Group Inc., a Stamford, Conn., consulting and research firm, says the outsourcing trend will grow by 20 percent per year through 2008 as more U.S. firms focus on cutting labor costs. Meta estimates that 60 percent of U.S. firms will send some technology work abroad by 2008 . . .
>
> "In the bigger picture, one job gain in India does not relate to one job in the United States," said Stan Lepeak of Meta Group.
>
> "The United States might employ fewer programmers here, but it will employ more managers and a variety of other new roles will be created to manage these new relationships."[25]

Also balancing the global jobs equation a bit are these two factors: (1) 5.1 million employees in the United States are employed by foreign-owned companies, such as Japan's Toyota and Germany's Siemens;[26] and (2) "insourcing." Insourcing occurs "when foreign multinationals open offices on U.S. soil and hire Americans, at a higher price, to do the very jobs they once lured overseas."[27] For example, at a 250-person call center in Reno, Ohio, India's Tata Group is striving "to give their U.S. customers a more culturally fluent, less frustrating 1-800 experience. (No more hearing someone read from a script ten time zones away.)"[28] Time will tell whether the United States is a net winner or loser in this global merry-go-round of jobs.

Today's model manager is one who is comfortable transacting business in multiple languages and cultures. There is a rapidly growing army of global managers from all corners of the world, and you can become a member of it through diligent effort and a clear sense of purpose. Chapter 4 is devoted to the topic of international management. The international cases and examples, and the Window on the World features throughout the text, are intended to broaden your awareness of international management.

H ewlett-Packard (HP) may be based in California's Silicon Valley, but it has a worldwide around-the-clock workforce. These call center employees work at HP's facility in Dalian, China. The "off-shoring" of jobs has stirred lively debate in the United States about its net benefits and costs.

THE EVOLUTION OF PRODUCT QUALITY. Managers have been interested in the quality of their products, at least as an afterthought, since the Industrial Revolution. But thanks to U.S. and Japanese quality gurus such as W. Edwards Deming and Kaoru Ishikawa[29] (more about them in Chapter 2), product/service quality has become both a forethought and a driving force in effective organizations of all kinds. Today's hospitals, hotels, universities, and government agencies are as interested in improving product/service quality as are factories, mines, airlines, and railroads.

In its most basic terms, the emphasis on quality has evolved through four distinct stages since World War II—from "fix it in" to "inspect it in" to "build it in" to "design it in." Progressive managers are moving away from the first two approaches and toward the build-it-in and design-it-in approaches.[30] Here are the key differences:

- *The fix-it-in approach to quality*
  Rework any defective products identified by quality inspectors at the end of the production process.

- *The inspect-it-in approach to quality*
  Have quality inspectors sample work in process and prescribe machine adjustments to avoid substandard output.

- *The build-it-in approach to quality*
  Make *everyone* who touches the product responsible for spotting and correcting defects. The emphasis is on identifying and eliminating *causes* of quality problems.

- *The design-it-in approach to quality*
  Intense customer and employee involvement drives the entire design-production cycle. The emphasis is on *continuous improvement* of personnel, processes, and product.

Notice how each stage of this evolution has broadened the responsibility for quality, turning quality improvement into a true team effort. Also, the focus has shifted from reactively fixing product defects to proactively working to prevent them and to satisfy the customer completely. Today's quality leaders strive to *exceed,* not just meet, the customer's expectations.[31]

A popular label for the build-it-in and design-it-in approaches to quality is *total quality management* (TQM).[32] TQM is discussed in detail in Chapter 16.

ENVIRONMENTALISM. Green issues such as deforestation; global warming; depletion of the ozone layer; toxic waste; food safety, and pollution of land, air, and water have gone mainstream.[33] This is evidenced by a recent worldwide survey of 45,000 people:

> *The Pew Research Center poll, taken in 46 countries and the Palestinian territories, found that people in countries as diverse as Canada, Peru, Ukraine, China and India identified environmental degradation as the greatest world danger, outranking concerns about nuclear weapons, ethnic hatred, and AIDS.*[34]

Managers around the world are picking up the environmental banner and putting their creative ideas to work. For example, Toyota's new 624,000-square-foot sales campus in Torrance, California, was designed and built with the environment in mind. Structural steel came primarily from recycled cars, solar panels generate enough electricity to power 500 homes, and recycled water is used to irrigate a drought-resistant landscape of native plants.[35] Managers are challenged to develop innovative ways to make a profit without unduly harming the environment in the process. Terms such as *industrial ecology, sustainable business,* and *eco-efficiency* are heard today under the general umbrella of sustainable development.

1c e-Waste

Americans currently dispose of 128 million cell phones a year, only 1% of which are diverted from landfills. This appalling number isn't even counted in the 2 million tons of used electronics we also discard annually. The waste from such devices contains, according to the EPA, substances that are toxic when burned. Worse, in landfills, they seep into the groundwater and never break down.

Source: Andrew Zoll, Business 3.0," *Fast Company*, no. 113 (March 2007): 68.

QUESTION:

What can *you* do about this problem?

Also, cleaning up the environment promises to generate whole new classes of jobs and robust profits in the future. The debate over jobs versus the environment has been rendered obsolete by recognition of the need for both a healthy economy *and* a healthy environment. Authors William McDonough and Michael Braungart, while calling for a new Industrial Revolution, recently offered this fresh new perspective:

> *We see a world of abundance, not limits. In the midst of a great deal of talking about reducing the human ecological footprint, we offer a different vision. What if humans designed products and systems that celebrate an abundance of human creativity, culture, and productivity? That are so intelligent and safe [that] our species leaves an ecological footprint to delight in, not lament?*
>
> *Consider this: All the ants on the planet, taken together, have a biomass greater than that of humans. Ants have been incredibly industrious for millions of years. Yet their productiveness nourishes plants, animals, and soil. Human industry has been in full swing for little over a century, yet it has brought about a decline in almost every ecosystem on the planet. Nature doesn't have a design problem. People do.*[36]

Encouragingly, researchers recently found 80 percent higher stock market valuations for multinational corporations adhering to strict environmental standards, compared with those taking advantage of the lax environmental standards often found in less-developed countries.[37] In short, investors tend to reward "clean" companies and to punish "dirty" ones.

AN ETHICAL REAWAKENING. Managers are under strong pressure from the public, elected officials, and respected managers to behave better. This pressure has resulted from years of headlines about discrimination, illegal campaign contributions, accounting fraud, price fixing, insider trading, the selling of unsafe products, and other unethical practices. Here is a sampling from just a single week of business news in 2007: the 82-year-old former chairman of Adelphia is going to jail for 15 years for $2.3 billion in securities fraud (in addition, his son got 20 years for his part) and British Airways is fined $550 million by the U.S. and British governments for fare-fixing.[38]

Traditional values such as honesty are being reemphasized in managerial decision making and conduct. A case in point: "When the *Economist* magazine published a Top 10 list of leadership qualities . . . , a sound ethical compass was No. 1."[39] Ethics and honesty are everyone's concern: *mine, yours,* and *ours.* Every day we have countless opportunities to be honest or dishonest. One survey of more than 4,000 employees uncovered the following ethical problems in the workplace (the percentage of employees observing the problem during the past year appears in parentheses).

- Lying to supervisors (56 percent)
- Lying on reports or falsifying records (41 percent)
- Stealing and theft (35 percent)
- Sexual harassment (35 percent)
- Abusing drugs or alcohol (31 percent)
- Conflict of interest (31 percent)[40]

Because of closer public scrutiny, ethical questions can no longer be shoved aside as irrelevant. The topic of managerial ethics is covered in depth in Chapter 5 and is explored in the Ethics: Character, Courage, and Values features throughout the text.

THE INTERNET AND E-BUSINESS REVOLUTION. In concept, the Internet began as a U.S. Department of Defense (DOD) research project during the Cold War era of the 1960s. The plan was to give university scientists a quick and inexpensive way to share their DOD research data. Huge technical problems, such as getting incompatible computers to communicate in a fail-safe network, were solved in 1969 at UCLA when researchers succeeded in getting two linked computers to exchange data. The Internet was born. Other universities were added to the Internet during the 1970s, and applications such as e-mail gradually emerged. By 1983, technology made it possible to share complex documents and graphics on the Internet, and the World Wide Web came into existence.[41] Time passed and improvements were made. During the early 1990s, individuals and businesses began to log on to

ETHICS: CHARACTER, COURAGE, AND VALUES

Take the High Road

USA Today: If you had a son or daughter graduating from college or high school this year, what advice would you give them?

Jim Quigley, CEO, Deloitte & Touche: Nearly half of all teens say they would act unethically to get ahead or make more money, if they knew for sure they would not get caught. I find that troubling and would advise any graduate to make ethical behavior the cornerstone of their career. The question is not, "Will I get caught?" or even, "Is it legal?" To be successful in business and in life, we must follow the higher standard of, "Is it right?" In my view, the people who follow this standard live richer, fuller lives and achieve success that lasts.

Source: Excerpted from Del Jones, "Just a Little Friendly Advice," USA Today (May 21, 2007): 7B.

FOR DISCUSSION

Is it necessary to cheat to get ahead today? Explain. Ultimately, who (or what) is responsible for your ethical/unethical behavior? What needs to be done to foster ethical behavior in society?

---

the "Web" to communicate via e-mail and to buy, sell, and trade things.

Growth of the **Internet**—the worldwide network of personal computers, routers and switches, powerful servers, and organizational computer systems—has been explosive. No one owns the Web in its entirety, and anyone with a computer modem can be part of it. Within its digital recesses are both trash and treasure. According to Computer Industry Almanac Inc., the number of Internet users worldwide topped 1 billion in 2005 and is expected to reach 2 billion in 2011.[42] *Business Week*'s recent depiction of a typical Internet transaction helps us bridge the gap between an abstract concept and a tangible communication system with many players and business opportunities:

> **Internet:** global network of servers and personal and organizational computers

After a student, say, at Rutgers University in New Brunswick, N.J., clicked on The Landlord, *one of hundreds of thousands of computer servers in Google's numerous California data centers pushed the video through Web networking gear from Cisco Systems and Juniper Networks. Last year [2006], Google, YouTube's parent company, spent $1.9 billion, or 18% of its sales, on technology systems and other capital expenditures to serve videos speedily and process search-engine queries.*

From Google's facility, the video shot across the U.S. on Level 3 Communications Inc.'s fiber-optic network, which encompasses 47,000 miles of cable. Reaching New Jersey, the clip was then handed off to a new fiber loop run by Verizon Communications Inc. Milliseconds later, Verizon served up the video to an apartment in New Brunswick through a broadband connection wired directly into the building.[43]

The implications of this nearly instantaneous global interconnectedness for all of us (especially managers) are profound and truly revolutionary. Legal, ethical, security, and privacy issues, however, remain largely unresolved.[44]

With the 2001 dot-com crash becoming a distant memory, the e-business revolution is proceeding in a more measured way and with more realistic expectations. Where their focus before the dot-com crash was primarily on business-to-consumer retailing, Internet strategists are now much more broadly focused. Thus, an **e-business** is one seeking efficiencies via the Internet in all basic business functions—production, marketing, and finance/accounting—and all support activities involving human, material, and financial resources.

> **e-business:** a business using the Internet for greater efficiency in every aspect of its operations

Craig Barrett, the chairman of Intel, the computer chip giant, explained how his firm evolved into what he calls an "Internet company":

> . . . for Intel, being an Internet company meant turning ourselves into a 100% e-business from front to back—not just in terms of selling and buying, but also in terms of information transfer, education, and customer interaction. We wanted to improve our competitiveness and our productivity, to streamline our internal operations, and to save some money. We also wanted to show that we can use the technology that we sell to the rest of the world.[45]

Aspects and implications of the Internet and e-business revolution are explored throughout this book, with detailed coverage of Internet strategy in Chapter 7.

Considering the variety of these sources of change in the general environment, managers are challenged to keep abreast of them and adjust and adapt as necessary.

WHAT DO MANAGERS DO?

Although nearly all aspects of modern life are touched at least indirectly by the work of managers, many people do not really understand what the management process involves. Management is much more, for example, than the familiar activity of telling employees what to do. Management is a complex and dynamic mixture of systematic techniques and common sense. As with any complex process, the key to learning about management lies in dividing it into readily understood pieces. There are two different ways in which we can analyze the management process for study and discussion. One approach, dating back to the early twentieth century, is to identify managerial functions. A second, more recent approach focuses more precisely on managerial skills.[46]

Managerial functions are general administrative duties that need to be carried out in virtually all productive organizations. **Managerial skills**, on the other hand, are specific observable behaviors that effective

managerial functions: general administrative duties that need to be carried out in virtually all productive organizations to achieve desired outcomes

managerial skills: specific observable behaviors that effective managers exhibit

managers exhibit.[47] When we shift the focus from functions to skills, we are moving from general to specific. To put it another way, functions tell us *what* managers generally do while skills tell us more precisely *how* they carry out those functions. We shall examine both perspectives more closely and then have a frank discussion of some managerial facts of life.

Managerial Functions

For nearly a century, the most popular approach to describing what managers do has been the functional view. It has been popular because it characterizes the management process as a sequence of rational and logical steps. Henri Fayol, a French industrialist turned writer, became the father of the functional approach in 1916 when he identified five managerial functions: planning, organizing, command, coordination, and control.[48] Fayol claimed that these five functions were the common denominators of all managerial jobs, whatever the purpose of the organization.[49] Over the years Fayol's original list of managerial functions has been updated and expanded by management scholars. This book, even though it is based on more than just Fayol's approach, is organized around eight different managerial functions: planning, decision making, organizing, staffing, communicating, motivating, leading, and controlling (see Figure 1.3).

FIGURE **1.3** Identifiable Functions in the Management Process

A brief overview of these eight managerial functions will describe what managers do and will preview what lies ahead in this text.

PLANNING. Commonly referred to as the primary management function, planning is the formulation of future courses of action. Plans and the objectives on which they are based give purpose and direction to the organization, its subunits, and contributing individuals.

DECISION MAKING. Managers choose among alternative courses of action when they make decisions. Making intelligent and ethical decisions in today's complex world is a major management challenge.

ORGANIZING. Structural considerations such as the chain of command, division of labor, and assignment of responsibility are part of the organizing function. Careful organizing helps ensure the efficient use of human resources.

STAFFING. Organizations are only as good as the people in them. Staffing consists of recruiting, training, and developing people who can contribute to the organized effort.

COMMUNICATING. Today's managers are responsible for communicating to their employees the technical knowledge, instructions, rules, and information required to get the job done. Recognizing that communication is a two-way process, managers should be responsive to feedback and upward communications.

MOTIVATING. An important aspect of management today is motivating individuals to pursue collective objectives by satisfying needs and meeting expectations with meaningful work and valued rewards. Flexible work schedules can be motivational for today's busy employees.

LEADING. Managers become inspiring leaders by serving as role models and adapting their management style to the demands of the situation. The idea of visionary leadership is popular today.

CONTROLLING. When managers compare desired results with actual results and take the necessary corrective action, they are keeping things on track through the control function. Deviations from past plans should be considered when formulating new plans.

Managerial Skills

Thanks to Clark L. Wilson's 30 years of research involving tens of thousands of managers, we have a very clear picture of what it takes to be an effective manager. It takes three skill categories—technical, teambuilding, and drive—that branch into the 12 specific managerial skills listed in Figure 1.4. Unfortunately, according to Wilson's research, about one-third of managers at all levels do not achieve an appropriate *balance* of managerial skills and are thus ineffective. He explains:

> *Too many managers try to exercise control without providing the Technical and Teambuilding skills needed to achieve their goals. They must see that they cannot exercise effective control without first exercising their up-front responsibilities for communicating goals and coordinating teams.*[50]

This conjures up the image of effective managers as jugglers struggling to keep three balls in the air at once. Those balls are labeled technical skills, teambuilding skills, and drive skills. Not an easy chore, but today's and tomorrow's managers are challenged to get the job done amid constant change.

Some Managerial Facts of Life (with No Sugar Coating)

Managing is a tough and demanding job today. The hours are long and, at first anyway, the pay may not be generous. Worse yet, managers are visible authority figures who get more than their fair share of criticism and ridicule from politicians and Scott Adams's Dilbert cartoons.[51] Nevertheless, managing can be a very rewarding occupation for those who develop

---

1d Managerial Functions and Dysfunctional Managers

In a study of 1,040 managers in 100 rapidly changing organizations, the two leading causes of managerial failure were "Ineffective communication skills/practices" and "Poor work relationships/interpersonal skills."

Source: Clinton O. Longenecker, Mitchell J. Neubert, and Laurence S. Fink, "Causes and Consequences of Managerial Failure in Rapidly Changing Organizations," Business Horizons, 50 (March–April 2007): 145–155.

QUESTION:
Which managerial functions and skills do these managers need to improve?

FIGURE **1.4** Wilson's Managerial Skills

SKILL CATEGORY	SKILLS	DESCRIPTION
TECHNICAL Applying your education, training, and experience to effectively organize a task, job, or project	**1. Technical expertise**	Skills you have acquired by education and experience; to understand and communicate key technical details
	2. Clarification of goals and objectives	Your ability to organize and schedule the work of your unit so it is achieved when expected, and meets established standards
	3. Problem solving	Your ability to resolve issues you confront in the day's work; to develop team collaboration in facing problems
	4. Imagination and creativity	You demonstrate an ability to originate ideas, to correct and develop ways to improve productivity
TEAMBUILDING Listening carefully and communicating clearly to develop and coordinate an effective group or team	**5. Listening for insights**	Keeping aware of activities of your team and units close to you; underpinning your ability to continue being a manager
	6. Directing and coaching	Meeting your goals and standards; keeping your team's skills up to target levels
	7. Solving problems as teams	An important role is helping your team contribute ideas to improve their performance
	8. Coordinating and cooperating	Demonstrating a willingness to work with others: your group, individuals, and units close to you
DRIVE Setting goals, maintaining standards, and evaluating performance to achieve effective outcomes involving costs, output, product quality, and customer service	**9. Standards of performance**	Your effort to keep your part of the organization moving, your willingness to be busy and keep aimed toward new accomplishments
	10. Control of details	Overseeing the performance of work at a close level, to meet performance goals and standards
	11. Energy	Demonstrating to your team and colleagues a readiness and willingness to work and that you expect their cooperation
	12. Exerting pressure	Urging others to perform, by shaping your activity to be perceived as teamwork, not domination

Source: Quoted and adapted from Clark L. Wilson, How and Why Effective Managers Balance Their Skills: Technical, Teambuilding, Drive, *2003, pp. 13, 18–20. Used by permission of the author.*

their skills and persist, as evidenced by American Management Association (AMA) research findings:

- Forty-six percent of U.S. managers say they feel more overwhelmed at work today than two years ago, and 22 percent more say they're "somewhat" more overwhelmed.
- Half of U.S. managers say they experience stress every day, but an even greater share—63 percent— say they feel enthusiasm for their jobs.[52]

A HECTIC PACE. According to Henry Mintzberg's classic observational studies of actual managers, the average manager is not the reflective planner and precise "orchestra leader" that the functional approach

suggests.[53] Mintzberg characterizes the typical manager as follows: "The manager is overburdened with obligations; yet he cannot easily delegate his tasks. As a result, he is driven to overwork and is forced to do many tasks superficially. Brevity, fragmentation, and verbal communication characterize his work."[54]

In addition, according to Mintzberg's research, constant interruptions are the order of the day. A more recent study supported Mintzberg's view and provided a somewhat surprising insight into the reality of nonstop interruptions. Stephanie Winston interviewed 48 top U.S. executives, including the late Katharine Graham, former chief executive of the *Washington Post,* and discovered that constant interruptions are not a threat to

Learning about management is a life-long quest. Just ask Ronald Friday, who recently retired as a Command-Sergeant Major after a 30-year career in the U.S. Army. He's building upon countless lessons from the school of hard knocks with an online degree in human resource management from the University of Maryland.

successful top executives. Indeed, interruptions are what the work of top managers is all about and actually constitute a valuable resource. Winston concluded, "They use a fluid time style to make abundant connections and draw in streams of information. . . . The torrent of questions, comments, updates, requests, and expectations is a rich resource to be mined."[55]

Thus, the typical manager's day involves a hectic schedule, with lots of brief interactions. Interruptions and fragmentation are the norm. Extended quiet periods for reflection and contemplation are rare. An even quicker pace is in store for future managers. However, in line with Wilson's advice to balance one's managerial skills, Mintzberg recently urged managers to balance reflective thought and action:

> *All effective managing has to be sandwiched between acting on the ground and reflecting in the abstract. Acting alone is thoughtless—we have seen enough of the consequences of that—just as reflecting alone is passive. Both are critical. But today, one—reflection—gets lost.*[56]

MANAGERS LOSE THEIR RIGHT TO DO MANY THINGS. Mention the word *manager,* and the average person will probably respond with terms such as *power, privilege, authority, good pay,* and so on. Although many managers eventually do enjoy some or all of these rewards, they pay a significant price for stepping to the front of the administrative parade.[57] According to one management expert, when you accept a supervisory or managerial position, you give up your right to do any of the following:

- Lose your temper
- Be one of the gang
- Bring your personal problems to work
- Vent your frustrations and express your opinion at work
- Resist change
- Pass the buck on tough assignments
- Get even with your adversaries
- Play favorites
- Put your self-interests first
- Ask others to do what you wouldn't do
- Expect to be immediately recognized and rewarded for doing a good job[58]

We tell you this not to scare you away from what could be a financially and emotionally rewarding career, but rather to present a realistic picture so you can choose intelligently. Management is not for everyone—it is not for the timid, the egomaniacal, or the lazy. Management requires clear-headed individuals who can envision something better and turn it into reality by working with and through others.

LEARNING TO MANAGE

Students of management are left with one overriding question: "How do I acquire the ability to manage?" This question has stimulated a good deal of debate among those interested in management education. What is the key, theory or practice? Some contend that future managers need a solid background in management theory acquired through formal education. Others argue that managing, like riding a bicycle, can be learned only by actually doing it.[59] We can leapfrog this debate by looking at how managers learn to manage, understanding how students learn about management, and considering how you can blend the two processes to your best advantage.

How Do Managers Learn to Manage?

We have an answer to this simple but intriguing question, thanks to the Honeywell study, which was conducted by a team of management development specialists employed by Honeywell.[60] In a survey, they asked 3,600 Honeywell managers, "How did you learn to manage?" Ten percent of the respondents were then interviewed for additional insights. Successful Honeywell managers reportedly acquired 50 percent of their management knowledge from job assignments (see Figure 1.5). The remaining 50 percent of what they knew about management reportedly came from relationships with bosses, mentors, and coworkers (30 percent) and from formal training and education (20 percent).

FIGURE **1.5** The Honeywell Study: How Managers Learn to Manage

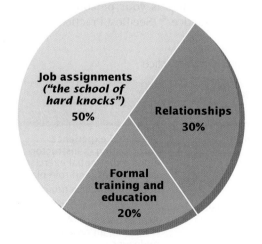

Source: Data from Ron Zemke, "The Honeywell Studies: How Managers Learn to Manage," Training, 22 (August 1985): 46–51.

Fully half of what the Honeywell managers knew about managing came from the so-called school of hard knocks. To that extent, at least, learning to manage is indeed like learning to ride a bike. You get on, you fall off and skin your knee, you get back on a bit smarter, and so on, until you're able to wobble down the road. But in the minds of aspiring managers, this scenario raises the question of what classes are held in the school of hard knocks. A second study, this one of British managers, provided an answer. It turns out that the following are considered *hard knocks* by managers:

- Making a big mistake
- Being overstretched by a difficult assignment
- Feeling threatened
- Being stuck in an impasse or dilemma
- Suffering an injustice at work
- Losing out to someone else
- Being personally attacked[61]

As someone once said, "If you're not making mistakes, then you're not learning." Nike, for example, is a successful athletic apparel company because its managers learn from their mistakes and hard knocks:

In the mid-80s, Nike ordered a bowling shoe with nonslip soles—perfect for flinging your body, along with the ball, into the gutter. When the company entered the women's apparel market, its first commercial featured triathlete Joanne Ernst telling women, "It wouldn't hurt to stop eating like a pig." (The joke didn't go over well.) Forays into the golf and skateboarding worlds in the mid-90s similarly misfired. Its first golf product, basically leather shoes with spikes drilled in, was so uncomfortable that embarrassed Nike staffers dubbed it "air-blister."...

Former Nike advertising VP Scott Bedbury ... says the key to the company's success is its willingness to embrace "a culture of screw-ups. It does learn from its mistakes."[62]

How Can Future Managers Learn to Manage?

As indicated in Figure 1.6, students can learn to manage by integrating theory and practice and observing role models. Theory can help you systematically analyze, interpret, and internalize the managerial significance of practical experience and observations.[63] Although formal training and education contributed only 20 percent to the Honeywell managers' knowledge, they nonetheless can provide needed conceptual foundations. Returning to our bicycle example, a cross-country trip on a high-tech bike requires more than the mere ability to ride a bike. It requires a sound

BEST PRACTICES

What Mountain Climbing Has Taught Jean Halloran About Good Management

High on Alaska's Mount McKinley, Jean Halloran and five climbing partners hunkered down in foul weather and waited for a chance to push to the 20,320-foot summit. They passed their time in the tent by brewing tea and reading. With all their gear, a climbing team can only carry a few books. During bivouacs, one person reads the first couple hundred pages of a book, rips them out and hands them to the next person. Books are shared like water, food, work, success and defeat.

"I've done a ton of mountaineering, and you become conscious that you cannot waste extra energy doing unnecessary stuff," explains Halloran, citing the use of books as an example. "You need to conserve your strength so you have enough to go from your high camp to the summit. The point is to stay focused. You can't carry extra stuff."

Halloran is senior vice president of HR [human resources] at Agilent Technologies Inc., a measurement technology company based in Santa Clara, Calif. She has a bachelor's degree in art history from Princeton and an MBA from Harvard Business School, and she studied at Oxford University. Yet mountaineering, not art or academics, is her analogy: "On the mountain, you threaten the success of meeting your goal if you carry superfluous stuff. It's the same in business. You avoid what slows you down and is distracting."

Share the load, avoid the superfluous and stay focused—these are among the principles from mountaineering that Halloran, one of Silicon Valley's most highly regarded HR executives, applies in guiding the development of nearly 19,000 employees, a diverse global mix of scientific, engineering and business talent.

Source: Excerpted from Bill Roberts, "HR at the Summit," HR Magazine, 52 (June 2007): 52–56. Copyright © 2007 by Society For Human Resource Management (SHRM). Reproduced with permission of Society for Human Resource Management (SHRM) in the format Textbook via Copyright Clearance Center.

foundation of knowledge about bicycle maintenance and repair, weather and road conditions, and road safety. So, too, new managers who have a good idea of what lies ahead can go farther and faster with fewer foolish mistakes. Learning valuable lessons in the school of hard knocks is inevitable. But you can foresee and avoid at least some of the knocks.

Ideally, an individual acquires theoretical knowledge and practical experience at the same time, perhaps through work-study programs or internships. Usually, though, full-time students get a lot of theory and little practice. This is when simulated experience and real experience become important. If you are a serious management student, you will put your newly acquired theories into practice wherever and whenever possible (for example, in organized sports; positions of leadership in fraternities, sororities, or clubs; part-time and summer jobs; and internships).[64] What really matters is your personal integration of theory and practice.[65] (See Best Practices.)

FIGURE **1.6** Acquiring the Ability to Manage by Merging Theory and Practice

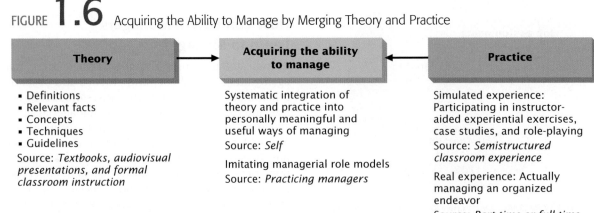

Theory	Acquiring the ability to manage	Practice
• Definitions • Relevant facts • Concepts • Techniques • Guidelines Source: *Textbooks, audiovisual presentations, and formal classroom instruction*	Systematic integration of theory and practice into personally meaningful and useful ways of managing Source: *Self* Imitating managerial role models Source: *Practicing managers*	Simulated experience: Participating in instructor-aided experiential exercises, case studies, and role-playing Source: *Semistructured classroom experience* Real experience: Actually managing an organized endeavor Source: *Part-time or full-time employment as a manager*

SMALL-BUSINESS MANAGEMENT

Small businesses have been called the "engine" of the U.S. economy. Consider, for example, the evolution of Wal-Mart. It began in 1945 as a single discount store in Arkansas run by Sam and Helen Walton.[66] Wal-Mart is now the largest company in the world, with annual revenues exceeding $351 *billion* and over 1.9 *million* employees.[67] Small businesses often are too small to attract much media attention, but collectively they (and their counterparts in other countries) are a huge and vibrant part of the global economy. As evidence, consider these facts about the millions of small businesses in the United States.

- Businesses with less than 500 employees make up 99.7 percent of all businesses and employ 50 percent of the civilian workforce.[68]
- Each year they account for more than one-quarter of the nation's $1.4 trillion in business capital investment.[69]

Interestingly, about 60 percent of them are "microbusinesses" with fewer than five employees, typically operating out of the owner's home[70] (1 out of every 13 workers in the United States is self-employed).[71] Free-enterprise capitalism is a rough-and-tumble arena where anyone can play, but only the very best survive.

1f Got a Good Business Idea? You've Got 45 Seconds

According to new-venture expert Elton B. Sherwin Jr., entrepreneurs who are trying to raise venture capital should be able to answer these "Seven Sacred Questions" in 45 seconds:

1. What is your product?
2. Who is the customer?
3. Who will sell it?
4. How many people will buy it?
5. How much will it cost to design and build?
6. What is the sales price?
7. When will you break even?

Source: Marc Ballon, "Hot Tips," Inc., 21 (April 1999): 104.

QUESTION:

Can you pass this 45-second test with your idea for a new business? Give details.

The only guaranteed result for those starting their own business is that they will be tested to their limit.

Few would dispute the facts and claims cited above, but agreement on the definition of a small business is not so easily reached. The many yardsticks used to distinguish small from large businesses include number of employees, level of annual sales, amount of owner's equity, and total assets. For our present purposes, a **small business** is defined as an independently owned and managed profit-seeking enterprise employing fewer than 100 people. (If the small business is incorporated, the owner/manager owns a significant proportion of the firm's stock.)

> **small business:** an independently owned and managed profit-seeking enterprise with fewer than 100 employees

The health of every nation's economy depends on how well its small businesses are managed. To get a better grasp of the realm of small-business management, we will clear up two common misconceptions, explore small-business career options, and discuss entrepreneurship.

Exploding Myths About Small Business

Mistaken notions can become accepted facts if they are repeated often enough. Such is the case with failure rates and job creation for small businesses. Fortunately, recent research sets the record straight.

THE 80-PERCENT-FAILURE-RATE MYTH. An often-repeated statistic says that four out of five small businesses will fail within five years.[72] This 80 percent casualty rate is a frightening prospect for anyone thinking about starting a business. But a study by Bruce A. Kirchhoff of the New Jersey Institute of Technology found the failure rate for small businesses to be *only 18 percent during their first eight years.*[73] Why the huge disparity? It turns out that studies by the U.S. government and others defined business failures much too broadly. Any closing of a business, even if it occurred because someone died, sold the business, or retired, was recorded as a business failure. In fact, only 18 percent of the 814,000 small businesses tracked by Kirchhoff for eight years went out of business with unpaid bills. This should be a comfort to would-be entrepreneurs.

THE LOW-WAGE-JOBS MYTH. When it came to creating jobs during the 1980s and 1990s, America's big businesses were put to shame by their small and mid-size counterparts. Eighty percent of the new job growth was generated by the smaller companies; massive layoffs were the norm at big companies.[74] Critics, meanwhile,

Entrepreneurs are driven by the mantra "Find a need and fill it (profitably)." Malaysian-born Shoba Purushothaman detected a need among news outlets for fast, high-quality video footage. Now, as CEO of her own company, NewsMarket, she provides free Web-based video feeds to broadcasters. Corporations and government agencies pay her fees, which range up to $100,000, to get their news footage on the air.

claimed that most of the new jobs in the small-business sector went to low-paid clerks and hamburger flippers. Such was not the case, according to a Cambridge, Massachusetts, study by researcher David Birch.

After analyzing new jobs created in the United States between 1987 and 1992, Birch found that businesses with fewer than 100 employees had indeed created most new jobs. Surprisingly, however, only 4 percent of those small firms produced 70 percent of that job growth.[75] Birch calls these rapidly growing small companies "gazelles," as opposed to the "mice" businesses that tend to remain very small. For the period studied, the gazelles added more high-paying jobs than big companies eliminated. Gazelles are not mom-and-pop operations. They tend to be computer software, telecommunications, and specialized engineering or manufacturing firms.[76] Thus, although small businesses on average pay less than big companies do and are about half as likely to offer health insurance benefits, they are *not* low-wage havens.[77]

Again, as in the case of failure rates, the truth about the prospects of starting or working for a small company is different—and brighter—than traditional fallacies suggest.

Career Opportunities in Small Business

Among the five small-business career options listed in Table 1.2, only franchises require definition. The other four are self-defining.[78] A franchise is a license to sell another company's products and/or to use another company's name in business. Familiar franchise operations include McDonald's, the National Basketball Association, and Holiday Inn.[79] Notice how each of the career options in Table 1.2 has positive and negative aspects. There is no one best option. Success in the small-business sector depends on the right combination of money, talent, hard work, luck, and opportunity.[80] Fortunately, career opportunities in small business are virtually unlimited.

Entrepreneurship

According to experts on the subject, "**entrepreneurship** is the process by which individuals—either on their own or inside organizations—pursue opportunities without regard to the resources they currently control."[81] In effect, entrepreneurs look beyond current resource constraints when they envision new possibilities. Entrepreneurs are preoccupied with "how to" rather than "why not." Entrepreneurs, as we discuss next, are risk takers—and all they want is a chance.

entrepreneurship: process of pursuing opportunities without regard to resources currently under one's control

1g What Is Your Tolerance for Risk?

Reed Hastings, founder and CEO of Netflix:

I was a Peace Corps volunteer right out of college in rural Africa, in Swaziland. Either that developed my risk tolerance or it was symptomatic of it. But once you have hitchhiked across Africa with ten bucks in your pocket, starting a business doesn't seem too intimidating.

Source: As quoted in Matthew Boyle, "Questions for . . . Reed Hastings," Fortune (May 28, 2007): 30.

QUESTIONS:
What accounts for your high, moderate, or low tolerance for risk? What impact would that tendency have on starting your own business?

A TRAIT PROFILE FOR ENTREPRENEURS. Exactly how do entrepreneurs differ from general managers or administrators? According to the trait profiles in Table 1.3, entrepreneurs tend to be high achievers who focus more on future possibilities, external factors, and technical details. Also, compared with general administrators, entrepreneurs are more comfortable with ambiguity and risk taking. It is important to note that entrepreneurs are not necessarily better or worse than other managers—they are just different.

Jeff Bezos, the founder and CEO of Amazon.com, had this to say in a recent interview with *Inc.* magazine:

Entrepreneurship is really more about a state of mind than it is about working for yourself. It's about being resourceful, it's about problem solving. If you meet people who seem like really good problem solvers, step back, and you'll see that they are self-reliant. I spent summers on my grandfather's ranch, in a small town in Texas; from age four to 16 I probably missed only two summers. One of the things that you learn in a rural area like that is self-reliance. People do everything themselves . . . . If something is broken, let's fix it.[82]

Bezos instructively calls himself a "realistic optimist." He explains:

I believe that optimism is an essential quality for doing anything hard—entrepreneurial endeavors or anything else. That doesn't mean that you're blind or unrealistic, it means that you keep focused on eliminating your risks, modifying your strategy, until it is a strategy about which you can be genuinely optimistic.[83]

Guy Kawasaki, a California venture capitalist and author of the book *The Art of the Start,* offers a slightly different portrait of the entrepreneur: "It's confidence; it's also a little bit of denial. Part of being an entrepreneur is ignoring things too, because if you listen to all the naysayers, no one would ever start a company."[84]

TABLE 1.2 Career Opportunities in Small Business

SMALL-BUSINESS CAREER OPTIONS	CAPITAL REQUIREMENTS	LIKELIHOOD OF STEADY PAYCHECK	DEGREE OF PERSONAL CONTROL	ULTIMATE FINANCIAL RETURN
1. Become an independent contractor/consultant	Low to moderate	None to low	Very high	Negative to high
2. Take a job with a small business	None	Moderate to high	Low to moderate	Low to moderate
3. Join or buy a small business owned by your family	Low to high	Low to high	Low to high	Moderate to high
4. Purchase a franchise	Moderate to high	None to moderate	Moderate to high	Negative to high
5. Start your own small business	Moderate to high	None to moderate	High to very high	Negative to very high

TABLE 1.3   Contrasting Trait Profiles for Entrepreneurs and Administrators

ENTREPRENEURS TEND TO	ADMINISTRATORS TEND TO
Focus on envisioned futures	Focus on the established present
Emphasize external/market dimensions	Emphasize internal/cost dimensions
Display a medium to high tolerance for ambiguity	Display a low to medium tolerance for ambiguity
Exhibit moderate to high risk-taking behavior	Exhibit low to moderate risk-taking behavior
Obtain motivation from a need to achieve	Obtain motivation from a need to lead others (i.e., social power)
Possess technical knowledge and experience in the innovative area	Possess managerial knowledge and experience

Source: Philip D. Olson, "Choices for Innovation-Minded Corporations," The Journal of Business Strategy, 11 (January–February 1990): Exhibit 1, p. 44. Reprinted from Journal of Business Strategy (New York: Warren, Gorham & Lamont). © 1990 Warren, Gorham & Lamont Inc. Used with permission.

ENTREPRENEURSHIP HAS ITS LIMITS. Many successful entrepreneurs have tripped over a common stumbling block. Their organizations outgrow the entrepreneur's ability to manage them. In fact, according to "a poll by PricewaterhouseCoopers, about 40% of CEOs at the fastest-growing companies said that their own ability to manage or reorganize their business could be an impediment to growth."[85] Some refer to this problem as "founder's disease."

1h What Comes First, People or Product?

Advice for entrepreneurs from best-selling author and mountain climber Jim Collins:

First figure out your partners, then figure out what ideas to pursue. The most important thing isn't the market you target, the product you develop, or the financing, but the founding team. Starting a company is like scaling an unclimbed face—you don't know what the mountain will throw at you, so you must pick the right partners, who share your values, on whom you can depend, and who can adapt.

Source: As quoted in Matthew Boyle, "Questions for Jim Collins," Fortune (February 19, 2007): 50.

QUESTION:
Is Collins right, or should an entrepreneur follow the more typical advice to start with an unmet customer need or a great new product idea?

Moreover, entrepreneurs generally feel stifled by cumbersome and slow-paced bureaucracies. One management consultant praised Microsoft's Bill Gates for knowing his limits in this regard:

In January [2000], Gates went from being CEO of the multibillion-dollar business he cofounded to naming himself "chief software architect" and handing over executive responsibility for his company to Steve Ballmer…. few people recognized it for what I think it was: a courageous leap into a self-esteem-threatening black hole.[86]

The trick, according to a recent study of great entrepreneurs such as Southwest Airlines' Herb Kelleher, is for company founders to keep some psychological distance between themselves and their companies:

… it's all in their heads. It's their ability to avoid thinking of themselves as one with their companies. "The most successful entrepreneurs think of their companies as a separate entity from themselves," says Nancy Koehn, a historian of entrepreneurship who is a professor at Harvard Business School. "It's incongruous, but they have a sense that if they have done their work well, the proof will be in their companies outgrowing, outpacing—and even outliving—them."[87]

Entrepreneurs who launch successful and growing companies face a tough dilemma: either grow with the company or have the courage to step aside and turn the reins over to professional managers who possess the administrative traits needed, such as those listed in Table 1.3.

SUMMARY

1. Formally defined, *management* is the process of working with and through others to achieve organizational objectives in a changing environment. Central to this process is the effective and efficient use of limited resources. An inability to work with people, not a lack of technical skills, is the main reason why some managers fail to reach their full potential. A manager is *effective* if he or she reaches a stated objective and *efficient* if limited resources are not wasted in the process.

2. Five overarching sources of change affecting the way management is practiced today are *globalization* (increased global commerce; controversy over offshoring of jobs to low-wage countries; greater need for global managers who can work effectively across cultures), *the evolution of product quality* (moving away from fix-it-in and inspect-it-in approaches; moving toward build-it-in and design-it-in approaches; emphasis on continuous improvement), *environmentalism* (greater emphasis on making money without destroying the natural environment; many profit opportunities in cleaning up the environment), *an ethical reawakening* (the public's low opinion of managers' ethical conduct is spurring renewed emphasis on honesty and ethical behavior), and *e-business on the Internet* (thanks to the Internet and the Web, e-commerce—buying and selling things over the Web—has evolved into e-business—using the Web to run the entire business).

3. Two ways to answer the question "What do managers do?" are the functional approach and the skills approach. *Managerial functions* generally describe *what* managers do, whereas *managerial skills* state in specific behavioral terms *how* they carry out those functions. This text is organized around eight managerial functions: planning, decision making, organizing, staffing, communicating, motivating, leading, and controlling.

4. Clark Wilson's three managerial skill categories are technical, teambuilding, and drive. His 30 years of research have uncovered an imbalance in managerial skills. About one-third of managers at all levels attempt to exercise control without first applying their technical and teambuilding skills. Thus, managers need to strive for an effective balance of skills.

5. Honeywell researchers found that managers learned 50 percent of what they know about managing from job assignments ("the school of hard knocks"). The remaining 50 percent of their management knowledge came from relationships (30 percent) and formal training and education (20 percent). A good foundation in management theory can give management students a running start and help them avoid foolish mistakes.

6. *Small businesses* (independently owned and managed profit-seeking companies with fewer than 100 employees) are central to a healthy economy. Contrary to conventional wisdom, 80 percent of new businesses do not fail within five years. In fact, one large study found only an 18 percent failure rate during the first eight years. The belief that small businesses create only low-wage jobs also has been shown to be a myth. Five career opportunities in the small-business sector are (1) becoming an independent contractor/consultant; (2) going to work for a small business; (3) joining or buying your family's business; (4) buying a franchise; and (5) starting your own business. Compared with general administrators, entrepreneurs tend to be high achievers who are more future-oriented, externally focused, ready to take risks, and comfortable with ambiguity.

TERMS TO UNDERSTAND

- **Management**, p. 5
- **Effectiveness**, p. 7
- **Efficiency**, p. 7
- **Offshoring**, p. 8
- **Internet**, p. 12
- **e-business**, p. 12
- **Managerial functions**, p. 13
- **Managerial skills**, p. 13
- **Small business**, p. 19
- **Entrepreneurship**, p. 20

MANAGER'S TOOLKIT

Career Tips for Today's and Tomorrow's Managers

How to Find the *Right* Job

1. **Assess yourself.**
   "Job seekers need to emphasize the things they do best," says Diane Wexler of Career Transition Management in Palo Alto, California. Wexler takes clients through a process of examining goals, interests, skills, and resources. Questions include: What are the 20 things you love to do, both alone and with others? What are the roles you fill, and which aspects would you like to incorporate into a career?

2. **Draft a mission statement.**
   Just as a company writes and adheres to a mission statement, create one for yourself. Thinking about your mission and putting it on paper will help define your job search.

3. **Brainstorm.**
   Ask others about what your ideal job would be, and how you should go about landing that position. Nancy Nagel invited eight people with a variety of interests and careers to dinner. "I got these great ideas, ranging from being a talk show host to leading adventure travel," she says. "I ended up tossing most of them out, but the session reminded me that there was a great big world out there."

4. **Network.**
   Conduct informational interviews. Yes, call those friends-of-friends and ask them for a few minutes of their time. Be prepared with some thoughtful questions.

5. **Research companies.**
   Job seekers often accept positions without adequately researching their employers, says Valerie Frankel, co-author of the *I Hate My Job Handbook*. "Inevitably, after a year or two, the job becomes intolerable," she says. Before talking to anyone at a company, research its history, values, and priorities.

6. **Be aware of your abilities and the realities of work.**
   "We have this entitlement problem, that we expect to be completely satisfied with our jobs," says Frankel. "I help people be humble when it comes to their job search," adds Elissa Sheridan of BSR. "You can't walk in with a BA or even an MBA and expect someone to be excited by your background without practical experience."

Source: *Excerpted from Mary Scott, "Finding the Perfect Job,"* Business Ethics, *10 (March–April 1996): 16. Reprinted with permission from Business Ethics Magazine, 52 South 10th Street, #110, Minneapolis, Minnesota 55403 (612-962-4700).*

Secrets to Success Once You've Found the Right Job

Investor's Business Daily has spent years analyzing leaders and successful people in all walks of life. Most have ten traits that, when combined, can turn dreams into reality.

1. How you think is everything. Always be positive. Think success, not failure. Beware of a negative environment.

2. Decide upon your true dreams and goals. Write down your specific goals and develop a plan to reach them.

3. Take action. Goals are nothing without action. Don't be afraid to get started now. Just do it.

4. Never stop learning. Go back to school or read books. Get training and acquire skills.

5. Be persistent and work hard. Success is a marathon, not a sprint. Never give up.

6. Learn to analyze details. Get all the facts, all the input. Learn from your mistakes.

7. Focus your time and money. Don't let other people or things distract you.

8. Don't be afraid to innovate; be different. Following the herd is a sure way to mediocrity.

9. Deal and communicate with people effectively. No person is an island. Learn to understand and motivate others.

10. Be honest and dependable; take responsibility. Otherwise, Numbers 1–9 won't matter.

Source: *"IBD's 10 Secrets to Success,"* Investor's Business Daily *(June 8, 2000): A4. © 2005 Investor's Business Daily, Inc. Reprinted with permission. All rights reserved. This material is protected by United States copyright law and may not be reproduced, distributed or displayed without the prior written permission of Investor's Business Daily, Inc.*

ACTION LEARNING EXERCISE

Do You Have the Right Stuff to Be an Entrepreneur?

Instructions: Entrepreneurship isn't just about a good business idea. It's a matter of temperament. Some have it, some don't. Do you? Test yourself. And be honest; there are no "right" answers.

1. Where do you think you'll be in 10 years' time?
   a. I don't think that far ahead; my short-term goals are clear, though.
   b. I have a career path in mind, and I'm going to stick to it.
   c. I live and work from day to day.
   d. I know where I want to be and have ideas on how to get there, but if a better idea comes along, I'll take it.

2. How would you describe your attitude toward competition?
   a. I relish it. Winning isn't everything, it's the only thing.
   b. I avoid it. Competition brings out the worst in people.
   c. I compete hard when I have to, but have been known to bluff my rivals.
   d. I compete hard, but my eye is always on the pay-off.

3. Your boss says, "That's the way we do things here." How do you react?
   a. I respect established procedures, but I know when to ignore them.
   b. I begin to think I should be working somewhere else.
   c. I accept it and proceed accordingly. After all, I want to keep my job.
   d. I may try to change his mind, but if I don't succeed quickly, I'll go along.

4. Which statement comes closest to describing your personal finances?
   a. My checkbook is always balanced, and I pay my bills when they come in.
   b. I have an interest-bearing bank account, and I wait until the end of the statement period to pay my bills. That way the bank doesn't get the interest.
   c. I have multiple credit cards, and every one of them is about maxed out.
   d. I separate my business and personal expenses by using different credit cards.

5. What gives you the greatest personal satisfaction at work?

   a. Having an idea and being allowed to run with it.
   b. Receiving praise for a job well done.
   c. Coming out ahead of an office rival.
   d. Knowing my office status is secure.

6. How do you handle criticism at work?
   a. It throws me off track and makes my next task more difficult.
   b. Other perspectives are often helpful, so I listen carefully and adjust if the criticism makes sense to me.
   c. While maintaining my dignity, I try to shift at least some of the blame to others.
   d. I don't like it, but what can I do? I absorb the criticism and move on.

7. What's best about your current job?
   a. My salary and perks. I do OK compared with people like me.
   b. The fine reputation of my company.
   c. I enjoy a certain amount of freedom to start my own projects.
   d. I get regular promotions, and there's a clear career path to the top.

8. Which statement best describes your attitude toward your projects at work?
   a. I like to start projects, but I tend to lose interest and delegate things to other people.
   b. I find myself moving on to new projects before I finish the current one.
   c. I always finish what I start. Personally.
   d. I've been known to put a project on hold if I run into difficulties.

9. How much time do you typically invest in your projects at work?
   a. I take pride in being on schedule, so I put in however many hours it takes. Then I take a breather.
   b. I work hard, but sometimes I'll take a day or two off in mid-project.
   c. I'm pretty much a 9-to-5er.
   d. My work is my life.

10. If you had what you thought was a good idea for a start-up, how would you finance it?
    a. A loan. That's why banks exist.
    b. To hold down my exposure, I'd hit up friends and family.
    c. I'd take out a second mortgage on my house.
    d. I'd *sell* my house if it came to that.

Scoring: Add up your score, using the following key.

1. a-2   b-3   c-1   d-4
2. a-3   b-1   c-2   d-4
3. a-3   b-4   c-1   d-2
4. a-1   b-3   c-4   d-2
5. a-4   b-2   c-3   d-1
6. a-1   b-4   c-3   d-2
7. a-2   b-1   c-4   d-3
8. a-2   b-3   c-4   d-1
9. a-4   b-2   c-1   d-3
10. a-1   b-2   c-3   d-4

Results

10 TO 19 POINTS
You are probably a responsible employee, but not a self-starter. You wait to be assigned tasks. Security is important to you. Your tolerance of risk is relatively low. You may derive too much of your sense of self-worth from factors outside yourself, such as the prestige of the company you work for. Stay put.

20 TO 29 POINTS
You are capable of initiative, even if it doesn't seem that way. You try to advance your career, but are careful not to offend people along the way. You understand office politics, but are reluctant to make bold moves. If you aren't already in middle management, you may be a good candidate.

30 TO 35 POINTS
Lack of ambition is not one of your shortcomings. Neither is a willingness to work hard, and outside normal office hours. You may, however, be somewhat impatient, and reluctant to seek advice from others. These are not good qualities in an entrepreneur. Go for top management instead.

36 TO 40 POINTS
You have the makings of an excellent entrepreneur. You have a high tolerance for risk—an essential ingredient. You are passionate about your ideas. Equally important, you are able to balance your own ambition with interest in others' thoughts and regard for their feelings. Go for it.

Source: From Newsweek, © 2000, Newsweek, Inc. May 29, 2000. All rights reserved. Used by permission and protected by the Copyright laws of the United States. The printing, copying, redistribution, or retransmission of the Material without express written permission is prohibited.

For Consideration/Discussion

1. Well, do you have the right stuff to be an entrepreneur? Is this a valid assessment tool? Why or why not?

2. Do you know someone who is a successful entrepreneur? If so, how well does the interpretation for an individual scoring 36 to 40 points characterize that person?

3. What would happen if everyone in the business world scored high on this quiz?

4. Is it an insult to score low on this quiz? Explain.

CLOSING CASE

Jennifer Reingold Samples a Day in the Life of a Manager

The lightning bolt wasn't a great sign. My first day on the job, and I was already losing control: A string of emails demanded split-second decisions for problems I had only just heard about; I needed to pull together a business-plan presentation for a product I had never laid eyes on; a rabid reporter lurked outside my door. Then, the single, jagged flash shot across my window. I gulped my Diet Dr Pepper. Maybe I wasn't meant to be an executive after all.

Not that I ever really thought I was. Sure, I've been covering management and leadership for 10 years, lambasting and lionizing executives, dismissing their best-laid plans with a few cutting words and anointing their successors with a few sparkling ones. But my actual experience with leading and managing has remained largely theoretical. Ironic? Sure, but I liked that.

Still, we all have to grow up sometime. So when Richard Wellins, an SVP at human-resources consulting firm Development Dimensions International (DDI), invited me to its intensive one-day "operational executive platform"—a simulation used to screen potential job candidates or identify and develop stars already in-house—I jumped at the chance. Over the course of one full day, I'd make strategic decisions, launch a new product, and deal with the challenges a boss typically faces. I'd be thrown curveballs by company brass, employees, customers, and media alike (all role-played by trained assessors). And then I'd receive an unvarnished evaluation of my work, a kind of psychographic leadership report card.

In the days running up to my visit, I logged on to DDI's Assessing Talent portal, which gave me financial and historical information about my fictitious company, Global Solutions, a robotics shop facing tough times in the year 2025. I also took a series of preliminary psych tests, or "leadership inventories," that would be analyzed in conjunction with my performance. Then I received my pseudo identity: Kelly Myers, a new VP whose predecessor at Global had just been canned.

Kelly and I, it turned out, had our work cut out for us: Margins were falling, inventories were rising, and the Jeeves—a robotic valet—had started doing odd things, such as cooking a client's favorite shoes and breaking into hotel rooms in the middle of the night.

The morning of the big day found me chugging coffee in my hotel room and trying to look the part, when the front desk called up to say my car had arrived. "But they're early!" I spat. "I'll be down when I can!" After I hung up on the poor woman, it occurred to me that I might have already blown my first test. Leadership? Yeah. In boot camp, maybe.

In the glass-skinned Pittsburgh headquarters of DDI, I was shown to my new "office." Ah! The faux-wood desk, the paper clips in the drawer, a suspicious box of tissues (would I be needing those?). A pleasant picture of boats distracted me from the view of the parking lot—and from the video camera recording my every move. I was disappointed to note that the workplace of 2025 was as drab as ever.

My email revealed a host of headaches, including a note about the Jeeves from a furious hotel manager and another from my boss: One of my direct reports was resisting the centralization of the sales and marketing functions. "It is imperative that you gain Marty's buy-in," he wrote.

Kelly and I dove in. First up was Marty, whom I motivated, I felt sure, with a deft application of both carrot and stick. Next came the hostile hotelier: I pulled out all the stops trying to placate her, offering a quick (and possibly nonexistent) fix that included temporarily substituting an earlier-generation robot. "This relationship is critical to our company, and we want to make you happy," I purred, adding an eye roll that was promptly captured by the now-forgotten camera.

I suddenly realized I hadn't gotten a single email in hours. "Oh, dear," said the coordinator. It seems there had been a computer glitch, not part of the simulation. When I rebooted, a good dozen emails lay festering in my inbox: Design an agenda for our off-site! Decide whether to move a guy from Asia to the inventory-reduction task force—today! Determine why all of our new-hire MBAs are quitting! Write a business plan by 4 P.M.! And, oh, by the way, you have a TV interview to address concerns that one of our security robots caused a teenager's death.

It was at about this time that the lightning bolt struck. "Not fair," I whined to myself, pining for my messy desk, my writer's block. No time for that now, though—I had a dead teenager on my hands. At least the interview would be a breeze, I figured, given my day job in real life. But when I tried to stay cool, explaining our position on the "unfortunate event," the jerk kept putting words in my mouth.

The rest of the day was a blur. More vile emails. An inspirational voice mail I had to record to introduce Kelly to the staff (in a brilliant, if unauthorized, initiative, I announced $1,000-to-$25,000 bonuses to anyone with "ideas that help the company"). I swore a lot under my breath. And then it was time for the business-plan presentation. Without a clue about how to crunch the production numbers, I had opted to concentrate on the marketing side of the Jeeves product launch—and to talk so much that my boss wouldn't miss the margin calculations or the ad budget. Amazingly, he actually seemed to buy it.

I left feeling like the white-collar equivalent of Lucille Ball in the chocolate factory. I didn't think I had been a complete loser, but that just raised the question: If this ink-stained—and un-trained—wretch could pass for management material, wasn't this whole exercise suspect? Could it really be worth the $4,000 to $12,000 that more than 1,000 companies have ponied up for DDI's full- or half-day assessments?

Kelly and I cuddled up together in the hotel for a brain-dead evening of reality TV, then returned to DDI the next morning for our results. . . .

To my delight and horror, the tests nailed me cold. My passion for new and different challenges, my hardworking, ambitious side, my love of socializing and interacting with others—all there. But so, too, were my tendency to get snappish at stressful moments and my "low interpersonal sensitivity" (i.e., extreme bluntness). DDI doesn't make yes-or-no job recommendations for candidates. Yet I came away with the strange—and somehow disturbing—conclusion that, warts and all, I could, with a lot of practice and probably a lot of therapy, be Kelly Myers. I didn't have much time to think about that, though. Thankfully, I had a story to write.

Source: Excerpted from Jennifer Reingold, "My (Long) Day at the Top," *Fast Company*, no. 106 (June 2006): 64-66. Copyright © 2006 by Mansueto Ventures LLC. Reproduced with permission of Mansueto Ventures LLC in the format Textbook via Copyright Clearance Center.

FOR DISCUSSION

1 How would you rate the effectiveness and efficiency of Jennifer Reingold (AKA Kelly Myers)? Explain.

2 Which of the eight managerial functions are evident in this case? Explain.

3 In what respects is this a manager's typical day?

4 Based on the trait profiles in Table 1.3, did Jennifer Reingold act more like an administrator or an entrepreneur? Explain.

TEST PREPPER

True/False Questions

_____ 1. If a company does not achieve its objective, it is effective but not efficient.

_____ 2. Offshoring is the controversial practice of drilling for oil in the ocean.

_____ 3. With the inspect-it-in approach to improving product quality, the emphasis is on continuous improvement of personnel and processes.

_____ 4. By definition, e-business involves much more than business-to-consumer retailing on the Internet.

_____ 5. Two managerial functions identified by French industrialist Henri Fayol in the early 1900s are planning and control.

_____ 6. One of the three managerial skill categories identified by Clark L. Wilson is leadership.

_____ 7. According to the Honeywell study, managers learned half of what they knew about managing from job assignments (the "school of hard knocks").

_____ 8. Ninety-nine percent of the employers in the United States are small businesses.

_____ 9. Eighty percent of small businesses fail within five years.

_____10. Entrepreneurs tend to be high achievers who dislike ambiguity.

Multiple-Choice Questions

1. Management is the process of working with and through others to achieve _____ in a changing environment.
   A. plans   B. strategies
   C. a mission   D. success
   E. organizational objectives

2. Which of these is(are) always required by organizational objectives or goals?
   A. Management approval   B. Job descriptions
   C. Collective action   D. Financial resources
   E. Information gathering

3. What does "offshoring" involve?
   A. Exporting goods to foreign countries
   B. Outsourcing jobs to lower-wage countries
   C. Hiring recent documented immigrants
   D. Hiring undocumented immigrants
   E. Sending employees on foreign assignments

4. The _____ stage in the evolution of product quality emphasizes _____.
   A. inspect-it-in; staffing and supervision
   B. fix-it-in; quality training
   C. design-it-in; continuous improvement
   D. build-it-in; product redesign
   E. work-it-in; engineering specifications

5. A business using the Internet for greater efficiency in every aspect is called a(n)
   A. global business.   B. integrated business.
   C. small business.   D. high-tech business.
   E. e-business.

6. Which of these functions is commonly referred to as the primary management function?
   A. Planning   B. Leading
   C. Controlling   D. Staffing
   E. Organizing

7. On the basis of his 30 years of research, Clark Wilson has identified the following three managerial skill categories:
   A. motivating, communicating, and leading.
   B. planning, checking, and regulating.
   C. communicating, inspecting, and control.
   D. teambuilding, motivating, and decision making.
   E. technical, teambuilding, and drive.

8. In the Honeywell study, managers learned the *least* (20 percent of what they learned) about managing from
   A. coworkers.
   B. internships.
   C. job assignments.
   D. formal training and education.
   E. role models.

9. Only _____ percent of small businesses tracked by Kirchhoff for _____ years went out of business with unpaid bills.
   A. 50; 5   B. 80; 2
   C. 25; 6   D. 75; 5
   E. 18; 8

10. Entrepreneurship, by definition, is the process by which individuals pursue opportunities without regard to
    A. risk.
    B. plans.
    C. the law.
    D. resources under one's control.
    E. the future.

See page T1 at the back of the text for answers to these questions. Want more questions? Visit the student Web site (see back cover for URL) and take the ACE quizzes for more practice.

2

The Evolution
of Management
Thought

OBJECTIVES

- **Identify** two key assumptions supporting the universal process approach, and briefly **describe** Henri Fayol's contribution.

- **Discuss** Frederick W. Taylor's approach to improving the practice of industrial management.

- **Identify** at least four key quality improvement ideas from W. Edwards Deming and the other quality advocates.

- **Describe** the general aim of the human relations movement, and **explain** the circumstances in which it arose.

- **Explain** the significance of applying open-system thinking to management.

- **Explain** the practical significance of adopting a contingency perspective.

- **Describe** what "management by best seller" involves, and **explain** what managers can do to avoid it.

THE CHANGING WORKPLACE

Craigie Zildjian Carries on a 14-Generation Tradition

The Zildjian Company, based in Norwell, Massachusetts, is the largest cymbal maker in the world and the oldest continuously family run business in the United States. Founded in Turkey in 1623 by Armenian alchemist Avedis Zildjian, the company, with 2006 revenues of $52 million, is now run by 14th-generation descendent Craigie Zildjian, who took the reins from her father in 1999, becoming the first woman to head up the business. We spoke with Zildjian about the challenges of leading her nearly four-century-old company into the future. The following are edited excerpts from that interview.

What's the secret to keeping a centuries-old business on the cutting edge? Many of the things we do are what any good company should do, whether it's thinking one year out or 100. We're guided by our core values—a focus on continuous quality improvement, innovation, craftsmanship, customer collaboration, empowering employees, avoiding complacency, and reinvesting in the company. We don't have a secret formula for our strategy. It's just good management practice. That said, there's no question that our legacy keeps us all focused on preserving the business for the long haul. As my niece Cady, part of the 15th generation, said, "We'd never want to be the ones who have to sell the company."

How do you balance the fear of being "the Zildjian who sold the business" with the need to take risks? A sure way to damage the business would be to stop innovating and risk taking. We have an estimated 65% of the world cymbal market, but that market share isn't a given. We have fierce competitors. So, on the one hand, we preserve the family jewels—the secret formulas we use that go back centuries—but we're always working on product innovations and other improvements. For instance, we introduced the first titanium-coated cymbal as a limited edition line, which was a risky R&D [research and development] project but paid off. And we're in the middle of a major plant expansion that will give us more capacity than we currently need. We're betting on the future.

Does this long-range focus affect how you relate to your customers?

We've always collaborated with customers on products—something a lot of companies are just catching on to now. My grandfather Avedis, who set up the U.S. company in 1929, became good friends with Gene Krupa, Chick Webb, and Papa Jo Jones, and he worked closely with them to develop the modern drum kit. . . . My father was a natural at this type of collaboration. Today, we continue the tradition of bringing artists into the plant so our R&D manager and marketing people can meet directly with them. We also take employees into stores so they can see customers buying Zildjians—and the competition. Careful listening is part of our corporate strategy.

Source: Excerpted from Gardiner Morse, "A Formula for the Future," *Harvard Business Review,* 86 (July–August 2007): p. 23. Reprinted by permission of HBS Publishing.

raigie Zildjian did not start with a blank slate at the company bearing her name. Her family tradition, corporate culture, and way of doing business continue to affect what she can and cannot do to keep Zildjian on the right course. In short, history matters at Zildjian Company. In a parallel sense, that is what this chapter is all about. Management historians believe that a better knowledge of the past will lead to a more productive future. They contend that students of management who fail to understand the evolution of management thought are destined to repeat past mistakes.[2] Moreover, historians and managers alike believe that one needs to know where management has been if one is to understand where it is going. While participating in a Harvard Business School roundtable discussion on the value of management history, a top-level executive put it this way:

> *It is always hard to communicate any sort of abstract idea to someone else, let alone get any acceptance of it. But when there is some agreement on the factual or historical background of that idea, the possibilities for general agreement expand enormously.*[3]

Historians draw a distinction between history and historical perspective. According to one management scholar,

> *Historical perspective is the study of a subject in light of its earliest phases and subsequent evolution. Historical perspective differs from history in that the object of historical perspective is to sharpen one's vision of the present, not the past.*[4]

This chapter qualifies as offering a historical perspective because it is part historical fact and part modern-day interpretation. Various approaches in the evolution of management thought are discussed relative to the lessons each can teach today's managers. The term *evolution* is appropriate here because management theory has developed in bits and pieces through the years. Moreover, pioneering contributors to management theory and practice have come from around the globe[5] (see Figure 2.1). A historical perspective puts these pieces together.

FIGURE **2.1** Management Is a Global Affair: Selected Contributors to Management Theory

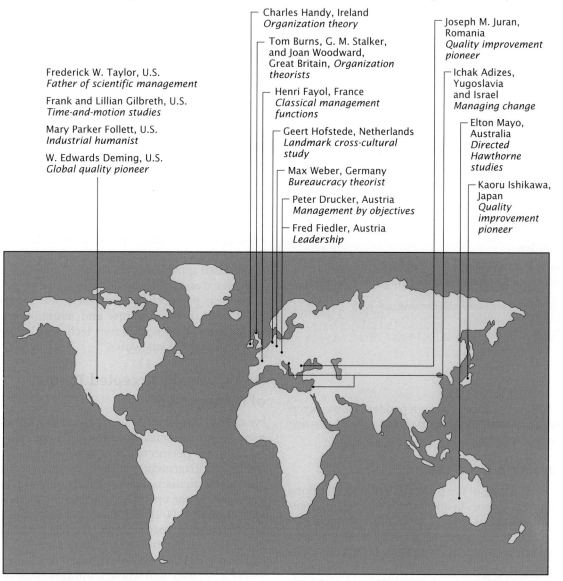

Charles Handy, Ireland
Organization theory

Tom Burns, G. M. Stalker,
and Joan Woodward,
Great Britain, *Organization
theorists*

Henri Fayol, France
*Classical management
functions*

Geert Hofstede, Netherlands
*Landmark cross-cultural
study*

Max Weber, Germany
Bureaucracy theorist

Peter Drucker, Austria
Management by objectives

Fred Fiedler, Austria
Leadership

Frederick W. Taylor, U.S.
Father of scientific management

Frank and Lillian Gilbreth, U.S.
Time-and-motion studies

Mary Parker Follett, U.S.
Industrial humanist

W. Edwards Deming, U.S.
Global quality pioneer

Joseph M. Juran,
Romania
*Quality improvement
pioneer*

Ichak Adizes,
Yugoslavia
and Israel
Managing change

Elton Mayo,
Australia
*Directed
Hawthorne
studies*

Kaoru Ishikawa,
Japan
*Quality
improvement
pioneer*

THE PRACTICE AND STUDY OF MANAGEMENT

The systemic study of management is relatively new. As an area of academic study, management is essentially a product of the twentieth century. Only three universities—Pennsylvania, Chicago, and California—offered business management courses before 1900.[6]

But the actual practice of management has been around for thousands of years. The pyramids of Egypt, for example, stand as tangible evidence of the ancient world's ability to manage. It reportedly took more than 100,000 individuals 20 years to construct the great pyramid honoring the Egyptian king Cheops nearly 5,000 years ago. This remarkable achievement was the result of systematically managed effort. Although the Egyptians' management techniques were crude by modern standards, many problems they faced are still around today. They, like today's managers, had to make plans, obtain and mobilize human and material

2a What About Factual Accuracy?

Apple cofounder Steve Wozniak:

I think it's time to set the record straight. So much of the information out there about me is wrong. I've come to hate books about Apple and its history so much because of that. For instance, there are stories that I dropped out of college (I didn't) or that I was thrown out of the University of Colorado (I wasn't), that Steve [Jobs, Apple's cofounder and CEO,] and I were high school classmates (we were several years apart in school) and that Steve and I engineered those first computers together (I did them alone).

Source: As quoted in a book review by Russ Juskalian, "Wozniak Sets Record Straight with Awkward, Charming Style," USA Today, (October 9, 2006): 5B.

QUESTIONS:

In general, how much do you trust the factual accuracy of historical accounts? What is the best way to get the *real* story?

For further information about the interactive annotations in this chapter, visit our student Web site.

resources, coordinate interdependent jobs, keep records, report their progress, and take corrective action as needed.

Information Overload

Since the building of the pyramids, entire civilizations have come and gone. In one form or another, management was practiced in each. Sadly, during those thousands of years of management experience, one modern element was missing: a systematically recorded body of management knowledge.[7] In early cultures, management was something one learned by word of mouth and by trial and error—not something one studied in school, read about in textbooks and on the Internet, theorized about, experimented with, or wrote about.

Thanks to modern print and electronic media, the collective genius of thousands of management theorists and practitioners has been compressed into a veritable mountain of textbooks, journals, research monographs, microfilms, movies, audio- and videotapes, and computer files. Never before have present and future managers had so much relevant information at their fingertips, as close as a Google search on the Web or the nearest library. As an indication of what is available, a 1990 study identified 54 journals dealing with just the behavioral side of management.[8] There are many, many others (see the Manager's Toolkit section at the end of this chapter). In fact, so much information on management theory and practice exists today that it is difficult, if not impossible, to keep abreast of all of it.[9]

An Interdisciplinary Field

A principal cause of the information explosion in management theory is its interdisciplinary nature. Scholars from many fields—including psychology, sociology, cultural anthropology, mathematics, philosophy, statistics, political science, economics, logistics, computer science, ergonomics, history, and various fields of engineering—have, at one time or another, been interested in management. In addition, administrators in business, government, religious organizations, health care, and education all have drawn from and contributed to the study of management. Each group of scholars and practitioners has interpreted and reformulated management according to its own perspective. With each new perspective have come new questions and assumptions, new research techniques, different technical jargon, and new conceptual frameworks.[10]

No Universally Accepted Theory of Management

We can safely state that no single theory of management is universally accepted today.[11] To provide a useful historical perspective that will guide our study of modern management, we shall discuss five different approaches to management: (1) the universal process approach, (2) the operational approach, (3) the behavioral approach, (4) the systems approach, and (5) the contingency approach. Understanding these general approaches to the theory and practice of management can help you appreciate how management has evolved, where it is today, and where it appears to be headed. Each of the five approaches to management represents a different conceptual framework for better understanding the practice of management. Cornell University professor Craig C. Lundberg explains the practical (and scientific) importance of conceptual frameworks:

When we have a known set of ideas, and the relationships among them are spelled out, we have a conceptual framework, or model. . . . In addition to helping us notice and comprehend something of interest as a frame of reference does, models also enable us to anticipate and discover relevant facts and to better

2b How Do You Handle the Information Overload in *Your* Life?

In a survey, 2,096 employees categorized their workspace habits as follows:

Neat freaks	33%
Pilers	27%
Filers	23%
Pack rats	12%
Slobs	2%
Don't know	3%

Source: Data from Cheryl Comeau-Kirschner, "Neatness Counts for Many Employees," Management Review, 88 (April 1999): 7.

QUESTIONS:

Are you experiencing information overload? Which category best describes your handling of the informational clutter in your life?

understand how things really work. Over time, with continuing experiences and/or confirmation from research, models are modified by being fine-tuned to better and better represent the phenomena of interest, or they are discarded and replaced.[12]

This chapter concludes with some cautionary words about slavishly following sure-fire success formulas in best-selling management books.

THE UNIVERSAL PROCESS APPROACH

The universal process approach is the oldest and one of the most popular approaches to management thought. It is also known as the universalist or functional approach. According to the **universal process approach**, the administration of all organizations, public or private and large or small,

universal process approach: assumes all organizations require the same rational management process

requires the same rational process. The universalist approach is based on two main assumptions. First, although the purpose of organizations may vary (for example, business, government, education, or religion), a core management process remains the same across all organizations. Successful managers, therefore, are assumed to be interchangeable among organizations of differing purpose. (This "universality of management" assumption drove the Pentagon's effort to recruit former corporate CEOs to help rebuild Iraq.)[13] The second assumption is that the universal management process can be reduced to a set of separate functions and related principles. Early universal process writers emphasized the specialization of labor (who does what), the chain of command (who reports to whom), and authority (who is ultimately responsible for getting things done).

Henri Fayol's Universal Management Process

In 1916, at the age of 75, Henri Fayol published his now-classic book *Administration Industrielle et Générale*, although it was not widely known in Britain and the United States until an English translation became available in 1949.[14] Despite its belated appearance in the English-speaking world and despite its having to compete with enthusiastic scientific management and human relations movements in the United States, Fayol's work left a permanent mark on twentieth-century management thinking.

Fayol was first an engineer and later a successful administrator in a large French mining and metallurgical concern, which is perhaps why he did not resort to theory in his pioneering management book. Rather, Fayol was a manager who attempted to translate his broad administrative experience into practical guidelines for the successful management of all types of organizations.

As we mentioned in Chapter 1, Fayol believed that the manager's job could be divided into five functions, or areas, of managerial responsibility—planning, organizing, command, coordination, and control—that are essential to managerial success. (Some educators refer to them as the POC³ functions.) His 14 universal principles of management, listed in Table 2.1, were intended to show managers how to carry out their functional duties. Fayol's functions and principles have withstood the test of time because of their widespread applicability. In spite of years of reformulation, rewording, expansion, and revision, Fayol's original management functions still can be found in nearly all management texts. In fact, after an extensive

TABLE **2.1** Fayol's 14 Universal Principles of Management

1. **Division of work.** Specialization of labor is necessary for organizational success.
2. **Authority.** The right to give orders must accompany responsibility.
3. **Discipline.** Obedience and respect help an organization run smoothly.
4. **Unity of command.** Each employee should receive orders from only one superior.
5. **Unity of direction.** The efforts of everyone in the organization should be coordinated and focused in the same direction.
6. **Subordination of individual interests to the general interest.** Resolving the tug of war between personal and organizational interests in favor of the organization is one of management's greatest difficulties.
7. **Remuneration.** Employees should be paid fairly in accordance with their contribution.
8. **Centralization.** The relationship between centralization and decentralization is a matter of proportion; the optimum balance must be found for each organization.
9. **Scalar chain.** Subordinates should observe the formal chain of command unless expressly authorized by their respective superiors to communicate with each other.
10. **Order.** Both material things and people should be in their proper places.
11. **Equity.** Fairness that results from a combination of kindliness and justice will lead to devoted and loyal service.
12. **Stability and tenure of personnel.** People need time to learn their jobs.
13. **Initiative.** One of the greatest satisfactions is formulating and carrying out a plan.
14. **Esprit de corps.** Harmonious effort among individuals is the key to organizational success.

Source: Adapted from Henri Fayol, General and Industrial Management, *trans. Constance Storrs (London: Isaac Pitman & Sons, 1949). Copyright © 1949 by Lake Publishing Company. Reprinted by permission.*

review of studies of managerial work, a pair of management scholars concluded:

> *The classical functions still represent the most useful way of conceptualizing the manager's job, especially for management education, and perhaps this is why it is still the most favored description of managerial work in current management textbooks. The classical functions provide clear and discrete methods of classifying the thousands of different activities that managers carry out and the techniques they use in terms of the functions they perform for the achievement of organizational goals.*[15]

Lessons from the Universal Process Approach

Fayol's main contribution to management thought was to show how the complex management process can be separated into interdependent areas of responsibility, or functions. Fayol's contention that management is a continuous process beginning with planning and ending with controlling also remains popular today. Contemporary adaptations of Fayol's functions offer students of management a useful framework for analyzing the management process. But as we noted in Chapter 1, this sort of rigid functional approach has been criticized for creating the impression that the management process is more rational and orderly than it really is. Fayol's functions, therefore, form a skeleton that needs to be fleshed out with concepts, techniques, and situational refinements from more modern approaches. The functional approach is useful because it specifies generally what managers *should* do, but the other approaches help explain *why* and *how*.

THE OPERATIONAL APPROACH

The term **operational approach** is a convenient description of the production-oriented area of management dedicated to improving efficiency, cutting waste, and improving quality. Since the turn of the twentieth century, it has had a number of labels, including scientific management, management science, operations research, production management, and operations management. Underlying this somewhat confusing evolution of terms has been a consistent purpose: to

operational approach: production-oriented field of management dedicated to improving efficiency and cutting waste

make person-machine systems work as efficiently as possible. Throughout its historical development, the operational approach has been technically and quantitatively oriented.

Frederick W. Taylor's Scientific Management

Born the son of a Philadelphia lawyer in 1856, Frederick Winslow Taylor was the epitome of the self-made man. Because a temporary problem with his eyes kept him from attending Harvard University, Taylor went to work as a common laborer in a small Philadelphia machine shop. In just four years he picked up the trades of pattern maker and machinist.[16]

Later, Taylor went to work at Midvale Steel Works in Philadelphia, where he quickly moved up through the ranks while studying at night for a mechanical engineering degree. As a manager at Midvale, Taylor was appalled at industry's unsystematic practices. He observed little, if any, cooperation between the managers and the laborers. Inefficiency and waste were rampant. Output restriction among groups of workers, which Taylor called "systematic soldiering," was widespread. Ill-equipped and inadequately trained workers were typically left on their own to determine how to do their jobs. Hence, the father of scientific management committed himself to the relentless pursuit of "finding a better way."[17] Taylor sought nothing less than what he termed a "mental revolution" in the practice of industrial management.[18]

According to an early definition, **scientific management** is "that kind of management which *conducts* a business or affairs by *standards* established by facts or truths gained through *systematic* observation, experiment, or reasoning."[19] The word *experiment* deserves special emphasis because it was Taylor's trademark. While working at Midvale and later at Bethlehem Steel, Taylor started the scientific management movement in industry in four areas: standardization, time and task study, systematic selection and training, and pay incentives.[20]

> **scientific management:** developing performance standards on the basis of systematic observation and experimentation

STANDARDIZATION. By closely studying metal-cutting operations, Taylor collected extensive data on the optimum cutting-tool speeds and the rates at which stock should be fed into the machines for each job. The resulting standards were then posted for quick reference by the machine operators. He also systematically catalogued and stored the expensive cutting tools that usually were carelessly thrown aside when a job was completed. Operators could go to the carefully arranged tool room, check out the right tool for the job at hand, and check it back in when finished. Taylor's approach caused productivity to jump and costs to fall.

Frederick W. Taylor, 1856–1915

TIME AND TASK STUDY. According to the traditional rule-of-thumb approach, there was no "science of shoveling." But after thousands of observations and stopwatch recordings, Taylor detected a serious flaw in the way various materials were being shoveled: each laborer brought his own shovel to work. Taylor knew the company was losing, not saving, money when a laborer used the same shovel for both heavy and light materials. A shovel load of iron ore weighed about 30 pounds, according to Taylor's calculations, whereas a shovel load of rice coal weighed only four pounds. Systematic experimentation revealed that a shovel load of 21 pounds was optimum (permitted the greatest movement of material in a day). Taylor significantly increased productivity by having workers use specially sized and shaped shovels provided by the company—large shovels for the lighter materials and smaller ones for heavier work.

SYSTEMATIC SELECTION AND TRAINING. Although primitive by modern standards, Taylor's experiments with pig iron handling clearly reveal the intent of this phase of scientific management. The task was to lift a 92-pound block of iron (in the steel trade, a "pig"), carry it up an incline (a distance of about 36 feet), and drop it into an open railroad car. Taylor observed that on the average, a pig iron handler moved about 12½ tons in a ten-hour day of constant effort. After careful study, Taylor found that if he selected the strongest men and instructed them in the proper techniques of lifting and carrying the pigs of iron, he could get each man to load 47 tons in a ten-hour day. Surprisingly, this nearly fourfold increase in output was achieved by having the pig iron handlers spend only 43 percent of their time actually hauling iron. The other 57 percent was spent either walking back empty-handed or sitting down. Taylor reported that the laborers liked

2c Piece-Rate Puzzle

Suppose you are a college student about to take a part-time job in the school library. The job involves taking books and bound periodicals from the sorting room and returning them on a hand cart to their proper shelves throughout the library. Library officials have observed that an average of 30 items can be reshelved during one hour of steady effort. You have the option of being paid $9 an hour or 30 cents per item reshelved. The quality of your work will be randomly checked, and 30 cents will be deducted from your pay for each item found to be improperly shelved.

QUESTIONS:

How do you want to be paid? Why? Which pay plan is probably better for the library? Why?

improved productivity. Under traditional piece-rate plans, an individual received a fixed amount of money for each unit of output. Thus, the greater the output, the greater the pay. In his determination to find a better way, Taylor attempted to improve the traditional piece-rate scheme with his differential piece-rate plan.

Figure 2.2 illustrates the added incentive effect of Taylor's differential plan. (The amounts are typical rates of pay in Taylor's time.) Under the traditional plan, a worker would receive a fixed amount (for example, 5 cents) for each unit produced. Seventy-five cents would be received for producing 15 units and $1.00 for 20 units. In contrast, Taylor's plan required that a time study be carried out to determine the company's idea of a fair day's work. Two piece rates were then put into effect. A low rate would be paid if the worker finished the day below the company's standard, a high rate if the day's output met or exceeded the standard. As the lines in Figure 2.2 indicate, a hard worker who produced 25 units would earn $1.25 under the traditional plan and $1.50 under Taylor's plan.

Taylor's Followers

Among the many who followed in Taylor's footsteps, Frank and Lillian Gilbreth and Henry L. Gantt stand out.

FRANK AND LILLIAN GILBRETH. Inspired by Taylor's time studies and motivated by a desire to expand human potential, the Gilbreths turned motion study into an exact science. In so doing, they pioneered the use of motion pictures for studying and streamlining work motions. They paved the way for modern work simplification by cataloguing 17 different hand motions, such as "grasp" and "hold." These they called "therbligs" (the name *Gilbreth* spelled backwards with

the new arrangement because they were less fatigued and took home 60 percent more pay.

Management historians recently have disputed Taylor's pig iron findings, suggesting his conclusions were unfounded and/or exaggerated.[21] As mentioned earlier, our present historical perspective is an evolving blend of fact and interpretation.

PAY INCENTIVES. According to Taylor, "What the workmen want from their employers beyond anything else is high wages."[22] This "economic man" assumption led Taylor to believe that piece rates were important to

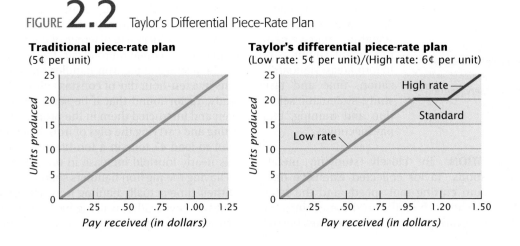

FIGURE **2.2** Taylor's Differential Piece-Rate Plan

illian M. Gilbreth, 1878–1972, at right, and Frank B. Gilbreth, 1868–1924, at left, with 11 of their dozen children.

the *t* and *h* reversed). Their success stories include the following:

> *In laying brick, the motions used in laying a single brick were reduced from eighteen to five—with an increase in output, from one hundred and twenty bricks an hour to three hundred and fifty an hour, and with a reduction in the resulting fatigue. In folding cotton cloth, twenty to thirty motions were reduced to ten or twelve, with the result that instead of one hundred and fifty dozen pieces of cloth, four hundred dozen were folded, with no added fatigue.*[23]

Frank and Lillian Gilbreth were so dedicated to the idea of finding the one best way to do every job that 2 of their 12 children wrote *Cheaper by the Dozen*, a humorous recollection of scientific management and motion study applied to the Gilbreth household.[24]

HENRY L. GANTT. Gantt, a schoolteacher by training, contributed to scientific management by refining production control and cost control techniques. As illustrated in Chapter 6, variations of Gantt's work-scheduling charts are still in use today.[25] He also humanized Taylor's differential piece-rate system by combining a guaranteed day rate (minimum wage) with an above-standard bonus. Gantt was ahead of his time in emphasizing the importance of the human factor

Henry L. Gantt, 1861–1919

and in urging management to concentrate on service rather than profits.[26]

The Quality Advocates

Today's managers readily attach strategic importance to quality improvement. The road to this enlightened view, particularly for U.S. managers, was a long and winding one. It started in factories and eventually made its way through service businesses, not-for-profit organizations, and government agencies. An international cast of quality advocates took much of the twentieth century to pave the road to quality. Not until 1980, when NBC ran a television documentary titled *If Japan Can . . . Why Can't We?* did Americans begin to realize fully that *quality* was a key to Japan's growing dominance in world markets. Advice from the following quality advocates finally began to sink in during the 1980s.[27]

WALTER A. SHEWHART. A statistician for Bell Laboratories, Shewhart introduced the concept of statistical quality control in his 1931 landmark text *Economic Control of Quality of Manufactured Product.*

KAORU ISHIKAWA. The University of Tokyo professor advocated quality before World War II and founded the Union of Japanese Scientists and Engineers (JUSE), which became the driving force behind Japan's quality revolution. Ishikawa proposed a preventive approach to quality. His expanded idea of the customer included both *internal and external customers.* Ishikawa's fishbone diagrams, discussed in Chapter 8, remain a popular problem-solving tool to this day.

W. EDWARDS DEMING.   This Walter Shewhart understudy accepted an invitation from JUSE in 1950 to lecture on his principles of statistical quality control. His ideas, detailed later in Chapter 16, went far beyond

what his Japanese hosts expected from a man with a mathematics Ph.D. from Yale. Japanese manufacturers warmly embraced Deming and his unconventional ideas about encouraging employee participation and striving for continuous improvement. His 1986 book *Out of the Crisis* is "a guide to the 'transformation of the style of American management,' which became a bible for Deming disciples."[28]

W. Edwards Deming,
1900–1993

JOSEPH M. JURAN.   Juran's career bore a striking similarity to Deming's. Both were Americans (Juran was a naturalized U.S. citizen born in Romania) schooled in statistics, both strongly influenced Japanese managers via JUSE, and both continued to lecture on quality into their nineties. Thanks to extensive training by the Juran Institute, the concept of internal customers is well established today.[29] Teamwork, partnerships with suppliers, problem solving, and brainstorming are all Juran trademarks. "A specific term associated with Juran is *Pareto analysis,* a technique for separating major problems from minor ones. A Pareto analysis looks for the 20 percent of possible causes that lead to 80 percent of all problems."[30] (The 80/20 rule is discussed in Chapter 6 under the heading "Priorities.")

ARMAND V. FEIGENBAUM.   While working on his doctorate at MIT, Feigenbaum developed the concept of *total quality control.* He expanded on his idea of an organizationwide program of quality improvement in his 1951 book *Total Quality Control.* He envisioned all functions of the business cycle—from purchasing and engineering, to manufacturing and finance, to marketing and service—as necessarily involved in the quest for quality. The *customer,* according to Feigenbaum, is the one who ultimately determines quality.[31]

PHILIP B. CROSBY.   The author of the 1979 best seller *Quality Is Free*, Crosby learned about quality improvement during his up-from-the-trenches career at ITT

(a giant global corporation in many lines of business). His work struck a chord with top managers because he documented the huge cost of having to rework or scrap poor-quality products. He promoted the idea of *zero defects,* or doing it right the first time.[32] (See Ethics: Character, Courage, and Values.)

Lessons from the Operational Approach

Scientific management often appears rather unscientific to those who live in a world of genetic engineering, piloted space flight, industrial robots, the Internet, and laser technology. *Systematic management* might be a more accurate label. Within the context of haphazard, turn-of-the-twentieth-century industrial practices, however, scientific management was indeed revolutionary. Heading the list of its lasting contributions is a much-needed emphasis on promoting production efficiency and combating waste. Today, dedication to finding a better way is more important than ever in view of uneven productivity growth and diminishing resources.

Nevertheless, Taylor and the early proponents of scientific management have been roundly criticized for viewing workers as unidimensional economic beings interested only in more money. These critics fear that scientific management techniques have dehumanized people by making them act like mindless machines. Not all would agree. According to one respected management scholar who feels that Taylor's work is widely misunderstood and unfairly criticized, Taylor actually improved working conditions by reducing fatigue and redesigning machines to fit people. A systematic analysis of Taylor's contributions led this same management scholar to conclude, "Taylor's track record is remarkable. The point is not, as is often claimed, that he was 'right in the context of his time' but is now outdated, but that *most of his insights are still valid today.*"[33]

Contributions by the quality advocates are subject to less debate today. The only question is, Why didn't we listen to them earlier? (See Chapter 16.)

An important post–World War II outgrowth of the operational approach is operations management. Operations management, like scientific management, aims at promoting efficiency through systematic observation and experimentation. However, operations management (sometimes called production/operations management) tends to be broader in scope and application than scientific management was. Whereas scientific management was limited largely to hand labor and machine shops, operations management specialists apply their expertise to all types of production and service operations, such as the purchase and

ETHICS: CHARACTER, COURAGE, AND VALUES

Taking Zero Defects to Heart

Bill George, Harvard Professor and former CEO of medical device maker Medtronic: Several years ago I visited Medtronic's heart-valve factory in southern California, where employees reconfigure valves from pig hearts to replace human heart valves. Because the process is more art than science, it requires extremely skilled workers. On the factory floor I met the top producer, a Laotian immigrant who made a thousand valves a year. When I asked her the key to her process, she looked at me with passion in her eyes and said, "Mr. George, my job is to make heart valves that save lives."

Before I sign my name to a completed valve, I decide whether it is good enough to put in my mother or my son. Unless it meets that standard, it does not pass. If just one of the valves I make is defective, someone may die. To the company 99.9 percent quality may be acceptable, but I could not live with myself if I caused someone's death. But when I go home at night, I fall asleep thinking about the five thousand people who are alive today because of heart valves I made.

Source: Bill George, with Peter Sims, True North: Discover Your Authentic Leadership *(San Francisco: Jossey-Bass, 2007), pp. 180–181.*

FOR DISCUSSION

How can managers foster this kind of ethical passion for excellence among employees whose work is not a life-or-death matter? What sort of self-management techniques would you recommend?

2d The Deming Legacy

Author and management consultant Gary Hamel:

If you asked managers 40 years ago where quality comes from, they would have said it came from either the inspector at the end of the production line or from an artisan who could make beautiful products. Deming sought instead to make quality a systemic capability, everywhere and all the time. He told companies to give ordinary employees the authority to stop a million-dollar production line. They thought he was nuts.

Source: As quoted in David Kirkpatrick, "Innovation Do's & Don'ts," Fortune (September 6, 2004): 239.

QUESTIONS:

So who is ultimately responsible for product quality, according to Deming? Explain your rationale. Why were American managers so reluctant to accept this approach?

storage of materials, energy use, product and service design, work flow, safety, quality control, and data processing. Thus, **operations management** is defined as the process of transforming raw materials, technology, and human talent into useful goods and services.[34] Operations managers could be called the frontline troops in the battle for productivity growth.

> **operations management:** the process of transforming material and human resources into useful goods and services

THE BEHAVIORAL APPROACH

Like the other approaches to management, the behavioral approach has evolved gradually over many years. Advocates of the behavioral approach to management point out that people deserve to be the central focus of organized activity. They believe that successful management depends largely on a manager's ability to understand and work with people who have a variety of backgrounds, needs, perceptions, and aspirations. The progress of this humanistic approach from the human relations movement to modern organizational behavior has greatly influenced management theory and practice.

The Human Relations Movement

The **human relations movement** was a concerted effort among theorists and practitioners to make managers more sensitive to employee needs. It came into being as a result of special circumstances that occurred during the first half of the twentieth century. As illustrated in Figure 2.3, the human relations movement may be compared to the top of a pyramid. Just as the top of a pyramid must be supported, the human relations movement was supported by three very different historical influences: (1) the threat of unionization, (2) the Hawthorne studies, and (3) the philosophy of industrial humanism.

> **human relations movement:**
> an effort to make managers more sensitive to their employees' needs

THREAT OF UNIONIZATION. To understand why the human relations movement evolved, one needs first to appreciate its sociopolitical background. From the late 1800s to the 1920s, American industry grew by leaps and bounds as it attempted to satisfy the many demands of a rapidly growing population. Cheap immigrant labor was readily available, and there was a seller's market for finished goods. Then came the Great Depression in the 1930s, and millions stood in bread lines instead of pay lines. Many held business somehow responsible for the depression, and public sympathy swung from management to labor. Congress consequently began to pass prolabor legislation. When the Wagner Act of 1935 legalized union-management collective bargaining, management began searching for ways to stem the tide of all-out unionization. Early human relations theory proposed an enticing answer: satisfied employees would be less inclined to join unions. Business managers subsequently began adopting morale-boosting human relations techniques in an effort to discourage unionization.

THE HAWTHORNE STUDIES. As the sociopolitical climate changed, a second development in industry took place. Behavioral scientists from prestigious universities began to conduct on-the-job behavior studies. Instead of studying tools and techniques in the scientific management tradition, they focused on people. Practical behavioral research such as the famous Hawthorne studies stirred management's interest in the psychological and sociological dynamics of the workplace.

The Hawthorne studies began in 1924 in a Western Electric plant near Chicago as a small-scale scientific management study of the relationship between light intensity and productivity. Curiously, the performance of a select group of employees tended to improve no matter how the physical surroundings were manipulated. Even when the lights were dimmed to mere moonlight intensity, productivity continued to climb! Scientific management doctrine could not account for what was taking place, and so a team of behavioral science researchers, headed by Elton Mayo, was brought in from Harvard to conduct a more rigorous study.

By 1932, when the Hawthorne studies ended, more than 20,000 employees had participated in one way or another. After extensive interviewing of the subjects, it became clear to researchers that productivity was much less affected by changes in work conditions than by the attitudes of the workers themselves. Specifically, relationships between members of a work

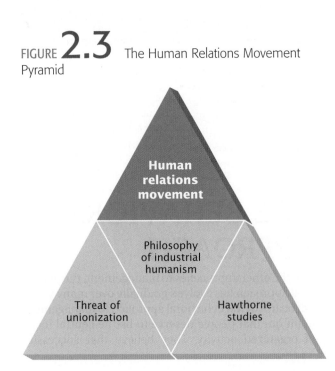

FIGURE **2.3** The Human Relations Movement Pyramid

Elton Mayo, 1880–1949

group and between workers and their supervisors were found to be more significant. Even though the experiments and the theories that evolved from them are criticized today for flawed methodology and statistical inaccuracies, the Hawthorne studies can be credited with turning management theorists away from the simplistic "economic man" model to a more humanistic and realistic view, the "social man" model.[35]

THE PHILOSOPHY OF INDUSTRIAL HUMANISM. Although unionization prompted a search for new management techniques and the Hawthorne studies demonstrated that people were important to productivity, a philosophy of human relations was needed to provide a convincing rationale for treating employees better. Elton Mayo, Mary Parker Follett, and Douglas McGregor, although from very different backgrounds, offered just such a philosophy.

Born in Australia, Elton Mayo was a Harvard professor specializing in psychology and sociology when he took over the Hawthorne studies. His 1933 book *The Human Problems of an Industrial Civilization*, inspired by what he had learned at Hawthorne, cautioned managers that emotional factors were a more important determinant of productive efficiency than physical and logical factors. Claiming that employees create their own unofficial yet powerful workplace culture complete with norms and sanctions, Mayo urged managers to provide work that fostered personal and subjective satisfaction. He called for a new social order designed to stimulate individual cooperation.[36]

Mary Parker Follett's experience as a management consultant and her background in law, political science, and philosophy shaped her strong conviction that managers should be aware that each employee is a complex collection of emotions, beliefs, attitudes, and habits. She believed that managers had to recognize the individual's motivating desires to get employees to work harder. Accordingly, Follett urged managers to motivate performance rather than simply demanding it. Cooperation, a spirit of unity, and self-control were seen as the keys to both productivity and a democratic way of life.[37] Historians credit Follett, who died in 1933, with being decades ahead of her time in terms of behavioral and systems management theory.[38]

Mary Parker Follett, 1868–1933

Her influence as a management consultant in a male-dominated industrial sector was remarkable as well.

A third philosophical rallying point for industrial humanism was provided by an American scholar named Douglas McGregor. In his 1960 classic *The Human Side of Enterprise*, McGregor outlined a set of highly optimistic assumptions about human nature.[39] McGregor viewed the typical employee as an energetic and creative individual who could achieve great things if given the opportunity. He labeled the set of assumptions for this optimistic perspective **Theory Y.**

McGregor's Theory Y assumptions are listed in Table 2.2, along with what he called the traditional Theory X assumptions. These two

> **Theory Y:** McGregor's optimistic assumptions about working people

sets of assumptions about human nature enabled McGregor to contrast the modern, or enlightened, view he recommended (Theory Y) with the prevailing traditional view (Theory X), which he criticized for being pessimistic, stifling, and outdated. Because of its relative recency (compared with Mayo's and Follett's work), its catchy labels, and its intuitive appeal, McGregor's description of Theory X and Theory Y has left an indelible mark on modern management thinking.[40] Some historians have credited McGregor with launching the field of organizational behavior.

Douglas McGregor, 1906–1964

Organizational Behavior

Organizational behavior is a modern approach to management that attempts to determine the causes of human work behavior and to translate the results into effective management techniques. Accordingly, it has a strong research orientation and a robust collection of theories. In fact, a recent review uncovered "73 established organizational behavior theories."[41] Organizational behaviorists have borrowed an assortment of theories and research techniques from all the behavioral sciences and

> **organizational behavior:** a modern approach seeking to discover the causes of work behavior and to develop better management techniques

TABLE **2.2**   McGregor's Theories X and Y

THEORY X: SOME TRADITIONAL ASSUMPTIONS ABOUT PEOPLE	THEORY Y: SOME MODERN ASSUMPTIONS ABOUT PEOPLE
1. Most people dislike work, and they will avoid it when they can.	1. Work is a natural activity, like play or rest.
2. Most people must be coerced and threatened with punishment before they will work. They require close direction.	2. People are capable of self-direction and self-control if they are committed to objectives.
3. Most people prefer to be directed. They avoid responsibility and have little ambition. They are interested only in security.	3. People will become committed to organizational objectives if they are rewarded for doing so.
	4. The average person can learn to both accept and seek responsibility.
	5. Many people in the general population have imagination, ingenuity, and creativity.

have applied them to people at work in modern organizations. The result is an interdisciplinary field in which psychology predominates.[42] In spite of its relatively new and developing state, organizational behavior has had a significant impact on modern management thought by helping to explain why employees behave as they do. Because human relations has evolved into a practical, how-to-do-it discipline for supervisors, organizational behavior amounts to a scientific extension of human relations. Many organizational behavior findings will be examined in Part Four of this text.

Lessons from the Behavioral Approach

Above all else, the behavioral approach makes it clear to present and future managers that *people* are the key to productivity.[43] According to advocates of the behavioral approach, technology, work rules, and standards do not guarantee good job performance. Instead, success depends on motivated and skilled individuals who are committed to organizational objectives.[44] Only a manager's sensitivity to individual concerns can foster the cooperation necessary for high productivity.

On the negative side, traditional human relations doctrine has been criticized as vague and simplistic. According to these critics, relatively primitive on-the-job behavioral research does not justify such broad conclusions. For instance, critics do not believe that supportive supervision and good human relations will lead automatically to higher morale and hence to better job performance. Also, recent analyses of the Hawthorne studies, using modern statistical techniques, have generated debate about the validity of the original conclusions.[45]

Fortunately, organizational behavior, as a scientific extension of human relations, promises to fill in some of the gaps left by human relationists, while at the same time retaining an emphasis on people. Today, organizational behaviorists are trying to piece together the multiple determinants of effective job performance in various work situations and across cultures.

THE SYSTEMS APPROACH

A **system** is a collection of parts operating interdependently to achieve a common purpose. Working from this definition, the systems approach represents a marked departure from the past; in fact, it requires a completely different style of thinking.

system: a collection of parts operating interdependently to achieve a common purpose

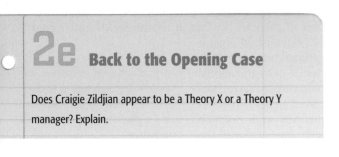

2e Back to the Opening Case

Does Craigie Zildjian appear to be a Theory X or a Theory Y manager? Explain.

Universal process, scientific management, and human relations theorists studied management by taking things apart. They assumed that the whole is equal to the sum of its parts and can be explained in terms of its parts. Systems theorists, in contrast, study management by putting things together and assume that the whole is greater than the sum of its parts. The difference is analytic versus synthetic thinking. According to one management systems expert, "Analytic thinking is, so to speak, outside-in thinking; synthetic thinking is inside-out. Neither negates the value of the other, but by synthetic thinking we can gain understanding that we cannot obtain through analysis, particularly of collective phenomena."[46]

Systems theorists recommend synthetic thinking because management is not practiced in a vacuum. Managers affect, and are in turn affected by, many organizational and environmental variables. Systems thinking has presented the field of management with an enormous challenge: to identify all relevant parts of organized activity and to discover how they interact. Two management writers predicted that systems thinking offers "a basis for understanding organizations and their problems which may one day produce a revolution in organizations comparable to the one brought about by Taylor with scientific management."[47]

Chester I. Barnard's Early Systems Perspective

In one sense, Chester I. Barnard followed in the footsteps of Henri Fayol. Like Fayol, Barnard established a new approach to management on the basis of his experience as a top-level manager. But the approach of the former president of New Jersey Bell Telephone differed from Fayol's. Rather than isolating specific management functions and principles, Barnard devised a more abstract systems approach. In his landmark 1938 book *The Functions of the Executive*, Barnard characterized all organizations as cooperative systems: "A cooperative system is a complex of physical, biological, personal, and social components which are in a specific systematic relationship by reason of the cooperation of two or more persons for at least one definite end."[48]

According to Barnard, willingness to serve, common purpose, and communication are the principal elements in an organization (or cooperative system).[49] He felt that an organization did not exist if these three elements were not present and working interdependently. As illustrated in Figure 2.4, Barnard viewed communication as an energizing force that bridges the natural gap between the individual's willingness to serve and the organization's common purpose.

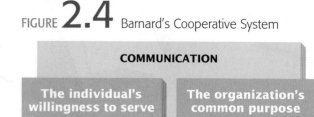

FIGURE **2.4** Barnard's Cooperative System

Barnard's systems perspective has encouraged management and organization theorists to study organizations as complex and dynamic wholes instead of piece by piece. Significantly, he was also a strong advocate of business ethics in his speeches and writings.[50] Barnard opened some important doors in the evolution of management thought.

General Systems Theory

General systems theory is an interdisciplinary area of study based on the assumption that everything is part of a larger, interdependent arrangement. According to Ludwig von Bertalanffy, a biologist and the founder of general systems theory, "In order to understand an organized whole we must know the parts and the relations between them."[51] This interdisciplinary perspective was eagerly adopted by Barnard's followers because it categorized levels of systems and distinguished between closed and open systems.

> **general systems theory:** an area of study based on the assumption that everything is part of a larger, interdependent arrangement

LEVELS OF SYSTEMS. Envisioning the world as a collection of systems was only the first step for general systems theorists. One of the more important recent steps has been the identification of hierarchies of systems, ranging from very specific systems to general ones. Identifying systems at various levels has helped translate abstract general systems theory into more concrete terms.[52] A hierarchy of systems relevant to management is the seven-level scheme of living systems shown in Figure 2.5. Note that each system is a subsystem of the one above it.

CLOSED VERSUS OPEN SYSTEMS. In addition to identifying hierarchies of systems, general systems theorists have distinguished between closed and open systems. A **closed system** is a self-sufficient entity,

> **closed system:** a self-sufficient entity

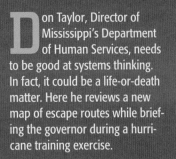

Don Taylor, Director of Mississippi's Department of Human Services, needs to be good at systems thinking. In fact, it could be a life-or-death matter. Here he reviews a new map of escape routes while briefing the governor during a hurricane training exercise.

whereas an **open system** depends on the surrounding environment for survival. In reality, these two kinds of systems cannot be completely separated. The key to classifying a system as relatively closed or relatively open is to determine the amount of interaction between the system and its environment. A battery-powered digital watch, for example, is a relatively closed system; after the battery is in place, the watch operates without help from the outside environment. In contrast, a solar-powered clock is a relatively open system; it cannot operate without a continuous supply of outside energy. The human body is a highly open system because life depends on the body's ability to import oxygen and energy and to export waste. In other words, the human body is highly dependent on the environment for survival.

open system: something that depends on its surrounding environment for survival

Along the same lines, general systems theorists say that all organizations are open systems because organizational survival depends on interaction with the surrounding environment. Just as no person is an island, no organization or organizational subsystem is an island, according to this approach. As a case in point, this is what Boeing's chief financial officer, James Bell, had to say about the giant aircraft maker:

> *To be a global player takes more than just building an airplane. You also have to have the global supply chain. You have to have the support around the world, because an airplane is a 30-year asset, and people aren't going to buy it if it can't be supported over its operating life.*[53]

New Directions in Systems Thinking

Two very different streams of thought are taking systems thinking in interesting new directions today. No one knows for sure where these streams will lead, but they promise to stimulate creative ideas about modern organizations.

ORGANIZATIONAL LEARNING AND KNOWLEDGE MANAGEMENT. An organizational learning perspective portrays the organization as a living and *thinking* open system. Like the human mind, organizations rely on feedback to adjust to changing environmental conditions. In short, organizations are said to learn from experience, just as humans and higher animals do. Organizations thus engage in complex mental processes such as anticipating, perceiving, envisioning, problem solving, and remembering. According to two organization theorists,

> *Some forms of organizational learning occur regularly in many organizations. Human resource development activities, strategic and other planning*

FIGURE **2.5** Levels of Living Systems

System level		Practical examples
Supranational	*General*	United Nations
National		Canada
Organizational		Wal-Mart
Group		Family, work group
Organismic		Human being
Organic		Heart
Cellular	*Specific*	Blood cell

2f Back to the Opening Case

Is Zildjian Company a closed or an open system? How can you tell?

activities, and the introduction and mastering of new technologies for doing work are three common learning processes. They often do not fulfill their potential for true organizational learning, however.

Organizational learning is more than the sum of the learning of its parts—more than cumulative individual learning. The training and development of individuals with new skills, knowledge bases, theories, and frameworks does not constitute organizational learning unless such individual learning is translated into altered organizational practices, policies, or design features. Individual learning is necessary but not sufficient for organizational learning.[54]

When organizational learning becomes a strategic initiative to identify and fully exploit valuable ideas from both inside and outside the organization, a *knowledge management* program exists.[55] You will find more about knowledge management and how it relates to decision making in Chapter 8.

CHAOS THEORY AND COMPLEX ADAPTIVE SYSTEMS. Chaos theory has one idea in common with organizational learning: systems are influenced by feedback. Work in the 1960s and 1970s by mathematicians Edward Lorenz and James Yorke formed the basis of modern chaos theory. So-called chaologists are trying to find order among the seemingly random behavior patterns of everything from weather systems to organizations to stock markets.[56] Behind all this is the intriguing notion that every complex system has a life of its own, with its own rule book. The challenge for those in the emerging field known as *complex adaptive systems theory* is to discover "the rules" in seemingly chaotic systems.

As indicated in Table 2.3, complex adaptive systems theory casts management in a very different

TABLE **2.3**	Complex Adaptive Systems Thinking Helps Managers Make Sense Out of Chaos
COMPLEX ADAPTIVE SYSTEMS THEORY	**CLASSICAL MANAGEMENT THEORY**
Change and transformation are inherent qualities of dynamic systems. The goal of management is to increase learning and self-organizing in continuously changing contexts.	Organizations exist in equilibrium, therefore change is a nonnormal process. The goal of management is to increase stability through planning, organizing, and controlling behavior.
Organizational behavior is inherently nonlinear, and results may be nonproportional to corresponding actions. New models and methods are needed to understand change.	Organizational behavior is essentially linear and predictable, and results are proportional to causes. Thus linear regression models explain most of the variance of organizational change.
Inputs do not cause outputs. The elements of a system are interdependent and mutually causal.	System components are independent and can be analyzed by separating them from the rest of the system, as well as from their outcomes.
An organization is defined, first of all, according to its underlying order and principles. These give rise to surface-level organizing structures, including design, strategy, leadership, controls, and culture.	An organization can be completely defined in terms of its design, strategy, leadership, controls, and culture.
Change should be encouraged through embracing tension, increasing information flow, and pushing authority downwards.	Change should be controlled by minimizing uncertainty and tension, limiting information, and centralizing decision making.
Long-term organizational success is based on optimizing resource flow and continuous learning. A manager's emphasis is on supporting structures that accomplish these goals.	Organizational success is based on maximizing resource utilization, to maximize profit and increase shareholder wealth. A manager's emphasis is on efficiency and effectiveness, and on avoiding both transformation and chaos.

Source: Academy of Management Executive: The Thinking Manager's Source *by Benjamin Bregmann Lichtenstein. Copyright © 2000 by Academy of Management (NY). Reproduced with permission of Academy of Management (NY) in the format Textbook via Copyright Clearance Center.*

light than do traditional models. Managers are challenged to be more flexible and adaptive than in the past.[57] They need to acknowledge the limits of traditional command-and-control management because complex systems have *self-organizing* tendencies. (For example, labor unions have historically thrived in eras when management was oppressive.) The twenty-first-century manager, profiled in the previous chapter (Table 1.1), is up to the challenge. Significantly, chaos theory and complex adaptive systems theory are launching pads for new and better management models, not final answers. Stay tuned.

Lessons from the Systems Approach

Because of the influence of the systems approach, managers now have a greater appreciation for the importance of seeing the whole picture. Open-system thinking does not permit the manager to become preoccupied with one aspect of organizational management while ignoring other internal and external realities. The manager of a business, for instance, must consider resource availability, technological developments, and market trends when producing and selling a product or service. Another positive aspect of the systems approach is how it tries to integrate various management theories. Although quite different in emphasis, both operations management and organizational behavior have been strongly influenced by systems thinking.

There are critics of the systems approach, of course. Some management scholars see systems thinking as long on intellectual appeal and catchy terminology and short on verifiable facts and practical advice.

THE CONTINGENCY APPROACH

A comparatively new line of thinking among management theorists has been labeled the contingency approach. Advocates of contingency management are attempting to take a step away from universally applicable principles of management and toward situational appropriateness. In the words of Fred Luthans, a noted contingency management writer, "The traditional approaches to management were not necessarily wrong, but today they are no longer adequate. The needed breakthrough for management theory and practice can be found in a contingency approach."[58] Formally defined, the **contingency approach** is an effort to determine through research which managerial practices and techniques are appropriate in specific situations. Imagine using Taylor's approach with a college-educated computer engineer! According to the contingency approach, different situations require different managerial responses.

> **contingency approach:**
> research effort to determine which managerial practices and techniques are appropriate in specific situations

Generally, the term *contingency* refers to the choice of an alternative course of action. For example, roommates may have a contingency plan to move their party indoors if it rains. Their subsequent actions are said to be contingent (or dependent) on the weather. In a management context, contingency management has become synonymous with situational management. As one contingency theorist put it, "The effectiveness of a given management pattern is contingent upon multitudinous factors and their interrelationship in a particular situation."[59] This means that the application of various management tools and techniques must be appropriate to the particular situation, because each situation presents unique problems. A contingency approach is especially applicable in intercultural dealings, where customs and habits cannot be taken for granted.

In real-life management, the success of any given technique is dictated by the situation. For example, researchers have found that rigidly structured organizations with many layers of management function best when environmental conditions are relatively stable. Unstable surroundings dictate a more flexible and streamlined organization that can adapt quickly to change. Consequently, traditional principles of management that call for rigidly structured organizations, no matter what the situation, have come into question.

Contingency Characteristics

Some management scholars are attracted to contingency thinking because it is a workable compromise between the systems approach and what can be called a purely situational perspective. Figure 2.6 illustrates this relationship. The systems approach is often criticized for being too general and abstract, while the purely situational view, which assumes that every real-life situation requires a distinctly different approach, has been called hopelessly specific. Contingency advocates have tried to take advantage of common denominators without lapsing into simplistic generalization. Three characteristics of the contingency approach are (1) an open-system perspective, (2) a practical research orientation, and (3) a multivariate approach.

FIGURE **2.6** The Contingency View: A Compromise

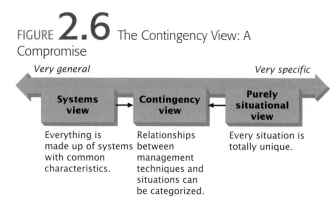

Very general   *Very specific*

Systems view	Contingency view	Purely situational view
Everything is made up of systems with common characteristics.	Relationships between management techniques and situations can be categorized.	Every situation is totally unique.

AN OPEN-SYSTEM PERSPECTIVE. Open-system thinking is fundamental to the contingency view. Contingency theorists are not satisfied with focusing on just the internal workings of organizations. They see the need to understand how organizational subsystems combine to interact with outside social, cultural, political, and economic systems.

A PRACTICAL RESEARCH ORIENTATION. Practical research is that which ultimately leads to more effective on-the-job management. Contingency researchers attempt to translate their findings into tools and situational refinements for more effective management.

A MULTIVARIATE APPROACH. Traditional closed-system thinking prompted a search for simple one-to-one causal relationships. This approach is called bivariate analysis. For example, the traditional human relations assumption that higher morale leads automatically to higher productivity was the result of bivariate analysis. One variable, morale, was seen as the sole direct cause of changes in a second variable, productivity. Subsequent multivariate analysis has shown that many variables, including the employee's personality, the nature of the task, rewards, and job and life satisfaction, collectively account for variations in productivity. **Multivariate analysis** is a research technique used to determine how a number of variables

multivariate analysis: research technique used to determine how a number of variables combine to cause a particular outcome

interact to cause a particular outcome. For example, if an employee has a conscientious personality, the task is highly challenging, and the individual is highly satisfied with his or her life and job, then analysis might show that productivity could be expected to be high. Contingency management theorists strive to carry out practical and relevant multivariate analyses.

Lessons from the Contingency Approach

Although still not fully developed, the contingency approach is a helpful addition to management thought because it emphasizes situational appropriateness. People, organizations, and problems are too complex to justify rigid adherence to universal principles of management. In addition, contingency thinking is a *practical* extension of the systems approach. Assuming that systems thinking is a unifying synthetic force in management thought, the contingency approach promises to add practical direction.

The contingency approach, like each of the other approaches, has its share of critics. One has criticized contingency theory for creating the impression that the organization is a captive of its environment.[60] If such were strictly the case, attempts to manage the organization would be in vain. In actual fact, organizations are subject to various combinations of environmental forces and management practices.

Whether the contingency management theorists have bitten off more than they can chew remains to be seen. At present they appear to be headed in a constructive direction. But it is good to keep in mind that the contingency approach is a promising step rather than the end of the evolution of conventional management thought.

THE ERA OF MANAGEMENT BY BEST SELLER: PROCEED WITH CAUTION

An interesting thing happened to the field of management over the last 25 years or so. It went mainstream. A fledgling field that had been pretty much limited to college classrooms and management development seminars began having a broader appeal. Peter F. Drucker, an Austrian-born management consultant,

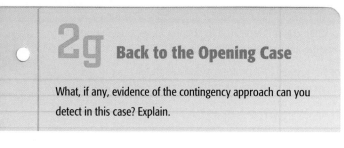

2g Back to the Opening Case

What, if any, evidence of the contingency approach can you detect in this case? Explain.

TABLE **2.4**   A Sampling of Business Management Best Sellers

NAME OF BOOK, AUTHOR(S), AND YEAR PUBLISHED	MAIN THEME/LESSONS
Theory Z: How American Business Can Meet the Japanese Challenge, William Ouchi, 1981	UCLA professor finds successful "Theory Z." U.S. firms such as IBM exhibit a blend of American and Japanese traits (e.g., participative decision making; teamwork + individual responsibility).
In Search of Excellence: Lessons from America's Best-Run Companies, Thomas J. Peters and Robert H. Waterman Jr., 1982	Consultants' analysis of 36 companies, including Johnson & Johnson and McDonald's, finds eight "attributes of excellence." Excellent companies reportedly focus on action, customers, entrepreneurship, people, values, the core business, simplicity, and balanced control and decentralization.
The One Minute Manager, Kenneth Blanchard and Spencer Johnson, 1982	Short parable of a young man who learns from experienced managers about the power of on-the-spot goals, praise, and reprimands.
High Output Management, Andrew S. Grove, 1983	Respected CEO of Intel Corp. urges managers to be output-oriented, team builders, and motivators of individual peak performance.
Iacocca: An Autobiography, Lee Iacocca (with William Novak), 1984	Legendary president of Ford and CEO of Chrysler details how being a master salesman helped him save Chrysler Corp.
The 7 Habits of Highly Effective People: Powerful Lessons in Personal Change, Stephen R. Covey, 1989	Professor/consultant charts pathway to personal growth in terms of good habits formed by balancing one's knowledge, skills, and desires.
Reengineering the Corporation: A Manifesto for Business Revolution, Michael Hammer and James Champy, 1993	Consultants recommend using information technology to radically redesign basic business practices to achieve lower costs, higher quality, and speed.
Built to Last: Successful Habits of Visionary Companies, James C. Collins and Jerry I. Porras, 1994	After studying 18 "visionary" companies, including American Express and Marriott, these professors/consultants urge managers to "preserve the core" (with strong cultures and internal promotions) and "stimulate progress" (with difficult goals and a hunger for continuous change).
The Death of Competition: Leadership & Strategy in the Age of Business Ecosystems, James F. Moore, 1996	Consultant advises firms to be as good at cooperating as they are at competing, especially with others in their ecosystem (e.g., Microsoft and Intel).
Who Moved My Cheese? Spencer Johnson, 1998	Coauthor of *The One Minute Manager* spins a short fable about two mice who learn to adapt to change by facing their fears and enjoying the trip.
Fish! Stephen C. Lundin, Harry Paul, and John Christensen, 2000	Short story of a manager who turns her department around by applying four lessons learned at Seattle's Pike Place fish market.
Good to Great: Why Some Companies Make the Leap . . . and Others Don't, Jim Collins, 2001	Coauthor of *Built to Last* returns with list of 11 companies, including Gillette and Walgreens, that jumped from good to great by hiring great people, confronting reality, and becoming the world's best.
Jack: Straight from the Gut, Jack Welch (with John A. Byrne), 2001	Legendary CEO of General Electric explains his concept of the "boundaryless" organization dedicated to sharing ideas, building people into winners, and fighting bureaucracy.
Execution: The Discipline of Getting Things Done, Larry Bossidy and Ram Charan (with Charles Burck), 2002	Retired CEO of Honeywell and professor/consultant tell how to get results by hiring good people who are taught to link strategy with operations.

writer, and teacher living in the United States, deserves to be considered the father of this trend.[61] His now-classic books, such as *The Concept of the Corporation* (1946), *The Practice of Management* (1954), and *The Effective Executive* (1967), along with his influential articles in *Harvard Business Review* and elsewhere, appealed to academics and practicing managers alike. Drucker became the first management guru whose sage advice was sought by executives trying to figure out how to manage in increasingly turbulent times. Others, such as quality advocates Juran and Deming, followed.

The popularization of management shifted into high gear in 1982 with the publication of Peters and Waterman's *In Search of Excellence*. This book topped the nonfiction best-seller lists for months, was translated into several foreign languages, and soon appeared in paperback. Just five years later, an astounding 5 million copies had been sold worldwide.[62] Other business management best sellers followed (see Table 2.4), and the popular appeal of management grew. The rest, as they say, is history. By 2004, best-selling authors such as Michael Hammer were collecting $82,000 per speaking engagement, worldwide sales of *The One Minute Manager* had reached 7 million copies,[63] and businessman Donald Trump was saying "You're fired!" on his reality TV hit *The Apprentice*.[64] Certain academics, meanwhile, worried about the instant gurus and their best sellers encouraging shoddy research and simplistic thinking, to say nothing of pandering to busy managers' desire for quick fixes.[65] Still, the era of management by best seller deserves serious discussion in any historical perspective on management thought, if for no other reason than the widespread acceptance among practicing managers of the books listed in Table 2.4.

What's Wrong with Management by Best Seller?

Craig M. McAllaster, the Business School Dean at Florida's Rollins College, recently offered this instructive critique of managing by best seller:

> *An executive reads a management book written by a guru listed on the* New York Times *Bestseller List and decides that the concepts presented therein represent the magic bullet. This bestseller's concepts will solve the current problems of the organization and position her/him for greatness. Many times the manager sees the approach as working with minimal change and disruption, especially for her/him. Fired up and sure of the prognosis and treatment, the executive returns to the organization and orders a thousand copies of the book and calls a management meeting to announce the change. No diagnosis or assessment takes place to determine the real organizational problems. The executive buys off on a well-written book that captures the essence of problems in someone else's company and applies the one-size-fits-all solution to the organization.[66]*

The inevitable disappointment is not the fault of popular management books, which typically do contain some really good ideas; rather, the hurried and haphazard application of those ideas is at fault. Our challenge, then, is to avoid the quick-fix mentality that makes management by best seller so tempting.

How to Avoid the Quick-Fix Mentality

In a follow-up study of Peters and Waterman's *In Search of Excellence*, Michael Hitt and Duane Ireland conducted a *comparative* analysis of "excellent" companies

Want to burn a couple of hours of extra time? Try browsing the business section at your local bookstore. You'll find a mountain of information with both trash and treasure. Be wary of quick fixes based on shoddy research while gathering those pearls of wisdom.

2h   Practical Take-Aways

Jeffrey Pfeffer, Stanford University management professor:

If companies act on the basis of simplistic and inaccurate theories of human behavior and organizational performance, their decisions will not be good ones and the results will be poor. Companies that are serious about overcoming this problem can spend more time getting informed about the facts, about history, and about alternative theories of behavior. Yes, this requires an investment of time and effort. But some forethought and learning can prevent some expensive errors.

Source: Jeffrey Pfeffer, *What Were They Thinking? Unconventional Wisdom About Management (Boston: Harvard Business School Press, 2007), pp. 7–8.*

QUESTION:

What specific take-away lessons have you learned from studying this chapter that can help you avoid common "rookie" mistakes as a manager?

and industry norms. Companies that satisfied all of Peters and Waterman's excellence criteria turned out to be no more effective than a random sample of *Fortune* 1000 companies.[67] This outcome prompted Hitt and Ireland to offer five tips for avoiding what they termed "the quick-fix mentality" (see Table 2.5).[68]

Putting What You Have Learned to Work

We need to put the foregoing historical overview into proper perspective. The topical tidiness of this chapter, while providing useful conceptual frameworks for students of management, generally does not carry over to the practice of management. Managers are, first and foremost, pragmatists. They use whatever works. Instead of faithfully adhering to a given school of management thought, successful managers tend to use a "mixed bag" approach. This chapter is a good starting point for you to begin building your own personally relevant and useful approach to management by blending theory, the experience and advice of others, and your own experience. A healthy dose of common sense would help as well.

TABLE **2.5**   How to Avoid the Quick-Fix Mentality in Management

Our research suggests that practicing managers should embrace appealing ideas when appropriate but anticipate that solutions typically are far more complex than the type suggested by Peters and Waterman's search for excellence. To avoid the quick-fix mentality, managers should:

1. Remain current with literature in the field, particularly with journals that translate research into practice.
2. Ensure that concepts applied are based on science or, at least, on some form of rigorous documentation, rather than purely on advocacy.
3. Be willing to examine and implement new concepts, but first do so using pilot tests with small units.
4. Be skeptical when simple solutions are offered; analyze them thoroughly.
5. Constantly anticipate the effects of current actions and events on future results.

Source: Michael A. Hitt and R. Duane Ireland, "Peters and Waterman Revisited: The Unended Quest for Excellence," *Academy of Management Executive, Vol. 2, no. 2 (May 1987): p. 96. Reprinted by permission.*

SUMMARY

1. Management is an interdisciplinary and international field that has evolved in bits and pieces over the years. Five approaches to management theory are (1) the universal process approach, (2) the operational approach, (3) the behavioral approach, (4) the systems approach, and (5) the contingency approach. Useful lessons have been learned from each.

   Henri Fayol's universal process approach assumes that all organizations, regardless of purpose or size, require the same management process. Furthermore, it assumes that this rational process can be reduced to separate functions and principles of management. The universal approach, the oldest of the various approaches, is still popular today.

2. Dedicated to promoting production efficiency and reducing waste, the operational approach has evolved from scientific management to operations management. Frederick W. Taylor, the father of scientific management, and his followers revolutionized industrial management through the use of standardization, time-and-motion study, selection and training, and pay incentives.

3. The quality advocates taught managers about the strategic importance of high-quality goods and services. Shewhart pioneered the use of *statistics* for quality control. Japan's Ishikawa emphasized *prevention* of defects in quality and drew management's attention to *internal* as well as external *customers*. Deming sparked the Japanese quality revolution with calls for *continuous improvement* of the entire production process. Juran trained many U.S. managers to improve quality through *teamwork, partnerships with suppliers*, and *Pareto analysis* (the 80/20 rule). Feigenbaum developed the concept of *total quality control*, thus involving all business functions in the quest for quality. He believed that the *customer* determined quality. Crosby, a champion of *zero defects*, emphasized how costly poor-quality products could be.

4. Management has turned to the human factor in the human relations movement and organizational behavior approach. Emerging from such influences as unionization, the Hawthorne studies, and the philosophy of industrial humanism, the human relations movement began as a concerted effort to make employees' needs a high management priority. Today, organizational behavior theorists try to identify the multiple determinants of job performance.

5. Advocates of the systems approach recommend that modern organizations be viewed as open systems.

Open systems depend on the outside environment for survival, whereas closed systems do not. Chester I. Barnard stirred early interest in systems thinking in 1938 by suggesting that organizations are cooperative systems energized by communication. General systems theory, an interdisciplinary field based on the assumption that everything is systematically related, has identified a hierarchy of systems and has differentiated between closed and open systems. New directions in systems thinking are organizational learning and chaos theory.

6. A comparatively new approach to management thought is the contingency approach, which stresses situational appropriateness rather than universal principles. The contingency approach is characterized by an open-system perspective, a practical research orientation, and a multivariate approach to research. Contingency thinking is a practical extension of more abstract systems thinking.

7. "Management by best seller" occurs when managers read a popular book by a management guru and hastily try to implement its ideas and one-size-fits-all recommendations without proper regard for their organization's unique problems and needs. The quick-fix mentality that fosters this problem can be avoided by staying current with high-quality management literature, requiring rigorous support for claims, engaging in critical thinking, and running pilot studies.

TERMS TO UNDERSTAND

- **Universal process approach**, p. 35
- **Operational approach**, p. 36
- **Scientific management**, p. 37
- **Operations management**, p. 41
- **Human relations movement**, p. 42
- **Theory Y**, p. 43
- **Organizational behavior**, p. 43
- **System**, p. 44
- **General systems theory**, p. 45
- **Closed system**, p. 45
- **Open system**, p. 46
- **Contingency approach**, p. 48
- **Multivariate analysis**, p. 49

MANAGER'S TOOLKIT

Recommended Publications for Staying Current in the Field of Management

Academic Journals (with a research orientation)
Academy of Management Journal
Academy of Management Review
Administrative Science Quarterly
Human Relations
Journal of Applied Psychology
Journal of Management
Journal of Organizational Behavior
Journal of Vocational Behavior

Journal of World Business
Nonprofit Management & Leadership

Scholarly Journals (with a practical orientation)
Academy of Management Perspectives (formerly *Academy of Management Executive*)
Business Horizons
Harvard Business Review
Journal of Organizational Excellence

MIT Sloan Management Review
Organizational Dynamics
Public Administration Review
The Leadership Quarterly

General Periodicals
Business 2.0
Business Week
Canadian Business
The Economist
Fast Company
Forbes
Fortune
Industry Week
The Wall Street Journal

Practitioner Journals (special interest)
Black Enterprise
Business Ethics
CIO (information technology)
Entrepreneur
Healthcare Executive

Health Care Management Review
Hispanic Business
HR Magazine (human resource management)
Inc. (small business)
Information Week (information technology)
Inside Supply Management
Macworld (Apple computer users)
Money (personal finance and investing)
NAFE Magazine (women executives)
Nonprofit World (not-for-profit organizations)
PC World (personal computing and Internet)
Technology Review (new technology)
Training
Training + Development
Web Bound (Web site directory)
Working Mother (work/family issues)

Blogs
800ceoread.com/blog
www.cenekreport.com

ACTION LEARNING EXERCISE

Open-System Thinking and Recycling

Instructions: Open-system thinking involves trying to better understand (and manage) complicated situations. It requires one to connect the dots, so to speak, and see the big picture. The idea is to comprehend the interconnectedness of things and to anticipate (and ideally avoid) possible unintended consequences. Corrective actions can then be taken on the basis of your new, broader understanding. This exercise challenges you to tackle the twin problems of too much solid waste and too little recycling. For a 24-hour period, keep a log of all the tangible items you buy or consume (such as a meal, DVD, cell phone, candy bar, book or magazine, bottle of water, can of soda, and the like) and jot down what you did with any resulting material waste or leftovers. Was the waste recycled, thrown away (where?), or poured down the drain? Be prepared to discuss your log in class, if requested by the instructor.

The Problem

When done right, recycling saves energy, preserves natural resources, reduces greenhouse-gas emissions, and keeps toxins from leaking out of landfills.

So why doesn't everyone do it? Because it's often cheaper to throw things away. The economics of recycling depends on landfill fees, the price of oil and other commodities, and the demand for recycled goods. Paper, for example, works well: About 52% of paper consumed in the U.S. is recovered for recycling, and 36% of the fiber that goes into new paper comes from recycled sources. By contrast, less than 25% of plastic bottles are recycled, and we use five billion (!) a year.

Americans generated an average of 4.5 pounds of garbage per person per day in 2005, the EPA reports. About 1.5 pounds were recycled. That's a national recycling rate for municipal solid waste of just 32%. (Source: Marc Gunther, Fortune.*)*[69]

For Consideration/Discussion

1. Viewing yourself as part of a natural open system, how wasteful are you? What are the broader environmental implications of your consumption habits?

2. Did this exercise spur you to do a better job of recycling?

3. Should recycling be a high priority for business? Explain.

4. On local, national, and global scales, what needs to be done to significantly reduce the solid waste stream?

5. Why is open-system thinking useful for issues as complex as solid waste reduction?

6. What other tough societal problems could managers and government leaders better understand and manage through open-system thinking? Discuss.

CLOSING CASE
History Matters at This Wisconsin Boat Builder

Production manager Rich Auth stood at the boatyard gate and watched his 166 colleagues, some tearful, leave behind the work that had sustained many of their families for generations. On that day, in November 1990, Burger Boat's absentee owner had faxed a message to the staff: the yard would close. Twenty minutes later, at the shift's end, the yard was shut down. Burger's owner had stopped paying employees' health insurance premiums and had run up $13 million in debt. Still, Auth's coworkers "went out like gentlemen," he says. "There was no foul language, no threats. That's just the way people are here." Or maybe they just knew they'd be back.

Manitowoc's boatyards were famous for building first-class schooners and for constructing submarines and other military vessels. Burger Boat, founded in 1863 and family run until 1986, had constructed boats for three wars when, in the early 1960s, the company repositioned itself as a builder of luxury aluminum motor yachts. The yachts quickly became known for quality craftsmanship.

By 1970, though, all the other shipbuilders in Manitowoc had moved or shut down, and Burger had been sold to its second out-of-towner, an ailing ship-building company based in Tacoma, Washington, that used Burger as a cash cow. When the yard closed, says Mayor Kevin Crawford, "everyone felt a ripple go through the community."

Luckily for Burger and Manitowoc, the ripple was felt as far away as Chicago, where David Ross, an entrepreneur who had sold his $55-million commercial-photo-labs company in 1989, heard of Burger's plight. Ross had always admired Burgers—coveted them, even. Now there appeared to be an opportunity to buy the company itself.

As Ross gathered information about Burger, what impressed him even more than the boats were the people who made them. Shortly after the yard closed, 18 Burger employees crawled through a hole in the fence to get the tools and materials they needed to finish a boat they'd been working on. Later a customer with an unfinished boat in the yard—*The Lady Iris*—would help Rich Auth and 70 other employees set up a shell corporation to try to revive the company. There was not only boat-building to be done but also a retirement plan to rescue, an employee stock ownership plan to develop, and a blatant violation of state plant-closing laws to redress.

Burger's yard had been filled with men whose fathers and grandfathers had practiced the same craftsmanship before them, who had fashioned gracefully curved bows from sheets of aluminum. The instinct to preserve that tradition was overpowering. "When I met Rich, I determined that this company was zero without the people who made it famous," says Ross. For more than a year, Burger's employees had struggled unsuccessfully to save the company.

Ross, along with his partner, Jim Ruffolo, offered the wary craftspeople a second chance. "They weren't ready to put their trust in just anyone," Ross recalls. "I told them I was going to move here and that I could offer them something they didn't have—a hands-on owner who could speak directly to clients, who could bring strong advertising, marketing, and sales skills."

Ross flew Auth to Chicago to speak with employees of Ross's former company and to examine its financial statements. "We didn't want another silver spoon coming into the yard," says Auth. Ross, he discovered, was genuinely respected by his old employees. By 1992, Burger's former workers decided to throw their lot in with Ross. Most, like Burger designer Don Fogltanz, had landed good jobs elsewhere. But, says Fogltanz, "I wanted to finish off my working years at the company where I had spent my life. I wanted to build boats."

In January 1993, after more than a year of negotiations, a dramatic appearance before a U.S. Bankruptcy Court judge, and more than $250,000 in legal fees, Ross and Ruffolo were permitted to buy Burger. They promised to keep the company in Manitowoc for at least 20 years. "We never would have done the deal if David were staying in Chicago," says Auth. But Ross never had any intention of staying there. What he saw at Burger—a company bonded to its community, and workers impassioned by their craft—had drawn him in.

Today Burger has a three-year backlog of orders, steady revenue growth, and four years of profits on the books. Half of the company's 200 employees are people who returned to Burger when the gates reopened in 1993; Ross keeps them and the company focused around their skills and passions. "In May we launched hull number 491, and it's an 85-foot flush-deck motor-yacht cruiser," says Ross. "In 1901 we launched our first motor yacht, and do you know what it was? It was an 80-foot flush-deck motor-yacht cruiser."

The launch of hull number 491—like most of Burger's launches—was a public event. Twelve hundred admirers crowded the yard to watch the maiden voyage. "It's just a beautiful ceremony," says Auth. "This company was started when Lincoln was president, and today we're building boats on the same shoreline. I know a lot of people here who take great pride in that."

Source: Donna Fenn, "Rescuing Tradition," *Inc.*, 23 (August 2001): 48–49. Copyright © 2001 by Mansueto Ventures LLC. Reproduced with permission of Mansueto Ventures LLC in the format Textbook via Copyright Clearance Center.

FOR DISCUSSION

1 Which of Fayol's 14 universal principles of management in Table 2.1 are evident in the Burger Boat case? Explain your reasoning for each principle selected.

2 What would Mary Parker Follett probably say about David Ross's management style? Explain.

3 Is David Ross a Theory X or a Theory Y manager? Explain.

4 Is Burger Boat a closed or an open system? Explain.

5 If you were responsible for designing and conducting a management training program for Burger Boat's managers, which of the management best sellers listed in Table 2.4 would you have them read? Why?

TEST PREPPER

True/False Questions

_____ 1. The actual practice of management has been around for thousands of years.

_____ 2. According to the universal process approach, a successful military commander should be able to run a business successfully.

_____ 3. Henri Fayol was the father of scientific management.

_____ 4. The idea of Pareto analysis, or doing it right the first time, was promoted by Elton Mayo.

_____ 5. Taylor and the early proponents of scientific management have been praised for viewing workers as complex human beings who work for more than just money.

_____ 6. McGregor's Theory Y assumes that people are capable of self-control.

_____ 7. According to general systems theory, everything we know belongs to only one system—the earth's ecosystem.

_____ 8. It is appropriate to characterize organizations as closed systems because they are managed internally.

_____ 9. The most significant contribution of contingency theory has been its search for the one best way to manage.

_____10. Peters and Waterman's book _In Search of Excellence_ played a key role in the era of management by best seller.

Multiple-Choice Questions

1. Sharpening one's vision of _____ is the purpose of _____.
   A. management theory; managerial practice
   B. the present; historical perspective
   C. management theory; what could be
   D. history; the past
   E. management; technology

2. _____ is _not_ one of Fayol's 14 universal principles of management.
   A. Esprit de corps   B. Empowerment
   C. Authority   D. Equity
   E. Centralization

3. When performance standards are developed on the basis of systematic observation and experimentation, what is involved?
   A. Fayol's universal principle   B. Therbligs

C. A Gantt chart   D. Total quality control
E. Scientific management

4. Which of these did Taylor's differential pay plan call for when the daily standard was met or exceeded?
   A. Inclusion in a bonus pool
   B. A higher per-unit rate
   C. Permission to go home early
   D. A ticket to a weekly prize drawing
   E. A minimum wage

5. Which of these is also known as the 80/20 rule?
   A. Linear programming   B. Contingency planning
   C. Pareto analysis   D. Fishbone analysis
   E. Strategic scanning

6. What did Mary Parker Follett urge managers to do?
   A. Motivate rather than simply demand performance.
   B. Adopt a Theory X view of workers.
   C. Ignore the findings of the Hawthorne studies.
   D. Get rid of the traditional hierarchy of authority.
   E. Share profits equally with workers.

7. Organizations can _best_ be described as which of these?
   A. Closed systems   B. Specialized systems
   C. Open systems   D. Functional systems
   E. Independent systems

8. Which of the following _best_ describes the contingency approach?
   A. Differential management
   B. Managerial uniformity
   C. Continuous improvement
   D. Situational management
   E. A search for the one best way to manage

9. Craig M. McAllaster criticizes "management by best seller" because
   A. management books are not theory-driven.
   B. only three authors have written all of the best sellers.
   C. management books exhibit too much reliance on survey data.
   D. Drucker's ideas keep being repeated over and over.
   E. management books offer too many "one-size-fits-all" solutions.

10. Managers can avoid the quick-fix mentality by reading which sort of management journals?
    A. Those that report nonquantitative studies
    B. Those that report highly controlled laboratory studies
    C. Those that report the results of public-opinion polls
    D. Those that specify how-to-do-it procedures
    E. Those that translate research into practice

See page T1 at the back of the text for answers to these questions. Want more questions? Visit the student Web site and take the ACE quizzes for more practice.

3

The Changing Environment of Management

Diversity, Global Economy, and Technology

> *The best way to predict the future is to create it.*[1]
> —ALAN KAYE

OBJECTIVES

- **Summarize** the demographics of the new American workforce.

- **Explain** how the social contract between employer and employee has changed in recent years.

- **Define** the term *managing diversity,* and **explain** why it is particularly important today.

- **Discuss** how the changing political-legal environment is affecting the practice of management.

- **Discuss** why business cycles and the global economy are vital economic considerations for modern managers.

- **Describe** the three-step innovation process, and **define** the term *intrapreneur*.

THE CHANGING WORKPLACE

You Raised Them, Now Manage Them

Nadira A. Hira, twenty-something reporter for Fortune *magazine:* Nearly every businessperson over 30 has done it: sat in his office after a staff meeting and—reflecting upon the 25-year-old colleague with two tattoos, a piercing, no watch, and a shameless propensity for chatting up the boss—wondered, What is *with* that guy?! . . .

Generation Y: Its members are different in many respects, from their upbringing to their politics. But it might be their effect on the workplace that makes them truly noteworthy—more so than other generations of twenty-somethings that writers have been collectively profiling since time immemorial. They're ambitious, they're demanding and they question everything, so if there isn't a good reason for that long commute or late night, don't expect them to do it. When it comes to loyalty, the companies they work for are last on their list—behind their families, their friends, their communities, their coworkers and, of course, themselves. But there are a whole lot of them. And as the baby-boomers begin to retire, triggering a ballyhooed worker shortage, businesses are realizing that they may have no choice but to accommodate these curious Gen Y creatures. . . .

Some 64 million skilled workers will be able to retire by the end of this decade, according to the Conference Board, and companies will need to go the extra mile to replace them, even if it means putting up with some outsized expectations. There is a precedent for this: In April 1969, *Fortune* wrote, "Because the demand for their services so greatly exceeds the supply, young graduates are in a strong position to dictate terms to their prospective employers. Young employees are demanding that they be given productive tasks to do from the first day of work, and that the people they work for notice and react to their performance." Those were the early baby-boomers, and—with their '60s sensibility and navel-gazing—they left their mark on just about every institution they passed through. Now come their children, to confound them. The kids—self-absorbed, gregarious, multitasking, loud, optimistic, pierced—are exactly what the boomers raised them to be, and now they're being themselves all over the business world.

It's going to be great.

"This is the most high-maintenance workforce in the history of the world," says Bruce Tulgan, the founder of leading generational-research firm Rainmaker Thinking. "The good news is they're also going to be the most high-performing workforce in the history of the world. They walk in with more information in their heads, more information at their fingertips—and, sure, they have high expectations, but they have the highest expectations first and foremost for themselves."

So just who is this fair bird? . . .

Boomers, know this: You are outnumbered. There are 78.5 million of you, according to Census Bureau figures, and 79.8 million members of Gen Y (for our purposes, those born between 1977 and 1995). . . .

More than a third of 18- to 25-year-olds surveyed by the Pew Research Center for the People and the Press have a tattoo, and 30 percent have a piercing somewhere besides their earlobe. But those are considered stylish, not rebellious. . . .

When it comes to Gen Y's intangible characteristics, the lexicon is less than flattering. Try "needy," "entitled." Despite a consensus that they're not slackers, there is a suspicion that they've avoided that moniker only by creating enough commotion to distract from the fact that they're really not that into "work." Never mind that they often need an entire team—and a couple of cheerleaders—to do anything. For some of them the concept "work ethic" needs rethinking. "I had a conversation with the CFO [chief financial officer] of a big company in New York," says Tamara Erickson, coauthor of the 2006 book *Workforce Crisis,* "and he said, 'I can't find anyone to hire who's willing to work 60 hours a week. Can you talk to them?' And I said, 'Why don't I start by talking to you? What they're really telling you is that they're sorry it takes you so long to get your work done.'" . . .

Race is even less of an issue for Gen Yers, not just because they're generally accustomed to diversity, but because on any given night they can watch successful mainstream shows featuring everyone from the Oscar-winning rap group Three 6 Mafia to wrestler Hulk Hogan. It all makes for a universe where anything—such as, say, being a bodybuilding accountant—seems possible.

Of course, Gen Yers have been told since they were toddlers that they can be anything they can imagine. It's an idea they clung to as they grew up and as their outlook was shaken by the Columbine shootings and 9/11. More than the nuclear threat of their parents' day, those attacks were immediate, potentially personal, and completely unpredictable. And each new clip of Al Gore spreading inconvenient truths or of polar bears drowning from lack of ice told Gen Yers they were not promised a healthy, happy tomorrow. So they're determined to live their best lives now.

. . . I've come to realize that the most significant characteristic of the Gen Y bird is that we are unapologetic. From how we look, to how spoiled we are, to what we want—even demand—of work, we do think we are special. And what ultimately makes us different is our willingness to talk about it, without much shame and with the expectation that somebody—our parents, our friends, our managers—will help us figure it all out.

Source: Excerpted from Nadira A. Hira, "You Raised Them, Now Manage Them," *Fortune* (May 28, 2007): 38–46. © 2007 Time Inc. All rights reserved.

Companies successfully integrating members of the new generation into their operations do more than merely cope with change; they learn to thrive on it.[2] Accordingly, present and future managers need to be aware of *how* things are changing in the world around them.

Ignoring the impact of general environmental factors on management makes about as much sense as ignoring the effects of weather and road conditions on high-speed driving. The general environment of management includes social, political-legal, economic, and technological dimensions. Changes in each area present managers with unique opportunities and obstacles that will shape not only the organization's strategic direction but also the course of daily operations. This challenge requires forward-thinking managers who can handle change and accurately see the greater scheme of things.

The purpose of this chapter, then, is to prepare you for constant change and help you see the *big picture* by identifying key themes in the changing environment of management.[3] It builds on our discussion in Chapter 1 of the five overarching sources of change for today's managers: globalization, the evolution of product quality, environmentalism, an ethical reawakening, and the e-business revolution.

THE SOCIAL ENVIRONMENT

According to sociologists, society is the product of a constant struggle between the forces of stability and change. Cooperation promotes stability, whereas conflict and competition upset the status quo. The net result is an ever-changing society. Keeping this perspective in mind, we shall discuss four important dimensions of the social environment: demographics, the new social contract, inequalities, and managing diversity. Each presents managers with unique challenges.

Demographics of the New Workforce

Demographics—statistical profiles of population characteristics—are a valuable planning tool for managers. Managers with foresight who study demographics can make appropriate adjustments

demographics: statistical profiles of human populations

in their strategic, human resource, and marketing plans. Selected demographic shifts reshaping the U.S. workforce are presented in Figure 3.1. (Other countries have their own demographic trends.) The projections in Figure 3.1 are not "blue sky" numbers. They are based on people already born, most of whom are presently working. In short, the U.S. workforce demonstrates the following trends:

- *It is getting larger.* As in the previous two decades, the U.S. labor force will continue to grow more

FIGURE **3.1** The Changing U.S. Workforce: 2004–2014

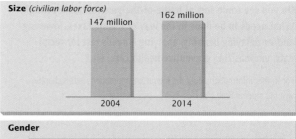

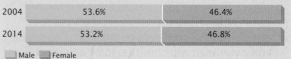

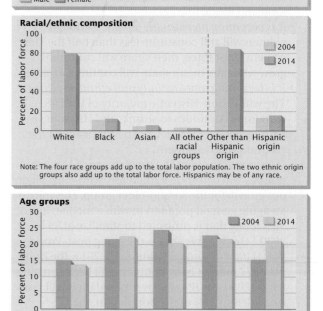

*Source: Data and bottom two figures from U.S. Department of Labor, Bureau of Labor Statistics, "Tomorrow's Jobs," Occupational Outlook Handbook, 2006–2007 edition, **www.bls.gov.***

3a The U.S. Social *In*security System?

[Unless significant reform legislation is passed. . .] starting somewhere around 2017 or 2019, the Social Security program will pay out more money in benefits than it takes in from taxes. Then by around 2041 to 2046, the Social Security trust fund will run dry. . . . Medicare starts drawing down its reserves a whole lot sooner—in 2010. If the national debt sounds staggering, at $8.5 trillion, try Medicare's projected short-fall of $32.4 trillion over 75 years.

Source: Excerpted from Silla Brush, "A Nation in Full," U.S. News & World Report, 141 (October 2, 2006): 57.

QUESTIONS:

Do you see some sort of battle-of-the-generations brewing? What needs to be done in the way of raising taxes, lowering and/or delaying benefits, applying a needs test for recipients, emphasizing preventive health care, etc.?

For further information about the interactive annotations in this chapter, visit our student Web site.

rapidly than the national population. The resulting labor shortage will continue to be a magnet for legal and illegal immigration.

- *It is becoming increasingly female.* Although women will still constitute less than half the U.S. civilian labor force, their share will continue to grow while the men's share will continue to shrink.
- *It is becoming more racially and ethnically diverse.* The white, non-Hispanic majority of the U.S. workforce continues to shrink, and Hispanics/Latinos have replaced African Americans as the second-largest segment.
- *It is becoming older.* The median age of U.S. employees will continue to increase, with most vigorous growth for the 55-and-older group. This mirrors an aging general population with a median age of 36.5 today that is projected to stabilize at 39 by 2030.[4] Driving this shift is the aging post–World War II baby-boom generation: "In 2011, the bubble of 77 million baby boomers will begin turning 65. By 2050, the 65-and-over population will grow from 12% to 21% of the population, the U.S. Census Bureau predicts."[5] (Japan and Italy hit the 20% threshold for citizens 65 and older in 2008!)[6] This trend has major (some say troubling) implications for the viability of old-age assistance

programs in developed countries, including the U.S. Social Security System.[7]

Parallel demographic shifts in the overall U.S. population have manufacturers redesigning products. Take refrigerators, for example:

Just 4% of refrigerators are sold with freezers on the bottom, but GE appliances is betting that the models are poised for a sales surge.

The bottom freezers are gaining in popularity with two important demographic groups: retirees and Gen Xers, GE says.

Older people like them because the food they reach for most often is up high, where they can see it and get at it. According to GE, consumers open their freezer once for every seven times they open their refrigerator. So having the freezer on the bottom actually means less bending over.

Gen Xers like them because they're different.

"They like the style and the look," says Robert Rogers, marketing manager for GE's refrigerator division."[8]

Similarly, products, services, and advertising are being tailored to the rapidly growing Hispanic/Latino population. Many banks, including Bank of America and Wells Fargo, offer Spanish-language services at their teller windows, ATMs, and telephone and Internet service centers. Businesses cannot afford to ignore the estimated $1.1 trillion in buying power that the U.S. Hispanic/Latino community will have by 2010.[9]

NEEDED: ON-THE-JOB REMEDIAL EDUCATION. While demographics foretell possible labor shortages in the near term,[10] the picture for employers grows worse when the issue of labor force *quality* is considered. *Fortune* magazine's Geoff Colvin recently offered this blunt assessment:

A steadily rising living standard has been vital to America's political and social stability. To keep that standard rising, our workers have to be worth what they cost in a global labor market. The only way they can do that is by getting an education that's world-class and constantly improving. The education that many U.S. kids get today is neither.[11]

In a 2004 survey of 119 manufacturers by the Federal Reserve Bank of Philadelphia, employers found 40 percent of their job applicants lacking in basic reading, math, and writing skills.[12]

Experts say about one out of every 20 adults in the United States is *functionally illiterate*, meaning that they have difficulty with basic life skills such as reading a newspaper, completing a job application, and

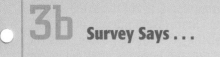

3b Survey Says . . .

Nine in 10 employed adults, or 92 percent, agree that strengthening the education system should be a top priority for the U.S. in the next decade.

Source: Margery Weinstein, "Unprepared," Training, 44 (May 2007): 10.

QUESTION:

As a "consumer" of many years in the educational system, what do you think needs to be done to improve it?

interpreting a bus schedule. In other words, 11 million U.S. adults could not comprehend the paragraph you are now reading.[13] Millions more would struggle to do so. According to the National Jewish Coalition for Literacy, "illiteracy costs the USA about $225 billion a year in lost productivity."[14] Consequently, many businesses, often in partnership with local schools and colleges, have launched remedial education programs. A *Training* magazine survey of 1,652 companies with 100 or more employees found a broad corporate commitment to remedial education; the following skills were being taught at the indicated percentages of the companies surveyed:

- Basic life/work skills (71 percent)
- English as a second language (41 percent)
- Remedial math (42 percent)
- Remedial reading (37 percent)
- Remedial writing (41 percent)
- Welfare-to-work transition (35 percent)[15]

These remedial programs typically involve an intensive schedule of small-group sessions emphasizing practical, work-related instruction. Knowledge is the entry ticket to today's computerized service economy.

MYTHS ABOUT OLDER WORKERS. As we have noted, the U.S. workforce is getting older. Bolstering this trend is the ongoing redefinition of the concept of retirement: "Sixty-eight percent of workers between the ages of 50 and 70 plan to work in retirement or never retire."[16] While we're on the subject, how old is old? According to a nationwide survey of 2,503 Americans between the ages of 18 and 75, the answer depends on how old *you* are! "Among those over 65, only 8 percent think of people under 65 as old, while 30 percent of those under 25 say 'old' is anywhere from 40 to 64."[17] Older workers, defined by the U.S. Department of

Labor as those aged 55 and up, tend to be burdened by a negative image in America's youth-oriented culture.[18] Researchers have identified and disproved five stubborn myths about older workers.

Myth: Older workers are less productive than the average worker.

Fact: Research shows that productivity does not decline with a worker's age. Older employees perform as well as younger workers in most jobs. Moreover, older workers meet the productivity expectations.

Myth: The costs of employee benefits outweigh any possible gain from hiring older workers.

Fact: The costs of health insurance increase with age, but most other fringe benefits do not, because they are tied to length of service and level of salary. A study at The Travelers Companies found that it was not safe to assume that older workers cost either more or less than younger workers.

Myth: Older workers are prone to frequent absences because of age-related infirmities and above-average rates of sickness.

Fact: Data show that workers age 65 and over have attendance records that are equal to or better than most other age groups of workers. Older people who are *not* working may have dropped out of the workforce because of their health. Older workers who stay in the labor force may well represent a self-selected healthier group of older people.

Myth: Older workers have an unacceptably high rate of accidents at work.

Fact: Data show that older workers account for only 9.7 percent of all workplace injuries, whereas they make up 13.6 percent of the labor force.

Myth: Older workers are unwilling to learn new jobs and [are] inflexible about the hours they will work.

Fact: The truth depends on the individual. Studies of older employees' interest in alternative work arrangements found that many were interested in altering their work hours and their jobs. They were particularly interested in part-time work.[19]

Enlightened employers view older workers as an underutilized and valuable resource in an aging society

3c   Back to the Opening Case

Generations follow observable historical patterns and thus offer a very powerful tool for predicting future trends. To anticipate what 40-year-olds will be like 20 years from now, don't look at today's 40-year-olds; look at today's 20-year-olds.

Source: Neil Howe and William Strauss, "The Next 20 Years: How Customer and Workforce Attitudes Will Evolve," Harvard Business Review, 85 (July–August 2007): 42.

QUESTION:

Generally, how do you envision the management style and priorities of today's 20-year-olds when they are in upper management 20 years from now?

facing a potential labor shortage.[20] Like all employees, older workers need to be managed according to their individual abilities, not as members of a demographic group.

A New Social Contract Between Employer and Employee

Between World War II and the 1970s there was an implicit cultural agreement, a social contract, in the United States between employers and employees: "Be loyal to the company and the company will take care of you until retirement." But then the 1980s and 1990s brought restructuring, downsizing, and layoffs. With the dawn of the twenty-first century came a recession that only made matters worse. In 2001, 2.5 million employees in the United States were put out of work by "mass layoffs" involving 50 or more people.[21] As the economy bottomed out and began to grow again, the mass layoffs continued (involving more than 9.3 million people from 2002 to mid-2007).[22] The traditional social contract between employers and employees has been broken. In its place is a new social contract, framed in the following terms.

> *In short, the rules of the game have changed, and they go something like this: Your career depends on you, and you had better work at increasing your own long-term value, because nobody is going to do it for you. Employers, in turn, have accepted this reality: In the new marketplace for talent, we must provide opportunities, resources, and rewards for the continual development of our workforce or risk losing our greatest competitive asset.[23]*

Thus, the **new social contract** is based not on the notion of lifetime employment with a single employer but rather on shorter-term relationships of convenience and mutual benefit.[24] The senior vice president of human resources at AT&T, Harold Burlingame, put it more bluntly:

new social contract: assumption that the employer-employee relationship will be a shorter-term one based on convenience and mutual benefit, rather than for life

> *There was a time when someone would come to the front door of AT&T and see an invisible sign that said, AT&T: a job for life. . . . That's over. Now it's a shared kind of thing. Come to us. We'll invest in you, and you invest in us. Together, we'll face the market, and the degree to which we succeed will determine how things work out.[25]*

Nagging Inequalities in the Workplace

Can the United States achieve full and lasting international competitiveness if a large proportion of its workforce suffers nagging inequalities?[26] Probably not. Unfortunately, women, minorities, and part-timers often encounter barriers in the workplace. Let's open our discussion by focusing on women, because all minorities share their plight to some degree.

UNDER THE GLASS CEILING.   As a large and influential minority, women are demanding—and

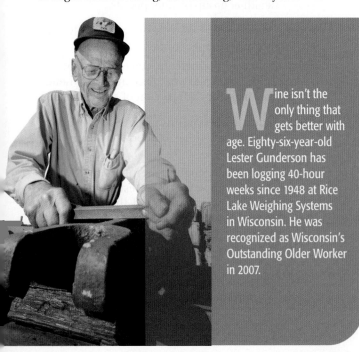

Wine isn't the only thing that gets better with age. Eighty-six-year-old Lester Gunderson has been logging 40-hour weeks since 1948 at Rice Lake Weighing Systems in Wisconsin. He was recognized as Wisconsin's Outstanding Older Worker in 2007.

getting—a greater share of workplace opportunities. Women occupy 50 percent of the managerial and professional positions in the U.S. workforce.[27] Still, a large inequity remains. *USA Today* summed up the situation:

> *For every dollar a man made in 2003, women made 75.5 cents, the Census Bureau said in its annual report on income. That was down from the record 76.6 cents that women earned vs. men's $1 in 2002. The median income for men working full time in 2003 was $40,668, not significantly different from the prior year, while the median income for women working full time was $30,724, down 0.6% from 2002.*
>
> *While the drop might appear minor, it was the first statistically significant decline in women's incomes since 1995, the Census Bureau said.*[28]

Also, according to a recent study, lifetime earnings for women in the United States equal, on average, 44 percent of the lifetime earnings for their male counterparts.[29] Across all job categories—from top business executives to lawyers, physicians, and office workers—the same sort of gender pay gap can be found.[30] This gap has expanded and contracted at various times since the 1950s in the United States, with the shortfall actually *growing* for women managers between 1995 and 2000.[31] In the United States, the gender pay gap can be summed up in two words: *large* and *persistent*. Comparatively well-paid men can grasp the significance of the gender wage gap by pondering the impact on their standard of living of a 25 percent pay cut. Moreover, men who share household expenses with a woman wage earner are also penalized by the gender wage gap.

In addition to suffering a wage gap, women (and other minorities) bump up against the so-called glass ceiling when climbing the managerial ladder.[32] "The **glass ceiling** is a concept popularized in the 1980s to describe a barrier so subtle that it is transparent, yet so strong that it prevents women and minorities from moving up in the management hierarchy."[33] It is not unique to the United States.

> **glass ceiling:** the transparent but strong barrier keeping women and minorities from moving up the management ladder

Consider the situation going into 2007:

- Companies in the *Fortune* 500, America's largest corporations, were headed by 491 men and nine women.[34]
- The percentage of women serving as *Fortune* 500 corporate directors slid to 14.6 percent from 14.7 percent the year before. Fifty-eight of the *Fortune* 500 companies had *no* female directors, including Honeywell, Apple, Toys 'R' Us, and Yahoo!.[35]
- Among industry groups, non-profit organizations had the most female CEOs (30 percent), followed by health care (22 percent).[36]

Why is there a glass ceiling? According to *Working Woman* magazine, women are being held back by "the lingering perception of women as outsiders, exclusion from informal networks, male stereotyping and lack of experience."[37] Other recent research suggests women are too often placed in precarious leadership positions, where *anyone* would have a higher probability of failure.[38] (See Valuing Diversity for some constructive steps.)

Another force is also at work here, siphoning off some of the best female executive talent part way up the corporate ladder. Many women are leaving the corporate ranks to start their own businesses. According to the U.S. Small Business Administration, "America's 9.1 million women-owned businesses employ 27.5 million people and contribute $3.6 trillion to the economy."[39]

CONTINUING PRESSURE FOR EQUAL OPPORTUNITY. Persistent racial inequality is underscored by the fact that the unemployment rate for African Americans generally is about twice as high as that for whites during both good and bad economic times.[40] Women, African Americans, Hispanics/Latinos, Native Americans, the physically challenged, and other minorities who are overrepresented in either low-level, low-paying jobs or the unemployment line can be expected to press harder

3d Is Race the Issue?

Kenneth Chenault, on being named CEO of American Express Corp.:

From a societal standpoint, it's a big deal; I won't minimize it. . . . But I want them to say, "He's a terrific CEO," not "He's a terrific black CEO."

Source: As quoted in Nelson D. Schwartz, "What's in the Cards for AMEX?" Fortune (January 22, 2001): 60.

QUESTION:
What is the real message here?

VALUING DIVERSITY
Leaders of the Pack

First up is Reynolds American. The tobacco giant is the only *Fortune* 500 company to have women in the CEO and CFO positions, as well as a female COO running its largest subsidiary. Then there's DuPont, where two women run three of the company's five business segments, bringing in $18 billion of DuPont's $27 billion in annual revenues. And Honeywell is unlike any of its competitors in having an equal number of men and women—two apiece—as divisional chief executive officers.

What's going on here? For a start, all three companies are fanatical about measurable results. "We're a performance culture," says Nance Dicciani, president and CEO of Specialty Materials at Honeywell. "The results and how you get them are judged and rewarded accordingly." All companies say they value performance, but Reynolds, DuPont and Honeywell go further, creating the conditions—empirical standards, clear goals, frequent reviews—that enable them to identify and reward high performers, regardless of sex. . . .

Highfliers are not just recognized. They're asked to take the kinds of tough assignments that give them the chance to leap beyond middle management. Reynolds CEO Susan Ivey says her big break came in 1990, when she was asked to take an overseas assignment and given 48 hours to decide. She went for it. The experience, Ivey says, was "broadening in every way." . . .

Then there's the chain-reaction effect. High-level female executives can inspire women throughout the organization and draw new talent. Ivey says Reynolds's new general counsel, E. Julia "Judy" Lambeth, was attracted to the job in part because there were so many women at the top. "It's easy for companies to say they don't have a glass ceiling," says Ivey, "but when you walk in the door here, it's eminently clear that we don't."

Source: Excerpted from Eugenia Levenson, "Leaders of the Pack," Fortune (October 16, 2006): 189. © 2006 Time Inc. All rights reserved.

to become full partners in the world of work.[41] Equal employment opportunity (EEO) and affirmative action are discussed in Chapter 10.

PART-TIMER PROMISES AND PROBLEMS. An increasing percentage of the U.S. labor force is now made up of **contingent workers**. According to the U.S. Bureau of Labor Statistics, there are more than 2 million contingent workers in the United States.[42] This "just-in-time" or "flexible" workforce includes a diverse array of part-timers, temporary workers, on-call employees, and independent contractors. "Their common denominator is that they do not have a long-term implicit contract with their ultimate employers, the purchasers of the labor and services they provide."[43] Employers are relying more on part-timers for two basic reasons. First, because they are paid at lower rates and often do not receive the full range of employer-paid benefits, part-timers are much less costly to employ than full-time employees. Second, as a flexible workforce, they can be let go when times are bad, without the usual repercussions of a general layoff. Starbucks

contingent workers: part-timers and other employees who do not have a long-term implicit contract with their ultimate employers

and Costco are notable exceptions to this state of affairs, as detailed in the Ethics feature later in this chapter.

On the down side, a recent comprehensive analysis of 38 studies involving 51,231 employees found lower "job involvement" among part-timers, compared with their full-time coworkers. (There were no significant differences in job satisfaction and organizational commitment, however.)[44] Also, critics warn of the risk of creating a permanent underclass of employees burdened by low pay, inadequate health and retirement benefits, and low status. Although some highly skilled professionals do enjoy good pay and greater freedom by working part time,[45] most part-timers do not. The plight of part-timers could become a major social and political issue worldwide in the years to come.

Managing Diversity

The United States, a nation of immigrants, is becoming even more racially and ethnically diverse. The evidence is compelling and controversial:

- "Foreign-born workers make up about 11% of the U.S. population and 14% of the labor force. But their impact is outsized, accounting for more than half of total workforce growth from 1996 to

2002. In the western Midwest, New England, and Mid-Atlantic regions, foreign-born workers accounted for more than 90% of employment growth from 1996 to 2002."[46]

- "In 303 counties [in the U.S.]—nearly one of 10—the share of whites has slipped below 50%. Eight more counties joined the list since 2005, and 205 others are nearing the mark with more than 40% minorities, nearly all in the South and West."[47]
- "The country will become a nation of minorities. Whites accounted for about 71% of the population . . . [in 2000,] but by 2050, the number will drop to 53%, blacks will increase one percentage point (to 13.2%), Asians will more than double to 8.9% (from 3.9%), and Hispanics will jump to 24.3% (from 11.8%)."[48]
- With a population growth rate seven times greater than that of any other group, Hispanics/Latinos passed African Americans in 2003 to become the country's largest minority.[49]
- An estimated 12 million undocumented people are living in the U.S. illegally, with half from Mexico.[50]

Accordingly, the U.S. workforce is becoming more culturally diverse. For example, the employees at some Marriott Hotels speak 30 different languages.[51] Some Americans decry what they consider to be an invasion of "their" national and organizational "territories." But many others realize that America's immigrants and minorities have always been a vitalizing, creative, hardworking force.[52] Progressive organizations are taking steps to better accommodate and more fully utilize America's more diverse workforce. **Managing diversity** is the process of creating an organizational culture that enables *all* employees, including women and minorities, to realize their full potential.[53]

> **managing diversity:** the process of helping all employees, including women and minorities, reach their full potential

MORE THAN EEO. Managing diversity builds on equal employment opportunity (EEO) and affirmative action programs (discussed in Chapter 10). EEO and affirmative action are necessary to get more women and minorities into the workplace. But getting them in is not enough. Comprehensive diversity programs are needed to create more *flexible* organizations where *everyone* has a fair chance to thrive and succeed.[54] These programs need to include white males who have sometimes felt slighted or ignored by EEO and affirmative action; they, too, have individual differences (opinions, lifestyles, age, and schedules) that deserve fair accommodation. Managing diversity requires many of us to adjust our thinking. According to sociologist Jack McDevitt, "We don't want to have as a goal just tolerating people. We have to *value* them."[55] In addition to being the ethical course of action, managing diversity is a necessity; a nation cannot waste human potential and remain globally competitive.

PROMISING BEGINNINGS. Among the diversity programs in use today are the following:

- Teaching English as a second language
- Creating mentor programs (an experienced employee coaches and sponsors a newcomer)
- Providing immigration assistance
- Fostering the development of support groups for minorities
- Training minorities for managerial positions
- Training managers to value and skillfully manage diversity
- Encouraging employees to contribute to and attend cultural celebrations and events in the community
- Creating, publicizing, and enforcing discrimination and harassment policies
- Actively recruiting minorities[56]

The scope of managing diversity is limited only by management's depth of commitment and imagination. For example, a supervisor learns sign language to communicate with a hearing-impaired employee. Or a married male manager attends a diversity workshop and becomes aware of the difficulties of being a single working mother. Perhaps a younger manager's age bias is

3e Does Diversity Need a Push?

Anne Fisher, *Fortune* magazine:

Researchers surveyed more than 5,500 American workers, including managers and CEOs, and the results are thought-provoking. Just 32% of U.S. employees think their companies do a decent job of hiring and promoting people other than white males. Their bosses' view isn't much rosier: Fewer than half of executives (47%) think their own diversity efforts are working, and the majority (59%) say it's partly their fault for not being involved enough.

Source: Anne Fisher, "How You Can Do Better on Diversity," Fortune (November 15, 2004): 60.

QUESTIONS:

Do you agree that diversity programs are coming up short? Explain. What needs to be done to strengthen diversity programs?

ETHICS: CHARACTER, COURAGE, AND VALUES

The Senator from Starbucks

On a freezing winter day in 1961, 7-year-old Howard Schultz came home from school in Brooklyn to find his parents in tears. His dad, a deliveryman, had broken his ankle and was out of a job, with no health insurance. His family's fear scarred Schultz. Later, as he grew Starbucks [where he is CEO], he vowed to build "the kind of company my father never got a chance to work for." Schultz was a leader in offering comprehensive benefits to part-timers—and the loyal talent Starbucks has thus attracted, he says, has been central to its success.

Now Starbucks' benevolent coffee republic is at risk. Like every business, it has seen double-digit increases in health costs. But the trouble goes beyond spending. "We can't be the kind of society we aspire to be when we have 50 million people uninsured," Schultz says. "It's a blemish on what it means to be an American."

And so Schultz has reached out to like-minded leaders, like Jim Sinegal of Costco, who also gives benefits to part-timers. Both men asked, What if this benefit becomes unsustainable? Reneging wasn't an option; they'd do whatever it took to keep their commitment to employees. . . . Meanwhile, in the 36 other countries where Starbucks operates, health care is basically funded by the government.

Such questions led Schultz to make the rounds in Washington, but he came away discouraged. "It's all great when you're there," he says. "Then you leave, and nothing happens." His next idea was to convene a summit on CNBC to call attention to the issue. He pulled it off [in 2005].

. . . as more CEOs realize that nothing they do inside their firms can fix what ails health care, the shadow Senator from Starbucks is well positioned to catalyze the business-led conversation we need.

Source: Excerpted from "The Senator from Starbucks," Fortune (August 7, 2006): 36.

FOR DISCUSSION

Is Schultz on the right track, or has he been unnecessarily distracted from his duty to provide Starbucks' shareholders with the best return on their investment? Should the United States follow other developed nations in shifting responsibility for providing health care insurance from business to government?

---

blunted after reading a research report documenting that older employees tend to be absent less often and to have lower accident rates than younger ones.[57] Maybe other companies begin to follow Corning's diversity policy, whereby "new employees are no longer encouraged to adopt the dress, style, and social activities of the white male majority."[58]

THE POLITICAL-LEGAL ENVIRONMENT

In its broadest terms, *politics* is the art (or science) of public influence and control. Laws are an outcome of the political process that differentiate good and bad conduct. An orderly political process is necessary because modern society is the product of an evolving consensus among diverse individuals and groups, often with conflicting interests and objectives. Although the list of special-interest groups is long and is still growing, not everyone can have his or her own way. The political system tries to balance competing interests in a generally acceptable manner.

Ideally, elected officials pass laws that, when enforced, control individual and collective conduct for the general good. Unfortunately, as we all know, variables such as hollow campaign promises, illegal campaign financing, and voter apathy throw sand into a democracy's political gears. Managers, as both citizens and caretakers of socially, politically, and economically powerful organizations, have a large stake in the political-legal environment. Two key pressure points for managers in this area are the politicization of management and increased personal legal accountability.

The Politicization of Management

Prepared or not and willing or not, today's managers often find themselves embroiled in issues with clearly political overtones (see Ethics: Character, Courage, and Values). Google is a good case in point. The young high-tech firm has had to quickly develop some political savvy in the face of calls for Web censorship around the world:

> The online search giant is taking a novel approach to the problem by asking U.S. trade officials to treat Internet restrictions as international trade barriers, similar to other hurdles to global commerce, such as tariffs.
>
> Google sees the dramatic increase in government Net censorship, particularly in Asia and the Middle East, as a potential threat to its advertising-driven business model, and wants government officials to consider the issue in economic, rather than just political terms.[59]

This sort of political climate has spurred the growth of a practice called *issues management.*

ISSUES MANAGEMENT.   **Issues management** (IM) is the ongoing organizational process of identifying, evaluating, and responding to relevant and important social and political issues. According to a pair of experts on the subject,

> **issues management:** ongoing process of identifying, evaluating, and responding to important social and political issues

> The purpose of IM is twofold. First, it attempts to minimize "surprises" which accompany social and political change by serving as an early warning system for potential environment threats and opportunities. IM analyzes the past development of an issue and assesses its importance for the firm. Second, IM attempts to prompt more systematic and effective responses to particular issues by serving as a coordinating and integrating force within the corporation. Once the issue has been analyzed, IM constructs alternative responses to deal with competing internal and external demands.[60]

IM is not an exact science. It has been carried out in various ways in the name of strategic planning, public relations, community affairs, and corporate communications, among others. IM's main contribution to good management is its emphasis on systematic preparedness for social and political action. Take Wal-Mart, for example. In the face of a record class-action sex discrimination lawsuit on behalf of 1.6 million past and present female employees and a growing wave of local opposition to its "big box" stores,[61] Wal-Mart's CEO Lee Scott outlined a more proactive response:

> "We have got to eliminate this constant barrage of negatives that cause people . . . to wonder if Wal-Mart will be allowed to grow," Scott said. "Our

Source: © 2004 Gary Markstein. Courtesy of the Milwaukee Journal Sentinel.

> message has not gotten out to the extent that it should. I think that's management's failure. We thought we could sit in Bentonville, take care of customers, take care of associates, and the world would leave us alone."
>
> He said Wal-Mart must be "more sophisticated" than it was in the days of founder Sam Walton, who shunned politics and public speaking.[62]

Indeed, Wal-Mart now has five lobbyists in Washington, D.C., and CEO Scott and other company executives give speeches and interviews. The company also has become a top campaign contributor (85 percent to Republicans in the 2004 election cycle).[63]

With this background in mind, let us turn our attention to three general political responses and four specific political strategies.

GENERAL POLITICAL RESPONSES.   The three general political responses available to management can be plotted on a continuum, as illustrated in Figure 3.2. Managers who are politically inactive occupy the neutral zone in the middle and have a "wait and see" attitude. But few managers today can afford the luxury of

FIGURE **3.2** Management's Political Response Continuum

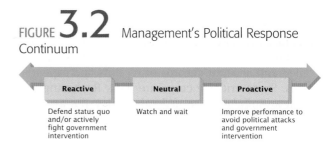

a neutral political stance. Those on the extreme left of the continuum are politically active in defending the status quo and/or fighting government intervention. In contrast, politically active managers on the right end of the continuum try to identify and respond constructively to emerging political/legal issues.

In recent years, more and more business managers have swung away from being reactive and have become proactive. Why? In short, they view prompt action as a way to avoid additional governmental regulation. The wisdom of choosing a proactive stance is clearly illustrated by the experiences of Microsoft and Intel. Both are dominant players in their respective fields of software and computer chips. According to the *Harvard Business Review,*

> For years now, Microsoft has been mired in court, facing charges of predatory behavior by the U.S. Department of Justice and the attorneys general of more than a dozen states. It has seen its name and business practices dragged through the mud, its senior executives distracted and embarrassed, and its very future as a single company thrown into doubt. . . .
>
> Intel, in stark contrast, has managed to avoid prolonged, high-profile antitrust cases. It's remained above the fray, its business focus largely undisturbed by trustbusters.
>
> Intel's success is not a matter of luck. It's a matter of painstaking planning and intense effort. The company's antitrust compliance program, refined over many years, may not receive a lot of attention from the press and the public, but it's been an integral element in the chip maker's business strategy.[64]

SPECIFIC POLITICAL STRATEGIES. Whether acting reactively or proactively, managers can employ four major strategies.[65]

1. *Campaign financing.* Although federal law prohibits U.S. corporations from backing a specific candidate or party with the firm's name, funds, or free labor, a legal alternative is available. Corporations can form political action committees (PACs) to solicit volunteer contributions from employees biannually for the support of preferred candidates and parties. Significantly, PACs are registered with the Federal Election Commission and are required to keep detailed and accurate records of receipts and expenditures. Some criticize corporate PACs for having too great an influence over federal politics. But a recent MIT study found no positive correlation between corporate political giving and subsequent profitability.

The researchers concluded that companies should spend their money in more productive ways.[66] Meanwhile, legislators are reluctant to tamper with a funding mechanism that tends to favor those already in office.

2. *Lobbying.* Historically, lobbying has been management's most popular and successful political strategy. Secret and informal meetings between hired representatives and key legislators in smoke-filled rooms have largely been replaced by a more forthright approach. Today, formal presentations by well-prepared company representatives are the preferred approach to lobbying for political support. For example, consider this trip to Washington by eBay's then-CEO Meg Whitman:

> . . . Whitman and 51 eBay customers held 36 meetings with politicians in a single day. They had breakfast with Rep. Jesse Jackson Jr., D-Ill., lunch with Rep. David Dreier, R-Calif., and dinner with Sen. John McCain, R-Ariz. Their goal: keeping Internet sales tax-free.
>
> "We need to make sure the government understands and supports what we're doing," says eBay government relations head Tod Cohen.[67]

Despite reform legislation from the U.S. Congress intended to correct abuses, loopholes, and weak penalties for inappropriate gifts, it is pretty much business as usual for corporate lobbyists. For example, phone companies AT&T and Verizon spent $22.4 million and $21.8 million, respectively, lobbying in Washington in 2006.[68]

3. *Coalition building.* In a political environment of countless special-interest groups, managers are finding that coalitions built around common rallying points are required for political impact.

4. *Indirect lobbying.* Having learned a lesson from unions, business managers now appreciate the value of grassroots lobbying. Members of legislative bodies tend to be more responsive to the desires of their constituents than to those of individuals who vote in other districts. Employee and consumer letter-writing, telephone, and e-mail campaigns have proved effective. **Advocacy advertising**, the controversial practice of promoting a cause or point of view along with a product or service, is another form of indirect lobbying that has grown in popularity in recent years. But it may not be as effective as hoped, judging from a recent survey of 1,066 adults: "Only 14% said they intentionally paid more for a product that

> **advocacy advertising:**
> promoting a point of view along with a product or service

3f   Greasing the Wheels

The price of persuasion in Washington continued to climb last year, with companies, unions, advocacy groups and trade associations spending $2.6 billion lobbying, 11 percent more than a year earlier.

The U.S. Chamber of Commerce and its affiliates led the way by spending a record $73 million, or $135,888 per member of Congress.

Source: Jonathan D. Salant, "The Cost to Lobby in D.C. Up in '06," Arizona Republic (March 30, 2007): D1.

QUESTION:

Is the intensive and costly lobbying of lawmakers good, bad, a necessary evil, or something else? Explain.

supports a cause."[69] The Internet is also becoming an effective indirect lobbying tool.

Auto makers launched saveleasing.com to defeat laws allowing companies to be held liable for damages caused by drivers in leased cars. By buying banner ads at local newspaper sites in Rhode Island, Connecticut, and New York, auto makers generated over 18,000 e-mails to legislators in those states. Connecticut and Rhode Island outlawed the suits.[70]

Increased Personal Legal Accountability

Recent changes in the political and legal climate have made it increasingly difficult for managers to take refuge in the bureaucratic shadows when a law has been broken. Managers in the United States who decide to take illegal courses of action stand a good chance of being held personally accountable in a court of law.

Things got even tougher in July 2002, when President George W. Bush signed the Sarbanes-Oxley Act into law. This sweeping corporate fraud bill, called SarbOx by many, garnered an unusually high degree of bipartisan support. The lawmakers were prodded into decisive action by public disgust over the fraud-tainted failures of corporate giants, including Enron, Andersen, WorldCom, and Adelphia.

The law, which passed the Senate by 99–0 and the House by 423–3, quadruples sentences for accounting fraud, creates a new felony for securities fraud that carries a 25-year prison term, places new restraints on corporate officers, and establishes a federal oversight board for the accounting industry.

"No more easy money for corporate criminals, just hard time," the president said. "The era of low standards and false profits is over, no boardroom in America is above or beyond the law."[71]

This increases the likelihood of managers being held *personally responsible* for the illegal actions of their companies. Anyone who is skeptical about rich and powerful executives being held accountable for their misdeeds should consider this roster of prison inmates: Jeffrey Skilling, former Enron CEO (serving 24 years); Bernard Ebbers, former CEO of WorldCom (25 years); Dennis Kozlowski, former CEO of Tyco (8 years); and Sanjay Kumar, former CEO of Computer Associates (12 years).[72] The personal accountability trend is spreading to other countries as well. In 2007, China executed the former head of its food and drug agency for accepting bribes for speedy approval of medicines.[73] So much for American managers complaining about SarbOx being too tough!

Misguided folks who do not heed this warning can take some comfort in a Dallas, Texas, consulting service.

The company is the nation's only felon-run consulting service that preps newly convicted white-collar crooks on what to expect once they get to prison, coaching them about how to make their hard time easier—a sort of school for scoundrels. . . .

[According to the consultant, a three-time loser for investment scams,] a lot of white-collar crooks, represented by some of the nation's best lawyers, were utterly clueless about life behind bars. . . .[74]

Guilty on all counts: Bernard Ebbers, the man who built a small Mississippi phone company into giant WorldCom, was convicted of massive accounting fraud in 2005. The jury didn't accept Ebbers's defense that he didn't know what was going on at his company when he was CEO. Ebbers could very well spend the rest of his life in prison.

Political-Legal Implications for Management

Managers will continue to be forced into becoming more politically astute, whether they like it or not. Support appears to be growing for the idea that managers can and should try to shape the political climate in which they operate. And the vigilant media and a wary public can be expected to keep a close eye on the form and substance of managerial politics to ensure that the public interest is served. Managers who abuse their political power and/or engage in criminal conduct while at work will increasingly be held accountable.

On the legal side, managers are attempting to curb the skyrocketing costs of litigation. Suing large companies with so-called deep pockets is a common practice in the United States, a country with more than 1 million lawyers. In a survey of large-company CEOs, 24 percent said litigation costs were their primary economic concern.[75] Indicative of the current legal climate is the 2002 class-action suit against McDonald's. The fast-food giant was sued for advertising and selling to children food that tends to make them more likely to become overweight and plagued by diabetes and heart disease. Regardless of the outcome of the suit, *Fortune* issued this warning to the food industry:

> *Seasoned lawyers from both sides of past mass-tort disputes agree that the years ahead hold serious tobacco-like litigation challenges that extend beyond fast foods to snack foods, soft drinks, packaged goods, and dietary supplements.*[76]

Not surprisingly, U.S. business leaders are pushing hard for tort (noncriminal) reform in which some sort of legislated cap is put on jury awards and damage claims.[77] Trial lawyers are pushing equally hard to squelch any such limitations, citing the need to protect the public. Meantime, managers can better prepare their companies and, it is hoped, avoid costly legal problems by performing legal audits. "A **legal audit** reviews all aspects of a firm's operations to pinpoint possible liabilities and other legal problems."[78] For example, a company's job application forms need to be carefully screened by the human resources department to eliminate any questions that could trigger a discriminatory-hiring lawsuit. Another approach, called **alternative dispute resolution**

legal audit: review of all operations to pinpoint possible legal liabilities or problems

alternative dispute resolution: avoiding courtroom battles by settling disputes with less costly methods, including arbitration and mediation

(ADR), strives to curb courtroom costs by settling disagreements out of court through techniques such as arbitration and mediation.

> *The modern ADR phenomenon has led to much greater use of older methods such as arbitration and mediation, as well as the creation of many new methods such as mini-trial, summary jury trial, private judging, neutral evaluation, and regulatory negotiation. Variations and hybrids of these techniques are also commonly found today.*[79]

As a technical point, a third-party arbitrator makes a binding decision, whereas a mediator helps the parties reach their own agreement.

THE ECONOMIC ENVIRONMENT

As we noted in Chapter 1, there is a close relationship between economics and management. Economics is the study of how scarce resources are used to create wealth and how that wealth is distributed. Managers, as trustees of our resource-consuming productive organizations, perform an essentially economic function. Unfortunately, economics is not a strong subject for the average American. In a recent nationwide survey by the University of Buffalo School of Management, "12th-graders answered only 52.3 percent of questions about personal finance and economics correctly."[80] A slight improvement over the 2002 results (50.2 percent of questions correctly answered) led the researcher to characterize U.S. high schoolers' knowledge of economics and finance as "dismal but improving."

Three aspects of the economic environment of management that deserve special consideration are jobs, business cycles, and the global economy.

The Job Outlook in Today's Service Economy, Where Education Counts

As in other important aspects of life, you have no guarantee of landing your dream job. However, as you move through college and into the labor force, one assumption is safe: you will probably end up with a job in the service sector. Why? According to the U.S. Bureau of Labor Statistics,

> *The long-term shift from goods-producing to service-providing employment is expected to continue. Service-providing industries are expected to account for approximately 18.7 million of the 18.9 million new wage and salary jobs generated over the 2004–2014 period.*[81]

For those concerned about having their future jobs outsourced to India, China, and elsewhere, the three fastest-growing job categories in the United States are education and health services, professional and business services, and leisure and hospitality (all are resistant to being offshored).

The traditional notion of the service sector as a low-wage haven of nothing but hamburger flippers and janitors is no longer valid. Well-paid doctors and dentists, lawyers, airline pilots, engineers, scientists, consultants, architects, and other professionals are all service-sector employees enjoying the fruits of a good education. Economists at the U.S. Bureau of Labor Statistics see it this way: "Occupations that require a bachelor's degree are projected to grow the fastest, nearly twice as fast as the average for all occupations. All of the 20 occupations with the highest earnings require at least a bachelor's degree. . . . Education is essential in getting a high paying job."[82]

Coping with Business Cycles

The **business cycle** is the up-and-down movement of an economy's ability to generate wealth; it has a predictable structure but variable timing. Historical economic data from industrialized economies show a clear pattern of alternating expansions and recessions. In between have been peaks and troughs of varying magnitude and duration.

> **business cycle:** the up-and-down movement of an economy's ability to generate wealth

According to Nobel Prize–winning economist Paul Samuelson, the four phases are like the changing seasons: "Each phase passes into the next. Each is characterized by different economic conditions. For example, during expansion we find that employment, production, prices, money, wages, interest rates, and profits are usually rising, with the reverse true in recession."[83] Long-term, the U.S. economy seems to have gotten a bit less volatile:

From 1900 through 1982, the economy slipped into 20 recessions that lasted an average of 15 months. But in the 24-plus years since, the economy has stumbled into a recession just twice, with each of those downturns lasting a mild eight months.[84]

CYCLE-SENSITIVE DECISIONS. Important decisions depend on the ebb and flow of the business cycle (see Figure 3.3). These decisions include ordering inventory, borrowing funds, increasing staff, and spending capital for land, equipment, and energy.

Timing is everything when it comes to making good cycle-sensitive decisions. Just as a baseball batter

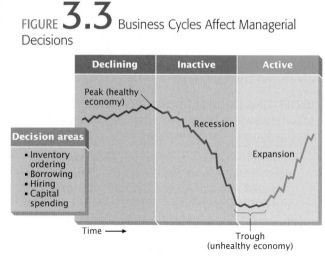

FIGURE **3.3** Business Cycles Affect Managerial Decisions

needs to start swinging before the ball reaches home plate, managers need to make appropriate cutbacks prior to the onset of a recession. Failure to do so, in the face of decreasing sales, leads to bloated inventories and idle productive resources—both costly situations. On the other hand, managers cannot afford to get caught short during a period of rapid expansion. Prices and wages rise sharply when everyone is purchasing inventories and hiring at the same time, and thus fueling inflation.

The trick is to stay slightly ahead of the pack. This is particularly true during recessions, when corporate strategy is tested to the fullest. According to a leading management consultant, "Successful players in a downturn place counterintuitive bets in order to dramatically transform their market positions, but these bets are not lucky gambles that miraculously win big against the odds. Instead they are rigorous and systematic moves that shift the odds in management's favor."[85] Consider, for example, the strategy described by Wolfgang Hultner, CEO of Mandarin Oriental Hotel Group's North American properties.

> *The hotel business, like others, is cyclical, with the cycle lasting anywhere between four and seven years. You want to build hotels when the cycle is a little bit down. Of course, you can't always choose the timing, but to build in the downtime is good for a number of reasons. Number one, construction costs are normally 20% to 25% lower than at the height of the market. Two, it's easier to find a good staff, and today in the hotel business, it's all about finding the right staff. By the time the hotel opens— and most hotels take between three and five years from the time you sign a contract to the day the doors open—hopefully you are out of the cycle and ready for some good news.*[86]

Hultner's strategy is simple: take market share from more timid competitors. Time will tell whether it is a good cycle-sensitive strategy. As mentioned repeatedly in this text, successful managers are *foresighted* rather than hindsighted. Accurate economic forecasts can be very helpful in this regard.

BENEFITING FROM ECONOMIC FORECASTS.   Thanks to some widely publicized bad calls, economic forecasting has come under fire in recent years. A case in point:

> *In the fourth quarter of 2000 the 36 forecasters surveyed [by the Federal Reserve Bank of Philadelphia] predicted that the economy would grow at a 3.3% rate in the first quarter of 2001; it shrank by 0.6%. In late 2001 the gang that couldn't predict straight said the economy in the first quarter of 2002 would grow by just 0.1%; it expanded at a whopping 5% pace.*[87]

One wit chided economic forecasters by claiming they have predicted eight out of the last four recessions! How can managers get some value from the hundreds of economic forecasts they encounter each year?

A pair of respected forecasting experts recommends a *consensus approach*.[88] They urge managers to survey a wide variety of economic forecasts, taking the forecasters' track records into consideration, and to look for a consensus or average opinion. Cycle-sensitive decisions can then be made accordingly, and slavish adherence to a single forecast can be avoided. One sure formula for failure is naïvely to assume that the future will simply be a replication of the past. In spite of their imperfection, professional economic forecasts are better than no forecasts at all.

One economist puts it this way: "Forecasters are very useful, in fact indispensable, because they give you plausible scenarios to help you think about the future in an organized way."[89]

The Challenge of a Global Economy

Nintendo's popular Wii game machine symbolizes the dynamic nature of today's truly globalized economy. *Fortune* magazine had an electronics expert disassemble a Wiimote, the system's remote-control device, and this is what he found: parts for the Japanese company's product were designed in Japan, the United States, Italy, and the Philippines; manufactured in the United States, Italy, Japan, Thailand, India, and Taiwan; and assembled in China.[90] So where *did* the product come from? It came from the global economy.

Each of us is challenged to better understand the workings and implications of the global economy in light of its profound impact on our lives and work.

A SINGLE GLOBAL MARKETPLACE.   Money spent on imported Japanese cars, French perfumes, Colombian coffee, New Zealand meat and produce, German beers, and Italian shoes may be evidence of an increasingly global economy. Deeper analysis, however, reveals more profound changes. First, according to observers, "The new global economy . . . must be viewed as the world moving from trade among countries to a single economy. One economy. One marketplace."[91] The North American Free Trade Agreement (NAFTA) among Mexico, Canada, and the United States, the 25-nation European Union, and the 150-nation World Trade Organization (WTO) represent

This giant container ship entering the Panama Canal from the Atlantic side is just a tiny cog in today's huge and growing economy. You are part of the global economy, too.

3g   A Global Brand Quiz

Name the home country for each of these well-known brands.

Brand	Home country*
Nokia	_____
Lego	_____
Samsung	_____
Ericsson	_____
Adidas	_____

*See Chapter 3 endnote 91 for the correct answers and the results of a 1,000-student survey.[92]

Source: Elizabeth Woyke, "Flunking Brand Geography" Business Week *(June 18, 2007): 14.*

QUESTIONS:

When you buy something, is a product's country of origin more or less important than price and value? What implications does your answer have for the global economy and for the U.S. economy?

GLOBALIZATION IS PERSONAL. Economic globalization is a huge concept, stretching the limits of the imagination. For instance, try to grasp what it means that more than $1.5 trillion moves through the global banking network in a single day![95] Ironically, globalization is also a very personal matter affecting where we work, how much we're paid, what we buy, and how much things cost. Let us explore two personal aspects of the global economy.

1. ***Working for a foreign-owned company.*** One of the most visible and controversial signs of a global economy is the worldwide trend toward foreign ownership. Consider the case of Toyota Motor as of 2007, for example. It is the sixth-biggest company in the world, employing nearly 300,000 people around the globe. Toyota employs 34,675 Americans (with an annual U.S. payroll of $2.9 billion) and "purchases $28 billion in parts, materials and services annually from hundreds of suppliers in over 30 states." After fifty years of doing business in the United States, Toyota's direct investment in facilities has grown to over $15 billion. An estimated 386,000 American jobs have been created by Toyota's presence in the United States.[96] This sort of cross-border ownership raises fundamental questions. For instance, has the increase in foreign-owned companies in the United States been a positive or a negative? Economists have found evidence on the positive side:

> *Americans who work in the USA for foreign companies typically make about 10% more than those who work for U.S. companies, just as foreigners who work for U.S. companies abroad make 10% more than domestic workers there, says Gary Hufbauer, senior economist with the Institute for International Economics.*
>
> *The reason, Hufbauer says, is that companies with the might to expand globally are the most productive, want the best workers and are willing to pay a premium.*[97]

2. ***Meeting world standards.*** One does not have to work for a foreign-owned company to be personally affected by the global economy. Many people today complain of having to work harder for the same (or perhaps less) money. Whether they realize it or not, they are being squeezed by two global economic trends: higher quality and lower wages. The "offshoring" of jobs discussed in Chapter 1 is a major byproduct of these trends. Only companies striking the right balance between quality and costs can be globally competitive.

steps toward that single global marketplace. Second, the size of the global economy has expanded dramatically. *Fortune* explains why:

> *. . . the commercial world has been swelled by the former Soviet empire, China, India, Indonesia, and much of Latin America—billions of people stepping out from behind political and economic walls. This is the most dramatic change in the geography of capitalism in history.*[93]

Third, and an ominous sign to some, the business cycles of countries around the world show signs of converging in concert with the U.S. economy. International Monetary Fund economists recently documented this trend after studying 20 years of economic data from 170 countries. "They found that an increase of one percentage point in the growth of U.S. output per capita was associated with an increase of 0.8 to 1.0 percentage point in the average growth of other countries. Decreases in U.S. output likewise lowered growth elsewhere."[94] The prospect of global expansions and recessions gives new meaning to the old saying "We're all in the same boat."

THE TECHNOLOGICAL ENVIRONMENT

Technology is a term that ignites passionate debates in many circles these days. Some blame technology for environmental destruction and cultural fragmentation. Others view technology as the key to economic and social progress. No doubt there are important messages in both extremes. See Table 3.1 for technologies likely to have significant effects on our lives in the future.

For our purposes, **technology** is defined as all the tools and ideas available for extending the natural physical and mental reach of humankind. A central theme in technology is the practical application of new ideas, a theme that is clarified by the following distinction between science and technology:

technology: all the tools and ideas available for extending the natural physical and mental reach of humankind

"Science is the quest for more or less abstract knowledge, whereas technology is the application of organized knowledge to help solve problems in our society."[98] According to the following historical perspective, technology is facilitating the evolution of the industrial age into the information age, just as it once enabled the agricultural age to evolve into the industrial age.

Stephen R. Barley, a professor at Cornell's School of Industrial and Labor Relations, builds on the work of others to argue that until recently, "the economies of the advanced industrial nations revolved around electrical power, the electric motor, the internal combustion engine, and the telephone." The development of these "infrastructural technologies" made possible the shift from an agricultural to a manufacturing economy, in the process precipitating "urbanization, the growth of corporations, the rise of professional management...."

Now, Barley writes, the evidence suggests that another shift is taking place, with implications likely to be just as seismic: "Our growing knowledge of how to convert electronic and mechanical impulses into digitally encoded information (and vice

TABLE **3.1**	Science Fiction Is Becoming Reality with These Seven New Technologies

- **Plastic solar cells:** "The new photovoltaics use tiny solar cells embedded in thin sheets of plastic to create an energy-producing material that is cheap, efficient, and versatile."

- **Printable mechatronics:** Researchers are "developing processes that adapt ink-jet printing technology to build ready-to-use products, complete with working circuitry, switches, and movable parts."

- **Memory drugs:** These drugs aim to help people with Alzheimer's and boost healthy people's memories by enhancing the brain's neural connections and functions.

- **Perpendicular magnetic storage:** "Today's hard drives store bits of data horizontally, like stalks of freshly cut corn. PMR stores them vertically, like cornstalks standing in a field. With perpendicular storage, each bit occupies less space on the surface of the disc, so more data can be stuffed into a smaller area." This technology also uses less power, thus prolonging battery life.

- **Microfluidic testing:** "Microfluidics is the science of moving fluids through tiny channels the thickness of a human hair. In microfluidic tests, blood, saliva, or urine samples are analyzed after coming into contact with tiny amounts of a chemical reagent."

- **Micro-opticals:** Combining the functions of several present-day chips on one integrated optical chip will make telecommunication faster and less expensive.

- **Software radio:** The goal of this new software is to create wireless communication devices that will work on all mobile networks—anywhere, anytime.

Source: Adapted from G. Pascal Zachary, Om Malik, David Pescovitz, and Matthew Maier, "Seven New Technologies That Change Everything," Business 2.0, 5 (September 2004): 82–90.

versa) and how to transmit such information across vast distances is gradually enabling industry to replace its electromechanical infrastructure with a computational infrastructure."[99]

Consequently, *information* has become a valuable strategic resource. Organizations that use appropriate information technologies to get the right information to the right people at the right time will enjoy a competitive advantage (Internet strategies are discussed in Chapter 7).

Two aspects of technology with important implications for managers are the innovation process and *intra*preneurship.

The Innovation Process

Technology comes into being through the **innovation process**, the systematic development and practical application of a new idea.[100] According to a recent survey of 250 executives, this important area needs improvement: ". . . nearly seven out of ten cited innovation as a top priority and said they plan to hike R&D [research and development] spending. Yet 57% also said they aren't satisfied with the return on their innovation investments."[101]

innovation process: the systematic development and practical application of a new idea

A great deal of time-consuming work is necessary to develop a new idea into a marketable product or service. And many otherwise good ideas do not become technologically feasible, let alone marketable and profitable. According to one innovation expert, "only one of every 20 or 25 ideas ever becomes a successful product—and of every 10 or 15 new products,

only one becomes a hit."[102] Nowhere is this uphill battle more apparent than in pharmaceutical research and development:

> *Drug discovery is a costly slog in which hundreds of scientists screen tens of thousands of chemicals against specific disease targets. After a remorseless round of testing, most of those compounds will prove to be unstable, unsafe, or otherwise unsuitable for human use. Pfizer spends $152 million a week funding 479 early-stage, preclinical discovery projects; 96% of those efforts will ultimately bomb.*[103]

A better understanding of the innovation process can help improve management's chances of turning new ideas into profitable goods and services.

A THREE-STEP PROCESS. The innovation process has three steps (see Figure 3.4). First is the conceptualization step, when a new idea occurs to someone. Development of a working prototype is the second step, called **product technology**. This involves actually creating a product that will work as intended. The third and final step is developing a production process to create a profitable relationship among quantity, quality, and price. This third step is labeled **production technology**. Successful innovation depends on the right combination of new ideas, product

product technology: second stage of the innovation process, involving the creation of a working prototype

production technology: third stage of the innovation process, involving the development of a profitable production process

Sometimes innovation comes with a face—and a name. Meet Zeno, a 6-pound, 17-inch-tall robotic boy being built at the Hanson Robotics facility in Richardson, Texas. Hmm, do you think the engineers can program Zeno to brush his teeth, be nice to his sister, and pick up his dirty clothes?

FIGURE **3.4** The Three-Step Innovation Process

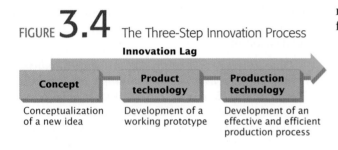

technology, and production technology. A missing or deficient step can ruin the innovation process.

INNOVATION LAG. The time it takes for a new idea to be translated into satisfied demand is called **innovation lag**. The longer the innovation lag, the longer society must wait to benefit from a new idea. For example, fax machines came into wide use in the early 1990s. But the fax concept was patented by a Scottish clockmaker named Alexander Bain in 1843—an innovation lag of nearly a century and a half.[104] Over the years, the trend has been toward shorter innovation lags. Consider CEO Steve Jobs's story about the birth of the Apple iPhone:

> **innovation lag:** time it takes for a new idea to be translated into satisfied demand

We started with the iPhone three years ago. We're product folks. We wanted to create a phone we loved. When we started this, none of us loved our phones. We wanted to make a phone so great, you couldn't imagine going anywhere without it.[105]

After a three-year innovation lag, from concept to marketplace, Apple had a hit on its hands.

SHORTENING INNOVATION LAG. Reducing innovation lags should be a high priority for modern managers. Innovative companies generally rely on two sound management practices: *goal setting* and *empowerment*. These practices create the sense of urgency necessary for speedier innovation. Medtronic, the Minnesota-based leader in manufacturing heart pacemakers, uses goal setting skillfully. A powerful message is sent to its 25,000-plus employees worldwide about promptly getting new ideas to market when top management restates the "annual goal of gathering 70% of its sales from products introduced within the past two years."[106] That is a bold commitment!

Empowerment, discussed in Chapter 14, involves pushing decision-making authority down to levels where people with the appropriate skills can do the most good. Software giant Microsoft is strong in this regard, as illustrated by the following story told by the firm's recently retired chief operating officer.

> *I was in a meeting where Bill Gates was quizzing a young manager—dressed in cutoffs, sandals, and a well-worn Microsoft T-shirt—about a new product proposal. After the meeting, I asked Bill, for whom this had been the first significant briefing on the product, what the next step would be. Would the manager prepare a memo summarizing the arguments, something top management could review before suggesting modifications to his proposal and granting final approval? Bill looked at me and smiled. "No, that's it. The key decisions got made,"* *he said. "Now his group better hustle to implement things—or else."*[107]

Another step in the right direction is a practice called *concurrent engineering*. Also referred to as parallel design, **concurrent engineering** is a team approach to product design. Such an approach lets research, design, production, finance, and marketing specialists have a direct say in the product design process from the very beginning. This contrasts with the traditional, and much slower, practice of having a product move serially from research to design, from design to manufacturing, and so on down the line toward the marketplace. The time to hear about possible marketing problems is while a product is still in the conceptualization stage, not after it has become a warehouse full of unsold goods.

> **concurrent engineering:** team approach to product design involving specialists from all functional areas, including research, production, and marketing

Promoting Innovation Through Intrapreneurship

When we hear someone called an entrepreneur, we generally think of a creative individual who has risked everything while starting his or her own business. Indeed, as we saw in Chapter 1, entrepreneurs are a vital innovative force in the economy. A lesser-known but no less important type of entrepreneur is the so-called intrapreneur.

Gifford Pinchot, author of the book *Intrapreneuring*, defines an **intrapreneur** as an employee who takes personal "hands-on responsibility" for pushing any type of innovative idea, product, or process through a large organization. Pinchot

> **intrapreneur:** an employee who takes personal responsibility for pushing an innovative idea through a large organization

3h Advice for Future Intrapreneurs

Among Gifford Pinchot's ten commandments for intrapreneurs are the following:

- "Come to work each day willing to be fired."
- "Do any job needed to make your project work, regardless of your job description."
- "Remember it is easier to ask for forgiveness than for permission."

Source: Excerpted from Gifford Pinchot III, Intrapreneuring: Why You Don't Have to Leave the Corporation to Become an Entrepreneur (New York: Harper & Row, 1985), 22.

QUESTIONS:

How can these ideas enhance innovation in large organizations? Is this advice a formula for career success or sudden unemployment?

calls intrapreneurs "dreamers who do." But unlike traditional entrepreneurs, who tend to leave the organizational confines to pursue their dreams, intrapreneurs strive for innovation *within* existing organizations. Intrapreneurs tend to have a higher need for security than entrepreneurs, who strike out on their own. They pay a price for being employees rather than owners. Pinchot explains:

Corporate entrepreneurs [or intrapreneurs], despite prior successes, have no capital of their own to start other ventures. Officially, they must begin from zero by persuading management that their new ideas are promising. Unlike successful independent entrepreneurs, they are not free to guide their next ventures by their own intuitive judgments; they still have to justify every move.[108]

Kathleen Synnott, a division marketing manager for Pitney Bowes Inc., is the classic intrapreneur. After seeing the potential of the versatile new Mail Center 2000, a computerized mail-handling and -stamping machine, Synnott became its enthusiastic champion. Just two things stood in her way: change-resistant managers and satisfied customers.

During the design process, for instance, Synnott helped protect the original blueprint from execs who wanted to break up the Mail Center 2000 and sell it as upgrading components to Pitney's existing mail-metering machines. She also guided it through a technical maze, insisting on 22 simulations to make sure potential customers liked what they saw. "There were naysayers who didn't think we were ready" for such a system, says Synnott. . . . "But they got religion."[109]

If today's large companies are to achieve a competitive edge through innovation, they need to foster a supportive climate for intrapreneurs like Synnott. According to experts on the subject, an organization can foster intrapreneurship if it does four things:

- Focuses on results and teamwork
- Rewards innovation and risk taking
- Tolerates and learns from mistakes
- Remains flexible and change-oriented[110]

Our discussions of creativity, participative management, and organizational cultures in later chapters contain ideas about how to encourage intrapreneurship of all types.

SUMMARY

1. Demographically, the U.S. workforce is becoming larger, older, more culturally diverse, and increasingly female. Remedial education programs are needed to improve the quality of the U.S. workforce. Researchers have disproved persistent myths that older workers are less productive and more accident-prone than younger coworkers.

2. A new social contract between employers and employees is taking shape because the tradition of lifetime employment with a single organization is giving way to shorter-term relationships of convenience and mutual benefit. The traditional paternalistic social contract between employer and employee, whereby lifetime job security was exchanged for loyalty, has been replaced by a shorter-term relationship of convenience. Today's employees are assumed to be responsible for their own employability.

3. The persistence of opportunity and income inequalities (and the so-called glass ceiling) among women and minorities is a strong stimulus for change. With part-timers playing a greater role in the U.S. workforce, there is genuine concern about

creating a disadvantaged underclass of employees. Managing-diversity programs attempt to go a step beyond equal employment opportunity. The new goal is to tap *every* employee's *full* potential in today's diverse workforce.

4. Because of government regulations and sociopolitical demands from a growing list of special-interest groups, managers are becoming increasingly politicized. More and more believe that if they are going to be affected by political forces, they should be more active politically. Some organizations rely on issues management to systematically identify, evaluate, and respond to important social and political issues. Managers can respond politically in one of three ways: by being reactive, neutral, or proactive. Four political strategies that managers have found useful for pursuing active or reactive political goals are campaign financing, lobbying, coalition building, and indirect lobbying. There is a strong trend toward managers being held personally accountable for the misdeeds of their organizations. Alternative dispute resolution tactics such as arbitration and mediation can help trim management's huge litigation bill.

5. Managers can make timely decisions about inventory, borrowing, hiring, and capital spending during somewhat unpredictable business cycles by taking a consensus approach to economic forecasts. Business is urged to compete actively and creatively in the emerging global economy. By influencing jobs, prices, quality standards, and wages, the global economy affects virtually *everyone*.

6. Consisting of conceptualization, product technology, and production technology, a healthy innovation process is vital to technological development. Innovation lags must be shortened. An organizational climate that fosters intrapreneurship can help. An intrapreneur is an employee who champions an idea or innovation by pushing it through the organization.

TERMS TO UNDERSTAND

- **Demographics,** p. 61
- **New social contract,** p. 64
- **Glass ceiling,** p. 65
- **Contingent workers,** p. 66
- **Managing diversity,** p. 67
- **Issues management,** p. 69
- **Advocacy advertising,** p. 70
- **Legal audit,** p. 72
- **Alternative dispute resolution,** p. 72
- **Business cycle,** p. 73
- **Technology,** p. 76
- **Innovation process,** p. 77
- **Product technology,** p. 77
- **Production technology,** p. 77
- **Innovation lag,** p. 78
- **Concurrent engineering,** p. 78
- **Intrapreneur,** p. 78

MANAGER'S TOOLKIT

How Business Leaders Can Help Women Break Through the Glass Ceiling

Businesses need as much leadership, talent, quality, competence, productivity, innovation, and creativity as possible as they face more effective worldwide competition. Following are ten actions that companies can take to ensure maximum use of women's business capability:

1. **Provide feedback on job performance.**
   Give frequent and specific appraisals. Women need and want candid reviews of their work. Clearly articulated suggestions for improvement, standards for work performance, and plans for career advancement will make women feel more involved in their jobs and help make them better employees.

2. **Accept women.**
   Welcome them as valued members of your management team. Include women in every kind of communication. Listen to their needs and concerns, and encourage their contributions.

3. **Ensure equal opportunities.**
   Give women the same chances you give talented men to grow, develop, and contribute to company profitability. Give them the responsibility to direct major projects, to plan and implement systems and programs. Expect them to travel and relocate and to make the same commitment to the company as do men who aspire to leadership positions.

4. **Provide career counseling.**
Give women the same level of counseling on professional career advancement opportunities as you give to men.

5. **Identify potential.**
Identify women as possible future managers early in their employment, and encourage their advancement through training and other developmental activities.

6. **Encourage assertiveness.**
Assist women in strengthening their assertion skills. Reinforce strategic career planning to encourage women's commitment to their careers and long-term career plans.

7. **Accelerate development.**
Provide "fast track" programs for qualified women. Either formally or informally, these programs will give women the exposure, knowledge and positioning they need for career advancement.

8. **Offer mentoring opportunities.**
Give women the chance to develop mentoring relationships with other employees. The overall goal should be to provide advice, counsel, and support to promising female employees from knowledgeable, senior-level men and women.

9. **Encourage networking.**
Promote management support systems and networks among employees of both genders. Sharing experiences and information with other men and women who are managers provides invaluable support to peers. These activities give women the opportunity to meet and learn from men and women in more advanced stages of their careers—a helpful way of identifying potential mentors or role models.

10. **Increase women's participation.**
Examine the feasibility of increasing the participation of women in company-sponsored planning retreats, use of company facilities, social functions, and so forth. With notable exceptions, men are still generally more comfortable with other men, and as a result, women miss many of the career and business opportunities that arise during social functions. In addition, women may not have access to information about the company's informal political and social systems. Encourage male managers to include women when socializing with other business associates.

Source: Excerpted from Rose Mary Wentling, "Breaking Down Barriers to Women's Success," HR Magazine, *40 (May 1995). Reprinted with the permission of* HR Magazine, *published by the Society for Human Resource Management, Alexandria, Virginia.*

ACTION LEARNING EXERCISE

Crystal Ball Gazing

Instructions: Read these predictions from *The Futurist* magazine and rate how probable each is, according to the scale below. (*Note:* Use the year 2020 if a specific time frame is not mentioned.)

No chance   **Virtually guaranteed**

0%	10%	20%	30%	40%	50%	60%	70%	80%	90%	100%

Prediction   **Probability of occurrence**

1. **Globalization could make foods less safe to eat.** As more food is imported from far-flung local producers, national food-safety standards will become harder to enforce. Growing demand for fresh foods year-round makes refrigeration and other safe-transport issues more of a concern.   _____

2. **Falling language barriers could spur more travel.** Automated translation systems could enable most of the world's people to communicate directly with one another—each speaking and hearing in his or her own language—by about 2020.   _____

3. **No more textbooks?** Printed and bound textbooks may disappear as more interactive coursework goes online.   _____

4. **"Internet Universities" could lead to the demise of traditional institutions.** Web-linked education services that offer franchised software and "college-in-a-box" courses from superstar teachers could lead to educational monopolies. Such "virtual" universities would have rigidly standardized curricula that undersell traditional courses in brick-and-mortar institutions.
         _____

5. **The era of cheap oil is NOT over.** Not only is the world not running out of oil, but prices are likely to fall again and remain around $20 per barrel for the next decade. Reason: The current high prices make intensive exploration and development of new oil sources more attractive, thus ultimately increasing supply and lowering prices.
         _____

6. **Water shortages will become more frequent and severe.** Most of the major cities in the developing world will face severe water shortages in the next two decades, as will one-third of the population of Africa. By 2040, at least 3.5 billion people will run short of water—almost 10 times as many as in 1995—and by 2050, two-thirds of the world's population could be living in regions with chronic, widespread shortages of water.
         _____

7. **Tissue engineers may one day grow a "heart in a bottle."** Using a fibrous "scaffold" that is seeded with stem cells, researchers could coax the cells to grow into the needed organ. Skin and cartilage have already been grown this way. In the future, organ generation could help the tens of thousands of patients in need of organ transplants, predicts Vladimir Mironov, chief scientific officer with Cardiovascular Tissues Technology, Inc.
         _____

8. **Nanomachines will enhance our brains.** Nanocomputers may soon be placed inside human brains to enhance memory, thinking ability, visualization, and other tasks, according to futurist consultant Michael Zey, author of *The Future Factor*. Technologies will also be developed that allow us to connect our brains to a computer and either download or upload data.
         _____

9. **Touch-sensitive robots may make virtual reality more realistic.** The ability to collect and transmit tactile data—such as the way it feels to kick a soccer ball—could add to humans' ability to experience events.
         _____

10. **Hardware will soften up**. Instead of pounding on hard, plastic keyboards to do your computing, you'll soon be able to gently caress soft electronic fabrics. Among potential applications for smart textiles: tablecloths with piano keyboards and furniture slipcovers with TV remote controls.
         _____

Source: *Originally published in the November–December 2001 issue of* The Futurist. *Used with permission from the World Future Society, 7910 Woodmont Avenue, Suite 450, Bethesda, Maryland 20814. Telephone: 301-656-8274; Fax: 301-951-0394;* **http://www.wfs.org.**

For Consideration/Discussion

1. When you compare your ratings with those of others, do you envision things changing more rapidly or more slowly than they do? What does this imply about the way you, as a manager, would tend to deal with organizational and external changes?

2. What, if any, potentially profitable business ideas do you see in any of these predictions? Explain.

3. What are two or three of your own 10-year predictions for our sociocultural, political-legal, economic, or technological future?

4. What needs to be done to prepare for two or three selected predictions from *The Futurist's* list (or from your own predictions)?

CLOSING CASE

Xerox's Inventor-in-Chief: Sophie Vandebroek

Xerox has become an innovation power again, producing new technologies that can read, understand, route, and protect documents, among other things. Leading that effort is Vandebroek, 45, the company's chief technology officer since late 2005. Her task is to keep Xerox at the leading edge of infotech progress in ways that make shareholders richer.

Born and raised in Belgium, Vandebroek has a doctorate in electrical engineering from Cornell; she first joined Xerox in 1991. Before an invited audience in New York City, she talked with *Fortune*'s Geoff Colvin about the difference between invention and innovation; why Xerox employs anthropologists; how to make girls passionate about engineering; and much else. Edited excerpts:

COLVIN: Innovation may be the hottest topic in business. How can it be a competitive advantage for Xerox?

VANDEBROEK: It's a matter of making sure that our customers constantly want to buy our products and services. Ultimately innovation is about delighting the customer, and that results in great economic returns for Xerox. If you innovate and it doesn't end up as something that the customer benefits from, then it's not innovation.

How does Xerox make sure that what it comes up with is not just what the engineers think is cool but what customers actually want?

It's tough. Innovation has two elements. No. 1, there is the creative piece, the "Aha!" moment. These are our own scientists and researchers and engineers, and our partners. A lot of what we do early on is dreaming and innovating with the customers. These are the early moments of understanding and seeing what nobody else has seen before that could result in a great product or service. The second piece is the "intrapreneurial" role within Xerox, making sure that this creative idea goes through the whole value chain and becomes the right product for the customer. . . .

Some companies renowned for innovation, such as Google and 3M, tell employees to spend a certain percentage of time on projects of their own without any guidance. Is that a good idea?

Within the broader scope of the vision, we encourage our researchers to spend time on their own — and that vision is articulated with help from the researchers. For example, we have a lot of blogging in the research center, and we created a Wiki to help articulate the strategy that we want to execute. So it's not top down. A lot of the brightest ideas and the best articulations come from within.

So what is your vision?

It's helping our customers deal with their document-intensive processes. That means making sure they have the information they need when and where they need it, with the history and the context of the information they need. It also means seamlessly bridging the digital and physical, and making it easy and fast to get to information. I want the document to be smart enough so I don't need to worry about it. . . .

In your research centers you have anthropologists, ethnographers, sociologists, psychologists. What's that all about?

A big piece of our business is mass customization. How could we personalize *Fortune* so that every one of your customers gets a personalized copy? People who have conventionally used offset printing have a whole work process in place. So we send in a bunch of sociologists—we call them "work practice specialists"—to observe how people do it. That way, when we come out with our digital presses, it matches the work flow, and the people who will have to start using this completely disruptive technology understand how it works. Otherwise we get all this great invention, and it hits the customers and they don't want to use it. I differentiate between invention and innovation. Innovation is when ultimately this service is rolled out and you actually can use it.

What's another example of innovation that came from observing the customer?

PARC, our Palo Alto Research Center, has work-practice specialists. They went to observe a typical office customer and noticed that 40% of the paper printed during the day went in the garbage at night, which is very bad. Based on that observation, we invented reusable paper. You print it. You have the notes today.

Tonight your paper is blank. You can print on it again tomorrow. The next day it's blank. It's reusable, so it's good for the environment. We're big into being green. It's still an invention. It's not yet an innovation because we now have to figure out how to get an idea like that into the market. . . .

You are president of the Xerox Innovation Group. Does it make sense to have such a thing? The name suggests that innovation happens there rather than everywhere.

I agree with you 100%—innovation is only innovation when the creative idea makes a difference to our customers and when they purchase it or work with Xerox to help them with their businesses. Innovation has to cover the whole company, the whole value chain—from research to development to manufacturing, through marketing, sales and service, and consultants. The Innovation Group consists of four research centers: one in Toronto in materials; the Palo Alto Research Center; one in Rochester, New York, focused on next-generation systems; and one in Grenoble, France, which does all the intelligent-document research. Within research you play three roles. There's an explorer role, where we push the limits of the technology and constantly look at how we can come up with these bright new ideas, either within the company or working with partners. Then we have the partnership role. You work with the business-group engineers to make sure these cool technologies actually end up in a product or a service. The third role, in the middle, is the incubator. Some of these novel technologies might work in the labs, but before the business groups will take them on you need to make sure no more invention is required. In this phase we try to understand fully the business value of these ideas and incubate them to a level where the business group says, "Yes, I want to invest in that."

I gather you're doing something innovative in the way you manage the researchers.

We launched a research center on Second Life earlier this year. We bought an island. Our CFO liked it a lot because now the researchers from all the different research centers are meeting in Second Life instead of getting on airplanes. It's really cool because not only can you envision the future today, you can show future concepts and thinking to your customers. We have done our first press release in Second Life and taken some industry analysts and shown them the new products. What is a document in a virtual world? What are the next-generation systems? We do these in Second Life now.

When you were getting your doctorate in electrical engineering at Cornell, how many other women were in your class?

In my research group, none. When I was getting my master's degree in Belgium, we were 500 students, 15 women.

Is the scarcity of women in engineering and related disciplines a problem for innovation?

I think it's a major problem. You're excluding half the population from being able to innovate. Girls lose interest in science in middle school. It's not cool. So you have to keep girls and minorities interested in science and technology all through middle school and high school, and especially with girls you have to talk about the social impact an engineer can make. There wouldn't be clean water, there wouldn't be the Internet, there wouldn't be iPods, there wouldn't be airplanes, there wouldn't be the stock market—all these things would disappear if you [took] away what engineers have done.

Source: Excerpted from Geoff Colvin, "Xerox's Inventor-in-Chief," *Fortune* (July 9, 2007): 65–72. © 2007 Time Inc. All rights reserved. Also see Nanette Byrnes, "Xerox' New Design Team: Customers," Business Week (May 7, 2007): 72.

FOR DISCUSSION

1 How is Vandebroek's distinction between invention and innovation related to the three-step innovation process shown in Figure 3.4?

2 What, if any, legal factors does Xerox need to consider when innovating new information technologies?

3 Which stages of the three-stage innovation process in Figure 3.4 are evident in this case? Explain.

4 Why is intrapreneurship an important part of Xerox's quest for innovative products and services?

5 What can businesses do to get more girls and women interested in math and sciences?

TEST PREPPER

True/False Questions

_____ 1. The U.S. workforce is getting older, more diverse, and increasingly female.

_____ 2. In 2004, only 24 *Fortune* 500 companies had female CEOs.

_____ 3. Hispanics/Latinos are now the largest minority group in the United States.

_____ 4. Managing diversity, by definition, is limited in scope to advancing women and minorities.

_____ 5. A "defend status quo" attitude is adopted by managers on the neutral portion of the political response continuum.

_____ 6. Settling legal disputes outside of court is referred to as legal auditing.

_____ 7. Economic forecasts are a waste of time for managers because they have a poor track record.

_____ 8. Researchers have found that in the United States, employees of foreign-owned companies earn less than employees of domestic companies.

_____ 9. The three steps in the innovation process are inspiration, development, and exploitation.

_____ 10. Intrapreneurs typically do not quit their present job to pursue an innovative idea.

Multiple-Choice Questions

1. Demographics involves the study of
   A. regional pay rates.
   B. managerial influence.
   C. male-female pay gaps.
   D. work schedule variations.
   E. population characteristics.

2. How does *Fortune* magazine's Geoff Colvin characterize the education American kids are getting?
   A. Not world-class
   B. Below average, but rapidly improving
   C. About average
   D. World-class
   E. Average, but steadily improving

3. Which phrase *best* sums up the new social contract between employers and employees?
   A. Mutual distrust
   B. Lifetime employment
   C. Cautious optimism

D. Shorter-term relationship of convenience
E. Loyalty and long-term obligations

4. The subtle yet strong barrier that has kept women and minorities from assuming top executive positions is called the
   A. dual-track syndrome.   B. black hole.
   C. glass ceiling.   D. wall.
   E. career canyon.

5. _____ is the process of creating an organizational culture that enables all employees to realize their full potential.
   A. Human asset accounting B. Managing diversity
   C. Constructive conflict   D. Issues management
   E. Protectionism

6. When a chemical company replaced its underground storage tanks six years before the government's deadline, it demonstrated that it occupied which position on the political response continuum?
   A. Neutral   B. Proactive
   C. Anticipatory   D. Reactive
   E. Entrenched

7. Which of the following is *not* one of the four political strategies available to management?
   A. Indirect lobbying   B. Watchful waiting
   C. Coalition building   D. Campaign financing
   E. Lobbying

8. The global economy, generally speaking, has raised _____ and lowered _____.
   A. financial standards; human tolerance
   B. the cost of capital; prices
   C. wages; tariff barriers
   D. quality standards; wage standards
   E. wages; protectionism

9. The three-step innovation process begins with
   A. gathering necessary resources.
   B. conducting a break-even analysis.
   C. developing a working prototype.
   D. doing a feasibility study.
   E. conceptualization of a new idea.

10. Which of these phrases *best* describes concurrent engineering?
    A. One-person product development cycle
    B. Continuous improvement
    C. Functional specialization
    D. Garbage in, garbage out
    E. Team approach to product design

See page T1 at the back of the text for answers to these questions. Want more questions? Visit the student Web site and take the ACE quizzes for more practice.

4

International Management and Cross-Cultural Competence

OBJECTIVES

- **Describe** the six-step internationalization process, and **distinguish** between a global company and a transnational company.

- **Identify** at least four of the nine cross-cultural competencies of global managers, and **contrast** ethnocentric, polycentric, and geocentric attitudes toward foreign operations.

- **Explain** from a cross-cultural perspective the difference between high-context and low-context cultures, and **identify** at least four of the GLOBE cultural dimensions.

- **Discuss** Hofstede's conclusion about the applicability of American management theories in foreign cultures, and **explain** the practical significance of the international study of work goals.

- **Summarize** the leadership lessons from the GLOBE Project.

- **Identify** the four leading reasons why U.S. expatriates fail to complete their assignments, and **discuss** the nature and importance of cross-cultural training in international management.

- **Summarize** the situation of North American women on foreign assignments.

THE CHANGING WORKPLACE

A Global Small-Business Manager Works at the Beach in the Dominican Republic

When working in the tropical sun becomes too much for Ivko Maksimovic, the lanky Serbian heads to one of the Dominican Republic's pristine white-sand beaches. He first gathers up a black hat, mosquito repellent, and a bottle of drinking water. Along with those essentials, he starts stuffing his black backpack with a tangle of computer cords, an extra laptop battery, a spare 160-gigabyte hard drive, and an EVDO card to connect to the Caribbean country's 3G broadband network. Finally, he adds a battered ThinkPad, a Skype-ready headset, and a cable lock to lash all the gear to a tree when he decides to take a swim. "It's very cool to think about important stuff while you fight the waves," Maksimovic says.

Maksimovic, 29, is the CTO [chief technology officer] of Vast.com, a startup search company based in San Francisco. He lives in the Dominican Republic because it's warm and far from Serbia's troubles. He works for Vast because his bosses think he's the best person for the job, and it doesn't matter much where he is physically as long as he has a broadband connection.

Between sessions in the surf pondering the arcana of coding on a May afternoon, Maksimovic chats with Vast's main development team in Belgrade by instant message and checks in with a colleague in Ireland through e-mail. The rest of the executive team dials in from San Francisco for a rare spoken conversation using a Skype-enabled speakerphone. Recently back from a trip to the Dominican Republic himself, Vast CEO Naval Ravikant can't resist asking his CTO what he's wearing. "Short pants," Maksimovic says. "And nothing else." The three people in the fogbound San Francisco office let out a collective groan. "I wish we were there too," says Ravikant, a serial entrepreneur who cofounded comparison-shopping service Epinions.

Vast launched a year ago in its present form and now employs 25 people who work across five time zones, four nations, and two continents—all of which makes it a particularly striking example of a growing breed of startup that can best be described as a micro-multinational. According to the United Nations, in 1990 there were about 30,000 multinational companies. Today there are more than 60,000, and while the number of multinational companies continues to grow, their average size is falling. As micro-multinationals proliferate, they're creating an entirely new form of corporate organization—one with powerful advantages for startups and entrepreneurs.

Like ExxonMobil or IBM, these multinational startups operate all over the world, pursuing talent and markets wherever they find them. Unlike their corporate big brothers, which historically expanded internationally via acquisitions or after tapping out markets close to home, micro-multinationals are global from day one. A big reason is money, but the benefits go beyond building a company on the cheap. Micro-multinationals are designing new corporate cultures and processes to compete in an increasingly global economy. Bound together by broadband and jet planes, they're startups all the same, run with the same fervor and energy as any garage-born company.

This is not offshoring as the term is commonly understood, although it is an outgrowth of it. Micro-multinationals aren't just moving operations from high-rent locales like Silicon Valley to Bangalore and other bargain-rate boomtowns. From the get-go, micro-multinationals open up shop and recruit skilled workers where it makes sense to do so. Are the ace coders in Estonia? Hire 'em. The COO [chief operating officer] would rather live in Sydney than Sunnyvale? So be it. The visionaries see Mongolia as a natural market for the planned product? Sign up some sales reps on the steppes. In short, these are true distributed companies; they're not merely handing off the scut work to overseas electronics sweatshops. "This is core stuff, very advanced technology," Ravikant says. "We are building a company in a way that wouldn't have been possible even two years ago."

Source: Excerpted from Michael V. Copeland, "The Mighty Micro-Multinational," *Business 2.0*, 7 (July 2006): 106–114.

Profit opportunities, such as those being exploited by the far-flung techies at Vast.com, are moving from country to country as never before, intensifying international competition.[2] At the heart of this swirl of commerce, technology, and talent is a global business tradition dating back farther than one might think:

In the antique shops of Shanghai's old French quarter, amid the German cameras, American radios, Russian crystal and other relics of a vanished past, lie tarnished reminders of just how long the world economy has been a global economy: rough-cast taels of South American silver and smooth-worn Mexican silver dollars.

It was in 1571 that modern global commerce began, argues Dennis O. Flynn, head of the economics department of the University of the Pacific in Stockton, Calif. That year, the Spanish empire founded the city of Manila in the Philippines to receive its silver-laden galleons that made their way across the vast Pacific Ocean from the New World. The metal was bound not for Spain, but for imperial China. For the first time, all of the world's populated continents were trading directly—Asia with the Americas, Europe, and Africa, and each with the others. They were highly interdependent: when silver depreciated in later decades, worldwide inflation ensued.

"Some economists think the global economy is a World War II thing," says Prof. Flynn. "That just demonstrates an ignorance of history."[3]

As documented in Chapters 1 and 3, striking evidence of the modern global marketplace is everywhere today. Take a trip to your local supermarket and you likely will find grapes from Chile, oranges from Australia, meat from Argentina, wines from France and South Africa, cheese from Italy, and cereals and cooking oil from Canada. "Darden Restaurants Inc., owner of the Red Lobster chain, buys fish in 30 countries."[4] A look at the labels on your clothes is yet another geography lesson, with countries of origin such as Mexico, Vietnam, Bangladesh, India, and China. Indeed, world trade has grown from $4 trillion in 1994 to over $12.5 trillion by 2006.[5] But, as the headlines tell us, this growth in economic interconnectedness has come with tough problems. Among them: record trade deficits for the United States, foreign labor abuses and sweatshops, offshoring of jobs, infringement of intellectual property rights, and unsafe and unhealthy imported goods and foods.[6] Meanwhile, the challenge to be competitive on the global stage looms large for today's business managers. "According to the Office of the United States Trade Representative, 95 percent of the world's consumers reside outside the United States."[7]

Like any other productive venture, an international corporation must be effectively and efficiently managed. Consequently, **international management**, the pursuit of organizational objectives in international and intercultural settings, has become an important discipline. Nancy Adler, a leading international management scholar at Canada's McGill University, sees it this way: "Managing the global enterprise and modern business management have become synonymous."[8] The purpose of this chapter is to define and discuss multinational and global corporations, stimulate global and cultural awareness, explore comparative management insights, and discuss the need for cross-cultural training.

> **international management:** pursuing organizational objectives in international and cross-cultural settings

---

4a General Electric's Global Game Plan

GE's CEO, Jeff Immelt, spends 12 weeks a year outside the United States.

Last fall he took a list created by Boston Consulting Group of the 100 most important companies in developing economies and arrayed it into four camps: customers, suppliers, competitors, and nonaligned. "I tell my leadership team, 'Our goal for this group is to have lots of customers, lots of suppliers—and no competitors,'" he says.

Source: Rik Kirkland, "The Greatest Economic Boom Ever," Fortune (July 23, 2007): 126, 128.

QUESTION:

What does this say about the changing landscape of the global economy?

For further information about the interactive annotations in this chapter, visit our student Web site.

GLOBAL ORGANIZATIONS FOR A GLOBAL ECONOMY

Many labels have been attached to international business ventures over the years. They have been called international companies, multinational companies, global companies, and transnational companies. This section clarifies the confusion about terminology by reviewing the six-stage internationalization process as a foundation for contrasting global and transnational companies.

The Internationalization Process

There are many ways to do business across borders.[9] At one extreme, a company may merely buy goods from a foreign source, or, at the other, it may actually buy the foreign company itself. In between is an internationalization process with identifiable stages.[10]

Companies may skip steps when pursuing foreign markets, so the following sequence should *not* be viewed as a lock-step sequence.

STAGE 1: LICENSING. Companies in foreign countries are authorized to produce and/or market a given product within a specified territory in return for a fee.[11] For example, under the terms of a 10-year licensing agreement, South Korea's Samsung Electronics will get to use Texas Instruments' patented semiconductor technology for royalty payments exceeding $1 billion.[12]

STAGE 2: EXPORTING. Goods produced in one country are sold to customers in foreign countries. Exports amount to a large and growing slice of the U.S. economy.

STAGE 3: LOCAL WAREHOUSING AND SELLING. Goods produced in one country are shipped to the parent company's storage and marketing facilities located in one or more foreign countries.

STAGE 4: LOCAL ASSEMBLY AND PACKAGING. Components, rather than finished products, are shipped to company-owned assembly facilities in one or more foreign countries for final assembly and sales.

STAGE 5: JOINT VENTURES. A company in one country pools resources with one or more companies in a foreign country to produce, store, transport, and market products, with resulting profits/losses shared appropriately. Joint ventures, also known as *strategic alliances* or *strategic partnerships*, have become very popular in recent years.[13] For example, consider this win-win alliance:

> *Industrial giants Honda Motor and General Electric are teaming up to produce an engine to power a new generation of smaller, lower-cost business jets. . . .*

> *GE, one of the largest makers of engines for big jets, would gain access to a market segment where it has been without a product: smaller business jets. Honda would fulfill a long-held plan to break into aviation.*[14]

International joint ventures/strategic alliances have tended to be fruitful for Japanese companies but disappointing for American and European partners.

> *Gary Hamel, a professor at the London Business School, regards partnerships as "a race to learn": The partner that learns fastest comes to dominate the relationship and can then rewrite its terms. Thus, an alliance becomes a new form of competition. The Japanese excel at learning from others, Hamel says, while Americans and Europeans are not so good at it.*[15]

Experts offer the following recommendations for successful international joint ventures/strategic alliances. First, exercise *patience* when selecting and building trust with a partner that has compatible (but not directly competitive) products and markets. Second, *learn* as fast and as much as possible without giving away core technologies and secrets. Third, establish firm *ground rules* about rights and responsibilities at the outset.[16]

STAGE 6: DIRECT FOREIGN INVESTMENTS. Typically, a company in one country produces and markets products through wholly owned subsidiaries in foreign countries. Global corporations are expressions of this last stage of internationalization.

Cross-border mergers are an increasingly popular form of direct foreign investment.[17] A cross-border merger occurs when a company in one country buys an entire company in another country. Unfortunately, cross-border mergers are not a quick and easy way to go global.

> *On top of the usual challenges of acquiring a company—paying a fair price, melding two management teams, and capturing the elusive "synergy" that's supposed to light up the bottom line—special risks and costs attach to cross-border mergers. They often involve wide differences in distance, language, and culture that can lead to serious misunderstandings and conflicts. . . .*
>
> *According to a study of cross-border mergers among large companies by consultants McKinsey & Co., nearly 40% end in total failure, with the acquiring company never earning back its cost of capital.*[18]

From Global Companies to Transnational Companies

The difference between these two types of international ventures is the difference between actual and theoretical. That is to say, transnational companies are evolving and represent a futuristic concept. Meanwhile, global companies, such as the giants in Table 4.1, do business in many countries simultaneously. They have

TABLE **4.1**	Corporate Giants Worldwide		
COMPANY	**HOME COUNTRY**	**INDUSTRY**	**2006 SALES (U.S. $, BILLIONS)**
Petrobrás	Brazil	Petroleum products	72
BP	Britain	Petroleum products	274
Nokia	Finland	Electronics	52
AXA	France	Insurance	140
Siemens	Germany	Electronics and industrial equipment	107
Fiat	Italy	Motor vehicles	65
Toyota Motor	Japan	Motor vehicles	205
Pemex	Mexico	Petroleum products	97
ING	Netherlands	Insurance	158
Samsung Electronics	South Korea	Electronics	89
UBS	Switzerland	Banking and financial services	108
Wal-Mart	United States	General retail and groceries	351

Source: Adapted from data in Telis Demos, "Global 500: The World's Largest Corporations," Fortune (July 23, 2007): 130–151.

4b A War in Iran—Cola War, That Is

Isn't corporate America prohibited by Washington's sanctions from doing business in Iran? Yes, for the most part, says U.S. Treasury spokeswoman Molly Millerwise. But Treasury has bent the rules for foodstuffs, a loophole through which American drinks giants Coca-Cola and PepsiCo have been able to pour thousands of gallons of concentrate into Iran via Irish subsidiaries. And that has allowed these brands, so much a symbol of America—and so much an affront to Iran's conservative clerics—to open another front in their global cola war. After just a few years back in Iran, Coke and Pepsi have grabbed about half the national soft drink sales in what is one of the Middle East's biggest drinks market.

Source: Eric Ellis, "Iran's Cola War," Fortune (March 5, 2007): 35.

QUESTION:

Technically, it may be legal for Coke and Pepsi do business in Iran, but is it right? Explain.

global strategies for product design, financing, purchasing, manufacturing, and marketing. By definition, a **global company** is a multinational venture centrally managed from a specific country.[19] For example, even though Coca-Cola earns most of its profit outside the United States, it is viewed as a U.S. company because it is run from a powerful headquarters in Atlanta, Georgia. The same goes for McDonald's, Ford, IBM, and Wal-Mart, with their respective U.S. headquarters.

global company: a multinational venture centrally managed from a specific country

A **transnational company**, in contrast, is a global network of productive units with a decentralized authority structure and no distinct national identity.[20] Transnationals rely on a blend of global and local strategies, as circumstances dictate. Local values and practices are adopted whenever possible, because in the end, all *customer contacts* are local. Ideally, managers of transnational organizations "think globally, but act locally." Managers of foreign operations are encouraged to interact freely with

transnational company: a futuristic model of a global, decentralized network with no distinct national identity

their colleagues from around the world. Once again, this type of international business venture exists mostly in theory, although some global companies are moving toward transnationalism. For example, consider L.M. Ericsson, the Swedish telecommunications equipment manufacturer. As reported in *Business Week*, "Ericsson . . . moved its European headquarters to London to escape Sweden's high personal-income taxes, and to be closer to investors and customers."[21] Ericsson's decision to relocate its headquarters was not constrained by national identity but, rather, guided by business and financial considerations.

Significantly, many experts are alarmed at the prospect of immense "stateless" transnational companies because of unresolved political, economic, and tax implications. If transnational companies become more powerful than the governments of countries in which they do business, who will hold them accountable in cases of fraud, human rights violations, and environmental degradation?[22]

TOWARD GREATER GLOBAL AWARENESS AND CROSS-CULTURAL EFFECTIVENESS

Americans in general and American business students and managers in particular are often considered too narrowly focused for the global stage. Boris Yavitz, former dean of Columbia University's Graduate School of Business, observed that "unlike European and Asian managers, who grow up expecting to see international service, U.S. executives are required to prepare only for domestic experience, with English as their only language."[23] This state of affairs is slowly changing amid growth of international business and economic globalization. To compete successfully in a dynamic global economy, present and future managers need to develop their international and cross-cultural awareness. In this section, we discuss the need for global managers with cultural intelligence and specific cross-cultural competencies, examine attitudes toward international operations, and explore key sources of cultural diversity.

TABLE **4.2**   Competencies Needed to Work Effectively Across Cultures

CROSS-CULTURAL COMPETENCY CLUSTER	KNOWLEDGE OR SKILL REQUIRED
1. Building relationships	Ability to gain access to and maintain relationships with members of host culture
2. Valuing people of different cultures	Empathy for difference; sensitivity to diversity
3. Listening and observation	Knows cultural history and reasons for certain cultural actions and customs
4. Coping with ambiguity	Recognizes and interprets implicit behavior, especially nonverbal cues
5. Translating complex information	Knowledge of local language, symbols, or other forms of verbal language and written language
6. Taking action and initiative	Understands intended and potential unintended consequences of actions
7. Managing others	Ability to manage details of a job including maintaining cohesion in a group
8. Adaptability and flexibility	Views change from multiple perspectives
9. Managing stress	Understands own and other's mood, emotions, and personality

Source: Academy of Management Learning & Education *by Yoshitaka Yamazaki and D. Christopher Kayes. Copyright © 2004 by Academy of Management (NY). Reproduced with permission of Academy of Management (NY) in the format Textbook via Copyright Clearance Center.*

Needed: Global Managers with Cultural Intelligence and Cross-Cultural Competencies

Successful global managers possess a characteristic called **cultural intelligence (CQ)**, the ability of an outsider to read individual behavior, group dynamics, and situations in a foreign culture as well as the locals do. (The initials CQ are a variation of the familiar label IQ, for intelligence quotient.) Just as a chameleon changes colors to blend in with its surroundings, a person with high CQ quickly analyzes an unfamiliar cultural situation and then acts appropriately and confidently. In short, CQ involves seeing the world as someone else sees it. CQ combines two topics we cover later—*impression management* (Chapter 13) and *emotional intelligence* (Chapter 14)—and puts them into a cross-cultural context. While noting that only 5 percent of managers studied possess high CQ, a pair of researchers shared this cautionary tale of a manager with low CQ:

cultural intelligence (CQ): ability to interpret and act in appropriate ways in unfamiliar cultural surroundings

Consider the example of the French manager transferred to the USA. After meeting his secretary

(a woman) the first time, he greeted her with a European "hello" (an effusive and personal cheek-to-cheek kiss greeting). This greeting was, however, met with obvious discomfort. His secretary later filed a complaint for harassment.[24]

You can boost your cultural intelligence by mastering the nine cross-cultural competencies listed in Table 4.2 and understanding the concepts in this chapter.

Contrasting Attitudes Toward International Operations

Can a firm's degree of internationalization be measured? Some observers believe it can, and they claim a true global company must have subsidiaries in at least six nations. Others say that to qualify as a multinational or global company, a firm must have a certain percentage of its capital or operations in foreign countries. However, Howard Perlmutter insists that these measurable guidelines tell only part of the story and suggests that it is management's *attitude* toward its foreign operations that really counts.

The more one penetrates into the living reality of an international firm, the more one finds it is necessary to give serious weight to the way executives think about doing business around the world. The

TABLE **4.3** | Three Different Attitudes Toward International Operations

ORGANIZATION DESIGN	ETHNOCENTRIC	POLYCENTRIC	GEOCENTRIC
Identification	Nationality of owner	Nationality of host country	Truly international company but identifying with national interests
Authority; decision making	High in headquarters	Relatively low in headquarters	Aim for a collaborative approach between headquarters and subsidiaries
Evaluation and control	Home standards applied for person and performance	Determined locally	Find standards that are universal and local
Communication; information flow	High volume to subsidiaries; orders, commands, advice	Little to and from headquarters; little between subsidiaries	Both ways and between subsidiaries; heads of subsidiaries part of management team
Perpetuation (recruiting, staffing, development)	Recruit and develop people of home country for key positions everywhere in the world	Develop people of local nationality for key positions in their own country	Develop best people everywhere in the world for key positions everywhere in the world

Source: Excerpted from Howard V. Perlmutter, "The Tortuous Evolution of the Multinational Corporation," Columbia Journal of World Business, 4 (January–February 1969): 12. Used with permission.

orientation toward "foreign people, ideas, resources," in headquarters and subsidiaries, and in host and home environments, becomes crucial in estimating the multinationality of a firm.[25]

Perlmutter identified three managerial attitudes toward international operations, which he labeled ethnocentric, polycentric, and geocentric.[26] Each attitude is presented here in its pure form, but all three are likely to be found in a single multinational or global corporation (see Table 4.3). The key question is "Which attitude predominates?"

ETHNOCENTRIC ATTITUDE. Managers with an **ethnocentric attitude** are home-country-oriented. Home-country personnel, ideas, and practices are viewed as inherently superior to those from abroad. Foreign nationals are not trusted with key decisions or technology. Home-country procedures and evaluation criteria are applied worldwide without variation. Proponents of ethnocentrism say that it makes for a simpler and more tightly controlled organization. Critics believe this attitude makes for poor planning and ineffective operations because of inadequate feedback, high turnover of

ethnocentric attitude: view that the home country's personnel and ways of doing things are best

subsidiary managers, reduced innovation, inflexibility, and social and political backlash.

In U.S.–Japanese business relations, ethnocentrism cuts both ways. Procter & Gamble failed to do its cultural homework when it ran a series of advertisements for Pampers in Japan. Japanese customers were bewildered by the ads, in which a stork carried a baby, because storks have no cultural connection to birth in Japan.[27] Similarly, Japanese companies operating in the United States seem to be out of touch with the expectations of American managers. In a survey of American managers employed by 31 such companies, the common complaint was too few promotions and too little responsibility.[28]

Ethnocentric attitudes can also cause problems in ethnically diverse countries, such as the United States. (Hispanics/Latinos are projected to make up nearly one-quarter of the U.S. population by 2050, and more than 28 million U.S. residents currently speak Spanish.)[29]

When it comes to Hispanic marketing, a little knowledge is a dangerous thing. . . . Tropicana advertised jugo de china in Miami. China means orange to Puerto Ricans, but Miami's Cubans thought it was juice from the Orient. Jack in the Box goofed with a commercial featuring a band of Mexican *mariachis accompanying a Spanish flamenco dancer. "That's like having Willie Nelson sing while Michael Jackson does the moonwalk," says Bert Valencia, a marketing professor at the American Graduate School of International Management in Glendale, Arizona.*

Why do companies sometimes end up looking like idiots? *Because learning this market takes more than a few lessons at Berlitz. An occasional blunder is forgivable. But many companies are designing advertising for the nation's . . . [more than 40] million Hispanics without understanding the differences among Mexicans, Puerto Ricans, Cubans, and the rich array of other nationalities that make up the U.S. Hispanic population.*[30]

In fact, U.S. Hispanics and Latinos trace their roots to 22 different countries.

POLYCENTRIC ATTITUDE. This host-country orientation is based on the assumption that because cultures are so different, local managers know what is best for their operations. A **polycentric attitude** leads to a loose confederation of comparatively independent subsidiaries rather than to a highly integrated structure. Because foreign operations are measured in terms of ends (instead of means), methods, incentives, and training procedures vary widely from location to location.

polycentric attitude: view that local managers in host countries know best how to run their own operations

On the negative side, wasteful duplication of effort occurs at the various units within the confederation precisely because they are independent. Such duplication can erode the efficiency of polycentric organizations. Moreover, global objectives can be undermined by excessive concern for local traditions and success. But there is a positive side: "The main advantages are an intensive exploitation of local markets, better sales since local management is often better informed, more local initiative for new products, more host-government support, and good local managers with high morale."[31]

GEOCENTRIC ATTITUDE. Managers with a **geocentric attitude** are world-oriented. For example, it is easy to detect a geocentric attitude in this recent Q&A with David Rothkopf, a former high-ranking U.S. Commerce Department official.

geocentric attitude: world-oriented view that draws on the best talent from around the globe

Q: If you were starting a business today, what steps would you take to be competitive in a global economy?
A: My approach would be not to look at geography as a limitation on my business. The tiniest businesses today can be completely global, and if you are looking for the best people only in the next town over, or you're looking for the best prices only in your community, or you're looking for who your competitors are only by looking to see who's down the street from you, you're making a mistake.

The best people and the best prices, the competitors, the markets of tomorrow . . . whatever it is you're doing, it very likely is someplace else. You need to be constantly searching for that.[32]

Skill, not nationality, determines who gets promoted or transferred to key positions around the globe in geocentric companies. Local and worldwide objectives are balanced in all aspects of operation. Collaboration between headquarters and subsidiaries is high, but an effort is made to maintain a balance between global standards and local discretion. Thus, a geocentric attitude is essential in the transnational model discussed earlier. At Germany's Siemens, the industrial giant with 475,000 employees worldwide,[33] CEO Klaus Kleinfeld has a more geocentric attitude than his predecessor:

Kleinfeld downplays the influence of his three years in the U.S., a stint ordinary Germans view as a blot on his résumé. There's no question, though, that he counts those years among his best. "I liked it over there," says Kleinfeld, who served as CEO of Siemens' U.S. operations in 2002 and 2003. "Wherever I went, I made friends." And to this day, Kleinfeld's style is decidedly less German-centric than that of his predecessor, Heinrich von Pierer. Von Pierer played tennis with the Chancellor. Kleinfeld runs the New York Marathon. Von Pierer served on a half-dozen boards of German companies. Kleinfeld does so for Citigroup, Alcoa, and the New York Metropolitan Opera. Von Pierer speaks English well but prefers German. Kleinfeld is totally fluent in English.[34]

Of these three contrasting attitudes, only a geocentric attitude can help management take a long step toward success in today's vigorously competitive global marketplace.

The Cultural Imperative

Culture has a powerful impact on people's behavior. For example, consider the everyday activity of negotiating a business contract.

4c Back to the Opening Case

Is Vast.com an ethnocentric, a polycentric, or a geocentric company? Explain.

To Americans, a contract signals the conclusion of negotiations; its terms establish the rights, responsibilities, and obligations of the parties involved. However, to the Japanese, a company is not forever bound to the terms of the contract. In fact, it can be renegotiated whenever there is a significant shift in the company's circumstances. For instance, an unexpected change in governmental tax policy, or a change in the competitive environment, are considered legitimate reasons for contract renegotiation. To the Chinese, a signatory to an agreement is a partner with whom they can work, so to them the signing of a contract is just the beginning of negotiations.[35]

Cross-cultural business negotiators who ignore or defy cultural traditions do so at their own risk. That means the risk of not making the sale or of losing a contract or failing to negotiate a favorable deal. Therefore, a sensitivity to cross-cultural differences is imperative for people who do business in other countries.

In this section, we define the term *culture* and address the fear of an "Americanized" world culture. Then, drawing primarily from the work of pioneering cultural anthropologist Edward T. Hall, we explore key sources of cross-cultural differences.

CULTURE DEFINED. **Culture** is the pattern of taken-for-granted assumptions about how a given collection of people should think, act, and feel as they go about their daily affairs.[36] Regarding the central aspect of this definition, *taken-for-granted assumptions,* Hall noted that

> **culture:** a population's taken-for-granted assumptions, values, beliefs, and symbols that foster patterned behavior

> *Much of culture operates outside our awareness; frequently, we don't even know what we know. . . . This applies to all people. The Chinese or the Japanese or the Arabs are as unaware of their assumptions as we are of our own. We each assume that they're part of human nature. What we think of as "mind" is really internalized culture.*[37]

In Chapter 9, *organizational culture* is called the social glue binding members of an organization together. Similarly, at a broader level, *societal culture* acts as a social glue. That glue is made up of norms, values, attitudes, role expectations, taboos, symbols, heroes, beliefs, morals, customs, and rituals. Cultural lessons are imparted from birth to death via role models, formal education, religious teachings, and peer pressure.

Cultural undercurrents make international dealings immensely challenging. According to Fons Trompenaars and Charles Hampden-Turner, the Dutch and English authors of the landmark book *Riding the Waves of Culture,*

> *International managers have it tough. They must operate on a number of different premises at any one time. These premises arise from their culture of*

Some American brands travel well because management "thinks globally, but acts locally." This KFC restaurant in Vietnam's Ho Chi Minh City (Saigon) is successful because the food and service standards have been adapted to local tastes and expectations.

origin, the culture in which they are working, and the culture of the organization which employs them.

In every culture in the world such phenomena as authority, bureaucracy, creativity, good fellowship, verification, and accountability are experienced in different ways. That we use the same words to describe them tends to make us unaware that our cultural biases and our accustomed conduct may not be appropriate, or shared.[38]

ARE U.S. GLOBAL CORPORATIONS TURNING THE WORLD INTO A SINGLE "AMERICANIZED" CULTURE?

Protesters at World Trade Organization and global economic summit meetings in recent years have decried the growing global reach of McDonald's (in over 100 countries) and other American corporate giants. They predict a homogenizing of the world's unique cultures into a so-called McWorld, where American culture prevails. Although they evoke much emotion, these concerns are *not* supported by University of Michigan researchers who have been tracking cultural values in 65 societies for more than 20 years. Citing evidence from their ongoing World Values Survey, the researchers reached the following conclusions:

The impression that we are moving toward a uniform "McWorld" is partly an illusion. The seemingly identical McDonald's restaurants that have spread throughout the world actually have different social meanings and fulfill different social functions in different cultural zones. Eating in a McDonald's restaurant in Japan is a different social experience from eating in one in the United States, Europe, or China.

Likewise, the globalization of communication is unmistakable, but its effects may be overestimated. It is certainly apparent that young people around the world are wearing jeans and listening to U.S. pop music; what is less apparent is the persistence of underlying value differences.

In short, economic development will cause shifts in the values of people in developing nations, but it will not produce a uniform global culture. The future may look like McWorld, but it won't feel like one.[39]

Cultural roots run deep, have profound effects on behavior, and are not readily altered.

Understanding Cultural Diversity

Dealing effectively with both coworkers and customers in today's diverse workplaces requires a good deal of cultural intelligence. For instance, the standard all-too-revealing hospital gown caused a unique cross-cultural problem for the Maine Medical Center in Portland, Maine. When the hospital's staff realized that Muslim women were canceling appointments to avoid the shame of being inadequately clothed, they created gowns for modest patients who desire coverage of their legs and backside.[40] Making this sort of cultural accommodation is a little easier when you know about the following important sources of cultural diversity.

HIGH-CONTEXT AND LOW-CONTEXT CULTURES. People from European-based cultures typically assess people from Asian cultures such as China and Japan as quiet and hard to figure out. Conversely, Asians tend to view Westerners as aggressive, insensitive, and even rude. True, language differences are a significant barrier to mutual understanding. But something more fundamental is involved, something cultural. Anthropologist Edward T. Hall prompted better understanding of cross-cultural communication by distinguishing between high-context and low-context cultures.[41] The difference centers on how much meaning one takes from what is actually said or written versus who the other person is.

In **high-context cultures**, people rely heavily on nonverbal and subtle situational messages when communicating with others. The other person's official status, place in society, and

> **high-context cultures:** cultures in which nonverbal and situational messages convey primary meaning

---

4d | A Little United Nations at Auralog Inc. in Phoenix

The company, which develops software for learning foreign languages, counts two Germans, two Frenchman, a Mexican, a Canadian, and a Belgian on its staff of 21 in Phoenix . . . . The 19-year-old company counts more than 5 million users worldwide and 200 employees globally.

Source: Russ Wiles, "Firm Flush with Cup Fever," Arizona Republic (July 4, 2006): D2.

QUESTIONS:

How do you rate your own awareness of global issues and preparedness to work in cross-cultural situations? How world-wise is your college coursework?

WINDOW ON THE WORLD

Context Matters When It Comes to Muslim Names

The sequence of a Muslim's name appears complicated for most Westerners but the name should be regarded, for practical purposes, as being in three parts: (1) Own name, (2) Father's name and (3) Family name, e.g., Abdullah bin Mohammad al-Talal (Abdullah, son of Mohammad of the Talal family). This person is known as "Abdullah." His own name—his given name—is "Abdullah." He is not known as "Mr. Al-Talal," but most well-traveled Arabs are used, for example, to hotel or airline staff registering them under their family name only, e.g., "Mr. A.B.M.A. Talal." These experienced Arabs are resigned to this frequent Western mistake and usually react helpfully if paged or addressed incorrectly. In certain cases, the adoption of a surname, in the Western sense of the word, has become almost normal in business. . . .

Where there are many Mohammads and Abdullahs . . . in an organization (which is frequently the case) there can be confusion. Usually the context or situation indicates which particular person is under discussion. For example, if both a doctor and a translator are called Mohammad and the conversation is about medicine, everyone will know which Mohammad is meant. Where context or situation does not remove doubt, the father's name can be added, as the following telephone conversation demonstrates: "Where's Mohammad?" "Who?" "Mohammad bin Abdullah." "He is not . . . [in his office]—call back in five minutes."

Source: Excerpted from Jeremy Williams, Don't They Know It's Friday? Cross-Cultural Considerations for Business and Life in the Gulf *(Dubai, UAE: Motivate Publishing, 1998), pp. 52–53.*

reputation say a great deal about the person's rights, obligations, and trustworthiness. In high-context cultures, people do not expect to talk about such "obvious" things. Conversation simply provides general background information about the other person. Thus, in high-context Japan, the ritual of exchanging business cards is a social necessity, and failing to read a card you have been given is a grave insult. The other person's company and position determine what is said and how. Arab, Chinese, and Korean cultures also are high-context[42] (see Window on the World).

People from **low-context cultures** convey essential messages and meaning primarily with words. Low-context cultures in Germany, Switzerland, Scandinavia, North America, and Great Britain expect people to communicate their precise intended meaning. Low-context people do read so-called body language, but its messages are secondary to spoken and written words. Legal contracts with precisely worded expectations are important in low-context countries such as the United States. However, according to international communications experts, "in high-context cultures the process of forging a business relationship is as important as, if not more important than, the written details of the actual deal."[43] This helps explain why Americans tend to be frustrated with the apparently slow pace of business dealings in Japan. For the Japanese, the many rounds of meetings and social gatherings are necessary to collect valuable contextual information as a basis for judging the other party's character. For the schedule-driven American, anything short of actually signing the contract is considered largely a waste of time. *Patience* is a prime virtue for low-context managers doing business in high-context cultures.

NINE DIMENSIONS OF CULTURE FROM THE GLOBE PROJECT. The GLOBE (Global Leadership and Organizational Behavior Effectiveness) project was conceived by Robert J. House, a University of Pennsylvania researcher. Beginning with a 1994 meeting in Calgary, Canada, the GLOBE project has grown to encompass an impressive network of over 150 researchers from 62 countries. It is a massive ongoing effort in which researchers assess organizations in their own cultures and languages with standardized instruments to collect data from around the world,

low-context cultures: cultures in which words convey primary meaning

building a comprehensive model. If things go as intended, the resulting database will yield important new insights about both similarities and differences across the world's cultures.[44] More important, it promises to provide practical guidelines for international managers. Thanks to the first two phases of the GLOBE project, we have a research-based list of key cultural dimensions (see Table 4.4).

Interestingly, according to one GLOBE research report, mid-level managers in the United States scored high on assertiveness and performance orientation

and moderately on uncertainty avoidance and institutional collectivism.[45]

OTHER SOURCES OF CULTURAL DIVERSITY. Managers headed for a foreign country need to do their homework on the following cultural variables to avoid awkwardness and problems.[46] There are no rights or wrongs here, only cross-cultural differences.

Individualism versus Collectivism. This distinction between "me" and "we" cultures deserves closer attention, because it encompasses two of the

TABLE 4.4 — Nine Cultural Dimensions from the GLOBE Project

DIMENSION	DESCRIPTION	COUNTRIES SCORING HIGHEST	COUNTRIES SCORING LOWEST
Power distance	Should leaders have high or low power over others?	Morocco, Argentina, Thailand	Denmark, Netherlands, South Africa (black sample)
Uncertainty avoidance	How much should social norms and rules be used to reduce future uncertainties?	Switzerland, Sweden, Germany (former West)	Russia, Hungary, Bolivia
Institutional collectivism	To what extent should society and institutions reward loyalty?	Sweden, South Korea, Japan	Greece, Hungary, Germany (former East)
In-group collectivism	To what extent do individuals value loyalty to their family or organization?	Iran, India, Morocco	Denmark, Sweden, New Zealand
Assertiveness	How aggressive and confrontational should one be with others?	Germany (former East), Austria, Greece	Sweden, New Zealand, Switzerland
Gender equality	How nearly equal are men and women?	Hungary, Poland, Slovenia	South Korea, Egypt, Morocco
Future orientation	How much should one work and save for the future, rather than just live for the present?	Singapore, Switzerland, Netherlands	Russia, Argentina, Poland
Performance orientation	How much should people be rewarded for excellence and improvement?	Singapore, Hong Kong, New Zealand	Russia, Argentina, Greece
Humane orientation	How much should people be encouraged to be generous, kind, and fair to others?	Philippines, Ireland, Malaysia	Germany (former West), Spain, France

Source: Adapted from discussions in Mansour Javidan and Robert J. House, "Cultural Acumen for the Global Manager: Lessons from Project GLOBE," Organizational Dynamics, 29 (Spring 2001): 289–305; Robert House, Mansour Javidan, Paul Hanges, and Peter Dorfman, "Understanding Cultures and Implicit Leadership Theories Across the Globe: An Introduction to Project GLOBE," Journal of World Business, 37 (Spring 2002): 3–10; and Mansour Javidan, Robert J. House, and Peter W. Dorfman, "A Nontechnical Summary of GLOBE Findings," in Robert J. House, Paul J. Hanges, Mansour Javidan, Peter W. Dorfman, and Vipin Gupta, eds., Culture, Leadership, and Organizations: The GLOBE Study of 62 Societies (Thousand Oaks, Calif.: Sage, 2004), pp. 29–48.

nine GLOBE cultural dimensions in Table 4.4. People in **individualistic cultures** focus primarily on individual rights, roles, and achievements. The United States and Canada are highly individualistic cultures.

individualistic cultures: cultures that emphasize individual rights, roles, and achievements

People in **collectivist cultures**—such as Egypt, Mexico, India, and Japan—rank duty and loyalty to family, friends, organization, and country above self-interests. Group goals and shared achievements are paramount to collectivists; personal goals and desires are suppressed. It is important to remember that individualism and collectivism are extreme ends of a continuum, along which people and cultures are variously distributed and mixed. For example, in the United States, one can find pockets of collectivism among Native Americans and recent immigrants from Latin America and Asia. This helps explain why a top-notch engineer born in China would be reluctant to attend an American-style recognition dinner where individual award recipients are asked to stand up for a round of applause.[47]

collectivist cultures: cultures that emphasize duty and loyalty to collective goals and achievements

Time. Hall referred to time as a silent language of culture. He distinguished between monochronic and polychronic time.[48] **Monochronic time** is based on the perception that time is a unidimensional straight line divided into standard units, such as seconds, minutes, hours, and days. In monochronic cultures, including North America and Northern Europe, everyone is assumed to be on the same clock, and time is treated as money. The general rule is to use time efficiently, to be on time, and (above all) not to waste time. Toy maker Hasbro has gone so far as to help time-starved Americans speed up their *play* time. "The Pawtucket, R.I.–based company . . . is introducing three 'Express' versions of classic board games this year: Monopoly Express, Scrabble Express and Sorry Express."[49] In contrast, **polychronic time** involves the perception of time as flexible, elastic, and multidimensional. Latin American, Mediterranean, and Arab cultures are polychronic. Managers in poly-

monochronic time: a perception of time as a straight line broken into standard units

polychronic time: a perception of time as flexible, elastic, and multidimensional

chronic cultures tend to view schedules and deadlines in relative rather than absolute terms. Different perceptions of time have caused many cultural collisions. For example, as the deadline for completion of the 2004 Olympic facilities in Athens approached, monochronic Americans fretted about the Greeks moving too slowly and missing the August deadline. But Brett Heyl, a U.S. kayaker who trained in Greece and became familiar with the local work habits, was not worried.

> *"You never see them working hard, but things seem to get done," Heyl says. "Don't ask me how."*
>
> *In April, Heyl took note of a seemingly idle crew of road workers, near the Athens airport.*
>
> *"You come back in a month, and you're driving on a new highway." Heyl says. "It's just astounding how quickly they can get things done. When I was here in April, I saw a city that could not possibly be ready for the Olympics. Now I see one that will be ready on Friday."*[50]

Sure enough, the Greeks pulled it off to rave reviews.

It is important to reset your mental clocks (and expectations) when living and working in a culture with a different time orientation or when working globally on a virtual team. (Virtual teams are discussed in Chapter 13.)[51]

Interpersonal Space. People in a number of cultures prefer to stand close when conversing. Many Arabs, Asians, and Pacific Islanders fall into this group. An interpersonal distance of only six inches is very disturbing to a Northern European or an American who is accustomed to conversing at arm's length. Cross-cultural gatherings in the Middle East often involve an awkward dance as Arab hosts strive to get closer while their American and European guests shuffle backwards around the room to maintain what they consider a proper social distance.

Language. Foreign-language skills are the gateway to true cross-cultural understanding. Translations are not an accurate substitute for conversational ability in the local language. Consider, for example, the complexity of the Japanese language:

> *Japanese is a situational language and the way something is said differs with the relationship between speaker, listener, or the person about whom they are speaking; their respective families, ages, professional statuses, and companies all affect the way they express themselves.*
>
> *In this respect, Japanese isn't one language but a group of them, changing with a dizzying array of social conventions with which Americans have no*

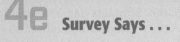

4e Survey Says . . .

More than half of all [U.S.] consumers, at all income levels, say lack of time is a bigger problem for them than lack of money in a poll by consulting company Yankelovich. . . .

The 56% citing a significant time deficit put a median price on their personal time of $1.50 a minute—$90 an hour (half said less, half said more). Even the 44% feeling less stress put a median value on their minutes of $1.

Source: Laura Petrecca, "Stores, Banks Go Speedy to Win Harried Customers," USA Today (December 1, 2006): 1B.

QUESTIONS:

What is your time worth? How much of a multitasker are you and how is that related to monochromic behavior? What are the secrets to being fast *and* effective, as opposed to "quick and dirty"?

experience. Japanese people are raised dealing with the shifting concepts of in-group/out-group, male and female speech patterns, appropriate politeness levels, and humble and honorific forms of speech. An unwary student, armed only with a few years of classroom Japanese, can pile up mistakes in this regard very quickly.[52]

Language instructors who prepare Americans for foreign assignments say it takes from 150 to 350 hours of classroom work, depending on the difficulty of the language, to reach minimum proficiency (e.g., exchanging greetings, shopping and ordering meals, and asking for directions). The American Society for Testing and Materials has ranked the difficulty of learning foreign languages for native English speakers:

> *The easiest to learn are the Romance and Germanic languages, such as Spanish, German and Swedish. Next are African and Eastern European languages, such as Russian. Finally, the hardest languages are Middle Eastern and Asian languages, such as Arabic, Chinese and Japanese.*[53]

Historically, foreign languages have not been a strong suit for Americans. Indeed, almost 81 percent speak only English, and although 200 million Chinese are studying English, a paltry 24,000 American children are trying to master Chinese.[54]

Religion. Awareness of a business colleague's religious traditions is essential for building a lasting relationship.[55] Those traditions may dictate dietary restrictions, religious holidays, and Sabbath schedules, which are important to the devout and represent cultural minefields for the uninformed. For instance, the official day of rest in Iran is Thursday; in Kuwait and Pakistan it is Friday.[56] In Israel, where the official day off is Saturday, "Burger King restaurants—unlike McDonald's—do not offer cheeseburgers in order to conform to Jewish dietary laws forbidding mixing milk products and meat."[57]

Of course, it is important to be aware of and follow applicable laws regarding religion in the workplace.

As always, these are turbulent and exciting times in the Middle East, where ethnic, religious, and cultural traditions collide with modern ways. Here Kuwaiti women demonstrate for broader rights in front of their nation's Parliament in Kuwait City. Expatriates working in countries such as Kuwait need to be fully aware of cross-cultural and religious differences if they are to get the job done.

COMPARATIVE MANAGEMENT INSIGHTS

Comparative management is the study of how organizational behavior and management practices differ across cultures. In this relatively new field of inquiry, as in other fields, there is disagreement about theoretical frameworks and research methodologies.[58] Nevertheless, some useful lessons have been learned. This research-based foundation of understanding can come in handy for managers such as Nancy McKinstry, who lives and works across cultures. McKinstry, an American, is the CEO of Wolters Kluwer, a $4.3-billion-a-year Dutch publishing company based in Amsterdam. This is the sort of cultural mix she deals with daily as she oversees operations in 25 countries:

> *Cultures vary from country to country, so the most important thing is to have local management on the ground that understands the markets. There are actually more similarities between the U.S., Germany and Holland than there are between those countries and southern Europe. In southern Europe, decision making is more collaborative, and developing long-term business relationships is essential to success.*[59]

In this section, we focus on (1) the applicability of American management theories in other cultures, (2) work-goal diversity across cultures, and (3) a GLOBE matrix of leadership styles.

comparative management: study of how organizational behavior and management practices differ across cultures

Made-in-America Management Theories Require Translation

In the 1970s, Geert Hofstede, a Dutch organizational behavior researcher, surveyed 116,000 IBM employees from 40 different countries.[60] He classified each of his 40 national samples according to four different cultural dimensions. Hofstede found a great deal of cultural diversity among the countries he studied. For example, employee needs were ranked differently from country to country. The need for self-actualization was tops in the United States, Great Britain, and members of the former British Empire (Canada, Hong Kong, India, Australia, New Zealand, and South Africa). Social needs ranked the highest in Singapore, the Netherlands, and the Scandinavian countries. Countries ranking security needs the highest included Switzerland, Germany, Italy, Mexico, Japan, and Argentina.

The marked cultural differences among the 40 countries led Hofstede to recommend that American management theories be adapted to local cultures rather than imposed on them. As we saw in Chapter 2, many popular management theories were developed within the U.S. cultural context. Hofstede believes that it is naive to expect those theories to apply automatically in significantly different cultures. For example, American-made management theories that reflect Americans' preoccupation with individualism are out of place in countries such as Mexico, Brazil, and Japan, where individualism is discouraged.

Hofstede's research does not attempt to tell international managers *how* to apply various management techniques in different cultures. However, it does provide a useful cultural typology and presents a convincing case for the cultural adaptation of American management theory and practice.[61] In turn, Americans would do well to culturally adapt any management theories and practices acquired from other cultures.

A Cross-Cultural Study of Work Goals

What do people want from their work? A survey of 8,192 employees from seven countries found general disagreement about the relative importance of 11 different work goals.[62] Respondents to the survey represented a broad range of professions and all levels of the organizational hierarchy. They were asked to rank 11 work goals. Those work goals are listed in Table 4.5, along with the average rankings for five countries. "Interesting work" got a consistently high ranking. "Opportunity for promotion" and "working conditions" consistently were at or very near the bottom of each country's rankings. Beyond those few consistencies, general disagreement prevailed.

The main practical implication of these findings is that managers need to adapt their motivational programs to local preferences.[63] Throughout this text, we consistently stress the importance of the contingency approach to management. In this case, an international contingency approach to motivation is called for. For instance, pay is less important in Japan than in the other four countries. And job security is much less important to Israelis than to American, British, German, and Japanese employees.

TABLE **4.5** Work Goals Vary from Country to Country

WORK GOALS	MEAN RANKINGS (BY COUNTRY)				
	U.S.	BRITAIN	GERMANY*	ISRAEL	JAPAN
Interesting work	1	1	3	1	2
Pay	2	2	1	3	5
Job security	3	3	2	10	4
Match between person and job	4	6	5	6	1
Opportunity to learn	5	8	9	5	7
Variety	6	7	6**	11	9
Interpersonal relations	7	4	4	2	6
Autonomy	8	10	8	4	3
Convenient work hours	9	5	6**	7	8
Opportunity for promotion	10	11	10	8	11
Working conditions	11	9	11	9	10

*Formerly West Germany.
**Two goals tied for sixth rank.
Source: Data from Itzhak Harpaz, "The Importance of Work Goals: An International Perspective," Journal of International Business Studies, 21 (First Quarter 1990): 81. Reprinted with permission.

Lessons in Leadership from the GLOBE Project

The huge 62-society database compiled by the GLOBE researchers provides valuable insights into the applicability of leadership styles around the world. As listed along the top of the matrix in Figure 4.1, the GLOBE researchers focused on the following five different leadership styles:

- *Charismatic/Value-based:* a visionary person who inspires high performance by exhibiting integrity and decisiveness
- *Team-oriented:* an administratively competent person and team builder who diplomatically emphasizes common purposes and goals
- *Participative:* a person who actively involves others in both making and carrying out decisions
- *Humane-oriented:* a compassionate, generous, considerate, and supportive person
- *Self-protective:* a self-centered and status-conscious person who tends to save face and stir conflict[64]

The matrix in Figure 4.1 rates these five leadership styles as most acceptable, moderately acceptable, or least acceptable for ten cultural clusters.

According to the matrix, the charismatic/value-based and team-oriented leadership styles have the greatest cross-cultural applicability. The self-protective leadership style definitely is *not* acceptable, regardless of the cultural setting. Humane-oriented leadership is perceived around the world as being only moderately acceptable, except within the southern Asian cultural cluster. This is probably because humane-oriented leaders are perceived in most cultures as not pushing hard enough to achieve goals and solid results. The picture for participative leadership is mixed, despite its general popularity in North and South America and in Germanic, Latin, and Nordic Europe.

A completely different study of employees in Russia's largest textile factory confirms the limited applicability of participative leadership in Eastern Europe. That study documented how participative leadership triggered a *decrease* in output. Why? The researchers felt the Russians were influenced by their lack of faith in participative schemes that had proved untrustworthy during the communist era.[65] It takes time for people in new democracies to get used to participative management. For example, American entrepreneur Michael Smolens took one step at a time at Danube Knitware Ltd., the textile mill he cofounded in

FIGURE **4.1** GLOBE Leadership Matrix

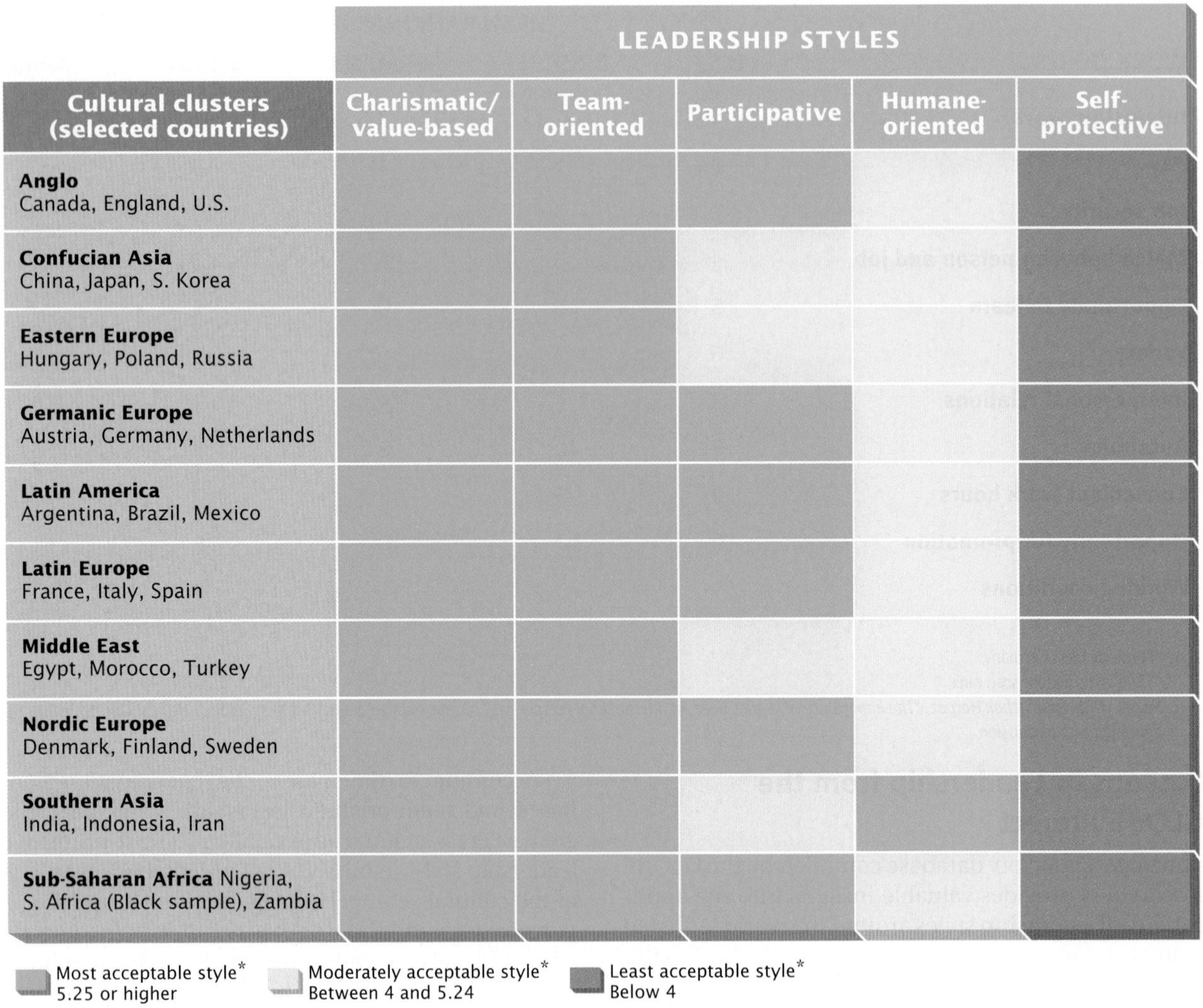

Cultural clusters (selected countries)	LEADERSHIP STYLES				
	Charismatic/ value-based	Team-oriented	Participative	Humane-oriented	Self-protective
Anglo Canada, England, U.S.					
Confucian Asia China, Japan, S. Korea					
Eastern Europe Hungary, Poland, Russia					
Germanic Europe Austria, Germany, Netherlands					
Latin America Argentina, Brazil, Mexico					
Latin Europe France, Italy, Spain					
Middle East Egypt, Morocco, Turkey					
Nordic Europe Denmark, Finland, Sweden					
Southern Asia India, Indonesia, Iran					
Sub-Saharan Africa Nigeria, S. Africa (Black sample), Zambia					

Most acceptable style* 5.25 or higher   Moderately acceptable style* Between 4 and 5.24   Least acceptable style* Below 4

*Mean score on 1–7 scale of acceptability

Source: Adapted from data in Peter W. Dorfman, Paul J. Hanges, and Felix C. Brodbeck, "Leadership and Cultural Variation: The Identification of Culturally Endorsed Leadership Profiles," in Robert J. House, Paul J. Hanges, Mansour Javidan, Peter W. Dorfman, and Vipin Gupta, Culture, Leadership, and Organizations: The GLOBE Study of 62 Societies (Thousand Oaks, Calif.: Sage, 2004), pp. 669–719; and Vipin Gupta and Paul J. Hanges, "Regional and Climate Clustering of Societal Cultures," in Ibid., pp. 178–218.

Hungary. It was a learning experience for all involved at the 950-employee company, which later opened a sewing factory in neighboring Romania.

The first step was getting workers used to high Western production standards and motivating them to accept the company's priorities. Hungary's low wage base was seen as a big plus when the company was being formed, but absenteeism has been an ongoing problem . . . . Smolens realized he'd have to strengthen his wage structure to keep his workers from abandoning the company for the family farms or the black market. He also moved from awarding attendance bonuses to providing other job incentives—in particular, cultivating a more comfortable, open work environment.

"We're actively soliciting comments from the workers day to day," says [cofounder Phil] Lightly. "They know what the problems are, but because of the way things used to be in this country, they're not always comfortable sharing them."

"It's a good approach," Smolens adds, "and we do see progress. They're starting to realize that what they say is being taken seriously."[66]

ETHICS: CHARACTER, COURAGE, AND VALUES

Leading by Example—All the Way to China

Shayne McQuade's company, Voltaic Systems, makes backpacks and messenger bags faced with solar panels that can charge things such as cell phones and PDAs. They're made in China. McQuade would like to explain why that is an environmentally progressive approach.

It's precisely because so many things are made in China. By sourcing his bags there, McQuade accrued a little influence. He told his manufacturer that he wanted the bags to be made from recycled PET plastic—soda bottles, essentially. The manufacturer couldn't find a supplier. So McQuade went to Taiwan and found the supplier himself. And here's the thing: Now his manufacturer makes products of recycled PET for lots of clients. Big clients, including Nike.

"By working with these factories, we have a hope of changing the manufacturing systems and making those materials and that fabric available through mainstream channels," says McQuade. "And that's where you change the world. If I'm doing some artisanal project in the U.S., it's not the same." . . .

Next up: bags with light-harvesting technology to charge a laptop.

Source: Larry Kanter, "The Eco-Advantage: The Green 50," Inc., 28 (November 2006): 87.

FOR DISCUSSION

What is the ethical lesson in this global business example? How would you respond to the cynic who says, "You can't change the world, so why bother"?

International managers need a full repertoire of leadership styles that they can use flexibly in a culturally diverse world[67] (see Ethics: Character, Courage, and Values).

STAFFING FOREIGN POSITIONS

In our global economy, successful foreign experience is becoming a required stepping stone to top management.

At PricewaterhouseCoopers, employees with as little as three years' experience can apply to spend up to two years in an international assignment—considered a key component to résumé building.[68]

Unfortunately, American expatriates reportedly have a higher-than-average failure rate. Failure in this context means foreign-posted employees perform so poorly that they are sent home early or voluntarily go home early. Estimates vary widely, from a modest 3.2 percent failure rate to an alarming 25 percent.[69] Whatever the failure rate, *any* turnover among employees on foreign assignments is expensive, considering that it costs an average of $1 to $2 million to send someone on a three-to-four-year foreign assignment.[70] Predeparture training for the employee and education allowances for children can drive the bill much higher. Managers are challenged not to waste this sort of investment. They need to do a better job of preparing employees for foreign assignments. Toward that end, let us examine why employees fail abroad and what can be done about it.

Why Do U.S. Expatriates Fail?

Although it has historically been a term for banishment or exile from one's native country, *expatriate* today refers to those who live and work in a foreign country. Living outside the comfort zone of one's native culture and surroundings can be immensely challenging—even overwhelming. Expatriates typically experience some degree of **culture shock**—feelings of anxiety, self-doubt, and isolation brought about by a mismatch between one's expectations and reality. Psychologist

culture shock: negative feelings triggered by a mismatch between expectations and reality

TABLE **4.6** — Research Findings on Why U.S. Expatriates Go Home Early

REASON	PERCENTAGE IN AGREEMENT
Not performing job effectively	48.4
Received other, more rewarding offers from other companies	43.7
Expatriate or family not adjusting to culture	36.6
Expatriate or family missing contact with family and friends at home	31.0
Received other, more rewarding offers from our company	12.2
Unable to adjust to deprived living standards in country of assignment	10.3
Concerned with problems of safety and/or health care in foreign location	10.3
Believed children's education was suffering	7.1
Feared that assignment would slow career advancement	7.1
Spouse wanted career	6.1
Compensation package was inadequate	0.0

Source: Reprinted from Business Horizons, *45 (November–December 2002), Gary S. Insch and John D. Daniels, "Causes and Consequences of Declining Early Departures from Foreign Assignments," Table 2, p. 41, Copyright © 2002 with permission from Elsevier.*

4f — A *Crash* Course in the Dangers of a Foreign Assignment

The Fears: In a survey of 1,129 MBA students, the leading reason (59 percent) for rejecting a foreign assignment involved fears about political instability, hostility toward foreigners, poverty, war, and violence.*

The Reality:

*Motor vehicle crashes—not crime or terrorism—are the No. 1 killer of healthy Americans in foreign countries. And the threat to travelers is poised to increase dramatically as worldwide economic growth gives more people access to motor vehicles. . . . [Researchers] predict that [annual] traffic fatalities worldwide will increase to 2.3 million in 2020, nearly double today's fatalities.***

Sources: *Data from Nancy J. Adler with Allison Gundersen,* International Dimensions of Organizational Behavior, *5th edition (Mason, Ohio: Thomson South-Western, 2008), Table 12-2, p. 356. **Gary Stoller, "Foreign Roads Can Be Deadly for Travelers,"* USA Today *(August 14, 2007): 1B–2B.*

QUESTION:
Does this perspective make you more or less fearful of taking a foreign assignment? Explain.

Elisabeth Marx offered these insights: "On average, managers in my study experienced culture shock symptoms for about seven weeks: 70 percent of managers reported these lasting up to five weeks and 30 percent had symptoms for up to ten weeks."[71]

Those who view culture shock as a natural part of living and working in a foreign country are better equipped to deal with it. More precise knowledge of why U.S. expatriates fail also is helpful. Thanks to a survey of 74 large U.S. companies, encompassing a total of 3.6 million employees and 12,500 expatriates, we have a clearer picture[72] (see Table 4.6). Job performance—either so poor that it prompted recall (48.4 percent) or so good that it attracted outside job offers (43.7 percent)—was the leading reason U.S. expatriates went home early. Also high on the list were factors related to culture shock (36.6 percent) and homesickness (31 percent). Other factors trailed in relative importance. It behooves candidates for foreign assignments to prepare themselves not just to avoid failure as an expatriate but to be stimulated and productive in a foreign assignment.

Cross-Cultural Training

As we have defined it, culture is the unique system of values, beliefs, and symbols that fosters patterned behavior in a given population. It is difficult to distinguish the individual from his or her cultural context. Consequently, people tend to be very protective of their cultural identity. Careless defiance or ignorance of cultural norms or traditions by outsiders can result in grave personal insult and put important business dealings at risk. Fortunately, cultural sensitivity can be learned through appropriate cross-cultural training. **Cross-cultural training** is any form of guided experience aimed at helping people live and work successfully in another culture. Experts say successful cross-cultural adaptation requires practice and mastery of the nine competencies listed in Table 4.2, in our earlier discussion of cultural intelligence.

> **cross-cultural training:** guided experience that helps people live and work successfully in foreign cultures

SPECIFIC TECHNIQUES. The nine cross-cultural competencies involve the *what* of cross-cultural training. Let us now consider *how* those competencies can be taught. Following is a list of five basic cross-cultural training techniques, ranked in order of increasing complexity and cost.[73]

Documentary programs. Trainees read about a foreign country's history, culture, institutions, geography, and economics. Videotaped and Web-based presentations are often used. For example, this is how Ambergris Solutions makes sure its 1,400 call center employees in the Philippines can comfortably converse with American clients of Texas-based companies:

> . . . *workers are given* USA Today *and the most recent Texas travel guide to read between calls. They watch the previous day's TV news from Texas during breaks*

in case conversation with a customer veers to current events.

> *Operations manager Katherine Ann Fernando said it can help knowing the weather, the top stories—even how the Dallas Cowboys or Texas Rangers are doing.*
>
> *"We can't afford to sound like we don't know anything about Texas," she said.*[74]

Culture assimilator. Cultural familiarity is achieved through exposure to a series of simulated intercultural incidents, or typical problem situations. This technique has been used to quickly train those who are given short notice of a foreign assignment.[75]

Language instruction. Conversational language skills are taught through a variety of methods. Months, sometimes years, of study are required to master difficult languages. But as a cross-cultural communications professor noted, "To speak more than one language is no longer a luxury, it is a necessity."[76] A good role model is Tupperware's top management team, made up of nine executives (all with foreign experience) who speak from two to four languages each.[77]

Sensitivity training. Experiential exercises teach awareness of the impact of one's actions on others in cross-cultural situations.[78]

Field experience. Extensive firsthand exposure to ethnic subcultures in one's own country or to foreign cultures can build cultural intelligence.[79] PricewaterhouseCoopers, the major accounting and consulting company mentioned earlier, has developed an inspiring leadership development program involving cross-cultural field experience. The Ulysses Program sends mid-career employees to developing

Say *Ni hao* (Hello) to Home Depot in China. This is the first store in Beijing for the world's largest home improvement retailer. Lots of cultural adaptation and training will be needed if Home Depot's made-in-America business model is to thrive in China.

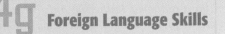

4g Foreign Language Skills

Fact: Native English speakers are projected to be only 5 percent of the world's population by 2050, down from 9 percent in 1995.

Fact: Senior executives in the Netherlands speak an average of 3.9 languages. Their counterparts in both the United Kingdom and the United States speak an average of 1.5 languages.

Learning a foreign language is easier for some than for others. International business experts say it is worth the time and effort in order to

- **Enhance the traveler's sense of mastery, self-confidence, and safety**
- **Show respect for foreign business hosts or guests**
- **Help build rapport and trust with foreign hosts or guests**
- **Improve the odds of a successful foreign business venture**
- **Build a base of confidence for learning other languages**
- **Promote a deeper understanding of other cultures**
- **Help travelers obtain the best possible medical care during emergencies**
- **Minimize culture shock and the frustrations of being an outsider**

Sources: Data from "English Declining as World Language," USA Today (February 27, 2004): 7A; Data from "Bilingual Business," USA Today (April 11, 2000): 1B. Adapted from Gary P. Ferraro, "The Need for Linguistic Proficiency in Global Business," Business Horizons, 39 (May–June 1996): 39–46.

QUESTIONS:

Could you conduct a business meeting in one or more foreign languages? What has been your experience with trying to learn foreign languages? How strong is your desire to speak a foreign language? Which language(s)? Why? Would a strong second language help you get a better job? Explain.

countries for eight-week community service projects. Here, for example, is the experience of Tahir Ayub:

> *His job: helping village leaders in the Namibian outback grapple with their community's growing AIDS crisis. Faced with language barriers, cultural differences, and scant access to electricity, Ayub, 39, and two colleagues had to scrap their PowerPoint presentations in favor of a more low-tech approach: face-to-face discussion. The village chiefs learned that they needed to garner community support for*

programs to combat the disease, and Ayub learned important lessons as well: Technology isn't always the answer, "You better put your beliefs and biases to one side and figure out new ways to look at things," he said.[80]

PricewaterhouseCoopers considers the $15,000 per-person cost of the Ulysses Program to be a sound investment in human and social capital.

IS ONE TECHNIQUE BETTER THAN ANOTHER? A study of 80 (63 male, 17 female) managers from a U.S. electronics company attempted to assess the relative effectiveness of two different training techniques.[81] A documentary approach was compared with an interpersonal approach. The latter combined sensitivity training and local ethnic field experience. These techniques were judged equally effective at promoting cultural adjustment, as measured during the managers' three-month stay in South Korea. The researchers recommended a *combination* of documentary and interpersonal training. The importance of language training was diminished in this study because the managers dealt primarily with English-speaking Koreans.

Considering that far too many U.S. companies have no formal expatriate training programs, the key issue is not which type of training is better, but whether companies offer any systematic cross-cultural training at all.

AN INTEGRATED EXPATRIATE STAFFING SYSTEM. Cross-cultural training, in whatever form, should not be an isolated experience. Rather, it should be part of an integrated, selection-orientation-repatriation process focused on a distinct career path.[82] The ultimate goal should be a positive and productive experience for the employee and his or her family and a smooth professional and cultural re-entry back home.

During the selection phase, the usual interview should be supplemented with an orientation session for the candidate's family. This session gives everyone an opportunity to "select themselves out" before a great deal of time and money has been invested. Experience has shown that upon the expatriate's arrival at the foreign assignment, family sponsors or assigned mentors are effective at reducing culture shock.[83] Sponsors and mentors ease the expatriate family through the critical first six months by answering naive but important questions and by serving as cultural translators.[84]

Finally, repatriation should be "a forethought" rather than an afterthought.[85] Candidates for foreign assignments deserve a firm commitment from their

4h Ready to Pack Your Bags?

Survey of 516 senior executives: "Half of the executives would take a job in China, 34 percent said they would work in India, and the same number would accept a position in Russia."

Survey of 1,000 employees: When asked whether they would move if their mate were given a foreign assignment, 68 percent said "No," 30 percent said "Yes," and 2 percent weren't sure.

Sources: Ann Pomeroy, "Have Job, Will Travel," HR Magazine, 49 (June 2004): 20; and data from "Most Mates Not Willing to Move Abroad," USA Today (July 21, 2004): 1B.

QUESTION:
How would you respond to these two surveys? Explain.

organization that a successful tour of duty will lead to a step up the career ladder upon their return. Expatriates who spend their time worrying about being leapfrogged while they are absent from headquarters are less likely to succeed.

What About North American Women on Foreign Assignments?

Historically, companies in Canada and the United States have sent very few women on foreign assignments. Between the early 1980s and the late 1990s, the representation of women among North American expatriates grew from 3 percent to a still small 14 percent.[86] Conventional wisdom—that women could not be effective because of foreign prejudice—has turned

out to be a myth.[87] Recent research and practical experience have given us these insights:

- North American women have enjoyed above-average success on foreign assignments.
- The greatest barriers to foreign assignments for North American women have been self-disqualification and prejudice among *home-country* managers. A recent survey led to this conclusion: "We found that American women in management and executive roles in foreign countries can do just as well as American men. Their biggest problem was convincing their companies to give them the assignments."[88]
- Culture is a bigger hurdle than gender. In other words, North American women on foreign assignments are seen as North Americans first and as women second.[89]

Testimonial evidence suggests that these last two factors are also true for African Americans, many of whom report smoother relations abroad than at home.[90] Thus, the best career advice for *anyone* seeking a foreign assignment is this: carefully prepare yourself, *go for it*, and don't take "no" for an answer![91]

Relying on Local Managerial Talent

In recent years, the expensive problem of expatriate failure and general trends toward geocentrism and globalism have resulted in a greater reliance on managers from host countries. Foreign nationals already know the language and culture and do not require huge relocation expenditures.[92] In addition, host-country governments tend to look favorably on a greater degree of local control. On the negative side, local managers may not have adequate knowledge of home-office goals and procedures. The staffing of foreign positions is necessarily a case-by-case proposition.

SUMMARY

1. The study of international management is more important than ever as the huge global economy continues to grow. Doing business internationally typically involves much more than importing and/or exporting goods. The six stages of the internationalization process are licensing, exporting, local warehousing and selling, local assembly and packaging, joint ventures, and direct foreign investments. There are three main guidelines for success in international joint ventures: (a) Be patient while

building trust with a carefully selected partner; (b) learn as much as fast as possible without giving away key secrets; and (c) establish clear ground rules for rights and responsibilities. Global companies are a present-day reality, whereas transnational companies are a futuristic vision. A global company does business simultaneously in many countries but pursues global strategies administered from a strong home-country headquarters. In contrast, a transnational company is envisioned as a decentralized global network of productive units with no distinct national identity. There is growing concern about the economic and political power that such stateless enterprises may acquire as they eclipse the power and scope of their host nations.

2. Cultural intelligence (CQ) is defined as the ability of an outsider to "read" individual behavior, group dynamics, and situations in a foreign culture as well as the locals do. Those with high CQ are cross-cultural chameleons who blend in with the local cultural situation. Global managers with high cultural intelligence possess these nine cross-cultural competencies: 1. building relationships; 2. valuing people of different cultures; 3. listening and observation; 4. coping with ambiguity; 5. translating complex information; 6. taking action and initiative; 7. managing others; 8. adaptability and flexibility; and 9. managing stress. According to Howard Perlmutter, management tends to exhibit one of three general attitudes about international operations: an ethnocentric attitude (home-country-oriented), a polycentric attitude (host-country-oriented), or a geocentric attitude (world-oriented). Perlmutter claims that a geocentric attitude will lead to better product quality, improved use of resources, better local management, and more profit than the other attitudes.

3. In high-context cultures such as Japan, communication is based more on nonverbal and situational messages than it is in low-context cultures such as the United States. The nine cultural dimensions identified by the GLOBE project are power distance, uncertainty avoidance, institutional collectivism, in-group collectivism, assertiveness, gender equality, future orientation, performance orientation, and humane orientation.

4. Comparative management is a new field of study concerned with how organizational behavior and management practices differ across cultures. A unique study by Geert Hofstede of 116,000 IBM employees in 40 nations classified each country by its prevailing attitude toward four cultural variables. In view of significant international differences on

these cultural dimensions, Hofstede suggests that American management theory and practice be adapted to local cultures rather than imposed on them. The cross-cultural study of work goals uncovered a great deal of diversity. Thus, motivational programs need to be tailored to the local culture.

5. Across 62 societies in the GLOBE study, the charismatic/value-based (goal-directed visionary) and team-oriented (competent team builder) leadership styles were found to be widely applicable. The self-protective (self-centered) leadership style was not acceptable in any culture. The participative leadership style (involving others in making and implementing decisions) had mixed applicability across cultures, as did the humane-oriented (supportive and nurturing) style. Global managers need to use a contingency approach to leadership, adapting their styles to the local culture.

6. Culture shock is a normal part of expatriate life. Job performance issues, family and/or individual culture shock, and homesickness are the leading reasons why U.S. expatriates go home early (a costly problem). Systematic cross-cultural training—ideally including development of interpersonal, observational, language, and stress management competencies—is needed. Expatriates also must be flexible and able to handle ambiguity. Specific cross-cultural training techniques include documentary programs, training via a culture assimilator, language instruction, sensitivity training, and field experience.

7. North American women fill a growing but still small share of foreign positions. The long-standing assumption that women will fail on foreign assignments because of foreigners' prejudice has turned out to be false. Women from the United States and Canada have been successful on foreign assignments but face two major hurdles at *home:* self-disqualification and prejudicial managers. Culture, not gender, is the primary challenge for women on foreign assignments. The situation for African Americans parallels that for women.

TERMS TO UNDERSTAND

MANAGER'S TOOLKIT

Pat McGovern's Tips for Business Travelers

Background: Pat McGovern is the CEO of IDG, a company he founded in Boston in 1964. The $3 billion-a-year firm's Web site offers the following corporate profile.

> *International Data Group (IDG) is the world's leading technology media, events, and research company. IDG's online network includes more than 450 Web sites spanning business technology, consumer technology, digital entertainment, and video games worldwide. IDG publishes more than 300 magazines and newspapers in 85 countries including CIO, CSO, Computerworld, GamePro, InfoWorld, Macworld, Network World, and PC World. IDG's lead-generation service, IDG Connect, matches technology companies with an audience of engaged, high-quality IT [information technology] professionals, influencers, and decision makers.*[93]

Mr. McGovern recently wrote in *Inc.* magazine that "I have spent an average of four months a year for the past 40 years launching our technology publications, events, and research and online services from Antarctica to Zimbabwe. . . . Today IDG operates in 85 countries; 80 percent of our profits come from outside the United States."[94] Here are his tips for today's globe-trotting businesspeople:

Make Packing a Reflex Action. As much as possible, I pack the same items in the same way for each trip. I can pack my bags for a two-week trip in five minutes.

Get Briefed. I prepare a briefing book with the latest economic and business information on countries I am about to visit. I cull most of the information from the Internet.

Stick to Top Business Hotels. I'm perfectly happy to fly business class on commercial airlines. But when it comes to lodging, I seek out the best international hotels. Their business centers are a great resource; they usually have well-equipped health clubs; and their prestige tells the locals I'm going first-class.

Arrive Early. For first-time visits, I like to arrive in a country on Saturday and spend the weekend wandering around observing people's behavior. I gain a sense of the pace and the culture: how fast people walk, how they gesture when they talk, what they wear, what they read. It puts me in sync for my Monday meetings.

Bear Gifts. In Asia, Latin America, and Africa it's good form to present your host with a gift. It needn't be lavish: a book about the city you live in, an engraved paperweight, or a silver business card holder will do just fine.

Practice Humility. In many cultures it's considered impolite to boast about yourself or your company's accomplishments. However, talking about your children and asking about those of your hosts is a great way to bond. Also, work in references to your philanthropic activities. It suggests you will share your success with local worthy causes.

Source: Inc. staff, "Pat McGovern's Tips for Business Travelers," Inc., 29 (April 2007): 114. Copyright © 2007 by Mansueto Ventures LLC. Reproduced with permission of Mansueto Ventures LLC in the format Textbook via Copyright Clearance Center.

ACTION LEARNING EXERCISE

Look into the Cultural Mirror

Instructions: Culture, as defined in this chapter, involves *taken-for-granted* assumptions about how we should think, act, and feel (relative to both ourselves and the world in general). Here is an opportunity to bring those assumptions to the surface. Remember, there are no right or wrong answers. Moreover, because this exercise has no proven scientific validity, it is intended for instructional purposes only. The idea is to see where you stand in the world's rich mosaic of cultural diversity by rating yourself on the cultural variables discussed in this chapter.

Low-context   High-context
("Put it in writing.")   ("The situation is more important than words.")

1. 2. . . . . 3. . . . . 4. 5

Individualistic   Collectivist
("Me first.")   ("It's all about us.")

1. 2. . . . . 3. . . . . 4. 5

Monochronic   Polychronic
("Do one thing at a time and be on time.")   ("There's a time to go fast and a time to go slow. Do more than one thing at a time.")

1. 2. . . . . 3. . . . . 4. 5

Power Distance

Low   High
("Leaders are no better than anyone else.")   ("Authority and power of leaders should be respected.")

1. 2. . . . . 3. . . . . 4. 5

Uncertainty Avoidance

Low   High
("Take chances, bend the rules.")   ("Take no chances, follow the rules.")

1. 2. . . . . 3. . . . . 4. 5

Future Orientation

Low   High
("Live for today; instant gratification.")   ("Think long-term; save for the future.")

1. 2. . . . . 3. . . . . 4. 5

Performance Orientation

Low   High
("Loyalty and belonging are what really count.")   ("Take the initiative; have a sense of urgency about getting results.")

1. 2. . . . . 3. . . . . 4. 5

Humane Orientation

Low   High
("Look out for yourself.")   ("Help others, especially the weak and vulnerable.")

1. 2. . . . . 3. . . . . 4. 5

Masculinity   Femininity
("Winning and material wealth are what count.")   ("Relationships and quality of life are what really matter.")

1. 2. . . . . 3. . . . . 4. 5

For Consideration/Discussion

1. Did this exercise help you better understand any of the cultural variables discussed in this chapter? Explain.

2. Does your cultural profile help you better understand some of your family's traditions, values, rituals, or customs?

3. How does your cultural profile compare with that of others (spouse, friends, classmates)? Could the seeds of conflict and misunderstanding grow from any cultural differences with them?

4. Which of your positive cultural traits could become a negative if taken to extremes?

CLOSING CASE
Tell the Kids We're Moving to Kenya

Dale Pilger, General Motors Corp.'s new managing director for Kenya, wonders if he can keep his Kenyan employees from interrupting his paperwork by raising his index finger.

"The finger itself will offend," warns Noah Midamba, a Kenyan. He urges that Mr. Pilger instead greet a worker with an effusive welcome, offer a chair and request that he wait. It can be even trickier to fire a Kenyan, Mr. Midamba says. The government asked one German auto executive to leave Kenya after he dismissed a man—whose brother was the East African country's vice president.

Mr. Pilger, his adventurous wife and their two teenagers, miserable about moving, have come to . . . [Boulder, Colorado,] for three days of cross-cultural training. The Cortland, Ohio, family learns to cope with being strangers in a strange land as consultants Moran, Stahl & Boyer International give them a crash immersion in African political history, business practices, social customs and nonverbal gestures. The training enables managers to grasp cultural differences and handle culture-shock symptoms such as self-pity.

Cross-cultural training is on the rise everywhere because more global-minded corporations moving fast-track executives overseas want to curb the cost of failed expatriate stints. . . .

But as cross-cultural training gains popularity, it attracts growing criticism. A lot of the training is garbage, argues Robert Bontempo, assistant professor of international business at Columbia University. Even customized family training offered by companies like Prudential Insurance Co. of America's Moran Stahl—which typically costs $6,000 for three days—hasn't been scientifically tested. "They charge a huge amount of money, and there's no evidence that these firms do any good" in lowering foreign-transfer flops, Prof. Bontempo contends.

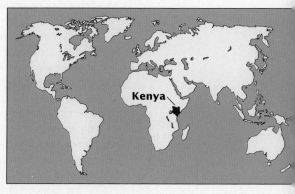

"You don't need research," to prove that cross-cultural training works because so much money has been wasted on failed overseas assignments, counters Gary Wederspahn, director of design and development at Moran Stahl.

General Motors agrees. Despite massive cost cutting lately, the auto giant still spends nearly $500,000 a year on cross-cultural training for about 150 Americans and their families headed abroad. "We think this substantially contributes to the low [premature] return rate" of less than 1 percent among GM expatriates, says Richard Rachner, GM general director of international personnel. . . .

The Pilgers' experience reveals the benefits and drawbacks of such training. Mr. Pilger, a 38-year-old engineer employed by GM for 20 years, sought an overseas post but never lived abroad before. He finds the sessions "worthwhile" in readying him to run a vehicle-assembly plant that is 51 percent owned by Kenya's government. But he finds the training "horribly empty . . . in helping us prepare for the personal side of the move."

Dale and Nancy Pilger have just spent a week in Nairobi. But the executive's scant knowledge of Africa becomes clear when trainer Jackson Wolfe, a former Peace Corps official, mentions Nigeria. "Is that where Idi Amin was from?" Mr. Pilger asks. The dictator ruled Uganda. With a sheepish smile, Mr. Pilger admits, "We don't know a lot about the world."

The couple's instructors don't always know everything about preparing expatriates for Kenyan culture, either. Mr. Midamba, an adjunct international-relations professor at Kent State University and son of a Kenyan political leader, concedes that he neglected to caution Mr. Pilger's predecessor against holding business dinners at Nairobi restaurants.

As a result, the American manager "got his key people to the restaurant and expected their wives to be there," Mr. Midamba recalls. But "the wives didn't show up." Married women in Kenya view restaurants "as places where you find prostitutes and loose morals," notes Mungai Kimani, another Kenyan trainer.

The blunder partly explains why Mr. Midamba goes to great lengths to teach the Pilgers the art of entertaining at home. Among his tips: Don't be surprised if guests arrive an hour early, an hour late, or announce their departure four times.

The Moran Stahl program also zeros in on the family's adjustment (though not to Mr. Pilger's satisfaction). A family's poor adjustment causes more foreign-transfer failures than a manager's work performance. That is the Pilgers' greatest fear because 14-year-old Christy and 16-year-old Eric bitterly oppose the move. The lanky, boyish-looking Mr. Pilger remembers Eric's tearful reaction as: "You'll have to arrest me if you think you're going to take me to Africa."

While distressed by his children's hostility, Mr. Pilger still believes living abroad will be a great growth experience for them. But he says he promised Eric that if "he's miserable" in Kenya, he can return to Ohio for his last year of high school next year.

To ease their adjustment, Christy and Eric receive separate training from their parents. The teens' activities include sampling Indian food (popular in Kenya) as well as learning how to ride Nairobi public buses, speak a little Swahili and juggle, of all things.

By the training's last day, both youngsters grudgingly accept being uprooted from friends, her swim team and his brand-new car. Going to Kenya "no longer seems like a death sentence," Christy says. Eric mumbles that he may volunteer at a wild-game reserve.

But their usually upbeat mother has become increasingly upset as she hears more about a country troubled by drought, poverty, and political unrest—where foreigners live behind walled fortresses. Now, at an international parenting session, she clashes with youth trainer Amy Kaplan over whether her offspring can safely ride Nairobi's public buses, even with Mrs. Pilger initially accompanying them.

"All the advice we've gotten is that it's deadly" to ride buses there, Mrs. Pilger frets. Ms. Kaplan retorts, "It's going to be hard" to let teenagers do their own thing in Kenya, but then they'll be less likely to rebel. The remark fails to quell Mrs. Pilger's fears that she can't handle life abroad. "I'm going to let a lot of people down if I blow this," she adds, her voice quavering with emotion.

FOR DISCUSSION

1 Does the Pilgers' son Eric seem to have an ethnocentric, polycentric, or geocentric attitude? Explain.

2 Would you label Kenya a monochronic or a polychronic culture, based on the evidence in this case? Explain.

3 Using Figure 4.1 as a guide, indicate which of the GLOBE leadership styles Pilger should use (and which he should avoid) in Kenya. Explain.

4 What were the positive and negative aspects of the Pilgers' predeparture training?

5 Do you think the Pilger family will end up having a productive and satisfying foreign assignment? Explain.

TEST PREPPER

True/False Questions

_____ 1. The first stage in the internationalization process is direct foreign investment.

_____ 2. Geocentric companies staff all positions with the best available talent in the world.

_____ 3. People from high-context countries such as Switzerland and the United States rely heavily on nonverbal cues when communicating.

_____ 4. Individuals and countries scoring high on Project GLOBE's "future orientation" prefer to work and save for the future rather than just living for the present.

_____ 5. Hofstede found American management theories to be universally applicable around the world.

_____ 6. In a cross-cultural study of work goals, "interpersonal relations" got a consistently high ranking.

_____ 7. GLOBE project researchers found the team-oriented leadership style to have wide cross-cultural applicability.

_____ 8. The number one reason why Americans fail in foreign assignments is "lack of motivation to work in another country."

_____ 9. "Coping with ambiguity" and "managing stress" are among the nine competencies needed for successful cross-cultural adaptation.

_____10. North American women have enjoyed above-average success on foreign assignments.

Multiple-Choice Questions

1. What is the final stage of the internationalization process?
   A. Direct foreign investment
   B. Exporting
   C. Licensing
   D. Local assembly and packaging
   E. A joint venture

2. Because of unresolved political, economic, and tax implications, many experts are alarmed at the prospect of immense "stateless" _____ companies.
   A. joint venture   B. transnational
   C. global   D. multinational
   E. cross-border

3. Which one of these creatures best characterizes someone with high cultural intelligence?
   A. An elephant   B. A tiger
   C. A chameleon   D. An eagle
   E. A butterfly

4. Which type of organization relies heavily on home-country personnel, ideas, and practices?
   A. Polycentric   B. Polychronic
   C. Ethnocentric   D. Geocentric
   E. Monochronic

5. _____ is(are) vital to communication in high-context cultures.
   A. Being on time
   B. Nonverbal and situational cues
   C. Being polite
   D. Having family ties
   E. Written contracts

6. Which of these is not one of the nine GLOBE project cultural dimensions?
   A. Assertiveness   B. Power distance
   C. Gender equality   D. Historical perspective
   E. Institutional collectivism

7. The perception of time as flexible, elastic, and multidimensional represents _____ time.
   A. polychronic   B. monochronic
   C. natural   D. low-context
   E. traditional

8. The GLOBE project researchers found the _____ leadership style to be widely applicable across cultures.
   A. charismatic/value-based   B. self-protective
   C. competence-based   D. humane-oriented
   E. participative

9. According to a recent survey, what was the number one reason why U.S. employees go home early from foreign assignments?
   A. Family not adjusting to culture
   B. Not performing job effectively
   C. Better offer from another company
   D. Safety concerns
   E. Inadequate compensation

10. Which of these phrases best sums up the status of North American women on foreign assignments?
    A. Rapidly approaching gender parity
    B. Better pay equality than at home
    C. Underrepresented but successful
    D. Greater administrative status than at home
    E. Lower satisfaction with foreign experiences than male counterparts report

See page T1 at the back of the text for answers to these questions. Want more questions? Visit the student Web site and take the ACE quizzes for more practice.

5

Management's Social and Ethical Responsibilities

OBJECTIVES

- **Define** the term *corporate social responsibility* (CSR), and **specify** the four levels in Carroll's global CSR pyramid.

- **Contrast** the classical economic and socioeconomic models of business, and **summarize** the arguments for and against CSR.

- **Identify** and **describe** the four social responsibility strategies, and **explain** the concept of enlightened self-interest.

- **Summarize** the four practical lessons from business ethics research.

- **Distinguish** between instrumental and terminal values, and **explain** their relationship to business ethics.

- **Identify** and **describe** at least four of the ten general ethical principles.

- **Discuss** what management can do to improve business ethics.

THE CHANGING WORKPLACE

A Texas Outfit in Sudan

The house on a side street in Khartoum, like others in Sudan's capital, is newly built, with a wall blocking its occupants from view. But these occupants might want the privacy: The red logo inside is that of Houston-based oilfield-services firm Weatherford International.

What's a Texas company doing renting drilling gear and other equipment in a country whose Islamic government has been under U.S. sanctions since 1997? Outraged over [the genocide in] Darfur, Congress has prohibited U.S. transactions with Sudan's oil industry, while President Bush has banned 30 Sudanese companies from using the U.S. financial system. Texas's own legislature recently voted to divest its pension funds [of] companies operating in Sudan.

The answer is there's a loophole big enough for a $6.5 billion company. "We report only to Dubai," said Tarek Khalil, who runs Weatherford Oil Tool Middle East in Khartoum, when *Fortune* visited his office recently. "We have nothing to do with the U.S." Indeed, according to Treasury spokeswoman Molly Millerwise, foreign subsidiaries of U.S. firms can operate in Sudan if "there is no involvement by the U.S. parent or any other U.S. person."

The main reason more don't try: The resulting PR isn't very good. "It creates a pretty bad rap for your company," says Michael Jacobson, a former Treasury official and now a fellow at the Washington Institute for Near East Policy. (Another former Treasury official, Nicholas Brady, who served as Secretary [of the Treasury] from 1988 to 1993, sits on Weatherford's board.)

Last year Weatherford competitor Baker Hughes pulled its foreign subsidiary out of Sudan. "There was near unanimity and condemnation of what was going on in Sudan," says spokesperson Gary Flaharty.

Activists might soon lobby firms with subsidiaries there for divestment. "These companies have been flying under the radar," says Jason Miller, policy advisor to the Sudan Divestment Task Force in Washington. "They are not abiding by the spirit of the law. If the public were made aware of it, there would be an outcry."

Carine Bouery, a spokeswoman at the Weatherford subsidiary's Dubai office, says, "We can't say anything in any publication about being in Sudan. This is too sensitive." In Houston, Weatherford CFO [chief financial officer] Andy Becnel says he's aware of the sensitivities but insists the company abides by the law. He added that activist pressure could force a change. "If something were really unpopular," he says. "the shareholders could request the company to no longer operate there."

Source: From Vivienne Walt, "A Texas Outfit in Sudan," *Fortune* (August 6, 2007): 18. © 2007 Time Inc. All rights reserved.

In terms of business ethics, is Weatherford International right or wrong? To whom are they primarily accountable, the firm's shareholders or public opinion? Is it enough to simply follow the law, or is more required? This chapter will help you deal with these tough questions.

As the social, political, economic, and technological environments of management have changed, the practice of management itself has changed. This is especially true for managers in the private business sector. Today, in the wake of the Enron, Tyco, and WorldCom debacles, it is far less acceptable for someone in business to stand before the public and declare that his or her sole job is to make as much profit as possible.[2] The public is wary of the abuse of power and the betrayal of trust, and business managers—indeed, managers of all types of organizations—are expected to make a wide variety of economic and social contributions. Demands on business that would have been considered patently unreasonable 30 or 40 years ago have become the norm today. Stuart Graham, the American CEO of Skanska, a giant Swedish construction company with 12,000 projects worldwide, recently framed the challenge this way:

> *The future is that there will be no letup in the demands of shareholders for financial performance. There will also be no letup in the demands of society that businesses behave responsibly. Management just has to get better.*[3]

The purpose of this chapter is to examine management's broader social and ethical responsibilities.

SOCIAL RESPONSIBILITY: DEFINITION AND PERSPECTIVES

When John D. Rockefeller was at the zenith of his power as the founder of Standard Oil Company, he handed out dimes to rows of eager children who lined the street. Rockefeller did this on the advice of a public relations expert who believed the dime campaign would counteract his widespread reputation as a monopolist who had ruthlessly eliminated his competitors in the oil industry. The dime campaign was not a complete success, however, because Standard Oil was broken up under the Sherman Antitrust Act of 1890.[4] Conceivably, Rockefeller believed he was fulfilling some sort of social responsibility by passing out dimes to hungry children. Since Rockefeller's time, the concept of social responsibility has grown and matured to the point where many of today's companies are intimately involved in social programs that have no direct connection with the bottom line. These programs include everything from support of the arts and urban renewal to education reform and environmental protection. But like all aspects of management, social responsibility needs to be carried out in an effective and efficient manner.

What Does Corporate Social Responsibility (CSR) Involve?

Social responsibility, as defined in this section, is a relatively new concern of the business community. Like a child maturing through adolescence on the way to adulthood, the idea of corporate social responsibility is evolving. One expert defined **corporate social responsibility (CSR)** as "the notion that corporations have an obligation to constituent groups in society other than stockholders and beyond that prescribed by law or union contract."[5] As might be expected for any emerging area, disagreement remains over the exact nature and scope of management's *social* responsibilities.[6]

> **corporate social responsibility (CSR):** the idea that business has social obligations above and beyond making a profit

Nancy Lockwood, a researcher for the Society for Human Resource Management, recently characterized CSR this way:

> *Simply put, the business case for CSR—establishing a positive company reputation and brand in the public eye through good work that yields a competitive edge while at the same time contributing to others—demands that organizations shift from solely focusing on making a profit to including financial, environmental and social responsibility in their core business strategies. Despite what the phrase* corporate social responsibility *suggests, the concept is not restricted to corporations but rather is intended for most types of organizations, such as associations, labor unions, organizations that serve the community for scientific, educational, artistic, public health or charitable purposes, and governmental agencies.*[7]

Thus, Lockwood has expanded the domain of CSR. The global economy is expanding it even more.

CSR FOR GLOBAL AND TRANSNATIONAL CORPORATIONS.
Business ethics scholar Archie B. Carroll believes the burgeoning global economy requires a more encompassing perspective on CSR. According to his model in Figure 5.1, today's global and transnational companies have four main areas of responsibility: economic, legal, ethical, and philanthropic. Working

FIGURE **5.1** Carroll's Global Corporate Social Responsibility Pyramid

Source: Academy of Management Executive: The Thinking Manager's Source *by Archie B. Carroll. Copyright 2004 by Academy of Management (NY). Reproduced with permission of Academy of Management (NY) in the format Textbook via Copyright Clearance Center.*

from bottom to top, this means the global corporation should

- *Make a profit* consistent with expectations for international businesses
- *Obey the law* of host countries as well as international law
- *Be ethical in its practices*, taking host-country and global standards into consideration
- *Be a good corporate citizen*, especially as defined by the host country's expectations[8]

Carroll emphasizes that this is not a pick-and-choose approach to CSR. All four responsibilities are intertwined and need to be fulfilled if a global corporation—or *any* company in any situation, for that matter—is to be called socially responsible. However, over the long term, a company must consistently satisfy the bottom three levels before exercising philanthropic responsibility. Carroll describes *philanthropic responsibilities* as "social activities that are not mandated by law nor generally expected of business in an ethical sense."[9] Of course, expectations regarding philanthropic responsibilities vary from country to country.[10] This global perspective on CSR is summed up very nicely by Tachi Kiuchi, managing director of Japan's Mitsubishi Electric Corp.:

> *People talk about businesses needing to be responsible as if it's something new we need to do on top of everything else. But the whole essence of business should be responsibility. My philosophy is, we don't run companies to earn profits. We earn profits to run companies. Our companies need meaning and purpose if they're to fit into the world, or why should they live at all?*[11]

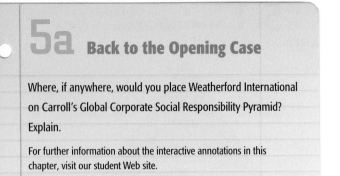

5a   Back to the Opening Case

Where, if anywhere, would you place Weatherford International on Carroll's Global Corporate Social Responsibility Pyramid? Explain.

For further information about the interactive annotations in this chapter, visit our student Web site.

CSR REQUIRES VOLUNTARY ACTION. An implicit feature of the above definition and perspective is that an action must be *voluntary* to qualify as socially responsible. For example, consider the actions of Paul Dolan at California's Fetzer Vineyards:

> [He says,] "it's the way we farm. Everything is organic." Indeed, every single one of the 2,000 acres owned by Fetzer is certified organic. Dolan has sworn to convert all of his 200 outside grape growers to organic methods by the year 2010. And Fetzer is considered a "zero waste" business by the State of California. "It's just how business needs to be done," he says. . . .
>
> [In his book on "sustainable business," True to Our Roots: Fermenting a Business Revolution], Dolan urges all businesses to commit to the "triple bottom line," a measure of corporate success that takes into account not just profit and loss but also

social and environmental impact, and he offers the story of Fetzer's own transformation as an example.

> To those who say that going organic, using alternative power sources, providing living wages for workers, and eliminating waste (all of which Fetzer does) are nice, fuzzy goals that don't make financial sense, Dolan simply points to his own success in a tough industry.[12]

Fetzer Vineyards is socially responsible because Dolan has *voluntarily* taken a creative and inspiring leadership role in the wine-making business to strike a workable balance between profit and the greater good. His actions did not involve reluctant compliance with new laws or court orders, nor are his actions a cynical public relations ploy to keep regulators at bay.

What Is the Role of Business in Society?

Much of the disagreement over what social responsibility involves can be traced to a fundamental debate about the exact purpose of a business. Is a business an economic entity responsible only for making a profit for its stockholders? Or is it a socioeconomic entity obligated to make both economic and social contributions to society?[13] Depending on one's perspective, social responsibility can be interpreted either way.

THE CLASSICAL ECONOMIC MODEL. The classical economic model can be traced to the eighteenth century, when businesses were owned largely by entrepreneurs or owner-managers. Competition was vigorous among small operations, and short-run profits were the sole concern of these early entrepreneurs.

The green movement is testing the limits of corporate social responsibility. Companies trumpet their energy-saving and earth-friendly initiatives while cynics call it "greenwashing." These Philippine school children taking part in a Greenpeace demonstration want action, not just slogans.

5b — Does the End Justify the Means?

Stanford University management professor Jeffrey Pfeffer:

There was a time when companies and people took pride in what they did and how they did it—not just in the results toted up on some financial Ouija board but in the processes that produced those results. Returning to the idea that what *people and companies do, not just what they* achieve, *matters is the first and most important step on the road to more ethical clarity and higher standards of behavior.*

Source: Jeffrey Pfeffer, What Were They Thinking? Unconventional Wisdom About Management *(Boston: Harvard Business School Press, 2007), p. 194.*

QUESTIONS:

If you get great grades in school, does it really matter *how* you got them? If a company is highly profitable, does it really matter *how* those profits were earned? Explain.

Of course, the key to attaining short-run profits was to provide society with needed goods and services. According to Adam Smith, father of the classical economic model, an "invisible hand" promoted the public welfare. Smith believed the efforts of competing entrepreneurs had a natural tendency to promote the public interest when each tried to maximize short-run profits. In other words, Smith believed the public interest was served by individuals pursuing their own economic self-interests.[14]

This model has survived into modern times. For example, *Business Week* quoted Robert J. Eaton, former chairman of Chrysler Corporation prior to the creation of DaimlerChrysler, as saying, "The idea of corporations taking on social responsibility is absolutely ridiculous. . . . You'll simply burden industry to a point where it's no longer competitive."[15] Thus, according to the classical economic model of business, short-run profitability and social responsibility are the same thing.

THE SOCIOECONOMIC MODEL. Reflecting society's broader expectations for business (for example, safe and meaningful jobs, clean air and water, charitable donations, safe products), many think the time has come to revamp the classical economic model, which they believe to be obsolete. Enron, the company that took a spectacular tumble from number 7 on the 2001

Fortune 500[16] list to a scandalous bankruptcy in 2002, has been cited as a prime case in point. Economist Robert Kuttner bluntly explained:

The deeper scandal here is ideological. Enron epitomized an entire philosophy about the supposed self-cleansing nature of markets. . . .

Enron, as a trading enterprise, claimed to be the quintessence of a pure free market. In practice, it was up to its ears in cronyism, influence-peddling, rigging the rules to favor insiders, and undermining the transparency on which efficient markets depend. . . .

Enron is to the menace of market fundamentalism what September 11 was to the peril of global terror—a very costly wake-up call.[17]

Enron's 21,000 former employees—most of whom lost their life's savings along with their jobs—would probably agree.[18] According to the socioeconomic model proposed as an alternative to the classical economic model, business is just one subsystem among many in a highly interdependent society.

Advocates of the socioeconomic model point out that many groups in society besides stockholders have a stake in corporate affairs. Creditors, current and retired employees, customers, suppliers, competitors, all levels of government, the community, and society in general have expectations, often conflicting, for management. Some companies go so far as to conduct a **stakeholder audit**.[19] This growing practice involves systematically identifying all parties that might possibly be affected by the company's performance (for an example,[20] see Figure 5.2). According to the socioeconomic view, business has an obligation to respond to the needs of all stakeholders while pursuing a profit.[21] Debra Dunn, senior vice president of corporate affairs at Hewlett-Packard, speaks to the difficulty of this balancing act:

> **stakeholder audit:** identification of all parties that might be affected by the organization

It begins with the way a company thinks about its role in the world. Does it simply exist to make as much money as possible? At Hewlett-Packard, the question we ask ourselves is this: How do we consistently address multiple stakeholders, including customers, employees, and the communities we're a part of?

Collaboration between sectors [e.g., government, business, and nonprofits] is critical, and it's also the biggest challenge we face.[22]

FIGURE **5.2** A Sample Stakeholder Audit for Wal-Mart, the World's Largest Retailer

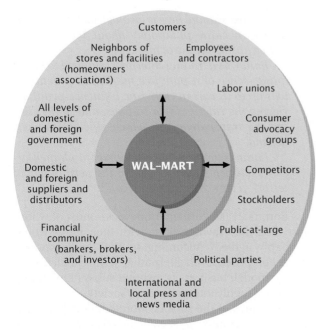

Arguments For and Against Corporate Social Responsibility

As one might suspect, the debate about the role of business has spawned many specific arguments both for and against corporate social responsibility.[23] A sample of four major arguments on each side will reveal the principal issues.

ARGUMENTS FOR.   Convinced that a business should be more than simply a profit machine, proponents of social responsibility have offered the following arguments.

1. *Business is unavoidably involved in social issues.* As social activists like to say, business is either part of the solution or part of the problem. There is no denying that private business shares responsibility for such societal problems as unemployment, inflation, and pollution. Like everyone else, corporate citizens must balance their rights and responsibilities.
2. *Business has the resources to tackle today's complex societal problems.* With its rich stock of technical, financial, and managerial resources, the private business sector can play a decisive role in solving society's more troublesome problems. After all, without society's support, business could not have built its resource base in the first place.
3. *A better society means a better environment for doing business.* Business can enhance its long-run profitability by making an investment in society today. Today's problems can turn into tomorrow's profits.
4. *Corporate social action will prevent government intervention.* As evidenced by waves of antitrust, equal employment opportunity, and pollution-control legislation, government will force business to do what it fails to do voluntarily.

Arguments like these four give business a broad socioeconomic agenda (see Window on the World).

ARGUMENTS AGAINST.   Remaining faithful to the classical economic model, opponents of corporate social responsibility rely on the first two arguments below. The third and fourth arguments have been voiced by those who think business is already too big and powerful.

1. *Profit maximization ensures the efficient use of society's resources.* By buying goods and services, consumers collectively dictate where assets

---

5c   Capitalism and CSR

Jack Welch, former CEO of General Electric, and Suzy Welch, former editor of *Harvard Business Review*:

Companies live or die because of engaged employees and satisfied customers. Obviously, both have to be heard. . . . companies reside in communities, are part of society, and must accept the responsibilities of good citizenship.

Capitalism, with its shareholder owners, reinforces all that. Why? Because capitalism is based on the principle that shareholders want their companies to be profitable over the long haul. And sustained profitability leads to . . . satisfied customers, engaged employees, thriving communities, and healthy societies.

Source: Jack Welch and Suzy Welch, "Whose Company Is It Anyway?" Business Week (October 9, 2006): 122.

QUESTIONS:

How is this interpretation of capitalism related to the distinction between the classical economic and socioeconomic models of business? Do you agree or disagree with the Welches? Explain.

WINDOW ON THE WORLD

India's Tata Steel Builds Communities Along with Profits

Tata Steel highlights the challenges of balancing Old World ways with New Economy realities. Jamshedpur, the company's home base in northern India, resembles a time capsule of a more paternalistic industrial age, a leafy city of genteel colonial-era structures and wide boulevards hacked from the jungle in 1908. Tata spends some $40 million a year supplying all civic services and schools, even though it employs just 20,000 of Jamshedpur's 700,000

residents. And in its downsizing program, workers who agreed to early retirement got full pay until age 60 and lifelong health care.

Tata Steel also spends millions annually on education, health, and agricultural development projects in 800 nearby villages. . . . [In the tiny village of Sidhma Kudhar,] children now attend classes in the refurbished school, and the village has three televisions, powered by Tata solar units that also supply enough juice for electric lights and clocks.

Source: Excerpted from Pete Engardio, "The Last Rajah," Business Week (August 13, 2007): 50.

should be deployed. Social expenditures amount to theft of stockholders' equity.

2. *As an economic institution, business lacks the ability to pursue social goals.* Gross inefficiencies can be expected if managers are forced to divert their attention from their pursuit of economic goals.

3. *Business already has enough power.* Considering that business exercises powerful influence over where and how we work and live, what we buy, and what we value, more concentration of social power in the hands of business is undesirable.

4. *Because managers are not elected, they are not directly accountable to the people.* Corporate social programs can easily become misguided. The market system effectively controls business's economic performance but is a poor mechanism for controlling business's social performance.

These arguments are based on the assumption that business should stick to what it does best—pursuing profit by producing marketable goods and services. Social goals should be handled by other institutions, such as the family, schools, religious organizations, or government.

TOWARD GREATER SOCIAL RESPONSIBILITY

Is it inevitable that management will assume greater social responsibility? Some scholars believe so. It has been said that business is bound by an **iron law of responsibility**, which states that "in the long run, those who do not use power in a way that society considers responsible will tend to lose it."[24] This is an important concept, considering that cynicism about business runs deep today, despite a more pro-business political climate worldwide. As *Training* magazine recently observed, "We are living in a time of low trust and high suspicion. 'Trusted leader' is an oxymoron."[25] The demand for business to act more responsibly is clear. If this challenge is not met voluntarily, government reform

> **iron law of responsibility:** those who do not use power in a socially responsible way will eventually lose it

FIGURE **5.3** A Continuum of Social Responsibility Strategies

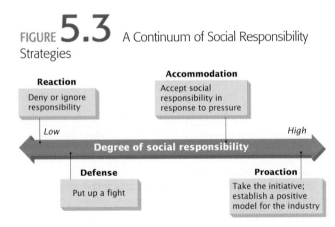

legislation is likely to force business to meet it. In this section, we look at four alternative social responsibility strategies and some contrasting expressions of corporate social responsibility.

Social Responsibility Strategies

Similar to management's political response continuum, discussed in Chapter 3, is its social responsibility continuum (see Figure 5.3), which is marked by four strategies: reaction, defense, accommodation, and proaction.[26] Each involves a distinctly different approach to demands for greater social responsibility.

REACTION. A business that follows a **reactive social responsibility strategy** will deny responsibility while striving to maintain the status quo. This strategy has been a favorite one for the tobacco industry, intent on preventing any legal liability linkage between smoking and cancer. When European countries showed signs of adopting U.S.-style bans on secondhand smoke, Philip Morris launched a rather odd reactive strategy:

> **reactive social responsibility strategy:** denying responsibility and resisting change

> *In a Western European ad campaign that backfired, Philip Morris suggested that inhaling secondhand smoke is less dangerous than eating a cookie or drinking milk. The campaign was banned from France after the National Union of Biscuit Makers and the National Committee Against Tobacco Use filed separate suits against Philip Morris.*[27]

> **defensive social responsibility strategy:** resisting additional responsibilities with legal and public relations tactics

DEFENSE. A **defensive social responsibility strategy** uses legal maneuvering and/or a public relations campaign to avoid assuming additional responsibilities. A case in point is this recent news item in *BusinessWeek*:

> *[A] 30-second radio spot [mocking the idea of having pickup trucks meet the same fuel standards as cars] is part of a campaign by the Alliance of Automobile Manufacturers to rally support against tougher fuel efficiency rules. Kicked off on Memorial Day weekend, the ads—with their folksy, almost grassroots feel—come as Congress considers legislating the first major boost to car fuel economy since 1975.*[28]

ACCOMMODATION. The organization must be pressured into assuming additional responsibilities when it follows an **accommodative social responsibility strategy**. Some outside stimulus, such as pressure from a special-interest group or threatened government action, is usually required to trigger an accommodative strategy. For example, consider this turn of events:

> **accommodative social responsibility strategy:** assuming additional responsibilities in response to pressure

> *[Office supply] superstore Staples agreed to stop purchasing paper that originated in endangered forests and to increase the fraction of recycled paper in its products to 30 percent. Activists had picketed Staples stores, heckled executives at shareholder meetings, and issued critical reports and press releases in a campaign led by ForestEthics and the Dogwood Alliance.*[29]

PROACTION. A **proactive social responsibility strategy** involves taking the initiative with a progressive program that serves as an inspiring role model for the industry. Sportswear maker Patagonia is a prime example. Founder Yvon Chouinard describes one recent initiative.

> **proactive social responsibility strategy:** taking the initiative with new programs that serve as models for the industry

> *We did an analysis of all the different fibers that we use in making clothes and found that the most damaging was just plain old industrial cotton—dripping with pesticides. I gave the company 18 months to get out of making any product out of industrial-grown cotton—25% of our business. We had to reinvent the way we made clothing to accomplish it, but what the switchover to organically*

5d Fast Food Without the Animal Cruelty?

Animal-rights advocates praised Burger King for its new commitment to begin buying eggs and pork from suppliers that do not keep their animals in cages or crates.

"We certainly hope that people will order the BK Veggie Burger when they go into Burger King," said Matt Prescott, spokesman for People for the Ethical Treatment of Animals [PETA]. "But the fact that Burger King has made positive changes for some of the animals killed for its restaurants will send a ripple effect through the fast-food industry and show other companies that animal welfare cannot be ignored."

PETA has been critical of the fast-food giant in the past.

Source: The Associated Press, "Burger King Gets Animal-Friendly," USA Today (March 29, 2007): 4B.

QUESTION:

Which of the four social responsibility strategies does this exemplify? Explain your choice.

grown cotton did was mobilize the company in a direction, and it's been more profitable because it puts us in a unique position. The Gap is coming here this week to learn how they can get more into organic cotton; we've influenced Nike, Levi's, and a bunch of companies to begin switching because we worked to make the stuff available. Now we're in the forefront of a new way of making clothes.[30]

Proponents of corporate social responsibility would like to see proactive strategies become management's preferred response in both good times and bad.

Who Benefits from Corporate Social Responsibility?

Is it accurate to say of social responsibility what used to be said about home medicine, "It has to taste bad to be good"? In other words, does social responsibility have to be a hardship for the organization? Those who answer *yes* believe that social responsibility should be motivated by **altruism**, an unselfish devotion to the interests of others.[31] This implies that businesses that are not socially responsible are motivated strictly by self-interest.

altruism: unselfish devotion to the interests of others

In short-run economic terms, the tobacco industry's foot dragging has saved it billions of dollars. In contrast, 3M's decision to pull its popular Scotchgard fabric protector spray cans from the marketplace as soon as the company became aware of a possible health hazard cost the company an estimated $500 million in annual sales.[32] On the basis of this evidence alone, one would be hard pressed to say that social responsibility pays. But research paints a brighter picture.

- A study of 243 companies for two years found a positive correlation between industry leadership in environmental protection/pollution control and profitability. The researchers concluded, "It pays to be green."[33]
- A second study found a good reputation for corporate social responsibility to be a competitive advantage in recruiting talented people.[34]

ENLIGHTENED SELF-INTEREST. Enlightened self-interest, the realization that business ultimately helps itself by helping to solve societal problems, involves balancing short-run costs and long-run benefits. Advocates of enlightened self-interest contend that social responsibility expenditures are motivated by profit. Research into **corporate philanthropy**, the charitable donation of company resources ($12.7 billion in the United States in 2006),[35] supports this contention.

enlightened self-interest: a business ultimately helping itself by helping to solve societal problems

corporate philanthropy: charitable donation of company resources

After analyzing Internal Revenue Service statistics for firms in 36 industries, researchers concluded that corporate giving is a form of *profit-motivated advertising*. They went on to observe that "it would seem ill-advised to use philanthropy data to measure altruistic responses of corporations."[36] This theory of profit-motivated advertising was further supported by a study of 130 large manufacturing firms in the United States. Companies that had committed significant crimes but donated a good deal of money had better responsibility ratings than companies that had committed no crimes but donated very little money.[37]

As U.S. companies earn increasingly more from foreign operations, their philanthropy has gone global. Here are some recent examples of global enlightened self-interest in action.

Intel Corp. now has computer clubhouses providing Internet access and technology training to children

These are not your grandfather's Louisville Sluggers! As part of a partnership between Major League Baseball and the Susan G. Komen for the Cure foundation, this Hillerich & Bradsby employee puts the finishing touches on pink versions of the firm's iconic baseball bats for a "Bats Against Breast Cancer" fundraiser. A well-designed corporate social responsibility program can be a win-win situation.

in 32 countries, including South Africa, India, and, in the West Bank, the Ramallah Clubhouse. Avon Products Inc. provides breast cancer programs in 50 countries, sponsoring research, donating medical gear, and subsidizing mammograms. This year, General Electric Co. pledged $20 million to construct 11 hospitals in Ghana. Total corporate giving abroad rose 13.82% from 2002 to 2003, according to the Conference Board's annual report on corporate contributions. International programs now account for 16% of U.S. corporate giving.[38]

What benefits are these companies likely to reap from their global philanthropy?

AN ARRAY OF BENEFITS FOR THE ORGANIZATION. In addition to the advertising effect, other possible long-run benefits for socially responsible organizations include

- Tax-free incentives to employees (such as buying orchestra tickets and giving them to deserving employees).
- Retention of talented employees by satisfying their altruistic motives.
- Help in recruiting talented and socially conscious personnel.
- Swaying public opinion against government intervention.
- Improved community living standards for employees.
- Attracting socially conscious investors.
- A nontaxable benefit for employees in which company funds are donated to their favorite causes. Many companies match employees' contributions to their college alma maters, for example.

Social responsibility can be a win-win proposition; both society and the socially responsible organization can benefit in the long run.[39] Meanwhile, in today's age of increased corporate accountability, efforts are under way to assess the benefits of philanthropy. According to one consultant, "Giving is an investment and it should be every bit as strategic as, say, marketing or a new business development."[40]

THE ETHICAL DIMENSION OF MANAGEMENT

There is widespread cynicism about business ethics these days.[41] Subsequent public disgust has surfaced in opinion pools: in one annual survey of corporate reputations, 74 percent said "corporate America's reputation is 'not good' or 'terrible.'"[42] Managers seem to be getting the message. A recent survey of 1,600

5f When Is "Cheating" Cheating?

On April 27 [2007], the dean of Duke's business school had the unfortunate task of announcing that nearly 10% of the [MBA] Class of 2008 had been caught cheating on a take-home final exam. . . .

Before going to B-school, they worked in corporations for an average of six years . . . .

Teaming up on a take-home exam: That's not academic fraud, it's postmodern learning, wiki style. Text-messaging exam answers or downloading essays onto iPods: That's simply a wise use of technology.

One can understand the confusion. This is a generation that came of age nabbing music off Napster and watching bootlegged Hollywood blockbusters in their dorm rooms.

. . . in this wired world, maybe the very notion of what constitutes cheating has to be reevaluated. The scandal at Duke points to how much the world has changed, and how academia and corporations are confused about it all, sending split messages.

Source: Excerpted from Michelle Conlin, "Cheating—or Postmodern Learning?" Business Week (May 14, 2007): 42.

QUESTIONS:
So what *does* constitute unethical cheating in school? Can students cheat their way through school and then suddenly transform into ethical decision makers on the job? Explain.

executives found 57 percent paying more attention to manager and supervisor ethics.[43] Indeed, the subject of ethics certainly deserves serious attention in management circles these days.[44]

Ethics is the study of moral obligation involving the distinction between right and wrong.[45] *Business ethics,* sometimes referred to as management ethics or organizational ethics, narrows the frame of reference to productive organizations.[46] However, as a pair of ethics experts noted, business ethics is not a simple matter.

> **ethics:** study of moral obligation involving right versus wrong

Just being a good person and, in your own way, having sound personal ethics may not be sufficient to handle the ethical issues that arise in a business organization. Many people who have limited business experience suddenly find themselves making decisions about product quality, advertising, pricing, hiring practices, and pollution control. The values they learned from family, church, and school may not provide specific guidelines for these complex business decisions. For example, is a particular advertisement deceptive? Should a gift to a customer be considered a bribe, or is it a special promotional incentive? . . . Many business ethics decisions are close calls. Years of experience in a particular industry may be required to know what is acceptable.[47]

With this realistic context in mind, we turn to a discussion of business ethics research, personal values, ethical principles, and steps that management can take to foster ethical business behavior.

Practical Lessons from Business Ethics Research

Empirical research is always welcome in a socially relevant and important area such as business ethics.[48] It permits us to go beyond mere intuition and speculation to determine more precisely who, what, and why. On-the-job research of business ethics among managers has yielded practical insights in four areas: (1) ethical hot spots, (2) pressure from above, (3) discomfort with ambiguity, and (4) the rationalization of unethical conduct.

ETHICAL HOT SPOTS.   In a survey of 1,324 U.S. employees from all levels across several industries, 48 percent admitted to having performed (during the prior year) at least one illegal or unethical act from a list of 25 questionable practices. The list included everything from calling in sick when feeling well through cheating on expense accounts, forging signatures, and giving or accepting kickbacks, to ignoring violations of environmental laws. Also uncovered in the study were the top ten workplace hot spots responsible for triggering unethical and illegal conduct:

- Balancing work and family
- Poor internal communications
- Poor leadership
- Work hours, workload
- Lack of management support
- Need to meet sales, budget, or profit goals
- Little or no recognition of achievements
- Company politics
- Personal financial worries
- Insufficient resources[49]

PRESSURE FROM ABOVE.   A number of studies have uncovered the problem of perceived pressure to achieve results. As discussed in Chapter 13, pressure from superiors can lead to unhealthful conformity. How widespread is the problem? Very widespread, according to the ethical hot spots survey just discussed:

- Most workers feel some pressure to act unethically or illegally on the job (56 percent), but far fewer (17 percent) feel a high level of pressure to do so. . . .
- Mid-level managers most often reported a high level of pressure to act unethically or illegally (20 percent). Employees of large companies cited such pressure more than those at small businesses (21 percent versus 14 percent).
- High levels of pressure were reported more often by those with a high school diploma or less (21 percent) versus college graduates (13 percent).[50]

By being aware of this problem of pressure from above, managers can (1) consciously avoid putting undue pressure on others and (2) prepare to deal with excessive organizational pressure.

An instructive case in point is Walt Pavlo, a former MCI employee who spent 18 months in prison for his part in a fraudulent scheme.

> *Working as a collection manager for high-risk accounts, Pavlo discovered that MCI executives, who were loading up on stock options, didn't want anything to happen that would cause the stock price to drop. So, Pavlo says, when he brought them bad news, they didn't want to hear it; Pavlo says he felt he was being told to fudge the numbers, which he did . . . .*
>
> *"I was under a lot of pressure," Pavlo recalls. "Thinking about doing something wrong, but wanting to be accepted by my bosses, a team member, part of the inner circle."*[51]

Excessive pressure to achieve results is a serious problem because it can cause otherwise good and decent people to take ethical shortcuts just to keep their jobs. The challenge for managers is to know where to draw the line between creating motivation to excel and exerting undue pressure.[52]

AMBIGUOUS SITUATIONS. In a survey of 111 executives (27 percent female) from a diverse array of large companies, 78 percent said the existence of "ambiguous rules" was a common rationale for "bending the rules."[53] Surveys of purchasing managers and field sales personnel showed that respondents were uncomfortable with ambiguous situations in which there were no clear-cut ethical guidelines. As one research team noted, "A striking aspect of the responses to the questionnaire is the degree to which the purchasing managers desire a stated policy."[54] In other words,

"THE DOG ATE OUR QUARTERLY STATEMENT? I LIKE IT."

Source: John Caldwell/*Harvard Business Review.*

those who often face ethically ambiguous situations want formal guidelines to help sort things out. Ethical codes, discussed later, can satisfy this need for guidelines.

RATIONALIZATION: HOW GOOD PEOPLE END UP DOING BAD THINGS. Rationalization is a fundamental part of everyday life. "They say chocolate is good for you. I think I'll have another big piece of that delicious chocolate cake." "Of course I cheat a little on my expense report, doesn't everybody? Besides, the company owes me." Such rationalizations involve perceiving an objectively questionable action as normal and acceptable. Rationalization may occur before and/or after the fact. A team of management researchers recently reviewed the behavioral science literature and came up with a list of six rationalization strategies that employees commonly use to justify misdeeds in the workplace (see Table 5.1). Those misdeeds can range from slightly wrong (e.g., exaggerating your knowledge of a software program to your coworkers) to absolutely criminal (e.g., accepting a bribe from a vendor). Both managers and nonmanagers need to be aware of these common rationalizations and resist the temptation to invoke them too often. New employees are particularly vulnerable to socialization tactics and influences infected with unhealthful rationalizations. The researchers' conclusion:

> *The pressure and temptations to cut ethical corners and to continue questionable practices instigated*

TABLE **5.1**

How Employees Tend to Rationalize Unethical Conduct

STRATEGY	DESCRIPTION	EXAMPLES
Denial of responsibility	The actors engaged in corrupt behaviors perceive that they have no other choice than to participate in such activities.	"What can I do? My arm is being twisted." "It is none of my business what the corporation does in overseas bribery."
Denial of injury	The actors are convinced that no one is harmed by their actions; hence the actions are not really corrupt.	"No one was really harmed." "It could have been worse."
Denial of victim	The actors counter any blame for their actions by arguing that the violated party deserved whatever happened.	"They deserved it." "They chose to participate."
Social weighting	The actors assume two practices that moderate the salience of corrupt behaviors: 1. Condemn the condemner, 2. Selective social comparison.	"You have no right to criticize us." "Others are worse than we are."
Appeal to higher loyalties	The actors argue that their violation of norms is due to their attempt to realize a higher-order value.	"We answered to a more important cause." "I would not report it because of my loyalty to my boss."
Metaphor of the ledger	The actors rationalize that they are entitled to indulge in deviant behaviors because of their accrued credits (time and effort) in their jobs.	"We've earned the right." "It's all right for me to use the Internet for personal reasons at work. After all, I do work overtime."

Source: Academy of Management Executive: The Thinking Manager's Source *by Vikas Anand, Blake Ashforth, and Mahendra Jo. Copyright 2004 by Academy of Management (NY). Reproduced with permission of Academy of Management (NY) in the format Textbook via Copyright Clearance Center.*

by others are strong indeed. And given the ambiguity, complexity, and dynamism that pervade contemporary environments, there is often ample room to rationalize such transgressions as unavoidable, commonplace, and even laudable. In this context, organizations need to be especially conscious in guarding against the onset of such tactics within the organization. Employee education and the establishment of independent ethics ombudspersons could go a long way toward protecting against the onset of rationalization/socialization tactics.[55]

A CALL TO ACTION. Corporate misconduct and the foregoing research findings underscore the importance of the following call to action. It comes from Bill George, the highly respected former CEO of Medtronic, manufacturer of heart pacemakers and other medical devices: "Each of us needs to determine . . . where our ethical boundaries are and, if asked to violate (them), refuse. . . . If it means refusing a direct order, we must be prepared to resign."[56] George's call is *personal*. It requires *courage*.[57] His words suggest that each of us can begin the process of improving business ethics by looking in a mirror.[58]

Personal Values as Ethical Anchors

Values are too often ignored in discussions of management.[59] This oversight is serious because personal values can play a pivotal role in managerial decision making and ethics. Take J.M. Smucker Co., for example.

Timothy P. and Richard K. Smucker, the brothers who serve as co-chief executives of J.M. Smucker Co., are unabashedly old-fashioned. The deeply

5g Survey Says . . .

Survey of 1,077 U.S. adults: 39 percent said "Yes" and 61 percent said "No" to the question "Have you ever called in sick to enjoy a day off during the summer?"

Survey of 2,137 working U.S. adults: "Have you ever taken office supplies for personal use?" About 13 percent of those with a high school diploma or less answered "Yes," while 27 percent of college graduates answered "Yes."

Sources: Adapted from "Calling in Sick When Well," USA Today (June 28, 2007): 1B; and "Education and Workplace Ethics," USA Today (August 22, 2007): 1B.

QUESTIONS:

Does one or both of these situations amount to stealing from one's employer? Explain. What rationalizations would those answering "Yes" probably offer? What does this say about the impact of higher education on ethics? Do you think people tend to answer ethics surveys honestly?

religious pair refuse to advertise their jams, jellies, peanut butter, and cooking oil on some of television's biggest hits because they deem the content offensive.[60]

Contemporary social observers complain that many managers lack character and have turned their backs on ethical values such as honesty. MIT management scholar Michael Schrage agrees:

If there's a single issue that frightens me about the workplace future, it's the rising willingness of people to blame institutional imperatives for betraying their own values. . . . There's no shortage of talent and intelligence; character may be the scarcer and more valuable commodity. That's the one to watch.[61]

Defined broadly, **values** are abstract ideals that shape an individual's thinking and behavior.[62] Let's explore two different types of values that act as anchors for our ethical beliefs and conduct.

values: abstract ideals that shape one's thinking and behavior

INSTRUMENTAL AND TERMINAL VALUES. Each manager, indeed each person, values various means

and ends in life. Recognizing this means-ends distinction, behavioral scientists have identified two basic types of values. An **instrumental value** is an enduring belief that a certain way of behaving is appropriate in all situations. For example, the time-honored saying "Honesty is the best policy" represents an instrumental value. A person who truly values honesty will probably behave in an honest manner under all circumstances. A **terminal value**, in contrast, is an enduring belief that a certain end-state of existence is worth striving for and attaining.[63] Whereas one person may strive for eternal salvation, another may strive for social recognition and admiration. Instrumental values (modes of behavior) help people achieve terminal values (desired end-states).

instrumental value: enduring belief in a certain way of behaving

terminal value: enduring belief in the attainment of a certain end-state

Because a person can hold a number of different instrumental and terminal values in various combinations, individual value systems are somewhat like fingerprints: each of us has a unique set. No wonder managers who face the same ethical dilemma often differ in their interpretations and responses.

IDENTIFYING YOUR OWN VALUES. To help you discover your own set of values, refer to the Rokeach value survey in the Action Learning Exercise at the end of this chapter. Take a few moments now to complete this survey. (As a reality check on the "fit" between your intentions and your actual behavior, have a close friend, relative, or spouse evaluate you later with the Rokeach survey.)

If your results surprise you, it is probably because we tend to take our basic values for granted. We seldom stop to arrange them consciously according to priority. For the sake of comparison, compare your top five instrumental and terminal values with the value profiles uncovered in a survey of 220 eastern U.S. managers. On average, those managers ranked their instrumental values as follows: (1) honest, (2) responsible, (3) capable, (4) ambitious, and (5) independent. The most common terminal value rankings were (1) self-respect, (2) family security, (3) freedom, (4) a sense of accomplishment, and (5) happiness.[64] These managerial value profiles are offered for purposes of comparison only; they are not necessarily an index of desirable or undesirable priorities. When addressing specific ethical issues,

Students at the Indian Institute of Management (IIM) recently tapped into a higher power for advice about business ethics when the Dalai Lama (right) gave a talk on the subject. Tibet's exiled spiritual leader is seen here sharing a laugh with IIM's chairman Vijaypat Singhania.

managers need to consider each individual's personal values.[65]

General Ethical Principles

Like your highly personalized value system, your ethical beliefs have been shaped by many factors, including family and friends, the media, culture, schooling, religious instruction, and general life experiences.[66] This section brings taken-for-granted ethical beliefs, generally unstated, out into the open for discussion and greater understanding. It does so by exploring ten general ethical principles. Even though we may not necessarily know how ethics scholars label them, we use ethical principles both consciously and unconsciously when dealing with ethical dilemmas.[67] Each of the ten ethical principles is followed by a brief behavioral guideline.

1. *Self-interests.* "Never take any action that is not in the *long-term* self-interests of yourself and/or of the organization to which you belong."
2. *Personal virtues.* "Never take any action that is not honest, open, and truthful and that you would not be proud to see reported widely in national newspapers and on television."
3. *Religious injunctions.* "Never take any action that is not kind and that does not build a sense of community, a sense of all of us working together for a commonly accepted goal."
4. *Government requirements.* "Never take any action that violates the law, for the law represents the minimal moral standards of our society."
5. *Utilitarian benefits.* "Never take any action that does not result in greater good than harm for the society of which you are a part."
6. *Universal rules.* "Never take any action that you would not be willing to see others, faced with the same or a closely similar situation, also be free to take."
7. *Individual rights.* "Never take any action that abridges the agreed-upon and accepted rights of others."
8. *Economic efficiency.* "Always act to maximize profits subject to legal and market constraints, for maximum profits are the sign of the most efficient production."
9. *Distributive justice.* "Never take any action in which the least [fortunate people] among us are harmed in some way."
10. *Contributive liberty.* "Never take any action that will interfere with the right of all of us [to] self-development and self-fulfillment."[68]

Source: Excerpted from Hosmer, Moral Leadership in Business, *pp. 39–41, © 1994, McGraw-Hill. Reproduced with permission of The McGraw-Hill Companies.*

Which of these ethical principles appeals most to you in terms of serving as a guide for making important decisions? Why? The best way to test your ethical standards and principles is to consider a *specific* ethical question and see which of these ten principles is most likely to guide your *behavior*. Sometimes, in complex situations, a combination of principles would be applicable (see Ethics: Character, Courage, and Values).

ETHICS: CHARACTER, COURAGE, AND VALUES

Human Guinea Pigs?

China's immense patient populations suffering from cancer, diabetes, cardiovascular illnesses, and a wide range of infectious diseases have captured the attention of drug and medical device companies across Europe and America. They are expanding research and testing facilities in China, not only because costs are low and it is relatively easy to recruit patients, but also because Beijing insists new drugs be tested locally before going on sale. . . .

Yet working inside China's sprawling, often under-supervised health-care system may raise complex ethical questions. . . . people recruited into trials don't always understand what they have signed up for, but they rush to join because it may be their only chance to see a doctor. . . .

Much of the appeal comes down to money. Running a trial in China may cost as little as 15% of what a company would pay in the West.

Source: Excerpted from Bruce Einhorn, "The Rush to Test Drugs in China," Business Week *(May 28, 2007): 60–61.*

FOR DISCUSSION

Is this an ethical or an unethical situation? Which of the ten ethical principles would you use to support your position?

ENCOURAGING ETHICAL CONDUCT

Simply telling managers and other employees to be good will not work. Both research evidence and practical experience tell us that words must be supported by action. Four specific ways to encourage ethical conduct within the organization are ethics training, ethical advocates, codes of ethics, and whistle-blowing. Each can make an important contribution to an integrated ethics program.

Ethics Training

Managers lacking ethical awareness have been labeled *amoral* by CSR and ethics researcher Archie B. Carroll. **Amoral managers** are neither moral nor immoral but indifferent to the ethical implications of their actions. Carroll contends that managers in this category far outnumber moral or immoral managers.[69] If his contention is correct, there is a great need for ethics training and education, a need

> **amoral managers:** managers who are neither moral nor immoral, but ethically lazy

that too often is not adequately met. Consider these recent research findings:

- According to a survey of human resource executives, only 27 percent of large U.S. companies provide ethics training for corporate directors.[70]
- Only 28 percent of a sample of 1,001 employees in the U.S. had received any ethics training during the prior year.[71]
- An analysis of the core curricula at 50 leading U.S. business schools "found only 40% require an ethics or social responsibility course."[72]

These are surprising and disappointing statistics, in view of the tidal wave of corporate misconduct in recent years.

Some say ethics training is a waste of time because ethical lessons are easily shoved aside in the heat of competition. For example, Dow Corning's model ethics program included ethics training but did not keep the company from getting embroiled in costly charges of selling leaky breast implants.[73] Ethics training is often halfhearted and intended only as window dressing. Hard evidence that ethics training actually improves behavior is lacking.[74] Nonetheless, carefully designed and administered ethics training courses can make a positive contribution. Key features of effective ethics training programs include

- Top-management support
- Open discussion of realistic ethics cases or scenarios

TABLE 5.2	Twelve Questions for Examining the Ethics of a Business Decision

1. Have you defined the problem accurately?
2. How would you define the problem if you stood on the other side of the fence?
3. How did this situation occur in the first place?
4. To whom and to what do you give your loyalty as a person and as a member of the corporation?
5. What is your intention in making this decision?
6. How does this intention compare with the probable results?
7. Whom could your decision or action injure?
8. Can you discuss the problem with the affected parties before you make your decision?
9. Are you confident that your position will be as valid over a long period of time as it seems now?
10. Could you disclose without qualm your decision or action to your boss, your CEO, the board of directors, your family, society as a whole?
11. What is the symbolic potential of your action if understood? If misunderstood?
12. Under what conditions would you allow exceptions to your stand?

Source: Exhibit from "Ethics Without the Sermon," by Laura L. Nash (November–December 1981). Reprinted by permission of HBS Publishing.

- A clear focus on ethical issues specific to the organization
- Integration of ethics themes into all training
- A mechanism for anonymously reporting ethical violations (Companies have had good luck with e-mail and telephone hot lines.)
- An organizational climate that rewards ethical conduct[75]

Ethical Advocates

An **ethical advocate** is a business ethics specialist who is a full-fledged member of the board of directors and acts as the board's social conscience.[76] This person may also be asked to sit in on top-management decision deliberations. The idea is to assign someone the specific role of critical questioner (see Table 5.2 for recommended questions). Problems with groupthink and blind conformity, discussed in Chapter 13, are less likely to arise when an ethical advocate tests management's thinking about ethical implications during the decision-making process.

ethical advocate: ethics specialist who plays a role in top-management decision making

Codes of Ethics

An organizational code of ethics is a published statement of moral expectations for employee conduct. Some codes specify penalties for offenders. As in the case of ethics training, growth in the adoption of company codes of ethics has stalled in recent years.

Recent experience has shown codes of ethics to be a step in the right direction, but not a cure-all.[77] To encourage ethical conduct, formal codes of ethics for organization members must satisfy two requirements. First, they should refer to specific practices, such as kickbacks, payoffs, receiving gifts, record falsification, and misleading claims about products. For example, Xerox Corporation's 15-page ethics code says, "We're honest with our customers. No deals, no bribes, no secrets, no fooling around with prices. A kickback in any form kicks anybody out. Anybody."[78] General platitudes about good business practice or professional conduct are ineffective—they do not provide specific guidance, and they offer too many tempting loopholes.

The second requirement for an organizational code of ethics is that it be firmly supported by top management and equitably enforced through the reward-and-punishment system. Selective or uneven enforcement is the quickest way to undermine the effectiveness of an ethics code. The effective development of ethics codes and monitoring of compliance are more important than ever in today's complex legal environment.[79]

Whistle-Blowing

Detailed ethics codes help managers deal swiftly and effectively with employee misconduct. But what should a manager do when a superior or an entire

N o doubt it took ethical courage for CPA Sherron Smith Watkins to confront Enron's leadership with her concerns about accounting irregularities and questionable financial deals. She even passed her concerns along to the firm's auditor, Arthur Andersen, to little avail. Unfortunately, Enron soon unraveled and took Andersen with it. Although rightly praised in the popular media for being an honest "whistle-blower," Watkins technically wasn't a whistle-blower, as the term is defined in this chapter. Whistle-blowers report corporate misdeeds to *outsiders* such as the media and government watchdog agencies.

organization is engaged in misconduct? Yielding to the realities of organizational politics, many managers simply turn their backs or claim they were "just following orders." (Nazi war criminals who based their defense at the Nuremberg trials on the argument that they were following orders ended up with ropes around their necks.) Managers with leadership and/or political skills may attempt to work within the organizational system for positive change.[80] Still others will take the boldest step of all, whistle-blowing. **Whistleblowing** is the practice of reporting perceived unethical practices to outsiders such as the news media, government agencies, or public-interest groups. Several whistle-blowers made headlines in recent years. Sherron Smith Watkins foresaw Enron's financial collapse, and FBI agent Coleen Rowley went public with allegations of a mishandled terrorist lead. Noreen Harrington blew the whistle on illegal trading at Canary Capital Partners, resulting in a scandal that rocked the entire mutual fund industry. Military policeman Joseph Darby blew the whistle on the abuse of Iraqi prisoners by his fellow U.S. soldiers.[81]

Not surprisingly, whistle-blowing is a highly controversial topic among managers, many of whom believe that whistle-blowing erodes their authority and

> **whistle-blowing:** reporting perceived unethical organizational practices to outside authorities

decision-making prerogatives. Because loyalty to the organization is still a cherished value in some quarters, whistle-blowing is criticized as the epitome of disloyalty. Consumer advocate Ralph Nader disagrees: "The willingness and ability of insiders to blow the whistle is the last line of defense ordinary citizens have against the denial of their rights and the destruction of their interests by secretive and powerful institutions."[82] Still, critics worry that whistle-blowers may be motivated by revenge.

Whistle-blowing generally means putting one's job and/or career on the line, even though the federal government and many states have passed whistle-blower protection acts.[83] A few whistle-blowers strike gold, such as the former Warner-Lambert employee who was awarded $26.6 million,[84] but most do not. After reviewing a wide variety of whistle-blower cases, *USA Today* reached the following conclusion.

> *Whistle-blowers might be heroes to people tired of the scandals that have swept Corporate America, but they often find themselves near-penniless, their home lives and emotional well-being in shambles, and followed by private investigators.*
>
> *Whistle-blowers persist because that's the way they are—a breed apart, driven by a desire to expose dirty executives, protect consumers or avenge wrongs they feel have been done to them.*[85]

5h An Uphill Battle?

Stephen Covey, former professor and best-selling author:

I'm convinced that 90% of failures in life are character failures, not ability failures.

After studying the ethical principles and ethical behavior of 674 business students at a U.S. university, a pair of researchers drew this rather somber conclusion:

While ethical behavior can be taught to our business students in the classroom, their resolve will be challenged on the job. Faced with pressure from above, platitudinous ethical codes, spotty enforcement, and no discernible link to the reward system, many will revert to expedience.

Sources: As quoted in "This Week's Question," *USA Today* (February 6, 2004): 4B; and Larry R. Watts and Joseph G. Ormsby, "Ethical Frameworks and Ethical Behavior: A Survey of Business Students," *International Journal of Value-Based Management, 73, no. 3 (1994): 233.*

QUESTIONS:

Is it a waste of time to teach business ethics to college students? Explain. How can colleges and universities do a better job of improving business ethics? What does the business community need to do to improve ethics in the workplace?

The challenge for today's management is to create an organizational climate in which the need to blow the whistle is reduced or, ideally, eliminated. Constructive steps include the following:

- Encourage the free expression of controversial and dissenting viewpoints.
- Streamline the organization's grievance procedure so that those who point out problems receive a prompt and fair hearing.
- Find out what employees think about the organization's social responsibility policies, and make appropriate changes.
- Let employees know that management respects and is sensitive to their individual consciences.
- Recognize that the harsh treatment of a whistle-blower will probably lead to adverse public opinion.[86]

In the final analysis, individual behavior makes organizations ethical or unethical. Organizational forces can help bring out the best in people by clearly identifying and rewarding ethical conduct.[87]

SUMMARY

1. Corporate social responsibility is the idea that management has broader responsibilities than just making a profit. A strict interpretation holds that an action must be voluntary to qualify as socially responsible. Accordingly, reluctant submission to court orders or government coercion is not an example of social responsibility. Carroll's global corporate social responsibility pyramid encompasses, from bottom to top, four responsibilities: economic, legal, ethical, and philanthropic.

2. The debate over the basic purpose of the corporation is long-standing. Those who embrace the classical economic model contend that business's social responsibility is to maximize profits for stockholders. Proponents of the socioeconomic model disagree, saying that business has a responsibility, above and beyond making a profit, to improve the general quality of life. The arguments *for* corporate responsibility say businesses are members of society with the resources and motivation to improve society and avoid government regulation. Those arguing *against* call for profit maximization because businesses are primarily economic institutions run by unelected officials who have enough power already.

3. Management scholars who advocate greater corporate social responsibility cite the iron law of responsibility. This law states that if business does not use its socioeconomic power responsibly, society will take away that power. A continuum of social responsibility includes four strategies: reaction, defense, accommodation, and proaction. The reaction strategy involves *denying* social responsibility, whereas the defense strategy involves actively *fighting* additional responsibility with political and public relations tactics. Accommodation occurs when a

company must be *pressured into* assuming additional social responsibilities. Proaction occurs when a business *takes the initiative* and becomes a positive model for its industry. In the short run, proactive social responsibility usually costs the firm money. But according to the notion of enlightened self-interest, both society and the company will gain in the long run. Research indicates that corporate philanthropy actually is a profit-motivated form of advertising.

4. Business ethics research has taught these four practical lessons: (1) 48 percent of surveyed workers reported engaging in illegal or unethical practices; (2) perceived pressure from above can erode ethics; (3) employees desire clear ethical standards in ambiguous situations, and (4) rationalization sometimes enables good people to do bad things. The call for better business ethics is clearly a *personal* challenge.

5. Managers cannot afford to overlook each employee's personal value system; values serve as anchors for one's beliefs and conduct. Instrumental values are related to desired behavior, whereas terminal values involve desired end-states. Values provide an anchor for one's ethical beliefs and conduct.

6. The ten general ethical principles that consciously and unconsciously guide behavior when ethical questions arise are self-interests, personal virtues, religious injunctions, government requirements, utilitarian benefits, universal rules, individual rights, economic efficiency, distributive justice, and contributive liberty.

7. The typical manager is said to be *amoral*—neither moral nor immoral—just ethically lazy or indifferent. Management can encourage ethical behavior in the following four ways: conduct ethics training; use ethical advocates in high-level decision making; formulate, disseminate, and consistently enforce specific codes of ethics; and create an open climate for dissent in which whistle-blowing becomes unnecessary.

TERMS TO UNDERSTAND

MANAGER'S TOOLKIT

An International Code of Ethics

Developed in 1994 by the Caux Round Table in Switzerland, these Principles for Business are believed to be the first international ethics code. This code was created through the collaboration of business leaders in Europe, Japan, and the United States.

Principle 1

The Responsibility of Businesses: Beyond Shareholders Toward Stakeholders. The value of a business to society is the wealth and employment it creates and the marketable products and services it provides to consumers at a reasonable price commensurate with quality. To create such value, a business must maintain its own economic health and viability, but survival is not a sufficient goal.

Businesses have a role to play in improving the lives of all their customers, employees, and shareholders by sharing with them the wealth they have created. Suppliers and competitors as well should expect businesses to honor their obligations in a spirit of honesty and fairness. As responsible citizens of the local, national, regional, and global communities in which they operate, businesses share a part in shaping the future of those communities.

Principle 2

The Economic and Social Impact of Business: Toward Innovation, Justice, and World Community. Businesses established in foreign countries to develop, produce, or sell should also contribute to the social advancement of those countries by creating productive employment and helping to raise the purchasing power of their citizens. Businesses also should contribute to human rights, education, welfare, and vitalization of the countries in which they operate.

Businesses should contribute to economic and social development not only in the countries in which they operate, but also in the world community at large, through effective and prudent use of resources, free and fair competition, and emphasis upon innovation in technology, production methods, marketing, and communications.

Principle 3

Business Behavior: Beyond the Letter of Law Toward a Spirit of Trust. While accepting the legitimacy of trade secrets, businesses should recognize that sincerity, candor, truthfulness, the keeping of promises, and transparency contribute not only to their own credibility and stability but also to the smoothness and efficiency of business transactions, particularly on the international level.

Principle 4

Respect for Rules. To avoid trade frictions and to promote freer trade, equal conditions for competition, and fair and equitable treatment for all participants, businesses should respect international and domestic rules. In addition, they should recognize that some behavior, although legal, may still have adverse consequences.

Principle 5

Support for Multilateral Trade. Businesses should support the multilateral trade systems of the World Trade Organization and similar international agreements. They should cooperate in efforts to promote the progressive and judicious liberalization of trade, and to relax those domestic measures that unreasonably hinder global commerce, while giving due respect to national policy objectives.

Principle 6

Respect for the Environment. A business should protect and, where possible, improve the environment, promote sustainable development, and prevent the wasteful use of natural resources.

Principle 7

Avoidance of Illicit Operations. A business should not participate in or condone bribery, money laundering, or other corrupt practices; indeed, it should seek cooperation with others to eliminate them. It should not trade in arms or other materials used for terrorist activities, drug traffic, or other organized crime.

Source: *Excerpted from "Principles for Business,"* Business Ethics, *10 (May–June 1996): 16–17. Reprinted with permission from* Business Ethics Magazine, *52 South 10th Street, #110, Minneapolis, MN 55403. 612/962–4700.*

ACTION LEARNING EXERCISE

The Rokeach Value Survey

Instructions: Study the following two lists of values, then rank the instrumental values in order of importance to you (1 = most important, 18 = least important). Do the same with the list of terminal values.

Instrumental values	Terminal values

Rank   **Rank**

_____ Ambitious (hardworking, aspiring)   _____ A comfortable life (a prosperous life)

_____ Broadminded (open-minded)   _____ An exciting life (a stimulating, active life)

_____ Capable (competent, effective)   _____ A sense of accomplishment (lasting contribution)

_____ Cheerful (lighthearted, joyful)   _____ A world at peace (free of war and conflict)

_____ Clean (neat, tidy)   _____ A world of beauty (beauty of nature and the arts)

_____ Courageous (standing up for your beliefs) _____ Equality (brotherhood, equal opportunity for all)

_____ Forgiving (willing to pardon others)   _____ Family security (taking care of loved ones)

_____ Helpful (working for the welfare of others) _____ Freedom (independence, free choice)

_____ Honest (sincere, truthful)   _____ Happiness (contentedness)

_____ Imaginative (daring, creative)   _____ Inner harmony (freedom from inner conflict)

_____ Independent (self-sufficient)   _____ Mature love (sexual and spiritual intimacy)

_____ Intellectual (intelligent, reflective)   _____ National security (protection from attack)

_____ Logical (consistent, rational)   _____ Pleasure (an enjoyable, leisurely life)

_____ Loving (affectionate, tender)   _____ Salvation (saved, eternal life)

_____ Obedient (dutiful, respectful)   _____ Self-respect (self-esteem)

_____ Polite (courteous, well-mannered)   _____ Social recognition (respect, admiration)

_____ Responsible (dependable, reliable)   _____ True friendship (close companionship)

_____ Self-controlled (restrained, self-disciplined) _____ Wisdom (a mature understanding of life)

Source: _Copyright 1967, by Milton Rokeach, and reproduced by permission of Halgren Tests, 873 Persimmon Avenue, Sunnyvale, CA. 94087._

For Consideration/Discussion

1. How does this value survey help you better understand yourself? Or others?

2. Do you believe that values drive behavior (including ethical and unethical behavior)? Explain.

3. Value _conflict_ can make life troublesome in three ways. First, there can be incompatibility among one's highly ranked instrumental values (e.g., honest vs. polite; courageous vs. obedient). Second, it may be difficult to achieve one's top terminal values via one's highly ranked instrumental values (e.g., ambitious and responsible vs. happiness and an exciting life). Third, your important instrumental and terminal values may clash with those of significant others—such as friends, spouse, coworkers, or an organization. What sorts of potential or actual value conflict do you detect in your survey responses? Explain. What can you do to minimize these conflicts?

CLOSING CASE
The Housewife Who Got Up Off the Couch

Each fall Eleanor Josaitis addresses the incoming class of MBA students at the University of Michigan in Ann Arbor and offers a challenge: "Every single person in this room," she says, "is going to help me change the world." The tiny 72-year-old may look like your grandmother, but her voice is steely and she is tough as titanium. Pacing the stage in one of her trademark navy-blue suits, Josaitis unfolds some of the hate mail she has received over the years in her capacity as CEO and cofounder of the Detroit civil-rights group Focus: HOPE. The "love letters," as she calls them, are vile. Josaitis fixes the audience with her steady gaze. "Does anyone in this room think I'm going to be intimidated for one minute by this?" she asks. "It's only going to make me work harder."

And how. Since cofounding Focus: HOPE in 1968 as a food program serving pregnant women, new mothers, and their children, Josaitis has built the organization from a basement operation run by a handful of friends into a sprawling 40-acre campus in Detroit that now employs over 500 people, boasts more than 50,000 volunteers and donors, and has helped over 3,000 more become gainfully employed.

Josaitis quickly learned that hunger was merely a symptom of a larger problem. "You end racism by making sure people enter the economic mainstream and ensuring that they can support their own families," she says. So Josaitis and her team set to work. They developed a technical school to help job seekers rack up certifications in IT support. They operate a machinists' training program that funnels people into the employment pipeline at local automotive companies. The organization also teams up with local universities to help disadvantaged students get college educations, and [it] runs a child-care center to make sure all these opportunities are available to working and single parents.

In racially divided Detroit, however, not everyone has wanted to see Josaitis succeed in bridging the economic and ethnic divides that run through the city. In addition to her stack of love letters, she also remembers the day in 1974 when the Focus: HOPE offices were fire-bombed at the beginning of a 13-year lawsuit the group pursued—and won—against the American Automobile Association for employment discrimination. Josaitis has a simple mantra for getting through dark times: "You can deck the SOBs, or you can outclass them," she says. "I choose to outclass them." And she relentlessly focuses on the positive: On the day she received what she recalls as her most hateful piece of mail, she also remembers receiving a check for $11,000.

Josaitis has stared down the detractors who have threatened her with bodily harm for more than 30 years. And she has dared anyone on her staff, in her community, in the businesses with which she interacts to tell her that she will not succeed in achieving her vision. But most important, she has had the imagination, the optimism, and the fortitude to overcome that helplessness we all have felt in the face of overwhelming odds.

In 1962, as she sat watching a television program about the Nuremberg trials, Josaitis—then a housewife with five children—asked herself what she would have done if atrocities were taking place in her own backyard. When a breaking news report interrupted the program to show images of Mississippi police turning dogs and fire hoses on civil-rights protesters, Josaitis knew her moment of truth had arrived. She started supporting Martin Luther King Jr., but when race riots burned through her hometown of Detroit in 1967, Josaitis knew that marching wasn't enough. She cofounded Focus: HOPE with Reverend William T. Cunningham the following year. "You have to have the guts to try *something*," she says. "Because you won't change a damn thing by sitting in front of the TV with the clicker in your hand." It was perhaps her most courageous act of all: Thirty-six years ago, Eleanor Josaitis turned off her television, got up off the couch, and decided to do something. And she has never looked back.[88]

Source: From Alison Overholt, "The Housewife Who Got Up Off the Couch," *Fast Company*, no. 86 (September 2004): 9. Reprinted by permission.

FOR DISCUSSION

1 What direct or indirect evidence of enlightened self-interest can you find in this case? Explain.

2 Judging on the basis of the Rokeach Value Survey in the Action Learning Exercise at the end of this chapter, what do you think Josaitis's primary instrumental and terminal values are? Explain your selections.

3 Which general ethical principles, as listed in this chapter, appear to drive Josaitis? Explain.

4 Does a not-for-profit organization such as Focus: HOPE need a formal code of ethics? If you think not, explain your reasoning. If you think so, what general areas should it cover?

5 What valuable ethics lessons can today's business executives learn from Eleanor Josaitis?

6 What is your personal opinion of Eleanor Josaitis?

TEST PREPPER

True/False Questions

_____ 1. The top level of Carroll's global corporate social responsibility pyramid is ethical responsibility.

_____ 2. An argument in favor of corporate social responsibility is that business is unavoidably involved in social issues.

_____ 3. By definition, a stakeholder audit identifies all parties with financial ties to the organization.

_____ 4. When an organization follows an accommodative social responsibility strategy, it must be pressured into assuming additional responsibilities.

_____ 5. Helping others is what altruistic people and organizations strive to do.

_____ 6. Managers who believe in enlightened self-interest think that, ultimately, the best way to help themselves is to help create a better society.

_____ 7. According to research, the number one workplace "hot spot" responsible for triggering unethical and illegal conduct is trying to meet unrealistic deadlines.

_____ 8. According to researchers, one way in which people rationalize their unethical conduct is to say that their victims deserved what they got.

_____ 9. Economic efficiency is one of the ten general ethical principles.

_____10. An effective code of ethics does not get bogged down in the details of specific behavior but, rather, needs to be stated in general terms.

Multiple-Choice Questions

1. Socially responsible acts, by definition, generally
   A. are not voluntary.
   B. are performed in response to legal pressure.
   C. take the form of a public relations campaign.
   D. are a reaction to public pressure.
   E. are voluntary and above and beyond the stockholders' needs.

2. _____ responsibility is *not* one of the four levels in Carroll's global corporate social responsibility pyramid.
   A. Economic   B. Ethical
   C. Legal   D. Philanthropic
   E. Cultural

3. Systematically identifying all parties that might be affected by a company's actions is the goal of performing a(n)
   A. social responsibility   B. stakeholder audit.
   profile.

C. corporate audit.   D. internal audit.
E. SWOT analysis.

4. Which of these is an argument in favor of corporate social responsibility?
   A. Ensuring the most efficient use of society's resources
   B. Profitability improvement
   C. Preventing government intervention
   D. Giving business more power
   E. Management accountability

5. Say a Swiss drug company denies responsibility for the dangerous side effects of a profitable new drug for anxiety, despite convincing scientific evidence of problems with the drug. Which social responsibility strategy is this company following?
   A. Proactive   B. Accommodating
   C. Traditional   D. Political/legal
   E. Reactive

6. What type of self-interest do businesses acknowledge when they realize that they ultimately help themselves by helping to solve society's problems?
   A. Progressive   B. Proactive
   C. Enlightened   D. Sociocentric
   E. Neo-economic

7. Which one of these is *not* among the top ten workplace "hot spots" for triggering unethical or illegal conduct?
   A. Work hours, workload
   B. Employees with undisclosed criminal records
   C. Lack of management support
   D. Personal financial worries
   E. Poor leadership

8. According to research, which one of these is a strategy that people tend to use to rationalize unethical conduct?
   A. Reverse logic   B. Inductive reasoning
   C. Denial of injury   D. Metaphor of the clock
   E. Groupthink

9. "Honesty is the best policy" reflects which type of personal value?
   A. Instrumental   B. Procedural
   C. Behavioral   D. Terminal
   E. Cultural

10. _____ is what an employee does if he or she reports his or her employer's falsified safety records to government regulators.
    A. Social auditing   B. Whistle-blowing
    C. Amoralizing   D. Exhibiting civil disobedience
    E. Indulging in moral
    deconstruction

See page T1 at the back of the text for answers to these questions. Want more questions? Visit the student Web site and take the ACE quizzes for more practice.

MANAGERS-IN-ACTION VIDEOS

1a

The Bakers' Best Story

Michael Baker, founder and co-owner of the Bakers' Best café and catering business in Newton, Massachusetts, explains how he built a business good enough to be in the "Best of Boston Hall of Fame." Various members of his management team provide insights about this entrepreneur's formula for success. It is an interesting and inspiring story of how a one-location restaurant with only word-of-mouth advertising came to be a $7.5 million-a-year business with 75 full-time employees.

Learning Objective

To see how a people-oriented entrepreneur energizes a business and its employees.

Links to Textual Material

Chapter 1: Management defined; The twenty-first century manager; Managerial functions and roles; Small-business management and entrepreneurship; **Chapter 10:** Employee selection; **Chapter 12:** Motivation; **Chapter 13:** Teamwork; **Chapter 14:** Leadership

Discussion Questions

1 How does Michael Baker exemplify the definition of management?

2 Which characteristics of the twenty-first-century manager (see Table 1.1) are evident in this video profile?

3 Which of the eight managerial functions (Figure 1.3) and which of Wilson's twelve managerial skills (Figure 1.4) are evident in this video profile? Explain.

4 How well does Michael Baker fit the entrepreneurial trait profile in Table 1.3? Explain, trait by trait.

1b

Hewlett-Packard Leverages Global Diversity

Three global managers at HP—Christian Foerg, Daisy Ng, and Gerard Brossard—discuss the unique challenges of communicating, evaluating performance, and leading across cultures. HP seeks to make its rich diversity a strategic advantage by focusing on character, capability, and collaboration within various cultural contexts.

Learning Objective

To show how a large global corporation strives to make the diversity of its employees a competitive advantage.

Links to Textual Material

Chapter 1: Managerial roles and skills; **Chapter 3:** Managing diversity; **Chapter 4:** Cross-cultural competence; **Chapter 10:** Performance appraisal; **Chapter 14:** Leadership

Discussion Questions

1 Which of the eight managerial functions (Figure 1.3) and which of Wilson's twelve managerial skills (Figure 1.4) are evident in this video profile? Explain.

2 Why is it important for HP's management to focus on character, capability, and collaboration?

3 If you were one of the three HP managers in this video, how would you explain to a group of visitors why managing diversity is important?

4 Which of the GLOBE leadership styles (Figure 4.1) appear to be most apparent in this video? Explain.

PART 2

Planning and Decision Making

6

The Basics

of Planning

and Project

Management

OBJECTIVES

- **Distinguish** among state, effect, and response uncertainty.
- **Identify** and **define** the three types of planning.
- **Write** good objectives, and **discuss** the role of objectives in planning.
- **Describe** the four-step management by objectives (MBO) process, and **explain** how it can foster individual commitment and motivation.
- **Discuss** project planning within the context of the project life cycle, and **list** six roles played by project managers.
- **Compare** and **contrast** flow charts and Gantt charts, and **discuss** the value of PERT networks.
- **Explain** how break-even points can be calculated.

THE CHANGING WORKPLACE

Nintendo: "Wii Will Rock You"

Nintendo's legendary videogame designer Shigeru Miyamoto is lying face down on the floor in Kyoto, Japan, hobbled by a right cross and struggling to regain his composure. The man some credit with the very existence of the $30 billion videogame industry, the Walt Disney of our generation, has taken one blow to the face too many. I'm standing over the creative force behind Donkey Kong, Super Mario, Nintendogs and his latest worldwide sensation, the Wii. I goad him to get up for the rest of his beating.

Clearly, one of us is taking our boxing match a bit too seriously. After all, it's not really Miyamoto who has crumbled but rather his avatar—his Mii, in Nintendo parlance. "Ohhh" is about all the man can muster as the clock runs out. Miyamoto puts down his controller and concedes defeat to finish a photo shoot. I may have beaten him at his own game, but we both know who's the real winner here. Nintendo's newest contraption has performed exactly as designed, creating yet another Wiivangelist, this time a gloating *gaijin* 5,000 miles from home who not only got up off the couch to play a videogame but actually worked up a sweat. With this little victory Miyamoto and company gather more momentum in their quest to conquer worthier competition. . . .

Nintendo is churning out over a million units a month and still can't meet demand. At the Nintendo World store in New York City's Rockefeller Center, shipments arrive nightly. In the wee hours customers begin lining up around the block. Doors open at nine, and a few hours later the consoles are gone. In the world's gadget epicenter, Tokyo's Akihabara district, shopkeepers complain about the lack of inventory. Wii displays are covered with SOLD OUT signs, while piles of PlayStation3 boxes carry a different message: 5 percent OFF. Even the Nintendo of America company store near Seattle sees lines of employees, visitors and contractors. . . .

It's not unusual for a new game console to sell out during its pre-Christmas introduction, only to see sales dwindle come January. But six months after the Wii's launch, sales are accelerating. Nintendo sold 360,000 boxes in the U.S. in April [2007], 100,000 more than in March. That's two Wiis for every Xbox 360 and four for every PlayStation3. While Sony and Microsoft lose money on hardware in hopes of seeding the market with their consoles, analysts say Nintendo makes about $50 on every unit. It may not sound like much, but the company plans to sell 35 million of these things over the next few years. That's $1.75 billion in potential profit. . . .

More difficult to comprehend is how a company founded 118 years ago as a maker of playing cards in Kyoto came to be pummeling Microsoft and Sony. The answer has something to do with reinvention. From industry-changing arcade machines to handhelds, 3-D graphics to immersive game play, Nintendo has shown a knack for leapfrogging its industry. Sure, some initiatives failed—a toy vacuum cleaner, a taxi service, a chain of "love hotels"—but the company rarely fails to surprise. And if the Wii shortage demonstrates anything, it's that this time, in changing perceptions of gaming, Nintendo has surprised even itself.

In a quieter moment Miyamoto ponders that ability to chart a new course. "How Nintendo has been able to create one surprise after another is a big question even for me," he says. "I'd like to know the answer."

The word "Nintendo" is an amalgamation of three symbols: *nin*, meaning "leave to"; *ten*, for "heaven"; and *do*, "company." The most common translation in Kyoto is "the company that leaves to heaven." What that means is open to debate. It could be a resignation to fate, as in "The company's destiny is in heaven's hands." But it's clear from a series of exclusive interviews with several executives over three months in Japan and the U.S. that little is left to chance. Another translation might be "Take care of every detail, and heaven will take care of the rest."

The man who oversees every detail is president and CEO Satoru Iwata. Iwata, 47, started as a developer for a firm Nintendo bought in 2000. Since taking over in 2002 he has westernized Nintendo, instituting performance-based raises and a retirement age of 65. To hear suppliers and contractors talk, working with Nintendo is both frustrating and inspirational. It can be Wal-Mart-esque, driving down prices by playing parts manufacturers against one another while challenging them to be more creative. Employees talk breathlessly about loving their jobs while grumbling about hectic schedules. Everyone flies commercial. The one person permitted in first class, Iwata himself, has been known to slog to London and back in one day for a press conference. No hotel required.

In short, Iwata has made Nintendo as efficient as a bullet train and as stingy as a bento box. The company's 3,400 employees generated $8.26 billion in revenue last year, or $2.5 million each. While exchange rates and fiscal calendars complicate comparisons to U.S. companies, let's do it anyway. Over roughly the same time frame, Microsoft employees generated $624,000 each; Google's performed 50 percent better, at $994,000, though still less than half as well as Nintendo employees. Nintendo's profits reached almost $1.5 billion, or $442,000 per employee, last year, compared with Microsoft's $177,000 and Google's $288,000.

Such gaudy numbers aren't the result of mere penny-pinching. Mainly they're a product of the strategic course Iwata has set. When he took over, PlayStation2 was king, and Microsoft, with its Xbox, was challenging Sony in a technological arms race. But Iwata felt his competitors were fighting the wrong battle. Cramming more technology into consoles would only make the games more expensive, harder to use, and worst of all, less fun. "We decided that Nintendo was going to take another route—game expansion," says Iwata, seated on the edge of a leather chair, leaning over green tea in a three-piece suit, a strip of gray emerging along the part in his thick hair. He has an easy command of English but speaks through an interpreter. "We are not competing against Sony or Microsoft. We are battling the indifference of people who have no interest in videogames."

Source: Excerpted from Jeffrey M. O'Brien, "Wii Will Rock You," *Fortune* (June 11, 2007): 82–92. © 2007 Time Inc. All rights reserved.

There is an old saying in management circles about the need to plan: "Organizations that fail to plan, plan to fail." Nintendo is a consistent winner because it formulates detailed plans and carries them out with diligence. But even Nintendo can't eliminate uncertainty in the global marketplace, as evidenced by inventory shortages in the face of unexpectedly high demand for its Wii game systems. Yes, amid all the uncertainty, even *success* can be a problem for today's planners.

Planning is the process of coping with uncertainty by formulating future courses of action to achieve specified results. Planning enables humans to achieve great things by envisioning a pathway from concept to reality. The greater the mission, the longer and more challenging the pathway. For example, imagine the challenges awaiting Starbucks. In 2006, *Fortune* magazine reported Howard Schultz's ambitious growth plan: "the head of the world's largest coffee-shop chain said he plans to more than triple the number of stores, to 40,000, with half in the U.S. and half overseas."[2] Planning is a never-ending process because of constant change, uncertainty, new competition, unexpected problems, and emerging opportunities.[3]

Because planning affects all downstream management functions (see Figure 6.1), it has been called the primary management function. With this model in mind, we shall discuss uncertainty, highlight five essential aspects of the planning function, and take a close look at management by objectives and project

> **planning:** coping with uncertainty by formulating courses of action to achieve specified results

planning. We shall also introduce four practical tools (flow charts, Gantt charts, PERT networks, and break-even analysis).

COPING WITH UNCERTAINTY

Ben Franklin said the only sure things in life are death and taxes. Although this is a gloomy prospect, it does capture a key theme of modern life. We are faced with a great deal of uncertainty. Organizations, like individuals, are continually challenged to accomplish something in spite of general uncertainty.[4] Organizations meet this challenge largely through planning. As a context for our discussion of planning in this and the following chapter, let us explore environmental uncertainty from two perspectives: (1) types of uncertainty and (2) organizational responses to environmental uncertainty.

Three Types of Uncertainty

Through the years, *environmental uncertainty* has been a catch-all term among managers and researchers. However, research indicates that people actually perceive three types of environmental uncertainty: state uncertainty, effect uncertainty, and response uncertainty. **State uncertainty** occurs when the environment, or a portion of the environment, is considered unpredictable. A manager's attempt to predict the *effects* of specific environmental changes or

> **state uncertainty:** environment is unpredictable

FIGURE **6.1** Planning: The Primary Management Function

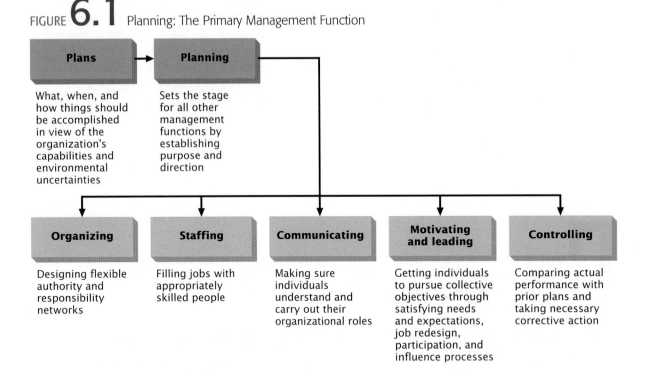

Plans	Planning
What, when, and how things should be accomplished in view of the organization's capabilities and environmental uncertainties	Sets the stage for all other management functions by establishing purpose and direction

Organizing	Staffing	Communicating	Motivating and leading	Controlling
Designing flexible authority and responsibility networks	Filling jobs with appropriately skilled people	Making sure individuals understand and carry out their organizational roles	Getting individuals to pursue collective objectives through satisfying needs and expectations, job redesign, participation, and influence processes	Comparing actual performance with prior plans and taking necessary corrective action

events on his or her organization involves **effect uncertainty**. **Response uncertainty** is inability to predict the *consequences* of a particular decision or organizational response.[5]

effect uncertainty: impacts of environmental changes are unpredictable

response uncertainty: consequences of decisions are unpredictable

A simple analogy can help us conceptually sort out these three types of uncertainty. Suppose you are a golfer, and on your way to the course you wonder whether it is going to rain; this is *state uncertainty*. Next, you experience *effect uncertainty* because you are not sure whether it will rain hard enough, if it does rain, to make you quit before finishing nine holes. Soon you begin weighing your chances of making par if you have to adjust your choice of golf clubs to poor playing conditions; now you are experiencing *response uncertainty*. Each of the three types of perceived uncertainty could affect your golfing attitude and performance. Similarly, managers are affected by their different perceptions of environmental factors. Their degree of uncertainty may vary from one type of uncertainty to another. A manager may, for example, be unsure about whether a key employee is about to quit (considerable state uncertainty) but very sure that productivity would suffer without that individual (little effect uncertainty).[6]

Organizational Responses to Uncertainty

Some organizations do a better job than others of planning amid various combinations of uncertainty. This is due in part to differing patterns of response to environmental factors beyond the organization's immediate control. As outlined in Table 6.1, organizations cope with environmental uncertainty by adopting one of four positions vis-à-vis the environment in which they operate. These are the positions taken by

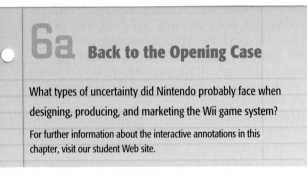

6a **Back to the Opening Case**

What types of uncertainty did Nintendo probably face when designing, producing, and marketing the Wii game system?

For further information about the interactive annotations in this chapter, visit our student Web site.

O uch! Lightning strikes such as this one during a severe storm in Clifton Park, New York, are a major source of both "state" and "effect" uncertainty for everyone, including business owners, airlines, and electric utilities. Indeed, this storm was responsible for regional power outages.

DEFENDERS. A defender can be successful as long as its primary technology and narrow product line remain competitive. But defenders can become stranded on a dead-end road if their primary market seriously weakens. A prime example of a defender is Harley-Davidson, which sold its recreational vehicle division and other nonmotorcycle businesses to get back to basics. Harley-Davidson enjoys such fierce brand loyalty among Hog riders that many sport a tattoo of the company's logo. Can you imagine a Coca-Cola or a Wal-Mart tattoo? But Harley-Davidson runs the risk of having its narrow focus miss the mark in an aging America. Specifically, the median age of Harley buyers rose from 35 in 1987 to 46 in 2002. Harley-Davidson is therefore seeking to lure younger riders who prefer sleek bikes away from Honda and other Japanese rivals.[8]

defenders, prospectors, analyzers, and reactors,[7] and each position has its own characteristic impact on planning.

PROSPECTORS. Prospector organizations are easy to spot because they have a reputation for aggressively making things happen rather than waiting for them to

TABLE **6.1**	Different Organizational Responses to an Uncertain Environment
TYPE OF ORGANIZATIONAL RESPONSE	**CHARACTERISTICS OF RESPONSE**
1. Defenders	Highly expert at producing and marketing a few products in a narrowly defined market
	Opportunities beyond present market not sought
	Few adjustments in technology, organization structure, and methods of operation because of narrow focus
	Primary attention devoted to efficiency of current operations
2. Prospectors	Primary attention devoted to searching for new market opportunities
	Frequent development and testing of new products and services
	Source of change and uncertainty for competitors
	Loss of efficiency because of continual product and market innovation
3. Analyzers	Simultaneous operations in stable and changing product/market domains
	In relatively stable product/market domain, emphasis on formalized structures and processes to achieve routine and efficient operation
	In changing product/market domain, emphasis on detecting and copying competitors' most promising ideas
4. Reactors	Frequently unable to respond quickly to perceived changes in environment
	Make adjustments only when finally forced to do so by environmental pressures

Source: Adapted from Organizational Strategy, Structure, and Process, *by Raymond E. Miles and Charles C. Snow. Copyright © 1978, McGraw-Hill Book Company, p. 29. Used with permission of McGraw-Hill Book Company.*

happen. But life is challenging for prospectors such as Amazon.com Inc.:

In some ways, Amazon is the ultimate example of transformation. Despite constant criticism, Amazon CEO Jeffrey P. Bezos quickly moved the company beyond books to other media, then to electronics, and just about everything else. Now Bezos is working on his next diversification play: offering other businesses spare computing and storage capacity, as well as leftover space in Amazon's huge distribution centers. The strategy has yet to deliver meaningful revenues, or any profits. But as Bezos will tell you, it reflects a never-ending need to search for the next source of tech growth.[9]

Prospectors (or pioneers) traditionally have been admired for their ability to gain what strategists call a *first-mover advantage*. In other words, the first one to market wins. Following the Internet crash, when many dot-com pioneers were the first to go bankrupt, the first-mover advantage was given a second look. Two researchers, one from the United States and the other from France, recently offered this insight about both industrial and consumer goods companies: ". . . we found that over the long haul, early movers are considerably *less* profitable than later entrants. Although pioneers do enjoy sustained revenue advantages, they also suffer from persistently *high* costs, which eventually overwhelm the sales gains."[10] Prospectors need to pick their opportunities very carefully, selecting those with the best combination of feasibility and profit potential. This is especially true for entrepreneurs starting small businesses.[11]

ANALYZERS.   An essentially conservative strategy of following the leader marks an organization as an analyzer. It is a "me too" response to environmental uncertainty. Analyzers let market leaders take expensive R&D risks and then imitate or build upon what works. This slower, more studied approach can pay off when the economy turns down and prospectors stumble. A classic example is Israel's Teva Pharmaceuticals, a maker of generic drugs that sell for much less than brand-name drugs:

You may never have heard of the Israeli company. But you could very well be taking one of its drugs. One in every 15 prescriptions in the U.S. is a Teva product, making the company this country's largest drug supplier. With $3.3 billion in revenues, it sells more than 450 drugs in North America, Europe, and Israel—everything from antibiotics to heart medicines. . . .

Chief executive Israel Makov doesn't have any illusions about turning Teva into a brand-name producer. . . . His goal is to double sales every four years by remaining largely a maker of me-too medications.[12]

Although analyzers such as generic drug companies may not get a lot of respect, they perform the important economic function of breaking up overly concentrated industries. Customers appreciate the resulting lower prices, too.

REACTORS.   The reactor is the exact opposite of the prospector. Reactors wait for adversity, such as declining sales, before taking corrective steps. They are slow to develop new products to supplement their tried-and-true ones. Their strategic responses to changes in the environment are often late. An instructive example in this area is Kodak:

Kodak continues to grapple with one of the harshest corporate transitions of the past decade. Its 100-year-old film business is waning in the face of digital photography, which exploded [in 2003]. . . .

The company cautiously moved into digital photography in the mid-1990s but never made the transition away from film. Now, it might be too late.

"Kodak saw this coming," says Michael Raynor, co-author of management best-seller The Innovator's Solution. *But instead of driving a transition earlier and building up a digital business, it's now "leaping on a train when it's going 70 miles per hour," Raynor says.*[13]

Not surprisingly, Kodak's global workforce has been cut by one-third (about 31,000 employees) over the last decade.[14] According to one field study, reactors tended to be less profitable than defenders, prospectors, and analyzers.[15]

Balancing Planned Action and Spontaneity in the Twenty-First Century

In the obsolete command-and-control management model, plans were considered destiny. Top management formulated exacting plans for every aspect of operations and then kept everything under tight control to "meet the plan." All too often, however, plans were derailed by unanticipated events, and success was dampened by organizational inflexibility. Today's progressive managers see plans as general guidelines for action, based on imperfect and incomplete information. Planning is no longer the exclusive domain of top management; it now typically involves those who carry out the plans because they are closer to the customer. Planning experts, who recommend *strategic*

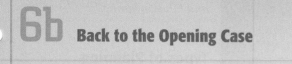

6b Back to the Opening Case

Would you categorize Nintendo as a defender, prospector, analyzer, or reactor? Explain.

agility,[16] say managers need to balance planned action with the flexibility to take advantage of surprise events and unexpected opportunities. A good analogy is to an improvisational comedy act.[17] The stand-up comic has a plan for the introduction, structure of the act, some tried-and-true jokes, and closing remarks. Within this planned framework, the comic will play off the audience's input and improvise as necessary. Accordingly, 3M Corporation had a plan for encouraging innovation that allowed it to capitalize on the spontaneous success of the Post-it Note.[18] Planning should be a springboard to success, not a barrier to creativity.

THE ESSENTIALS OF PLANNING

Planning is an ever-present feature of modern life, although there is no universal approach. Virtually everyone is a planner, at least in the informal sense. We plan leisure activities after school or work; we make career plans. Personal or informal plans give purpose to our lives. In a similar fashion, more formalized plans enable managers to mobilize their intentions to accomplish organizational purposes. A **plan** is a specific, documented intention consisting of an objective and an action statement. The objective portion is the end, and the action statement represents the means to that end. Stated another way, objectives give management targets to shoot at, whereas action statements provide the arrows for hitting the targets. Properly conceived plans tell *what, when*, and *how* something is to be done.

plan: an objective plus an action statement

In spite of the wide variety of formal planning systems that managers encounter on the job, we can identify some essentials of sound planning. Among these common denominators are organizational mission, types of planning, objectives, priorities, and the planning/control cycle.

Organizational Mission

To some, defining an organization's mission might seem to be an exercise in the obvious. But exactly the opposite is true. Some organizations drift along without a clear mission. Others lose sight of their original mission. Sometimes an organization, such as the U.S. Army Corps of Engineers, finds its original mission no longer acceptable to key stakeholders. In fact, the Corps is stepping back from its tradition of building dams and levees, in favor of more environmentally sensitive projects. It has tackled "a 30-year, $7.8 billion restoration of the Florida Everglades"[19] that will involve tearing down levees to restore the natural flow of the Kissimmee River. Periodically redefining an organization's mission is both common and necessary in an era of rapid change.

A clear, formally written, and publicized statement of an organization's mission is the cornerstone of any planning system that will effectively guide the organization through uncertain times. The satirical definition by Scott Adams, the Dilbert cartoonist, tells us how *not* to write an organizational mission statement: "A Mission Statement is defined as a long, awkward sentence that demonstrates management's inability to think clearly."[20] This sad state of affairs, too often true, can be avoided by a well-written mission statement that does the following things:

1. *Defines* your organization for key stakeholders
2. Creates an *inspiring vision* of what the organization can be and can do
3. Outlines *how* the vision is to be accomplished
4. Establishes key *priorities*
5. States a *common goal* and fosters a sense of togetherness
6. Creates a *philosophical anchor* for all organizational activities
7. Generates *enthusiasm* and a "can do" attitude
8. *Empowers* present and future organization members to believe that *every* individual is the key to success[21]

A good mission statement provides a focal point for the entire planning process. When Vincent A. Sarni took the top job at PPG, the large glass and paint company, he created a document he called "Blueprint for the Decade." In it he specified the company's mission and corporate objectives for such things as service, quality, and financial performance.

I f you want a Big Mac, fries, a chocolate shake, and a prayer of forgiveness, this is the man to see. He's the Reverend Joe Ratliff, senior pastor of the Brentwood Baptist Church in Houston, Texas. Reverend Ratliff saw McDonald's outlets popping up in unusual places such as gas stations, schools, and hospitals. So why not have one for the church's 10,000-member congregation? After all, on-site dining fit the church's mission of helping people and a restaurant fit nicely into the plans for a huge new multi-purpose building. "Good idea," said McDonald's, and the rest is history. Did you say, "Hold the onions?"

Sarni ... trudged from plant to plant preaching the virtues in his Little Blue Book. "My first two or three years I always started with a discussion of the Blueprint," he says. "I don't have to do that anymore.

The Blueprint's on the shop floor, and it has meaning."[22]

Types of Planning

Ideally, planning begins at the top of the organizational pyramid and filters down. The rationale for beginning at the top is the need for coordination. It is top management's job to state the organization's mission, establish strategic priorities, and draw up major policies. After these statements are in place, successive rounds of strategic, intermediate, and operational planning can occur. Figure 6.2 presents an idealized picture of the three types of planning, as carried out by different levels of management.

STRATEGIC, INTERMEDIATE, AND OPERATIONAL PLANNING. **Strategic planning** is the process of determining how to pursue the organization's long-term goals with the resources expected to be available.[23] A well-conceived strategic plan communicates much more than general intentions about profit and growth. It specifies *how* the organization will achieve a competitive advantage, with profit and growth as necessary by-products. **Intermediate planning** is the process of determining the contributions that subunits can make with allocated resources. Finally, **operational planning** is the process of determining how specific tasks can best be accomplished on time with available resources. Each level of planning is vital to an organization's success and cannot effectively stand alone without the support of the other two levels.

strategic planning: determining how to pursue long-term goals with available resources

intermediate planning: determining what contributions subunits can make with allocated resources

operational planning: determining how to accomplish specific tasks with available resources

PLANNING HORIZONS. As Figure 6.2 illustrates, planning horizons vary for the three types of planning.

FIGURE **6.2** Types of Planning

THE MANAGERIAL PYRAMID	PLANNING HORIZONS
Top management Chief executive officer, president, vice president, general managers, division heads	*Strategic planning:* One to ten years
Middle management Functional managers, product-line managers, department heads	*Intermediate planning:* Six months to two years
Lower management Unit managers, first-line supervisors	*Operational planning:* One week to one year

The term **planning horizon** refers to the time that elapses between the formulation and the execution of a planned activity. As the planning process evolves from strategic to operational, planning horizons shorten and plans become increasingly specific. Naturally, management can be more confident—and hence more specific—about the near future than about the distant future.

> **planning horizon:** time that elapses between planning and execution

Note, however, that the three planning horizons overlap, their boundaries being elastic rather than rigid. The trend today is toward involving employees from all levels in the strategic planning process. Also,

" Sure, it's easy for <u>you</u> to plan for the long haul . . with your <u>nine lives</u> ! "

it is not uncommon for top and lower managers to have a hand in formulating intermediate plans. Middle managers often help lower managers draw up operational plans as well. Hence Figure 6.2 is an ideal instructional model with countless variations in the workplace.

Objectives

Just as a distant port is the target or goal for a ship's crew, objectives are targets that organization members steer toward. Although some theorists distinguish between goals and objectives, managers typically use the terms interchangeably. A goal or an **objective** is defined as a specific commitment to achieve a measurable result within a given time frame. Many experts view objectives as the single most important feature of the planning process. They help managers and entrepreneurs build a bridge between their dreams, aspirations, and visions and an achievable *reality*. Dan Sullivan, a consultant for entrepreneurs, explains:

> **objective:** commitment to achieve a measurable result within a specified period

> *[Objectives and goals] should be achievable by definition. If you are setting functional goals, at useful increments, they should be both real and realizable. The distance between where you actually are now and your goal can be measured objectively, and when you achieve your goal, you know it. Think of the distinction this way: no matter how fast you run toward the horizon, you'll never get there, but if you run more quickly toward a goalpost, you will get there faster. Sounds simplistic, but I'm constantly amazed at how many people—and entrepreneurs in particular—confuse their goals with their ideals.*[24]

It is important for present and future managers to be able to write good objectives, to be aware of their importance, and to understand how objectives combine to form a means-ends chain.

WRITING GOOD OBJECTIVES.   An authority on objectives recommends that "as far as possible, objectives [should be] expressed in quantitative, measurable, concrete terms, in the form of a written statement of desired results to be achieved within a given time period."[25] In other words, objectives represent a firm commitment to accomplish something specific. A well-written objective should state what is to be accomplished and when it is to be accomplished. In the following sample objectives, note that the desired results are expressed *quantitatively*, in units of output, dollars, or percentage of change.

- To increase subcompact car production by 240,000 units during the next production year
- To reduce bad-debt loss by $50,000 during the next six months
- To achieve an 18 percent increase in Brand X sales by December 31 of the current year

For actual practice in writing good objectives and plans, see the Action Learning exercise at the end of this chapter.

THE IMPORTANCE OF OBJECTIVES. From the standpoint of planning, carefully prepared objectives benefit managers by serving as targets and measuring sticks, fostering commitment, and enhancing motivation.[26]

- *Targets.* As mentioned earlier, objectives provide managers with specific targets. Without objectives, managers at all levels would find it difficult to make coordinated decisions. People quite naturally tend to pursue their own ends in the absence of formal organizational objectives.
- *Measuring sticks.* An easily overlooked, after-the-fact feature of objectives is that they are useful for measuring how well an organizational subunit or individual has performed. When appraising performance, managers need an established standard against which they can measure performance. Concrete objectives enable managers to weigh performance objectively on the basis of accomplishment, rather than subjectively on the basis of personality or prejudice.

- *Commitment.* The very process of getting an employee to agree to pursue a given objective gives that individual a personal stake in the success of the enterprise. Thus objectives can be helpful in encouraging personal commitment to collective ends. Without individual commitment, even well-intentioned and carefully conceived strategies are doomed to failure.
- *Motivation.* Good objectives represent a challenge—something to reach for. Accordingly, they have a motivational aspect. People usually feel good about themselves and what they do when they successfully achieve a challenging objective. Moreover, objectives give managers a rational basis for rewarding performance. Employees who believe they will be equitably rewarded for achieving a given objective will be motivated to perform well.

THE MEANS-ENDS CHAIN OF OBJECTIVES. Like the overall planning process, objective setting is a top-to-bottom proposition. Top managers set broader objectives with longer time horizons than do successively lower levels of managers. In effect, this downward flow of objectives creates a means-ends chain. Working from bottom to top in Figure 6.3, supervisory-level objectives provide the means for achieving middle-level objectives (ends) that, in turn, provide the means for achieving top-level objectives (ends).

The organizational hierarchy in Figure 6.3 has, of course, been telescoped and narrowed at the middle and lower levels for illustrative purposes. Usually, two or three layers of management would separate the president and the product-line managers.

Another layer or two would separate product-line managers from area sales managers. But the telescoping helps show that lower-level objectives provide the means for accomplishing higher-level ends or objectives.

FIGURE **6.3** A Typical Means-Ends Chain of Objectives

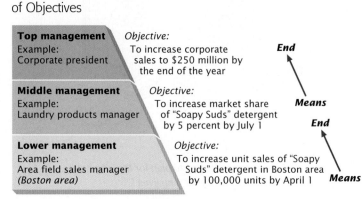

Priorities (Both Strategic and Personal)

Defined as a ranking of goals, objectives, or activities in order of importance, **priorities** play a special role in planning. By listing long-range organizational objectives in order of their priority, top management prepares to make later decisions regarding the allocation of resources. Limited time, talent, and financial and material resources need to be channeled into more important endeavors and away from other areas in proportion to the relative priority of the areas. Establishment of priorities is a key factor in managerial and organizational effectiveness. Strategic priorities give both insiders and outsiders answers to the questions "Why does the organization exist?" and "How should it act and react during a crisis?" An inspiring illustration of the latter occurred for American Express after the September 11, 2001, terrorist attacks:

> The hundreds of ad hoc decisions made by [new CEO Kenneth I.] Chenault and his team were guided by two overriding concerns: employee safety and customer service. AmEx helped 560,000 stranded cardholders get home, in some cases chartering airplanes and buses to ferry them across the country. It waived millions of dollars in delinquent fees on late-paying cardholders and increased credit limits to cash-starved clients. . . .
>
> Most telling, Chenault gathered 5,000 American Express employees at the Paramount Theater in New York on Sept. 20 for a highly emotional "town hall meeting." During the session, Chenault demonstrated . . . poise, compassion, and decisiveness.[27]

priorities: goals, objectives, or activities ranked in order of importance

THE A-B-C PRIORITY SYSTEM. Despite time-management seminars, day planners, and computerized "personal digital assistants," establishing priorities remains a subjective process affected by organizational politics and value conflicts.[28] Although there is no universally acceptable formula for carrying out this important function, the following A-B-C priority system is helpful.

A: "Must do" objectives *critical* to successful performance. They may be the result of special demands from higher levels of management or other external sources.

B: "Should do" objectives *necessary* for improved performance. They are generally vital, but their achievement can be postponed if necessary.

C: "Nice to do" objectives *desirable* for improved performance, but not critical to survival or improved performance. They can be eliminated or postponed to achieve objectives of higher priority.[29]

Home Depot uses an interesting and effective color-coded variation of this approach. According to *Business Week*: ". . . when a to-do list for managers arrives electronically, it is marked in green. If it isn't done by the set date, it changes to red—and district managers can pounce."[30]

THE 80/20 PRINCIPLE. Another proven priority-setting tool is the 80/20 principle (or Pareto analysis, as mentioned in Chapter 2). "The **80/20 principle** asserts that a minority of causes, inputs, or effort usually leads to a majority of the results, outputs, or rewards."[31] Care needs to be taken not to interpret the 80/20 formula too literally—it is approximate. Managers can leverage their time by focusing on the *few* people, problems, or opportunities with the *greatest* impact. Consider this situation, for example:

80/20 principle: a minority of causes, inputs, or effort that tends to produce a majority of results, outputs, or rewards

> Market Line Associates, an Atlanta financial consultancy, estimates that the top 20% of customers at a typical commercial bank generate up to six times

ETHICS: CHARACTER, COURAGE, AND VALUES

Wells Fargo Helps Its Business Customers Control Fraud and Identity Theft

Wells Fargo & Co.'s Treasury Management University (TMU) provides training to employees on the wholesale-banking side—the people who handle commercial loans and many other services for business customers. Since 2002 TMU has offered training to customers as well.

"We saw it as an opportunity to help commercial customers improve the way they use the bank's services: 'Here's how to use us better to save you time and money,'" says Luann Woneis, vice president and manager of Treasury Management University in San Francisco. . . .

One popular online seminar, offered monthly, concerns preventing fraud and lowering the risk of identity theft. . . .

The advice includes tips such as: Be careful which employees have access to which information. Use dual controls for writing and reconciling checks; don't have the same person perform both functions. If you send a wire over a certain dollar amount, have someone else verify the wire.

Source: Excerpted from Jack Gordon, "Take That to the Bank," Training, 43 (June 2006): 40, 42.

FOR DISCUSSION

Relative to our coverage of corporate social responsibility in Chapter 5, is this a case of enlightened self-interest? Explain. Why is this an example of good business ethics?

as much revenue as they cost, while the bottom fifth cost three to four times more than they make for the company.[32]

For profit-minded banks and other businesses, all customers are not alike. Indeed, ING Bank, the U.S. subsidiary of the Dutch insurance giant ING, "'fires' about 3,600 of its 2 million customers every year. Ditching clients who are too time-consuming saves the company at least $1 million annually."[33] How would business purists who say, "The customer is always right," feel about this practice?

AVOIDING THE "BUSYNESS" TRAP. These two simple yet effective tools for establishing priorities can help managers avoid the so-called *busyness trap.*[34] In these fast-paced times, managers should not confuse being busy with being effective and efficient. *Results* are what really count. Activities and speed, without results, are an energy-sapping waste of time. By slowing down a bit, having clear priorities, and taking a strategic view of daily problems, busy managers can be successful *and* "get a life."[35]

Finally, managers striving to establish priorities amid lots of competing demands would do well to heed Peter Drucker's advice—that the most important skill for setting priorities and managing time is simply learning to say "no."

The Planning/Control Cycle

To put the planning process in perspective, it is important to show how it is connected with the control function. Figure 6.4 illustrates the cyclical relationship between planning and control. Planning gets things headed in the right direction, and control keeps them headed in the right direction (see Ethics: Character, Courage, and Values). Because of the importance of the control function, it is covered in detail in Chapter 16. Basically, each of the three levels of planning is a two-step sequence followed by a two-step control sequence.

FIGURE **6.4** The Basic Planning/Control Cycle

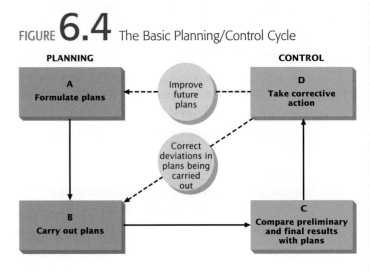

The initial planning/control cycle begins when top management establishes strategic plans. When those strategic plans are carried out, intermediate and operational plans are formulated, thus setting in motion two more planning/control cycles. As strategic, intermediate, and operational plans are carried out, the control function begins. Corrective action is necessary when either the preliminary or the final results deviate from plans. For planned activities still in progress, the corrective action can get things back on track before it is too late. Deviations between final results and plans, on the other hand, are instructive feedback for the improvement of future plans. The broken lines in Figure 6.4 represent the important sort of feedback that makes the planning/control cycle a dynamic and evolving process. Our attention now turns to some practical planning tools.

MANAGEMENT BY OBJECTIVES AND PROJECT PLANNING

In this section we examine a traditional planning technique and a modern planning challenge. Valuable lessons about planning can be learned from each.

Management by Objectives

Management by objectives (MBO) is a comprehensive management system based on measurable and participatively set objectives. MBO has come a long way since it was first suggested by Peter Drucker in 1954 as a means of promoting managerial self-control.[36] MBO theory[37] and practice subsequently mushroomed and spread around the world. In one form or another, and under various labels, MBO has been adopted by most public and private organizations of any significant size. For example, at Cypress Semiconductor Corporation, the San Jose, California, electronics firm, computerization paved the way for high-tech MBO. T. J. Rodgers, the company's founder and chief executive officer, explains:

> *All of Cypress's 1,400 employees have goals, which, in theory, makes them no different from employees at most other companies. What makes our people different is that every week they set their own goals, commit to achieving them by a specific date, enter them into a database, and report whether or not they completed prior goals. Cypress's computerized goal system is an important part of our managerial infrastructure. It is a detailed guide to the future and an objective record of the past. In any given week, some 6,000 goals in the database come due. Our ability to meet those goals ultimately determines our success or failure . . . .*
>
> *I developed the goal system long before personal computers existed. It has its roots in management-by-objectives techniques I learned in the mid-1970s at American Microsystems.*[38]

The common denominator that has made MBO programs so popular in management theory and practice is the emphasis on objectives that are both *measurable* and *participatively set.*

THE MBO CYCLE. Because MBO combines planning and control, the four-stage MBO cycle corresponds to the planning/control cycle outlined in Figure 6.4. Steps 1 and 2 make up the planning phase of MBO, and steps 3 and 4 are the control phase.

1. *Step 1: Setting objectives.* A hierarchy of challenging, fair, and internally consistent objectives is the necessary starting point for the MBO cycle and serves as the foundation for all that follows. All objectives, according to MBO theory, should be reduced to writing and put away for later reference during steps 3 and 4. Consistent with what was said earlier about objectives, objective setting in MBO begins at the top of the managerial pyramid and filters down, one layer at a time.

   MBO's main contribution to the objective-setting process is its emphasis on the participation and involvement of people at lower levels. There is no place in MBO for the domineering manager ("Here are the objectives I've written for you") or for the passive manager ("I'll go along with whatever objectives you set"). MBO calls for a give-and-take negotiation of objectives between the manager and those who report directly to him or her.[39]

2. *Step 2: Developing action plans.* With the addition of action statements to the participatively set objectives, the planning phase of MBO is complete. Managers at each level develop plans that incorporate objectives established in step 1. Higher managers are responsible for ensuring that their direct assistants' plans complement one another and do not work at cross-purposes.

management by objectives (MBO): comprehensive management system based on measurable and participatively set objectives

3. *Step 3: Periodic review.* As plans turn into action, attention turns to step 3, monitoring performance. Advocates of MBO usually recommend face-to-face meetings between a manager and his or her people at three-, six-, and nine-month intervals. (Some organizations, such as Cypress, rely on shorter cycles.) These periodic checkups permit those who are responsible for a particular set of objectives to reconsider them, checking their validity in view of unexpected events—added duties or the loss of a key assistant—that could make them obsolete. If an objective is no longer valid, it is amended accordingly. Otherwise, progress toward valid objectives is assessed. Periodic checkups also afford managers an excellent opportunity to give their people needed and appreciated feedback.

4. *Step 4: Performance appraisal.* At the end of one complete cycle of MBO, typically one year after the original goals were set, final performance is compared with the previously agreed-upon objectives. The pairs of superior and subordinate managers who mutually set the objectives one year earlier meet face to face once again to discuss how things have turned out. MBO emphasizes results, not personalities or excuses. The control phase of the MBO cycle is completed when success is rewarded with promotion, merit pay, or other suitable benefits and when failure is noted for future corrective action.

After one round of MBO, the cycle repeats itself, with each cycle contributing to the learning process. A common practice in introducing MBO is to start at the top and to pull a new layer of management into the MBO process each year. Experience has shown that plunging several layers of management into MBO all at once often causes confusion, dissatisfaction, and failure. In fact, even a moderate-sized organization usually takes five or more years to evolve a full-blown MBO system that ties together such areas as planning, control, performance appraisal, and the reward system. MBO programs can be facilitated by using off-the-shelf software programs. Such programs offer helpful spreadsheet formats for goal setting, timelines, at-a-glance status boards, and performance reports. MBO proponents believe that effective leadership and greater motivation—through the use of realistic objectives, more effective control, and self-control—are the natural by-products of a proper MBO system.[40]

STRENGTHS AND LIMITATIONS OF MBO. Any widely used management technique is bound to generate debate about its relative strengths and weaknesses,

FIGURE **6.5** MBO's Strengths and Limitations

Strengths	Limitations
• MBO blends planning and control into a rational system of management.	• MBO is too often sold as a cure-all.
• MBO forces an organization to develop a top-to-bottom hierarchy of objectives.	• MBO is easily stalled by authoritarian (Theory X) managers and inflexible bureaucratic policies and rules.
• MBO emphasizes end results rather than good intentions or personalities.	• MBO takes too much time and effort and generates too much paperwork.
• MBO encourages self-management and personal commitment through employee participation in setting objectives.	• MBO's emphasis on measurable objectives can be used as a threat by overzealous managers.

and MBO is no exception.[41] Present and future managers will have more realistic expectations for MBO if they are familiar with both sides of this debate. The four primary strengths of MBO and four common complaints about it are compared in Figure 6.5.

This debate will probably not be resolved in the near future. Critics of MBO, such as the late quality expert W. Edwards Deming, point to both theoretical and methodological flaws.[42] Meanwhile, MBO advocates insist that it is the misapplication of MBO, not the MBO concept itself, that leads to problems. In the final analysis, MBO will probably work when organizational conditions are favorable and will probably fail when those conditions are unfavorable. A favorable climate for MBO includes top-management commitment, openness to change, Theory Y management, and employees who are willing and able to shoulder greater responsibility.[43] Research justifies putting *top-management commitment* at the top of the list. In a review of 70 MBO studies, researchers found that "when top-management commitment was high, the average gain in productivity was 56 percent. When such commitment was low, the average gain in productivity was only 6 percent."[44] A strong positive relationship was also found between top-management commitment to MBO program success and employee job satisfaction.[45] The greater management's commitment, the greater the satisfaction.

Project Planning and Management

Project-based organizations are becoming the norm today. Why? Concept-to-market times are being honed to the minimum in today's technology-driven world.[46] Typically, cross-functional teams of people with different technical skills are brought together on a temporary basis to complete a specific project as swiftly as possible. According to the 240,000-member Project Management Institute, "A **project** is a temporary endeavor undertaken to achieve a particular aim."[47] Projects, like all other activities within the management domain, need to be systematically planned and managed. What sets project planning/management apart is the *temporary* nature of projects, as contrasted to the typical ongoing or continuous activities in organizations. Projects may be pursued within the organization or performed for outside clients. When the job is done, project members disband and move on to other projects or return to their usual work routines. Time is usually of the essence for project managers because of tight schedules and deadlines. For example, put yourself in the shoes of the executive project manager at book publisher Scholastic faced with the following challenge:

> *Print 12 million copies of the highly anticipated* Harry Potter and the Deathly Hallows—*a record first printing in publishing—and deliver them to thousands of retailers around the U.S.*
>
> *The daunting part was synchronizing shipments to arrive no more than a day (or hours) before the scheduled July 21 [2007] 12:01 a.m. release—to minimize the risk of someone's leaking the book's ending.*
>
> *Even before author J. K. Rowling delivered the manuscript . . . [in early 2007], Scholastic was in full battle planning. Executives from its manufac-*

project: a temporary endeavor undertaken to achieve a particular aim

turing and logistics divisions were meeting with printers and trucking companies to make sure they could deliver on the tight turnaround required to get the book to fans before summer vacation ended.[48]

Project management is the usual thing on Hollywood movie sets and at construction companies building homes, roads, and skyscrapers. But it is newer to manufacturers, banks, insurance companies, hospitals, and government agencies. Unfortunately, much of this Internet-age project management leaves a lot to be desired. For example, consider the dismal track record for information technology (IT) projects, typically involving conversion of an old computer system to new hardware, software, and work methods.

> *Most large IT projects are delivered late and over budget because they are inefficiently managed. A study by the Hackett Group, a Hudson, Ohio–based benchmarking firm, found that the average company completes only 37 percent of large IT projects on time and only 42 percent on budget.*[49]

A broader and deeper understanding of project management is in order.

Project managers face many difficult challenges. First and foremost, they work outside the normal organizational hierarchy or chain of command because projects are ad hoc and temporary. Consequently, they must rely on excellent "people management skills" instead of on giving orders.[50] Those skills include, but are not limited to, communication, motivation, leadership, conflict resolution, and negotiation (see Chapters 11–15).

Project *planning* deserves special attention in this chapter because project managers have the difficult job of being both intermediate/tactical and operational

Now here's a project to curb your sweet tooth. These three German confectioners from Berlin made their delicious contribution to the goal of selling 15,000 pieces of cake from bakeries in 27 European Union countries during a 2007 EU summit in Berlin. How would you have managed that project?

6f Look Before You Leap

James P. Hackett, CEO of office furniture maker Steelcase in Grand Rapids, Michigan:

Companies celebrate their "can-do" culture. Later on, after the errors show up, we all wish we had been more rigorous in scouting out the territory before we sprinted down the execution path.

Source: James P. Hackett, "Preparing for the Perfect Product Launch," Harvard Business Review, 85 (April 2007): 46.

QUESTION:

What "school of hard knocks" lessons have you learned from inadequate project planning in your everyday life?

planners. They are responsible for both the big picture and the little details of their project. A project that is not well planned is a project doomed to failure. So let us take a look at the project life cycle, project management software, the six roles project managers play, and guidelines for project managers.

THE PROJECT LIFE CYCLE. Every project, from developing a new breakfast cereal to staging a benefit rock concert, has a predictable four-stage life cycle. As shown in Figure 6.6, the four stages are conceptualization, planning, execution, and termination. Although they are shown equally spaced in Figure 6.6, the four stages typically involve varying periods of time. Sometimes the borders between stages blur. For example, project goal setting actually begins in the conceptualization stage and often carries over to the planning stage. During this stage, project managers turn their attention to facilities and equipment, personnel and task assignments, and scheduling. Work on the project begins in the execution stage, and additional resources are acquired as needed. Budget demands are highest during the execution stage because everything is in motion. To some, the label "termination" in stage 4 might suggest a sudden end to the project. But more typically, the completed project is turned over to an end user (for example, a new breakfast cereal is turned over to manufacturing) and project resources are phased out.[51]

PROJECT MANAGEMENT SOFTWARE. Recall from our earlier discussion of the basic planning/control cycle (Figure 6.4) how planning and control are inter-

twined. One cannot occur without the other. The same is true for project planning. Making sure planned activities occur when and where appropriate and taking corrective action when necessary can be an overwhelming job for the manager of a complex project. Fortunately, a host of computer software programs can make the task manageable. But which one of the many available programs—such as Microsoft Project for Windows—should a project manager use? Thanks to project management experts, we have a handy list of screening criteria for selecting the right tool. Judging from the list that follows, the overriding attributes of good project management software packages are *flexibility* and *transparency* (meaning quick and up-to-date status reports on all important aspects of the project).[52]

- Identify and ultimately schedule need-to-do activities
- Ability to dynamically shift priorities and schedules, and view resulting impact
- Provide critical path analysis
- Provide flexibility for plan modifications
- Ability to set priority levels
- Flexibility to manage all resources: people, hardware, environments, cash
- Ability to merge plans
- Management alerts for project slippage
- Automatic time recording to map against project
- Identification of time spent on activities[53]

SIX ROLES PLAYED BY PROJECT MANAGERS. In a recent study, interviews with 40 project managers (and their clients) revealed what it takes to be effective.[54] The managers studied were working with outside clients on IT projects involving software development, systems integration, and technical support. In addition to the key role of "implementer," effective project managers played the roles of entrepreneur, politician, friend, marketer, and coach (see Table 6.2 on page 162). Each role has its own set of challenges and appropriate strategies for meeting those challenges. It takes a highly skilled and motivated person to play all these roles successfully in today's business environment. As one project management educator put it,

In today's harsh business economy, executives want to know one thing about any project management initiative: "What's the value?" More than ever, every dollar invested must be justified, and every initiative must deliver tangible results.[55]

FIGURE **6.6** The Project Life Cycle and Project Planning Activities

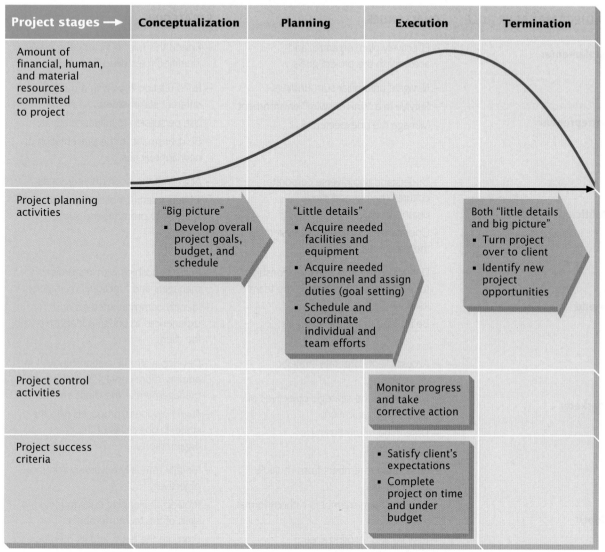

Source: Adapted in part from Figure 1.2 and discussion in Jeffrey K. Pinto and O. P. Kharbanda, Successful Project Managers: Leading Your Team to Success (New York: Van Nostrand Reinhold, 1995), pp. 17–21.

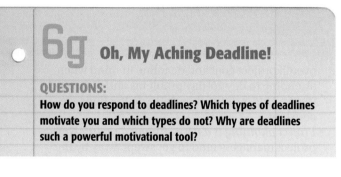

6g **Oh, My Aching Deadline!**

QUESTIONS:
How do you respond to deadlines? Which types of deadlines motivate you and which types do not? Why are deadlines such a powerful motivational tool?

PROJECT MANAGEMENT GUIDELINES. Project managers need a working knowledge of basic planning concepts and tools, as presented in this chapter (see Window on the World). Beyond that, they need to be aware of the following special planning demands of projects.

- *Projects are schedule-driven and results-oriented.* By definition, projects are created to accomplish

TABLE **6.2** Roles, Challenges, and Strategies for Effective Project Managers

PROJECT MANAGER ROLE	CHALLENGES	STRATEGIES
Implementer	– Effectively plan, organize, and accomplish the project goals.	– Extend this role to include the newly identified roles described.
Entrepreneur	– Navigate unfamiliar surroundings. – Survive in a "sink or swim" environment. – Manage the unexpected.	– Build relationships with a number of different stakeholders. – Use persuasion to influence others. – Be charismatic in the presentation of new approaches.
Politician	– Understand two diverse corporate cultures (parent and client organizations). – Operate within the political system of the client organization.	– Align with the powerful individuals. – Obtain a senior/politically savvy client sponsor to promote and support the project.
Friend	– Determine the important relationships to build and sustain outside the team itself. – Be a friend to the client.	– Build friendships with key project managers and functional managers. – Identify common interests and experiences to bridge a friendship with the client.
Marketer	– Access client corporate strategic information. – Understand the strategic objectives of the client organization. – Determine future business opportunities.	– Develop a strong relationship with the primary client contact and with top management in the client organization. – Align new ideas/proposals with the strategic objectives of the client organization.
Coach	– Blend team members from multiple organizations. – Motivate team members without formal authority. – Reward and recognize team accomplishments with limited resources.	– Identify mutually rewarding common objectives. – Provide challenging tasks to build the skills of the team members. – Promote the team and its members to key decision makers.

Source: Academy of Management Executive: The Thinking Manager's Source by Sheila Simsarian Webber and Maria Torti. Copyright 2004 by Academy of Management (NY). Reproduced with permission of Academy of Management (NY) in the format Textbook via Copyright Clearance Center.

something specific by a certain time. Project managers require a positive attitude about making lots of quick decisions and doing things in a hurry. They tend to value results more than process.

• *The big picture and the little details are of equal importance.* Project managers need to keep the overall project goal and deadline in mind when attending to day-to-day problems and personnel issues. This is difficult because distractions are constant.

• *Project planning is a necessity, not a luxury.* Novice project managers tend to get swept away by the

WINDOW ON THE WORLD

How a Global Investment Bank Avoids E-mail Overload on Projects with a Wiki*

Dresdner Kleinwort Wasserstein uses a Socialtext wiki to create meeting agendas and post training videos for new hires. Participants in a project can avoid endless e-mail exchanges and instead post documents, schedules, and other materials on a wiki Web site, which anyone else on the project can then append with changes or comments. Six months after launching it, traffic on the 2,500-plus-page wiki, used by a quarter of the bank's workforce, has surpassed that of the company's intranet. And there has been a 75% drop in the number of e-mails on projects using wikis.

*"A wiki is a collaborative website which can be directly edited by anyone with access to it."

Sources: Robert D. Hof, "Web 2.0: The New Guy at Work," Business Week (June 19, 2006): 59; and **wikipedia.org.**

pressure for results and fail to devote adequate time and resources to project planning.

- *Project managers know the motivational power of a deadline.* A challenging (but not impossible) project deadline is the project manager's most powerful motivational tool. The final deadline serves as a focal point for all team and individual goal setting.[56]

GRAPHICAL PLANNING/ SCHEDULING/ CONTROL TOOLS

Management science specialists have introduced needed precision into the planning/control cycle through graphical analysis. Three graphical tools for planning, scheduling, and controlling operations are flow charts, Gantt charts, and PERT networks. They can be found in project management software programs.

Sequencing with Flow Charts

Flow charts have been used extensively by computer programmers for identifying task components and by TQM (total quality management) teams for *work simplification* (eliminating wasted steps and activities). Beyond that, flow charts are a useful sequencing tool with broad application.[57] Sequencing is simply arranging events in the order of their actual or desired occurrence. For instance, this book had to be purchased before it could be read. Thus the event "purchase book" would come before the event "read book" in a flow chart for completing assignments in this course.

A sample flow chart is given in Figure 6.7. Note that the chart consists of boxes and diamonds in addition to the start and stop ovals. Each box contains a major event, and each diamond contains a yes-or-no decision.

Managers at all levels and in all specialized areas can identify and properly sequence important events and decisions with flow charts of this kind. User-friendly computer programs make flow-charting fun and easy today. Flow charts force people to consider all relevant links in a particular endeavor, as well as their proper sequence. This is an advantage because it encourages analytical thinking. But flow charts have two disadvantages. First, they do not indicate the time dimension—that is, the varying amounts of time

FIGURE **6.7** A Sample Flow Chart

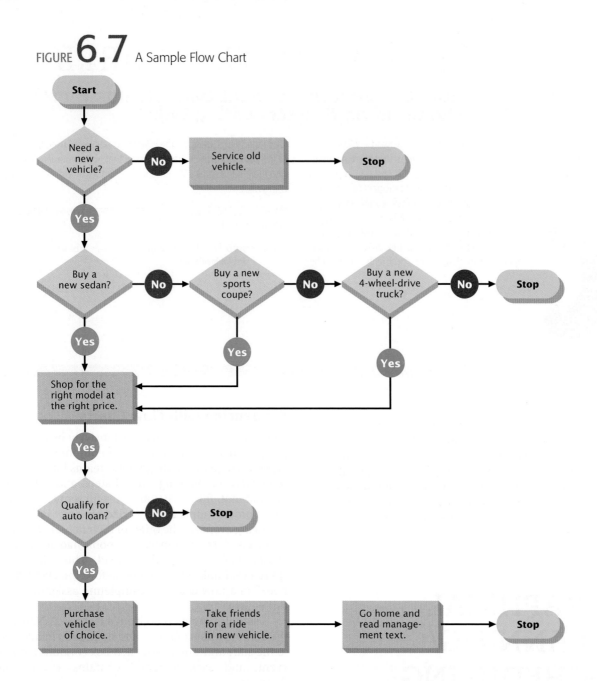

required to complete each step and make each decision. Second, the use of flow charts is not practical for complex endeavors in which several activities take place at once.

Scheduling with Gantt Charts

Scheduling is an important part of effective planning. When later steps depend on the successful completion of earlier steps, schedules help managers determine when and where resources are needed. Without schedules, inefficiency creeps in as equipment and people stand idle. Also, like any type of plan or budget, schedules provide management with a measuring stick for corrective action. Gantt charts, named for Henry L. Gantt, who developed the technique, are a convenient scheduling tool for managers.[58] Gantt worked with Frederick W. Taylor at Midvale Steel beginning in 1887 and, as discussed in Chapter 2, helped refine the practice of scientific management.

FIGURE **6.8** A Sample Gantt Chart

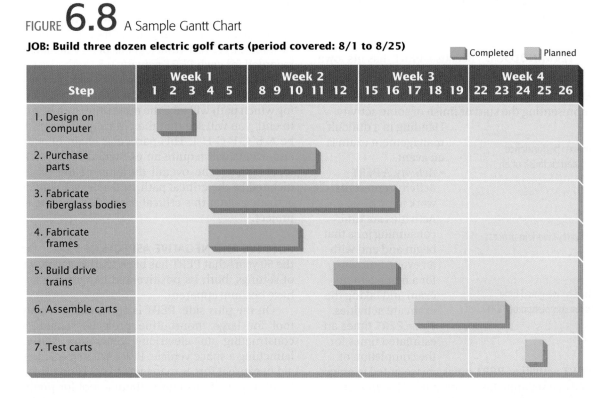

JOB: Build three dozen electric golf carts (period covered: 8/1 to 8/25)

Completed | Planned

Step	Week 1 1 2 3 4 5	Week 2 8 9 10 11 12	Week 3 15 16 17 18 19	Week 4 22 23 24 25 26
1. Design on computer				
2. Purchase parts				
3. Fabricate fiberglass bodies				
4. Fabricate frames				
5. Build drive trains				
6. Assemble carts				
7. Test carts				

A **Gantt chart** is a graphical scheduling technique historically used in production operations. Things have changed since Gantt's time, and so have Gantt chart applications. Updated versions like the one in Figure 6.8 are widely used today for planning and scheduling all sorts of organizational activities. They are especially useful for large projects such as moving into a new building or installing a new computer network.[59]

Gantt chart: graphical scheduling technique

Figure 6.8 also shows how a Gantt chart can be used for more than just scheduling the important steps of a job. Filling in the timelines of completed activities makes it possible to assess *actual* progress at a glance. Like flow charts, Gantt charts force managers to be analytical as they reduce jobs or projects to separate steps. Moreover, Gantt charts improve on flow charts by allowing the planner to specify the time to be spent on each activity. A disadvantage Gantt charts share with flow charts is that overly complex endeavors are cumbersome to chart.

PERT Networks

The more complex the project, the greater the need for reliable sequencing and scheduling of key activities. Simultaneous sequencing and scheduling amounts to programming. One of the most widely recognized programming tools used by managers is a technique referred to simply as PERT. An acronym for **Program Evaluation and Review Technique (PERT)** is a graphical sequencing and scheduling tool for large, complex, and nonroutine projects.

Program Evaluation and Review Technique (PERT): graphical sequencing and scheduling tool for complex projects

HISTORY OF PERT. PERT was developed in 1958 by a team of management consultants for the U.S. Navy Special Projects Office. At the time, the navy was faced with the seemingly insurmountable task of building a weapon system that could fire a missile from the deck of a submerged submarine. PERT not only contributed to the development of the Polaris submarine project but also was credited with helping to bring the system to combat readiness nearly two years ahead of schedule. News of this dramatic administrative feat caught the attention of managers around the world. But, as one user of PERT reflected, "No management technique has ever caused so much enthusiasm, controversy, and disappointment as PERT."[60] Realizing that PERT is not a panacea, but rather a specialized planning and control tool that can be appropriately or inappropriately applied, helps managers accept it at face value.[61]

PERT TERMINOLOGY.   Because PERT has its own special language, four key terms must be understood.

- *Event.* A **PERT event** is a performance milestone representing the start or finish of some activity. Handing in a difficult management exam is an event.

PERT event: performance milestone; start or finish of an activity

- *Activity.* A **PERT activity** represents work in process. Activities are time-consuming jobs that begin and end with an event. Studying for a management exam and taking the exam are activities.

PERT activity: work in process

- *Time.* **PERT times** are estimated times for the completion of PERT activities. PERT times are weighted averages of three separate time estimates: (1) *optimistic time* (T_o)—the time an activity should take under the best of conditions; (2) *most likely time* (T_m)—the time an activity should take under normal conditions; and (3) *pessimistic time* (T_p)—the time an activity should take under the worst possible conditions. The formula for calculating estimated PERT time (T_e) is

PERT times: weighted time estimates for completion of PERT activities

$$T_e = \frac{T_o + 4T_m + T_p}{6}$$

- *Critical path.* The **critical path** is the most time-consuming chain of activities and events in a PERT network. In other words, the longest path through a PERT network is critical because if any of the activities along it are delayed, the entire project will be delayed accordingly.[62]

critical path: most time-consuming route through a PERT network

PERT IN ACTION.   A PERT network is shown in Figure 6.9. The task in this example, the design and construction of three dozen customized golf carts for use by physically challenged adults, is relatively simple for instructional purposes. PERT networks are usually reserved for more complex projects with hundreds or even thousands of activities. PERT events are coded by circled letters, and PERT activities, shown by the arrows connecting the PERT events, are coded by number. A PERT time (T_e) has been calculated and recorded for each PERT activity.

Before reading on, see if you can pick out the critical path in the PERT network in Figure 6.9. By calculating which path will take the most time from beginning to end, you will see that the critical path turns out to be A-B-C-F-G-H-I. This particular chain of activities and events will require an estimated 21.75 workdays to complete. The overall duration of the project is dictated by the critical path, and a delay in any of the activities along this critical path will delay the entire project.

POSITIVE AND NEGATIVE ASPECTS OF PERT.   During the 50 years that PERT has been used in a wide variety of settings, both its positive and its negative aspects have become apparent.

On the plus side, PERT is an excellent scheduling tool for large, nonroutine projects, ranging from constructing an electricity generation station to launching a space vehicle. PERT is a helpful planning aid because it forces managers to envision projects in their entirety. It also gives them a tool for predicting resource needs, potential problem areas, and the impact of delays on project completion. If an activity runs over or under its estimated time, the ripple effect of lost or gained time on down-stream activities can be calculated. PERT also gives managers an opportunity, through the calculation of optimistic and pessimistic times, to factor in realistic uncertainties about planning horizons.

On the minus side, PERT is an inappropriate tool for repetitive assembly-line operations in which scheduling is dictated by the pace of machines. PERT also shares with other planning and decision-making aids the disadvantage of being only as good as its underlying assumptions. False assumptions about activities and events and miscalculations of PERT times can render PERT ineffective. Despite the objective impression of numerical calculations, PERT times are derived rather subjectively. Moreover, PERT's critics say it is too time-consuming: A complex PERT network prepared by hand may be obsolete by the time it is completed, and frequent updates can tie PERT in knots. Project management software with computerized PERT routines is essential for complex projects because it can greatly speed the graphical plotting process and updating of time estimates.

FIGURE **6.9** A Sample PERT Network

TASK: Build three dozen customized golf carts for use by physically challenged adults

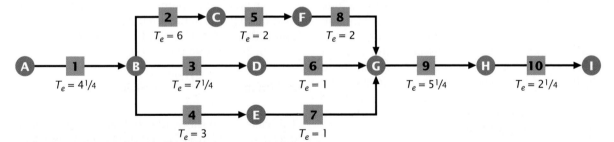

PERT events		PERT activities and times				
	Activities	T_o	T_m	T_p	T_e*
A. Receive contract	1. Prepare final design	3	4	6	$4^1/_4$
B. Begin construction	2. Purchase parts	4	5	12	6
C. Receive parts	3. Fabricate bodies	5	$7^1/_2$	9	$7^1/_4$
D. Bodies ready for testing	4. Fabricate frames	$2^1/_2$	3	4	3
E. Frames ready for testing	5. Build drive trains	$1^1/_2$	2	3	2
F. Drive trains ready for testing	6. Test bodies	$^1/_2$	1	$1^1/_2$	1
G. Components ready for assembly	7. Test frames	$^1/_2$	1	$1^1/_2$	1
H. Carts assembled	8. Test drive trains	1	$1^1/_2$	5	2
I. Carts ready for shipment	9. Assemble carts	3	5	9	$5^1/_4$
	10. Test carts	1	2	5	$2^1/_4$

*Rounded to nearest $^1/_4$ workday

BREAK-EVEN ANALYSIS

In well-managed businesses, profit is a forethought rather than an afterthought. A widely used tool for projecting profits relative to costs and sales volume is break-even analysis. In fact, break-even analysis is often referred to as cost-volume-profit analysis. By using either the algebraic method or the graphical method, planners can calculate the **break-even point**, the level of sales at which the firm neither suffers a loss nor realizes a profit. In effect, the break-even point is the profit-making threshold. If sales are below that point, the organization loses money. If sales go beyond the break-even point, it makes a profit. Break-even points, as discussed later, are often expressed in units. An example is Europe's Airbus Industrie's huge 555-passenger commercial airliner that went into service in 2007. The break-even point for the $300 million double-deck A380 reportedly is about 250 units.[63]

From a procedural standpoint, a critical part of break-even analysis is separating fixed costs from variable costs.

Fixed versus Variable Costs

Some expenses, called fixed costs, must be paid even if a firm fails to sell a single unit. Other expenses, termed variable costs, are incurred only as units are produced and sold. **Fixed costs** are contractual costs that must be paid regardless of the level of output or sales. Typical examples include rent, utilities, insurance premiums, managerial and professional staff salaries,

> **break-even point:** level of sales at which there is no loss or profit

> **fixed costs:** contractual costs that must be paid regardless of output or sales

property taxes, and licenses. **Variable costs** are costs that vary directly with the firm's production and sales. Common variable costs include costs of production (such as labor, materials, and supplies), sales commissions, and product delivery expenses. As output and sales increase, fixed costs remain the same but variable costs accumulate. Looking at it another way, fixed costs are a function of *time* and variable costs are a function of *volume*. You can now calculate the break-even point.

variable costs: costs that vary directly with production and sales

The Algebraic Method

Where the following abbreviations are used,

 FC = total fixed costs
 P = price (per unit)
 VC = variable costs (per unit)
 BEP = break-even point

the formula for calculating break-even point (in units) is

$$BEP(\text{in units}) = \frac{FC}{P - VC}$$

The difference between the selling price P and per-unit variable costs VC is referred to as the **contribution margin**. In other words, the contribution margin is the portion of the unit selling price that falls above and beyond the variable costs and that

contribution margin: selling price per unit minus variable costs per unit

can be applied to fixed costs. Above the break-even point, the contribution margin contributes to profits.

Variable costs are normally expressed as a percentage of the unit selling price. As a working example of how the break-even point (in units) can be calculated, assume that a firm has total fixed costs of $30,000, a unit selling price of $7, and variable costs of 57 percent (or $4 in round numbers).

$$BEP(\text{in units}) = \frac{30,000}{7 - 4} = 10,000$$

This calculation shows that 10,000 units must be produced and sold at $7 each if the firm is to break even on this particular product.

PRICE PLANNING. Break-even analysis is an excellent "what-if" tool for planners who want to know what impact price changes will have on profit. For instance, what would the break-even point be if the unit selling price were lowered to match a competitor's price of $6?

$$BEP(\text{in units}) = \frac{30,000}{6 - 4} = 15,000$$

In this case, the $1 drop in price to $6 means that 15,000 units must be sold before a profit can be realized.

PROFIT PLANNING. Planners often set profit objectives and then work backwards to determine the required level of output. Break-even analysis greatly assists such planners. The modified break-even formula for profit planning is

$$BEP(\text{in units}) = \frac{FC + \text{desired profit}}{P - VC}$$

Dairy farming is an endless struggle with break-even analysis. Lisa Kaiman, seen here with some heifers on her 33-acre farm in Chester, Vermont, is being squeezed by higher costs and lower milk prices. It's no surprise that Vermont's 11,206 dairy farms in 1947 are now down to fewer than 1,500 today.

Assuming that top management has set a profit objective for the year at $30,000 and that the original figures above apply, the following calculation results:

$$BEP(\text{in units}) = \frac{30{,}000 + 30{,}000}{7 - 4} = 20{,}000$$

To meet the profit objective of $30,000, the company would need to sell 20,000 units at $7 each.

The Graphical Method

If you place the dollar value of costs and revenues on a vertical axis and unit sales on a horizontal axis, you can calculate the break-even point by plotting fixed costs, total costs (fixed + variable costs), and total revenue. As illustrated in Figure 6.10, the break-even point is where the total costs line and the total sales revenue line intersect.

Although the algebraic method does the same job, some planners prefer the graphical method because it presents the various cost-volume-profit relationships at a glance, in a convenient visual format.

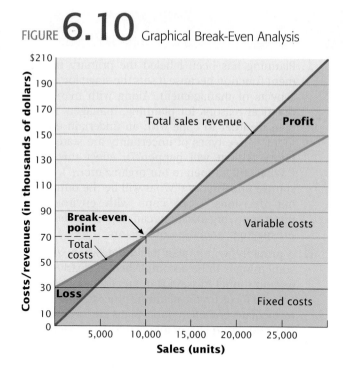

FIGURE **6.10** Graphical Break-Even Analysis

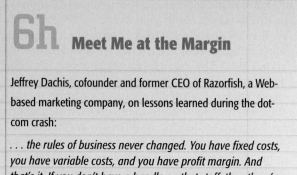

6h Meet Me at the Margin

Jeffrey Dachis, cofounder and former CEO of Razorfish, a Web-based marketing company, on lessons learned during the dot-com crash:

. . . the rules of business never changed. You have fixed costs, you have variable costs, and you have profit margin. And that's it. If you don't have a handle on that stuff, then there's nothing else to talk about. If there is no profit margin, you're in trouble.

Source: As quoted in Fast Company, no. 80 (March 2004): 51.

QUESTION:
What is the connection between this statement and break-even analysis?

Break-Even Analysis: Strengths and Limitations

Like the other planning tools discussed in this chapter, break-even analysis is not a cure-all. It has both strengths and limitations.

On the positive side, break-even analysis forces planners to acknowledge and deal realistically with the interrelatedness of cost, volume, and profit. All three variables are connected such that a change in one sends ripples of change through the other two. As mentioned earlier, break-even analysis allows planners to ask what-if questions concerning the impact of price changes and varying profit objectives.

The primary problem with break-even analysis is that neatly separating fixed and variable costs can be very difficult. General managers should enlist the help of accountants to isolate relevant fixed and variable costs. Moreover, because of complex factors in supply and demand, break-even analysis is not a good tool for setting prices. It serves better as a general planning and decision-making aid.

SUMMARY

1. Planning has been labeled the primary management function because it sets the stage for all other aspects of management. Along with many other practical reasons for planning, managers need to plan in order to cope with an uncertain environment. Three types of uncertainty are state uncertainty ("What will happen?"), effect uncertainty ("What will happen to our organization?"), and response uncertainty ("What will be the outcome of our decisions?"). To cope with environmental uncertainty, organizations can respond as defenders, prospectors, analyzers, or reactors.

2. A properly written plan tells what, when, and how something is to be accomplished. A clearly written organizational mission statement tends to serve as a useful focus for the planning process. Strategic, intermediate, and operational plans are formulated by top, middle, and lower management, respectively.

3. Objectives have been called the single most important feature of the planning process. Well-written objectives spell out, in measurable terms, what should be accomplished and when it is to be accomplished. Good objectives help managers by serving as targets, acting as measuring sticks, encouraging commitment, and strengthening motivation. Objective setting begins at the top of the organization and filters down, thus forming a means-ends chain. Priorities affect resource allocation by assigning relative importance to objectives. Plans are formulated and executed as part of a more encompassing planning/control cycle.

4. Management by objectives (MBO), an approach to planning and controlling, is based on measurable and participatively set objectives. MBO basically consists of four steps: (1) setting objectives participatively, (2) developing action plans, (3) periodically reevaluating objectives and plans and monitoring performance, and (4) conducting annual performance appraisals. Objective setting in MBO flows from top to bottom. MBO has both strengths and limitations and requires a supportive climate favorable to change, participation, and the sharing of authority.

5. Project planning occurs throughout the project life cycle's four stages: conceptualization, planning, execution, and termination. "Big-picture" tactical planning—project goal, budget, and schedule—occurs during stage 1 and into stage 2. During stage 2 and into the execution phase in stage 3, project planning deals with the "little details" of facilities and equipment, personnel and job assignments, and scheduling. Starting near the end of stage 3 and carrying into the termination stage, both little-details and big-picture planning are required to pass the project along and identify new project opportunities. Planning is central to project success because projects are schedule-driven and results-oriented. Project planners need to keep constantly abreast of both the big picture and the little details. Novice project managers too often shortchange planning. Challenging but realistic project deadlines are project managers' most powerful motivational tool. Six roles performed by effective project managers are implementer, entrepreneur, politician, friend, marketer, and coach.

6. Flow charts, Gantt charts, and PERT networks, found in project management software packages, are three graphical tools for more effectively planning, scheduling, and controlling operations. Flow charts visually sequence important events and yes-or-no decisions. Gantt charts, named for Frederick W. Taylor's disciple Henry L. Gantt, are a graphical scheduling technique used in a wide variety of situations. Both flow charts and Gantt charts have the advantage of forcing managers to be analytical. But Gantt charts realistically portray the time dimension, whereas flow charts do not. PERT, which stands for Program Evaluation and Review Technique, is a sequencing and scheduling tool appropriate for large, complex, and nonroutine projects. Weighted PERT times enable managers to factor in their uncertainties about time estimates.

7. Break-even analysis, or cost-volume-profit analysis, can be carried out algebraically or graphically. Either way, it helps planners gauge the potential impact of price changes and profit objectives on sales volume. A major limitation of break-even analysis is that specialized accounting knowledge is required to identify relevant fixed and variable costs.

TERMS TO UNDERSTAND

- **Planning,** p. 147
- **State uncertainty,** p. 147
- **Effect uncertainty,** p. 148
- **Response uncertainty,** p. 148
- **Plan,** p. 151
- **Strategic planning,** p. 152
- **Intermediate planning,** p. 152
- **Operational planning,** p. 152
- **Planning horizon,** p. 153

- **Objective,** p. 153
- **Priorities,** p. 155
- **80/20 principle,** p. 155
- **Management by objectives (MBO),** p. 157
- **Project,** p. 159
- **Gantt chart,** p. 165
- **Program Evaluation and Review Technique (PERT),** p. 165

- **PERT event,** p. 166
- **PERT activity,** p. 166
- **PERT times,** p. 166
- **Critical path,** p. 166
- **Break-even point,** p. 167
- **Fixed costs,** p. 167
- **Variable costs,** p. 168
- **Contribution margin,** p. 168

MANAGER'S TOOLKIT

Ten Common Errors to Avoid When Writing a Plan for a New Business

Here are errors in business plan preparation that almost certainly will result in denial of a loan application by a bank.

- Submitting a "rough copy," perhaps with coffee stains on the pages and crossed-out words in the text, tells the banker that the owner doesn't take his idea seriously.
- Outdated historical financial information or industry comparisons will leave doubts about the entrepreneur's planning abilities.
- Unsubstantiated assumptions can hurt a business plan; the business owner must be prepared to explain the "whys" of every point in the plan.
- Too much "blue sky"—a failure to consider prospective pitfalls—will lead the banker to conclude that the idea is not realistic.
- A lack of understanding of the financial information is a drawback. Even if an outside source is used to prepare the projections, the owner must fully comprehend the information.
- Absence of any consideration of outside influences is a gap in a business plan. The owner

needs to discuss the potential impact of competitive factors as well as the economic environment prevalent at the time of the request.

- No indication that the owner has anything at stake in the venture is a particular problem. The lender will expect the entrepreneur to have some equity capital invested in the business.
- Unwillingness to personally guarantee any loans raises a question: If the business owner isn't willing to stand behind his or her company, then why should the bank?
- Introducing the plan with a demand for unrealistic loan terms is a mistake. The lender wants to find out about the viability of the business before discussing loan terms.
- Too much focus on collateral is a problem in a business plan. Even for a cash-secured loan, the banker is looking toward projected profits for repayment of the loan. The emphasis should be on cash flow.

Source: J. Tol Broome Jr., "Mistakes to Avoid in Drafting a Plan," Nation's Business, 81 (February 1993): 30. Reprinted by permission, uschamber.com, April 2008. Copyright 1993, U.S. Chamber of Commerce.

ACTION LEARNING EXERCISE

How to Write Good Objectives and Plans (Plan = What + When + How)

Instructions: Well-written objectives are the heart of effective planning. An objective should state *what* is to be accomplished (in measurable terms) and *when* it will be accomplished. An objective becomes a plan when the *how* is added. Here is an everyday example of a well-written plan: "I will ("what?") lose 5 pounds ("when?") in 30 days ("how?") by not eating desserts and walking a mile four days a week."

Remember the following handy three-way test to assess how well your plans are written.

- Test 1: Does this plan specify *what* the intended result is, and is it stated in *measurable* terms?
- Test 2: Does this plan specify *when* the intended result is to be accomplished?
- Test 3: Does this plan specify *how* the intended result is to be accomplished?

Write a plan that passes all three tests for each of the following areas of your life.

Self-improvement plan: What? _____

When? _____

How? _____

Work-related plan: What? _____

When? _____

How? _____

Community-service plan: What? _____

When? _____

How? _____

For Consideration/Discussion

1. In terms of the above three-way test, which of your plans is the best? Why? Which is the worst? Why?

2. What is the hardest part of writing good plans? Explain.

3. From a managerial standpoint, why is it important to have plans written in measurable terms?

4. What is the managerial value of formally written plans, as opposed to verbal commitments?

5. Why would some employees resist writing plans according to the specifications in this exercise? Explain.

CLOSING CASE
Ford's Hybrid SUV Team Races to the Finish

In the spring of 2003, Phil Martens saw trouble down the road. As head of product development for Ford, he was supervising the creation of what could be one of the most important vehicles in company history. While the car wasn't due to come out until the fall of 2004, the team needed to be in launch mode right then to stay on schedule.

It wasn't. It was still pulling marathon hours just trying to get the thing running properly.

The vehicle was the much-anticipated gas-electric hybrid that CEO Bill Ford Jr. had been touting for a couple of years as emblematic of the new, environmentally friendly Ford. The Ford Escape Hybrid would be the first hybrid SUV; it would handle like a muscular V-6, yet sip gas—36 miles per gallon, about 50% better than a standard Escape; its emissions would be minuscule. It was the most technically advanced product the automaker had ever attempted to put into mass production.

The hybrid team was packed with PhDs, but for all of their technical prowess, the brainiacs had one weakness: little launch experience. Martens needed someone to crack the whip without destroying morale, someone to persuade the scientists to stop perfecting and start finishing the vehicle. That someone was Mary Ann Wright—part spark plug, part disciplinarian, and all Ford.

A self-described "car nut," Wright, 42, has launched Sables, Tauruses, and Lincolns. Her discipline is legendary. Twelve-plus-hour days. Five hours of sleep. Four A.M. workouts. She has blond bangs, blue eyes, a firm handshake, and the confidence of someone who doesn't miss deadlines. "My launches are really, really good," she says. Somehow this doesn't come across as a boast.

Even with Wright on board, staying on schedule wasn't a sure thing. Introducing one major technology is a challenge. The Escape Hybrid contains nine such technologies. By the time Ford sends it to dealers in September, this SUV will have been in the works for a little more than five years. In addition to overcoming herculean technical hurdles, Ford collaborated with suppliers around the globe. "This is an unusually complex team with little or no experience with hybrid technology," says Martens, "and they're introducing this unusually complex technology into a mainstream manufacturing system without any flaws." . . .

Creating a dramatically different product is a staggering challenge for any organization, but for the oldest and second-largest American automaker, it's a higher, steeper mountain to scale. Ford Motor Co. has been making cars for 101 years—cars with one motor. Open the hood of a hybrid, and you'll find two: one gas, the other electric.

As a "full" hybrid, the Escape can run on either motor. Its network monitors an array of computers to determine which motor can drive the wheels most efficiently. In an instant, the vehicle balances the dueling demands for power and acceleration and for high mileage and low emissions. For team member Tom Gee, Ford's announcement of a mass-produced hybrid was "the equivalent of Kennedy saying, 'We're going to the moon by the end of the decade.'" At Ford, vehicle programs are typically ranked 1 to 10, according to the complexity of the power train. "This was a 20," says longtime researcher Mike Tamor.

The stakes are particularly high because Honda and Toyota introduced their hybrids in the United States first—in 1999 and 2000, respectively. Although they lacked the power and roominess of conventional cars, the first gas-electric models found a niche audience. Last year, Toyota released a zippier Prius, but Ford insists that its Escape is going where no hybrid has gone before: into the mainstream. The pitch? No compromises on acceleration, towing capacity, cargo space, fuel economy, or emissions. Not only is it the first hybrid manufactured by an American automaker, but it's also the first hybrid SUV. Ford has plenty of competition in the rearview mirror, though; over the next three years, the major automakers plan to release 20 new hybrids, many of them SUVs and trucks. . . .

Ford's Escape Hybrid program got its start in a Toyota Prius, of all places. After being tapped to head the team in late 1998, Prabhaker Patil went for a test drive with then-chairman Alex Trotman. As the two had suspected, the soon-to-be-released Prius sacrificed too much performance. Trotman insisted that Ford's hybrid do better.

To develop its unconventional vehicle, Ford created an unconventional team. Typically, researchers and product engineers don't work closely together. At Ford, in fact, they work in different buildings. Researchers act as consultants; they share their expertise while commuting from the Ford Scientific Research Laboratory. But Ford's team would itself be a hybrid: scientists and product engineers inventing and building software and hardware together, then shepherding their creation through production. "The people story is as interesting as the technology story," says Wright.

Patil, 54, was a hybrid himself, a PhD scientist who worked in Ford's lab for more than 15 years and then in product development for the past four. He sought team members he knew would be open to collaboration. They included Anand Sankaran, 39, who holds a doctorate in electrical engineering and is a nine-year veteran of the research lab. "It has always been my wish to take something into product production," he says. Still, Sankaran was curious about the fit. "There was a little bit of concern, because I come from a background where I deal more with solving problems technically but it's not fine-tuned to be put easily into production."

The creative tension often centered on deadlines. "On one side, you have people with program discipline who said, 'This has to happen at this point and at this point,'" Patil says, "and the other side would say, 'Oh you want to time an invention?'" . . .

Internally, the hybrid team is simply Team U293. It occupies a long stretch of gray cubicles a one-minute walk from the tinted glass door of one of Bill Ford's offices. The bulletin board celebrates new babies and new patents ("Method for controlling an internal combustion engine during engine shutdown to reduce evaporative emissions"). Schedules wallpaper the conference room, along with a banner that says, "By When?"

The office feels ordinary, but for Ford it is revolutionary. Engineers and scientists work in adjacent cubicles. "Before, it might have been a half a mile apart, but even one building away is a barrier compared with what we have now," says Gee. "It makes a huge difference." Group lunches in the nearby cafeteria evolve into meetings. Hallway chats lead to impromptu problem solving. Once, a couple of engineers at the soda machine discovered a discrepancy in a power-train specification and corrected the issue before the code was written. With thousands of tasks on the to-do list, preventing a problem is as sweet as solving one.

The hybrid group has become the envy of other Ford engineers. "I have engineers who say, 'I wish I could be on that team,'" says Craig Rigby, a technical support supervisor. "Then I tell them the hours." As a way of motivating his weary team, Patil would remind them how fortunate they were. "This was a product that if you did it right, it was going to do a great deal for customers and the company and the country and the environment," he says. "You rarely get a chance to go after something like this in your career. It's what I call the nobility of the cause." . . .

After putting his foot down in the spring of 2003 about the Escape Hybrid's launch, Martens gave the team a rare gift: no outside interruptions. From May through December, it wouldn't have to do management reviews and other presentations. Martens would check in periodically and test-drive the latest prototype so he could keep his bosses informed. "I was getting questions from above," he says. "Weekly." A grin. "Daily."

During this "dark period," Martens says, "I allowed them to be entrepreneurial, and they doubled their productivity." Issues that had been stalled for months got resolved: reaching the fuel economy goal and building the first preproduction model. "The same people who had been coming into my office saying, 'I don't know how we're going to get there,' were saying within weeks and months, 'My God, we can get there,'" Wright recalls. . . .

Wright put the pedal to the metal. "Every day is a lost day," she would tell the team. She quickly established a launch plan and a "meeting cadence": daily get-togethers at 8 A.M. for two hours, with suppliers in Germany and Japan participating by video. There were also weekly meetings with chief engineers and technical forums to tackle specific issues. Wright devoured the details. "Most chiefs won't do that. I find it helps motivate people and helps educate me."

Launch mode meant acting as an even more integrated team. During the design phase, small groups had focused on each system to master its separate technology. Now the challenge was orchestrating the interaction between systems. "I told them, 'If one person is struggling, we're all struggling,'" says Wright. She could be tough, but Martens believed she was what the team needed, just as Patil and his more collegial style had been effective in development. She was the hybrid team's second motor; if Patil's job was to inspire invention, hers was to wrap it up.

Letting go didn't come naturally to scientists like Sankaran. One of his goals was eliminating extraneous engine noise. Like a conductor with extraordinary hearing, he could detect an occasional, almost imperceptible high-pitched tone even though the transmission met the noise requirements. Technically—officially—it was good to go. But, Sankaran says, "as an engineer I wanted to say, 'What are the physics behind this sound? I can do better.'" Ultimately, though, he was persuaded to let it go by taking consolation in another of Wright's reminders: "This isn't the only one we'll do." There will be more hybrids down the road.

Source: Excerpted from Chuck Salter, "Ford's Escape Route," *Fast Company,* no. 87 (October 2004): 106–110. Reprinted by permission.

FOR DISCUSSION

1 Which stages of the project life cycle in Figure 6.6 are evident in this case? Explain.

2 Was it a good idea for Phil Martens, head of product development, to have two project managers—first Prabhaker Patil and then Mary Ann Wright—to head the Escape Hybrid project? Explain.

3 From a project manager's standpoint, what are the toughest challenges with this sort of high-visibility, high-risk project? Explain.

4 Which of the project manager roles in Table 6.2 did Mary Ann Wright play in this case? Explain.

5 Would you like to have been a member of this team? Why or why not?

TEST PREPPER

True/False Questions

_____ 1. State, effect, and response uncertainty are three types of environmental uncertainty that people perceive, according to research.

_____ 2. Analyzer organizations have a reputation for aggressively making things happen, rather than waiting for them to happen.

_____ 3. Mission statements have little practical value today because everything is changing so fast.

_____ 4. By definition, an objective deals with achieving a measurable result without regard to time.

_____ 5. "C" objectives are in the "nice to do" category in the A-B-C priority system.

_____ 6. Monitoring performance, step 2 in the MBO cycle, is the most important step.

_____ 7. Among the six roles that project managers play are friend and marketer.

_____ 8. Planned as well as actual progress can be plotted on a Gantt chart.

_____ 9. Work in process is represented by a PERT event.

_____10. Both fixed costs and variable costs need to be calculated when doing a break-even analysis.

Multiple-Choice Questions

1. Which sort of uncertainty is related to being unable to predict the consequences of a particular decision?
   A. Effect   B. State
   C. Response   D. Economic
   E. Macro

2. A good example of a(n) _____ is motorcycle maker Harley-Davidson, because it successfully produces and markets a few products in a narrowly defined market.
   A. reactor   B. prospector
   C. defender   D. opportunist
   E. analyzer

3. Two key components of a plan are
   A. an objective and an action statement.
   B. a budget and an alternative plan.
   C. a strategy and an estimated budget.
   D. a sales forecast and an operations analysis.
   E. a time line and an action statement.

4. Which type of planning involves determining how specific tasks can best be accomplished on time with available resources?
   A. Budgetary   B. Operational
   C. Strategic   D. Intermediate
   E. Contingency

5. Objectives are both targets and
   A. barriers.   B. measuring sticks.
   C. threats.   D. priorities.
   E. flow charts.

6. The _____ asserts that a minority of causes, inputs, or effort usually is responsible for a majority of the results, outputs, or rewards.
   A. MBO cycle
   B. principle of diminishing returns
   C. project life cycle
   D. PERT network
   E. 80/20 principle

7. _____ is the second step in the MBO process.
   A. Reviewing plans
   B. Performance appraisal
   C. Task analysis
   D. Developing action plans
   E. Setting objectives

8. _____ is not one of the roles played by project managers.
   A. Entrepreneur   B. Friend
   C. Politician   D. Scheduler
   E. Marketer

9. The boxes on a flow chart contain
   A. cost estimates.   B. time estimates.
   C. major events.   D. potential barriers.
   E. key decisions.

10. If a candle factory has fixed costs of $40,000, a unit selling price of $10, and a variable cost per unit of $6, its break-even point in units is
    A. 13,000.
    B. 3,000.
    C. 10,000.
    D. impossible to determine without more data.
    E. 2,500.

See page T1 at the back of the text for answers to these questions. Want more questions? Visit the student Web site and take the ACE quizzes for more practice.

7

Strategic

Management

Planning for

Long-Term

Success

The minute you've developed a new business model, it's extinct, because somebody is going to copy it.[1]
—INDRA NOOYI, CEO, PepsiCo

THE CHANGING WORKPLACE

The Cheese Queen's Bid for a Bigger Slice

Moments after finishing a rousing speech to thousands of employees on her return to Kraft Foods . . . [in 2006], Irene Rosenfeld walked upstairs from the company's sprawling Northfield, Ill., headquarters cafeteria to the wood-paneled executive suite. There the new CEO discovered that a special passkey was needed for employees to access the floor. Kraft's reenergized staffers literally couldn't follow her into battle.

So in her first official act Rosenfeld unlocked the doors, and in doing so ushered in (she hopes) a new era at a company in dire need of a shakeup. "It was a metaphor for what this company can become—and needs to become," she says. If only it were that easy. Rosenfeld, 53, who spent 22 years at Kraft before leaving to run Frito-Lay in 2004, now has to unlock the potential of a $34 billion behemoth once the envy of the food industry for its profitable stable of beloved brands—Oscar Mayer, Jell-O, Oreo—and a management bench headhunters drooled over.

In 1988, Philip Morris bought Kraft as a hedge against a then-shrinking U.S. tobacco market; it had already acquired General Foods in 1985. When Big Mo (now called Altria) took 16% of Kraft public in 2001 to pay down debt from its acquisition of Nabisco, one analyst titled his report on Kraft "The Juggernaut" and called Kraft's stock—which debuted at $31—a must-have.

As it turns out, investors would have been better off with an interest-bearing checking account. Kraft's stock today trades at its IPO [initial public offering] price. The company has been lapped by smaller, nimbler rivals like Kellogg, has suffered an embarrassing exodus of top talent, and has seen ballyhooed innovations like Tassimo, a pricey coffeemaker, fall flat. Rising packaging costs and private-label products have eaten at Kraft's profit margins and market share.

"The challenges they face seem gargantuan," says Wendy Liebmann, president of consultancy WSL Strategic Retail. "I'm not sure [former General Electric CEO] Jack Welch could turn this company around," adds a longtime industry consultant.

Rosenfeld, a onetime high school basketball player, knows that Kraft, the world's second-largest food company (Nestlé is No. 1), has no fouls left to give. But she is confident her newly independent company—Altria spun Kraft out completely to its shareholders March 30 [2007]—is poised to rebound. . . . Her plan calls for repositioning familiar products like processed-cheese slices into larger, faster-growing markets, while unclogging Kraft's notoriously sclerotic decision making. The linchpin is fixing cheese, a crucial business for Kraft. . . .

Rosenfeld has made a living by breathing new life into tired brands. Can she do it again? "She's always had that constant turnaround mentality," says her former General Foods boss Jim Kilts, who went on to run Gillette and knows a thing or two about bringing companies back from the brink. "She reminds me of me."

Sipping Maxwell House coffee (a Kraft brand, of course) in her spacious office about 20 miles north of Chicago, Irene Rosenfeld recalls her upbringing in suburban Long Island: "We grew up on Kraft mac-and-cheese and Jell-O." She still seems to be that sort of person: unpretentious and direct.

Rosenfeld enjoys getting inside people's heads. "I've always been fascinated by how people think," she says. That fascination led her to major in psychology at Cornell, where she explored the psychology of advertising. After getting a doctorate in marketing and statistics— "which makes it harder for people to snow me with numbers"—she joined the market research department at General Foods in 1981.

One day, Rosenfeld gave a presentation to Jim Kilts about Kool-Aid, which was struggling at the time, since moms were growing hesitant to serve the sugary drink to their kids. Kilts was impressed and eventually asked Rosenfeld to work for him. She later repositioned Kool-Aid as a healthier alternative to Coke and Pepsi, and sales improved. More prominent assignments followed: head of beverages in 1991, then desserts in 1994, where she rejuvenated Jell-O with sugar-free snack cups. "I've been reframing categories my whole life," she says.

Source: Excerpted from Matthew Boyle, "The Cheese Queen's Bid for a Bigger Slice," *Fortune* (April 30, 2007): 108–111. © 2007 Time Inc. All rights reserved.

Strategic management drives the effort to succeed amid constant change, uncertainty, and obstacles. No one knows this more than Kraft's Irene Rosenfeld, who is charged with developing and implementing a turnaround strategy at a company with "more than 90,000 employees and 159 manufacturing and processing facilities worldwide."[2] Without the discipline of a strategic management orientation, Kraft's employees would work at cross-purposes, with no unified direction.[3] In fact, a statistical analysis of 26 published studies documented the positive impact of strategic planning on business performance.[4]

Executives responding to a recent Gallup Poll said they spend the largest proportion of their time (39 percent) on "strategic thinking/planning."[5] For instance, this is Michael Dell's assessment of his role at the computer company he founded in his college dorm room over 20 years ago:

I spend more time thinking about the future and the challenges and how to avoid making mistakes, how to keep growing and how to conquer new markets and succeed in places where we haven't.[6]

Accordingly, many people assume that strategy is the exclusive domain of top-level management. But that simply is not true.[7] Its relevance for those lower in the organization may not be as apparent, but it is relevant for *everyone* in the organization. A management student who is 10 to 20 years away from a top-level executive position might reasonably ask, "If top managers formulate strategies and I'm headed for a supervisory or staff position, why should I care about strategic management?" There are three good reasons

why staff specialists and managers at all levels need a general understanding of strategic management.

First, in view of widespread criticism that American managers tend to be shortsighted,[8] a strategic orientation encourages farsightedness (see Table 7.1). Second, employees who think in strategic terms tend to understand better how top managers think and why they make the decisions they do. In other words, the rationale behind executive policies and decisions is more apparent when things are viewed from a strategic perspective. Unfortunately, as a recent survey of 143 strategic management professionals revealed, things seem to be headed in the wrong direction: Only 5 percent of the companies represented in the survey share their strategy with their employees.[9]

TABLE **7.1** Key Dimensions of Strategic Farsightedness

	SHORTSIGHTED	FARSIGHTED
1. Organizational strategy	No formally documented strategies.	A formally written and communicated statement of long-term organizational mission.
2. Competitive advantage	"Follow the leader." No attention devoted to long-term competitive edge.	"Be the leader." Emphasis on gaining and holding a strategic competitive edge.
3. Organizational structure	Rigid structure emphasizing status quo, downward communication, and predictability.	Flexible structure encouraging change, upward and lateral communication, adaptability, and speed.
4. Research and development	Emphasis on applying competitors' good ideas.	Heavy emphasis on developing new products and services and on innovations in production, marketing, and human resource management.
5. Return	Emphasis on short-term profits.	Emphasis on increased market share, growth, and future profit potential.
6. Human resources	Emphasis on stopgap hiring and training. Labor viewed as a commodity. Layoffs common.	Emphasis on long-term development of employees. Labor viewed as a valuable human resource. Layoffs seen as a last resort.
7. Problem solving	Emphasis on chasing symptoms and blaming scapegoats.	Emphasis on finding solutions to emerging problems.
8. Management style	Emphasis on day-to-day firefighting, owing to short-term orientation.	Multilevel strategic thinking that encourages managers to consider long-term implications of their actions and decisions.

7a Quick Quiz

Maurice Lévy, CEO of Paris-based advertising agency Publicis Groupe:

Most of the ideas discussed at Publicis Groupe in Paris originate from the agencies in the field. The executive committee is not always the best place to smell the future, and we should accept that. Our job is to listen and to interpret what we hear from people working and talking in the field.

Source: Maurice Lévy, "Look to Your Front Line for the Future," Harvard Business Review, 85 (July–August 2007): 56.

QUESTION:
Which of the strategy-making modes in Table 7.2 does this exemplify? Explain.

For further information about the interactive annotations in this chapter, visit our student Web site.

cycle are eroding the traditional distinction between those who plan and those who implement plans. In terms of the five strategy-making modes shown in Table 7.2, there is a clear trend *away from* the command, symbolic, and rational modes and *toward* the transactive and generative modes.[10] In other words, the traditional idea of top-management strategists as commanders, coaches, or bosses is giving way to a view of them more as participative facilitators and sponsors. In each of the traditional modes, people below the top level must be obedient, passive, and reactive. In the *transactive* strategy-making mode, continuous improvement is the order of the day, as middle- and lower-level managers and staff specialists actively participate in the process. They go a step further, becoming risk-taking entrepreneurs, in the *generative* mode. Here is a case in point:

J. M. Smucker Co., the Ohio-based maker of jams and jellies, . . . enlisted a team of 140 employees— 7 percent of its workforce—who devoted nearly 50 percent of their time to a major strategy exercise for more than six months. "Instead of having just 12 minds working it, we really used the team of 140 as ambassadors to solicit input from all 2,000 employees," says President [now co-CEO] Richard K. Smucker. "It gave us a broader perspective, and it brought to the surface a lot of people with special talents." The company, which has struggled to grow

A third reason for promoting a broader understanding of strategic management is related to a recent planning trend. Specifically, greater teamwork and cooperation throughout the planning/control

TABLE **7.2** Five Different Strategy-Making Modes

	TRADITIONAL MODES			MODERN MODES	
	COMMAND	**SYMBOLIC**	**RATIONAL**	**TRANSACTIVE**	**GENERATIVE**
Style	*Imperial* Strategy driven by leader or small top team	*Cultural* Strategy driven by mission and a vision of the future	*Analytical* Strategy driven by formal structure and planning systems	*Procedural* Strategy driven by internal process and mutual adjustment	*Organic* Strategy driven by organizational actors' initiative
Role of Top Management	*Commander* Provide direction	*Coach* Motivate and inspire	*Boss* Evaluate and control	*Facilitator* Empower and enable	*Sponsor* Endorse and support
Role of Organizational Members	*Soldier* Obey orders	*Player* Respond to challenge	*Subordinate* Follow the system	*Participant* Learn and improve	*Entrepreneur* Experiment and take risks

Source: Adapted from Stuart L. Hart, "An Integrative Framework for Strategy-Making Processes," Academy of Management Review, 17 (April 1992): 334. Reprinted by permission.

in a mature market, now has a dozen viable initiatives that could double its $635 million revenues over the next five years.[11]

This strategic exercise certainly paid off because some key purchases, including Crisco oil and Jif peanut butter from Procter & Gamble, helped boost Smucker's annual sales to over $2 billion eight years later.[12]

Thus you, today's management student, are not as far away from the strategic domain as you may think. The time to start thinking strategically is *now*. This chapter defines strategic management, looks at ways to think strategically (including e-business strategy), explores the strategic management process, and discusses forecasting.

STRATEGIC MANAGEMENT = STRATEGIC PLANNING + IMPLEMENTATION + CONTROL

Strategic management is the ongoing process of ensuring a competitively superior fit between an organization and its changing environment.[13] In a manner of speaking, strategic management is management on a grand scale, management of the "big picture." Accordingly, **strategy** has been defined as an integrated and externally oriented perception of how the organization will achieve its mission.[14] The strategic management perspective is the product of a historical evolution and is now understood to include budget control, long-range planning, and strategic planning.[15]

strategic management: seeking a competitively superior organization-environment fit

strategy: integrated, externally oriented perception of how to achieve the organization's mission

Significantly, strategic management does not do away with earlier, more restricted approaches. Instead, it synthesizes and coordinates them all in a more systematic fashion. For example, consider the relationship between strategic planning, as defined in Chapter 6, and strategic management. Recall that *strategic planning* is the process of determining how to pursue the organization's long-term goals with the resources expected to be available. Note that nothing is said in this definition about adjustment or control. But just as astronauts and space scientists need to make midflight corrections to ensure that space shuttles reach their distant destinations, strategic adjustment and control are necessary. The more encompassing strategic management concept is useful today because it effectively merges strategic planning, implementation, and control.

Managers who adopt a strategic management perspective appreciate that strategic plans are living documents. They require updating and fine-tuning as conditions change. They also need to draw on all available talent in the organization. Regarding the human component of strategic management, Stephen R. Covey recently had this advice for corporate trainers:

Training people need to think strategically and talk the language of the top decision makers and help them realize the importance of empowering people throughout the entire organization, as Toyota has done. It's one of the reasons why the Big 3 automobile companies in Detroit are in big trouble.[16]

The strategic management process is discussed in greater detail later in this chapter. But first we need to consider alternative ways to encourage strategic thinking.

THINKING STRATEGICALLY (INCLUDING E-BUSINESS STRATEGIES)

Effective strategic management involves more than just following a few easy steps. It requires *every* employee, on a daily basis, to consider the "big picture" and think strategically about gaining and keeping a competitive edge. ABB Power Technologies, based in

Alamo, Tennessee, uses a teambulding business simulation to get its employees to think strategically:

> ABB, along with its management consultancy, The Hayes Group, created "Learn or Burn: Making the Right Business Decisions," a one-day workshop required of all employees. Working in teams of four, employees participate in a simulation in which they must run a manufacturing business for three years. They purchase materials, move products through production, pay for overhead, complete profit and loss statements and analyze financial ratios. The idea is that employees will be able to more clearly see the direct impact that their decisions have on an organization.
>
> "It's everyone's responsibility to make decisions, not just management," says Eduardo Miller, ABB manager and workshop co-instructor. "If all of us are not learning to make the right decisions, we can burn the business."[17]

This section presents four alternative perspectives for thinking innovatively about strategy in today's fast-paced global economy: synergies, Porter's generic strategies, business ecosystems, and e-business strategies.

Synergy

Although not necessarily a familiar term, *synergy* is a well-established and valuable concept. **Synergy** occurs when two or more variables (for example, chemicals, drugs, people, and organizations) interact to produce an effect greater than the sum of the effects of all of the variables acting independently. Some call this the $1 + 1 = 3$ effect; others prefer to say that with synergy, the whole is greater than the sum of its parts. Either definition is acceptable as long as one appreciates the bonus effect in synergistic relationships. In strategic management, managers are urged to achieve as much *market, cost, technology,* and *management synergy*[18] as possible when making strategic decisions. Those decisions may involve mergers,[19] acquisitions, new products, new technology or production processes, or executive replacement. When Procter & Gamble bought pet-food maker Iams, executives trumpeted the potential synergies. Five years later, unique synergies materialized and the acquisition proved to have been a wise one.

> **synergy:** the concept that the whole is greater than the sum of its parts

> P&G, being P&G, flexed its marketplace muscle immediately: Using 3,000 trucks to move Iams into 25,000 mass retail outlets, it increased distribution nearly 50% overnight. Then, armed with research indicating that pet owners fear that their four-footed family members will die before they do, Iams's R&D folks began collaborating with Procter's scientists who study human hearts, bones, muscles, teeth, and gums. Iams unleashed a stream of new foods aimed at lengthening pets' lives—weight-control formulas, antioxidant blends, tartar-fighting "dental defense" ingredients.
>
> It paid off: Iams has moved from the nation's No. 5 pet-food brand to No. 1. Worldwide sales have doubled to $1.6 billion; profits have tripled.[20]

MARKET SYNERGY. When one product or service fortifies the sales of one or more other products or services, market synergy has been achieved. Examples of market synergy are common in the business world. For instance, it has proved profitable for

Johnson Controls recently showed off a bit of technological synergy at the Detroit Auto Show with its Home Recharging Station. If plug-in electric vehicles become the norm, Johnson Controls will be ready with this handy extension to your home electrical system. But remember to unplug it before driving away.

7b Back to the Opening Case

Go to Kraft's Web site (**www.kraft.com**), click on the "Brands" tab, and explore the company's many brands for possible synergies. As a case in point, many people think Reese's Peanut Butter Cups are a tasty synergy of peanut butter and chocolate. How many tasty synergies can you dream up for Kraft that would fortify the sales of two or more of its products?

Costco to build 268 gas stations alongside its retail warehouses:

> Costco gas stations (unbranded, of course) are self-service only and don't take Visa or MasterCard, whose fees hammer a gas station's profitability. There's nary a squeegee in sight. . . .
>
> Costco's gas business now accounts for well over $3 billion in revenues, about 5% of the warehouse chain's $62 billion total.[21]

COST SYNERGY. This second type of synergy can occur in almost every dimension of organized activity. When two or more products can be designed by the same engineers, produced in the same facilities, distributed through the same channels, or sold by the same salespeople, overall costs will be lower than they would be if each product received separate treatment. In an interesting example of cost synergy, major hotels are trying to squeeze more value from their costly real estate. "At Miami Airport, Marriott has three hotels on the same plot of land. There's the Marriott Hotel, a full-service hotel. Behind the hotel are a Courtyard by Marriott, a midprice hotel, and a Fairfield Inn, an economy brand."[22] Cost synergy also can be achieved by recycling by-products and hazardous wastes that would normally be thrown away.[23] Human imagination is the only limit to creating cost synergies through recycling. Cost synergy through waste reduction and recycling is good business ethics, too (see Ethics: Character, Courage, and Values).

TECHNOLOGICAL SYNERGY. The third variety of synergy involves transferring technology from one application to another, thus opening up new markets. For example, consider this marriage of technologies from two very different industries:

> Oil company ConocoPhillips and meat producer Tyson Foods said . . . they're joining forces to pro-duce diesel fuel for U.S. vehicles using beef, pork and poultry fat.
>
> The companies said they have collaborated over the past year on ways to combine Tyson's expertise in protein chemistry and production with Conoco-Phillips' processing and marketing knowledge to introduce a renewable diesel fuel with lower carbon emissions than petroleum-based fuels.[24]

Thanks to this sort of technological synergy, profitable new markets can be tapped with existing equipment and technical know-how.

MANAGEMENT SYNERGY. This fourth type of synergy occurs when a management team is more productive because its members have complementary rather than identical skills. For example, the top two corporate officers of global mining giant Freeport-McMoRan Copper & Gold, chairman James R. Moffett and CEO Richard C. Adkerson, are a strong team. Says Adkerson, "We complement each other's skills. . . . He knows geology and I know finance."[25] Management synergy also is achieved when an individual with multiple skills or talents is hired for an administrative position.

You may find it difficult, if not impossible, to take advantage of all four types of synergy when developing new strategies. Nonetheless, your strategies are more likely to be realistic and effective if you give due consideration to all four types of synergy as early as possible.[26]

Porter's Generic Competitive Strategies

In 1980 Michael Porter, a Harvard University economist, developed a model of competitive strategies. During a decade of research, Porter's model evolved to encompass these four generic strategies: (1) cost leadership, (2) differentiation, (3) cost focus, and (4) focused differentiation.[27] As shown in Figure 7.1, Porter's model combined two variables, *competitive advantage* and *competitive scope*.

On the horizontal axis is competitive advantage, which can be achieved via low costs or differentiation. A competitive advantage based on low costs, which means lower prices, is self-explanatory. **Differentiation**, according to Porter, "is the ability to provide unique and superior value to the buyer in terms of product quality, special features, or after-sale service."[28] Differentiation helps explain why consumers willingly pay more for branded products such as Sunkist oranges and Lexus motor vehicles.[29] On the vertical axis is competitive scope. Is the firm's target market

differentiation: buyer perceives unique and superior value in a product

ETHICS: CHARACTER, COURAGE, AND VALUES

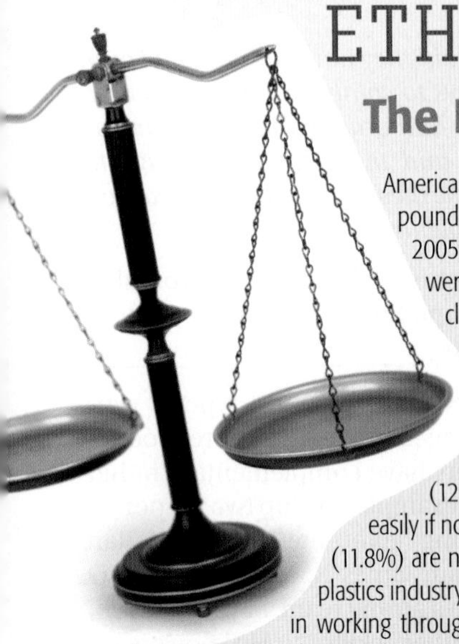

The End of Garbage?

Americans generated an average of 4.5 pounds of garbage per person per day in 2005, the EPA reports. About 1.5 pounds were recycled. That's a national recycling rate for municipal solid waste of just 32%.

What's in our garbage? Paper and cardboard (34%), yard trimmings (13%), and food scraps (12%) are the three biggies. All can be easily if not always profitably recycled. Plastics (11.8%) are next and are harder to recycle. "The plastics industry hasn't been as interested as others in working through its problems," says Gary Liss, a California zero-waste consultant. "They have fought bottle bills all over the country for 30 years."

Bottle bills are an example of "extended producer responsibility," a key tenet of zero-waste. It puts the onus for safely disposing of products on the companies that make them. Yes, it's a controversial concept. (In this country. In the EU [European Union], makers of household appliances are obliged to take them back.)

The deeper purpose here is to change the way things are made. "From our perspective, waste doesn't need to exist," says San Francisco's (environment department director) Jared Blumenfeld. "It's a design flaw." Carpet companies Interface, BASF, and Milliken, furniture makers Herman Miller and Steelcase, and clothing firms Nike and Patagonia have all redesigned products to make them easier to recycle.

Over time the economics of recycling should improve. The costs of virgin commodities are likely to rise as supplies dwindle; fees will climb at landfills as they fill up. Landfills also release methane, a greenhouse gas that could be taxed because it contributes to global warming. Meanwhile, recycling has become a $238 billion business, employing 1.1 million people, according to the EPA.

Despite all that, recycling rates have flattened lately. "We have to reengage the consumer," says Kate Krebs, executive director of the National Recycling Coalition, a trade group whose board includes executives of Dell, Coca-Cola, and Time Inc. . . . "If we don't, then all the commitments that Wal-Mart and Dell and others have been making will be difficult to keep."

Source: Marc Gunther, "The End of Garbage," Fortune (March 19, 2007): 162. © 2007 Time Inc. All rights reserved.

FOR DISCUSSION

Is the greening of American business for real, or just a public relations smoke screen? What is the business ethics case for reducing and recycling waste?

---

broad or narrow? Dell, which sells many types of computers all around the world, serves a very broad market. A neighborhood pizza parlor offering one type of food in a small geographic area has a narrow target market.

Like the concept of synergy, Porter's model helps managers think strategically: it enables them to see the big picture as it affects the organization and its changing environment. Each of Porter's four generic strategies deserves a closer look.

COST LEADERSHIP STRATEGY. Managers pursuing this strategy have an overriding concern for keeping costs, and therefore prices, lower than those of competitors. Normally, this means extensive production or service facilities with efficient economies of scale (low unit costs of making products or delivering services). Productivity improvement is a high priority for managers following the cost leadership strategy. Wal-Mart Stores, Inc., is a prime example of the cost leadership strategy.

The Wal-Mart formula is deceptively simple: Sell good-quality, name-brand, modestly priced merchandise in a clean, no-frills setting that offers one-stop family shopping. Rather than entice shoppers with an ever-changing array of discounts and sales, Wal-Mart operates from an "everyday low price" philosophy.[30]

FIGURE **7.1** Porter's Generic Competitive Strategies

		COMPETITIVE ADVANTAGE	
		Lower cost	Differentiation
COMPETITIVE SCOPE	Broad target	Cost leadership	Differentiation
	Narrow target	Cost focus	Focused differentiation

Source: Adapted with permission of The Free Press, a Division of Simon & Schuster Adult Publishing Group, from The Competitive Advantage of Nations by Michael E. Porter. Copyright © 1990, 1998 by Michael E. Porter. All rights reserved.

7c Back to the Opening Case

Under Irene Rosenfeld's leadership, which of Porter's four generic competitive strategies is Kraft pursuing? Explain your rationale.

Wal-Mart's computerized warehousing network gives it an additional cost advantage over its less efficient competitors. When rival Kmart declared bankruptcy in 2002, a retail industry consultant bluntly observed, "Kmart is simply another piece of retail roadkill in Wal-Mart's march to dominance."[31]

In manufacturing firms, the preoccupation with minimizing costs flows beyond production into virtually all areas: purchasing, wages, overhead, R&D, advertising, and selling. A relatively large market share is required to accommodate this high-volume, low-profit-margin strategy.

DIFFERENTIATION STRATEGY. For this strategy to succeed, a company's product or service must be considered unique by most of the customers in its industry. Advertising and promotion help the product to stand out from the crowd. Specialized design (BMW automobiles), a widely recognized brand (Crest toothpaste), leading-edge technology (Intel), or reliable service (Caterpillar) also may serve to differentiate a product in the industry. Because customers with brand loyalty will usually spend more for what they perceive to be a superior product, the differentiation strategy can yield larger profit margins than the low-cost strategy. But if a brand's image is not carefully nurtured and protected, brand loyalty and customers' willingness to pay a premium price can erode. For businesses sticking to a differentiation strategy, it is important to note that cost reduction is not ignored; it simply is not the highest priority.

COST FOCUS STRATEGY. Organizations with a cost focus strategy attempt to gain a competitive edge in a narrow (or regional) market by exerting strict control. For instance, Foot Locker has become a powerhouse in athletic footwear and apparel by selling off unrelated businesses, such as San Francisco Music Box, and focusing on what it does best.

> With an 18% (and growing) share of the athletic retail market—nearly twice that of its nearest competitor—Foot Locker uses its weight to negotiate advantageous deals with manufacturers like Nike and Reebok. It gets the hottest products earlier and cheaper than its peers.[32]

Foot Locker plans to increase its 2,000-store chain internationally in the years ahead.

FOCUSED DIFFERENTIATION STRATEGY. This generic strategy involves achieving a competitive edge by delivering a superior product and/or service to a limited audience. The Mayo Clinic's world-class health care facilities—in Rochester, Minnesota; Jacksonville, Florida; and Scottsdale, Arizona—are an expression of this strategy.[33]

A contingency management approach is necessary for determining which of Porter's generic strategies is appropriate. Research on Porter's model indicates a positive relationship between long-term earnings growth and a good fit between strategy and environment.[34]

Business Ecosystems

Researchers recently have given new meaning to the saying "It's a jungle out there." They have extended the concept of ecosystems from nature to business. In his bestseller *The Death of Competition: Leadership and Strategy in the Age of Business Ecosystems*, James F. Moore writes, "It is my view that executives need to think of themselves as part of organisms participating in an ecosystem in much the same way that biological organisms participate in a biological ecosystem."[35] A **business ecosystem** is an economic community of organizations and all their stakeholders, including suppliers and customers.[36] This evolving model makes one very important contribution to modern strategic thinking: *organizations need to be as good at cooperating as they are at competing if they are to succeed.*

> **business ecosystem:** economic community of organizations and all their stakeholders

A BUSINESS ECOSYSTEM IN ACTION. Within a business ecosystem, key organizations selectively cooperate and compete to achieve both their individual and their collective goals. A prime example is the next generation of wireless Internet technology called WiMAX. Whereas current Wi-Fi hot spots extend hundreds of yards, WiMAX promises a 30-mile range—and five times faster! *Business Week* recently traced the evolution of the WiMAX ecosystem:

> *WiMAX, which stands for Worldwide Interoperability for Microwave Access, grew out of work in the 1990s by engineers at dozens of companies. It remained on the back burner for years, until by happenstance several major tech companies were looking at the same time for a wireless technology that could help them boost sales. Intel was looking*

for something that would prompt consumers to buy new computers running its chips. Sprint needed an edge to set it apart from larger rivals Verizon and AT&T. Mobile handset maker Nokia wanted to expand into providing communications services. And Samsung Group wanted to get into the networking equipment business. The interests of these four companies resulted in a pooling of patents and money to create the WiMAX phenomenon.[37]

By 2007, the WiMAX ecosystem had grown to over 400 companies worldwide, and competition was stirring.[38] Only time will tell if WiMAX goes mainstream in the next few years. Another evolving business ecosystem to watch is Apple's computer/telephone/entertainment combination.[39] In the meantime, things won't be dull in the business jungle.

NEEDED: MORE STRATEGIC COOPERATION. Through the years, the terms *strategy* and *competition* have become synonymous.[40] Business ecologists now call for greater cooperation, even among the toughest of competitors. Moore puts it this way: "The major factor today limiting the spread of realized innovation is not a lack of good ideas, technology, or capital. It is the inability to command cooperation across broad, diverse communities of players who must become intimate parts of a far-reaching process of coevolution."[41] In ecosystem terms, companies need to "coevolve" with key strategic partners (and sometimes even with their competitors) if they are to thrive today. A prime example is OnStar, the 24-hour emergency satellite communication system developed by General Motors. Chet Huber, president of OnStar, originally startled his bosses at GM when he suggested offering the service to other auto companies, rather than keeping it a GM exclusive. "Huber's mold-breaking strategy worked. Today, OnStar provides its service to Lexus, Audi, Isuzu, Acura, Volkswagen, and Subaru cars, in addition to GM's own lines. OnStar now controls 70% of the market."[42]

E-Business Strategies for the Internet

The Internet is not a fixed thing. It is a complex bundle of emerging technologies at various stages of development.[43] Corporate strategists and entrepreneurs are challenged to build business models based on *where they expect these technologies to be* X years down the road. This exercise is akin to hitting a moving target from a moving platform—very difficult, at best. But Amazon.com's founder and CEO Jeff Bezos proved it can be done:

> *. . . he was one of the few dot-com leaders to understand that sweating the details of Internet technologies would make all the difference. Amazon wasn't the first store on the Web. But Bezos beat rivals in inventing or rolling out new Internet technologies that made shopping online faster, easier, and more personal than traditional retail. He offered customized recommendations based on other buyers' purchases, let people buy an item with just one mouse click, and created personalized storefronts for each customer.*[44]

E-business experts predict major changes ahead for several industries, including software development and distribution, real estate, telecommunications, bill payment, jewelry, and advertising.[45]

TABLE **7.3** Seven Basic Internet Business Models

TYPE	FEATURES AND CONTENT	SOURCES OF COMPETITIVE ADVANTAGE
Commission-based	Commissions charged for brokerage or intermediary services. Adds value by providing expertise and/or access to a wide network of alternatives.	Search Evaluation Problem solving Transaction
Advertising-based	Web content paid for by advertisers. Adds value by providing free or low-cost content—including customer feedback, expertise, and entertainment programming—to audiences that range from very broad (general content) to highly targeted (specialized content).	Search Evaluation
Markup-based	Reselling marked-up merchandise. Adds value through selection, distribution efficiencies, and the leveraging of brand image and reputation. May use entertainment programming to enhance sales.	Search Transaction
Production-based	Selling manufactured goods and custom services. Adds value by increasing production efficiencies, capturing customer preferences, and improving customer service.	Search Problem solving
Referral-based	Fees charged for referring customers. Adds value by enhancing a company's product or service offering, tracking referrals electronically, and generating demographic data. Expertise and customer feedback are often included with referral information.	Search Problem solving Transaction
Subscription-based	Fees charged for unlimited use of service or content. Adds value by leveraging strong brand name, providing high-quality information to specialized markets or access to essential services. May consist entirely of entertainment programming.	Evaluation Problem solving
Fee-for-service-based	Fees charged for metered services. Adds value by providing service efficiencies, expertise, and practical outsourcing solutions.	Problem solving Transaction

Source: Reprinted from Organizational Dynamics, *33, no. 2, G. T. Lumpkin and Gregory G. Dess, "E-Business Strategies and the Internet Business Models: How the Internet Adds Value," p. 169, Copyright 2004, with permission from Elsevier.*

Recall from our definition in Chapter 1 that e-business involves using the Internet to make *all* business functions—from sales to human resource management—more efficient, more responsive, and speedier. The purpose of this section is to build a framework of understanding for squeezing maximum value from the Internet.

BASIC INTERNET BUSINESS MODELS. Relative to buying, selling, and trading things on the Internet, it is possible to fashion a strategy around one or a combination of seven basic business models (see Table 7.3).[46] eBay, for example, has been hugely successful with the commission-based model.[47]

Google, on the other hand, makes its money via an advertising-based model.[48] As indicated in Table 7.3, each of the Internet business models has its own unique set of opportunities for strategic competitive advantage. Our challenge is to take what we have learned about synergy, Porter's competitive strategies, and business ecosystems and develop a winning strategy. Guiding us in the right direction are the following four Internet strategy lessons learned in recent years.

THERE IS NO ONE-SIZE-FITS-ALL INTERNET STRATEGY. Harvard's Michael Porter, whose generic competitive strategies we just covered, cautions us to avoid putting

Internet strategies into one basket. Instead, he sees two major categories:

> At this critical juncture in the evolution of Internet technology, dot-coms and established companies face different strategic imperatives. Dot-coms must develop real strategies that create economic value. They must recognize that current ways of competing are destructive and futile and benefit neither themselves nor, in the end, customers. Established companies, in turn, must stop deploying the Internet on a stand-alone basis and instead use it to enhance the distinctiveness of their strategies.[49]

These two types of businesses have been called dot-coms and dot-corps. Porter urges established "bricks-and-mortar" businesses to weave the Internet into the very fabric of their operations—in short, to become true e-businesses.

CUSTOMER LOYALTY IS BUILT WITH RELIABLE BRAND NAMES AND "STICKY" WEB SITES. Web surfers have proved to have very short attention spans. Seemingly attractive Web sites can have many visitors ("hits"), but few or no sales. When doing business at Internet speed, Web sites need to satisfy three criteria: (1) high-quality layout and graphics; (2) fast, responsive service; and (3) complete and up-to-date information.[50] A trusted brand name can further enhance what e-business people call the *stickiness* of a Web site—that is, the ability to draw the same customer back again and again. A great deal of work is needed in this area, considering the results of one study: two-thirds of the visitors to online stores did not return within a year.[51] Even though e-retailing might appear to be a quick-and-easy and impersonal process, loyal customers still expect a personal touch and some "hand holding" when they have questions, problems, or suggestions.

BRICKS AND CLICKS: BLENDING THE BEST OF TWO WORLDS. Popular accounts of e-business conjure up visions of "virtual organizations" where an entrepreneur and a handful of employees run a huge business with little more than an Internet hookup and a coffee maker. Everything—including product design, production, marketing, shipping, billing, and accounting—is contracted out. As discussed in Chapter 9, these network or virtual organizations *do* exist, but they are more the exception than the rule. More typically, companies with bricks-and-mortar facilities such as factories, warehouses, retail stores, and showrooms are blending the Internet into their traditional business models. In fact, some retailers are using a so-called "three-tailing"[52] concept whereby a retailer such as Lands' End (acquired by Sears in 2002) serves the customer in three ways—mail-order catalog, Web site, and stores. With the *clicks-and-bricks* strategy used by Lands' End, customers have a lot of freedom in how and when they shop. Conceivably, after seeing something they liked in the Lands' End mail catalog, customers could place an order over the phone, by mail, or over the Internet. Later, if dissatisfied with the purchase, they could mail it back or take it back to the nearest Sears store for a refund or exchange. Lands' End now does over one-third of its business via the Internet.[53]

E-BUSINESS PARTNERING SHOULD NOT DILUTE STRATEGIC CONTROL OR ETHICAL STANDARDS. Whenever uncompetitive assets are sold and tasks contracted out, care needs to be taken to maintain ethical and quality standards. Do both domestic and foreign subcontractors follow applicable labor laws and ethical labor practices, or do sweatshop conditions prevail? Are subcontractors ruining the natural environment to reduce costs? Is a product designed properly before it is manufactured by an outside

7d Are You Ready for the 3D Web?

Google, Second Life creator Linden Lab, IBM, and a bevy of additional companies are moving toward the day when you can stroll around a 3D Web . . . using a virtual replica of yourself. . . .

In this future scenario, you could go mall shopping with a gang of friends during a lunch break, even while you remain miles apart. In reality, you'd all be pinned to your work terminals, but on that screen you would be transported to a digital replica of the shopping center. As you walk by a sale at a virtual jeans store, Web cameras in the real store let you see how crowded it actually is, in case a popular item is selling out. Your avatar, set to your body's measurements, tries on the jeans and spins around to show them to your pals. You might buy the pants online or visit the physical store later.

Source: Aili McConnon, "Just Ahead: The Web as a Virtual World," Business Week (August 13, 2007): 62.

QUESTIONS:
From an e-business standpoint, what promises and problems do you foresee for the 3D Web? What is your own personal vision for the Web in five years?

contractor? Are product quality standards faithfully met? These ethical and technical questions can be answered only through systematic monitoring and strategic oversight. Tough sanctions are also needed. Informed consumers are holding the sellers of goods and services to higher standards these days. And in doing so, they include a company's *entire* supply chain, foreign and domestic. Sweatshop-produced goods and/or substandard goods sold via sophisticated e-business networks are still dirty business.[54]

THE STRATEGIC MANAGEMENT PROCESS

Strategic plans are formulated during an evolutionary process with identifiable steps. In line with the three-level planning pyramid covered in Chapter 6, the strategic management process is broader and more general at the top and filters down to narrower and more specific terms. Figure 7.2 outlines the four major steps of the strategic management process: (1) formulation of a grand strategy, (2) formulation of strategic plans, (3) implementation of strategic plans, and (4) strategic control. Corrective action based on evaluation and feedback takes place throughout the entire strategic management process to keep things headed in the right direction.[55]

It is important to note that this model represents an ideal approach for instructional purposes. Because

FIGURE **7.2** The Strategic Management Process

of organizational politics, as discussed in Chapter 13, and different planning orientations among managers, a somewhat less systematic process typically results.

Nevertheless, it is helpful to study the strategic management process as a systematic and rational sequence in order to better understand what it involves. Although he noted that rational strategic planning models should not be taken literally, Henry Mintzberg acknowledged their profound instructional value. They teach necessary vocabulary and implant the notion "that strategy represents a fundamental congruence between external opportunity and internal capability."[56]

The folks at JetBlue Airways will be the first to tell you how challenging it is to find a profitable strategy in the commercial airline business. It requires thinking outside the box, such as a co-sponsorship with The Simpsons Movie and the launch of this specialty aircraft. Please don't let Homer get his hands on the controls!

Formulation of a Grand Strategy

As pointed out in Chapter 6, a clear statement of organizational mission serves as a focal point for the entire planning process. Key stakeholders inside and outside the organization are given a general idea of why the organization exists and where it is headed. Working from the mission statement, top management formulates the organization's **grand strategy**, a general explanation of *how* the organization's mission is to be accomplished. Grand strategies are not drawn out

grand strategy: how the organization's mission will be accomplished

of thin air. They are derived from a careful *situational analysis* of the organization and its environment. A clear vision of where the organization *is* headed and of where it *should be* headed is the gateway to competitive advantage.[57]

SITUATIONAL ANALYSIS. A **situational analysis** is a technique for matching organizational strengths and weaknesses with environmental opportunities and threats to determine the right niche for the organization (see Figure 7.3). Many strategists refer to this

situational analysis: finding the organization's niche by performing a SWOT analysis

process as a SWOT analysis. SWOT stands for **S**trengths, **W**eaknesses, **O**pportunities, and **T**hreats. (You can perform an actual SWOT analysis in the Action Learning Exercise at the end of this chapter.) Every organization should be able to identify the purpose for which it is best suited. But this matching process is more difficult than it may first appear. Strategists are faced not with snapshots of the environment and the organization but with a video of rapidly changing events. As one researcher said, "The task is to find a match between opportunities that are still unfolding and resources that are still being acquired."[58] For example, Google CEO Eric Schmidt explains how his company tackles this task:

> There's tremendous opportunity before us, so we're organized around taking advantage of . . . technology discontinuities as they occur. And therefore we spend a lot of time trying to make sure that we're busy seeing them. And that's our competitive advantage. You have to be set up to shift your focus quickly so that you spend most of your energies inventing the new business instead of blindly optimizing the old one.[59]

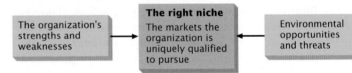

FIGURE **7.3** Determining Strategic Direction Through Situational (SWOT) Analysis

Forecasting techniques, such as those reviewed later in this chapter, help managers cope with uncertainty about the future while conducting situational analyses.

Strategic planners, whether top managers, key operating managers, or staff planning specialists, have many ways to scan the environment for opportunities and threats. They can study telltale shifts in the economy, recent technological innovations, growth and movement among competitors, market trends, labor availability, and demographic patterns.[60]

Unfortunately, according to a survey of executives at 100 U.S. corporations, not enough time is spent looking outside the organization: "Respondents said they spend less than half of their planning time (44 percent) evaluating external factors—competition and markets—compared with 48 percent on internal analysis—budget, organizational factors, human resources. 'That's the corporate equivalent of contemplating one's navel,'"[61] says the researcher.

Environmental opportunities and threats need to be sorted out carefully. A perceived threat may turn out to be an opportunity, or vice versa. Steps can be taken to turn negatives into positives. Pitney Bowes is an interesting case in point:

> In February [2004], after eBay went looking for a company to create a system for online postage, it didn't turn to Stamps.com or any other dotcom whippersnapper. Rather, the nine-year-old Internet upstart tapped 84-year-old graybeard Pitney Bowes, a firm based in Stamford, Conn., that dominates the world of postal meters. Now millions of sellers on eBay download postage and print it out—with Pitney Bowes earning a click fee each time.
>
> It's the latest ratification of Pitney's business model, which many believed would be rendered obsolete by e-mail and the Internet. Instead, the $4.6 billion company has bolstered its 80 percent share of the domestic postal-meter market with new revenue streams from the digital world. Profits are growing at a clip of 13 percent a year.[62]

7e Back to the Opening Case

Based on the facts of this case and any reasonable assumptions you might make about Kraft, what would a situational (SWOT) analysis suggest that the future strategic direction of Kraft should be? *Hint:* First arrange your evidence under these four headings: organizational strengths, organizational weaknesses, environmental opportunities, and environmental threats.

CAPABILITY PROFILE. After scanning the external environment for opportunities and threats, management's attention turns inward to identifying the organization's strengths and weaknesses.[63] This subprocess is called creating a **capability profile**. The following are key capabilities for today's companies:

capability profile: identifying the organization's strengths and weaknesses

- Quick response to market trends
- Rapid product development
- Rapid production and delivery
- Continuous cost reduction
- Continuous improvement of processes, human resources, and products
- Greater flexibility of operations[64]

Diversity initiatives are an important way to achieve continuous improvement of human resources.[65] Also note the clear emphasis on *speed* in this list of key organizational capabilities.

THE STRATEGIC NEED FOR SPEED. Speed has become an important competitive advantage. Warren Holtsberg, a Motorola corporate vice president, offered this perspective:

> *I find the impatience of the new economy refreshing. The concept that fast is better than perfect bodes well, particularly for the technology industry. At Motorola, we used to be able to introduce a cellular telephone, and it would have a life expectancy in the marketplace of about two years. Now we face cycle times of four to six months. People continue to demand new things. They demand change. They're impatient. Bringing that into a big corporation is invigorating.[66]*

Accordingly, the new strategic emphasis on speed involves more than just doing the same old things faster. It calls for rethinking and radically redesigning the entire business cycle, a process called **reengineering**[67] (see the Manager's Toolkit at the end of this chapter). The idea is to have cross-functional teams develop a whole new—and better—production process, one that does not let time-wasting mistakes occur in the first place. (The related topic of horizontal organizations is covered in Chapter 9.)

reengineering: radically redesigning the entire business cycle for greater strategic speed

Formulation of Strategic Plans

In the second major step in the strategic management process, general intentions are translated into more concrete and measurable strategic plans, policies, and budget allocations.[68] This translation is the responsibility of top management, although staff planning specialists and middle managers often provide input. From our discussion in the last chapter, we recall that a well-written plan consists of both an objective and an action statement. Plans at all levels need to specify by whom, what, when, and how things are to be accomplished and for how much. Many managers prefer to call these specific plans "action plans" to emphasize the need to turn good intentions into action. Even though strategic plans may have a time horizon of one or more years, they must meet the same criteria that shorter-run intermediate and operational plans meet. They should do the following:

1. Develop clear, results-oriented objectives in measurable terms.
2. Identify the particular activities required to accomplish the objectives.
3. Assign specific responsibility and authority to the appropriate personnel.
4. Estimate times to accomplish activities and their appropriate sequencing.
5. Determine resources required to accomplish the activities.
6. Communicate and coordinate the above elements and complete the action plan.[69]

All of this does not happen in a single quick-and-easy session. Specific strategic plans usually evolve over a period of months as top management consults with key managers in all areas of the organization to gather their ideas and recommendations and, one hopes, to win their commitment.

STRATEGIC IMPLEMENTATION AND CONTROL

As illustrated earlier in Figure 7.2, the third and fourth stages of the strategic management cycle involve implementation and control. The entire process is only as strong as these two traditionally underemphasized areas.

Implementation of Strategic Plans

Because strategic plans are too often shelved without adequate attention to implementation, top managers need to do a better job of facilitating the implementation process and building middle-manager commitment.[70]

A SYSTEMATIC FILTERING-DOWN PROCESS. Strategic plans require further translation into successively lower-level plans. Top-management strategists can do some groundwork to ensure that the filtering-down process occurs smoothly and efficiently. Planners need answers to four questions, each tied to a different critical organizational factor:

1. *Organizational structure.* Is the organizational structure compatible with the planning process, with new managerial approaches, and with the strategy itself?
2. *People.* Are people with the right skills and abilities available for key assignments, or must attention be given to recruiting, training, management development, and similar programs?
3. *Culture.* Is the collective viewpoint on "the right way to do things" compatible with strategy, must it be modified to reflect a new perspective, or must top management learn to manage around it?
4. *Control systems.* Is the necessary apparatus in place to support the implementation of strategy and to permit top management to assess performance in meeting strategic objectives?[71]

Strategic plans that successfully address these four questions have a much greater chance of helping the organization achieve its intended purpose than those that do not. In addition, field research indicates the need to *sell* strategies to all affected parties. New strategies represent change, and people tend to resist change for a variety of reasons. "The strategist thus faces a major selling job; that is, trying to build and maintain support among key constituencies for a plan that is freshly emerging."[72] FedEx founder and CEO Fred Smith explains how strategy is "sold" throughout his company:

> We have meetings each year to review our strategy, to make sure we're not drifting out of our core competencies, and to make sure we're correctly seeing where the markets are going. Once we've bought into that as a senior management team, we then communicate that in every way we can think of. We put it in the mission statement. We put it in the employee handbooks. We tie our business plans to it. We tie our incentive plans to it. We have one of the biggest industrial TV networks in the world, and we use it to make sure our employees understand what we're trying to do and why we're trying to do it.[73]

This brings us to the challenge of obtaining commitment among middle managers.

BUILDING MIDDLE-MANAGER COMMITMENT. Resistance among middle managers can kill an otherwise excellent strategic management program. A study of 90 middle managers who wrote 330 reports about instances in which they had resisted strategic decisions documented the scope of this problem. It turned out that to protect their own self-interests, the managers in the study frequently derailed strategies. This finding prompted the researchers to conclude as follows:

> If general management decides to go ahead and impose its decisions in spite of lack of commitment, resistance by middle management can drastically lower the efficiency with which the decisions are

Winter in Yellowstone National Park, where the buffalo (more precisely, American bison) roam. Actually, that's the problem—the buffalo do indeed *roam,* into neighboring private and public grazing lands. Sometimes they carry diseases harmful to cattle. A comprehensive strategic control program attempts to maintain a healthy herd within the Park and minimize damage elsewhere. Predictably, no stakeholders—including ranchers, hunters, and environmentalists—are totally happy with the program.

The ultimate goal of a strategic control system is to detect and correct downstream problems in order to keep strategies updated and on target, without stifling creativity and innovation in the process. A survey of 207 planning executives found that in high-performing companies there was no tradeoff between strategic control and creativity. Rather, the two were delicately balanced.[78]

Corrective Action Based on Evaluation and Feedback

As illustrated in Figure 7.2, corrective action makes the strategic management process a dynamic cycle. A rule of thumb is that negative feedback should prompt corrective action at the step immediately before.[79] Should the problem turn out to be more deeply rooted, then the next earlier step also may require corrective action. The key is to detect problems and initiate corrective action, such as updating strategic assumptions, reformulating plans, rewriting policies, making personnel changes, or modifying budget allocations, as soon as possible. In the absence of prompt corrective action, problems can rapidly worsen (see Best Practices).

Let us now turn to forecasting. Without the ability to obtain or develop reliable environmental forecasts, managerial strategists have little chance of successfully negotiating their way through the strategic management process.

implemented, if it does not completely stop them from being implemented. Particularly in dynamic, competitive environments, securing commitment to the strategy is crucial because rapid implementation is so important.[74]

Participative management (see Chapter 12) and influence tactics (see Chapter 14) can foster middle-management commitment.[75]

Strategic Control

Strategic plans, like our more informal daily plans, can go astray, so a formal control system is needed to keep strategic plans on track.[76] Software programs that synchronize and track all contributors' goals in real time are indispensable today. And strategic control systems need to be carefully designed ahead of time, not merely tacked on as an afterthought.[77] Before strategies are translated downward, planners should set up and test channels for information on progress, problems, and strategic assumptions about the environment or organization that have proved to be invalid. If a new strategy varies significantly from past ones, then new production, financial, or marketing reports will probably have to be drafted and introduced.

FORECASTING

An important aspect of strategic management is anticipating what will happen in the years ahead. **Forecasts** may be defined as predictions, projections, or estimates of future events or conditions in the environment in which the organization operates. The idea is to sketch a rough outline of the future to enable better strategic decision making *today.*[80] Forecasts may be little more than educated guesses, or they may be the result of highly sophisticated statistical analyses. They vary in reliability, as we all know from off-the-mark weather forecasts.[81]

forecasts: predictions, projections, or estimates of future situations

BEST PRACTICES

Google's "Fail Fast" Strategy

One of Silicon Valley's best companies at managing failure also happens to be its hottest: Google. "Fundamentally, everything we do is an experiment," says Douglas Merrill, a Google vice president for engineering. "The thing with experimentation is that you have to get data and then be brutally honest when you're assessing it." When introducing new features, Google has remained true to a "fail fast" strategy: launch, listen, improve, launch again. . . . Even when a feature is a full-blown failure, Google prefers to view it as an experiment that yielded useful information. That's what happened with Google Answers, a four-year effort to build an expert answer service that was shuttered in November [2006]. "I don't think Answers was a failure, because we incorporated a lot of what we learned into our new custom search engine," Merrill says. "The failures are the things where you don't learn anything."

Source: Excerpted from Tom McNichol, "A Startup's Best Friend? Failure," Business 2.0, *8 (March 2007): 40.*

They may be relatively short run—a few hours to a year—or long run—five or more years. A combination of factors determines a forecast's relative sophistication, time horizon, and reliability. These factors include the type of forecast required, management's knowledge of forecasting techniques, and how much money management is willing to invest.[82]

Types of Forecasts

There are three types of forecasts: (1) event outcome forecasts, (2) event timing forecasts, and (3) time series forecasts.[83] Each type answers a different general question (see Table 7.4). **Event outcome forecasts** are used when strategists want to predict the outcome of highly probable future events. For example: "How will an impending strike affect output?"

Event timing forecasts predict when, if ever, given events will occur. Strategic questions in this area might include "When will the prime interest rate begin to fall?" or "When will our primary competitor introduce a certain product?" Timing questions such as these typically can be answered by identifying leading indicators that historically have preceded the events in question. For instance, a declining inflation rate often prompts major banks to lower their prime interest rate, or a competitor may flag the introduction of a new product

> **event outcome forecasts:** predictions of the outcome of high probable future events

> **event timing forecasts:** predictions of when a given event will occur

---

TABLE **7.4**	Types of Forecasts	
TYPE OF FORECAST	**GENERAL QUESTION**	**EXAMPLE**
1. Event outcome forecast	"What will happen when a given event occurs?"	"Who will win the next Super Bowl?"
2. Event timing forecast	"When will a given event occur?"	"When will a human set foot on Mars?"
3. Time series forecast	"What value will a series of periodic data have at a given point in time?"	"What will the Dow Jones Industrial Average stock index close at on January 5, 2012?"

by conducting market tests or ordering large quantities of a new raw material.

Time series forecasts seek to estimate future values in a sequence of periodically recorded statistics. A common example is the sales forecast for a business. Sales forecasts need to be as accurate as possible because they affect decisions all along the organization's supply chain.[84] As Cisco Systems learned the hard way, sales forecasts based on poor input can be very costly.

> *In May 2001, Cisco Systems announced the largest inventory write-down in history: $2.2 billion erased from its balance sheet for components it ordered but couldn't use. . . .*
>
> *To lock in supplies of scarce components during the [Internet] boom, Cisco ordered large quantities well in advance, based on demand projections from the company's sales force. What the forecasters didn't notice, however, was that many of their projections were inflated artificially. With network gear hard to come by, many Cisco customers also ordered similar equipment from Cisco's competitors, knowing that they'd ultimately make just one purchase—from whoever could deliver the goods first.[85]*

time series forecasts: estimates of future values in a statistical sequence

Forecasting Techniques

Modern managers may use one or a combination of four techniques to forecast future outcomes, timing, and values. These techniques are informed judgment, scenario analysis, surveys, and trend analysis.

INFORMED JUDGMENT. Limited time and money often force strategists to rely on their own intuitive judgment when forecasting. Judgmental forecasts are both fast and inexpensive, but their accuracy depends on how well informed the strategist is. Frequent visits with employees—in sales, purchasing, and public relations, for example—who regularly tap outside sources of information are a good way of staying informed. A broad reading program to stay in touch with current events and industry trends, and refresher training through management development programs, are also helpful. Additionally, customized news clipping services (delivered by e-mail), spreadsheet forecasting software, and a competitive intelligence-gathering operation can help keep strategic decision makers up to date. The trick is to separate key bits of information from extraneous background noise. For example, "Apple watchers used Hitachi's announcement of its 1-inch hard drive to accurately predict the arrival of the iPod mini."[86]

Of course, informed judgment is no panacea. It generally needs to be balanced with data from other forecasting techniques and formal market research.[87]

SCENARIO ANALYSIS. This technique also relies on informed judgment, but it is more systematic and disciplined than the approach just discussed. **Scenario analysis** (also called scenario planning) is the preparation and study of written descriptions of *alternative* but *equally likely* future conditions.[88] Scenarios are visions of what "could be." The late futurist Herman Kahn is said to have first used the term *scenario* in conjunction with forecasting during the 1950s. The two types of scenarios are longitudinal and cross-sectional.

scenario analysis: preparing written descriptions of equally likely future situations

7h Calling All Oddball Curiosities and Failures

More often than not, indicators look like mere oddball curiosities or, worse, failures, and just as we dislike uncertainty, we shy away from failures and anomalies. But if you want to look for the thing that's going to come whistling in out of nowhere in the next years and change your business, look for interesting failures—smart ideas that seem to have gone nowhere.

Source: Paul Saffo, "Six Rules for Effective Forecasting," Harvard Business Review, 85 (July–August 2007): 128.

QUESTION:

Among the failed businesses and product flops you have observed recently, which ones are "interesting failures" that, given the right conditions, could be profitable ideas? Explain.

Longitudinal scenarios describe how the present is expected to evolve into the future. **Cross-sectional scenarios,** the most common type, simply describe possible future situations at a given time.

> **longitudinal scenarios:** describing how the future will evolve from the present

> **cross-sectional scenarios:** describing future situations at a given point in time

While noting that *multiple forecasts* are the cornerstone of scenario analysis, one researcher offered the following perspective:

> *Scenario writing is a highly qualitative procedure. It proceeds more from the gut than from the computer, although it may incorporate the results of quantitative models. Scenario writing is based on the assumption that the future is not merely some mathematical manipulation of the past, but the confluence of many forces, past, present and future, that can best be understood by simply thinking about the problem.*[89]

The same researcher recommends developing two to four scenarios (three being optimal) for narrowly defined topics. Likely candidates for scenario analysis are specific products, industries, markets, or catastrophic events.[90] For example, a grain-exporting company's strategists might look five years into the future by writing scenarios for three different likely situations: (1) above-average grain harvests, (2) average harvests, and (3) below-average harvests. These scenarios could serve as focal points for strategic plans concerning construction of facilities, staffing and training, and so on. As the future unfolds, the strategies written to accompany the more realistic scenario would be followed.

This approach has been called "no surprise" strategic planning. The results of a poll uncovered a crying need for such an approach: "fully two-thirds of 140 corporate strategists . . . admitted that their organizations had been surprised by as many as three high-impact events in the past five years."[91] Amazingly, 97 percent of the respondents "stated that their companies have no early warning system in place."[92] *Business Week* framed the case for scenario planning this way:

> *If you envision multiple versions of the future and think through their implications, you will be better prepared for whatever ends up happening. In effect, you won't be seeing the future for the first time. You'll be remembering it. The alternative won't cut it: Those who cannot remember the future are condemned to be taken by surprise.*[93]

The key to good scenario writing is to focus on the few readily identifiable but unpredictable factors that will have the greatest impact on the topic in question. Because scenarios look far into the future, typically five or more years, they need to be written in general and rather imprecise terms.[94]

SURVEYS. Surveys are a forecasting technique involving face-to-face or telephone interviews and mailed, fax, or e-mail questionnaires. They can be used to pool expert opinion or to fathom consumer tastes, attitudes, and opinions. When carefully constructed and properly administered to representative samples, surveys can give management comprehensive and fresh information. They suffer the disadvantages, however, of being somewhat difficult to construct, time-consuming to administer and interpret, and expensive. Although costs can be trimmed by purchasing an off-the-shelf or "canned" survey, standardized instruments too often either fail to ask precisely the right questions or ask unnecessary questions.

TREND ANALYSIS. Essentially, a **trend analysis** is the hypothetical extension of a past pattern of events or time series into

> **trend analysis:** hypothetical extension of a past series of events into the future

"We're looking for a more comprehensive research strategy than simply 'Google it.' "

the future. An underlying assumption of trend analysis is that past and present tendencies will continue into the future.[95] Of course, surprise events such as the September 11, 2001, terrorist attacks can destroy that assumption. Trend analysis can be fickle and cruel to reactive companies. As a case in point, Chrysler's commitment to fuel-efficient, four-cylinder cars in the early 1980s was based on the assumption that the 1970s trend toward higher gas prices would continue. However, when the price of gasoline stabilized during the 1980s, Chrysler came up short as U.S. car buyers demanded more horsepower.[96] By the time Chrysler had geared up its production of more powerful V-6

engines, Iraq's 1990 invasion of Kuwait had sent the price of gasoline skyward—and car buyers scrambling for four-cylinder cars. Again Chrysler had tripped over a faulty trend analysis. If sufficient valid historical data are readily available, then barring disruptive surprise events, trend analysis can be a reasonably accurate, fast, and inexpensive strategic forecasting tool. An unreliable or atypical database, however, can produce misleading trend projections.

Each of these forecasting techniques has inherent limitations. Consequently, strategists are advised to cross-check each source of forecast information with one or more additional sources.

SUMMARY

1. Strategic management sets the stage for virtually all managerial activity. Managers at all levels need to think strategically and to be familiar with the strategic management process for three reasons: far-sightedness is encouraged, the rationale behind top-level decisions becomes more apparent, and strategy formulation and implementation are more decentralized today. Strategic management is defined as the ongoing process of ensuring a competitively superior fit between the organization and its ever-changing environment. Strategic management effectively merges strategic planning, implementation, and control.

2. Strategic thinking, the ability to look ahead and spot key organization-environment interdependencies, is necessary for successful strategic management and planning. Four perspectives that can help managers think strategically are synergy, Porter's model of competitive strategies, the concept of business ecosystems, and e-business models and lessons. Synergy has been called the $1 + 1 = 3$ effect because it focuses on situations where the whole is greater than the sum of its parts. Managers are challenged to achieve four types of synergy: market synergy, cost synergy, technological synergy, and management synergy.

3. According to Porter's generic competitive strategies model, four strategies are (1) cost leadership, (2) differentiation, (3) cost focus, and (4) focused differentiation. Porter's model helps managers create a profitable "fit" between the organization and its environment.

4. Contrary to the traditional assumption that strategy automatically equates to competition, the business ecosystems model emphasizes that organizations need to be as good at *cooperating* as they are at competing. By balancing competition and cooperation, competitors can *coevolve* into a dominant economic community (or business ecosystem).

5. Seven basic Internet business models are the commission-based, advertising-based, markup-based, production-based, referral-based, subscription-based, and fee-for-service-based models. Each model affords its own opportunities for competitive advantage. Four Internet strategy lessons have been learned in recent years: (1) there is no one-size-fits-all strategy; (2) reliable brand names and "sticky" Web sites are needed to build customer loyalty, (3) a bricks-and-clicks strategy effectively blends the old (bricks-and-mortar facilities such as stores and warehouses) with the new (a presence on the Web), and (4) strategic control and high ethical standards are more important than ever with today's virtual global partnerships on the Web.

6. The strategic management process consists of four major steps: (1) formulation of a grand strategy, (2) formulation of strategic plans, (3) implementation of strategic plans, and (4) strategic control. Corrective action based on evaluation of progress and feedback helps keep the strategic management process on track. Results-oriented strategic plans that specify what, when, and how are then formulated and translated downward into more specific and shorter-term intermediate and operational plans. Participative management can build needed middle-manager commitment during implementation. Problems encountered along the way should be detected by the strategic control mechanism or by ongoing evaluation and subjected to corrective action.

7. Strategists formulate the organization's grand strategy after conducting a SWOT analysis. The organization's key capabilities and appropriate niche in the marketplace become apparent when the organization's strengths (S) and weaknesses (W) are cross-referenced with environmental opportunities (O) and threats (T). Strategic speed has become an important capability today, sometimes necessitating radical reengineering of the entire business cycle.

8. Event outcome, event timing, and time series forecasts help strategic planners anticipate and prepare for future environmental circumstances. Popular forecasting techniques among today's managers include informed judgment, scenario analysis, surveys, and trend analysis. Each technique has its own limitations, so forecasts need to be cross-checked against one another.

TERMS TO UNDERSTAND

MANAGER'S TOOLKIT

Reengineering

Reengineering, a.k.a. process innovation and core process redesign, is the search for, and implementation of, radical change in business processes to achieve breakthrough results. Its chief tool is a clean sheet of paper. Most change efforts start with what exists and fix it up. Reengineering, adherents emphasize, is not tweaking old procedures and certainly not plain-vanilla downsizing. Nor is it a program for bottom-up continuous improvement. Reengineers start from the future and work backward, as if unconstrained by existing methods, people, or departments. In effect they ask, "If we were a new company, how would we run this place?" Then, with a meat ax and sandpaper, they conform the company to their vision.

That's how GTE looks at its telephone operations, which account for four-fifths of the company's $20 billion in annual revenues. Facing new competitive threats, GTE figured it had to offer dramatically better customer service. Rather than eke out steady gains in its repair, billing, and marketing departments, the company examined its operations from the outside in. Customers, it concluded, wanted one-stop shopping—one number to fix an erratic dial tone, question a bill, sign up for call waiting, or all three, at any time of day.

GTE set up its first pilot "customer care center" in Garland, Texas, [in late 1992] and began to turn vision into fact. The company started with repair clerks, whose job had been to take down information from a customer, fill out a trouble ticket, and send it on to others who tested lines and switches until they found and fixed the problem. GTE wanted that done while the customer was still on the phone—something that happened just once in 200 calls. The first step was to move testing and switching equipment to the desks of the repair clerks—now called "front-end technicians"—and train them to use it. GTE stopped measuring how fast they handled calls and instead tracked how often they cleared up a problem without passing it on. Three out of ten now, and GTE is shooting for upward of seven.

The next step was to link sales and billing with repair, which GTE is doing with a push-button phone menu that allows callers to connect directly to any service. It has given operators new software so their computers can get into databases that let the operators handle virtually any customer request. In the process, says GTE vice president Mark Feighner, "we eliminated a tremendous amount of work—in the pilots, we've seen a 20 percent or 30 percent increase in productivity so far."

GTE's rewired customer-contact process—one of eight similar efforts at the company—displays most of the salient traits of reengineering: It is occurring in a dramatically altered competitive landscape; it is a major change, with big results; it cuts across departmental lines; it requires hefty investment in training and information technology; and layoffs result. . . .

It ain't cheap, and it ain't easy. At Blue Cross of Washington and Alaska, where redesigning claims processing raised labor productivity 20 percent in 15 months, CEO Betty Woods says the resource she drew on most was courage: "It was more difficult than we ever imagined, but it was worth it."

Therein lies the most important lesson from business's experience with reengineering: Don't do it if you don't have to. Says Thomas H. Davenport, head of research for Ernst & Young: "This hammer is incredibly powerful, but you can't use it on everything." Don't reengineer your buggy whip business; shut it. If you're in decent shape but struggling with cost or quality problems or weak brand recognition, by all means juice up your quality program and fire your ad agency, but don't waste money and energy on reengineering. Save reengineering for big processes that really matter, like new-product development or customer service, rather than test[ing] the technique someplace safe and insignificant.

Source: From Thomas A. Stewart, "Reengineering: The Hot New Managing Tool," Fortune *(August 23, 1993): 41–42.* © *1993 Time Inc. All rights reserved.*

ACTION LEARNING EXERCISE

Thinking Strategically: A SWOT Analysis

Instructions: This exercise is suitable for either an individual or a team. First, pick an organization as the focal point of the exercise. It can be a large company, a unit of a large company, a small business, or a nonprofit organization such as a college, government agency, or religious organization. Next, look inward and list the organization's strengths and weaknesses. Turning the analysis outward, list opportunities and threats in the organization's environment. Finally, envision workable strategies for the organization by cross-referencing the two sets of factors. Be sure to emphasize organizational strengths that can exploit environmental opportunities and neutralize or overcome outside threats. Also think about what needs to be done to correct organizational weaknesses. The general idea is to create the best possible fit between the organization and its environment (the "right niche").

Note: A SWOT analysis also can be a powerful career guidance tool. Simply make *yourself* the focus of the exercise and go from there.

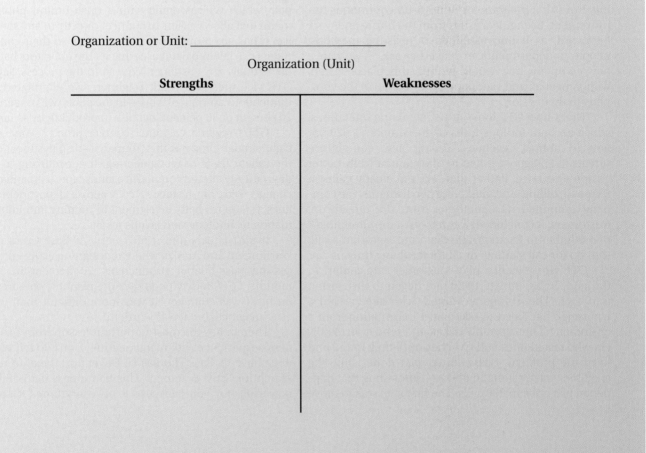

Organization or Unit: _____

Organization (Unit)

Strengths	Weaknesses

Environment (Unit's Situation)

Opportunities	Threats

For Consideration/Discussion

1. Which of the four elements—strengths, weaknesses, opportunities, threats—turned out to be the most difficult to develop? Why? Which was the easiest? Why?

2. What valuable insights about your focal organization did you gain during your SWOT analysis?

3. Why should every manager know how to do a SWOT analysis?

4. What "right niche" did your SWOT analysis yield?

5. How can a personal SWOT analysis improve your career prospects?

CLOSING CASE
Sally Jewel's Market-Driven Strategy at REI

Sally Jewel knows there are a thousand other places where outdoor enthusiasts can buy trail boots, maybe even at a better price. But Jewel, the CEO of outdoor-gear retailer Recreational Equipment Inc., also knows there's simply nowhere else hikers will find the REI experience: testing boots on an indoor mountain to see how much their toes hurt when they tromp downhill, or trying them on a climbing wall to check traction. At REI's flagship store in Seattle, hikers do just that, and at REIs across the country, shoppers also test gas stoves, practice setting up tents, and ask real explorers—who happen to be store clerks—which sleeping bags they would use on a mountain trek.

The in-store learning works both ways. When women shoppers looking to get active began flooding stores in recent years, REI responded with a new line of products based on what they asked for: tops with built-in bras for hiking and sleeping bags with extra room at the hips and extra warmth at the feet. When its staff heard complaints from shoppers about being pressed for time, REI responded with more gear for activities that can be done in a day, instead of focusing only on multiday adventures.

In a world where customer service is routinely terrible, REI has created a customer experience that is unique in retail. "We used to be product-driven—assuming we have the experience in gear and relying on customers to trust us to pick the right products," Jewel says. "Our breakthrough four years ago was to shift to being market-driven—paying attention to who these customers are and how we can adapt to the way they want to recreate."

If indoor mountains and climbing walls sound gimmicky, don't be fooled. It's not the individual pieces but the combined effect that's important. In his most recent book, *The Future of Competition* (Harvard Business School Press, 2004), University of Michigan professor C. K. Prahalad writes that developing brand value by increasing the quality, not just the frequency, of interactions with customers is a strategic imperative in a market overcrowded with too many brands for customers to care about. No longer content with the emotional imagery of advertising campaigns, shoppers now demand experiences in exchange for brand loyalty. As Prahalad puts it, "Experience is the brand."

The REI experience extends beyond its store walls. REI's Web site stocks thousands of products; customers can access it from kiosks in stores, and clerks can use it to place orders at checkout. The site was profitable in its second year and contributed $84 million in revenue in 2003. That successful multichannel strategy, with seamless click-and-mortar operations, is a part of REI's success. So too is its effective vertical integration as both a manufacturer of original products and a reseller of other brands, which kept overall sales growth at 9% during a tough retail year. And so is its active base of co-op members who pushed the company to nearly double its stores to 70 since 1996. But in the end, perhaps REI's success relates back to Prahalad's insight. Says Kate Delhagen, who follows retailing for Forrester Research: "People care about the REI experience."

Source: By Alison Overholt, © 2005 Gruner & Jahr USA Publishing. First published in *Fast Company Magazine*. Reprinted by permission.

FOR DISCUSSION

1 Which of Porter's four generic competitive strategies does REI seem to be using? Explain.

2 Drawing on your own experience, what businesses can you identify that attempt to turn the customer's experience into a brand? Explain how they do it, and rate their effectiveness.

3 Which of the seven basic Internet business models is REI using? Explain.

4 Is REI using any of the four Internet strategy lessons presented in this chapter? Explain.

5 Using your imagination and making reasonable assumptions, indicate what opportunities and threats (the O and T portions of a SWOT analysis) you can envision for REI.

TEST PREPPER

True/False Questions

_____ 1. Finding solutions to emerging problems reveals a farsighted management style.

_____ 2. In the two modern modes of strategy making, top managers act as commander and coach rather than as sponsor or facilitator.

_____ 3. Synergy has been called the 2 + 1 = 3 effect.

_____ 4. Competitive advantage and competitive scope are the two major variables in Porter's generic competitive strategies model.

_____ 5. Two of the seven basic Internet business models are advertising-based models and entertainment-based models.

_____ 6. Writing a formal code of ethics is the first step in the strategic management process.

_____ 7. The "O" in a SWOT analysis stands for "outlook."

_____ 8. Strategic planning is a bottom-up process, as opposed to a top-down process.

_____ 9. Time series forecasts seek to estimate future values in a sequence of periodically recorded statistics.

_____ 10. The key to good scenario writing is to focus on the few readily identifiable but unpredictable factors that will have the greatest impact on the topic in question.

Multiple-Choice Questions

1. _____ is *not* a key dimension of strategic farsightedness.
   A. Emphasizing the development of new products
   B. Emphasizing increased market share
   C. Writing a formal mission statement
   D. Viewing labor as a commodity
   E. Relying on upward communication

2. There is a trend away from the _____ mode and toward the _____ mode in strategy making.
   A. command; rational   B. symbolic; rational
   C. transactive; symbolic   D. symbolic; generative
   E. generative; command

3. Strategic management =
   A. operational planning + intermediate planning + strategic planning.
   B. resources + opportunities + results.
   C. top-management commitment + results.

D. strategic planning + implementation + control.
   E. strategic planning.

4. What does the term *synergy* refer to?
   A. The 1 + 1 = 2 effect   B. Situational analysis
   C. The additive effect   D. The 1 + 1 = 3 effect
   E. Forecasting

5. Which of these, according to Porter, is the ability to provide unique and superior value to the buyer in terms of product quality, special features, or after-sales service?
   A. Competitive scope   B. Cost leadership
   C. Market segmentation   D. Economies of scale
   E. Differentiation

6. The seven basic Internet business models include all *except* which one of these?
   A. Transaction-based models
   B. Commission-based models
   C. Referral-based models
   D. Subscription-based models
   E. Markup-based models

7. One of four key lessons that managers have learned about Internet strategy is that when doing business on the Internet, it is especially important to ensure that e-business partnering does not dilute
   A. profitability.
   B. strategic control and ethical standards.
   C. executive leadership.
   D. employee morale.
   E. communication and teamwork.

8. _____ serves as the focal point for the entire planning process.
   A. Product/service quality
   B. A performance appraisal system
   C. The customer
   D. A code of ethics
   E. A mission statement

9. The "W" in a SWOT analysis stands for
   A. weaknesses.   B. workers.
   C. window of opportunity.   D. workability.
   E. willingness.

10. _____ analysis has been called "no surprise" strategic planning.
   A. Rational   B. Trend
   C. Market   D. Scenario
   E. Economic

See page T1 at the back of the text for answers to these questions. Want more questions? Visit the student Web site and take the ACE quizzes for more practice.

8

Decision Making and Creative Problem Solving

Every now and then, I'm reminded that the difference between success and failure in business is often one decision. You make the right one, and you survive. You make the wrong one, and you don't.[1]

—NORM BRODSKY, ENTREPRENEUR

OBJECTIVES

- **Specify** at least five sources of decision complexity for modern managers.

- **Explain** what a *condition of risk* is and what managers can do to cope with it.

- **Define** and **discuss** the three decision traps: framing, escalation of commitment, and over-confidence.

- **Discuss** why programmed and nonprogrammed decisions require different decision-making procedures, and **distinguish** between the two types of knowledge in knowledge management.

- **Explain** the need for a contingency approach to group-aided decision making.

- **Identify** and briefly **describe** five of the ten "mental locks" that can inhibit creativity.

- **List** and **explain** the four basic steps in the creative problem-solving process.

- **Describe** how causes of problems can be tracked down with fishbone diagrams.

THE CHANGING WORKPLACE

The Human Game Boy

With his quirky attitude and unconventional management style, Richard Tait, a former Microsoft executive, has shaken up the once-sleepy board-game industry with Cranium, his clever line of products and activities for kids and adults. The Seattle company has sold over 22 million games, toys, and books since it launched in 1998. In less than a decade Cranium has won more than 130 awards, including Toy of the Year—the equivalent of an industry Oscar—five out of the past six years. Tait, 43, who continues to expand his toy and game empire, shared his work strategy with *Fortune's* Jenny Mero.

Take the product to the customer. We seek out unique ways to reach our customers that allow them to experience our products. Cranium started by exclusively selling games at Starbucks, because we knew that's where our core customer base was. And we sold our first million games by word-of-mouth.

Design a decision-making space. While fun is always at the core of our culture, there are times management needs to buckle down and focus on critical issues. I wanted a room specifically for these important discussions, and that became the Red Dot room. Calling it a War Room didn't fit our culture. Red Dot conveys a sense of focus, which is exactly what we do in these meetings. There are no seats—we all stand—and there are red dots on the carpet to remind us of our focus.

Smell the competition. I go on anthropological visits to check out other companies and see what I can bring back. John Lasseter's office [at Pixar] is the only office I've seen that has more toys than me. I have to catch up. But these visits help us. Earlier I had to choose among 12 scents for our clay in the original Cranium game. We picked lemon, because we noticed that it's what P&G [Procter & Gamble] used to launch new products.

Make titles meaningful. People get to choose their own title. When Whit Alexander and I first created Cranium, we wanted to make sure everything about our company was fun, so we decided to give ourselves creative job titles—I am the Grand Poo Bah, and he's the Chief Noodler. Now all new employees we hire are empowered to develop their own special title. Our CFO is Professor Profit, and our head of the toy business is the Viceroy of Toy.

Add color to the workplace. I find it very frustrating when I go to the offices of other toymakers, and I see they've chosen to paint their walls beige. It costs the same to paint them red. It's perplexing to me. You have to create an environment for people to be creative and innovative. My office has a glass wall, and I'm right near the front door, so I'm the official greeter. The walls are brightly colored, and we have music playing everywhere. Even the way the offices are arranged is incredibly collaborative—there's no sense of departments.

Listen to your kids. These days playing games has become everything in life for me. It's part of who I am and how I live. As Grand Poo Bah, I participate in game play at Cranium Central, as we develop new products and test them. Then I go home to my "real" job—father of three—where I infuse game play into our time together. We don't just pull out our Cranium games. I find myself creating new ones with my kids. In fact, just last week I created a game with my son while we were at the gas station, of all places!

Source: Jenny Mero, "The Human Game Boy," *Fortune* (March 19, 2007): 50. © 2007 Time Inc. All rights reserved.

Decision making is the process of identifying and choosing among alternative courses of action in a manner appropriate to the demands of the situation.[2] The act of choosing implies that alternative courses of action must be identified, weighed, and weeded out. That is precisely what Richard Tait and his team at Cranium do as they sift through all sorts of wild ideas to create marketable board games. They need to make sound decisions amid

decision making: identifying and choosing among alternative courses of action

lots of change and uncertainty, including incomplete information about competitors, the economy, and future customers. Thus judgment and discretion are fundamental to decision making. Moreover, today's organizational decision making requires courage and steady nerves, as in the case of Google's CEO Eric Schmidt. According to Schmidt, who holds a commercial pilot's license,

I can tell you that flight training is very useful. You are taught to make quick decisions, take command, know when to relinquish command, and move quickly. In jets, bad things can happen very quickly. I've benefited from that training as an executive.[3]

8a What Do You Stand For?

Michael Useem, Director, Center for Leadership and Change Management, University of Pennsylvania:

When you have to make a fast decision with significant stakes, you better know what you stand for, because the temptation to violate your basic commitments in life can be large because of the stress of the moment.

Source: Michael Useem, "How Do Values Relate to Courage?" Fast Company, no. 86 (September 2004): 102.

QUESTIONS:

Is this a major ethics problem for today's managers? Explain. How about in your own personal life? Explain.

For further information about the interactive annotations in this chapter, visit our student Web site.

This chapter highlights major challenges for decision makers, introduces a general decision-making model, discusses group-aided decision making, and examines creativity and problem solving.

CHALLENGES FOR DECISION MAKERS

Decision making has never been easy, but it is especially challenging for today's managers. In an era of accelerating change, the pace of decision making also has accelerated. According to a survey of 479 managers, 77 percent reported making *more decisions* during the previous three years, and 43 percent said they had *less time* to make each of those decisions.[4] A stunning example of this second trend occurred when AT&T was in the middle of a bidding war for its wireless unit.

> *With time running out in the high-stakes poker match for AT&T wireless, the CEOs for BellSouth and SBC Communications agreed . . . to throw one last chip on the table. At just past 2 A.M. . . ., the telecom giants authorized their investment bankers to increase their all-cash offer for AT&T to $41 billion with just one condition: AT&T's board had one minute to decide. . . . Finally, after a flurry of e-mail messages, AT&T said yes to the gambit, then yes to the offer.[5]*

In addition to having to cope with this acceleration, today's decision makers face a host of tough challenges. Those that we will discuss here are (1) complex streams of decisions, (2) uncertainty, (3) information-processing styles, and (4) perceptual and behavioral decision traps.

Dealing with Complex Streams of Decisions

Above all else, today's decision-making contexts are not neat and tidy. A pair of experts lent realism to the subject by using the analogy of a stream:

> *If decisions can be viewed as streams—streams containing countless bits of information, events, and choices—then how should decision makers be viewed? . . . The streams flowing through the organization do not wait for them; they flow around them. The streams do not serve up problems neatly wrapped and ready for choice. Rather, they deliver the bits and pieces, the problems and choices, in no particular order. . . .*
>
> *In short, decision makers in an organization are floating in the stream, jostled capriciously by problems popping up, and finding anchors through action at a given time in a given place.[6]*

It is important to note that the foregoing is a recognition of complexity, *not* an admission of hopelessness. A working knowledge of eight intertwined factors contributing to decision complexity can help decision makers successfully navigate the stream (see Figure 8.1).

1. ***Multiple criteria.*** Typically, a decision today must satisfy a number of often-conflicting criteria representing the interests of different groups. For example, the Denver International Airport was designed and built with much more than airplanes in mind:

> *Denver's is the first airport to be built for maximum accessibility for the disabled. During construction, the city took blind people, deaf people and those who use wheelchairs and canes through the terminal and concourses to road-test the layout.*
>
> *"They wanted to make sure a sign wasn't too low or a drinking fountain sticking out too far," says Thom Walsh, project manager at Fentress Bradburn. "It's a completely accessible building and uses Braille and voice paging."[7]*

Identifying stakeholders and balancing their conflicting interests is a major challenge for today's decision makers.

FIGURE **8.1** Sources of Complexity for Today's Managerial Decision Makers

Anderson pushed ahead, making one of the *[greatest] strategic decisions in U.S. oil history.*

The day after Christmas, oil historian Daniel Yergin recounts, a sound like four jumbo jets flying just overhead announced a plume of spewing natural gas. Prudhoe Bay turned out to be the largest petroleum discovery ever in North America.[8]

Because of the importance of this particular aspect of decision complexity, we shall devote special attention to it in the next section.

4. ***Long-term implications.*** Major decisions generally have a ripple effect, with today's decisions creating the need for later rounds of decisions. For example, remember the European Airbus's 555-seat A380 jetliner, mentioned in our Chapter 6 discussion of break-even analysis? Consider these long-term implications for the world's largest commercial airplane now being put into service:

> *The Airbus A380 is so large that it cannot park at a terminal designed for a row of Boeing 747s. It is so long that it will handle some taxiways like a tractor-trailer truck turning into a suburban driveway. It is so heavy that it cannot taxi across some culverts and bridges.*
>
> *Its engines are spaced so far apart that their exhaust could fry a runway's guide lights. Its body is so wide and tall that tower controllers may have to ban aircraft from nearby runways and taxiways before the plane lands or takes off.*[9]

Airports will have to be significantly updated to accommodate the A380.

5. ***Interdisciplinary input.*** Decision complexity is greatly increased when technical specialists such as lawyers, consumer advocates, tax advisers, accountants, engineers, and production and marketing experts are consulted before making a decision.

2. ***Intangibles.*** Factors such as customer goodwill, employee morale, increased bureaucracy, and aesthetic appeal (for example, negative reaction to a billboard on a scenic highway), although difficult to measure, often determine decision alternatives.

3. ***Risk and uncertainty.*** Along with every decision alternative goes the chance that it will fail in some way. Poor choices can prove costly. Yet the right decision, as illustrated in this legendary example, can open up whole new worlds of opportunity:

> *In 1967, seven dry holes on Alaska's harsh North Slope had left Atlantic Richfield Chairman Robert O. Anderson facing a costly choice. Should he try one more? The consummate wildcatter,*

keep Louisville weird.

This oddball Kentucky billboard conveys a very serious message from the owners of local small businesses. They fear being driven out of business by look-alike, big-box stores. The giant mass-retail chains, in turn, consider the failure of some local businesses to be an unintended consequence of their low-price strategy. Where do you stand on this issue?

VALUING DIVERSITY
Are You a Biased Decision Maker?

Are you willing to bet that you feel the same way toward European Americans as you do toward African Americans? How about women versus men? Or older people versus younger ones? Think twice before you take that bet. Visit **implicit.harvard.edu** or **www.tolerance.org/hidden_bias** to examine your unconscious attitudes.

The Implicit Association Tests available on these sites reveal unconscious beliefs by asking takers to make split-second associations between words with positive or negative connotations and images representing different types of people. The various tests on these sites expose the differences—or the alignment—between test takers' conscious and unconscious attitudes toward people of different races, sexual orientation, or physical characteristics. Data gathered from over 2.5 million online tests and further research tell us that unconscious biases are

- **widely prevalent.** At least 75% of test takers show an implicit bias favoring the young, the rich, and whites.
- **robust.** The mere conscious desire not to be biased does not eliminate implicit bias.
- **contrary to conscious intention.** Although people tend to report little or no conscious bias against African Americans,

Arabs, Arab Americans, Jews, gay men, lesbians, or the poor, they show substantial biases on implicit measures.
- **different in degree depending on group status.** Minority group members tend to show less implicit preference for their own group than majority group members show for theirs. For example, African Americans report strong preference for their group on explicit measures but show relatively less implicit preference in the tests. Conversely, white Americans report a low explicit bias for their group but [show] a higher implicit bias.
- **consequential.** Those who show higher levels of bias on the IAT are also likely to behave in ways that are more biased in face-to-face interactions with members of the group they are biased against and in the choices they make, such as hiring decisions.
- **costly.** Research currently under way in our lab suggests that implicit bias generates a "stereotype tax"—negotiators leave money on the table because biases cause them to miss opportunities to learn about their opponent and thus create additional value through mutually beneficial tradeoffs.

Source: Reprinted by permission of the Harvard Business Review. *An exhibit from "How (Un)Ethical Are You?" vol. 81, p. 59. Reprinted by permission of HBS Publishing.*

This process can become even more complex and time-consuming in traditional societies such as China, for example, where it is common practice to consult *feng shui* experts about superstitious beliefs. "*Feng shui* (pronounced 'fung schway') literally means wind (*feng*) and water (*shui*) and refers to the ancient Chinese art of creating harmony between inhabitants and their environment."[10] Perhaps a tree needs to be removed, the roof painted a different color, or the alignment of doorways changed. Foreigners who ignore what they deem to be superstitious nonsense do so at the peril of their business dealings with their Chinese partners.[11]

6. ***Pooled decision making.*** Rarely is a single manager totally responsible for the entire decision process. For example, consider the approach of Brian Ruder, the successful president of Heinz's U.S. unit:

> [He] has collected a number of mentors and advisers over the course of his career. Ruder, in fact, has elected a group of people, including his father,

to a personal board of directors. He canvasses them whenever he's faced with a major decision, such as introducing plastic ketchup bottles. . . . "I rely on them," he says, "for total frankness and objectivity." Obviously, it's helped.[12]

After pooled input, complex decisions wind their way through the organization, with individuals and groups interpreting, modifying, and sometimes resisting. Minor decisions set the stage for major decisions, which in turn are translated back into local decisions. Typically, many people's fingerprints are on final decisions in the organizational world.

7. ***Value judgments.*** As long as decisions are made by people with differing backgrounds, perceptions, aspirations, and values, the decision-making process will be marked by disagreement over what is right or wrong, good or bad, and ethical or unethical[13] (see Valuing Diversity). For example, following the Virginia Tech massacre in 2007, Facebook made a value judgment about its policy of removing the

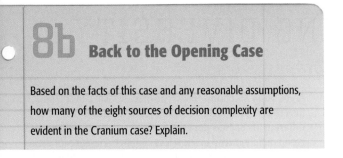

8b   Back to the Opening Case

Based on the facts of this case and any reasonable assumptions, how many of the eight sources of decision complexity are evident in the Cranium case? Explain.

pages of deceased users. As reported by *USA Today* at the time:

> The decision follows online protests and a letter-writing campaign by friends and other members of the social-networking website who heard that the pages were to be removed. . . . The company's past policy had been to delete profiles as a way of respecting the privacy rights of those who had died.
>
> "Until the Virginia Tech tragedy, we had a very simplistic policy in place, and that event made us re-evaluate," says Facebook's Brandee Barker. "We rely on our users to help educate us."
>
> Victims' profile pages have become places where friends and family swap favorite memories and post messages to their lost loved one.[14]

8. *Unintended consequences.* The **law of unintended consequences**, according to an expert on the subject, "states that you cannot always predict the results of

law of unintended consequences: results of purposeful actions are often difficult to predict

purposeful action."[15] In other words, there can be a disconnect between intentions and actual results. Although unintended consequences can be positive, negative ones are most troublesome and have been called the Frankenstein monster effect.[16] For example, consider this dilemma during the second war in Iraq:

> The Pentagon has launched an urgent effort to develop radio systems immune to the jamming signals that troops use to foil homemade bombs planted by insurgents in Iraq.
>
> The jammers, which block signals that detonate improvised explosive devices (IEDs), have become so powerful they can "cause the loss of all communications" for U.S. troops, a Pentagon solicitation to contractors says. It calls for information on devices that will let troops use jammers and radios at the same time.[17]

And therein lies the crux of the problem of unintended consequences. Namely, *hurried and/or narrowly focused decision makers typically give little or no consideration to the full range of likely consequences of their decisions.* Unintended consequences cannot be altogether eliminated in today's complex world.[18] Still, they can be moderated to some extent by giving them creative and honest consideration when making important decisions.

Coping with Uncertainty

Among the valuable contributions of decision theorists are classification schemes for types and degrees of uncertainty. (Recall our discussion in Chapter 6 about state, effect, and response uncertainty.)

Bad weather is a major source of uncertainty for supply chain managers. A record snowfall in January 2008 stranded these truckers and many motorists overnight on Interstate 5, a primary link between Los Angeles, Sacramento, and northern California.

Unfortunately, life is filled with varying degrees of these types of uncertainties. Managers are continually asked to make the best decisions they can, despite uncertainties about both present and future circumstances. For example, this is how Richard Branson, the flamboyant British founder and CEO of Virgin, recently described a key strategic decision:

> *When we did Virgin Mobile four years ago, it was a big investment for us—$300 million. I looked at the percentage of people in America with prepaid phones, and it was 8%. Yet in England it was 83%, in France 78%, and so on. And yet we had long debates before making the decision. I decided to push on with it—and it's been one of the best investment decisions we've ever made. So sometimes you just have to go on gut feeling. To start Virgin Mobile, I sold assets that I loved, that I'd had since I was 20 years old, in order to take one opportunity.[19]*

Managers who are able to assess the degrees of certainty in a situation—whether conditions are certain, risky, or uncertain—are able to make more effective decisions. As illustrated in Figure 8.2, there is a negative correlation between uncertainty and the decision maker's confidence in a decision. In other words, the more uncertain a manager is about the principal factors in a decision, the less confident he or she will be about the successful outcome of

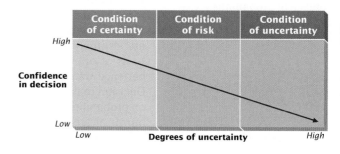

FIGURE **8.2** The Relationship Between Uncertainty and Confidence

that decision. The key, of course, lies not in eliminating uncertainty, which is impossible, but rather in learning to work within an acceptable range of uncertainty.[20]

CERTAINTY. A **condition of certainty** exists when there is no doubt about the factual basis of a particular decision, and its outcome can be predicted accurately. Much like the economic concept of pure competition, the concept of certainty is useful mainly as a theoretical anchor point for a continuum. In a world filled with uncertainties, certainty is relative rather than absolute. For example, the decision to order more rivets for a manufacturing firm's fabrication department is based on the relative certainty that the current rate of use will exhaust the rivet inventory on a specific date. But even in this case, uncertainties about the possible misuse or theft of rivets creep in to reduce confidence. Because nothing is truly certain, conditions of risk and uncertainty are the general rule for managers, not the exception.

> **condition of certainty:** solid factual basis allows accurate prediction of decision's outcome

RISK. A **condition of risk** is said to exist when a decision must be made on the basis of incomplete but reliable factual information.[21] Reliable information, though incomplete, is still useful to managers coping with risk because they can use it to calculate the probability that a given event will occur and then to select a decision alternative with favorable odds.

> **condition of risk:** decision made on basis of incomplete but reliable information

The two basic types of probabilities are objective and subjective probabilities. **Objective probabilities** are derived mathematically from reliable historical data, whereas **subjective probabilities** are estimated on the basis of one's past experience or judgment. Decision making based on probabilities is common in all areas of management today. For instance, laundry product manufacturers would not think of launching a new detergent without determining the probability of its acceptance via consumer panels and test marketing. A number of inferential statistical techniques can help managers objectively assess risks.[22]

objective probabilities: odds derived mathematically from reliable data

subjective probabilities: odds based on judgment

UNCERTAINTY. A **condition of uncertainty** exists when little or no reliable factual information is available. Still, judgmental or subjective probabilities can be estimated. Decision making under conditions of uncertainty can be both rewarding and nerve-racking for managers. Just ask executives in the biotechnology industry: "It costs tens of millions of dollars and can take five to 15 years to get a drug from the test tube to the clinic—and many drugs simply don't make it."[23] Decision confidence is lowest when a condition of uncertainty prevails because decisions are then based on educated guesses rather than on hard factual data.

condition of uncertainty: no reliable factual information available

Information-Processing Styles

Thinking is one of those activities we engage in constantly yet seldom pause to examine systematically. But within the context of managerial decision making and problem solving, it is important that one's thinking not get into an unproductive rut. The quality of our decisions is a direct reflection of how we process information.

Researchers have identified two general information-processing styles: the thinking style and the intuitive style.[24] One is not superior to the other. Both are needed during organizational problem solving. Managers who rely predominantly on the *thinking* style tend to be logical, precise, and objective. They prefer routine assignments requiring attention to detail and systematic implementation. Conversely, managers who are predominantly *intuitive* find comfort in rapidly changing situations in which they can be creative and follow their hunches and visions. Intuitive managers see things in complex patterns rather than as logically ordered bits and pieces. They typically rely on their own mental shortcuts and detours.[25] An interesting example of intuitive thinking involves Jann Wenner, the man who founded *Rolling Stone* magazine forty years ago:

> *Wenner, who helped found the Rock and Roll Hall of Fame, says he has thrived by trusting his gut. Instead of basing editorial and business decisions on readership surveys or financial reports, he considers what he likes and—as important—what would be fun.[26]*

Of course, not every manager falls neatly into one of these two categories; many people process information through a combination of the two styles. For example, Bonnie Reitz, a senior vice president for sales at Continental Airlines, told *Fast Company* magazine, "I believe in unshakable facts. Get as many facts as you can. Don't spend forever on it, but if you have enough facts and the gut intuition, you're going to get it right most of the time."[27] (See Table 8.1.)

The important thing to recognize here is that managers can approach decision making and problem solving in very different ways, depending on their information-processing styles.[28] It is a matter of

TABLE **8.1**   How to Sharpen Your Intuition

RECOMMENDATION	DESCRIPTION
1. Open up the closet	To what extent do you: experience intuition; trust your feelings; count on intuitive judgments; suppress hunches; covertly rely upon gut feel?
2. Don't mix up your I's	Instinct, insight, and intuition are not synonymous; practice distinguishing between your instincts, your insights, and your intuitions.
3. Elicit good feedback	Seek feedback on your intuitive judgments; build confidence in your gut feel; create a learning environment in which you can develop better intuitive awareness.
4. Get a feel for your batting average	Benchmark your intuitions; get a sense for how reliable your hunches are; ask yourself how your intuitive judgment might be improved.
5. Use imagery	Use imagery rather than words; literally visualize potential future scenarios that take your gut feelings into account.
6. Play devil's advocate	Test out intuitive judgments; raise objections to them; generate counter-arguments; probe how robust gut feel is when challenged.
7. Capture and validate your intuitions	Create the inner state to give your intuitive mind the freedom to roam; capture your creative intuitions; log them before they are censored by rational analysis.

Source: Academy of Management Executive: The Thinking Manager's Source *by Eugene Sadler-Smith and Erella Shefy. Copyright 2004 by Academy of Management (NY). Reproduced with permission of Academy of Management (NY) in the format Textbook via Copyright Clearance Center.*

diversity. Their approaches, perceptions, and recommendations vary because their minds work differently. In traditional pyramid work organizations, where the thinking style tends to prevail, intuitive employees may be criticized for being imprecise and rocking the boat. A concerted effort needs to be made to tap the creative skills of "intuitives" and the implementation abilities of "thinkers." An appreciation for alternative information-processing styles needs to be cultivated because they complement one another.

Avoiding Perceptual and Behavioral Decision Traps

Behavioral scientists have identified some common human tendencies that are capable of eroding the quality of decision making. Three well-documented ones are framing, escalation, and overconfidence. Awareness and conscious avoidance of these traps can give decision makers a competitive edge.

FRAMING ERROR. One's judgment can be altered and shaped by how information is presented or labeled. In other words, labels create frames of reference with the power to bias our interpretations.

Framing error is the tendency to evaluate positively presented information favorably and negatively presented information unfavorably.[29] Those evaluations, in turn, influence one's behavior. A study with 80 male and 80 female University of Iowa students documented the framing-interpretation-behavior linkage. Half of each gender group was told about a cancer treatment with a 50 percent success rate. The other two groups heard about the same cancer treatment but were told it had a 50 percent failure rate. The researchers summed up the results of the study as follows:

framing error: how information is presented influences one's interpretation of it

> *Describing a medical treatment as having a 50 percent success rate led to higher ratings of perceived effectiveness and higher likelihood of recommending the treatment to others, including family members, than describing the treatment as having a 50 percent failure rate.*[30]

Framing thus influenced both interpretations and intended behavior. Given the importance of the information in this study (cancer treatment), ethical questions arise about the potential abuse of framing error.

FIGURE **8.3**   Why Escalation of Commitment Is So Common

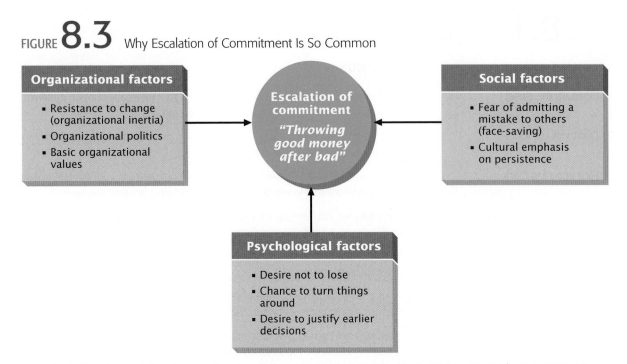

Source: Adapted from discussion in Barry M. Staw and Jerry Ross, "Understanding Behavior in Escalation Situations," Science, 246 (October 13, 1989): 216–220.

In organizations, framing error can be used constructively or destructively. Advertisers, for instance, take full advantage of this perceptional tendency when attempting to sway consumers' purchasing decisions. A leading brand of cat litter boasts of being 99 percent dust-free. Meanwhile, a shampoo claims to be fortified with 1 percent natural protein. Thanks to framing error, we tend to perceive very little dust in the cat litter and a lot of protein in the shampoo. Managers who couch their proposals in favorable terms hope to benefit from framing error. And who can blame them? On the negative side, prejudice and bigotry thrive on framing error.[31] A male manager who believes women can't manage might frame an interview report so that Max looks good and Maxine looks bad.

ESCALATION OF COMMITMENT.   Why are people slow to write off bad investments? Why do people stay in bad relationships? Why do companies stick to unprofitable strategies? And why are government officials reluctant to scrap over-budget and behind-schedule programs? Escalation of commitment is a possible explanation for these diverse situations.[32] **Escalation of commitment** is the

escalation of commitment: people get locked into losing courses of action to avoid the embarrassment of quitting or admitting error

tendency of individuals and organizations to get locked into losing courses of action because *quitting is personally and socially difficult.* This decision-making trap has been called the "throwing good money after bad" dilemma. Those victimized by escalation of commitment are often heard talking about "sunk costs" and "too much time and money invested to quit now." Within the context of management, psychological, social, and organizational factors conspire to encourage escalation of commitment[33] (see Figure 8.3).

In their weekly column in *Business Week*, Jack and Suzy Welch recently addressed the issue of why large diversified companies too often fail to unload broken businesses:

Big companies hold on to failing businesses for all kinds of reasons: sentimental value, false hope, and culture, to name just three. . . .

In most cases, though, inertia is what stops companies from letting go of broken companies. It's just so hard to sell an old operation—so messy. After all, getting rid of a fixer-upper takes patience and often the willingness to take a loss. Who has the time or wherewithal for that?

Which is why letting go of a business has to be a corporate discipline for it to happen at all. Companies should only keep trying to fix businesses as long as they serve a strategic purpose. And they should face reality and "give up hope" . . . as soon as they don't.[34]

Specifically, reality checks, in the form of comparing actual progress with goals and timetables, can help keep escalation in check.[35]

OVERCONFIDENCE. The term *overconfidence* is commonplace and requires no formal definition. We need to comprehend the psychology of overconfidence because it can expose managers to unreasonable risks. For example, in his book *Why Smart Executives Fail—and What You Can Learn from Their Mistakes*, Sydney Finkelstein offers this helpful caution:

Movies, television shows, and journalists all offer us instantly recognizable vignettes of the dynamic executive making a dozen decisions a minute, snapping out orders that will redirect huge enterprises, dealing with numerous crises at once, and taking only seconds to size up situations that have obviously stumped everyone else for days. . . .

The problem with this picture of executive competence is that it is really a fraud. In a world where business conditions are constantly changing and innovations often seem to be the only constant, no one can "have all the answers" for long. Leaders who are invariably crisp and decisive tend to settle issues so quickly that they have no opportunity to grasp the ramifications. Worse, because these leaders need to feel that they already have all the answers, they have no way to learn new answers. Their instinct, whenever something truly important

is at stake, is to push for rapid closure, allowing no periods of uncertainty, even when uncertainty is appropriate.[36]

Ironically, researchers have found a positive relationship between overconfidence and task difficulty. In other words, the more difficult the task, the greater the tendency for people to be overconfident.[37] Easier and more predictable situations foster confidence, but generally not unrealistic overconfidence. People may be overconfident about one or more of the following: accuracy of input data; individual, team, or organizational ability; and the probability of success. There are various theoretical explanations for overconfidence. For example, overconfidence may often be necessary to generate the courage needed to tackle difficult situations.

As with the other decision traps, managerial awareness of this problem is the important first step toward avoiding it. Careful analysis of situational factors, critical thinking about decision alternatives, and honest input from stakeholders can help managers avoid overconfidence. Yet another remedy is to make what management consultants call *deliberate mistakes*.

Inexperienced managers make many mistakes and learn from them. Experienced managers may become so good at the game they're used to playing that they no longer see ways to improve significantly. They may need to make deliberate mistakes to test the limits of their knowledge.[38]

MAKING DECISIONS

It stands to reason that if the degree of uncertainty varies from situation to situation, there can be no single way to make decisions.[39] Managers do indeed make decisions in every conceivable way. One of the oddest examples is how the stacked potato chips we know as Pringles got their name. It seems that employees at Procter & Gamble pulled it out of a phone book.[40] Even doing nothing can qualify as decision making. Behavioral economists explain: "Postponement, delay, procrastination. They may seem like the path of least resistance, but they are in their own way as consequential as any other choice."[41] How often a particular decision is made is another important consideration. Some decisions are made frequently, perhaps several times a day. Others are made infrequently or just once. Consequently, decision

---

8e The Best Mistakes

Carlos Slim Helú, Mexican businessman and one of the world's richest people:

If we have to make mistakes, we make small mistakes. . . . We prefer no mistakes, of course, but small mistakes are the best mistakes.

Source: As quoted in Stephanie N. Mehta, "Carlos Slim: The Richest Man in the World," Fortune (August 20, 2007): 29.

QUESTIONS:

How good are you at learning from your mistakes? Is admitting one's mistakes a good way for managers to avoid overconfidence? Explain.

theorists have distinguished between programmed and nonprogrammed decisions.[42] Each of these types of decisions requires a different procedure.

Making Programmed Decisions

Programmed decisions are those that are repetitive and routine. Examples include hiring decisions, billing decisions in a hospital, supply reorder decisions in a purchasing department, consumer loan decisions in a bank, and pricing decisions in a university bookstore. Managers tend to devise fixed procedures for handling these everyday decisions. Most decisions made by the typical manager on a daily basis are of the programmed variety.

programmed decisions: repetitive and routine decisions

At the heart of the programmed decision procedure are decision rules. A **decision rule** is a statement that identifies the situation in which a decision is required and specifies how the decision will be made. Behind decision rules is the idea that standard, recurring problems need to be solved only once. Decision rules enable busy managers to make routine decisions quickly without having to go through comprehensive problem solving over and over again.[43]

decision rule: tells when and how programmed decisions should be made

Generally, decision rules should be stated in "if-then" terms. A decision rule for a consumer loan officer in a bank, for example, might be: *If* the applicant is employed, has no record of loan default, and can put up 20 percent collateral, *then* a loan not to exceed $50,000 can be authorized."[44] Carefully conceived decision rules can streamline the decision-making process by allowing lower-level managers to shoulder the responsibility for programmed decisions and freeing higher-level managers for relatively more important, nonprogrammed decisions.

Making Nonprogrammed Decisions

Nonprogrammed decisions are those made in complex, important, and nonroutine situations, often under new and largely unfamiliar circumstances. This kind of decision is made much less frequently than programmed decisions. Examples of nonprogrammed decisions include deciding whether to merge with another company, how

nonprogrammed decisions: decisions made in complex and nonroutine situations

to replace an executive who died unexpectedly, whether a foreign branch should be opened, and how to market an entirely new kind of product or service. The following six questions need to be asked prior to making a nonprogrammed decision:

1. What decision needs to be made?
2. When does it have to be made?
3. Who will decide?
4. Who will need to be consulted prior to the making of the decision?
5. Who will ratify or veto the decision?
6. Who will need to be informed of the decision?[45]

The decision-making process becomes more sharply focused when managers take the time to answer these questions.

One respected decision theorist has described nonprogrammed decisions as follows: "There is no cut-and-dried method for handling the problem because it hasn't arisen before, or because its precise nature and structure are elusive or complex, or because it is so important that it deserves a custom-tailored treatment."[46]

Nonprogrammed decision making calls for creative problem solving. The four-step problem-solving process introduced later in this chapter helps managers make effective and efficient nonprogrammed decisions.

A General Decision-Making Model

Although different decision procedures are required for different situations, it is possible to construct a general decision-making model. Figure 8.4 shows an idealized, logical, and rational model of organizational decision making. Significantly, it describes how decisions can be made, but it does not portray how managers actually make decisions.[47] In fact, on-the-job research found that managers did not follow a rational and logical series of steps when making decisions.[48] Why, then, should we even consider a rational, logical model? Once again, as in the case of the strategic management process in Chapter 7, a rational descriptive model has instructional value because it identifies key components of a complex process.[49] It also suggests a better way of doing things.

The first step, a scan of the situation, is important, although it is often underemphasized or ignored altogether in discussions of managerial decision making. Scanning answers the question "How do I know a decision should be made?" Seventy years ago, Chester I. Barnard gave one of the best answers to this question, stating that "the occasions for decision originate in three distinct fields: (a) from authoritative communications from superiors; (b) from cases referred for decision by subordinates; (c) from cases originating in

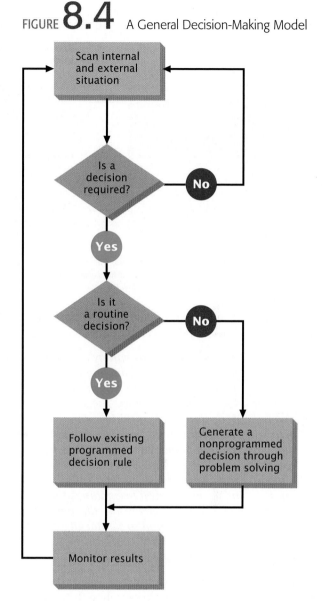

FIGURE **8.4** A General Decision-Making Model

the initiative of the [manager] concerned."[50] In addition to signaling when a decision is required, scanning reveals the degree of uncertainty and provides necessary information for pending decisions.

When the need for a decision has been established, the manager should determine whether the situation is routine. If it is routine and there is an appropriate decision rule, the rule is applied. But if it turns out to be a new situation demanding a nonprogrammed decision, comprehensive problem solving begins. In either case, the results of the final decision need to be monitored to see whether any follow-up action is necessary.

Knowledge Management: A Tool for Improving the Quality of Decisions

An army of academics, consultants, and managers have rallied around the concept of knowledge management during the last dozen years. Although some may dismiss it as a passing fad, knowledge management is a powerful and robust concept that deserves a permanent place in management theory and practice.[51] Authorities on the subject define **knowledge management** (KM) as "the development of tools, processes, systems, structures, and cultures explicitly to improve the creation, sharing, and use of knowledge critical for decision-making."[52] KM is at the heart of what organizational theorists call *learning organizations*, a topic we cover in the next chapter. Our purpose here is to explore the basics of KM, with an eye toward better orga-

knowledge management: developing a system to improve the creation and sharing of knowledge critical for decision making

nizational decisions. After all, decisions are only as good as the information on which they are based.

TWO TYPES OF KNOWLEDGE. KM specialists draw a fundamental distinction between two types of knowledge: tacit knowledge and explicit knowledge (see Figure 8.5). **Tacit knowledge** is personal, intuitive, and undocumented information about how to skillfully perform tasks, solve problems, and make decisions. People who are masters

tacit knowledge: personal, intuitive, and undocumented information

FIGURE **8.5** Key Dimensions of Knowledge Management

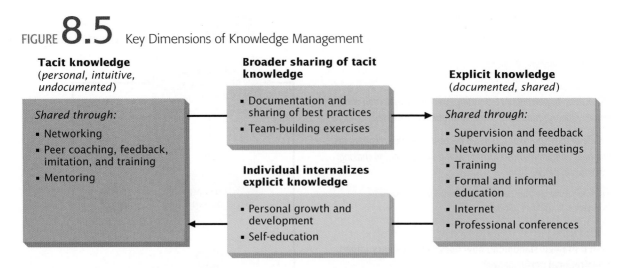

Source: Adapted from discussion in Kiujiro Nonaka, "The Knowledge-Creating Company," Harvard Business Review on Knowledge Management (Boston: Harvard Business School Publishing, 1998), pp. 21–45; and Roy Lubit, "Tacit Knowledge and Knowledge Management: The Key to Sustainable Competitive Advantage," Organizational Dynamics, 29 (Winter 2001): 164–178.

of their craft have tacit knowledge (or "deep smarts") accumulated through years of experience.

> *Experts who encounter a wide variety of situations over many years accumulate a storehouse of knowledge and, with it, the ability to reason swiftly and without a lot of conscious effort. Those with keen managerial or technical intuition can rapidly determine whether current cases fit any patterns that have emerged in the past; they're also adept at coherently (though not always consciously) assembling disparate elements into a whole that makes sense. . . . In fact, when asked to explain a decision, experts often cannot re-create all the pathways their brains checked out and so cannot give a carefully reasoned answer. They chalk up to gut feel what is really a form of gut* knowledge.[53]

Experts with deep smarts simply "do" the task; they have a "feel" for the job; they know when they are "in the zone." For example, ask really good golfers how they know their swing is right.[54]

Meanwhile, **explicit knowledge** is readily sharable information because it is in verbal, textual, visual, or numerical form. It can be found in presentations and lectures, books and magazines (both hard copy and online), policy manuals, technical specifications, training programs, databases, and software programs. In short, explicit knowledge is public (to varying degrees), whereas tacit knowledge is private.

explicit knowledge: documented and sharable information

IMPROVING THE FLOW OF KNOWLEDGE.   As indicated in Figure 8.5, knowledge resides in different places and needs to be shared. Each type of knowledge is important in its own way. Each needs to be carefully cultivated. The sharing of constructive tacit knowledge between coworkers is a top priority, as indicated in Figure 8.5. Organizational support is needed to help individuals feel comfortable about giving and receiving useful task-related knowledge on demand.[55]

Sophisticated new KM software is proving very useful and cost-effective in large organizations for sharing both tacit and explicit knowledge.[56] For example, consider the experience of Werner Hinz, a lead engineer at defense contractor Northrop Grumman:

> *[He] had to prepare a design bid for a next-generation unmanned airplane for the Pentagon—one that travels at several times the speed of sound. To do this, Hinz needed some high-level expertise on hypersonics. But no one he knew, or knew of, had what he needed.*
>
> *So Hinz turned to [ActiveNet, a KM software application Northrup had purchased]. . . . The program combs through thousands of employee profiles and millions of internal documents—from e-mails to PowerPoint slides—and suggests synergistic matchups between workers, based on what the software's algorithms perceive as someone's interests and expertise. After Hinz typed in a few phrases and keywords, the program fired back a message listing two colleagues in his building—people Hinz had met, but whose backgrounds he didn't know—who might be good sources. Hinz called the first one; two minutes later he knew he'd found the right person.[57]*

KM software is sort of like an Internet dating service—but for informational rather than romantic purposes. According to KM advocates, it is important to know what you know, to know what you don't know, and to know how to find what you need to know. The result: better and more timely decisions.

You will encounter many topics in this book to improve the various knowledge flows in Figure 8.5. Among them are organizational cultures, training, communication, empowerment, participative management, virtual teams, transformational leadership, and mentoring.

GROUP-AIDED DECISION MAKING: A CONTINGENCY PERSPECTIVE

Decision making, like any other organizational activity, does not take place in a vacuum. Typically, decision making is a highly social activity with committees, study groups, review panels, or project teams contributing in a variety of ways.

Collaborative Computing

Computer networks, the Internet, and the advent of **collaborative computing** guarantee even broader participation in the decision-making process.

> **collaborative computing:** teaming up to make decisions via a computer network programmed with groupware

Collaborative computing is a catchphrase for a new body of software and hardware that helps people work better together. A collaborative system creates an environment in which people can share information without the constraints of time and space.

Network groupware applications link workgroups across a room or across the globe. The software gives the group a common, online venue for meetings, and it lets all members labor on the same data simultaneously.

Collaborative applications include calendar management, video teleconferencing, computer teleconferencing, integrated team support, and support for business meetings and group authoring. Messaging and e-mail systems represent the most basic type of groupware.[58]

Unfortunately, according to research, groupware is typically plagued by low-quality implementation. Sixty-five percent of the survey respondents used it simply as a communication tool, to send and receive e-mail, which is analogous to using a personal computer for

Some creative group-aided decision making between the Little Traverse Bay Bands of Odawa Indians and Harbor Springs Public Schools led to an interesting nonprogrammed decision. Harbor Springs is the only public school system in Michigan to offer a for-credit course in a Native American language. Here Cheyenne Worthington writes in her native Odawa language, *Anishinaabemowin*.

word processing only. Groupware users need to be taught how to *collaborate* via computer (for instance, jointly identifying and solving problems). "When [Groupware is] implemented correctly, the benefits are astounding. Groupware had twice the impact on individual job performance and nearly three times the impact on customer satisfaction at the organizations with the highest-quality implementation compared with the organization with the lowest."[59]

Group Involvement in Decisions

Whether the situation is a traditional face-to-face committee meeting or a global e-meeting, at least five aspects of the decision-making process can be assigned to groups:

1. Analyzing the problem
2. Identifying components of the decision situation
3. Estimating components of the decision situation (for example, determining probabilities, feasibilities, time estimates, and payoffs)
4. Designing alternatives
5. Choosing an alternative[60]

Assuming that two (or more) heads may be better than one and that managers can make better use of their time by delegating various decision-making chores, there is a strong case for turning to groups when making decisions. But before bringing others into the decision process, managers need to be aware of the problem of dispersed accountability and consider the tradeoff between the advantages and disadvantages of group-aided decision making. In view of these problems and of research evidence comparing individual and group performance, a contingency approach is recommended.

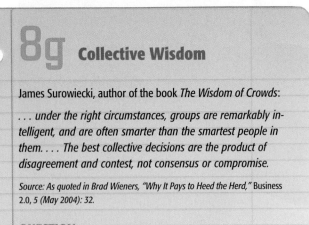

8g Collective Wisdom

James Surowiecki, author of the book *The Wisdom of Crowds*:

. . . under the right circumstances, groups are remarkably intelligent, and are often smarter than the smartest people in them. . . . The best collective decisions are the product of disagreement and contest, not consensus or compromise.

Source: As quoted in Brad Wieners, "Why It Pays to Heed the Herd," Business 2.0, 5 (May 2004): 32.

QUESTION:
Do you agree or disagree? Explain.

The Problem of Dispersed Accountability

There is a critical difference between group-aided decision making and group decision making. In the first instance, the group does everything except make the final decision. In the second instance, the group actually makes the final decision. Managers who choose the second route face a dilemma. Although a decision made by a group will probably reflect the collective experience and wisdom of all those involved, personal accountability is lost. Blame for a joint decision that fails is too easily passed on to others. For example, Robert Palmer, hired to turn Digital Equipment around, inherited the following situation: "This was a company run by committee, by consensus. No one actually made a decision. When things went well, there would be a number of people willing to take credit. But when things went wrong, it was impossible to fix responsibility on anyone."[61] This legacy of dispersed accountability proved too much for Palmer, and Digital was sold to Compaq Computer, which eventually became part of Hewlett-Packard.

The traditional formula for resolving this problem is to make sure that a given manager is personally accountable for a decision when the responsibility for it has to be traced. According to this line of reasoning, even when a group is asked to recommend a decision, the responsibility for the final outcome remains with the manager in charge. For managers who want to maintain the integrity of personal accountability, there is no such thing as group decision making; there is only group-*aided* decision making. There are three situations in which individual accountability for a decision is necessary:

- The decision will have significant impact on the success or failure of the unit or organization.
- The decision has legal ramifications (such as possible prosecution for price-fixing, antitrust, or product safety violations).
- A competitive reward is tied to a successful decision. (For example, only one person can get a promotion.)

In less critical areas, the group itself may be responsible for making decisions.

Advantages and Disadvantages of Group-Aided Decision Making

Various combinations of positive and negative factors are encountered when a manager brings others into

TABLE **8.2**   Advantages and Disadvantages of Group-Aided Decision Making and Problem Solving

ADVANTAGES	DISADVANTAGES
1. **Greater pool of knowledge.** A group can bring much more information and experience to bear on a decision or problem than can an individual acting alone.	1. **Social pressure.** Unwillingness to "rock the boat" and pressure to conform may combine to stifle the creativity of individual contributors.
2. **Different perspectives.** Individuals with varied experience and interests help the group see decision situations and problems from different angles.	2. **Domination by a vocal few.** Sometimes the quality of group action is reduced when the group gives in to those who talk the loudest and longest.
3. **Greater comprehension.** Those who personally experience the give-and-take of group discussion about alternative courses of action tend to understand the rationale behind the final decision.	3. **Logrolling.** Political wheeling and dealing can displace sound thinking when an individual's pet project or vested interest is at stake.
4. **Increased acceptance.** Those who play an active role in group decision making and problem solving tend to view the outcome as "ours" rather than "theirs."	4. **Goal displacement.** Sometimes secondary considerations such as winning an argument, making a point, or getting back at a rival displace the primary task of making a sound decision or solving a problem.
5. **Training ground.** Less experienced participants in group action learn how to cope with group dynamics by actually being involved.	5. **"Groupthink."** Sometimes cohesive "in groups" let the desire for unanimity override sound judgment when generating and evaluating alternative courses of action. (Groupthink is discussed in Chapter 13.)

the decision-making process. The advantages and disadvantages are listed in Table 8.2. If there is a conscious effort to avoid or at least minimize the disadvantages, managers can gain a great deal by sharing the decision-making process with peers, outside consultants, and team members.[62] However, some important contingency factors need to be taken into consideration.

A Contingency Approach Is Necessary

Are two or more heads actually better than one? The answer depends on the nature of the task, the ability of the contributors, and the form of interaction (see Figure 8.6). An analysis of dozens of individual-versus-group performance studies conducted over a 61-year period led one researcher to the following conclusions: (1) groups tend to do quantitatively and qualitatively better than the *average* individual; and (2) *exceptional* individuals tend to outperform the group, particularly when the task is complex and the group is made up of relatively low-ability people.[63]

Consequently, busy managers need to delegate aspects of the decision-making process (specified earlier) according to the contingencies in Figure 8.6. More is said about delegation in the next chapter.

FIGURE **8.6** Individual versus Group Performance: Contingency Management Insights from 61 Years of Research

Nature of task	Insights from research
Problem-solving task	Individuals are faster, but groups tend to produce better results
Complex task	Best results achieved by polling the contributions of individuals working alone
Brainstorming task	Same as for complex task
Learning task	Groups consistently outperform individuals
Concept mastery/ creative task	Contributions from average-ability group members tend to improve when they are teamed with high-ability group members

Source: Based in part on research conclusions found in Gayle W. Hill, "Group versus Individual Performance: Are N + 1 Heads Better than One?" Psychological Bulletin, 91 (May 1982): 517–539.

MANAGERIAL CREATIVITY

Demands for creativity and innovation make the practice of management endlessly exciting (and often extremely difficult).[64] Nearly all managerial problem solving requires a healthy measure of creativity as managers mentally take things apart, rearrange the pieces in new and potentially productive configurations, and look beyond normal frameworks for new solutions. This process is like turning the kaleidoscope of one's mind. Thomas Edison used to retire to an old couch in his laboratory to do his creative thinking. Henry Ford reportedly sought creative insights by staring at a blank wall in his shop. Although the average manager's attempts at creativity may not be as dramatically fruitful as Edison's or Ford's, workplace creativity needs to be understood and nurtured.[65] As a steppingstone to the next section on creative problem solving, this section defines creativity, discusses the management of creative people, and identifies barriers to creativity.

What Is Creativity?

Creativity is a rather mysterious process known chiefly by its results and is therefore difficult to define. About as close as we can come is to say that **creativity** is the reorganization of experience into new configurations.[66] According to a management consultant specializing in creativity, "Creativity is a function of *knowledge,*

creativity: the reorganization of experience into new configurations

imagination, and *evaluation.* The greater our knowledge, the more ideas, patterns, or combinations we can achieve. But merely having the knowledge does not guarantee the formation of new patterns; the bits and pieces must be shaken up and interrelated in new ways. Then, the embryonic ideas must be evaluated and developed into usable ideas."[67] Donna Kacmar, an architect in Houston, Texas, exemplifies our definition of creativity:

> *My creativity lies in trying to explore new possibilities for what might be considered a dumb or mundane problem. We all think we know how to make an office building or a townhouse or some run-of-the-mill thing like that. Well, do we? Let's question the assumptions that we have and see if there are some new things we can try. . . .*
>
> *What I'm able to do is help people see things a different way. I think I'm able to see things a little bit more openly—to find relationships between things that aren't as readily apparent and then make something of those relationships. My version of creativity is more like a quest for understanding.*[68]

Creativity is often subtle and may not be readily apparent to the untrained eye. But the combination and extension of seemingly insignificant day-to-day breakthroughs lead to organizational progress.

Identifying general types of creativity is easier than explaining the basic process. One pioneering writer on the subject isolated three overlapping domains of creativity: art, discovery, and humor.[69] These have been called the "ah!" reaction, the "aha!" reaction, and the "haha!" reaction, respectively.[70]

The discovery ("aha!") variation is the most relevant to management. Entirely new businesses can

From left to right, Samantha Richey of DeSoto, Texas; Sarah Fakhraldeen of Kuwait; and Sajid Mehmood of Somerset, New Jersey, tackle a creative problem-solving exercise at the Seeds of Peace summer camp in Otisfield, Maine. Whether they realize it or not, they are developing cross-cultural communication skills that are vital to success in the global economy.

8h A Quick Test of Your Creativity

You have a candle, some matches, and a box of tacks. How can you affix the burning candle to the wall without dripping any wax on the wall or the floor?

Source: Puzzle adapted from and answer quoted from Janet Paskin, "Happily Ever After," Money, 35 (June 2006): 28.

QUESTIONS:

How quickly did you solve this puzzle? What was right or wrong about your approach? What does it say about your creativity? (See endnote 71 for the answer.)[71]

spring from creative discovery. Here is a prime example:

> *Gary Goldberg's aha! moment came in the spring of 2004, when Dr. Robert Klein, a pediatrician at Rhode Island Hospital, told him how difficult it was to combat allergen-related illnesses. Those conversations, coupled with Goldberg's own 8-year-old son's struggles with allergies, left the third-generation textile specialist convinced there was a big market for products to serve the 60 million U.S. allergy sufferers.*
>
> *Today, 37-year-old Goldberg is president of East Providence (R.I.)–based CleanBrands, which has developed a unique line of mattress and pillow covers, called CleanRest encasements, that prevents sleepers from inhaling allergens, like dust mites, that live in their beddings naturally.[72]*

Goldberg's success has been nothing to sneeze at, with his products in all 850 Bed, Bath, & Beyond stores by 2006 and revenues of $2.9 million by mid 2007.[73]

Workplace Creativity: Myth and Modern Reality

Recent research has shattered a long-standing myth about creative employees. According to the myth, creative people are typically nonconformists. But Alan Robinson's field research paints a very different picture:

> *"We went to 450 companies in 13 countries and spoke to 600 people who'd done highly creative things, from big new innovations to tiny improvements," he explains. Only three out of the 600 were*

true nonconformists. The rest were more like your average corporate Joe, much more "plodding and cautious" than most managers would expect. Other creativity studies have had similar results, he says.

> *One reason for the mismatch between popular perception and reality, he believes, is that so many steps are needed to bring most new ideas to fruition. Those who succeed must be able to build support for the idea among other team members, and they sometimes need a lot of patience as well. Corporate nonconformists may not have a great deal of either.[74]*

Thus, creative self-expression through unconventional dress and strange behavior does not necessarily translate into creative work.

Today's managers are challenged to create an organizational culture and climate capable of evoking the often hidden creative talents of *every* employee.[75] Consider, for instance, the birth of Frappuccino at Starbucks, as related by founder and CEO Howard Schultz:

> *Frappuccino was created by a store manager in West L.A. This person was fooling around one day in our store, blending beverages with a blender she bought on her own. We started sampling that, and the people in our Southern California region were very intrigued. We tested it, named it, and Frappuccino today is a multi-hundred-million-dollar business in our stores. A ready-to-drink joint venture with Pepsi-Cola is a $500 million business unto itself. The employee who came up with it? She is now god. She still works with Starbucks.[76]*

Learning to Be More Creative

Some people naturally seem to be more creative than others. But that does not mean that those who feel the need cannot develop their creative capacity. It does seem clear that creative ability can be learned, in the sense that our creative energies can be released from the bonds of convention, lack of self-confidence, and narrow thinking. We all have the potential to be more creative.

The best place to begin is by trying consciously to overcome what creativity specialist Roger von Oech calls *mental locks*. The following mental locks are attitudes that get us through our daily activities but tend to stifle our creativity*:

1. ***Looking for the "right" answer.*** A given problem may have several right answers, depending on one's perspective.

*Source: List adapted from A Whack on the Side of the Head *by Roger von Oech, Warner Books, 1983. Reprinted by permission.*

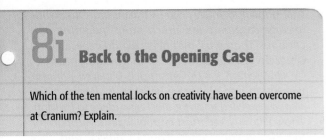

8i Back to the Opening Case

Which of the ten mental locks on creativity have been overcome at Cranium? Explain.

2. ***Always trying to be logical.*** Logic does not always prevail, given human emotions and organizational inconsistencies, ambiguity, and contradictions.
3. ***Strictly following the rules.*** If things are to be improved, arbitrary limits on thinking and behavior need to be questioned.
4. ***Insisting on being practical.*** Impractical answers to "what-if" questions can become steppingstones to creative insights.
5. ***Avoiding ambiguity.*** Creativity can be stunted by too much objectivity and specificity.
6. ***Fearing and avoiding failure.*** Fear of failure can paralyze us into not acting on our good ideas. This is unfortunate because we learn many valuable and lasting lessons from our mistakes.
7. ***Forgetting how to play.*** The playful experimentation of childhood too often disappears by adulthood.
8. ***Becoming too specialized.*** Cross-fertilization of specialized areas helps in defining problems and generating solutions.
9. ***Not wanting to look foolish.*** Humor can release tensions and unlock creative energies. Seemingly foolish questions can enhance understanding.
10. ***Saying "I'm not creative."*** By nurturing small and apparently insignificant ideas, we can convince ourselves that we are indeed creative.[77]

(Try the creativity exercise in the Action Learning Exercise at the end of this chapter.) If these mental locks are conquered, the creative problem-solving process discussed in the next section can be used to its full potential.

CREATIVE PROBLEM SOLVING

We are all problem solvers. But this does not mean that all of us are good problem solvers or even, for that matter, that we know how to solve problems systematically. Most daily problem solving is done on a haphazard, intuitive basis. A difficulty arises, so we

look around for an answer, jump at the first workable solution to come along, and move on to other things. In a primitive sense, this sequence of events qualifies as a problem-solving process, and it works quite well for informal daily activities. But in the world of management, a more systematic problem-solving process is required for tackling difficult and unfamiliar nonprogrammed decisions. In the context of management, **problem solving** is the conscious process of bringing the actual situation closer to the desired situation.[78] Managerial problem solving consists of a four-step sequence: (1) identifying the problem, (2) generating alternative solutions, (3) selecting a solution, and (4) implementing and evaluating the solution (see Figure 8.7).

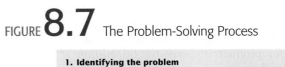

problem solving: conscious process of closing the gap between actual and desired situations

Identifying the Problem

As strange as it may seem, the most common problem-solving difficulty lies in the identification of problems. Busy managers have a tendency to rush into generating

FIGURE **8.7** The Problem-Solving Process

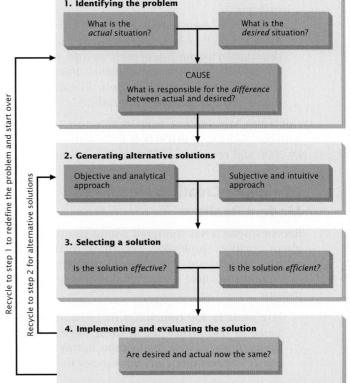

ETHICS: CHARACTER, COURAGE, AND VALUES

Stephen Siegel Does Well By Doing Good

When people tell me something is a bad idea, that makes me think it's a good idea. In 2003, the real estate market in California heated up and it was harder to get good deals. One day, I found a 132-unit building in Las Vegas on the Internet. It was in a real rough neighborhood, but the location was great because it was attached to the Las Vegas Convention Center.

I parked across the street from the building and stared at it, visualizing what I could do to improve it. The building was full of drug dealers and prostitutes. I went inside to do an inspection and some police officers were there. They said I would never be able to clean it up. Everyone said I was crazy. That was my trigger. If someone tells me I can't do it, I'm doing it. I bought the building for $6 million.

I started with the neighborhood. I made friends with the people who hung out on the streets. I met a family living in the bushes across from the building. I gave them a free apartment and put the husband to work. I paid other people to keep an eye on the building. We removed pay phones to discourage drug dealing. That's how I secured the neighborhood.

People who are doing the wrong thing like to hide with the lights off. When you turn on the lights and make a building look good, they take off. It took about a year to rehab the building and get rid of the bad people. At that point, I sold it to the convention center for $10.2 million.

Source: Excerpted from Stephen Siegel, "How I Did It," Inc., 29 (September 2007): 182. Copyright 2007 by Mansueto Ventures LLC. Reproduced with permission of Mansueto Ventures LLC in the format Textbook via Copyright Clearance Center.

FOR DISCUSSION

Would you call Siegel an *ethical* businessman, or just a *good* businessman because he probably made a handsome profit on this community improvement project?

---

and selecting alternative solutions before they have actually isolated and understood the real problem. According to Peter Drucker, the respected management scholar, "The greatest source of mistakes in top management is to ask the same questions most people ask. They all assume that there are the same 'right answers' for everyone. But one does not begin with answers. One begins by asking, 'What are our questions?'"[79] When problem finding, managers should probe with the right questions.[80] Only then can the right answers be found.

Problem finding can be a great career booster, too, as Michael Iem discovered. It all started with his love of tough challenges.

> *This bricklayer's son has no formal job title and no office, but his career at Tandem Computers [now part of Hewlett-Packard] is on a tear. He personifies the advice that executive recruiter Robert Horton offers all who want to advance: "Find the biggest business problem your employer faces for which you and your skills are the solution."... [Iem's problem-solving ability] made him known throughout Tandem, bringing promotions and a doubling of his $32,000 starting salary.... The company lets him decide what projects to take on, making him the youngest of perhaps a dozen employees with the broad mandate.*[81]

WHAT IS A PROBLEM? Ask half a dozen people how they identify problems, and you are likely to get as many answers. Consistent with the definition given earlier for problem solving, a **problem** is defined as the difference between an actual state of affairs and a desired state of affairs. In other words, a problem is the gap between where one is and where one wants to be. Problem solving is meant to close this gap (see Ethics: Character, Courage, and Values). For example, a person in New York who has to make a presentation in San Francisco in 24 hours has a problem. The problem is not being in New York (the actual state of affairs), nor is it presenting in San Francisco in 24 hours (the desired state of affairs). Instead, the problem is the distance between New York and San Francisco. Flying would be an obvious solution. But thanks to modern communications technology such as videoconferencing, there are ways to overcome the 2,934-mile gap without having to travel.

> **problem:** the difference between an actual and a desired state of affairs

Managers need to define problems according to the gaps between the actual and the desired situations. A production manager, for example, would be wise to concentrate on the gap between the present level of weekly production and the desired level. This focus is much more fruitful than complaining about the current low production or wishfully thinking about high production. The challenge is discovering a workable alternative for closing the gap between actual and desired production.[82]

STUMBLING BLOCKS FOR PROBLEM FINDERS. There are three common stumbling blocks for those attempting to identify problems:

1. ***Defining the problem according to a possible solution.*** One should be careful not to rule out alternative solutions in the way one states a problem. For example, a manager in a unit plagued by high absenteeism who says, "We have a problem with low pay," may prevent management from discovering that tedious and boring work is the real cause. By focusing on how to close the gap between actual and desired attendance, instead of simply on low pay, management stands a better chance of finding a workable solution.

2. ***Focusing on narrow, low-priority areas.*** Successful managers are those who can weed out relatively minor problems and reserve their attention for problems that really make a difference. Formal organizational goals and objectives provide a useful framework for determining the priority of various problems. Don't be concerned with cleaning the floor when the roof is caving in.

3. ***Diagnosing problems in terms of their symptoms.*** As a short-run expedient, treating symptoms rather than underlying causes may be appropriate. Buying a bottle of aspirin is cheaper than trying to find a less stressful job, for example. In the longer run, however, symptoms tend to reappear and problems tend to get worse. There is a two-way test for discovering whether one has found the cause of a problem: "If I *introduce* this variable, will the problem (the gap) disappear?" or "If I *remove* this variable, will the problem (the gap) disappear?" **Causes** are variables that, because of their presence in or absence from the situation, are primarily responsible for the difference between the actual and the desired conditions. For example, the *absence* of a key can cause a problem with a locked door, and the *presence* of a nail can cause a problem with an inflated tire.[83]

causes: variables responsible for the difference between actual and desired conditions

PINPOINTING CAUSES WITH FISHBONE DIAGRAMS. Fishbone diagrams, discussed in Chapter 16 as a TQM process improvement tool, are a handy way to track down causes of problems. They work especially well in group problem-solving situations. Construction of a

Harvard Business Review, May 2006

"THIS ENSURES THAT WE DON'T OVERANALYZE."

fishbone diagram begins with a statement of the problem (the head of the fish skeleton). "On the bones growing out of the spine one lists possible causes of . . . problems, in order of possible occurrence. The chart can help one see how various separate problem causes might interact. It also shows how possible causes occur with respect to one another, over time, helping start the problem-solving process."[84] (A sample fishbone diagram appears in the Manager's Toolkit at the end of this chapter.)

Generating Alternative Solutions

After the problem and its most probable cause have been identified, attention turns to generating alternative solutions. This is the creative step in problem solving. Unfortunately, as the following statement points out, creativity is often shortchanged.

> *The natural response to a problem seems to be to try to get rid of it by finding an answer—often taking the first answer that occurs and pursuing it because of one's reluctance to spend the time and mental effort needed to conjure up a rich storehouse of alternatives from which to choose.*[85]

It takes time, patience, and practice to become a good generator of alternative solutions: a flexible combination of analysis and intuition is helpful. A good sense of humor can aid the process as well. Several popular and useful techniques can stimulate

8j Creating a Questioning Culture. Any Questions?

When we ask questions of others and invite them to search for answers with us, we are not just sharing information, we are sharing responsibility. A questioning culture is a culture in which responsibility is shared. And when responsibility is shared, ideas are shared, problems are shared (problems are not yours or mine, but ours), and ownership of results is shared. When an organization develops a questioning culture, it also creates a culture of we, rather than a culture of you versus me, or management versus employees.

Source: Michael Marquardt, Leading with Questions: How Leaders Find the Right Solutions by Knowing What to Ask *(San Francisco: Jossey-Bass, 2005), p. 28.*

QUESTIONS:

What are the barriers to creating a questioning culture in today's work organizations? What can be done to overcome them?

individual and group creativity. Among them are the following approaches:

- *Brainstorming.* This is a group technique in which any and all ideas are recorded, in a *nonjudgmental* setting, for later critique and selection. Brainstorming on computer network systems is proving worthwhile now that sophisticated groupware is available.[86] IBM's CEO Samuel J. Palmisano believes in the creative potential of brainstorming and does it on a truly grand scale:

  > He is pulling people together for the online equivalent of a town meeting. His hope: The opinions of some 100,000 minds will lead to catalytic innovations so powerful they will transform industries, alter human behavior, and lead to new businesses for IBM. He calls the project an Innovation Jam. . . .
  >
  > To prepare those invited to participate, the company built an interactive Web site that includes sound clips, virtual guided tours, and video snippets with background information.[87]

- *Free association.* Analogies and symbols are used to foster unconventional thinking. For example, think of your studies as a mountain requiring special climbing gear and skills.
- *Edisonian method.* Named for Thomas Edison's tedious and persistent search for a durable light

bulb filament, this technique involves trial-and-error experimentation.

> On a Sunday evening in 1897, Thomas Edison and his assistants powered up an electric bulb and took turns watching it. Over the past 18 months their quest for a workable filament had generated nothing but 1,200 failures and $40,000 in expenses. But this time the carbonized sewing thread inside was still glowing more than 13 hours later.[88]

The rest, as they say, is history.

- *Attribute listing.* Ideal characteristics of a given object are collected and then screened for useful insights.
- *Scientific method.* Systematic hypothesis testing, manipulation of variables, situational controls, and careful measurement are the essence of this rigorous approach.
- *Creative leap.* This technique involves thinking up idealistic solutions to a problem and then working back to a feasible solution.

Selecting a Solution

Simply stating that the best solution should be selected in step 3 (refer to Figure 8.7) can be misleading. Because of time and financial constraints and political considerations, *best* is a relative term. Generally, alternative solutions should be screened for the most appealing balance of effectiveness and efficiency in view of relevant constraints and intangibles. Russell Ackoff, a specialist in managerial problem solving, contends that three things can be done about problems: they can be resolved, solved, or dissolved.[89]

RESOLVING THE PROBLEM. When a problem is resolved, a course of action that is good enough to meet the minimum constraints is selected. The term **satisfice** has been applied to the practice of settling for solutions that are good enough rather than the best possible.[90] A badly worn spare tire may satisfice as a replacement for a flat tire for the balance of the trip, although getting the flat repaired is the best possible solution. According to Ackoff, most managers rely on problem resolving. This nonquantitative, subjective approach is popular because managers claim they do not have the information or time necessary for the other approaches. Satisficing, however, has been criticized as a shortsighted and passive technique

satisfice: to settle for a solution that is good enough

emphasizing expedient survival instead of improvement and growth.

SOLVING THE PROBLEM.   A problem is solved when the best possible solution is selected. Managers are said to **optimize** when, through scientific observation and quantitative measurement, they systematically research alternative solutions and select the one with the best combination of benefits.

> **optimize:** to systematically identify the solution with the best combination of benefits

DISSOLVING THE PROBLEM. A problem is dissolved when the situation in which it occurs is changed so that the problem no longer exists. Problem dissolvers are said to **idealize** because they actually change the nature of the system in which a problem resides. Managers who dissolve problems rely on whatever combination of nonquantitative and quantitative tools is needed to get the job done. The replacement of automobile assembly-line welders with robots, for instance, has dissolved the problem of costly absenteeism among people in that job category.

> **idealize:** to change the nature of the situation in which a problem has arisen

Whatever approach a manager chooses, the following advice from Ackoff should be kept in mind: "Few if any problems . . . are ever permanently resolved, solved, or dissolved; every treatment of a problem generates new problems."[91] A Japanese manager at the General Motors-Toyota joint venture auto plant in California put it this way: "No problem is a problem."[92] And, as pointed out by the co-founder of a successful import business, an administrative life made up of endless problems is cause for optimism, not pessimism: "Spare yourself some grief. Understand that, in business, you will always have problems. They are where the opportunities lie."[93] Hence the need for continuous improvement.

Implementing and Evaluating the Solution

Time is the true test of any solution. Until a particular solution has had time to prove its worth, the manager can rely only on his or her judgment concerning its effectiveness and efficiency. Ideally, the solution selected will completely eliminate the difference between the actual and the desired in an efficient and timely manner. Should the gap fail to disappear, two options are open. If the manager remains convinced that the problem has been correctly identified, he or she can recycle to step 2 to try another solution that was identified earlier. This recycling can continue until all feasible solutions have been given a fair chance or until the nature of the problem changes to the extent that the existing solutions are obsolete. If the gap between actual and desired persists in spite of repeated attempts to find a solution, then it is advisable to recycle to step 1 to redefine the problem and engage in a new round of problem solving.

SUMMARY

1. Decision making is a fundamental part of management because it requires choosing among alternative courses of action. In addition to having to cope with an era of accelerating change, today's decision makers face the challenges of dealing with complexity, uncertainty, the need for flexible thinking, and decision traps. Eight factors that contribute to decision complexity are multiple criteria, intangibles, risk and uncertainty, long-term implications, interdisciplinary input, pooled decision making, value judgments, and unintended consequences.

2. Managers must learn to assess the degree of certainty in a situation—whether conditions are certain, risky, or uncertain. Confidence in one's decisions decreases as uncertainty increases. Managers can respond to a condition of risk—incomplete but reliable factual information—by calculating objective or subjective probabilities. Today's managers need to tap the creative potential of intuitive employees and the implementation skills of those who process information as thinkers.

3. Researchers have identified three perceptual and behavioral decision traps that can undermine the quality of decisions. Framing error occurs when people let labels and frames of reference sway their interpretations. People fall victim to escalation of commitment when they get locked into losing propositions for fear of quitting and looking bad. Oddly, researchers find that overconfidence tends to grow with the difficulty of the task.

4. Decisions, generally, are either programmed or nonprogrammed. Because programmed decisions are relatively clear-cut and routinely encountered, fixed decision rules can be formulated for them. In contrast, nonprogrammed decisions require creative problem solving because they are novel and unfamiliar. Decision making can be improved with a knowledge management (KM) program. KM is a systematic approach to creating and sharing critical information throughout the organization. Two types of knowledge are *tacit* (personal, intuitive, and undocumented) and *explicit* (documented and sharable) knowledge.

5. Managers may choose to bring other people into virtually every aspect of the decision-making process. However, when a group rather than an individual is responsible for making the decision, personal accountability is lost. Dispersed accountability is undesirable in some key decision situations. Group-aided decision making has both advantages and disadvantages. Because group performance does not always exceed individual performance, a contingency approach to group-aided decision making is advisable.

6. Creativity requires the proper combination of knowledge, imagination, and evaluation to reorganize experience into new configurations. The domains of creativity may be divided into art, discovery (the most relevant to management), and humor. Contrary to myth, researchers have found only a weak link between creativity and nonconformity. A fun and energizing workplace climate can tap *every* employee's creativity. By consciously overcoming ten mental locks, we can become more creative.

7. The creative problem-solving process consists of four steps: (1) identifying the problem, (2) generating alternative solutions, (3) selecting a solution, and (4) implementing and evaluating the solution. Inadequate problem finding is common among busy managers. By seeing problems as gaps between an actual situation and a desired situation, managers are in a better position to create more effective and efficient solutions. Depending on the situation, problems can be resolved, solved, or dissolved. It is important to remember that today's solutions often become tomorrow's problems.

8. A clear and concise statement of the problem forms the "head" of the fishbone skeleton. Each of the "bones" extending out from the backbone of the fishbone diagram represents a possible cause of the problem. More likely causes are located closer to the head of the diagram. Possible explanations for each cause are attached to each particular "bone."

TERMS TO UNDERSTAND

- **Decision making,** p. 206
- **Law of unintended consequences,** p. 210
- **Condition of certainty,** p. 211
- **Condition of risk,** p. 211
- **Objective probabilities,** p. 212
- **Subjective probabilities,** p. 212
- **Condition of uncertainty,** p. 212

- **Framing error,** p. 213
- **Escalation of commitment,** p. 214
- **Programmed decisions,** p. 216
- **Decision rule,** p. 216
- **Nonprogrammed decisions,** p. 216
- **Knowledge management,** p. 217
- **Tacit knowledge,** p. 217
- **Explicit knowledge,** p. 218

- **Collaborative computing,** p. 219
- **Creativity,** p. 222
- **Problem solving,** p. 224
- **Problem,** p. 225
- **Causes,** p. 226
- **Satisfice,** p. 227
- **Optimize,** p. 228
- **Idealize,** p. 228

MANAGER'S TOOLKIT

How to Construct a Fishbone Diagram

Tips

- Reduce a complex web of problems to a distinct, high-priority problem.
- Create fishbones for the main categories of causes.
- Chart the most recent causes nearest the head (problem).
- Fill in specific causes.

POSSIBLE CAUSES

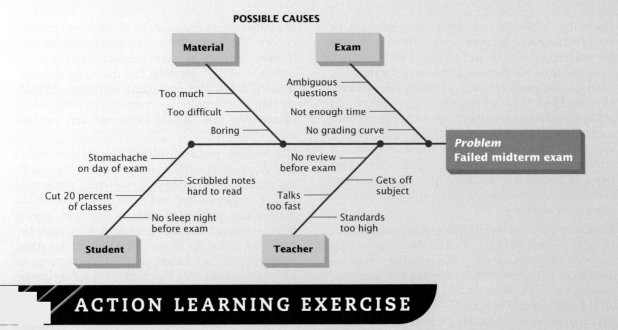

ACTION LEARNING EXERCISE

How Creative Are You?

Instructions: This exercise is for both individuals and teams. Assume that a steel pipe is embedded in the concrete floor of a bare room as shown below. The inside diameter is .06 inch larger than the diameter of a ping-pong ball (1.50 inches) which is resting gently at the bottom of the pipe. You are one of a group of six people in the room, along with the following objects:

- 100 feet of clothesline
- Carpenter's hammer

- Chisel
- Box of Wheaties
- File
- Wire coat hanger
- Monkey wrench
- Light bulb

List as many ways you can think of (in five minutes) to get the ball out of the pipe without damaging the ball, tube, or floor.

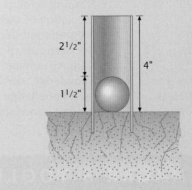

Source: From Conceptual Blockbusting *by James L. Adams. Reprinted by permission of Da Capo Press, a member of Perseus Books Group.*

For Consideration/Discussion

1. In terms of the definition in this chapter, what is the "problem" here?

2. What assumptions did you make about any of the objects?

3. How would you rate your creativity on this exercise on a scale of 1 = low to 10 = high?

4. How many of the eight resource objects did you manage to employ? Which was the most useful? Why?

5. How many solutions did you develop? Which one is the "best"? Why?

CLOSING CASE
The Phantasmagoria Factory

To understand what a Cirque du Soleil circus is like, you first have to forget every childhood memory of ring-masters, clown cars, and lion tamers. Get ready instead for a dancing headless man carrying an umbrella and a bowler hat (in *Quidam,* one of Cirque's five touring shows). Or a clown acting a pantomime of lost love, then disappearing in an elaborately staged blizzard (in *Alegria,* another touring show). Or trapeze artists dropping into a huge indoor lake that then "evaporates" before the audience's eyes (in *O,* Cirque's resident show at the Bellagio in Las Vegas).

Cirque du Soleil (French for "circus of the sun") is one of the rare companies that utterly redefine their industries. It takes the circus's raw materials—trapeze artists, contortionists, strong men, clowns—combines them with surreal costumes, nonstop New Age music, and dazzling stagecraft, and then ties it all together with a vaguely profound theme, like "a tribute to the nomadic soul" (*Varekaï*) or "a phantasmagoria of urban life" (*Saltimbanco*). The result is a spectacle that leaves audiences cheering—and flailing for metaphors. "It's like a tour of Dante's Inferno designed and cast by Federico Fellini," reads one review of *O.*

Though considerably less surreal than its shows, Cirque's business model is another crowd pleaser. Bobby Baldwin, CEO of Mirage Resorts, whose Treasure Island casino in Las Vegas hosts Cirque's *Mystère,* calls Cirque "the most successful entertainment company in the world." He isn't referring strictly to profits: The private, Montreal-based company nets more than $100 million a year on $500 million in revenue; that's not peanuts, but it's no more than Disney's live entertainment division.

Instead, Baldwin is talking about the power of the brand. In two decades and 15 separate productions, Cirque du Soleil has never had a flop. By comparison, 9 out of 10 shows on Broadway—productions aimed at the same sophisticated, big-ticket audience as Cirque—fail to earn back the money invested in them. Cirque's reputation for never missing is so strong that, in exchange for half the profits, four Las Vegas resorts, as well as Disney World, each agreed to spend tens of millions of dollars to build a custom theater to house a Cirque show and foot half the show's production costs, which can hit $25 million. No traditional circus has ever inspired such an outpouring of capital from business partners. And who can blame them? According to a recent survey, some 5 percent of all Las Vegas tourists—1.8 million a year—cite Cirque's shows as their main reason for visiting.

Much of the credit goes, appropriately, to the company's performers and artists—especially Franco Dragone, the Belgian director who headed the creative team for six of Cirque's nine current productions. Cirque's president for shows and new ventures, Daniel Lamarre, is only too happy to agree. A 50-year-old former television executive who seems slightly amused to find himself in the constant company of world-class acrobats, contortionists, designers, and musicians, Lamarre says he knows exactly why his business works: "We let the creative people run it." . . .

Cirque du Soleil was hatched in 1984 by two high school dropouts—Guy Laliberté, a 23-year-old Montreal fire breather, and Daniel Gauthier, 24, a youth hostel manager. In what had to be one of the entertainment industry's most audacious acts of persuasion, they talked the Quebec government into granting them just over $1 million to develop a show around local street performers as part of a festival celebrating the 450th anniversary of Montreal's founding. The pair hired Dragone in 1985, and what he calls the "transdisciplinary experience" of circus blended with stagecraft, live music, and song became Cirque's trademark and a hit across Canada.

The moment of truth arrived in 1987 when Laliberté and Gauthier took their act to the L.A. Arts Festival. The pair knew that if the show flopped, they couldn't afford to fly the cast and equipment home. They needn't have worried, however: The standing ovation went on for five minutes, and by the time the box office opened the next morning, 500 people were standing in line. Cirque du Soleil was no longer a nonprofit organization.

The new business was less than four years old when the founders made perhaps their most crucial decision. As word had spread of Cirque's blockbuster success, offers flooded in from other production companies eager to license touring versions of the show. No doubt the road shows could have made money. Ringling Bros. and Barnum & Bailey Circus, for example, has built its business on touring shows that have been offering up basically the same trained-lions-and-traditional-trapeze fare for generations. And for a Broadway musical, tours can be the main source of profit. But Gauthier and Laliberté refused. World-class circus performers are simply too scarce a resource, they reasoned, and a wave of road shows could only dilute the genius of the original. Rather than compromise on quality, they decided that every show bearing the Cirque name would be created in-house and be unlike any show that went before. "We said, 'Each show is a new member of the family, and we never want twins,'" Gauthier says. (Gauthier left Cirque in 2001, but Laliberté, now CEO and sole proprietor of Cirque, has never budged from that resolution.)

Lamarre freely admits that the decision has restricted the company's growth. "People tell me we're leaving a lot of money on the table by not duplicating our shows," he says. "And you know what? They're right." But he says he has no regrets, adding that Cirque's success is the best proof that the founders were right to choose quality over quick profits. The same holds for the company's deliberate pace of production. Cirque will release just one new show a year through 2007. Since the company builds each show from scratch—a three-year process—a faster schedule would spread creative resources too thin, as the company learned in 1998 when it produced both *La Nouba* and *O.*

At the moment, five Cirque shows tour the world, each a one-of-a-kind production accompanied by its own 2,500-seat tent. Another four play in permanent venues built exclusively for Cirque in Las Vegas and Orlando. Such arrangements are not cheap. To launch *Zumanity*, for example, New York-New York owner MGM Mirage put up $51 million, including the cost of building the theater, while Cirque kicked in $7.5 million.

So far, though, Cirque has repaid its partners' investments—and then some. The brand draws a decidedly upscale college-educated audience, skewing toward women. Such patrons appreciate Cirque's ambitious themes and, just as important, don't blink at ticket prices that range from $45 to $150. The company sells 97 percent of available seats. . . .

True to Lamarre's assertion that the creative minds lead the company, he and his business staff never get involved with a show's three-year-long creative gestation. At conception, Lamarre meets with the team of director, circus director, choreographer, composer, and set and lighting designers and agrees on a production budget and an opening date. After that, the director can spend the budget—typically on the order of $10 million to $25 million—as he or she sees fit. "Cirque allows you to approach shows with the artistic priority first," Dragone confirms. "I never had to worry about the money or the business and instead could focus on the show." While it seems hard to believe, Lamarre says no director has ever come begging for more money.

That doesn't mean, of course, that the business office is irrelevant. Indeed, one key to each new show's electrifying originality is Lamarre's massive investment in research and development. While he won't be specific, Lamarre hints at an annual outlay of some $40 million. The payback: astonishing effects like a swirling snowstorm in *Alegria*. Perhaps the most amazing invention is *O*'s indoor lake, which can shrink from a 25-foot-deep pool to a puddle in a matter of seconds, thanks to a hydraulically powered floor that rises through the water. The specially equipped theater cost $70 million alone, paid for entirely by MGM Mirage, which also shouldered nearly half the $22 million in production costs. . . .

Ideas on the drawing board include a nightclub called Club Cirque and a Cirque Resort in Vegas that would feature New Age music, brightly colored furniture, and theatrical lighting throughout the building. Cirque's entertainers would also have roles; Lamarre says he envisions jugglers as room service waiters. "We want to challenge our creative people to work in new mediums," he says.

Source: From Geoff Keighley, "The Phantasmagoria Factory," *Business 2.0,* (January–February 2004): 103–107. © 2004 Time Inc. All rights reserved.

FOR DISCUSSION

1 Which of the eight sources of complexity for today's decision makers (Figure 8.1) are evident in this case? Explain your choices.

2 Is most of the decision making discussed in this case programmed or nonprogrammed? Explain.

3 What was "the key decision" in this case? Could it have any unintended consequences? Explain.

4 What does Cirque du Soleil do to foster a healthy climate for creativity? What else could they do?

5 How does Cirque du Soleil create a profitable balance between artistic creativity and business discipline?

6 What is the secret of Cirque du Soleil's success?

TEST PREPPER

True/False Questions

_____ 1. One of the eight intertwined factors that contribute to decision complexity is governmental regulation.

_____ 2. By definition, a condition of risk exists when there is little or no reliable factual information available.

_____ 3. One way to sharpen your intuition is to get good feedback on your intuitive judgments.

_____ 4. Throwing good money after bad is involved in escalation of commitment.

_____ 5. "If-then" decision rules are used when one is making programmed decisions.

_____ 6. There are two types of knowledge: implicit knowledge and tactical knowledge.

_____ 7. "Logrolling" is a disadvantage of group-aided decision making.

_____ 8. According to recent field research, creative people tend to be extreme nonconformists.

_____ 9. A problem is defined as any sort of deficiency.

_____10. "Satisficing" involves finding a solution to a problem that is "good enough," rather than finding the best possible solution.

Multiple-Choice Questions

1. As defined, decision making involves
   A. eliminating uncertainty.
   B. leadership.
   C. information technology.
   D. choosing.
   E. overcoming fears.

2. Which of these, according to the author, is a contributor to decision complexity?
   A. Culture   B. Personality conflict
   C. Poor leadership   D. Interdisciplinary input
   E. Government regulation

3. Which one of these is *not* among the seven recommendations for sharpening your intuition?
   A. Play devil's advocate.
   B. Use imagery.
   C. Open up the closet.
   D. Get a feel for your batting average.
   E. Engage in circular reasoning.

4. _____ is the tendency to evaluate positively presented information favorably and negatively presented information unfavorably.
   A. Short-term thinking   B. Overconfidence
   C. Framing error   D. Escalation of commitment
   E. Satisficing

5. _____ are those that are repetitive and routine.
   A. Reality checks
   B. Nonprogrammed decisions
   C. Programmed decisions
   D. Semiprogrammed decisions
   E. Contingent decisions

6. _____ knowledge is personal, intuitive, and undocumented information about how to skillfully perform tasks, solve problems, and make decisions.
   A. Explicit   B. Tacit
   C. Job   D. Conditional
   E. Implicit

7. Which of the following is *not* cited as an advantage of group-aided decision making?
   A. More ethical decisions
   B. Training ground
   C. Greater pool of knowledge
   D. Increased acceptance
   E. Greater comprehension

8. _____ is defined as the reorganization of experience into new configurations.
   A. Forecasting   B. Groupthink
   C. Conceptualization   D. Decision making
   E. Creativity

9. Which of the following is *not* among the ten mental locks on creativity?
   A. Strictly following the rules
   B. Not being logical or rational
   C. Insisting on being practical
   D. Avoiding ambiguity
   E. Not wanting to look foolish

10. When the situation in which a problem occurs is changed so that the problem no longer exists, the problem is
   A. dissolved.   B. created.
   C. optimized.   D. resolved.
   E. satisfied.

See page T1 at the back of the text for answers to these questions. Want more questions? Visit the student Web site and take the ACE quizzes for more practice.

MANAGERS-IN-ACTION VIDEOS

2a

Strategic Leadership: Life is Good

Brothers Bert and John Jacobs started their apparel business in 1989 hawking t-shirts out of their van on streets and college campuses. Like true entrepreneurs, they took risks and learned as they went along—and had fun in the process. That spirit of fun is evident today in the name of their thriving company (Life is Good), Bert's CEO title (Chief Executive Optimist), and the whimsical stick figures that adorn their clothing and recreational products. But behind all the fun are serious businesspeople with big plans. For more background, visit **www.lifeisgood.com.**

Learning Objectives

To learn more about the strategies and planning behind growing an entrepreneurial venture into a thriving business. To understand how to blend general management, vision, priorities, intuition, and creativity into a successful business formula.

Links to Textual Material

Chapter 1: Entrepreneurs; **Chapter 6:** Essentials of planning; **Chapter 7:** Porter's generic competitive strategies; **Chapter 8:** Decision complexity; Intuition; Creativity

Discussion Questions

1 How well do Bert and John Jacobs exemplify the entrepreneurial characteristics in Table 1.3? Explain.

2 How important have organizational vision/mission and priorities been to the success of Life is Good?

3 Which of Porter's generic competitive strategies (see Figure 7.1) is Life is Good using?

4 Which sources of decision complexity (see Figure 8.1) are evident in this video case? Explain your choices.

5 What roles have intuition and creativity played in Life is Good's formula for success?

2b

New Balance

According to the firm's Web site (**www.newbalance.com**): "New Balance began as a Boston-based arch support company in the early 1900s, developed into a specialized shoe manufacturer in the 1970s, and has grown to become a leading global athletic products company. Today New Balance is a family of brands including New Balance, Dunham, PF Flyers, Aravon, Warrior and Brine." In this video case, company executives explain key strategic considerations such as product development, core competencies, pricing, and offshoring.

Learning Objective

To learn more about strategic management.

Links to Textual Material

Chapter 6: Organizational responses to uncertainty; **Chapter 7:** Porter's generic competitive strategies; Situational analysis (SWOT); **Chapter 8:** Decision complexity; Creativity

Discussion Questions

1 Is New Balance a defender, prospector, analyzer, or reactor (see Table 6.1)? Explain.

2 Which of Porter's generic competitive strategies has New Balance been following? Explain.

3 As part of a SWOT analysis, what are New Balance's key capabilities?

4 Which of the eight sources of decision complexity (Figure 8.1) play a role in product pricing decisions at New Balance?

5 How important is creativity at New Balance? As a company executive, what would you do to foster creativity?

PART 3

Organizing, Managing Human Resources, and Communicating

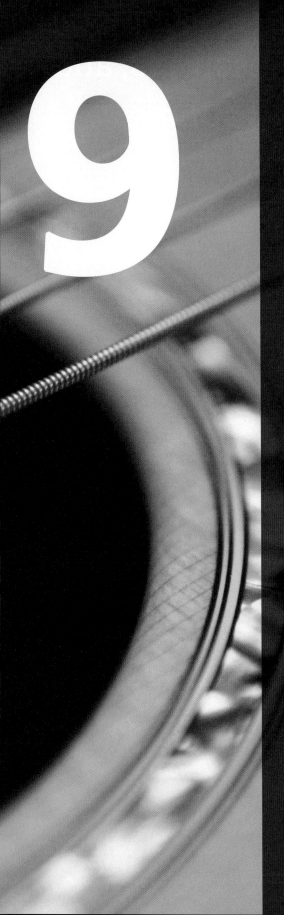

9

Organizations:
Effectiveness,
Design, and
Cultures

You have to think small
to grow big.[1]
—SAM WALTON

OBJECTIVES

- **Identify** and **describe** four characteristics common to all organizations, and **distinguish** between line and staff positions.

- **Describe** a business organization in terms of the open-system model, and **explain** the time dimension of organizational effectiveness.

- **Explain** the concept of contingency organization design, and **distinguish** between mechanistic and organic organizations.

- **Identify** and briefly **describe** the five basic departmentalization formats.

- **Describe** how a highly centralized organization differs from a highly decentralized one.

- **Define** the term *delegation*, and **list** at least five common barriers to delegation.

- **Explain** how the traditional pyramid organization is being reshaped.

- **Describe** at least three characteristics of organizational cultures, and **explain** the cultural significance of stories.

THE CHANGING WORKPLACE

Eileen Fisher Inc. Is Driven by Founder's Passion and Obsession

Passion for the business is integrated into the culture and the creative process at Eileen Fisher Inc., a women's clothing designer and manufacturer ranked No. 7 among the 2007 Best Medium Companies to Work for in America.

An obsession with the "Eileen Fisher Way" radiates from the founder ("passion" and "obsession" are this entrepreneur's favorite words) and permeates the organization.

Eileen Fisher herself is a self-described "quantum leap girl" who started the company in 1984 with four designs, $350 and complete confidence that "I know how to do this." She brought it off, creating a successful company that "encourages people to discover their passions and who they are, and helps them create their own place here."

The firm's collaborative leadership style is the opposite of top-down management. "For us, [leadership] comes from the center," says Susan Schor, the "chief culture officer" who co-leads the company while Fisher concentrates on creating new designs.

Fisher, who met Schor at a party, says she "came in and created her own place," helping to develop a "fluid structure" that defies translation into traditional corporate terms.

Schor guides the "People and Culture" areas: leadership, learning and development, social consciousness, human resources, and internal communications. Working in partnership, she and two colleagues are charged with "holding the whole," a responsibility akin to that of a chief operating officer.

Everyone works in teams, says Schor, and "no one reports to anyone. Instead, we 'connect into' someone else." Leadership teams are run by facilitators, who are "not necessarily the ones who make the decisions," she adds.

HR [human resource] director Shari Simberkoff says that hiring, too, is a collaborative process that includes multiple team interviews. HR's job begins with "hiring the right people for this organization," keeping in mind that the company is not right for everyone. Once a good match has been made, "We try to give people reasons to stay by providing terrific benefits and services, and by helping them develop personally."

The company's hiring and retention efforts seem to be working. Simberkoff says it averaged about 15 percent turnover companywide last year, compared with a national turnover rate of 25 percent to 40 percent in the retail industry. She has been with the company for nine years, and many others have been there longer, she says.

Although the eccentric and highly original culture is "not an easy environment to succeed in," says Schor, it offers excitement and opportunity to those who "get it." . . .

A successful "citizen of Eileen Fisher" is a person who is open and flexible and does not "hold on too tightly to what has been," says Vice President of Communications Hilary Old. "Eileen is good at galvanizing people, and that helps you take off the ego coat when you come in the door."

Source: Excerpted from Ann Pomeroy, "Passion, Obsession Drive the 'Eileen Fisher Way,'" *HR Magazine,* 52 (July 2007): 55. Copyright 2007 by Society for Human Resource Management (SHRM). Reproduced with permission of Society for Human Resource Management (SHRM) in the format Textbook via Copyright Clearance Center.

Organizations are an ever-present feature of modern society. We look to organizations for food, clothing, education, employment, entertainment, health care, transportation, and protection of our basic rights. Eileen Fisher Inc., for its part, strives to meet the need for stylish women's clothing both online and in department stores, boutiques, and outlets across the United States.[2] For better or for worse, virtually every aspect of modern life is influenced in one way or another by organizations. Douglas Smith, a management consultant/author who is concerned about ethics and values in our era of giant global corporations, offers this perspective on organizations:

Organizations are not just places where people have jobs. They are our neighborhoods, our communities. They are where we join with other people to make a difference for ourselves and others. If we think of them only as the places where we have jobs, we not only lose the opportunity for meaning, but we endanger the planet.[3]

Smith calls for increased corporate transparency and accountability to make sure the greater good is served.

In Chapter 1 we said the purpose of the management process is to achieve *organizational* objectives in an effective and efficient manner. Organizations are social entities that enable people to work together to achieve objectives they normally could not achieve alone. This chapter explores the organizational context in which managers and all other employees operate. It examines the structure, effectiveness, and design of organizations. The importance of delegation and the changing shape of organizations are discussed. The chapter concludes with the interesting topic of organizational cultures.

ORGANIZATIONAL STRUCTURE AND EFFECTIVENESS

An **organization** is defined as a cooperative social system involving the coordinated efforts of two or more people pursuing a shared purpose.[4] In other words, when people gather and formally agree to combine their efforts for a common purpose, an organization is the result.

organization: cooperative and coordinated social system of two or more people with a common purpose

There are exceptions, of course, such as when two strangers agree to push a car out of a ditch. This task is a one-time effort based on temporary expediency. But if the same two people decided to pool their resources to create a towing service, an organization would be created. The "coordinated efforts" portion of our definition, which implies a degree of formal planning and division of labor, is present in the second instance but not in the first.

Characteristics Common to All Organizations

According to Edgar Schein, an organizational psychologist, all organizations share four characteristics: (1) coordination of effort, (2) common goal or purpose, (3) division of labor, and (4) hierarchy of authority.[5]

COORDINATION OF EFFORT.   As we noted in the last chapter, two heads are sometimes better than one. Individuals who join together and coordinate their mental and/or physical efforts can accomplish great and exciting things. Building the great pyramids, conquering polio, sending astronauts to the moon—all these achievements far exceeded the talents and abilities of any single individual. Coordination of effort multiplies individual contributions.

COMMON GOAL OR PURPOSE.   Coordination of effort cannot take place unless those who have joined together agree to strive for something of mutual interest. A common goal or purpose gives the organization focus and its members a rallying point. For instance, as mentioned in Chapter 6, Starbucks' Chairman Howard Schultz has big plans for his coffee giant: "By 2012, Schultz aims to nearly triple annual sales, to $23.3 billion."[6] That's a lot of lattes, and it will take an army of well-trained employees to reach the goal!

DIVISION OF LABOR.   By systematically dividing complex tasks into specialized jobs, an organization can use its human resources efficiently. Division of labor permits each organization member to become more proficient by repeatedly doing the same specialized task. (But, as is discussed in Chapter 12, overspecialized jobs can breed boredom and alienation.)

The advantages of dividing labor have been known for a long time. One of its early proponents was the pioneering economist Adam Smith. While touring an eighteenth-century pin-manufacturing plant, Smith observed that a group of specialized laborers could produce 48,000 pins a day. This was an astounding figure, considering that each laborer could produce only 20 pins a day when working alone.[7]

HIERARCHY OF AUTHORITY.   According to traditional organization theory, if anything is to be accomplished through formal collective effort, someone should be given the authority to see that the intended goals are carried out effectively and efficiently. Organization theorists have defined **authority** as the right to direct the actions of others. Without a clear hierarchy of authority, coordination of effort is difficult, if not impossible, to achieve.[8] Accountability is also enhanced by having people serve in what is often called, in military language, the *chain of command.* For instance, a grocery store manager has authority over the assistant manager, who has authority over the produce department head, who in turn has authority over the employees in the produce department. Without such a chain of command, the store manager would have the impossible task of directly overseeing the work of every employee in the store.

authority: right to direct the actions of others

The idea of hierarchy has many critics, particularly among those who advocate flatter organizations with fewer levels of management.[9] One organization theorist answered those critics as follows:

At first glance, hierarchy may seem difficult to praise. Bureaucracy is a dirty word even among bureaucrats, and in business there is a widespread view that managerial hierarchy kills initiative, crushes creativity, and has therefore seen its day. Yet 35 years of research have convinced me that managerial

Harvard Business Review, April 2004

DAVE Carpenter

"YOU KNOW, EVER SINCE I STARTED WORKING HERE, I'VE HAD THIS CRAVING FOR CHEESE."

Source: Published by Harvard Business Review, *April 2004. Permission by Dave Carpenter.*

hierarchy is the most efficient, the hardiest, and in fact the most natural structure ever devised for large organizations. Properly structured, hierarchy can release energy and creativity, rationalize productivity, and actually improve morale.[10]

PUTTING ALL THE PIECES TOGETHER. All four of the foregoing characteristics are necessary before an organization can be said to exist. Many well-intentioned attempts to create organizations have failed because something was missing. In 1896, for example, Frederick Strauss, a boyhood friend of Henry Ford, helped Ford set up a machine shop, supposedly to produce gasoline-powered engines. But while Strauss was busy carrying out his end of the bargain by machining needed parts, Ford was secretly building a horseless carriage in a workshop behind his house.[11] Although Henry Ford eventually went on to become an automobile-industry giant, his first attempt at organization failed because not all of the pieces of an organization were in place. Ford's and his partner's efforts were not coordinated, they worked at cross-purposes, their labor was vaguely divided, and they had no hierarchy of authority. In short, they had organizational intentions, but no organization.

Organization Charts

An **organization chart**, such as the one in Figure 9.1, is a diagram of an organization's official positions and formal lines of authority. In effect, an organization chart is a visual display of an organization's structural skeleton. With their familiar pattern of boxes and connecting lines, these charts (some call them tables) are a useful management tool because they offer an organizational blueprint for deploying human resources.[12] Organization charts are common in both profit and nonprofit organizations.

organization chart: visual display of an organization's positions and lines of authority

These ancient ruins atop the Acropolis in Athens, Greece, remind us that the four characteristics common to all organizations are timeless. It took incredible coordination of effort, a common goal, division of labor, and a hierarchy of authority to construct this façade that still stands thousands of years later.

FIGURE **9.1** A Simplified Sample Organization Chart

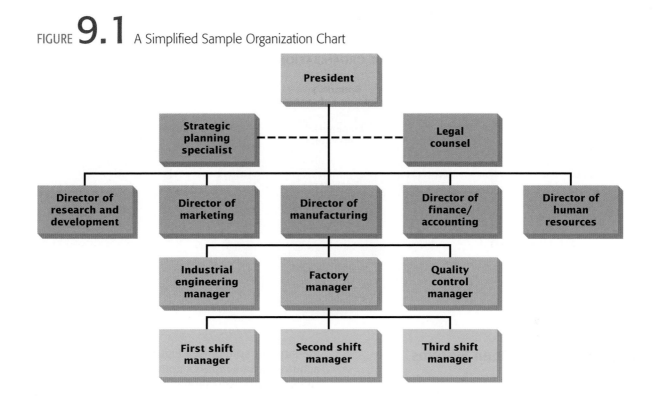

VERTICAL AND HORIZONTAL DIMENSIONS. Every organization chart has two dimensions, one representing *vertical hierarchy* and one representing *horizontal specialization*. Vertical hierarchy establishes the chain of command, or who reports to whom. The five directors in Figure 9.1 report directly to the president. Also note the unmistakable chain of command from the president, down through the director of manufacturing and factory manager, to the shift managers who oversee the factory workers. Horizontal specialization establishes the division of labor. For example, the directors of marketing and finance/accounting in Figure 9.1 have very different specialized skill sets.

LINE VERSUS STAFF POSITIONS. Technically, Figure 9.1 is a line and staff organization. In a **line and staff organization**, a distinction is made between line positions, those in the formal chain of command (connected by solid lines), and staff positions, those serving in an advisory capacity outside the formal chain of command (indicated by broken lines). Line managers have the authority to make decisions and give orders to those lower in the chain of command. In contrast, those who occupy staff positions merely advise and support line managers. Staff authority is normally restricted to immediate assistants (for example, Figure 9.1 shows that the legal counsel directs his or her staff).

line and staff organization: organization in which line managers make decisions and staff personnel provide advice and support

FIGURE **9.2** Open-System Model of a Business

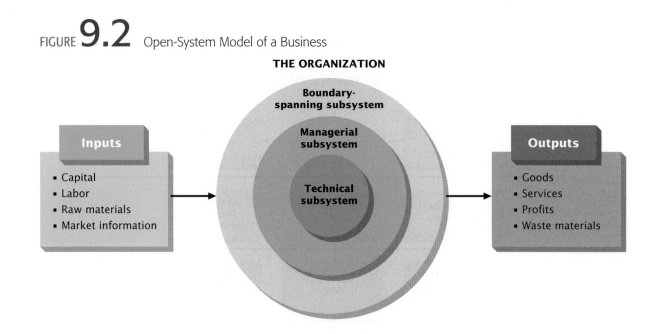

THE ORGANIZATION

Boundary-spanning subsystem

Managerial subsystem

Technical subsystem

Inputs
- Capital
- Labor
- Raw materials
- Market information

Outputs
- Goods
- Services
- Profits
- Waste materials

Organizations as Open Systems

Open-system thinking puts the concepts we have been discussing in motion by considering the dynamic interaction between an organization and its environment.[13] (Recall our discussion of general systems theory in Chapter 2.) An open-system model encourages managers to think about the organization's life-support system (see Figure 9.2). A business must acquire various *inputs:* capital, either through selling stock or borrowing; labor, through hiring people; raw materials, through purchases; and market information, through research. On the *output* side of the model, goods and services are marketed, profits (or losses) are realized, and waste materials are discarded (if not recycled).[14] There are other inputs and outputs as well. This open-system model, although descriptive of a business organization, readily generalizes to all types of organizations.

By using the open-system premise that systems are made up of interacting subsystems, we can identify three prominent organizational subsystems: technical, boundary-spanning, and managerial. Sometimes called the production function, the technical subsystem physically transforms raw materials into finished goods and services. But the ability to turn out a product does not in itself guarantee organizational survival. Other supporting subsystems working in concert are also needed.

Whereas technical subsystems may be viewed as being at an organization's very core, boundary-spanning subsystems are directed outward toward the general environment. Most boundary-spanning jobs, or interface functions, as they are sometimes

One major takeaway from viewing organizations and the world as open systems is that we're all in this together. For example, the Hurricane Katrina-ravaged Gulf Coast continues to draw volunteers from around the world. Cheryl "Salt" James, half of the rap duo Salt-N-Pepa, pitched in to help rebuild a home in Violet, Louisiana, in 2008 for a VH1 reality show.

9b Back to the Opening Case

Using Figure 9.2 as a guide (and drawing on your general knowledge and creativity), how would you graphically depict Eileen Fisher Inc. as an open system?

called, are easily identified by their titles. Purchasing and supply-chain specialists are responsible for making sure the organization has a steady and reliable flow of raw materials and subcomponents.[15] Public relations staff are in charge of developing and maintaining a favorable public image of the organization. Strategic planners have the responsibility of surveying the general environment for actual or potential opportunities and threats. Sales personnel probe the environment for buyers for the organization's goods or services. Purchasing agents, public relations staff, strategic planners, and sales personnel have one common characteristic: they all facilitate the organization's interaction with its environment. Each, so to speak, has one foot inside the organization and one foot outside.[16]

Although the technical and boundary-spanning subsystems are important and necessary, one additional subsystem is needed to tie the organization together. As Figure 9.2 indicates, the managerial subsystem serves as a bridge between the other two subsystems. The managerial subsystem controls and directs the other subsystems in the organization. It is within this subsystem that the subject matter of this book is practiced as a blend of science and art.

Organizational Effectiveness

The practice of management, as defined in Chapter 1, challenges managers to use organizational resources effectively and efficiently. Effectiveness is a measure of whether organizational objectives are accomplished. In contrast, efficiency is the relationship between outputs and inputs. In an era of diminishing resources and increasing concern about civil rights, society is reluctant to label "effective" any organization that wastes scarce resources or tramples on civil rights. Management's definition of organizational effectiveness therefore needs to be refined.

NO SILVER BULLET. According to one management scholar, "no single approach to the evaluation of effectiveness is appropriate in all circumstances or for all

organizational types."[17] More and more, the effectiveness criteria for modern organizations are being prescribed by society in the form of explicit expectations, regulations, and laws. In the private sector, profitability is no longer the sole criterion of effectiveness.[18] Winslow Buxton, CEO of Pentair, Inc., a Minnesota manufacturing company with $2 billion in annual revenue and 10,000 employees, offered this perspective:

> *One of the most challenging aspects of my job is balancing the differing expectations of employees, management, customers, financial analysts, and investors. The common denominator for all these groups is growth. But this seemingly simple term has different connotations for each constituency, and a successful company must satisfy all of those meanings.*[19]

Moreover, today's managers are caught up in an enormous web of laws and regulations covering employment practices, working conditions, job safety, pensions, product safety, pollution, and competitive practices. To be truly effective, today's productive organizations need to strike a generally acceptable balance between organizational and societal goals. Direct conflicts, such as higher wages for employees versus lower prices for customers, are inevitable (see Ethics: Character, Courage, and Values). Therefore, the process of determining the proper weighting of organizational effectiveness criteria is an endless one that requires frequent review and updating.[20]

A TIME DIMENSION. To build a workable definition of organizational effectiveness, we shall introduce a time dimension. As indicated in Figure 9.3, the organization needs to be effective in the near, intermediate, and distant future. Consequently, **organizational effectiveness** can be defined as meeting organizational objectives and prevailing societal expectations in the near future, adapting and developing in the intermediate future, and surviving into the distant future.[21]

> **organizational effectiveness:** being effective, efficient, and satisfying today; adapting and developing in the intermediate future; and surviving in the long term

Most people think only of the near future. It is in the near future that the organization has to produce goods or render services, use resources efficiently, and satisfy both insiders and outsiders with its activity. But this is just the beginning, not the end. To grow and be effective, an organization must adapt to new environmental demands and must mature and learn in the intermediate future (two to four years).

ETHICS: CHARACTER, COURAGE, AND VALUES

Should We Admire Wal-Mart?

There is an evil company in Arkansas, some say. It's a discount store—a very, very big discount store—and it will do just about anything to get bigger. You've seen the headlines. Illegal immigrants mopping its floors. Workers locked inside overnight. A big gender discrimination suit. Wages low enough to make other companies' workers go on strike. And we know what it does to weaker suppliers and competitors. Crushing the dream of the independent proprietor—an ideal as American as Thomas Jefferson—it is the enemy of all that's good and right in our nation.

There is another big discount store in Arkansas, yet this one couldn't be more different from the first. Founded by a folksy entrepreneur whose notions of thrift, industry, and the square deal were pure Ben Franklin, this company is not a tyrant but a servant. Passing along the gains of its brilliant distribution system to consumers, its far-sighted managers have done nothing less than democratize the American dream. Its low prices are spurring productivity and helping win the fight against inflation. . . .

Weirdest part is, both these companies are named Wal-Mart Stores Inc.

The more America talks about Wal-Mart, it seems, the more polarized its image grows. Its executives are credited with the most expansive of visions and the meanest of intentions; its CEO is presumed to be in league with Lex Luthor *and* St. Francis of Assisi. It's confusing. Which should we believe in: good Wal-Mart or evil Wal-Mart? . . .

Where you stand on Wal-Mart, then, seems to depend on where you sit. If you're a consumer, Wal-Mart is good for you. If you're a wage earner, there's a good chance it's bad. If you're a Wal-Mart shareholder, you want the company to grow. If you're a citizen, you probably don't want it growing in your backyard. So, which one are you?

And that's the point: Chances are, you're more than one. And you may think each role is important. Yet America has elevated one above the rest. . . .

Wal-Mart swore fealty to the consumer and rode its coattails straight to the top. Now we have more than just a big retailer on our hands, though. We have a servant-king—one powerful enough to place everyone else in servitude to the consumer too. Gazing up at this new order, we wonder if our original choices made so much sense after all. . . .

Now Wal-Mart has been brought face to face with its own contradiction: Its promises of the good life threaten to ring increasingly hollow if it doesn't pay its workers enough to have that good life.

It's important that this debate continue. But in holding the mirror up to Wal-Mart, we would do well to turn it back on ourselves. Sam Walton created Wal-Mart. But we created it, too.

Source: From Jerry Useem, "Should We Admire Wal-Mart?" Fortune *(March 8, 2004): 118–120.* © 2004 Time Inc. All rights reserved.

FOR DISCUSSION

How are judgments about organizational effectiveness and ethical considerations intertwined in this case? How would you rate Wal-Mart's effectiveness? Explain.

FIGURE **9.3** The Time Dimension of Organizational Effectiveness

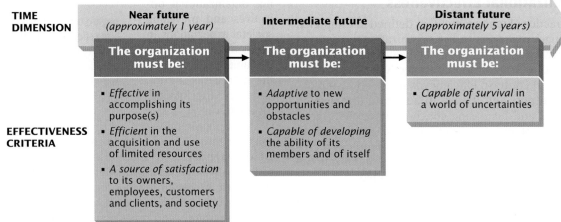

TIME DIMENSION	**Near future** *(approximately 1 year)*	**Intermediate future**	**Distant future** *(approximately 5 years)*
	The organization must be:	**The organization must be:**	**The organization must be:**
EFFECTIVENESS CRITERIA	• *Effective* in accomplishing its purpose(s) • *Efficient* in the acquisition and use of limited resources • *A source of satisfaction* to its owners, employees, customers and clients, and society	• *Adaptive* to new opportunities and obstacles • *Capable of developing* the ability of its members and of itself	• *Capable of survival* in a world of uncertainties

Source: Adapted from James L. Gibson, John M. Ivancevich, and James H. Donnelly Jr., Organizations: Behavior, Structure, Processes, *5th ed. (Homewood, Ill.: Richard D. Irwin, Inc.), p. 37.* © 1991.

Organizational effectiveness got the spotlight when millions of Chinese-made toys were recalled in the United States because of toxic lead-tainted paint. Enter smaller but more effective European toy companies such as this one in Bad Rodach, Germany. These days, nervous parents are willing to pay more for European toys made from safe, natural materials.

CONTINGENCY DESIGN

Recall from our discussion in Chapter 2 that contingency thinking amounts to situational thinking. Specifically, the contingency approach to organizing involves taking special steps to make sure the organization fits the demands of the situation. In direct contrast to traditional thinking, contingency design is based on the assumption that there is no single best way to structure an organization. **Contingency design** is the process of determining the degree of environmental uncertainty and adapting the organization and its subunits to the situation. This does not mean that all contingency organizations necessarily differ from each other. Instead, it means that managers who take a contingency approach select from a number of standard design alternatives to create the most situationally effective organization possible. Contingency managers typically start with the same basic collection of design alternatives but end up with unique combinations of them as dictated by the demands of their situations.

> **contingency design:** fitting the organization to its environment

The contingency approach to designing organizations boils down to two questions: (1) How much environmental uncertainty is there? (See Table 9.1 for a handy way to answer this question.) (2) What combination of structural characteristics is most appropriate? Let us set the stage by examining a landmark contingency model to establish the validity of the contingency approach.

The Burns and Stalker Model

Tom Burns and G. M. Stalker, both British behavioral scientists, proposed a useful typology for categorizing organizations by structural design.[22] They distinguished between mechanistic and organic organizations. **Mechanistic organizations** tend to be rigid in design and have strong bureaucratic qualities. In contrast, **organic organizations** tend to be quite flexible in structure and adaptive to change. Actually, these two organizational types are the extreme ends of a single continuum. Pure types are difficult to find, but it is fairly easy to check off the characteristics listed in Table 9.2 to determine whether a particular organization (or subunit) is relatively mechanistic or relatively organic. It is notable that a field study found distinctly different communication patterns in mechanistic and organic organizations. Communication tended to be the formal

> **mechanistic organizations:** rigid bureaucracies

> **organic organizations:** flexible, adaptive organization structures

TABLE **9.1** Determining Degree of Environmental Uncertainty

	LOW	MODERATE	HIGH
1. How strong are social, political, and economic pressures on the organization?	Minimal	Moderate	Intense
2. How frequent are technological breakthroughs in the industry?	Infrequent	Occasional	Frequent
3. How reliable are resources and supplies?	Reliable	Occasional, predictable shortages	Unreliable
4. How stable is the demand for the organization's product or service?	Highly stable	Moderately stable	Unstable

TABLE **9.2** Mechanistic versus Organic Organizations

CHARACTERISTIC	MECHANISTIC ORGANIZATIONS	ORGANIC ORGANIZATIONS
1. Task definition for individual contributors	Narrow and precise	Broad and general
2. Relationship between individual contribution and organization purpose	Vague	Clear
3. Task flexibility	Low	High
4. Definition of rights, obligations, and techniques	Clear	Vague
5. Reliance on hierarchical control	High	Low (reliance on self-control)
6. Primary direction of communication	Vertical (top to bottom)	Lateral (between peers)
7. Reliance on instructions and decisions from superior	High	Low (superior offers information and advice)
8. Emphasis on loyalty and obedience	High	Low
9. Type of knowledge required	Narrow, technical, and task-specific	Broad and professional

Source: Adapted from Tom Burns and G. M. Stalker, The Management of Innovation *(London: Tavistock, 1961), pp. 119–125. Reprinted by permission.*

command-and-control type in the mechanistic factory and to be participative in the organic factory.[23]

TELLING THE DIFFERENCE. Here is a quick test of how well you understand the distinction between mechanistic and organic organizations. Read the following description of how an Emeryville, California, company maximizes the security of its clients' Web site data, and then attach a mechanistic or organic label.

SiteROCK employees . . . are required to read through several three-inch-thick binders of standard operating procedures before they can work in the command center. As each shift turns over, the staff must shuffle through 90 minutes of paperwork

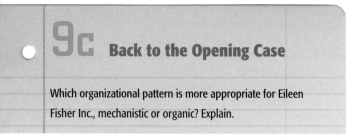

9c Back to the Opening Case

Which organizational pattern is more appropriate for Eileen Fisher Inc., mechanistic or organic? Explain.

before handing over the keys. "Not everyone would be able to do this job. You have to be able to follow directions and follow the processes," says Lori Perrine, a customer-support specialist at siteROCK.[24]

If you said mechanistic, you're right. Using Table 9.2 as a guide, we see evidence of precise task definition, low task flexibility, clear definition of techniques, and high emphasis on obedience. Indeed, siteROCK is staffed mostly by former military personnel and is run with military precision.

An organic organization would have basically the opposite characteristics. George Lucas, the creative genius behind *Star Wars*, knows how organic design can stimulate collaboration and creativity. For example, this is the scene at Industrial Light & Magic (ILM), Lucasfilm Ltd.'s special effects operation in San Francisco:

The digital artists at ILM sit in a pool of cubes positioned in the center of the building, most of them away from the sunlight so they can get precise readings of the colors on their screens. "We do our best work in black boxes," says Scott Farrar, an Oscar-winning visual effects supervisor who most recently oversaw work on the film Transformers. *Typical office hierarchies don't apply. Managers like Farrar, who oversee teams of hundreds of artists on big films, are rootless. They move through office suites scattered around the central pool of artists, depending on whose talents are needed for the movie.*[25]

SITUATIONAL APPROPRIATENESS. Burns and Stalker's research uncovered distinct organization-environment patterns indicating the relative appropriateness of both mechanistic and organic organizations. It revealed that *successful organizations in relatively stable and certain environments tended to be mechanistic.* Conversely, Burns and Stalker also discovered that *relatively organic organizations tended to be the successful ones when the environment was unstable and uncertain.*

For practical application, this means that mechanistic design is appropriate for environmental stability, and organic design is appropriate for high environmental uncertainty. Today, the trend necessarily is toward more organic organizations because uncertainty is the rule. *Management Review* summed up the situation this way:

Products, companies, and industries all have shorter life cycles, which means that product launches, corporate realignments, and other initiatives may take place in months rather than years. The global span of today's companies, which have employees, customers, and suppliers throughout

In the language of Burns and Stalker, do you want your espresso mechanistic or organic? While "organic" is a popular option among those wanting healthier foods and beverages today, you would be better off choosing "mechanistic." These baristas at Caffe Vita Coffee Roasting Co., a small Seattle chain, strive to outdo Starbucks by giving you precisely what you want, not some weird concoction they dreamed up. This means following exacting specifications for preparation and service; hence, a "mechanistic" espresso.

the world, also multiplies the complexities of change. And let us not forget another complicator—technology. Companies must constantly upgrade systems, evaluate new technology, and adopt new ways of doing business.[26]

This is not to say that organic is good and mechanistic is bad. Mechanistic organizations have their place. SiteROCK's mechanistic structure, for example, makes it highly resistant to human error, technical failures, and attacks by hackers and terrorists.

Basic Departmentalization Formats

Aside from the hierarchical chain of command, one of the most common ways to coordinate an organization is departmentalization. It is through **departmentalization** that related jobs, activities, or processes are grouped into major organizational subunits. For example, all jobs involving staffing activities such as recruitment, hiring, and training are often grouped into a human resources department. Grouping jobs through the formation of departments, according to management author James D. Thompson, "permits coordination to be handled in the least costly manner."[27] A degree of coordination is achieved through departmentalization because members of the department work on interrelated tasks, are guided by the same departmental rules, and report to the same department head. It is important to note that although the term *departmentalization* is used here, it does not always literally apply; managers commonly use labels such as *division*, *group*, or *unit* in large organizations.

> **departmentalization:** grouping related jobs or processes into major organizational subunits

Five basic types of departmentalization are functional departments, product-service departments, geographic location departments, customer classification departments, and work flow process departments.[28]

FUNCTIONAL DEPARTMENTS. Functional departments categorize jobs according to the activity performed. Among profit-making businesses, variations of the functional production-finance-marketing arrangement in Figure 9.4A are the most common forms of departmentalization. Functional departmentalization is popular because it permits those with similar technical expertise to work in a coordinated subunit. Of course, functional departmentalization is not restricted to profit-making businesses. Functional departments in a nonprofit hospital might be administration, nursing, housekeeping, food service, laboratory and x-ray, admission and records, and accounting and billing.

A negative aspect of functional departmentalization is that it creates "technical ghettos," in which local departmental concerns and loyalties tend to override strategic organizational concerns. For example, look what Bruce L. Claflin, head of IBM's newly formed mobile computing division, ran into when he called a planning meeting for the Think-Pad 700C.

> *Everybody cared more about how their own area—say, marketing—would fare than [about] what was best for IBM. The marketing people knew [the 700C] would be competitive, but they had made commitments to sell only 6,000 worldwide. They didn't believe the development group would build it anyway. The development people knew they could design it, but they said, "Well, marketing won't sell it, and anyway, manufacturing can't build it." And manufacturing figured it would never be developed. It was complete gridlock.*[29]

Situations like this prompted a major reorganization at IBM and the eventual sale of its PC unit to a Chinese company in 2004.[30]

PRODUCT-SERVICE DEPARTMENTS. Because functional departmentalization has been criticized for encouraging specialization at the expense of coordination, a somewhat more organic alternative has evolved. It is called product-service departmentalization because a product (or service), rather than a functional category of work, is the unifying theme. As diagrammed in Figure 9.4B, the product-service approach permits each of, say, two products to be managed as semiautonomous businesses. Organizations rendering a service instead of turning out a tangible product might find it advantageous to organize around service categories. In reality, however, many of today's companies turn out *bundles* of products and services for customers. General Electric, for example, was recently reorganized around these major product/service categories: energy (power generation equipment), transportation (aircraft engines and rail locomotives), NBC-Universal (television and films), health care (diagnostic equipment), and consumer and industrial products and services.[31] Ideally, those working in this sort of product-service structure have a broad "business" orientation rather than a narrow functional perspective. As Figure 9.4B shows, it is the general manager's job to ensure that these minibusinesses work in a complementary fashion, rather than competing with one another.[32]

FIGURE **9.4** Alternative Departmentalization Formats

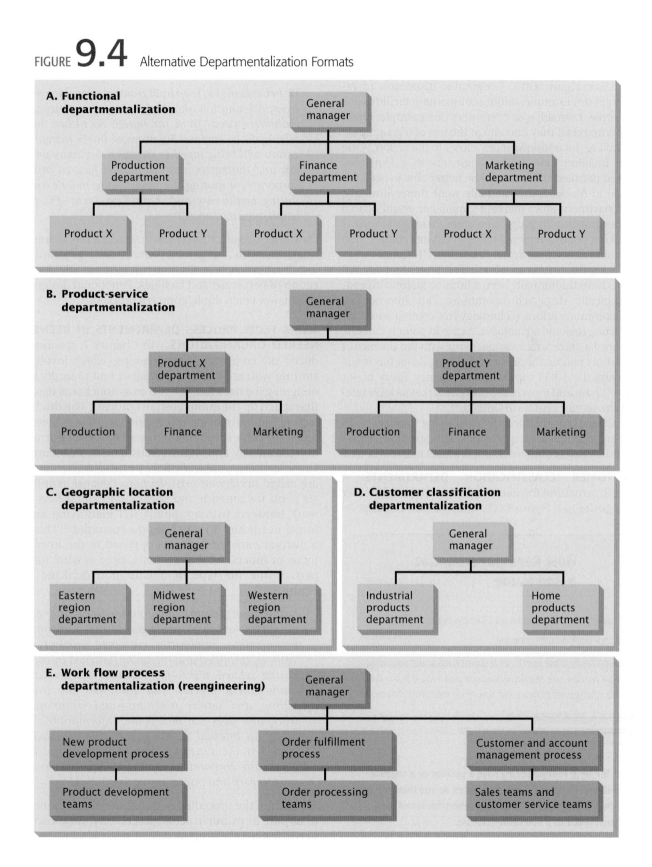

GEOGRAPHIC LOCATION DEPARTMENTS. Sometimes, as in the case of organizations with nationwide or worldwide markets, geography dictates structural format (see Figure 9.4C). Geographic dispersion of resources (for example, mining companies), facilities (for example, railroads), or customers (for example, chain supermarkets) may encourage the use of a geographic format to put administrators "closer to the action." One can imagine that drilling engineers in a Houston-based petroleum firm would be better able to get a job done in Alaska if they actually went there. Similarly, a department-store marketing manager would be in a better position to judge consumer tastes in Florida if working out of a regional office in Orlando rather than out of a home office in Salt Lake City or Toronto.

Long lines of communication among organizational units have traditionally been a limiting factor with geographically dispersed operations. But Internet-age telecommunications technology has created some interesting regional advantages. A case in point is Omaha, Nebraska. Its central location, along with the absence of a distinct regional accent among Nebraskans, has made Omaha the 1-800 capital of the country. Every major hotel chain and most of the big telemarketers have telephone service centers in Omaha.[33]

Global competition is pressuring managers to organize along geographic lines. This structure allows multinational companies to serve local markets better.

CUSTOMER CLASSIFICATION DEPARTMENTS. A fourth structural format centers on various customer categories (see Figure 9.4D). Intel is a case in point. As Paul Otellini was getting ready to assume the CEO post at Intel in 2005, he reorganized the computer-chip maker to sharpen its focus on the customer:

> *He believes that to keep Intel growing, every idea and technical solution should be focused on meeting customers' needs from the outset. So rather than relying on its engineering prowess, Intel's reorganization will bring together engineers, software writers, and marketers into five market-focused units: corporate computing, the digital home, mobile computing, health care, and channel products—PCs for small manufacturers.*[34]

Customer classification departmentalization shares a weakness with the product-service and geographic location approaches: all three can create costly duplication of personnel and facilities. Functional design is the answer when duplication is a problem.

WORK FLOW PROCESS DEPARTMENTS IN REENGINEERED ORGANIZATIONS. In Chapter 7, we introduced the concept of reengineering, which involves starting with a clean sheet of paper and radically redesigning the organization into cross-functional teams that speed up the entire business process. The driving factors behind reengineering are lower costs, better quality, greater speed, better use of modern information technology, and improved customer satisfaction.[35] Organizations with work flow process departments are called *horizontal organizations* because emphasis is on the smooth and speedy horizontal flow of work between two key points: (1) identifying customer needs and (2) satisfying the customer.[36] This is a distinct *outward* focus, as opposed to the inward focus of functional departments. Here is what happens inside the type of organization depicted in Figure 9.4E:

> *Rather than focusing single-mindedly on financial objectives or functional goals, the horizontal organization emphasizes customer satisfaction. Work is simplified and hierarchy flattened by combining related tasks—for example, an account-management process that subsumes the sales, billing, and service functions—and eliminating work that does not add value. Information zips along an internal superhighway. The knowledge worker analyzes it, and technology moves it quickly across the corporation instead of up and down, speeding up and improving decision making.*[37]

Each of the preceding design formats is presented in its pure form, but in actual practice, hybrid versions occur frequently. For example, Coca-Cola created a

---

9d — How Reengineering Got a Bad Name

A manager reportedly told James Champy, coauthor of the landmark book on reengineering,

We don't really know how to do reengineering in our company; so what we do is, we regularly downsize and leave it to the three people who are left to figure out how to do their work differently.

Source: As quoted in "Anything Worth Doing Is Worth Doing from Scratch," Inc. (20th Anniversary Issue), 21 (May 18, 1999): 51–52.

QUESTIONS:

Does the term *reengineering* have a positive or a negative connotation for you? Explain. How often do you think misapplication or misinterpretation gives otherwise sound management practices a bad name? Explain.

mix of three geographic location units and a functional unit in 2001 to make the global company more responsive to both customers and product trends. The four units: "Americas, Asia, Europe/Africa, and New Business Ventures."[38] From a contingency perspective, the five departmentalization formats are useful starting points rather than final blueprints for organizers. A number of structural variations show how the basic formats can be adapted to meet situational demands.

Span of Control

The number of people who report directly to a manager represents that manager's **span of control**. (Some prefer the term *span of management*.) Managers with a narrow span of control oversee the work of a few people, whereas those with a wide span of control have many people reporting to them (see Figure 9.5). Generally, narrow spans of control foster tall organizations (many levels in the hierarchy). In contrast, flat organizations (few hierarchical levels) have wide spans of control. Everything else being equal, it stands to reason that an organization with narrow spans of control needs more managers than one with wide spans. For many years, the question was "What is the ideal span

span of control: number of people who report directly to a given manager

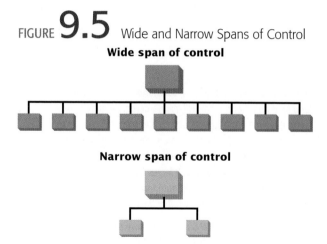

FIGURE **9.5** Wide and Narrow Spans of Control

of control?"[39] But today's emphasis on contingency organization design, combined with evidence that wide spans of control can be effective, has made the question of an ideal span obsolete. The relevant question today is "How wide *can* one's span of control be?" Wider spans of control mean less administrative expense and more self-management, both popular notions today. Overly wide spans, however, can mean inadequate supervision and loss of control. Clearly, a rationale is needed for striking a workable balance.

Situational factors such as those listed in Figure 9.6 are a useful starting point. The narrow, moderate, and

FIGURE **9.6** Situational Determinants of Span of Control

	Wide span of control appropriate (10 or more)	Moderate span of control appropriate (5 to 9)	Narrow span of control appropriate (2 to 4)
1. Similarity of work performed by subordinates	Identical		Distinctly different
2. Dispersion of subordinates	Same work area		Geographically dispersed
3. Complexity of work performed by subordinates	Simple and repetitive		Highly complex and varied
4. Direction and control required by subordinates	Little and/or infrequent		Intensive and/or constant
5. Time spent coordinating with other managers	Little		A great deal
6. Time required for planning	Little		A great deal

9e Wider Is Better, for the Head of Cisco Systems

Says John Chambers, CEO of Cisco Systems Inc.: "I learned a long time ago that a team will always defeat an individual. And if you have a team of superstars, then you have a chance to create a dynasty." That's one reason why Chambers has two to three times as many people reporting to him as does the average executive in his company: It forces him to empower those directly under him with greater autonomy, because he can't possibly keep up with every detail of their work.

Source: John Byrne, "The Global Corporation Becomes the Leaderless Corporation," Business Week (August 30, 1999): 90.

QUESTION:

What is the key to making Chambers's wide span of control work?

wide span-of-control ranges in Figure 9.6 are intended to be illustrative benchmarks rather than rigid limits. Each organization must do its own on-the-job experimentation. At Federal Express, for example, the span of control varies with different areas of the company. Departments that employ many people doing the same job or very similar jobs—such as customer service agents, handlers/sorters, and couriers—usually have a span of control of 15 to 20 employees per manager. Groups performing multiple tasks, or tasks that require only a few people, are more likely to have spans of control of five or fewer.[40] No ideal span of control exists for all kinds of work.

Centralization and Decentralization

Where are the important decisions made in an organization? Are they made strictly by top management or by middle- and lower-level managers? These questions are at the heart of the decentralization design alternative. Centralization is at one end of a continuum, and at the other end is decentralization. **Centralization** is defined as the relative retention of decision-making authority by top management. Nearly all decision-making authority is retained by top management in highly centralized organizations. In contrast,

centralization: the retention of decision-making authority by top management

decentralization is the granting of decision-making authority by management to lower-level employees. Decentralization increases as the degree, importance, and range of lower-level decision making *increase* and the amount of checking up by top management *decreases* (see Figure 9.7).

decentralization: management's sharing of decision-making authority with lower-level employees

When we speak of centralization or decentralization, we are describing a comparative degree, not an absolute. The challenge for managers, as one management consultant observed, is to strike a workable balance between two extremes.

> *The modern organization in transition will recognize the pull of two [poles]: a need for greater centralization to create low-cost shared resources; and, a need to improve market responsiveness with greater decentralization. Today's winning organizations are the ones that can handle the paradox and tensions of both pulls. These are the firms that analyze the optimum organizational solution in each particular circumstance, without prejudice for one type of organization over another. The result is, almost invariably, a messy mixture of decentralized units sharing cost-effective centralized resources.[41]*

Support for greater decentralization in the corporate world has come and gone over the years in faddish waves. Today, the call is for the type of balance just discussed. The case against extreme decentralization can be summed up in three words: *lack of control.* Balance helps neutralize this concern. Again, the contingency approach dictates which end of the continuum needs to be emphasized.[42] Centralization, because of its mechanistic nature, generally works best for organizations in relatively stable situations.[43] A more decentralized approach is appropriate for firms in complex and changing conditions. As an extreme example, health care giant Johnson & Johnson actually is a collection of over 200 operating units, each acting as a stand-alone profit center.[44]

EFFECTIVE DELEGATION

Delegation is an important common denominator that runs through virtually all relatively organic design alternatives. It is vital to successful decentralization.

FIGURE **9.7** Factors in Relative Centralization/Decentralization

	Highly centralized organization	Highly decentralized organization
How many decisions are made at lower levels in the hierarchy?	Very few, if any	Many or most
How important are the decisions that are made at lower levels (*i.e., do they impact organizational success or dollar values*)?	Not very important	Very important
How many different functions (*e.g., production, marketing, finance, human resources*) rely on lower-level decision making?	Very few, if any	All or most
How much does top management monitor or check up on lower-level decision making?	A great deal	Very little or not at all

Formally defined, **delegation** is the process of assigning various degrees of decision-making authority to lower-level employees.[45] As this definition implies, delegation is not an all-or-nothing proposition. There are at least five different degrees of delegation[46] (see Figure 9.8).

delegation: assigning various degrees of decision-making authority to lower-level employees

A word of caution about delegation is necessary, because there is one thing it does *not* include. Former President Harry Truman is said to have had a little sign on his White House desk that read, "The Buck Stops Here!"[47] Managers who delegate should keep this idea in mind because, although authority may be passed along to people at lower levels, ultimate responsibility cannot be passed along. Thus delegation is the sharing of authority, not the abdication of responsibility. Chrysler's former CEO Lee Iacocca admittedly fell victim to this particular lapse:

> When the company started to make money, it spent its cash on stock buybacks and acquisitions. For his part, Iacocca was distracted by nonautomotive concerns. [Iacocca] concedes that while he kept his finger on finance and marketing, he should have paid closer attention to new model planning. "If I made one mistake," he says now, "it was delegating all the product development and not going to one single meeting."[48]

Iacocca corrected this mistake prior to his retirement, and customers liked Chrysler's bold new designs.

FIGURE **9.8** The Delegation Continuum

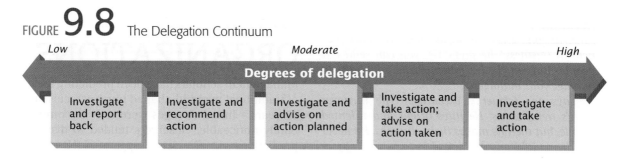

Low		Moderate		High
		Degrees of delegation		
Investigate and report back	Investigate and recommend action	Investigate and advise on action planned	Investigate and take action; advise on action taken	Investigate and take action

9f   One More Reason to Delegate: You Need a Vacation

Former NASA scientists, working on behalf of Air New Zealand and using testing tools normally reserved for astronauts, recently found that vacationers experienced an 82% increase in job performance post-trip.

Source: Michelle Conlin, "Do Us a Favor, Take a Vacation," Business Week (May 21, 2007): 88.

QUESTION:

Why are overloaded workaholic managers who refuse to delegate not as indispensable as they think?

The Advantages of Delegation

Managers stand to gain a great deal by adopting the habit of delegating. By passing along well-defined tasks to lower-level people, managers can free more of their time for important chores such as planning and motivating. Regarding the question of exactly *what* should be delegated, Intel's former chairman, Andy Grove, made the following recommendation: "Because it is easier to monitor something with which you are familiar, if you have a choice you should delegate those activities you know best."[49] Grove cautions that delegators who follow his advice will experience some psychological discomfort because they will quite naturally want to continue doing what they know best.

In addition to freeing valuable managerial time,[50] delegation is also a helpful management training and development tool. Moreover, lower-level managers who desire more challenge generally become more committed and satisfied when they are given the opportunity to tackle significant problems. Conversely, a lack of delegation can stifle initiative. Consider the situation of a California builder:

> [The founder and chairman] personally negotiates every land deal. Visiting every construction site repeatedly, he is critical even of details of cabinet construction. "The building business is an entrepreneurial business," he says. "Yes, you can send out people. But you better follow them. You have to manage your managers."
>
> Says one former . . . executive: "The turnover there's tremendous. He hires bright and talented people, but then he makes them eunuchs. He never lets them make any decisions."[51]

Perfectionist managers who avoid delegation have problems in the long run when they become overwhelmed by minute details.

Barriers to Delegation

There are several reasons why managers generally do not delegate as much as they should:

- Belief in the fallacy expressed in the advice "If you want it done right, do it yourself"
- Lack of confidence and trust in lower-level employees
- Low self-confidence
- Fear of being called lazy
- Vague job definition
- Fear of competition from those below
- Reluctance to take the risks involved in depending on others
- Lack of controls that provide early warning of problems with delegated duties
- Poor example set by bosses who do not delegate[52]

Managers can go a long way toward effective delegation by recognizing and correcting these tendencies both in themselves and in their fellow managers. Because successful delegation is habit-forming, the first step usually is the hardest. Properly trained and motivated people who know how to take initiative in challenging situations (see the Manager's Toolkit at the end of this chapter) often reward a delegator's trust with a job well done.[53]

Once managers have developed the habit of delegating, they need to remember this wise advice from Peter Drucker: "Delegation . . . requires that delegators follow up. They rarely do—they think they have delegated, and that's it. But they are still accountable for performance. And so they have to follow up, have to make sure that the task gets done—and done right."[54] (See Valuing Diversity.)

THE CHANGING SHAPE OF ORGANIZATIONS

Management scholars have been predicting the death of traditional pyramid-shaped bureaucracies for over 40 years.[55] Initial changes were slow in coming and barely noticeable. Observers tended to dismiss the predictions as naïve and exaggerated. However, the

VALUING DIVERSITY
Don't Take Your Superstars for Granted

Never make the mistake of thinking that some employees are so talented, skilled and motivated that you don't need to manage them. Like everyone else, superstars have bad days, sometimes go in the wrong direction, and have lapses in judgment or integrity. Even superstars need guidance, direction, support and encouragement. They need to be challenged and developed. What's more, superstars often want to know that someone is keeping track of their great work and looking for ways to reward them.

Sometimes managers will say, "This superstar is different. She is so talented, skilled and motivated that I have nothing to offer her." If that's truly the case, it doesn't mean the employee doesn't need a boss. It just means that maybe you should promote her, move her to a boss who does have something to offer her, or change your relationship with her so that you work together as partners or collaborators. . . .

You need to manage this superstar because she challenges you in ways you don't expect. You need to check in regularly to make sure things are going as well as you think. Regardless of her talents, you need to verify that the work is getting done.

Source: Excerpted from Bruce Tulgan, "Superstars Need Managers," HR Magazine, 52 (June 2007): 135. Copyright 2007 by Society for Human Resource Management (SHRM). Reproduced with permission of Society for Human Management (SHRM) in the format Textbook via Copyright Clearance Center.

pace and degree of change have picked up dramatically since the 1980s. All of the social, political-legal, economic, and technological changes discussed in Chapter 3 threaten to make traditional organizations obsolete. Why? Because they are too slow, unresponsive, uncreative, costly, and hard to manage. It is clear today that no less than a reorganization revolution is under way. Traditional pyramid organizations, though still very much in evidence, are being questioned as never before. General Electric's legendary CEO Jack Welch put it this way:

> *The old organization was built on control, but the world has changed. The world is moving at such a pace that control has become a limitation. It slows you down. You've got to balance freedom with some control, but you've got to have more freedom than you ever dreamed of.*[56]

Consequently, to be prepared for tomorrow's workplace, we need to take a look at how organizations are evolving. Figure 9.9 illustrates three different ways in which the traditional pyramid organization is being reshaped. They are the hourglass organization, the cluster organization, and the virtual organization. To varying extents, these new configurations embody three current organizational trends:

- Fewer layers (For example, CEO Andrea Jung recently streamlined Avon's hierarchy by 7 layers—from 15 layers down to 8—to enable the beauty

FIGURE **9.9** Reshaping the Traditional Pyramid Organization

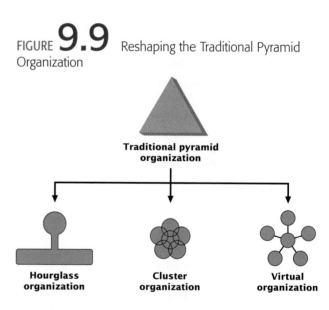

products firm to respond more quickly to rapidly changing consumer tastes.)[57]
- Greater emphasis on teams
- Smallness within bigness (For example, in 2002, "Nokia split its monolithic $21 billion mobile-phone unit into nine profit-and-loss centers, each charged with bolstering the company's position in a particular market."[58])

The new configurations may overlap, as when an hourglass organization relies extensively on teams. The new

9g A Radical Approach to Virtual Organizations

Advice from management guru Michael Hammer:

See your business not as a self-contained company but as part of an extended enterprise of companies that work together to create customer value.

Source: Michael Hammer, The Agenda: What Every Business Must Do to Dominate the Decade *(New York: Crown Business, 2001), p. 221.*

QUESTIONS:
But what about quaint notions such as loyalty and company pride? How prepared are you to work in this sort of fluid and uncertain environment? Explain.

structures have important implications for both the practice of management and the quality of work life. Let us examine them and take an imaginary peek into the not-too-distant future of work organizations.

Hourglass Organizations

The **hourglass organization** consists of three layers, with the middle layer distinctly pinched. A strategic elite is responsible for formulating a vision for the organization and making sure it becomes reality. A significantly shrunken middle-management layer carries out a coordinating function for diverse lower-level activities. Thanks to computer networks that flash information directly from the factory floor or retail outlet to the executive suite and back again, middle managers are no longer simply conduits for warmed-over information. Also unlike traditional middle managers, hourglass middle managers are generalists rather than narrow specialists. They are comfortable dealing with complex inter-functional problems. A given middle manager might deal with an accounting problem one day, a product design issue the next, and a marketing dilemma the next—all within cross-functional team settings.

At the bottom of the hourglass is a broad layer of technical specialists who act as their own supervisors much of the time. Consequently, the distinction between supervisors and rank-and-file personnel is blurred. Employees at this operating level complain about a very real lack of promotion opportunities.

> **hourglass organization:** three-layer structure with a constricted middle layer

Management tries to keep them motivated with challenging work assignments, lateral transfers, skill-training opportunities, and pay-for-performance schemes. Union organizers attempt to exploit complaints about employees "having to act like managers, but not being paid like managers."

Cluster Organizations

Another new configuration shown in Figure 9.9 is the **cluster organization**. This label is appropriate because teams are the primary structural unit.[59]

> **cluster organization:** collaborative structure in which teams are the primary unit

For instance, Oticon Inc., a Danish hearing-aid manufacturer that also has operations in Somerset, NJ, abolished its formal organizational structure several years ago as part of a strategic turnaround. The old way of doing things has been replaced with a flexible work environment and project-based work processes. Self-directed teams have become the defining unit of work, disbanding and forming again as the work requires. Oticon typically has 100 projects running at any time, and most of its 1,500 employees work on several projects at once.[60]

Imagining ourselves working in a cluster organization, we see multiskilled people moving from team to team as projects dictate. Pay for knowledge is a common practice. Motivation seems to be high, but some complain about a lack of job security because things are constantly changing. Stress levels rise when the pace of change quickens. Special training efforts, involving team-building exercises, are aimed at enhancing everyone's communication and group involvement skills.[61]

Virtual Organizations

From the time of the Industrial Revolution until the Internet age, the norm was to build an organization capable of designing, producing, and marketing products. Bigger was assumed to be better. And this approach worked as long as large batches of look-alike products were acceptable to consumers. But then along came the Internet, e-business, and mass customization, discussed in Chapters 1 and 7. *Speed*—in the form of faster market research, faster product development, faster production, and faster delivery—became more important than organizational size. Meanwhile, global competition kept a lid on prices. Suddenly, consumers realized they could get exactly what they wanted, at a good price, and fast. Many lumbering organizational giants of the past were not up to the task. Enter **virtual organizations**, flexible networks of value-adding subcontractors, linked by the Internet, e-mail, fax machines, and telephones.[62] Probably the most extreme example of a virtual organization that we can find today is Linux. What started in 1991 as Linus Torvalds's student project at Finland's University of Helsinki has evolved into a huge global enterprise with a product competing head-to-head with Microsoft's Windows operating system. *Business Week* explained:

virtual organizations: Internet-linked networks of value-adding subcontractors

There's no headquarters, no CEO, and no annual report. And it's not a single company. Rather, it's a cooperative venture in which employees at about two dozen companies [including industry giants IBM, Intel, and Hewlett-Packard], along with thousands of individuals [including volunteers], work together to improve Linux software. The tech companies contribute sweat equity to the project, largely by paying programmers' salaries, and then make money by selling products and services around the Linux operating system. They don't charge for Linux itself, since under the cooperative's rules the software is available to all comers for free. . . .

Distributors, including Red Hat Inc. and Novell Inc., package Linux with helpful user manuals, *regular updates, and customer service, and then charge customers annual subscription fees for all the extras. . . .*

IBM, HP, and others capitalize on the ability to sell machines without any up-front charge for an operating-system license, which can range up to several thousand dollars for some versions of Windows. . . .[63]

Torvalds studiously monitors the quality of changes to his open-source software from his home in Oregon via the Internet. Aside from the Torvalds legacy, what holds this far-ranging virtual organization together is a common passion for creating world-class software.[64]

Other virtual organizations are taking shape as large companies strive to cut costs by outsourcing functions ranging from manufacturing and shipping to payroll and accounting.[65]

From a personal perspective, life in virtual organizations is *hectic*. Everything moves at Internet speed. Change and learning are constant. Cross-functional teams are the norm, and job reassignments are frequent. Project specialists rarely see a single project to completion because they are whisked off to other projects. Unavoidable by-products of constant change are stress and burnout. Unexpectedly, the need for face-to-face contact increases as geographically dispersed team members communicate via e-mail, instant messaging, groupware, and voice mail.[66] Only face-to-face interaction, both on and off the job, can build the rapport and trust necessary to get something done quickly with people you rarely see. The growing gap

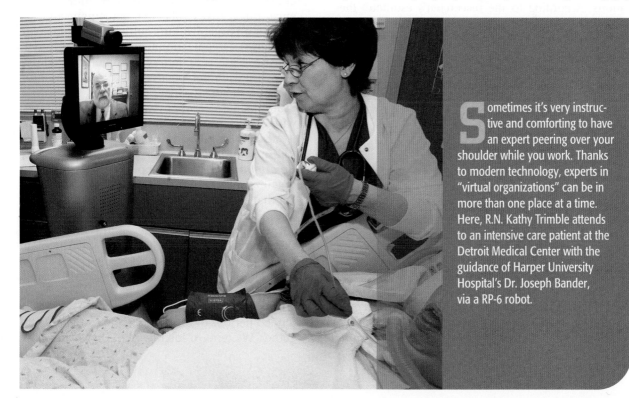

Sometimes it's very instructive and comforting to have an expert peering over your shoulder while you work. Thanks to modern technology, experts in "virtual organizations" can be in more than one place at a time. Here, R.N. Kathy Trimble attends to an intensive care patient at the Detroit Medical Center with the guidance of Harper University Hospital's Dr. Joseph Bander, via a RP-6 robot.

between information haves and have-nots produces resentment and alienation among low-paid workers employed by factory, data-processing, and shipping subcontractors.

ORGANIZATIONAL CULTURES

The notion of organizational culture is rooted in cultural anthropology.[67] **Organizational culture** is the collection of shared (stated or implied) beliefs, values, rituals, stories, myths, and specialized language that foster a feeling of community among organization members.[68] Culture, although based largely on taken-for-granted or "invisible" factors, exerts a potent influence on behavior. For example, a six-year study of more than 900 newly hired college graduates found significantly lower turnover among those who joined public accounting firms with cultures emphasizing respect for people and teamwork. New hires working for accounting firms whose cultures emphasized detail, stability, and innovation tended to quit 14 months sooner than their counterparts in the more people-friendly organizations. According to the researcher's estimate, the companies with people-friendly cultures saved $6 million in human resource expenses because of lower turnover rates.[69]

Unfortunately, there is a dark side to organizational cultures as well. Dysfunctional cultures anchored to irresponsible values and supportive of (or blind to) unethical conduct have been blamed for the collapse of Enron, Arthur Andersen, and WorldCom and for the crash of NASA's space shuttle *Columbia* that took the lives of its seven crew members.[70] The problem of "groupthink," discussed in Chapter 13, is associated with cultural misdirection. Today's managers need to understand the subtle yet powerful influence of organizational culture and appropriately manage it. For example, this is how *Business Week* recently framed the challenge faced by Ford's new CEO Alan R. Mulally:

> ...*fixing Ford will require more than simply whacking expenses. One way or another, the company will also have to figure out how to produce more vehicles that consumers actually want.*

> *And doing that will require addressing the most fundamental problem of all: Ford's dysfunctional, often defeatist culture.*[71]

Some call organizational (or corporate) culture the "social glue" that binds an organization's members together. Accordingly, this final section binds together all we have said about organizations in this chapter. Without an appreciation for the cultural aspect, an organization is just a meaningless collection of charts, people, and job assignments. An anthropologist-turned-manager offered these cautionary words:

> *Corporate culture is not an ideological gimmick to be imposed from above by management or management consulting firms but a stubborn fact of human social organization that can scuttle the best of corporate plans if not taken into account.*[72]

Characteristics of Organizational Cultures

Given the number of variables involved, organizational cultures can vary widely from one organization to the next. Even so, authorities on the subject have identified six characteristics that most organizational cultures exhibit.[73] Let us briefly examine these common characteristics to gain a fuller understanding of organizational cultures.

1. ***Collective.*** Organizational cultures are *social* entities. An individual may exert a cultural influence, but it takes collective agreement and action for an organization's culture to assume a life of its own. Organizational cultures are truly synergistic (1 + 1 = 3). Jeffrey R. Immelt offered this companywide perspective soon after becoming the new head of General Electric: "We run a multibusiness company with common cultures, with common management . . . where the whole is always greater than the sum of its parts. Culture counts."[74]

2. ***Emotionally charged.*** People tend to find their organization's culture a comforting security blanket that enables them to deal with (or sometimes mask) their insecurities and uncertainties. Not surprisingly, people can develop a strong emotional attachment to their cultural security blanket. They will fight to protect it, often refusing to question its basic values. Corporate mergers often get bogged down in culture conflicts.[75]

3. ***Historically based.*** Shared experiences, over extended periods of time, bind groups of people together. We tend to identify with those who have

organizational culture: shared values, beliefs, and language that create a common identity and sense of community

This is no Mickey Mouse operation. Disney has been so successful at creating a productive and fun organizational culture at its Magic Kingdom theme parks that it conducts training sessions for other companies. Rob Morton (center), a Disney Institute business consultant, instructs a pair of Miami Airport employees at Florida's Walt Disney World. There's nothing Goofy about learning from the best.

had similar life experiences. Trust and loyalty, two key components of culture, are earned by consistently demonstrating predictable patterns of words and actions.[76]

4. ***Inherently symbolic.*** Actions often speak louder than words. Memorable symbolic actions are the lifeblood of organizational culture.[77] For instance, consider what has been going on at Procter & Gamble:

> *From the outside, Procter & Gamble Co's Cincinnati headquarters looks unchanged. But on the top floor—the haunt of P&G's top brass for 50 years—there's a major overhaul under way. Wood paneling and an executive cafeteria are making way for a training center that will bring employees from around the world within earshot of CEO Alan G. Lafley. "I have made a lot of symbolic, very physical changes so people understand we are in the business of leading change," says Lafley.[78]*

The changes at P&G symbolically tell top executives to focus less on power and privilege and more on employee development and open communication.

5. ***Dynamic.*** In the long term, organizational cultures promote predictability, conformity, and stability. Just beneath this apparently stable surface, however, change boils as people struggle to communicate and comprehend subtle cultural clues.[79] A management trainee who calls the president by her first name after being invited to do so may be

embarrassed to learn later that "no one actually calls the president by her first name, even if she asks you to."

6. ***Inherently fuzzy.*** Ambiguity, contradictions, and multiple meanings are fundamental to organizational cultures. Just as a photographer cannot capture your typical busy day in a single snapshot, it takes intense and prolonged observation to capture the essence of an organization's culture.

Forms and Consequences of Organizational Cultures

Figure 9.10 lists major forms and consequences of organizational cultures. To the extent that people in an organization share symbols, a common language, stories, and practices, they will tend to experience the four consequences. The degree of sharing and the intensity of the consequences determine whether the organization's culture is strong or weak.

Shared values are a pivotal factor. Unlike instrumental and terminal values, discussed in Chapter 5 as *personal* beliefs, **organizational values** are *shared* beliefs about what the organization stands for.[80] Shared values, when deeply embedded in the organization's culture, become the equivalent of its DNA. Just as DNA in the cells of our bodies

organizational values: shared beliefs about what the organization stands for

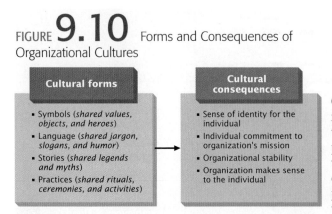

FIGURE **9.10** Forms and Consequences of Organizational Cultures

Source: Forms adapted from Harrison M. Trice and Janice M. Beyer, The Cultures of Work Organizations (Englewood Cliffs, N.J.: Prentice-Hall, 1993), pp. 77–128. Consequences adapted from Linda Smircich, "Concepts of Culture and Organizational Analysis," Administrative Science Quarterly, 28 (September 1983): 339–358.

determines who we are, shared values define an organization. For example, Houston-based Bridgeway Funds stood out as a positive role model in the recent mutual fund trading scandal. Founder and president John Montgomery explained why:

> *The biggest safeguard is a very strong culture . . . of integrity. We have four business values we've had from day one, in order: integrity, investment performance, low cost and service. Another guideline we have is answering the question "What's in the long-term interest of current shareholders?"*[81]

Not surprisingly, Bridgeway does not own any tobacco stocks, and half the firm's profits are donated to charity.

The Process of Organizational Socialization

Organizational socialization is the process through which outsiders are transformed into accepted insiders.[82] In effect, the socialization process helps newcomers make sense of their new situation and integrate into the organization's culture.

organizational socialization: process of transforming outsiders into accepted insiders

> *The culture asserts itself when the taken-for-granted cultural assumptions are in some way violated by the uninitiated and provoke a response. As the uninitiated bump into one after another taken-for-granted assumption, more acculturated*

> *employees respond in a variety of ways (tell stories, offer advice, ridicule, lecture, shun, and so forth) that serve to mold the way in which the newcomer thinks about his or her role and about "how things are done around here."*[83]

ORIENTATIONS. *Orientation programs*—in which newly hired employees learn about their organization's history, culture, competitive realities, and compensation and benefits—are an important first step in the socialization process. Too often today, however, orientations are hurried or nonexistent, and new employees are left to "sink or swim."[84] This is a big mistake, according to workplace research:

> *One study at Corning Glass Works (in Corning, New York) found that new employees who went through a structured orientation program were 69 percent more likely to be with the company after three years than those who were left on their own to sort out the job. A similar two-year study at Texas Instruments concluded that employees who [were] carefully oriented to both the company and their jobs reached full productivity two months sooner than those who weren't.*[85]

STORYTELLING. *Stories* deserve special attention here because, as indicated in Figure 9.10, they are a central feature of organizational socialization and culture. Company stories about heroic or inspiring deeds let newcomers know what "really counts."[86] For example, 3M's eleventh commandment—"Thou shalt not kill a new product idea"—has been ingrained in new employees through one inspiring story about the employee who invented transparent cellophane tape.

> *According to the story, an employee accidentally discovered the tape but was unable to get his superiors to buy the idea. Marketing studies predicted a relatively small demand for the new material. Undaunted, the employee found a way to sneak into the board room and tape down the minutes of board members with his transparent tape. The board was impressed enough with the novelty to give it a try and experienced incredible success.*[87]

Upon hearing this story, a 3M newcomer has believable, concrete evidence that innovation and persistence pay off at 3M. It has been said that stories are "social roadmaps" for employees, telling them where to go and where not to go and what will happen when they get there. Moreover, stories are remembered longer than abstract facts or rules and regulations. How many times have you recalled a professor's colorful story but forgotten the rest of the lecture?

9h An American Indian Art Form Goes Corporate Mainstream

As a child, retired Citgo CEO David Tippeconnic sat on the porch of his Oklahoma farmhouse and listened to the stories of his Comanche elders.

Tippeconnic, 64, recalls a lesson handed down to his grandfather, to his father and then to himself that he says can be summarized: "Don't trust a red-faced white man."

In business, Tippeconnic has interacted primarily with white men. But he's interpreted the boyhood lesson to mean that he should avoid dealing with anyone, of any race, who angers easily, and that he should maintain his cool. It has served him well . . . .

Companies in their never-rest quest for the hot strategy have inadvertently backed into the art of Indian storytelling.

Source: Del Jones, "Indian Art of Storytelling Seeps into Boardroom," USA Today (September 20, 2004): 1B.

QUESTIONS:

What family stories that were passed on to you during your childhood have served you well (or not so well) in life? Why are stories such a powerful form of communication?

Strengthening Organizational Cultures

Given the inherent fuzziness of organizational cultures, how can managers identify cultural weak spots that need improvement? Symptoms of a weak organizational culture include the following:

- ***Inward focus.*** Has internal politics become more important than real-world problems and the marketplace?
- ***Morale problems.*** Are there chronic unhappiness and high turnover?
- ***Fragmentation/inconsistency.*** Is there a lack of "fit" in the way people behave, communicate, and perceive problems and opportunities?
- ***Ingrown subcultures.*** Is there a lack of communication among subunits?
- ***Warfare among subcultures.*** Has constructive competition given way to destructive conflict?
- ***Subculture elitism.*** Have organizational units become exclusive "clubs" with restricted entry?

Have subcultural values become more important than the organization's values?[88] Evidence of these symptoms may encourage a potential recruit to look elsewhere. Each of these symptoms of a weak organizational culture can be a formidable barrier to organizational effectiveness. Organizations with strong cultures do a good job of avoiding these symptoms.[89]

SUMMARY

1. Organizations need to be understood and intelligently managed because they are an ever-present feature of modern life. Whatever their purpose, all organizations exhibit four characteristics: (1) coordination of effort, (2) common goal or purpose, (3) division of labor, and (4) hierarchy of authority. If even one of these characteristics is absent, an organization does not exist. Line managers are in the formal chain of command and have decision-making authority, whereas staff personnel provide advice and support.

2. In open-system terms, business organizations are made up of interdependent technical, boundary-spanning, and managerial subsystems. As an open system, a business is dependent on its environment and has inputs and outputs. Because there is no single criterion for organizational effectiveness, for-profit as well as nonprofit organizations need to satisfy different effectiveness criteria in the near, intermediate, and distant future. In the near term, effective organizations accomplish their purposes, are efficient, and are a source of satisfaction to all stakeholders. They are adaptive and developing in the intermediate term. Ultimately, in the long term, effective organizations survive.

3. The idea behind contingency design is structuring the organization to fit situational demands. Consequently, contingency advocates contend that there is no one best organizational setup for all situations. Diagnosing the degree of environmental uncertainty is an important first step in contingency design. Field studies have confirmed the validity of the assumption that organization structure should vary according to the situation. Burns and Stalker discovered that mechanistic (rigid) organizations are effective when the environment is relatively stable and that organic (flexible) organizations are best when unstable conditions prevail.

4. There are five basic departmentalization formats, each with its own combination of advantages and

disadvantages. Functional departmentalization is the most common approach. The others are product-service, geographic location, customer classification, and work flow process departmentalization. In actual practice, these pure types of departmentalization are usually combined in various ways.

5. As we have come to realize that situational factors dictate how many people a manager can directly supervise, the notion of an ideal span of control has become obsolete. In a centralized organization, top management retains all major decision-making authority and does a lot of checking up on subordinates. Decentralization, the delegation of decision authority to lower-level managers, has been praised as being democratic and has been criticized for reducing top management's control.

6. Delegation of authority, although generally resisted for a variety of reasons, is crucial to decentralization. Effective delegation permits managers to tackle higher-priority duties while helping train and develop lower-level managers. Although delegation varies in degree, it never means abdicating primary responsibility. Successful delegation requires that lower-level managers display plenty of initiative. Among the barriers to delegation are doing everything yourself, lack of confidence and trust in others, low self-confidence, fear of competition, reluctance to risk depending on others, and poor role models who do not delegate.

7. Many factors, with global competition leading the way, are forcing management to reshape the traditional pyramid bureaucracy. These new organizations are characterized by fewer layers, extensive use of teams, and manageably small subunits. Three emerging organizational configurations are the hourglass organization, the cluster organization, and the virtual organization. Each has its own advantages and pitfalls.

8. Organizational culture is the "social glue" binding people together through shared symbols, language, stories, and practices. Organizational cultures can commonly be characterized as collective, emotionally charged, historically based, inherently symbolic, dynamic, and inherently fuzzy (or ambiguous). Diverse outsiders are transformed into accepted insiders through the process of organizational socialization. Orientations and stories are powerful and lasting socialization techniques. Systematic observation can reveal symptoms of a weak organizational culture.

TERMS TO UNDERSTAND

- **Organization,** p. 239
- **Authority,** p. 239
- **Organization chart,** p. 240
- **Line and staff organization,** p. 241
- **Organizational effectiveness,** p. 243
- **Contingency design,** p. 245

- **Mechanistic organizations,** p. 245
- **Organic organizations,** p. 245
- **Departmentalization,** p. 248
- **Span of control,** p. 251
- **Centralization,** p. 252
- **Decentralization,** p. 252
- **Delegation,** p. 253

- **Hourglass organization,** p. 256
- **Cluster organization,** p. 256
- **Virtual organizations,** p. 257
- **Organizational culture,** p. 258
- **Organizational values,** p. 259
- **Organizational socialization,** p. 260

MANAGER'S TOOLKIT

If You Want to Be Delegated Important Duties, Then Demonstrate a Lot of Initiative

Instructions: Assess yourself with this checklist for taking initiative. What areas need improvement?

Going Beyond the Job
- I make the most of my present assignment.
- I do more than I am asked to do.

- I look for places where I might spot problems and fix them.
- I fix bugs that I notice in programs or at least tell someone about them.
- I look for opportunities to do extra work to help the project move along more quickly.

New Ideas and Follow-Through
- I try to do some original work.
- I look for places where something that's already done might be done better.
- I have ideas about new features and other technical projects that might be developed.
- When I have an idea, I try to make it work and let people know about it.
- I try to document what my idea is and why it's a good idea.
- I think about and try to document how my idea would save the company money or bring in new business.
- I seek advice from people who have been successful in promoting ideas.
- I construct a plan for selling my idea to people in the company.

Dealing Constructively with Criticism
- I tell colleagues about my ideas to get their reactions and criticisms.

- I use their comments and criticisms to make my ideas better.
- I consult the sources of criticisms to help find solutions.
- I continue to revise my ideas to incorporate my colleagues' concerns.

Planning for the Future
- I spend time planning what I'd like to work on next.
- I look for other interesting projects to work on when my present work gets close to the finish line.
- I talk to people to find out what projects are coming up and will need people.

Source: An exhibit from "How Bell Labs Creates Star Performers," by Robert Kelley and Janet Caplan, 71 (July–August 1993). Copyright © 1993 by the President and Fellows of Harvard College; all rights reserved. Reprinted by permission of HBS Publishing.

ACTION LEARNING EXERCISE

An Organizational X Ray: Capturing the "Feel" of an Organization's Culture

Instructions: Working either alone or as part of a team, select an organization you are personally familiar with (such as your college or university or a place of present or past employment). Alternatively, you may choose to interview someone about an organization of their choice. The key is to capture a knowledgeable "insider's" perspective. Complete Parts A and B of this exercise with your target organization in mind. (*Notes:* This instrument is for instructional purposes only, because it has not been scientifically validated. Also, you may want to disguise the organization in any class discussion if your cultural profile could offend someone or is strongly negative.)

Part A
For each of the following adjective pairs, circle the number that best describes the "feel" of the organization, and then calculate a sum total.

Rejecting	1·····2·····3·····4·····5·····6·····7·····8·····9·····10	Accepting
Destructive	1·····2·····3·····4·····5·····6·····7·····8·····9·····10	Constructive
Uncomfortable	1·····2·····3·····4·····5·····6·····7·····8·····9·····10	Comfortable
Unfair	1·····2·····3·····4·····5·····6·····7·····8·····9·····10	Fair
Unsupportive	1·····2·····3·····4·····5·····6·····7·····8·····9·····10	Supportive
Demeaning	1·····2·····3·····4·····5·····6·····7·····8·····9·····10	Empowering
Dishonest	1·····2·····3·····4·····5·····6·····7·····8·····9·····10	Honest
Dull, boring	1·····2·····3·····4·····5·····6·····7·····8·····9·····10	Challenging
Declining	1·····2·····3·····4·····5·····6·····7·····8·····9·····10	Improving
Untrustworthy	1·····2·····3·····4·····5·····6·····7·····8·····9·····10	Trustworthy

Total score = _____

Interpretive scale

1. 10–39 = Run for your life!
2. 40–69 = Needs a culture transplant.
3. 70–100 = Warm and fuzzy!

Part B

Write a brief statement for each of the following:

1. What are the organization's key values (as enacted, not simply as written or stated)?

2. What story (or stories) best convey(s) what the organization is "really" like?

3. Does the organization have legends or heroes that strongly influence how things are done? Describe.

4. What traditions, practices, or symbols make the organization's culture stronger?

5. Does the organization have a larger-than-life reputation or mythology? Explain.

For Consideration/Discussion

1. Is the organization's culture strong or weak? How can you tell?

2. Is the organization's culture people-friendly? Explain.

3. Does the strength (or weakness) of the culture help explain why the organization is thriving (or suffering)? Explain.

4. Will the organization's culture attract or repel high-quality job applicants? Explain.

5. What can or should be done to improve the organization's culture?

CLOSING CASE

Toyota: "America's Best Car Company"

Two tinny sedans left the port of Yokohama in August 1957, bound for California—the first exports from Toyota. The four-door clunkers flopped. The car, which looked like a brick with a roof on top, was prone to overheating and vibrated at speeds of more than 60 miles per hour. By late 1960, Toyota realized it had made a mistake and pulled the Toyopet Crown off the market. A less determined company might never have returned after this humiliation. But Toyota came back a few years later with a better car and has gone from strength to strength ever since.

The world's most profitable automaker—and soon to be its biggest—now has a 15% market share in the U.S., where it sold 2.5 million cars and trucks . . . [in 2006]. Because Toyota is already bigger than Chrysler in the U.S. and is about to pass Ford, *Automotive News*, the industry bible, has retired the "Big Three" moniker; GM, Ford, and Chrysler will henceforth be known as the Detroit Three. Toyota's presence in the U.S. is now so routine that the 3,322 business leaders *Fortune* surveyed named Toyota one of America's Most Admired Companies for the second year in a row—boosting it to third place overall, behind two American perennials, General Electric and Starbucks. Toyota has returned the compliment, making an entrance into that most American of sports—we're talking NASCAR—and introducing a full-sized, Texas-built pickup truck, the Tundra.

As the story of the tarnished Crown hints, nothing was inevitable about Toyota's success. It has managed to survive discriminatory taxes, import restraints, and the occasional xenophobic hissy fit—U.S. workers taking sledgehammers to imported cars—to become something of a model citizen. There's no question that coming in fresh, Toyota had some advantages over Detroit: It was unburdened by retiree obligations, union contracts that had been bid up over decades, and brands like Oldsmobile that refused to make money (or die). And yes, it was lucky to have small cars ready to sell when the first oil shocks hit in the 1970s. But the most important reason that Toyota became America's most prestigious automaker is that this quintessentially Japanese company has been better than Detroit at reading the American car psyche. Toyota has never been a style leader. It has never created a car as iconic as, say, the Ford Mustang. But it discerned correctly that many car buyers don't need the next hot thing. They just want a trouble-free product that looks fine—and they will pay a premium for it.

One way Toyota reads the public mind is the think tank at Toyota Motor Sales in Torrance, Calif., where a research department staffed by 116 people monitors the industry and keeps tabs on demographic and economic developments. Its mission: to predict consumer trends and create a lineup of cars and trucks to capitalize on them. Each professional is expected to spend time out in the field talking to car buyers. The Japanese have a name for it: *genchi genbutsu*—go to the scene and confirm the actual happenings.

Most big companies have something like it; what distinguishes Toyota is that its executives actually listen and have turned those insights into profits. When researchers found in the mid-1990s that Toyota was losing young buyers to hipper brands like VW, its marketers dreamed up the hugely successful Scion. Another case: GM was fooling around with electric cars as far back as the 1980s, but it was Toyota that tapped into the appeal of the green revolution with the hybrid-powered Prius. The Prius accounts for less than 5% of U.S. sales, but Toyota has won a fortune in good publicity. . . .

Beginning in 1988, when it started production in its first assembly plant in Georgetown, Ky., Toyota has been careful to locate each new assembly plant in a different state, partly to maximize congressional clout. "It is better to be spread as broadly as we can be spread," says Josephine Cooper, who runs Toyota's Washington, D.C., office. Toyota has no political action committee, but it has built an effective lobbying operation. "Toyota is a public relations case study—a masterpiece of managing the message," says marketing consultant George Peterson of AutoPacific. "People refer to it as the Teflon car company." In 1989, for example, when the new Lexus had to be recalled to fix the high-mounted brake light, Toyota still emerged with its new-car smell unsullied when it returned the cars fixed, washed, and with a full tank of gas.

Toyota has sunk deep roots in the U.S., especially in the middle of the country, where it has built parts and assembly plants and technical centers in a north-south corridor stretching along I-75. The latest, a $1.3 billion assembly plant in Mississippi to make the Highlander SUV, is due to open in 2010. Toyota employs 34,600 Americans directly and 400,000 more indirectly at suppliers and dealers. Every year, Toyota buys $28.5 billion in parts and materials from U.S. suppliers, most of which goes into the 1.2 million cars and trucks that it builds here—about half the total it sells domestically. And when it is time to clear inventory, Toyota can be as brassy as any Yank.

In this sense Toyota can look as American as baseball, hot dogs, apple pie—and yes, Chevrolet. But in terms of how it's managed, that is not quite the case. Every U.S. function—sales and marketing, R&D, manufacturing—reports to Japan. U.S. managers sometimes endure 20-hour roundtrip flights to attend a single meeting. Japanese "coordinators" in the U.S. shadow each operation and make their own reports to headquarters. Organizationally it looks like a nightmare, but somehow the two-language, two-culture hybrid works.

Source: Excerpted from Alex Taylor III, "America's Best Car Company," *Fortune* (March 19, 2007): 98–104. © 2007 Time Inc. All rights reserved.

FOR DISCUSSION

1 What evidence can you identify, in this case, of Toyota's being an open system?

2 Which approach, mechanistic or organic, would be better for a company like Toyota that designs, manufactures, and sells technically sophisticated products such as cars and trucks? Explain.

3 What evidence of centralization or decentralization can you find in this case?

4 From the standpoint of Toyota's culture, what does the story of the failed Toyopet Crown symbolically say to both new and long-term employees?

TEST PREPPER

True/False Questions

_____ 1. By definition, it takes at least seven people to make an organization.

_____ 2. It is possible for an organization to be effective in the near future but not in the distant future.

_____ 3. According to contingency design, there is no single best way to structure an organization.

_____ 4. Mechanistic organizations are characterized by high task flexibility and low emphasis on obedience.

_____ 5. A company with production, marketing, and finance departments is organized around functions.

_____ 6. An entrepreneur who insists on making all decisions in her 200-person company has created a centralized organization.

_____ 7. Delegation is central to the concept of decentralization.

_____ 8. Hourglass organizations, by definition, are based on teams.

_____ 9. An organization's culture is clearly spelled out in its mission statement.

_____ 10. Symbolism plays a large part in organizational culture.

Multiple-Choice Questions

1. _____ is *not* a characteristic common to all organizations.
   A. Coordination of effort
   B. Division of labor
   C. Hierarchy of authority
   D. Equal authority and responsibility
   E. Common goal or purpose

2. What are the two dimensions of an organization chart?
   A. People and tasks
   B. Vertical hierarchy and horizontal specialization
   C. Economic and social power
   D. Division of labor and coordination
   E. Boxes and lines

3. Which of the following must the organization be if it is to be effective specifically in the intermediate term?
   A. A source of satisfaction for employees and customers
   B. Efficient
   C. Adaptive and developing
   D. Large and growing
   E. Capable of survival

4. The _____ approach permits the custom tailoring of organizations to meet unique situational demands.
   A. organic
   B. contingency
   C. differentiation
   D. traditional
   E. integration

5. Communication tends to be _____ in the organic organization and _____ in the mechanistic organization.
   A. top-down; bottom-up
   B. vertical; lateral
   C. lateral; participative
   D. command-and-control; vertical
   E. lateral; top-to-bottom

6. Horizontal organizations have _____ departments.
   A. geographic location
   B. work flow process
   C. customer classification
   D. product-service
   E. line and staff

7. _____ is *not* a situational determinant of spans of control.
   A. Dispersion of subordinates
   B. Time required for planning
   C. Dominant technology
   D. Complexity of work performed by subordinates
   E. Time spent coordinating with other managers

8. In a highly decentralized lamp shade factory, who makes many of the important decisions?
   A. Middle and lower managers
   B. Top management
   C. Outside consultants
   D. Customers
   E. The corporate board of directors

9. _____ are Internet-linked networks of value-adding subcontractors.
   A. Virtual organizations   B. Matrix systems
   C. Hourglass structures   D. Cluster organizations
   E. Functional structures

10. Which of these is *not* a characteristic of organizational cultures?
   A. Dynamic   B. Inherently symbolic
   C. Collective   D. Focused on the future
   E. Emotionally charged

See page T1 at the back of the text for answers to these questions. Want more questions? Visit the student Web site and take the ACE quizzes for more practice.

10

Human

Resource

Management

Business is a game, and as with all games, the team that puts the best people on the field and gets them playing together wins. It's that simple.[1]

—JACK AND SUZY WELCH

OBJECTIVES

- **Explain** what human resource management involves.

- **Define** the term *human capital,* and **identify** at least four of Pfeffer's people-centered practices.

- **Identify** and briefly **explain** the seven steps in the PROCEED model of employee selection.

- **Distinguish** among equal employment opportunity, affirmative action, and managing diversity.

- **Explain** how managers can be more effective interviewers.

- **Discuss** how performance appraisals can be made legally defensible.

- **Compare** and **contrast** the ingredients of good training programs for both skill and factual learning.

- **Specify** the essential components of an organization's policies for dealing with sexual harassment and alcohol and drug abuse.

THE CHANGING WORKPLACE

Emphasis on People Makes Holder No. 1

Executives at Holder Construction Co. in Atlanta are happy to share the secret of their company's success with anyone—even competitors. Their secret is a fairly simple and straightforward idea—hire the best and brightest and give them the opportunity to excel.

"People are our No. 1 asset, and that's something all of us here firmly believe and practice every day," says Tommy Holder, chairman and CEO of Holder Construction.

Holder says he learned long ago that people truly make the difference in how a business performs. He even goes so far as to say that he's happy to share any of his company's procedures, software, training tools and policies with other companies.

"I know without a doubt that a competitor can use any of the same tools or processes that we use but still have a much different result, because our people and their dedication to doing the best job possible [are] the real key," Holder says.

Holder Construction's commitment to making sure its 400 full-time employees have the tools and skills they need has earned the company the top spot on this year's list of the Best Medium Companies to Work for in America. A perennial on the list, Holder moved up from No. 2 last year.

"It's no surprise to me that Holder has been recognized for being a great place to work," says Tom Nichols, superintendent for mechanical, electrical and plumbing services. "There's no other construction company that I would work for, and I've received calls and offers [from competitors] before, but my answer is always the same: 'You better have one huge tub full of money to offer—and I mean huge—because I'm extremely happy where I am.'"

When Nichols was hired six years ago, his boss asked him to figure out what he wanted to do and how he could best help the company—in other words, create his own job.

"I was pretty much blown away by that idea. I've never had an employer suggest such an idea to me before. It really was a complete breath of fresh air for me to think that way about a job," Nichols says.

Nichols found the company to be true to its word, and he has formed his job to best match his skills. His sense of empowerment and the opportunity to excel is shared by other Holder associates.

"This is such a great place to work because of the willingness and cooperation to give me what I need to do my job," says Jackie McGarity, project manager. "And then they let me do my job the way that I want, which I love."

Most of the skills and tools Holder provides to its associates come through the organization's top-notch training program. Nearly all of the training at Holder is developed in-house by associates who see a need and then design a training course.

Most training sessions are well attended in the headquarters' new training and conference center. Any Holder associate can participate through online video and audio links. And with construction projects in 12 states and regional offices in Phoenix and Herndon, Va., teleconferencing is very popular among Holder staff members, according to Lee Johnston, executive vice president for Holder Construction.

"We are always trying to make the connections better and give all our associates the opportunity to participate in any training session that interests them," Johnston says.

Johnston has worked with Holder Construction for 27 years, and her long tenure is typical for the company's senior management. She heads the organization's human resource function and reports directly to the CEO.

"Lee has a connection to every associate. She has had a hand in hiring nearly every person here," says Tommy Holder. "You hear people say all the time that HR should have a place at the table. Well, HR has long had a place at the table at Holder Construction, and that has made us a much stronger organization and just a great place to work."

Staffing has long been an integral part of the management process. Like other traditional management functions, such as planning and organizing, the domain of staffing has grown throughout the years. This growth reflects increasing environmental complexity and greater organizational sophistication, as the Holder Construction case illustrates. Early definitions of staffing focused narrowly on hiring people for vacant positions. Today, the traditional staffing function is just one part of the more encompassing human resource management process. **Human resource management** involves the acquisition, retention, and development of human resources necessary for organizational success. This broader definition underscores the point

> **human resource management:** acquisition, retention, and development of human resources

that people are valuable *resources* requiring careful nurturing. In fact, what were once called personnel departments are now called human resource departments. In a more folksy manner, the top human resources executive at Wal-Mart is called the "senior vice president of people."[2] This people-centered human resource approach emphasizes the serious moral and legal issues involved in viewing labor simply as a commodity to be bought, exploited to exhaustion, and discarded when convenient. Moreover, global opportunities and competitive pressures have made the skillful management of human resources more important than ever.[3]

Progressive and successful organizations treat all employees as valuable human resources. They go out of their way to accommodate their employees' full range of needs. A prime example is Analytical Graphics Inc. in Exton, Pennsylvania:

> Its aerospace, electrical and software engineers develop mission-critical software that helps analyze and visualize data from missiles, jets, rockets and satellites for commercial and military aerospace uses, including NASA's space shuttle. . . .
>
> The company serves [free] daily breakfasts, lunches and dinners, to which family members are invited. Its kitchen and pantries offer free snack foods and drinks. The entire headquarters staff meets Friday for hot lunches and "story time"— during which the CEO and other employees update everyone on company performance figures, activities and news.
>
> The free-flowing food encourages teamwork and camaraderie, employees say, while making their work lives easier and more productive.
>
> Other free family-style perks include a laundry room with free washers, dryers and supplies; a well-equipped fitness room; and free holiday gift wrapping. For nominal fees, employees can take advantage of other services, such as dry cleaning, oil changes, car washes, flower delivery and shoeshines.[4]

Field research indicates that employees tend to return the favor when they are treated with dignity and respect. For instance, one study compared steel mills with either "control" or "commitment" human resource systems. Emphasis at the control-oriented steel mills was on cost cutting, rule compliance, and efficiency. Meanwhile, the other steel mills encouraged psychological commitment to the company with a climate of trust and participation. "The mills with commitment systems had higher productivity, lower

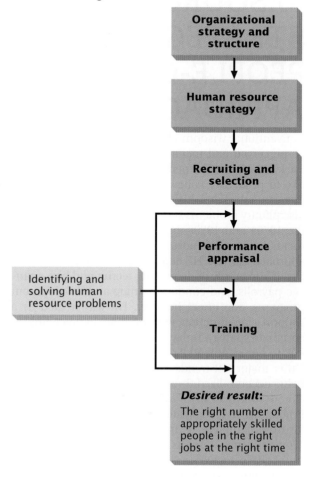

FIGURE **10.1** A General Model for Human Resource Management

scrap rates, and lower employee turnover than those with control systems."[5]

Figure 10.1 presents a model for the balance of this chapter; it reflects this strategic orientation. Note that a logical sequence of human resource management activities—human resource strategy, recruiting, selection, performance appraisal, and training—all derive from organizational strategy and structure. Without a strategic orientation, the management of people becomes haphazardly inefficient and ineffective. Also, as indicated in Figure 10.1, an ongoing process following the hiring decision involves identifying and solving human resource problems. Two contemporary human resource problems, explored in the last section of this chapter, are discouraging sexual harassment and controlling alcohol and drug abuse.

HUMAN RESOURCE STRATEGY: A PEOPLE-CENTERED APPROACH

Conventional wisdom about how employees should be perceived and managed has evolved greatly over the last 60 years. The pendulum has swung from reactive to proactive. Following World War II, personnel departments filled hiring requisitions and handled disciplinary problems submitted by managers. During the 1970s and 1980s, human resource (HR) departments became the norm, and a more encompassing approach evolved. HR departments attempted to forecast labor supply and demand, recruit and hire, manage payrolls, and conduct training and development programs. Too often, however, HR was treated as a support-staff function with only an indirect link to corporate strategy. Today, in well-managed companies, HR is being embedded in organizational strategy.[6] Other major HR trends: traditional HR functions are being decentralized throughout the enterprise and, in a more controversial move, being outsourced;[7] and HR is adapting to globalization.[8] But these transitions are far from complete, as indicated by this observation: "Some business pundits have likened the current status of HR to an awkward adolescent. The profession is just beginning to come of age but isn't quite sure where it's heading."[9] This section outlines a strategic agenda for human resource management.

The Age of Human Capital

This perspective requires open-system thinking, as discussed in Chapters 2 and 9. It is a "big picture" approach to managing people and staying competitive. According to the authors of *The HR Scorecard: Linking People, Strategy, and Performance,*

> *We're living in a time when a new economic paradigm—characterized by speed, innovation, short cycle times, quality, and customer satisfaction—is highlighting the importance of intangible assets, such as brand recognition, knowledge, innovation, and particularly human capital.*[10]

The term **human capital** encompasses all present and future workforce participants and emphasizes the need to develop their fullest potential for the benefit of everyone. Central to this perspective is the assumption that every employee is a valuable asset, not merely an expense item.[11] This broad concern for possible *future* employees is a marked departure from traditional "employees-only" perspectives.

human capital: the need to develop all present and future employees to their fullest potential

Intel, the Santa Clara, California–based maker of computer microprocessors, is committed to developing human capital. The company "adopts" primary and secondary schools—providing computers, teaching talent, and money—and encourages its employees to help. "For every 20 hours [that] workers volunteer at local schools, Intel donates $200."[12] As might be expected from a high-tech company, the emphasis is on math and science. Additionally, Intel matches employees' donations to their college alma maters up to $10,000 a year and awards $1,250,000 in school grants and scholarships each year to winners in a national science competition for high school seniors. Most of those who benefit from these initiatives will *not* end up working for Intel. That's what developing the *world's* human capital is all about—thinking big!

People-Centered Organizations Enjoy a Competitive Advantage

In an era of nonstop layoffs, the oft-heard slogan "Employees are our most valuable asset" rings hollow. In fact, Dilbert cartoonist Scott Adams calls that statement "The First Great Lie of Management."[13] But such cynicism can be countered by looking at how leading companies build a bridge from progressive human resource practices to market success. Take, for instance, Southwest Airlines. Cofounder and former CEO Herb Kelleher told *Fortune* magazine, "My mother taught me that your employees come first. If you treat them well, then they treat the customers well, and that means your customers come back and your shareholders are

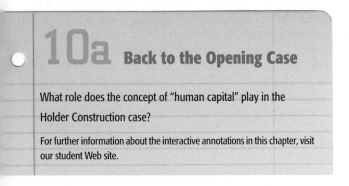

10a Back to the Opening Case

What role does the concept of "human capital" play in the Holder Construction case?

For further information about the interactive annotations in this chapter, visit our student Web site.

ETHICS: CHARACTER, COURAGE, AND VALUES

Traci Bell Gets a Helping Hand from Her Coworkers at Houston-based David Weekley Homes

. . . [I]t was the way her bosses and coworkers supported her after she was diagnosed with Hodgkin's disease that really cinched her loyalty to the company. Bell had to be out two days every other week for six months, followed by two rounds of stem cell transplants. Everyone worked around her schedule and pitched in to help, and then she found out two days before Christmas that her team members in Charlotte, N.C., and Charleston, S.C., had donated 117 of their personal vacation days to her. "I will probably never work anyplace else," she says.

Source: Nancy Hatch Woodward, "Uplifting Employees," HR Magazine, 52 (August 2007): 81.

FOR DISCUSSION

What do companies need to do to set the moral tone for this type of unselfish helping behavior? How would you respond to a manager who complained about today's employees that "Nobody's loyal to the company anymore"?

---

happy."[14] Well, Herb's mom was right! Solid research support for this approach comes from Stanford's Jeffrey Pfeffer, who reported a strong connection between *people-centered practices* and higher profits and lower employee turnover. Pfeffer identified the following seven people-centered practices:

- Protection of job security (including a no-layoff policy)
- Rigorous hiring process
- Employee empowerment through decentralization and self-managed teams
- Compensation linked to performance
- Comprehensive training
- Reduction of status differences
- Sharing of key information

Pfeffer sees these practices as an integrated package and cautions against implementing them piecemeal. Unfortunately, according to Pfeffer's calculations, only about 12 percent of today's organizations qualify as being systematically people-centered.[15] Thus, we have

a clear developmental agenda for human resource management. Ideas about how to enact people-centered practices can be found throughout the balance of this book (see, for instance, Ethics: Character, Courage, and Values).

RECRUITMENT AND SELECTION

Jim Collins, in his best-seller *Good to Great: Why Some Companies Make the Leap . . . and Others Don't,* uses the metaphor of a bus when referring to the organization and its employees.[16] He believes a busload of great people can go just about anywhere it wants.[17] But a bus filled with confused and unruly passengers is destined for the ditch. A survey of CEOs reinforces the importance of getting the right people on the bus and keeping them there. When the CEOs were asked what they probably will look back on five years from now as the key to their success, the number one response was "Getting and retaining talent."[18] This section deals with that important challenge.

Recruiting for Diversity in the Internet Age

The ultimate goal of recruiting is to generate a pool of qualified applicants for new and existing jobs. Everyday

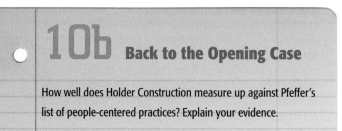

10b Back to the Opening Case

How well does Holder Construction measure up against Pfeffer's list of people-centered practices? Explain your evidence.

recruiting tactics include internal job postings, referrals by present and past employees, campus recruiters, newspaper ads, Web sites, public and private employment agencies, so-called headhunters, job fairs, temporary-help agencies, and union halls. Meanwhile, an underlying reality makes today's recruiting extremely challenging. Specifically, applicant pools need to be demographically representative of the population at large if diversity is to be achieved. One *Fortune* 500 company CEO stated the business case for diversity this way:

> *What's most important is understanding that having a long-term commitment to diversity isn't an option. It's a requirement. It isn't something that you can turn on and off. It has to be built into the fabric of the business. Diversity is a business objective with real payoff, not a "nice-to-do." As soon as people get it into their heads that diversity is a "nice-to-do," I think it's the kiss of death. Diversity is the right thing to do, but it also is an imperative for businesses that intend to be successful over the long term. So you do it because it's a have-to-do.*[19]

Researchers have turned up some surprises about recruiting for diversity in the Internet age. Interestingly,

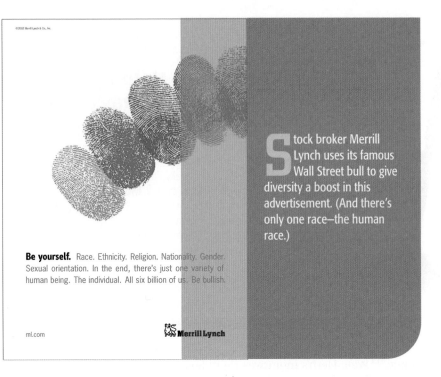

Be yourself. Race. Ethnicity. Religion. Nationality. Gender. Sexual orientation. In the end, there's just one variety of human being. The individual. All six billion of us. Be bullish.

ml.com   **Merrill Lynch**

Stock broker Merrill Lynch uses its famous Wall Street bull to give diversity a boost in this advertisement. (And there's only one race—the human race.)

one study turned the tables and took a *job hunter's* perspective (see Table 10.1). Within the top five categories of search methods, corporate Web sites[20] had the distinction of being the most frequently used but *least successful* job-hunting method. Referrals turned out to be the best way to land a job. Job hunters who go the referral route need to polish their networking skills. "To network effectively, start with friends, family, and others who know you well and can help present your case, says Bob Critchley, executive VP for global relationships at outplacement firm Drake Beam Morin."[21]

Another research surprise came from the employers' side of the equation. A 2007 study of companies using e-recruitment tools such as trade group listings, social networking sites, and blogs uncovered disappointment about attracting high-quality and diverse candidates.[22] One bright spot for online recruiting because of its global reach, however, is finding skilled people in far-flung places. Consider this case in point:

> *Organizations can bolster their staffs by using social networks to find just the right skills wherever they are needed. For example, Ning, a Silicon Valley startup with 10 nationalities represented among its 27 employees, follows blog postings and other cyber-trails to find the most qualified candidates. The company provides software tools for consumers to build their own social networking sites, and it was through its own software that Ning located Fabricio Zuardi, living in remote São Carlos, Brazil. He had*

TABLE **10.1**	How Diverse Candidates Search for and Find Jobs

Top 5 Search Methods	
1. Corporate Web sites	70%
2. General job-listing sites	67
3. Classified ads	53
4. Referrals	52
5. Headhunters/agencies	35
Top 5 Ways Candidates Found Jobs	
1. Referrals	25%
2. General job-listing sites	17
3. Headhunters/agencies	17
4. Classified ads	15
5. Corporate Web sites	6

Source: HR Magazine *by Ruth Thaler-Carter. Copyright 2001 by Society for Human Resource Management (SHRM). Reproduced with permission of Society for Human Resource Management (SHRM) in the format Textbook via Copyright Clearance Center.*

used Ning's tools to build a social networking site for people interested in music. This was May 2006. Ning engineers liked what he was doing and engaged him in an online conversation. One day, Zuardi had the very pleasant surprise of finding a job offer from co-founder Marc Andreessen in his e-mail inbox. "For anyone in the world, the American dream is more accessible now," says Zuardi.[23]

Before we leave the subject of recruiting on the Internet, the following caution about the growing practice of online video résumés needs to be emphasized.

Garry Mathiason, a senior partner at leading employment firm Littler Mendelson in San Francisco, says that employers should never require video résumés from candidates. That's tantamount, he says, to asking questions about race or age, "[which] at this stage in the process are unlawful."[24]

The Selection Process: An Overview

HR experts commonly compare the screening and selection process to a hurdle race. Equal employment opportunity (EEO) legislation in the United States and elsewhere attempts to ensure a fair and unprejudiced race for all job applicants.[25] The first two hurdles are résumé screening and reference checking. Both are very important because of discouraging evidence such as this:

ADP Screening and Selection Services, a unit of the Roseland, N.J.–based ADP payroll and benefits

managing company, says that in performing 2.6 million background checks in 2001, it found that 44 percent of applicants lied about their work histories, 41 percent lied about their education, and 23 percent falsified credentials or licenses.[26]

Background checks for criminal records and citizenship/immigration status are more crucial than ever amid concerns about workplace violence and international terrorism. Consider this: "Between January 1998 and October 2000, American Background Information Services Inc. (ABI), based in Winchester, Va., found undisclosed criminal backgrounds on 12.6 percent of the people it screened."[27] In 2004, Wal-Mart began to perform criminal background checks on all of its job applicants.[28] Other hurdles may include psychological tests, physical examinations, interviews, work-sampling tests, and drug tests. The whole selection process can become quite complex and drawn out at companies such as Google, where rapid growth means steady hiring:

A team of nearly 50 recruiters divided by specialty combs through résumés, which applicants must submit online, then dumps them into a program that routes those selected for interviews to the proper hiring committee and throws the rest in the electronic trash. Interviewing for a job is a grueling process that can take months. Every opening has a hiring committee of seven to nine Googlers who must meet you. Engineers may be asked to write software or debug a program on the spot. Marketers are often required to take a writing test. No matter how long you have been out of school, Google requires that you submit your transcripts to be considered. The rigorous process is important partly for the obvious reason that in high tech, as on Wall Street, being the smartest and the cleverest at what you do is a critical business advantage.[29]

Speaking of Google, job seekers are cautioned about the risk of having embarrassing material posted to their social networking sites such as Facebook turn up in a Web search by a potential employer.[30]

Del J. Still, a respected author and trainer, summarizes the overall employee selection process with the acronym PROCEED, where each letter represents one of the seven steps involved (see Table 10.2). This model encourages managers to take a systems perspective, all the way from preparation to the final hiring decision. Before examining key elements of the PROCEED model in depth, we need to clarify what is involved in the first three action items for step 1. This is where job analysis and job descriptions come into play.

Job analysis is the process of identifying basic task and skill requirements for specific jobs by studying superior performers. A **job description** is a concise document outlining the role expectations and skill requirements for a specific job. Some say they have become obsolete in today's fast-paced world, but up-to-date job descriptions foster discipline in selection and performance appraisal by offering a formal measuring stick.[31]

> **job analysis:** identifying task and skill requirements for specific jobs by studying superior performers

> **job description:** document outlining role expectations and skill requirements for a specific job

Equal Employment Opportunity

Although earlier legislation selectively applies, the landmark EEO law in the United States is Title VII of the Civil Rights Act of 1964. Subsequent amendments, presidential executive orders, and related laws have

TABLE **10.2**	The Employee Selection Process: Still's PROCEED Model

Step 1: PREPARE
- Identify existing superior performers.
- Create a job description for the position.
- Identify the competencies or skills needed to do the job.
- Draft interview questions.

Step 2: REVIEW
- Review questions for legality and fairness.

Step 3: ORGANIZE
- Select your interview team and your method of interviewing.
- Assign roles to your team and divide the questions.

Step 4: CONDUCT
- Gather data from the job candidate.

Step 5: EVALUATE
- Determine the match between the candidate and the job.

Step 6: EXCHANGE
- Share data in a discussion meeting.

Step 7: DECIDE
- Make the final decision.

Source: Del J. Still, High Impact Hiring: How to Interview and Select Outstanding Employees, *2nd edition, revised (Dana Point, CA.: Management Development Systems, 2001), pp. 43–44. Reprinted by permission.*

expanded EEO's coverage. EEO law now provides a broad umbrella of employment protection for certain categories of disadvantaged individuals:

> *The result of this legislation has been that in virtually all aspects of employment, it is unlawful to discriminate on the basis of race, color, sex, religion, age, national origin, . . . [disabilities], being a disabled veteran, or being a veteran of the Vietnam Era.*[32]

What all this means is that managers cannot refuse to hire, promote, train, or transfer employees simply on the basis of the characteristics listed above. Nor can they lay off or discharge employees on these grounds. Sexual preference and gender identity have been added to the list in some local and state jurisdictions.[33] Selection and all other personnel decisions must be made solely on the basis of objective criteria, such as ability to perform or seniority. Lawsuits and fines by agencies such as the U.S. Equal Employment Opportunity Commission (EEOC) are a powerful incentive to comply with EEO laws. In fact, racial discrimination settlements cost Texaco $176 million in 1996 and Coca-Cola $192.5 million in 2000.[34] In 2004, Boeing agreed to pay $72.5 million to settle a class-action lawsuit covering 29,000 women who claimed the aircraft maker discriminated against them when making pay and promotion decisions.[35]

AFFIRMATIVE ACTION. A more rigorous refinement of EEO legislation is affirmative action. An **affirmative action program (AAP)** is a plan for actively seeking out, employing, and developing the talents of those groups historically discriminated against in employment.[36] Affirmative action amounts to a concerted effort to make up for *past* discrimination. EEO, in contrast, is aimed at preventing *future* discrimination. Typical AAPs attack employment discrimination with the following four methods: (1) *active* recruitment of women and minorities, (2) elimination of prejudicial questions on employment application forms, (3) establishment of specific goals and timetables for minority hiring, and (4) statistical validation of employment testing procedures.

> **affirmative action program (AAP):** making up for past discrimination by actively seeking and employing minorities

Like any public policy with legal ramifications, the EEO/AAP area is fraught with complexity.[37] Varying political and legal interpretations and inconsistent court decisions have sometimes frustrated and confused managers.[38] Researchers have uncovered both negative and positive findings about affirmative action. On the negative side, "people [who are] believed to be hired through affirmative action programs carry a stigma of incompetence no matter how qualified they are for the job."[39] On the positive side, a study based on nationwide U.S. Census Bureau data found that affirmative action had enhanced the promotion opportunities of black workers in both government and business organizations. In fact, according to the researcher, "with the exception of women in the public sector, women and blacks enjoyed better promotion opportunities than equally qualified and situated white male workers."[40] These findings disturb some white males, who claim to be the victims of "reverse discrimination."[41] At the same time, some minority employees complain of swapping one injustice for another when they take advantage of affirmative action. Legislated social change, however necessary or laudable, is not without pain. Much remains to be accomplished to eliminate the legacy of unfair discrimination in the workplace.

FROM AFFIRMATIVE ACTION TO MANAGING DIVERSITY. As discussed in Chapter 3, the "managing-diversity" movement promises to raise the discussion of equal employment opportunity and affirmative action to a higher plane. One authority on the subject, R. Roosevelt Thomas Jr., put it this way:

> *Managers usually see affirmative action and equal employment opportunity as centering on minorities*

10d What About Those Tattoos and Piercings?

Fact: 22 Percent of Americans have a tattoo.

A staffing professional:

Daria Juran, office manager for Express Personnel staffing agency in Phoenix, said her company directly addresses body art. "We absolutely never ignore tattoos or piercings," she says.

"Typically, people aren't resistant to hearing they need to cover up a tattoo, or to remove piercing jewelry," she said. "But it does limit job opportunities."

Sources: Data from Michelle Archer, "Tome Tracks Our Trends, from Tattoos to Snipers," USA Today (September 10, 2007): 9B. As quoted in Patricia Bathurst, "Workplace Policies on Body Art Differ," Arizona Republic (October 22, 2006): EC1.

QUESTION:
Where should employers draw the line at dictating how employees should look? Explain.

VALUING DIVERSITY

Dealing with Religion in the U.S. Workplace

For employers wanting to offer a more open environment for employees, it's important to know the laws and regulations. With some 97 percent of religious people practicing one of 20 religions and more than 2,200 individual religions and sects, according to Business for Social Responsibility, it's no wonder religious discrimination complaints to the U.S. Equal Employment Opportunity Commission have risen by 50 percent since 1991.

Complaints are often about restrictions placed on workers who want to bring a small part of their religion into the workplace—whether it be a prayer time or particular garments. Simultaneously, employees complain about too much tolerance—special treatment because of a particular religion or employees proselytizing.

Employers are prohibited from discriminating against individuals because of their religion (among other things) in hiring, firing, and other parts of employment, according to Title VII of the Civil Rights Act of 1964. Employers are also expected to make reasonable accommodations for employees' religious practices.

In 1998, the Clinton administration, along with a religious coalition including the Christian Legal Society and the American Jewish Congress, sought to clarify Title VII in regard to religion. New guidelines stated that personal expression should be allowed as long as workplace productivity was not at risk. Employees, for example, can keep the Koran or Bible on their desks, talk to coworkers about religion, and pray during breaks.

But like many laws, vagueness and uncertainty still exist. Business for Social Responsibility offers a few helpful hints to employers who want to stay accepting but legal of religion in the workplace.

Spread the word. Either through employee orientation materials, bulletin boards or meetings, let employees know that your company is willing to make reasonable accommodations for their religious practices.

Be specific about what is reasonable and unreasonable.

Be fair. Don't exclude religions because they are new or widely unknown.

Review company policies for phrases that could be considered discriminating.

Educate yourself. Learn about other religions, along with their beliefs, holidays, and customs. Then share this information with employees.

Seek individualized solutions. Take time to work with employees on an individual basis to find the answers to specific problems.

Don't forget the nonreligious. Rather than offering time off for religious holidays, offer time off for personal needs.

Source: From Heather Johnson, "Spiritually Responsible," Training, 41 (April 2004): 26. © VNU Business Media, Inc. Reprinted with permission.

---

and women, with very little to offer white males. The diversity I'm talking about includes not only race, gender, creed, and ethnicity but also age, background, education, function, and personality differences. The objective is not to assimilate minorities and women into a dominant white male culture but to create a dominant heterogeneous culture.[42]

In short, diversity advocates want to replace all forms of bigotry, prejudice, and intolerance with tolerance and, ideally, *appreciation* of interpersonal differences.[43] (See Valuing Diversity.) They also want to broaden the message of *inclusion* to make it globally applicable in multinational organizations.

ACCOMMODATING THE NEEDS OF PEOPLE WITH DISABILITIES. From the perspective of someone in a wheelchair, the world can be a very unfriendly place. Curbs, stairways, and inward-swinging doors in small public toilet stalls all implicitly say, "You're not welcome here; you don't fit in." Prejudice and discrimination worsen the situation. Cheri Blauwet, a world-class wheelchair racer from Larchwood, Iowa, who was paralyzed below the waist in a farm accident at 15 months of age, offered this perspective:

The thing that bothers me most is the low expectations strangers have of me. The first thing people see is not a 24-year-old woman who's strong and capable. They don't see a Stanford medical school student. What they see is the wheelchair.[44]

Human disabilities vary widely, but historically, disabled people have had one thing in common— unemployment. Consider these telling statistics:

Today, more than 54 million Americans are disabled, nearly 20 percent of the U.S. population. One

The world changed for Carmen Jones when a car accident during her junior year at Virginia's Hampton University left her in a wheelchair for life. After months of painful rehabilitation, an inspiring boost from the University's president helped her eliminate deep self-doubts and earn a marketing degree with honors. It's been onward and upward ever since. Now she's the founding president of Solutions Marketing Group in Arlington, Virginia. The company helps businesses reach and better serve disabled people—a group Jones believes is seriously underserved.

in five disabled adults has not graduated from high school, and more than 70 percent of disabled people between ages 18 and 55 are unemployed.[45]

Reducing the unemployment rate for people with disabilities is not just about jobs and money. It is about self-sufficiency, hopes, and dreams.[46] With enactment of the Americans with Disabilities Act of 1990 (ADA), disabled Americans hoped to get a real chance to take their rightful place in the workforce.[47] But according to research, this hope remains unfulfilled. In fact, added government regulation reportedly has discouraged some employers from hiring disabled people. The disappointing findings: "analysis of Census Bureau survey data from 1987 to 1996 indicates that the act's impact on employment of the disabled was negative."[48] Also, in a 2004 survey of 2,000 disabled Americans, "64% said the Americans with Disabilities Act has made no difference in their lives, up from 58% in 2000."[49]

The ADA, enforced by the EEOC, requires employers to make *reasonable* accommodations to the needs of present and future employees with physical and mental disabilities. As the ADA was being phased in to cover nearly all employers, many feared their businesses would be saddled with burdensome expenses and many lawsuits. But a 1998 White House–sponsored survey "determined that the mean cost of helping disabled workers to overcome their impairments was a mere $935 per person."[50]

New technology is also making accommodation easier.[51] Large-print computer screens for the partially blind, braille keyboards and talking computers for the blind, and telephones with visual readouts for the deaf are among today's helpful technologies. Here are some general policy guidelines for employers:

- Audit all facilities, policies, work rules, hiring procedures, and labor union contracts to eliminate barriers and bias.
- Train all managers in ADA compliance and all employees in how to be sensitive to coworkers and customers with disabilities.[52]
- Do not hire anyone who cannot safely perform the basic duties of a particular job with reasonable accommodation.

10e The Word *Ability* Is the Most Important Part of Disability

Don't call people without disabilities 'normal.' They're 'nondisabled.' Indeed, some would add that those without disabilities are 'temporarily nondisabled.'

Source: Marc Hequet, "ADA Etiquette," Training, 30 (April 1993): 33.

QUESTIONS:

What are the implications of these word choices for people with disabilities? What sorts of accommodations to disabled people have you observed recently? How do any of these accommodations affect your life?

With lots of low-tech ingenuity, a touch of high tech, and support from coworkers, millions of disabled people can help their employers win the battle of global competition.

Employment Selection Tests

EEO guidelines in the United States have broadened the definition of an **employment selection test** to include any procedure used as a basis for an employment decision. This means that in addition to traditional pencil-and-paper tests, numerous other procedures qualify as tests, such as unscored application forms; informal and formal interviews; performance tests; and physical, educational, or experience requirements.[53] This definition of an employment test takes on added significance when you realize that in the United States, the federal government requires all employment tests to be statistically valid and reliable predictors of job success.[54] Historically, women and minorities have been victimized by invalid, unreliable, and prejudicial employment selection procedures. Similar complaints have been voiced about the use of personality tests, polygraphs, drug tests, and AIDS and DNA screening during the hiring process[55] (see Table 10.3). Despite questions about the practice, and despite its potential drawbacks, the Association of Test Publishers recently noted that "overall employment testing, including personality tests, has been growing at a rate of 10% to 15% in each of the past three years."[56]

employment selection test: any procedure used in the employment decision process

Effective Interviewing

Interviewing warrants special attention here because it is the most common employee selection tool.[57] Line managers at all levels are often asked to interview candidates for job openings and promotions and should be aware of the weaknesses of the traditional unstructured interview. The traditional unstructured or informal interview, which has no fixed question format or systematic scoring procedure, has been criticized on grounds such as the following:

- It is highly susceptible to distortion and bias.
- It is highly susceptible to legal attack.
- It is usually indefensible if legally contested.
- It may have apparent validity, but no real validity.
- It is rarely totally job-related and may incorporate personal items that infringe on privacy.
- It is the most flexible selection technique, thereby being highly inconsistent.
- There is a tendency for the interviewer to look for qualities he or she prefers, and then to justify the hiring decision based on these qualities.
- Often the interviewer does not hear about the selection mistakes.
- There is an unsubstantiated confidence in the traditional interview.[58]

THE PROBLEM OF CULTURAL BIAS. Traditional unstructured interviews are notorious for being culturally insensitive. Evidence of this problem surfaced in a study of the interviewing practices of 38 general managers employed by nine different fast-food chains. According to the researcher,

Considering the well-known demographics of today's workforce, it's amazing that 9 percent of those receiving a negative hiring decision are turned down for inappropriate eye contact. To give a firm handshake and look someone straight in the eyes is a very important lesson taught by Dad to every middle-class male at a tender age. Not only do nonmainstream groups miss the lesson from Dad, some are taught that direct eye contact is rude or worse. Girls are frequently taught that direct eye contact is unbecoming in a female. In reality, having averted or shifty eyes may indicate mostly that the job applicant is not a middle-class male.[59]

These job seekers lined up in front of Con Edison, a New York public utility, share a common desire for a job. What they don't have in common are their demographic categories, work histories, skills, and abilities. This is where skilled interviewers asking structured interview questions are required to find the right talent in an unbiased and fair manner.

TABLE **10.3** Employment Testing Techniques: An Overview

TYPE OF TEST	PURPOSE	COMMENTS
Pencil-and-paper psychological and personality tests	Measure attitudes and personality characteristics such as emotional stability, intelligence, and ability to deal with stress.	Renewed interest based on claims of improved validity. Can be expensive when scoring and interpretations are done by professionals. Validity varies widely from test to test.
Pencil-and-paper honesty tests (integrity testing)	Assess the degree of risk of a candidate's engaging in dishonest behavior.	Inexpensive to administer. Promising evidence of validity. Growing in popularity since recent curtailment of polygraph testing. Women tend to do better than men.
Job skills tests (clerical and manual dexterity tests, math and language tests, assessment centers, and simulations)	Assess competence in actual "hands-on" situations.	Generally good validity if carefully designed and administered. Assessment centers and simulations can be very expensive.
Polygraph (lie detector) tests	Measure physical signs of stress, such as rapid pulse and perspiration.	Growing use in recent years severely restricted by federal (Employee Polygraph Protection Act of 1988), state, and local laws. Questionable validity.
Drug tests	Check for controlled substances through urine, blood, or hair samples submitted to chemical analysis.	Rapidly growing in use despite strong employee resistance and potentially inaccurate procedures.
Handwriting analysis (graphoanalysis)	Infer personality characteristics and styles from samples of handwriting.	Popular in Europe and growing in popularity in the United States. Sweeping claims by proponents leave validity in doubt.
AIDS/HIV antibody tests	Find evidence of AIDS virus through blood samples.	An emerging area with undetermined legal and ethical boundaries. Major confidentiality issue.
Genetic/DNA screening	Use tissue or blood samples and family history data to identify those at risk of costly diseases.	Limited but growing use strongly opposed on legal and moral grounds. Major confidentiality issue.

Managers can be taught, however, to be aware of and to overcome cultural biases when interviewing. This is particularly important in today's era of managing diversity and greater sensitivity to disabled people.

STRUCTURED INTERVIEWS. Structured interviews are the recommended alternative to traditional unstructured or informal interviews.[60] A **structured interview** is a set of job-related questions with standardized answers applied consistently across all interviews for a specific job.[61] Structured interviews are constructed, conducted, and scored by a committee of three to six members to try to eliminate individual bias. The systematic format and scoring of structured interviews eliminate the weaknesses inherent in unstructured interviews. Four types of questions typically characterize structured interviews: (1) situational, (2) job knowledge, (3) job sample simulation, and (4) worker requirements (see Table 10.4).

BEHAVIORAL INTERVIEWING. Behavioral scientists tell us that past behavior is the best predictor of future behavior. We are, after all, creatures of habit. Situational-type interview questions can be greatly strengthened by anchoring them to actual past behavior (as opposed to hypothetical situations).[62] Structured, job-related, behaviorally specific interview questions

structured interview: set of job-related questions with standardized answers

TABLE **10.4**   Types of Structured Interview Questions

TYPE OF QUESTION	METHOD	INFORMATION SOUGHT	SAMPLE QUESTION
Situational	Oral	Can the applicant handle difficult situations likely to be encountered on the job?	"What would you do if you saw two of your people arguing loudly in the work area?"
Job knowledge	Oral or written	Does the applicant possess the knowledge required for successful job performance?	"Do you know how to do an Internet search?"
Job sample simulation	Observation of actual or simulated performance	Can the applicant actually do essential aspects of the job?	"Can you show us how to compose and send an e-mail message?"
Worker requirements	Oral	Is the applicant willing to cope with job demands such as travel, relocation, or hard physical labor?	"Are you willing to spend 25 percent of your time on the road?"

Source: Updated from "Structured Interviewing: Avoiding Selection Problems," by Elliott D. Pursell, Michael A. Campion, and Sarah R. Gaylord, copyright November 1980. Reprinted with permission of Personnel Journal, *Costa Mesa, California; all rights reserved.*

10f Caution! Tough Interview Questions Ahead

1. **What was the last product or service you saw that took your breath away?**
2. **Is the customer always right?**
3. **Have you learned more from your mistakes or your successes?**
4. **On what occasions are you tempted to lie?**
5. **Tell me about yourself in words of one syllable.**

Source: Excerpted from John Kador, How to Ace the Brainteaser Interview *(New York: McGraw-Hill, 2005), pp. 213–214.*

QUESTIONS:

How would you handle these "think-on-your-feet" questions in a job interview? Playing the interviewer's role, what kinds of answers would you like to hear?

keep managers from running afoul of the problems associated with unstructured interviews, as listed earlier.

In a **behavior-based interview**, candidates are asked to recall specific actions they have taken in past job-related situations and describe them in detail. . . .

behavior-based interview:
detailed questions about specific behavior in past job-related situations

Behavior-based interviews are rich with verifiable data. Candidates are required to include details such as names, dates, times, locations, and numbers.

Candidates are reminded to use the word "I" rather than using "we" or "they" as they describe past experiences. This helps the candidates remain focused on their role in each situation and helps the interviewer evaluate the presence or absence of specific competencies.[63]

If the questions are worded appropriately, the net result should be a good grasp of the individual's relevant skills, initiative, problem-solving ability, and ability to recover from setbacks and learn from mistakes. (For practice, see the Action Learning Exercise at the end of this chapter.)

PERFORMANCE APPRAISAL

Annual performance appraisals are such a common part of modern organizational life that they qualify as a ritual. As with many rituals, the participants repeat the historical pattern without really asking the important questions: "Why?" and "Is there a better way?" Both appraisers and appraisees tend to express general dissatisfaction with performance appraisals. According to HR specialist Susan Jespersen, "Giving performance feedback is the No. 1 dreaded task of managers."[64] This is a major threat to productivity because, according to a recent survey, "more than 70% of managers admit they have trouble giving a tough performance review to an underachieving employee."[65] Not surprising, in view of the following observation:

> *The annual performance review process, touted by some as the gateway to future prosperity, is, in reality for many companies, nothing more than a fill-in-the-blank, form-completing task that plots an individual's performance against a sanitized list of often generic corporate expectations and required competencies.*[66]

Considering that experts estimate the average cost of a *single* performance appraisal to be $1,500, the waste associated with poorly administered appraisals is mind-boggling.[67]

Performance appraisal can be effective and satisfying if systematically developed and implemented techniques replace haphazard methods. For our purposes, **performance appraisal** is the process of evaluating individual job performance as a basis for making objective personnel decisions.[68] This definition intentionally excludes occasional coaching, in which a supervisor simply checks an employee's work and gives immediate feedback. Although personal coaching is fundamental to good management, formally documented appraisals are needed both to ensure equitable distribution of opportunities and rewards and to avoid prejudicial treatment of protected minorities.[69]

performance appraisal: evaluating job performance as a basis for personnel decisions

In this section, we will examine two important aspects of performance appraisal: (1) legal defensibility and (2) alternative techniques.

Making Performance Appraisals Legally Defensible

Lawsuits challenging the legality of specific performance appraisal systems and resulting personnel actions have left scores of human resource managers asking themselves, "Will my organization's performance appraisal system stand up in court?" From the standpoint of limiting legal exposure, it is better to ask this question in the course of developing a formal appraisal system than after it has been implemented. Managers need specific criteria for legally defensible performance appraisal systems. Fortunately, researchers have discerned some instructive patterns in court decisions.

After studying the verdicts in 66 employment discrimination cases in the United States, one pair of researchers found that employers could successfully defend their appraisal systems if these systems satisfied four criteria:

1. A *job analysis* was used to develop the performance appraisal system.
2. The appraisal system was *behavior-oriented*, not trait-oriented.
3. Performance evaluators followed *specific written instructions* when conducting appraisals.
4. Evaluators *reviewed the results* of the appraisals with the ratees.[70]

Each of these conditions has a clear legal rationale. Job analysis, discussed earlier relative to employee selection, anchors the appraisal process to specific job duties, not to personalities. Behavior-oriented appraisals properly focus management's attention on *how* the individual actually performed his or her job.[71] Performance appraisers who follow specific written instructions are less likely to be plagued by vague performance standards and/or personal bias. Finally, by reviewing performance appraisal results with those who have been evaluated, managers provide the feedback necessary for learning and improvement. Managers who keep these criteria for legal defensibility and the elements in Table 10.5 in mind are better equipped to select a sound appraisal system from alternative approaches and techniques.

Alternative Performance Appraisal Techniques

The list of alternative performance appraisal techniques is long and growing. Appraisal software programs also are proliferating. Unfortunately, many are simplistic, invalid, and unreliable. In general terms, an *invalid* appraisal instrument does not accurately measure what it is supposed to measure. *Unreliable* instruments do not measure criteria in a consistent manner. Many other performance appraisal techniques are so complex that they are impractical and burdensome to use. But armed with a working knowledge of the most popular appraisal techniques, a good manager can distinguish the strong from the weak. Once again, the strength of an appraisal technique is gauged by its conformity to the criteria for legal defensibility discussed previously. The following are some of the techniques used through the years.

- *Goal setting.* Within an MBO framework, performance is typically evaluated in terms of formal objectives set at an earlier date. This is a

TABLE **10.5** | Elements of a Good Performance Appraisal

Appraisals can be used to justify merit increases, document performance problems or simply "touch base" with employees. Experts say HR first must decide what it wants the appraisal to accomplish [and] then customize the form and the process to meet that goal.

Elements to consider:

1. Objectives set by the employee and manager at the last appraisal.
2. List of specific competencies or skills being measured, with examples of successful behaviors.
3. Ratings scale appropriate to the organization.
4. Space for employee's self-appraisal.
5. Space for supervisor's appraisal.
6. Space for specific comments from the supervisor about the employee's performance.
7. Suggestions for employee development.
8. Objectives to meet by the next appraisal date.

Source: HR Magazine *by Carla Johnson. Copyright 2001 by Society for Human Resource Management (SHRM). Reproduced with permission of Society for Human Resource Management (SHRM) in the format Textbook via Copyright Clearance Center.*

10g Survey Says . . . I'm a Star!

In a recent survey of "2,000 U.S. executives and middle managers, . . . an impossible 90% of respondents believe they're in the top 10% of performers."

Source: Peter Coy, "The Poll: Ten Years from Now," Business Week *(August 20–27, 2007): 42.*

QUESTIONS:

Why is this a major roadblock for honest performance appraisals? Does this help explain the widespread dissatisfaction with performance appraisal systems? Explain.

comparatively strong technique if desired outcomes are clearly linked to specific behavior. For example, a product design engineer's "output" could be measured in terms of the number of product specifications submitted per month.

- *Written essays.* Managers describe the performance of employees in narrative form, sometimes in response to predetermined questions. Evaluators often criticize this technique for consuming too much time. This method is also limited by the fact that some managers have difficulty expressing themselves in writing.[72]
- *Critical incidents.* Specific instances of inferior and superior performance are documented by the supervisor when they occur. Accumulated incidents then provide an objective basis for evaluations at appraisal time. The strength of critical incidents is enhanced when evaluators document specific behavior in specific situations and ignore personality traits.[73]
- *Graphic rating scales.* Various traits or behavior are rated on incremental scales. For example, "initiative" could be rated on a 1(= low)—2—3—4—5(= high) scale. This technique is among the weakest when personality traits are employed. However, **behaviorally anchored rating scales (BARS)**, defined as performance rating scales divided into increments of observable job behavior determined through job analysis, are considered one of the strongest performance appraisal techniques. For example, managers at credit card issuer Capital One use performance rating scales with behavioral anchors such as "Do you get things done well through other people? Do you play well as a team member?"[74]

behaviorally anchored rating scales (BARS): performance appraisal scales with notations about observable behavior

- *Weighted checklists.* Evaluators check appropriate adjectives or behavioral descriptions that have predetermined weights. The weights, which gauge the relative importance of the randomly mixed items on the checklist, are usually unknown to the evaluator. Following the evaluation, the weights of the checked items are added or averaged to permit interpersonal comparisons. As with the other techniques, the degree of behavioral specificity largely determines the strength of weighted checklists.

"I work best when someone is looking over my shoulder and telling me that I'm a screw-up."

• *Rankings/comparisons.* Coworkers in a subunit are ranked or compared in head-to-head fashion according to specified accomplishments or job behavior. A major shortcoming of this technique is that the absolute distance between ratees is unknown. For example, the employee ranked number one may be five times as effective as number two, who in turn is only slightly more effective than number three. Rankings/comparisons are also criticized for causing resentment among lower-ranked, but adequately performing, coworkers. *Fortune* offered this overview:

> *In companies across the country, from General Electric to Hewlett-Packard, such grading systems—in which all employees are ranked against one another and grades are distributed along some sort of bell curve—are creating a firestorm of controversy. In the past 15 months employees have filed class-action suits against Microsoft and Conoco as well as Ford, claiming that the companies discriminate in assigning grades. In each case, a different group of disaffected employees is bringing the charges: older workers at Ford, blacks and women at Microsoft, U.S. citizens at Conoco.[75]*

Ford and Microsoft have since dropped their forced ranking systems.[76] This technique can be strengthened by combining it with a more behavioral technique, such as critical incidents or BARS.

• *Multirater appraisals.* This is a general label for a diverse array of nontraditional appraisal techniques involving more than one rater for the focal person's performance. The rationale for multirater appraisals is that "two or more heads are less biased than one." One approach that enjoyed faddish popularity in recent years involves 360-degree feedback. In a **360-degree review**, a manager is evaluated by his or her boss, peers, and subordinates. The results may or may not be statistically pooled and are generally fed back anonymously.[77] The use of 360-degree reviews as a performance appraisal tool has produced mixed results.[78] A recent cross-cultural study found 360-degree feedback to be more effective in individualistic ("me") cultures than in collectivist ("we") cultures.[79] Researchers also found that 360-degree *feedback* is an effective management development technique, especially when paired with coaching.[80] Consider, for example, how 360-degree feedback is used at Wachovia, the Charlotte, North Carolina–based bank:

360-degree review: pooled, anonymous evaluation by one's boss, peers, and subordinates

> *For the past year, [extensively trained internal and external] coaches have been supporting participants in the company's 360 Assessment Process, which is based on Wachovia's executive leadership competency model. The coaches deliver the 360 feedback, assist participants in understanding the results, support them in developing individual development plans, and provide ongoing coaching and support for a four-month period after the 360 in conjunction with the participant's manager and human resource business partner.[81]*

TRAINING

No matter how carefully job applicants are screened and selected, typically a gap remains between what employees *do* know and what they *should* know. Training is needed to fill in this knowledge gap. In 2006, companies in the United States spent $55.8 billion on training.[82] Huge as this number sounds, it still is not nearly enough for two reasons: first, administrative expenses can eat up as much as 50 percent of a company's training budget;[83] and second, as we will see in a moment, a skills shortage looms in the United States.

Not all training takes place in offices and factories. This session is occurring under a tree near Cerro Grande Peak in New Mexico. Students from the Southwest Fire Use Training Academy (FUTA) are learning how to fight fire with fire from assistant fire management officer Julian Affuso. If they have to fight a wildfire in rough terrain someday, their lives could depend on how much they learned during this training session.

Formally defined, **training** is the process of changing employee behavior and/or attitudes through some type of guided experience. We now focus on a skills gap in the United States and on current training methods, the ingredients of a good training program, and the important distinction between skill and factual learning.

A Shortage of Skilled Workers?

Could a shortage of skilled workers in the United States be around the corner? *Yes*, because experts say the U.S. labor force will come up short in terms of both numbers and quality in the years ahead. Driving this situation is a "perfect storm" of demographic and technological trends. Demographically, the huge post–World War II baby-boom generation is hitting retirement age. Jeff Taylor, founder of Monster.com, the Internet job-search leader, frames the demographic dilemma this way: "About 70 million baby boomers, some highly skilled, will exit the workforce over the next 18 years with only 40 million workers coming in."[84] Meanwhile, technological change will continue to increase the need for so-called "knowledge workers," people who are comfortable with math, science, and technology. Consequently, education and training are more important than ever. Edward E. Gordon, author of *The 2010 Crossroad: The New World of People and Jobs*, explains the unfolding situation:

> In the short term (2005–2010), U.S. business will likely move more jobs offshore, keep some older workers for a few extra years, and continue replacing people with technology. But none of these strategies are long-term solutions.
>
> U.S. employers must begin to ramp up their training investment in the current workforce—and they must do it now. By 2015 the situation may become so critical that the United States will have little choice but to support massive career preparation efforts that will still lag far behind new employment opportunities.[85]

Sadly, most corporate leaders appear to have their heads in the sand on this issue. According to *Fortune*, "even though surveys show that 70% to 80% of executives at big companies are concerned about the coming brain drain, fewer than 20% have begun to do anything about it."[86] Some farsighted companies, such as David Weekley Homes, the Houston firm featured earlier in the Ethics box, have made training a top strategic priority. The 1,234-employee homebuilder "spends at least $4,500 a year per employee on training; that's more than $5 million each year."[87]

Today's Training: Content and Delivery

Training magazine's annual survey of companies with at least 100 employees gives us a revealing snapshot of current training practices. The top portion of Figure 10.2 lists the nine most common types of training. How that training was delivered is displayed in the bottom portion of the figure. Surprisingly, despite all we read and hear about computer-based training and e-learning over the Internet, the majority of today's training is remarkably low-tech. We anticipate growth in e-learning and other nontraditional methods as the technology

FIGURE **10.2** The Content and Delivery of Today's Training

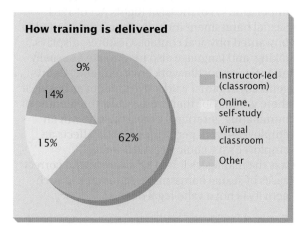

Which program areas will receive the most funding resources in the coming year?

Sales training	33%
Management/Supervisory training	29%
IT/Systems training	24%
Mandatory/Compliance training	19%
Customer service training	19%
Profession/Industry-specific training	17%
Interpersonal skills	13%
Desktop application training	10%
Executive development	7%

How training is delivered

- 62% Instructor-led (classroom)
- 15% Online, self-study
- 14% Virtual classroom
- 9% Other

Source: Data in top portion and graphic in bottom portion from Tammy Galvin, "2006 Industry Report," Training, 43, December 2006, pp. 25–26. Copyright © Nielsen Business Media, Inc. Reprinted with permission from Training.

becomes more user-friendly and more affordable. Consider, for example, this breakthrough application:

> *Dublin, Ireland–based Intuition, a provider of technology-enabled learning, has announced the deployment of what it calls "the world's first fully trackable mobile e-learning course" for PDAs such as BlackBerry. The course, which has been developed for financial services institutions, and enables users' progress to be tracked and recorded automatically, is intended to make mandatory training easier to deploy, more convenient, and fully auditable.*[88]

Meanwhile, the old standbys—classroom PowerPoint presentations, workbooks/manuals, DVDs, and seminars—are still the norm. For better or for worse, the typical college classroom is still a realistic preview of what awaits you in the world of workplace training.

Which instructional method is best? There are probably as many answers to this question as there are trainers. Given variables such as interpersonal differences, budget limitations, and instructor capabilities, it is safe to say that there is no one best training technique. For example, the lecture method, though widely criticized for being dull and encouraging learner passivity, was still widely used in the study just discussed. Whatever method is used, trainers need to do their absolute best because they are key facilitators for people's hopes and dreams.

The Ingredients of a Good Training Program

Although training needs and approaches vary, managers can get the most out of their training budgets by following a few guidelines. According to two training specialists, every training program should be designed along the following lines to maximize retention and transfer learning to the job.

1. Maximize the similarity between the training situation and the job situation.
2. Provide as much experience as possible with the task being taught.
3. Provide for a variety of examples when teaching concepts or skills.
4. Label or identify important features of a task.
5. Make sure that general principles are understood before expecting much transfer.
6. Make sure that the trained behaviors and ideas are rewarded in the job situation.
7. Design the training content so that the trainees can see its applicability.
8. Use adjunct questions to guide the trainee's attention.[89]

Skill versus Factual Learning

The ingredients of a good training program vary according to whether skill learning or factual learning is involved.

> *Effective skill learning should incorporate four essential ingredients: (1) goal setting, (2) modeling, (3) practice, and (4) feedback. Let's take as an example the task of training someone to ride horseback. How would you do it? It basically must entail telling someone specifically what you want them to do (goal setting), showing them how you want them to do it (modeling), giving them the opportunity to*

10h   Life-Long Learning

Learning is based on experience, but experience doesn't guarantee learning. . . . People who, knowing their own learning style, are able to coax learning out of their experiences will have a leg up over others.

Source: Don Moyer, "The Stages of Learning," Harvard Business Review, 85 (May 2007): 148.

QUESTIONS:

Do you learn best by seeing, by hearing, by doing, or by engaging in some combination of these? How could you become a more effective life-long learner?

try out what you have told them and shown them (practice), and then telling them what they are doing correctly (feedback).[90]

When factual learning is involved, the same sequence is used, except that in step 2, "meaningful presentation of the materials" is substituted for modeling. Keep in mind that the object of training is *learning*. Learning requires thoughtful preparation, carefully guided exposure to new ideas or behavior, and motivational support.[91] Let us turn our attention to modern human resource management problems that have serious implications for the well-being of today's organizations and employees.

CONTEMPORARY HUMAN RESOURCE CHALLENGES AND PROBLEMS

Modern organizations are a direct reflection of society in general. People take societal influences to work (such as attitudes toward the opposite sex). Along with these predispositions, they take their social, emotional, behavioral, and health-related problems to work. Like it or not and prepared or not, managers face potential problems such as sexual harassment and alcohol and drug abuse. Today's challenge to deal effectively with human resource problems of this

nature cannot be ignored because organizational competitiveness is at stake.

Discouraging Sexual Harassment

A great deal of misunderstanding surrounds the topic of sexual harassment because of sexist attitudes, vague definitions, differing perceptions,[92] and inconsistent court findings. **Sexual harassment**, defined generally as unwanted sexual attention or conduct, has both behavioral and legal dimensions (see Table 10.6). Important among these are the following:

> **sexual harassment:** unwanted sexual attention that creates an offensive or intimidating work environment

- Although it is typically female employees who are the victims of sexual harassment, both women and men (in the United States) are protected under Title VII of the Civil Rights Act of 1964.
- Sexual harassment includes, but is not limited to, unwanted physical contact. Gestures, displays, joking, and language also may create a sexually offensive or hostile work environment. "Courts generally regard a work environment as hostile if there is behavior that is physically threatening or humiliating, interferes unreasonably with an employee's work performance, and affects an employee's psychological well-being."[93]
- It is the manager's job to be aware of and correct cases of sexual harassment. Ignorance of such activity is not a valid legal defense.[94]

Research evidence indicates that sexual harassment is commonplace. In one recent survey, 35 percent of women and 17 percent of men reported having been sexually harassed at work.[95] Employees who use e-mail systems must also contend with problems of sexual harassment in the form of rape threats and obscene words and graphics. In 2000, "Dow Chemical fired 50 employees and disciplined 200 others after an e-mail investigation turned up hard-core pornography and violent subject matter. . . . 'This sort of activity creates a harassment environment that we can't tolerate,' [said a company official]."[96] Sexual harassment begins early, with 83 percent of high school girls and 60 percent of high school boys reportedly experiencing it.[97] According to research, people generally agree that unwanted sexual propositions, promises, or threats tied to sexual favors, lewd comments/gestures/jokes, and touching/grabbing/brushing qualify as sexual harassment. Beyond that, opinions differ.[98] Personal tastes and sensibilities vary widely from individual to

TABLE **10.6**   Behavioral and Legal Dimensions of Sexual Harassment

What exactly is sexual harassment? The Equal Employment Opportunity Commission (EEOC) says that unwelcome sexual advances, requests for sexual favors, and other verbal or physical conduct of a sexual nature constitute sexual harassment when submission to such conduct is made a condition of employment; when submission to or rejection of sexual advances is used as a basis for employment decisions; or when such conduct creates an intimidating, hostile, or offensive work environment. These EEOC guidelines interpreting Title VII of the Civil Rights Act of 1964 further state that employers are responsible for the actions of their supervisors and agents and that employers are responsible for the actions of other employees if the employer knows or should have known about the sexual harassment.

individual. In view of the foregoing evidence, corrective action needs to be taken both by the victims of sexual harassment and by management.

WHAT CAN THE VICTIM DO?   Employees who believe they are victims of sexual harassment can try to live with it, fight back, complain to higher-ups, find another job, or sue their employer. Those who choose to file a lawsuit need to know how to arrange the odds in their favor. An analysis of sexual harassment cases revealed that the following five factors are likely to lead to success. Victims of sexual harassment tended to win their lawsuits when

- the harassment was severe.
- there were witnesses.
- management had been notified.
- there was supporting documentation.
- management had failed to take action.[99]

The more of these factors that apply, the greater the chances that a sexual harassment lawsuit will be successful. Courtrooms are the last line of defense for victims of sexual harassment. Preventive and remedial actions are also needed. Harassers need to be told by their victims, coworkers, and supervisors that their actions are illegal, unethical, and against company policy. As more organizations develop and enforce sexual harassment policies, the problem can be greatly reduced without costly court battles and the loss of valued employees.

WHAT CAN THE ORGANIZATION DO?   Starting with top management, an organizationwide commitment to eliminating sexual harassment should be established. A clear policy statement, with behavioral definitions of sexual harassment and associated penalties, is essential. Like all policies, sexual harassment policies need to be disseminated and uniformly enforced if they are to have the desired impact. Appropriate training, particularly for new employees, can alert people to the problem and consequences of sexual harassment.[100] Finally, in accordance with EEOC

As at any co-ed college or university, sexual harassment is a potential problem at the U.S. Naval Academy in Annapolis, Maryland. Part of the Academy's response is the SHAPE program, a peer education program about sexual harassment. Midshipmen Josh Foxton and Joy Dewey are seen here jointly conducting one of the sessions.

ETHICS: CHARACTER, COURAGE, AND VALUES

Call a Cab!

An employee in New York:

"Letting off steam is part of the culture in my high-pressure industry. But one colleague—a great guy, well-liked—drinks so much at our after-work get-togethers that we've all become uncomfortable. He doesn't get obnoxious, just really drunk. I'm worried and would like to say something. But I don't know if I'm being prudish and I don't want to single myself out from the group."

Source: Excerpted from Kerry Sulkowicz, "(Not) the Life of the After-Work Party," Business Week (June 4, 2007): 18.

FOR DISCUSSION

What is the *right* thing for this employee to do about his colleague? Should this problem be brought to management's attention? Is this after-hours behavior any of the employer's business? If it is, what should management do?

---

guidelines, management can remain adequately informed of any sexual harassment in the organization by establishing a grievance procedure. Harassed employees should be able to get a fair hearing of their case without fear of retaliation.

Controlling Alcohol and Drug Abuse

Statistics tell a grim story about the number one drug problem—alcohol.

More than 30% of adults in the USA have abused alcohol or had alcoholism at some point in their lives, and few have received treatment, a government study reports. Alcoholics who received treatment first got help, on average, at about age 30—eight years after they developed a dependence on drinking, researchers find. "That's a big lag," especially combined with the fact that only 24% of alcoholics reported receiving any treatment at all, says study co-author Bridget Grant of the National Institute on Alcohol Abuse and Alcoholism.[101]

Once believed to be a character disorder, **alcoholism** is now considered a disease in which an individual's normal social and economic roles are disrupted by the consumption of alcohol. Very few alcoholics are actually bums on skid

alcoholism: a disease in which alcohol abuse disrupts one's normal life

row; the vast majority are average citizens with jobs and families. (See Ethics: Character, Courage, and Values.) Alcoholism cuts across all age, gender, racial, and ethnic categories. Experts say a glance in the mirror shows what the average alcoholic looks like.

Close on the heels of employee alcoholism as a growing problem is workplace drug abuse. As a general point of reference, a survey of people 12 and older by the U.S. Department of Health and Human Services found that 46 percent had used illicit drugs during their lifetime. "Illicit drugs include marijuana, hashish, cocaine, crack, heroin, hallucinogens, inhalants, or any prescription-type psychotherapeutic (non-medical usage)."[102]

Because drug fads come and go, the drug problem is a moving target. For example, when one workplace drug-testing company began an ecstasy-screening program, "the number of positives in the methamphetamine category (where ecstasy resides) almost doubled."[103] A 2004 drug use study by the U.S. Department of Health and Human Services found that "10.5 percent of full-time employed adults and 11.9 percent of part-time employed adults were classified with dependence or abuse."[104] Compared with nonabusers, alcoholic employees and drug abusers are one-third less productive, ten times more likely to be absent, three times more likely to be involved in an accident, and responsible for 300 percent higher health care costs.[105]

One way employers are attempting to curb this costly erosion of human resources is with the controversial practice of drug testing for job applicants and employees. But does this tactic work? At least in part, the answer is "yes," according to Quest Diagnostics, which performs 7.3 million drug tests annually. Between 1988 and 2006, the rate for "positives" dropped from 13.6 percent to 3.8 percent (a 72 percent decline). Marijuana remained by far the most common cause for a positive test result.[106] Because drug testing is not necessarily a cure, however, the issue of employee drug abuse remains. Additional tactics are needed.

THE LEGAL SIDE OF WORKPLACE SUBSTANCE ABUSE. Businesses doing contract work for the U.S. government are squeezed on two sides by the law. On the one side, alcoholics and drug addicts are protected from employment discrimination by the Vocational Rehabilitation Act of 1973. They are presumed to have the same employment rights as any disabled person.[107] On the other side, employers with federal contracts exceeding $25,000 are subject to the Federal Drug-Free Workplace Act of 1988. These employers "must certify that they will maintain a drug-free workplace."[108] The idea is to rid federal contractors' workplaces of the production, distribution, and possession of controlled substances. Alcohol is not considered a controlled substance by the 1988 act. Companies found to be in violation of the act may lose their right to do business with the U.S. government.

Do these two legal thrusts work in opposite directions? Actually, the two laws work in combination because they make *rehabilitation* the best option.

REFERRAL AND REHABILITATION. Alcoholism and drug abuse typically reveal themselves to the manager in the form of increased absenteeism, tardiness, sloppy work, and complaints from coworkers. As soon as a steady decline in performance is observed, the manager should confront the individual with his or her poor performance record. Experts advise supervisors *not* to make accusations about alcohol or drug abuse. It is the employee's challenge to admit having such a problem. Management's job is to refer troubled employees to appropriate sources of help. Managers are cautioned against "playing doctor" when trying to help the alcohol- or drug-abusing employee. If the organization has an *employee assistance program (EAP)*, counselors, or a company doctor, an in-house referral can be made.[109] One study, "which tracked 25,000 employees over a four-year period, showed that the company's EAP saved $4 in health claims and absentee rates for every dollar it spent."[110]

Managers in small organizations without sophisticated employee services can refer the alcoholic employee to community resources such as Alcoholics Anonymous. Similar referral agencies for drug abusers exist in most communities. The overriding objective for the manager is to put troubled employees in touch with trained rehabilitation specialists as soon as possible.

SUMMARY

1. Human resource management involves human resource acquisition, retention, and development. Four key human resource management activities necessarily linked to organizational strategy and structure are (1) human resource strategy, (2) recruitment and selection, (3) performance appraisal, and (4) training. After an employee has joined the organization, part of the human resource management process involves dealing with human resource problems such as sexual harassment and alcohol and drug abuse.

2. A systems approach to human resource strategy views both present and future employees as human capital that needs to be developed to its fullest potential. Pfeffer's seven people-centered practices can serve as a strategic agenda for human resource management. The seven practices are provision of job security, rigorous hiring practices, employee empowerment, performance-based compensation, comprehensive training, reduction of status differences, and sharing of key information.

3. Managers need to recruit for diversity to increase their appeal to job applicants and customers alike. The hurdle-like selection process can be summed up in the seven-step PROCEED model. The seven steps are (1) prepare (job analysis, job descriptions, and interview questions), (2) review (ensure the legality and fairness of the questions), (3) organize (assign the questions to an interview team), (4) conduct (collect information from the candidate), (5) evaluate (judge the candidate's qualifications), (6) exchange (meet and discuss information about the candidate), and (7) decide (extend a job offer or not).

4. Federal equal employment opportunity laws require managers to make hiring and other personnel decisions on the basis of ability to perform rather than personal prejudice. Affirmative action (making up for past discrimination) is evolving into managing diversity. Appreciation of interpersonal differences within a heterogeneous organizational culture is the

goal of managing-diversity programs. The Americans with Disabilities Act of 1990 (ADA) requires employers to make reasonable accommodations so that disabled people can enter the workforce.

5. All employment tests must be valid predictors of job performance. Because interviews are the most popular employee screening device, experts recommend structured rather than traditional, informal interviews.

6. Legally defensible performance appraisals enable managers to make objective personnel decisions. Four key legal criteria are job analysis, behavior-oriented appraisals, specific written instructions, and discussion of results with ratees. Seven common performance appraisal techniques are goal setting, written essays, critical incidents, graphic rating scales, weighted checklists, rankings/comparisons, and 360-degree reviews.

7. Today, training is a huge business in itself. Unfortunately, most training dollars are being spent where they are least needed: to train well-educated managers and professionals. Managers can ensure that their training investment pays off by using techniques appropriate to the situation. Training programs should be designed with an eye toward maximizing the retention of learning and its transfer to the job. Successful skill learning and factual learning both depend on goal setting, practice, and feedback. But skills should be modeled, whereas factual information should be presented in a logical and meaningful manner.

8. Sexual harassment and alcohol and drug abuse are contemporary human resource problems that require top-management attention and strong policies. A sexual harassment policy needs to define the problem behaviorally, specify penalties, and be disseminated and enforced. Useful ways to fight substance abuse in the workplace include drug testing for job applicants and employees and referral to professional help and rehabilitation.

TERMS TO UNDERSTAND

- **Human resource management,** p. 270
- **Human capital,** p. 272
- **Job analysis,** p. 276
- **Job description,** p. 276
- **Affirmative Action Program (AAP),** p. 277
- **Employment selection test,** p. 280
- **Structured interview,** p. 281
- **Behavior-based interview,** p. 282
- **Performance appraisal,** p. 283
- **Behaviorally Anchored Rating Scales (BARS),** p. 284
- **360-degree review,** p. 285
- **Training,** p. 286
- **Sexual harassment,** p. 288
- **Alcoholism,** p. 290

MANAGER'S TOOLKIT

How to Handle the Job Interview Successfully

1. **Thoroughly pre-scout the employer.**
   Spy discreetly on the company to learn about its activities, characteristics, strengths, trends, and market position. Review newsletters, product literature, financial and annual reports, brochures, news articles, and anything else you can find about the company in the library or on the Internet. For personal accounts, visit the company on a pre-interview day or arrive early for your appointment and casually converse with departing or arriving employees. . . .

2. **Ask permission to take notes.**
   Your interviewer won't refuse this request, so have paper and a pen handy for jotting down important facts during the meeting. Not only will this help you make a good impression, but it also will provide ammunition for your interview summary and follow-up letter.

   Examples of what you should write down include the final hiring deadline, details about the job description, information about the company and its policies, the name of your prospective manager, product information, and advice on next steps you can take.

3. **Ask pertinent questions.**
   This underutilized strategy may, in fact, be the most valuable of all to candidates. By asking questions,

you'll show what you've learned about the company and find out more about the job requirements and where you stand. Questions you might want to ask include the following:

"Would you take a few moments to give me a more comprehensive description of the job requirements?"

"What do you think are the most important qualities that candidates for this job should have?"

"What opportunities exist in the future for someone who performs successfully in this position?" . . .

4. **Ask the interviewer to rate your qualifications for the job.**

From this reply, you'll learn which way the wind is blowing and possibly uncover a potentially fatal problem or weakness the interviewer didn't plan to discuss with you. . . .

You've made an impression, gained information, and set the stage to politely and briefly summarize the strengths and assets you'd bring to the job. This is where the notes you've taken during the interview come in handy.

Quoting the interviewer's job description and specifications whenever possible, repeat each requirement for the position as you understand them. Then cite the strengths, experience, and values you'd bring to each area. Candidly admit to any weaknesses, but promise to embark on a vigorous training program to overcome them. State that the company's training strengths and your attitude are a winning combination.

As you finish your summary, be sure to ask for the job confidently and pleasantly. If you're enthusiastic and polite, you won't be labeled as overly aggressive. Employers prefer you to be results-oriented because they think you'll act the same way on the job. . . .

5. **Always follow up.**

Write and mail a follow-up letter to the interviewer within 12 to 24 hours of your meeting, with a copy to any other executives who are involved in the decision. [An e-mail can get lost in the clutter, unless the interviewer expressly prefers to communicate via e-mail.]

Your letter should state:

- What you liked most about the company.
- The assets you'd bring to the position.
- Your availability and enthusiasm.
- Your hope of meeting other decision makers as soon as possible.

Source: National Business Employment Weekly *[Only Staff-Produced Materials May Be Used] by Milton Gralla. Copyright 1997 by Dow Jones & Company, Inc. Reproduced with the permission of Dow Jones & Company, Inc. in the format Textbook via Copyright Clearance Center.*

ACTION LEARNING EXERCISE

Writing Behavioral Interview Questions

Instructions: Working either alone or as a member of a team, select a specific job and write *two* behavioral interview questions for at least *five* of these categories.

Being a self-starter and demonstrating initiative

Being a leader

Being an effective communicator

Being ethical

Being able to make a hard decision

Being a team player

Being able to handle conflict

Being able to handle a setback, disappointment, or failure

Tips: If you pick a higher-level job, this exercise will be easier because people at higher levels have more responsibility and engage in a broader range of behavior.

Be sure to prepare by rereading the Behavioral Interviewing section in this chapter.

For Consideration/Discussion

1. How well will each of your questions uncover *actual past job-related behavior?*

2. Would any of your questions put the candidate at a disadvantage because of his or her gender, race, ethnicity, religion, disability, marital status, or sexual preference?

3. When others hear your questions, are they judged to be *fair* questions?

4. Which question is your absolute best? Why? Which is your weakest? Why?

5. What (if anything) do you like about behavioral interviews? What (if anything) do you dislike about them?

CLOSING CASE
How UPS Delivers Objective Performance Appraisals

Determining whether a supervisor is using enough objectivity during the employee review is one of the most difficult aspects of any company's employee evaluation process.

With this in mind, the United Parcel Service (UPS), based in Washington D.C., is deploying personal digital assistants (PDAs) to its supervisors to use in on-road driver evaluations. The PDAs are equipped with proprietary software that standardizes the evaluation process, helping to ensure that each driver review is as objective as possible.

"Our supervisors do ride-alongs to see if the driver is following procedures and adhering to our health and safety policies," says Cathy Callagee, vice president of applications development for UPS's operations portfolio. "But this is problematic because supervisors have to write notes on paper, then bring their notes back to the office and type them into reports."

Paper is eliminated with the help of PDAs, which display a series of checklists for the supervisor to use during the evaluation. The checklists guide the supervisors through a list of duties the driver should be performing. The supervisor simply checks off each duty as the driver completes it. Additionally, the checklists are uniform across the UPS network, so each driver receives the same evaluation, regardless of who is conducting the review.

The new PDAs also are helpful for supervisors because they serve as a remote office, allowing supervisors to receive e-mail and check the status of other activities while they are on the road with drivers. Currently, UPS has 1,400 PDAs in the field, with plans to deploy an additional 600 this year.

"Supervisors can now electronically write how their drivers are doing and if they are following procedures," Callagee says. "If not, the supervisor can bring the applied methods right up on the PDA and walk the driver through it."

Before PDAs, drivers and supervisors were forced to memorize these instructions or put notes in their back pocket, but since the data is transmitted electronically, they can simply plug the PDA into their PC and it automatically uploads the information to the PC.

"The use of PDAs eliminates paperwork, makes the rides more consistent and complete, improves the accountability of UPS supervisors and also increases the professionalism for the group," Callagee says. "This is going to become a way of life for UPS supervisors."

The PDAs also identify training needs, which will be particularly helpful to new drivers who might need additional safety training. "Our objective is to have drivers follow procedures that will help make their job safer, [make them] more efficient and provide better service for customers," Callagee says. "From a workforce perspective, the use of PDAs will make training easier so we can accomplish these goals."

Source: From Gail Johnson, "Online Objectivity," *Training*, 41 (July 2004): 18. © VNU Business Media, Inc. Reprinted with permission.

FOR DISCUSSION

1 Would Jeffrey Pfeffer be likely to call UPS a people-centered company? Why or why not?

2 Which one (or what combination) of the performance appraisal techniques discussed in this chapter is UPS using? Explain.

3 How would you rate the legal defensibility of UPS's driver evaluation program? Explain.

4 From an ethical standpoint, there is a thin line between supervision and "snoopervision." In your opinion, has UPS crossed that line? Explain.

5 How could UPS improve its driver evaluation program?

TEST PREPPER

True/False Questions

_____ 1. The human capital perspective is a "big picture" approach to managing people and staying competitive.

_____ 2. According to Jeffrey Pfeffer, only about 12 percent of today's organizations qualify as being systematically people-centered.

_____ 3. The process of identifying basic task and skill requirements for specific jobs by studying superior performers is called job analysis.

_____ 4. Title VII of the Civil Rights Act of 1964 is the landmark equal employment opportunity law in the United States.

_____ 5. Disabled Americans and nondisabled citizens have the same unemployment rate.

_____ 6. Today, polygraphs (lie detectors) are in wide use in the United States because of strong government support.

_____ 7. From a legal standpoint, trait-oriented performance appraisals are more defensible than behavior-oriented appraisals.

_____ 8. Despite what is published about computer-based training and e-learning via the Internet, the vast bulk of today's training is remarkably low-tech.

_____ 9. Verbal misconduct cannot be considered sexual harassment.

_____ 10. Employee assistance programs for substance abusers can end up saving companies money.

Multiple-Choice Questions

1. What did researchers find when comparing "control" human resource systems and "commitment" human resource systems?
   A. Employees preferred control systems over commitment systems.
   B. Productivity was high and employee turnover was low with commitment systems.
   C. Employee turnover was much higher with commitment systems.
   D. Productivity was the same under both systems.
   E. Productivity and turnover were significantly lower with control systems.

2. Which of the following is *not* one of the seven people-centered practices identified by Pfeffer?
   A. Sharing of key information
   B. Compensation linked to performance
   C. Protection of job security
   D. Rigorous hiring process
   E. Emphasis on status differences

3. _____, according to research, is(are) the most frequently used but least successful job-hunting method.
   A. Corporate Web sites   B. Internal job posting
   C. Referrals   D. Job fairs
   E. Temporary-help agencies

4. What does the R stand for in the PROCEED model of employee selection?
   A. Repeat interview   B. Request references
   C. Review interview questions   D. Register with EEOC
   E. Reject unqualified applicants

5. Research suggests that affirmative action programs in the United States
   A. actually helped white males the most.
   B. doubled female employment between 1965 and 1985.
   C. helped black workers get promoted in government and business.
   D. had the greatest positive impact on Native Americans.
   E. tripled the percentage of Asian Americans in the workforce.

6. A(n) _____ interview is subject to distortion and bias and open to legal attack.
   A. traditional unstructured   B. structured
   C. virtual   D. lengthy   E. objective

7. Which of the following is *not* a criterion for legally defensible performance appraisals in the United States?
   A. Specific written instructions for evaluators
   B. Results reviewed with ratees
   C. Based on job analysis
   D. Results linked with compensation decisions
   E. Behavior-oriented

8. A convergence of demographic and technological trends is predicted to have which impact on the U.S. labor force?
   A. Too many job seekers   B. Unemployment
   C. Shortage of skilled workers D. Racism
   E. Proportionately fewer women

9. Individuals who believe they are being sexually harassed at work and would like to file a lawsuit should follow which bit of advice?
   A. Find witnesses.
   B. Threaten the harasser with dire consequences.
   C. Wait until you're physically assaulted.
   D. Just ignore it.
   E. Make sure a manager is the aggressor.

10. What is the preferred strategy for dealing with employee substance abusers?
   A. Ignoring the problem   B. Referral and rehabilitation
   C. Imprisonment   D. Stiff fines
   E. Peer pressure

See page T1 at the back of the text for answers to these questions. Want more questions? Visit the student Web site and take the ACE quizzes for more practice.

11

Communicating

in the Internet

Age

It is a luxury to be understood.[1]
—RALPH WALDO EMERSON

OBJECTIVES

- **Identify** each major link in the communication process.

- **Explain** the concept of media richness and the Lengel-Daft contingency model of media selection.

- **Identify** the five communication strategies, and **specify** guidelines for using them.

- **Discuss** why it is important for managers to know about grapevine and nonverbal communication.

- **Explain** ways in which management can encourage upward communication.

- **Identify** and **describe** four barriers to communication.

- **List** two practical tips for each of the three modern communication technologies (e-mail, cell phones, and videoconferences), and **summarize** the pros and cons of telecommuting.

- **List** at least three practical tips for improving each of the following communication skills: listening, writing, and running a meeting.

THE CHANGING WORKPLACE

Bruce Moeller's *Mostly Digital Communication Style*

Bruce Moeller is the CEO of DriveCam, a $23 million company, based in San Diego, that sells and installs video recorders that monitor the behavior of commercial drivers.

The first thing I do when I get up—before I even go to the restroom or anything—I'll grab my BlackBerry and see what the issues are. Then I'll take it with me to the bathroom and go through all my e-mails. I get 80 or 100 a day, and I have to know what's okay or what isn't okay. Then I'll brush my teeth and take a shower. Some mornings it's a struggle to get dressed before you're writing back different e-mails on the BlackBerry.

I get to work about 7:30. I've had to really force myself not to read the BlackBerry while I'm driving, though I don't always even succeed at that. And I'm the guy that's supposed to be about driver safety.

When I get in, I put my PC, which I've brought from home, into the docking station. I'm compulsive about my e-mail. That's my primary communication with the rest of the enterprise. It's a one-to-many communication so it's more efficient.

Then I'll start walking around and going to visit each of my direct reports: marketing, sales, engineering, operations, finance. The COO [chief operating officer] and I also have a meeting that lasts half an hour or an hour every morning—it might be, there's a compliment about this level of service, or somebody dropped the ball on this. I might also meet with the CFO [chief financial officer]. We just raised a round [of funding]—$28 million—so there's plenty of cash, but there might be a receivables issue. Usually he's just making me aware of issues so I see the little warning flags if someone's not paying. Sometimes he's escalating it to me, saying could you call their CEO and request the payment, or ask their COO under what conditions they could pay. It's really just what's going on in everyone's world; all of us debrief on anything that's new. This is a pretty fast-paced place. We joke here if you miss half a day you've got to get caught back up.

I'm a kind of hub-and-spoke guy, so it's me with this person or me with that one. But because of that hub and spoke, various guys were having difficulty communicating with each other. I'm feeling totally in the loop, of course, getting updates on everything and everybody, but it became apparent that the different functions might not be aware of what the others were doing. So I just agreed to do a meeting with my direct reports every week. We go off-site from 3 P.M. to 8 P.M. We call it Tuesdays with Moeller.

I like to keep my schedule fairly open so that I can be in the moment with whatever the hot issue is—a customer problem or some opportunity. During the day I'll typically have only two or three scheduled meetings. I just like to be very fluid and to force the organization to stay externally focused. If you spend a lot of scheduled time, you get fooled into thinking you're working when you're just playing with each other on internal stuff. When you could've been externally focused on the marketplace.

I like one-on-one meetings anyway. I like to be able to read people, read their eyes, and probe if I'm sensing they're pulling back on something or afraid of something. I'm reading signals all the time. Group meetings are problematic because people perform for audiences. Especially with the CEO in the room, it hampers full-flowing conversation because people don't want to look stupid and you tend to get managed information. To combat that, I tell them you never shoot the messenger. Whatever you're feeling, you don't show it. By reacting emotionally you're putting a brand on that news, and you're subliminally shaping behavior. Even when I'm happy, I try to control my emotions. Otherwise I would be telling people not to come to me unless it's with good news.

I encourage free-flowing conversation with other little things, too. A lot of times I'll dress really casually and speak very casually with the employees, trying to be just one of the

guys—of course, realizing that I'm not and they don't see me that way. I also have an open-door policy, and my office tends to be a gathering place. I put candy and nuts in here to encourage people to come in, grab a handful of M&M's, and communicate. Everyone here knows that even if there are three people in here talking about something, you can come in and join the meeting, too. If we're talking about marketing and you're an engineer, you might have a good idea. If someone walks in, especially if I think he would be interested or could enhance the conversation, I'll take a quick 60 seconds to update him on what we're talking about. And if he's not interested or doesn't have time to talk, that's okay.

I've always resisted having a secretary. I like to do all the stuff myself and not have somebody keep me insulated from anyone else. Unless I'm really busy, I do my own travel. Expense reports—that's the one liberty I do take. I don't do expense reports. I take all my receipts and walk them down to accounting and say, here, this is from a speech I gave in New Orleans. And that's as far as I go.

I'm almost fully digital, so there's no paper at all on my desk. I do have a little desk calendar with a different French word every day . . . where I can jot down a name and number. But I'm not a big note-taker. I think it distracts from really listening to and absorbing what somebody said. If notes are required, I make sure our COO or somebody else is there to take them. I just listen, engage, and remember what the salient points are. I find I'd miss certain nuances of the inflection in the voice, or body language, if I were taking notes.

I'm a loner and I'm an introvert. So when I'm dealing with all these people, they're taking every ounce of my being and my energy; when I'm engaged, I'm engaged, I'm passionately in-volved. So at lunch I typically go out by myself and grab some fast food or something, and sit and listen to political radio. I force myself to use that to recharge my batteries, to get out of here and think of something different. Though while I'm doing that, if that BlackBerry buzzes I'm right on it.

It's not that I'm shy. My definition of an introvert is someone who seeks solitude to get his batteries recharged, whereas extroverts seek the company of others. People think I'm kidding when I say I'm an introvert; I'm always the dominant one in a meeting, taking on difficult prob-lems or people, setting a hard course, or being flippant and making a joke.

Source: Excerpted from Stephanie Clifford, "The Way I Work," *Inc.*, 29 (July 2007): 88–91. Copyright 2007 by Mansueto Ventures LLC. Reproduced with permission of Mansueto Ventures LLC in the format Textbook via Copyright Clearance Center.

ne of the most difficult challenges for management is getting individuals to understand and voluntarily pursue organizational objectives. Effective communication, as used by Bruce Moeller to get everyone at DriveCam on the same page, is vital to meeting this challenge. Organizational communication takes in a great deal of territory—virtually every management function and activity can be considered communica-tion in one way or another. Planning and controlling require a good deal of communicating, as do organi-zation design and development, decision making and problem solving, leadership, and staffing. Organizational cultures would not exist without communication. Studies have shown that both orga-nizational and individual performance improve when managerial communication is effective.[2] Given today's team-oriented organizations, where things need to be accomplished with and through people over whom a manager has no direct authority, com-munication skills are more important than ever. In fact, a survey of 133 executives revealed that

The most-desired management skill is good com-munication, followed by a sense of vision, honesty,

decisiveness, and ability to build good relationships with employees.[3]

Thanks to modern technology, we can communi-cate more quickly and less expensively. But the ensuing torrent of messages has proved to be a mixed blessing for managers and nonmanagers alike. Complaints of information overload are common today. Marketing executive Hilary Billings has observed,

There's a growing realization that we're all becom-ing victims of the technological devices that were supposed to make our lives simpler. The prolifera-tion of laptops, PDAs, and pagers means that we're working harder and harder to keep up with our own inventions. The price of being available 24-7 is the loss of time for reflection, creative thinking, and connections with our loved ones—the things that are really important for our emotional and spiri-tual lives.[4]

Worse yet, managers have a growing suspicion that more communication is not necessarily better. Research bears out this suspicion: "Executives say 14 percent of each 40-hour work-week is wasted be-cause of poor communication between staff and managers. . . . That amounts to a staggering seven

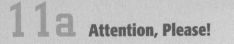

11a Attention, Please!

Microsoft vice president Linda Stone:

You're in a conference room, and all the people around the table are glancing—frequently and surreptitiously—at the cell phones or BlackBerrys they're holding just below the table. . . . This constant checking of handheld electronic devices has become epidemic, and it illustrates what I call "continuous partial attention."

Source: Linda Stone, "Living with Continuous Partial Attention," Harvard Business Review, 85 (February 2007): 28.

QUESTIONS:

How well does this describe you? What positive and negative effects has continuous partial attention had on communication in the workplace?

For further information about the interactive annotations in this chapter, visit our student Web site.

THE COMMUNICATION PROCESS

Management scholar Keith Davis defined **communication** as "the transfer of information and understanding from one person to another person."[6] Communication is inherently a social process. Whether one communicates face to face with a single person or with a group of people via television, it is still a social activity involving two or more people. By analyzing the communication process, one discovers that it is a chain made up of identifiable links (see Figure 11.1). Links in this process include sender, encoding, medium, decoding, receiver, and feedback.[7] The essential purpose of this chainlike process is to send an idea from one person to another in a way that will be understood by the receiver. Like any other chain, the communication chain is only as strong as its weakest link.[8]

> **communication:** interpersonal transfer of information and understanding

Encoding

Thinking takes place within the privacy of your brain and is greatly affected by how you perceive your environment. But when you want to pass along a thought to someone else, an entirely different process begins. This second process, communication, requires that you, the sender, package the idea for understandable transmission. Encoding starts at this point. The purpose of encoding is to translate internal thought

workweeks of squandered productivity a year."[5] The challenge to improve this situation is both immense and immediate. But before managers, or anyone else for that matter, can become more effective communicators, they need to appreciate that communication is a complex process subject to a great deal of perceptual distortion and many problems. This is especially true for the apparently simple activity of communicating face to face.

FIGURE **11.1** The Basic Communication Process

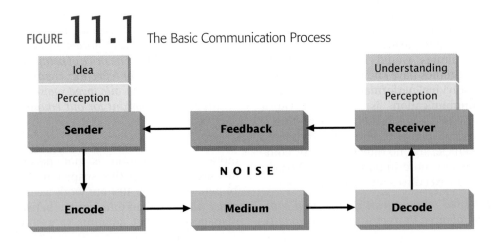

ommunication greases the wheels of organizational life. Nothing can happen without it. Effective communicators, such as this manager, get the desired response by skillfully using each link in the basic communication process. Sometimes, a little appropriate humor can help, too.

patterns into a language or code that the intended receiver of the message will probably understand.

Managers usually rely on words, gestures, or other symbols for encoding. Their choice of symbols depends on several factors, one of which is the nature of the message itself. Is it technical or nontechnical, emotional or factual? Perhaps it could be expressed better with colorful PowerPoint slides than with words, as in the case of a budget report. To express skepticism, merely a shrug might be enough. More fundamentally, will the encoding help get the attention of busy and distracted people?[9]

Greater cultural diversity in today's global workplace also necessitates careful message encoding[10] (see Valuing Diversity). E-mail translation programs promise to make the encoding process a bit easier when communicating across cultures.

Selecting a Medium

Managers can choose among a number of media: face-to-face conversations, telephone calls, e-mails, memos, letters, computer reports and networks, photographs, bulletin boards, meetings, organizational publications, and others. Communicating with those outside the organization opens up further possibilities, such as news releases, press conferences, and advertising on television and radio or in magazines, in newspapers, and on the Internet.

MEDIA SELECTION IN CROSS-CULTURAL SETTINGS. The importance of selecting an appropriate medium is magnified when one moves from internal to cross-cultural dealings. Recall the distinction between low-context and high-context cultures that we made in Chapter 4; managers moving from low-context cultures to high-context cultures need to select communication media with care.

The United States, Canada, and northern European nations are defined as low-context cultures, meaning that the verbal content of a message is more important than the medium—the setting through which the message is delivered. In such cultures, a videoconference or an e-mail is usually accepted as an efficient substitute for an in-person meeting.

But in other countries—including many in Asia and the Middle East—context, or setting, with its myriad nonverbal cues, can convey far more meaning than the literal words of a given message. In such high-context cultures, business transactions are ritualized, and the style in which the rituals are enacted matters more than the words. A high value is placed on face-to-face interaction, and after-hours socialization with customers and colleagues is almost a daily occurrence.[11]

A CONTINGENCY APPROACH. A contingency model for media selection was developed by Robert Lengel and Richard Daft.[12] It pivots on the concept of media richness. **Media richness** describes the capacity of a given medium to convey information and promote learning. As illustrated

> **media richness:** a medium's capacity to convey information and promote learning

VALUING DIVERSITY

The Diversity Advantage in a Global Economy

The seasoned banker from Rhode Island and the junior banker from Brazil seemed to be worlds apart on the surface. But when Merrill Lynch managing director Kerry Cannella and young associate Selma Bueno joined forces on their first deal, they made a potent cross-cultural duo.

Merrill Lynch was representing Brazilian investors selling their stake in a multibillion-dollar Latin American company to potential U.S. investors. The deal was moving slowly, with both sides cautious.

Then Cannella and Bueno stepped up the pace. They jetted between New York and Brazil many times. Bueno analyzed financial papers in Portuguese. She put together an offering document for investors. She picked classy hotels and restaurants, translated during negotiations, and made both sides feel more at ease with each other.

With the help of Bueno's business and social skills, the bankers finally closed the deal—in the hundreds of millions of dollars—to everyone's satisfaction.

Source: Edward Iwata, "Companies Find Gold Inside Melting Pot," USA Today (July 9, 2007): 1B–2B.

---

in the top portion of Figure 11.2, media vary in richness from high (or rich) to low (or lean). Face-to-face conversation is a rich medium because it (1) simultaneously provides *multiple information cues,* such as message content, tone of voice, facial expressions, and so on; (2) facilitates immediate *feedback;* and (3) is *personal* in focus. In contrast, bulletins and general computer reports are lean media; that is, they convey limited information and foster limited learning. Lean media, such as general e-mail bulletins, provide a single cue, do not facilitate immediate feedback, and are impersonal.

Management's challenge, indicated in the bottom portion of Figure 11.2, is to match media richness with the situation. Nonroutine problems are best handled with rich media such as face-to-face, telephone, or video interactions. John Chambers, the highly-respected CEO of Cisco Systems, recently explained why he prefers richer media.

> *I'm a voice person. I communicate with emotion that way. I like to listen to emotion too. It's a lot easier to listen to a key customer if I hear how they're describing a problem to me. I'll leave 40 or 50 voicemails a day. I do them on the way to work and coming back from work. The newest thing for me is video on demand, which is my primary communication vehicle today. We have a small studio downstairs. We probably tape 10 to 15 videos a quarter. That way employees, and customers, can watch them when they want.*[13]

Lean media are appropriate for routine problems. Examples of mismatched media include reading a corporate annual report at a stockholders' meeting (data glut) or announcing a layoff with an impersonal e-mail (data starvation). The latter situation has major ethical implications, as these examples illustrate:

> *In August [2006], RadioShack Corp. notified about 400 employees at its Texas headquarters by e-mail that their positions had been eliminated. And just a few weeks earlier, a London-based body-piercing and jewelry shop reportedly fired one of its sales assistants via a text message.*[14]

Imagine being on the receiving end of these poor media-selection decisions.

Decoding

Even the most expertly fashioned message will not accomplish its purpose unless it is understood. After physically receiving the message, the receiver needs to comprehend it. If the message has been properly encoded, decoding is supposed to take place rather routinely. But perfect decoding is nearly impossible in our world of many languages and cultures. Jerry Adriano, an official with the Hispanic Contractors of America, says the language barrier is a major reason why workplace deaths among Hispanic workers jumped 53 percent between 1992 and 2000.

> *Many Hispanic laborers are Mexican immigrants who don't speak English. Their supervisors often don't speak Spanish. That makes safety training harder. Translating training materials into Spanish doesn't always help, because many immigrants don't read Spanish, Adriano says.*[15]

FIGURE **11.2** The Lengel-Daft Contingency Model of Media Selection

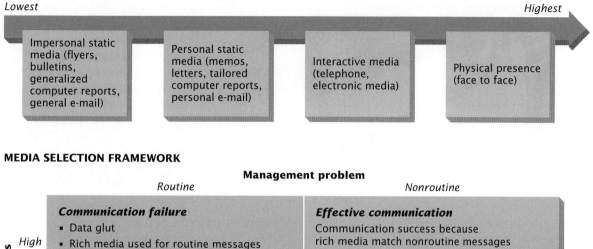

MEDIA RICHNESS HIERARCHY

Lowest → Highest

- Impersonal static media (flyers, bulletins, generalized computer reports, general e-mail)
- Personal static media (memos, letters, tailored computer reports, personal e-mail)
- Interactive media (telephone, electronic media)
- Physical presence (face to face)

MEDIA SELECTION FRAMEWORK

Management problem

	Routine	Nonroutine
High (Media richness)	**Communication failure** • Data glut • Rich media used for routine messages • Excess cues cause confusion and surplus meaning	**Effective communication** Communication success because rich media match nonroutine messages
Low (Media richness)	**Effective communication** Communication success because media low in richness match routine messages	**Communication failure** • Data starvation • Lean media used for nonroutine messages • Too few cues to capture message complexity

Source: Based on Robert H. Lengel and Richard L. Daft, "The Selection of Communication Media as an Executive Skill," Academy of Management Executive, 2 (August 1988): 226, 227, exhibits 1 and 2. Reprinted by permission.

Successful decoding also is more likely if the receiver knows the jargon and terminology used in the message. American sports jargon is particularly troublesome in cross-cultural business dealings. Take baseball jargon, for instance:

Executives from Qingdao to São Paulo must know what it means to "make a pitch," and if they don't know what it takes to develop a "home-run" product, they had better know how to "manufacture runs" by "choking up" and "playing small ball in the late innings."

Huh? Business is so rife with the jargon that it makes foreigners wonder what Americans are smoking when they throw around baseball in a business context, like "throwing smoke." "Around the horn" has nothing to do with shipping. "Pickles" don't come from a Vlasic jar. "Chin music" doesn't come from an iPod, and "ringing someone up" has nothing to do with an iPhone.[16] (*Note*: A baseball-loving classmate can translate this jargon, if needed.)

It helps, too, if the receiver understands the sender's purpose and background situation. Effective listening is given special attention later in this chapter.

Feedback

Some sort of verbal or nonverbal feedback from the receiver to the sender is required to complete the communication process. Appropriate forms of feedback are determined by the same factors that govern the sender's encoding decision. Without feedback, senders have no way of knowing whether their ideas

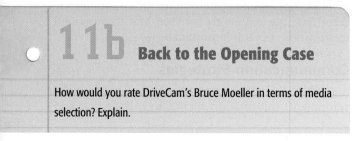

11b **Back to the Opening Case**

How would you rate DriveCam's Bruce Moeller in terms of media selection? Explain.

It's a noisy world. Just ask this little girl as she blocks out construction noise in New York City, prior to a comprehensive noise ordinance recently going into effect. When communicating, we need to take all possible sources of noise into consideration, tailoring our messages and selecting our media accordingly.

have been accurately understood (see the Manager's Toolkit feature at the end of this chapter). Knowing whether others understand us significantly affects both the form and the content of our follow-up communication.

Employee surveys consistently underscore the importance of timely and personal feedback from management. For example, one survey of 500,000 employees from more than 300 firms contrasted satisfaction with "coaching and feedback from boss" for two groups of employees: (1) committed employees who planned to stay with their employer for at least five years and (2) those who intended to quit within a year. Satisfaction with coaching and feedback averaged 64 percent among the committed employees, whereas it dropped to 34 percent among those ready to quit.[17] Accounting firm PricewaterhouseCoopers has taken the following constructive steps:

A few years ago the company resolved to let employees themselves decide when during their first 90 days they would sit down with their boss for a performance review. (After that, they could do so every month if they chose to.) And, get this, a second reader is supposed to review the initial written review to make sure it is sufficiently clear.[18]

Noise

Noise is not an integral part of the chainlike communication process, but it may influence the process at any or all points. As the term is used here, **noise** is any interference with the normal flow of understanding

noise: any interference with the normal flow of communication

from one person to another. This is a very broad definition. Thus, a speech impairment, garbled technical transmission, a negative attitudes, lies,[19] misperception, illegible print or pictures, telephone static, partial loss of hearing, and poor eyesight all qualify as noise. Understanding tends to diminish as noise increases. In general, the effectiveness of organizational communication can be improved in two ways. Steps can be taken to make verbal and written messages more understandable. And at the same time, noise can be minimized by foreseeing and neutralizing sources of interference.

DYNAMICS OF ORGANIZATIONAL COMMUNICATION

As a writer on the subject pointed out, "civilization is based on human cooperation and without communication, no effective cooperation can develop."[20] Accordingly, effective communication is essential for cooperation within productive organizations. At least four dynamics of organizational communication—communication strategies, the grapevine, nonverbal communication, and upward communication—largely determine the difference between effectiveness and ineffectiveness in this important area.

Communication Strategies

A good deal of effort goes into plotting product development, information technology, financial, and

FIGURE **11.3** Clampitt's Communication Strategy Continuum

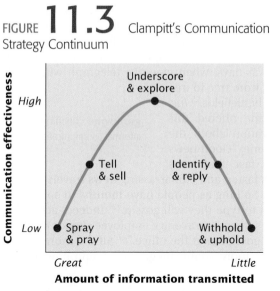

Source: Academy of Management Executive: The Thinking Manager's Source by Phillip Clampitt. Copyright 2000 by Academy of Management (NY). Reproduced with permission of Academy of Management (NY) in the format Textbook via Copyright Clearance Center.

marketing strategies these days. Much less attention, if any, is devoted to organizational communication strategies.[21] Hence, organizational communication tends to be haphazard and often ineffective. A more systematic approach is needed. This section introduces five basic communication strategies, with an eye toward improving the overall quality of communication.

A COMMUNICATION CONTINUUM WITH FIVE STRATEGIES. A team of authors led by communication expert Phillip G. Clampitt created the useful communication strategy continuum shown in Figure 11.3. Communication effectiveness is the vertical dimension of the model, ranging from low to high. A message communicated via any of the media discussed earlier is effective if one's intended meaning is conveyed fully and accurately to the receiver. The horizontal dimension of Clampitt's model is the amount of information transmitted, which may range from great to little. Plotted on this quadrant are five common communication strategies. Let us examine each one more closely.

- *Spray & Pray.* This is the organizational equivalent of a large lecture section where passive receivers are showered with information in the hope that some of it will stick. Managers employing the Spray & Pray strategy assume "more is better." Unfortunately, as employees who are swamped by corporate e-mail directives and announcements will attest, more is *not* necessarily better. This

strategy suffers from being one-way, impersonal, and unhelpful because it leaves receivers to sort out what is actually important or relevant.

- *Tell & Sell.* This strategy involves communicating a more restricted set of messages and taking time to explain their importance and relevance. Top executives often rely on Tell & Sell when introducing new strategies, merger plans, and reorganizations. A potentially fatal flaw arises when more time is spent polishing the presentation than assessing the receivers' actual needs.
- *Underscore & Explore.* Key information and issues closely tied to organizational success are communicated with this give-and-take strategy. Priorities are included and justifications are offered. Unlike the first two strategies, this one is two-way. Receivers are treated as active rather than passive participants in the process. Feedback is generated by "allowing employees the creative freedom to explore the implications of those ideas in a disciplined way."[22] Listening, resolving misunderstandings, building consensus and commitment, and addressing actual or potential obstacles are fundamental to success with the Underscore & Explore strategy.
- *Identify & Reply.* This is a reactive and sometimes defensive strategy. Employee concerns about prior communications are the central focus here. Employees are not only viewed as active participants; they essentially drive the process because they are assumed to know the key issues. According to Clampitt and his colleagues, "Employees set the agenda, while executives respond to rumors, innuendoes, and leaks."[23] Those using the Identify & Reply strategy need to be good listeners.
- *Withhold & Uphold.* With this communication strategy, you tell people what you think they need to know only when you believe they need to know it. Secrecy and control are paramount. Because information is viewed as power, it is rationed and restricted. Those in charge cling to their rigid and narrow view of things when challenged or questioned. If you think this sounds like the old Theory X command-and-control style of management, you're right. The Withhold & Uphold communication strategy virtually guarantees rumors and resentment.

In organizational life, one can find hybrid combinations of these five strategies. But usually there is a dominant underlying strategy that may or may not be effective.

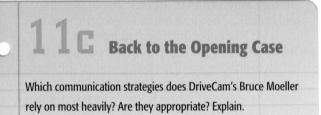

11c   Back to the Opening Case

Which communication strategies does DriveCam's Bruce Moeller rely on most heavily? Are they appropriate? Explain.

SEEKING A MIDDLE GROUND.   Both ends of the continuum in Figure 11.3 are problematic.

> On one extreme, employees receive all the information they could possibly desire, while at the other, they are provided with little or no communication. Strategies at the extremes have a similar quality: employees have difficulty framing and making sense out of organizational events. Discovering salient information, focusing on core issues, and creating the proper memories are left to employees' personal whims.[24]

Accordingly, managers need to follow this set of guidelines when selecting a communication strategy appropriate to the situation: (1) avoid Spray & Pray and Withhold & Uphold; (2) use Tell & Sell and Identify & Reply sparingly; and (3) use Underscore & Explore as much as possible.

MERGING COMMUNICATION STRATEGIES AND MEDIA RICHNESS.   Present and future managers who effectively blend lessons from Figure 11.2 (media selection) and Figure 11.3 (communication strategies) are on the path toward improved organizational communication. The trick is to select the richest medium possible (given resource constraints) when employing the Tell & Sell, Identify & Reply, and Underscore & Explore strategies.

The Grapevine

In every organization large or small, there are actually two communication systems, one formal and the other informal. Sometimes these systems complement and reinforce each other; at other times they come into direct conflict. Although theorists have found it convenient to separate the two, distinguishing one from the other in real life can be difficult. Information required to accomplish official objectives is channeled throughout the organization via the formal system. By definition, official or formal communication flows in accordance with established lines of authority and structural boundaries. Media for official communication include all those channels discussed earlier. But intertwined with this formal network is the **grapevine**, the unofficial and informal communication system. The term *grapevine* can be traced back to Civil War days, when vine-like telegraph wires were strung from tree to tree across battlefields.[25] *Inc.* magazine offered this observation about the grapevine: "Good news travels fast, bad news travels faster, and embarrassing news travels at warp speed. So long as people have mouths to speak and fingers to type they will gossip."[26] Indeed, according to one survey, "the average employee spends 65 hours a year gossiping at the office."[27] All the more reason to learn more about the grapevine and how to deal with it.

> **grapevine:** unofficial and informal communication system

WORDS OF CAUTION ABOUT THE E-GRAPEVINE. The Internet has been a boon to the grapevine, vastly and instantly extending its reach via e-mail and other Web tools. According to a recent survey, 20 percent of large company employees "say they contribute regularly to blogs, social networks, wikis, and other Web 2.0 services."[28] But this new communication landscape holds some nasty surprises for the unwary. Consider these words of caution about e-mail, which have even broader implications for blogging and online social networking:

> E-mail allows workplace tales to spread faster than ever. But without the opportunity for nonverbal cues and interactivity, e-mail makes it even harder for employees to accurately interpret the message. Because in many if not most work environments e-mail messages are stored and subject to inspection (by people for whom the message was not intended), the savviest employees will not engage in e-gossip. Indeed, companies have pursued legal action to deal with some of the more harmful aspects of their e-grapevines.[29]

So a bit of gossip shared by the water cooler is not the same as a bit of gossip shared online, because the latter leaves an electronic trail that could be read by anyone. The same goes for blogs (short for "Web logs") and online social networking sites such as MySpace, Facebook, and LinkedIn. About 1,000 Microsoft employees reportedly have blogs, and an estimated 11,000 employees at accounting giant Ernst & Young have information on Facebook.[30] The e-grapevine is one more area where lawmakers, ethics specialists, and company policy makers are racing to catch up with new technology.

eet Sanya Richards, who has run 400 meters in under 49 seconds, making her the fastest woman in U.S. history. Not only is she fast on the track, her Internet blog allows the Olympic gold medalist to broadcast her accomplishments worldwide in seconds. This "global e-grapevine" is both good and bad news for organizations and managers.

According to legal experts, policies to get workplace blogging (and social networking) under control need to take the following issues into account.

- *How much blogging [and online social networking] is acceptable during work hours?*
- *All company-posted blogs should clearly state that the employee's opinions are not necessarily shared by the company.*
- *Protect confidentiality. Ensure that employees know what corporate or personal information is not to be disclosed.*[31]

MANAGERIAL ATTITUDES TOWARD THE GRAPEVINE. One survey of 341 participants in a management development seminar uncovered predominantly negative feelings among managers toward the grapevine. Moreover, first-line supervisors perceived the grapevine to be more influential than did middle managers. This second finding led the researchers to conclude that "apparently the grapevine is more prevalent, or at least more visible, at lower levels of the managerial hierarchy where supervisors can readily feel its impact."[32] Finally, the survey found that employees of relatively small organizations (fewer than 50 people) viewed the grapevine as less influential than did those from larger organizations (more than 100 people). A logical explanation for this last finding is that smaller organizations are usually more informal.

In spite of the negative attitude that many managers harbor toward it, the grapevine does have a positive side. In fact, experts estimate that grapevine communication is about 75 percent accurate.[33] Even though the grapevine has a reputation among managers as a bothersome source of inaccurate information and gossip, it helps satisfy a natural desire to know what is really going on and gives employees a sense of belonging. The grapevine also serves as an emotional outlet for employee fears and apprehensions.[34] Consider, for example, what happened when investor Laurence A. Tisch became chairman of CBS:

> *Tisch's reputation as a ferocious cost cutter, which he despises, forces him to watch every word and gesture. Simple questions—such as why a department needs so many people—are sometimes interpreted as orders to slash. One day Tisch and [the CBS News department head] were talking outside CBS's broadcast center on Manhattan's West 57th Street when Tisch pointed to a tower atop the building, asking what it was. Apparently staffers at a window saw him pointing in their general direction, and the next day newspaper reporters called CBS checking out a rumor that Tisch planned to sell the building.*[35]

Nevertheless, grapevine communication can carry useful information through the organization with amazing speed. Moreover, grapevine communication can help management learn how employees truly feel about policies and programs.

COPING WITH THE GRAPEVINE. Considering how the grapevine can be an influential and sometimes

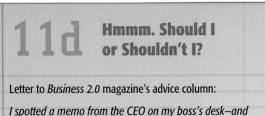

11d Hmmm. Should I or Shouldn't I?

Letter to *Business 2.0* magazine's advice column:

I spotted a memo from the CEO on my boss's desk—and proceeded to find out who will be the targets of downsizing. I don't need a lecture about wandering eyes, but I wonder if I should tell my co-worker that he's on the list.

Source: As quoted in Evelyn Nussenbaum, "I Know Something I Shouldn't Know," Business 2.0, 5 (January–February 2004): 115.

QUESTIONS:
What is the *ethical* thing to do here? What would *you* do? Explain your rationale.

negative force, what can management do about it? First and foremost, the grapevine *cannot be extinguished*. In fact, attempts to stifle grapevine communication may serve instead to stimulate it. Subtly monitoring the grapevine and officially correcting or countering any potentially damaging misinformation is about all any management team can do.[36] "Management by walking around" is an excellent way to monitor the grapevine in a nonthreatening manner. Some managers selectively feed information into the grapevine. For example, a health care administrator has admitted, "Sure, I use the grapevine. Why not? The employees sure use it. It's fast, reaches everyone, and employees believe it—no matter how preposterous. I limit its use, though."[37] Rumor-control hotlines and Web sites with answers to frequently asked questions (FAQs) have proved useful for neutralizing disruptive and inaccurate rumors and grapevine communication.[38]

For their part, individuals would do well to follow this time-honored advice from *Training* magazine's editor-in-chief, Tammy Galvin:

Whether it's something you're hearing or something you're telling, ask yourself: Is it the truth? Is it fair to all concerned? Will it build goodwill and better friendships? And finally, will it be beneficial to all concerned? If you answer "no" to even one of those questions, don't open your mouth. If you're on the receiving end, you are equally responsible. You should decline to participate in the conversation, and the onus is also on you to try to cut it off at the source.[39]

Nonverbal Communication

In today's hurried world, our words are often taken to have meanings that were not intended. Facial expressions and body movements that accompany our words can either enhance communication or worsen matters. This nonverbal communication, sometimes referred to as **body language**, is an important part of the communication process.[40] In fact, one expert contends that only 7 percent of the impact of our face-to-face communication comes from the words we utter; the other 93 percent comes from our vocal intonations, facial expressions, posture, and appearance.[41] Even periods of silence can carry meaning. Consider this advice:

> **body language:** nonverbal communication based on facial expressions, posture, and appearance

Your job as a manager is to learn to hear not only what people are saying, but also what they may not be saying in a conversation. So the next time you encounter someone's silence during an interview or a meeting, don't interrupt unless the person is clearly anxious or having a hard time responding.[42]

Silence may indicate doubt, lack of understanding, or polite disagreement. Even the whole idea of "dressing for success" is an attempt to send a desired nonverbal message about oneself.[43] (See Ethics: Character, Courage, and Values.) Image consultants have developed a thriving business helping aspiring executives look the part:

Vanda Sachs had a problem. The 35-year-old senior marketing executive for a well-known fashion magazine had her sights set on the publisher's office. Her trouble? Projecting enough authority to be considered for the job. "I'm petite and blonde and I'm baby-faced," she says, "none of which goes over very well in a world of 45-year-old men who are 6-foot-2." Being short, in particular, is a "major liability," she adds, "more so than being a woman."

Beyond wearing high heels, Sachs (a pseudonym) couldn't do much about her height, but she decided she could improve on her appearance. The first step was to hire a personal image consultant. Her choice: Emily Cho, founder of New Image, a respected New York City personal-image shopping service that for 19 years has been helping women choose clothes compatible with their private and professional aspirations. Four days and $3,000 later, Sachs had a knockout wardrobe and a newly

ETHICS: CHARACTER, COURAGE, AND VALUES

What Are the Practical and Ethical Boundaries of "Business Casual"?

Jennifer Cohen thought she had a good understanding of her company's policy allowing business casual attire.

So the 24-year-old was stunned when an older colleague pulled her aside to tell her she was dressing inappropriately by donning Bermuda shorts, sleeveless tops and capris.

"Each generation seems to have a different idea of what is acceptable in the workplace, and in this situation I was highly offended," says Cohen, who works at a marketing firm in Philadelphia. "I was actually not allowed to attend a meeting because my attire was deemed 'inappropriate.' People my age are taught to express themselves, and

saying something negative about someone's fashion is saying something negative about them."

Business casual has become a staple of the office, but more companies are trying to enforce rules that set at least a minimum standard of dress.

Source: Stephanie Armour, "'Business Casual' Causes Confusion," USA Today (July 10, 2007): 1B–2B.

FOR DISCUSSION

What does "business casual" mean to you? What is the ethical argument for (or against) telling people what to wear at work? What, if any, workplace dress code do you recommend?

---

acquired savvy that would help her look the part of a publisher. "Like it or not," she explains, "we're a society that's built on first impressions."[44]

TYPES OF BODY LANGUAGE. There are three kinds of body language: facial, gestural, and postural.[45] Without the speaker or listener consciously thinking about it, seemingly insignificant changes in facial expressions, gestures, and posture send various messages. A speaker can tell whether a listener is interested by monitoring a combination of nonverbal cues, including an attentive

gaze, an upright posture, and confirming or agreeing gestures. Unfortunately, many people in positions of authority—parents, teachers, and managers—ignore or misread nonverbal feedback. When this happens, they become ineffective communicators.

RECEIVING NONVERBAL COMMUNICATION. Like any other interpersonal skill, sensitivity to nonverbal cues can be learned (see Table 11.1).

Listeners need to be especially aware of subtleties, such as the fine distinctions between an attentive gaze

These Habitat for Humanity volunteers in Port Huron, Michigan, know the importance of nonverbal communication when getting instructions from the team leader. Ear plugs, sawing and hammering, and roaring electric generators and air compressors all conspire to make verbal communication very difficult.

TABLE **11.1** Reading Body Language

UNSPOKEN MESSAGE	BEHAVIOR
"I want to be helpful."	Uncrossing legs Unbuttoning coat or jacket Unclasping hands Moving closer to other person Smiling face Removing hands from pockets Unfolding arms from across chest
"I'm confident."	Avoiding hand-to-face gestures and head scratching Maintaining an erect stance Keeping steady eye contact Steepling fingertips below chin
"I'm nervous."	Clearing throat Expelling air (such as "Whew!") Placing hand over mouth while speaking Hurried cigarette smoking
"I'm superior to you."	Peering over tops of eyeglasses Pointing a finger Standing behind a desk and leaning palms down on it Holding jacket lapels while speaking

Source: Adapted from William Friend, "Reading Between the Lines," Association Management, 36 (June 1984): 94–100. Reprinted by permission of the publisher.

and a glaring stare and between an upright posture and a stiff one. Knowing how to interpret a nod, a grimace, or a grin can be invaluable to managers.[46] If at any time the response seems inappropriate to what one is saying, it is time to back off and reassess one's approach. It may be necessary to explain things more clearly, adopt a more patient manner, or make other adjustments.

Nonverbal behavior can also give managers a window on deep-seated emotions. For example, consider the situation Michael C. Ruettgers encountered shortly after joining EMC Corp., a leading manufacturer of computer data storage equipment.

Four months into Ruettgers' new job as head of operations and customer service, EMC's product quality program erupted into a full-blown crisis. Every piece of equipment the company sold was crashing because EMC engineers [had] failed to detect faulty disk drives supplied by NEC Corp. Ruettgers made a series of marathon swings across the country to meet personally with customers. In Denver and Salt Lake City, he came face to face with the scope of the catastrophe when managers broke down in *tears because their computer operations were in shambles. "Nothing can really prepare you for that," Ruettgers says.[47]*

After his promotion to CEO, Ruettgers helped make EMC a leader in product quality. No doubt his face-to-face interaction with frustrated customers, who conveyed powerful nonverbal emotional messages, drove home the need for improvement.

GIVING NONVERBAL FEEDBACK. What about the nonverbal feedback that managers give rather than receive? A research study carried out in Great Britain suggests that nonverbal feedback from authority figures significantly affects employee behavior. Among the people who were interviewed, those who received nonverbal approval from the interviewers in the form of smiles, positive head nods, and eye contact behaved quite differently from those who received nonverbal disapproval through frowns, head shaking, and avoidance of eye contact. Those receiving positive nonverbal feedback were judged by neutral observers to be significantly more relaxed, more friendly, more talkative, and more successful in creating a good impression.[48]

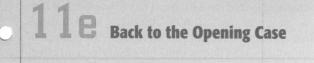

11e   Back to the Opening Case

Does DriveCam's Bruce Moeller use nonverbal communication effectively? Explain.

Positive nonverbal feedback to and from managers is a basic building block of good interpersonal relations. A smile or nod of the head in the appropriate situation tells the individual that he or she is on the right track and to keep up the good work. Such feedback is especially important for managers, who must avoid participating in the subtle but powerful nonverbal discrimination experienced by women in leadership positions.[49] When samples of men and women leaders in one study offered the same arguments and suggestions in a controlled setting, the women leaders received more negative and less positive nonverbal feedback than the men.[50] Managing-diversity workshops target this sort of "invisible barrier" to women and minorities. Similarly, cross-cultural training alerts employees bound for foreign assignments to monitor their nonverbal gestures carefully. For example, the familiar thumbs-up sign tells American employees to keep up the good work. Much to the embarrassment of poorly informed expatriates, that particular nonverbal message does not travel well. The same gesture would be a vulgar sign in Australia, would say "I'm winning" in Saudi Arabia, and would signify the number one in Germany and the number five in Japan. Malaysians use the thumb, instead of their forefinger, for pointing.[51]

Two other trends in nonverbal communication are offering etiquette classes for students and management trainees[52] and teaching sign language to coworkers of deaf employees.

Upward Communication

As used here, the term **upward communication** refers to a process of systematically encouraging employees to share their feelings and ideas with management. Although upward communication is more important than ever, a recent survey of 25,000 employees at 17 companies in the United States found it lacking: "Less than half of workers, 45 percent,

upward communication: encouraging employees to share their feelings and ideas with management

said their senior managers both talk and listen. And almost half said there was no procedure to raise questions and answers with upper management."[53] A refreshing exception is IBM's CEO, Sam Palmisano:

> [His lofty position as the head of a company with 355,766 employees worldwide] doesn't stop him from reading every single e-mail message sent to him by IBM employees, aides say, or from calling midlevel managers just to ask them what they think.[54]

At least seven different options are open to managers who want to improve upward communication.

FORMAL GRIEVANCE PROCEDURES. When unions represent rank-and-file employees, provisions for upward communication are usually spelled out in the collective bargaining agreement. Typically, unionized employees utilize a formal grievance procedure for contesting managerial actions and oversights. Grievance procedures usually consist of a series of progressively more rigorous steps.[55] For example, union members who have been fired may talk with their supervisor in the presence of the union steward. If the issue is not resolved at that level, the next step may be a meeting with the department head. Sometimes the formal grievance process includes as many as five or six steps, with a third-party arbitrator as the last resort. Formal grievance procedures are also found in nonunion situations.

A promising alternative to the traditional grievance process is the *peer review* program. Originally developed in the early 1980s by General Electric at its Appliance Park factory in Columbia, Maryland, peer reviews have been adopted by a growing number of organizations. At GE, the three specially trained coworkers and two managers on the panel listen to the grievance, conduct a majority-rule secret ballot, and render a final decision. Certain issues, including those involving work rules, performance appraisal results, and pay rates, are not handled by GE's peer review panels. GE created this process as a union-avoidance tactic.[56]

EMPLOYEE ATTITUDE AND OPINION SURVEYS. Both in-house and commercially prepared surveys can bring employee attitudes and feelings to the surface. Thanks to commercial software packages, time-saving and paperless electronic surveys are popular in today's workplaces.[57] Employees will usually complete surveys if they are convinced that meaningful changes will result. Consider this chain of events, for example:

> Taking time to implement action plans based on survey results "translates into big bucks", says Gregg

Campa, director of client relations at the Business Research Lab in Houston, which conducts about 70 employee surveys a year. He cites a financial services client that had a turnover rate of 55 percent. After the company acted on results from a survey that pinpointed the source of its retention problems, the turnover rate the next year dropped to 22 percent and then down to 14 percent following a second survey. The firm documented savings of $2 million annually by reducing turnover, Campa says.[58]

Surveys with no feedback or follow-up action tend to alienate employees, who feel the surveys are just wasting their time.[59] On the other hand, a researcher found that unionized companies conducting regular attitude surveys were less likely to experience a labor strike than companies that failed to survey their employees.[60]

SUGGESTION SYSTEMS. Who knows more about a job than someone who performs that job day in and day out? This rhetorical question is the primary argument for suggestion systems, which can be a wellspring of good ideas. At Ernst & Young, the New York-based accounting firm, "a new confidential ethics hotline came from an employee suggestion."[61] Fairness and prompt feedback are keys to successful suggestion systems. Monetary incentives can help, too. Take, for example, this success story at Winnebago Industries, the recreational vehicle maker in Forest City, Iowa:

The program works because employees take it seriously. All reasonable suggestions submitted—an impressive 10,355 since the program began in 1991—are investigated by two full-time employees. The company has ended up implementing fully a third of these ideas, and employees have won more than $500,000 (they receive 10 percent of what the company saves in the first year). Winnebago says the program's first-year savings have added up to $5.8 million.[62]

Nice return on investment! (The 10 percent rule is also used at Chicago's famous chewing gum and candy company, Wm. Wrigley Jr.)[63] And a study of U.S. government employees found a positive correlation between suggestions and productivity.[64]

OPEN-DOOR POLICY. The open-door approach to upward communication has been both praised and criticized. Proponents say problems can be nipped in the bud when managers keep their doors open and employees feel free to walk in at any time and talk with them. But critics contend that an open-door policy encourages employees to leapfrog the formal chain of command (something that happens a lot these days because of e-mail and blogs). They argue further that it is an open invitation to annoying interruptions when managers can least afford them. A limited open-door policy—afternoons only, for example—can effectively remedy this particular problem. Another problem that needs to be overcome is the tendency for hard-charging managers and entrepreneurs to be too defensive. *Inc.* magazine explains:

. . . research shows that entrepreneurs are adept at "internalizing" success, taking full personal credit when things go right, and "externalizing" failure, blaming setbacks on outside factors. This psychological dynamic leads to certain less than helpful responses: Some managers become defensive and lash out; others find themselves wracked with self-doubt.

There's only one way to approach the problem and it's pretty simple: Remind yourself that even if the feedback feels personal, your reaction to it has to be anything but. Tell yourself . . . that a business mistake is not the same thing as a moral failing. [California Internet entrepreneur Christine] White, for example, has now created an "open door" policy to invite negative feedback. When she feels herself getting defensive, she remembers that it's all just part of doing business.[65]

INFORMAL MEETINGS. Employees may feel free to air their opinions and suggestions if they are confident that management will not criticize or penalize them for being frank. But they need to be given the right opportunity.[66] Here is an excellent case in point:

Employees at the Lodge at Vail are instructed to treat guests like treasured friends, anticipating and meeting their needs with the hope that they return season after season. HR director Mandy Wulfe's job is to ensure that the Vail, Colo., hotel's 280 workers feel the same way about their employer.

To bolster employee relations, Wulfe and her boss, hotel manager Wolfgang Triebnig, last spring started a "lunch with the boss" program to give each employee the opportunity to interact with Triebnig in a casual setting.

. . . Wulfe developed "Wolfgang's Lunch Gang," a series of monthly employee lunches in which eight staff members are invited to dine with Triebnig in the hotel's five-star restaurant. Over time, each employee will have a turn at the table.[67]

INTERNET CHAT ROOMS. In the Internet age, a convenient way for management to get candid feedback is to host a meeting place on the Web. These so-called "virtual water coolers" give employees unprecedented

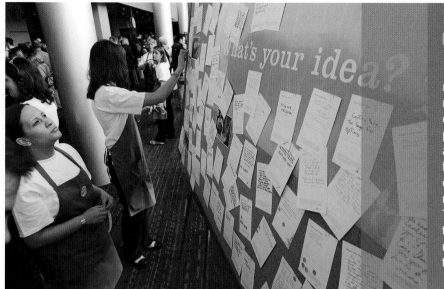

This scene from Starbucks's annual stockholder meeting in Seattle in 2008 reminds us of the importance of making customer feedback part of the upward communication process. Starbucks employees are seen here selecting their favorites from customer comment cards during the launch of the mystarbucksidea.com Web site. Think of it as a corporate suggestion system with potentially millions of participants. Now, that's a good idea!

freedom of speech. Dave Barram, head of the huge General Services Administration (GSA) in Washington, D.C., offered this assessment:

> . . . GSA has set up a Web-based "chat line," in which employees exchange uncensored thoughts and ideas. "If we have honest conversations about what's working and what isn't, we can become really good," Barram says. "If we don't, we'll never help each other."[68]

This approach takes lots of managerial courage, if the rough-and-tumble "cyberventing" on unauthorized Web sites aimed at specific companies is any indication.[69]

EXIT INTERVIEWS. An employee leaving the organization, for whatever reason, no longer fears possible recrimination from superiors and so can offer unusually frank and honest feedback, obtained in a brief, structured **exit interview**.[70] For example, Bill Klingelsmith, an executive at the Quad/Graphics printing plant in Martinsburg, Virginia, was tasked with helping to reduce turnover.

exit interview: brief, structured interview with a departing employee

> One of the first things Klingelsmith did was to call people who had left to ask them why. Though he couldn't fix one big complaint (rising home prices), the second was a surprise: Ex-employees said they hadn't gotten enough training and had quit in frustration. Quad stepped up its training efforts, and

> Klingelsmith says, "We haven't heard that complaint from anybody in eight or nine months."[71]

On the other hand, exit interviews have been criticized for eliciting artificially negative feedback because the employee may have a sour-grapes attitude toward the organization. Research finds the use of exit interviews to be spotty and haphazard, although many employers claim to use them. "If done well, managers and consultants said, exit interviews can show trends and point to potential problems that need to be addressed."[72]

Systematic use of exit interviews is recommended, not only for feedback purposes, but also for "harvesting" valuable knowledge from retiring experts. This needs to be done within the context of a comprehensive *knowledge management* (KM) program, as discussed in Chapter 8. In the following recommendation from *Business 2.0* magazine, we discover how Halliburton, the oil-services contractor, collects and shares vital knowledge from exit interviews.

> Target the gurus in a particular field, prolific inventors, or people in charge of a set of relationships either inside or outside the company. In particular, seize those who haven't groomed obvious successors. Halliburton's knowledge harvesters focused on a chemical division manager who had juggled suppliers and bundled contracts. He'd never shown anyone else his tricks of the trade. . . .
>
> Halliburton picks key lessons and designs online flowcharts that are so rich in graphics that viewing them is like playing a game of Chutes and Ladders.[73]

11f Straight Talk at CarMax

Employees at this chain of used-car superstores know their opinions count: CEO Austin Ligon opens frequent Q&A sessions with them by asking, "What are we doing that is stupid, unnecessary, or doesn't make sense?"

Source: Robert Levering and Milton Moskowitz, "The 100 Best Companies to Work For," Fortune (January 24, 2005): 78.

QUESTIONS:

If your present (or a former) boss asked you these questions, what would you say? How many of today's executives would be comfortable with this upward communication technique? Explain.

This use of exit interviews for KM is especially important in view of the coming wave of post–World War II baby boom retirees, discussed in Chapter 10.

In general, attempts to promote upward communication will be successful only if employees truly believe that their contributions will have a favorable impact on their employment. Halfhearted or insincere attempts to get employees to open up and become involved will do more harm than good.

COMMUNICATION PROBLEMS AND PROMISES IN THE INTERNET AGE

Because communication is a complex, give-and-take process, problems will occur. Managers who are aware of common barriers to communication and who are sensitive to the problems of sexist and racist communication are more likely to be effective communicators. In addition, managers who want to be effective communicators need to be aware of opportunities and obstacles in Internet-age communication systems.

Barriers to Communication

Do intended messages actually have the desired impact on employee behavior? This is the true test of organizational communication. Emerson Electric, the successful maker of electric motors, has a simple but effective way of testing how well its organizational communication is working. According to the head of the company,

> As a measure of communication at Emerson, we claim that every employee can answer four essential questions about his or her job:
>
> 1. What cost reduction are you currently working on?
> 2. Who is the "enemy" (who is the competition)?
> 3. Have you met with your management in the past six months?
> 4. Do you understand the economics of your job?
>
> When I repeated to a business journalist the claim that every employee can answer these questions, he put it to the test by randomly asking those questions of different employees at one of our plants. Each employee provided clear and direct answers, passing both the journalist's test and ours.[74]

Emerson Electric evidently has done a good job of overcoming the four main types of communication barriers: (1) process barriers, (2) physical barriers, (3) semantic barriers, and (4) psychosocial barriers.

PROCESS BARRIERS. Every step in the communication process is necessary for effective communication. Blocked steps become barriers. Consider the following situations:

- **Sender barrier.** A management trainee with an unusual new idea fails to speak up at a meeting for fear of criticism.
- **Encoding barrier.** This is a growing problem in today's culturally diverse workplace:

  > William D. Fleet, human-resources director at the Seattle Marriott, where employees speak 17 languages, once fired a Vietnamese kitchen worker for wrongly accusing a chef of assault. Only after another employee was attacked by a kitchen worker did Fleet figure out that the Vietnamese employee had used the word "chef" to refer to all kitchen workers with white uniforms. The misunderstanding had led to the firing of a good staffer and delayed the arrest of a dangerous one. . . .
  >
  > That's why . . . [Fleet] instituted a comprehensive ESL [English as a second language] program for staffers to take on company time. After all, workers who know English interact better with guests.[75]

- **Medium barrier.** After getting no answer three times and a busy signal twice, a customer concludes that a store's consumer hot line is a waste of time.

- ***Decoding barrier.*** A restaurant manager does not understand unfamiliar computer jargon during a sales presentation for laptop computers.
- ***Receiver barrier.*** A manager who is preoccupied with the preparation of a budget asks a team member to repeat an earlier statement.
- ***Feedback barrier.*** During on-the-job training, the failure of the trainee to ask any questions causes a manager to wonder whether any real understanding has been achieved.

The complexity of the communication process itself is a potentially formidable barrier to communication. Malfunctions anywhere along the line can singly or collectively block the transfer of understanding.

PHYSICAL BARRIERS. Sometimes a physical object blocks effective communication. For example, a riveter who wears ear protectors probably could not hear someone yelling "Fire!" Distance is another physical barrier. Thousands of miles and differing time zones traditionally made international business communication difficult. So today's global managers appreciate how the Internet and modern telecommunications technology have made the planet a seemingly smaller place. Although people often take physical barriers for granted, they can sometimes be removed. Perhaps an inconveniently positioned wall in an office can be torn out. Architects and office layout specialists called "organizational ecologists" are trying to redesign buildings and offices with more effective communication in mind. An interesting example is Timex's eye-catching headquarters building in Middlebury, Connecticut:

> *All of the 275 employees—including the CEO—work in a single, open room roughly the size of a football field: No walls, no partitions, no cubes divide them. . . .*
>
> *By opening up space, Timex hopes to promote all of the usual behavior expected from workspace design these days: collaboration, interaction, spontaneous meetings.*[76]

SEMANTIC BARRIERS. Formally defined, **semantics** is the study of the meaning of words. Words are indispensable, although they can cause a great deal of trouble. In a well-worn army story, a growling drill sergeant once ordered a frightened recruit to go out and paint his entire jeep. Later, the sergeant was shocked to find that the private had painted his *entire* jeep, including the headlights, windshield, seats, and dashboard gauges. Obviously, the word *entire* meant something different to the recruit than it did to the sergeant.

semantics: study of the meaning of words

In today's highly specialized world, managers and professionals in such fields as accounting, computer science, advertising, medicine, and law may become so accustomed to their own technical jargon that they forget that people outside their field may not understand them. (For instance, viewers of Donald Trump's television show, *The Apprentice*, are bombarded with business jargon such as "bottom line," "synergy," "face time," "scenario," "proactive," and "on the same page.")[77] Unexpected reactions or behavior by others may signal a semantic barrier when jargon is used. It may become necessary to reencode the message using more familiar terms. Sometimes, if the relationship among specialists in different technical fields is an ongoing one, remedial steps can be taken. For example, hospital administrators often take a special course in medical terminology to better understand the medical staff.

PSYCHOSOCIAL BARRIERS. Psychological and social barriers are probably responsible for more blocked communication than any other type of barrier.[78] People's backgrounds, perceptions, values, biases, needs, and expectations differ. Childhood experiences may result in negative feelings toward authority figures

Has modern telecommunications technology made communicating easier or harder? Both, really. This young woman in Bangkok, Thailand, could be talking to anyone, anywhere on the planet. But language barriers, inappropriate media, and incompatible equipment remain problematic.

(such as supervisors), racial prejudice, distrust of the opposite sex, or lack of self-confidence. Family and personal problems (including poor health, alcoholism, lack of sleep, and emotional strain) may be so upsetting that an employee is unable to concentrate on work. Experience on present or past jobs may have created anger, distrust, and resentment that speak more loudly in the employee's mind than any work-related communication. Sincere sensitivity to the receiver's needs and personal circumstances goes a long way toward overcoming psychosocial barriers to communication.

Sexist and Racist Communication

In recent years the English language has been increasingly criticized for being sexist and racist. Words such as *he, chairman, brotherhood, mankind,* and the like have traditionally been used in reference to both men and women. The usual justification is that everyone understands that these words refer to both sexes, and it is simpler to use the masculine form. Critics maintain that wholly masculine wording subtly denies women a place and image worthy of their equal status and importance in society.[79] This criticism is largely based on psychological and sociological considerations. Calling the human race *mankind,* for instance, is seldom a real barrier to understanding. But a Stanford University researcher found that "males appear to use 'he' in response to male-related imagery, rather than in response to abstract or generic notions of humanity."[80] In other words, *he* is commonly interpreted to mean literally *he* (a man), not *they* (men and women).

For both ethical and legal reasons, these same cautions carry over to the problem of racist communication.

> *Words spoken at work that aren't literally racist— such as "you people," "poor people," and "that one in there"—now can be grounds for employment discrimination lawsuits [in the United States].*
> *They're called "code words." . . .*
> *It's not just the words, says Herman Cain, the black CEO of Godfather's Pizza and author of* Leadership Is Common Sense. *"It's body language. Tone of voice. How people talk to you. Over the years you can develop a sixth sense."*[81]

Progressive and ethical managers are weeding sexist and racist language out of their vocabularies and correspondence to eliminate both intentional and inadvertent demeaning of women and racial minorities.[82]

Communicating in the Online Workplace

Computers speak a simple digital language of 1s and 0s. Today, every imaginable sort of information—including text, numbers, still and moving pictures, and sound—is being converted into a digital format. This process has meant nothing short of a revolution for the computer, telecommunications, consumer electronics, publishing, and entertainment industries. Organizational communication, already significantly reshaped by computer technology, is undergoing its own revolutionary change. This section does *not* attempt the impossible task of describing all the emerging communication technologies, ranging from speech recognition software through wireless broadband Internet to virtual reality.[83] Rather, it explores the impact of some established digital-age technologies on workplace communications. Our goal is to more effectively use the technologies we have and to prepare for those to come.

GETTING A HANDLE ON E-MAIL AND INSTANT MESSAGING. E-mail via the Internet has precipitated a communication revolution akin to those brought about by the printing press, telephone, radio, and television. If you are on the Internet, you are ultimately linked to each of the hundreds of millions of people on Earth capable of sending and receiving e-mail. Both on and off the job, e-mail is more than a way of communication—it is a lifestyle! Jim Keyes, CEO of the 7-Eleven convenience store chain, "burns three to four hours of his day on 200 e-mails and is

11g Survey Says . . . A Digital Brain Drain?

Our reliance on stored passwords and speed dialing may be dimming our recall. . . . Since memory grows weaker when it's not used, this vicious cycle leads to forgetfulness. A quarter of the 3,000 people surveyed, for example, couldn't recite their home phone numbers. On average, the respondents were burdened with five passwords, five PINS, five security IDs, three bank account numbers, and two license plate combinations. . . .

Technology-induced memory atrophy seems to hit the techno-smug young harder. In the over-50 set, 87% could recall family birthdays, vs. 40% of the under-30s.

Source: Excerpted from Adam Aston, "High-Tech Memory Loss," Business Week (July 30, 2007): 10.

QUESTIONS:
Have communication devices with memory functions dimmed your own memory or freed up your mind for more important things? Have mobile communication devices helped or hindered your work-and-life balance? Explain.

such a heavy user that if a top field executive or licensee were to phone him, he might not recognize the voice."[84] Shifting the focus from individual to organization, we run into astonishing numbers. After discovering that many of its 88,000 employees worldwide were spending about 2½ hours each day exchanging 3 million e-mails, Intel decided to act:

The chipmaker recently started classes on how to manage e-mail. Some tips: Put short messages in the subject line so recipients don't have to open it to read the note. Intel also is asking workers to sparingly use graphics and attachments and get off unnecessary distribution lists.

"We're not discouraging e-mail, just [encouraging] better use," spokesman Chuck Mulloy says.[85]

E-mail is a two-headed beast: easy and efficient, while at the same time grossly abused and mismanaged.[86] By managing e-mail effectively, the organization can take a big step toward properly using the Internet. An organizational e-mail policy, embracing the following recommendations from experts, can help.

- The e-mail system belongs to the company, which has the legal right to monitor its use. (*Never* assume privacy with company e-mail.)[87]
- Workplace e-mail is for business purposes only.
- Harassing and offensive e-mail will not be tolerated.
- E-mail messages should be concise (see Table 11.2). As in all correspondence, grammar and spelling count because they reflect on your diligence and credibility. Typing in all capital letters makes the message hard to read and amounts to SHOUTING in cyberspace. (All capital letters can be appropriate, for contrast purposes, when adding comments to an existing document.)

- Lists of bullet items (similar to the format you are reading now) are acceptable because they tend to be more concise than paragraphs.
- Long attachments defeat the quick-and-easy nature of e-mail.
- Recipients should be told when a reply is *unnecessary*.
- An organization-specific priority system should be used for sending and receiving all e-mail. *Example:* "At Libit, a company in Palo Alto, Calif., that makes silicon products for the cable industry, e-mail is labeled as either informational or action items to avoid time wasting."[88]
- "Spam" (unsolicited and unwanted e-mail) that gets past filters should be deleted without being read. Despite passage of a federal anti-spam law in the United States, spam still constitutes about 60 to 70 percent of all e-mail.[89] So-called spy-ware and adware should be blocked and should be uninstalled when a system has been infected.
- To avoid file clutter, messages unlikely to be referred to again should not be saved.[90]

IBM has responded to e-mail overload by encouraging the use of *instant messaging* (IM), because it is faster and supposedly less of a burden on the network. But instant messaging, especially when it is not managed by the organization, has its own drawbacks. A survey of 840 companies, conducted by the American Management Association, uncovered some disturbing information about the uses and abuses of IM:

. . . only 11 percent of organizations have IM gateway/management software to control the 31 percent of employees who IM in the office.

TABLE 11.2 How to Compose a CLEAR E-Mail Message

Concise. A brief message in simple conversational language is faster for you to write and more pleasant for your readers to read.

Logical. A message in logical steps, remembering to include any context your readers need, will be more easily understood.

Empathetic. When you identify with your readers, your message will be written in the right tone and in words they will readily understand.

Action-oriented. When you remember to explain to your readers what you want them to do next, they are more likely to do it.

Right. A complete message, with no important facts missing, with all the facts right, and with correct spelling, will save your readers having to return to you to clarify details.

Source: Joan Tunstall, Better, Faster Email: Getting the Most Out of Email *(St. Leonards, Australia: Allen & Unwin, 1999), p. 37. Reprinted by permission.*

That's a dangerous prospect, given that 70 percent of these IMers have downloaded free IM software from the Internet, increasing legal, compliance, productivity and security issues.

The survey, "2004 Workplace E-Mail and Instant Messaging Survey," also reveals that of those who IM at work, 58 percent engage in personal chats. Within these chats, 19 percent send attachments; 16 percent send jokes, gossip, rumors or disparaging remarks; 9 percent share confidential information about the company, coworkers or clients; and 6 percent exchange sexual, romantic or pornographic content.[91]

Like e-mail, IM requires standards, policy guidelines, and management oversight.

HELLO! CAN WE TALK ABOUT CELL PHONE ETIQUETTE? According to industry data, there were over 243 million wireless subscribers in the United States in late 2007.[92] The market penetration rate for cell phones in the United States is around 80 percent, with much higher figures for other countries, such as Italy.[93] As a sign of the times, an entire 8,000-person engineering group at Ford Motor Company recently traded in their desktop phones for cell phones.[94] Like e-mail, cell phones have proved to be both a blessing and a curse. Offsetting the mobility and convenience are concerns about distracted drivers and loud and obnoxious phone conversations in public places.[95] Managers need to be particularly sensitive to the risk of inadvertently broadcasting proprietary company information, names, and numbers. Competitors could be standing in the same airport line or sitting in the next restaurant booth. Table 11.3 offers some practical tips to help make the use of cell phones more effective, secure, and courteous.

Camera phones also require restrictions in the workplace because of concerns about privacy and information security. At Chrysler, for example, neither visitors nor employees are allowed to have camera phones on company property.[96]

VIDEOCONFERENCES. A **videoconference** is a live television or broadband Internet video exchange between people in different locations. The decreasing cost of steadily improving videoconferencing technologies and the desire to reduce costly travel time have fostered wider use of this approach to organizational communication.[97] Consider this case in point:

> **videoconference:** live television or broadband Internet video exchange between people in different locations

As part of its knowledge-management initiative, British Petroleum rolled out some videoconferencing technology for rapidly sharing ideas. Soon after, one of their gas drills broke down in the North Slope of Alaska. BP's leading expert in gas turbines was working in the North Sea; it would have taken him 20 hours to fly to Alaska. Instead of putting him on a plane, BP patched him into the North Slope via videoconference, and he worked with on-site technicians to pinpoint the problem and get the drill back onstream. They finished the job in just 30 minutes.[98]

Communication pointers for videoconference participants include the following:

- Test the system before the meeting convenes.
- Dress for the occasion. The video image is distorted by movement of wild patterns and flashy

---

TABLE 11.3 Five Commandments of Cell Phone Etiquette

1. *Thou shalt not subject defenseless others to cell phone conversations.* Cell phone etiquette, like all forms of etiquette, centers on having respect for others.

2. *Thou shalt not set thy ringer to play La Cucaracha every time thy phone rings.* It's a phone, not a public address system.

3. *Thou shalt turn thy cell phone off during public performances.* Set your phone on vibrate when in meetings or in the company of others and, if necessary, take or return the call at a polite distance.

4. *Thou shalt not dial while driving.* If you must engage in cell phone conversations while driving, use a hands-off device.

5. *Thou shalt not speak louder on thy cell phone than thou would on any other phone.* It's called "cell yell" and it's very annoying to others.

Source: Five basic commandments in bold excerpted from Dan Briody, "The Ten Commandments of Cell Phone Etiquette," InfoWorld, February 5, 2005, www.infoworld.com.

jewelry. Solid white clothing tends to "glow" on camera.

- Make sure everyone is introduced.
- Check to make sure everyone can see and hear the content of the meeting.
- Do not feel compelled to direct your entire presentation to the camera or monitor. Directly address those in the same room.
- Speak loudly and clearly. Avoid slang and jargon in cross-cultural meetings where translations are occurring.
- Avoid exaggerated physical movements that tend to blur on camera.
- Adjust your delivery to any transmission delay, pausing longer than usual when waiting for replies.
- Avoid side conversations, which are disruptive.
- Do not nervously tap the table or microphone or shuffle papers.[99]

TELECOMMUTING. Years ago, futurist Alvin Toffler used the term *electronic cottage* to refer to the practice of working at home on a personal computer connected—typically by telephone in those days—to an employer's place of business. More recently, this practice has been labeled **telecommuting** because work, rather than the employee, travels between a central office and the employee's home, reaching the computer via telephone or cable modem. The advent of overnight delivery services, low-cost facsimile (fax)

telecommuting: sending work to and from one's office via computer modem while working at home

machines, e-mail, and broadband Internet, combined with wireless communication devices, has broadened the technical potential for telecommuting. Yet the growth of telecommuting has stalled, according to a recent study by the Society for Human Resource Management: "About 19 percent of companies permit telecommuting by full-time employees, down from the peak of 23 percent three years ago."[100] Despite some compelling advantages, telecommuting has enough drawbacks to make it unsuitable for many employees as well as employers (see Table 11.4). Telecommuting can disrupt the normal social and communication patterns in the workplace, as this manager has discovered:

> *Jack Kramer, sales vice president at Pathlore Software, a provider of online learning systems, works from home in Chester Springs, Pa., rather than corporate headquarters in Columbus, Ohio. Family was a key reason for his [reluctance] to move: After relocating previously for work, he'd promised his children . . . they wouldn't have to move again.*
>
> *Technology also enables the setup. Through virtual technology, his employees can view a desktop at the same time he does, despite the distance: Before a recent national kickoff event, he was able to show them all a PowerPoint presentation even though he was nearly 400 miles away. "The biggest challenge is 'face time.' We have to schedule in cups of coffee remotely," [he says].*[101]

Telecommuting will not become the prevailing work mode any time soon, but it certainly is more than a passing fad.[102]

TABLE **11.4** Telecommuting: Promises and Problems

PROMISES	POTENTIAL PROBLEMS
1. Significantly boosts individual productivity.	1. Can cause fear of stagnating at home.
2. Saves commuting time and travel expenses (lessens traffic congestion).	2. Can foster sense of isolation due to lack of social contact with coworkers.
3. Taps broader labor pool (such as mothers with young children, disabled and retired persons, and prison inmates).	3. Can result in competition or interference with family duties, thus causing family conflict.
4. Eliminates office distractions and politics.	4. Can disrupt traditional manager-employee relationship.
5. Reduces employer's cost of office space.	5. Can cause fear of being "out of sight, out of mind" at promotion time.

BECOMING A BETTER COMMUNICATOR

Three communication skills as important as ever in today's rapidly changing world are listening, writing, and running meetings. Managers who master these skills generally have fewer interpersonal relations problems. Moreover, effective communicators tend to move up the hierarchy faster than poor ones do. *Training* magazine recently summed up the importance of communication this way:

> One of the biggest challenges managers face is communication . . . [and] communication is also one of the most critical aspects of leadership. Without good communication, managers can fail to gain commitment from employees, fail to achieve business goals and fail to develop rapport with the people on their team. In short, they can fail as leaders no matter how good their intentions may be.[103]

Effective Listening

Nearly all training in oral communication in high school, college, and management development programs is in effective speaking. But what about listening, the other half of the communication equation? Listening is the forgotten factor in communication skills training. This is unfortunate because the most glowing oration is a waste of time if it is not heard.

Interestingly, a Cornell University researcher asked 827 employees in the hospitality industry to rate their managers' listening ability. The managers whom the employees considered good listeners tended to be female, under 45 years of age, and relatively new to their position.[104]

Listening takes place at two steps in the verbal communication process. First, the receiver must listen in order to decode and understand the original message. Then the sender becomes a listener when attempting to decode and understand subsequent feedback. Identical listening skills come into play at both ends. Xerox's CEO Anne Mulcahy calls listening "one of those things that is easy to talk about, difficult to do. . . . I'm talking about listening in a way that actually treasures and absorbs criticism and makes a point of getting honest feedback."[105]

We can hear and process information much more quickly than the normal speaker can talk. According to researchers, our average rate of speaking is about 125 words per minute, whereas we are able to listen to about 400 to 600 words a minute.[106] Thus, listeners have up to 75 percent slack time during which they can daydream or, alternatively, analyze the information and plan a response. Effective listeners know how to put that slack time to good use. Here are some practical tips for more effective listening:

- Tolerate silence. Listeners who rush to fill momentary silences cease being listeners.
- Ask stimulating, open-ended questions that require more than merely a yes-or-no answer.

How would you handle this tough communication situation? Suppose you're an oil industry executive addressing these truck drivers protesting high fuel prices in Harrisburg, Pennsylvania, in 2008. Hint: do more listening than talking.

- Encourage the speaker with attentive eye contact, alert posture, and verbal encouragers such as "umhum," "yes," and "I see." Occasionally repeating the speaker's last few words also helps.
- Paraphrase. Periodically restate in your own words what you have just heard.
- Show emotion to demonstrate that you are a sympathetic listener.
- Know your biases and prejudices and attempt to correct for them.
- Avoid premature judgments about what is being said.
- Summarize. Briefly highlight what the speaker has just finished saying to bring out possible misunderstandings.[107]

For their part, speakers need to randomly insert comprehension checks. John Baldoni, a Michigan communication consultant, offers this tip: "Implement the 'brief-back.' Make sure people understand what you say. Ask your listeners to tell you what you have just told them."[108]

"Oh, vowels are so 2006!"

Effective Writing

Managers often complain about poor writing skills. Here's an example:

> Larry Kensington, president of Kentwood, Mich.– based Bananza Air Management Systems, sifted through scores of résumés to hire three workers this year. One of his biggest gripes: Job applications riddled with spelling errors. "They can't even express themselves in a simple sentence," he says, noting employees need to be able to write so they can fill out quality-control data and other reports.[109]

Writing difficulties stem from an educational system that requires students to do less and less writing. Essay tests have given way in many classes to the multiple-choice variety, and term papers are being pushed aside by team activities and projects. Quick-and-dirty e-mails, instant messages, and cell phone text messaging at home, school, and the workplace also have contributed to the erosion of writing quality in recent years. *USA Today* noted this in 2007, on the 15th anniversary of the first text message:

> OMG! TXT MSG turns 15!
>
> Cellphone-accessorized teens may think that's just GR8. But as the lexicon spawned by a 160-character message limit starts to spill off the cellphone screen into written work, some of their English teachers aren't exactly ROFL. Nor does seeing text abbreviations crop up in essays bring a smiley face to college admission officers.[110]

Moreover, spelling and grammar checkers used by those who compose at the computer keyboard are not cure-alls. (There really is no adequate substitute for careful proofreading.) As a learned skill, effective writing is the product of regular practice. Students who do not get the necessary writing practice in school are at a disadvantage when they enter the job market.

Good writing is a key form of encoding in the basic communication process. If it is done skillfully, potentially troublesome semantic and psychosocial barriers can be surmounted. Caterpillar's publications editor offered four helpful reminders.

1. ***Keep words simple.*** Simplifying the words you use will help reduce your thoughts to essentials; keep your readers from being "turned off" by the complexity of your letter, memo, or report; and make it more understandable.
2. ***Don't sacrifice communication to rules of composition.*** Most of us who were sensitized to the rules of grammar and composition in school never quite recovered from the process. As proof, we keep trying to make our writing conform to rigid rules and customs without regard to style or the ultimate

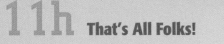

11h That's All Folks!

John Clemens, management professor and author:

. . . managers have to develop a sixth sense as to when a major moment is at hand so that employees walk out [of a meeting] jazzed up–and never discount the natural high of exiting a meeting early.

Source: Patrick J. Sauer, "What Time Is the Next Meeting?" Inc., 26 (May 2004): 75.

QUESTIONS:

How does a manager develop such a sixth sense? Taking the role of a management consultant, discuss how often (and when) the early-finish tactic should be used.

---

purpose of the communication. (Of course, employees need to be sensitive to the stylistic preferences of their bosses.)

3. ***Write concisely.*** This means expressing your thoughts, opinions, and ideas in the least number of words consistent with effective composition and smoothness. But don't confuse conciseness with mere brevity; otherwise, you may write briefly without being clear or complete.

4. ***Be specific.*** Vagueness is one of the most serious flaws in written communication because it destroys accuracy and clarity, leaving the reader to wonder about your meaning or intent.[111]

Also, avoid irritating your readers with useless phrases such as "to be perfectly honest," "needless to say," "as you know," and "please be advised that."[112]

Running a Meeting

Meetings are an ever-present feature of modern organizational life. Whether they are convened to find facts, solve problems, or pass along information, meetings typically occupy a good deal of a manager's time. Sadly, much of that time is wasted. Management consultant Stuart R. Levine recently summed up what he learned from a study of mid- and upper-level managers' experiences with meetings:

It turns out they were spending approximately 70 percent of their time in meetings, the meetings had clear objectives only about 40 percent of the time, and they achieved their objectives only about 28 percent of the time.[113]

A good first step toward better meetings, according to author Patrick M. Lencioni, is to categorize meetings for a sharper focus. Four general categories that he recommends using are:

> ***Daily check-in.*** *A five-minute morning huddle to report on activities that day.*
>
> ***Weekly tactical.*** *A 45- to 90-minute meeting to review the firm's critical metrics (revenue, expenses, etc.) and solve problems.*
>
> ***Monthly strategic.*** *Executives wrestle with, debate, analyze and decide the big critical issues that will affect the bottom line.*
>
> ***Quarterly off-site review.*** *These reviews focus on four areas—strategy, team, personnel, and competitors—to help avoid turning into the "touchy-feely boondoggle" that such meetings can become.*[114]

Whatever the reason for a meeting, managers who convene meetings owe it to themselves and their organization to use everyone's time and talent efficiently. Here are ten pointers for conducting successful meetings:

- Meet for a specific purpose, not simply as a ritual.
- Create an agenda and distribute it at least one day in advance.
- Communicate expectations for attendees to help them come prepared with proper data and documentation.
- Limit attendance to essential personnel.
- Open the meeting with a brief overview of what has been accomplished and what lies ahead.
- Deal with the most difficult/challenging agenda items quite early in the meeting while the energy level is still high.
- Encourage broad participation, while sticking to the agenda.
- Selectively use stimulating visual aids to make key points and, according to one expert, do not use more than three PowerPoint slides for every 10 minutes of presentation.[115]
- Make sure everyone understands what action items they are responsible for after the meeting.
- Begin and end the meeting on time, and follow up as necessary.[116]

With practice, these guidelines will become second nature. Running a meeting brings into focus all the components of the communication process, including coping with noise and barriers. Effective meetings are important to organizational communication and, ultimately, to organizational success in today's team-oriented workplaces.

SUMMARY

1. Modern technology has made communicating easier and less costly but has had the unintended side effect of information overload. Managers are challenged to improve the *quality* of their communication because it is a core process for everything they do. Communication is a social process involving the transfer of information and understanding. Links in the communication process include sender, encoding, medium, decoding, receiver, and feedback. Noise is any source of interference.

2. According to the Lengel-Daft contingency model, media richness is determined by the amount of information conveyed and the amount of learning promoted. Rich media such as face-to-face communication are best for nonroutine problems. Lean media such as impersonal bulletins are suitable for routine problems.

3. Organizational communication is typically too haphazard. Clampitt's communication continuum indicates that the five basic strategies are not equally effective. The Spray & Pray and Withhold & Uphold strategies are generally ineffective and should be avoided. The Tell & Sell and Identify & Reply strategies should be used sparingly. Managers need to use the Underscore & Explore strategy as much as possible. Media richness needs to be as high as possible if the preferred communication strategies are to be effective.

4. The unofficial and informal communication system that sometimes complements and sometimes disrupts the formal communication system has been labeled the grapevine. A sample of managers surveyed had predominantly negative feelings toward it. Recognizing that the grapevine cannot be suppressed, managers are advised to monitor it constructively. Nonverbal communication (including facial, gestural, and postural body language) accounts for most of the impact of face-to-face communication. Managers can become more effective communicators by doing a better job of receiving and giving nonverbal communications.

5. Upward communication can be stimulated by using formal grievance procedures, employee attitude and opinion surveys, suggestion systems, an open-door policy, informal meetings, Internet chat rooms, and exit interviews.

6. Managers need to identify and overcome four barriers to communication. Process barriers can occur at any one of the basic links in the communication process. Physical barriers, such as walls and distance between two points, can block effective communication. Semantic barriers are encountered when there is confusion about the meaning of words. Psychosocial barriers to communication involve the full range of human perceptions, prejudices, and attitudes that can interfere with understanding. Care needs to be taken to eliminate subtle forms of sexist and racist communication.

7. E-mail, supposedly a real time saver, has quickly become a major time waster. Organizations need to create and enforce a clear e-mail policy to improve message quality and curb abuses. Cell phone users need to be discreet and courteous to avoid broadcasting privileged information and/or offending others. Videoconferencing restricts how people communicate because televised contacts are more mechanical than face-to-face meetings. Although telecommuting can reduce travel time and expense and can offer employment to nontraditional employees, it restricts normal social contact and face-to-face communication in the workplace.

8. Listening does not get sufficient attention in communications training. Active, cooperative listening is to be encouraged. Writing skills are no less important in the computer age. Written messages need to be specific, simply worded, and concise. Meetings, an ever-present feature of organizational life, need to be focused and agenda-driven if time is to be used wisely.

TERMS TO UNDERSTAND

- **Communication**, p. 300
- **Media richness**, p. 301
- **Noise**, p. 304
- **Grapevine**, p. 306
- **Body language**, p. 308
- **Upward communication**, p. 311
- **Exit interview**, p. 313
- **Semantics**, p. 315
- **Videoconference**, p. 318
- **Telecommuting**, p. 319

MANAGER'S TOOLKIT

How to Give and Receive Feedback

Giving feedback to employees—and receiving feedback yourself—is one of the most misunderstood and poorly executed human resource processes, according to ClearRock, an outplacement and executive coaching firm based in Boston. To point you in the right direction, the firm has some feedback dos and don'ts:

- **Focus on the positive first.** "Feedback should start with positive observations about the contributions an employee is making before detailing areas that need improvement," says Annie Stevens, managing partner with ClearRock.
- **Stay nonjudgmental and don't personalize feedback.** "Focus on the behavior that needs to be changed, and not the person," says ClearRock managing partner Greg Gostanian.
- **Limit feedback to those areas the employee has the ability to change.** "Feedback that is irrelevant will not be accepted by the recipient, and may even be detrimental," says Stevens.

- **Use "I," and not "We."** Say, "I observed you, rather than, "We observed you."
- **Avoid "over-dumping" on someone.** "Often, one behavioral example is all that's needed to help someone understand," says Gostanian.
- **Give the recipient a chance to respond.** "Listen as openly as possible, even if all you expect to receive are rationalizations," says Stevens. "At least you will find out if your feedback has been understood."
- **Keep received feedback in perspective.** "Try not to dwell on perceived negative comments," says Gostanian, "and balance it with what you know about yourself."
- **Provide your reaction when given the chance to respond:** "Don't suffer in silence," says Stevens. "Respond to feedback by focusing on the comments without personalizing your reaction."

Source: Margery Weinstein, "Friendly Feedback," Training, 44 (May 2007): 11.

ACTION LEARNING EXERCISE

Oh, No! What Have I Done?

Situation: It's almost 6 P.M. and you're back at your office putting the finishing touches on next week's annual presentation to top management. Your stomach is churning, partly from hunger and partly from the stress of having missed another one of your twins' soccer matches. As the corporate director of product design at a large multinational company, you don't need to be reminded about the importance of next week's presentation. Between 3 P.M. and a few minutes ago, you had hidden out in a remote conference room fine-tuning it. Your cell phone was with you but had a dead battery, as you just noticed.

Right now, you are staring in disbelief at an e-mail message on your computer screen. The three-word message "WHERE WERE YOU!" burns into your mind. This particular e-mail is from your firm's director of marketing. She e-mailed an hour ago from her home after a late-afternoon meeting with two executives from a company that has been a customer for over ten years. During a quick chat in the hallway yesterday, you had promised the marketing director you'd attend today's meeting to provide technical support. This customer is one of your smaller accounts, but there is potential for a big jump in business this year. The marketing director's idea was to have a brief "let's explore possibilities" meeting.

The plain truth is you simply forgot about the meeting. You've been on major overload. You never bothered to put it on your electronic calendar because the commitment was made just yesterday and you thought you'd surely remember it. Well, you didn't!

Your mind races, weighing the situation and what to do about it. Losing this customer would be very bad for your career because your CEO is a table-pounder about customer service. Whom should you contact first—the marketing director, your boss, the customer, your family? And how should you communicate with them? It's dinnertime now. What about calling later tonight? Can everything but your family wait until tomorrow? What about e-mails? You know both your boss and the marketing director check their BlackBerry e-mails later each evening at home. Should you stop by anybody's home tonight to deliver a personal apology and explanation? What should you do? What should you say? How should you say it? Your stomach tightens a couple more notches.

Instructions: Working either alone or as a member of a team, quickly develop a communication plan for this awkward situation. Your plan should involve (1) specifying your assumptions and objectives, (2) choosing an appropriate medium for each message (face-to-face, cell phone, telephone/voice mail, or e-mail), and (3) composing messages to the relevant parties.

For Consideration/Discussion

1. What assumptions did you make in this case? How did they influence your response?
2. What were your priorities in this situation? How did they influence your actions?
3. Whom did you contact first? How and why?
4. How did you communicate with each party? Why did you choose that way?
5. What practical lessons about communication did you learn from this exercise? Explain.

CLOSING CASE
Found in Translation: How to Make the Multicultural Workforce Work

At City Fresh Foods, CEO Glynn Lloyd likes to hire from the neighborhood. And because the 12-year-old food-service company is headquartered in Boston's polyglot Dorchester neighborhood, Lloyd's payroll resembles a mini–United Nations. Some 70 percent of his 65 employees are immigrants, from places like Trinidad, Brazil, Nigeria, the Dominican Republic, and Cape Verde, off the West Coast of Africa. They speak half a dozen languages, not to mention the myriad cultural differences. "Visitors can see that we're a community of people from all over. They pick up on it right away," says Lloyd, 38. "You walk in, and you can feel the vibe of all those places."

Immigrants will account for nearly two-thirds of the country's population growth between now and 2050, according to the U.S. Department of Labor. Minority groups will constitute almost half of the population by then, meaning that successful managers will have to understand how to develop and retain employees who come from more cultures than any CEO could master. Indeed, while policymakers struggle to find an acceptable posture on border security, Lloyd has been working hard to figure out his own urgent question: How can managers best ensure that employees from so many different cultures work side by side productively?

He's come up with an ad hoc series of practices and processes that are achieving that aim. The highest hurdle, of course, has been communication. Lloyd tried overcoming it by providing about 40 hours of ESL [English as a second language] classes to his workers so that all 65 of them would use English. But that bar seemed too high, so Lloyd has lowered it. Instead, he requires his employees to learn the more limited language of City Fresh Foods—terms like "delivery ticket," "checkout sheet," and "ice packs." "I spend a little extra time trying to help them read what they need to know," says Kurt Stegenga, the company's logistics manager, who grew up in Mexico. "It takes a bit of clarification so that they can reach into the refrigerator and know what it is they are grabbing—say, cream cheese and not cheese sticks." But once they know those terms, productivity begins humming, Lloyd says.

At monthly companywide meetings, meanwhile, multilingual employees volunteer to serve as translators. Rosemary De la Cruz, a 26-year-old administrator from the Dominican Republic, sits next to employees who need the Spanish version and translates. Delivery manager Jose Tavares makes notes about his department meetings; his assistant translates them into Portuguese and Spanish for the company's 26 drivers. He's also ready to jump on the phone and solve any problems that might occur when an immigrant driver cannot answer a customer's question. Cotumanama "Toby" Peña—many employees adopt nicknames to further the cause of simplification—learned English words such as "safe" and "out" by watching baseball in his native Dominican Republic and picked up the alphabet from *Sesame Street*. "The English I speak is broken," says Peña, a cook. "For me, it's sometimes better to write things down." (Nonetheless, he often finds himself translating for one of his fellow cooks who is among the 40 percent of employees who don't speak English.)

When it comes to company material that is typically communicated with words—training manuals, say—Lloyd sticks mainly to visual tools, an outgrowth of the knack he had to develop for using gestures to make himself understood. To learn how to stack a cooler, for instance, employees study photos of how the contents can be arranged so that drivers don't have to reach deep inside to grab any drinks. How does City Fresh pack bread? Employees take turns using a machine that pumps air into a bag, slipping a loaf inside the bag, and then using another machine to tape it up. "A demonstration is better than words," says Lloyd.

City Fresh also counts on numbers to serve as a universal language. For instance, Lloyd worked with his managers to design a checklist that employees use to keep track of how many meals still need to be produced—the company ships out 4,000 daily, mostly to institutional customers ranging from charter schools to nursing homes—and for which accounts. The bulk packers can tell how many pounds of green beans they'll need. The expediters who match the beverages and desserts to each meal know what time it has to leave and who will be delivering it. Everybody can use the document, no matter what language they speak, says Lloyd.

But anybody with designs on rising into a management position has to master English. City Fresh will contribute up to $1,000 per person a year to help; it allocates $12,000 a year for education. These days, one assistant manager is getting 90 minutes of private tutoring a week. Rather than hauling everyone into a classroom, "we're going to start using this kind of learning more strategically," Lloyd says. "It will be a reward for the people who we think will get the most value from it." Otherwise, he says, ESL classes come and go without much to show for them. Nobody gets sufficiently immersed in English at work because "they don't need to know it," he says. "They can talk to each other in whatever language they want."

Lloyd goes to such lengths not just to ease communication but also because it's good for his customers. Many, especially the elderly, are from ethnic communities themselves and have "a taste for the authentic," as he puts it. Chefs from the Caribbean know how to whip up such specialties as mondongo (cow intestine), stewed goat, and salted codfish. And if employees sometimes run into problems with customers because they do not speak English, they've also been known to save the day when an English-speaking staffer encounters a customer from another country.

FOR DISCUSSION

1 What role does the basic communication process in Figure 11.1 play in this case? Explain.

2 Which of the five communication strategies in Figure 11.3 does CEO Glynn Lloyd rely on the most at City Fresh Foods? Explain.

3 How should Glynn Lloyd stimulate upward communication at City Fresh Foods? Explain.

4 How would you rate Glynn Lloyd as a listener? Explain.

5 How comfortable would you be managing this type of multicultural organization? Explain.

TEST PREPPER

True/False Questions

_____ 1. Feedback is one of the links in the basic communication process.

_____ 2. According to the Lengel-Daft model, e-mail communication ranks highest on the media richness scale.

_____ 3. In the "Withhold & Uphold" communication strategy, managers tell what they think people need to know only when they believe people need to know it.

_____ 4. The organizational grapevine is an even bigger problem today, thanks to e-mail, blogs, and online social networking.

_____ 5. Most of the impact of our communication comes from the implied meaning of our words.

_____ 6. With an open-door policy, an employee is free to leave the workplace at any time.

_____ 7. Psychological and social barriers are responsible for most blocked communication.

_____ 8. Videoconference participants should look directly at the camera when speaking.

_____ 9. Effective listeners ask simple yes-or-no questions.

_____ 10. One key to conducting a successful meeting is to create an agenda and distribute it at least one day in advance.

Multiple-Choice Questions

1. Which of these *best* describes the basic communication process?
   A. A chain with identifiable links
   B. Noninstructive
   C. Inherently flawed
   D. A computer network
   E. A burning bush

2. Media richness involves the capacity to
   A. achieve organizational results.
   B. justify decisions.
   C. convince and persuade.
   D. convey information and promote learning.
   E. build personal relationships.

3. Which of the following is *not* one of the basic communication strategies?
   A. Spray & Pray   B. Underscore & Say More
   C. Identify & Reply   D. Withhold & Uphold
   E. Tell & Sell

4. Judging on the basis of what you read in this chapter, what advice would you give a bookstore manager about the grapevine?
   A. Uproot it as soon as possible.
   B. Pretend it doesn't exist.
   C. Don't try to kill it.
   D. Make it the official communication network.
   E. Weed out the troublemakers.

5. In a recent survey of 25,000 employees in the United States, _____ said that their senior managers both talk *and* listen.
   A. 45 percent   B. slightly more than half
   C. only 7 percent   D. 75 percent
   E. about 25 percent

6. Which of these is *most* effective in making employees more willing to complete attitude and opinion surveys?
   A. Promise of specific results
   B. Early time off with pay
   C. Money
   D. Likelihood of meaningful changes
   E. None of these; employees are very resistant to surveys today.

7. All of the following are suggestions by Joan Tunstall for composing a clear e-mail message *except*
   A. making the message action-oriented.
   B. sending copies to all parties involved.
   C. ensuring that the message unfolds in logical steps.
   D. expressing empathy with readers through appropriate tone and choice of words.
   E. keeping the message concise.

8. The text sums up the future of telecommuting as
   A. a serious threat to productivity.
   B. just a passing fad.
   C. already obsolete.
   D. more than a passing fad.
   E. certain to be the standard work routine in 20 years.

9. Asking _____ questions is among the practical tips for effective listening.
   A. easy-to-answer   B. yes-or-no
   C. many   D. open-ended
   E. no more than two

10. The _____ is *not* among the four types of meetings discussed in this chapter.
    A. quarterly off-site review
    B. monthly strategic meeting
    C. weekly tactical meeting
    D. daily check-in
    E. annual employee recognition

See page T1 at the back of the text for answers to these questions. Want more questions? Visit the student Web site and take the ACE quizzes for more practice.

MANAGERS-IN-ACTION VIDEOS

3a

Organization Structures at Green Mountain Coffee Roasters

CEO and chairman Bob Stiller and his executive team provide a strategic overview of this 670-employee business based in Waterbury, Vermont. Functional departments are effectively blended with cross-functional teams. A culture of collaboration and cooperation, driven by principles and values, is a point of pride at this leading specialty coffee company. Decentralization is encouraged despite the company's growth. The organization is kept as flat as possible by relying on virtual teamwork via e-mail. For more background, see **www.greenmountaincoffee.com.**

Learning Objective

To show the importance of organization structure and design to overall organizational success.

Links to Textual Material

Chapter 9: Organizational characteristics; Mechanistic and organic organizations; Decentralization; Characteristics of the "new organizations;" Organizational culture; **Chapter 11:** E-mail communication

Discussion Questions

1 Which of the four common characteristics of organizations, presented in Chapter 9, are evident in this video? Explain.

2 Where does Green Mountain Coffee fit on the mechanistic-organic continuum? Explain.

3 What are the arguments for and against decentralization, as practiced at Green Mountain Coffee?

4 Which characteristics of the "new organizations," discussed in Chapter 9, can you detect in this video? Explain.

5 Explain how the culture at Green Mountain Coffee acts as a "social glue," as the term is used in Chapter 9.

3b

Managing Human Capital at Accenture

Gill Rider, chief leadership officer at the 100,000-employee consulting and computer outsourcing firm, explains her role as head of all corporate human resource functions. The strategic goal is to deploy the right people with the right skills at the right time. We learn about the company's fluid and virtual organization structure. An overriding goal is to put in place "authentic leaders" who are value creators, good at developing people, and good business operators. For more background, visit: **www.accenture.com.**

Learning Objective

To appreciate the central importance of effective human resource management.

Links to Textual Material

Chapter 9: Organic organizations; New organizations; **Chapter 10:** Human capital; Human resource management; **Chapter 14:** Leadership

Discussion Questions

1 Which organic characteristics (Table 9.2) are evident in this video? What difficulties might they cause?

2 What evidence of a "virtual organization" can you detect at Accenture? What associated problems might be encountered?

3 How are the concepts of human capital and authentic leaders interrelated at Accenture?

PART 4 Motivating and Leading

12

Motivating Job Performance

OBJECTIVES

- **Explain** the motivational lessons taught by Maslow's theory, Herzberg's theory, and expectancy theory.

- **Describe** how goal setting motivates performance.

- **Discuss** how managers can improve the motivation of personnel who perform routine tasks.

- **Explain** how job enrichment can be used to enhance the motivating potential of jobs.

- **Distinguish** extrinsic rewards from intrinsic rewards, and **list** four rules for administering extrinsic rewards effectively.

- **Explain** how quality control circles, open-book management, and self-managed teams promote employee participation.

- **Explain** how companies are striving to motivate today's diverse workforce with quality-of-work-life programs.

THE CHANGING WORKPLACE

Best Buy Smashes the Time Clock

Jason Dehne's brother called him one day in March and asked if he might like to have lunch and then visit the annual auto show in downtown Minneapolis. Without even checking his schedule, Dehne—a human resource manager of retirement and wealth strategies at Best Buy—agreed to the plan. The brothers spent a blissful Tuesday afternoon walking through showrooms full of the latest vehicles.

The story might not seem unusual if it were not for the fact that Dehne did not need to inform his boss of his whereabouts—he knew his boss could not care less. Nor did he feel guilty about it, since his job allows him to work wherever and whenever he wants as long as he completes projects on a timely basis.

Dehne participates in the consumer electronics retailer's novel Results-Only Work Environment (ROWE) program, which allows almost all of its 4,000 corporate employees to have the same freedom.

"Three years ago, if I was going to go to the car show I would have felt so guilty about it, I would have probably first worked the entire day and then left after 6 p.m. to get to the show [for] an hour or two" before closing time, Dehne says. Now, he continues, "people I work with don't know where I am all the time, but they know how to reach me—I have e-mail; I have a cell phone; I have voice mail. I don't report all of my activities, and I don't feel guilty about it anymore."

Begun four years ago at Best Buy's suburban Minneapolis campus, ROWE has been so successful that the company created a division, CultureRx, to promote it to other companies.

Meanwhile, Best Buy has started rolling out ROWE to the 100,000 employees in its retail stores. Figuring out just how that will work remains to be seen, however, since retail requires time clocks—anathema to the program's operating philosophy. . . .

ROWE was created by Jody Thompson and Cali Ressler when they were Best Buy employees; both now serve as principals of CultureRx. They share a passion for shaking up the American workplace and replacing the 9-to-5 paradigm with one that emphasizes freedom for employees and results for employers.

In a time when many white-collar Americans complain of being chained to desks for 50 to 70 hours a week and of having too little time for families and hobbies, CultureRx offers a remedy for the prevailing zeitgeist—a prescription that has attracted the attention of national media such as "60 Minutes," National Public Radio, the *New York Times* and *BusinessWeek*.

ROWE [offers] Best Buy employees whose departments participate in it the opportunity to do their work wherever and whenever they wish. They might play tennis in the morning, go windsurfing on a lake one afternoon, take a two-hour lunch or run a couple of days a week, as Dehne does.

Best Buy supervisors have been retrained to think less about line-of-sight management (Jim is at his desk, so he must be working) and more about the results of employees' work. Some employees work outside the office just one day a week, while others spend the majority of their time at home or other locations.

Thompson likens ROWE to the college lifestyle, in which studying and writing papers can be done anytime and anywhere—the library, the dorm room or a coffeehouse. "Going from college to the workforce is like going back to elementary school—you have no control," she says. "The conundrum is that managers are always trying to manage people—instead of results. Think about it. People come into the workforce as adults, and they're treated like children." . . .

Results from and reactions to ROWE have been encouraging. Productivity has increased an average of 35 percent within six to nine months in Best Buy units implementing ROWE, a figure based on metrics reported or estimated by managers using the new system. Voluntary turnover has dropped between 52 percent and 90 percent in three Best Buy divisions that CultureRx has studied. The three divisions were chosen because they were otherwise unaffected by company reorganizations or other initiatives.

Ressler cites this voluntary turnover figure as an indication that employees who once would have left Best Buy decided to stay put after ROWE was implemented. Thompson says one procurement division, an early adopter, saw voluntary turnover drop from 36.6 percent a year to less than 6 percent annually.

A CultureRx study of attitudes of ROWE participants found that feelings of pressure and a sense of working too hard have changed. "They feel happier about work. They feel more ownership of their work. They feel more clear about what they're doing for the company, and they see it [ROWE] as a benefit that's almost more important than any other," says Thompson. "They talk about it as if to say, 'Someone else could offer me more money, but I wouldn't go because I now have control over my time.'"

Phyllis Moen, sociology professor at the University of Minnesota, is studying ROWE and has looked at other work arrangements around the country. She finds the favorable results no surprise. Her own studies, and a large body of related workplace research, show "schedule control" leads to lower turnover, increased productivity and employee wellness. Having control over work schedules enhances "health, life quality and productiveness," she wrote in an e-mail interview. . . .

Managers "are scared to death" when the training process begins, Thompson says, but they soon come to realize freedom is rewarded with exceptional work. "Everyone wants the benefit, everyone is jazzed up about it, and no one wants to screw it up," she says. "Managers get better work and more work out of people because they've allowed employees their freedom. Managers find out pretty quickly they can trust people."

Source: Excerpted from Frank Jossi, "Clocking Out," *HR Magazine,* 52 (June 2007): 46–50. Copyright 2007 by Society for Human Resource Management (SHRM). Reproduced with permission of Society for Human Resource Management (SHRM) in the format Textbook via Copyright Clearance Center.

The complex webs of factors that motivate our work efforts are as varied as our occupations. Innovative initiatives such as Best Buy's ROWE program are needed today. As used here, the term **motivation** refers to a psychological process that gives behavior purpose and direction. By appealing to this process, managers attempt to get individuals to pursue organizational objectives willingly and persistently. Motivation theories are generalizations about the "why" and "how" of purposeful behavior.[2]

motivation: psychological process giving behavior purpose and direction

Figure 12.1 is an overview model for this chapter. The final element in this model, job performance, is the product of a combination of an individual's motivation and ability. Both are necessary. All the motivation in the world, for example, will not enable a computer-illiterate person to sit down and create a computer spreadsheet. Ability and skills, acquired through training and/or on-the-job experience, are also required. The individual's motivational factors—needs, satisfaction, expectations, and goals—are affected by challenging work, rewards, and participation.[3] We need to take a closer look at each key element in this model. A review of four basic motivation theories is a good starting point.

MOTIVATION THEORIES

Although there are dozens of different theories of motivation, four have emerged as the most influential: Maslow's theory of the hierarchy of needs, Herzberg's two-factor theory, expectancy theory, and goal-setting theory. Each approaches the motivation process from a different angle, each has supporters and detractors, and each teaches important lessons about motivation to work.

Maslow's Hierarchy of Needs Theory

In 1943 psychologist Abraham Maslow proposed that people are motivated by a predictable five-step hierarchy of needs.[4] Little did he realize at the time that his tentative proposal, based on an extremely limited clinical study of neurotic patients, would become one of the most influential concepts in the field of management. Perhaps because it is so straightforward and intuitively appealing, Maslow's theory has strongly influenced those interested in work behavior. Maslow's message was simply this: people always have needs, and when one need is relatively fulfilled, others emerge in a predictable sequence to take its place. From bottom to top, Maslow's needs hierarchy includes physiological, safety, love, esteem, and self-actualization

FIGURE **12.1** Individual Motivation and Job Performance

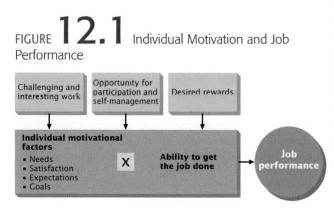

12a Quick Quiz

Howard Schultz, chairman of Starbucks, explains his company's formula for "exceeding employee expectations" so that they, in turn, will do the same for customers:

We provided comprehensive health care as well as equity in the form of stock options to all employees. For the first time in America's history, not only did part-time workers have a stake in the financial outcome of the company, but they had the kind of health-care programs that gave them the sense of security and a psychological contract with the company that the company was not going to leave people behind.

Source: As quoted in Jeremy B. Dann, "How to Find a Hit as Big as Starbucks," Business 2.0, 5 (May 2004): 66.

QUESTIONS:

Starbucks is trying to satisfy which particular needs in Maslow's hierarchy? Explain. Is this an effective approach to motivating today's employees?

For further information about the interactive annotations in this chapter, visit our student Web site.

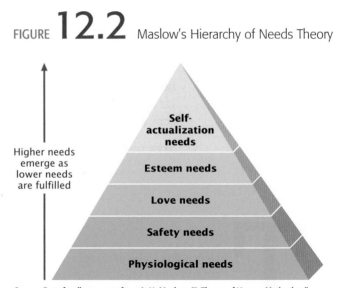

FIGURE **12.2** Maslow's Hierarchy of Needs Theory

Higher needs emerge as lower needs are fulfilled

Self-actualization needs

Esteem needs

Love needs

Safety needs

Physiological needs

Source: Data for diagram are from A. H. Maslow, "A Theory of Human Motivation," Psychological Review, 50 (July 1943): 370–396.

needs (see Figure 12.2). According to Maslow, most individuals are not consciously aware of these needs, yet we all supposedly proceed up the hierarchy of needs, one level at a time.

PHYSIOLOGICAL NEEDS. At the bottom of the hierarchy are needs based on physical drives, including the need for food, water, sleep, and sex. Fulfillment of these lowest-level needs enables the individual to survive, and nothing else is important when these bodily needs have not been satisfied. As Maslow observed, "It is quite true that man lives by bread alone—when there is no bread."[5] But today the average employee experiences little difficulty in satisfying physiological needs. Figuratively speaking, the prospect of eating more bread is not motivating when one has plenty of bread to eat.

SAFETY NEEDS. After our basic physiological needs have been relatively well satisfied, we next become concerned about our safety from the elements, enemies, and other threats. For reasons that are not entirely clear (terrorism? workplace violence?), researchers have documented a recent jump in the need for "feeling safe

at work."[6] Yet most of us, by virtue of earning a living, achieve a reasonable degree of fulfillment in this area. Unemployment assistance is a safety net for those between jobs. Insurance also helps fulfill safety needs, a point not lost on Coca-Cola Femsa, Mexico's primary bottler of Coke:

Many of the store owners in Mexico, Coke's second-biggest market, turned out to be single mothers and retirees who couldn't afford health insurance. Armed with that intelligence, Femsa was able to create an incentive program that rewards shopkeepers who sell enough Cokes with access to group insurance—a move that helped boost Coke's sales volume in Mexico 13 percent last year.[7]

LOVE NEEDS. A physiologically satisfied and secure person focuses next on satisfying needs for love and affection. This category is a powerful motivator of human behavior. People typically strive hard to achieve a sense of belonging with others. As with the first two levels of needs, relative satisfaction of love needs paves the way for the emergence of needs at the next higher level.

ESTEEM NEEDS. People who perceive themselves as worthwhile are said to possess high self-esteem.[8] Self-respect is the key to esteem needs. Much of our self-respect, and therefore our esteem, comes from being accepted and respected by others. It is important for those who are expected to help achieve organizational objectives to have their esteem needs relatively well fulfilled. But esteem needs cannot emerge if lower-level needs go unattended.

SELF-ACTUALIZATION NEEDS. At the very top of Maslow's hierarchy is the open-ended category *self-actualization needs*. It is open-ended because, as Maslow pointed out, it reflects the need "to become more and more what one is, to become everything that one is capable of becoming."[9] One may satisfy this need by striving to become a better homemaker, plumber, rock singer, or manager. For example, this is what Grammy Award–winning singer and song writer Alicia Keys told an interviewer who asked how she would follow up her hit *Fallin'* that got a lot of radio play:

> *I have to find the truth in everything I do, and I have to make sure it means something for me. . . . That's how I write, and that's who I am. I can't say, "Oh, let's get this radio song." All I know how to do is what I feel and what I love.*[10]

According to one management writer, the self-actualizing manager has the following characteristics:

1. Has warmth, closeness, and sympathy.
2. Recognizes and shares negative information and feelings.
3. Exhibits trust, openness, and candor.
4. Does not achieve goals by power, deception, or manipulation.
5. Does not project own feelings, motivations, or blame onto others.
6. Does not limit horizons; uses and develops body, mind, and senses.
7. Is not rationalistic; can think in unconventional ways.
8. Is not conforming; regulates behavior from within.[11]

Granted, this is a rather tall order to fill. It has been pointed out that "a truly self-actualized individual is more of an exception than the rule in the organizational context."[12] Whether productive organizations need more self-actualized individuals is subject to debate. On the positive side, self-actualized employees might help break down barriers to creativity and steer the organization in new directions. On the negative side, too many unconventional nonconformists could wreak havoc with the typical administrative setup dedicated to predictability.

RELEVANCE OF MASLOW'S THEORY FOR MANAGERS. Behavioral scientists who have attempted to test Maslow's theory in real life claim it has some deficiencies.[13] Even Maslow's hierarchical arrangement has been questioned. Practical evidence points toward a two-level rather than a five-level hierarchy. In this competing view, physiological and safety needs are arranged in hierarchical fashion, as Maslow contends. But beyond that point, any one of a number of needs may emerge as the single most important need, depending on the individual. Edward Lawler, a leading motivation researcher, observed, "Which higher-order needs come into play after the lower ones are satisfied and in which order they come into play cannot be predicted. If anything, it seems that most people are simultaneously motivated by several of the same-level needs."[14]

Although Maslow's theory has not stood up well under actual testing, it teaches managers one important lesson: a *fulfilled* need does not motivate an individual. For example, the promise of unemployment benefits may partially fulfill an employee's need for economic security (the safety need). But the added security of additional unemployment benefits will probably not motivate fully employed individuals to

12b Survey Says . . . Job Satisfaction Is Declining.

According to the Conference Board's annual survey of 5,000 households in the United States, the percent of employees who reported being satisfied with their jobs has dropped steadily between 1987 (61%) and 2006 (47%).

Source: Data from "U.S. Job Satisfaction Declines," USA Today (April 9, 2007): 1B.

QUESTION:
What, in your opinion, is responsible for this downward trend? Explain.

work any harder. Effective managers anticipate each employee's personal need profile and provide opportunities to fulfill *emerging* needs. Because challenging and worthwhile jobs and meaningful recognition tend to enhance self-esteem, the esteem level presents managers with the greatest opportunity to motivate better performance.

Herzberg's Two-Factor Theory

During the 1950s, Frederick Herzberg proposed a theory of employee motivation based on satisfaction.[15]

His theory implied that a satisfied employee is motivated from within to work harder and that a dissatisfied employee is not self-motivated. Herzberg's research uncovered two classes of factors associated with employee satisfaction and dissatisfaction (see Table 12.1). As a result, his concept has come to be called Herzberg's two-factor theory.

DISSATISFIERS AND SATISFIERS. Herzberg compiled his list of dissatisfiers by asking a sample of about 200 accountants and engineers to describe job situations in which they felt exceptionally bad about their jobs. An analysis of their responses revealed a consistent pattern. Dissatisfaction tended to be associated with complaints about the job context or factors in the immediate work environment.

Herzberg then drew up his list of satisfiers, factors responsible for self-motivation, by asking the same accountants and engineers to describe job situations in which they had felt exceptionally good about their jobs. Again, a patterned response emerged, but this time different factors were described: the opportunity to experience achievement, receive recognition, work on an interesting job, take responsibility, and experience advancement and growth. Herzberg observed that these satisfiers centered on the nature of the task itself. Employees appeared to be motivated by *job content*—that is, by what they actually did all day long. Consequently, Herzberg concluded that

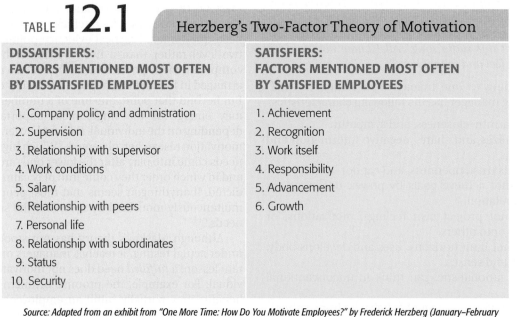

TABLE **12.1** Herzberg's Two-Factor Theory of Motivation

DISSATISFIERS: FACTORS MENTIONED MOST OFTEN BY DISSATISFIED EMPLOYEES	SATISFIERS: FACTORS MENTIONED MOST OFTEN BY SATISFIED EMPLOYEES
1. Company policy and administration	1. Achievement
2. Supervision	2. Recognition
3. Relationship with supervisor	3. Work itself
4. Work conditions	4. Responsibility
5. Salary	5. Advancement
6. Relationship with peers	6. Growth
7. Personal life	
8. Relationship with subordinates	
9. Status	
10. Security	

Source: Adapted from an exhibit from "One More Time: How Do You Motivate Employees?" by Frederick Herzberg (January–February 1968). Copyright © 1968 by the President and Fellows of Harvard College; all rights reserved. Reprinted by permission of HBS Publishing.

enriched jobs were the key to self-motivation. The work itself—not pay, supervision, or some other environmental factor—was the key to satisfaction and motivation.

IMPLICATIONS OF HERZBERG'S THEORY. By insisting that satisfaction is not the opposite of dissatisfaction, Herzberg encouraged managers to think carefully about what actually motivates employees. According to Herzberg, "the opposite of job satisfaction is not job dissatisfaction, but rather *no* job satisfaction; and similarly, the opposite of job dissatisfaction is not job satisfaction, but *no* dissatisfaction,"[16] Rather, the dissatisfaction-satisfaction continuum contains a zero midpoint at which both dissatisfaction and satisfaction are absent. An employee stuck on this midpoint, although not dissatisfied with pay and working conditions, is not particularly motivated to work hard because the job itself lacks challenge. Herzberg believes that the most managers can hope for when attempting to motivate employees with pay, status, working conditions, and other contextual factors is to reach the zero midpoint. But the elimination of dissatisfaction is not the same as truly motivating an employee. To satisfy and motivate employees, an additional element is required: meaningful, interesting, and challenging work. Herzberg believed that money is a weak motivational tool because, at best, it can only eliminate dissatisfaction.

Like Maslow, Herzberg triggered lively debate among motivation theorists. His assumption that job performance improves as satisfaction increases has been criticized for having a weak empirical basis. But a recent analysis of studies encompassing a total of 7,939 business units at 36 companies lends weight to Herzberg's model. The researchers' conclusion: "One implication is that changes in management practices that increase employee satisfaction may increase business-unit outcomes, including [greater productivity, fewer accidents, less turnover, and more] profit."[17] On the negative side, other researchers found that one person's dissatisfier may be another's satisfier (for example, money).[18] Nonetheless, Herzberg made a major contribution to motivation theory by emphasizing the motivating potential of enriched work. (Job enrichment is discussed in detail in the next section.)

Expectancy Theory

Both Maslow's and Herzberg's theories have been criticized for making unsubstantiated generalizations about what motivates people. Practical experience shows that people are motivated by lots of different things. Fortunately, expectancy theory, based largely on Victor H. Vroom's 1964 classic *Work and Motivation*, effectively deals with the highly personalized rational choices individuals make when faced with the prospect of having to work to achieve rewards. Individual perception, though secondary in the Maslow and Herzberg models, is central to expectancy theory. Accordingly, **expectancy theory** is a motivation model based on the assumption that motivational strength is determined by perceived probabilities of

> **expectancy theory:** model that assumes that motivational strength is determined by perceived probabilities of success

Our expectations affect our motivation to engage in all sorts of work and non-work behavior. For example, if you were jockey Tony McCoy and you had suffered a fractured vertebrae in a riding accident, what would be your expectations about riding again and possibly winning? As seen here, Tony did ride again, placing second aboard Kruguyrova in this major Irish steeplechase race.

> **expectancy:** the belief or expectation that one thing will lead to another

success. The term **expectancy** refers to the subjective probability (or expectation) that one thing will lead to another. Work-related expectations, like all other expectations, are shaped by ongoing personal experience. For instance, an employee's expectation of a raise, diminished after a request for a raise has been turned down, later rebounds when the supervisor indicates a willingness to reconsider the matter.

A BASIC EXPECTANCY MODEL.   Although Vroom and other expectancy theorists developed their models in somewhat complex mathematical terms, the descriptive model in Figure 12.3 is helpful for basic understanding. In this model, one's motivational strength increases as one's perceived effort-performance and performance-reward probabilities increase. All this is not as complicated as it sounds. For example, estimate your motivation to study if you expect to do poorly on a quiz no matter how hard you study (low effort-performance probability) and you know the quiz will not be graded (low performance-reward probability). Now contrast that estimate with your motivation to study if you believe that you can do well on the quiz with minimal study (high effort-performance probability) and that doing well on the quiz will significantly improve your grade in the course (high performance-reward probability). Like students, employees are motivated to expend effort when they believe it will ultimately lead to rewards they themselves value. This expectancy approach not only appeals strongly to common sense; it also has received encouraging empirical support from researchers.[19]

RELEVANCE OF EXPECTANCY THEORY FOR MANAGERS. According to expectancy theory, effort → performance → reward expectations determine whether motivation will be high or low. Although these expectations are in the mind of the employee, they can be influenced by managerial action and organizational experience. Training, combined with challenging but realistic objectives, gives people reason to believe that they can get the job done if they put forth the necessary effort. But perceived effort-performance probabilities are only half the battle. Listening skills enable managers to discover each individual's perceived performance-reward probabilities. Employees tend to work harder when they believe they have *a good chance* of getting *personally meaningful* rewards. Both sets of expectations require managerial attention. Each is a potential barrier to work motivation.

Goal-Setting Theory

Think of the three or four most successful people you know personally. Their success may have come via business or professional achievement, politics, athletics, or community service. Chances are they got where they are today by being goal-oriented. In other words, they committed themselves to (and achieved) progressively more challenging goals in their professional and personal affairs.[20] A prime example is Martina Navratilova, the Hall of Fame tennis star and champion of 18 Grand Slam tournaments:

> *Now that I am playing doubles, I want to be the best doubles player I can be right now. And that means doing everything I can to get to that point. You set your goals and then break it down and try to figure out how to get there. Then it becomes a palatable, doable daily routine.*
>
> *You say, "OK, how was my serve?" This is where I can make it better. "How is my level of fitness?" Well, I am in shape, but I could have better endurance. And then you get into the solution. Maybe I need to start running more long distance or I need to practice more of my backhand down the line or I need to think more about strategy.*[21]

FIGURE **12.3** A Basic Expectancy Model

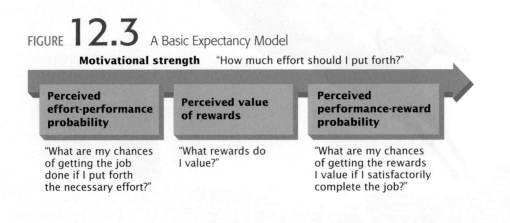

Motivational strength   "How much effort should I put forth?"

Perceived effort-performance probability	Perceived value of rewards	Perceived performance-reward probability
"What are my chances of getting the job done if I put forth the necessary effort?"	"What rewards do I value?"	"What are my chances of getting the rewards I value if I satisfactorily complete the job?"

Biographies and autobiographies of successful people in all walks of life generally attest to the virtues of goal setting. Accordingly, goal setting is acknowledged today as a respected and useful motivation theory.

Within an organizational context, **goal setting** is the process of improving individual or group job performance with formally stated objectives, deadlines, or quality standards.[22] Management by objectives (MBO), discussed in Chapter 6, is a specific application of goal setting that advocates participative and measurable objectives. Also, recall from Chapter 6 that managers tend to use the terms *goal* and *objective* interchangeably.

goal setting: process of improving performance with objectives, deadlines, or quality standards

A GENERAL GOAL-SETTING MODEL. Thanks to motivation researchers such as Edwin A. Locke and Gary P. Latham, there is a comprehensive body of knowledge about goal setting.[23] Goal setting has been researched more rigorously than the three motivation theories just discussed.[24] Locke and Latham pinpointed the power of goals in their recent summary of goal-setting research evidence:

> *Why are goals so effective? A goal is a level of performance proficiency that we wish to attain, usually within a specified time period. Thus goal setting is first and foremost a discrepancy-creating process, in that the goal creates constructive discontent with our present performance.*[25]

Important lessons from goal-setting theory and research are incorporated in the general model in Figure 12.4. This model shows how properly conceived goals trigger a motivational process that improves performance. Let us explore the key components of this goal-setting model, while keeping in mind that a Franklin Covey survey of workers in the United States found that only 19 percent had "clearly defined work goals."[26]

PERSONAL OWNERSHIP OF CHALLENGING GOALS. In Chapter 6, the discussion of MBO and writing good objectives stressed how goal effectiveness is enhanced by *specificity, difficulty,* and *participation.* Measurable and challenging goals encourage an individual or group to stretch while trying to attain progressively more difficult levels of achievement. For instance, parents who are paying a college student's tuition and expenses are advised to specify a challenging grade point goal rather than simply to tell their son or daughter, "Just do your best." Otherwise, the student could show up at the end of the semester with two Cs and three Ds, saying, "Well, I did my best!" It is important to note that goals need to be difficult enough to be challenging, but they should not be impossible. Impossible goals hamper performance; they are a handy excuse for not even trying.[27]

Participation in the goal-setting process gives the individual *personal ownership.* From the employee's viewpoint, it is "something I helped develop, not just my boss's wild idea." Feedback on performance operates in concert with well-conceived goals. Feedback lets the person or group know if things are on track or if corrective action is required to reach the goal. An otherwise excellent goal-setting program can be compromised by lack of timely and relevant feedback from managers. Researchers have documented the motivational value of matching *specific goals* with *equally specific feedback.*[28] Sam Walton, the founder of Wal-Mart, was a master of blending goals and feedback. For example, consider this exchange between

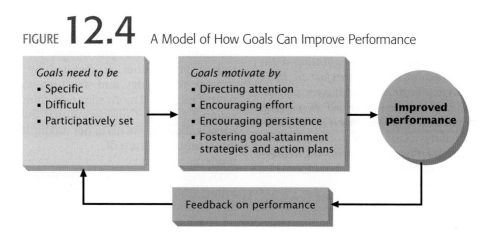

FIGURE **12.4** A Model of How Goals Can Improve Performance

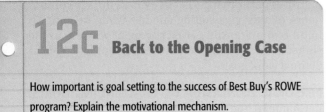

12c   Back to the Opening Case

How important is goal setting to the success of Best Buy's ROWE program? Explain the motivational mechanism.

Sam Walton and an employee during one of his regular store visits.

A manager rushes up with an associate in tow.

"Mr. Walton, I want you to meet Renee. She runs one of the top ten pet departments in the country."

"Well, Renee, bless your heart. What percentage of the store [sales] are you doing?"

"Last year it was 3.1 percent," Renee says, "but this year I'm trying for 3.3 percent."

"Well, Renee, that's amazing," says Sam. "You know our average pet department only does about 2.4 percent. Keep up the great work."[29]

HOW DO GOALS ACTUALLY MOTIVATE?   Goal-setting researchers say goals perform a motivational function by doing the four things listed in the center of Figure 12.4. First, a goal is an exercise in selective perception because it directs one's *attention* to a specific target. Second, a goal encourages one to exert *effort* toward achieving something specific. Third, because a challenging goal requires sustained or repeated effort, it encourages *persistence*. Fourth, because a goal creates the problem of bridging the gap between actual and desired, it fosters the creation of *strategies and action plans* (prompted by the "constructive discontent" Locke and Latham mentioned earlier). Consider, for example, how all these motivational components were activated by the following program at Marriott's hotel chain.

For years, Marriott's room-service business didn't live up to its potential. But after initiating a 15-minute-delivery guarantee for breakfast in 1985, Marriott's breakfast business—the biggest portion of its room-service revenue—jumped 25 percent. [Hotel guests got their breakfast free if it was delivered late.] Marriott got employees to devise ways to deliver the meals on time, including having deliverers carry walkie-talkies so they [could] receive instructions more quickly.[30]

Marriott's goal, increased room-service revenue, was the focal point for this program. In effect, the service-guarantee program told Marriott employees that prompt room service was important, and they rose to the challenge with persistent and creative effort. Clear, reasonable, and challenging goals, reinforced by specific feedback and meaningful rewards, are indeed a powerful motivational tool.[31]

PRACTICAL IMPLICATIONS OF GOAL-SETTING THEORY.   Because the model in Figure 12.4 is a generic one, the performance environment may range from athletics to academics to the workplace. The motivational mechanics of goal setting are the same, regardless of the targeted performance. If you learn to be an effective goal setter in school, that ability will serve you faithfully throughout life.

Anyone tempted to go through life without goals should remember the smiling Cheshire Cat's good advice to Alice when she asked him to help her find her way through Wonderland.

"Would you tell me, please, which way I ought to walk from here?"

"That depends a good deal on where you want to get to," replied the Cat.

"I don't much care where—" said Alice.

"Then it doesn't matter which way you walk," said the Cat.

"—so long as I get somewhere," Alice added as an explanation.

"Oh, you're sure to do that," said the Cat, "if you only walk long enough."[32]

MOTIVATION THROUGH JOB DESIGN

A job serves two separate but intertwined functions. It generates value for the organization and income for the individual. Thus **job design**, the delineation of task responsibilities as dictated by organizational strategy, technology, and structure, is a key determinant of individual motivation and ultimately of organizational success. Considering that the average adult spends about half of his or her waking life at work, jobs are a central feature of modern existence. A challenging and interesting job can add zest and meaning to one's life. Boring and tedious

job design: creating task responsibilities based on strategy, technology, and structure

jobs, on the other hand, can become a serious threat to one's motivation to work hard, not to mention their negative effect on one's physical and mental health. Concern about uneven productivity growth, product quality, and declining employee satisfaction has persuaded managers to consider two job design strategies.[33]

Strategy One: Fitting People to Jobs

For technological or economic reasons, work sometimes must be divided into routine and repetitive tasks. Imagine, for example, doing Paula Villalta's job at Chung's Gourmet Foods in Houston, Texas:

> *Quickly wrapping one egg roll after another, Paula Villalta becomes rapt herself.*
>
> *Her fingers move with astonishing speed, placing a glutinous vegetable mixture on a small sheet of pastry before rolling it closed in one smooth stroke. But the secret to her swiftness lies not just in her nimble hands.*
>
> *The real key, says Ms. Villalta, pointing to her head, is staying completely focused throughout an eight-hour shift. . . .*
>
> *The results are stunning. The average wrapper at Chung's Gourmet churns out about 4,000 shrimp, pork, vegetable, or chicken egg rolls per shift. Ms. Villalta typically tops 6,000.*[34]

In routine tasks, steps can be taken to avoid chronic dissatisfaction and bolster motivation.[35] Three proven alternatives are realistic job previews, job

rotation, and limited exposure. Each involves adjusting the person rather than the job in the person-job equation. Hence, each entails creating a more compatible fit between an individual and a routine or fragmented job. (In line with this approach is the employment of mentally disadvantaged workers, often in sheltered workshops.)

REALISTIC JOB PREVIEWS. Unrealized expectations are a major cause of job dissatisfaction, low motivation, and turnover. Managers commonly create unrealistically high expectations in job applicants to entice them to accept a position. This has proved particularly troublesome with regard to routine tasks. Dissatisfaction too often sets in when lofty expectations are brought down to earth by dull or tedious work. **Realistic job previews** (RJPs), honest explanations of what a job actually entails, have been successful in helping to avoid employee dissatisfaction resulting from unrealized expectations. On-the-job and laboratory research have demonstrated the practical value of giving a realistic preview of both positive and negative aspects to applicants for highly specialized and/or difficult jobs.

> **realistic job previews:** honest explanations of what a job actually entails

A recent statistical analysis of 40 different RJP studies revealed these patterns: fewer dropouts during the recruiting process, lower initial expectations, and lower turnover and higher performance once on the job. The researcher recommended a

ans of the Discovery Channel's *Dirty Jobs* are familiar with the wild and crazy situations Mike Rowe gets himself into while performing not-so-glamorous everday jobs. Aside from being fun entertainment, *Dirty Jobs* should motivate college students to stay in school and get good grades. *Dirty Jobs* also helps us empathize with the folks who perform the dirty work that makes modern life possible. Don't even ask what Mike's up to here.

contingency approach to the form and timing of RJPs. *Written* RJPs are better for reducing the dropout rate during the recruiting process, whereas *verbal* RJPs more effectively reduce post-hiring turnover (quitting). "RJPs given just *before* hiring are advisable to reduce attrition [dropouts] from the recruitment process and to reduce . . . turnover, but organizations wishing to improve employee performance should provide RJPs *after* job acceptance, as part of a realistic socialization effort."[36]

JOB ROTATION.   As the term is used here, **job rotation** involves periodically moving people from one specialized job to another. Such movement prevents stagnation. Other reasons for rotating personnel include compensating for a labor shortage, enhancing safety, training, and preventing fatigue.[37] *Carpal tunnel syndrome* and other painful and disabling injuries stemming from repetitive-motion tasks can be reduced significantly through job rotation. For example, Nissan, at its U.S. vehicle assembly plants, "has workers do four different jobs during a typical eight-hour shift, to try to cut down on repetitive-motion injuries. Nissan claims that injury rates have fallen 60% in the past two years."[38] Meanwhile, the FBI rotates its agents off the drug squad periodically to discourage corruption.[39] If highly repetitive and routine jobs are unavoidable, job rotation, by introducing a modest degree of novelty, can help prevent boredom and resulting alienation.

> **job rotation:** moving people from one specialized job to another

Of course, a balance needs to be achieved—people should be rotated often enough to fight boredom and injury and acquire valuable cross-training, but not so often that they feel unfairly manipulated or disoriented. *Business Week* recently summed up the problem of too-rapid job rotation in the management ranks at Ford Motor Company:

> *Ford has a long tradition of rapidly cycling executives through new posts every two years or so. In fact, managers refer to their posts as "assignments" rather than jobs. But one consequence of employees' need to make their mark in such a short time was to discourage cooperation with other divisions and regions, whose products were often on a different timetable. And no engineer ever got noticed by carrying over his predecessor's design or idea—even if it saved big money.[40]*

Ford's new CEO Alan R. Mulally has slowed the job-rotation cycle to foster cooperation.

LIMITED EXPOSURE.   Another way of coping with the need to staff a highly fragmented and tedious job is to limit the individual's exposure to it. A number of organizations have achieved high productivity among personnel doing routine tasks by allowing them to earn an early quitting time.[41] This technique, called **contingent time off** (CTO) or earned time off, involves establishing a challenging yet fair daily performance standard, or quota, and letting employees go home when it is reached. The following CTO plan was implemented at a large manufacturing plant where the employees were producing about 160 units a day with 10 percent rejects.

> **contingent time off:** rewarding people with early time off when they get the job done

> *If the group produced at 200 units with three additional good units for each defective unit, then they could leave the work site for the rest of the day. Within a week of implementing this CTO intervention, the group was producing 200+ units with an average of 1.5 percent rejects. These employees, who had formerly put in an 8-hour day, were now working an average of 6.5 hours per day and, importantly, they increased their performance by 25 percent.[42]*

Some employees find the opportunity to earn eight hours of pay for six hours of steady effort extremely motivating.

Companies using contingent time off report successful results. Impressive evidence comes from a large-scale survey of 1,598 U.S. companies employing about 10 percent of the civilian workforce. Among nine nontraditional reward systems, "earned time off" ranked only eighth in terms of use (5 percent of the companies). But among those using it, earned time off ranked *second* in terms of positive impact on job performance—an 85 percent approval rating.[43] Thus, the use of contingent time off has not yet reached its excellent potential as a motivational tool.

Strategy Two: Fitting Jobs to People

The second job-design strategy calls for managers to consider changing the job instead of the person. Two job-design experts have proposed that managers address the question "How can we achieve a fit between persons and their jobs that fosters *both* high work productivity and a high-quality organizational experience for the people who do the work?"[44] Two techniques for moving in this direction are job enlargement and job enrichment.

JOB ENLARGEMENT. As used here, **job enlargement** is the process of combining two or more specialized tasks in a work flow sequence into a single job. Aetna used this technique to give some of its office employees a measure of relief from staring at a video display terminal (VDT) all day:

> **job enlargement:** combining two or more specialized tasks to increase motivation

> *Aetna Life & Casualty in Hartford . . . reorganized its payroll department to combine ten full-time data-entry jobs with ten jobs that involve paper-work and telephoning. Now nobody in the depart-ment spends more than 70 percent of [the] day on a VDT. Morale and productivity have gone up dra-matically since the change, says Richard Assunto, Aetna's payroll services manager.*[45]

A moderate degree of complexity and novelty can be introduced in this manner. But critics claim that two or more potentially boring tasks do not necessarily make one challenging job. Furthermore, organized labor has criticized job enlargement as a devious ploy for getting more work for the same amount of money. But if pay and performance are kept in balance, bore-dom and alienation can be kept somewhat at bay by job enlargement.

JOB ENRICHMENT. In general terms, **job enrichment** is redesigning a job to increase its motivating poten-tial.[46] Job enrichment increases the challenge of one's work by reversing the trend toward greater spe-cialization. Unlike job enlargement, which merely combines equally sim-ple tasks, job enrich-ment builds more com-plexity and depth into jobs by introducing planning and decision-making responsibility normally carried out at higher levels. Thus, enriched jobs are said to be *vertically loaded,* whereas enlarged

> **job enrichment:** redesigning jobs to increase their motivational potential

jobs are *horizontally loaded.* Managing an entire project can be immensely challenging and motivat-ing thanks to vertical job loading. Scott Nichols, a home construction foreman, had this to say about his job:

> *I find it very rewarding. Just building something, creating something, and actually seeing your work. . . . You start with a bare, empty lot with grass growing up and then you build a house. A lot of times you'll build a house for a family, and you see them move in, that's pretty gratifying. . . . I'm proud of that.*[47]

Jobs can be enriched by upgrading five core dimensions of work: (1) skill variety, (2) task identity, (3) task significance, (4) autonomy, and (5) job feed-back. Each of these core dimensions deserves a closer look.

- *Skill variety.* The degree to which the job requires a variety of different activities in carrying out the work, involving the use of a number of different skills and talents of the person
- *Task identity.* The degree to which the job requires completion of a "whole" and identifiable piece of work; that is, doing a job from beginning to end with a visible outcome
- *Task significance.* The degree to which the job has a substantial impact on the lives of other people, whether those people are in the immedi-ate organization or in the world at large
- *Autonomy.* The degree to which the job provides substantial freedom, independence, and discre-tion to the individual in scheduling the work and in determining the procedures to be used in carrying it out
- *Job feedback.* The degree to which carrying out the work activities required by the job provides the individual with direct and clear information about the effectiveness of his or her performance[48]

Figure 12.5 shows the theoretical connection be-tween enriched core job characteristics and high motivation and satisfaction. At the heart of this job-enrichment model are three psychological states that highly specialized jobs usually do not satisfy: mean-ingfulness, responsibility, and knowledge of results.

It is important to note that not all employees respond favorably to enriched jobs. Personal traits and motives influence the connection between core job characteristics and desired outcomes. Only those with the necessary knowledge and skills plus a desire for personal growth will be motivated by enriched

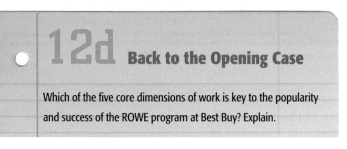

12d Back to the Opening Case

Which of the five core dimensions of work is key to the popularity and success of the ROWE program at Best Buy? Explain.

FIGURE **12.5** How Job Enrichment Works

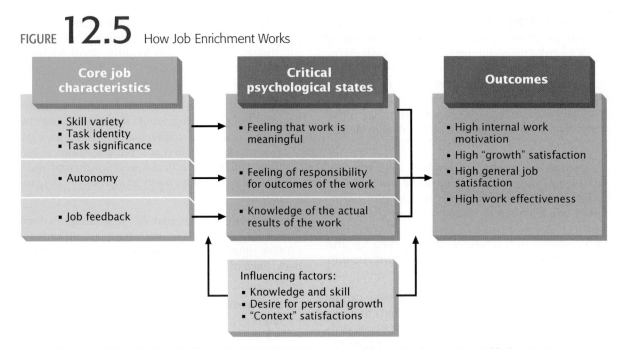

Source: J. Hackman/G. Oldham, Work Redesign (Figure 4.6). © 1980. Reprinted by permission of Pearson Education, Inc., Upper Saddle River, New Jersey.

work. Furthermore, in keeping with Herzberg's two-factor theory, dissatisfaction with factors such as pay, physical working conditions, or supervision can neutralize enrichment efforts. Researchers have reported that fear of failure, lack of confidence, and lack of trust in management's intentions can stand in the way of effective job enrichment. But job enrichment can and does work when it is carefully thought out, when management is committed to its long-term success, and when employees desire additional challenge.[49]

MOTIVATION THROUGH REWARDS

All workers, including volunteers who donate their time to worthy causes, expect to be rewarded in some way for their contributions. **Rewards** can be defined broadly as the material and psychological payoffs for performing tasks in the workplace. Managers have found

rewards: material and psychological payoffs for working

that job performance and satisfaction may be improved by properly administered rewards. Today, rewards vary greatly in both type and scope, depending on one's employer and geographic location. One indicator of the vastness of this topic is the book *The 1001 Rewards & Recognition Fieldbook.*[50]

In this section, we distinguish between extrinsic and intrinsic rewards, review alternative employee compensation plans, and discuss the effective management of extrinsic rewards.

Extrinsic versus Intrinsic Rewards

There are two different categories of rewards. **Extrinsic rewards** are payoffs granted to the individual by other people. Examples include money, employee benefits, promotions, recognition, status symbols, and praise. The second category consists of **intrinsic rewards**, which are self-granted and internally experienced payoffs. Among intrinsic rewards are a sense of accomplishment, self-esteem, and self-actualization.[51] For example, Audrey Tsao, a surgeon in

extrinsic rewards: payoffs, such as money, that are granted by others

intrinsic rewards: self-granted and internally experienced payoffs, such as a feeling of accomplishment

This assistant pastry chef aboard Cunard's luxury ocean liner Queen Mary 2 is putting the finishing touches on a tray of tasty desserts. Pay and recognition are welcome extrinsic rewards for this work, but the pastry staff gets powerful intrinsic rewards from knowing that a detailed recipe, ingredients, and preparation have come together to perfection. As a pastry chef once noted, if a chef overcooks a steak it can end up in tomorrow's stew. If a dessert is a flop it ends up in the garbage can.

Arizona who specializes in hip and knee replacements, says,

> My patients keep me going. . . . They arrive in pain, lacking mobility, and afterward they can walk again and enjoy life. There are very few professions where you can make such a big impact on someone's life, even in other fields of medicine.[52]

Usually, on-the-job extrinsic and intrinsic rewards are intermingled. For instance, employees often experience a psychological boost, in addition to reaping material benefits, when they complete a big project. Harvard Business School's Abraham Zaleznik offered this perspective:

> I think a paycheck buys you a baseline level of performance. But one thing that makes a good leader is the ability to offer people intrinsic rewards, the tremendous lift that comes from being aware of one's own talents and wanting to maximize them.[53]

(For an example of another effective kind of reward, see Best Practices.)

Employee Compensation

Compensation deserves special attention at this point because money is the universal extrinsic reward.[54] Managers need to be effective and efficient in this area because, when nonwage benefits are added in, "labor costs are about two-thirds of total business expenses."[55] Employee compensation is a complex area fraught with legal, ethical, and tax implications.[56] Although an exhaustive treatment of employee compensation plans is beyond our present purpose, we can

identify major types. Table 12.2 lists and briefly describes ten different pay plans. Two are nonincentive plans, seven qualify as incentive plans, and one plan is in a category of its own. Each type of pay plan has advantages and disadvantages. Therefore, there is no single best plan suitable for all employees. Indeed, two experts at the U.S. Bureau of Labor Statistics say the key words in compensation for the next 25 years will be *flexible* and *varied*. A diverse workforce will demand an equally diverse array of compensation plans.[57]

Improving Performance with Extrinsic Rewards

Extrinsic rewards, if they are to motivate job performance effectively, need to be administered in ways that (1) satisfy operative needs, (2) foster positive expectations, (3) ensure equitable distribution, and (4) reward results. Let us see how these four criteria can be met relative to the ten different pay plans in Table 12.2.

REWARDS MUST SATISFY INDIVIDUAL NEEDS. Whether it is a pay raise or a pat on the back, a reward has no motivational impact unless it satisfies an operative need.[58] Not all people need the same things, and one person may need different things at different times. Money is a powerful motivator for those who seek security through material wealth. But the promise of more money may mean little to a financially secure person who seeks ego gratification from challenging work. People's needs concerning when and how they want to be paid also vary.

BEST PRACTICES
Pat McGovern Motivates Through Respect

The genius of Pat McGovern is the way he makes things all about you. That impressed me hugely, because when I first met Pat back in 1989 I wasn't the sort of person anything was all about. I was a new copy editor at *CIO* magazine; Pat was (still is) the founder and chairman of *CIO's* parent, International Data Group, a then $400 million technology publishing and research empire. It hadn't occurred to me that the twain would meet, so I was startled (confused, marginally freaked) when a tall, ruddy man loomed in the entrance to my cubicle a few weeks before Christmas.

Pat thanked me for my contributions. He asked how things were going and looked vaguely disappointed when all I could muster was an unilluminating "Fine." Then he complimented me on a column I had ghostwritten for some technology honcho. The column was my most substantive accomplishment to date and the thing I was proudest of. But my name didn't appear on it anywhere, so how did he know? After three or four minutes, he handed me my bonus and proceeded to the next cubicle.

The formula for Pat's Christmas calls—expression of gratitude/request for feedback/congratulations on specific achievement/delivery of loot—never varied, even as IDG grew into the $2.4 billion global behemoth it is today. To personally thank most every person in every business unit in the U.S., more than 1,500 employees, takes almost four weeks, he told me years later: Managers provide him with a list of accomplishments for all their reports, and Pat memorizes them the night before his visits. He does this because he wants employees to know that he sees them—really sees them—as individuals, and that he considers what they do all day to be meaningful.

Not only does Pat care about his people; he also believes in them. His commitment to decentralization has created a constellation of motivated business units that make their own decisions about everything from how to reward staff to what new businesses to launch.

Source: From Leigh Buchanan, "For Knowing the Power of Respect," Inc. Magazine, 26, April 2004, p. 143. Reprinted by permission of the author.

Because cafeteria compensation is unique and particularly promising, we shall examine it more closely. **Cafeteria compensation** (also called life-cycle benefits) is a plan that allows each employee to determine the make-up of his or her benefit package.[59] Because today's nonwage benefits are a significant portion of total compensation, the motivating potential of such a privilege can be sizable.

cafeteria compensation: plan that allows employees to select their own mix of benefits

> Under these plans, employers provide minimal "core" coverage in life and health insurance, vacations, and pensions. The employee buys additional benefits to suit [his or her] own needs, using credit based on salary, service, and age.
>
> The elderly bachelor, for instance, may pass up the maternity coverage he would receive, willy-nilly, under conventional plans and "buy" additional pension contributions instead. The mother whose children are covered by her husband's employee health insurance policy may choose legal and dental care insurance instead.[60]

Although some organizations have balked at installing cafeteria compensation because of added administrative expense, the number of programs in effect in the United States has grown steadily. Cafeteria compensation enhances employee satisfaction, according to at least one study,[61] and represents a revolutionary step toward fitting rewards to people, rather than vice versa.

EMPLOYEES MUST BELIEVE EFFORT WILL LEAD TO REWARD. According to expectancy theory, an employee will not strive for an attractive reward unless it is perceived as being attainable. For example, the promise of an expenses-paid trip to Hawaii for the leading salesperson will prompt additional efforts at sales only among those who feel they have a decent chance of winning. Those who believe they have little chance of winning will not be motivated to try any

TABLE **12.2** Guide to Employee Compensation Plans

PAY PLAN	DESCRIPTION/CALCULATION	MAIN ADVANTAGE	MAIN DISADVANTAGE
Nonincentive			
Hourly wage	Fixed amount per hour worked	Time is easier to measure than performance	Little or no incentive to work hard
Annual salary	Contractual amount per year	Easy to administer	Little or no incentive to work hard
Incentive			
Piece rate	Fixed amount per unit of output	Pay tied directly to personal output	Negative association with sweatshops and rate-cutting abuses
Sales commission	Fixed percentage of sales revenue	Pay tied directly to personal volume of business	Morale problem when sales personnel earn more than other employees
Merit pay	Bonus granted for outstanding performance	Gives salaried employees incentive to work harder	Fairness issue raised when tied to subjective appraisals
Profit sharing	Distribution of specified percentage of bottom-line profits	Individual has a personal stake in firm's profitability	Profits affected by more than just performance (for example, by prices and competition)
Gain sharing	Distribution of specified percentage of productivity gains and/or cost savings	Encourages employees to work harder *and* smarter	Calculations can get cumbersome
Pay-for-knowledge	Salary or wage rates tied to degrees earned or skills mastered	Encourages lifelong learning	Tends to inflate training and labor costs
Stock options	Selected employees earn right to acquire firm's stock free or at a discount	Gives individual a personal stake in firm's financial performance	Can be resented by ineligible personnel; morale tied to stock price
Other			
Cafeteria compensation (life-cycle benefits)	Employee selects personal mix of benefits from an array of options	Tailored benefits package fits individual needs	Can be costly to administer

harder than usual. Incentive pay plans, especially merit pay, profit sharing, gain sharing, and stock options, need to be designed and communicated in a way that will foster believable effort-reward linkages.[62]

REWARDS MUST BE EQUITABLE. Something is equitable if people perceive it to be fair and just. Each of us carries in our head a pair of scales upon which we weigh equity.[63] Figure 12.6 shows one scale for *personal equity* and another for *social equity*. The personal equity scale tests the relationship between effort expended and rewards received. The social equity scale, in contrast, compares our own effort-reward ratio with that of someone else in the same situation. We are motivated to seek personal and social equity and to avoid inequity.[64] An interesting aspect of

FIGURE **12.6** Personal and Social Equity

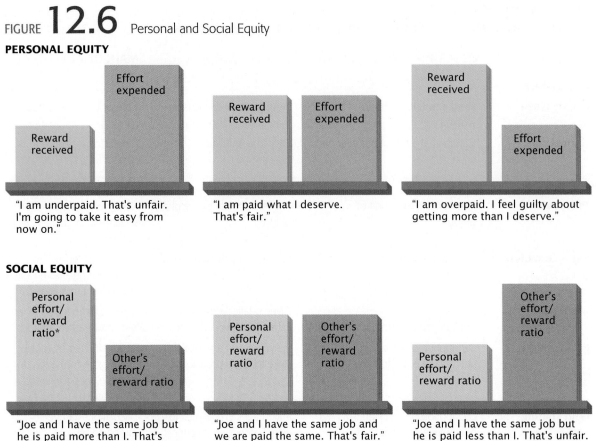

PERSONAL EQUITY

"I am underpaid. That's unfair. I'm going to take it easy from now on."

"I am paid what I deserve. That's fair."

"I am overpaid. I feel guilty about getting more than I deserve."

SOCIAL EQUITY

"Joe and I have the same job but he is paid more than I. That's unfair. I'm going to take it easy. Is Joe special?"

"Joe and I have the same job and we are paid the same. That's fair."

"Joe and I have the same job but he is paid less than I. That's unfair. He's going to wonder why I receive special treatment."

* The lower the effort/reward ratio, the greater the motivation.

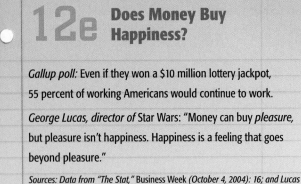

12e Does Money Buy Happiness?

Gallup poll: Even if they won a $10 million lottery jackpot, 55 percent of working Americans would continue to work.

George Lucas, director of Star Wars: "Money can buy *pleasure,* but pleasure isn't happiness. Happiness is a feeling that goes beyond pleasure."

Sources: Data from "The Stat," Business Week (October 4, 2004): 16; and Lucas as quoted in Craig Wilson, "How Much Would Make You Smile?" USA Today (December 27, 2004): 2B.

QUESTIONS:
Some management theorists say money isn't a motivator. Do you agree or disagree? Why? When it comes to motivating you to do your best, what role does money play?

research on this topic is its demonstration that inequity is perceived by those who are *overpaid* as well as by those who are underpaid.[65] Because perceived inequity is associated with feelings of dissatisfaction and anger, jealousy, or guilt, inequitable reward schemes tend to be counterproductive and are ethically questionable. Record-setting executive pay in recent years of painful downsizings, massive layoffs, and stock market underperformance has been roundly criticized as inequitable and unfair. Take Terry Semel, for instance. The CEO of Yahoo took home $71.7 million in 2006, a year when Yahoo's stock took a 38 percent dive.[66] In fact, when 400 college-educated people were recently asked, "What has undermined your trust in companies?" 60 percent said "Excessive compensation for executives."[67] One notable exception to this trend occurred at Xilinx, the San Jose, California, semiconductor maker: "Xilinx survived the recent tech downturn by cutting salaries across the board—the CEO took a 27% hit—instead of resorting to mass layoffs."[68]

REWARDS MUST BE LINKED TO PERFORMANCE. Ideally, there should be an if-then relationship between task performance and extrinsic rewards. Traditional hourly wage and annual salary pay plans are weak in this regard. They do little more than reward the person for showing up at work. Managers can strengthen motivation to work by making sure that those who give a little extra get a little extra. In addition to piece-rate and sales-commission plans, merit pay, profit sharing, gain sharing, and stock option plans are popular ways of linking pay and performance.[69] Cash bonuses, when paid promptly to maximize the *positive reinforcement* effect, can boost motivation:

> *If an employee's performance has been exceptional—such as filling in for a sick colleague, perhaps, or working nights or weekends or cutting costs for the company—the employer may reward the worker with a one-time bonus of $50, $100 or $500 shortly after the noteworthy actions.*
>
> *"Your boss walking by and saying, 'That's a great job,' and showing up the next day with a check or gift certificate really underscores the specific thing you just did," says Salary.com's [senior vice president of compensation Bill] Coleman. That differentiates spot bonuses from more structured programs such as annual bonuses: While those larger yearly awards can be a crucial part of an overall compensation package, annual bonuses are often distributed so long after the fact that employees have forgotten the impressive behavior for which they're being paid, he says.*[70]

Harvard Business Review, September 2006

"HIGGINS, BOTH YOU AND FERGUSON WILL BE GOING AFTER THE SAME CARROT."

Positive reinforcement is discussed in Chapter 14, in the context of behavior modification.

The concept of team-based incentive pay as a way of rewarding teamwork and cooperation has been slow to take hold in the United States for two reasons: (1) it goes against the grain of an individualistic culture, and (2) poorly conceived and administered plans have given team-based pay a bad reputation.[71]

All incentive pay plans should be carefully conceived because undesirable behavior may inadvertently be encouraged. Consider, for example, what the head of Nucor Corporation, a successful minimill steel company, had to say about his firm's bonus system:

> *[Nucor's] bonus system . . . is very tough. If you're late even five minutes, you lose your bonus for the day. If you're late more than 30 minutes, or you're absent because of sickness or anything else, you lose your bonus for the week. Now, we do have what we call four "forgiveness" days during the year when you can be sick or you have to close on a house or your wife is having a baby. But only four. We have a melter, Phil Johnson, down in Darlington, and one of the workers came in one day and said that Phil had been in an automobile*

12f Survey Says . . . Pay for *What* Performance?

A survey of 10,000 employees asked the question: "Do employees who do a better job receive more money and benefits than those in the same position who do a poor job?"

Responses: 47 percent said "No," 41 percent said "Yes," and 12 percent said "Not sure."

Source: Quoted and adapted from "Good Performance May Not Mean Good Pay," USA Today (August 29, 2007): 1B.

QUESTIONS:
What are the general motivational implications of this situation? What pay-for-performance recommendations would you make to improve matters?

accident and was sitting beside his car off of Route 52, holding his head. So the foreman asked, "Why didn't you stop and help him?" And the guy said, "And lose my bonus?"[72]

Like goals, incentive plans foster selective perception.[73] Consequently, managers need to make sure goals and incentives point people in ethical directions.

MOTIVATION THROUGH EMPLOYEE PARTICIPATION

While noting that the term *participation* has become a "stewpot" into which every conceivable kind of management fad has been tossed, one management scholar helpfully identified four key areas of participative management. Employees may participate in (1) setting goals, (2) making decisions, (3) solving problems, and (4) designing and implementing organizational changes.[74] Thus, **participative management** is defined as the process of empowering employees to assume greater control of the workplace.[75] When personally and meaningfully involved, above and beyond just doing assigned tasks, employees are said to be more motivated and productive. In fact, a study of 164 New Zealand companies with at least 100 employees found lower employee turnover and higher organizational productivity among firms using participative management practices.[76]

participative management: empowering employees to assume greater control of the workplace

This section focuses on three approaches to participation. They are quality control circles, open-book management, and self-managed teams. After taking a closer look at each, we consider four keys to successful employee participation programs.

Quality Control Circles

Developed in Japan during the early 1960s, this innovation took the U.S. industrial scene by storm during the late 1970s and early 1980s. Today, thousands of quality control circles (carrying all sorts of names) can be found in hundreds of North American and European companies. **Quality control circles**, commonly referred to as QC circles or simply quality circles, are voluntary problem-solving groups of five to ten employees from the same work area who meet regularly to discuss quality improvement and ways to reduce costs.[77] A weekly one-hour meeting, during company time, is common practice. By relying on *voluntary* participation, QC circles attempt to tap the creative potential every employee possesses. Although QC circles do not work in every situation, benefits such as direct cost savings, improved worker-management relations, and greater individual commitment have been reported.[78]

quality control circles: voluntary problem-solving groups committed to improving quality and reducing costs

QC circles should be introduced in evolutionary fashion rather than by management edict. Training, supportive supervision, and team building are all part of this evolutionary development. The idea is to give those who work day in and day out at a specific job the tools, group support, and opportunity to have a say in nipping quality problems in the bud. Each QC circle is responsible not only for recommending solutions but also for actually implementing and evaluating those solutions. According to one observer, "The invisible force behind the success of QC's [quality circles] is its ability to bring the psychological principles of Maslow, McGregor, and Herzberg into the workplace through a structured process."[79]

Open-Book Management

Open-book management (OBM) involves "opening a company's financial statements to all employees and providing the education that will enable them to understand how the company makes money and how their actions affect its success and bottom line."[80] Clearly, this is a bold break from traditional management practice. Many companies claim to practice OBM, but few actually do.[81] Why? OBM asks managers to correct three typical shortcomings by (1) displaying a high degree of trust in employees, (2) having a deep and unwavering commitment to

open-book management: sharing key financial data and profits with employees who are trained and empowered

employee training, and (3) being patient when waiting for results.[82] Once again, as we saw earlier with his masterful blending of goals and feedback, Wal-Mart's founder Sam Walton was a pioneer in open-book management and employee participation. Here is how former Wal-Mart CEO David Glass remembers it:

> *Sam felt we were all partners, and he wanted to share everything. And he was absolutely right. He believed that everyone should be an entrepreneur. If you ran the toy department in Harrison, Ark., you'd have all your financial information. So you're just like the toy entrepreneur of Harrison: You know what your sales are, what your margins are, what your inventory is. And then we had another philosophy where we had grass-roots meetings in every store. And there was an absolute belief that the best ideas ever at Wal-Mart came from the bottom up. Ideas would come up from those meetings and be implemented companywide. The door greeter, for example, was the idea of a hourly associate in Louisiana.*[83]

A four-step approach to OBM is displayed in Figure 12.7. The STEP acronym stands for *share, teach, empower,* and *pay.* Skipping or inadequately performing a step virtually guarantees failure. A systematic process is needed. Experts tell us it takes at least two complete budget cycles (typically two years) to see positive results. In step 1, employees are exposed to eye-catching public displays of key financial data. Sales, expense, and profit data for both the organization and relevant business units are shared in hallways, in cafeterias, and on internal Web sites. Of course, without step 2, step 1 would be meaningless. Comprehensive, ongoing training gives *all* employees a working knowledge of the firm's business model. Here is what Jelly Belly Candy Co. does:

> *Through Jelly Belly University, employees from the uppermost management level to administrative support personnel learn the art of candymaking, evaluate the results and conduct product evaluations, production scheduling and inventory control.*[84]

Thus, Jelly Belly's employees not only learn how to make great jelly beans; they also learn what it takes to make a profit in the process. In OBM companies, finance specialists teach other employees how to read and interpret basic financial documents such as profit-loss statements. Entertaining and instructive business board games and computer simulations have proved effective. Remedial education is provided when needed. Armed with knowledge about the company's workings and financial health, employees are ready for step 3. Managers find it easier to trust empowered employees to make important decisions when the employees are adequately prepared (more on empowerment in Chapter 14). In step 4, employees enjoy the fruits of their efforts by sharing profits and/or receiving bonuses and incentive compensation. There is no magic to OBM. It simply involves doing *important* things in the *right* way.[85]

Self-Managed Teams

According to the logic of this comprehensive approach to participation, self-management is the best management because it taps people's full potential. Advocates say self-management fosters creativity, motivation, and productivity. **Self-managed teams**, also known as autonomous work groups or high-performance work teams, take on traditional managerial tasks

> **self-managed teams:** high-performance teams that assume traditional managerial duties such as staffing and planning

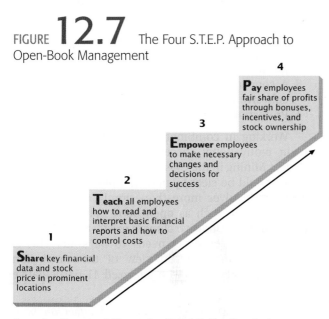

FIGURE **12.7** The Four S.T.E.P. Approach to Open-Book Management

4
Pay employees fair share of profits through bonuses, incentives, and stock ownership

3
Empower employees to make necessary changes and decisions for success

2
Teach all employees how to read and interpret basic financial reports and how to control costs

1
Share key financial data and stock price in prominent locations

Source: Based in part on Raj Aggarwal and Betty J. Simkins, "Open Book Management—Optimizing Human Capital," Business Horizons, 44 (September–October 2001): 5–13.

as part of their normal work routine.[86] They can have anywhere from 5 to more than 30 members, depending on the job. Unlike QC circles, which are staffed with volunteers, employees are assigned to self-managed teams. Cross-trained team members typically rotate jobs as they turn out a complete product or service. Any supervision tends to be minimal, with managers acting more as *facilitators* than as order givers.

VERTICALLY LOADED JOBS. In the language of job enrichment, team members' jobs are vertically loaded. This means nonmanagerial team members assume duties traditionally performed by managers. But specifically which duties? A survey of industry practices at 1,456 U.S. companies by *Training* magazine gave us some answers. Over 60 percent of the companies using self-managed teams let team members determine work schedules, deal directly with customers, and conduct training. Between 30 and 40 percent of the teams were allowed to manage budgets, conduct performance appraisals, and hire people. Only 15 percent of the teams were permitted to fire coworkers. The researchers concluded that *true* self-managed teams are still in the early growth stage.[87] Still, Google Inc., the Internet search and advertising giant, shows how far the concept can go:

> When [chief engineer Wayne] Rosing started at Google in 2001, "we had management in engineering. And the structure was tending to tell people, No you can't do that." So Google got rid of the managers. Now most engineers work in teams of three, with project leadership rotating among team members. If something isn't right, even if it's in a product that has already gone public, teams fix it without asking anyone.
>
> "For a while," Rosing says, "I had 160 direct reports. No managers. It worked because the teams knew what they had to do. That set a cultural bit in people's heads: You are the boss. Don't wait to take the hill. Don't wait to be managed."
>
> And if you fail, fine. On to the next idea. "There's faith here in the ability of smart, well-motivated people to do the right thing," Rosing says. "Anything that gets in the way of that is evil."[88]

Consequently, Google hires very carefully, putting applicants through a rigorous screening process. *Fortune* quoted the head of Texas Instruments as saying, "No matter what your business, these teams are the wave of the future."[89]

MANAGERIAL RESISTANCE. Not surprisingly, managerial resistance is the number one barrier to self-managed teams. More than anything else, self-managed teams represent *change*, and lots of it.

> *Adopting the team approach is no small matter; it means wiping out tiers of managers and tearing down bureaucratic barriers between departments. Yet companies are willing to undertake such radical changes to gain workers' knowledge and commitment—along with productivity gains that exceed 30 percent in some cases.*[90]

Traditional authoritarian supervisors view autonomous teams as a threat to their authority and job security. For this reason, *new* facilities built around the concept of self-managed teams, so-called greenfield sites, tend to fare better than reworked existing operations.

Managers who take the long view and switch to self-managed teams are finding it well worth the investment of time and money. Self-managed teams even show early promise of boosting productivity in the huge service sector. (Teamwork is discussed in the next chapter.)

Keys to Successful Employee Participation Programs

According to researchers, four factors build the *employee* support necessary for any sort of participation program to work:

1. A profit-sharing or gain-sharing plan
2. A long-term employment relationship with good job security
3. A concerted effort to build and maintain group cohesiveness
4. Protection of the individual employee's rights[91]

Working in combination, these factors help explain motivational success stories such as that of Badger Mining in the Closing Case for this chapter.

It should be clear by now that participative management involves more than simply announcing a new program, such as open-book management. To make sure a supportive climate exists, a good deal of background work often needs to be done. This is particularly important in view of the conclusion drawn by researchers who analyzed 41 participative management studies:

> *Participation has ... [a positive] effect on both satisfaction and productivity, and its effect on satisfaction is somewhat stronger than its effect on productivity. ... Our analysis indicates specific*

Participation in key decisions can be a powerful motivator for today's employees. However, researchers tell us that a key ingredient of successful employee participation programs is a profit-sharing plan. That's why these executives and employees at Britain's John Lewis department store are cheering. Thanks to an annual 19 percent growth in profits, 69,000 John Lewis employees recently split a $362 million bonus pool.

organizational factors that may enhance or constrain the effect of participation. For example, there is evidence that a participative climate has a more substantial effect on workers' satisfaction than participation in specific decisions.[92]

In the end, effective participative management is as much a managerial attitude about sharing power as it is a specific set of practices. In some European countries, such as Germany, the supportive climate is reinforced by government-mandated participative management.[93]

MOTIVATION THROUGH QUALITY-OF-WORK-LIFE PROGRAMS

Workforce diversity has made *flexibility* and *accommodation* top priorities for managers today. This chapter concludes with a look at ways of accommodating emerging employee needs. For example, a big concern these days involves striking a proper balance between work and life beyond the workplace. The dilemmas facing Dan Rosensweig, Yahoo's chief operating officer, and teacher Carmen Alvarez are typical today:

> ***Rosensweig:*** *The biggest challenge is, when you're given an opportunity like this, how do you give it everything you have because it deserves it, and also recognize and appreciate that the most important things in your life are your wife and daughters. I'm envious of people who have been able to find better balance.*[94]
>
> ***Alvarez:*** *Each day after teaching fourth graders, Carmen Alvarez, 35, cooks for her three daughters, helps them with their homework and finds time to attend at least one of their games. "I feel responsible for everything." Alvarez, who is separated from the girls' father, finished Ph.D. coursework at Boston College. Now she's trying to complete her dissertation. "How do you find time to put yourself first?"*[95]

Harvard's Rosabeth Moss Kanter believes employers need to be part of the solution: "If we don't make it possible for people to have highly flexible lives, I think we won't get the mutual benefits to our society of all the talent there is. At least now there are role-model companies that offer more flexibility, sabbaticals, family leaves, and the like. But a lot more needs to be done."[96] By meeting these needs in creative ways, such

as flexible work schedules, family support services, wellness programs, and sabbaticals, managers hope to enhance motivation and job performance.[97]

Flexible Work Schedules

The standard 8 A.M. to 5 P.M., 40-hour workweek has come under fire as dual-income families, single parents, and others attempt to juggle hectic schedules. One alternative is **flextime**, a work-scheduling plan that allows employees to determine their own arrival and departure times within specific limits.[98] All employees must be present during a fixed core time (see the center portion of Figure 12.8). If an eight-hour day is required, as in Figure 12.8, an early bird can put in the required eight hours by arriving at 7:00 A.M., taking half an hour for lunch, and departing at 3:30 P.M. Alternatively, a late starter can come in at 9:00 A.M. and leave at 5:30 P.M. Some progressive organizations, such as Mitre, in McLean, Virginia, take flextime to an extreme: "The nonprofit technology consultant for the Pentagon allows the most flexible of schedules: Create your own as long as you hit 40 hours in a seven-day period."[99] (Best Buy's ROWE program, in the chapter-opening case, also goes far beyond flextime.) When given the choice between "flexible work hours" and an "opportunity to advance" in a survey, 58 percent of the women opted for flexible hours. Forty-three percent of the men chose that option.[100] The growing use of flextime and other alternative work arrangements, such as telecommuting, is partly due to employer self-interest. Employers want to cut the cost of unscheduled absenteeism. One survey found the average annual cost for each employee's unscheduled absenteeism (68 percent of which was *not* for illness) to be $775.[101] Flextime can also be used to accommodate the special needs of disabled employees.[102]

flextime: allows employees to choose their own arrival and departure times within specified limits

FIGURE **12.8** Flextime in Action

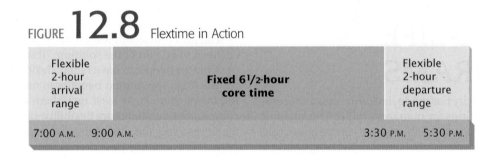

Flexible 2-hour arrival range	Fixed 6½-hour core time		Flexible 2-hour departure range
7:00 A.M. 9:00 A.M.			3:30 P.M. 5:30 P.M.

BENEFITS. In addition to many anecdotal reports citing the benefits of flextime, research studies have uncovered promising evidence. Flextime has several documented benefits:

- Better employee-supervisor relations
- Reduced absenteeism
- Selective positive impact on job performance (for example, a 24 percent improvement for computer programmers over a two-year period but no effect on the performance of data-entry workers)[103]

Flextime, though very popular among employees because of the degree of freedom it brings, is not appropriate for all situations. Problems reported by adopters include greater administrative expense, supervisor resistance, and inadequate coverage of jobs.

ALTERNATIVES.   According to organizations promoting a better quality of work life—such as Alliance for Work-Life Progress and Families and Work Institute—the concept of flextime is taking on a much broader meaning:

> *Traditionally, flexibility means being allowed to start and end work at employee-determined times, usually within a preset band of times. Nowadays, it's a bigger concept involving reduced time, options for moving between part- and full-time, paid leave for family or personal reasons, telecommuting and more. One new idea is career flexibility, or the ability to move in and out of active work, entering and re-entering the workforce over the course of a working life.*[104]

A good case in point is Brenda Barnes. In 1997, she quit as CEO of PepsiCo's North America division to spend more time with her three children, a career-ending move according to some observers at the time. Such was not the case, however, and Barnes was named the new CEO of Sara Lee, the $20 billion-a-year food and apparel company, in 2005.[105] Other work-scheduling variations include *compressed workweeks* (40 or more hours in fewer than five days)[106] and *permanent part-time* (workweeks with fewer than 40 hours). *Job sharing* (complementary scheduling that allows two or more part-timers to share a single full-time job), yet another work-scheduling innovation, is growing in popularity among employers of working parents.[107]

Under the heading of unintended consequences, a European study suggests that employees may be paying a price for the freedom of flexible work scheduling. Compared with a control group of employees on fixed schedules, employees with compressed workweeks, rotating shifts, irregular schedules, and part-time jobs experienced significantly more health, psychological, and sleeping problems.[108]

Family Support Services

Family-friendly companies recognize that employees have lives and priorities outside the workplace and make appropriate accommodations.   They strive to help their employees achieve a productive and satisfying balance between work and life with supportive policies, programs, and culture. This last factor—culture—is particularly important because it is driven by the organization's core values. A company that claims to be family-friendly, yet promotes only those who log 60-hour weeks, values total dedication more than work/life balance. A study by the Society for Human Resource Management identified "the top five family-friendly benefits": 1. "Dependent care flexible spending accounts" (71 percent); 2. "Flextime" (55 percent); 3. "Family leave above required leave of the federal Family and Medical Leave Act" (39 percent); 4. "Telecommuting on a part-time basis" (34 percent); and 5. "Compressed workweeks" (31 percent).[109] It is important to note that the U.S. Family and Medical Leave Act (FMLA), which took effect in 1993, has significant holes and limitations. First, only companies with 50 or more employees are required to comply with the law mandating up to 12 weeks of *unpaid* leave per year for family events such as births, adoptions, and sickness. Because the vast majority of U.S. businesses (95 percent) employ fewer than 50 people, millions of working Americans (43 percent) are left

> **family-friendly companies:** companies that recognize and accommodate employees' nonwork lives and priorities

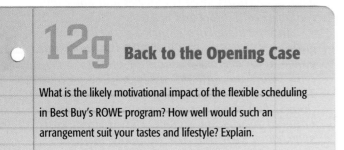

12g Back to the Opening Case

What is the likely motivational impact of the flexible scheduling in Best Buy's ROWE program? How well would such an arrangement suit your tastes and lifestyle? Explain.

12h How Family-Friendly Are U.S. Labor Laws?

- **Fathers in 66 countries receive or have a right to paid paternity leave. The United States does not guarantee paternity leave.**

- **168 out of 173 countries studied guarantee paid maternity leave, but the United States, Lesotho, Liberia, Papua New Guinea and Swaziland do not. Ninety-eight countries offer 14 or more weeks of paid leave.**

Source: Kathy Gurchiek, "U.S. Lags in Policies That Are Worker-Friendly," HR Magazine, 52 (April 2007): 29, 32.

QUESTIONS:

What is your assessment of this situation? How far should companies go in terms of being family-friendly?

unprotected by FMLA. Second, employees can be required by their employer to exhaust their sick leave and vacation allotments before taking FMLA leave. Fortunately, states and businesses have plugged some of the holes in FMLA.[110]

True family-friendly companies go way beyond the legal minimum, as these recent inspiring examples show.

- **Container Store, Coppell, Texas:** "Nearly one-tenth of all employees take advantage of 'family-friendly' shift, from 9 A.M. to 2 P.M., allowing for school dropoffs and pickups."
- **Starbucks Coffee, Seattle:** "Though 85 percent of 'partners' (Starbucks-speak for employees) are part-timers, they're still eligible for full benefits if they work 240 hours a quarter."
- **Station Casinos, Las Vegas:** "[Employees] get discounted child care as long as the casino is open—24 hours a day, seven days a week."
- **Northwest Community Hospital, Arlington Heights, Illinois:** "Employees enjoy benefits not commonly found in hospitals: $3,500 tuition reimbursement, enhanced loans for nursing or radiology school, concierge service, and a $5,000 forgivable loan to buy a new home."
- **Paychex, Rochester, New York:** "This payroll specialist, serving 543,000 small and medium-sized companies, recently added new benefits

such as two extra holidays, $4,000 in adoption aid, new flex schedules, and an increase in tuition reimbursement."[111]

As more and more companies offer family-friendly benefits,[112] cost-conscious managers properly ask, "What is the return on our investment?" Recent studies of companies with family-friendly practices have documented financial payoffs from easier recruitment, lower absenteeism and turnover, and greater productivity.[113] In fact, Big Four accounting and consulting firm Deloitte & Touche claims that its flexible work schedule programs "helped the company avoid $41.5 million in turnover-related costs in 2003."[114]

Wellness Programs

Stress and burnout are all too common consequences of modern work life.[115] (See the Manager's Toolkit feature at the end of this chapter.) Family-versus-work conflict, long hours, overload, hectic schedules, deadlines, frequent business travel, and accumulated workplace irritations are taking their toll. Progressive companies are coming to the rescue with *wellness programs* featuring a wide range of offerings. Among them are stress reduction, healthy eating and living clinics, quit-smoking and weight-loss programs, exercise facilities, massage breaks, behavioral health counseling, and health screenings. The ultimate objective is to help employees achieve a sustainable balance between their personal lives and work lives, with win-win benefits all around[116] (see Ethics: Character, Courage, and Values). A good example is Fieldale Farms, a chicken processor in Baldwin, Georgia, where the $50,000 tab each time an employee had a heart attack was making health insurance unaffordable.

> . . . the company went on a campaign to make its 4,600 employees healthier. It paid for gym memberships and offered free health screenings, one-on-one nutritional counseling and educational sessions at work about heart disease, diabetes and other preventable health problems. . . .
>
> Since Fieldale Farms started its wellness program in 1992, its cost for health insurance has grown at an average annual rate of just 2.5 percent, below the national average of 12 percent. The company health insurance plan spends less than $3,000 a year per employee, compared to the national average of $5,800. The program costs $200,000 a year, but the company insists it is worth it.[117]

ETHICS: CHARACTER, COURAGE, AND VALUES

Get Healthy, or Else . . .

Here's how the program works: Employers offer a high-deductible insurance plan through UnitedHealth, such as a policy that requires single workers to pay their first $2,500 in annual health costs before insurance kicks in; families $5,000.

Workers who want to lower their annual deductible can volunteer to have blood tests and other evaluations once a year to see if they smoke and if they meet target goals for blood pressure, cholesterol and height/weight ratio. For each of the four goals they meet, workers would qualify for a $500 credit as individuals or $1,000 as families toward the deductible. If they qualify for all four—and UnitedHealth estimates that few will initially meet all four—their annual deductible would fall to $500 for individuals or $1,000 for families.

Source: Julie Appleby, "Insurance Rewards Healthy Workers," USA Today (July 11, 2007): 1B.

FOR DISCUSSION

Do you see any ethical red flags in this program? Explain. Overall, do you approve or disapprove of this approach to employee wellness? Explain.

Sabbaticals

Some progressive companies in the United States (about 2 percent) give selected employees paid sabbaticals after a certain number of years of service. Here is a sampling to illustrate the many variations:

- **Adobe Systems and Men's Wearhouse:** Three weeks every five years.
- **Silicon Graphics:** Six weeks every four years.
- **Genentech**: Six weeks every six years.
- **American Century:** Four weeks every seven years.
- **Intel**: Eight weeks every seven years.[118]
- **Timberland:** "It offers a six-month, fully paid sabbatical for those who want 'to pursue a personal dream that benefits the community in a meaningful way.'"[119]

An extended period of paid time off gives the employee time for family, recreation, service, or travel. The idea is to refresh dedicated employees and, it is hoped, bolster their motivation and loyalty in the process.[120]

Laat op vrijdag de files achter je en... heradem.

FRIDAY BIKEDAY

Le vendredi, faites sauter les bouchons et... respirez pur.

www.fridaybikeday.be

Here's a great idea that combines Earth-friendly transportation and employee fitness. Employees at the European Commission's (EC) headquarters in Brussels, Belgium, have free access to a fleet of 200 bicycles for short work-related trips. The EC bikes have been used as much as 20,000 times a year, which meshes nicely with Brussels' "Friday Bikeday" program.

SUMMARY

1. Maslow's five-level hierarchy of needs, though criticized on the basis of empirical evidence of deficiencies, makes it clear to managers that people are motivated by emerging rather than fulfilled needs. Assuming that job satisfaction and performance are positively related, Herzberg believed that the most that wages and working conditions can do is eliminate sources of dissatisfaction. According to Herzberg, the key to true satisfaction, and hence motivation, is an enriched job that provides an opportunity for achievement, responsibility, and personal growth. Expectancy theory is based on the idea that the strength of one's motivation to work is the product of perceived probabilities of acquiring personally valued rewards. Both effort-performance and performance-reward probabilities are important in expectancy theory.

2. Goals can be an effective motivational tool when they are specific, difficult, participatively set, and accompanied by feedback on performance. Goals motivate performance by directing attention, encouraging effort and persistence, and prompting goal-attainment strategies and action plans.

3. Managers can counteract the boredom associated with routine-task jobs through realistic job previews, job rotation, and limited exposure. This third alternative involves letting employees earn an early departure time.

4. Job enrichment vertically loads jobs to meet individual needs for meaningfulness, responsibility, and knowledge of results. Personal desire for growth and a supportive climate must exist for job enrichment to be successful.

5. Both extrinsic (externally granted) and intrinsic (self-granted) rewards, when properly administered, can have a positive impact on performance and satisfaction. There is no single best employee compensation plan. A flexible and varied approach to compensation will be necessary in the coming years because of workforce diversity. The following rules can help managers maximize the motivational impact of extrinsic rewards: (1) rewards must satisfy individual needs, (2) one must believe that one's effort will lead to reward, (3) rewards must be equitable, and (4) rewards must be linked to performance. Gain-sharing plans have great motivational potential because they emphasize participation and link pay to actual productivity.

6. Participative management programs foster direct employee involvement in one or more of the following areas: goal setting, decision making, problem solving, and change implementation. Quality control circles are teams of volunteers who meet regularly on company time to discuss ways to improve product/service quality. The S.T.E.P. model of open-book management encourages employee participation when managers (1) *share* key financial data with all employees, (2) *teach* employees how to interpret financial statements and control costs, (3) *empower* employees to make improvements and decisions, and (4) *pay* a fair share of profits to employees. Employees assigned to self-managed teams participate by taking on tasks that have traditionally been performed by management. Profit sharing or gain sharing, job security, cohesiveness, and protection of employee rights are keys to building crucial employee support for participation programs.

7. Quality-of-work-life programs are being used to accommodate and motivate today's diverse workforce. Flextime, a flexible work-scheduling scheme that allows employees to choose their own arrival and departure times, has been effective in improving employee-supervisor relations while reducing absenteeism. Employers are increasingly providing family-friendly services such as child care, elder care, parental leaves, and adoption benefits. Employee wellness programs and sabbaticals are offered by some companies to reduce health insurance costs, build loyalty, and boost motivation.

TERMS TO UNDERSTAND

- **Motivation**, p. 335
- **Expectancy theory**, p. 339
- **Expectancy**, p. 340
- **Goal setting**, p. 341
- **Job design**, p. 342
- **Realistic job previews**, p. 343
- **Job rotation**, p. 344
- **Contingent time off**, p. 344
- **Job enlargement**, p. 345

MANAGER'S TOOLKIT

Stress Management 101

Feeling burned out? You're not alone. According to a survey of 7,000 senior executives in the United States and 12 other countries, burnout is on the rise in the executive ranks, and many companies fail to handle the problem properly.

"All leaders are at risk for burnout, but too often companies are embarrassed by the phenomenon and have no idea how to address it," says Andrew Kakabadse, director of the survey and professor of management at the Cranfield University School of Management, Bedford, UK.

Even if companies aren't addressing the issue of burnout, there are some steps individuals can take on their own. Lois Tamir, vice president of Personnel Decisions International in Minneapolis, Minnesota, offers a number of suggestions for the busy executive who needs to stay focused during a tough time. In a nutshell, managers can reduce stress by thinking big and treating themselves better.

How to Avoid Burnout

- *Pace yourself.* Don't put in extra hours because you probably won't get much done anyway.

- *Laugh more.* Humor relieves a great deal of physiological and psychological stress.
- *Be good to yourself.* Do something that you enjoy, such as going to the movies.
- *Keep it simple.* Separate your work into small tasks that can be accomplished easily. It's important to feel a sense of achievement.
- *Stay true to your values.* Think about the larger values in your work and personal life. Integrity, family priorities, and kindness to others will keep you grounded and put things in perspective.
- *Keep expectations in check.* Forget about changing the world or achieving your greatest goal at work. Some things will have to be postponed until you are better equipped to handle your own situation.
- *Don't try to be perfect.* Everyone experiences difficult times in his or her professional and personal life.

Source: Management Review *by Cheryl Comeau-Kirschner. Copyright 1999 by* American Management Association. *Reproduced with permission of* American Management Association *in the format Textbook via Copyright Clearance Center.*

ACTION LEARNING EXERCISE

Quality-of-Work-Life Survey

Instructions: Think of your present job, or one you had in the past, and circle one number for each of the following items. Add the circled numbers to get a total quality-of-work-life score. Alternatively, you can use this survey to interview another jobholder to determine his or her quality of work life. (*Note:* This survey is for instructional purposes only because it has not been scientifically validated.)

General Job Satisfaction
Most of the time, my job satisfaction is

Very low						Very high
1	2	3	4	5	6	7

Quality of Supervision
The person I report to respects me, listens to me, and supports me.

Never						Always
1	2	3	4	5	6	7

Quality of Communication
The organization keeps me well informed about its mission and pending changes.

Never						Always
1	2	3	4	5	6	7

Organizational Climate
My workplace generally feels like

A cold, rainy day						A warm, sunny day
1	2	3	4	5	6	7

Job Design
The work I do is

Routine and boring						Varied and challenging
1	2	3	4	5	6	7

Unimportant						Important
1	2	3	4	5	6	7

Feedback and Compensation
I am given timely and constructive feedback.

False						True
1	2	3	4	5	6	7

I am paid fairly for what I do.

False						True
1	2	3	4	5	6	7

Coworkers
My coworkers are

Negative and unfriendly						Positive and friendly
1	2	3	4	5	6	7

Work Hours and Schedules
My work hours and schedules are flexible and accommodate my lifestyle.

Never						Always
1	2	3	4	5	6	7

Organizational Identification
I have a strong sense of commitment and loyalty to my work organization.

False						True
1	2	3	4	5	6	7

Stress
The degree of unhealthy stress in my workplace is

Very high						Very low
1	2	3	4	5	6	7

Total quality-of-work-life score = _____

Scale

12–35 = Warning—this job could be hazardous to your health
36–60 = Why spend half your waking life settling for average?
61–84 = T.G.I.M. (Thank goodness it's *Monday!*)

For Consideration/Discussion

1. Which of these various quality-of-work-life factors is of overriding importance to you? Why? Which are least important? Why?

2. How strongly does your quality-of-work-life score correlate with the amount of effort you put into your job? Explain the connection.

3. How helpful would this survey be in your search for a better job? Explain.

4. How much does your total score reflect your attitude about life in general?

5. What should your managers do to improve the quality-of-work-life scores for you and your coworkers?

6. How important is quality of work life to your overall lifestyle and happiness? Explain.

CLOSING CASE
The Small Company with a Big-Time Motivation Program

They've made some changes at Badger Mining Corp. over the past year—expanded a production site, revamped the interior at company headquarters in Berlin, Wisconsin, and enhanced the wellness program.

But the collaborative culture and the core values such as trust and mutual respect remain unchanged. And so does Badger Mining's No. 1 ranking on the list of the Best Small Companies to Work for in America.

The family-owned, privately held company, which produces more than 1.5 million tons of industrial-use sand yearly, stands out for, among other things, the richness of its rewards for its 180 employees—called associates—and the inclusiveness it fosters throughout the enterprise.

"I knew this place was different," benefits specialist Barbara Swanson, SPHR, says in recalling an interview as a job applicant a few years ago. "I immediately felt that this was a place that cared about who they wanted to hire."

Signs of Badger Mining's abiding focus on employees are pervasive: flexible scheduling, freedom to take time-off for family matters, a company match of 401(k) plan contributions up to 3 percent of salary, and generous profit-sharing payouts that Swanson says have been rising every quarter. The company also pays employees' full premium for standard health coverage, and the wellness program now includes personalized health coaching.

As with other company initiatives, safety training is a collaborative exercise. Linda Arzt, a resource data associate, encourages mining workers' suggestions when she develops such programs. After all, she says, "they're the experts." What's more, she adds, it sends the right message—that the associates are valued for their input.

When the mining facility at Taylor, Wisconsin, underwent a major expansion, boosting production by 25 percent, Dan Valiquette, vice president for operations at Taylor, made sure he kept everyone—"the guys who have to run the equipment and maintain it"—involved in designing the processes, coordinating the contractors, and selecting vendors and equipment.

It promoted workers' buy-in for the project, he says. "This wasn't just a Taylor project. We had the support of the whole company."

It's just that sort of approach that underlies the company's achievements, says President Timothy J. Wuest. "Each and every one of our associates, working as a team," he says, has made the company "the leader in the industrial minerals industry."

Source: Excerpted from Terence F. Shea, "Badger Mining Stages an Encore," *HR Magazine*, 52 (July 2007): 44–45. Copyright 2007 by Society for Human Resource Management (SHRM). Reproduced with permission of Society for Human Resource Management (SHRM) in the format Textbook via Copyright Clearance Center.

FOR DISCUSSION

1 On the basis of what you have read in this chapter, how strong do you think the overall employee motivation program at Badger Mining is? Explain.

2 What evidence of participative management can you detect in this case?

3 How well do you think open-book management would work at Badger Mining? Why?

4 Which of the keys to successful employee participation programs are evident in this case? Does Badger Mining have the right climate for participative management? Explain.

5 Would you like to work at a small company like Badger Mining? Why or why not?

TEST PREPPER

True/False Questions

_____ 1. On Maslow's hierarchy of needs, social needs rank above self-actualization needs.

_____ 2. According to Herzberg's theory of motivation, salary and supervision are dissatisfiers.

_____ 3. Rewards play a role in the expectancy model of motivation.

_____ 4. Participative goals are less effective than imposed goals.

_____ 5. Contingent time off involves letting employees go home when they do not feel like working.

_____ 6. A critical psychological state in the job enrichment model is "Feeling that the work is meaningful."

_____ 7. Perceived inequity can be experienced by employees who are either underpaid or overpaid.

_____ 8. The S.T.E.P. acronym, in open-book management, stands for share, teach, empower, and perform.

_____ 9. In a flextime program, workers can arrive at work whenever they choose.

_____ 10. By definition, family-friendly companies help employees achieve a productive and satisfying balance between work and life outside the workplace.

Multiple-Choice Questions

1. What needs rank at the very top of Maslow's hierarchy of needs?
   A. Esteem   B. Love
   C. Physiological needs   D. Safety
   E. Self-actualization

2. Which of the following motivate(s) employees *most* effectively, according to Herzberg?
   A. Good working conditions   B. The work itself
   C. Money   D. Supportive supervision
   E. Supportive coworkers

3. How do rewards influence motivational strength in the expectancy model?
   A. Rewards do not play a role in expectancy theory.
   B. They erode intrinsic motivation.
   C. They have little impact on motivation.
   D. They motivate effort but not results.
   E. Through the perception that effort will lead to valued rewards.

4. Goals motivate performance by doing all of the following *except*
   A. directing attention.
   B. fostering action plans.
   C. fostering teamwork.
   D. encouraging effort.
   E. encouraging persistence.

5. _____ involve(s) telling recruits about both the good and the bad aspects of a particular job.
   A. Realistic job previews   B. Job enlargement
   C. Job enrichment   D. Job rotation
   E. Cafeteria compensation

6. Doing a "whole" piece of work from beginning to end is the defining characteristic of which of the following?
   A. Job feedback   B. Task significance
   C. Autonomy   D. Skill variety
   E. Task identity

7. According to the experts at the U.S. Bureau of Labor Statistics, the term(s) _____ will apply to future compensation plans.
   A. time-based   B. lean and uniform
   C. flexible and varied   D. uniform and standardized
   E. skill-based

8. The equity of rewards is said to be weighed by people on which two scales?
   A. Intrinsic and extrinsic
   B. Short-term and long-term
   C. Personal and organizational
   D. Technical and social
   E. Personal and social

9. The "S" in the S.T.E.P. approach to open-book management stands for
   A. share.   B. separate.
   C. sales.   D. strength.
   E. success.

10. How does the text characterize the U.S. Family and Medical Leave Act that took effect in 1993?
   A. Long overdue universal coverage
   B. More generous than state laws
   C. The first law to require paid leave for everyone
   D. Probably unconstitutional
   E. Marred by significant holes and limitations

See page T1 at the back of the text for answers to these questions. Want more questions? Visit the student Web site and take the ACE quizzes for more practice.

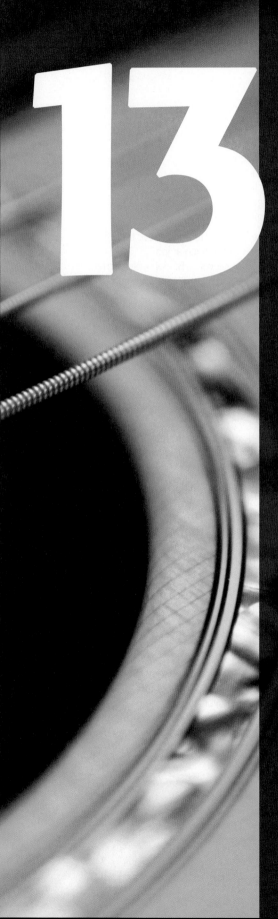

13

Group Dynamics
and Teamwork

OBJECTIVES

- **Define** the term *group.*
- **Explain** the significance of cohesiveness, roles, norms, and ostracism in regard to the behavior of group members.
- **Identify** and briefly **describe** the six stages of group development.
- **Define** *organizational politics,* and **summarize** relevant research insights.
- **Explain** how groupthink can lead to blind conformity.
- **Define** and **discuss** the management of virtual teams.
- **Discuss** the criteria and determinants of team effectiveness.
- **Explain** why trust is a key ingredient of teamwork, and **discuss** what management can do to build trust.

THE CHANGING WORKPLACE

My Boss Wants to Be My Online Friend

Paul Dyer always was able to hold off his boss's invitations to party by employing that arm's-length response: "We'll have to do that sometime," he'd say.

But when his boss, in his 30s, invited Dyer, 24, to be friends on the social-networking sites MySpace and Facebook, dodging wasn't so easy.

On the one hand, accepting a person's request to be friends online grants them access to the kind of intimacy never meant for office consumption, such as recent photos of keggers and jibes from friends ("Still wearing that lampshade?").

But declining a "friend" request from a colleague or a boss is a slight. So Dyer accepted the invitation, then removed any inappropriate or incriminating photos of himself—"I'd rather speak vaguely about them," he says.

Dyer, it turns out, wasn't the one who had to be embarrassed. His boss had photos of himself attempting to imbibe two drinks at once, ostensibly, Dyer ventures, to send the message: "I'm a crazy, young party guy." The boss also wore a denim suit ("I'd never seen anything like it," Dyer says) and posed in a photo flashing a hip-hop backward peace sign.

It was painful to watch. "I hurt for him," Dyer said.

Like e-mail and "buddy lists" before them, social networking sites, such as Facebook and MySpace, provide a definition of the word "friend" so expansive that it includes perfect strangers. Yet, strangers are the easy part. It can be a lot creepier to interact intimately with someone you sort of know than [with] someone you don't know at all.

"Nothing changes when a stranger invites you to be a friend," said Nina Singh, a market-research consultant. But when one of her clients "friended" her, she saw a semi-erotic photo of him topless, posed and softly lit. "When you see your client's pubic bone, something has changed."

Victor Sanchez, 54, a senior development director, was once invited to join a site and was surprised to see a photograph of a younger colleague's seahorse tattoo.

"Sometimes it's good to learn things about a colleague much later—or never at all," he said.

These networking sites assist existing social relationships, letting people easily plan events, share pictures and keep up-to-date with far-flung friends. Once they penetrate the office, however, such sites can create awkward moments, particularly with colleagues who commit the social felony of attempted hipness.

When it comes to the boss, there is a real dilemma. You're caught between a career-limiting rejection of virtual friendship [and] a career-limiting access to photos of yourself glassy-eyed at a party.

Source: Jared Sandberg, "OMG—My Boss Wants to 'Friend' Me on my Online Profile," *Wall Street Journal* (Eastern Edition) (July 14, 2007). Copyright 2007 by Dow Jones & Company, Inc. Reproduced with permission of Dow Jones & Company, Inc. in the format Textbook via Copyright Clearance Center.

As in daily life itself, relationships rule in modern organizations. The more managers know about building and sustaining good working relationships, the better. In fact, in a recent study involving 1,040 managers and 208 focus groups, the two leading causes of managerial failure were ineffective communication skills/practices (81 percent) and poor work relationships/interpersonal skills (78 percent).[2] What is involved here is the concept of **social capital**, "productive potential resulting from strong relationships, goodwill, trust, and cooperative effort."[3] In line with our discussion of human capital in Chapter 10, managers need to build social capital by working on strong, constructive, and mutually beneficial relationships. This often involves delicate balancing acts, such as deciding whether to engage in online social networking with coworkers and bosses. The purpose of this chapter is to build a foundation of understanding about how groups and teams function in today's organizations.

> **social capital:** productive potential of strong relationships, goodwill, trust, and cooperation

FUNDAMENTAL GROUP DYNAMICS

According to one organization theorist, "All groups may be collections of individuals, but all collections of individuals are not groups."[4] This observation is more than a play on words; mere togetherness does not automatically create a group. Consider, for example, this situation. Half a dozen people who worked for different companies in the same building often shared the same elevator in the morning. As time passed, they introduced themselves and exchanged pleasantries. Eventually, four of the elevator riders discovered that they all lived in the same suburb. Arrangements for a car pool were made, and they began to take turns picking up and delivering one another. A group technically came into existence only when the car pool was formed. To understand why this is so, we need to examine the definition of the term *group*.

What Is a Group?

From a sociological perspective, a **group** can be defined as two or more freely interacting individuals who share a common identity and purpose.[5] Careful analysis of this definition reveals four important dimensions (see Figure 13.1). First, a group must be made up of two or more people if it is to be considered a social unit. Second, the individuals must freely interact in some manner. An organization may qualify

> **group:** two or more freely interacting individuals with a common identity and purpose

as a sociological group if it is small and personal enough to permit all its members to interact regularly with each other. Generally, however, larger organizations with bureaucratic tendencies are made up of many overlapping groups. Third, the interacting individuals must share a common identity. Each must recognize himself or herself as a member of the group.

FIGURE **13.1** What Does It Take to Make a Group?

Group

Two or more people	Free interaction among members	Common identity	Common purpose

Fourth, these interacting individuals who have a common identity must also have a common purpose. That is, there must be at least a rough consensus on why the group exists.

Types of Groups

Human beings belong to groups for many different reasons. Some people join a group as an end in itself. For example, an accountant may enjoy the socializing that is part of belonging to a group at a local health club. That same accountant's membership in a work group is a means to a professional end. Both the exercise group and the work group satisfy the sociological definition of a group, but they fulfill very different needs. The former is an informal group, and the latter is a formal group.

INFORMAL GROUPS. As Abraham Maslow pointed out, a feeling of belonging is a powerful motivator. People generally have a great need to fit in, to be liked, to be one of the gang. Whether a group meets at work or during leisure time, it is still an **informal group** if the

informal group: collection of people seeking friendship

principal reason for belonging is friendship.[6] Informal groups usually evolve spontaneously. They serve to satisfy esteem needs because one develops a better self-image when one is accepted, recognized, and liked by others. Sometimes, as in the case of a group of friends forming an investment club, an informal group may evolve into a formal group.

Managers cannot afford to ignore informal groups, because grassroots social networks can either advance or threaten the organization's mission.[7] As experts on the subject have explained,

> These informal networks can cut through formal reporting procedures to jump-start stalled initiatives and meet extraordinary deadlines. But informal networks can just as easily sabotage companies' best-laid plans by blocking communication and fomenting opposition to change unless managers know how to identify and direct them. . . .
>
> If the formal organization is the skeleton of a company, the informal [organization] is the central nervous system driving the collective thought processes, actions, and reactions of its business units. Designed to facilitate standard modes of production, the formal organization is set up to handle easily anticipated problems. But when unexpected

Purdue University's Professor Dan Raftery (second from right) and a team of students prepare to do an analysis on a mass spectrometer in their search for bio-markers for early stage cancer. If the students socialize apart from their schoolwork, this formal group would also qualify as an informal group. What are the advantages and drawbacks of being friends with your co-workers?

problems arise, the informal organization kicks in. Its complex web of social ties forms every time colleagues communicate and solidif[ies] over time into surprisingly stable networks. Highly adaptive, informal networks move diagonally and elliptically, skipping entire functions to get work done.[8]

FORMAL GROUPS. A **formal group** is a group created for the purpose of doing productive work. It may be called a team, a committee, or simply a work group. Whatever its name, a formal group is usually formed for the purpose of contributing to the success of a larger organization. Formal groups tend to be more rationally structured and less fluid than informal groups. Rather than joining formal task groups, people are assigned to them

formal group: collection of people created to do something productive

according to their talents and the organization's needs. One person normally is granted formal leadership responsibility to ensure that the members carry out their assigned duties. Informal friendship groups, in contrast, generally do not have officially appointed leaders, although informal leaders often emerge by popular demand. For the individual, the formal group and an informal group at the place of employment may or may not overlap. In other words, one may or may not be friends with one's coworkers.

The overlapping of formal and informal groups brings us to the issue of whether managers should be friends with those who report to them. This is a problematic issue, made even more complicated by the breaking down of traditional social barriers by innovations such as online social networking[9] (as noted in the Opening Case). A useful perspective was offered recently by Jack and Suzy Welch in their *Business Week* column:

> *[Being friends with your direct reports is] certainly nothing to be afraid of! Of course, you don't need to be friends with your subordinates, as long as you share the same values for the business. But if you are friends with them, lucky you. Working with people you really like for 8 to 10 hours a day adds fun to everything.*
>
> *That said, remember that boss-subordinate friendships live or die because of one thing: complete, unrelenting candor. Candor is imperative in any working relationship, but it's especially necessary when there's a social aspect involved. You don't want your liking someone's personality to automatically communicate that you like his or her performance.*[10]

Attraction to Groups

What attracts a person to one group but not to another? And why do some groups' members stay whereas members of other groups leave? Managers who can answer these questions can take steps to motivate people to join and remain members of a formal work group. Individual commitment to either an informal or a formal group hinges on two factors. The first is *attractiveness*, the outside-looking-in view.[11] A nonmember will want to join a group that is attractive and will shy away from a group that is unattractive. The second factor is **cohesiveness**, the tendency of group members to follow the group and resist outside influences. This is the inside-looking-out view. In a highly

cohesiveness: tendency of a group to stick together

13a Back to the Opening Case

Fact about Facebook networks:

Work networks are exploding, with 14,000 at IBM, 10,000 at Ernst & Young, 8,100 at the BBC [British Broadcasting Corporation], and 6,300 at General Electric. The U.S. Army network has 43,000 members.

Stanley Bing, *Fortune* magazine columnist:

I called my daughter.

"Nora," I said, "I have decided to join a social network. I hear Facebook is the coolest. Should I join that?"

"Dad," said my child, "anybody over 25 who is on Facebook is a dork."

Sources: David Kirkpatrick, "Facebook's Plan to Hook Up the World," Fortune (June 11, 2007): 130; and Stanley Bing, "My Network, Myself," Fortune (October 1, 2007): 202.

QUESTIONS:

Is Nora right? Where should a manager draw the line between business and friendship in the workplace? Are the "rules" different in the age of online social networking? Explain.

For further information about the interactive annotations in this chapter, visit our student Web site.

A re you a dog lover? If so, you would be attracted to this fundraising group at Pierce College in Southern California. The annual Nuts for Mutts dog show benefits New Leash on Life Animal Rescue, a non-profit animal rescue and placement organization. Speaking of attraction, who wouldn't be attracted to Lola, the too-cute-for-words pooch in the middle?

cohesive group, individual members tend to see themselves as "we" rather than "I." Cohesive group members stick together.[12]

Factors that either enhance or destroy group attractiveness and cohesiveness are listed in Table 13.1. It is important to note that each factor is a matter of degree. For example, a group may offer the individual little, moderate, or great opportunity for prestige and status. Similarly, group demands on the individual may range from somewhat disagreeable to highly disagreeable. What all this means is that both the decision to join a group and the decision to continue being a member depend on a net balance of the factors in Table 13.1. Naturally, the resulting balance is colored by one's perception and frame of reference, as it was in

the case of Richard Dale, a former manager of distribution at Commodore International, during his first meeting with the company's founder, Jack Tramiel.

Dale's first meeting with Tramiel began with a summons to appear at Tramiel's office. Dale flew from his office in Los Angeles to Santa Clara . . . , only to find that Tramiel had decided to visit him instead.

Terrified, Dale caught a plane back to find his secretary shaking in her shoes and the burly Tramiel sitting at his desk. For an hour Tramiel grilled Dale on his philosophy of business, pronounced it all wrong, and suggested a tour of the warehouse. When they passed boxes of . . . [computers] waiting for shipment, recalls Dale, Tramiel seemed to "go crazy,"

TABLE 13.1 Factors That Enhance or Detract from Group Attractiveness and Cohesiveness

FACTORS THAT ENHANCE	FACTORS THAT DETRACT
1. Prestige and status	1. Unreasonable or disagreeable demands on the individual
2. Cooperative relationship	2. Disagreement over procedures, activities, rules, and the like
3. High degree of interaction	3. Unpleasant experience with the group
4. Relatively small size	4. Competition between the group's demands and preferred outside activities
5. Similarity of members	5. Unfavorable public image of the group
6. Superior public image of the group	6. Competition for membership by other groups
7. A common threat in the environment	

Source: Table adapted from Group Dynamics: Research and Theory, *2nd ed., by Dorwin Cartwright and Alvin Zander. New York: HarperCollins Publishers, Inc.*

13b Toward a Sense of *Community* in the Workplace

Carolyn Schaffer and Kristin Anundsen, authors of the book *Creating Community Anywhere: Finding Support and Connection in a Fragmented World:*

Community is a dynamic whole that emerges when a group of people:

- *Participate in common practices;*
- *Depend upon one another;*
- *Make decisions together;*
- *Identify themselves as part of something larger than the sum of their individual relationships; and*
- *Commit themselves for the long term to their own, one another's, and the group's well-being.*

Source: Quoted in Ron Zemke, "The Call of Community," *Training, 33* (March 1996): 27.

QUESTIONS:

How important is it to build this sense of community in today's work groups and organizations? Explain. What is your personal experience with a genuine feeling of community? Are we naïve to expect a sense of community in today's hurried and rapidly changing workplace? Explain.

pounding the boxes with his fists and yelling, "Do you think this is bourbon? Do you think it gets better with age?"[13]

Dale's departure within a few months of this episode is not surprising in view of the fact that Tramiel's conduct utterly destroyed work group attractiveness and cohesiveness.

Roles

According to Shakespeare, "All the world's a stage, and all the men and women merely players." In fact, Shakespeare's analogy between life and play-acting can be carried a step further—to organizations and their component formal work groups. Although employees do not have scripts, they do have formal positions in the organizational hierarchy, and they are expected to adhere to company policies and rules. Furthermore, job descriptions and procedure manuals spell out how jobs are to be done. In short, every employee has one or more organizational roles to play. An organization that is appropriately structured, in which everyone plays his or her role(s) effectively and efficiently, will have a greater chance for organizational success.

A social psychologist has described the concept of *role* as follows:

The term role is used to refer to (1) a set of expectations concerning what a person in a given position must, must not, or may do, and (2) the actual behavior of the person who occupies the position. A central idea is that any person occupying a position and filling a role behaves similarly to anyone else who could be in that position.[14]

A **role**, then, is a socially determined prescription for behavior in a *specific* position. Roles evolve out of the tendency for social units to perpetuate themselves, and roles are socially enforced. Role models are a powerful influence. They are indispensable to those trying to resolve the inherent conflicts between work and family roles, for example.[15]

> **role:** socially determined way of behaving in a specific position

Norms

Norms define "degrees of acceptability and unacceptability."[16] More precisely, **norms** are general standards of conduct that help individuals judge what is right or wrong or good or bad in a given social setting (such as work, home, play, or religious organization). Because norms are culturally derived, they vary from one culture to another. For example, public disagreement and debate, which are normal in Western societies, are often considered rude in Eastern countries such as Japan.

> **norms:** general standards of conduct for various social settings

Norms have a broader influence than roles, which focus on a specific position. Although usually unwritten, norms influence behavior enormously.[17]

Every mature group, whether informal or formal, generates its own pattern of norms that constrains and directs the behavior of its members. Norms are enforced for at least four different reasons:

1. To facilitate survival of the group
2. To simplify or clarify role expectations
3. To help group members avoid embarrassing situations (protect self-images)
4. To express key group values and enhance the group's unique identity[18]

FIGURE **13.2** Norms Are Enforced for Different Reasons

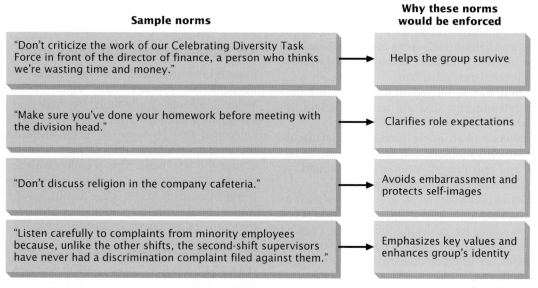

Sample norms	Why these norms would be enforced
"Don't criticize the work of our Celebrating Diversity Task Force in front of the director of finance, a person who thinks we're wasting time and money."	Helps the group survive
"Make sure you've done your homework before meeting with the division head."	Clarifies role expectations
"Don't discuss religion in the company cafeteria."	Avoids embarrassment and protects self-images
"Listen carefully to complaints from minority employees because, unlike the other shifts, the second-shift supervisors have never had a discrimination complaint filed against them."	Emphasizes key values and enhances group's identity

As illustrated in Figure 13.2, norms tend to go above and beyond formal rules and written policies. Compliance is shaped with social reinforcement in the form of attention, recognition, and acceptance.[19] Those who fail to comply with the norm may be criticized or ridiculed. For example, consider the pressure Gwendolyn Kelly experienced in medical school:

The word among students is that if you've got any brains, "tertiary" medicine—which involves complex diagnostic procedures and comprehensive care—is where it's at. Instructors often refer to the best students as "future surgeons" and belittle the family-practice specialty. These attitudes trickle down. I've heard my peers say the reason so many women choose pediatrics is that "they want to be mommies." And students who take a family-practice residency may be maligned by colleagues who say the choice is a sign of sub-par academic credentials.[20]

Reformers of the U.S. health care system, who want to increase the number of primary care (family-practice) doctors from one-third to one-half, need to begin by altering medical school norms.

Worse than ridicule is the threat of being ostracized. **Ostracism**, or rejection from the group, is figuratively the capital punishment of group dynamics. Informal groups derive much of their power over individuals through the ever-present threat of ostracism. Thus, informal norms play a pivotal role in on-the-job ethics.[21] Police officers, for example, who honor the traditional "code of silence" norm that demands *total* loyalty to one's fellow officers, face a tough moral dilemma when they encounter a "bad cop."

ostracism: rejection from a group

GROUP DEVELOPMENT

Like inept youngsters who mature into talented adults, groups undergo a maturation process before becoming effective. We have all experienced the uneasiness associated with the first meeting of a new group, be it a class, club, or committee. Initially, there is little mutual understanding, trust, or commitment among the new group members, and their uncertainty about objectives, roles, and leadership doesn't help. The prospect of cooperative action seems unlikely in view of defensive behavior and differences of opinion about who should do what. Someone steps forward to assume a leadership role, and the group is off and running toward eventual maturity (or perhaps premature demise). A working knowledge of the characteristics of a mature group can help managers envision a goal for the group development process.

Characteristics of a Mature Group

If and when a group takes on the following characteristics, it can be called a mature group.

1. Members are aware of their own and each other's assets and liabilities vis-à-vis the group's task.
2. These individual differences are accepted without being labeled as good or bad.
3. The group has developed authority and interpersonal relationships that are recognized and accepted by the members.
4. Group decisions are made through rational discussion. Minority opinions and dissension are recognized and encouraged. Attempts are not made to force decisions or a false unanimity.
5. Conflict is over substantive group issues such as group goals and the effectiveness and efficiency of various means for achieving those goals. Conflict over emotional issues regarding group structure, processes, or interpersonal relationships is at a minimum.
6. Members are aware of the group's processes and their own roles in them.[22]

Effectiveness and productivity should increase as the group matures. Recent research with groups of school teachers found positive evidence in this regard. The researchers concluded, "Faculty groups functioning at higher levels of development have students who perform better on standard achievement measures."[23] This finding could be fruitful for those seeking to reform and improve the American education system.

A hidden but nonetheless significant benefit of group maturity is that individuality is strengthened, not extinguished.[24] Protecting the individual's right to dissent is particularly important in regard to the problem of blind obedience, which we shall consider later in this chapter. Also, as indicated in the fifth item on the list, members of mature groups tend to be emotionally mature.[25] This paves the way for building much-needed social capital.

Six Stages of Group Development

Experts have identified six distinct stages in the group development process[26] (see Figure 13.3). During stages 1 through 3, attempts are made to overcome the obstacle of uncertainty over power and authority. Once this first obstacle has been surmounted, addressing uncertainty over interpersonal relations becomes the challenge. This second obstacle must be cleared during stages 4 through 6 if the group is to achieve maturity. Each stage confronts the group's leader and contributing members with a unique combination of problems and opportunities.

STAGE 1: ORIENTATION.   Attempts are made to "break the ice." Uncertainty about goals, power, and interpersonal relationships is high. Members generally want and accept any leadership at this point. Emergent leaders often misinterpret this "honeymoon period" as a mandate for permanent control. According to a recent survey of 900 executives, 42 percent of team members said "their team rarely, if ever, gets off to the right start."[27]

STAGE 2: CONFLICT AND CHALLENGE.   As the emergent leader's philosophy, objectives, and policies become apparent, individuals or subgroups advocating alternative courses of action struggle for control. This second stage may be prolonged while members strive to clarify and reconcile their roles as part of a complete redistribution of power and authority. Many groups never continue past stage 2 because they get

Group development is both important and a bit more challenging in today's diverse workplaces. People from different backgrounds bring different perspectives, values, and issues to the table. Here, Nike's Ethnic Diversity Council meets to gather ideas and plot strategy.

FIGURE **13.3** Group Development from Formation to Maturity

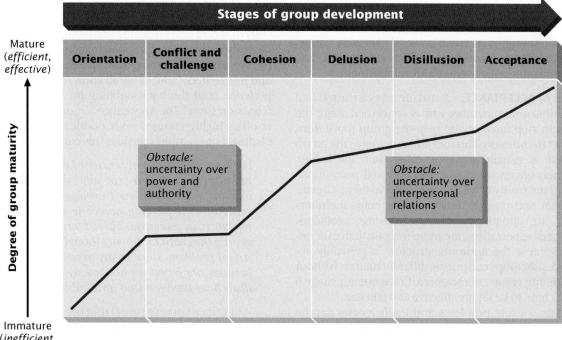

Source: Group Effectiveness in Organizations, *by Linda N. Jewell and H. Joseph Reitz, p. 20. Used with permission of the authors.*

13c The Business of Golf

Ask people why they golf with business associates, and the answer is always the same: It's a great way to build relationships. They say this far more about golf than about going to dinner or attending a baseball game, and for good reason. Indeed, this may be the central fact about corporate golf, though it's rarely said: When people golf together, they see one another humiliated. At least 95% of all golfers are terrible, which means that in 18 holes everyone in the foursome will hit a tree, take three strokes in one bunker, or four-putt, with everyone else watching. Bonding is simply a matter of people jointly going through adversity, and a round of golf will furnish plenty of it.

Source: Geoffrey Colvin, "Why Execs Love Golf," Fortune (April 30, 2001): 46.

QUESTIONS:

Why does shared adversity foster strong relationships and bonding? How can managers get task group members to bond like this without playing golf?

bogged down as a consequence of emotionalism and political infighting. Organizational committees often bear the brunt of jokes (we've all heard that a camel is a horse designed by a committee) because their frequent failure to mature beyond stage 2 prevents them from accomplishing their goals.[28]

STAGE 3: COHESION. The shifts in power started in stage 2 are completed, under a new leader or the original leader, with a new consensus on authority, structure, and procedures. A "we" feeling emerges as everyone becomes truly involved. Any lingering differences over power and authority are resolved quickly. Stage 3 is usually of relatively short duration. If not, the group is likely to stall.

STAGE 4: DELUSION. A feeling of "having been through the worst of it" prevails after the rather rapid transition through stage 3. Issues and problems that threaten to break this spell of relief are dismissed or treated lightly. Members seem committed to fostering harmony at all costs. Participation and camaraderie run high because members believe that all the difficult emotional problems have been solved.

STAGE 5: DISILLUSION. Subgroups tend to form as the illusion of unlimited goodwill wears off, and there is a growing disenchantment with how things are turning out. Those with unrealized expectations challenge the group to perform better and are prepared to reveal their personal strengths and weaknesses if necessary. Others hold back. Tardiness and absenteeism are symptomatic of diminishing cohesiveness and commitment.[29]

STAGE 6: ACCEPTANCE. It usually takes a trusted and influential group member who is concerned about the group to step forward and help the group move from conflict to cohesion. This individual, acting as the group catalyst, is usually someone other than the leader. Members are encouraged to test their self-perceptions against the reality of how others perceive them. Greater personal and mutual understanding helps members adapt to situations without causing problems. Members' expectations are more realistic than ever before. Because the authority structure is generally accepted, subgroups can pursue different matters without threatening group cohesiveness. Consequently, stage 6 groups tend to be highly effective and efficient.[30]

Time-wasting problems and inefficiencies can be minimized if group members are consciously aware of this developmental process. Just as it is impossible for a child to skip being a teenager on the way to adulthood, committees and other work groups will find there are no shortcuts to group maturity. Some emotional stresses and strains are inevitable along the way.

ORGANIZATIONAL POLITICS

Only in recent years has the topic of organizational politics (also known as impression management) begun to receive serious attention from management theorists and researchers.[31] But as we all know from practical experience (and the back-stabbing on Donald Trump's television show "The Apprentice"),[32] organizational life is often highly charged with political wheeling-and-dealing. For example, consider this complaint:

I've been working at my current job as a marketing manager for about a year now, and one thing is bugging me. Every time I propose a strategy or a solution in a meeting, someone else at the table repeats it, in somewhat altered form—and ends up getting the credit for having thought of it. This is no trivial problem, since in my department, year-end bonuses are based on how many of each person's ideas have been put into (profitable) practice.[33]

Workplace surveys reveal that organizational politics can hinder effectiveness and be an irritant to employees. A three-year study of 46 companies attempting to establish themselves on the Internet "found that poor communication and political infighting were the No. 1 and No. 2 causes, respectively, for slowing down change."[34] Meanwhile, 44 percent

The consequences of organizational politics can be productive or counterproductive, depending upon the players and the circumstances. However, managers can be fairly certain that major organizational changes will set political wheels in motion. Some political maneuvering is likely at Procter & Gamble's headquarters as Edgar Sandoval (right) deals with the integration of the Puerto Rico-based Hispanic marketing unit into the North American multicultural team in Cincinnati.

of full-time employees and 60 percent of independent contractors listed "freedom from office politics" as extremely important to their job satisfaction.[35]

Whether they themselves are politically motivated or not, managers need to be knowledgeable about organizational politics because their careers will be affected by it.[36] New managers, particularly, should be aware of the political climate in their organization and develop important networking skills without becoming shameless politicians.[37] As "new kids on the job," they might be more easily taken advantage of than other, more experienced managers. Certain political maneuvers also have significant ethical implications[38] (see Ethics: Character, Courage, and Values).

What Does Organizational Politics Involve?

As the term implies, self-interest is central to organizational politics. In fact, **organizational politics** has been defined as "the pursuit of self-interest at work in the face of real or imagined opposition."[39] Political maneuvering is said to encompass all self-serving behavior above and beyond competence, hard work, and luck.[40] For example, consider this clip from the *Wall Street Journal*:

> **organizational politics:** the pursuit of self-interest in response to real or imagined opposition

A former Wall Street analyst, a veteran of several investment banks who knows the value of that most ludicrous of achievements—performing "better than expected"—advises us to list easy goals and just make them sound hard. That way next year you can say you "achieved 100% of goals" last year.

All year long, she would collect kudos as ammo, dumping them into folders she named "Success" and "Yay." The latter was for praise from colleagues. "Getting messages from my boss's boss—or anyone else he respected and was also slightly intimidated by—was even better," she confides.

Brownie points, we all know, come from personally saving a few pennies. "Point out in the [annual performance] review—not in writing!—that the rest of the team stayed at the Four Seasons and flew American," the analyst says. Then wipe your fingerprints from the knives you stuck in everyone's backs.[41]

Although self-serving people such as this have given the term *organizational politics* a negative connotation, researchers have identified both positive and negative aspects:

> *Political behaviors widely accepted as legitimate would certainly include exchanging favors, "touching bases," forming coalitions, and seeking sponsors at upper levels. Less legitimate behaviors would include whistle-blowing, revolutionary coalitions, threats, and sabotage.[42]*

Recall our discussion of whistle-blowing in Chapter 5.[43]

Employees resort to political behavior when they are unwilling to trust their career solely to competence, hard work, and luck. One might say that organizational politicians help luck along by relying on political tactics. Whether employees will fall back on political tactics has a lot to do with an organization's climate or culture. A culture that presents employees with unreasonable barriers to individual and group success tends to foster political maneuvering. Consider this situation, for example: "A cadre of Corvette lovers inside General Motors lied, cheated, and stole to keep the legendary sports car from being eliminated during GM's management turmoil and near-bankruptcy in the late 1980s and early 1990s."[44] The redesigned Corvette finally made it to market in 1997, thanks in part to the Corvette team giving high-level GM executives thrilling unauthorized test rides in the hot new model.

Research on Organizational Politics

Researchers in one widely cited study of organizational politics conducted structured interviews with 87 managers employed by 30 electronics firms in southern California. Included in the sample were 30 chief

---

13d Are You Ready for Virtual Impression Management?

IBM—once known for its unwritten white-shirt-and-wingtip [shoes] dress code—has issued etiquette guidelines for employees visiting Second Life, where it has a business presence, and other online worlds. Created collectively by SL-savvy IBMers, the document asks colleagues to be "sensitive to the appropriateness of your avatar or persona's appearance when you are meeting with IBM clients."

Source: Aili McConnon, "And Now, a Virtual Dress Code," *Business Week* (August 13, 2007): 10.

QUESTION:

Within the context of impression management, is this a good idea or is it a futile attempt to control the appearance of employees in the anything-goes virtual world?

ETHICS: CHARACTER, COURAGE, AND VALUES

How Do You Feel About "Hard Ball" Organizational Politics?

Circle one number for each item, total your responses, and compare your score with the scale below:

	Unacceptable attitude/conduct			*Acceptable attitude/conduct*	
1. The boss is always right.	1	2	3	4	5
2. If I were aware that an executive in my company was stealing money, I would use that information against him or her in asking for favors.	1	2	3	4	5
3. I would invite my boss to a party in my home even if I didn't like that person.	1	2	3	4	5
4. Given a choice, take on only those assignments that will make you look good.	1	2	3	4	5
5. I like the idea of keeping a "blunder (error) file" about a company rival for future use.	1	2	3	4	5
6. If you don't know the correct answer to a question asked by your boss, bluff your way out of it.	1	2	3	4	5
7. Why go out of your way to be nice to any employee in the company who can't help you now or in the future?	1	2	3	4	5
8. It is necessary to lie once in a while in business in order to look good.	1	2	3	4	5
9. Past promises should be broken if they stand in the way of one's personal gain.	1	2	3	4	5
10. If someone compliments you for a task that is another's accomplishment, smile and say thank you.	1	2	3	4	5

Scale

10–20 = Straight arrow with solid ethics.

21–39 = Closet politician with elastic ethics.

40–50 = Hard ball politician with no ethics.

Total score = _____

Source: "Measuring Your Political Tendencies," adapted from Winning Office Politics *by Andrew J. DuBrin, copyright © 1990 by Prentice-Hall, Inc. Used by permission of Portfolio, an imprint of Penguin Group (USA) Inc.*

FOR DISCUSSION

What are the on-the-job ethical implications of your score? Is it necessary to fight dirty to win pay raises and promotions in today's organizations? Explain.

executive officers, 28 middle managers, and 29 supervisors. Significant results included the following:

- The higher the level of management, the greater the perceived amount of political activity.
- The larger the organization, the greater the perceived amount of political activity.
- Personnel in staff positions were viewed as more political than those in line positions.
- People in marketing were the most political; those in production were the least political.
- "Reorganization changes" reportedly prompted more political activity than any other type of change.
- A majority (61 percent) of those interviewed believed that organizational politics helps advance one's career.
- Forty-five percent believed that organizational politics distracts from organizational goals.[45]

Regarding the last two findings, it was clear that political activities were seen as helpful to the individual. On the other hand, the interviewed managers were split on the question of the value of politics to the organization. Managers who believed political behavior had a positive impact on the organization cited the following reasons: "gaining visibility for ideas, improving coordination and communication, developing teams and groups, and increasing *esprit de corps*. . . ."[46] The most-often-cited negative effect of politics in the study was its distraction of managers from organizational goals. Misuse of resources and conflict were also mentioned as typical problems.

Political Tactics

As defined earlier, organizational politics takes in a lot of behavioral territory. The following six political tactics are common expressions of politics in the workplace:

- *Posturing.* Those who use this tactic look for situations in which they can make a good impression. "One-upmanship" and taking credit for other people's work are included in this category.
- *Empire building.* Gaining and keeping control over human and material resources is the principal motivation behind this tactic. Those with large budgets usually feel more safely entrenched in their positions and believe they have more influence over peers and superiors.
- *Making the supervisor look good.* Traditionally referred to as "apple polishing," this political strategy is prompted by a desire to favorably influence those who control one's career ascent. Anyone with an oversized ego is an easy target for this tactic.
- *Collecting and using social IOUs.* Reciprocal exchange of political favors can be done in two ways: (1) helping someone look good or (2) preventing someone from looking bad by ignoring or covering up a mistake. Those who rely on this tactic feel that all favors are coins of exchange rather than expressions of altruism or unselfishness.
- *Creating power and loyalty cliques.* Because there is power in numbers, the idea here is to face superiors and competitors as a cohesive group rather than alone.
- *Engaging in destructive competition.* As a last-ditch effort, some people will resort to character assassination through suggestive remarks, vindictive gossip, or outright lies. This tactic also includes sabotaging the work of a competitor.[47]

Obvious illegalities notwithstanding, one's own values and ethics, as well as organizational sanctions, are the final arbiters of whether these tactics are acceptable. (See Table 13.2 for a practicing manager's advice on how to win at office politics.)

Antidotes to Political Behavior

The foregoing political tactics vary in degree. The average person will probably acknowledge using at least one of these strategies. But excessive political maneuvering can become a serious threat to productivity

13e Happy Birthday, Boss, Bring It On!

Responses to a survey of 1,000 employees asking whether they buy a birthday gift for their boss: 57 percent said "Yes;" 42 percent said "No."

Letter to *Fortune* magazine:

I am a 31-year-old executive at a company headed by a friendly but fiercely competitive CEO. We get along fine, but here's the thing: We both play racquet-ball, and he's mentioned repeatedly that we should play sometime. I keep putting off setting a date for a game because I'm an excellent player and I'm pretty sure I would crush him, which I'm afraid would be career suicide. Should I agree to play? If so, should I play to win?—Killer Backhand

Sources: "Do You Buy Your Boss a Birthday Gift?" USA Today (May 16, 2007): 1B; and Anne Fisher, "Will I Lose If I Beat the Boss at Racquetball?" Fortune (January 24, 2005): 36.

QUESTIONS:

How would you handle these situations? How "political" are your answers?

TABLE **13.2**   One Manager's Rules for Winning at Office Politics

1. Find out what the boss expects.
2. Build an information network. Knowledge is power. Identify the people who have power and the extent and direction of it. Title doesn't necessarily reflect actual influence. Find out how the grapevine works. Develop good internal public relations for yourself.
3. Find a mentor. This is a trusted counselor who can be honest with you and help train and guide you to improve your ability and effectiveness as a manager.
4. Don't make enemies without a very good reason.
5. Avoid cliques. Keep circulating in the office.
6. If you must fight, fight over something that is really worth it. Don't lose ground over minor matters or petty differences.
7. Gain power through allies. Build ties that bind. Create IOUs, obligations, and loyalties. Do not be afraid to enlist help from above.
8. Maintain control. Don't misuse your cohorts. Maintain the status and integrity of your allies.
9. Mobilize your forces when necessary. Don't commit your friends without their approval. Be a gracious winner when you do win.
10. Never hire a family member or a close friend.

Source: Adapted from David E. Hall, "Winning at Office Politics," Credit & Financial Management, *86 (April 1984): 23. Reprinted with permission from* Credit & Financial Management. *Copyright April 1984, published by the National Association of Credit Management, 475 Park Avenue South, New York, NY 10016.*

when self-interests clearly override the interests of the group or organization. Organizational politics can be kept within reasonable bounds by applying the following five tips:

- Strive for a climate of openness and trust.
- Measure performance results rather than dwelling on personalities.
- Encourage top management to refrain from exhibiting political behavior that will be imitated by employees.
- Strive to integrate individual and organizational goals through meaningful work and career planning.
- Practice job rotation to encourage broader perspectives and understanding of the problems of others.[48]

CONFORMITY AND GROUPTHINK

Conformity means complying with the role expectations and norms perceived by the majority to be appropriate in a particular situation. Conformity enhances predictability, which is generally thought to be good for rational planning and productive enterprise. How can anything be accomplished if people cannot be counted

conformity: complying with prevailing role expectations and norms

on to perform their assigned duties? On the other hand, why do so many employees actively participate in or passively condone illegal and unethical organizational practices involving discrimination, environmental degradation, accounting fraud, and unfair competition?[49] The answers to these questions lie along a continuum with anarchy at one end and blind conformity at the other. Socially responsible management is anchored to a point somewhere between them.[50]

Research on Conformity

Social psychologists have discovered much about human behavior by studying individuals and groups in controlled laboratory settings. One classic laboratory study conducted by Solomon Asch was designed to answer the following question: How often will an individual take a stand against a unanimous majority that is obviously wrong?[51] Asch's results were both intriguing and unsettling.

THE HOT SEAT.   Asch began his study by assembling groups of seven to nine college students, supposedly to work on a perceptual problem. Actually, though, Asch was studying conformity. All but one member of each group were Asch's confederates, and Asch told them exactly how to behave and what to say. The experiment was really concerned with the reactions of the remaining student—called the naïve subject—who didn't know what was going on.

All the students in each group were shown cards with lines similar to those in Figure 13.4. They were

"Everyone in favor raise your right hand." This vote took place at Beijing's Great Hall of the People in late 2007 as the 17th Communist Party Congress drew to a close. Thanks to general conformity and stifled dissent, Chinese President Hu Jintao was able to consolidate his power base. In your world view, how much conformity is too much?

instructed to match the line on the left with the one on the right that was closest to it in length. The differences in length among the lines on the right were obvious. Each group went through 12 rounds of the matching process, with a different set of lines for every round. The researcher asked one group member at a time to announce his or her choice to the group. Things proceeded normally for the first two rounds as each group member voiced an opinion. Agreement was unanimous. Suddenly, on the third round only one individual, the naïve subject, chose the correct pair of lines. All the other group members chose a different (and obviously wrong) pair. During the rounds in which there was disagreement, all of Asch's confederates conspired to select an incorrect pair of lines. It was the individual versus the rest of the group.

FOLLOWING THE IMMORAL MAJORITY. Each of the naïve subjects was faced with a personal dilemma. Should he or she fight the group or give in to the obviously incorrect choice of the overwhelming majority? Among 31 naïve subjects who made a total of 217 judgments, two-thirds of the judgments

FIGURE **13.4** The Asch Line Experiment

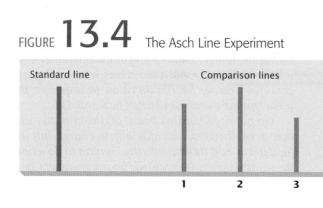

were correct. The other one-third were incorrect; that is, they were consistent with the majority opinion. Individual differences were great, with some subjects yielding to the incorrect majority opinion more readily than others. *Only 20 percent of the naïve subjects remained entirely independent in their judgments.* All the rest turned their backs on their own perceptions and went along with the group at least once. In other words, 80 percent of Asch's subjects knuckled under to the pressure of group opinion at least once, even though they knew the majority was dead wrong.

Replications of Asch's study in the Middle East (Kuwait) and in Japan have demonstrated that this tendency toward conformity is not unique to American culture.[52] Indeed, a statistical analysis of 133 Asch conformity studies across 17 countries concluded that blind conformity is a greater problem in collectivist ("we") cultures than in individualist ("me") cultures. Japan is strongly collectivist, whereas the United States and Canada are highly individualistic cultures.[53] (You may find it instructive to ponder how you would act in such a situation.)[54]

Because Asch's study was a contrived laboratory experiment, it failed to probe the relationship between cohesiveness and conformity. Asch's naïve subjects were outsiders. But more recent research on "groupthink" has shown that a cohesive group of insiders can fall victim to blind conformity.

Groupthink

After studying the records of several successful and several unsuccessful American foreign policy decisions, psychologist Irving Janis uncovered an undesirable by-product of group cohesiveness. He labeled this problem **groupthink** and defined it as a "mode of thinking that people engage in when they are deeply involved in a cohesive in-group, when the members' strivings for unanimity override their motivation to realistically appraise alternative courses of action."[55] Groupthink helps explain how intelligent policymakers, in

both government and business, can sometimes make incredibly unwise decisions.

One dramatic result of groupthink in action was the Vietnam War. Strategic advisers in three successive administrations rubber-stamped battle plans laced with false assumptions. Critical thinking, reality testing, and moral judgment were temporarily shelved as decisions to escalate the war were enthusiastically railroaded through. Although Janis acknowledges that cohesive groups are not inevitably victimized by groupthink, he warns group decision makers to be alert for the signs of groupthink—the risk is always there.

SYMPTOMS OF GROUPTHINK. According to Janis, the onset of groupthink is foreshadowed by a definite pattern of symptoms. Among these are excessive optimism, an assumption of inherent morality, suppression of dissent, and an almost desperate quest for unanimity.[56] Given such a decision-making climate, the probability of a poor decision is high. Managers face a curious dilemma here. While a group is still in stage 1 or stage 2 of development, its cohesiveness is too low for it to get much accomplished in the face of emotional and time-consuming power struggles. But by the time, in stage 3, that the group achieves enough cohesiveness to make decisions promptly, the risk of groupthink is high. The

"Damn it, Hopkins, didn't you get yesterday's memo?"

trick is to achieve needed cohesiveness without going to the extreme of groupthink.

PREVENTING GROUPTHINK. According to Janis, one of the group members should periodically ask, "Are we allowing ourselves to become victims of groupthink?"[57] More fundamental preventive measures include

- Avoiding the use of groups to rubber-stamp decisions that have already been made by higher management.
- Urging each group member to be a critical evaluator.
- Bringing in outside experts for fresh perspectives.
- Assigning someone the role of devil's advocate to challenge assumptions and alternatives.[58]
- Taking time to consider possible side effects and the consequences of alternative courses of action.[59]

Ideally, decision quality improves when these steps become second nature in cohesive groups. But groupthink remains a constant threat in management circles.

One major area ripe for abuse is corporate governance. Corporate boards of directors are supposed to represent the interests of stockholders and to hold top executives accountable for results. Too often, however, domineering CEOs and pliable boards create the perfect environment for groupthink.[60] For example, consider Al Dunlap, as profiled in the book *Bad Leadership*, by Harvard's Barbara Kellerman. Dunlap, nicknamed "chainsaw Al" and "Rambo in pinstripes" by the business press, was hired as CEO of Sunbeam Corporation in 1996 to turn the company around. Less than two years later, after Dunlap had slashed 40 percent of Sunbeam's payroll while richly rewarding himself, the company was deeply in debt and on the verge of bankruptcy. Dunlap was fired amid claims of financial trickery. Kellerman explains how Dunlap fostered a climate conducive to groupthink:

> *Dunlap's original contract gave him the right to immediately select three new board members and eventually to replace nearly every director with one of his own choosing. Consequently, until nearly the end of his reign, the majority of board members supported him; they were not overly curious, nor did they seek to interfere with the way he ran the business. Sunbeam's board unanimously approved his plans for restructuring, no matter [what] its draconian measures. And whatever their personal reservations, board members continued nearly for the duration to acquiesce in what Dunlap wanted and when he wanted it. . . .*
>
> *On paper, Sunbeam's board of directors, like all boards of directors, was officially in charge, but in fact, it was not. By empowering Dunlap to do what he wanted when he wanted, board members became followers, even groupies.[61]*

13f It's My Way or the Highway

Letter to *Fast Company* magazine:

I'm a lawyer, and I have just joined my first corporate board. The chairman, a client of mine, runs meetings as if only his ideas matter; he seems more interested in impressing us than in using our counsel.

Source: Kerry J. Sulkowicz, "The Corporate Shrink," Fast Company, no. 82 (May 2004): 54.

QUESTIONS:

What is the risk of groupthink in this type of situation? Explain. How would you handle the situation if you were the lawyer? What are the ethical implications of your answer?

Disturbing? Yes. Unusual? Not really, especially when groupthink prevails.

Managers who cannot imagine themselves being victimized by blind conformity are prime candidates for groupthink.[62] Dean Tjosvold at Lingnan University in Hong Kong recommends "cooperative conflict" (see the Manager's Toolkit feature at the end of this chapter). The constructive use of conflict is discussed further in Chapter 15.

13g Survey Says . . .

Respondents in a survey of 305 executives said teamwork was the most important skill (44 percent).

Respondents in a survey of 510 recent college graduates said teamwork was the skill they believed employers most wanted (38 percent).

Source: Adapted from Mary Beth Marklein, "Panel Urges Collegians to Focus on Liberal Arts," USA Today (January 11, 2007): 9D.

QUESTIONS:

How would you rate yourself as a team player? Which teamwork skills—such as communication, group problem solving, conflict management, negotiation, leadership, and persuasion—do you need to develop?

TEAMS, TEAMWORK, AND TRUST

Teams are the organizational unit of choice today, especially teams that mix and match people with different talents and perspectives. For instance. IBM's CEO, Samuel J. Palmisano, has staked the future of his giant corporation on teams, starting at the top.

> *For generations, ... [the] 12-person body presiding over IBM's strategy and initiatives represented the inner sanctum for every aspiring Big Blue executive. . . . [In 2003], the CEO hit the send button on an e-mail to 300 senior managers announcing that this venerable committee was finito, kaput. Palmisano instead would work directly with three teams he had put in place the year before—they comprised people from all over the company who could bring the best ideas to the table. The old committee, with its monthly meetings, just slowed things down.*[63]

Thus, teams and teamwork are vital group dynamics in the modern workplace.[64] Unfortunately, team skills in today's typical organization tend to lag far behind technical skills.[65] It is one thing to be a creative software engineer, for example. It is quite another for that software specialist to be able to team up with other specialists in accounting, finance, and marketing to beat the competition to market with a profitable new product. In this final section, we explore teams and teamwork by discussing cross-functional teams, virtual teams, a model of team effectiveness, and the importance of trust.

Cross-Functional Teams

A **cross-functional team** is a task group staffed with a mix of specialists focused on a common objective. This structural innovation deserves special attention here because cross-functional teams are becoming commonplace.[66] They may or may not be self-managed, although self-managed teams (as discussed in Chapter 12) generally are cross-functional. Cross-functional teams are based on assigned rather than voluntary membership. Quality control (QC) circles made up of volunteers, also discussed in Chapter 12, technically are in a different category. Cross-functional teams stand in sharp

cross-functional team: task group staffed with a mix of specialists pursuing a common objective

BEST PRACTICES

Cross-Functional Teamwork Fosters Creativity at Microsoft

MEDX [Mobile and Embedded Devices Experience design center] has long, shared desks equipped with computer monitors, also for sharing, on 360-degree swivels. The gleaming, white walls are actually floor-to-ceiling white boards intended to foster collaborative brainstorming.

On a recent day, general manager Ira Snyder broached a favorite topic with researcher Bryan Agnetta: how to make the notifications that alert a phone user about appointments or missed calls more prominent, without being obtrusive. A wandering engineer joined in, then a product manager and a statistician. The group drifted over to a corner furnished with a couch and easy chairs. Someone started to scribble on the wall. An hour later the blank wall was festooned with a sprawling flow chart.

"We may have 100 little pieces we're working on," Snyder says. "The ability to pop folks out and place them in different groups is invaluable. Whoever can help out, we let them play."

Source: Byron Acohido, "Microsoft Cultures Creativity in Unique Lab," USA Today (July 11, 2007): 3B.

---

contrast to the tradition of lumping specialists into functional departments, thereby creating the problem of integrating and coordinating those departments. For example, ArcelorMittal, the world's largest steel company, relies on cross-functional teams to integrate its various specialists in East Chicago, in Indiana, and at other plants around the world.

The company has a five-part process, from idea through launch, that is closely monitored and reviewed. Cross-functional teams, which range from scientists to plant managers to salespeople, are crucial—because unless all parts of the process work, the whole thing will flop. Communication is constant.[67]

Cross-functional teams have exciting potential. But they present management with the immense challenge of getting technical specialists to be effective boundary spanners (see Best Practices).

Talk about teamwork and trust! The effectiveness of NASCAR driver Kyle Busch's pit crew is measured in fractions of a second. Risks to life and limb are huge. Everyone in this cross-functional team consisting of driver, pit crew, support personnel, and owner and sponsors is focused on a single goal—a safe trip to the checkered flag.

Virtual Teams

Along with the move toward virtual organizations, discussed in Chapter 9, have come virtual teams. A **virtual team** is a physically dispersed task group linked electronically.[68] A researcher elaborates:

A virtual team, similar to face-to-face teams, is a group of people who interact to achieve a common purpose. However, unlike face-to-face teams, virtual teams operate across space, time, culture, and organizational boundaries using electronic means.[69]

Face-to-face contact is usually minimal or nonexistent. E-mail, voice mail, videoconferencing, Web-based project software, and other forms of electronic interchange allow members of virtual teams from anywhere on the planet to accomplish a common goal.[70] It is commonplace today for virtual teams to have members from different organizations, different time zones, and different cultures.[71] Because virtual organizations and teams are so new, paced as they are by emerging technologies, managers are having to learn from the school of hard knocks rather than from established practice.

Just as we noted (in Chapter 9) about virtual organizations, one reality of managing virtual teams is clear. *Periodic face-to-face interaction, trust building, and team building are more important than ever when team members are widely dispersed in time and space.* Although faceless interaction may work in Internet chat rooms, it can doom a virtual team with a crucial task and a pressing deadline. Additionally, special steps need to be taken to clearly communicate role expectations, performance norms, goals, and deadlines (see Table 13.3). Virtual teamwork may be faster than the traditional face-to-face kind, but it is by no means easier[72] (see this chapter's Closing Case).

TABLE 13.3 The Basics of Managing a Virtual Team

Forming the Team

- Develop a team mission statement along with teamwork expectations and norms, project goals, and deadlines
- Recruit team members with complementary skills and diverse backgrounds who have the ability and willingness to contribute
- Get a high-level sponsor to champion the project
- Post a skill, biographical sketch, contact information, and "local time" matrix to familiarize members with each other and their geographic dispersion

Preparing the Team

- Make sure everyone has a broadband connection and is comfortable with virtual teamwork technologies (e.g., e-mail, instant messaging, conference calls, online meeting and collaboration programs such as WebEx, and videoconferencing)
- Establish hardware and software compatibility
- Make sure everyone is comfortable with *synchronous* (interacting at the same time) and *asynchronous* (interacting at different times) teamwork
- Get individuals to buy-in on team goals, deadlines, and individual tasks

Building Teamwork and Trust

- Make sure everyone is involved (during meetings and overall)
- Arrange periodic face-to-face work meetings, team-building exercises, and leisure activities
- Encourage collaboration between and among team members on sub-tasks
- Establish an early-warning system for conflicts (e.g., gripe sessions)

Motivating and Leading the Team

- Post a scoreboard to mark team progress toward goals
- Celebrate team accomplishments both virtually and face-to-face
- Begin each virtual meeting with praise and recognition for outstanding individual contributions
- Keep team members' line managers informed of their accomplishments and progress

Sources: Based on discussions in Jack Gordon, "Do Your Virtual Teams Deliver Only Virtual Performance?" Training, 42 (June 2005): 20–26; Deborah L. Duarte and Nancy Tennant Snyder, Mastering Virtual Teams, 3rd edition (San Francisco: Jossey-Bass, 2006); and Arvind Malhotra, Ann Majchrzak, and Benson Rosen, "Leading Virtual Teams," Academy of Management Perspectives 21 (February 2007): 60–70.

FIGURE **13.5** A Model of Team Effectiveness

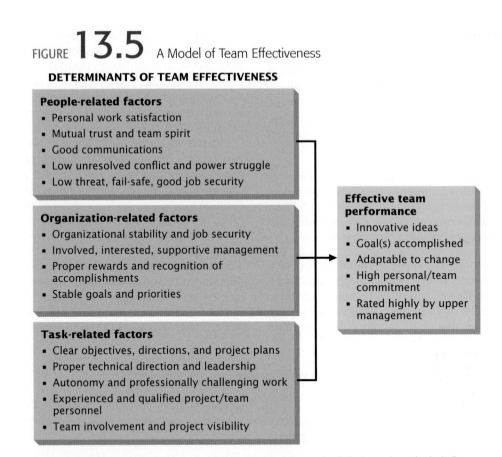

DETERMINANTS OF TEAM EFFECTIVENESS

People-related factors
- Personal work satisfaction
- Mutual trust and team spirit
- Good communications
- Low unresolved conflict and power struggle
- Low threat, fail-safe, good job security

Organization-related factors
- Organizational stability and job security
- Involved, interested, supportive management
- Proper rewards and recognition of accomplishments
- Stable goals and priorities

Task-related factors
- Clear objectives, directions, and project plans
- Proper technical direction and leadership
- Autonomy and professionally challenging work
- Experienced and qualified project/team personnel
- Team involvement and project visibility

Effective team performance
- Innovative ideas
- Goal(s) accomplished
- Adaptable to change
- High personal/team commitment
- Rated highly by upper management

Source: Reprinted from Journal of Product Innovation Management, 7, Hans J. Thamhain, "Managing Technologically Innovative Team Efforts Toward New Product Success," pp. 5–18. Copyright 1990, with permission from Elsevier Science.

What Makes Workplace Teams Effective?

Widespread use of team formats—including quality circles, self-managed teams, cross-functional teams, and virtual teams—necessitates greater knowledge of team effectiveness.[73] A model of team effectiveness criteria and determinants is presented in Figure 13.5. This model is the product of two field studies involving 360 new-product-development managers employed by 52 high-tech companies.[74] It is a generic model that applies equally well to all workplace teams.[75]

The five criteria for effective team performance in Figure 13.5 parallel the criteria for organizational effectiveness discussed in Chapter 9. Thus, team effectiveness feeds organizational effectiveness.

Determinants of team effectiveness, shown in Figure 13.5, are grouped into people-, organization-, and task-related factors. Considered separately, these factors involve rather routine aspects of good management. But the collective picture reveals each factor to be part of a complex and interdependent whole.

Managers cannot maximize just a few of them, ignore the rest, and hope to have an effective team. In the spirit of the Japanese concept of *kaizen*, managers and team leaders need to strive for "continuous improvement" on all fronts. Because gains on one front will inevitably be offset by losses in another, the pursuit of team effectiveness and teamwork is an endless battle with no guarantees of success.

Let's focus on trust, one of the people-related factors in Figure 13.5 that can make or break work teams.

Trust: A Key to Team Effectiveness

Trust, a belief in the integrity, character, or ability of others, is essential if people are to achieve anything together in the long run.[76] Participative management programs are very dependent on trust.[77] According to Stanford's Jeffrey Pfeffer, "one of the most important factors in employee retention and motivation is trust in

trust: belief in the integrity, character, or ability of others

management."[78] Sadly, trust is not one of the hallmarks of the current U.S. business scene. Harris Interactive polls in the United States in 2000 and 2004 found that the public's "confidence in executives" had plunged from an already low 28 percent to 12 percent.[79] To a greater extent than they may initially suspect, managers determine the level of trust in the organization and its component work groups and teams. Experts in the area of social capital tell us that

> *No one can manufacture trust or mandate it into existence. When someone says, "You can trust me," we usually don't, and rightly so. But leaders can make deliberate investments in trust. They can give people reasons to trust one another instead of reasons to watch their backs. They can refuse to reward successes that are built on untrusting behavior. And they can display trust and trustworthiness in their own actions, both personally and on behalf of the company.*[80]

ZAND'S MODEL OF TRUST.   Trust is not a free-floating variable. It affects, and in turn is affected by, other group processes. Dale E. Zand's model of work group interaction puts trust into proper perspective (see Figure 13.6). Zand believes that trust is the key to establishing productive interpersonal relationships.[81]

Primary responsibility for creating a climate of trust falls on the manager. Team members usually look to the manager, who enjoys hierarchical advantage and greater access to key information, to set the tone for interpersonal dealings. Threatening or intimidating actions by the manager will probably encourage the group to bind together in cohesive resistance. Therefore, trust needs to be developed right from the beginning, when team members are still receptive to positive managerial influence.

Trust is initially encouraged by a manager's openness and honesty. Trusting managers talk *with* their people rather than *at* them. A trusting manager, according to Zand's model, demonstrates a willingness to be influenced by others and to change if the facts indicate a change is appropriate. Mutual trust between a manager and team members encourages *self-control,* as opposed to control through direct supervision.

Paradoxically, managerial control actually expands when committed group or team members enjoy greater freedom in pursuing consensual goals. Those who trust each other generally avoid taking advantage of others' weaknesses or shortcomings.[82]

SIX WAYS TO BUILD TRUST.   Trust is a fragile thing. As most of us know from personal experience, trust grows at a painfully slow pace yet can be destroyed in an instant with a thoughtless remark. Mistrust can erode the long-term effectiveness of work teams and organizations. According to management professor and consultant Fernando Bartolomé, managers need

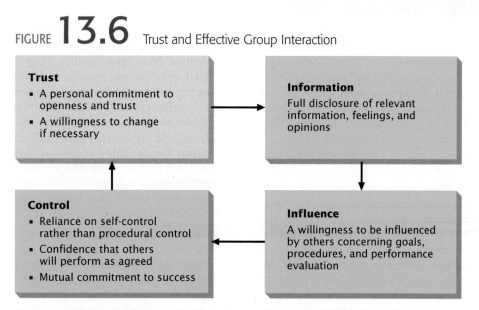

FIGURE **13.6**   Trust and Effective Group Interaction

Trust
- A personal commitment to openness and trust
- A willingness to change if necessary

Information
Full disclosure of relevant information, feelings, and opinions

Control
- Reliance on self-control rather than procedural control
- Confidence that others will perform as agreed
- Mutual commitment to success

Influence
A willingness to be influenced by others concerning goals, procedures, and performance evaluation

Source: Reprinted from "Trust and Managerial Problem Solving," by Dale E. Zand and published in Administrative Science Quarterly, *17, no. 2 (June 1972), by permission of* Administrative Science Quarterly. © *1972 by Cornell University.*

13h No Team Is an Island

Martha Rogers, partner, Peppers and Rogers Group, Bowling Green, Ohio:

You can't say, "teams work because of this" or "teams don't work because of that"—because it depends. But if you're looking for one quality that most good teams share, I'd have to say that it's the culture of the company in which the team exists. Is the culture one that rewards groups? Is it one that rewards individuals? Or is it a culture where no one gets rewarded? Look around. Watch how people act and interact, regardless of whether they're on a team. Do people do things for one another? Do they pick up coffee for others when they're going out? If the culture is full of give and take—if it's supportive and trusting—there's a good chance that you'll see successful teams at work.

Source: As quoted in Regina Fazio Maruca, "What Makes Teams Work?" Fast Company, no. 40 (November 2000): 109.

QUESTIONS:

Do you agree? Explain. How can management build a supportive and trusting organizational culture?

to concentrate on six areas: communication, support, respect, fairness, predictability, and competence.

- *Communication.* Keep your people informed by providing accurate and timely feedback and explaining policies and decisions. Be open and honest about your own problems. Do not hoard information or use it as a political device or reward.
- *Support.* Be an approachable person who is available to help, encourage, and coach your people. Show an active interest in their lives and be willing to come to their defense.
- *Respect.* Delegating important duties is the sincerest form of respect, followed closely by being a good listener.
- *Fairness.* Evaluate your people fairly and objectively and be liberal in giving credit and praise.
- *Predictability.* Be dependable and consistent in your behavior and keep all your promises.
- *Competence.* Be a good role model by exercising good business judgment and being technically and professionally competent.[83]

Managers find that trust begets trust. In other words, those who feel they are trusted tend to trust others in return.[84]

SUMMARY

1. Managers need a working understanding of group dynamics because groups are the basic building blocks of organizations. Generating social capital through strong, constructive, and win-win relationships is essential to success today. Both informal (friendship) and formal (work) groups are made up of two or more freely interacting individuals who have a common identity and purpose.

2. After someone has been attracted to a group, cohesiveness—a "we" feeling—encourages continued membership. Roles are social expectations for behavior in a specific position, whereas norms are more general standards for conduct in a given social setting. Norms are enforced because they help the group survive, clarify role expectations, protect self-images, and enhance the group's identity by emphasizing key values. Compliance with role expectations and norms is rewarded with social reinforcement; noncompliance is punished by criticism, ridicule, and ostracism.

3. Mature groups are characterized by mutual acceptance, encouragement of minority opinion, and minimal emotional conflict. They are the product of a developmental process with identifiable stages. During the first three stages—orientation, conflict and challenge, and cohesion—power and authority problems are resolved. Groups are faced with the obstacle of uncertainty over interpersonal relations during the last three stages—delusion, disillusion, and acceptance. Committees have a widespread reputation for inefficiency and ineffectiveness because they tend to get stalled in an early stage of group development.

4. Organizational politics centers on the pursuit of self-interest. Research shows greater political activity to be associated with higher levels of management, larger organizations, staff and marketing personnel, and reorganizations. Political tactics such as posturing, empire building, making the boss look good, collecting and using social IOUs,

creating power and loyalty cliques, and engaging in destructive competition need to be kept in check if the organization is to be effective.

5. Although a fairly high degree of conformity is necessary if organizations and society in general are to function properly, blind conformity is ultimately dehumanizing and destructive. Research shows that individuals have a strong tendency to bend to the will of the majority, even if the majority is clearly wrong. Cohesive decision-making groups can be victimized by groupthink when unanimity becomes more important than critical evaluation of alternative courses of action.

6. Teams are becoming the structural format of choice. Today's employees generally have better technical skills than team skills. Cross-functional teams are particularly promising because they facilitate greater strategic speed. Although members of virtual teams by definition collaborate via electronic media, there is still a need for periodic face-to-face interaction and team building. Three sets of factors—relating to people, organization, and task—combine to determine the effectiveness of a work team.

7. Trust, a key ingredient of effective teamwork, is disturbingly low in the American workplace today. When work group members trust one another, there will be a more active exchange of information, more interpersonal influence, and hence greater self-control. Managers can build trust through communication, support, respect (primarily in the form of delegation), fairness, predictability, and competence.

TERMS TO UNDERSTAND

- Social capital, p. 368
- Group, p. 368
- Informal group, p. 369
- Formal group, p. 370
- Cohesiveness, p. 370
- Role, p. 372
- Norms, p. 372
- Ostracism, p. 373
- Organizational politics, p. 377
- Conformity, p. 380
- Groupthink, p. 382
- Cross-functional team, p. 383
- Virtual team, p. 385
- Trust, p. 386

MANAGER'S TOOLKIT

How to Use *Cooperative Conflict* to Avoid Groupthink

Guides for Action
- Elaborate positions and ideas.
- List facts, information, and theories.
- Ask for clarification.
- Clarify opposing ideas.
- Search for new information.
- Challenge opposing ideas and positions.
- Reaffirm your confidence in those who differ.
- Listen to all ideas.
- Restate opposing arguments that are unclear.
- Identify strengths in opposing arguments.
- Change your mind only when confronted with good evidence.
- Integrate various information and reasoning.
- Create alternative solutions.
- Agree to a solution responsive to several points of view.
- Use a new round of cooperative conflict to develop and refine the solution.

Pitfalls to Avoid
- Assume your position is superior.
- Prove your ideas are right and must be accepted.
- Interpret opposition to your ideas as a personal attack.
- Refuse to admit weaknesses in your position.
- Pretend to listen.
- Ridicule to weaken the others' resolve to disagree.
- Try to win over people to your position through charm and exaggeration.
- See accepting another's ideas as a sign of weakness.

Source: Reprinted from Learning to Manage Conflict: Getting People to Work Together Productively *by Dean Tjosvold. Copyright © 1993 Dean Tjosvold. First published by Lexington Books. All rights reserved. All correspondence should be sent to Lexington Books, 4720 Boston Way, Lanham, MD, 20706.*

ACTION LEARNING EXERCISE

Management Teamwork Survey

Instructions: Think of your present job (or a past one) and check one box for each of the following 10 questions. Alternatively, you can ask a manager to complete this survey. The idea is to assess the organization's commitment to building cooperation and teamwork among managers. This instrument also pinpoints weak spots needing attention.

TO WHAT EXTENT DO ...	Never	To a Limited Extent	To a Great Extent	Always
1. Our managers pursue common goals that focus on our customers and profitability?	☐	☐	☐	☐
2. We have team-based performance measurements and feedback devices?	☐	☐	☐	☐
3. Our top managers demonstrate and foster cooperation in their approach to leadership?	☐	☐	☐	☐
4. We provide incentives and rewards that encourage management cooperation?	☐	☐	☐	☐
5. We engage in ongoing team-building activities and skill development among our managers?	☐	☐	☐	☐
6. We identify and resolve problems/conflicts among managers in a timely fashion?	☐	☐	☐	☐
7. We create management team ownership of decision processes and outcomes?	☐	☐	☐	☐
8. We clarify each manager's roles and goals to each other?	☐	☐	☐	☐
9. We integrate planning, problem-solving, and communication activities among managers?	☐	☐	☐	☐
10. We build consensus and understanding around work processes and systems?	☐	☐	☐	☐

Interpretation: Scores in Columns 1 and 2 represent areas that damage management cooperation and teamwork; these areas should be systematically addressed to enhance organizational performance. Scores in Columns 3 and 4 represent practices that can and should be continued and improved to increase management cooperation and teamwork.

Source: Clinton O. Longenecker and Mitchell Neubert, "Barriers and Gateways to Management Cooperation and Teamwork." Reprinted with permission from Business Horizons, 43 *(September–October 2000). Copyright 2000 by the Trustees at Indiana University, Kelley School of Business.*

For Consideration/Discussion

1. Why are cooperation and teamwork among managers so important today?

2. Overall, how does this organization measure up in terms of fostering managerial cooperation and teamwork?

3. Which areas are strongest? How can they be made even stronger?

4. Which areas are weakest and what needs to be done?

5. Which factors in this survey are most critical to organizational success today? Explain.

CLOSING CASE
Thirteen Time Zones Can't Keep Lucent's Virtual Team from Succeeding

Note: After this case study was written, Lucent merged with France's Alcatel to form Alcatel-Lucent, a global company with 79,000 employees in 130 countries. The executive offices are in Paris and the CEO is an American, Patricia Russo.[85]

Imagine designing the most complex product in your company's history. You need 500 engineers for the job. They will assemble the world's most delicate hardware and write more than a million lines of code. In communicating, the margin for error is minuscule.

Now, scatter those 500 engineers over 13 time zones. Over three continents. Over five states in the United States alone. The Germans schedule to perfection. The Americans work on the fly. In Massachusetts, they go to work early. In New Jersey, they stay late.

Now you have some idea of what Bill Klinger and Frank Polito have been through in the past 18 months. As top software-development managers in Lucent Technologies' Bell Labs division, they played critical roles in creating a new fiber-optic phone switch called the Bandwidth Manager, which sells for about $1 million. . . . The high-stakes development was Lucent's most complex undertaking by far since its spin-off from AT&T in 1996.

Managing such a far-flung staff ("distributed development," it's called) is possible only because of technology. But as the two Lucent leaders painfully learned, distance still magnifies differences, even in a high-tech age. "You lose informal interaction—going to lunch, the water cooler," Mr. Klinger says. "You can never discount how many issues get solved that way."

The product grew as a hybrid of exotic, widely dispersed technologies: "lightwave" science from Lucent's Merrimack Valley plant, north of Boston, where Mr. Polito works; "cross-connect" products here in New Jersey, where Mr. Klinger works; timing devices from the Netherlands; and optics from Germany.

Development also demanded multiple locations because Lucent wanted a core model as a platform for special versions for foreign and other niche markets. Involving overseas engineers in the flagship product would speed the later development of spin-offs and impress foreign customers.

And rushing to market meant tapping software talent wherever it was available—ultimately at Lucent facilities in Colorado, Illinois, North Carolina, and India. "The scary thing, scary but exciting, was that no one had really pulled this off on this scale before," says Mr. Polito.

Communication technology was the easy part. Lashing together big computers in different cities [ensured that] . . . everyone was working on the same up-to-date software version. New project data from one city were instantly available on Web pages everywhere else. Test engineers in India could tweak prototypes in New Jersey. The project never went to sleep.

Technology, however, couldn't conquer cultural problems, especially acute between Messrs. Klinger's and Polito's respective staffs in New Jersey and Massachusetts. Each had its own programming traditions and product histories. Such basic words as "test" could mean different things. A programming chore requiring days in one context might take weeks in another. Differing work schedules and physical distance made each location suspect the other of slacking off. "We had such clashes," says Mr. Klinger.

Personality tests revealed deep geographic differences. Supervisors from the sleek, glass-covered New Jersey office, principally a research facility abounding in academics, scored as "thinking" people who used cause-and-effect analysis. Those from the old, brick facility in Massachusetts, mainly a manufacturing plant, scored as "feeling" types who based decisions on subjective, human values. Sheer awareness of the differences ("Now I know why you get on my nerves!") began to create common ground.

Amid much cynicism, the two directors hauled their technical managers into team exercises—working in small groups to scale a 14-foot wall and solve puzzles. It's corny, but such methods can accelerate trust building when time is short and the stakes are high. At one point Mr. Klinger asked managers to show up with the product manuals from their previous projects— then, in a ritualistic break from technical parochialism, instructed everyone to tear the covers to pieces.

More than anything else, it was sheer physical presence—face time—that began solidifying the group. Dozens of managers began meeting fortnightly in rotating cities, socializing as much time as their technical discussions permitted. (How better to grow familiar than over hot dogs, beer, and nine innings with the minor league Durham Bulls?) Foreign locations found the direct interaction especially valuable. "Going into the other culture is the only way to understand it," says Sigrid Hauenstein, a Lucent executive in Nuremberg, Germany. "If you don't have a common understanding, it's much more expensive to correct it later."

Eventually the project found its pace. People began wearing beepers to eliminate time wasted on voice-mail tag. Conference calls at varying levels kept everyone in the loop. Staffers posted their photos in the project's Web directory. Many created personal pages. "It's the ultimate democracy of the Web," Mr. Klinger says.

The product is now shipping—on schedule, within budget, and with more technical versatility than Lucent expected. Distributed development "paid off in spades," says Gerry Butters, Lucent optical-networking chief.

Even as it helps build the infrastructure of a digitally connected planet, Lucent is rediscovering the importance of face-to-face interaction. All the bandwidth in the world can convey only a fraction of what we are.

Source: *Wall Street Journal* (Eastern Edition) by Thomas Petzinger. Copyright 1999 by Dow Jones & Company, Inc. Reproduced with permission of Dow Jones & Company, Inc. in the format Textbook via Copyright Clearance Center.

FOR DISCUSSION

1 Which team effectiveness criteria in Figure 13.5 are apparent in this case?

2 How big a problem do you suppose organizational politics was during this project? Explain.

3 What practical lessons does this case teach managers about managing a virtual team?

4 Would you be comfortable working on this sort of global virtual team? Explain.

TEST PREPPER

True/False Questions

_____ 1. Jean is a member of both a formal group and an informal group if she socializes with her coworkers.

_____ 2. Members of a cohesive group tend to see themselves as "we" rather than "I."

_____ 3. Roles have a broader influence than norms, which focus on behavior in a specific position.

_____ 4. The first stage in the six-stage group development process is acceptance.

_____ 5. According to research, people in marketing were the least political, whereas people in production were the most political.

_____ 6. According to research, the more conformity in organizations, the better.

_____ 7. Too often, domineering CEOs and pliable corporate boards create the perfect environment for groupthink.

_____ 8. Quality control circles and cross-functional teams are the same thing.

_____ 9. Much more than goal accomplishment is involved in the model of team effectiveness.

_____10. According to a management professor and consultant who has suggested six ways in which managers can build trust, one of the best ways to show respect for subordinates is to delegate important duties.

Multiple-Choice Questions

1. Which of the following is *not* one of the four definitional dimensions of a group?
   A. Trust   B. Common identity
   C. Free interaction   D. Two or more people
   E. Common purpose

2. How do people become members of formal groups in the workplace?
   A. Volunteering   B. Demotion
   C. Lottery drawing   D. Luck
   E. Assignment

3. The tendency of group members to follow the group and resist outside influences is called
   A. attractiveness.   B. cohesiveness.
   C. ostracism.   D. conformity.
   E. groupthink.

4. Which of the following is the *best* description of norms?
   A. General standards of conduct
   B. Prescriptions for behavior in specific positions
   C. Individually determined principles
   D. Laws
   E. Culturally neutral principles

5. A "we" feeling becomes apparent during the _____ stage of the group development process.
   A. delusion   B. acceptance
   C. orientation   D. agreement
   E. cohesion

6. How do experts describe political behavior at work?
   A. Universally positive   B. Inevitably destructive
   C. Usually negative   D. Both positive and negative
   E. At first neutral but eventually positive

7. Which one of these was *not* found by researchers to be associated with increased political activity?
   A. Smaller organizations
   B. People in marketing
   C. Higher levels of management
   D. Reorganizations
   E. Staff personnel

8. What was the major finding in Asch's line experiments?
   A. Employees engage in organizational politics when they fear for their jobs.
   B. Americans hold stronger opinions than Japanese.
   C. People tend to yield to the majority opinion, even when it is wrong.
   D. Groupthink is not a problem in smaller companies.
   E. Women tend to make more ethical decisions than men.

9. A cross-functional team can *best* be described as
   A. a mix of employees and outside consultants.
   B. people assigned to play the role of devil's advocate.
   C. containing no more than three members.
   D. both managers and nonmanagers from the same department.
   E. a mix of specialists.

10. Which of the following is *not* among the areas that managers should concentrate on as they attempt to build trust?
   A. Predictability   B. Competence
   C. Fairness   D. Communication
   E. Friendship

See page T1 at the back of the text for answers to these questions. Want more questions? Visit the student Web site and take the ACE quizzes for more practice.

14

Influence, Power, and Leadership

Leaders, by definition, cannot do the work of the enterprise; they can only communicate what needs to be done, inspire trust and motivate others to execute the plans.[1]

—SUZANNE BATES

OBJECTIVES

- **Identify** and **describe** eight generic influence tactics used in modern organizations.

- **Identify** the five bases of power, and **explain** what it takes to make empowerment work.

- **Explain** the concept of emotional intelligence in terms of Goleman's four leadership traits.

- **Summarize** what the Ohio State model and the Leadership Grid® have taught managers about leadership.

- **Describe** the path-goal theory of leadership, and **explain** how the assumption on which it is based differs from the assumption on which Fiedler's contingency theory is based.

- **Describe** a transformational leader, and **explain** Greenleaf's philosophy of the servant leader.

- **Identify** the two key functions that mentors perform, and **explain** how a mentor can develop a junior manager's leadership skills.

- **Explain** the management of antecedents and consequences in behavior modification.

THE CHANGING WORKPLACE

"No Holds Barred:" An Interview with American Express CEO Ken Chenault

American Express had plenty of management-training programs in place before CEO Ken Chenault started making leadership development more intensive and disciplined over the past few years. It's a pattern more companies are following. Chenault sat down recently with *Fortune*'s Geoff Colvin to talk about what he's doing, why, and what he has learned. Edited excerpts:

You've recently taken several steps to improve leadership development at American Express. Is there a strategy behind what you're doing?

What's important about our approach is that it's a comprehensive and integrated one based on where I'm trying to take the company. So I start from two aspirations I've set for the company: We want to be one of the most successful companies in terms of financial and business performance, and we want to be one of the most respected and admired companies. Then, given the times we're in—and the fact that we're in the service business—people are our greatest asset. We need rationally and emotionally engaged people to be outstanding leaders.

One of the ways you pursue that goal is the sessions you lead with high-potential and senior-level managers. How do they work?

Every [new] senior vice president goes through an onboarding process. It's very important not only that we impart the strategies and business objectives of the company but also that they understand our culture and our leadership requirements. I always meet with them for several hours and have dinner with them. One of the most constructive parts of the session is a no-holds-barred Q&A. Also, wherever I travel around the world, I generally have an informal group of employees where we sit down and talk about leadership.

For sessions like those to be effective, the culture has to include a high level of straight talk. What's your assessment of candor at American Express?

I think the level is high. Is it high everywhere? That would be disingenuous to say. But one of the things I talk about often is constructive confrontation. I want to be confronted with the issues, the facts. I really want that engagement. The first time I did one of these sessions with the new senior VPs, they were a little tentative. But then word spread that I really want a no-holds-barred discussion.

What's increasingly clear is that when you are open to a discussion of leadership, and you're relating it to your company, it is much easier to get people to become open. There's not a lot of room to hide. So [our leadership development] has substantially increased the level of openness, which frankly was an unintended consequence.

A related issue is feedback. As leaders develop, you want them to get continual feedback, but at most companies they hardly get any. How's that going?

I was just talking to a group of our managers about that. Regular feedback is one of the hardest things to drive through an organization. Over the past several years the level of informal feedback has certainly increased—[but] not to a level I'm satisfied with.

You've recently started rating people on a grid showing performance on one axis and potential on the other—and telling people where they stand. Organizationally that must have been a very big deal.

It was a very big deal. It has resulted in some people understanding how they're viewed and deciding they should go elsewhere. But our employee-survey scores continue to improve as a result of, in my view, giving more honest and candid feedback.

Looking back on your own development, which experiences were most valuable?

The first was in the early '80s—I took over a division called merchandise services. It sold jewelry, stereos, electronics through the mail. It was a business that was outcast, a dispirited unit. People in the card business just hated it. I had to put together a strategy that was not just galvanizing to the business but also connected it to the broader business. I had to make some major leadership changes, do it quickly, and . . . motivate and engage the employees. We went from $100 million in sales to close to $700 million in three years. The pride of the organization just skyrocketed. What was terrific was that at a young age I had to confront all the elements of a business in crisis. That was an incredible developmental experience.

Another very formative experience was obviously 9/11. [American Express headquarters is directly across the street from the World Trade Center site.] We saw this was obviously a crisis, but we said, "We have to remember that reputations are won or lost in a crisis."

The most valuable experiences always seem to be crises.

Right. And one thing you learn is to understand thoroughly the attributes that are really important and focus on them so you're not just doing them unconsciously—you're conscious about it. It gives you an advantage. I say this all the time: Everyone can make a conscious choice to be a leader.

Source: Geoff Colvin, "No Holds Barred," *Fortune* (October 1, 2007): 102–103. © 2007 Time Inc. All rights reserved.

What do the following situations have in common?

- A magazine editor praises her supervisor's new outfit shortly before asking for the afternoon off.
- A milling-machine operator tells a friend that he will return the favor if his friend will watch out for the supervisor while he takes an unauthorized cigarette break.
- An office manager attempts to head off opposition to a new Internet-use policy by carefully explaining how it will be fair and will increase productivity.

Aside from the fact that all of these situations take place on the job, the common denominator is "influence." In each case, someone is trying to get his or her own way by influencing someone else's behavior. American Express's Ken Chenault is an inspiring role model for the skillful and responsible use of influence, power, and leadership.

Influence is any attempt by a person to change the behavior of superiors, peers, or lower-level employees. Influence is not inherently good or bad. As the foregoing situations illustrate, influence can be used for purely selfish reasons, to subvert organizational objectives, or to enhance organizational effectiveness. Managerial success is firmly linked to the ability to exercise the right sort of influence at the right time. A good

influence: any attempt to change another's behavior

example is Andrea Jung, CEO of Avon, as she was working her way up the executive ladder:

> *Jung had little business experience in foreign markets, but as the daughter of immigrants from Hong Kong and China (she was born in Toronto), she had a feel for different cultures. . . . She once flew to Mexico to unveil a new line of products. [Former CEO Jim] Preston recalls that Avon's executive team in Latin America expected her to bomb, that her Manhattan-glam look would make it hard for her to connect with the local sales staff. But Jung sprinkled a little Spanish into her talk and connected, says Preston, who heard glowing reports back from the team.*[2]

Jung's influence skills eventually paid off when she was named the first woman CEO of Avon in its 118-year history.

The purpose of this chapter is to examine different approaches to influencing others. We focus specifically on influence tactics, power, leadership, mentoring, and behavior modification.

INFLUENCE TACTICS IN THE WORKPLACE

A replication and refinement of an earlier groundbreaking study provides useful insights about on-the-job influence.[3] Both studies asked employees basically the same question: "How do you get your boss,

Could you be influenced to shave your head? These and 104 other Basin Electric Power Cooperative employees in Bismarck, North Dakota, did just that recently as part of a fundraising event. The worthy cause was for children's cancer research. Studying influence tactics makes us more aware of the powerful give and take of influence in our daily lives.

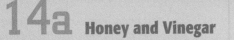

14a Honey and Vinegar

If there is one thing people care about, it is being taken seriously and treated as if they are important. So, behavior that treats others with discourtesy and disrespect is certainly no way to win friends.

Source: Jeffrey Pfeffer, What Were They Thinking? Unconventional Wisdom About Management *(Boston: Harvard Business School Press, 2007), p. 110.*

QUESTIONS:

In your daily affairs both inside and outside the workplace, which influence tactics do you rely on the most? Are you an effective influencer? Which approach to influence generally works best for managers, a positive (honey) approach or a negative (vinegar) approach? Explain.

For further information about the interactive annotations in this chapter, visit our student Web site.

coworker, or subordinate to do something you want?" The following eight generic influence tactics emerged:

1. *Consultation.* Seeking someone's participation in a decision or change
2. *Rational persuasion.* Trying to convince someone by relying on a detailed plan, supporting information, reasoning, or logic

3. *Inspirational appeals.* Appealing to someone's emotions, values, or ideals to generate enthusiasm and confidence
4. *Ingratiating tactics.* Making someone feel important or good before making a request; acting humble or friendly before making a request
5. *Coalition tactics.* Seeking the aid of others to persuade someone to agree
6. *Pressure tactics.* Relying on intimidation, demands, or threats to gain compliance or support
7. *Upward appeals.* Obtaining formal or informal support of higher management
8. *Exchange tactics.* Offering an exchange of favors; reminding someone of a past favor; offering to make a personal sacrifice[4]

These influence tactics are *generic* because they are used by various organizational members to influence lower-level employees (downward influence), peers (lateral influence), or superiors (upward influence). Table 14.1 indicates what the researchers found out about patterns of use for the three different directions of influence. Note that consultation, rational persuasion, and inspirational appeals were the three most popular tactics, regardless of the direction of influence.[5] Meanwhile, pressure tactics, upward appeals, and exchange tactics consistently were the least-used influence tactics. Ingratiating and coalition tactics fell in the midrange of use.[6] This is an encouraging pattern from the standpoint of getting things done through collaborative problem solving rather

TABLE **14.1**	Use of Generic Organizational Influence Tactics		
	RANK ORDER (BY DIRECTION OF INFLUENCE)		
TACTIC	**DOWNWARD**	**LATERAL**	**UPWARD**
Consultation	1	1	2
Rational persuasion	2	2	1
Inspirational appeals	3	3	3
Ingratiating tactics	4	4	5
Coalition tactics	5	5	4
Pressure tactics	6	7	7
Upward appeals	7	6	6
Exchange tactics	8	8	8

Source: Adapted from discussion in Gary Yukl and Cecilia M. Falbe, "Influence Tactics and Objectives in Upward, Downward, and Lateral Influence Attempts," Journal of Applied Psychology, 75 (April 1990): 132–140.

than through intimidation and conflict in today's team-oriented workplaces.

> For example, Frank Squillante, an IBM vice president, has only four direct reports. To do his job—devising the strategy for the company's intranet, and then developing and deploying applications for 325,000 people and 100,000 business partners—he must be a master at cajoling people over whom he has no real power. "I use 'collaborative influence' every minute of every day," he says. "If I tried to pull one of these 'I'm in charge so you have to do this' maneuvers, the whole thing would break down."[7]

Do women and men tend to rely on different influence tactics? Available research evidence reveals no systematic gender-based differences relative to influencing others.[8] In contrast, the tactics used by employees to influence their bosses were found to vary with different leadership styles. Employees influencing authoritarian managers tended to rely on ingratiating tactics and upward appeals. Rational persuasion was used most often to influence participative managers.[9]

POWER

Power is inevitable in modern organizations. According to one advocate of the positive and constructive use of power,

> Power must be used because managers must influence those they depend on. Power also is crucial in the development of managers' self-confidence and willingness to support subordinates. From this perspective, power should be accepted as a natural part of any organization. Managers should recognize and develop their own power to coordinate and support the work of subordinates; it is powerlessness, not power, that undermines organizational effectiveness.[10]

As a manager, if you understand power, its bases, and empowerment, you will have an advantage when it comes to getting things accomplished with and through others.[11]

What Is Power?

Power is "the ability to marshal the human, informational, and material resources to get something done."[12] Power affects organizational members in the following three areas:

> **power:** ability to marshal resources to get something done

1. **Decisions.** A packaging engineer decides to take on a difficult new assignment after hearing her boss's recommendations.
2. **Behavior.** A hospital lab technician achieves a month of perfect attendance after receiving a written warning about absenteeism from his supervisor.
3. **Situations.** The productivity of a product design group increases dramatically following the purchase of project management software.[13]

Another instructive way of looking at power is to distinguish among "power over" (ability to dominate), "power to" (ability to act freely), and "power from" (ability to resist the demands of others).[14]

By emphasizing the word *ability* in our definition and discussion of power, we can contrast power with authority. As defined in Chapter 9, authority is the "right" to direct the activities of others.[15] Authority is an officially sanctioned privilege that may or may not get results. In contrast, power is the demonstrated *ability* to get results. As illustrated in Figure 14.1, one may possess authority but have no power, possess no authority yet have power, or possess both authority and power. The first situation, authority but no power, was experienced by Albanian police in 1997, when Europe's poorest nation fell into anarchy over dissatisfaction with a corrupt government. According to *Newsweek*, "An angry mob surrounded one group of police, stripped them to their underpants, and burned their gear."[16] At the other end of the model in Figure 14.1, it is possible for an individual to have power but no authority. For example, employees may respond

IT WAS ABOUT HERE, WASN'T IT, ED, WHEN YOU CAME ONBOARD AS SALES MANAGER?"

Harvard Business Review, March 2007

FIGURE **14.1** The Relationship Between Authority and Power

Authority but no power
The *right* but not the *ability* to get subordinates to do things

Authority plus power
The *right* and the *ability* to get subordinates to do things

Power but no authority
The *ability* but not the *right* to get other people to do things

to the wishes of the supervisor's spouse.[17] Finally, a manager who gets employees to work hard on an important project has both authority and power.

The Five Bases of Power

Essential to the successful use of power in organizations is an understanding of the various bases of power. One widely cited classification of power bases identifies five types of power: reward, coercive, legitimate, referent, and expert.[18]

REWARD POWER. One's ability to grant rewards to those who comply with a command or request is the key to **reward power**. Management's reward power can be strengthened by linking pay raises, merit pay, and promotions to job performance. Sought-after expressions of friendship or trust also enhance reward power.

reward power: gaining compliance through rewards

COERCIVE POWER. Rooted in fear, **coercive power** is based on threatened or actual punishment. For example, a manager might threaten a habitually tardy employee with a demotion if he or she is late one more time.

coercive power: gaining compliance through threats or punishment

LEGITIMATE POWER. **Legitimate power** is achieved when a person's superior position alone prompts another person to act in a desired manner. This type of power closely parallels formal authority, as discussed above. Parents, teachers, religious leaders, and managers who expect or demand obedience by virtue of their superior social position are attempting to exercise legitimate power. Note, however, the following warning about legitimate power.

legitimate power: gaining compliance on the basis of one's formal position

Trying to control others solely by directing them and on the basis of the power associated with one's position simply will not work—first, because managers are always dependent on some people over whom they have no formal authority, and second, because virtually no one in modern organizations will passively accept and completely obey a constant stream of orders from someone just because he or she is the "boss."[19]

One might reasonably conclude that legitimate power has been eroded by its frequent abuse (or overuse) through the years.[20] Moreover, legitimate power may exact a price that fewer are willing to pay these days. According to a recent survey, "60 percent of executives don't want to be CEO. That's double the number (27 percent) who had no interest in the top job in 2001."[21]

REFERENT POWER. An individual has **referent power** over those who identify with him or her if they comply on that basis alone. Personal attraction is an elusive thing to define, let alone consciously cultivate. *Charisma* is a term often used in conjunction with referent power. Although leaders with the personal magnetism of Abraham Lincoln, John Kennedy, or Martin Luther King Jr. are always in short supply, charisma in the workplace can be problematic. *Fortune* magazine offered this perspective:

referent power: gaining compliance on the basis of charisma or personal identification

Used wisely, it's a blessing. Indulged, it can be a curse. Charismatic visionaries lead people ahead—and sometimes astray. They can be impetuous, unpredictable, and exasperating to work for, like [media mogul Ted] Turner. [Donald] Trump. Steve Jobs. Ross Perot. Lee Iacocca. "Often what begins as a mission becomes an obsession," says John Thompson, president of Human Factors, a leadership consulting service in San Rafael, California. "Leaders can cut corners on values and become driven by self-interest. Then they may abuse anyone who makes a mistake."

Like pornography, charisma is hard to define. But you know it when you see it. And you don't see much of it in the Fortune 500.[22]

Still, as we will see in our discussion of transformational leadership later in this chapter, charisma does have its positive side.

Religion exercises a powerful influence over the lives of many people around the world. This mosque minaret towering high above Dubai Creek, bustling with water taxis, calls the Islamic faithful to prayer five times a day. Business is not conducted on Fridays in Dubai, United Arab Emirates; it is a day for worship and rest. What, if any, religious traditions have power in your life?

EXPERT POWER. Those who possess and can dispense valued information generally exercise **expert power** over those in need of such information. Information technology experts, for instance, are in a position today to wield a great deal of expert power. Anyone who has ever been taken advantage of by an unscrupulous computer technician knows what expert power in the wrong hands can mean.

expert power: gaining compliance on the basis of one's ability to dispense valued information

Empowerment

Empowerment occurs when employees are adequately trained, provided with all relevant information and the best possible tools, fully involved in key decisions, and fairly rewarded for results.[23] Those who endorse this key building block of progressive management view power as an unlimited resource. Frances Hesselbein, the widely respected former head of the Girl Scouts of the USA, offered this perspective: "The more power you give away, the more you have."[24] This can be a difficult concept to grasp for traditional authoritarian managers who see empowerment

empowerment: making employees *full* partners in the decision-making process and giving them the necessary tools and rewards

as a threat to their authority and feeling of being in control. Today, the issue is not empowerment versus no empowerment. Rather, the issue is how empowerment should take place. As indicated in the Manager's Toolkit at the end of this chapter, employee empowerment is like a seed requiring favorable growing conditions. Consider this recent example from Best Buy's CEO Brad Anderson.

We've got a wonderful team of eccentric people working in our Manhattan store on 44th Street and Fifth Avenue. Now, there's a large Brazilian community near the store, and the manager said, "Hey, we don't do anything to cater to them." So he hired folks who spoke the [Brazilian Portuguese] language in the store. They wound up discovering that there are cruise ships of Brazilians that come to New York City, so they contacted the travel company and found that the store was a desirable stop for them. So all of a sudden we have buses of tour groups pulling up on Sundays. If we waited for someone in Minnesota [headquarters] to come up with that idea, we'd still be waiting.[25]

Much of the burden for successful empowerment falls on the *individual*. No amount of empowerment and supportive management can overcome dishonesty, untrustworthiness, selfishness, and inadequate skills.[26] Moreover, as we learned in the Enron case, empowerment without proper oversight can lead to very bad consequences.

Young people, many just out of undergraduate or MBA programs, were handed extraordinary authority, able to make $5 million decisions without higher approval. . . .

At Enron, however, the pressure to make the numbers often overwhelmed the pretext of "tight" controls. "The environment was ripe for abuse," says a former manager in Enron's energy services unit. "Nobody at corporate was asking the right questions.

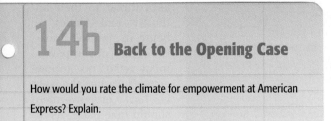

14b Back to the Opening Case

How would you rate the climate for empowerment at American Express? Explain.

It was completely hands-off management. A situation like that requires tight controls. Instead, it was a runaway train."[27]

Once again, rigorous employee selection and training and ethics training, as discussed in Chapters 5 and 10, come to the forefront.

LEADERSHIP

Leadership has fascinated people since the dawn of recorded history. The search for good leaders has been a common thread running through human civilization.[28] In view of research evidence that effective leadership is associated with both better performance and more ethical performance, the search for ways to identify (or develop) good leaders needs to continue.[29] Indeed, when 800 training and development managers were surveyed recently, 63 percent ranked "Developing potential leaders" as the number one management challenge.[30] As Peter Drucker pointed out, leadership is a difficult topic because great leaders come in all sizes, shapes, and temperaments. The

14c Lead Me!

Mads Kamp, director of human resources at Danish hearing aid maker Oticon:

"People want to be led."

Source: As quoted in Jack Ewing, "No-Cubicle Culture," Business Week (August 20–27, 2007): 60.

QUESTIONS:

For people in general, do you agree or disagree? What about you, personally? What about free-spirited entrepreneurs? Explain.

legendary management scholar helpfully offered the following leader *effectiveness* criteria:

> *. . . some of the best business and nonprofit CEOs I've worked with over a 65–year consulting career were not stereotypical leaders. They were all over the map in terms of their personalities, attitudes, values, strengths, and weaknesses. They ranged from extroverted to nearly reclusive, from easygoing to controlling, from generous to parsimonious.*
>
> *What made them all effective is that they followed the same eight practices:*
>
> * *They asked, "What needs to be done?"*
> * *They asked, "What is right for the enterprise?"*
> * *They developed action plans.*
> * *They took responsibility for decisions.*
> * *They took responsibility for communicating.*
> * *They were focused on opportunities rather than problems.*
> * *They ran productive meetings.*
> * *They thought and said "we" rather than "I."*[31]

Let us keep these effectiveness criteria in mind as we explore the topic of leadership, while resisting the temptation to embrace a one-size-fits-all leadership model.[32]

Leadership Defined

Research on leadership has produced many definitions of the term. Much of the variation is semantic; the definition offered here is a workable compromise. **Leadership** is the process of inspiring, influencing, and guiding others to participate in a common effort.[33] In today's highly interconnected world, leadership extends beyond the office door or factory gate.

leadership: social influence process of inspiring and guiding others in a common effort

> *Leaders bear the responsibility of guiding a host of constituents toward the accomplishment of an overarching goal, whether this be leading employees toward greater productivity, guiding suppliers toward a better understanding of ways to cooperate in order to better serve the firm's customers, or helping investors appreciate the firm's strategy and how achievement of that strategy will result in enhanced shareholder value. All require a solid grounding in a vision that guides the leader and, ultimately, the organization toward better performance.*[34]

To encourage such broad participation, leaders supplement any authority and power they possess with their personal attributes, imagination, and social skills. Colin Powell, a leader admired in both military and civilian circles, offers his own definition: "Leadership is the art of accomplishing more than the science of management says is possible."[35]

Formal and Informal Leaders

Experts on leadership distinguish between formal and informal leadership. **Formal leadership** is the process of influencing relevant others to pursue official organizational objectives. **Informal leadership**, in contrast, is the process of influencing others to pursue unofficial objectives that may or may not serve the organization's interests. Formal leaders generally have a measure of legitimate power because of their formal authority, whereas informal leaders typically lack formal authority. Beyond that, both types rely on expedient combinations of reward, coercive, referent, and expert power. Informal leaders who identify with the job to be done are a valuable asset to an organization. Conversely, an organization can be brought to its knees by informal leaders who turn cohesive work groups against the organization.

formal leadership: the process of influencing others to pursue official objectives

informal leadership: the process of influencing others to pursue unofficial objectives

The Issue of Leaders versus Managers: A Middle Ground

A long-standing debate about the differences between leaders and managers sprang from Abraham Zaleznik's 1977 article in *Harvard Business Review* titled "Managers and Leaders: Are They Different?" Over the years, stereotypes developed characterizing leaders and managers in very different ways. Leaders are typically viewed as farsighted and even heroic visionaries who boldly blaze new trails. They can't be bothered with details. In contrast, a less-flattering portrayal of the manager is that of a facilitator who tends to the details of turning the leader's vision into reality. Accordingly, it has been said that leaders make chaos out of order and managers make order out of chaos. This dueling-stereotypes debate may be an amusing academic exercise, but it misses one important *practical* point: Today's leaner and continuously evolving organizations require people who can both lead *and* manage—in other words, the total package.[36] The future belongs to those who can effectively blend the characteristics in Table 14.2. JetBlue Airways founder and chairman David Neeleman explains how his airline strives to strike the right balance:

> JetBlue's officers don't act aloof and sit at their desks all day. We roll up our sleeves to understand what's going on, because our leaders shouldn't treat others as inferiors. A couple of years ago, we promoted our middle managers without giving them leadership training. They became little dictators, and favoritism started to creep in.
>
> So we had to create a leadership program to reset the expectations of what leaders should do. But we didn't hire a bunch of slick facilitators to talk about principles. Instead, the people who were actually living [those principles] at JetBlue were the ones teaching the courses. Now 40 of our top managers spend two days a year leading the group.[37]

No one ever said leadership was easy.

Leadership has many faces and directions today. Take this diverse group of powerful women, for example. From left to right are Andrea Jung, CEO of Avon Products; actress and Avon Global Ambassador Reese Witherspoon; Joanne Sandler, executive director of UNIFEM (United Nations Development Fund for Women); and personal finance expert/television personality Suze Orman. Avon donated $1 million to the UN Trust Fund to End Violence Against Women.

TABLE **14.2**   Lead or Manage? Good Leaders Must Do Both

BEING A LEADER MEANS	BEING A MANAGER MEANS
Motivating, influencing and changing behavior.	Practicing stewardship, directing and being held accountable for resources.
Inspiring, setting the tone, and articulating a vision.	Executing plans, implementing and delivering the goods and services.
Managing people.	Managing resources.
Being charismatic.	Being conscientious.
Being visionary.	Planning, organizing, directing and controlling.
Understanding and using power and influence.	Understanding and using authority and responsibility.
Acting decisively.	Acting responsibly.
Putting people first. The leader knows, responds to, and acts for his or her followers.	Putting customers first. The manager knows, responds to, and acts for his or her customers.
Leaders can make mistakes when: 1. they choose the wrong goal, direction or inspiration, due to incompetence or bad intentions; or 2. they over-lead; or 3. they are unable to deliver on [or] implement the vision due to incompetence or a lack of follow-through commitment.	Managers can make mistakes when: 1. they fail to grasp the importance of people as the key resource; or 2. they under-lead; they treat people like other resources [or like] numbers; or 3. they are eager to direct and to control but are unwilling to accept accountability.

Source: Reprinted from Organizational Dynamics, *Vol. 33, Peter Lorenzi, "Managing for the Common Good: Prosocial Leadership," p. 286, Copyright 2004, with permission from Elsevier.*

The study of leadership has evolved as theories have been developed and refined by successive generations of researchers.[38] Something useful has been learned at each stage of development. We now turn to significant milestones in the evolution of leadership theory by examining the trait, behavioral styles, situational, and transformational approaches (see Figure 14.2).

Trait Theory

During most of recorded history, the prevailing assumption was that leaders are born and not made. Leaders such as Alexander the Great, Napoleon Bonaparte, and George Washington were said to have been blessed with an inborn ability to lead. This so-called great-man approach to leadership[39] eventually gave way to trait theory. According to one observer,

FIGURE **14.2**   The Evolution of Leadership Theory

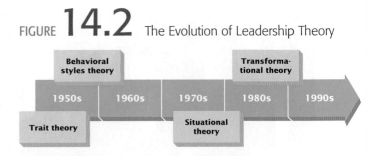

"under the influence of the behavioristic school of psychological thought, the fact was accepted that leadership traits are not completely inborn but can also be acquired through learning and experience. Attention turned to the search for universal traits possessed by leaders."[40]

As the popularity of the trait approach mushroomed during the second quarter of the twentieth century, literally hundreds of physical, mental, and personality traits were said to be the key determinants of successful leadership. Unfortunately, few theorists agreed on the most important traits of a good leader. The predictive value of trait theory was severely limited because traits tend to be a chicken-and-egg proposition: Was George Washington a good leader because he had self-confidence, or did he have self-confidence because he was thrust into a leadership role at a young age? In spite of inherent problems, trait profiles provide a useful framework for examining what it takes to be a good leader.

AN EARLY TRAIT PROFILE. Not until 1948 was a comprehensive review of competing trait theories conducted. After comparing more than 100 studies of leader traits and characteristics, the reviewer uncovered moderate agreement on only five traits. In the reviewer's words, "the average person who occupies a position of leadership exceeds the average member of his group in the following respects: (1) intelligence, (2) scholarship, (3) dependability in exercising responsibilities, (4) activity and social participation, and (5) socioeconomic status."[41]

A MODERN TRAIT PROFILE: LEADERS WITH EMOTIONAL INTELLIGENCE. Daniel Goleman's 1995 book *Emotional Intelligence* popularized a concept that psychologists had talked about for years.[42] Whereas standard intelligence (IQ) deals with thinking and reasoning, emotional intelligence (EQ) deals more broadly with building social relationships and controlling one's emotions. **Emotional intelligence** has been defined as

> **emotional intelligence:** the ability to monitor and control one's emotions and behavior in complex social settings

. . . good old street smarts—knowing when to share sensitive information with colleagues, laugh at the boss's jokes or speak up in a meeting. In more scientific terms, . . . [emotional intelligence] can be defined as an array of noncognitive skills, capabilities and competencies that influence a person's ability to cope with environmental demands and pressures.[43]

Higher EQ scores indicate more polished social skills and greater emotional maturity (try the Action Learning Exercise at the end of this chapter). Interestingly, Goleman says that emotional intelligence should be evaluated by others because it is difficult to be objective about oneself in such an important domain.

Goleman and his colleagues recently cast emotional intelligence in terms of four leadership traits:

- *Self-awareness.* This essential component of emotional intelligence involves the ability to read one's own emotions and hence be better equipped to assess one's strengths and limitations.
- *Self-management.* Those who possess this trait do not let their moods and emotions disrupt honest and straightforward relationships.
- *Social awareness.* Those who possess this trait are able to read others' emotions and reactions and subsequently adapt in a constructive and caring fashion.
- *Relationship management.* Leaders who possess this trait are clear, enthusiastic, and convincing communicators who can defuse conflicts. They rely on kindness and humor to build strong relationships.[44]

Each of these traits can be learned, according to Goleman. A big step in the right direction is for managers to fully appreciate how their emotional outbursts and foul moods can poison the work environment. Leaders and followers alike need to exhibit greater emotional intelligence in order to build social capital in today's hectic and often stressful workplaces.[45] (See Ethics: Character, Courage, and Values.)

THE CONTROVERSY OVER FEMALE AND MALE LEADERSHIP TRAITS. A second source of renewed interest in leadership traits is the ongoing debate about female versus male leadership traits. In an often-cited survey by Judy B. Rosener, female leaders were found to be better than their male counterparts at sharing power and information.[46] Critics have chided Rosener for reinforcing this traditional feminine stereotype.[47] Actually, a comprehensive review of 162 different studies found *no significant difference* in leadership styles exhibited by women and men. In real-life organizational settings, women did *not* fit the feminine stereotype of being more relationship-oriented, and men did *not* fit the masculine stereotype of being more task-oriented.[48] As always, it is bad practice to make prejudicial assumptions about individuals on the basis of their membership in a particular demographic category.

Behavioral Styles Theory

During World War II, the study of leadership took on a significant new twist. Rather than concentrating on the personal traits of successful leaders, researchers

ETHICS: CHARACTER, COURAGE, AND VALUES

Is Courage an Important Leader Trait?

In Hebrew, *omets lev* means "strength of heart." In English, it's known as courage, something Morem Klein is passionate about. "It's about building a sense of community and the strength to pull together to face adversity," he says. Klein is the executive director of the Courage Institute, an international training consortium based in Western Galilee, Israel, specializing in building the inner strength—the courage—of teams and leaders.

Klein spent years studying why some teams succeed despite adversity, and asked if it was possible to teach those characteristics that are necessary to excel. He believes the answer to this question is yes and that the single most important attribute to sustain is courage.

The Courage Institute, which also has an office in Elkins, Pa., has a five-part definition for courage:

- **Purpose:** everyone clearly understanding the goals of the company;
- **Will:** confidence, enthusiasm, and determination;
- **Rigor:** constantly improving and learning new skills;
- **Candor:** always being honest; and
- **Risks:** the ability to relinquish control for the interest of the team.

Source: Excerpted from Heather Johnson, "Strength of Heart," Training, 41 (July 2004): 16. Reprinted by permission of Billboard. Also see Kathleen K. Reardon, "Courage as a Skill," Special Issue: The Tests of a Leader, Harvard Business Review, 85 (January 2007): 58–64.

FOR DISCUSSION

How does this contrast with your beliefs about courage? What is the linkage between courage and ethical conduct in the workplace? Which of the five dimensions of courage are evident in Ken Chenault's remarks in the chapter-opening case? Explain.

working with the military began turning their attention to patterns of leader behavior (called leadership styles). In other words, attention turned from who the leader was to how the leader actually behaved. One early laboratory study of leader behavior demonstrated that followers overwhelmingly preferred managers who had a democratic style to those with an authoritarian style or a laissez-faire (hands-off) style.[49] An updated review of these three classic leadership styles can be found in Table 14.3.

For a number of years, theorists and managers hailed democratic leadership as the key to productive and happy employees. Eventually, however, their enthusiasm was dampened when critics noted how the original study relied on children as subjects and virtually ignored productivity. Although there is general agreement that these basic styles exist, debate has been vigorous over their relative value and appropriateness. Practical experience has shown, for example, that the democratic style does not always stimulate better performance. Some employees prefer to be told what to do rather than participating in decision making. This can be the result of cultural differences, as was the case recently when the world's largest television maker was created by the merger of China's TCL Corp. and France's Thomson.

In China, says one TCL official, "if the leader says something is right, even if he is wrong, employees will agree with him. But in foreign companies, they will not agree with him. We have two different cultures."[50]

14d Through the Eyes of a Woman CEO

Abbe Raven, president and CEO of A&E Television Networks:

I always want to be known as a good executive, not as a good female executive. But I do have camaraderie with other women in my position and have learned from them, and we have our own special issues that we have to deal with.

Source: As quoted in Richard M. Smith, "Staying Power," Newsweek (October 15, 2007): E4.

QUESTIONS:

What unique issues and challenges do women in high leadership positions face?

TABLE **14.3**   The Three Classic Styles of Leadership

	AUTHORITARIAN	**DEMOCRATIC**	**LAISSEZ-FAIRE**
Nature	Leader retains all authority and responsibility	Leader delegates a great deal of authority while retaining ultimate responsibility	Leader grants responsibility and authority to group
	Leader assigns people to clearly defined tasks	Work is divided and assigned on the basis of participatory decision making	Group members are told to work things out themselves and do the best they can
	Primarily a downward flow of communication	Active two-way flow of upward and downward communication	Primarily horizontal communication among peers
Primary strength	Stresses prompt, orderly, and predictable performance	Enhances personal commitment through participation	Permits self-starters to do things as they see fit without leader interference
Primary weakness	Approach tends to stifle individual initiative	Democratic process is time-consuming	Group may drift aimlessly in the absence of direction from leader

THE OHIO STATE MODEL. While the democratic style of leadership was receiving attention, a slightly different behavioral approach to leadership emerged. This second approach began in the late 1940s when a team of Ohio State University researchers defined two independent dimensions of leader behavior.[51] One dimension, called "initiating structure," was the leader's efforts to get things organized and get the job done.

The second dimension, labeled "consideration," was the degree of trust, friendship, respect, and warmth that the leader extended to subordinates. By making a matrix out of these two independent dimensions of leader behavior, the Ohio State researchers identified four styles of leadership (see Figure 14.3).

This particular scheme proved to be fertile ground for leadership theorists, and variations of the original

FIGURE **14.3** Basic Leadership Styles from the Ohio State Study

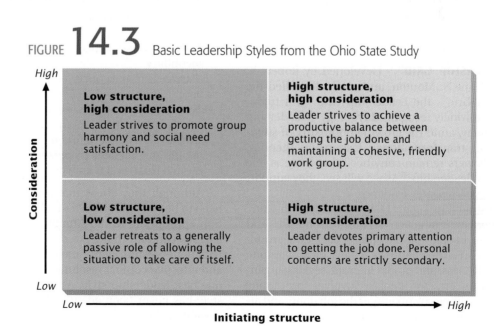

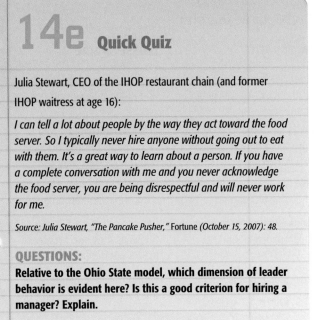

FIGURE **14.4** Blake and McCanse's Leadership Grid®

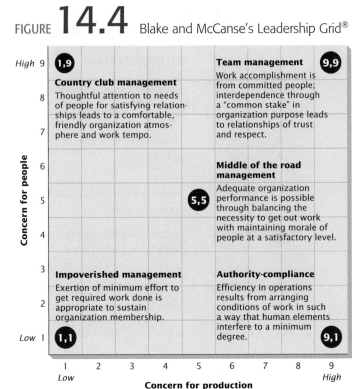

Source: From Blake, R. R. & A. A. McCanse. Leadership Dilemmas–Grid Solutions. Houston: Gulf Publishing, 1991.

Ohio State approach soon appeared.[52] Leadership theorists began a search for the "one best style" of leadership. The high-structure, high-consideration style was generally hailed as the best all-around style. This "high-high" style has intuitive appeal because it embraces the best of both categories of leader behavior. But one researcher cautioned in 1966 that although there seemed to be a positive relationship between consideration and employee satisfaction, a positive link between the high-high style and work group performance had not been proved conclusively.[53]

THE LEADERSHIP GRID®. Developed by Robert R. Blake and Jane S. Mouton, and originally called the Managerial Grid®, the Leadership Grid® is a trademarked and widely recognized typology of leadership styles.[54] Today, amid the growing popularity of situational and transformational leadership theories, Blake's followers remain convinced that there is one best style of leadership.[55] As we will see, they support this claim with research evidence.

As illustrated in Figure 14.4, the Leadership Grid® has "concern for production" on the horizontal axis and "concern for people" on the vertical axis. Concern for production involves a desire to achieve greater output, cost-effectiveness, and profits in profit-seeking organizations. Concern for people involves promoting friendship, helping coworkers get the job done, and attending to things that matter to people, such as pay and

working conditions. When a scale from 1 to 9 is marked on each axis, five major styles emerge on the grid:

9,1 style: primary concern for production; people secondary

1,9 style: primary concern for people; production secondary

1,1 style: minimal concern for either production or people

5,5 style: moderate concern for both production and people to maintain the status quo

9,9 style: high concern for both production and people as evidenced by personal commitment, mutual trust, and teamwork

Although they stress that managers and leaders need to be versatile enough to select the courses of action appropriate to the situation, Blake and his colleagues contend that a 9,9 style correlates positively with better results, better mental and physical health, and effective conflict resolution. They believe there *is* one best leadership style. As they see it, the true 9,9 style has never been adequately tested by the situationalists. In a more recent study by Blake and

14f Back to the Opening Case

Where would you plot American Express's Ken Chenault on Blake and McCanse's Leadership Grid®? Why?

Mouton, 100 experienced managers overwhelmingly preferred the 9,9 style, regardless of how the situation varied.[56] Consequently, Blake's management training and organization development programs were designed to help individuals and entire organizations move into the 9,9 portion of the Leadership Grid®.

A 9,9 leadership style certainly worked well for Lawrence R. Johnston, CEO of grocery giant Albertsons Inc., when he worked for Jack Welch at General Electric:

> Welch dispatched him to Paris in 1997 to fix the [medical and hospital services] business, which was losing $100 million a year, or dump it.
>
> In less than three years, the division was making a $100 million operating profit. According to Welch, Johnston succeeded because he quickly realized his chief task was reenergizing the employees. "This was a cynical group of French and German engineers," Welch recalls. "But he engaged them incredibly." Every month Johnston traveled to a different European city, conducting sales meetings in the mornings and taking his team to visit hospitals in the afternoons. And at nights he studied French. "Larry can lead people over the hill," Welch says. "He put us on the map in Europe."[57]

Situational Theory

Convinced that no one best style of leadership exists, some management scholars have advocated situational or contingency thinking. Although a number of different situational-leadership theories have been developed, they all share one fundamental assumption: successful leadership occurs when the leader's style matches the situation. Situational-leadership theorists stress the need for flexibility. They reject the notion of a universally applicable style. Research is under way to determine precisely when and where various styles of leadership are appropriate. Fiedler's contingency theory and the path-goal theory are introduced and discussed here because they represent distinctly different approaches to situational leadership.

FIEDLER'S CONTINGENCY THEORY. Among the various leadership theories proposed so far, Fiedler's is the most thoroughly tested. It is the product of more than 30 years of research by Fred E. Fiedler and his associates. Fiedler's contingency theory gets its name from the following assumption:

> The performance of a leader depends on two interrelated factors: (1) the degree to which the situation gives the leader control and influence—that is, the likelihood that [the leader] can successfully accomplish the job; and (2) the leader's basic motivation—that is, whether [the leader's] self-esteem depends primarily on accomplishing the task or on having close supportive relations with others.[58]

Regarding the second factor, the leader's basic motivation, Fiedler believes leaders are either task-motivated or relationship-motivated. These two motivational

How transferable are leadership skills from one industry to another? Alan Mulally had a stellar career at aircraft-maker Boeing before taking the CEO post at Ford Motor Company. Auto industry analysts bemoaned Mulally's total lack of experience in his new industry and predicted problems. Time will tell if he can make the jump. Meanwhile, he is learning the auto business at the showroom level as he spends time here selling vehicles at Galpin Ford in North Hills, California.

FIGURE **14.5**   Fiedler's Contingency Theory of Leadership

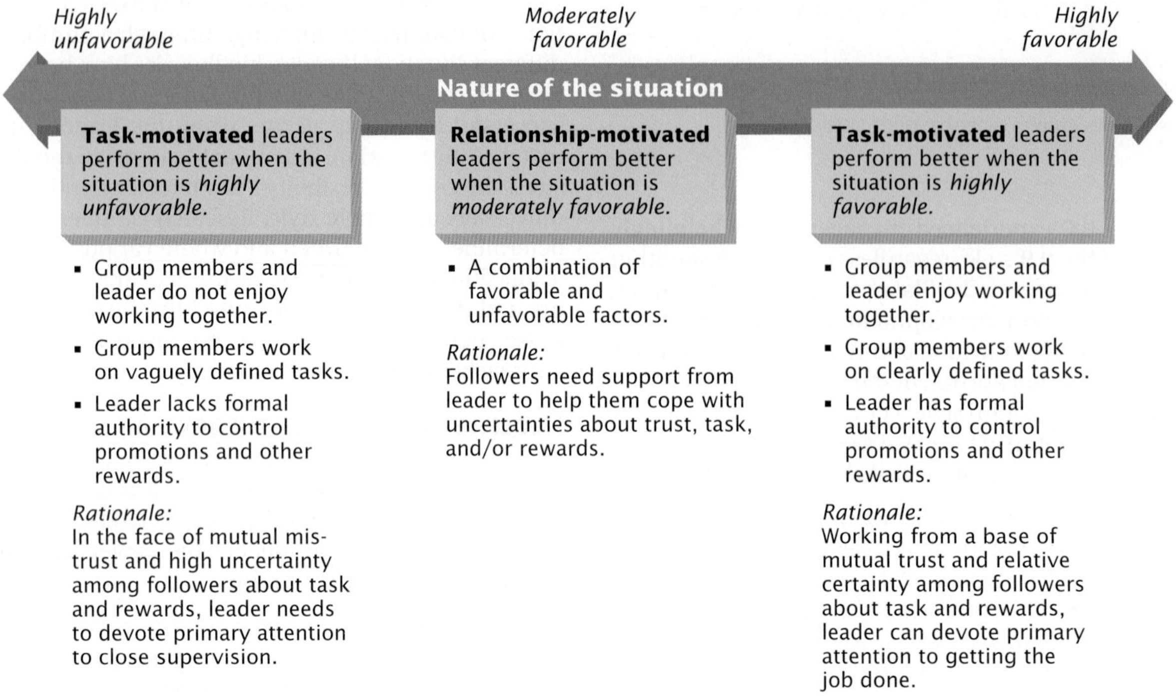

Highly unfavorable	*Moderately favorable*	*Highly favorable*

Nature of the situation

Task-motivated leaders perform better when the situation is *highly unfavorable*.	**Relationship-motivated** leaders perform better when the situation is *moderately favorable*.	**Task-motivated** leaders perform better when the situation is *highly favorable*.
▪ Group members and leader do not enjoy working together. ▪ Group members work on vaguely defined tasks. ▪ Leader lacks formal authority to control promotions and other rewards. *Rationale:* In the face of mutual mistrust and high uncertainty among followers about task and rewards, leader needs to devote primary attention to close supervision.	▪ A combination of favorable and unfavorable factors. *Rationale:* Followers need support from leader to help them cope with uncertainties about trust, task, and/or rewards.	▪ Group members and leader enjoy working together. ▪ Group members work on clearly defined tasks. ▪ Leader has formal authority to control promotions and other rewards. *Rationale:* Working from a base of mutual trust and relative certainty among followers about task and rewards, leader can devote primary attention to getting the job done.

profiles are roughly equivalent to initiating structure (or concern for production) and consideration (or concern for people).

A consistent pattern has emerged from the many studies of effective leaders carried out by Fiedler and others.[59] As illustrated in Figure 14.5, task-motivated leaders seem to be effective in extreme situations when they have either very little control or a great deal of control over situational variables. In moderately favorable situations, however, relationship-motivated leaders tend to be more effective. Consequently, Fiedler and one of his colleagues summed up their findings by noting that "everything points to the conclusion that there is no such thing as an ideal leader."[60] Instead, there are leaders, and there are situations. The challenge, according to Fiedler, is to analyze a leader's basic motivation and then match that leader with a suitable situation to form a productive combination. He believes it is more efficient to move leaders to a suitable situation than to tamper with their personalities by trying to get task-motivated leaders to become relationship-motivated, or vice versa.

HOUSE'S UPDATED PATH-GOAL THEORY. Another situational-leadership theory is the path-goal theory, a derivative of expectancy motivation theory (see Chapter 12). Path-goal theory gets its name from the assumption that effective leaders can enhance employee motivation by (1) clarifying the individual's perception of work goals, (2) linking meaningful rewards to goal attainment, and (3) explaining how goals and desired rewards can be achieved. In short, leaders should motivate their followers by providing clear goals and meaningful incentives for reaching them. Path-goal theorists believe that motivation is essential to effective leadership.

According to path-goal theorists Robert J. House and Terence R. Mitchell, leaders can enhance motivation by "increasing the number and kinds of personal payoffs to subordinates for work-goal attainment and making paths to these payoffs easier to travel by clarifying the paths, reducing roadblocks and pitfalls, and increasing the opportunities for personal satisfaction en route."[61] The path-goal perspective is clearly evident in the following profile, offered by best-selling author Marcus Buckingham, who has studied leaders for 20 years.

As a leader, your job is to make people more confident about the future you're dragging them into. To that end, you need to tell them why they're going to win. There are many competitors out there. Why will we beat them? There are many obstacles in our path. Why will we overcome them? The more clearly you can answer these questions, the more confident we will be, and therefore the more resilient, the more persistent, and the more creative.[62]

Personal characteristics of employees, environmental pressures, and demands on employees will all vary from situation to situation. Thus, House's updated path-goal model advises managers to rely contingently on eight categories of leader behavior:

- **Path-goal clarifying behaviors** (Make it clear how goal attainment is linked with meaningful rewards.)
- **Achievement-oriented behaviors** (Set challenging goals, emphasize excellence, and seek continuous improvement while maintaining a high degree of confidence that employees will meet difficult challenges in a responsible manner.)
- **Work facilitation behaviors** (Plan and coordinate work, make decisions, provide feedback and coaching, provide resources, remove roadblocks, and empower employees.)
- **Supportive behaviors** (Be friendly and approachable, and show concern for employees' well-being.)

- **Interaction facilitation behaviors** (Resolve disputes and encourage collaboration, diverse opinions, and teamwork.)
- **Group decision behaviors** (Encourage group input, problem solving, and participation.)
- **Networking behaviors** (Build bridges to influential people and represent the group's best interests to others.)
- **Value-based behaviors** (Self-confidently formulate and passionately support a vision.)[63]

The assumption that managers can and do shift situationally from one behavior pattern to another clearly sets path-goal theory apart from Fiedler's model. Recall that Fiedler claims managers cannot and do not change their basic leadership styles.

Limited research on the path-goal model has yielded mixed results.[64] One valuable contribution of path-goal theory is its identification of achievement-oriented leadership behavior. As managers deal with an increasing number of highly educated and self-motivated employees in advanced-technology industries, they will need to become skilled facilitators rather than just order givers or hand holders.

Transformational Leadership Theory

In his 1978 book *Leadership*, James McGregor Burns drew a distinction between transactional and transformational leadership. Burns characterized **transformational leaders** as visionaries who challenge people to achieve exceptionally high levels of morality, motivation, and performance.[65] Only transformational leaders, Burns argued, are capable of charting necessary new courses for modern organizations. Why? Because they are masters of change (see Valuing Diversity).[66] They can envision a better future, effectively communicate that vision, and get others to willingly make it a reality.

> **transformational leaders:** visionaries who challenge people to do exceptional things

TRANSACTIONAL VERSUS TRANSFORMATIONAL LEADERS. Extending the work of Burns, Bernard Bass emphasized the importance of charisma in transformational leadership. Transformational leaders rely heavily on referent power. Wendy's Dave Thomas, Wal-Mart's Sam Walton, and Southwest Airlines' Herb Kelleher exemplify charismatic leaders who engineered great success at their respective companies.[67] While acknowledging that transformational leaders exhibit widely different styles and tend to stir their fair share of controversy, Bass rounded out

---

14g Quick Quiz: How Do You Lead Creative People?

Leading people who often don't think of themselves as employees of anyone or anything, let alone followers embedded in an organization consisting of levels, layers, and moving parts, is about as far from Management 101 as you can get. In fact, it's an art, drawing on all sorts of soft skills, like empathy, an ability to nurture, and ad hoc psychological counseling. But what a mistake if you lead creative people from your heart and stop there. Managing creative people also requires—it even demands—a measure of authority. Nothing heavy-handed, of course. You don't want your resident out-of-the-box thinkers running for the exits. . . . Still, creative people must know that boundaries and values exist, and they have to respect them.

Source: Jack Welch and Suzy Welch, "Wielding the Velvet Hammer," Business Week (September 24, 2007): 116.

QUESTION:
Which combination of path-goal leader behaviors would you use to manage your creative employees? Explain your rationale.

VALUING DIVERSITY

A Native American's Vision for a Better Future

It started as a simple business matter: The people needed jobs and nobody was providing them. Nothing is simple, though, when your community is wilting under endemic poverty, when your ancestors left their footprints on forced removals from Wisconsin to Iowa to Minnesota to South Dakota to Nebraska, when your people have few options outside the federal government, when tribal politicians pull the strings on the local economy, and when the only available start-up funds come one pull of a handle, one rake of the chips, at a time. Or is it? Can a driven visionary entrepreneur change the fate of his people? In the case of Lance Morgan, the answer is yes.

"We've done it," says Morgan, "and other tribes have just as much talent as the Winnebagos, but they don't have the model . . . yet." The model is Ho-Chunk Inc., the $100 million tribe-owned corporation that employs 355 people in a variety of businesses, including housing construction, hotels, convenience stores, e-commerce hot spot Allnative.com, Web design, tobacco distribution, community development, and Indianz.com, a news site for all things Native American. After graduating from Harvard Law School and spending two unhappy years at a corporate firm in Minneapolis, Morgan returned to the Winnebago reservation in 1995 to start Ho-Chunk with $8 million in seed money from a casino (although the company hasn't taken a nickel of gaming money since). "I don't think much of gaming," says Morgan, "but it was a means to an end."

The idea is no less than to create an economy, and it wouldn't have taken off if Morgan hadn't convinced the tribal council to break with the norm and allow Ho-Chunk to operate somewhat autonomously. (Ho-Chunk and the Winnebago tribal council meet quarterly and are partners in a business whose model is being studied and adopted by tribes across the country.) Morgan is currently embedded in an ambitious project to literally build a better community from the ground up. Houses and businesses are being erected in Ho-Chunk Village, a new urbanism/small town combination created to replace dilapidated, random government housing and where, Morgan says, "we can have a warm, safe place to raise a family, like any other neighborhood, except nicer and everyone will be brown."

Like most go-getters, Morgan, 35, has time for work and family and not much else—[University of Nebraska] Cornhuskers football is one of his few diversions from building a 21st-century economic model for Indian peoples nationwide who have been shut out of the entrepreneurial arena. "We've taken control of our destiny, gotten a taste of independence, and don't plan on giving it up," says Morgan. "Government-led economies have been a total failure. I refuse to believe the Winnebagos are Karl Marx's last hope."

Ho-Chunk (which loosely translates to "the people") has spoken.

Source: By Patrick J. Sauer, first published in Inc. *Magazine. Copyright 2004 by Mansueto Ventures LLC. Reproduced with permission of Mansueto Ventures LLC in the format Textbook via Copyright Clearance Center.*

Burns's distinction between transactional and transformational leaders (see Table 14.4). Transactional leaders monitor people so that they do the expected, according to plan. In contrast, transformational leaders inspire people to do the unexpected, above and beyond the plan. This distinction can mean the difference between maintaining the status quo and fostering creative and productive growth.

POSITIVE EVIDENCE. It is important to note that the distinction in Table 14.4 is not between bad and good leaders—both transactional and transformational leaders are needed today. This is where transformational leadership theory effectively combines the behavioral styles and situational approaches just discussed. To the traditional behavioral patterns of initiating structure and consideration have been added charismatic and other behaviors.[68] Transformational leadership also needs to be situationally appropriate. Specifically, transformational leadership is needed in rapidly changing situations; transactional leaders can best handle stable situations.[69]

Available laboratory and field research evidence generally supports the transformational-leadership pattern. Followers of transformational leaders tend to perform better and to report greater satisfaction than followers of transactional leaders.[70]

Putting to Work What You've Learned by Using "Practical Intelligence" and Becoming a "Servant Leader"

Finding ways to practice leadership both on and off the job can help present and future managers develop their abilities. Serving in campus, community, or religious

Steve Jobs is a true transformational leader and he has the résumé to prove it. His vision, charisma, and communication skills are legendary in Silicon Valley. In the 1970s, he co-founded Apple with buddy Steve Wozniak. In the 1980s, he bought Pixar, the animated movie studio that would be responsible for such hits as *Finding Nemo*. In the 1990s, he rejoined Apple as CEO and launched the iPod. Then came the iPhone in the new millenium. What's next?

PRACTICAL INTELLIGENCE. Yale University's Robert J. Sternberg believes that good leaders effectively blend three things: wisdom, intelligence, and creativity. What sort of intelligence? He explains:

Practical intelligence is the ability to solve everyday problems by utilizing knowledge gained from experience in order to purposefully adapt to, shape, and select environments. It thus involves changing oneself to suit the environment (adaptation), changing the environment to suit oneself (shaping), or finding a new environment within which to work (selection). One uses these skills to (a) manage oneself, (b) manage others, and (c) manage tasks.[71]

Because practical intelligence is a broad concept—involving both relationships and tasks—it includes and goes beyond emotional intelligence, discussed earlier. Significantly, Sternberg rejects the notion of "born leaders." Leadership is learned, he contends, because wisdom, practical intelligence, and creativity all can be learned.

SERVANT LEADERS. In addition to a working knowledge of the various leadership theories we have discussed in this chapter, aspiring leaders need a

organizations, for example, will give you an opportunity to experiment with different leadership styles in a variety of situations. Leading effectively, like riding a bike, is learned only by doing. This section offers some inspiration for polishing your leadership abilities.

TABLE **14.4** Transactional versus Transformational Leaders

TRANSACTIONAL LEADER		TRANSFORMATIONAL LEADER	
Contingent reward	Contracts exchange of rewards for effort, promises rewards for good performance, recognizes accomplishments.	**Charisma**	Provides vision and sense of mission, instills pride, gains respect and trust.
Management by exception (active)	Watches and searches for deviations from rules and standards, takes corrective action.	**Inspiration**	Communicates high expectations, uses symbols to focus efforts, expresses important purposes in simple ways.
Management by exception (passive)	Intervenes only if standards are not met.	**Intellectual stimulation**	Promotes intelligence, rationality, and careful problem solving.
Laissez-faire	Abdicates responsibilities, avoids making decisions.	**Individualized consideration**	Gives personal attention, treats each employee individually, coaches, advises.

Source: Reprinted from Organizational Dynamics *(Winter 1990). Bernard M. Bass et al., "From Transactional to Transformational Leadership: Learning to Share the Vision," Copyright 1990, with permission from Elsevier Science.*

14h Misled Leaders

Bill George, former CEO of Medtronic, Harvard professor, and author of the book *True North*:

Leaders who fail often do so because they fall prey to the pressures and seductions they face. It isn't that they lack leadership skills, style, or power—but that their egos, their greed, their craving for public adulation, and their fear of loss of power overwhelm their responsibility to build their institutions. In contrast, authentic leaders understand that leading is about serving others and bringing them together around a common cause.

Source: As quoted in "Open Debate," Fast Company, no. 114 (April 2007): 112.

QUESTION:
How is this quotation related to transformational and servant leadership?

philosophical anchor point.[72] This is where Robert K. Greenleaf's philosophy of the *servant leader* enters the picture as an instructive and inspiring springboard. The servant leader is an ethical person who puts *others*—not herself or himself—in the foreground. As a devout Quaker with years of real-world experience at AT&T, Greenleaf wove humility and a genuine concern for the whole person into his philosophy of leadership.[73] He portrayed the servant leader as one who, in addition to putting others first, has a clear sense of purpose in life, is a good listener, is trustworthy, and accepts others at face value. The servant leader tries to

improve the world, first and foremost, through *self-improvement*. One person who embodies the servant leader philosophy is John Wooden, who coached the UCLA men's basketball team to an astounding ten national championships: "The great thing about Coach Wooden is that he is what he is," former player Bill Walton says. "This is a man with no pretensions. He is a humble, giving person who wants nothing in return but to see other people succeed."[74]

MENTORING

In spite of mountains of leadership research, much remains to be learned about why some people are good leaders whereas many others are not.[75] One thing is clear, though: mentors can make an important difference. Take Michael Dell, for example. How was he able to take a personal computer business he started in his dorm room at the University of Texas and build it into a giant company with $50 billion in annual sales? And all before his 40th birthday! *Business Week* offered this insight: ". . . most amazing of all to his peers is Dell's near egoless management. From the start, he has sought out gray-haired mentors to help show him the way."[76] Let us explore this interesting process whereby leadership skills are acquired by exposure to role models.

Learning from a Mentor

The many obstacles and barriers blocking the way to successful leadership make it easy to understand why there is no simple formula for developing leaders. Abraham Zaleznik, the respected sociologist mentioned earlier, insists that leaders must be

Anyone who has had a mentor knows how valuable the experience can be for all involved. As part of Ohio's mandate that all first-year teachers have mentors during their critical first year, Paula Hodson (background) observes Rachel Daw, a first-year teacher, as she helps fifth graders with fractions in Brunswick, Ohio.

14i Mentoring Turned Upside Down

Procter & Gamble, Cincinnati, Ohio:

The consumer-products giant pairs junior female employees with a senior manager for reverse mentoring to help the mostly male higher-ups understand the issues women face.

Source: Robert Levering and Milton Moskowitz, "The 100 Best Companies to Work For," Fortune (January 24, 2005): 74.

QUESTIONS:

What are the pros and cons of this approach to mentoring? On balance, do you endorse this practice? Explain.

nurtured under the wise tutelage of a mentor. A **mentor** is an individual who systematically develops another person's abilities through intensive tutoring, coaching, and guidance.[77] Zaleznik explains the nature of this special relationship:

> **mentor:** someone who develops another person through tutoring, coaching, and guidance

Mentors take risks with people. They bet initially on talent they perceive in [junior] people. Mentors also risk emotional involvement in working closely with their juniors. The risks do not always pay off, but the willingness to take them appears crucial in developing leaders.[78]

A survey of 246 health care industry managers found higher satisfaction, greater recognition, and more promotion opportunities among managers with mentors than among those without.[79] Additionally, a recent study of turnover among more than 15,000 employees led the researchers to conclude, "People with mentors are twice as likely to stay as those without."[80] Other research suggests that *informal* relationships that arise naturally work better than formally structured pairings.[81] Still, major accounting firm KPMG prefers this carefully structured approach:

> *. . . [E]very junior staffer is expected to have a mentor, every manager a protégé, and those in the middle often have both. There's a website to facilitate the formal process, and social activities—happy hours, softball games, group lunches—are organized to encourage informal networking.[82]*

Whatever approach is taken to mentoring, a survey of senior executives revealed a major shortfall. "Just one in nine had a mentor or buddy to help them get acclimated to the position and the company."[83] Not surprisingly, 61 percent expressed dissatisfaction with their integration into their new positions.

Dynamics of Mentoring

According to Kathy Kram, who conducted intensive biographical interviews with both members in 18 different senior manager–junior manager mentor relationships, mentoring fulfills two important functions: (1) a career enhancement function and (2) a psychological and social support function (see Table 14.5). Mentor relationships were found to average about five years in length.[84] Thus, a manager might have a series of mentors during the course of an organizational career. Also, as explained recently by a team of

TABLE **14.5** **Mentors Serve Two Important Functions**

CAREER FUNCTIONS*	PSYCHOSOCIAL FUNCTIONS**
Sponsorship	Role modeling
Exposure and visibility	Acceptance and confirmation
Coaching	Counseling
Protection	Friendship
Challenging assignments	

*Career functions are those aspects of the relationship that primarily enhance career advancement.
**Psychosocial functions are those aspects of the relationship that primarily enhance a sense of competence, clarity of identity, and effectiveness in the managerial role.
Source: Kathy E. Kram, "Phases of the Mentor Relationship," *Academy of Management Journal, 26 (December 1983): 614 (Exhibit 1). Reprinted by permission.*

researchers, there is a growing need for having more than one mentor at a time.

> *Forces such as rapidly changing technology, shifting organizational structures, and global marketplace dynamics have transformed mentoring into a process that by necessity extends beyond the services of a single mentor. As knowledge continuously changes and evolves, it becomes difficult if not impossible for individuals—or individual mentors—to possess all the requisite knowledge within themselves. Having multiple mentors facilitates the building of knowledge in the people who then become the primary assets and sources of competitive advantage to the firm.*[85]

Interestingly, the junior member of a mentor relationship is not the only one to benefit. Mentors often derive great intrinsic pleasure from seeing their protégés move up through the ranks and conquer difficult challenges. Moreover, by passing along their values and their technical and leadership skills to promising junior managers, mentors can wield considerable power. Mentor relationships do sometimes turn sour, however.[86] A mentor can become threatened by a protégé who surpasses him or her. Also, cross-gender[87] and cross-race mentor relationships can fall victim to bias and social pressures.[88]

BEHAVIOR MODIFICATION

This last approach to influencing behavior can be traced to two psychologists, John B. Watson and Edward L. Thorndike, who did their work in the early twentieth century. From Watson came the advice to concentrate on observable behavior. Accordingly, the philosophy of **behaviorism** maintains that observable behavior is more important than hypothetical inner states such as needs, motives, and expectations.[89] From Thorndike came an appreciation of the way in which consequences control behavior. According to Thorndike's classic law of effect, favorable consequences encourage behavior, whereas unfavorable consequences discourage behavior.[90] However, it remained for B. F. Skinner, the late Harvard psychologist, to integrate Watson's and Thorndike's contributions into a precise technology of behavior change.

behaviorism: belief that observable behavior is more important than inner states

What Is Behavior Modification?

Skinner was the father of *operant conditioning*, the study of how behavior is controlled by the surrounding environment.[91] Although some find Skinner's substitution of environmental control for self-control repulsive and dehumanizing,[92] few deny that operant conditioning actually occurs. Indeed, much of our behavior is the product of environmental shaping. Rather, the debate centers on whether or not natural shaping processes should be systematically managed to alter the course of everyday behavior.[93] Advocates of behavior modification in the workplace believe they should be.[94]

Behavior modification is the practical application of Skinnerian operant-conditioning techniques to everyday behavior problems. **Behavior modification** (B. Mod.) involves systematically managing environmental factors to get people to do the right things more often and the wrong things less often. This is accomplished by managing the antecedents and/or consequences of observable behavior.

behavior modification: systematic management of the antecedents and consequences of behavior

Managing Antecedents

An **antecedent** is an environmental cue that prompts an individual to behave in a given manner. Antecedents do not automatically *cause* the person to behave in a predictable manner, as a hot stove causes you to withdraw your hand reflexively when you touch it. Rather, we learn through experience to interpret antecedents as signals telling us it is time to behave in a certain way if we are to get what we want or to avoid what we do not want. This process is sometimes referred to as *cue control.* Domino's Pizza Inc. makes effective use of cue control for maintaining product quality.

antecedent: an environmental cue for a specific behavior

> *[Every Domino's] features a myriad of strategically placed, visually appealing posters displaying helpful, job-related tips and reminders. . . .*
>
> *Centrally located, particularly for the benefit of the oven tender who slices and boxes the just-baked pizza, are two photos, one of "The Perfect Pepperoni" pizza, the other showing a pizza with ten common flaws, one per slice.*[95]

Although it is often overlooked, the management of antecedents is a practical and simple way of encouraging good performance. As Table 14.6 indicates,

TABLE **14.6**	Managing Antecedents
BARRIERS: REMOVE BARRIERS THAT PREVENT OR HINDER THE COMPLETION OF A GOOD JOB. FOR EXAMPLE:	**AIDS: PROVIDE HELPFUL AIDS THAT ENHANCE THE OPPORTUNITY TO DO A GOOD JOB. FOR EXAMPLE:**
Unrealistic objectives, plans, schedules, or deadlines	Challenging yet attainable objectives
Uncooperative or distracting coworkers	Clear and realistic plans
Training deficiencies	Understandable instructions
Contradictory or confusing rules	Constructive suggestions, hints, or tips
Inadequate or inappropriate tools	Clear and generally acceptable work rules
Conflicting orders from two or more managers	Realistic schedules and deadlines
	Friendly reminders
	Posters or signs with helpful tips
	Easy-to-use forms
	Nonthreatening questions about progress
	User-friendly computer software and hardware

there are two ways to manage antecedents. Barriers can be removed, and helpful aids can be offered. These steps ensure that the path to good performance is clearly marked and free of obstacles (which meshes with the path-goal theory of leadership).

Managing Consequences

Managing the consequences of job performance is more complex than dealing strictly with antecedents, because there are four different classes of consequences. Each type of consequence involves a different process. Positive reinforcement and negative reinforcement both encourage behavior, but they do so in different ways. Extinction and punishment discourage behavior but, again, in different ways. These four terms have precise meanings that are often confused by casual observers.

POSITIVE REINFORCEMENT. Positive reinforcement encourages a specific behavior by immediately following it with a consequence the individual finds pleasing. For example, a machine operator who maintains a clean work area because he or she is praised for doing so has responded to positive reinforcement. As the term implies, positive reinforcement reinforces or builds behavior in a positive way.

positive reinforcement: encouraging a behavior with a pleasing consequence

NEGATIVE REINFORCEMENT. *Negative reinforcement* encourages a specific behavior by immediately withdrawing or terminating something a particular person finds displeasing. Children learn the power of negative reinforcement early in life when they discover that the quickest way to get something is to cry and scream until their parents give them what they want. In effect, the parents are negatively reinforced for complying with the child's demand by the termination of the crying and screaming. In other words, the termination or withdrawal of an undesirable state of affairs (for example, the threat of being fired) has an incentive effect. In a social context, negative reinforcement amounts to blackmail. "Do what I want, or I will continue to make your life miserable" are the bywords of the person who relies on negative reinforcement to influence behavior.

EXTINCTION. Through *extinction*, a specific behavior is discouraged by ignoring it. For example, managers sometimes find that the best way to keep employees from asking redundant questions is simply not to answer them. Just as a plant will wither and die without water, behavior will fade away without occasional reinforcement.

PUNISHMENT. *Punishment* discourages a specific behavior by the immediate presentation of an undesirable consequence or the immediate removal of something desirable. For example, a manager may punish a tardy employee by either assigning the individual to a dirty job or docking the individual's pay.

It is important to remember that positive and negative reinforcement, extinction, and punishment all entail the manipulation of the *immediate* or *direct* consequences of a desired or undesired behavior. If action is taken before the behavior, behavior control is unlikely. For instance, if a manager gives an employee a cash bonus *before* a difficult task is completed, the probability of the task being completed declines because the incentive effect has been removed. In regard to managing consequences, behavior modification works only when there is a contingent ("if . . . then") relationship between a specific behavior and a given consequence.

Positively Reinforce What Is Right About Job Performance (the Art of "Bucket Filling")

Proponents of behavior modification prefer to build up desirable behaviors rather than tearing down undesirable ones. Every undesirable behavior has a desirable counterpart that can be reinforced. For example, someone who comes in late once a week actually comes in on time four days a week. To encourage productive behaviors, managers are advised to focus on the positive aspects of job performance when managing consequences. Thus, positive reinforcement is the preferred consequence strategy.[96] This positive approach was effectively taken to heart by Preston Trucking, a Maryland shipping company.

> *Preston, years ago, had terrible relations between management and labor. Then, one day, top management resolved to bury the hatchet. All sorts of reforms were announced, including the Four-to-One Rule: For every criticism a manager made about a driver's performance, he had to give him four compliments. You can imagine how this went over. "It was like a . . . like a marriage encounter," says Teamster Nick Costa, rolling his eyes. Eventually, though, drivers discovered that the rule really did reflect a change of heart.[97]*

This positive approach to modifying behavior is the central theme in the longstanding best-seller *The One Minute Manager,* which extols the virtues of "catching people doing something *right!"*[98] Positive reinforcement also is the core message in Tom Rath and Donald O. Clifton's best-selling book *How Full Is*

Talk about positive reinforcement! Presidential hopeful Barack Obama was bathed in it during this 2007 rally in Cedar Rapids, Iowa—cheering throngs, supportive placards, and Oprah Winfrey clapping enthusiastically. Of course, in a democracy, politicians are ultimately reinforced (or not) on Election Day. In the day-to-day workplace, meanwhile, positive reinforcement in the form of praise and recognition can be a bit scarce.

BEST PRACTICES

Grant Makers: $50 Isn't Much—Unless it Comes from a Coworker

Here's what Kimley-Horn and Associates, a big civil-engineering company in Cary, North Carolina, does with $50: At any time, for any reason, without permission, any employee can award a bonus of that amount to any other employee. No strings.

"It works because it's real time, and it's not handed down from management," says Barry Barber, Kimley-Horn's human-resources director. "Any employee who does something exceptional receives recognition from their peers within minutes." Everyone feels good, in real time.

To make an award, an employee downloads a form, explains his thinking, signs it, and—if possible—delivers it to the recipient in person. The awardee sends the form to payroll to cash it in. There's very little oversight and virtually no abuse. And "when we think of what our clients received for that $55 [the extra $5 is to cover taxes]," Barber says, "we know it's money well spent."

Source: Excerpted from Alex C. Pasquariello, "Grant Makers," Fast Company, no. 114 (April 2007): 32. Copyright 2007 by Mansueto Ventures LLC. Reproduced with permission of Mansueto Ventures LLC in the format Textbook via Copyright Clearance Center.

Your Bucket? Positive Strategies for Work and Life. Rath and his now-deceased grandfather use the metaphor of a *bucket* to represent how a person feels and acts. One's bucket is filled by praise and other forms of positive reinforcement. Criticism and negativity empty one's bucket. On the basis of their Gallup surveys of a worldwide sampling of over 4 million employees, Rath and Clifton claim that "regular recognition and praise" boost productivity and satisfaction while reducing accidents and turnover. But they caution managers to use "positive interactions" to an appropriate extent— not too little, not too much. Citing recent research evidence, they recommend a ratio of positive to negative interactions (both at work and at home) of between 3 to 1 and 13 to 1. Less than a 3-to-1 ratio is flirting with corrosive negativity. A ratio greater than 13 to 1 communicates false optimism and lacks realism. Their conclusion: ". . . most of us don't have to worry about breaking the upper limit. The positive-to-negative ratios in most organizations are woefully inadequate and leave substantial room for improvement."[99]

Schedule Positive Reinforcement Appropriately

Both the type and the timing of consequences are important in successful B. Mod. When a productive behavior is first tried out by an employee, a continuous schedule of reinforcement is appropriate. Under **continuous reinforcement** every instance of the desired behavior is reinforced. For example, a bank manager who is training a new loan officer to handle a difficult type of account should praise the loan officer after every successful transaction until the behavior is firmly established. After the loan officer is able to handle the transaction, the bank manager can switch to a schedule of intermittent reinforcement. As the term implies, **intermittent reinforcement** calls for reinforcing some, rather than all, of the desired responses.

continuous reinforcement: rewarding every instance of a behavior

intermittent reinforcement: rewarding some, but not all, instances of a behavior

The more unpredictable the payoff schedule is, the better the results will be. One way to appreciate the power of intermittent reinforcement is to think of the enthusiasm with which people play slot machines; these gambling devices pay off on an unpredictable intermittent schedule. In the same way, occasional reinforcement of established productive behaviors with meaningful positive consequences is an extremely effective management technique.[100] To spark your imagination, see Best Practices.

(Now go do something nice for yourself as positive reinforcement for reading this chapter.)

SUMMARY

1. Influence is fundamental to management because individuals must be influenced to pursue collective objectives. Researchers have identified eight generic influence tactics used on the job: consultation (seeking participation of others), rational persuasion (reasoning with logic), inspirational appeals (appealing to someone's values or ideals), ingratiating tactics (using flattery or humility prior to a request), coalition tactics (seeking help in persuading others), pressure tactics (using intimidation, demands, or threats), upward appeals (seeking the support of higher management), and exchange tactics (trading favors).

2. The five basic types of power are reward, coercive, legitimate, referent, and expert power. Empowerment cannot work without a supporting situation, which may include a skilled individual, an organizational culture of empowerment, an emotionally mature individual with a well-developed character, and empowerment opportunities such as delegation, participation, and self-managed teams.

3. Formal leadership consists of influencing relevant others to voluntarily pursue organizational objectives. Informal leadership can work for or against the organization. Leadership theory has evolved through four major stages: trait theory, behavioral styles theory, situational theory, and transformational theory. A promising trait approach is based on Goleman's four dimensions of emotional intelligence: self-awareness, self-management, social awareness, and relationship management.

4. Researchers who differentiated among authoritarian, democratic, and laissez-faire leadership styles concentrated on leader behavior rather than personality traits. Leadership studies at Ohio State University isolated four styles of leadership based on two categories of leader behavior: initiating structure and consideration. A balanced high-structure, high-consideration style was recommended. According to Blake and his colleagues, a 9,9 style (high concern for both production and people) is the best overall style because it emphasizes teamwork.

5. Situational-leadership theorists believe there is no single best leadership style; rather, different situations require different styles. Many years of study led Fiedler to conclude that task-motivated leaders are more effective in either very favorable or very unfavorable situations, whereas relationship-motivated leaders are better suited to moderately favorable situations. The favorableness of a situation is dictated by the degree of the leader's control and influence in getting the job done. Path-goal leadership theory, an expectancy perspective, assumes that leaders are effective to the extent that they can motivate followers by clarifying goals and clearing the paths to achieving those goals and valued rewards. Unlike Fiedler, path-goal theorists believe that managers can and should adapt their leadership behavior to the situation.

6. In contrast to transactional leaders who maintain the status quo, transformational leaders are visionary, charismatic leaders dedicated to change. Greenleaf's philosophy of the servant leader helps aspiring leaders integrate what they have learned about leadership. The servant leader is motivated to serve rather than lead. Clear goals, trust, good listening skills, positive feedback, foresight, and self-development are the characteristics of a servant leader.

7. Mentors help develop less experienced people by fulfilling career and psychosocial functions. Mentors engage in intensive tutoring, coaching, and guiding. Mentors are role models for aspiring leaders.

8. Behavior modification (B. Mod.) is the practical application of Skinner's operant conditioning principles. B. Mod. involves managing antecedents (removing barriers and providing helpful aids) and consequences to strengthen desirable behavior and weaken undesirable behavior. Proponents of B. Mod. prefer to shape behavior through positive reinforcement rather than negative reinforcement, extinction, and punishment. Continuous reinforcement is recommended for new behavior and intermittent reinforcement for established behavior.

TERMS TO UNDERSTAND

- **Influence**, p. 397
- **Power**, p. 399
- **Reward power**, p. 400
- **Coercive power**, p. 400
- **Legitimate power**, p. 400
- **Referent power**, p. 400
- **Expert power**, p. 401
- **Empowerment**, p. 401
- **Leadership**, p. 402

MANAGER'S TOOLKIT

Putting the Empowerment Puzzle Together

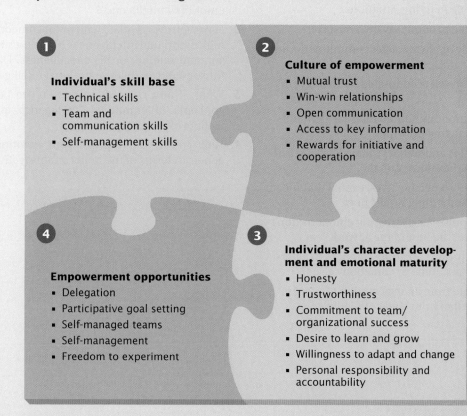

1

Individual's skill base
- Technical skills
- Team and communication skills
- Self-management skills

2

Culture of empowerment
- Mutual trust
- Win-win relationships
- Open communication
- Access to key information
- Rewards for initiative and cooperation

4

Empowerment opportunities
- Delegation
- Participative goal setting
- Self-managed teams
- Self-management
- Freedom to experiment

3

Individual's character development and emotional maturity
- Honesty
- Trustworthiness
- Commitment to team/ organizational success
- Desire to learn and grow
- Willingness to adapt and change
- Personal responsibility and accountability

Source: *Adapted in part from discussion in Stephen R. Covey,* Principle-Centered Leadership *(New York: Simon & Schuster, 1991), pp. 212–216.*

ACTION LEARNING EXERCISE

What Is Your Emotional Intelligence (EQ)?[101]

Instructions: Evaluate each statement about your emotional intelligence on a scale of 1 = "not at all like me" to 10 = "very much like me." Try to be objective by viewing yourself through the eyes of key people in your life such as family members, close friends, coworkers, and classmates. (*Note:* This instrument is for instructional purposes only because it was derived from a 25-item survey of unknown validity.)

_____ 1. I usually stay composed, positive, and unflappable in trying situations.

_____ 2. I am able to admit my own mistakes.

_____ 3. I usually or always meet commitments and keep promises.

_____ 4. I hold myself accountable for meeting my goals.

_____ 5. I can smoothly handle multiple demands and changing priorities.

_____ 6. Obstacles and setbacks may delay me a little, but they don't stop me.

_____ 7. I seek fresh perspectives, even if that means trying something totally new.

_____ 8. My impulses or distressing emotions don't often get the best of me at work.

_____ 9. I usually don't attribute setbacks to a personal flaw (mine or somebody else's).

_____10. I operate from an expectation of success rather than from a fear of failure.

Total = _____

Interpretation: A score below 70 indicates a need for improvement. With sincere effort, one's emotional intelligence can be improved. It is part of a natural process of "growing up" and becoming mature in challenging social situations. People with low EQ scores are like porcupines—they're hard to hug.

For Consideration/Discussion

1. What do you like or dislike about the concept of emotional intelligence?

2. Have you ever worked with or for someone who had high emotional intelligence? If so, describe that person and rate her or his effectiveness. Do the same for someone with low emotional intelligence.

3. What, if any, connection do you see between the concepts of emotional intelligence and servant leader? Explain.

4. How could you improve your emotional intelligence, in terms of the items on this test?

CLOSING CASE
Leadership Development GE-Style

As companies evolve, so do their leadership philosophies. And General Electric's John F. Welch Leadership Center at Crotonville has had more time to evolve than any other corporate university, as . . . [2006 marked] its 50th anniversary. In that half century, the center, in Ossining, N.Y., 30 miles outside of Manhattan, has turned out internal and external leaders ready to take on global-scale business challenges—and there's no sign of a slowdown.

"Crotonville is embedded in the GE culture and the GE values," GE Chief Learning Officer Bob Corcoran says. "All of our major change initiatives—cultural change and business change processes—have either originated at Crotonville as a result of best practice assessments and evaluations or executive leadership summits, or they have been broadcast, trained, amplified or rolled out with Crotonville as the change agent."

Corcoran himself is a 27-year GE veteran in human resources and executive leadership, and holds the distinction of being the first CLO and head of Crotonville who is a graduate of all of the executive development programs. . . .

Nominated executives stay in the Residence Building, a 190-bed facility where each room is a carbon copy of the next, reinforcing the level playing field Corcoran says he wants all attendees to be playing on. "Every person who comes here wears a little nametag; it doesn't say you're the [head] of health care, it doesn't say you're a junior finance accountant. It says your name and your business." He says employees are there to discuss values, processes and change initiatives, regardless of position. "It really is a place that fundamentally reinforces the concepts and principles of a meritocracy."

And while students are there, they'll be treated to lectures from not only leadership experts in the academic world (the late Peter Drucker taught there), but also GE leaders. In 25 years, [former CEO Jack] Welch and current Chairman and CEO Jeffrey Immelt have spoken at 329 of the last 330 executive-level courses at the facility, which is 60 miles from the GE headquarters in Fairfield, Conn. Welch, who missed one when he had heart bypass surgery, was known to speak up to six hours to students.

But lest one think taking leadership courses at Crotonville is a cushy reward for good behavior or a golf-centric retreat, Corcoran stresses that students, who represent each GE business, are there to work. "Our classes don't just go 8 to 5," he says, explaining project work, evening lectures and roundtable discussions take up participants' time.

In the first of the three progressive courses, Manager Development Course (MDC), 75 to 80 students compete in an artificial intelligence marketplace via computer simulation following lectures that teach them business management basics. Instructors, who Corcoran says are two-thirds internal, one-third external, stress both theory and practical application. The format of the course, given eight times a year, Corcoran explains, is "concept, application, practice." And although it's the first of the top three courses, a GE executive won't be eligible for the program until 10 to 20 years into his or her career.

In the second and third courses, Business Manager Course (BMC) and Executive Development Course (EDC), respectively, not only do participants get assigned a real problem GE is facing, but also must present their findings to Immelt, who hand selects the problem. In BMC, given three times a year to 50 to 60 participants who are eligible about three to four years after MDC, the focus is on assessing and evaluating change with action-learning techniques, Corcoran says. The program typically involves a week of world travel, as many of the problems students are given hinge on staying competitive in a global market. The students conduct interviews and merge that into a recommendation for Immelt and his team.

EDC, meanwhile, focuses on changing GE's culture. The annual course is given to 35 individuals among the top 300 in the company and could potentially become one of the 170 GE corporate officers. "They get big issues to deal with," Corcoran says. There are guest lecturers, and students wrestle with broad-based solutions. Lectures are given in "The Pit" at Crotonville, which is a 100-seat amphitheater that Corcoran says truly puts the speaker in the spotlight. "When lecturers are there at the bottom, our classes don't sit quietly and say, 'Thank you very much,' and then talk badly about them when they leave. They smack them around live, and it doesn't matter if it's a vice president or not of GE." Participants also present their findings to Immelt and corporate officers.

While all this learning is happening under Immelt's scrutiny, Corcoran stresses that participants' experiences, successes and failures are not reported to supervisors. "We create a very, very safe learning environment. We fundamentally said Crotonville is a safe haven," Corcoran says. "You have to be free to make mistakes. The reality is that in the real world, in real life when you're not in the classroom, people learn most when they make mistakes. We encourage people to take risks; we encourage them to try."

There is no grading process during the courses, Corcoran says, stressing that it's more important that students take the lessons learned and apply [them] and create value in their jobs. "Potential's good, but results are better."

Source: Excerpted from Jacqueline Durett, "GE Hones Its Leaders at Crotonville," *Training*, 42 (May 2006): 25–27. Reprinted by permission of Billboard.

FOR DISCUSSION

1 Referring to the section titled "Learning to Manage" in Chapter 1, do you think this is an effective way to teach leadership? Explain.

2 Is GE's Crotonville a better learning environment than the typical college classroom? Why or why not?

3 If you were a GE employee and were nominated to attend Crotonville, what would you look forward to the most (and what would you fear the most) about the experience? Explain.

4 How would you integrate a formal mentoring program with the Crotonville course work?

5 All things considered, can leadership be taught or do some people just naturally have what it takes? Explain.

TEST PREPPER

True/False Questions

_____ 1. According to research, consultation and rational persuasion are the most widely used influence tactics on the job.

_____ 2. Negative power, based on threatened or actual punishment, is one of the five bases of power.

_____ 3. Despite differing characteristics between leaders and managers, we need people who can lead _and_ manage today.

_____ 4. Higher EQ scores indicate more polished social skills and greater emotional maturity.

_____ 5. Blake and Mouton, through their research with the Leadership Grid®, came to believe that no one best style of leadership exists.

_____ 6. The ideal leader is relationship-motivated, according to Fiedler's contingency theory.

_____ 7. Transactional leaders characteristically offer a lot of personal attention and advice to employees.

_____ 8. Within the context of practical intelligence, Yale's Robert J. Sternberg rejects the notion of "born leaders."

_____ 9. One of the psychosocial functions of mentoring is role modeling.

_____10. Both positive and negative reinforcement can be used to encourage specific target behaviors.

Multiple-Choice Questions

1. Which of the following is _not_ among the generic influence tactics described in the text?
   A. Upward appeals   B. Exchange tactics
   C. Coalition tactics   D. Participative tactics
   E. Consultation

2. _____ power closely parallels formal authority.
   A. Rational   B. Referent
   C. Legitimate   D. Traditional
   E. Functional

3. All _except_ which one of these are among Peter Drucker's criteria for assessing the effectiveness of leaders?
   A. They knew when to say "no."
   B. They asked, "What needs to be done?"
   C. They developed action plans.
   D. They ran productive meetings.
   E. They took responsibility for communicating.

4. _____ leadership involves influencing others to pursue objectives that may or may not serve the organization's interests.
   A. Corollary   B. Formal
   C. Informal   D. Ad hoc
   E. Decentralized

5. _____ can be defined as an array of noncognitive skills, capabilities, and competencies that influence a person's ability to cope with environmental demands and pressures.
   A. Self-management   B. Emotional intelligence
   C. Behavior modification D. Empowerment
   E. IQ

6. In the Ohio State leadership model, the term _____ _best_ characterizes "consideration."
   A. trust   B. goals
   C. results   D. techniques
   E. authority

7. According to Fiedler's contingency theory, _____ leaders tend to perform better when the situation is _____ favorable.
   A. achievement-oriented; moderately
   B. authoritarian; highly
   C. relationship-motivated; moderately
   D. social; highly
   E. task-motivated; moderately

8. Which of the following is _not_ one of the eight categories of leader behavior in House's updated path-goal theory?
   A. Work facilitation behaviors
   B. Group decision behaviors
   C. Achievement-oriented behaviors
   D. Value-based behaviors
   E. Mentoring behaviors

9. _____ is(are) the center of attention in Greenleaf's servant-leadership theory.
   A. Others   B. God
   C. The leader   D. Top management
   E. The mission

10. In their best-selling book _How Full Is Your Bucket?_ Rath and Clifton point to research evidence that the right ratio of positive to negative interactions with others is somewhere between _____ to 1 and _____ to 1.
    A. 2; 4   B. 3; 13
    C. 5; 10   D. 6; 12
    E. 2; 8

See page T1 at the back of the text for answers to these questions. Want more questions? Visit the student Web site and take the ACE quizzes for more practice.

15

Change, Conflict, and Negotiation

OBJECTIVES

- **Identify** and **describe** four types of organizational change, according to the Nadler-Tushman model.

- **Explain** how people tend to respond differently to changes they like and those they dislike.

- **List** at least six reasons why employees resist change, and **discuss** what management can do about resistance to change.

- **Describe** how the unfreezing-change-refreezing metaphor applies to organization development (OD).

- **Describe** tempered radicals, and **identify** the 5Ps in the checklist for grassroots change agents.

- **Contrast** the competitive and cooperative conflict styles.

- **Identify** and **describe** five conflict resolution techniques.

- **Identify** and **describe** the elements of effective negotiation, and **explain** the advantage of added value negotiating (AVN).

THE CHANGING WORKPLACE

Bell Canada: Energizing a Sluggish Culture

In 2002, Bell Canada's new CEO, Michael Sabia, inherited a struggling 122-year-old company that needed to banish its monopolist mentality in order to compete.

To make his employees more outward-looking, dynamic, and productive, Sabia started with traditional business moves, such as implementing a Six Sigma [quality improvement] program and cutting costs. They weren't enough. Culture change can start in the corner office, but it cannot end there: "We needed to get to the front lines of the organization," says Sabia, "and my view is that it's very hard to do that through formal programs."

Working with [author and consultant Jon] Katzenbach, as well as chief talent officer Leo Houle and Mary Anne Elliott, SVP [senior vice president] for human resources, Bell Canada decided to try to cultivate change from within. Using surveys, performance reviews, and recommendations from executives, it scoured its nearly 50,000 employees to find 14 low- and mid-level managers who embodied the mentality the company sought: committed, passionate, and competitive. Katzenbach and staffers in the HR department interviewed the 14 extensively. They found that the subjects shared the ability to get people to trust them and to solve problems rather than complain about them. "These people have incredible influence," says Elliott. "It's like the [Life cereal] commercial—Will Mikey eat it?" The initial group then recommended another 40 associates.

In September 2004, Bell Canada organized an all-day meeting in Toronto for these "Pride Builders," including a session with Sabia, who bluntly asked them to lead a cultural transformation. "When we were brought into this environment," says Valerie Belzile, one of the original 54 and now associate director for corporate client care in the wireless unit Bell Mobility, "there was no more hierarchy. I felt, 'Oh, my God, this is real.'" The group gradually grew to 150 people, who created their own "community of practice" in which they shared ideas. They also worked on problems identified during company-organized gripe sessions and determined future conference topics themselves, such as managing people from different generations. At one, they handed Sabia a list of "pain points" he was unaware of, such as the bureaucracy associated with bringing in new hires. The Pride Builders helped shorten the process from as much as six weeks to five days.

Ironically, the Pride Builders' success has made it a much more formal organization. Today it has morphed into a veritable army of 2,500 people in 25 local chapters; three full-time staffers take care of administrative tasks. Belzile is co-coordinator of a chapter and organizes a monthly lunch to share best practices.

Has it made any difference? There are some quantifiable results. Starting in the fall of 2005, the company measured the impact of "pride behaviors" on customer and employee satisfaction in its small and medium-sized business call centers. Relative to the control group, employee satisfaction rose dramatically, as much as 71 percentage points. Customer satisfaction jumped too: Percentage increases ranged from 35% to 245%. "A formal organization is responsive to the exertion of power," says Sabia, "but an informal organization is responsive to persuasion. It's changed the way I think about management." Investors' views of the company have changed too: At the end of June [2007], Bell Canada's parent went private in a $33 billion deal—the largest such transaction in Canadian history.

Source: From Jennifer Reingold and Jia Lynn Yang, "The Hidden Workplace," *Fortune* (July 23, 2007): 100, 102. © 2007 Time Inc. All rights reserved.

Being competitive in today's fast-paced global economy means managers must be able to understand and manage constant change. High among the top ten challenges for CEOs, according to a worldwide survey, was "Speed, flexibility and adaptability to change."[2] Case in point:

Every year, PepsiCo adds more than 200 product variations to its global portfolio of brands that includes Frito-Lay snacks, Pepsi-Cola sodas, Gatorade sports drinks, and Tropicana juice. Many are aimed at wooing ethnic tastes as well as satisfying health-conscious consumers.[3]

As Bell Canada's leadership team now knows, rapid revolutionary changes and more deliberate evolutionary changes need to be balanced so that people both inside and outside the organization can handle them.[4] Also, as Xerox's CEO Anne Mulcahy learned from the school of hard knocks, it helps to be proactive rather than reactive. She told an interviewer, "It's hard to know exactly when change is needed, but better early than

late."[5] The purpose of this chapter, then, is to explore the dynamics of organizational change and its natural by-product, conflict. We discuss change from organizational and individual perspectives, address resistance to change, and examine how to make change happen. We then consider the nature and management of conflict and conclude with a discussion of negotiation.

CHANGE: ORGANIZATIONAL AND INDIVIDUAL PERSPECTIVES

Researchers report a constant tension between opposing forces for stability and change in today's work organizations.[6] A productive balance is required. Too much stability and organizational decline begins.

Too much change and the mission blurs and employees burn out. Today's managers need a robust set of concepts and skills to juggle stability and change. Let us tackle this major challenge for managers by looking at four types of organizational change and also at how individuals tend to respond to significant changes. These twin perspectives are important because organizational changes unavoidably have personal impacts.

Types of Organizational Change

Consultant David A. Nadler and management professor Michael L. Tushman together developed an instructive typology of organizational change (see Figure 15.1). On the vertical axis of their model, change is characterized as either anticipatory or reactive. **Anticipatory changes** are any systematically planned changes intended to take advantage of expected situations. By contrast, **reactive changes** are those necessitated by unexpected environmental events or pressures. The horizontal axis deals with the scope of a particular change, either incremental or strategic. **Incremental changes** involve subsystem adjustments needed to keep the organization on its chosen path. **Strategic changes** alter the overall shape or direction of the organization. For instance, adding a night shift to meet unexpectedly high demand for the company's product is an incremental change. Switching from building houses to building high-rise apartment complexes would be a strategic change. Four resulting types of organizational change in the Nadler-Tushman model are tuning, adaptation, re-orientation, and re-creation.[7] These types of organizational changes—here listed and discussed in order of increasing complexity, intensity, and risk—require a closer look.

FIGURE **15.1** Four Types of Organizational Change

	Incremental	Strategic
Anticipatory	Tuning	Re-orientation
Reactive	Adaptation	Re-creation

Source: David A. Nadler and Michael L. Tushman, "Beyond the Charismatic Leader: Leadership and Organizational Change." Copyright ©1990 by the Regents of the University of California. Reprinted from the California Management Review, vol. 32, no. 2. By permission of the Regents. All rights reserved.

anticipatory changes: planned changes based on expected situations

reactive changes: changes made in response to unexpected situations

incremental changes: subsystem adjustments required to keep the organization on course

strategic changes: altering the overall shape or direction of the organization

TUNING. Tuning is the most common, least intense, and least risky type of change. Other names for it include preventive maintenance and the Japanese concept of *kaizen* (continuous improvement).[8] The key to effective tuning is to actively anticipate and avoid problems rather than passively waiting for things to go wrong before taking action. For example, Du Pont tuned its marketing efforts by developing an Adopt-a-Customer program. The program "encourages blue-collar workers to visit a customer once a month, learn his needs, and be his representative on the factory floor."[9] This is a refreshing alternative to the traditional practice of waiting for customer complaints and only then trying to figure out how to fix them.

ADAPTATION. Like tuning, adaptation involves incremental changes. But this time, the changes are in reaction to external problems, events, or pressures. For example, in response to a declining market share, Dell deviated from its direct-to-the-customer sales model in 2007 by selling its computers through Wal-Mart. As *USA Today* reported at the time,

> *Dell's deal with the world's biggest retailer is a huge about-face. Dell dominated the PC industry for years because its direct-sales model kept costs low and customers close. Now, an evolving market is forcing Dell to adjust. "It's not an easy transition," . . . [one industry observer] says. "You've got to change your mind-set and your culture."*[10]

RE-ORIENTATION. This type of change is anticipatory and strategic in scope. Nadler and Tushman call re-orientation "frame bending" because the organization is significantly redirected. Significantly, there is not a complete break with the organization's past. Consider this example of frame bending at Cisco

These ancient ruins from past civilizations in what is now Rome, Italy, remind us that change is relentless. Today's great idea is tomorrow's taken-for-granted reality. Today's young up-start is tomorrow's old pro. People, organizations, nations, and civilizations that attempt to stand still get left behind in a fast-changing world.

Systems, the leading maker of Internet gear, after it had reported a 21 percent jump in sales in 2006:

> *Much of the jump came from Cisco's $6.9 billion acquisition of Scientific-Atlanta, a company that makes cable TV set-top boxes for Time Warner, Comcast and others. The deal . . . was a major strategic shift.*
>
> *Cisco's core business is pricey networking gear used by big businesses. But the company hopes that the growth of digital movies, music, television and telephony will give it an entry into consumer sales. Cisco's ultimate goal is a complete line of networking products, from back-end systems used by telephone companies to consumer gear used at home.*[11]

Cisco's frame bending is motivated by a desire to broaden its customer base to avoid getting hurt as it was when the Internet bubble burst in 2001.

RE-CREATION. Competitive pressures normally trigger this most intense and risky type of organizational change. Nadler and Tushman say it amounts to "frame breaking." A stunning example of frame breaking is the software giant Microsoft. Cofounder and then-CEO Bill Gates tied his company's future to the Internet in the mid-1990s after initially dismissing it as a passing fad. According to observers at the time,

> *Indeed, in just six months, Gates has done what few executives have dared. He has taken a thriving, $8 billion, 20,000-employee company and done a massive about-face. "I can't think of one corporation that has had this kind of success and after 20 years, just stopped and decided to reinvent itself from the ground up," says Jeffrey Katzenberg, a principal of DreamWorks SKG, which has a joint venture with Microsoft. "What they're doing is decisive, quick, breathtaking."*[12]

Frame breaking helped Bill Gates to re-create Microsoft's strategy and products around the Internet.

Individual Reactions to Change

Ultimately, workplace changes of all types become a *personal* matter for employees. A merger, for example, means a new job assignment for one person and a new boss for another. The first person may look forward to the challenge of a new assignment, whereas the second may dread the prospect of adjusting to a new boss. Researchers tell us these two people will tend to exhibit distinctly different response patterns.[13] Specifically, people tend to respond to changes they *like* differently than they do to changes they *dislike*. Let us explore these two response patterns with the goal of developing a contingency model for managers. It is important to note that both models are generic; that is, they apply equally to on-the-job and off-the-job changes. (See Window on the World.)

15a Back to the Opening Case

Relative to Figure 15.1, which type (or combination of types) of change took place at Bell Canada? Explain.

For further information about the interactive annotations in this chapter, visit our student Web site.

WINDOW ON THE WORLD

Globe-Trotting Employees Face Accelerating Change

Insurance executive Irene Dec moved to Warsaw in February [2007] for an exciting year-long assignment launching Prudential's operations in Poland.

It's the latest in a series of country-hopping work orders for Dec, 56. Since 2000, she has spent weeks or months on Prudential projects in Shanghai, Tokyo, Mexico City, London and Seoul. This is her longest international posting, and she hopes it won't be her last. . . .

Dec's career path places her squarely in the center of a growing trend in international corporate travel. Where international assignments almost universally used to last two or three years, companies increasingly are deploying valued employees outside their home countries in assignments that last less than 12 months. . . .

Companies like shorter assignments because they don't have to pay for big-ticket, family-related expenses such as private school tuition, international health insurance and a spousal allowance.

Source: Excerpted from Barbara DeLollis, "International Business Assignments Getting Shorter," USA Today (October 16, 2007): 8B.

HOW PEOPLE RESPOND TO CHANGES THEY LIKE. According to Figure 15.2, a three-stage adjustment is typical when people encounter a change they like. New college graduates, for instance, often see their unrealistic optimism (stage A) give way to the reality shock (stage B) of earning a living before getting their life and career on track (stage C). Key personal factors—including attitude, morale, and desire to make the change work—dip during stage B. Sometimes the dip is so severe or prolonged that the person gives up, as, say, when newlyweds head for the divorce court. Stage B is thus a critical juncture where leadership can make a difference.[14]

HOW PEOPLE RESPOND TO CHANGES THEY FEAR AND DISLIKE. Although exact statistics are not available, the situation in Figure 15.3 is probably more common in the workplace than the one in Figure 15.2. In other words, on-the-job change generally is more feared than welcomed. Changes, particularly sudden ones, represent the unknown. Most of us fear the unknown. We can bring the model in Figure 15.3 to life by walking through it with Maria, a production supervisor at a dairy products cooperative. She and her coworkers face a major reorganization involving a switch to team-based production.

FIGURE **15.2** How People Tend to Respond to Changes They *Like*

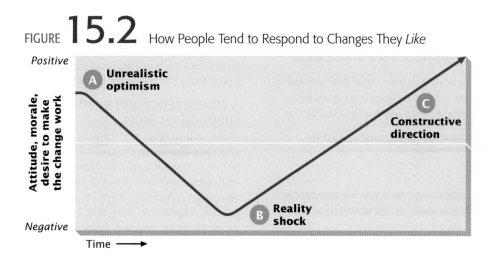

FIGURE **15.3** How People Tend to Respond to Changes They *Fear* and *Dislike*

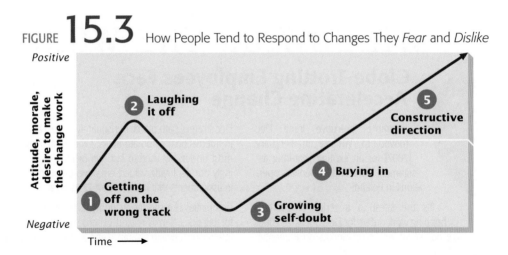

In stage 1, Maria feels a bit unsure and somewhat overwhelmed by the sudden switch to teams. She needs a lot more information to decide whether she really likes the idea. She feels twinges of fear. Stage 2 finds Maria joking with the other supervisors about how upper management's enthusiasm for teams will blow over in a few days, so there's no need to worry. Her attitude, mood, and desire for change improve a bit. After an initial training session on team-based management and participation, Maria begins to worry about her job security. Even if she keeps her job, she wonders whether she is up to the new way of doing things. Her morale drops sharply in stage 3. In stage 4, after a stern but supportive lecture from her boss about being a team player, Maria comes to grips with her resistance to the team approach. She resolves to stop criticizing management's "fad of the week" and to help make the switch to teams a success. Her attitude turns positive, and her morale takes an upswing in stage 5, as she tries participative management techniques and gets positive results. Additional training and some personal research and reading on team-based management convince Maria that this approach is the wave of the future.

Ten months after the switch to teams was announced, Maria has become an outspoken advocate for teams and participative management. Her job security is strengthened by a pending promotion to the training department, where she will coordinate all team training for supervisors. Unbeknownst to upper management, Maria has even toyed with the idea of starting her own consulting business, specializing in team management. Maria's transition from fear to full adaptation has taken months and has not been easy. But the experience has been normal and positive, including a timely boost from her manager between stages 3 and 4.

A CONTINGENCY MODEL FOR GETTING EMPLOYEES THROUGH CHANGES. Contingency managers, once again, adapt their techniques to the situation. The response patterns in Figures 15.2 and 15.3 call for different managerial actions. Managerial action steps for both situations are listed in Table 15.1. When employees understand that stages B and 3 are normal and expected responses, they will be less apt to panic and more likely to respond favorably to managerial guidance through action steps C and 4 and 5.

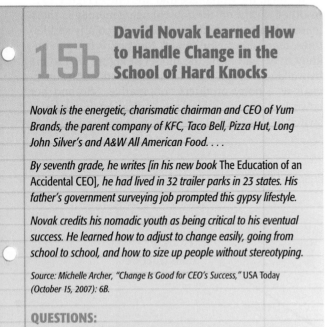

15b

David Novak Learned How to Handle Change in the School of Hard Knocks

Novak is the energetic, charismatic chairman and CEO of Yum Brands, the parent company of KFC, Taco Bell, Pizza Hut, Long John Silver's and A&W All American Food. . . .

By seventh grade, he writes [in his new book The Education of an Accidental CEO*], he had lived in 32 trailer parks in 23 states. His father's government surveying job prompted this gypsy lifestyle.*

Novak credits his nomadic youth as being critical to his eventual success. He learned how to adjust to change easily, going from school to school, and how to size up people without stereotyping.

Source: Michelle Archer, "Change Is Good for CEO's Success," USA Today (October 15, 2007): 6B.

QUESTIONS:

How well do you handle change? Have your life experiences helped (or hindered) your ability to deal effectively with change? Explain.

TABLE **15.1**	How to Help Individuals Deal with Change: A Contingency Approach

Situation: The person *likes* the change.

STAGE	MANAGERIAL ACTION STEPS
A. Unrealistic optimism "What a great idea! It will solve all our problems."	Encourage enthusiasm while directing attention to potential problems and to the cooperation and work necessary to get the job done.
B. Reality shock "This is going to be a lot harder than it seemed."	Listen supportively to negative feelings and neutralize unreasonable fears. Set realistic short-term goals. Build self-confidence. Recognize and reward positive comments and progress.
C. Constructive direction "This won't be easy, but we can do it."	Set broader and longer-term goals. Encourage involvement. Emphasize group problem solving and learning. Celebrate individual and group achievements. Prepare for bigger and better things.

Situation: The person *fears* and *dislikes* the change.

STAGE	MANAGERIAL ACTION STEPS
1. Getting off on the wrong track "What a dumb idea!"	Be a positive role model for the vision of a better way. Be a supportive listener and correct any misunderstanding.
2. Laughing it off "Just another wild idea that won't go anywhere. Don't worry about it."	Same as action step A above.
3. Growing self-doubt "I don't think I have what it takes."	Same as action step B above.
4. Buying in "Okay, I'll give this thing a try."	Encourage the person to let go of the past and look forward to a better future. Build personal commitment. Recognize and reward positive words and actions.
5. Constructive direction "This won't be easy, but we can do it."	Same as action step C above.

OVERCOMING RESISTANCE TO CHANGE

Dealing with change is an integral part of modern management. Change expert Ichak Adizes puts it this way:

Living means solving problems, and growing up means being able to solve bigger problems.

The purpose of management, leadership, parenting, or governing is exactly that: to solve today's problems and get ready to deal with tomorrow's problems. This is necessary because there is change. No management is needed when there are no problems, and there are no problems only when we are dead. To manage is to be alive, and to be alive means to experience change with the accompanying problems it brings.[15]

Within the change typology just discussed, organizational change comes in all sizes and shapes. Often it's new and unfamiliar technology, such as the second-generation Internet.[16] It could be a reorganization, a merger, a new pay plan, or perhaps a new performance appraisal program. Whatever its form, change is like a stone tossed into a still pond. The initial impact causes ripples to radiate in all directions, often with unpredictable consequences. A common consequence of change in organizations is resistance from those whose jobs are directly affected. Both rational and irrational resistance can bring the wheels of progress to a halt. Management faces the challenge of foreseeing and neutralizing resistance to change. The question is, how? To answer that question, we need to examine why employees resist change.

Why Do Employees Resist Change?

Employees resist change for many reasons.[17] The following are the most common.

SURPRISE. Significant changes that are introduced on the spur of the moment or with no warning can create a threatening sense of imbalance in the workplace. Regarding this problem, an executive task force at J. C. Penney Co., the well-known retailer, had this recommendation: "Schedule changes in measurable, comfortable stages. Too much, too soon can be counterproductive."[18]

INERTIA. Many members of the typical organization desire to maintain a safe, secure, and predictable status quo. The bywords of this group are "But we don't do things that way here." Technological inertia also is a common problem. Consider, for example, the history of the standard typewriter keyboard (referred to as the Qwerty keyboard because Q, W, E, R, T,

and Y are the first six letters in the upper-left-hand corner).

> *The ungainly layout of the Qwerty keyboard was introduced in 1873 to slow down typists so they wouldn't jam keys. That design imperative quickly disappeared, yet Qwerty has turned back all attempts—including one by its own inventor—to replace it with something faster. The productive cost? Undoubtedly billions of dollars.*[19]

Thanks to resistance to change, the latest high-tech marvels in personal computing come out of the box today complete with an 1873-style keyboard! Supervisors and middle managers who fall victim to unthinking inertia can effectively kill change programs.

MISUNDERSTANDING/IGNORANCE/LACK OF SKILLS. Without adequate introductory or remedial training, an otherwise positive change may be perceived in a negative light. This is precisely the situation Ann Fudge encountered in 2003 when she was hired as chair and CEO of Young & Rubicam, a troubled ad agency known for its turf battles. Fudge envisioned a more collaborative, efficient, and client-focused organization. But, as reported by *Business Week*, the transition hit some potholes:

> *Fudge's message of discipline is . . . bruising [senior managers'] egos. Many openly snicker at her attempts to introduce Six Sigma, the rigid and almost religious quality-control program long associated with General Electric Co. (where Fudge sits on the board). They call it Sick Sigma. She calls the initiative FIT—for focus, innovation, and teamwork—and says it's tailored to simplifying processes in the ad industry. She now has staffers trained as Six Sigma "green belts," who tackle everything from sourcing supplies to honing the process for developing creative strategies. Despite resistance, several converts are already excited about the results, with Y&R account manager Kathryn Burke arguing: "This really needed to be done."*[20]

However, three and a half years later, resistance to change won out. With Fudge's change program stalled and clients dissatisfied, she retired to focus her attention on nonprofit work.[21]

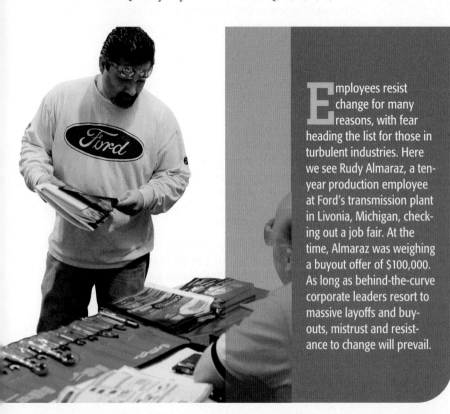

Employees resist change for many reasons, with fear heading the list for those in turbulent industries. Here we see Rudy Almaraz, a ten-year production employee at Ford's transmission plant in Livonia, Michigan, checking out a job fair. At the time, Almaraz was weighing a buyout offer of $100,000. As long as behind-the-curve corporate leaders resort to massive layoffs and buyouts, mistrust and resistance to change will prevail.

EMOTIONAL SIDE EFFECTS.   Those who are forced to accept on-the-job changes can experience a sense of powerlessness and even anger. The subsequent backlash can be passive (stalling, pretending not to understand) or active (vocal opposition, sabotage, or aggression).

LACK OF TRUST.   Promises of improvement are likely to fall on deaf ears when employees do not trust management. Conversely, managers are unlikely to permit necessary participation if they do not trust their people.

FEAR OF FAILURE.   Just as many college freshmen have doubts about their chances of ever graduating, challenges presented by significant on-the-job changes can also be intimidating.

PERSONALITY CONFLICTS.   Managers who are disliked by their people are poor conduits for change.

POOR TIMING.   In every work setting, internal and/or external events can conspire to create resentment about a particular change. For example, an otherwise desirable out-of-state transfer would only make things worse for an employee with an ailing elderly parent.

LACK OF TACT.   As we all know, it is not necessarily what is said that shapes our attitude toward people and events. *How* it is said is often more important. Tactful and sensitive handling of change is essential.

THREAT TO JOB STATUS/SECURITY.   Because employment fulfills basic needs, employees can be expected to resist changes with real or imaginary impacts on job status or job security.

BREAKUP OF WORK GROUP.   Significant changes can tear the fabric of on-the-job social relationships.[22] Accordingly, members of cohesive work groups often exert peer pressure on one another to resist changes that threaten to break up the group.[23]

PASSIVE-AGGRESSIVE ORGANIZATIONAL CULTURE. This subtle but potent form of resistance hides behind smiling faces. Passive-aggressive behavior becomes a major barrier to change when it becomes embedded in the organization's culture.

> *Meetings are a good way for employees to determine if they work for a passive-aggressive company. They go like this: Everyone is pleasant and agreeable. There's little debate. Heads nod when someone with power says it's time to introduce something new.*
>
> *The meeting ends with everyone seemingly on the same page, but then the quips begin about the flavor of the month. Most go back and do their jobs as they always have, or procrastinate, hoping the proposed change will blow over.*[24]

COMPETING COMMITMENTS.   Employees may not have a problem with the change itself, but rather with how it disrupts their pursuit of other goals. Such competing commitments are often unconscious and need to be skillfully brought to the surface to make progress. Consider this situation: "[Y]ou find that the person who won't collaborate despite a passionate and sincere commitment to teamwork is equally dedicated to avoiding the conflict that naturally attends any ambitious team activity."[25]

These reasons for resisting change help demonstrate that participation is not a panacea. For example, imagine the futility of trying to gain the enthusiastic support of a team of assembly-line welders for a robot that will eventually take over their jobs. In extreme form, each reason for resisting change can become an insurmountable barrier to genuine participation. Therefore, managers need a broad array of methods for dealing with resistance to change.

Strategies for Overcoming Resistance to Change

Only in recent years have management theorists begun to give serious attention to alternative ways of overcoming resistance to change.[26] At least six options, including participation, are available in this area.

1. ***Education and communication.*** This strategy is appealing because it advocates prevention rather than cure. The idea here is to help employees understand the true need for a change as well as the

The North American Free Trade Agreement (NAFTA) is a political hot potato in the United States. But that doesn't mean people in other participating countries are happy. These agricultural protestors in Mexico City worry that the removal of import tariffs on farm products under NAFTA will make them uncompetitive with U.S. farmers, who they say are subsidized by the government. Those responsible for NAFTA could have done a better job preparing the citizens of Canada, the United States, and Mexico for change.

logic behind it. Various media may be used, including face-to-face discussions, formal group presentations, or special reports or publications.

2. ***Participation and involvement.*** Once again, personal involvement through participation tends to defuse both rational and irrational fears about a workplace change. By participating in both the design of a change and its implementation, one acquires a personal stake in its success.

3. ***Facilitation and support.*** When fear and anxiety are responsible for resistance to doing things in a new and different way, support from management in the form of special training, job stress counseling, and compensatory time off can be helpful. According to the CEO of Medtronic, this is how the heart pacemaker company facilitates employees' acceptance of a constant stream of product innovations:

> *We set up venture teams of people who aren't emotionally invested in the old product. Once the new one has enough strength to stand on its own, we reintegrate the doubters. That's key. If you just tell them that "here's the new product," it demoralizes people. You have to go from the venture team to integrating it into the mainstream business.*[27]

4. ***Negotiation and agreement.*** Sometimes management can neutralize potential or actual resistance by exchanging something of value for cooperation. An hourly clerical employee may, for instance, be put on a salary in return for learning how to operate a new Internet workstation.

5. ***Manipulation and co-optation.*** Manipulation occurs when managers selectively withhold or dispense information and consciously arrange events to increase the chance that a change will be successful. Co-optation normally involves token participation. Those who are co-opted with token participation cannot claim they have not been consulted, yet the ultimate impact of their input is negligible.

6. ***Explicit and implicit coercion.*** Managers who cannot or will not invest the time required for the other strategies can try to force employees to go along with a change by threatening them with termination, loss of pay raises or promotions, transfer, and the like.

As shown in Table 15.2, each of these strategies for overcoming resistance to change has advantages and drawbacks. Appropriateness to the situation is the key to success.

Now we turn our attention to implementing changes in organizations.

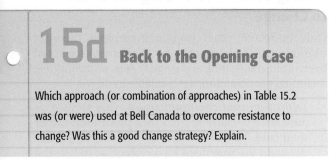

15d Back to the Opening Case

Which approach (or combination of approaches) in Table 15.2 was (or were) used at Bell Canada to overcome resistance to change? Was this a good change strategy? Explain.

TABLE 15.2   Dealing with Resistance to Change

APPROACH	COMMONLY USED IN SITUATIONS	ADVANTAGES	DRAWBACKS
1. Education + communication	Where there is a lack of information or inaccurate information and analysis	Once persuaded, people will often help with the implementation of the change	Can be very time-consuming if lots of people are involved
2. Participation + involvement	Where the initiators do not have all the information they need to design the change, and where others have considerable power to resist	People who participate will be committed to implementing change, and any relevant information they have will be integrated into the change plan	Can be very time-consuming if participators design an inappropriate change
3. Facilitation + support	Where people are resisting because of adjustment problems	No other approach works as well with adjustment problems	Can be time-consuming, expensive, and still fail
4. Negotiation + agreement	Where someone or some group will clearly lose out in a change, and where that group has considerable power to resist	Sometimes it is a relatively easy way to avoid major resistance	Can be too expensive in many cases if it alerts others to negotiate for compliance
5. Manipulation + co-optation	Where other tactics will not work or are too expensive	It can be a relatively quick and inexpensive solution to resistance problems	Can lead to future problems if people feel manipulated
6. Explicit + implicit coercion	Where speed is essential, and the change initiators possess considerable power	It is speedy and can overcome any kind of resistance	Can be risky if it leaves people mad at the initiators

Source: From "Choosing Strategies for Change," by John P. Kotter and Leonard A. Schlesinger, Harvard Business Review *(March–April 1979, p. 111). Reprinted by permission of HBS Publishing.*

MAKING CHANGE HAPPEN

In these fast-paced times, managers need to be active agents of change rather than passive observers or, worse, victims of circumstances beyond their control. This active role requires foresight, responsiveness, flexibility, and adaptability.[28] In this section, we focus on two approaches to making change happen: (1) organization development, a formal top-down approach, and (2) grassroots change, an unofficial and informal bottom-up approach.

Planned Change Through Organization Development (OD)

Organization development has become a convenient label for a host of techniques and processes aimed at making sick organizations healthy and healthy organizations healthier.[29] According to experts in the field,

> *Organization development (OD) consists of planned efforts to help persons work and live together more effectively, over time, in their organizations. These goals are achieved by applying behavioral science principles, methods, and theories adapted from the fields of psychology, sociology, education, and management.*[30]

organization development (OD): planned change programs intended to help people and organizations function more effectively

Others simply call OD *planned change*. Regarding the degree of change involved, OD consultant and writer Warner Burke contends that

> *Organization development is a process of fundamental change in an organization's culture. By*

Americans love their national parks. In fact, they're loving many of them to death. Yosemite National Park ranger Jesse McGahey (right) talks to a pair of rock climbers below Cathedral Peak about the damage being done and litter left behind by neophyte rock climbers who lack wilderness ethics. Education is a big part of making change happen. As they say in the wilds: "Pack it in, pack it out. Take nothing but pictures and leave nothing but footprints."

fundamental change, as opposed to fixing a problem or improving a procedure, I mean that some significant aspect of the organization's culture will never be the same.[31]

OD programs generally are facilitated by hired consultants,[32] although inside OD specialists can also be found.[33]

THE OBJECTIVES OF OD. OD programs vary because they are tailored to unique situations. What is appropriate for one organization may be totally out of place in another. In spite of this variation, certain objectives are common to most OD programs. In general, OD programs develop social processes such as trust, problem solving, communication, and cooperation to facilitate organizational change and enhance personal and organizational effectiveness. More specifically, the typical OD program tries to achieve the following seven objectives:

1. Deepen the sense of organizational purpose (or vision) and align individuals with that purpose.
2. Strengthen interpersonal trust, communication, cooperation, and support.
3. Encourage a problem-solving rather than a problem-avoiding approach to organizational problems.
4. Develop a satisfying work experience capable of building enthusiasm.
5. Supplement formal authority with authority based on personal knowledge and skill.
6. Increase personal responsibility for planning and implementing.
7. Encourage personal willingness to change.[34]

Critics of OD point out that there is nothing really new in this list of objectives. Directly or indirectly,

each of these objectives is addressed by one or another general management technique. OD advocates respond by saying general management lacks a systematic approach. They claim that the usual practice of teaching managers how to plan, solve problems, make decisions, organize, motivate, lead, and control contributes to a haphazard, bits-and-pieces management style. According to OD thinking, organization development gives managers a vehicle for systematically introducing change by applying a broad selection of management techniques as a unified and consistent package. This, they claim, leads to greater personal, group, and organizational effectiveness.

THE OD PROCESS. A simple metaphor helps introduce the three major components of OD.[35] Suppose someone hands you a coffee cup filled with clear, solid ice. You look down through the ice and see a penny lying tails up on the bottom of the cup. Now suppose that for some reason you want the penny to be frozen in place in a heads-up position. What can you do? There is really only one practical solution. You let the ice in the cup melt, reach in and flip the penny over, and then refreeze the cup of water. This is precisely how social psychologist Kurt Lewin recommended that change be handled in social systems. Specifically, Lewin told change agents to unfreeze, change, and then refreeze social systems.[36]

Unfreezing prepares the members of a social system for change and then helps neutralize initial resistance. Sudden, unexpected change, according to Lewin, is socially disruptive.[37] For example, Brooklyn Union Gas held a mock

unfreezing: neutralizing resistance by preparing people for change

15e Your Change, My Loss?

Effective change leadership requires attention to the linkages between loss and change.

Source: Joan Didion, as paraphrased in Joan V. Gallos, "Book Review: The Year of Magical Thinking," Academy of Management Learning and Education, 6 (June 2007): 286–292.

QUESTION:

How can the OD process be used to overcome the problem of perceived loss during a major organizational change?

funeral when it became KeySpan. Deregulation had forced the former monopoly to reinvent itself to compete in the marketplace, a wrenching change. Corporate ombudsman Kenny Moore, a former priest who came up with the funeral idea, explains what took place with about 70 key managers in the room:

In one corner, I put two tombstones from our Halloween display and a funeral urn. I wore my priestly stole and played a tape of Gregorian chants. "Dearly beloved," I said, "we are gathered here today to bid farewell to the Brooklyn Union Gas of old." Then I asked people to write what was over for the company on index cards and put them in the urn. People wrote things like "lifetime employment" and "monopoly." . . .

In the next corner was a steamer trunk for the things we needed to keep on our journey. We wrote things like "great people," and "dedication to the community" on cards and threw them in. Finally,

I had a stork from our Valentine's display to symbolize our birth as KeySpan. I made everyone draw what the future of the company might look like with crayons on poster paper. By then, everyone was participating.[38]

Once the change has been introduced, **refreezing** is necessary to follow up on problems, complaints, unanticipated side effects, and any lingering resistance. This seemingly simple approach to change spells the difference between systematic and haphazard change.

> **refreezing:** systematically following up a change program for lasting results

The OD model introduced here is based on Lewin's approach to handling change (see Figure 15.4). Diagnosis is carried out during the unfreezing phase. Change is then carefully introduced through tailor-made intervention. Finally, a systematic follow-up refreezes the situation. Each phase is critical to successful organizational change and development. Still, it takes continual recycling through this three-phase sequence to make OD an ongoing system of planned change.

Unofficial and Informal Grassroots Change

OD is rationally planned, formal, systematic, and initiated by top management. As a sign of the times, many of today's organizations cannot be described in those terms. They tend to be spontaneous, informal, experimental, and driven from within. (Interestingly, employees in some of these modern organizations were empowered by earlier OD programs.) Unusual things can happen when empowered employees start

FIGURE **15.4** A General Model of OD

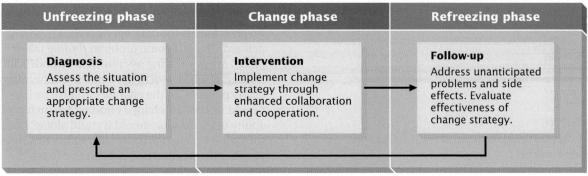

Unfreezing phase	Change phase	Refreezing phase
Diagnosis Assess the situation and prescribe an appropriate change strategy.	**Intervention** Implement change strategy through enhanced collaboration and cooperation.	**Follow-up** Address unanticipated problems and side effects. Evaluate effectiveness of change strategy.

to take the initiative. Consider the unconventional language in this description of change:

> *Change starts with finding a backer—someone who can sell your plan to the senior team. Change dies without a fighter—someone smart enough and skilled enough to win over the opposition. Change kicks in when people start to trust—in the plan and in one another. Trust is the glue that invariably holds a change effort together. Change just might work when people are focused—on the goal, and on each step that's necessary to achieve it.*
>
> *Getting the buy-in. Overcoming resistance. Building trust. Zeroing in on the objective. These are the critical skills that every change team must leverage if it is to have any hope of succeeding.[39]*

This is not top-down change in the tradition of OD. Rather, it involves change from inside the organization. Let us explore two perspectives on unofficial and informal grassroots change: tempered radicals and the 5P model.

TEMPERED RADICALS. This intriguing term and the concept it embraces come from Stanford professor Debra E. Meyerson. She defines **tempered radicals** as

> *people who want to succeed in their organizations yet want to live by their values or identities, even if [these] are somehow at odds with the dominant culture of their organizations. Tempered radicals want to fit in and they want to retain what makes them different. They want to rock the boat, and they want to stay in it.[40]*

tempered radicals: people who quietly try to change the dominant organizational culture in line with their convictions

Meyerson's research has found many "square pegs in round holes" who identify powerfully with her concept of the tempered radical. They tend to work quietly yet relentlessly to advance their vision of a better organization. If progressive managers are to do a good job of managing diversity, then they need to handle their tempered radicals in win-win fashion (see Valuing Diversity). Too often those with different ideas are marginalized and/or trivialized. When this happens, the organization's intellectual and social capital suffer greatly.

Four practical guidelines for tempered radicals stem from Meyerson's research:

1. ***Think small for big results.*** Don't try to change the organization's culture all at once. Start small and build a string of steadily larger victories. Learn as you go. Encourage small, nonthreatening experiments. Trust and confidence in you and your ideas will grow with the victories.
2. ***Be authentic.*** Base your actions on your convictions and thoughtful preparation, not on rash emotionalism. Anger, aggression, and arrogance give people an easy excuse to dismiss you and your ideas.
3. ***Translate.*** Build managerial support by explaining the business case for your ideas.
4. ***Don't go it alone.*** Build a strong support network of family, friends, and coworkers to provide moral support and help advance your cause.[41]

THE 5P CHECKLIST FOR GRASSROOTS CHANGE AGENTS (TURNING IDEAS INTO ACTION). The 5P model consists of an easy-to-remember list for anyone interested in organizational change: *preparation, purpose, participation, progress,* and *persistence* (see Figure 15.5). The model is generic, which means that it applies to all levels in profit and nonprofit organizations of all sizes. Let us examine each item more closely.

- ***Preparation:*** Is the concept or problem clearly defined? Has adequate problem *finding* taken place? Are underlying assumptions sound? Will the end result be worth the collective time, effort, and expense? Can the change initiative be harnessed to another change effort with a high probability of success, or should it stand alone? Does the proposed change have a *champion* or a *driver* who has the passion and persistence to see the process through to completion?

15f Celebrating the Unexpected

Legendary management writer and consultant Peter F. Drucker:

If you start out by looking at change as threats, you will never innovate. Don't dismiss something simply because this is not what you had planned. The unexpected is often the best source of innovation.

Source: As quoted in James Daly, "Sage Advice," Business 2.0, 1 (August 22, 2000): 142.

QUESTION:

What does this perspective teach us about dealing with tempered radicals?

VALUING DIVERSITY
Tempered Radicals as Everyday Leaders

In the course of their daily actions and interactions, tempered radicals teach important lessons and inspire change. In so doing, they exercise a form of leadership within organizations that is less visible than traditional forms—but just as important.

The trick for organizations is to locate and nurture this subtle form of leadership. Consider how Barry Coswell, a conservative, yet open-minded lawyer who headed up the securities division of a large, distinguished financial services firm, identified, protected, and promoted a tempered radical within his organization. Dana, a left-of-center, first-year attorney, came to his office on her first day of work after having been fingerprinted—a standard practice in the securities industry. The procedure had made Dana nervous: What would happen when her new employer discovered that she had done jail time for participating in a 1960s-era civil rights protest? Dana quickly understood that her only hope of survival was to be honest about her background and principles. Despite the difference in their political proclivities, she decided to give Barry the benefit of the doubt. She marched into his office and confessed to having gone to jail for sitting in front of a bus.

"I appreciate your honesty," Barry laughed, "but unless you've broken a securities law, you're probably okay." In return for her small confidence, Barry shared stories of his own about growing up in a poor county and about his life in the military. The story swapping allowed them to put aside ideological disagreements and to develop a deep respect for each other. Barry sensed a budding leader in Dana. Here was a woman who operated on the strength of her convictions and was honest about it but was capable of discussing her beliefs without self-righteousness. She didn't pound tables. She was a good conversationalist. She listened attentively. And she was able to elicit surprising confessions from him.

Barry began to accord Dana a level of protection, and he encouraged her to speak her mind, take risks, and, most important, challenge his assumptions. In one instance, Dana spoke up to defend a female junior lawyer who was being evaluated harshly and, Dana believed, inequitably. Dana observed that different standards were being applied to male and female lawyers, but her colleagues dismissed her "liberal" concerns. Barry cast a glance at Dana, then said to the staff, "Let's look at this and see if we are being too quick to judge." After the meeting, Barry and Dana held a conversation about double standards and the pervasiveness of bias. In time, Barry initiated a policy to seek out minority legal counsel, both in-house and at outside legal firms. And Dana became a senior vice president.

In Barry's ability to recognize, mentor, and promote Dana there is a key lesson for executives who are anxious to foster leadership in their organizations. It suggests that leadership development may not rest with expensive external programs or even with the best intentions of the human resources department. Rather, it may rest with the open-minded recognition that those who appear to rock the boat may turn out to be the most effective of captains.

Source: From Debra E. Meyerson, "Radical Change the Quiet Way," Harvard Business Review, 79, October 2001: 98. Reprinted by permission of HBS Publishing.

- *Purpose:* Can the objective or goal of the change initiative be expressed in clear, measurable terms? Can it be described quickly to busy people? What are the specific progress milestones and critical deadlines?
- *Participation:* Have key people been involved in refining the change initiative to the extent of having personal "ownership" and willingness to fight for it? Have potential or actual opponents been offered a chance to participate? Have powerful people in the organization been recruited as advocates and defenders?
- *Progress:* Are performance milestones and intermediate deadlines being met? If not, why? Is support for the initiative weakening? Why? Have

unexpected roadblocks been encountered? How can they be removed or avoided?
- *Persistence:* Has a reasonable sense of urgency been communicated to all involved? (*Note:* Extreme impatience can fray relationships and be stressful.) Has the change team drifted away from the original objective as time has passed? Does everyone on the team have realistic expectations about how long the change process will take?

With situational adjustments for unique personalities and circumstances, the 5P approach can help ordinary employees create extraordinary change.[42] So sharpen your concept and take your best shot!

FIGURE **15.5**   The 5P Checklist for Change Agents

Key action steps	
✓ **P**reparation	Develop concept; test assumptions; weigh costs and benefits; identify champion or driver.
✓ **P**urpose	Specify measurable objectives, milestones, deadlines.
✓ **P**articipation	Refine concept while building broad and powerful support.
✓ **P**rogress	Keep things moving forward despite roadblocks.
✓ **P**ersistence	Foster realistic expectations and a sense of urgency while avoiding impatience.

MANAGING CONFLICT

Conflict is intimately related to change and interpersonal dealings. Harvard's Abraham Zaleznik offered this perspective:

> *Because people come together to satisfy a wide array of psychological needs, social relations in general are awash with conflict. In the course of their interactions, people must deal with differences as well as similarities, with aversions as well as affinities. Indeed, in social relations, Sigmund Freud's parallel of humans and porcupines is apt: like porcupines, people prick and injure one another if they get too close; they will feel cold if they get too far apart.*[43]

The term *conflict* has a strong negative connotation, evoking words such as *opposition, anger, aggression,* and *violence.*[44] But conflict does not have to be a negative experience. Based on research evidence that most organizational conflict occurs within a cooperative context, Dean Tjosvold offered this more positive definition: "**Conflict** involves incompatible behaviors; one person interfering, disrupting, or in some other way making another's actions less effective."[45] This definition sets the scene for an important distinction between *competitive* (or destructive) conflict and *cooperative* (or constructive) conflict. Cooperative conflict is based on the win-win negotiating attitude discussed later in this chapter. Also, recall our discussion, in Chapter 13, of cooperative conflict as a tool for avoiding groupthink.

conflict: incompatible behaviors that make another person less effective

Students who want to argue for a higher grade may not want to tackle this particular professor. He's Bruce Patton, who teaches conflict management seminars in Harvard Law School's Program on Negotiation. For better or for worse, he calls conflict "a growth industry." He advises managers to not waste their time minimizing conflict, but rather to harness it in creative and constructive ways. Now, about that grade . . .

Dealing with the Two Faces of Conflict

Tjosvold contrasts competitive and cooperative conflict as follows:

The assumption that conflict is based on opposing interests leads to viewing conflict as a struggle to see whose strength and interests will dominate and whose will be subordinated. We must fight to win, or at least not lose. The assumption that you have largely cooperative goals leads to viewing the conflict as a common problem to be solved for mutual benefit, which in turn makes it more likely that the conflict will be constructive and that people will improve their abilities to deal with conflict.[46]

Figure 15.6 graphically illustrates the difference between competitive and cooperative conflict. In the competitive mode, the parties pursue directly opposite goals. Each mistrusts the other's intentions and disbelieves what the other party says. Both parties actively avoid constructive dialogue and have a win-lose attitude. Unavoidably, the disagreement persists and they go their separate ways.[47] Does this self-defeating cycle sound familiar? Probably, because most of us at one time or another have suffered through a broken relationship or destructive conflict with someone else.

In sharp contrast, the *cooperative* conflict cycle in Figure 15.6 is a mutually reinforcing experience serving the best interests of both parties. Cooperative conflict is standard practice at Anheuser-Busch, brewer of Budweiser beer:

When the policy committee of that company considers a major move—getting into or out of a business, or making a big capital expenditure—it sometimes assigns teams to make the case for each side of the question. There may be two teams or even three. Each is knowledgeable about the subject; each has

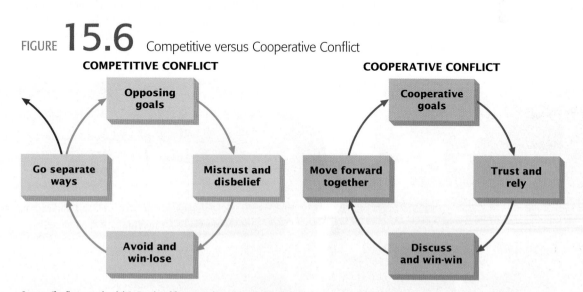

FIGURE **15.6** Competitive versus Cooperative Conflict

COMPETITIVE CONFLICT

- Opposing goals
- Mistrust and disbelief
- Avoid and win-lose
- Go separate ways

COOPERATIVE CONFLICT

- Cooperative goals
- Trust and rely
- Discuss and win-win
- Move forward together

Source: (for figure on the right): Reprinted from Learning to Manage Conflict: Getting People to Work Together Productively by Dean Tjosvold. Copyright © 1993 by Dean Tjosvold. First published by Lexington Books. All rights reserved. All correspondence should be sent to Lexington Books, 4720 Boston Way, Lanham, MD 20706.

access to the same information. Occasionally some-one in favor of the project is chosen to lead the dis-sent, and an opponent to argue for it. Pat Stokes, who heads the company's beer empire, describes the result: "We end up with decisions and alternatives we hadn't thought of previously," sometimes repre-senting a synthesis of the opposing views. "You be-come a lot more anticipatory, better able to see what might happen, because you have thought through the process."[48]

When *Business Week* recently recognized Intel as a Silicon valley legend, it pointed out the semiconduc-tor maker's use of cooperative conflict: "The process, dubbed 'disagree and commit,' encouraged engineers to constantly think of new ways of doing things faster, cheaper, and more reliably."[49] Cooperative conflict thus can give creativity and innovation a boost.

As a skill-building exercise, you might want to use the cooperative conflict model in Figure 15.6 to sal-vage a personal relationship mired in competitive conflict. Show the cooperative model to the other party and suggest starting over with a new set of ground rules. Cooperative goals are the necessary starting point. This process can be difficult, yet very rewarding (see the Action Learning Exercise at the end of this chapter). Win-win conflict is not just a good idea; it is one of the keys to a better world. (See the Manager's Toolkit section at the end of this chapter for tips on how to express anger.)[50]

There are two sets of tools available for manag-ing conflict.[51] The first we call conflict triggers, for stimulating conflict; the second involves conflict resolution techniques, used when conflict becomes destructive.

Conflict Triggers

A **conflict trigger** is a circumstance that increases the chances of intergroup or interpersonal conflict. As long as a conflict trigger appears to stimulate con-structive conflict, it can be allowed to continue. But as soon as the symptoms of destructive conflict[52] become apparent, steps need to be taken to re-move or correct the of-fending conflict trigger. Major conflict triggers include the following:

> **conflict trigger:** any factor that increases the chances of conflict

- *Ambiguous or overlapping jurisdictions.* Unclear job boundaries often create competition for re-sources and control. Reorganization can help to clarify job boundaries if destructive conflict be-comes a problem (refer to the organization design alternatives discussed in Chapter 9).
- *Competition for scarce resources.* As the term is used here, *resources* include funds, personnel, authority, power, and valuable information. In other words, anything of value in an organiza-tional setting can become a competitively sought-after scarce resource. Sometimes, as in the case of money and people, destructive competition for scarce resources can be avoided by enlarging the resource base (such as increasing competing managers' budgets or hiring additional personnel).[53]
- *Communication breakdowns.* Because commu-nication is a complex process beset by many barriers, these barriers often provoke conflict. It is easy to misunderstand another person or group

Is money the ultimate conflict trigger? Just ask German Interior Minister Wolfgang Schäuble, seen here giving a statement in Potsdam prior to wage negotiations with Germany's government employees' associa-tion. The demand was for an 8 percent pay hike. When you think about it, money has value precisely because it is a scarce resource. Let the conflict and negotiations begin.

of people if two-way communication is hampered in some way. The battle for clear communication never ends.

- ***Time pressure.*** Deadlines and other forms of time pressure can stimulate prompt performance or trigger destructive emotional reactions. When imposing deadlines, managers should consider individuals' ability to cope.
- ***Unreasonable standards, rules, policies, or procedures.*** These triggers generally lead to dysfunctional conflict between managers and the people they manage. The best remedy is for the manager to tune into employees' perceptions of fair play and correct extremely unpopular situations before they mushroom.
- ***Personality clashes.*** It is very difficult to change one's personality on the job. Therefore, the practical remedy for serious personality clashes is to separate the antagonistic parties by reassigning one or both to a new job.[54]
- ***Status differentials.*** As long as productive organizations continue to be arranged hierarchically, this trigger is unavoidable. But managers can minimize dysfunctional conflict by showing a genuine concern for the ideas, feelings, and values of lower-level employees.[55]
- ***Unrealized expectations.*** Dissatisfaction grows when expectations are not met. Conflict is another by-product of unrealized expectations. Destructive conflict can be avoided in this area by taking time to discover, through frank discussion, what people expect from their employment. Unrealistic expectations can be countered before they become a trigger for dysfunctional conflict.

15h Research Says . . .

Couples who routinely trade nasty or controlling remarks during marital spats might be harming their hearts—and not just emotionally, a study suggests.

The findings fit in with a body of research suggesting that hostile and domineering men and women are at risk of developing heart disease, the No. 1 killer in the USA.

Source: Kathleen Fackelmann, "Arguing Hurts the Heart in More Ways Than One," *USA Today* (March 6, 2006): 10D.

QUESTION:
What is the general life lesson here about handling conflict?

Managers who understand these conflict triggers will be in a much better position to manage conflict in a proactive and systematic fashion. Those who passively wait for things to explode before reacting will find conflict managing them. Worst case scenarios involve workplace bullying,[56] aggression, and violence (see Ethics: Character, Courage, and Values).

Resolving Conflict

Even the best managers sometimes find themselves in the middle of destructive conflict, whether it is due to inattention or to circumstances beyond their control. In such situations, they may choose to do nothing (some call this an *avoidance* strategy) or try one or more of the following conflict resolution techniques.[57]

PROBLEM SOLVING. When conflicting parties take the time to identify and correct the source of their conflict, they are engaging in problem solving. This approach is based on the assumption that causes must be rooted out and attacked if anything is really to change. Problem solving (refer to our discussion of creative problem solving in Chapter 8) encourages managers to focus their attention on causes, factual information, and promising alternatives rather than on personalities or scapegoats. The major shortcoming of the problem-solving approach is that it takes time, but the investment of extra time can pay off handsomely when the problem is corrected instead of ignored and allowed to worsen.

SUPERORDINATE GOALS. "Superordinate goals are highly valued, unattainable by any one group [or individual] alone, and commonly sought."[58] When a manager relies on superordinate goals to resolve destructive conflict, he or she brings the conflicting parties together and, in effect, says, "Look, we're all in this together. Let's forget our differences so we can get the job done." For example, a company president might remind the production and marketing department heads who have been arguing about product design that the competition is breathing down their necks. Although this technique often works in the short run, the underlying problem tends to crop up later to cause friction once again.

COMPROMISE. This technique generally appeals to those living in a democracy. Advocates of compromise say everyone wins because compromise is based on negotiation, on give-and-take.[59] However, as discussed in the next section, most people do not have good negotiating skills. They approach compromise situations with a win-lose attitude. Thus compromises tend to be disappointing, leaving one or both parties

ETHICS: CHARACTER, COURAGE, AND VALUES

The Issue of Weapons-Free Workplaces

In states that let employers ban guns in cars, if you choose to ban guns, how comprehensive should your policy be? And how far should you go to enforce the policy? . . .

Even when a gun is spotted, there's usually wiggle room, says Philip Deming, SPHR, president of Philip S. Deming and Associates, a security risk management consulting firm, and former member of the Society for Human Resource Management's Employee Health, Safety and Security Special Expertise Panel. "If you've got a 'no-guns' policy, it's Monday after Thanksgiving, and you see the rifle and ammo in Joe's car, you could say, 'Joe, you're fired.' Instead, most employers say, 'Joe you'll have to leave. Come back tomorrow.'"

Safety expert Paul Viollis, president of Risk Control Systems in New York, and a safety expert who often appears as an expert witness for employers in legal proceedings, says the standard of care employers must meet to fulfill their legal obligations to keep the workplace safe for employees is based on "reasonableness." The U.S. Occupational Safety and Health Administration and the courts expect employers to be able to respond affirmatively to three questions:

- Do you have a stand-alone workplace policy that addresses weapons and all aspects of workplace violence, including domestic violence?
- Do you professionally train your employees on workplace violence, including how to identify, defuse and report incidents?
- Do you meet best practices relating to physical security and monitoring how people gain access to workplaces?

Viollis says employers serious about keeping guns off premises must search cars. "I advise random searches for all of my clients unless [such searches] would violate state laws. Where any weapons are found, the owners should be fired immediately." The wording he recommends: "To mitigate the risk of potential violence and to ensure a weapons-free workplace, the company reserves the right to search vehicles on a random basis."

Viollis adds, "Security officers implement the policy by identifying vehicles randomly, notifying [each owner] that they'll be searching his or her car today. Some people do every third car." He concedes, however, that "very few" of his clients agree to conduct vehicle searches, suspecting that they may be an invasion of privacy.

Employment lawyers are divided on the merits of proactive searches of vehicles. Many believe it's too heavy-handed. "Reserve the right to search cars to the extent you have information," says W. Kirk Turner, a partner in Newton, O'Connor, Turner & Ketchum PC in Tulsa, Okla. "You shouldn't do it willy-nilly. In my opinion, when you engage in blanket or random searching, you've crossed the line from taking reasonable steps to becoming Big Brother."

On the other hand, employers already take other steps that employees may find intrusive. "Why would searching a car be different [from] checking handbags?" asks Richard Ross, a partner at Fredrickson & Byron PC in Minneapolis.

Source: Excerpted from Robert J. Grossman, "Enforcing Policies," HR Magazine, 52 (September 2007): 55. Copyright 2007 by Society for Human Resource Management (SHRM). Reproduced with permission of Society for Human Resource Management (SHRM) in the format Textbook via Copyright Clearance Center.

FOR DISCUSSION

How far should employers go in creating and enforcing weapons-free workplace policies? What should be considered a weapon?

---

feeling cheated. Conflict is only temporarily suppressed when people feel cheated. Successful compromise requires skillful negotiation.

FORCING. Sometimes, especially when time is important or a safety issue is involved, management must simply step into a conflict and order the conflicting parties to handle the situation in a particular manner. Reliance on formal authority and the power of a superior position is at the heart of forcing. Consider this example involving Burger King's former CEO Gregory D. Brenneman: "After hearing of nasty e-mails flying between feuding execs, he told perpetrators to cut it out or they would be fired."[60] As one might suspect, forcing does not resolve the conflict and, in fact, may serve to compound it by hurting feelings and/or fostering resentment and mistrust.

SMOOTHING. A manager who relies on smoothing says to the conflicting parties something like "Settle down. Don't rock the boat. Things will work out by themselves." This approach may tone down conflict in the short run, but it does not solve the underlying problem. Just like each of the other conflict resolution techniques, smoothing has its place. It can be useful when management is attempting to hold things together until a critical project is completed or when there is no time for problem solving or compromise and forcing is deemed inappropriate.

Problem solving and skillfully negotiated compromises are the only approaches that remove the actual sources of conflict. They are the only resolution techniques capable of improving things in the long run. The other approaches amount to short-run, stopgap measures. And managers who fall back on an avoidance strategy are simply running away from the problem. Nonetheless, as we have noted, problem solving and full negotiation sessions can take up valuable time—time that managers may not be willing or able to spend at the moment. When this is the case, management may choose to fall back on superordinate goals, forcing, or smoothing, whichever seems most suitable.[61]

NEGOTIATING

Negotiating is a fact of everyday life. Our negotiating skills are tested when we begin a new job, rent an apartment, live with a roommate, buy a house, buy or lease a car, ask for a raise or promotion, live with a spouse, divorce a spouse, or fight for custody of a child. Managers have even more opportunities to negotiate. Salespeople, employees, labor unions, other managers, and customers all have wishes that the organization may not be able to grant without some give-and-take. Sadly, most of us are rather poor negotiators. Negotiating skills, like any other crucial communication skill, need to be developed through diligent study and regular practice.[62] In fact, subjects in a study who had been trained in negotiating tactics negotiated more favorable outcomes than did those with no such training.[63]

Experts from Northwestern University define **negotiation** as "a decision-making process among interdependent parties who do not share identical preferences." They go on to say, "It is through negotiation that the parties decide what each will give and take in their relationship."[64] The scope of negotiations spans all levels of human interaction, from individuals to organizations to nations.

negotiation: decision-making process among interdependent parties with different preferences

" NEVER EVER PURR DURING THE NEGOTIATING PROCESS, DERWOOD ! "

Two common types of negotiation are *two-party* and *third-party negotiation*. This distinction is evident in common real estate transactions. If you sell your home directly to a buyer after settling on a mutually agreeable price, that is a two-party negotiation. It becomes a third-party negotiation when a real estate broker acts as a go-between for seller and buyer. Regardless of the type of negotiation, the same basic negotiating concepts apply. This final section examines three elements of effective negotiation and introduces a useful technique called *added value negotiating.*

Elements of Effective Negotiation

A good way to learn about proper negotiation is to start from zero. This means confronting and neutralizing one's biases and faulty assumptions. Sports and military metaphors, for example, are usually inappropriate. Why? Because effective negotiators are not bent on beating the opposition or wiping out the enemy.[65] They have a much broader agenda. For instance, effective negotiators not only satisfy their own needs, they also enhance the other party's readiness to negotiate again. Trust is important in this regard.[66] Using this "clean slate" approach to learning, let us explore three common elements of effective negotiation.

ADOPTING A WIN-WIN ATTITUDE. Culture, as discussed in Chapter 4, has a powerful influence on individual behavior. In America, for example, the prevailing culture places a high value on winning and

15i Negotiating a Pay Raise

... suggests [ExecuNet CEO] Dave Opton, "Pull together the data you need to position yourself, including what your peers else-where are making and what you've contributed to the company. Think of yourself as a brand you have to sell. Explain the fea-tures." Many managers, he says, make the mistake of waiting to bring up money during a formal evaluation. "It's never a good idea, because those discussions tend to focus on how you can improve. Start a discussion about pay a few months beforehand."

Source: Anne Fisher, "How to Ask for–and Get–a Raise Now," Fortune *(December 27, 2004): 47.*

QUESTIONS:
Do you dislike asking for a pay raise? Why? How well would this advice work for you? Explain.

shames losing. You can be number one or be a loser, with little or nothing in between. America's cultural preoccupation with winning, while sometimes an ad-mirable trait, can be a major barrier to effective nego-tiation.[67] A win-win attitude is preferable.

Stephen R. Covey, author of the best-selling books *The Seven Habits of Highly Effective People* and *The 8th Habit*, offered this instructive perspective:

Win/Win is a frame of mind and heart that con-stantly seeks mutual benefit in all human interac-tions. Win/Win means that agreements or solutions are mutually beneficial, mutually satisfying. With a Win/Win solution, all parties feel good about the decision and feel committed to the action plan. Win/Win sees life as a cooperative, not a competi-tive, arena. Most people tend to think in terms of di-chotomies: strong or weak, hardball or softball, win or lose. But that kind of thinking is basically flawed. It's based on power and position rather than on principle. Win/Win is based on the paradigm that there is plenty for everybody, that one person's suc-cess is not achieved at the expense or exclusion of the success of others.

Win/Win is a belief in the Third Alternative. It's not your way or my way; it's a better way, a higher way.[68]

Replacing a culturally based win-lose attitude with a win-win attitude is quite difficult; deeply in-grained habits are hard to change. But change they must if American managers are to be more effective

negotiators in today's global marketplace.[69] Tom's of Maine, famous for its toothpaste and other all-natural products, is a good role model. Founder and CEO Tom Chappell has built a values-driven company that pays its manufacturing employees in Maine 15 per-cent above the going rate and donates 10 percent of pretax profits to charity. He relies on a win-win atti-tude to grow his business:

... rather than compromising as it grows, Tom's has figured out how to convince mass-market retailers [such as Wal-Mart and Rite-Aid] that its values-centered business practices are good for the bottom line—a clever tactic that has helped the company expand its reach steadily over the course of three decades. ...

To create new opportunities, Chappell and COO [chief operating officer] Tom O'Brien approach po-tential distributors by going right to the top, meet-ing with the retailer's CEO or COO. To prepare for these sessions, they dig through annual reports and press releases to find statements that describe the retailer's values—goals that can be cited during the meetings to establish a foundation of shared beliefs. Tom's execs then describe their customers, making the pitch that these shoppers—who O'Brien says spend more and shop more frequently than the av-erage consumer—are looking for retailers who share their values.[70]

KNOWING YOUR BATNA. This odd-sounding label represents the anchor point of effective negotiations. It is an abbreviation for *best alternative to a negotiated agreement*. In other words, what will you settle for if negotiations do not produce your desired outcome(s)? Members of the Harvard Negotiation Project, which is responsible for the concept, call BATNA "the standard against which any proposed agreement should be measured. That is the only standard which can protect you both from accepting terms that are too unfavor-able and from rejecting terms it would be in your inter-est to accept."[71] In today's popular language, it adds up to "What is your bottom line?" For example, a business seller's BATNA becomes the measuring stick for ac-cepting or rejecting offers.

A realistic BATNA is good insurance against the three decision-making traps discussed in Chapter 8: framing error, escalation of commitment, and over-confidence. To negotiate without a BATNA is to stum-ble along aimlessly in the dark.

IDENTIFYING THE BARGAINING ZONE. Negotiation is useless if the parties involved have no common ground (see the top portion of Figure 15.7). At the

FIGURE **15.7** The Bargaining Zone for Negotiators

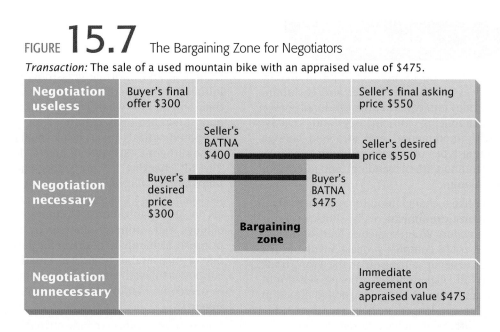

Transaction: The sale of a used mountain bike with an appraised value of $475.

Negotiation useless	Buyer's final offer $300			Seller's final asking price $550
Negotiation necessary	Buyer's desired price $300	Seller's BATNA $400 **Bargaining zone**	Buyer's BATNA $475	Seller's desired price $550
Negotiation unnecessary				Immediate agreement on appraised value $475

other extreme, negotiation is unnecessary if both parties are satisfied with the same outcome. Midway, negotiation is necessary when there is a degree of overlap in the ranges of acceptable outcomes. Hence, the **bargaining zone** can be defined as the gap between the two BATNAs—the area of overlapping interests where agreement is possible[72] (see the middle portion of Figure 15.7). Because negotiators keep their BATNAs secret, each party needs to *estimate* the other's BATNA when identifying the likely bargaining zone.

bargaining zone: the gap between two parties' BATNAs

Added Value Negotiating

Win-win negotiation[73] is a great idea that can be difficult to implement on a daily basis. Managers and others tend to stumble when they discover that a win-win attitude, though necessary, is not all they need to get through a tough round of negotiations. A step-by-step process is also essential. Karl and Steve Albrecht's added value negotiating process bridges the gap between win-win theory and practice. **Added value negotiating** (AVN) is a five-step process involving the development of *multiple deals* that add value to the negotiating process.[74] This approach is quite different from traditional

added value negotiating: five-step process involving development of multiple deals

"single-outcome" negotiating that involves "taking something" from the other party. AVN comprises the following five steps:

1. *Clarify interests.* Both subjective (judgmental) and objective (observable and measurable) interests are jointly identified and clarified by the two parties. The goal is to find some *common ground* as a basis for negotiation.
2. *Identify options.* What sorts of value—in terms of money, property, actions, rights, and risk reduction—can each party offer the other? This step creates a *marketplace of value* for the negotiators.
3. *Design alternative deal packages.* Rather than tying the success of the negotiation to a single win-win offer, create a number of alternatives from various combinations of value items. This vital step, which distinguishes AVN from other negotiation strategies, fosters *creative agreement.*
4. *Select a deal.* Each party tests the various deal packages for value, balance, and fit. Feasible deals are then discussed jointly, and a *mutually acceptable deal* is selected.
5. *Perfect the deal.* Unresolved details are hammered out by the negotiators. Agreements are put in writing. *Relationships* are strengthened for future negotiations. Added value negotiating, according to the Albrechts, "is based on openness, flexibility, and a mutual search for the successful exchange of value. It allows you to build strong relationships with people over time."[75]

SUMMARY

1. Managers need to do a much better job of managing the process of change. Nadler and Tushman's model identifies four types of organizational change by cross-referencing anticipatory and reactive change with incremental and strategic change. Four resulting types of change are tuning, adaptation, re-orientation (frame bending), and re-creation (frame breaking).

2. People who like a change tend to go through three stages: unrealistic optimism, reality shock, and constructive direction. When someone fears or dislikes a change, a more complex process involving five stages tends to occur: getting off on the wrong track, laughing it off, experiencing growing self-doubt, buying in, and moving in a constructive direction. Managers are challenged to help employees deal effectively with reality shock and self-doubt.

3. Inevitable resistance to change must be overcome if the organization is to succeed. Employees resist change for many different reasons, including (but not limited to) surprise, inertia, ignorance, lack of trust, fear of failure, passive-aggressive behavior, and competing commitments. Modern managers facing resistance to change can select from several strategies, including education and communication, participation and involvement, facilitation and support, negotiation and agreement, manipulation and co-optation, and explicit and implicit coercion.

4. Organization development (OD) is a systematic approach to planned organizational change. The principal objectives of OD are increased trust, better problem solving, more effective communication, improved cooperation, and greater willingness to change. The typical OD program is a three-phase process of unfreezing, change, and refreezing.

5. Unofficial and informal grassroots change can be initiated by tempered radicals, who quietly follow their convictions when trying to change the dominant organizational culture. Four guidelines for tempered radicals are (1) think small for big results, (2) be authentic, (3) translate, and (4) don't go it alone. The 5P checklist for grassroots change agents—*preparation, purpose, participation, progress,* and *persistence*—is a generic model for people at all levels in all organizations. Ordinary employees can achieve extraordinary changes by having a clear purpose, a champion or driver for the change initiative, a measurable objective, broad and powerful support achieved through participation, an ability to overcome roadblocks, and a persistent sense of urgency.

6. Competitive conflict is characterized by a destructive cycle of opposing goals, mistrust and disbelief, and avoidance of discussion, coupled with a win-lose attitude. In contrast, cooperative conflict involves a constructive cycle of cooperative goals, trust and reliance, and discussion, coupled with a win-win attitude.

7. Conflict triggers can cause either constructive or destructive conflict. Destructive conflict can be resolved through problem solving, superordinate goals, compromise, forcing, or smoothing.

8. Three basic elements of effective negotiations are a win-win attitude, a BATNA (best alternative to a negotiated agreement) to serve as a negotiating standard, and the calculation of a bargaining zone to identify overlapping interests. Added value negotiating (AVN) improves on standard negotiation strategies by fostering a creative range of possible solutions.

TERMS TO UNDERSTAND

- **Anticipatory changes,** p. 429
- **Reactive changes,** p. 429
- **Incremental changes,** p. 429
- **Strategic changes,** p. 429
- **Organization development (OD),** p. 437
- **Unfreezing,** p. 438
- **Refreezing,** p. 439
- **Tempered radicals,** p. 440
- **Conflict,** p. 442
- **Conflict trigger,** p. 444
- **Negotiation,** p. 447
- **Bargaining zone,** p. 449
- **Added value negotiating,** p. 449

MANAGER'S TOOLKIT

How to Express Anger

Although not every angry feeling should be expressed to the person held accountable, this approach is direct and has the most potential to initiate a productive conflict. There are several rules to keep in mind when expressing anger.

- **Check assumptions.** No matter how convinced employees are that someone has deliberately interfered and tried to harm them, they may be mistaken. People can ask questions and probe. It may be that the other person had no [ill] intention and was unaware that others were frustrated. The incident may just dissolve into a misunderstanding.
- **Be specific.** People find being the target of anger stressful and anxiety provoking. They fear insults and rejection. The more specific the angry person can be, the less threatening and less of an attack on self-esteem the anger is. Knowing what angered the other can give the target of the anger concrete ways to make amends.
- **Be consistent.** Verbal and nonverbal messages should both express anger. Smiling [while] verbally expressing anger confuses the issue.
- **Take responsibility for anger.** Persons expressing anger should let the target know that they are angry and . . . [why they] feel unjustly frustrated.
- **Avoid provoking anger.** Expressing anger through unfair, insinuating remarks ("I can't believe someone can be as stupid as you!") can make the target of the anger angry too. Such situations can quickly deteriorate.
- **Watch for impulsivity.** Anger agitates, and people say things they later regret.

- **Be wary of self-righteousness.** People can feel powerful, superior, and right; angry people can play "Now I got 'ya and you will pay." But anger should be used to get to the heart of the matter and solve problems, not for flouting moral superiority.
- **Be sensitive.** People typically underestimate the impact their anger has on others. Targets of anger often feel defensive, anxious, and worried. It is not usually necessary to repeat one's anger to get people's attention.
- **Make the expression cathartic.** Anger generates energy. Telling people releases that energy rather than submerges it. Anger is a feeling to get over, not to hang on to.
- **Express positive feelings.** Angry people depend upon and usually like people they are angry with. People expect help from people who have proved trustworthy, and are angry when it is not forthcoming.
- **Move to constructive conflict management.** Feeling affronted, personally attacked, and self-righteous should not side-track you from solving the underlying problems. Use the anger to create positive conflict.
- **Celebrate joint success.** Anger tests people's skills and their relationship. Be sure to celebrate the mutual achievement of expressing and responding to anger successfully.

Source: Dean Tjosvold, The Conflict-Positive Organization *(pp. 133–134). © 1991. Reprinted by permission of Pearson Education, Inc., Upper Saddle River, New Jersey.*

ACTION LEARNING EXERCISE

Putting Conflict on Ice[76]

Instructions: Working alone or as a member of a team, read the following material on the iceberg of conflict. As instructed in the reading, focus on a specific conflict and then answer the seven sets of questions. Alternatively, both parties in a conflict can complete this exercise and then compare notes to establish interconnections and move toward resolution.

The Iceberg of Conflict
One way of picturing the hidden layers and complexities of conflict is through the metaphor of the iceberg, as depicted in the following chart. You may want to identify additional layers besides the ones we cite, to reveal what is below the surface for you.

ICEBERG OF CONFLICT

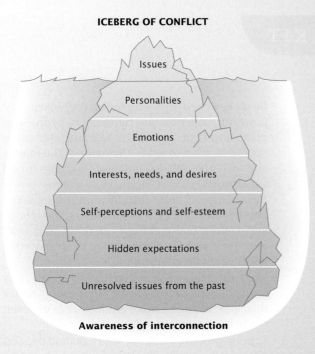

Awareness of interconnection

Exploring Your Iceberg

Each level of the iceberg represents something that does not appear on the surface, yet adds weight and immobility to our arguments when we are in conflict. Beneath the iceberg, the chart identifies an "awareness of interconnection," meaning that we all have the capacity, when we go deep enough and are not stuck on the surface of our conflicts, to experience genuine empathy and awareness of our interconnection with each other—including the person who is upsetting us.

To understand the deeper layers of your iceberg and get to an awareness of interconnection, consider a conflict in which you are now engaged. Try to identify the specific issues, problems, and feelings that exist for you at each level of the iceberg. As you probe deeper, notice whether your definition of the conflict changes, and how it evolves. Become aware of any emotions that emerge as you look deeper. Fear or resistance to these feelings can keep the conflict locked in place and block you from reaching deeper levels. Allow yourself to experience these feelings, whatever they are, and identify them to yourself or to someone you trust, so you can let them go. Try to answer the following questions for yourself and your opponent.

- *Issues:* What issues appear on the surface of your conflict?

- *Personalities:* Are differences between your personalities contributing to misunderstanding and tension? If so, what are they and how do they operate?

- *Emotions:* What emotions are having an impact on your reactions? How are they doing so? Are you communicating your emotions responsibly, or suppressing them?

- *Interests, needs, desires:* How are you proposing to solve the conflict? Why is that your proposal? What deeper concerns are driving the conflict? What do you really want? Why? What needs or desires, if satisfied, would enable you to feel good about the outcome? Why is that important? What does getting what you want have to do with the conflict?

- *Self-perceptions and self-esteem:* How do you feel about yourself and your behavior when you are engaged in the conflict? What do you see as your strengths and weaknesses?

- *Hidden expectations:* What are your primary expectations of your opponent? Of yourself? Have you clearly, openly, and honestly communicated your expectations to the other person? What would happen if you did? How might you release yourself from false expectations?

- *Unresolved issues from the past:* Does this conflict remind you of anything from your past relationships? Are there any unfinished issues remaining from the past that keep you locked in this conflict? Why?

For Consideration/Discussion

1. Did the issues and your perception of the conflict change as you worked through the iceberg? Explain.

2. Was there more (or less) to this conflict than you initially thought? Explain.

3. Which level of the iceberg was the most difficult to address? Why? Which was the easiest? Why?

4. What interconnections surfaced? How can they be used as a foundation for resolving the conflict?

5. How will this exercise affect the way you try to understand and resolve (or avoid) conflicts in the future?

Source: *From Kenneth Cloke and Joan Goldsmith,* Resolving Conflicts at Work: A Complete Guide for Everyone on the Job, *pp. 114–116. Copyright © 2000 by Jossey-Bass. Reprinted with permission of John Wiley & Sons, Inc.*

CLOSING CASE
Under the Knife

Emergency room physician John Halamka is on one of his evening shifts at Beth Israel Deaconess Medical Center in Boston. "Got a new admit for you, John," a nurse yells, as Halamka watches a heavyset middle-aged man heading toward him on a stretcher. The patient, Joe S., complains of labored breathing and occasional dizziness, but insists he's fine—his wife made him come in. "OK, let's get his chart," the doctor commands, and a young resident wheels over a cart bearing a laptop computer. Halamka logs in to the hospital's network and discovers that Joe had an EKG done at this hospital a year earlier.

The physician clicks open the old EKG, and a trace of Joe's heartbeat blooms on the screen. Halamka and other doctors peer closer, eyes darting from last year's scan to the squiggles scratched out by the electrocardiograph to which Joe is now hooked up. Halamka utters a new command: "Let's get him into the CCL. *Now.*" Despite Joe's protestations of health, he's having a heart attack. CCL is the cardiac catheterization lab, where physicians will race to save his life.

Joe is in deep trouble, but in one sense, he's a lucky man. He's at Beth Israel. Most hospitals don't have computer systems that let doctors instantly view a patient's past records, saving life-or-death seconds. According to trade publication *Health Affairs,* some 80 percent of hospitals and 95 percent of doctor's offices use the same methods for storing and accessing patient data that they did 50 years ago—which is to say, sheets of paper and film buried in huge metal cabinets. At those hospitals, a doctor who wants to see an EKG or other patient data must dispatch a request and wait anywhere from a few hours to an entire day for someone to retrieve it.

Even people who work for the federal government marvel at the inefficiency of such a system. "It's a brain-dead way to do things," says Carolyn Clancy, director of the government's Agency for Healthcare Research and Quality. Clancy calls the current state of affairs the "Marcus Welby system," after the '70s TV show about a doctor who writes everything on paper in a code no one else can understand.

In the real world, this situation carries a harrowing toll. Health-care costs are locked in a runaway spiral—up 20 percent since 2001, a time of near-zero inflation in the rest of the economy. While no one thinks technological backwardness is solely to blame, the dearth of IT [information technology] is clearly a major factor. Mind-numbing inefficiencies add hundreds of billions of dollars to employers' and employees' health-care bills, while medical errors, many of them preventable with even rudimentary IT, kill up to an estimated 98,000 people a year.

Any attempt to improve the pitiful state of health-care IT faces formidable obstacles. Money is perennially tight in an industry with puny profit margins and many high-profile basket cases, such as HealthSouth and Tenet Healthcare. As things stand, health-care IT investment runs at just 3.9 percent of revenue, which pales in comparison with that of other industries; telecom, for instance, spends an average of 7.9 percent. A deeply rooted technophobia among doctors and administrators further complicates any reform attempt. For example, in late 2002, Cedars Sinai Hospital in Los Angeles installed software it had spent years developing with Perot Systems, only to rip it out six months later when doctors refused to use it. And finally, hovering over everything is the politically explosive issue of patient privacy. One chief information officer actually received death threats for spearheading a plan to share medical records electronically among hospitals in Indianapolis.

Against that backdrop, Beth Israel stands out as something of a medical freak: a hospital that not only deploys the latest in high-tech medical machines but also manages information in a sophisticated way. Its online database, called CareWeb, contains records on 9 million patients. A computerized system automates orders for all prescriptions, lab tests, and IV drips.

Physician requests are checked against patient data to make sure there are no drug interactions or allergies, then are routed automatically to the pharmacy or lab. Illegible prescriptions, the bane of pharmacists everywhere, are a thing of the past. So are many medication-related errors, which have dropped 50 percent since the system was installed in 2001. "This system is designed to take out the guesswork," says Halamka, who should know—he designed it. In addition to being an emergency room physician, he's the CIO [chief information officer] at CareGroup, the company that owns Beth Israel and four other Boston-area hospitals.

A boyish 41-year-old, Halamka is part of a growing group of tech-savvy health-care insiders who are finally starting to change a stubborn industry. More and more hospitals are looking to places like Beth Israel as a model for how to provide better care and rein in costs. Indeed, Gartner Group predicts that the industry will be the fastest-growing sector of the economy for IT spending during the next four years.

But change won't come easily. There are no magic bullets for health care's condition. Indeed, as shown by any number of IT deployment disasters like Cedars Sinai's, hospital systems seem particularly resistant to costly, one-shot-cures-all tech fixes. Halamka's experience suggest a better, if no less arduous, course of treatment: dragging health care into the modern IT age, doctor by doctor, hospital by hospital. And even then, it can be touch and go.

Source: Excerpted from Melanie Warner, "Under the Knife," *Business 2.0*, 5 (January–February 2004): 84–89. © 2004 Time Inc. All rights reserved. For additional background information, see Carol Marie Cropper, "Between You, the Doctor, and the PC," *Business Week* (January 31, 2005): 90–91; and Timothy J. Mullaney and Arlene Weintraub, "The Digital Hospital," *Business Week* (March 28, 2005): 76–84.

FOR DISCUSSION

1 Why is Dr. Halamka uniquely qualified to be a change agent in the health care industry?

2 Why are doctors so resistant to change? Using Table 15.2 as a guide, indicate what you think needs to be done about it.

3 If you were Dr. Halamka, how would you "unfreeze" (in the language of OD) doctors and hospitals to prepare them for adopting modern information technology?

4 What lessons from the 5P checklist for change agents should guide Dr. Halamka's efforts? Explain.

5 Should Dr. Halamka polish his conflict management and negotiation skills? Explain.

TEST PREPPER

True/False Questions

_____ 1. Because the organization is significantly redirected, Nadler and Tushman call adaptation "frame bending."

_____ 2. Poor timing and lack of trust are among the reasons why employees resist change.

_____ 3. Managers can tell when resistance to change is caused by a passive-aggressive culture because everyone is unpleasant and disagreeable.

_____ 4. Organization development (OD) involves planned change.

_____ 5. Top-level managers are the only ones who should use the 5P checklist for change agents.

_____ 6. A practical guideline for tempered radicals is "think big for small results."

_____ 7. Mistrust and disbelief are involved in the cycle of competitive conflict.

_____ 8. The superordinate goals technique involves identifying the causes of problems.

_____ 9. Negotiation, by definition, is a decision-making process.

_____10. Added value negotiating (AVN) is useful because it forces the parties into single-outcome negotiating.

Multiple-Choice Questions

1. What type of change is planned and based on expected situations?
   A. Exponential   B. Incremental
   C. Anticipatory   D. Strategic
   E. Reactive

2. _____ is the low point of the response to change when employees are responding to changes they like.
   A. Self-doubt   B. Laughing it off
   C. Dissatisfaction D. Reality shock
   E. Attitude adjustment

3. _____ is typically an employee's first response when coping with a change that he or she dislikes or fears.
   A. Low self-esteem
   B. Unrealistic optimism
   C. Laughing it off
   D. Getting off on the wrong track
   E. Self-doubt

4. _____ is _not_ a strategy for overcoming resistance to change, as described in the text.
   A. Facilitation and support
   B. Manipulation and co-optation
   C. Participation and involvement
   D. Education and communication
   E. Divide and conquer

5. Which of the following is a good description of organization development (OD)?
   A. Frame bending   B. Employee renewal
   C. Expectation shaping D. Planned change
   E. Organizational modification

6. During what phase of OD does diagnosis occur?
   A. Preparation   B. Planning
   C. Research   D. Search
   E. Unfreezing

7. Relative to the 5P checklist for change agents, measurable objectives, milestones, and deadlines are specified in which P?
   A. Purpose   B. Persistence
   C. Participation D. Programming
   E. Preparation

8. Personality clashes, communication breakdowns, and time pressure are
   A. superordinate goals.
   B. OD trouble spots.
   C. OD failure factors.
   D. examples of constructive conflict.
   E. conflict triggers.

9. The attitude that effective negotiators need is _best_ described as
   A. compromising.   B. win-win.
   C. self-confident. D. single-minded.
   E. carefree.

10. According to the added value negotiating (AVN) model, the last step in the process should
    A. strengthen relationships for future negotiations.
    B. pinpoint the single best outcome.
    C. involve an exchange of BATNAs.
    D. involve selecting at least three possible alternatives.
    E. comfort the losing party.

See page T1 at the back of the text for answers to these questions. Want more questions? Visit the student Web site and take the ACE quizzes for more practice.

MANAGERS-IN-ACTION VIDEOS

4a

Alternative Work Arrangements at Hewlett-Packard

Three managers introduce us to the nature and benefits of flexible work scheduling and nontraditional work arrangements at HP. Sid Reel is vice president of diversity and work life. Kristy Ward is a marketing manager who formerly was in a job-sharing arrangement. Karen Lee is a real estate and workspace services delivery manager. By accommodating its employees' diverse and complex lives, HP hopes to reap motivational benefits. Among the alternative work arrangements illustrated are flextime, job sharing, telecommuting, and "free-address" offices. For more background, see **www.hp.com.**

Learning Objective

To demonstrate the rich array (and motivational impacts) of alternatives to the traditional 9-to-5 workday in a single location.

Links to Textual Material

Chapters 3 and 10: Valuing diversity; **Chapter 9:** Virtual organizations; **Chapter 12:** Motivation; Quality-of-work-life programs

Discussion Questions

1 What is the practical business linkage between the concepts of valuing diversity and alternative work arrangements?

2 What is the connection between virtual organizations and alternative work arrangements?

3 Briefly, what are the pros and cons of flextime, job sharing, and free-address offices?

4 What is the motivational case for alternative work arrangements?

5 Which alternative work arrangement appeals most to you? Why?

4b

Entrepreneurial Leadership

This inspiring 11-minute video introduces Jayson Goltz, president of Artist's Frame Service, based in Chicago, Illinois, and documents how an entrepreneur's leadership style must grow with the business. For more background, see **www.artistsframeservice.com.**

Learning Objective

To demonstrate how modern leaders must constantly learn and adapt to meet new challenges. To illustrate why successful inspirational leaders are not cookie-cutter imitations, but unique individuals who dare to be different.

Links to Textual Material

Chapter 1: Entrepreneurship; **Chapter 11:** Communication; **Chapter 12:** Motivating; **Chapter 14:** Influence tactics; Power; Leadership; **Chapter 15:** Managing change; **Chapter 16:** Product/service quality

Discussion Questions

1 How well does Jayson Goltz fit the entrepreneur trait profile in Table 1.3? Explain.

2 What influence tactics, as discussed in Chapter 14, are evident in this case?

3 In terms of House's updated path-goal leadership model in Chapter 14, which categories of leader behavior does Goltz seem to rely on the most?

4 Would you label Goltz a transactional or a transformational leader (see Table 14.4)? Explain.

5 Is Goltz a good leader? Explain. Would you like to work for him? Why or why not?

PART 5

Organizational Control Processes

CHAPTER 16   **Organizational Control and Quality Improvement**

16

Organizational

Control and

Quality

Improvement

OBJECTIVES

- **Identify** three types of control and the components common to all control systems.

- **Discuss** organizational control from a strategic perspective.

- **Identify** the four key elements of a crisis management program.

- **Identify** five types of product quality.

- **Explain** how providing a service differs from manufacturing a product, and **identify** the five service-quality dimensions.

- **Define** *total quality management (TQM)*, and **specify** the four basic TQM principles.

- **Describe** at least three of the seven TQM process improvement tools.

- **Explain** how Deming's PDCA cycle can improve the overall management process.

- **Specify** and **discuss** at least four of Deming's famous 14 points.

THE CHANGING WORKPLACE

"You Got Served" (T-Mobile's Sue Nokes)

"Marry me, Sue!" We've just pulled into the parking lot of Albuquerque's Jefferson Commons call center, home to 800 T-Mobile USA customer-service representatives, and outside there's mayhem. Hundreds of screaming, chanting people are standing in front of the building, bedecked in a wild array of hot-pink clothing (T-Mobile's signature color) ranging from T-shirts to cowboy hats to feather boas. They're waving signs, holding up camera phones, and generally acting like starstruck teenagers. One guy's wearing a fuchsia bathrobe; another, in a fluorescent-pink wig, is screaming, "We love you!" over and over.

All this booty shaking and flag waving might seem a bit extreme, given that technically today's event features a middle-aged woman on a routine visit from headquarters. But this isn't just any suit: It's Sue Nokes. She's the flashy, feisty spark plug of a woman who runs sales and customer service at T-Mobile USA, the fast-growing $17 billion subsidiary of Deutsche Telekom. In that capacity she's in charge of more than 15,000 employees around the U.S. Why the rousing welcome? Well, it has something to do with her outsized personality, an inspiring, wacky combination of Rosie O'Donnell, Evita Perón, and Auntie Mame. But mostly it's a result of her lifelong belief that making the customer happy is a lot easier to do when employees actually like their jobs and feel that what they do matters. "Sue's zeal for always putting the customer first is absolutely infectious," says René Obermann, CEO of Deutsche Telekom.

Serving a hot lunch to your employees, as Nokes usually does on her site visits—or repeating, like a mantra, "You are No. 1, and the customer is why"—could easily come across as meaningless corporate doublespeak. But not only does Nokes pull it off, she seems to have a blast doing it. "I'm just a kid from downstate Michigan who knows where I come from," she says. "I didn't start out wanting to be Sue Nokes, SVP [senior vice president] of anything. It just happened because I did what I loved."

Customers seem to love what she does too. À la Southwest Airlines or Nordstrom, T-Mobile's heavy service focus, led by CEO Robert Dotson, has become a key differentiating strategy, along with an emphasis on the "young and social" and smart branding. Though T-Mobile is ranked fourth, with 11% of the U.S. market, behind Verizon, AT&T, and Sprint Nextel, since the end of 2002 it has gained more than five share points, according to Mark Cardwell of Sanford C. Bernstein. Even more impressive, within two years of Nokes's arrival in 2002, the company catapulted to the top of J.D. Power's rankings of customer care in the wireless industry. It has now won the biannual title six times in a row. "It's pretty amazing, actually," says Kirk Parsons, senior director of wireless services at J.D. Power. "They have great customer care, they handle the folks they do have, and they're growing at a pretty good clip."

That's a huge turnaround from 2002, when T-Mobile ranked dead last according to internal surveys. (J.D. Power started its national wireless surveys in 2003.) Dotson, who had just been named CEO, reached out to Nokes, then at Wal-Mart.com, telling her that the company's customer organization needed a complete overhaul. Before committing to the job, Nokes visited a few call centers and was horrified by what she saw. Absenteeism averaged 12% daily; turnover was a staggering 100%-plus annually. The company used "neighborhood seating," a common technique at call centers in which employees don't have desks but instead drag their stuff from cubicle to cubicle. "I asked [managers], 'Are you losing any good people?' They said, 'Yeah,'" Nokes says. "I said, 'Anybody feeling bad about that?'" Karen Viola, general manager of the Menaul call center, also in Albuquerque, describes what happened next. "She walked up to the board and wrote Sue Nokes. Then she sat back down, put her feet up on the desk, and said, 'There's a new sheriff in town.'"

Although Nokes loves to talk, she actually spends much of her day listening. In a focus group in the Menaul center, dressed in a natty black jacket with white trim, tons of gold jewelry, and funky black-and-white-checked glasses to match, Nokes, 52, says what she says at virtually every such meeting (after, that is, making a bunch of wisecracks about her weight, age, and declining mental functions). "I have two questions: What's going well, and what's broken?"

One rep suggests a feature that lets customers turn off incoming text messages so that they don't have to be charged; another, Sergio Juardo, wonders why T-Mobile.com has no web page in Spanish. Nokes listens carefully, seemingly unfazed by the fact that Juardo's cheek is painted with the words I HEART SUE NOKES. In the focus groups and in the larger town hall meetings, Nokes is brutally honest, telling the group, for instance, that the company erred by not adding enough service reps to support T-Mobile's new pay-as-you-go service. Responding to a complaint that it's too time-consuming to log in to the system, she tells employees that a quick fix is impossible given the company's other technological priorities. "It's important that we build an environment where you can tell me my baby is ugly," Nokes says, her hard A's revealing her Midwestern roots. "And when you ask what's wrong, you'd better fix some stuff."

Sue Nokes's never-ending quest for top-quality service at T-Mobile teaches us an important management lesson. Strategies and plans, no matter how well conceived, are no guarantee of organizational success.[2] Those strategies and plans need to be updated and carried out by skilled and motivated employees amid changing circumstances and an occasional crisis. Adjustments and corrective action are inevitable. This final chapter helps present and future managers put this lesson to work by introducing fundamentals of organizational control, discussing crisis management, and exploring product and service quality.

FUNDAMENTALS OF ORGANIZATIONAL CONTROL

The word *control* suggests the operations of checking, testing, regulation, verification, or adjustment. As a management function, **control** is the process of taking the necessary preventive or corrective actions to ensure that the organization's

control: taking preventive or corrective actions to keep things on track

mission and objectives are accomplished as effectively and efficiently as possible. Objectives are yardsticks against which actual performance can be measured. If actual performance is consistent with the appropriate objective, things will proceed as planned. If not, changes must be made. Successful managers detect (and even anticipate) deviations from desirable standards and make appropriate adjustments.[3] Those adjustments can range from ordering more raw materials to overhauling a production line; from discarding an unnecessary procedure to hiring additional personnel; from containing an unexpected crisis to firing a defrauder. Although the possible adjustments exercised as part of the control function are countless, the purpose of the control function is always the same: *Get the job done despite environmental, organizational, and behavioral obstacles and uncertainties.* Here is how Michael Dell, founder of the computer powerhouse bearing his name, explains his company's secret to steady growth:

> We all make mistakes. It's not as though at any given time, Dell doesn't have some part of the business that's not working for us as it should. But we have a culture of continuous improvement. We train employees to constantly ask themselves: "How do we grow faster? How do we lower our cost structure? How do we improve service for customers?"[4]

Types of Control

Every open system processes inputs from the surrounding environment to produce a unique set of outputs. Natural open systems, such as the human body, are kept in life-sustaining balance through automatic feedback mechanisms. In contrast, artificial open

Passengers and crew on Cunard's new ocean liner Queen Victoria expect their food to be safe and tasty. As this truckload of fresh fish was being transferred aboard the ship in Puntarenas, Costa Rica, some high-tech and low-tech feedforward control occurred. A ship's officer (right) scanned the fish with an electronic toxic chemical sniffer and a chef sniffed the fish with his nose.

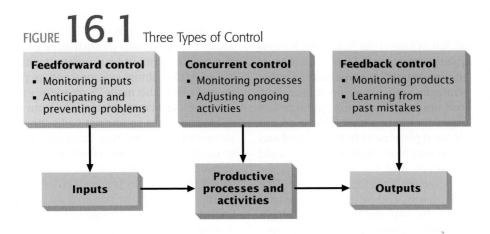

FIGURE **16.1** Three Types of Control

systems, such as organizations, do not have automatic controls. Instead, they require constant monitoring and adjustment to control for deviations from standards. Figure 16.1 illustrates the control function. Note the three different types of control: feedforward, concurrent, and feedback.

FEEDFORWARD CONTROL. According to two early proponents of feedforward control, "the only way [managers] can exercise control effectively is to see the problems coming in time to do something about them."[5] **Feedforward control** is the active anticipation of problems and their timely prevention, rather than after-the-fact reaction. Carpenters have their own instructive version of feedforward control: "Measure twice, cut once." It is important to note that planning and feedforward control are two related but different processes. Planning answers the question "Where are we going and how will we get there?" Feedforward control addresses the issue "What can we do ahead of time to help our plan succeed?" For many industries—including agriculture, insurance, and transportation—feedforward control involves keeping a close eye on the weather:

> *As typhoon Nanmadol spun across the South pacific . . . [in late 2004], few people monitored it as closely as FedEx's meteorologists in Memphis. The company runs its Asian flights out of a single-runway airport nestled on a narrow strip between a mountainside and the Philippines' Subic Bay. When a bad storm rolls through, it can shut the place down. On December 1, just 24 hours*

feedforward control: active anticipation and prevention of problems, rather than passive reaction

> *before the storm hit, managing director of global operations John Dunavant set his contingency plan in motion: Fourteen wide-body MD-11 airplanes and roughly 50 employees scrambled to Taipei [Taiwan], where FedEx could operate its hub without delays until the weather cleared. "Most of the time weather is forecasted," Dunavant says, calling weather the single greatest challenge in operating his 663 airplanes. "Since it is, we should always be able to proactively implement a solution."[6]*

Product design, preventive maintenance on machinery and equipment, and *due diligence* also qualify as feedforward control. On a personal level, think of due diligence as refusing to go on a blind date without first researching the person's background and reputation.

Of the three types of control, American managers tend to do the poorest job with feedforward control. Longer-term thinking and better cross-functional communication could help this situation.

CONCURRENT CONTROL. This second type of control might well be called real-time control because it deals with the present rather than with the future or past. **Concurrent control** involves monitoring and adjusting ongoing activities and processes to ensure compliance with standards.[7] When you adjust the water temperature while taking a shower, you are engaging in concurrent control. So, too, construction supervisors engage in concurrent control when they help electricians, carpenters, and plumbers with difficult tasks at the building site.

concurrent control: monitoring and adjusting ongoing activities and processes

FEEDBACK CONTROL. Feedback control is gathering information about a completed activity, evaluating that information, and taking steps to improve similar activities in the future. Feedback control permits managers to use information on past performance to bring future performance into line with planned objectives and acceptable standards. For example, consider the famous Aflac duck:

> **feedback control:** checking a completed activity and learning from mistakes

After spending nearly $200 million over the last four years on ads featuring a duck that quacks its name, Aflac has gained plenty of name recognition. Too bad name recognition isn't the same as product recognition: 60 percent of the people Aflac surveyed in a recent poll weren't sure what the company actually does (it sells insurance that pays the bills when an accident keeps you off the job). The fix? A new $50 million campaign that subtly lays blame at the feet of its mascot.[8]

Critics of feedback control say it is like closing the gate after the horse (or duck?) is gone. Because corrective action is taken after the fact, costs tend to pile up quickly, and problems and deviations persist.

On the positive side, feedback control tests the quality and validity of objectives and standards. Objectives found to be impossible to attain should be made more reasonable. Those that prove too easy need to be toughened.

In summary, successful managers exercise all three types of control in today's complex organizations and fast-changing circumstances.[9] Feedforward control helps managers avoid mistakes in the first place; concurrent control enables them to catch mistakes as they are being made; feedback control keeps them from repeating past mistakes. Interaction and a workable balance among the three types of control are desirable.

Components of Organizational Control Systems

The owner-manager of a small business such as a dry-cleaning establishment can keep things under control by personally overseeing operations and making necessary adjustments. An electrician can be called in to fix a broken pressing machine, poor workmanship can be improved through coaching, a customer's complaint can be handled immediately, or a shortage of change in the cash register can be remedied. A small organization directed by a single, highly motivated individual with expert knowledge of all aspects of the operation represents the ideal control situation. Unfortunately, the size and complexity of most productive organizations have made firsthand control by a single person obsolete. Consequently, multilevel, multidimensional organizational control systems have evolved.

A study of nine large companies in different industries sheds some light on the mechanics of complex organizational control systems.[10] After interviewing dozens of key managers, the researchers identified six distinct control subsystems (we have added a seventh).

1. ***Strategic plans.*** Qualitative analyses of the company's position within the industry
2. ***Long-range plans.*** Typically, five-year financial projections
3. ***Annual operating budgets.*** Annual estimates of profit, expenses, and financial indicators
4. ***Statistical reports.*** Quarterly, monthly, or weekly nonfinancial statistical summaries of key indicators such as orders received and personnel surpluses or shortages
5. ***Performance appraisals.*** Evaluation of employees through the use of management by objectives (MBO) or rating scales
6. ***Policies and procedures.*** Organizational and departmental standard operating procedures referred to on an as-needed basis

---

16a Quick Quiz

Microsoft acknowledged "an unacceptable number of repairs" [for its Xbox 360 video game consoles]. It said it had investigated the sources of hardware failures indicated by three red flashing lights. The software giant has made manufacturing and production changes to reduce the hardware failures, says Robbie Bach, president of the entertainment and devices division.

Source: Jon Swartz and Mike Snider, "Microsoft Extends Warranty on Xbox 360," USA Today *(July 6, 2007): 1B.*

QUESTION:

What sort of control—feedforward, concurrent, or feedback—occurred in this situation? Explain.

For further information about the interactive annotations in this chapter, visit our student Web site.

7. **The organization's culture.** As discussed in Chapter 9, stories, rituals, and company legends have a profound impact on how things are done in specific organizations.[11] Take Toyota, for example:

> *An old Toyota proverb goes something like this: To make a better product, get off your rear end and experience the marketplace. Charged with revamping the Sienna minivan for 2004, Toyota chief engineer Yuji Yokoya did just that. To improve on the previous Sienna—small and underpowered—Yokoya embarked on a 53,000–mile North American minivan road trip that included five cross-continent treks. . . . [When asked why, he simply said], "The road will tell us."*
>
> *. . . Yokoya had many epiphanies. In Santa Fe, N.M., narrow downtown streets convinced him that the new Sienna should have a tighter turning radius. On the gravel of the Alaskan Highway, he understood the need for all-wheel drive.*[12]

In more typical circumstances, employees who deviate from cultural norms are promptly straightened out with glances, remarks, or ridicule.

Complex organizational control systems such as these help keep things on the right track because they embrace three basic components that are common to all organizational control systems: objectives, standards, and an evaluation-reward system.[13]

OBJECTIVES. In Chapter 6, we defined an *objective* as a target signifying what should be accomplished and when. Objectives are an indispensable part of any control system because they provide measurable reference points for corrective action.[14] Yearly progress reports let managers know if they are on target or if corrective actions (such as creating a new advertising campaign) are necessary.

STANDARDS. Whereas objectives serve as measurable targets, standards serve as guideposts on the way to reaching those targets. Standards provide feedforward control by warning people when they are off track.[15] Golfers use par as a standard for gauging the quality of their game. When the objective is to shoot par, a golfer who exceeds par on a hole is warned that he or she must improve on later holes to achieve the objective. Universities exercise a degree of feedforward control over student performance by establishing and following admission standards for grades and test scores. Businesses rely on many different kinds of standards, including those in purchasing, engineering, time, safety, accounting, and quality.

A proven technique for establishing challenging standards is **benchmarking**—that is, identifying, studying, and imitating the *best practices* of market leaders.[16] The central idea in benchmarking is to be competitive by striving to be as good as or better than the *best* in the business (see Window on the World). The search for benchmarks is not necessarily restricted to one's own industry. Consider, for example, United Airlines' benchmarking efforts in Marina Del Rey, California:

benchmarking: identifying, studying, and building upon the best practices of organizational role models

> *In a bid to boost the quality of its overseas service, United Airlines is bringing some of its attendants to the best hotels, such as the Ritz-Carlton here, to learn the fine points of catering to the needs of the well-heeled.*

WINDOW ON THE WORLD

Benchmarking Helped Germany's Porsche Pull into the Fast Lane

[CEO Wendelin] Wiedeking's emphasis on churning out high-performance cars that are as durable as Japanese sedans is a key factor in Porsche's success. To revive the near-bankrupt company when he took over in 1993, Wiedeking dispatched his engineers to Japan to study Toyota Motor Corp.'s manufacturing processes, and it paid off with dramatic improvements in quality and cost. For the past two years the brand has ranked No. 1 in J.D. Power & Associates Inc.'s survey of initial quality (based on problems in the first three months of ownership). And this year [2007] the flagship 911 coupe had just 69 problems per 100 cars—the best in the industry.

Wiedeking, meanwhile, has maintained a Japanese-like grip on costs. A key strategy has been teaming up with other companies on research and development, helping Porsche boost innovation on the cheap.

Source: Gail Edmondson, "Pedal to the Metal at Porsche," Business Week (September 3, 2007): 68.

"They are very much recognized name-wise for a higher level of service," explains United trainer Christine Swanstrom. "The clientele we're trying to attract in international is the clientele that would stay at a Ritz."[17]

AN EVALUATION-REWARD SYSTEM. Because employees do not all achieve equal results, some sort of performance review is required to document individual and/or team contributions to organizational objectives. Extrinsic rewards need to be tied equitably to documented results[18] and improvement. A carefully conceived and clearly communicated evaluation-reward scheme can shape favorable effort-reward expectancies, thus motivating better performance. This is how CEO Paul R. Charron got Liz Claiborne Inc., the large apparel company, back on track:

> *. . . Charron changed the measure of performance and the trigger for bonuses to one common metric. The yardstick—direct operating profit—is reinforced through quarterly performance reviews and is now imprinted on the Claiborne culture.*[19]

When integrated systematically, objectives, standards, and an equitable evaluation-reward system constitute an invaluable control mechanism.

Strategic Control

Managers who fail to complement their strategic planning with strategic control, as recommended in Chapter 7, will find themselves winning some battles but losing the war.[20] The performance pyramid in Figure 16.2 illustrates the necessarily tight linkage between planning and control. It is a strategic model because everything is oriented toward the strategic peak of the pyramid. Objectives based on the corporate vision (or mission) are translated downward during planning. As plans become reality, control measures of activities and results are translated up the pyramid. The flow of objectives and measures requires a good information system.

Criteria related to external effectiveness and those related to internal efficiency are distinguished in Figure 16.2 by color coding. Significantly, all of the external effectiveness areas are focused on the marketplace in general and on the *customer* in particular. According to the performance pyramid, control measures are needed for cycle time, waste, flexibility, productivity, and financial results. *Cycle time* is the time it takes for a product to be transformed from raw materials or parts into a finished good. Note that *flexibility* is related to both effectiveness and efficiency. A garden tractor manufacturer, for example, needs to be externally flexible in adapting to changing customer

FIGURE **16.2** The Performance Pyramid for Strategic Control

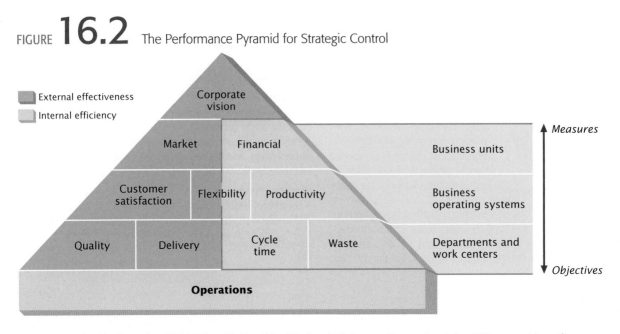

- External effectiveness
- Internal efficiency

Source: C. J. McNair, Richard L. Lynch, and Kelvin F. Cross, "Do Financial and Nonfinancial Performance Measures Have to Agree?" Management Accounting, published by the Institute of Management Accountants, Montvale, N.J., 72 (November 1990): 30. Copyright by Institute of Management Accountants. Reprinted by permission.

demands and internally flexible in training employees to handle new technology.

Identifying Control Problems

Control problems have a way of quietly snowballing to overwhelming proportions. Progressive managers can take constructive steps to keep today's complex operations under control.[21] Two very different approaches are executive reality checks and internal auditing.

EXECUTIVE REALITY CHECK. In the **executive reality check**, top-level managers periodically work "in the trenches" to increase their awareness of operations. Consider, for example, how this CEO stays in the thick of the action:

executive reality check: top managers periodically working at lower-level jobs to become more aware of operations

Many CEOs talk about spending time on the front lines. But few take it as seriously as Arkadi Kuhlmann. In early September [2007], the CEO of Internet bank ING Direct USA traded the quiet, spacious, warehouse-chic digs he shares with three other C-suite members for a noisy corner desk in the call center.

Kuhlmann's new "office"—an oval table at one end of a vast open room, complete with file cabinets, two halogen floor lamps, and a cubicle for his assistant—has energized the Wilmington (Del.) call center staff, say the floor's supervisors. And, of course, it keeps him close to customer issues. Overhearing one customer asking about CD rates reminds him he has to do more to discourage rate shoppers who probably won't turn out to be loyal.[22]

Executive reality checks not only alert top managers to control problems but also foster empathy for lower-level employees' problems and concerns.[23] In addition to firsthand reality checks, an internal audit can identify weak spots and problems in the organizational control system.

INTERNAL AUDITS. There are two general types of auditing, external and internal. External auditing, generally performed by certified public accountants (CPAs), is the verification of an organization's financial records and reports. In the United States, the protection of stockholders' interests is the primary rationale for objective external audits. Of course, the Internal Revenue Service (IRS) and the Securities and Exchange Commission (SEC) also have a stake in external auditors' watchdog function. Ideally, external auditors help keep organizations honest by double-checking to see whether reported financial results are derived through generally accepted accounting principles and are based on material fact, not fiction.[24] Thanks to the Enron/Arthur Andersen scandal (among

16b Back to the Opening Case

Does T-Mobile's Sue Nokes have the right management style for identifying control problems? Explain.

several others), external auditing has been put under the microscope, and needed financial reforms such as the Sarbanes-Oxley Act of 2002 are now in place. Managers who "cook the books" run a greater risk than ever of paying stiff fines and doing jail time.[25] One of Sarbanes-Oxley's most notable requirements forces chief executive officers and chief financial officers to personally sign and certify their company's periodic financial statements and reports.

> *The penalties for non-compliance are staggering. For example, a CEO or CFO who falsely represents company finances may be fined up to $1 million and/or imprisoned for up to 10 years. The penalty for willful violations is up to $5 million and/or 20 years imprisonment.*[26]

On the positive side, auditing is a hot job category these days.[27]

Internal auditing differs from external auditing in a number of ways. First, and most obviously, it is performed by an organization's staff rather than by outsiders. General Electric, for example, employs 500 internal auditors.[28] Second, internal auditing is intended to serve the interests of the organization as a whole. Also, as the following definition illustrates, internal auditing tends to be more encompassing than the external variety: "**Internal auditing** is the independent appraisal of the various operations and systems control within an organization to determine whether acceptable policies and procedures are followed, established standards are met, resources are used efficiently and economically, planned missions are accomplished effectively, and the organization's objectives are being achieved."[29]

> **internal auditing:** independent appraisal of organizational operations and systems to assess their effectiveness and efficiency

The product of internal auditing is called a *process audit* by some and a *management audit* by others. Internal audits certainly are necessary, as discovered in a survey of 203 auditors: 92 percent "identified various gaps in their companies' accounting controls."[30] To strengthen the objectivity of internal auditing, experts recommend that internal auditors report directly to the top person in the organization. In organization development terms, some "unfreezing" needs to be done to quiet the common complaint that internal auditing is a ploy used by top management for snooping and meddling.[31] Timely and valid internal audits are a primary safeguard against organizational decline, as well as against theft and fraud.

SYMPTOMS OF INADEQUATE CONTROL. When a comprehensive internal audit is not available, a general checklist of symptoms of inadequate control can be a useful diagnostic tool. Although every situation has some unusual problems, certain symptoms are common:

- An unexplained decline in revenues or profits
- A degradation of service (customer complaints)
- Employee dissatisfaction (complaints, grievances, excessive absenteeism, turnover)

Sure, Brad Pitt can act. But can he keep a big construction project under control? Each pink tent plots the location of an affordable eco-friendly home being built in the still devastated Lower 9th Ward in New Orleans. Brad reportedly does regular reality checks of progress and he should do some internal auditing to make sure donated money is spent wisely.

16c Is This a Good Way to Control Costly Absenteeism?

Problem: Every year, employee absenteeism costs U.S. businesses an estimated $74 billion in lost productivity.

Possible solution: *After he was out sick for two days, a Delphi laborer in Rochester, N.Y., named Stanley Straughter was asked to sign a waiver releasing his medical information to the company. Straughter, citing privacy concerns, refused and was fired, he claims. The Equal Employment Opportunity Commission, which says such requests for medical information for absent employees are standard at Delphi, has since filed suit against the automotive supplier on Straughter's behalf.*

Source: Data and excerpt from Michelle Conlin, "Shirking Working: The War on Hooky," Business Week (November 12, 2007): 72, 75.

QUESTIONS:
What are the pros and cons of this control technique? Is it ethical? Explain. What alternatives would you suggest for controlling absenteeism?

- Cash shortages caused by bloated inventories or delinquent accounts receivable
- Idle facilities or personnel
- Disorganized operations (workflow bottlenecks, excessive paperwork)
- Excessive costs
- Evidence of waste and inefficiency (scrap, rework)[32]

Problems in one or more of these areas may be a signal that things are getting out of control.

CRISIS MANAGEMENT

The September 11, 2001, terrorist attacks on America were a symbolic wake-up call for any managers who had a lax attitude toward organizational crisis management programs.[33] And companies that were already prepared stepped up their preparedness. FedEx, for example, now has "a dedicated security force that is more than 500 employees strong."[34] Beyond terrorism, managers need to be vigilant for a vast array of trouble spots, including everything from product tampering, to the death of a key executive, to data theft, to a factory explosion. An uncontained crisis can be fatal for the organization. Consider the following example.

> *It took 67 years to build Topps Meat into one of the country's largest suppliers of frozen beef patties; it took just six days to bring it down.*
>
> *Topps, which began grinding beef before the nation entered World War II and eventually had its products sold in stores across the country, announced . . . [in October 2007] that it was shutting down.*
>
> *Closure of the privately held, Elizabeth, N.J.-based company puts 87 employees out of work and comes after Topps was forced to issue the second-largest beef recall in U.S. history on Sept. 29 [2007].*
>
> *The culprit was 21.7 million pounds of frozen beef patties—an entire year of production—that may have been tainted with potentially fatal E. coli bacteria.*[35]

Even on a less dramatic scale, business-as-usual inevitably involves the occasional crisis that demands skillful crisis management and disaster recovery.[36]

Today, the diversity and scope of organizational crises stretch the imagination.[37] Experts on the subject define an *organizational crisis* this way:

> *An organizational crisis is a low-probability, high-impact event that threatens the viability of the organization and is characterized by ambiguity of cause, effect, and means of resolution, as well as by belief that decisions must be made swiftly.*[38]

Clearly, managers need to "manage the unthinkable" in a foresighted, systematic, and timely manner.[39] Enter the emerging discipline known as *crisis management*.

Crisis Management Defined

Traditionally, crisis management was viewed negatively, as "managerial firefighting"—waiting for things to go wrong and then scurrying to limit the damage. More recently, the term has taken on a more precise and proactive meaning. In fact, a body of theory and practice is evolving around the idea that managers should think about the unthinkable and expect the unexpected.[40] **Crisis management** is the systematic anticipation of and preparation for internal and external problems that could seriously threaten an organization's reputation, profitability, or survival.[41] Crisis management involves much

> **crisis management:** anticipating and preparing for events that could damage the organization

eologically speaking, Japan is a violent country. Devastating earthquakes and tsunamis are constant threats. These highly trained and well-equipped Tokyo firefighters are seen here participating in a drill conducted by the Fire and Disaster Management Agency. Thinking about and preparing for the unthinkable is what crisis management is all about.

more than an expedient public relations ploy or so-called spin control to make the organization look good amid bad circumstances. This new discipline is intertwined with strategic control.

Developing a Crisis Management Program

As illustrated in Figure 16.3, a crisis management program is made up of four elements. Disasters need to be anticipated, contingency plans need to be formulated, and crisis management teams need to be staffed and trained. Finally, the program needs to be perfected through realistic practice. Let us examine each of these elements.

CONDUCTING A CRISIS AUDIT.   A crisis audit is a systematic way of seeking out trouble spots and vulnerabilities. Disaster scenarios become the topic of discussion as managers ask a series of "What if?" questions.[42] Lists such as the one in Table 16.1 can be useful during this stage. Some crises, such as the untimely death of a key executive, are universal and hence readily identified. Others are industry-specific.

For example, crashes are an all-too-real disaster scenario for passenger airline companies.[43]

FORMULATING CONTINGENCY PLANS.   A **contingency plan** is a backup plan that can be put into effect when things go wrong.[44] Whenever possible, each contingency plan should specify early warning signals, actions to be taken, and expected consequences of those actions.

> **contingency plan:** a backup plan for emergencies

Attention to detail is a crucial component of most contingency plans. Dow has produced a 20-page program for communicating with the public during a disaster, right down to such particulars as who is going to run the copy machines. Many companies designate a single corporate spokesperson to field all inquiries from the press. A list may be drawn up of those executives to be notified in emergency situations, and the late-night phone numbers of local radio and television stations may be kept posted on office walls.[45]

FIGURE 16.3   Key Elements in a Crisis Management Program

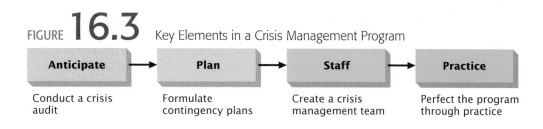

Anticipate	**Plan**	**Staff**	**Practice**
Conduct a crisis audit	Formulate contingency plans	Create a crisis management team	Perfect the program through practice

TABLE **16.1** **An Organizational Crisis Can Come in Many Different Forms**

- Extortion
- Hostile takeover
- Product tampering
- Vehicular fatality
- Copyright infringement
- Environmental spill
- Computer tampering
- Security breach
- Executive kidnapping
- Product/service boycott
- Work-related homicide
- Malicious rumor
- Natural disaster that disrupts a major product or service
- Natural disaster that destroys organizational information base

- Bribery
- Information sabotage
- Workplace bombing
- Terrorist attack
- Plant explosion
- Sexual harassment
- Escape of hazardous materials
- Personnel assault
- Assault of customers
- Product recall
- Counterfeiting
- Natural disaster that destroys corporate headquarters
- Natural disaster that eliminates key stakeholders

Both crisis audits and related contingency plans need to be updated at least annually and, if changing conditions dictate, more often.

CREATING A CRISIS MANAGEMENT TEAM. Organizational crisis management teams have been likened to the SWAT teams that police departments use for extraordinary situations such as hostage takings. Crisis management teams necessarily represent different specialties, depending on what kinds of crises are envisioned. For example, an electrical utility company might have a crisis management team made up of a media relations expert, an electrical engineer, a consumer affairs specialist, and a lawyer. As the case of Dow Chemical Canada illustrates, quick response and effective communication are the hallmarks of an effective crisis management team.

> *Dow Chemical Canada decided to improve its crisis plans after a railroad car carrying a Dow chemical derailed near Toronto in 1979, forcing the evacuation of 250,000 residents. Since then, Dow Canada has prepared information kits on the hazards of its products and [has] trained executives in interview techniques.*
>
> *. . . Another accident [years later] spilled toxic chemicals into a river that supplies water for several towns. Almost immediately, Dow Canada's emergency-response team arrived at the site and set up a press center to distribute information about the chemicals. They also recruited a neutral expert—the regional public health officer—to speak about the hazards and how to deal with them. The result: officials praised Dow's response.*[46]

Although an exact figure is not available, many companies have crisis management teams in place today.

PERFECTING THE PROGRAM THROUGH PRACTICE. Like athletic teams, crisis management teams can achieve the necessary teamwork, effectiveness, and speed of response only through diligent practice. Simulations, drills, and mock disasters provide this invaluable practice. Top-management support of such exercises is essential to provide good role models and underscore the importance of the activity. Reinforcing employee efforts in this area with an effective reward system can also encourage serious practice.

Experts say management's two biggest mistakes regarding organizational crises are (1) ignoring early warning signs and (2) denying the existence of a problem when disaster strikes. These mistakes cost Ford Motor Company "about $3 billion to replace 10.6 million Firestone tires. . . . More than 250 people were killed and hundreds more injured in accidents involving Bridgestone/Firestone tires."[47] A good crisis management program effectively eliminates these self-defeating mistakes. Nike, for example, is getting it right after some initial stumbles.

16d The Truth, and Nothing But the Truth

Howard Rubenstein, renowned public relations (PR) expert:

My first ground rule is always to tell the truth. A client will call and say, "This terrible thing happened to me. What should I say?" I say, "Wait a minute. First ask: What is the right thing to do? Then do it." Some of the people involved in the current corporate scandals thought they could talk their way out of a corner. They should have instead consulted their lawyer, talked to a PR person who would only deal in accurate statements, or [said] nothing at all.

Source: As quoted in Adam Haft, "How I Did It: Howard Rubenstein," Inc., 26 (March 2004): 88–90.

QUESTIONS:

Why do people in crisis situations consistently ignore this simple advice? How would you respond to a cynic who said, "Good PR people are just professional liars." How do you tend to respond to a crisis in your life?

When Nike was getting pummeled on the subject [of sweatshop conditions at its 900 or so independent foreign suppliers] in the 1990s, it typically had only two responses: anger and panic. Executives would issue denials, lash out at critics, and then rush someone to the offending supplier to put out the fire. But since 2002, Nike has built an elaborate program to deal with charges of labor exploitation. It allows random factory inspections by the Fair Labor Assn., a monitoring outfit that it founded with human rights groups and other big companies . . . that use overseas contractors. Nike also has an in-house staff of 97 which has inspected 600 factories in the past two years, grading them on labor standards. [Says a company official,]" You haven't heard about us recently because we have had our head down doing it the hard way. Now we have a system to deal with the labor issue, not a crisis mentality."[48]

THE QUALITY CHALLENGE

Not too many years ago, North American industry was roundly criticized for paying inadequate attention to the quality of goods and services. Today, many organizations have achieved a dramatic turnaround. There is even a national trophy for quality in the United States that means prestige and lots of free media exposure for winners: the Malcolm Baldrige National Quality Award. Named for a former U.S. secretary of commerce, it was launched by Congress in 1987 to encourage and reward world-class quality.[49] Some observers claim the drive for quality was a passing fad. Tom Peters, the well-known management writer and consultant, offered this instructive perspective in a question-and-answer session:

> *Q: Do you think the bloom is off the quality movement?*
> *A: I think it's in the genes. The quality movement has gone from hype to something people do. The average American manager, whether she or he is in accounting or purchasing or engineering, takes for granted that quality is a major thing you think about in life. You can't compete with shabby products.*[50]

Anyone tempted to dismiss quality as a once-hot topic past its prime should ponder the situation described in Ethics: Character, Courage, and Values. Quality is not always a life-or-death matter,[51] but it certainly is a major *quality-of-life* factor for each of us.

The balance of this chapter builds a foundation of understanding about quality. The following questions will be answered: How are product and service quality defined? What does total quality management (TQM) involve? What is Deming management?

Defining Quality

According to quality expert Philip Crosby, the basic definition of **quality** is "conformance to requirements."[52] But whose requirements? The sound quality of an MP3 player may seem flawless to its new owner, adequate to the engineer who helped design it, and terrible to an accomplished musician. In regard to *service* quality, being put on hold for 30 seconds when calling a computer company's hot line may be acceptable for one person but very irritating for another. Because quality is much more than a simple either/or proposition, both product and service quality need to be analyzed. To do this, we will explore five types of product quality, the unique challenges faced by service organizations, and the ways in which consumers judge service quality.

quality: conformance to requirements

ETHICS: CHARACTER, COURAGE, AND VALUES

Medical Device Maker Medtronic Gets Some Bad News

The Sprint Fidelis leads—wires implanted in patients' hearts and connected to defibrillators that shock abnormal heartbeats back to normal—have suffered a higher-than-expected rate of fractures, which can cause unwanted heart shocks or [administer] none if needed.

Medtronic, the leading maker of implantable cardiovascular defibrillators, or ICDs, asked doctors to stop implanting the Fidelis leads and return unused ones to Medtronic. It didn't call the action a "recall," but the Food and Drug Administration did.

Most Fidelis users, estimated at 235,000, won't need their leads replaced but should have their defibrillators reprogrammed so that they alert doctors to potential fractures, say Medtronic and the FDA.

At estimated failure rates, about 4,000 to 5,000 patients may need replacements. . . .

Medtronic said Fidelis lead fractures may have contributed to five patients' deaths. . . .

Medtronic . . . [is] not recommending patients have the leads automatically replaced because of the substantial risk associated with the surgery.

Source: Excerpted from Julie Schmit, "Medtronic Withdraws Leads for Heart Devices," USA Today (October 16, 2007): 3B.

FOR DISCUSSION

Did Medtronic mislead doctors and patients by not agreeing with the FDA that its actions constituted a product recall? What sort of feedforward control could have prevented this crisis? Explain.

Five Types of Product Quality

Other specialists in the field have refined Crosby's general perspective by identifying at least five different types of product quality: transcendent, product-based, user-based, manufacturing-based, and value-based.[53] Each represents a unique and useful perspective on product quality.

TRANSCENDENT QUALITY. Inherent value or innate excellence is apparent to the individual. Observing people's varied reactions to pieces of art in a museum is a good way to appreciate the subjectiveness of this type of quality. Beauty, as they say, is in the eye of the beholder.[54]

PRODUCT-BASED QUALITY. The presence or absence of a given product attribute is the primary determinant of this type of quality. Soft tissues, rough sandpaper, flawless glass, sweet candy, and crunchy granola exemplify product-based quality in very different ways. This is where the quality of key ingredients comes to the fore:

"Cashmere" sweaters, for example, that cost significantly less than . . . [$100] may be only partly cashmere, the ultrafine wool from the undercoat of the cashmere goat. . . .

Raw cashmere costs about $90 a kilogram (2.2 pounds) and a woman's sweater takes about 12 ounces.

Consumer Reports magazine recently became suspicious when $50 "cashmere" sweaters were spotted in food markets. Its tests of the fabric showed the sweaters had been blended with cheaper treated wool that appeared to be cashmere—except under a microscope.[55]

USER-BASED QUALITY. Here, the quality of a product is determined by its ability to meet the user's expectations, preferences, and tastes. Does it get the job done? Is it reliable? Does it taste good? Customer satisfaction surveys conducted by *Consumer Reports* magazine[56] give smart shoppers valuable input about user-based quality.

MANUFACTURING-BASED QUALITY. How well does the product conform to its design specifications or blueprint? The closer the match between the intended product and the actual one, the higher the quality. Car doors designed to close easily, quietly, and snugly

It's been said, "If you have to ask the price of a Bentley automobile, you probably can't afford it." Here, at the Bentley Motors Factory in Crewe, England, workers do a final quality inspection inside a glaring light tunnel, where imperfections can't hide. The quest for "transcendant quality," along with a world-class blend of the other four types of quality, helps explain a Bentley's six-figure price tag.

exhibit high quality if they do so. This category corresponds to Crosby's "conformance to requirements" definition of quality.

VALUE-BASED QUALITY. When you hear someone say, "I got a lot for my money," the speaker is describing value-based quality. Cost-benefit relationships are very subjective because they derive from human perception and personal preferences. About value, *Fortune* magazine observed that "[t]he concept can be nebulous because each buyer assesses value individually. In the end, value is simply giving customers what they want at a price they consider fair."[57] Discount retailers such as Big Lots and Family Dollar successfully exploit this important type of product quality.

Unique Challenges for Service Providers

Services are a rapidly growing and increasingly important part of today's global economy. Convincing evidence of this can be found in the annual *Fortune* 500 list of the largest U.S. companies by sales revenue. Among the top ten in 2007 were Wal-Mart (retailing), Citigroup and Bank of America (banking), and American International Group (insurance). Wal-Mart, a pure service business, topped the list, which has long been dominated by petroleum refiners and automobile companies. Wal-Mart, with annual revenues exceeding $350 billion, has nearly 2 million employees.[58] (If Wal-Mart were a city, it would be the fifth largest in the United States.) Indeed, the vast majority of the U.S. labor force now works in the service sector.

Because services are customer-driven, pleasing the customer is more important than ever.[59] Experts say it costs five times more to win a new customer than it does to keep an existing one.[60] Still, U.S. companies lose an average of about 20 percent of their customers each year.[61] Service-quality strategists emphasize that it is no longer enough simply to satisfy the customer. The strategic service challenge today is to *anticipate* and *exceed* the customer's expectations. Many managers of service operations, following the lead of Leon Leonwood Bean, the legendary founder of L.L. Bean Inc., regard customer satisfaction as an ethical responsibility.

> *The first product Leon Bean ever sold was a disaster. It was 1912, and Bean, a 40-year-old hunter and fisherman, had concocted for his own use a hybrid hunting boot with a leather top and a rubber bottom. He liked his invention so much he started selling the boots through the mail to fellow sportsmen, promising refunds if customers weren't satisfied. They weren't—90 of his first 100 pairs fell apart and were returned.*
>
> *. . . he kept his word and refunded the full price, but then what? Did he stop promising refunds? No. Bean went in the other direction: He borrowed $400—a lot of money for a partner in a small town clothing store in Maine—and used it to perfect the boot. Then he perfected the guarantee. His credo: "No sale is really complete until the product is worn out, and the customer is satisfied."[62]*

Leon Leonwood Bean surely would be proud that in a 2004 study of telephone service representatives (nearly 100 years after he founded the company), L.L. Bean's reps rated tops in friendliness.[63]

To varying extents, virtually every organization is a service organization. Pure service organizations (such as day-care centers) and manufacturers that provide not only products but also delivery and installation services face similar challenges. Specifically, they need to understand and manage the following five distinctive service characteristics.[64]

1. *Customers participate directly in the production process.* Whereas people do not go to the factory to help build the cars and refrigerators that they eventually buy, they do need to be present when their hair is styled or a broken bone is set in a hospital emergency room.
2. *Services are consumed immediately and cannot be stored.* Hairstylists cannot store up a supply of haircuts in the same way that electronics manufacturer Intel can amass an inventory of computer chips.
3. *Services are provided where and when the customer desires.* McDonald's does more business by building thousands of restaurants in convenient locations around the world than it would if everyone had to travel to its Oakbrook, Illinois, headquarters to get a Big Mac and fries. Accommodating customers'

sometimes odd schedules is a fact of life for service providers. Insurance salespersons generally work evenings and weekends during their clients' leisure periods.

4. *Services tend to be labor-intensive.* Although skilled labor has been replaced by machines such as automatic bank tellers in some service jobs, most services are provided by people to customers face to face. Consequently, the morale and social skills of service employees are vitally important. In fact, customer service has been called a *performing art* requiring a good deal of "emotional labor."[65] It isn't easy to look happy and work hard for an angry customer when you're having a bad day, but good customer service demands it.
5. *Services are intangible.* Objectively measuring an intangible service is more difficult than measuring a tangible good, but nonetheless it is necessary. For example, consider how a Pennsylvania electrical parts maker measures key services: during one observation period, the company reportedly shipped 93 percent of its orders on time and averaged a delay of 3.5 seconds in answering phone calls from customers.[66]

Because customers are more intimately involved in the service-delivery process than in the manufacturing process, we need to go directly to the customer for service-quality criteria. As service-quality experts tell us,

> *Quality control of a service entails watching a process unfold and evaluating it against the consumer's judgment. The only completely valid standard of comparison is the customer's level of satisfaction.*

16f Just One Question

Consumer behavior researchers studied the correlation between survey responses for 4,000 consumers and their loyalty to companies and products, as demonstrated by their actual purchases or recommendations to others. The best predictor across all industries was "How likely is it that you would recommend [company X] to a friend or colleague?"

Source: Frederick F. Reichheld, "The One Number You Need to Grow," Harvard Business Review, 81 (December 2003): 50. For more, see Darren Dahl, "Would You Recommend Us? Perfect Your Service by Asking the Only Question That Matters," Inc., 28 (September 2006): 40, 42.

QUESTIONS:

As a customer, is the answer to this question a key indicator of your satisfaction? Explain why or why not. What other considerations affect whether you are a satisfied customer?

That's a perception—something appreciably more slippery to measure than the physical dimensions of a product.[67]

How, then, do consumers judge service quality?

Defining Service Quality

Researchers at Texas A&M University uncovered valuable insights about customer perceptions of service quality.[68] They surveyed hundreds of customers of various types of service organizations. The following five service-quality dimensions emerged: *reliability, assurance, tangibles, empathy,* and *responsiveness.* (You may find it helpful to remember these with the acronym RATER.)[69] Customers apparently judge the quality of each service transaction in terms of these five dimensions. (To better understand each dimension and to gauge your own service-quality satisfaction, take a moment now to complete the Action Learning Exercise at the end of this chapter.)

Which of the five RATER dimensions is most important to you? In the Texas A&M study, *reliability* was the most important dimension of service quality, regardless of the type of service involved. Anyone who has waited impatiently for an overdue airplane knows firsthand the central importance of service reliability.[70]

Specific ways to improve product and service quality are presented throughout the rest of this chapter.

AN INTRODUCTION TO TOTAL QUALITY MANAGEMENT (TQM)

Definitions of TQM are many and varied, which is not surprising for an area that has been subject to intense discussion and debate.[71] For our present purposes, **total quality management (TQM)** is defined as creating an organizational culture committed to the continuous improvement of skills, teamwork, processes, product and service quality, and customer satisfaction.[72]

> **total quality management (TQM):** creating an organizational culture committed to continuous improvement in every regard

Consultant Richard Schonberger's shorthand definition calls TQM "continuous, customer-centered, employee-driven improvement."[73]

Our definition of TQM is anchored to *organizational culture* because successful TQM is deeply embedded in virtually every aspect of organizational life. As discussed in detail in Chapter 9, an organization's culture encompasses all the assumptions its employees take for granted about how people should think and act. In other words, personal commitment to systematic continuous improvement needs to become an everyday matter of "that's just the way we do things here." For example, Dr. Frank P. Carrubba, chief technical officer at Philips, the huge Dutch electronics firm, believes it is never too early to get people thinking about quality.

> *"It is not good enough to invent something new,"* he says. *"An elegant result that is not strategic or reproducible in a reliable, high-quality way is not worth much to the customer. Quality has to begin in research. We have to invent in an environment that reflects the same quality we want to achieve throughout the company."*[74]

As might be expected with a topic that received so much attention in a relatively short period of time, some unrealistic expectations were created. Unrealistic expectations inevitably led to disappointment and the need for a new quick fix.[75] However, managers with realistic expectations about the deep and long-term commitment necessary for successful TQM can make it work. TQM can have a positive impact if managers understand and enact these four principles of TQM:

1. Do it right the first time.
2. Be customer-centered.
3. Make continuous improvement a way of life.
4. Build teamwork and empowerment.[76]

Let us examine each of these TQM principles.

1. Do It Right the First Time

As noted in Chapter 1, the trend in recent practice has been toward designing and building quality into the product. This approach is much less costly than fixing or throwing away substandard parts and finished products, or experiencing a product recall crisis. Toy company Mattel learned the first lesson of TQM the hard way in 2007 when it had to recall millions of lead-tainted products that can cause serious injury or even death in children. The expense of lost revenues, damaged reputation, and potential government fines, in the long run, will no doubt outweigh the cost of ensuring the safety of materials used by Mattel's Chinese manufacturers and their subcontractors.[77] Schonberger, who studied many Japanese and U.S. factories firsthand, contends that "errors, if any, should be caught and corrected at the source, i.e., where the work is performed."[78] Consider, for example, the work of a pastry chef. This is what Kimberly Davis Cuthbert, owner of Sweet Jazmines, a Berwyn, Pennsylvania, made-to-order bakery, says:

> *"If the recipe is cream the butter for three minutes, cream the butter and the cream cheese for another three minutes, add the sugar four times for 2 1/2 [minutes], then that's what you have to do. It's very scientific, and that's the only way I found out that I could do this and train other people to do it and have it come out the same way every time."*
>
> *For the pastry chef, there is no room for error, unlike the culinary chef who can usually salvage something.*
>
> *"If we overcook a flank steak, we can cut it into strips and make fajitas. Spinach can always be made into cream of spinach," says Sylvia Smith, a culinary chef and caterer in Metropolitan Washington. "But baking is an exact art. Once you mess up, you have to throw it out.*[79]

A great many jobs in today's economy are like baking. Generally, comprehensive training in TQM tools and statistical process control is essential if employees are to accept personal responsibility for quality improvement.

2. Be Customer-Centered

Everyone has one or more customers in a TQM organization. They may be internal or external customers.

Total quality management (TQM) can be a life-and-death matter, as in the case of aircraft engine construction and field maintenance. These employees work for N3 Engine Overhaul Services in Arnstadt, Germany. They specialize in overhauling Rolls-Royce engines that power European-made Airbus aircraft. The next time you land safely on an airplane, whisper a "thank you" to skilled people such as these.

Internal customers are other members of the organization who rely on *your* work to get *their* job done.[80] For example, a corporate lawyer employed by Marriott does not directly serve the hotel chain's customers by changing beds, serving meals, or carrying luggage. But that lawyer has an internal customer when a Marriott manager needs to be defended in court.

> **internal customers:** anyone in your organization who cannot do a good job unless you do a good job

Regarding external customers, TQM requires all employees who deal directly with outsiders to be customer-centered. Being **customer-centered** means (1) anticipating the customer's needs, (2) listening to the customer, (3) learning how to satisfy the customer, and (4) responding appropriately to the customer.[81] Listening to the customer is a major stumbling block for many companies. But at Coach, known for its trendy women's handbags, listening to the customer is practically a religion.

> **customer-centered:** satisfying the customer's needs by anticipating, listening, and responding

Today Coach annually interviews at least 10,000 customers individually (primarily by telephone) to keep tabs on how the brand is faring in their minds. During the company's transformation, clerks intercepted shoppers to ask about specific products, whether they preferred chrome or nickel, or if they thought the length of the strap was right.

Coach also tests its products carefully in a limited number of its 174 stores in North America six months before a product comes out. . . . "It's street-level information, multiple angles, not just surveys and focus groups," says [a marketing consultant].[82]

Appropriate responses to customers depend upon the specific nature of the business.[83] For example, Table 16.2 lists good and bad customer service

---

TABLE **16.2** Turning a Supermarket into a Customer-Centered Organization

EMPLOYEES	BEHAVIORS BEFORE THE CHANGE	BEHAVIORS AFTER THE CHANGE
Bag packers	Ignore customers Lack of packing standards	Greet customers Respond to customers Ask for customers' preference
Cashiers	Ignore customers Lack of eye contact	Greet customers Respond to customers Assist customers Speak clearly Call customers by name
Shelf stockers	Ignore customers Don't know store	Respond to customers Help customers with correct product location information Knowledgeable about product location
Department workers	Ignore customers Limited knowledge	Respond to customers Know products Know store
Department managers	Ignore customers Ignore workers	Respond to customers Reward employees for responding to customers
Store managers	Ignore customers Stay in booth	Respond to customers Reward employees for service Appraise employees on customer service

Source: Reprinted from Organizational Dynamics, *Summer 1992, Randall S. Schuler, "Strategic Human Resource Management: Linking the People with the Strategic Needs of the Business," exhibit 4. Copyright 1992, with permission from Elsevier Science.*

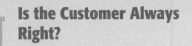

Is the Customer Always Right?

Jack Welch, retired CEO of General Electric:

We used to give speeches to our people: "No one can guarantee you a job other than satisfied customers." That's the only thing that works. Nothing creates work other than products and services you provide that create satisfied customers.

Source: As quoted in Stephen B. Shepard, "Life After GE? And How," Business Week (March 8, 2004): 77.

QUESTIONS:

Anyone who has worked serving the public knows that "customers" can be impatient, rude, dishonest, and shoplifters. So how can the customer *always* be right? Explain how this needs to be sorted out.

behaviors at a U.S. supermarket chain. Note that service-quality training led to very different patterns of behavior for the different jobs.

Vague requests to "be nice to the customer" are useless in TQM organizations. *Behavior*, not good intentions, is what really matters. As discussed in Chapter 14 in relation to behavior modification, desirable behavior needs to be strengthened with *positive reinforcement*. A good role model in this regard is Ohio Health:

> *Ohio's largest health-care provider rewards everything: customer service, community service, stars of the month, and perfect attendance.* [84]

3. Make Continuous Improvement a Way of Life

The Japanese word for "continuous improvement" is *kaizen*, which means improving the overall system by constantly improving the little details. TQM managers dedicated to *kaizen* are never totally happy with things. *Kaizen* practitioners view quality as an endless journey, not a final destination. They are always experimenting, measuring, adjusting, and improving. Rather than naïvely assuming that achieving zero defects necessarily means perfection has been attained, they search for potential and actual trouble spots. *Fortune* magazine

kaizen: a Japanese word meaning "continuous improvement"

recently explained how *kaizen* is a comprehensive concept at Toyota:

> *The soul of the Toyota production system is . . .* kaizen. *The word is often translated as "continuous improvement," but its essence is the notion that engineers, managers, and line workers collaborate continually to systematize production tasks and identify incremental changes to make work go more smoothly. Toyota strives to keep inventories as close to zero as possible, not only to minimize costs but also to ferret out inefficiencies the moment they occur. Toyota deliberately runs production lines at full tilt. And workers are given authority to stop the process and summon assistance at the first sign of trouble.* [85]

There are four general avenues for continuous improvement:

- Improved and more consistent product and service *quality*
- Faster *cycle times* (in cycles ranging from product development to order processing to payroll processing)
- Greater *flexibility* (for example, faster response to changing customer demands and new technology)
- Lower *costs* and less *waste* (for example, eliminating needless steps, scrap, rework, and non–value-adding activities) [86]

Significantly, these are not tradeoffs, as traditionally believed. In other words, TQM advocates reject the notion that a gain on one front must mean a loss on another. Greater quality, speed, and flexibility have to be achieved at lower cost and with less waste. This is an "all things are possible" approach to management. It requires diligent effort and creativity (see, for example, the Closing Case on Toyota at the end of this chapter).

4. Build Teamwork and Empowerment

Earlier, we referred to TQM as employee-driven. In other words, it empowers employees at all levels in order to tap their full creativity, motivation, and commitment. *Empowerment*, as defined in Chapter 14, occurs when employees are adequately trained, provided with all relevant information and the best possible tools, fully involved in key decisions, and fairly rewarded for results. [87] TQM advocates prefer to reorganize the typical hierarchy into teams of people from different specialties.

In earlier chapters you encountered many ways to promote teamwork and employee involvement:

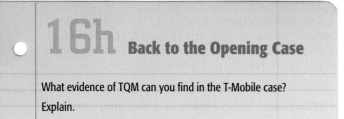

16h Back to the Opening Case

What evidence of TQM can you find in the T-Mobile case? Explain.

suggestion systems (Chapter 11), quality control circles and self-managed teams (Chapter 12), teamwork and cross-functional teams (Chapter 13), and participative leadership (Chapter 14). Each can be a valuable component of TQM.

The Seven Basic TQM Process Improvement Tools

Continuous improvement of productive processes in factories, offices, stores, hospitals, hotels, and banks requires lots of measurement. Skilled TQM managers have a large repertoire of graphical and statistical tools at their disposal. The beginner's set consists of the seven tools displayed in Figure 16.4. A brief overview of each will help promote awareness and establish a foundation for further study.

FLOW CHART. A **flow chart** is a graphical representation of a sequence of activities and decisions. Standard flow-charting symbols include boxes for events or activities, diamonds for key decisions, and ovals for start and stop points. Flow charts show, for instance, how a property damage claim moves through an insurance company. Armed with knowledge of who does what to the claim, and in which sequence, management can streamline the process by eliminating unnecessary steps or delays. Chapter 6 shows a sample flow chart as a planning and control tool. TQM teams have found flowcharting to be a valuable tool for increasing efficiency, reducing costs, and eliminating waste.

> **flow chart:** graphical display of a sequence of activities and decisions

CAUSE-AND-EFFECT ANALYSIS. The **fishbone diagram**, named for its rough resemblance to a fish skeleton, helps TQM teams visualize important cause-and-effect relationships. (Some refer to fishbone diagrams as Ishikawa diagrams, in tribute to the Japanese quality pioneer mentioned in Chapter 2.) For example, did a computer crash because of an operator error, an equipment failure, a power surge, or a software problem?

> **fishbone diagram:** a cause-and-effect diagram

FIGURE **16.4** Seven Basic TQM Tools

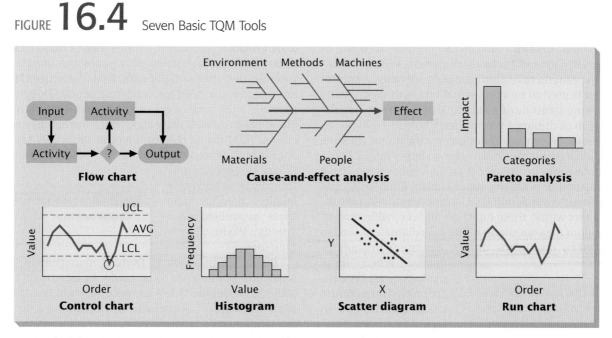

Source: Arthur R. Tenner and Irving J. DeToro, Total Quality Management: Three Steps to Continuous Improvement *(Figure 9.2, p. 113). © 1992 by Addison-Wesley Publishing Company, Inc. Reprinted by permission of Pearson Education, Inc. Publishing as Pearson Addison Wesley.*

A TQM team can systematically track down a likely cause by constructing a fishbone diagram. An illustrative fishbone diagram is presented in the Manager's Toolkit at the end of Chapter 8.

PARETO ANALYSIS.   This technique, popularized by quality expert Joseph M. Juran and discussed in Chapter 6, is named for the Italian economist Vilfredo Pareto (1848–1923). Pareto detected the so-called 80/20 pattern in many real-world situations: relatively few people or events (about 20 percent) account for most of the results or impacts (about 80 percent). It is thus most efficient to focus on the few things (or people) that make the biggest difference. The next time you are in class, for example, note how relatively few students offer the great majority of the comments in class. Likewise, a few students account for most of the absenteeism during the semester. In TQM, conducting a **Pareto analysis** involves constructing a bar chart by counting and tallying the number of times significant quality problems occur. The tallest bar on the chart, representing the most common problem, demands prompt attention. In a newspaper printing operation, for example, the most common cause of printing press stoppages for the week might turn out to be poor-quality paper. A quick glance at a Pareto chart would alert management of the need to demand better quality from the paper supplier.

Pareto analysis: bar chart indicating which problem needs the most attention

CONTROL CHART.   *Statistical process control* of repetitive operations helps employees keep key quality measurements within an acceptable range. A **control chart** is used to monitor actual versus desired quality measurements during repetitive operations. Consider the job of drilling a 2-centimeter hole in 1,000 pieces of metal. According to design specifications, the hole should have an inside diameter no larger than 2.1 centimeters and no smaller than 1.9 centimeters. These measurements are the upper control limit (UCL) and the lower control limit (LCL), respectively. Any hole diameters within these limits are of acceptable quality. Random measurements of the hole diameters need to be taken during the drilling operation to monitor quality. When these random measurements are plotted on a control chart, like the one in Figure 16.4, the operator has a handy visual aid that flags violations

control chart: visual aid showing acceptable and unacceptable variations from the norm for repetitive operations

of the control limits and signals the need for corrective action. Perhaps the drill needs to be cleaned, sharpened, or replaced. This sort of statistical process control is considerably less expensive than having to redrill or scrap 1,000 pieces of metal with wrong-sized holes.

HISTOGRAM.   A **histogram** is a bar chart showing whether repeated measurements of a given quality characteristic conform to a standard bell-shaped curve. Deviations from the standard signal the need for corrective action. The controversial practice of teachers "curving" grades when there is an abnormally high or low grade distribution can be implemented with a histogram.

histogram: bar chart indicating deviations from a standard bell-shaped curve

SCATTER DIAGRAM.   A **scatter diagram** is used to plot the correlation between two variables. The one illustrated in Figure 16.4 indicates a negative correlation. In other words, as the value of variable X increases, the value of variable Y tends to decrease. A design engineer for a sporting goods company would find this particular type of correlation while testing the relationship between various thicknesses of fishing rods and flexibility. The thicker the fishing rod, the lower the flexibility.

scatter diagram: diagram that plots the relationship between two variables

RUN CHART.   Also called a time series or trend chart, a **run chart** tracks the frequency or amount of a given variable over time. Significant deviations from the norm signal the need for corrective action. Hospitals monitor vital body signs such as temperature and blood pressure with daily logs, which are actually run charts. TQM teams can use them to spot "bad days." For example, automobiles made in U.S. factories on a Friday or Monday historically have had more quality defects than those assembled on a Tuesday, Wednesday, or Thursday.

run chart: a trend chart for tracking a variable over time

Before we move on to Deming management, an important point needs to be made. As experts on the subject remind us, "Tools are necessary but not sufficient for TQM."[88] Successful TQM requires a long-term, organizationwide drive for continuous improvement. The appropriate time frame is *years,* not days or months. Tools such as benchmarking and control charts are just one visible feature of that process. Invisible factors—such as values, learning, attitudes, motivation, and personal commitment—dictate the ultimate success of TQM.

DEMING MANAGEMENT

It is hard to overstate the worldwide impact of W. Edwards Deming's revolutionary ideas about management. His ideas have directly and indirectly created better and more productive work environments for countless millions of people. This section builds upon the historical sketch in Chapter 2 by examining basic principles of Deming management and Deming's famous 14 points.

Principles of Deming Management

Deming management is the application of W. Edwards Deming's ideas to revitalize productive systems by making them more responsive to the customer, more democratic, and more efficient. This approach qualifies as a revolution because, when first proposed by Deming in the 1950s, it directly challenged the legacy of Taylor's scientific management.[89] Scientific management led to rigid and autocratic organizations unresponsive to customers

> **Deming management:** application of W. Edwards Deming's ideas for more responsive, more democratic, and less wasteful organizations

and employees alike. Deming management proposed essentially the opposite approach. Some of the principles discussed below may not seem revolutionary today, precisely because Deming management has become ingrained in everyday *good* management.

QUALITY IMPROVEMENT DRIVES THE ENTIRE ECONOMY. Higher quality eventually means more jobs. Deming's simple yet convincing logic is presented in Figure 16.5. Quality improvement is a powerful engine driving out waste and inefficiency. Quality also generates higher productivity, greater market share, and new business and employment opportunities. In short, everybody wins when quality improves.[90]

THE CUSTOMER ALWAYS COMES FIRST. In his influential 1986 text *Out of the Crisis*, Deming wrote, "The consumer is the most important part of the production line. Quality should be aimed at the needs of the consumer, present and future."[91] Of course, these are just inspirational words until they are enacted faithfully by individuals on the job.

DON'T BLAME THE PERSON, FIX THE SYSTEM. Deming management chides U.S. managers for being preoccupied with finding someone to blame rather than with fixing problems. His research convinced him that "the system"—meaning management, work rules, technology, and the organization's structure and culture—typically is responsible for upwards of 85 percent of substandard quality. People can and will turn out superior quality, *if* the system is redesigned to permit them to do so. Deming management urges managers to treat employees as internal customers, listening

FIGURE **16.5** Everyone Benefits from Improved Quality

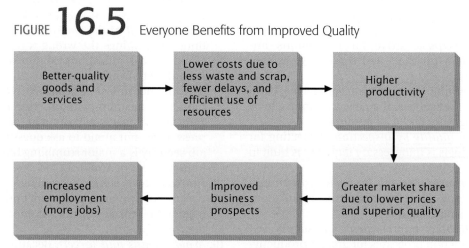

Source: Adapted from W. Edwards Deming, Out of the Crisis (Cambridge, Mass.: MIT Press, 1986), p. 3.

and responding to their ideas and suggestions for improvement. After all, who knows more about a particular job—the person who performs it for 2,000 hours a year or a manager who stops by now and again?

PLAN-DO-CHECK-ACT. Deming's approach calls for making informed decisions on the basis of hard data. His recommended tool for this process is what is popularly known as the **PDCA cycle** (plan-do-check-act cycle). Deming preferred the term *Shewhart cycle*,[92] in recognition of the father of statistical quality control, Walter A. Shewhart, who is mentioned in Chapter 2. (Japanese managers call it the Deming cycle.) Whatever the

> **PDCA cycle:** Deming's "plan-do-check-act" cycle that relies on observed data for continuous improvement of operations

label, the PDCA cycle reminds managers to focus on what is really important, use observed data, start small and build upon accumulated knowledge, and be research-oriented in observing changes and results (see Figure 16.6). The influence of Deming management was obvious at Intel when then-CEO Craig Barrett gave his employees a pep talk in a 2004 Webcast:

> *"There is nothing new in anything I'm saying," said Barrett, adding that the principles of quality— planning, doing, checking, and acting—were first elucidated some 70 years ago. "I expect everyone to adopt this system."*[93]

Deming's 14 Points

Deming formulated his 14 points to transform U.S. industry from what he considered to be its backward ways. Here is a summary of the 14 points that constitute the heart and soul of Deming management:[94]

1. *Constant purpose.* Strive for continuous improvement in products and services to remain competitive.
2. *New philosophy.* Western management needs to awaken to the realities of a new economic age by demanding wiser use of all resources.
3. *Give up on quality by inspection.* Inspecting for faulty products is unnecessary if quality is built in from the very beginning.
4. *Avoid the constant search for lowest-cost suppliers.* Build long-term, loyal, and trusting relationships with single suppliers.
5. *Seek continuous improvement.* Constantly improve production processes for greater productivity and lower costs.

FIGURE **16.6** Deming's PDCA Cycle

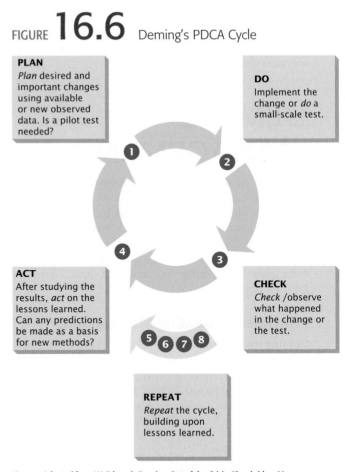

PLAN
Plan desired and important changes using available or new observed data. Is a pilot test needed?

DO
Implement the change or *do* a small-scale test.

ACT
After studying the results, *act* on the lessons learned. Can any predictions be made as a basis for new methods?

CHECK
Check /observe what happened in the change or the test.

REPEAT
Repeat the cycle, building upon lessons learned.

Source: Adapted from W. Edwards Deming, Out of the Crisis (Cambridge, Mass.: MIT Press, 1986), p. 88.

6. *Train everyone.* Make sure people have a clear idea of how to do their job. Informally learning a new job from coworkers entrenches bad work habits.
7. *Provide real leadership.* Leading is more than telling. It involves providing individualized help.
8. *Drive fear out of the workplace.* Employees continue to do things the wrong way when they are afraid to ask questions about why and how. According to Deming, "No one can put in his best performance unless he feels secure. *Se* comes from the Latin, meaning without, *cure* means fear or care. *Secure* means without fear, not afraid to express ideas, not afraid to ask questions."[95] Lack of job security is a major stumbling block for quality improvement in America.
9. *Promote teamwork.* Bureaucratic barriers between departments and functional specialists need to be broken down. Customer satisfaction is the common goal.
10. *Avoid slogans and targets.* Because the *system* is largely responsible for product quality, putting

pressure on individuals who feel they do not control the system breeds resentment. Posters with slogans such as "zero defects" and "take pride in quality" do nothing to help the individual measure and improve productive processes. Control charts and other process-control tools, in contrast, give employees direction and encouragement. Deming's approach tells managers that if they provide leadership and continually improve the system, the scoreboard will take care of itself.

11. ***Get rid of numerical quotas.*** When employees aggressively pursue numerical goals or quotas, they too often take their eyes off quality, continuous improvement, and costs. Hence, Deming

management strongly rejects the practice of management by objectives (MBO),[96] discussed in Chapter 6.

12. ***Remove barriers that stifle pride in workmanship.*** Poor management, inadequate instruction, faulty equipment, and pressure to achieve a numerical goal get in the way of continuous improvement.

13. ***Education and self-improvement are key.*** Greater knowledge means greater opportunity. Continuous improvement should be the number one career objective for everyone in the organization.

14. ***"The transformation is everyone's job."***[97] Virtually *everyone* in the organization plays a key role in implementing Deming management.

SUMMARY

1. Feedforward control is preventive in nature, whereas feedback control is based on the evaluation of past performance. Managers engage in concurrent control when they monitor and adjust ongoing operations to keep them performing up to standard. The three basic components of organizational control systems are objectives, standards, and an evaluation-reward system.

2. According to the performance pyramid, strategic control involves the downward translation of objectives and the upward translation of performance measures. Both external effectiveness and internal efficiency criteria need to be achieved.

3. The four elements of a crisis management program are (1) *anticipate* (conduct a crisis audit), (2) *plan* (formulate contingency plans), (3) *staff* (create a crisis management team), and (4) *practice* (perfect the program through practice).

4. Product quality involves much more than the basic idea of "conformance to requirements." Five types of product quality are transcendent, product-based, user-based, manufacturing-based, and value-based.

5. Service providers face a unique set of challenges that distinguish them from manufacturers. Because we live in a predominantly service economy, it is important to recognize these challenges: (1) direct customer participation, (2) immediate consumption of services, (3) provision of services at customers' convenience, (4) the tendency of services to be more labor-intensive than manufacturing, and (5) the intangibility of services, making them harder to measure. Consumer research uncovered five service-quality dimensions: reliability, assurance, tangibles,

empathy, and responsiveness (RATER). Consumers consistently rank *reliability* number one.

6. Total quality management (TQM) involves creating a culture dedicated to customer-centered, employee-driven continuous improvement. The four TQM principles are
   • Do it right the first time.
   • Be customer-centered.
   • Make continuous improvement a way of life.
   • Build teamwork and empowerment.

7. Seven basic TQM process improvement tools are flow charts, fishbone diagrams, Pareto analysis, control charts, histograms, scatter diagrams, and run charts.

8. Deming's plan-do-check-act (PDCA) cycle forces managers to make decisions and take actions on the basis of observed and carefully measured data. This procedure removes quality-threatening guesswork. The PDCA cycle also helps managers focus on what is really important. PDCA work never ends, because lessons learned from one cycle are incorporated into the next.

9. Deming formulated his famous 14 points in an effort to revolutionize Western management practices. In summary, they urge managers to seek continuous improvement through extensive training, leadership, teamwork, and self-improvement. The points call for *doing away with* mass quality inspections, selecting suppliers only on the basis of low cost, fear, slogans, numerical quotas, and barriers to pride in workmanship. This transformation, according to Deming, is *everyone's* job.

TERMS TO UNDERSTAND

- **Control,** p. 461
- **Feedforward control,** p. 462
- **Concurrent control,** p. 462
- **Feedback control,** p. 463
- **Benchmarking,** p. 464
- **Executive reality check,** p. 466
- **Internal auditing,** p. 467
- **Crisis management,** p. 468

- **Contingency plan,** p. 469
- **Quality,** p. 471
- **Total Quality Management (TQM),** p. 475
- **Internal customers,** p. 477
- **Customer-centered,** p. 477
- *Kaizen,* p. 478
- **Flow chart,** p. 479

- **Fishbone diagram,** p. 479
- **Pareto analysis,** p. 480
- **Control chart,** p. 480
- **Histogram,** p. 480
- **Scatter diagram,** p. 480
- **Run chart,** p. 480
- **Deming management,** p. 481
- **PDCA cycle,** p. 482

MANAGER'S TOOLKIT

How to Avoid a Public Relations Nightmare in a Crisis

1. **Prepare written organizational policies,** including:
   - an employee handbook
   - policies for screening potential employees (including volunteers)
   - anti-discrimination and -harassment policies
   - financial control systems
   - an ethics policy

2. **Be sure all employees** (including volunteers) understand the organization's policies.

3. **Create a written crisis plan,** clearly stating what will be done and who will do it in [the event] of a crisis. Make sure your plan includes:
   - names and contact numbers of people to contact in an emergency
   - a list of questions you're likely to be asked by the media and other stakeholders in a crisis
   - forms to record the details of what happens in a crisis
   - details on who will communicate what to whom
   - your goals for effective crisis communications— the outcomes you hope for and how you will measure success.

4. **Build trust and respect** with local media representatives.

5. **Appoint someone to communicate** with the media and someone to meet with victims' families in case of an emergency. Choose these people *before* a crisis occurs. They should know what's expected and be ready to swing into action at the first hint of a problem.

6. **Keep communication lines open** between your organization and its stakeholders at all times.

7. **Hold frequent brainstorming and role playing sessions.** Encourage all staff to participate, and be open to all their ideas.

8. **Accept the blame** when your organization makes an error. Let the public know what you're doing to be sure the problem isn't repeated.

9. **Always tell the truth.**

10. **Don't wait until a crisis occurs** before implementing these ideas. Begin today to prevent the preventable and prepare for the inevitable.

Source: *Lolita Hendrix, "Will You Be Ready When Disaster Strikes?"* Nonprofit World, *18 (May-June 2000): 37. Reprinted by permission.*

ACTION LEARNING EXERCISE

Measuring Service Quality

Think of the kind of treatment you have received in service establishments recently. Pick a specific restaurant, hair-styling salon, bank, airline, hospital, government agency, auto repair shop, department store, bookstore, or other service organization, and rate the kind of customer service you received, using the following five RATER factors. Circle one response for each factor and total them.

1. *Reliability:* ability to perform the desired service dependably, accurately, and consistently.

Very poor   1   2   3   4   5   6   7   8   9   10   Very good

2. *Assurance:* employees' knowledge, courtesy, and ability to convey trust and confidence.

Very poor   1   2   3   4   5   6   7   8   9   10   Very good

3. *Tangibles:* physical facilities, equipment, appearance of personnel.

Very poor   1   2   3   4   5   6   7   8   9   10   Very good

4. *Empathy:* provision of caring, individualized attention to customers.

Very poor   1   2   3   4   5   6   7   8   9   10   Very good

5. *Responsiveness:* willingness to provide prompt service and help customers.

Very poor   1   2   3   4   5   6   7   8   9   10   Very good

Total score = _____

Scoring Key

1. 5–10: Cruel and unusual punishment.
2. 11–20: You call this service?
3. 21–30: Average, but who wants average service?
4. 31–40: Close only counts in horseshoes.
5. 41–50: Service hall-of-fame candidate.

For Consideration/Discussion

1. If your service encounter was good (or bad), how many other people have you told about it? Why do people tend to pass along more stories about bad service than about good service?

2. Which of the five service-quality criteria was a major problem in the specific service situation you chose? What corrective actions should management take?

3. In the service situation you selected, which of the five criteria was most important to you? Why? Did you walk away satisfied? Why or why not?

4. If your present (or most recent) job involves rendering a service, how would you score yourself on the RATER factors? What needs to be done to improve your total score?

5. Does the most important RATER factor change for various types of service (for instance, a visit to the doctor versus flying on a commercial airliner)? Explain, with specific examples.

6. Generally speaking, which of the RATER factors is the weak link for today's service organizations? What remedies do you recommend?

CLOSING CASE
Continuous Improvement at Toyota

Deep inside Toyota's car factory in Georgetown, Kentucky, is the paint shop, where naked steel car bodies arrive to receive layers of coatings and colors before returning to the assembly line to have their interiors and engines installed. Every day, 2,000 Camrys, Avalons, and Solaras glide in to be painted one of a dozen colors by carefully programmed robots.

Georgetown's paint shop is vast and crowded, but in two places there are wide areas of open concrete floor, each the size of a basketball court. The story of how that floor space came to be cleared—tons of equipment dismantled and removed—is really the story of how Toyota has reshaped the U.S. car market.

It's the story of Toyota's genius: an insatiable competitiveness that would seem un-American were it not for all the Americans making it happen. Toyota's competitiveness is quiet, internal, self-critical. It is rooted in an institutional obsession with improvement that Toyota manages to instill in each one of its workers, a pervasive lack of complacency with whatever was accomplished yesterday.

The result is a startling contrast to the car business. At a time when the traditional Big Three are struggling, Toyota is thriving. Just this year [2006], Ford and GM have terminated 46,000 North American employees. Together, they have announced the closing of 26 North American factories over the next five years. Toyota has never closed a North American factory; it will open a new one in Texas this fall [2007] and another in Ontario [Canada] in 2008. Detroit isn't being bested by imports: 60% of the cars Toyota sells in North America are made here.

Toyota doesn't have corporate convulsions, and it never has. It restructures a little bit every work shift. That's what the open space in the Georgetown paint shop is all about.

Chad Buckner helped clear the space. Buckner, 35, has a soft Southern accent and an air of helpfulness. He is an engineering manager in the painting department, where he arrived straight out of the University of Kentucky 13 years ago. His whole career has been spent at Toyota.

As recently as 2004, a car body spent 10 hours in painting. Robots did much of the work, then as now, but they were supplied with paint through long hoses from storage tanks. "If we were painting a car red, before we could paint the next car white, we had to stop, flush the red paint out of the lines and the applicator tip, and reload the next color," Buckner says. Georgetown literally threw away 30% of the pricey car paint it bought, cleaning it out of equipment and supply hoses when switching colors.

Now, each painting robot, eight per car, selects a paint cylinder the size of a large water bottle. A whirling disk at the end of the robot arm flings out a mist of top-coat paint. When a car is painted—it takes just seconds—the paint cartridge is set back down, and a freshly filled cartridge is selected by each robot.

No hoses need to be flushed. There is no cleaning between cars. All the paint is in the cartridges, which are refilled automatically from reservoirs. Cars don't need to be batched by color—a system that saved paint but caused constant delays. Cars now spend 8 hours in paint, instead of 10. The paint shop at any moment holds 25% fewer cars than it used to. Wasted paint? Practically zero. What used to require 100 gallons now takes 70.

The benefits ripple out. Not only does Georgetown use less paint, it also buys less cleaning solvent and has dramatically reduced disposal costs for both. Together with new programming to make the robots paint more quickly, Buckner's group has increased the efficiency of its car-wash-sized paint booths from 33 cars an hour to 50.

"We're getting the same volume with two booths that we used to get with three," Buckner says. "So we shut down one of the booths." If you want to trim your energy bill, try unplugging

an oven big enough to bake 25 cars. Workers dismantled Top Coat Booth C, leaving the open floor space available for some future task.

So what do Buckner and his crew do with a triumphant operational improvement like that? By way of an answer, he walks to the second area of open space, where the sealer-application robots used to sit. They've been consolidated, too. Buckner points to another undercoating booth that the engineering staff is now working to eliminate.

Indeed, shutting down Top Coat Booth C liberated a handful of maintenance engineers—who turned their attention to accelerating the next round of changes. Success, in that way, becomes the platform for further improvement. By the end of this year, Buckner and his team hope to have cut almost in half the amount of floor space the paint shop needs—all while continuing to paint 2,000 cars a day.

For Buckner, the paint-shop improvements aren't "projects" or "initiatives." They are the work, his work, every day, every week. That's one of the subtle but distinctive characteristics of a Toyota factory. The supervisors and managers aren't "bosses" in any traditional American sense. Their job is to find ways to do the work better: more efficiently, more effectively.

"We're all incredibly proud of what we've accomplished," says Buckner, a little puzzled that his attitude might be considered unusual. "But you don't stop. You don't stop. There's no reason to be satisfied." . . .

What is so striking about Toyota's Georgetown factory is, in fact, that it only looks like a car factory. It's really a big brain—a kind of laboratory focused on a single mission: not how to make cars, but how to make cars better. The cars it does make—one every 27 seconds—are in a sense just a by-product of the larger mission. Better cars, sure; but really, better ways to make cars. It's not just the product, it's the process.

The process is, in fact, paramount—so important that "Toyota also has a process for teaching you how to improve the process," says Steven J. Spear, a senior lecturer at MIT who has studied Toyota for more than a decade. The work is really threefold: making cars, making cars better, and teaching everyone how to make cars better. At its Olympian best, Toyota adds one more level: It is always looking to improve the process by which it improves all the other processes.

There's a certain Zen sensibility to that—but also a relentlessly capitalistic, tenaciously competitive quality. If your factory is just making cars, once a day the whistle blows and it's quitting time, no more cars to make that day. If your factory is making a new way to make cars, the whistle never blows, you're never done.

Without fanfare, in fact, Toyota is confounding conventional wisdom about U.S. manufacturing. Toyota isn't outsourcing; it's creating jobs in the United States. It isn't having trouble manufacturing complicated products here—it's opening factories as quickly as its systems and quality standards allow. It's offering union wages and good health insurance (to avoid being unionized) and selling the products its American workers make to Americans, profitably and more inexpensively than its U.S. competitors.

So put aside everything you think you know about the current state of the car business in the United States. Sure, Toyota enjoys some structural advantages in the form of lower health care and pension costs. But the real reason it is thriving is because of people like Chad Buckner saying, "There's no reason to be satisfied." It's not just the way Toyota makes cars—it's the way Toyota thinks about making cars.

That thinking is hardly novel: Lean manufacturing and continuous improvement have been around for more than a quarter-century. But the incessant, almost mindless repetition of those phrases camouflages the real power behind the ideas. Continuous improvement is tectonic. By constantly questioning how you do things, by constantly tweaking, you don't outflank your competition next quarter. You outflank them next decade.

Toyota is far from infallible, of course. In the past two years, recalls for quality and safety problems have spiked dramatically—evidence of the strain that rapid growth puts on even the best systems. But those quality issues have seized the attention of Toyota's senior management. In the larger arena, when the strategy isn't to build cars but to build cars better, you create perpetual competitive advantage. By the time you best your competitors, they aren't just a bit behind you, in need of a reorganization and a sales surge to regain the lead. They are a decade behind. They just don't realize it. . . .

What happens every day at Georgetown, and throughout Toyota, is teachable and learnable. But it's not a set of goals, because goals mean there's a finish line, and there is no finish line. It's not something you can implement, because it's not a checklist of improvements. It's a way of looking at the world. You simply can't lose interest in it, shrug, and give up—any more than you can lose interest in your own future.

"People who join Toyota from other companies, it's a big shift for them," says John Shook, a faculty member at the University of Michigan, a former Toyota manufacturing employee, and a [highly] regarded consultant on how to use Toyota's ideas at other companies. "They kind of don't get it for a while." They do what all American managers do—they keep trying to make their management objectives. "They're moving forward, they're improving, and they're looking for a plateau. As long as you're looking for that plateau, it seems like a constant struggle. It's difficult. If you're looking for a plateau, you're going to be frustrated. There is no 'solution.'"

Even working at Toyota, you need that moment of Zen.

"Once you realize that it's the process itself—that you're not seeking a plateau—you can relax. Doing the task and doing the task better become one and the same thing," Shook says. "This is what it means to come to work."

Source: Excerpted from Charles Fishman, "No Satisfaction," *Fast Company*, no. 111 (December 2006/January 2007): 82–92. Copyright 2006 by Mansueto Ventures LLC. Reproduced with permission of Mansueto Ventures LLC in the format Textbook via Copyright Clearance Center.

FOR DISCUSSION

1 What roles (if any) do feedforward, concurrent, and feedback control play in Toyota's manufacturing strategy?

2 Which of the five types of product quality are evident in this case? Explain.

3 Which of the four principles of TQM are evident in this case? Explain.

4 Which of Deming's 14 points are evident in this case? Explain.

TEST PREPPER

True/False Questions

_____ 1. Objectives are yardsticks against which actual performance can be measured.

_____ 2. Two components of the performance pyramid for strategic control are flexibility and cycle times.

_____ 3. A high-probability, low-impact event with clear relationships among cause, effect, and resolution is an organizational crisis.

_____ 4. "Beauty is in the eye of the beholder" describes transcendent quality.

_____ 5. Services cannot be measured because they are intangible.

_____ 6. Calling TQM customer-centered and employee-driven is appropriate.

_____ 7. A French word meaning "put the customer first" is _kaizen._

_____ 8. Constructing a statistical process control chart is part of Pareto analysis.

_____ 9. In Deming's PDCA cycle, the "C" stands for "control."

_____10. One of Deming's 14 points is a recommendation to get rid of numerical quotas.

Multiple-Choice Questions

1. What type of control involves monitoring and adjusting ongoing activities and processes?
   A. Benchmarking   B. Feedback control
   C. Quality control   D. Concurrent control
   E. Feedforward control

2. _____ involves identifying, studying, and building upon the best practices of organizational role models.
   A. Benchmarking   B. _Kaizen_
   C. Pareto analysis   D. The PDCA cycle
   E. TQM

3. According to experts, to whom should internal auditors report their findings?
   A. The corporate treasurer
   B. The Internal Revenue Service
   C. All employees
   D. The head of accounting
   E. The organization's top manager

4. A back-up plan for emergencies is called a _____ plan.
   A. fall-back   B. contingency
   C. reserve   D. benchmark
   E. crisis

5. Which of the following is _not_ one of the five types of product quality?
   A. Value-based quality
   B. User-based quality
   C. Technology-based quality
   D. Manufacturing-based quality
   E. Product-based quality

6. The RATER service-quality dimension that is related to the provision of caring and individualized attention to customers is
   A. assurance.   B. reliability.
   C. responsiveness.   D. professionalism.
   E. empathy.

7. Which of the following terms refers to anyone within the organization who relies on your work to get her or his work done?
   A. Quality partner   B. Lateral associate
   C. _Kaizen_   D. Internal customer
   E. Downstream coworker

8. Which of the following do TQM advocates prefer, rather than the typical hierarchy?
   A. No middle managers
   B. Inverted organizations
   C. Leaderless three-person teams
   D. Teams of different specialists
   E. Circular organizations

9. An acceptable quality measurement, on a TQM control chart, should fall
   A. between the upper and lower control limits.
   B. below the lower control limit.
   C. outside the upper and lower control limits.
   D. above the upper control limit.
   E. on the median line.

10. According to Deming, _____ is the most important part of the production line.
   A. technology   B. the employee
   C. the supervisor   D. engineering
   E. the consumer

See page T1 at the back of the text for answers to these questions. Want more questions? Visit the student Web site and take the ACE quizzes for more practice.

MANAGERS-IN-ACTION VIDEOS

5a

Finagle A Bagel's Management, Organization, and Production Finesse

A skilled management team, headed by husband-and-wife managing partners Alan Litchman and Laura B. Trust, helps this Boston-area chain of bagel cafes succeed in a competitive marketplace. We see the complex inner workings of a combination wholesale and retail food operation. A hands-on corporate culture keeps things humming and product quality first-rate. For more background, see **www.finagleabagel.com.**

Learning Objective

To demonstrate how to organize and control all the working parts of a complex growing business to achieve high product/service quality and customer satisfaction.

Links to Textual Material

Chapter 8: Decision making; **Chapter 9:** Organizational structure and effectiveness; **Chapter 16:** Organizational control; Product and service quality; Total quality management (TQM)

Discussion Questions

1 Using Figure 8.1 as a guide, how many sources of decision complexity can you detect in this video case?

2 How important is feedforward control, as described in Chapter 16, at Finagle A Bagel?

3 Which one of the five types of product quality, discussed in Chapter 16, reigns supreme at Finagle A Bagel?

4 Which of the four principles of total quality management (TQM) can you find evidence of in this video case? Explain.

5 Which of Deming's 14 points are evident at Finagle A Bagel?

5b

Training a Sales Employee at REI

Store manager Bob Voltz introduces us to REI, a consumer cooperative outdoor sporting goods store started in 1938 in Seattle. REI has become one of the biggest stores in the sporting goods business in the United States. "REI is more than a store, it's a lifestyle," says director of training Steve Kittel. We follow the progress of new employee Susan Lee as she explains life at REI. A five-step customer service program is detailed. For more background, see the Closing Case in Chapter 7 and **www.rei.com.**

Learning Objective

To illustrate how a well-run retail company achieves good customer service and high customer satisfaction.

Links to Textual Material

Chapter 9: Organizational culture; **Chapter 10:** Training; **Chapter 12:** Motivation; **Chapter 16:** Organizational control; Product/service quality; Total quality management; Deming management

Discussion Questions

1 Judging on the basis of everything you have read in this textbook, how would you rate the management of REI? Explain.

2 What is the connection between training new employees in applying company values and service quality?

3 Which components of organizational control, discussed in Chapter 16, are evident in this video case?

4 Using the Action Learning Exercise for Chapter 16, what score would you give the customer service quality at REI?

5 Which total quality management (TQM) principles covered in Chapter 16 are most evident at REI? Explain their practical significance.

TEST PREPPER ANSWERS

CHAPTER 1

True/False: 1. False 2. False 3. False 4. True 5. True 6. False 7. True 8. True 9. False 10. False
Multiple-Choice: 1. E 2. C 3. B 4. C 5. E 6. A 7. E 8. D 9. E 10. D

CHAPTER 2

True/False: 1. True 2. True 3. False 4. False 5. False 6. True 7. False 8. False 9. False 10. True
Multiple-Choice: 1. B 2. B 3. E 4. B 5. C 6. A 7. C 8. D 9. E 10. E

CHAPTER 3

True/False: 1. True 2. False 3. True 4. False 5. False 6. False 7. False 8. False 9. False 10. True
Multiple-Choice: 1. E 2. A 3. D 4. C 5. B 6. B 7. B 8. D 9. E 10. E

CHAPTER 4

True/False: 1. False 2. True 3. False 4. True 5. False 6. False 7. True 8. False 9. True 10. True
Multiple-Choice: 1. A 2. B 3. C 4. C 5. B 6. D 7. A 8. A 9. B 10. C

CHAPTER 5

True/False: 1. False 2. True 3. False 4. True 5. True 6. True 7. False 8. True 9. True 10. False
Multiple-Choice: 1. E 2. E 3. B 4. C 5. E 6. C 7. B 8. C 9. A 10. B

CHAPTER 6

True/False: 1. True 2. False 3. False 4. False 5. True 6. False 7. True 8. True 9. False 10. True
Multiple-Choice: 1. C 2. C 3. A 4. B 5. B 6. E 7. D 8. D 9. C 10. C

CHAPTER 7

True/False: 1. True 2. False 3. False 4. True 5. False 6. False 7. False 8. False 9. True 10. True
Multiple-Choice: 1. D 2. D 3. D 4. D 5. E 6. A 7. B 8. E 9. A 10. D

CHAPTER 8

True/False: 1. False 2. False 3. True 4. True 5. True 6. False 7. True 8. False 9. False 10. True
Multiple-Choice: 1. D 2. D 3. E 4. C 5. C 6. B 7. A 8. E 9. B 10. A

CHAPTER 9

True/False: 1. False 2. False 3. True 4. False 5. True 6. True 7. True 8. False 9. False 10. True
Multiple-Choice: 1. D 2. B 3. C 4. B 5. E 6. B 7. C 8. A 9. A 10. D

CHAPTER 10

True/False: 1. True 2. True 3. True 4. True 5. False 6. False 7. False 8. True 9. False 10. True
Multiple-Choice: 1. B 2. E 3. A 4. C 5. C 6. A 7. D 8. C 9. A 10. B

CHAPTER 11

True/False: 1. True 2. False 3. True 4. True 5. False 6. False 7. True 8. False 9. False 10. True
Multiple-Choice: 1. A 2. D 3. B 4. C 5. A 6. D 7. B 8. D 9. D 10. E

CHAPTER 12

True/False: 1. False 2. True 3. True 4. False 5. False 6. True 7. True 8. False 9. False 10. True
Multiple-Choice: 1. E 2. B 3. E 4. C 5. A 6. E 7. C 8. E 9. A 10. E

CHAPTER 13

True/False: 1. True 2. True 3. False 4. False 5. False 6. False 7. True 8. False 9. True 10. True
Multiple-Choice: 1. A 2. E 3. B 4. A 5. E 6. D 7. A 8. C 9. E 10. E

CHAPTER 14

True/False: 1. True 2. False 3. True 4. True 5. False 6. False 7. False 8. True 9. True 10. True
Multiple-Choice: 1. D 2. C 3. A 4. C 5. B 6. A 7. C 8. E 9. A 10. B

CHAPTER 15

True/False: 1. False 2. True 3. False 4. True 5. False 6. False 7. True 8. False 9. True 10. False
Multiple-Choice: 1. C 2. D 3. D 4. E 5. D 6. E 7. A 8. E 9. B 10. A

CHAPTER 16

True/False: 1. True 2. True 3. False 4. True 5. False 6. True 7. False 8. False 9. False 10. True
Multiple-Choice: 1. D 2. A 3. E 4. B 5. C 6. E 7. D 8. D 9. A 10. E

REFERENCES

CHAPTER 1

1. **Opening Quote:** Henry Mintzberg, "Third-Generation Management Development," *Training & Development* (March 2004): 30. (emphasis added.)
2. Joan Magretta, *What Management Is: How It Works and Why It's Everyone's Business* (New York: The Free Press, 2002), p. 7.
3. As quoted in Kathryn Tyler, "The Boss Makes the Weather," *HR Magazine*, 49 (May 2004): 93. Also see Bill Leonard, "Study: Bully Bosses Prevalent in U.S." *HR Magazine*, 52 (May 2007): 22, 28; Stanley Bing, "Crazy Bosses," *Fortune* (May 28, 2007): 49–54; and Jack Welch and Suzy Welch, "Bosses Who Get It All Wrong," *Business Week* (July 23, 2007): 88.
4. For more, see Steven M. Nakashima, "Executive Exemption Construed Narrowly," *HR Magazine*, 51 (November 2006): 118; and A Kevin Troutman, "Deja Review," *HR Magazine*, 52 (February 2007): 58–62.
5. Ellen Van Velsor and Jean Brittain Leslie, "Why Executives Derail: Perspectives Across Time and Cultures," *Academy of Management Executive*, 9 (November 1995): 63. For related studies, see Frank Shipper and John E. Dillard Jr., "A Study of Impending Derailment and Recovery of Middle Managers Across Career Stages," *Human Resource Management*, 39 (Winter 2000): 331–345; Clinton O. Longenecker, Mitchell J. Neubert, and Laurence S. Fink, "Causes and Consequences of Managerial Failure in Rapidly Changing Organizations," *Business Horizons*, 50 (March–April 2007): 145–155; and Keith R. McFarland, "Lessons from the Anti-Mentor," *Business Week* (June 11, 2007): 86.
6. Jon Swartz, "Conway's Ethics Led to Firing," *USA Today* (October 5, 2004): 1B. For related research, see Bennett J. Tepper, "Consequences of Abusive Supervision," *Academy of Management Journal*, 43 (April 2000): 178–190.
7. Spencer E. Ante, "The Info Tech 100," *Business Week* (July 2, 2007): 63.
8. Employee data from **www.nokia.com,** August 5, 2007.
9. Marc Gunther, "The End of Garbage," *Fortune* (March 19, 2007): 166.
10. Robert J. Samuelson, "The Economic Mega-Worry," *Newsweek* (January 8, 2007): 51.
11. Timothy J. Mullaney, "The Doctor Is (Plugged) In," *Business Week* (June 26, 2006): 56.
12. Data from Victoria Markham, "America's Supersized Footprint," *Business Week* (October 30, 2006): 132. Also see Fareed Zakaria, "A Cure for Oil Addicts," *Newsweek* (August 6, 2007): 34.
13. For example, see John Carey and Adam Aston, "Put a Termite in Your Tank," *Business Week* (December 18, 2006): 132, 135; Paul Davidson, "Biomass Plants Find Power in Poop," *USA Today* (February 9, 2007): 4B; Eugene Linden, "From Peak Oil to Dark Age?" *Business Week* (June 25, 2007): 94; and David Whitford, "Going Nuclear," *Fortune* (August 6, 2007): 42–54.
14. Data from "How Much the Global Population Grows," *USA Today* (April 14, 2004): 1A. U.S. population data and projections are reported in Haya El Nasser, "U.S. Population Tops 290M, Could Reach 300M by 2007," *USA Today* (December 19, 2003): 3A; and "Growing Bigger by the Decade," *USA Today* (April 7, 2004): 1A.
15. Data from Margie Mason, "World Populace Will Max Out, Study Finds," *USA Today* (August 2, 2001): 8D.
16. See Elizabeth Weise, "Global Hunger Is Increasing, Report Says," *USA Today* (November 25, 2003): 13A.
17. Diane Brady, "Wanted: Eclectic Visionary with a Sense of Humor," *Business Week* (August 28, 2000): 143.
18. See Betsy Morris, "The New Rules," *Fortune* (July 24, 2006): 70–87; and Geoffrey Colvin, "Managing in Chaos," *Fortune* (October 2, 2006): 76–82.
19. **www.mcdonalds.com,** August 5, 2007.
20. Matt Krantz, "Dow Stampedes Past 14,000," *USA Today* (July 20, 2007): 1B. Also see Steve Hamm, "The Back Roads to IT Growth," *Business Week* (August 6, 2007): 78.
21. Data from Lou Dobbs, "Dangerously Dependent," *U.S. News & World Report* (February 9, 2004): 40.
22. Data from Julie Schmit, "Flow of Chinese Seafood into USA Slows," *USA Today* (July 17, 2007): 3B.
23. For good overviews of the offshoring controversy, see Diana Farrell, "Smarter Offshoring," *Harvard Business Review*, 84 (June 2006): 83–92; Ann E. Harrison and Margaret S. McMillan, "Dispelling Some Myths About Offshoring," *Academy of Management Perspectives*," 20 (November 2006): 6–22; and Michael Mandel, "The Real Cost of Offshoring," *Business Week* (June 18, 2007): 28–34.
24. See Pamela Babcock, "America's Newest Export: White-Collar Jobs," *HR Magazine*, 49 (April 2004): 50–57; Fara Warner, "Made in China," *Fast Company,* no. 114 (April 2007): 70–77; and Pete Engardio, "Blueprint from India," *Business Week* (April 2, 2007): 44.
25. Diane E. Lewis, "Jobs Offshoring Here to Stay," *Arizona Republic* (October 17, 2004): D1.
26. Employment data from Jia Lynn Yang, "Indian Call Center Lands in Ohio," *Fortune* (August 6, 2007): 23.
27. *Ibid.*
28. *Ibid.* Also see Steve Hamm, "Guess Who's Hiring in America,"*Business Week* (June 25, 2007): 47.
29. A good historical overview of the quality movement can be found in R. Ray Gehani, "Quality Value-Chain: A Meta-Synthesis of Frontiers of Quality Movement," *Academy of Management Executive,* 7 (May 1993): 29–42.
30. For recent product quality problems see Julie Schmit, "More Pet Food Recalled After Discovery," *USA Today* (May 4, 2007): 1B; and Jon Swartz and Mike Snider, "Microsoft Extends Warrranty on Xbox 360," *USA Today* (July 6, 2007): 1B.
31. For instructive reading about Toyota's admired quality program, see Charles Fishman, "No Satisfaction," *Fast Company,* no. 111 (January 2007): 82–92; and Thomas A. Stewart and Anand P. Raman, "Lessons from Toyota's Long Drive," *Harvard Business Review,* 85 (July–August 2007): 74–83.
32. See Kenneth R. Thompson, "Confronting the Paradoxes in a Total Quality Environment," *Organizational Dynamics,* 26 (Winter 1998): 62–74; and Thomas J. Douglas and William Q. Judge Jr., "Total Quality Management Implementation and Competitive Advantage: The Role of Structural Control and Exploration," *Academy of Management Journal,* 44 (February 2001): 158–169.
33. See the nine stories in Chris Taylor, "Go Green. Get Rich.," *Business 2.0,* 8 (January–February 2007): 68–79; Heather Green, "The Greening of America's Campuses," *Business Week* (April 9, 2007): 62–65; Rachel Mosteller, "Thinking Globally, Eating Locally in the USA," *USA Today* (May 4, 2007): 6D; Dan Vergano, "Global Carbon Levels Spiraling," *USA Today* (May 22, 2007): 1A; and Jean Chatzky, "Save a Buck, Save the World," *Money,* 36 (June 2007): 30, 32.
34. Susan Page, "Many in Global Poll See Pollution as Biggest Threat," *USA Today* (June 28, 2007): 10A.

35. Drawn from Alex Lash, "Toyota's Green Giant," *Business 2.0*, 5 (May 2004): 72. Also see Jonathan Lash and Fred Wellington, "Competitive Advantage on a Warming Planet," *Harvard Business Review*, 85 (March 2007): 94–102; Christopher Palmeri, "Up from the Onion Fields," *Business Week* (June 25, 2007): 76; Andrew King, "Cooperation Between Corporations and Environmental Groups: A Transaction Cost Perspective," *Academy of Management Review*, 32 (July 2007): 889–900; and Ben Elgin, "How 'Green' Is That Water?" *Business Week* (August 13, 2007): 68.

36. William McDonough and Michael Braungart, *Cradle to Grave: Remaking the Way We Make Things* (New York: North Point Press, 2002), pp. 15–16. For a brief overview, see Brian Dumaine, "Mr. Natural," *Fortune* (October 29, 2002): 184, 186.

37. Data from Gene Koretz, "On Wall Street, Green Is Golden," *Business Week* (January 8, 2001): 30.

38. Drawn from Leslie Cauley, "Rigas Tells His Side of the Adelphia Story," *USA Today* (August 6, 2007): 1B–2B; and Michael Arndt, "The Business Week," *Business Week* (August 13, 2007): 24.

39. Del Jones, "CEOs of the Future Get Formal Training to Take Giant Leap," *USA Today* (December 1, 2003): 2B. Also see Bill George and Peter Sims, *True North: Discover Your Authentic Leadership* (San Francisco: Jossey-Bass, 2007).

40. Julie Amparano, "As Ethics Crisis Grows, Businesses Take Action," *Arizona Republic* (November 24, 1996): D9.

41. See Janet Kornblum, "First U.S. Web Page Went Up 10 Years Ago," *USA Today* (December 11, 2001): 3D; Otis Port, "He Made the Net Work," *Business Week* (September 27, 2004): 20; and Otis Port, "Spinning the World's Web," *Business Week* (November 8, 2004): 16.

42. Data from a January 4, 2006 press release in **www.c-i-a.com.**

43. Spencer E. Ante, "Back from the Dead," *Business Week* (June 25, 2007): 49–50. Also see David Kirkpatrick, "Facebook's Plan to Hook Up the World," *Fortune* (June 11, 2007): 127–130; Steve Hamm, "Children of the Web," *Business Week* (July 2, 2007): 50–58; and Heather Green, "A Web That Thinks Like You," *Business Week* (July 9–16, 2007): 94–95.

44. See Jonathan Zittrain, "Saving the Internet," *Harvard Business Review*, 85 (June 2007): 49–59.

45. Quoted in Cheryl Dahle, "Putting Its Chips on the Net," *Fast Company*, no. 48 (July 2001): 154.

46. For example, see Nigel Andrews and Laura D'Andrea Tyson, "The Upwardly Global MBA," *Strategy + Business*, 36 (Fall 2004): 60–69; and Mike Morrison,

"The Very Model of a Modern Senior Manager," *Harvard Business Review*, Special Issue: The Tests of a Leader, 85 (January 2007): 27–39.

47. For related research, see Frank Shipper, "A Study of the Psychometric Properties of the Managerial Skill Scales of the Survey of Management Practices," *Educational and Psychological Measurement*, 55 (June 1995): 468–479; Frank Shipper and Charles S. White, "Mastery, Frequency, and Interaction of Managerial Behaviors Relative to Subunit Effectiveness," *Human Relations*, 52 (January 1999): 49–66; and Frank Shipper and Jeanette Davy, "A Model and Investigation of Managerial Skills, Employees' Attitudes, and Managerial Performance," *The Leadership Quarterly*, 13, no. 2 (2002): 95–120.

48. See Henri Fayol, *General and Industrial Management*, trans. Constance Storrs (London: Isaac Pitman & Sons, 1949).

49. For a modern example of the universality of managerial functions, see Tim Arango, "Bob Wright's Next Move," *Fortune* (March 5, 2007): 87–91.

50. Clark L. Wilson, *How and Why Effective Managers Balance Their Skills: Technical, Teambuilding, Drive* (Columbia, Md.: Rockatech Multimedia Publishing, 2003), pp. 13, 18–20.

51. See Scott Adams, *The Dilbert Principle* (New York: HarperBusiness, 1996); and Lisa A. Burke and Jo Ellen Moore, "Contemporary Satire of Corporate Managers: Time to Cut the Boss Some Slack?" *Business Horizons*, 42 (July–August 1999): 63–67.

52. "AMA Research," *Management Review*, 85 (July 1996): 10.

53. See Henry Mintzberg, "Managerial Work: Analysis from Observation," *Management Science*, 18 (October 1971): B97–B110.

54. Henry Mintzberg, "The Manager's Job: Folklore and Fact," *Harvard Business Review*, 53 (July–August 1975): 54. For Mintzberg's recent thoughts about managing, see Jonathan Gosling and Henry Mintzberg, "The Five Minds of a Manager," *Harvard Business Review*, 81 (November 2003): 54–63.

55. As quoted in Alan Deutschman, "The CEO's Secret of Managing Time," *Fortune* (June 1, 1992): 136.

56. Jonathan Gosling and Henry Mintzberg, "Reflect Yourself," *HR Magazine*, 49 (September 2004): 151–152.

57. See Martin M. Broadwell and Carol Broadwell Dietrich, "Culture Clash: How to Turn Blue-Collar Workers into Good Supervisors," *Training*, 37 (March 2000): 34–36; and Sam Grobart, "Congratulations, You're the Boss! Now What?" *Money*, 36 (June 2007): 38, 40.

58. Adapted from Earnest R. Archer, "Things You Lose the Right to Do When You Become a Manager," *Supervisory Management*, 35 (July 1990): 8–9. Also see "Do I Have To?" *Business Week* (July 7, 2003): 14; and Nadine Heintz, "Why Can't We Be Friends?" *Inc.*, 26 (January 2004): 31–32.

59. See Henry Mintzberg, "The MBA Menace," *Fast Company*, no. 83 (June 2004): 31–32; Jennifer Merritt, "Masters of Barely Anything," *Business Week* (July 12, 2004): 22; and Diana Middleton, "Is the Focus Too Fine?" *Business Week* (October 18, 2004): 92.

60. See Ron Zemke, "The Honeywell Studies: How Managers Learn to Manage," *Training*, 22 (August 1985): 46–51.

61. Adapted from Robin Snell, "Graduating from the School of Hard Knocks?" *Journal of Management Development*, 8, no. 5 (1989): 23–30. Also see Sidney Finkelstein, *Why Smart Executives Fail* (New York: Portfolio, 2003); Joseph Weber, "Stress Factors: Please Don't Promote Me," *Business Week* (May 14, 2007): 13; Kerry Sulkowicz, "Stressed for Success," *Business Week* (May 21, 2007): 18; and Ann Pomeroy, "Promotion a Major Life Stressor," *HR Magazine*, 52 (July 2007): 12, 16.

62. Brad Stone, "Nike's Short Game," *Newsweek* (January 26, 2004): 40–41.

63. See Craig C. Lundberg, "Is There Really Nothing So Practical as a Good Theory?" *Business Horizons*, 47 (September–October 2004): 7–14; Denise M. Rousseau and Sharon McCarthy, "Educating Managers from an Evidence-Based Perspective," *Academy of Management Learning and Education*, 6 (March 2007): 84–101; and Terence R. Mitchell, "The Academic Life: Realistic Changes Needed for Business School Students and Faculty," *Academy of Management Learning and Education*, 6 (June 2007): 236–251.

64. See Kerry Sulkowicz, "Tips for Interns—and Their Bosses," *Business Week* (July 2, 2007): 18.

65. See Linda A. Hill, "Becoming the Boss," *Harvard Business Review*, Special Issue: The Tests of a Leader, 85 (January 2007): 48–56; Mark Learmonth, "Critical Management Education in Action: Personal Tales of Management Unlearning," *Academy of Management Learning and Education*, 6 (March 2007): 109–113; and Aili McConnon, "The Games Managers Play," *Business Week* (June 25, 2007): 12.

66. Drawn from Jim Hopkins, "PCs, Immigrants Help Launch Millions of Little Firms," *USA Today* (October 30, 2002): 1B.

67. Data from Telis Demos, "Global 500: The World's Largest Corporations," *Fortune*

(July 23, 2007): 133, 143. For more on Wal-Mart, see Jon Birger, "The Unending Woes of Lee Scott," *Fortune* (January 22, 2007): 118–122; Robert Berner, "My Year at Wal-Mart," *Business Week* (February 12, 2007): 70–74; and Anthony Bianco, "Wal-Mart's Midlife Crisis," *Business Week* (April 30, 2007): 46–56.

68. Data from Jennifer Schramm, "Benefits at Risk?" *HR Magazine*, 52 (February 2007): 152.

69. Data from Jim Hopkins, "Small Businesses Hold Off on Big Purchases," *USA Today* (October 16, 2001): 1B.

70. Data from Jim Hopkins, "New Bosses Should Develop Management Skills," *USA Today* (September 12, 2001): 9B; and Jim Hopkins, "Micro-Businesses Targeted as Source of Sales Revenue," *USA Today* (April 3, 2001): 1B.

71. Data from Jim Hopkins, "More Self-Employed Bet on Not Getting Sick, Hurt," *USA Today* (August 23, 2004): 1B.

72. See George Gendron, "The Failure Myth," *Inc.* (January 2001): 13; and Ben Levinson, "And Now for That Dream Job," *Business Week* (July 9–16, 2007): 60, 62.

73. See David R. Francis, "Spiking Stereotypes About Small Firms," *Christian Science Monitor* (May 7, 1993): 9; Gene Koretz, "A Surprising Finding on New-Business Mortality Rates," *Business Week* (June 14, 1993): 22; and James Aley, "Debunking the Failure Fallacy," *Fortune* (September 6, 1993): 21. For related reading, see Sydney Finkelstein, "The Myth of Managerial Superiority in Internet Startups: An Autopsy," *Organizational Dynamics*, 30 (Fall 2001): 172–185.

74. Data from Larry Light, "Small Business: The Job Engine Needs Fuel," *Business Week* (March 1, 1993): 78.

75. Data from Charles Burck, "Where Good Jobs Grow," *Fortune* (June 14, 1993): 22. Also see David Neumark, Junfu Zhang, and Brandon Wall, "Where the Jobs Are: Business Dynamics and Employment Growth," *Academy of Management Perspectives*, 20 (November 2006): 79–94.

76. For more on Birch's research, see Alan Webber, "Business Race Isn't Always to the Swift, But Bet That Way," *USA Today* (February 3, 1998): 15A. Also see "The Gazelle Theory," *Inc.*, 23 (May 29, 2001): 28–29; and Magnus Aronsson, "Education Matters—But Does Entrepreneurship Education? An Interview with David Birch," *Academy of Management Learning and Education*, 3 (September 2004): 289–292.

77. For data on pay in big companies versus small companies, see Michael Mandel, "Big Players Offer Better Pay," *Business Week* (August 30, 1999): 30. For small business health insurance data, see

Howard Gleckman, "Whose Plan Is Healthier?" *Business Week* (May 24, 2004): 90, 92; and Jim Hopkins, "Rising Benefit Costs Hurt Small Businesses' Financial Health," *USA Today* (June 4, 2004): 1B–2B.

78. For interesting reading on partnerships, see Patrick J. Sauer, "How to Work with a Partner (Year After Year After Year)," *Inc.*, 26 (October 2004): 90–97; and Michael S. Hopkins, "How to Work (If You Must) with Your Spouse," *Inc.*, 26 (October 2004): 91. Consulting is discussed in Suzanne McGee, "Getting Started: Brains for Hire," *Inc.*, 26 (April 2004): 61, 63.

79. See Susan J. Wells, "Franchisors Walk a Fine Line," *HR Magazine*, 49 (August 2004): 48–53.

80. See recent issues of *Inc.* and *Fast Company* magazines for inspiring small-business success stories. Also see Oliver Ryan, "Chairman of the Board," *Fortune* (April 2, 2007): 30; Mindy Fetterman, "Russell Simmons Can't Slow Down," *USA Today* (May 14, 2007): 1B–2B; Steven Levy, "Meet the Next Billionaires," *Newsweek* (May 21, 2007): 61–69; and Max Chafkin, Stephanie Clifford, Sarah Goldstein, and Mike Hofman, "How to Launch a Cool, Profitable, Worth-All-the-Risk, Kick-Ass Start-Up," *Inc.*, 29 (July 2007): 77–86.

81. Howard H. Stevenson and J. Carlos Jarillo, "A Paradigm of Entrepreneurship: Entrepreneurial Management," *Strategic Management Journal*, 11 (Summer 1990): 23 (emphasis added). Also see Thomas K. McCraw, "Mapping the Entrepreneurial Psyche," *Inc.*, 29 (August 2007): 73–74.

82. As quoted in Rob Walker, "Because Optimism Is Essential," *Inc.*, 26 (April 2004): 150.

83. Ibid. Also see Robert D. Hof, "Jeff Bezos' Risky Bet," *Business Week* (November 13, 2006): 52–58.

84. As quoted in Bruce Rosenstein, "Inspiration for Entrepreneur Wannabes," *USA Today* (October 11, 2004): 9B. Also see Jim Hopkins, "Venture Capital 101: Entrepreneur Courses Increase," *USA Today* (January 5, 2004): 1B; Jim Hopkins, "Entrepreneurs Are Born, But Can They Be Taught?" *USA Today* (April 7, 2004): 1B–2B; and Dean A. Shepherd, "Educating Entrepreneurship Students About Emotion and Learning from Failure," *Academy of Management Learning and Education*, 3 (September 2004): 274–287.

85. Stephanie Armour, "UBUBU Boldly Launches Start-Up in Cyberspace," *USA Today* (June 19, 2000): 3B. Also see Marc Malone, "The Small Business Ego Trap," *Business Horizons*, 47 (July–August 2004): 17–22.

86. Steven Berglas, "GIs for Guts," *Inc.*, 22 (May 2000): 45.

87. Joshua Hyatt, "The Real Secrets of Entrepreneurs," *Fortune* (November 15, 2004): 186.

CHAPTER 2

1. **Opening Quote:** John W. Gardner, *Self-Renewal: The Individual and the Innovative Society* (New York: Harper & Row, 1964), chap. 11.

2. For interesting historical perspectives, see David Strutton, "The Courtly Path to Managerial Leadership," *Business Horizons*, 47 (January–February 2004): 7–18; Russ Juskalian, "History of Bronfmans Makes for a Spirited Tale," *USA Today* (July 10, 2006): 4B; and Robert J. Samuelson, "The Next Capitalism," *Newsweek* (October 30, 2006): 45.

3. Alonzo L. McDonald, as quoted in Alan M. Kantrow, ed., "Why History Matters to Managers," *Harvard Business Review*, 64 (January–February 1986): 82. Also see Arthur G. Bedeian, "The Gift of Professional Maturity," *Academy of Management Learning and Education*, 3 (March 2004): 92–98.

4. Barbara S. Lawrence, "Historical Perspective: Using the Past to Study the Present," *Academy of Management Review*, 9 (April 1984): 307. Also see Mary Beth Marklein, "Today's Students Don't Know Much About History," *USA Today* (September 26, 2006): 9D.

5. See Morgan Witzel, *Fifty Key Figures in Management* (London: Routledge, 2003). A review of this book by W. Jack Duncan can be found in "Book Reviews," *Academy of Management Review*, 29 (October 2004): 687–689.

6. For a discussion in this area, see "How Business Schools Began," *Business Week* (October 19, 1963): 114–116. Also see John Trinkaus, "Urwick on the Business Academy," *Business Horizons*, 35 (September–October 1992): 25–29; and David D. Van Fleet and Daniel A. Wren, "Teaching History in Business Schools: 1982–2003," *Academy of Management Learning and Education*, 4 (March 2005): 44–56.

7. The top ten most influential management thinkers of the twentieth century, as selected by the readers of *Business Horizons* magazine, are discussed in Dennis W. Organ, "And the Winners Are . . .," *Business Horizons*, 43 (March–April 2000): 1–3.

8. See Marian M. Extejt and Jonathan E. Smith, "The Behavioral Sciences and Management: An Evaluation of Relevant Journals," *Journal of Management*, 16 (September 1990): 539–551. For a list of 40 management-oriented periodicals, see Jonathan L. Johnson and Philip M. Podsakoff, "Journal Influence in the

Field of Management: An Analysis Using Salancik's Index in a Dependency Network," *Academy of Management Journal*, 37 (October 1994): 1392–1407.

9. For advice on dealing with information overload, see Suzy Wetlaufer, "Thanks for Asking," *Harvard Business Review*, 80 (February 2002): 10.

10. See the instructive timeline in "Management Ideas Through Time," *Management Review*, 87 (January 1998): 16–19. Also see Daniel A. Wren and Ronald G. Greenwood, *Management Innovators: The People and Ideas That Shaped Modern Business* (New York: Oxford University Press, 1998).

11. For ideas about the related area of management as a profession, see Rakesh Khurana, "You Got a License to Run That Company?" *Harvard Business Review*, 82 (February 2004): 14.

12. Craig C. Lundberg, "Is There Really Nothing So Practical as a Good Theory?" *Business Horizons*, 47 (September–October 2004): 10.

13. Based on Jennifer Alsever Beauprez, "Retired CEO Takes Expertise to Iraq," *Arizona Republic* (December 13, 2003): A26.

14. See Henri Fayol, *General and Industrial Management*, trans. Constance Storrs (London: Isaac Pitman & Sons, 1949). An interesting review by Nancy M. Carter of Fayol's book can be found in Allen C. Bluedorn, ed., "Special Book Review Section on the Classics of Management," *Academy of Management Review*, 11 (April 1986): 454–456.

15. Stephen J. Carroll and Dennis J. Gillen, "Are the Classical Management Functions Useful in Describing Managerial Work?" *Academy of Management Review*, 12 (January 1987): 48.

16. Frank B. Copley, *Frederick W. Taylor: Father of Scientific Management* (New York: Harper & Brothers, 1923), I: 3. Also see the brief profile of Taylor in "Taylorism," *Business Week*: 100 Years of Innovation (Summer 1999): 16.

17. For expanded treatment, see Frank B. Copley, *Frederick W. Taylor: The Principles of Scientific Management* (New York: Harper & Brothers, 1911). A good retrospective review of Taylor's classic writings may be found in Bluedorn, ed., "Special Book Review Section on the Classics of Management," pp. 443–447. Robert Kanigel's *One Best Way*, a modern biography of Taylor, is reviewed in Alan Farnham, "The Man Who Changed Work Forever," *Fortune* (July 21, 1997): 114.

18. For an interesting update on Taylor, see Christopher Farrell, "Micromanaging from the Grave," *Business Week* (May 15, 1995): 34.

19. George D. Babcock, *The Taylor System in Franklin Management*, 2nd ed. (New York: Engineering Magazine Company, 1917), p. 31.

20. Taylor's seminal 1911 book *The Principles of Scientific Management* was recently selected by a panel of management experts as the most influential management book of the twentieth century: See Arthur G. Bedeian and Daniel A. Wren, "Most Influential Management Books of the 20th Century," *Organizational Dynamics*, 29 (Winter 2001): 221–225. Also see Oswald Jones, "Scientific Management, Culture and Control: A First-Hand Account of Taylorism in Practice," *Human Relations*, 53 (May 2000): 631–653.

21. For an alternative perspective and detailed critique of Taylor's experiments with pig iron handlers, see Charles D. Wrege and Richard M. Hodgetts, "Frederick W. Taylor's 1899 Pig Iron Observations: Examining Fact, Fiction, and Lessons for the New Millennium," *Academy of Management Journal*, 43 (December 2000): 1283–1291. Also see Sigmund Wagner-Tsukamoto, "An Institutional Economic Reconstruction of Scientific Management: On the Lost Theoretical Logic of Taylorism," *Academy of Management Review*, 32 (January 2007): 105–117.

22. Frederick W. Taylor, *Shop Management* (New York: Harper & Brothers, 1911), p. 22.

23. Frank B. Gilbreth and Lillian M. Gilbreth, *Applied Motion Study* (New York: Sturgis & Walton, 1917), p. 42. A retrospective review of the Gilbreths' writings, by Daniel J. Brass, can be found in Bluedorn, ed., "Special Book Review Section on the Classics of Management," pp. 448–451.

24. See Frank B. Gilbreth Jr. and Ernestine Gilbreth Carey, *Cheaper by the Dozen* (New York: Thomas Y. Crowell, 1948).

25. For example, see the Gantt chart on p. 64 of Tom D. Conkright, "So You're Going to Manage a Project," *Training*, 35 (January 1998): 62–67.

26. For detailed coverage of Gantt's contributions, see H. L. Gantt, *Work, Wages, and Profits*, 2nd ed. (New York: Engineering Magazine Company, 1913). An interesting update on Gantt's contributions can be found in Peter B. Peterson, "Training and Development: The Views of Henry L. Gantt (1861–1919)," *SAM Advanced Management Journal*, 52 (Winter 1987): 20–23.

27. Good historical overviews of the quality movement include Ron Zemke, "A Bluffer's Guide to TQM," *Training*, 30 (April 1993): 48–55; R. Ray Gehani, "Quality Value-Chain: A Meta-Synthesis of Frontiers of Quality Movement,"

Academy of Management Executive, 7 (May 1993): 29–42; and Sangit Chatterjee and Mustafa Yilmaz, "Quality Confusion: Too Many Gurus, Not Enough Disciples," *Business Horizons*, 36 (May–June 1993): 15–18. A look back at the roots of the quality movement can be found in Geoffrey Colvin, "A Concise History of Management Hooey," *Fortune* (June 28, 2004): 166–176.

28. Mary Walton, *Deming Management at Work* (New York: Putnam, 1990), p. 13. See John Hillkirk, "World-Famous Quality Expert Dead at 93," *USA Today* (December 21, 1993): 1B–2B; Peter Nulty, "The National Business Hall of Fame: W. Edwards Deming," *Fortune* (April 4, 1994): 124; Keki R. Bhote, "Dr. W. Edwards Deming—A Prophet with Belated Honor in His Own Country," *National Productivity Review*, 13 (Spring 1994): 153–159; Anne Willette, "Deming Legacy Gives Firms Quality Challenge," *USA Today* (October 19, 1994): 2B; and M. R. Yilmaz and Sangit Chatterjee, "Deming and the Quality of Software Development," *Business Horizons*, 40 (November–December 1997): 51–58.

29. See Jack Gordon, "An Interview with Joseph M. Juran," *Training*, 31 (May 1994): 35–41. Deming and Juran are saluted in Otis Port, "The Kings of Quality," *Business Week* (August 30, 2004): 20.

30. Zemke, "A Bluffer's Guide to TQM," p. 51. Also see Joseph M. Juran, "Made in U.S.A.: A Renaissance in Quality," *Harvard Business Review*, 71 (July–August 1993): 42–50.

31. See Armand V. Feigenbaum, "How Total Quality Counters Three Forces of International Competitiveness," *National Productivity Review*, 13 (Summer 1994): 327–330. More of Feigenbaum's ideas can be found in Del Jones, "Employers Going for Quality Hires, Not Quantity," *USA Today* (December 11, 1997): 1B; and Armand Feigenbaum and Donald S. Feigenbaum, "What Quality Means Today," *MIT Sloan Management Review*, 46 (Winter 2005): 96.

32. Crosby's more recent ideas may be found in Philip B. Crosby, *Completeness: Quality for the 21st Century* (New York: Dutton, 1992).

33. Edwin A. Locke, "The Ideas of Frederick W. Taylor: An Evaluation," *Academy of Management Review*, 7 (January 1982): 22–23. Also see David H. Freedman, "Is Management Still a Science?" *Harvard Business Review*, 70 (November–December 1992): 26–38.

34. See Donald W. Fogarty, Thomas R. Hoffman, and Peter W. Stonebraker, *Production and Operations Management* (Cincinnati, Ohio:

South-Western Publishing Co., 1989), pp. 7–8; and Vincent A. Mabert, "Operations in the American Economy: Liability or Asset?" *Business Horizons*, 35 (July–August 1992): 3–5.

35. The Hawthorne studies are discussed in detail in F. J. Roethlisberger and William J. Dickson, *Management and the Worker* (Cambridge, Mass.: Harvard University Press, 1939). Dennis W. Organ's review of this classic book, in which he criticizes the usual textbook treatment of it, can be found in Bluedorn, ed., "Special Book Review Section on the Classics of Management," pp. 459–463.

36. See Ellen S. O'Connor, "The Politics of Management Thought: A Case Study of the Harvard Business School and the Human Relations School," *Academy of Management Review*, 24 (January 1999): 117–131.

37. See Henry C. Metcalf and L. Urwick, *Dynamic Administration: The Collected Papers of Mary Parker Follett* (New York: Harper & Brothers, 1942); Mary Parker Follett, *Freedom and Coordination* (London: Management Publications Trust, 1949). A review by Diane L. Ferry of *Dynamic Administration* can be found in Bluedorn, ed., "Special Book Review Section on the Classics of Management," pp. 451–454.

38. See L. D. Parker, "Control in Organizational Life: The Contribution of Mary Parker Follett," *Academy of Management Review*, 9 (October 1984): 736–745; Albie M. Davis, "An Interview with Mary Parker Follett," *Negotiation Journal*, 5 (July 1989): 223–225; and Dana Wechsler Linden, "The Mother of Them All," *Forbes* (January 16, 1995): 75–76.

39. See David Jacobs, "Book Review Essay: Douglas McGregor—The Human Side of Enterprise in Peril," *Academy of Management Review*, 29 (April 2004): 293–296.

40. For a case study of a military leader's transition from a Theory X style to a Theory Y style, see D. Michael Abrashoff, "Retention Through Redemption," *Harvard Business Review*, 79 (February 2001): 136–141.

41. John B. Miner, "The Rated Importance, Scientific Validity, and Usefulness of Organizational Behavior Theories: A Quantitative Review," *Academy of Management Learning and Education*, 2 (September 2003): 250–268.

42. For example, the new field of positive psychology has evolved into positive organizational behavior. See Martin E. P. Seligman and Mihaly Csikszentmihalyi, "Positive Psychology: An Introduction," *American Psychologist*, 55 (January 2000): 5–14; and Thomas A. Wright, "Positive Organizational Behavior: An Idea Whose Time Has Truly Come,"

Journal of Organizational Behavior, 24 (June 2003): 437–442.

43. The founders of Hewlett-Packard Co. are recognized for their pioneering efforts to put people first in Peter Burrows, "Architects of the Info Age," *Business Week* (March 29, 2004): 22.

44. An interesting and instructive timeline of human resource milestones can be found in "Training and Development in the 20th Century," *Training*, 35 (September 1998): 49–56.

45. For a statistical interpretation of the Hawthorne studies, see Richard Herbert Franke and James D. Kaul, "The Hawthorne Experiments: First Statistical Interpretation," *American Sociological Review*, 43 (October 1978): 623–643. Also see Stephen R. G. Jones, "Worker Interdependence and Output: The Hawthorne Studies Reevaluated," *American Sociological Review*, 55 (April 1990): 176–190.

46. Russell L. Ackoff, "Science in the Systems Age: Beyond IE, OR, and MS," *Operations Research*, 21 (May–June 1973): 664.

47. Charles J. Coleman and David D. Palmer, "Organizational Application of System Theory," *Business Horizons*, 16 (December 1973): 77.

48. Chester I. Barnard, *The Functions of the Executive* (Cambridge, Mass.: Harvard University Press, 1938), p. 65.

49. Ibid., p. 82. A retrospective review, by Thomas L. Keon, of Barnard's *The Functions of the Executive* can be found in Bluedorn, ed., "Special Book Review Section on the Classics of Management," pp. 456–459.

50. For details, see Lori Verstegen Ryan and William G. Scott, "Ethics and Organizational Reflection: The Rockefeller Foundation and Postwar 'Moral Deficits,' 1942–1954," *Academy of Management Review*, 20 (April 1995): 438–461.

51. Ludwig von Bertalanffy, "The History and Status of General Systems Theory," *Academy of Management Journal*, 15 (December 1972): 411.

52. For an example of an economic/industrial hierarchy of organizations, see Figure 2 (p. 774) in Philip Rich, "The Organizational Taxonomy: Definition and Design," *Academy of Management Review*, 17 (October 1992): 758–781.

53. Geoff Colvin, "Boeing Prepares for Takeoff," Fortune (June 11, 2007): 133–140.

54. Susan Albers Mohrman and Allan M. Mohrman Jr., "Organizational Change and Learning," in *Organizing for the Future: The New Logic for Managing Complex Organizations*, eds. Jay R. Galbraith, Edward E. Lawler III, and Associates (San Francisco: Jossey-Bass, 1993), p. 89. For an excellent overview

of organizational learning, see David A. Garvin, "Building a Learning Organization," *Harvard Business Review*, 71 (July–August 1993): 78–91. Also see Robert Aubrey and Paul M. Cohen, *Working Wisdom: Timeless Skills and Vanguard Strategies for Learning Organizations* (San Francisco: Jossey-Bass, 1995); and Timothy T. Baldwin and Camden C. Danielson, "Building a Learning Strategy at the Top: Interviews with Ten of America's CLOs," *Business Horizons*, 43 (November–December 2000): 5–14.

55. For an excellent collection of readings, see *Harvard Business Review on Knowledge Management* (Boston: Harvard Business School Publishing, 1998).

56. For example, see Gary Weiss, "Chaos Hits Wall Street—The Theory, That Is," *Business Week* (November 2, 1992): 138–140.

57. See Benyamin Bergmann Lichtenstein, "Self-Organized Transitions: A Pattern amid the Chaos of Transformative Change," *Academy of Management Executive*, 14 (November 2000): 128–141; and Polly LaBarre, "Organize Yourself," *Fast Company*, no. 50 (September 2001): 60.

58. Fred Luthans, *Introduction to Management: A Contingency Approach* (New York: McGraw-Hill, 1976), p. 28. Also see Henry L. Tosi Jr. and John W. Slocum Jr., "Contingency Theory: Some Suggested Directions," *Journal of Management*, 10 (Spring 1984): 9–26.

59. Y. K. Shetty, "Contingency Management: Current Perspective for Managing Organizations," *Management International Review*, 14, no. 6 (1974): 27.

60. See Joseph W. McGuire, "Management Theory: Retreat to the Academy," *Business Horizons*, 25 (July–August 1982): 37.

61. See Bruce Rosenstein, "Visionary Writer Mined the Mind," *USA Today* (November 14, 2005): 3B; Kevin Maney, "In 2003 Visit, Management Guru Drucker Told It Like It Was," *USA Today* (November 16, 2005): 3B; John A. Byrne, "The Man Who Invented Management," *Business Week* (November 28, 2005): 96–106; and Geoffrey Colvin, "Peter Drucker: 1909–2005," *Fortune* (November 28, 2005): 32. The influence of Peter Drucker on his grandson, a software entrepreneur, is discussed in Heather Green, "A Web That Thinks Like You," *Business Week* (July 9–16, 2007): 94–95.

62. Data from John A. Byrne, "How the Best Get Better," *Business Week* (September 14, 1987): 98–99.

63. Data from Ryan Underwood, "A *Field Guide* to the Gurus," *Fast Company*,

no. 88 (November 2004): 104. Also see Edward Iwata, "Naisbitt Turns Lust for Life into Mega Book Career," *USA Today* (September 25, 2006): 3B.

64. See Del Jones, "It's Nothing Personal? On 'Apprentice,' It's All Personal," *USA Today* (March 26, 2004): 6B; and Del Jones and Bill Keveney, "10 Lessons of 'The Apprentice,'" *USA Today* (April 15, 2004): 1A, 5A.

65. Academic management gurus are discussed in Eric W. Ford, W. Jack Duncan, Arthur G. Bedeian, and Peter M. Ginter, "People, Places, and Life Transitions: Consequential Experiences in the Lives of Management Laureates," *Academy of Management Learning and Education*, 5 (December 2006): 408–421.

66. Craig M. McAllaster, "The 5 P's of Change: Leading Change by Effectively Utilizing Leverage Points Within an Organization," *Organizational Dynamics*, 33, no. 3 (2004): 321.

67. See Michael A. Hitt and R. Duane Ireland, "Peters and Waterman Revisited: The Unended Quest for Excellence," *Academy of Management Executive*, 1 (May 1987): 91–98.

68. Regarding management fads, see Danny Miller, Jon Hartwick, and Isabelle Le Breton-Miller, "How to Detect a Management Fad—and Distinguish It from a Classic," *Business Horizons*, 47 (July–August 2004): 7–16; Stanley Bing, "Remembrance of Fads Past," *Fortune* (November 15, 2004): 244; Robert J. David and David Strang, "When Fashion Is Fleeting: Transitory Collective Beliefs and the Dynamics of TQM Consulting," *Academy of Management Journal*, 49 (April 2006): 215–233; Jack Gordon, "Yikes! Can Rah-Rah Survive?" *Training*, 43 (October 2006): 6; Michelle Archer, "Level-Headed Book Exposes Some Wrong Business Thinking," *USA Today* (February 19, 2007): 5B; and Jena McGregor, "Ladies and Gents . . . Marcus Buckingham!" *Business Week* (March 26, 2007): 44.

69. Marc Gunther, "The End of Garbage," *Fortune* (March 19, 2007): 162.

CHAPTER 3

1. **Opening Quote:** As quoted in R. Stanley Williams, "You Ain't Seen Nothin' Yet," *Business 2.0* (September 26, 2000): 168.

2. See Kathryn Tyler, "The Tethered Generation," *HR Magazine*, 52 (May 2007): 40–46; Holly Dolezalek, "X-Y Vision," *Training*, 44 (June 2007): 22–27; and Holly Dolezalek, "Biz Kids," *Training*, 44 (July–August 2007): 12–16.

3. For general trends and implications, see Jon Meacham, "What You Need to Know Now," *Newsweek* (July 2–9, 2007): 34–37; and Michael Mandel, "Which Way to the Future?" *Business Week* (August 20–27, 2007): 45–46.

4. Data from Silla Brush, "A Nation in Full," *U.S. News & World Report*, 141 (October 2, 2006): 46–57.

5. Janet Kornblum, "'A Nation of Caregivers,'" *USA Today* (April 6, 2004): 6D. Also see Holly Dolezalek, "Boomer Reality," *Training*, 44 (May 2007): 16–21.

6. Data from Robert J. Samuelson, "Protecting the Welfare State," *Newsweek* (March 8, 2004): 37.

7. For instructive reading, see Phillip Longman, "Fixing Social Security," *Fortune* (November 1, 2004): 78; Pat Regnier, "Can You Live Long and Prosper?" *Money*, 35 (October 2006): 96–104; Robert J. Samuelson, "'Boomsday' Is Approaching," *Newsweek* (April 16, 2007): 44; and Robert J. Samuelson, "When Silence Isn't Golden," *Newsweek* (August 6, 2007): 37.

8. Mark Yost, "GE Focuses of Fridges from Bottom Freezer Up," *USA Today* (November 29, 2002): 10B. Considering demographics when designing products also is discussed in David Welch, "Staying Paranoid at Toyota," *Business Week* (July 2, 2007): 80, 82.

9. Based on Dean Foust, "For Banks, Money Also Talks in Spanish," *Business Week* (January 13, 2003): 111. Buying power data from Stephanie N. Mehta, "The Man with the Golden Gut," *Fortune* (May 14, 2007): 92–98. Also see Andrea Stone, "More Officials in Midwest, South Adding Spanish Lessons to Training," USA Today (December 26, 2006): 1A; and Kerry Miller, "E-Commerce: A Missed *Oportunidad*," *Business Week* (July 9–16, 2007): 14.

10. See Ken Dychtwald, Tamara J. Erickson, and Robert Morison, *Workforce Crisis: How to Beat the Coming Shortage of Skills and Talent* (Boston: Harvard Business School Press, 2006); Peter Coy and Jack Ewing, "Where Are All the Workers?" *Business Week* (April 9, 2007): 28–31; and Jennifer Schramm, "Coping with Tight Labor," *HR Magazine*, 52 (June 2007): 192.

11. Geoff Colvin, "Failing the Test," *Fortune* (May 14, 2007): 39.

12. Data from Barbara Hagenbaugh, "Good Help Hard to Find for Manufacturers," *USA Today* (April 16, 2004): 1B. Also see Craig R. Taylor, "Retention Leadership," *T+D*, 58 (March 2004): 41–45; Gail Johnson, "The Tomorrow Team," *Training*, 41 (August 2004): 16; and Susan Meisinger, "Shortage of Skilled Workers Threatens Economy," *HR Magazine*, 49 (November 2004): 12.

13. Data from Greg Toppo, "One in 20 U.S. Adults Lack Basic English Skills," *USA Today* (December 16, 2005): 1A.

14. "Illiteracy Still a Problem," *USA Today* (November 29, 2000): 1A.

15. Data from Tammy Galvin, "2001 Industry Report," *Training*, 38 (October 2001): 40–75.

16. Russell Wild, "Great Jobs," *AARP: The Magazine*, 46 (November–December 2003): 52. Also see Peter Coy, "Golden Paychecks," *Business Week* (July 2, 2007): 13.

17. Mark Clements, "What We Say About Aging," *Parade Magazine* (December 12, 1993): 4. Also see Neil Howe and William Strauss, "The Next 20 Years: How Customer and Workforce Attitudes Will Evolve," *Harvard Business Review*, 85 (July–August 2007): 41–52.

18. See Kimberly A. Wrenn and Todd J. Maurer, "Beliefs About Older Workers' Learning and Development Behavior in Relation to Beliefs About Malleability of Skills, Age-Related Decline, and Control," *Journal of Applied Social Psychology*, 34 (February 2004): 223–242; and Ruth Kanfer and Phillip L. Ackerman, "Aging, Adult Development, and Work Motivation," *Academy of Management Review*, 29 (July 2004): 440–458.

19. Excerpted from Paul Mayrand, "Older Workers: A Problem or the Solution?" *Proceedings: Textbook Authors Conference* (AARP: Washington, D.C., October 21, 1992), pp. 28–29. © Reprinted by permission of AARP.

20. See Amy Dunkin, "You're Older? So Sell Your Wisdom," *Business Week* (February 19, 2007): 82; Kathryn Tyler, "Leveraging Long Tenure," *HR Magazine*, 52 (May 2007): 54–60; Anne Fisher, "Working for Your Kids," *Fortune* (June 25, 2007): 130–138; and Margaret Guroff, "The New Kid," *AARP: The Magazine*, 50 (September–October 2007): 54–58.

21. Data from "Mass Layoffs in USA Idle 2.5 Million in 2001," *USA Today* (January 30, 2002): 1B.

22. Data compiled from "Employment & Unemployment (Mass layoffs)," **www.bls.gov.**

23. Robert Aubrey and Paul M. Cohen, *Working Wisdom: Timeless Skills and Vanguard Strategies for Learning Organizations* (San Francisco: Jossey-Bass, 1995), p. 29.

24. See Michelle Conlin, "And Now, the Just-in-Time Employee," *Business Week* (August 28, 2000): 168–170; and Ann Pomeroy, "Not Your Parents' Workplace," *HR Magazine*, 52 (August 2007): 12, 14.

25. John Huey, "Where Managers Will Go," *Fortune* (January 27, 1992): 51.

26. See Robert J. Samuelson, "The Quagmire of Inequality," *Newsweek* (June 11, 2007): 48.

27. Data from **www.bls.gov.**

28. Barbara Hagenbaugh, "Women's Pay Suffers Setback vs. Men's," *USA Today* (August 27, 2004): 4B.

29. Data from Aaron Bernstein, "Women's Pay: Why the Gap Remains a Chasm," *Business Week* (June 14, 2004): 58–59.

30. For specific data, see Kimberly Blanton, "More Women in Top-Tier Jobs Earn 6 Figures," *Arizona Republic* (April 11, 2004): D1, D5; Emily Thornton, "Fed Up—and Fighting Back," *Business Week* (September 20, 2004): 100–101.

31. Data from "Female Managers Still Earn Less, GAO Says," *USA Today* (January 24, 2002): 1B. Also see Francine D. Blau and Lawrance M. Kahn, "The Gender Pay Gap: Have Women Gone as Far as They Can?" *Academy of Management Perspectives*, 21 (February 2007): 7–23; and Brian Hindo, "Mind If I Peek at Your Paycheck?" *Business Week* (June 18, 2007): 40, 42.

32. See Patricia Sellers, "It's Good to Be the Boss," *Fortune* (October 16, 2006): 134–142; Eve Conant, "Trying to Opt Back In," *Newsweek* (May 28, 2007): 42; and Leslie Bennetts and Vivian Steir Rabin, "Open Debate: Is Staying Home with Kids Career Suicide?" *Fast Company*, no. 117 (July–August 2007): 67.

33. Ann M. Morrison and Mary Ann Von Glinow, "Women and Minorities in Management," *American Psychologist*, 45 (February 1990): 200 (emphasis added).

34. Data from Del Jones, "Women-Led Firms Lift Stock Standing," *USA Today* (December 27, 2006): 3B.

35. Data from Diane Brady, "A Little Shame Goes a Long Way," *Business Week* (April 16, 2007): 34–35; and "2006 Census: Women Board Directors," **www.catalystwomen.org.**

36. Data from "Women in Leadership," *USA Today* (June 25, 2007): 1B. Also see Diane Brady, "Where More Women Are Bosses," *Business Week* (August 20–27, 2007): 14.

37. As quoted in Rhonda Richards, "More Women Poised for Role as CEO," *USA Today* (March 26, 1996): 2B. Also see Anna Fels, "Do Women Lack Ambition?" *Harvard Business Review*, 82 (April 2004): 50–60; and Matt Krantz, "More Women Take CFO Roles," *USA Today* (October 13, 2004): 3B.

38. Based on Michelle K. Ryan and S. Alexander Haslam, "The Glass Cliff: Exploring the Dynamics Surrounding the Appointment of Women to Precarious Leadership Positions," *Academy of Management Review*, 32 (April 2007): 549–572.

39. **www.sba.gov,** FAQ no. 27. Accessed August 7, 2007.

40. For specifics, see Stephanie Armour, "Minority Job Losses Shrink Gains Made in '90s," *USA Today* (January 14, 2002): 1B.

41. See Michelle Conlin and Aaron Bernstein, "Working . . . and Poor," *Business Week* (May 31, 2004): 58–68; Louise Marie Roth, "Women on Wall Street: Despite Diversity Measures, Wall Street Remains Vulnerable to Sex Discrimination Charges," *Academy of Management Perspectives*, 21 (February 2007): 24–35; and Stephanie Armour, "English-Only Workplaces Lead to Discrimination Suits," *USA Today* (May 7, 2007): 4B.

42. Data from Kathryn Tyler, "Making the Transition," *HR Magazine*, 49 (October 2004): 97–102.

43. Gene Koretz, "Taking Stock of the Flexible Work Force," *Business Week* (July 24, 1989): 12.

44. Data from Todd J. Thorsteinson, "Job Attitudes of Part-Time vs. Full-Time Workers: A Meta-Analytic Review," *Journal of Occupational and Organizational Psychology*, 76 (June 2003): 151–177.

45. See Martha Frase-Blunt, "Short-Term Executives," *HR Magazine*, 49 (June 2004): 110–114; and Lin Grensing-Pophal, "Committing to Part-Timers," *HR Magazine*, 52 (April 2007): 84–88.

46. Sue Kirchhoff and Barbara Hagenbaugh, "Immigration: A Fiscal Boon or Financial Strain?" *USA Today* (January 22, 2004): 2B.

47. Haya El Nasser and Brad Heath, "Hispanic Growth Extends Eastward," *USA Today* (August 9, 2007): 1A.

48. Tamara Henry, "Societal Shifts Could Alter Education by Midcentury," *USA Today* (February 26, 2001): 6D.

49. Data from Kate Bonamici, "Going Long on Latinos," *Fortune* (February 23, 2004): 153; and Brian Grow, "Hispanic Nation," *Business Week* (March 15, 2004): 58–70.

50. Data from Eamon Javers, "The Divided States of America," *Business Week* (April 16, 2007): 67; and Chris Hawley, "For Many Mexicans, Migration is a Two-Way Street," *USA Today* (July 26, 2007): 9A.

51. Data from Del Jones, "Setting Diversity's Foundation in the Bottom Line," *USA Today* (October 15, 1996): 4B.

52. See Haya El Nasser, "American Muslims Reject Extremes," *USA Today* (May 23, 2007): 1A–2A; and Lisa Miller, "American Dreamers," *Newsweek* (July 30, 2007): 24–33.

53. For more, see David A. Thomas, "Diversity as Strategy," *Harvard Business Review*, 82 (September 2004): 98–108; Robert Rodriguez, "Diversity Finds Its Place," *HR Magazine*, 51 (August 2006): 56–61; Ann Pomeroy, "Cultivating Female Leaders," *HR Magazine*, 52 (February 2007): 44–50; and Margery Weinstein, "Diversity Dilemma," *Training*, 44 (July–August 2007): 10.

54. See Bill Leonard, "Transgender Issues Test Diversity Limits," *HR Magazine*, 52 (June 2007): 32–34; and Rebecca R. Hastings, "The Forgotten Minority," *HR Magazine*, 52 (July 2007): 62–67.

55. As quoted in Jack McDevitt, "Are We Becoming a Country of Haters?" *USA Today* (September 2, 1992): 9A. Also see Leslie C. Aguilar, *Ouch! That Stereotype Hurts: Communicating Respectfully in a Diverse World* (Dallas: The Walk the Talk Company, 2006): and Loriann Roberson and Carol T. Kulik, "Stereotype Threat at Work," *Academy of Management Perspectives*, 21 (May 2007): 24–40.

56. Adapted from Sheryl Hilliard Tucker and Kevin D. Thompson, "Will Diversity = Opportunity + Advancement for Blacks?" *Black Enterprise*, 21 (November 1990): 50–60; and Lee Gardenswartz and Anita Rowe, "Important Steps for Implementing Diversity Training," *Mosaics*, 8 (July–August 2002): 5.

57. Research support can be found in Joseph J. Martocchio, "Age-Related Differences in Employee Absenteeism: A Meta-Analysis," *Psychology and Aging*, 4 (December 1989): 409–414.

58. Douglas T. Hall and Victoria A. Parker, "The Role of Workplace Flexibility in Managing Diversity," *Organizational Dynamics*, 22 (Summer 1993): 8.

59. Christopher Rugaber, "Google Uses Trade Tactic in Censorship Fight," *Arizona Republic* (June 24, 2007): D3. Also see Richard S. Dunham, "Excuse Me, Mr. Chairman," *Business Week* (February 12, 2007): 11; Laura Petrecca, "VW Reviews Complaints, Pulls Ad After All," *USA Today* (February 16, 2007): 1B; and Mike Hofman, "Legal Lemons, PR Lemonade," *Inc.*, 29 (June 2007): 25–26.

60. Steven L. Wartick and Robert E. Rude, "Issues Management: Corporate Fad or Corporate Function?" *California Management Review*, 29 (Fall 1986): 124–140. Also see "The Top Five Legal Challenges for Business Leaders," Special Advertising Section, *Fortune* (May 14, 2007): S1–S27; Diane Cadrain, "Setting the Records Straight," *HR Magazine*, 52 (June 2007): 82–86; Diane Cadrain, "Don't Let Dormant Policies Lie," *HR Magazine*, 52 (July 2007): 74–77; and Michael Orey, "In-House Attorneys, Watch Your Step," *Business Week* (August 6, 2007): 36.

61. See, for example, John Ritter, "California Tries to Slam Lid on Big Boxed Wal-Mart," *USA Today* (March 2, 2004): 1B–2B; Stephanie Armour, "'Rife with Discrimination,'" *USA Today* (June 24, 2004): 3B; and Cora Daniels, "Wal-Mart's Women Problem," *Fortune* (July 12, 2004): 28. Also see Robert Berner, "My Year at Wal-Mart," *Business Week* (February 12, 2007): 70–74.

62. Emily Kaiser, "Wal-Mart Looks to Reputation," *USA Today* (September 9, 2004): 5B. For updates, see Jon Birger,

"The Unending Woes of Lee Scott," *Fortune* (January 22, 2007): 118–122; and Anthony Bianco, "Wal-Mart's Midlife Crisis," *Business Week* (April 30, 2007): 46–56.

63. Based on Jim Hopkins, "Wal-Mart Widens Political Reach, Giving Primarily to GOP," *USA Today* (February 3, 2004): 1B.

64. David B. Yoffie and Mary Kwak, "Playing by the Rules," *Harvard Business Review*, 79 (June 2001): 119–120.

65. Drawn from S. Prakash Sethi, "Serving the Public Interest: Corporate Political Action for the 1980s," *Management Review*, 70 (March 1981): 8–11. Also see David J. Dent, "Hands On: Playing Politics," *Inc.*, 26 (September 2004): 29–30.

66. Based on James Mehring, "Soft Money's Flabby Return," *Business Week* (April 26, 2004): 30.

67. Michelle Kessler, "Techies Plug In to Capitol Hill Power," *USA Today* (June 23, 2004): 1B.

68. Data from Olga Kharif, "Tearing Down the Wireless Fortress," *Business Week* (August 13, 2007): 52–53.

69. Conrad Wilson, "Shopper Without a Cause," *Business Week* (July 9–16, 2007): 14.

70. Christopher Palmeri, "E-Advocacy: How to Make a Corporate Cause Click," *Business Week* (January 12, 2004): 14.

71. Sandra Sobiera, "Bush Signs Corporate Fraud Crackdown Bill," **www.azcentral.com** (July 31, 2002): 1. Also see David Henry, "Not Everyone Hates SarbOx," *Business Week* (January 29, 2007): 37; Dan R. Dalton and Catherine M. Dalton, "Sarbanes-Oxley and the Guidelines of the Listing Exchanges: What Have We Wrought?" *Business Horizons*, 50 (March–April 2007): 93–100; Ann Pomeroy, "Costs Dropping for Compliance with Sarbanes-Oxley Section 404," *HR Magazine*, 52 (July 2007): 12; and Joseph Weber, "SarbOx Isn't Really Driving Stocks Away," *Business Week* (July 2, 2007): 87.

72. Drawn from Nicholas Varchaver, "Long Island Confidential," *Fortune* (November 27, 2006): 172–186. Also see Bob Johnson, "Scrushy Gets Nearly 7 Years in Prison," *USA Today* (June 29, 2007): 2B; and Leslie Cauley, "Rigas Tells His Side of the Adelphia Story," *USA Today* (August 6, 2007): 1B–2B.

73. Based on "China Executes the Former Director of Food, Drug Safety," *USA Today* (July 11, 2007): 11A.

74. Michelle Conlin, "If the Pardon Doesn't Come Through . . . ," *Business Week* (April 2, 2001): 64–65. Also see Geoffrey Colvin, "White-Collar Crooks Have No Idea What They're in For," *Fortune* (July 26, 2004): 60.

75. Lawyer and survey data from Del Jones, "Lawyers, Wannabes on the Rise," *USA Today* (December 26, 2003): 5B.

76. Roger Parloff, "Is Fat the Next Tobacco?" *Fortune* (February 3, 2003): 52.

77. See Michael Orey, "How Business Trounced the Trial Lawyers," *Business Week* (January 8, 2007): 44–50.

78. Marianne M. Jennings and Frank Shipper, *Avoiding and Surviving Lawsuits* (San Francisco: Jossey-Bass, 1989), p. 118 (emphasis added).

79. John R. Allison, "Easing the Pain of Legal Disputes: The Evolution and Future of Reform," *Business Horizons*, 33 (September–October 1990): 15. For more, see Michael Orey, "Arbitration Aggravation," *Business Week* (April 30, 2007): 38–39.

80. Jeannine Aversa, "Financing Isn't Their Strong Subject," *Arizona Republic* (April 4, 2004): D7.

81. U.S. Bureau of Labor Statistics, "Tomorrow's Jobs," *Occupational Outlook Handbook*, 2006–2007 Edition, **www.bls.gov.** Also see Michael Arndt, "The Heavy Duty of the Factory Man," *Business Week* (August 20–27, 2007): 75–76.

82. Data from 1998–1999 *Occupational Outlook Handbook*, **www.bls.gov.** Also see Steve Hamm, "The Changing Talent Game," *Business Week* (August 20–27, 2007): 68–71.

83. Paul A. Samuelson, *Economics*, 10th ed. (New York: McGraw-Hill, 1976), p. 253. Also see Robert J. Samuelson, "The Upside of Recession?" *Newsweek* (April 30, 2007): 53; and Christopher Farrell, "Bubbles: Bring 'Em On," *Business Week* (June 11, 2007): 84.

84. Russ Wiles, "Market Fundamentals Still Appear Strong," *Arizona Republic* (July 29, 2007): D4.

85. Darrell Rigby, "Moving Upward in a Downturn," *Harvard Business Review*, 79 (June 2001): 100. Also see Amitabh S. Raturi and Eric P. Jack, "Creating a Volume-Flexible Firm," *Business Horizons*, 47 (November–December 2004): 69–78.

86. "Fast Talk," *Fast Company*, no. 82 (May 2004): 64.

87. Daniel Gross, "The Revenge of the Business Cycle," *Fortune* (July 26, 2004): 58.

88. For an informative discussion of the value of economic forecasting, see Peter L. Bernstein and Theodore H. Silbert, "Are Economic Forecasters Worth Listening To?" *Harvard Business Review*, 62 (September–October 1984): 32–40.

89. Lawrence S. Davidson, "Knowing the Unknowable," *Business Horizons*, 32 (September–October 1989): 7.

90. Drawn from Jeffrey M. O'Brien, "Wii Will Rock You," *Fortune* (June 11, 2007): 82–92. Also see Elizabeth Weise, "Buying American? It's Not in the Bag," *USA Today* (July 11, 2007): 1D–2D.

91. John Naisbitt and Patricia Aburdene, *Megatrends 2000* (New York: William Morrow, 1990), p. 21. Also see Michael Arndt, "Smog Across the Waters," *Business Week* (April 9, 2007): 10.

92. Nokia (Finland), Lego (Denmark), Samsung (Korea), Ericsson (Sweden), and Adidas (Germany). In a survey of 1,000 American college students, only 4.4 percent had the correct answer for Nokia (53.6 percent said Japan). Correct answers for the other four brands, respectively, were 8.4 percent, 9.8 percent, 9.9 percent, and 12.2 percent.

93. Thomas A. Stewart, "Welcome to the Revolution," *Fortune* (December 13, 1993): 67. Also see Sheridan Prasso, "China's New Cultural Revolution," *Fortune* (May 28, 2007): 90–96; and Sharon Silke Carty, "Big 3's Reign over Auto Sales Nears End," *USA Today* (July 6, 2007): 1B.

94. Michael J. Mandel, "From America: Boom—and Bust," *Business Week* (January 28, 2002): 26.

95. Data from **www.chips.org.**

96. Global data from Telis Demos, "The World's Largest Corporations," *Fortune* (July 23, 2007): 133, 143. U.S. data and quote from **www.toyota.com.** For more on Toyota, see Charles Fishman, "No Satisfaction," *Fast Company*, no. 111 (January 2007): 82–92; Alex Taylor III, "America's Best Car Company," *Fortune* (March 19, 2007): 98–104, and David Welch, "Staying Paranoid at Toyota," *Business Week* (July 2, 2007): 80–82.

97. Del Jones, "Foreign Firms Snap Up U.S. Rivals," *USA Today* (March 7, 2001): 6B.

98. Jerome B. Wiesner, "Technology and Innovation," in *Technological Innovation and Society*, ed. Dean Morse and Aaron W. Warner (New York: Columbia University Press, 1966), p. 11.

99. Walter Kiechel III, "How We Will Work in the Year 2000," *Fortune* (May 17, 1993): 39. Also see Jay Greene, "Where PCs Were Born," *Business Week* (February 26, 2007): 110.

100. For good reading on innovation, see Scott D. Anthony, Matt Eyring, and Lib Gibson, "Mapping Your Innovation Strategy," *Harvard Business Review*, 84 (May 2006): 104–113; Oliver Ryan et al., "Innovators at the Gate," *Fortune* (May 14, 2007): 73–80; Satish Nambisan and Mohanbir Sawhney, "A Buyer's Guide to the Innovation Bazaar," *Harvard Business Review*, 85 (June 2007): 109–118; Morten T. Hansen and Julian Birkinshaw, "The Innovation Value Chain," *Harvard Business Review*, 85 (June 2007): 121–130; and Scott Berkun, *The Myths of Innovation* (Sebastopol, CA.: O'Reilly Media, 2007).

101. Pete Engardio, "Scouring the Planet for Brainiacs," *Business Week* (October 11, 2004): 102.

102. Brian Dumaine, "Closing the Innovation Gap," *Fortune* (December 2, 1991): 57.

103. Bill Breen, "The Thrill of Defeat," *Fast Company*, no. 83 (June 2004): 77 (emphasis added).

104. Based on Stratford Sherman, "When Laws of Physics Meet Laws of the Jungle," *Fortune* (May 15, 1995): 193–194.

105. As quoted in Jefferson Graham, "Apple, AT&T CEOs See iPhone as Industry Game-Changer," *USA Today* (June 29, 2007): 6B.

106. David Whitford, "A Human Place to Work," *Fortune* (January 8, 2001): 110. Also see Michael Arndt, "3M: A Lab for Growth?" *Business Week* (January 21, 2002): 50–51.

107. Robert J. Herbold, "Inside Microsoft: Balancing Creativity and Discipline," *Harvard Business Review*, 80 (January 2002): 73–74.

108. Gifford Pinchot III, *Intrapreneuring* (New York: Harper & Row, 1985), p. xvii. Also see R. Duane Ireland and Justin W. Webb, "Strategic Entrepreneurship: Creating Competitive Advantage Through Streams of Innovation," *Business Horizons*, 50 (January–February 2007): 49–59.

109. Tim Smart, "Kathleen Synnott: Shaping the Mailrooms of Tomorrow," *Business Week* (November 16, 1992): 66.

110. Vince Luchsinger and D. Ray Bagby, "Entrepreneurship and Intra-preneurship: Behaviors, Comparisons, and Contrasts," *SAM Advanced Management Journal*, 52 (Summer 1987): 12. For intrapreneurs in action, see Christine Canabou, "Free to Innovate," *Fast Company*, no. 52 (November 2001): 60–62.

CHAPTER 4

1. **Opening Quote:** As quoted in Saren Starbridge, "Anita Roddick: Fair Trade," *Living Planet*, 3 (Spring 2001): 92.

2. See Laura D'Andrea Tyson, "A Resilient World Economy," *Business Week* (March 19, 2007): 108; Steve Hamm, "Children of the Web," *Business Week* (July 2, 2007): 50–58; and Cora Daniels, "Fast Talk: Olympic Trials: Going for China's Gold," *Fast Company*, no. 118 (September 2007): 27–34.

3. *Wall Street Journal*, from Marcus W. Brauchli, "Echoes of the Past," (September 26, 1996): R24. Wall Street Journal. Eastern Edition [only staff-produced materials may be used] by Marcus Brauchli. Copyright © 1996 by Dow Jones & Co., Inc. Reproduced with permission of Dow Jones & Co. Inc. in the format Textbook via Copyright Clearance Center. Also see Fareed Zakaria, "How Long Will America Lead the World?" *Newsweek* (June 12, 2006):

40–45; Jack Welch and Suzy Welch, "Who Will Rule the 21st Century?" *Business Week* (July 2, 2007): 112; and Jack Welch and Suzy Welch, "Don't Count Brand America Out," *Business Week* (August 6, 2007): 96.

4. Aaron Pressman, "Fished Out," *Business Week* (September 4, 2006): 60.

5. Data from "Snapshots of the Next Century," *Business Week: 21st Century Capitalism* (Special Issue, 1994): 194 and World Trade Organization, "International Trade Statistics 2006," **www.wto.org,** accessed August 16, 2007. Also see Rik Kirkland, "The Greatest Economic Boom Ever," *Fortune* (July 23, 2007): 120–128.

6. For specifics, see Dexter Roberts and Pete Engardio, "Secrets, Lies, and Sweatshops," *Business Week* (November 27, 2006): 50–58; Peggy E. Chaudhry, "Changing Levels of Intellectual Property Rights Protection for Global Firms: A Synopsis of Recent U.S. and EU Trade Enforcement Strategies," *Business Horizons*, 49 (November–December 2006): 463–472; David J. Lynch, "U.S. Trade Deficit Hits New High for Fifth Year in a Row," *USA Today* (February 14, 2007): 2B; Michael Mandel, "The Real Cost of Offshoring," *Business Week* (June 18, 2007): 28–34; Pete Engardio, Dexter Roberts, Frederik Balfour, and Bruce Einhorn, "Broken China," *Business Week* (July 23, 2007): 38–45; and Anne D'Innocenzio, "Mattel to Recall Toy from China," *USA Today* (August 14, 2007): 1B.

7. "Going Global," *Inc.*, 29 (April 2007): 88. Also see Gail Edmondson, "The Race to Build Really Cheap Cars," *Business Week* (April 23, 2007): 44–48.

8. Nancy J. Adler with Allison Gundersen *International Dimensions of Organizational Behavior*, 5th ed. (Mason, Ohio: Thomson South-Western, 2008), p. 5.

9. See Jack Stack with Bo Burlingham, "My Awakening," *Inc.*, 29 (April 2007): 92–97; Ian Bremmer, "How to Calculate Political Risk," *Inc.*, 29 (April 2007): 99–101; Nitasha Tiku, "How to Get Started," *Inc.*, 29 (April 2007): 107–110; and David Kirkpatrick, "How Microsoft Conquered China," *Fortune* (July 23, 2007): 78–84.

10. This six-step sequence is based on Alan M. Rugman, "A New Theory of the Multinational Enterprise: Internationalization versus Internalization," *Columbia Journal of World Business*, 15 (Spring 1980): 23–29.

11. See Sandra Mottner and James P. Johnson, "Motivations and Risks in International Licensing: A Review and Implications for Licensing to Transitional and Emerging Economies," *Journal of World Business*, 35 (Summer

2000): 171–188; and Thomas Y. Choi, Jaroslaw Budny, and Norbert Wank, "Intellectual Property Management: A Knowledge Supply Chain Perspective," *Business Horizons*, 47 (January–February 2004): 37–44.

12. Data from "Chip Licensing Deal," *USA Today* (November 27, 1996): 1B.

13. For related discussion, see James Bamford, David Ernst, and David G. Fubini, "Launching a World-Class Joint Venture," *Harvard Business Review*, 82 (February 2004): 90–100; Donald Gerwin, "Coordinating New Product Development in Strategic Alliances," *Academy of Management Review*, 29 (April 2004): 241–257; and Lourdes Urriolagoitia and Marcel Planellas, "Sponsorship Relationships as Strategic Alliances: A Life Cycle Model Approach," *Business Horizons*, 50 (March–April 2007): 157–166.

14. Chris Woodyard, "Honda, GE Build New Jet Engine," *USA Today* (February 17, 2004): 1B.

15. Jeremy Main, "Making Global Alliances Work," *Fortune* (December 17, 1990): 121–126.

16. Adapted from Ibid. and David Lei and John W. Slocum Jr., "Global Strategic Alliances: Payoffs and Pitfalls," *Organizational Dynamics*, 19 (Winter 1991): 44–62. Also see Srilata Zaheer and Akbar Zaheer, "Trust Across Borders," *Journal of International Business Studies*, 37 (January 2006): 21–29; Stewart Johnston and John W. Selsky, "Duality and Paradox: Trust and Duplicity in Japanese Business Practice," *Organization Studies*, 27 (February 2006): 183–205; and Yadong Luo, "The Independent and Interactive Roles of Procedural, Distributive, and Interactional Justice in Strategic Alliances," *Academy of Management Journal*, 50 (June 2007): 644–664.

17. See Brian Bremner, "Japan: A Tale of Two Mergers," *Business Week* (May 10, 2004): 42; and Jeffrey H. Dyer, Prashant Kale, and Harbir Singh, "When to Ally and When to Acquire," *Harvard Business Review*, 82 (July–August 2004): 108–115.

18. Joan Warner, "The World Is Not Always Your Oyster," *Business Week* (October 30, 1995): 132. Also see Ping Deng, "Outward Investment by Chinese MNCs: Motiva-tions and Implications," *Business Horizons*, 47 (May–June 2004): 8–16.

19. For example, see David Welch, "Why Toyota Is Afraid of Being Number One," *Business Week* (March 5, 2007): 42–50. Also see Tieying Yu and Albert A. Cannella Jr., "Rivalry Between Multinational Enterprises: An Event History Approach," *Academy of Management Journal*, 50 (June 2007): 665–686.

20. Based on Fons Trompenaars and Charles Hampden-Turner, *Riding the*

Waves of Culture: Understanding Cultural Diversity in Global Business, 2nd ed. (New York: McGraw-Hill, 1998), pp. 191–192; Marie-Claude Boudreau, Karen D. Loch, Daniel Robey, and Detmar Straud, "Going Global: Using Information Technology to Advance the Competitiveness of the Virtual Transnational Organization," *Academy of Management Executive*, 12 (November 1998): 120–128; and Anil K. Gupta and Vijay Govindarajan, "Converting Global Presence into Global Competitive Advantage," *Academy of Management Executive*, 15 (May 2001): 45–56.

21. Stanley Reed, "Busting Up Sweden Inc.," *Business Week* (February 22, 1999): 52, 54. For another example, see Sophie Hares, "'Unmistakably Australian' News Corp. Moves to NYC," *USA Today* (April 7, 2004): 6B.

22. For exwmple, see Mary Carmichael, "Troubled Waters," *Newsweek* (June 4, 2007): 52–56.

23. "Amidst Stiffer International Competition, U.S. Managers Need a Broader Perspective," *Management Review*, 69 (March 1980): 34.

24. P. Christopher Earley and Elaine Mosakowski, "Toward Culture Intelligence: Turning Cultural Differences into a Workplace Advantage," *Academy of Management Executive*, 18 (August 2004): 155. Also see the cultural intelligence exercise on page 143 of P. Christopher Earley and Elaine Mosakowski, "Cultural Intelligence," *Harvard Business Review*, 82 (October 2004): 139–146.

25. Howard V. Perlmutter, "The Tortuous Evolution of the Multinational Corporation," *Columbia Journal of World Business*, 4 (January–February 1969): 11. Also see Malika Richards and Michael Y. Hu, "U.S. Subsidiary Control in Malaysia and Singapore," *Business Horizons*, 46 (November–December 2003): 71–76.

26. Perlmutter and a colleague later added "regiocentric attitude" to their typology. Such an attitude centers on a regional identification (North America, Europe, and Asia, for example). See David A. Heenan and Howard V. Perlmutter, *Multinational Organization Development* (Reading, Mass.: Addison-Wesley, 1979).

27. Drawn from Brian Dumaine, "The New Turnaround Champs," *Fortune* (July 16, 1990): 36–44.

28. See Amy Borrus, "Can Japan's Giants Cut the Apron Strings?" *Business Week* (May 14, 1990): 105–106.

29. See Andrea Coombes, "Fluency in Foreign Language Called Plus for Workers," *Arizona Republic* (January 18, 2004): D1; Brian Grow, "Hispanic Nation," *Business Week* (March 15, 2004): 58–70;

Kathryn Tyler, "Financial Fluency," *HR Magazine*, 51 (July 2006): 76–81; Andrea Stone, "More Officials in Midwest, South Adding Spanish Lessons to Training," *USA Today* (December 26, 2006): 1A; and Stephanie Armour, "English-Only Workplaces Lead to Discrimination Suits," *USA Today* (May 7, 2007): 4B.

30. Julia Lieblich, "If You Want a Big, New Market . . . ," *Fortune* (November 21, 1988): 181. Population update from U.S. Census Bureau, **www.census.gov,** accessed August 18, 2007.

31. Perlmutter, "The Tortuous Evolution of the Multinational Corporation," p. 16.

32. Andrew Johnson, "Forces of Globalization Intrigue Policy Scholar," *Arizona Republic* (December 10, 2006): D2.

33. Data from Telis Demos, "The World's Largest Corporations," *Fortune* (July 23, 2007): 143.

34. Jack Ewing, "Siemens' Culture Clash," *Business Week* (January 29, 2007): 43.

35. Arvind V. Phatak and Mohammed M. Habib, "The Dynamics of International Business Negotiations," *Business Horizons*, 39 (May–June 1996): 34.

36. For more, see Adler with Gundersen, *International Dimensions of Organizational Behavior*, pp. 18–68; and Georgia T. Chao and Henry Moon, "The Cultural Mosaic: A Metatheory for Understanding the Complexity of Culture," *Journal of Applied Psychology*, 90 (November 2005): 1128–1140.

37. As quoted in "How Cultures Collide," *Psychology Today*, 10 (July 1976): 69.

38. Trompenaars and Hampden-Turner, *Riding the Waves of Culture*, p. 3.

39. Ronald Inglehart and Wayne E. Baker, "Modernization's Challenge to Traditional Values: Who's Afraid of Ronald McDonald?" *The Futurist*, 35 (March–April 2001): 18, 21. Also see Robert Levine, "Spoils of Warcraft," *Fortune* (March 19, 2007): 151–156; Jason Bush, "Mouse Ears Over Moscow," *Business Week* (June 11, 2007): 42; and William J. Holstein, "Why Wal-Mart Can't Find Happiness in Japan," *Fortune* (August 6, 2007): 73–78.

40. Drawn from "Maine Hospital Open to Gown Redesign," *USA Today* (August 18, 2004): 12B.

41. See "How Cultures Collide," pp. 66–74, 97; Edward T. Hall, *The Hidden Dimension* (Garden City, N.Y.: Doubleday, 1996); and Mary Munter, "Cross-Cultural Communication for Managers," *Business Horizons*, 36 (May–June 1993): 69–78.

42. See Sheridan Prasso, "China's New Cultural Revolution," *Fortune* (May 28, 2007): 90–96; and Stanley Reed, "The Master Builder of the Middle East," *Business Week* (July 2, 2007): 48–49.

43. Ronald E. Dulek, John S. Fielden, and John S. Hill, "International

Communication: An Executive Primer," *Business Horizons*, 34 (January–February 1991): 21.

44. For example, see Robert House, Mansour Javidan, Paul Hanges, and Peter Dorfman, "Understanding Cultures and Implicit Leadership Theories Across the Globe: An Introduction to Project GLOBE," *Journal of World Business*, 37 (Spring 2002): 3–10; Robert J. House, Paul J. Hanges, Mansour Javidan, Peter W. Dorfman, and Vipin Gupta, eds., *Culture, Leadership, and Organizations: The GLOBE Study of 62 Societies* (Thousand Oaks, Calif.: Sage, 2004); Jiing-Lih Farh, Rick D. Hackett, and Jian Liang, "Individual-Level Cultural Values as Moderators of Perceived Organizational Support-Employee Outcome Relationships in China: Comparing the Effects of Power Distance and Traditionality," *Academy of Management Journal*, 50 (June 2007): 715–729; and Mansour Javidan, "Forward-Thinking Cultures," *Harvard Business Review*, 85 (July–August 2007): 20.

45. For more, see Mansour Javidan and Robert J. House, "Cultural Acumen for the Global Manager: Lessons from Project GLOBE," *Organizational Dynamics*, 29 (Spring 2001): 289–305.

46. This list is based on Edward T. Hall, "The Silent Language in Overseas Business," *Harvard Business Review*, 38 (May–June 1960): 87–96; Rose Knotts, "Cross-Cultural Management: Transformations and Adaptations," *Business Horizons*, 32 (January–February 1989): 29–33; and Adler with Gundersen, *International Dimensions of Organizational Behavior*, pp. 22–62.

47. For related research, see Markus Kemmelmeier et al., "Individualism, Collectivism, and Authoritarianism in Seven Societies," *Journal of Cross-Cultural Psychology*, 34 (May 2003): 304–322; Shuyuan Wang and Catherine S. Tamis-LeMonda, "Do Child-Rearing Values in Taiwan and the United States Reflect Cultural Values of Collectivism and Individualism?" *Journal of Cross-Cultural Psychology*, 34 (November 2003): 629–642; and Juri Allik and Anu Realo, "Individualism-Collectivism and Social Capital," *Journal of Cross-Cultural Psychology*, 35 (January 2004): 29–49.

48. For detailed discussion, see Allen C. Bluedorn, Carol Felker Kaufman, and Paul M. Lane, "How Many Things Do You Like to Do at Once? An Introduction to Monochronic and Polychronic Time," *Academy of Management Executive*, 6 (November 1992): 17–26.

49. Michelle R. Smith, "When Play's the Thing, People are Choosing Speedier Games," Arizona Republic (March 30, 2007): D4. Also see Christopher Palmeri, "Pass Go. Collect $200. Hurry," *Business*

Week (February 19, 2007): 14. Multitasking is discussed in David H. Freedman, "Why Interruptions, Distraction, and Multitasking Are Not Such Awful Things After All," *Inc.*, 29 (February 2007): 67–68; Bruce Horovitz, "Alpha Moms Leap to Top of Trendsetters," *USA Today* (March 27, 2007): 1B–2B; and Ellen Nichols, "Hyper-Speed Managers," *HR Magazine*, 52 (April 2007): 107–110.

50. Tom Weir, "Four Days Out, Athens Confident It'll Be Ready," *USA Today* (August 9, 2004): 2A.

51. See Carol Saunders, Craig Van Slyke, and Douglas R. Vogel, "My Time or Yours? Managing Time Visions in Global Virtual Teams," *Academy of Management Executive*, 18 (February 2004): 19–31.

52. Jerry Shine, "More US Students Tackle Japanese," *Christian Science Monitor* (November 25, 1991): 14. Also see Mary Ann von Glinow, Debra L. Shapiro, and Jeanne M. Brett, "Can We *Talk*, and Should We? Managing Emotional Conflict in Multicultural Teams," *Academy of Management Review*, 29 (October 2004): 578–592; and Mary Yoko Brannen, "When Mickey Loses Face: Recontextualization, Semantic Fit, and the Semiotics of Foreignness," *Academy of Management Review*, 29 (October 2004): 593–616.

53. Kathryn Tyler, "I Say Potato, You Say *Patata*," *HR Magazine*, 49 (January 2004): 87.

54. Data from "Diverse Landscape of Newest Americans," *USA Today* (December 4, 2006): 8A; and "USA Today Snapshots: Learning the Lingo," *USA Today* (January 26, 2006): 1A.

55. See Nalini Tarakeshwar, Jeffrey Stanton, and Kenneth I. Pargament, "Religion: An Overlooked Dimension in Cross-Cultural Psychology," *Journal of Cross-Cultural Psychology*, 34 (July 2003): 377–394; Heather Johnson, "Taboo No More," *Training*, 41 (April 2004): 22–26; and Aijaz Ansari, "Buddhism Calls Many Low-Caste Indians," *Arizona Republic* (June 3, 2007): A25.

56. Based on Figure 2 in Gary Bonvillian and William A. Nowlin, "Cultural Awareness: An Essential Element of Doing Business Abroad," *Business Horizons*, 37 (November–December 1994): 44–50.

57. "Burger Boost," *USA Today* (October 11, 1995): 1B. Also see Michael Arndt, "A Misguided Beef with McDonald's," *Business Week* (May 21, 2001): 14.

58. See Peter B. Smith, "Nations, Cultures, and Individuals: New Perspectives and Old Dilemmas," *Journal of Cross-Cultural Psychology*, 35 (January 2004): 6–12.

59. Del Jones, "American CEO in Europe Blends Leadership Styles," *USA Today* (June 21, 2004): 4B.

60. See Geert Hofstede, *Culture's Consequences: Comparing Values, Behaviors, Institutions, and Organizations Across Nations*, 2nd ed. (Thousand Oaks, Calif.: Sage, 2001); Michael H. Hoppe, "An Interview with Geert Hofstede," *Academy of Management Executive*, 18 (February 2004): 75–79; John W. Bing, "Hofstede's Consequences: The Impact of His Work on Consulting and Business Practices," *Academy of Management Executive*, 18 (February 2004): 80–87; Harry C. Triandis, "The Many Dimensions of Culture," *Academy of Management Executive*, 18 (February 2004): 88–93; Bradley L. Kirkman, Kevin B. Lowe, and Cristina B. Gibson, "A Quarter Century of *Culture's Consequences*: A Review of Empirical Research Incorporating Hofstede's Cultural Values Framework," *Journal of International Business Studies*, 37 (May 2006): 285–320.

61. An extension of Hofstede's original work can be found in Geert Hofstede and Michael Harris Bond, "The Confucius Connection: From Cultural Roots to Economic Growth," *Organizational Dynamics*, 16 (Spring 1988): 4–21. Also see Geert Hofstede, "Problems Remain, but Theories Will Change: The Universal and the Specific in 21st-Century Global Management," *Organizational Dynamics*, 28 (Summer 1999): 34–44; Sang M. Lee and Suzanne J. Peterson, "Culture, Entrepreneurial Orientation, and Global Competitiveness," *Journal of World Business*," 35 (Winter 2000): 401–416; and Ashleigh Merritt, "Culture in the Cockpit: Do Hofstede's Dimensions Replicate?" *Journal of Cross-Cultural Psychology*, 31 (May 2000): 283–301.

62. See Itzhak Harpaz, "The Importance of Work Goals: An International Perspective," *Journal of International Business Studies*, 21 (First Quarter 1990): 75–93. Also see David A. Ralston, David J. Gustafson, Priscilla M. Elsass, Fanny Cheung, and Robert H. Terpstra, "Eastern Values: A Comparison of Managers in the United States, Hong Kong, and the People's Republic of China," *Journal of Applied Psychology*, 77 (October 1992): 664–671.

63. See "Pursuit of Happiness," *Harvard Business Review*, 85 (March 2007): 22; and Jack Ewing, "Will Travel for a Job," *Business Week* (August 20–27, 2007): 78.

64. Based on discussion in Peter W. Dorfman, Paul J. Hanges, and Felix C. Brodbeck, "Leadership and Cultural Variation: The Identification of Culturally Endorsed Leadership Profiles," in Robert J. House, Paul J. Hanges, Mansour Javidan, Peter W. Dorfman, and Vipin Gupta, eds., *Culture, Leadership, and Organizations: The*

GLOBE Study of 62 Societies (Thousand Oaks, Calif.: Sage, 2004), pp. 669–719. Also see Mansour Javidan, Peter W. Dorfman, Mary Sully de Luque, and Robert J. House, "In the Eye of the Beholder: Cross Cultural Lessons in Leadership from Project GLOBE," *Academy of Management Perspectives*, 20 (February 2006): 67–90; and David A. Waldman, Mary Sully de Luque, Nathan Washburn, Robert J. House, et al., "Cultural and Leadership Predictors of Corporate Social Responsibility Values of Top Management: A GLOBE Study of 15 Countries," *Journal of International Business Studies*, 37 (November 2006): 823–837.

65. Data from Dianne H. B. Welsh, Fred Luthans, and Steven M. Sommer, "Managing Russian Factory Workers: The Impact of U.S.-Based Behavioral and Participative Techniques," *Academy of Management Journal*, 36 (February 1993): 58–79. Also see Jack Welch and Suzy Welch, "The Riddle of Russia," *Business Week* (June 11, 2007): 88.

66. Kristin Dunlap Godsey, "Thread by Thread," *Success*, 43 (April 1996): 8.

67. See Stanley Reed, "Mittal & Son," *Business Week* (April 16, 2007): 44–52; Sharon Silke Carty, "Mercedes' New Insight Was Born in the USA," *USA Today* (June 20, 2007): 3B; and Pete Engardio, "The Last Rajah," *Business Week* (August 13, 2007): 46–51.

68. "Developing Them," *Fortune* (May 28, 2007): 46. For more, see Mason A. Carpenter, Wm. Gerard Sanders, and Hal B. Gregersen, "Building Human Capital with Organizational Content: The Impact of International Assignment Experience on Multicultural Firm Performance and CEO Pay," *Academy of Management Journal*, 44 (June 2001): 493–511; and "International Experience Aids Career," *USA Today* (January 28, 2002): 1B.

69. Data from J. Stewart Black and Hal B. Gregersen, "The Right Way to Manage Expats," *Harvard Business Review*, 77 (March–April 1999): 52–63; and Gary S. Insch and John D. Daniels, "Causes and Consequences of Declining Early Departures from Foreign Assignments," *Business Horizons*, 45 (November–December 2002): 39–48.

70. Data from Robert O'Connor, "Plug the Expat Knowledge Drain," *HR Magazine*, 47 (October 2002): 101–107; and Carla Joinson, "No Returns," *HR Magazine*, 47 (November 2002): 70–77. Also see Lisa Orndorff, "Taxing Expats, Poaching Talent, E-Newsletters," *HR Magazine*, 52 (May 2007): 33.

71. Elisabeth Marx, *Breaking Through Culture Shock: What You Need to Succeed in International Business* (London: Nicholas Brealey Publishing, 2001), p. 7.

72. Based on Insch and Daniels, "Causes and Consequences of Declining Early Departures from Foreign Assignments."

73. List based on Rosalie L. Tung, "Selection and Training of Personnel for Overseas Assignments," *Columbia Journal of World Business*, 16 (Spring 1981): 68–78; and Mark E. Mendenhall, Gunter K. Stahl, Ina Ehnert, Gary Oddou, Joyce S. Osland, and Torsten M. Kuhlmann, "Evaluation Studies of Cross-Cultural Training Programs: A Review of the Literature from 1988 to 2000," in Dan Landis, Janet M. Bennett, and Milton J. Bennett, eds., *Handbook of Intercultural Training*, 3rd ed. (Thousand Oaks, Calif.: Sage, 2004), pp. 129–143. Also see Martha Frase, "Show All Employees a Wider World," *HR Magazine*, 52 (June 2007): 98–102.

74. Oliver Teves, "Filipinos Embrace the 'In' Job," *Arizona Republic* (December 6, 2003): D5.

75. See P. Christopher Earley and Randall S. Peterson, "The Elusive Cultural Chameleon: Cultural Intelligence as a New Approach to Intercultural Training for the Global Manager," *Academy of Management Learning and Education*, 3 (March 2004): 100–115.

76. Robert Moran, "Children of Bilingualism," *International Management*, 45 (November 1990): 93. Also see "Online Conversations Build Language Skills," *Training*, 42 (April 2005): 9; Tom Price, "Talk Is Cheap," *Business 2.0*, 6 (March 2005): 110, 112; Beth Wilson, "Speak the Language of Youth," *USA Today* (January 10, 2007): 8D; and Barbara De Lollis, "Travel Firms Aim to Speak Customers' Language," *USA Today* (February 12, 2007): 1B.

77. Based on Joann S. Lublin, "An Overseas Stint Can Be a Ticket to the Top," *Wall Street Journal* (January 29, 1996): B1, B5.

78. See Andrew Molinsky, "Cross-Cultural Code-Switching: The Psychological Challenges of Adapting Behavior in Foreign Cultural Interactions," *Academy of Management Review*, 32 (April 2007): 622–640.

79. See Phyllis Tharenou, "The Initial Development of Receptivity to Working Abroad: Self-Initiated International Work Opportunities in Young Graduate Employees," *Journal of Occupational and Organizational Psychology*, 76 (December 2003): 489–515.

80. Jessi Hempel, "It Takes a Village—And a Consultant," *Business Week* (September 6, 2004): 76.

81. See P. Christopher Earley, "Intercultural Training for Managers: A Comparison of Documentary and Interpersonal Methods," *Academy of Management Journal*, 30 (December 1987): 685–698. A comprehensive overview of 18 different cross-cultural training methods can be found in Table 3.3 on page 79 of Sandra M. Fowler and Judith M. Bloom, "An Analysis of Methods for Intercultural Training," in Dan Landis, Janet M. Bennett, and Milton J. Bennett, eds., *Handbook of Intercultural Training* (Thousand Oaks, Calif.: Sage, 2004), pp. 37–84.

82. An excellent resource book is J. Stewart Black, Hal B. Gregersen, and Mark E. Mendenhall, *Global Assignments: Successfully Expatriating and Repatriating International Managers* (San Francisco: Jossey-Bass, 1992). Also see Juan I. Sanchez, Paul E. Spector, and Cary L. Cooper, "Adapting to a Boundaryless World: A Developmental Expatriate Model," *Academy of Management Executive*, 14 (May 2000): 96–106; and Susan Meisinger, "Going Global: A Smart Move for HR Professionals," *HR Magazine*, 49 (March 2004): 6.

83. See Elisabeth Marx, *Breaking Through Culture Shock: What You Need to Succeed in International Business* (London: Nicholas Brealey Publishing, 2001); and Annelies E. M. van Vianen, Irene E. De Pater, Amy L. Kristof-Brown, and Erin C. Johnson, "Fitting in: Surface- and Deep-Level Cultural Differences and Expatriates' Adjustment," *Academy of Management Journal*, 47 (October 2004): 697–709.

84. See Stephenie Overman, "Mentors Without Borders," *HR Magazine*, 49 (March 2004): 83–85; and Ann Pomeroy, "Protecting Expats Around the World," *HR Magazine*, 52 (April 2007): 16.

85. See Annette B. Bossard and Richard B. Peterson, "The Repatriate Experience as Seen by American Expatriates," *Journal of World Business*, 40 (February 2005): 9–28; and Kathryn Tyler, "Retaining Repatriates," *HR Magazine*, 51 (March 2006): 97–102.

86. Data from Rosalie L. Tung, "American Expatriates Abroad: From Neophytes to Cosmopolitans," *Journal of World Business*, 33 (Summer 1998): 125–144.

87. See Rosalie L. Tung, "Female Expatriates: The Model Global Manager?" *Organizational Dynamics*, 33, no. 3 (2004): 243–253.

88. David Stauffer, "No Need for Inter-American Culture Clash," *Management Review*, 87 (January 1998): 8. Also see Arup Varma, Linda K. Stroh, and Lisa B. Schmitt, "Women and International Assignments: The Impact of Supervisor-Subordinate Relationships," *Journal of World Business*, 36 (Winter 2001): 380–388.

89. See Louisa Wah, "Surfing the Rough Sea," *Management Review*, 87 (September 1998): 25–29; and Paula M. Caligiuri and Wayne F. Cascio, "Can We Send Her There? Maximizing the Success of Western Women on Global Assignments," *Journal of World Business*, 33 (Winter 1998): 394–416.

90. See Lynette Clemetson, "Soul and Sushi," *Newsweek* (May 4, 1998): 38–41.

91. For helpful tips, see Linda K. Stroh, Arup Varma, and Stacey J. Valy-Durbin, "Why Are Women Left Home: Are They Unwilling to Go on International Assignments?" *Journal of World Business*, 35 (Fall 2000): 241–255; and Brooke Kosofsky Glassberg, "10 Questions: Do Your Homework Before a Semester Abroad," *Budget Travel*, 9 (October 2006): 36, 38.

92. For more, see Timothy Dwyer, "Localization's Hidden Costs," *HR Magazine*, 49 (June 2004): 135–144; Michelle Tsai, "Shanghai Surprises: The Perils of Opening an Office in China," *Inc.*, 29 (March 2007): 47, 51; and Calum MacLeod, "Whirlpool Spins China Challenge into Turnaround," *USA Today* (April 5, 2007): 1B–2B.

93. "Corporate Profile," **www.idg.com,** July 27, 2007.

94. Excerpted from Pat McGovern, "How to Be a Local, Anywhere," *Inc.*, 29 (April 2007): 112–114.

CHAPTER 5

1. **Opening Quote:** Stephen R. Covey, *Principle-Centered Leadership* (New York: Simon & Schuster, 1991), p. 95.

2. For good reading, see Andrew Zolli, "Business 3.0," *Fast Company*, no. 113 (March 2007): 64–69.

3. As quoted in Del Jones, "American CEO's Take on Europe," *USA Today* (August 20, 2007): 5B.

4. For an interesting look back at Rockefeller, see Jerry Useem, "Entrepreneur of the Century," *Inc.* Twentieth anniversary issue, 21 (May 18, 1999): 159–173.

5. Thomas M. Jones, "Corporate Social Responsibility Revisited, Redefined," *California Management Review*, 22 (Spring 1980): 59–60. Also see Jeb Brugmann and C. K. Prahald, "Cocreating Business's New Social Compact," *Harvard Business Review*, 85 (February 2007): 80–90; and Oliver Falck and Stephen Heblich, "Corporate Social Responsibility: Doing Well by Doing Good," *Business Horizons*, 50 (May–June 2007): 247–254.

6. For example, see W. M. Greenfield, "In the Name of Corporate Social Responsibility," *Business Horizons*, 47 (January–February 2004): 19–28.

7. Nancy R. Lockwood, "Corporate Social Responsibility: HR's Leadership Role," 2004 Research Quarterly insert, *HR Magazine*, 49 (December 2004): 2.

8. Archie B. Carroll, "Managing Ethically with Global Stakeholders: A Present and Future Challenge," *Academy of Management Executive*, 18 (May 2004): 118.

9. Ibid., pp. 117–118.

10. See Petra Christmann, "Multinational Companies and the Natural Environment: Determinants of Global Environmental Policy Standardization," *Academy of Management Journal*, 47 (October 2004): 747–760.

11. Tachi Kiuchi, "Fast Talk," *Fast Company*, no. 78 (January 2004): 64.

12. Alison Overholt, "The Good Earth," *Fast Company*, no. 77 (December 2003): 86.

13. This distinction between the economic and the socioeconomic models is based partly on discussion in Courtney C. Brown, *Beyond the Bottom Line* (New York: Macmillan, 1979), pp. 82–83.

14. See Robert J. Samuelson, "The Spirit of Adam Smith," *Newsweek* (December 2, 1996): 63; Geoffrey Colvin, "Capitalists: Savor This Moment," *Fortune* (July 24, 2000): 64; and Anthony Bianco, "The Enduring Corporation," *Business Week* (August 28, 2000): 198–204.

15. As quoted in Keith H. Hammonds, "Writing a New Social Contract," *Business Week* (March 11, 1996): 60. Also see Jack Welch and Suzy Welch, "The Real Verdict on Business," *Business Week* (June 12, 2006): 100; and Geoff Colvin, "Business Is Back!" *Fortune* (May 14, 2007): 40–48.

16. Data from "Fortune 5 Hundred Largest U.S. Corporations," *Fortune* (April 16, 2001): F1.

17. Robert Kuttner, "Enron: A Powerful Blow to Market Fundamentals," *Business Week* (February 4, 2002): 20.

18. For more, see Daniel McGinn, "The Ripple Effect," *Newsweek* (February 18, 2002): 29–32; Jayne O'Donnell and Gary Strauss, "Enron Investigator Blasts Senior Managers," *USA Today* (February 5, 2002): 1B; and John Ellis, "Life After Enron's Death," *Fast Company*, no. 56 (March 2002): 118, 120.

19. See Alfred Rappaport, "10 Ways to Create Shareholder Value," *Harvard Business Review*, 84 (September 2006): 66–77; Thomas M. Jones, Will Felps, and Gregory A. Bigley, "Ethical Theory and Stakeholder-Related Decisions: The Role of Stakeholder Culture," *Academy of Management Review*, 32 (January 2007): 137–155; John Carey, "Hugging the Tree-Huggers," *Business Week* (March 12, 2007): 66–68; and Michael L. Barnett, "Stakeholder Influence Capacity and the Variability of Financial Returns to Corporate Social Responsibility," *Academy of Management Review*, 32 (July 2007): 794–816.

20. See Jayne O-Donnell, "Wal-Mart Includes Workers, Suppliers in Environment Efforts," *USA Today* (February 2, 2007): 7B.

21. See Edward Iwata, "Businesses Grow More Socially Conscious," *USA Today* (February 14, 2007): 3B; Geoff Colvin, "The 500 Gets Religion," *Fortune* (April 30, 2007): 72; J. J. Smith, "Globally, Companies Are Giving Back," *HR Magazine*, 52 (June 2007): 30; and Ruth V. Aguilera, Deborah E. Rupp, Cynthia A. Williams, and Jyoti Ganapathi, "Putting the S Back in Corporate Social Responsibility: A Multilevel Theory of Social Change in Organizations," *Academy of Management Review*, 32 (July 2007): 836–863.

22. "Fast Talk," *Fast Company*, no. 78 (January 2004): 62.

23. These arguments have been adapted in part from Jones, "Corporate Social Responsibility Revisited," p. 61; and Keith Davis and William C. Frederick, *Business and Society: Management, Public Policy, and Ethics*, 5th ed. (New York: McGraw-Hill, 1984), pp. 28–41.

24. Davis and Frederick, *Business and Society*, p. 34. Other theories of CSR are presented in Frank Den Hond and Frank G. A. De Bakker, "Ideologically Motivated Activism: How Activist Groups Influence Corporate Social Change Activities," *Academy of Management Review*, 32 (July 2007): 901–924; Christopher Marquis, Mary Ann Glynn, and Gerald F. Davis, "Community Isomorphism and Corporate Social Action," *Academy of Management Review*, 32 (July 2007): 925–945; and John L. Campbell, "Why Would Corporations Behave in Socially Responsible Ways? An Institutional Theory of Corporate Social Responsibility," *Academy of Management Review*, 32 (July 2007): 946–967.

25. Ron Zemke, "The Confidence Crisis," *Training*, 41 (June 2004): 22. Also see Sajnicole A. Joni, "The Geography of Trust," *Harvard Business Review*, 82 (March 2004): 82–88; Ben W. Heineman, Jr., "Avoiding Integrity Land Mines," *Harvard Business Review*, 85 (April 2007): 100–108; and F. David Schoorman, Roger C. Mayer, and James H. Davis, "An Integrative Model of Organizational Trust: Past, Present, and Future," *Academy of Management Review*, 32 (April 2007): 344–354.

26. Drawn from Ian Wilson, "What One Company Is Doing About Today's Demands on Business," in *Changing Business-Society Interrelationships*, ed. George A. Steiner (Los Angeles: UCLA Graduate School of Management, 1975). Other models are presented in Homer H. Johnson, "Does It Pay to Be Good? Social Responsibility and Financial Performance," *Business Horizons*, 46 (November–December 2003): 34–40; Simon Zadek, "The Path to Corporate Responsibility," *Harvard Business Review*, 82 (December 2004): 125–132; and

27. Michael E. Porter and Mark R. Kramer, "Strategy and Society," *Harvard Business Review*, 84 (December 2006): 78–92.

28. Mike France, "The World War on Tobacco," *Business Week* (November 11, 1996): 100. Also see John Carey, "Big Tobacco Blows Some Smoke," *Business Week* (August 14, 2000): 8; Paul Raeburn, "Blowing Smoke over Ventilation," *Business Week* (May 7, 2001): 72–73; and "Camel No. 9 Being Marketed to Adult Women, Maker Says," *Arizona Republic* (May 4, 2007): D3.

28. Moira Herbst, "Selling the SUV Status Quo," *Business Week* (June 11, 2007): 16.

29. Betsy Carpenter, "Fighting for a Forgotten Forest," *U.S. News & World Report* (February 9, 2004): 60. For related reading, see Larry Kanter, "Not Playing Around: A Skateboard Company with a Mission," *Inc.*, 28 (November 2006): 83. An accommodative CSR strategy is reported in Roger Yu, "Marriott Says Trans Fats Will Check Out," *USA Today* (February 1, 2007): 1B.

30. As quoted in Abrahm Lustgarten, "Warm, Fuzzy, and Highly Profitable," *Fortune* (November 15, 2004): 194. For another proactive CSR strategy, see Jeff Nachtigal, "It's Easy and Cheap Being Green," *Fortune* (October 16, 2006): 53.

31. See Vincent Jeffries, "Virtue and the Altruistic Personality," *Sociological Perspectives*, 41, no. 1 (1998): 151–166. The case against altruism is presented in Edwin A. Locke and Terry W. Noel, "Right Problem, Wrong Solution: A Rejoinder to Mitroff's & Swanson's Call to Action," *The Academy of Management News*, 35 (October 2004): 4.

32. Based on Joseph Weber, "3M's Big Cleanup," *Business Week* (June 5, 2000): 96–98.

33. Data from Michael V. Russo and Paul A. Fouts, "A Resource-Based Perspective on Corporate Environmental Performance and Profitability," *Academy of Management Journal*, 40 (June 1997): 534–559.

34. Based on Daniel B. Turban and Daniel W. Greening, "Corporate Social Performance and Organizational Attractiveness to Prospective Employees," *Academy of Management Journal*, 40 (June 1996): 658–672. Also see Johnson, "Does It Pay to Be Good? Social Responsibility and Financial Performance"; Louis Lavelle, "Playing Fair Pays Off," *Business Week* (February 23, 2004): 14; Abrahm Lustgarten, "Lean, Mean—and Green?" *Fortune* (July 26, 2004): 210; and Alison Mackey, Tyson B. Mackey, and Jay B. Barney, "Corporate Social Responsibility and Firm Performance: Investor Preferences and Corporate Strategies," *Academy of Management Review*, 32 (July 2007): 817–835.

35. Data from "2006 U.S. Corporate Giving Stronger Than Expected," **www.afpnet.org,** July 9, 2007.

36. Louis W. Fry, Gerald D. Keim, and Roger E. Meiners, "Corporate Contributions: Altruistic or For-Profit?" *Academy of Management Journal*, 25 (March 1982): 105.

37. For complete details, see Richard E. Wokutch and Barbara A. Spencer, "Corporate Saints and Sinners: The Effects of Philanthropic and Illegal Activity on Organizational Performance," *California Management Review*, 29 (Winter 1987): 62–77.

38. Jessi Hempel and Lauren Gard, "The Corporate Givers," *Business Week* (November 29, 2004): 100. For more examples, see Kerry Capell, "Vaccinating the World's Poor," *Business Week* (April 26, 2004): 65–69; Catherine Arnst, "Why Business Should Make AIDS Its Business," *Business Week* (August 2, 2004): 78, 80; Bruce Einhorn, "Intel Inside the Third World," *Business Week* (July 9–16, 2007): 38, 40.

39. Examples are reported in Pete Engardio, "Beyond the Green Corporation," *Business Week* (January 29, 2007): 50–64; Nicholas Varchaver, "Chemical Reaction," *Fortune* (April 2, 2007): 52–58; Wolfgang Puck, "Changing Tastes," *Newsweek* (May 7, 2007): 68; and Pete Engardio and Michael Arndt, "What Price Reputation?" *Business Week* (July 9–16, 2007): 70–79.

40. As quoted in Heather Johnson, "The ROI of ROPI," *Training*, 41 (February 2004): 18. For more on corporate philanthropy, see Craig M. Sasse and Ryan T. Trahan, "Rethinking the New Corporate Philanthropy," *Business Horizons*, 50 (January–February 2007): 29–38; Dean Foust, "Charity Begins . . . Online," *Business Week* (March 5, 2007): 10; and Jia Lynn Yang, "Buffett to Gates: Spend It!" *Fortune* (March 19, 2007): 38.

41. See Jack Welch and Suzy Welch, "The High Cost of Corruption," *Business Week* (January 8, 2007): 92; and Shaker A. Zahra, Richard L. Priem, and Abdul A. Rasheed, "Understanding the Causes and Effects of Top Management Fraud," *Organizational Dynamics*, 36, no. 2 (2007): 122–139.

42. Shoshana Zuboff, "From Subject to Citizen," *Fast Company*, no. 82 (May 2004): 104.

43. Data from Karen Colteryahn and Patty Davis, "8 Trends You Need to Know Now," *Training and Development*, 58 (January 2004): 28–36.

44. An excellent resource book is LaRue Tone Hosmer, *Moral Leadership in Business* (Burr Ridge, Ill.: Irwin, 1994). Also see the entire issue of *Organizational Dynamics*, 36, no. 2 (2007).

45. See Rushworth M. Kidder, "Tough Choices: Why It's Getting Harder to Be Ethical," *The Futurist*, 29 (September–October 1995): 29–32.

46. See the five-article series on business ethics in the May 2004 issue of *Academy of Management Executive;* Terry Thomas, John R. Schermerhorn, Jr., and John W. Dienhart, "Strategic Leadership of Ethical Behavior in Business," *Academy of Management Executive*, 18 (May 2004): 56–66; Dale Buss, "Corporate Compasses," *HR Magazine*, 49 (June 2004): 127–134; and Jennifer Schramm, "Perceptions on Ethics," *HR Magazine*, 49 (November 2004): 176.

47. O. C. Ferrell and John Fraedrich, *Business Ethics: Ethical Decision Making and Cases* (Boston: Houghton Mifflin, 1991), pp. 10–11.

48. Business ethics research findings are reviewed in Phillip V. Lewis, "Defining 'Business Ethics': Like Nailing Jell-O to a Wall," *Journal of Business Ethics*, 4 (October 1985): 377–383. Also see Lawrence J. Walker and Karl H. Hennig, "Differing Conceptions of Moral Exemplarity: Just, Brave, and Caring," *Journal of Personality and Social Psychology*, 86 (April 2004): 629–647; and John B. Cullen, K. Praveen Parboteeah, and Martin Hoegl, "Cross-National Differences in Managers' Willingness to Justify Ethically Suspect Behaviors: A Test of Institutional Anomie Theory," *Academy of Management Journal*, 47 (June 2004): 411–421.

49. Del Jones, "48% of Workers Admit to Unethical or Illegal Acts," *USA Today* (April 4, 1997): 1A. Also see Ann Pomeroy, "Beware the 'Boiling Frog Syndrome,'" *HR Magazine*, 52 (May 2007): 12, 14.

50. Ibid., p. 2A.

51. Robert J. Grossman, "The Five-Finger Bonus: The Fraud Triangle at Work," *HR Magazine*, 48 (October 2003): 41. For an update on MCI, see Joseph McCafferty, "Extreme Makeover," *CFO* (July 2004): 47–52.

52. For related research and discussion, see Maurice E. Schweitzer, Lisa Ordonez, and Bambi Douma, "Goal Setting as a Motivator of Unethical Behavior," *Academy of Management Journal*, 47 (June 2004): 422–432; and Marshall Schminke, Anke Arnaud, and Maribeth Kuenzi, "The Power of Ethical Work Climates," *Organizational Dynamics*, 36, no. 2 (2007): 171–186.

53. Data from John F. Veiga, Timothy D. Golden, and Kathleen Dechant, "Why Managers Bend Company Rules," *Academy of Management Executive*, 18 (May 2004): 84–90.

54. William Rudelius and Rogene A. Buchholz, "Ethical Problems of Purchasing Managers," *Harvard Business Review*, 57 (March–April 1979): 12. Also see Alan J. Dubinsky, Eric N. Berkowitz, and William Rudelius, "Ethical Problems of Field Sales Personnel," *MSU Business Topics*, 28 (Summer 1980): 11–16; James R. Davis, "Ambiguity, Ethics, and the Bottom Line," *Business Horizons*, 32 (May–June 1989): 65–70; and "Cheating Hearts," *USA Today* (February 15, 2001): 1B.

55. Vikas Anand, Blake E. Ashforth, and Mahendra Joshi, "Business as Usual: The Acceptance and Perpetuation of Corruption in Organizations," *Academy of Management Executive*, 18 (May 2004): 51. Also see Oliver Ryan, "By the Numbers," *Fortune* (November 15, 2004): 40; and Mark A. Barnett, Fred W. Sanborn, and Andrea C. Shane, "Factors Associated with Individuals' Likelihood of Engaging in Various Minor Moral and Legal Violations," *Basic and Applied Social Psychology*, 27 (March 2005): 77–84.

56. As quoted in Del Jones, "Military a Model for Execs," *USA Today* (June 9, 2004): 4B. Also see Bill George with Peter Sims, *True North: Discover Your Authentic Leadership* (San Francisco: Jossey-Bass, 2007).

57. For inspiring reading, see John McCain, "In Search of Courage," *Fast Company*, no. 86 (September 2004): 53–56.

58. See Kevin Gibson, "Excuses, Excuses: Moral Slippage in the Workplace," *Business Horizons*, 43 (November–December 2000): 65–72.

59. See Ben Cohen and Mal Warwick, *Values-Driven Business: How to Change the World, and Have Fun* (San Francisco: Berrett-Koehler, 2006).

60. Joseph Weber, "Keeping Out of a Jam," *Business Week* (October 4, 2004): 104.

61. Michael Schrage, "I Wasn't Fired," *Fortune* (January 21, 2002): 128.

62. For a landmark treatment of values, see Milton Rokeach, *Beliefs, Attitudes, and Values* (San Francisco: Jossey-Bass, 1968), p. 124; and Milton Rokeach and Sandra J. Ball-Rokeach, "Stability and Change in American Value Priorities, 1968–1981," *American Psychologist*, 44 (May 1989): 775–784. Also see Gregory R. Maio and James M. Olson, "Values as Truisms: Evidence and Implications," *Journal of Personality and Social Psychology*, 74 (February 1998): 294–311.

63. Rokeach, *Beliefs, Attitudes, and Values*, p. 124.

64. See Rick Wartzman, "Nature or Nurture? Study Blames Ethical Lapses on Corporate Goals," *Wall Street Journal* (October 9, 1987): 27. Two other Rokeach scale studies are reported in Maris G. Martinsons and Aelita Brivins Martinsons, "Conquering Cultural Constraints to Cultivate Chinese Management Creativity and

Innovation," *Journal of Management Development*, 15, no. 9 (1996): 18–35; and Ralph A. Rodriguez, "Challenging Demographic Reductionism: A Pilot Study Investigating Diversity in Group Composition," *Small Group Research*, 29 (December 1998): 744–759. Also see Shalom H. Schwarz and Galit Sagie, "Value Consensus and Importance: A Cross-National Study," *Journal of Cross-Cultural Psychology*, 31 (July 2000): 465–497; and "Generational Truths," *Training*, 44 (June 2007): 13.

65. See Jeanne Fleming and Leonard Schwarz, "What Would You Do for Money?" *Money*, 36 (June 2007): 98–104.

66. Marc Gunther, "God & Business," *Fortune* (July 9, 2001): 58–80; and Gary R. Weaver and Bradley R. Agle, "Religiosity and Ethical Behavior in Organizations: A Symbolic Interactionist Perspective," *Academy of Management Review*, 27 (January 2002): 77–97.

67. See Edward Soule, "Managerial Moral Strategies—In Search of a Few Good Principles," *Academy of Management Review*, 27 (January 2002): 114–124.

68. Excerpted from Hosmer, *Moral Leadership in Business*, pp. 39–41. © 1994, McGraw-Hill. Reproduced with permission of The McGraw-Hill Companies.

69. See Archie B. Carroll, "In Search of the Moral Manager," *Business Horizons*, 30 (March–April 1987): 7–15. Also see Gary R. Weaver, "Ethics and Employees: Making the Connection," *Academy of Management Executive*, 18 (May 2004): 121–125.

70. Data from "The Stat," *Business Week* (December 29, 2003): 16.

71. Data from "Ethics Training a Low Priority," *USA Today* (January 29, 2004): 1B.

72. Peter Navarro, "Why Johnny Can't Lead," *Harvard Business Review*, 82 (December 2004): 17. Also see Fara Warner, "Ethics? Ask a First Grader," *Fast Company*, no. 83 (June 2004): 45; Mica Schneider, "Poor Marks for Ethics Teaching," *Business Week* (June 14, 2004): 16; and Jennifer Merritt, "Welcome to Ethics 101," *Business Week* (October 18, 2004): 90.

73. For details, see John A. Byrne, "The Best-Laid Ethics Programs . . ." *Business Week* (March 9, 1992): 67–69.

74. See Margery Weinstein, "Survey Says: Ethics Training Works," Training, 42 (November 2005): 15.

75. Based on discussion in Brad Lee Thompson, "Ethics Training Enters the Real World," *Training*, 27 (October 1990): 82–94; "Top Execs Work with Corporate Boards on Ethics Programs," *HR Magazine*, 52 (January 2007): 16; and Margery Weinstein, "Executing Ethics," *Training*, 44 (March 2007): 8.

76. For ground-breaking material on ethical advocates, see Theodore V. Purcell, "Electing an 'Angel's Advocate' to the Board," *Management Review*, 65 (May 1976): 4–11; Theodore V. Purcell, "Institutionalizing Ethics into Top Management Decisions," *Public Relations Quarterly*, 22 (Summer 1977): 15–20. Also see Dov Seidman, "The Case for Ethical Leadership," *Academy of Management Executive*, 18 (May 2004): 134–138; Robert M. Fulmer, "The Challenge of Ethical Leadership," *Organizational Dynamics*, 33, no. 3 (2004): 307–317; and Michael E. Brown, "Misconceptions of Ethical Leadership: How to Avoid Potential Pitfalls," *Organizational Dynamics*, 36, no. 2 (2007): 140–155.

77. See Linda Klebe Trevino and Michael E. Brown, "Managing to Be Ethical: Debunking Five Business Ethics Myths," *Academy of Management Executive*, 18 (May 2004): 69–81.

78. "Business's Big Morality Play," *Dun's Review* (August 1980): 56.

79. See Margaret M. Clark, "New Sentencing Guidelines to Reward Ethical Culture, Compliance Commitment," *HR Magazine*, 49 (September 2004): 28.

80. See Richard P. Nielsen, "Changing Unethical Organizational Behavior," *Academy of Management Executive*, 3 (May 1989): 123–130. Relative to the Enron case, see Wendy Zellner, "A Hero—and a Smoking-Gun Letter," *Business Week* (January 28, 2002): 34–35; and Greg Farrell and Jayne O'Donnell, "Watkins Testifies Skilling, Fastow Duped Lay, Board," *USA Today* (February 15, 2002): 1B–2B.

81. See "Former Enron Vice President Sherron Watkins on the Enron Collapse," *Academy of Management Executive*, 17 (November 2003): 119–125; Amanda Ripley and Maggie Sieger, "The Special Agent," *Time* (January 6, 2003): 34–40; Christine Dugas, "Spotlight Hits Whistle-Blower," *USA Today* (December 10, 2003): 3B; and Alan Levin, "Pa. Home-town Proud of MP Who Blew Whistle on Scandal," *USA Today* (May 10, 2004): 4A.

82. Ralph Nader, "An Anatomy of Whistle Blowing," in *Whistle Blowing*, ed. Ralph Nader, Peter Petkas, and Kate Blackwell (New York: Bantam, 1972), p. 7. For a case study of whistle-blowing, see Ralph Hasson, "Why Didn't We Know?" *Harvard Business Review*, 85 (April 2007): 33–43.

83. The federal Whistleblowers Protection Act of 1989 is discussed in David Israel and Anita Lechner, "Protection for Whistleblowers," *Personnel Administrator*, 34 (July 1989): 106. Also see Jayne O'Donnell, "It's Tough to Get a Lawsuit Heard," *USA Today* (July 29, 2004): 2B; and Maria Greco Danaher, "Internal Complaints May Support Whistle-Blower Claim," *HR Magazine*, 49 (December 2004): 108.

84. Data from Jayne O'Donnell, "$26.6M Won't Change Me, Whistle-Blower Says," *USA Today* (May 14, 2004): 2B. Also see Neil Weinberg, "The Dark Side of Whistleblowing," *Forbes* (March 14, 2005): 90–98.

85. Jayne O'Donnell, "Complainants Take Risks Unfathomable to Most," *USA Today* (July 29, 2004): 1B. Also see Bill Leonard, "Blowing Whistle on Navy Recruitment Proves Costly," *HR Magazine*, 52 (March 2007): 25, 28.

86. Adapted from Kenneth D. Walters, "Your Employees' Right to Blow the Whistle," *Harvard Business Review*, 53 (July–August 1975): 26–34, 161–162.

87. See D. Christopher Kayes, David Stirling, and Tjai M. Nielsen, "Building Organizational Integrity," *Business Horizons*, 50 (January–February 2007): 61–70; and Steven P. Feldman, "Moral Business Cultures: The Keys to Creating and Maintaining Them," *Organizational Dynamics*, 36, no. 2 (2007): 156–170.

88. For more, go to **www.focushope.edu.**

CHAPTER 6

1. **Opening Quote:** As quoted in Brent Schlender, "Peter Drucker Takes the Long View," *Fortune* (September 28, 1998): 170.

2. David Stires, "A Darker View of Starbucks," *Fortune* (November 13, 2006): 197.

3. See Darrell Rigby, "A Growing Focus on Preparedness," *Harvard Business Review*, 85 (July-August 2007): 21–22.

4. For example, see John Carey, "Shell: The Case of the Missing Oil," *Business Week* (January 26, 2004): 45–46; and Sarah Bartlett, "What We Didn't Plan For," *Inc.*, 27 (January 2005): 74–81.

5. Based on discussion in Frances J. Milliken, "Three Types of Perceived Uncertainty About the Environment: State, Effect, and Response Uncertainty," *Academy of Management Review*, 12 (January 1987): 133–143. Also see Hugh Courtney, *20/20 Foresight: Crafting Strategy in an Uncertain World* (Boston: Harvard Business School Press, 2001): chp. 2. Uncertainty and fear are discussed in Jerry Useem, "A Brief History of Fear," *Fortune* (September 3, 2007): 84–86.

6. For related reading, see Peter Coy and Jack Ewing, "Where Are All the Workers?" *Business Week* (April 9, 2007): 28–31; and Jennifer Schramm, "Coping with Tight Labor," *HR Magazine*, 52 (June 2007): 192.

7. See Raymond E. Miles and Charles C. Snow, *Organizational Strategy,*

Structure, and Process (New York: McGraw-Hill, 1978), p. 29. A validation of the Miles and Snow model can be found in Stephen M. Shortell and Edward J. Zajak, "Perceptual and Archival Measures of Miles and Snow's Strategic Types: A Comprehensive Assessment of Reliability and Validity," *Academy of Management Journal*, 33 (December 1990): 817–832. Also see the four articles accompanying David J. Ketchen, Jr., "Introduction: Raymond E. Miles and Charles C. Snow's *Organizational Strategy, Structure, and Process*," *Academy of Management Executive*, 17 (November 2003): 95–96.

8. Data from Joseph Weber, "Harley Investors May Get a Wobbly Ride," *Business Week* (February 11, 2002): 65.

9. Spencer E. Ante, "The Info Tech 100," *Business Week* (July 2, 2007): 64. For related reading about prospectors, see Fernando F. Suarez and Gianvito Lanzolla, "The Role of Environmental Dynamics in Building a First Mover Advantage Theory," *Academy of Management Review*, 32 (April 2007): 377–392; Rita Gunther McGrath and Thomas Keil, "The Value Captor's Process: Getting the Most out of Your New Business Ventures," *Harvard Business Review*, 85 (May 2007): 128–136; and Cliff Edwards, "The Road to WiMax," *Business Week* (September 3, 2007): 58–64.

10. William Boulding and Markus Christen, "First-Mover Disadvantage," *Harvard Business Review*, 79 (October 2001): 20–21 (emphasis added). Also see Jim Collins, "Best Beats First," *Inc.*, 22 (August 2000): 48–52; and Kevin Maney, "Impregnable 'First Mover Advantage' Philosophy Suddenly Isn't," *USA Today* (July 18, 2001): 3B.

11. See Thomas Stemberg, "Treat People Right and They Will Eat Nails for You, and Other Lessons I learned Building Staples into a Giant Company," *Inc.*, 29 (January 2007): 75–77; Pat Regnier, "Getting Rich in America," *Money*, 36 (July 2007): 74–77; and Chuck Salter, "Girl Power," *Fast Company*, no. 118 (September 2007): 104–112.

12. David Stires, "Rx for Investors," *Fortune* (May 3, 2004): 170. For more on analyzers, see Eric Bonabeau, "The Perils of the Imitation Age," *Harvard Business Review*, 82 (June 2004): 45–54; and Owen Thomas, "The 800-Lb. Copycat," *Business 2.0*, 5 (September 2004): 100.

13. Kevin Maney, "Kodak to Lay Off 15,000, Cut Manufacturing Capacity," *USA Today* (January 23, 2004): 4B.

14. Based on data in Ben Dobbin, "Kodak Cutting More Workers," *Arizona Republic* (January 23, 2004): D1–D2.

15. For details, see Jeffrey S. Conant, Michael P. Mokwa, and P. Rajan Varadarajan, "Strategic Types, Distinctive Marketing Competencies and Organizational Performance: A Multiple Measures Based Study," *Strategic Management Journal*, 11 (September 1990): 365–383. Also see Shaker A. Zahra and John A. Pearce II, "Research Evidence on the Miles-Snow Typology," *Journal of Management*, 16 (December 1990): 751–768.

16. See Yves L. Doz and Mikko Kosonen, "The New Deal at the Top," *Harvard Business Review*, 85 (June 2007): 98–104.

17. Based on Mary M. Crossan, Henry W. Lane, Roderick E. White, and Leo Klus, "The Improvising Organization: Where Planning Meets Opportunity," *Organizational Dynamics*, 24 (Spring 1996): 20–35.

18. See Michael Arndt, "3M's Rising Star," *Business Week* (April 12, 2004): 62–74.

19. "$1.4B Authorized to Restore Everglades," *USA Today* (December 12, 2000): 15A. For an update, see Brian Skoloff, "Water Again Flowing into Florida's Big Lake," *USA Today* (July 26, 2007): 4A.

20. Scott Adams, "Dilbert's Management Handbook," *Fortune* (May 13, 1996): 104.

21. Based on R. Duane Ireland and Michael A. Hitt, "Mission Statements: Importance, Challenge, and Recommendations for Development," *Business Horizons*, 35 (May–June 1992): 34–42. Also see V. Kasturi Rangan, "Lofty Missions, Down-to-Earth Plans," *Harvard Business Review*, 82 (March 2004): 112–119.

22. Bill Saporito, "PPG: Shiny, Not Dull," *Fortune* (July 17, 1989): 107.

23. See George Stalk, Jr. "Curveball: Strategies to Fool the Competition," *Harvard Business Review*, 84 (September 2006): 114–122.

24. Dan Sullivan, "The Reality Gap," *Inc.*, 21 (March 1999): 119.

25. Anthony P. Raia, *Managing by Objectives* (Glenview, Ill.: Scott, Foresman, 1974), p. 24.

26. For an excellent and comprehensive treatment of goal setting, see Edwin A. Locke and Gary P. Latham, *Goal Setting: A Motivational Technique That Works!* (Englewood Cliffs, N.J.: Prentice-Hall, 1984). Also see Gary P. Latham and Edwin A. Locke, "Enhancing the Benefits and Overcoming the Pitfalls of Goal Setting," *Organizational Dynamics*, 35, no. 4 (2006): 332–340.

27. John A. Byrne and Heather Timmons, "Tough Times for a New CEO," *Business Week* (October 29, 2001): 66.

28. For example, see Eric Krell, "The Best of Times," *HR Magazine*, 52 (May 2007): 48–52.

29. Raia, *Managing by Objectives*, p. 54.

30. Brian Grow, "Thinking Outside the Big Box," *Business Week* (October 25, 2004): 70.

31. Richard Koch, *The 80/20 Principle: The Secret of Achieving More with Less* (New York: Currency Doubleday, 1998), p. 4. Also see Gail Johnson, "Squeaky Wheels," *Training*, 41 (June 2004): 20.

32. Diane Brady, "Why Service Stinks," *Business Week* (October 23, 2000): 126.

33. Elizabeth Esfahani, "How to Get Tough with Bad Customers," *Business 2.0*, 5 (October 2004): 52.

34. See Barbara Moses, "The Busyness Trap," *Training*, 35 (November 1998): 38–42; "The Time Trap," *Inc.*, 26 (June 2004): 42–43; and Nanci Hellmich, "Most People Multitask, So Most People Don't Sit Down to Eat," *USA Today* (September 30, 2004): 8D.

35. See Steven Berglas, "Chronic Time Abuse," *Harvard Business Review*, 82 (June 2004): 90–97; Michael C. Mankins, "Stop Wasting Valuable Time," *Harvard Business Review*, 82 (September 2004): 58–65; Catherine Arnst, "We'll Get Around to It Later," *Business Week* (January 29, 2007): 10; and Kerry Sulkowicz, "Your Procrastinatin' Heart," *Business Week* (March 12, 2007): 18.

36. See Peter F. Drucker, *The Practice of Management* (New York: Harper & Row, 1954). For a short update on Drucker, see Thomas A. Stewart, "Effective Immediately," *Harvard Business Review*, 82 (June 2004): 10.

37. As an indication of the widespread interest in MBO, more than 700 books, articles, and technical papers had been written on the subject by the late 1970s. For a brief history of MBO, see George S. Odiorne, "MBO: A Backward Glance," *Business Horizons*, 21 (October 1978): 14–24. An excellent collection of readings on MBO may be found in George Odiorne, Heinz Weihrich, and Jack Mendleson, *Executive Skills: A Management by Objectives Approach* (Dubuque, Iowa: Wm. C. Brown, 1980). Also see Henry H. Beam, "George Odiorne," *Business Horizons*, 39 (November-December 1996): 73–76.

38. T. J. Rodgers, "No Excuses Management," *Harvard Business Review*, 68 (July–August 1990): 87, 89.

39. For related reading, see Philippe Haspeslagh, Tomo Noda, and Fares Boulos, "It's Not Just About the Numbers," *Harvard Business Review*, 79 (July–August 2001): 65–73.

40. For example, see Jan P. Muczyk and Bernard C. Reimann, "MBO as a Complement to Effective Leadership," *Academy of Management Executive*, 3 (May 1989): 131–139.

41. An interesting study of the positive and negative aspects of MBO may be found in Robert C. Ford and Frank S. McLaughlin, "Avoiding Disappointment in MBO Programs," *Human Resource Management*, 21 (Summer 1982): 44–49.

Positive research evidence is summarized in Robert Rodgers and John E. Hunter, "Impact of Management by Objectives on Organizational Productivity," *Human Resource Management*, 76 (April 1991): 322–336.

42. For a critical appraisal of MBO core assumptions, see David Halpern and Stephen Osofsky, "A Dissenting View of MBO," *Public Personnel Management*, 19 (Fall 1990): 321–330. Deming's critical comments may be found in W. Edwards Deming, *Out of the Crisis* (Cambridge, Mass.: MIT Press, 1986), pp. 23–96; and Dennis W. Organ, "The Editor's Chair," *Business Horizons*, 39 (November-December 1996): 1.

43. See Richard Babcock and Peter F. Sorensen Jr., "An MBO Check-List: Are Conditions Right for Implementation?" *Management Review*, 68 (June 1979): 59–62.

44. Robert Rodgers and John E. Hunter, "Impact of Management by Objectives on Organizational Productivity," *Journal of Applied Psychology*, 76 (April 1991): 322.

45. See Robert Rodgers, John E. Hunter, and Deborah L. Rogers, "Influence of Top Management Commitment on Management Program Success," *Journal of Applied Psychology*, 78 (February 1993): 151–155.

46. For an excellent resource book, see James P. Lewis, *Fundamentals of Project Management*, 3rd ed. (New York: AMACOM, 2007).

47. Project Management Institute, "What Is a Project?" **www.pmi.org,** p. 1.

48. Dean Foust, "Harry Potter and the Logistical Nightmare," *Business Week* (August 6, 2007): 9. Also see Karen Stewart, "Planning a Conference?" *Training*, 44 (April 2007): 31–35.

49. Louisa Wah, "Most IT Projects Prove Inefficient," *Management Review*, 88 (January 1999): 7. Also see Jennifer Gill, "Smart Questions for Your Tech Consultant," *Inc.*, 29 (January 2007): 45.

50. See Dave Zielinski, "Soft Skills, Hard Truths," *Training*, 42 (July 2005): 18–23; Ed Gash, "More Training Than Camp," *Training*, 43 (December 2006): 7; and George B. Graen, Chun Hui, and Elizabeth A. Taylor, "Experience-Based Learning About LMX Leadership and Fairness in Project Teams: A Dyadic Directional Approach," *Academy of Management Learning and Education*, 5 (December 2006): 448–460.

51. For related insights, see Martin Walfisz, Peter Zackariasson, and Timothy L. Wilson, "Real-Time Strategy: Evolutionary Game Development," *Business Horizons*, 49 (November–December 2006): 487–498.

52. See recent issues of *Project Management Journal.*

53. Excerpted from a list of 26 attributes in "4.1 Software Attributes," **www. project-manager.com.**

54. Based on Sheila Simsarian Webber and Maria T. Torti, "Project Managers Doubling as Client Account Executives," *Academy of Management Executive*, 18 (February 2004): 60–71. Also see Sheila Simsarian Webber and Richard J. Klimoski, "Client-Project Manager Engagements, Trust, and Loyalty," *Journal of Organizational Behavior*, 25 (December 2004): 997–1013.

55. Jimmie West, "Show Me the Value," *Training*, 40 (September 2003): 62.

56. See Dan Carrison, "Fueling Deadline Urgency," *HR Magazine*, 48 (December 2003): 111–115; Tammy Galvin, "Managing Projects," *Training*, 41 (January 2004): 12; and Yukika Awazu, Kevin C. Desouza, and J. Roberto Evaristo, "Stopping Runaway IT Projects," *Business Horizons*, 47 (January–February 2004): 73–80.

57. One example of the application of a flow chart is Sharon M. McKinnon, "How Important Are Those Foreign Operations? A Flow-Chart Approach to Loan Analysis," *Financial Analysts Journal*, 41 (January–February 1985): 75–78.

58. For examples of early Gantt charts, see H. L. Gantt, *Organizing for Work* (New York: Harcourt, Brace and Howe, 1919), chp. 8.

59. Gantt chart applications can be found in Conkright, "So You're Going to Manage a Project," p. 64; and Andrew Raskin, "Task Masters," *Inc.* Tech 1999, no. 1 (1999): 62–72.

60. Ivars Avots, "The Management Side of PERT," *California Management Review*, 4 (Winter 1962): 16–27.

61. Additional information on PERT can be found in Nancy Madlin, "Streamlining the PERT Chart," *Management Review*, 75 (September 1986): 67–68; Eric C. Silverberg, "Predicting Project Completion," *Research Technology Review*, 34 (May–June 1991): 46–49; Robert L. Armacost and Rohne L. Jauernig, "Planning and Managing a Major Recruiting Project," *Public Personnel Management*, 20 (Summer 1991): 115–126; T. M. Williams, "Practical Use of Distributions in Network Analysis," *Journal of the Operational Research Society*, 43 (March 1992): 265–270; and Hooshang Kuklan, "Effective Project Management: An Expanded Network Approach," *Journal of Systems Management*, 44 (March 1993): 12–16.

62. Adapted in part from John Fertakis and John Moss, "An Introduction to PERT and PERT/Cost Systems," *Managerial Planning*, 19 (January–February 1971): 24–31.

63. See "Airbus Sees End to A380 Cancellations," *USA Today* (November 24, 2006): 5B.

CHAPTER 7

1. **Opening Quote:** As quoted in Eugenia Levenson, Christopher Tkaczyk, and Jai Lynn Yang, "Indra Rising," *Fortune* (October 16, 2006): 145.

2. "Profile: Fact Sheet," **www.kraft.com,** accessed August 27, 2007.

3. For good background reading on strategic management, see W. Chan Kim and Renee Mauborgne, "Blue Ocean Strategy," *Harvard Business Review*, 82 (October 2004): 76–84; Donald L. Laurie, Yves L. Doz, and Claude P. Sheer, "Creating New Growth Platforms," *Harvard Business Review*, 84 (May 2006): 80–90; Michael A. Hitt, "Spotlight on Strategic Management," *Business Horizons*, 49 (September–October 2006): 349–352; Pankaj Ghemawat, "Managing Differences: The Central Challenge of Global Strategy," *Harvard Business Review*, 85 (March 2007): 58–68; and José Santos, "Strategy Lessons from Left Field," *Harvard Business Review*, 85 (April 2007): 20–21.

4. Data from C. Chet Miller and Laura B. Cardinal, "Strategic Planning and Firm Performance: A Synthesis of More Than Two Decades of Research," *Academy of Management Journal*, 37 (December 1994): 1649–1665.

5. Data from "U.S. Executives Cite Main Issues," *USA Today* (October 8, 2004): 1A.

6. As quoted in Ron Insana, "Dell Knows His Niche and He'll Stick with It," *USA Today* (April 5, 2004): 3B.

7. See Michael C. Mankins, "Stop Wasting Valuable Time," *Harvard Business Review*, 82 (September 2004): 58–65.

8. See the first Q&A in Jack Welch and Suzy Welch, "That's Management!" *Business Week* (February 19, 2007): 94; Natalie Mizik and Robert Jacobson, "The Cost of Myopic Management," *Harvard Business Review*, 85 (July–August 2007): 22, 24; and Henry Mintzberg, "Productivity Is Killing American Enterprise," *Harvard Business Review*, 85 (July–August 2007): 25.

9. Data from "Most Employers Don't Share Company Strategy," *USA Today* (November 15, 2006): 1B.

10. Strategy making is discussed in Michael Beer and Russell A. Eisenstat, "How to Have an Honest Conversation About Your Business Strategy," *Harvard Business Review*, 82 (February 2004): 82–89; Kwaku Atuahene-Gima and Haiyang Li, "Strategic Decision Comprehensiveness and New Product Development Outcomes in New Technology Ventures," *Academy of Management Journal*, 47 (August 2004): 583–597; and the four articles by top

executives in "Who Owns the Long Term?" *Harvard Business Review,* 85 (July–August 2007): 54–60.

11. John A. Byrne, "Strategic Planning," *Business Week* (August 26, 1996): 52.

12. Data from Joseph Weber, "Keeping Out of a Jam," *Business Week* (October 4, 2004): 104–106. Also see Ellen Florian, "Six Lessons from the Fast Lane," *Fortune* (September 6, 2004): 156.

13. Based on a definitional framework found in David J. Teece, "Economic Analysis and Strategic Management," *California Management Review,* 26 (Spring 1984): 87. An alternative view calls for supplementing the notion of "fit" with the concept of "stretch," thus better accommodating situations in which a company's aspirations exceed its present resource capabilities. See Gary Hamel and C. K. Prahalad, "Strategy as Stretch and Leverage," *Harvard Business Review,* 71 (March–April 1993): 75–84. *Rule-breaking* strategy is discussed in Dodo zu Knyphausen-Aufsess, Nils Bickhoff, and Thomas Bieger, "Understanding and Breaking the Rules of Business: Toward a Systematic Four-Step Process, *Business Horizons,* 49 (September–October 2006): 369–377.

14. Based on discussion in Donald C. Hambrick and James W. Fredrickson, "Are You Sure You Have a Strategy?" *Academy of Management Executive,* 15 (November 2001): 48–59. Also see Christian Stadler, "The 4 Principles of Enduring Success," *Harvard Business Review,* 85 (July–August 2007): 62–72.

15. See Michael A. Hitt, Barbara W. Keats, and Samuel M. DeMarie, "Navigating in the New Competitive Landscape: Building Strategic Flexibility and Competitive Advantage in the 21st Century," *Academy of Management Executive,* 12 (November 1998): 22–42. For related reading, see Richard T. Watson, Pierre Berthon, Leyland F. Pitt, and George M. Zinkhan, "Marketing in the Age of the Network: From Marketplace to U-Space," *Business Horizons,* 47 (November–December 2004): 33–40.

16. Stephen R. Covey, "Paradigm Shift," *Training,* 44 (May 2007): 48.

17. Heather Johnson, "Learn or Burn," *Training,* 41 (April 2004): 19.

18. See William R. King and David I. Cleland, *Strategic Planning and Policy* (New York: Van Nostrand Reinhold, 1978), pp. 180–183; Laura Landro, "Giants Talk Synergy But Few Make It Work," *Wall Street Journal* (September 25, 1995): B1–B2; Thomas Osegowitsch, "The Art and Science of Synergy: The Case of the Auto Industry," *Business Horizons,* 44 (March–April 2001): 17–24; and Dominic Dodd and Ken Favaro,

"Managing the Right Tension," *Harvard Business Review,* 84 (December 2006): 62–74.

19. See J. Myles Shaver, "A Paradox of Synergy: Contagion and Capacity Effects in Mergers and Acquisitions," *Academy of Management Review,* 31 (October 2006): 962–976; and Ramin Setoodeh, "Channeling Angst," *Newsweek* (May 7, 2007): 50.

20. Patricia Sellers, "P&G: Teaching an Old Dog New Tricks," *Fortune* (May 31, 2004): 168.

21. Amy Feldman, "The Tiger in Costco's Tank," *Fast Company,* no. 117 (July–August 2007): 38. For additional examples of market synergy, see Robert Berner, "At the Car Wash," *Business Week* (February 5, 2007): 12; Gary Stoller, "Avis' Newest Rental Option: Chauffeur," *USA Today* (June 4, 2007): 1B; and Michael Arndt, "A Safeway with Tablecloths," *Business Week* (July 9–16, 2007): 12.

22. "Hotels Developing Multiple Personalities," *USA Today* (September 10, 1996): 4B. For an unusual example of cost synergy, see Kerry Miller, "Four Weddings and a Funeral," *Business Week* (May 14, 2007): 18.

23. See Marc Gunther, "The End of Garbage," *Fortune* (March 19, 2007): 158–166; Mark Pagell, Zhaohui Wu, and Nagesh M. Murthy, "The Supply Chain Implications of Recycling," *Business Horizons,* 50 (March–April 2007): 133–143; and Michelle Kessler, "Tech's Green Problems," *USA Today* (July 17, 2007): 1B–2B.

24. John Porretto, "Squeezing Diesel Out of Animal Fat," *USA Today* (April 17, 2007): 9B.

25. As quoted in Max Jarman, "Freeport CEO Stays Focused on Future," *Arizona Republic* (May 27, 2007): D2.

26. See Don Moyer, "The Sin in Synergy," *Harvard Business Review,* 82 (March 2004): 131.

27. See Michael E. Porter, *Competitive Strategy* (New York: Free Press, 1980), p. 35; and Michael E. Porter, *The Competitive Advantage of Nations* (New York: Free Press, 1990), p. 39. For updates on Michael Porter, see James Surowiecki, "The Return of Michael Porter," *Fortune* (February 1, 1999): 135–138; Richard M. Hodgetts, "A Conversation with Michael E. Porter: A 'Significant Extension' Toward Operational Improvement and Positioning," *Organizational Dynamics,* 28 (Summer 1999): 24–33; and Carolin Decker and Thomas Mellewigt, "Thirty Years After Michael E. Porter: What Do We Know About Business Exit?" *Academy of Management Perspectives,* 21 (May 2007): 41–55.

28. Porter, *The Competitive Advantage of Nations,* p. 37. Also see Keith H.

Hammonds, "Michael Porter's Big Ideas," *Fast Company,* no. 44 (March 2001): 150–156.

29. For more on brands, see Dave Ulrich and Norm Smallwood, "Building a Leadership Brand," *Harvard Business Review,* 85 (July–August 2007): 92–100; Leonard M. Lodish and Carl F. Mela, "If Brands Are Built over Years, Why Are They Managed over Quarters?" *Harvard Business Review,* 85 (July–August 2007): 104–112; and David Kiley, "Best Global Brands," *Business Week* (August 6, 2007): 56–64.

30. Ron Zemke and Dick Schaaf, *The Service Edge* (New York: New American Library, 1989), p. 360. For another example of a cost leadership strategy, see Elizabeth Woyke, "Hipster Appeal, Mall Prices," *Business Week* (February 12, 2007): 68.

31. As quoted in Bruce Horovitz and Theresa Howard, "With Image Crumbling, Kmart Files Chapter 11," *USA Today* (January 23, 2002): 1B. Also see Jerry Useem, "Should We Admire Wal-Mart?" *Fortune* (March 8, 2004): 118, 120; Jack Ewing, "The Next Wal-Mart?" *Business Week* (April 26, 2004): 60–62; and Nirmalya Kumar, "Strategies to Fight Low-Cost Rivals," *Harvard Business Review,* 84 (December 2006): 104–112.

32. Adrienne Carter, "Foot Locker," *Money,* 31 (January 2002): 69.

33. See Leonard L. Berry and Kent D. Seltman, "Building a Strong Services Brand: Lessons from Mayo Clinic," *Business Horizons,* 50 (May–June 2007): 199–209.

34. For details, see Luis Ma. R. Calingo, "Environmental Determinants of Generic Competitive Strategies: Preliminary Evidence from Structured Content Analysis of *Fortune* and *Business Week* Articles (1983–1984)," *Human Relations,* 42 (April 1989): 353–369. For related research, see Praveen R. Nayyar, "Performance Effects of Three Foci in Service Firms," *Academy of Management Journal,* 35 (December 1992): 985–1009.

35. James F. Moore, *The Death of Competition: Leadership and Strategy in the Age of Business Ecosystems* (New York: HarperBusiness, 1996), p. 25. For relevant background material, see Warren Boeker, "Organizational Strategy: An Ecological Perspective," *Academy of Management Journal,* 34 (September 1991): 613–635; and James F. Moore, "Predators and Prey: A New Ecology of Competition," *Harvard Business Review,* 71 (May–June 1993): 75–86. Also see Marco Iansiti and Roy Levien, "Strategy as Ecology," *Harvard Business Review,* 82 (March 2004): 68–78.

36. See Courtney Shelton Hunt and Howard E. Aldrich, "The Second Ecology: Creation and Evolution of

Organizational Communities," in *Research in Organizational Behavior,* vol. 20, ed. Barry M. Staw and L. L. Cummings (Greenwich, Conn.: JAI Press, 1998), pp. 267–301; Peter Coy, "Sleeping with the Enemy," *Business Week* (August 21–28, 2006): 96–97; and DaeSoo Kim, "Process Chain: A New Paradigm of Collaborative Commerce and Synchronized Supply Chain," *Business Horizons,* 49 (September–October 2006): 359–367.

37. Cliff Edwards, "The Road to WiMax," *Business Week* (September 3, 2007): 60. Also see Dovev Lavie, Christoph Lechner, and Harbir Singh, "The Performance Implications of Timing of Entry and Involvement in Multipartner Alliances," *Academy of Management Journal,* 50 (June 2007): 578–604.

38. Data from Ibid., p. 62.

39. See Peter Burrows, "Welcome to Apple World," *Business Week* (July 9–16, 2007): 88–92.

40. For example, see Patrick J. Sauer, "Are You Ready for Some Football Cliches?" *Inc.,* 25 (October 2003): 96–100.

41. Moore, *The Death of Competition,* p. 61.

42. "OnStar: Competitors Can Be Partners," *Fast Company,* no. 81 (April 2004): 68.

43. For more, see Erick Schonfeld, "Web 2.0 Around the World," *Business 2.0,* 7 (August 2006): 105–109; Heather Green, "A Web That Thinks Like You," *Business Week* (July 9–16, 2007): 94–95; and Aili McConnon, "Just Ahead: The Web as a Virtual World," *Business Week* (August 13, 2007): 62–63.

44. Robert D. Hof, "The Wizard of Web Retailing," *Business Week* (December 20, 2004): 18.

45. See Stephen Baker, "Wiser About the Web," *Business Week* (March 27, 2006): 54–58; Robert D. Hof, "My Virtual Life," *Business Week* (May 1, 2006): 72–82; David Kirkpatrick, "Life in a Connected World," *Fortune* (July 10, 2006): 98–100; David Kirkpatrick, "Facebook's Plan to Hook Up the World," *Fortune* (June 11, 2007): 127–130; and Steve Hamm, "Children of the Web," *Business Week* (July 2, 2007): 50–58.

46. Based on G. T. Lumpkin and Gregory G. Dess, "E-Business Strategies and Internet Business Models: How the Internet Adds Value," *Organizational Dynamics,* 33, no. 2 (2004): 161–173. Also see Richard T. Grenci and Charles A. Watts, "Maximizing Customer Value via Mass Customized E-consumer Services," *Business Horizons,* 50 (March–April 2007): 123–132.

47. See Erick Schonfeld, "How to Manage Growth: Meg Whitman, CEO, eBay," *Business 2.0,* 5 (December 2004): 99.

48. See Des Laffey, "Paid Search: The Innovation That Changed the Web," *Business Horizons,* 50 (May–June 2007): 211–218.

49. Michael E. Porter, "Strategy and the Internet," *Harvard Business Review,* 79 (March 2001): 76.

50. Based on Leyland Pitt, Pierre Berthon, and Richard T. Watson, "Cyberservice: Taming Service Marketing Problems with the World Wide Web," *Business Horizons,* 42 (January–February 1999): 11–18; Chris Charuhas, "How to Train Web-Site Builders," *Training,* 36 (August 1999): 48–53; John R. Graham, "How Can We Get More Visitors to Our Web Site?" *Canadian Manager,* 25 (Fall 2000): 16–17; Chip Heath and Dan Heath, "Give 'em Something to Talk About," *Fast Company,* no. 116 (June 2007): 58–59; and David H. Freedman, "Shout It Out Loud: Customers Need More Data. You Have More Data. It's Time to Start Sharing," *Inc.,* 29 (August 2007): 69–70.

51. Data from Jon Swartz, "E-Tailers Ring Up a Record Holiday Week," *USA Today* (December 27, 2001): 3B. Also see Jeanette Brown, "Shoppers Are Beating a Path to the Web," *Business Week* (December 24, 2001): 41.

52. Based on Jon Swartz, "Retailers Discover Leap to Web's a Doozy," *USA Today* (December 18, 2001): 3B.

53. Based on discussion in Lorrie Grant, "Lands' End Is an Ultimate Online Model," *USA Today* (December 3, 2004): 1B–2B. For another example, see Robert Berner, "J. C. Penney Gets the Net," *Business Week* (May 7, 2007): 70.

54. See Julie Schmit, "More Pet Food Recalled After Discovery," *USA Today* (May 4, 2007): 1B; David J. Lynch, "Made in China," *USA Today* (July 3, 2007): 1B–2B; and Elizabeth Weise, "Buying American? It's Not in the Bag," *USA Today* (July 11, 2007): 1D–2D.

55. For an alternative perspective, see Mahesh Gupta, Lynn Boyd, and Lyle Sussman, "To Better Maps: A TOC Primer for Strategic Planning," *Business Horizons,* 47 (March–April 2004): 15–26. Also see Geoffrey A. Moore, "Focus on the Middle Term," *Harvard Business Review,* 85 (July–August 2007): 84–90.

56. Henry Mintzberg, "The Design School: Reconsidering the Basic Premises of Strategic Management," *Strategic Management Journal,* 11 (March–April 1990): 192. Also see Daniel P. Forbes, "Reconsidering the Strategic Implications of Decision Comprehensiveness," *Academy of Management Review,* 32 (April 2007): 361–376.

57. See Jonathan Lash and Fred Wellington, "Competitive Advantage on a Warming Planet," *Harvard Business Review,* 85 (March 2007): 95–102; and Chris Zook, "Finding Your Next Core Business," *Harvard Business Review,* 85 (April 2007): 66–75.

58. Richard F. Vancil, "Strategy Formulation in Complex Organizations," *Sloan Management Review,* 17 (Winter 1976): 18. Also see Brian J. Huffman, "Why Environmental Scanning Works Except When You Need It," *Business Horizons,* 47 (May–June 2004): 39–48; and Norm Brodsky, "The Myths About Niches," *Inc.,* 26 (August 2004): 53–54.

59. As quoted in Fred Vogelstein, "It's Not Just Business, It's Personal," *Fortune* (November 15, 2004): 200.

60. For example, see Krysten Crawford, "The BIG Opportunity," *Business 2.0,* 7 (June 2006): 94–99.

61. "Is Your Company an Extrovert?" *Management Review,* 85 (March 1996): 7.

62. Duff McDonald, "Meet eBay's New Postman," *Business 2.0,* 5 (September 2004): 52.

63. See Dave Ulrich and Norm Smallwood, "Capitalizing on Capabilities," *Harvard Business Review,* 82 (June 2004): 119–127.

64. Adapted from Andrew Bartmess and Keith Cerny, "Building Competitive Advantage Through a Global Network of Capabilities," *California Management Review,* 35 (Winter 1993): 78–103. Also see Robert L. Cardy and T. T. Selvarajan, "Competencies: Alternative Frameworks for Competitive Advantage," *Business Horizons,* 49 (May–June 2006): 235–245.

65. See David A. Thomas, "Diversity as Strategy," *Harvard Business Review,* 82 (September 2004): 98–108.

66. As quoted in Alan Webber, "The Old Economy Meets the New Economy," *Fast Company,* no. 51 (October 2001): 74. For more on strategic speed, see "Is Your Company Up to Speed?" *Fast Company,* no. 71 (June 2003): 81–86; and Hau L. Lee, "The Triple-A Supply Chain," *Harvard Business Review,* 82 (October 2004): 102–112.

67. For essential reading in this area, see Michael and James Champy, *Reengineering the Corporation: A Manifesto for Business Revolution* (New York: HarperBusiness, 1993); and James Champy, *Reengineering Management: The New Mandate for Leadership* (New York: HarperBusiness, 1995). Also see Gail L. Rein, "FEEL IT—A Method for Achieving Sustainable Process Changes," *Business Horizons,* 47 (May–June 2004): 75–81; and Daniel McGinn, "Re-engineering 2.0," *Newsweek* (November 22, 2004): 59.

68. According to Henry Mintzberg, there are four reasons why organizations need strategies: (1) to set direction, (2) to focus effort of contributors, (3) to define the organization, and (4) to provide consistency. For more, see Henry Mintzberg, "The Strategy Concept II: Another Look at Why Organizations Need Strategies," *California Management Review,* 30 (Fall 1987): 25–32.

69. Waldron Berry, "Beyond Strategic Planning," *Managerial Planning,* 29 (March–April 1981): 14.

70. See Joseph L. Bower and Clark G. Gilbert, "How Managers' Everyday Decisions Create or Destroy Your Company's Strategy," *Harvard Business Review,* 85 (February 2007): 72–79.

71. Charles H. Roush Jr. and Ben C. Ball Jr., "Controlling the Implementation of Strategy," *Managerial Planning,* 29 (November–December 1980): 4.

72. Donald C. Hambrick and Albert A. Cannella Jr., "Strategy Implementation as Substance and Selling," *Academy of Management Executive,* 3 (November 1989): 282–283. Another good discussion of strategic implementation can be found in Orit Gadiesh and James L. Gilbert, "Transforming Corner-Office Strategy into Frontline Action," *Harvard Business Review,* 79 (May 2001): 72–79.

73. As quoted in "How to Keep Your Company's Edge," *Business 2.0,* 4 (December 2003): 93.

74. William D. Guth and Ian C. Macmillian, "Strategy Implementation versus Middle Management Self-Interest," *Strategic Management Journal,* 7 (July–August 1986): 321.

75. See Gail Johnson, "Brain Drain," *Training,* 40 (December 2003): 16.

76. See Robert S. Kaplan and David P. Norton, "Using the Balanced Scorecard as a Strategic Management System," *Harvard Business Review,* 85 (July–August 2007): 150–161.

77. See F. C. "Ted" Weston, Jr., "ERP II: The Extended Enterprise System," *Business Horizons,* 46 (November–December 2003): 49–55.

78. See Vasudevan Ramanujan and N. Venkatraman, "Planning and Performance: A New Look at an Old Question," *Business Horizons,* 30 (May–June 1987): 19–25.

79. See Ken McGee, "Give Me That Real-Time Information," *Harvard Business Review,* 82 (April 2004): 26; and Vaidyanathan Jayaraman and Yadong Luo, "Creating Competitive Advantages Through New Value Creation: A Reverse Logistics Perspective," *Academy of Management Perspectives,* 21 (May 2007): 56–73.

80. See Paul Saffo, "Six Rules for Effective Forecasting," *Harvard Business Review,* 85 (July–August 2007): 122–131.

81. See Pat Regnier, "Why You Can't Believe Predictions," *Money,* 35 (July 2006): 96–100; Joseph Stiglitz, "Good Numbers Gone Bad," *Fortune* (October 2, 2006): 68; Chuck Salter, "An Inconvenient Business," *Fast Company,* no. 111 (January 2007): 47; and Peter Coy, "Reality Check: At Least No One Predicted Peace in the Middle East," *Business Week* (January 8, 2007): 14.

82. An excellent overview of forecasting techniques may be found in David M. Georgoff and Robert G. Murdick, "Manager's Guide to Forecasting," *Harvard Business Review,* 64 (January–February 1986): 110–120.

83. Based on C. W. J. Granger, *Forecasting in Business and Economics* (New York: Academic Press, 1980), pp. 6–10.

84. See Robert B. Young and Rajshekhar G. Javalgi, "International Marketing Research: A Global Project Management Perspective," *Business Horizons,* 50 (March–April 2007): 113–122; and "Smart Questions: Data You Can Bank On," *Inc.,* 29 (July 2007): 39.

85. Paul Kaihla, "Inside Cisco's $2 Billion Blunder," *Business 2.0,* 3 (March 2002): 88–89.

86. Duncan Martell, "Rumors Fly About iPod Upgrade," *USA Today* (October 12, 2004): 2B.

87. See Corey Hajim, "Looking Beyond the Fundamentals," *Fortune* (June 12, 2006): 186; and Erick Schonfeld, "The Wisdom of the Corporate Crowd," *Business 2.0,* 7 (September 2006): 47–49.

88. See Steven Schnaars and Paschalina (Lilia) Ziamou, "The Essentials of Scenario Writing," *Business Horizons,* 44 (July–August 2001): 25–31; Hugh Courtney, "Scenario Planning," *20-20 Foresight: Crafting Strategy in an Uncertain World* (Boston: Harvard Business School Press, 2001), pp. 160–165; and Jeff Cares and Jim Miskel, "Take Your Third Move First," *Harvard Business Review,* 85 (March 2007): 20–21.

89. Steven P. Schnaars, "How to Develop and Use Scenarios," *Long Range Planning,* 20 (February 1987): 106.

90. See Doug Randall and Jesse Goldhammer, "Four Futures for China," *Business 2.0,* 7 (August 2006): 34, 36; Darrell Rigby, "A Growing Focus on Preparedness," *Harvard Business Review,* 85 (July–August 2007): 21–22; and Mike Eskew, "Stick with Your Vision," *Harvard Business Review,* 85 (July–August 2007): 56–57.

91. Leonard Fuld, "Be Prepared," *Harvard Business Review,* 81 (November 2003): 20.

92. Ibid.

93. Peter Coy and Neil Gross, "21 Ideas for the 21st Century," *Business Week* (August 30, 1999): 82.

94. See "Slipping into the Future," *Fast Company,* no. 89 (December 2004): 88.

95. See Nancy Chambers, "The Really Long View," *Management Review,* 87 (January 1998): 10–15; Karen Thomas, "Fashion Understatement: That's So 5 Minutes Ago," *USA Today* (March 23, 1999): 1D–2D; and H. Donald Hopkins, "Using History for Strategic Problem-Solving: The Harley-Davidson Effect," *Business Horizons,* 42 (March–April 1999): 52–60.

96. See Wendy Zellner, "Chrysler's Next Generation," *Business Week* (December 19, 1988): 52–57.

CHAPTER 8

1. **Opening Quote:** Norm Brodsky, "The Thin Red Line," *Inc.,* 26 (January 2004): 49.

2. See R. Duane Ireland and C. Chet Miller, "Decision-Making and Firm Success," *Academy of Management Executive,* 18 (November 2004): 8–12.

3. As quoted in Jefferson Graham, "Schmidt Says He Didn't Grasp the Power of Google at First," *USA Today* (May 16, 2007): 4B.

4. Data from "Hurry Up and Decide!" *Business Week* (May 14, 2001): 16.

5. Andrew Backover and Elliot Blair Smith, "AT&T Wireless Gambit Places Cingular at Top," *USA Today* (February 18, 2004): 1B. Also see Deone M. Zell. Alan M. Glassman, and Shari A. Duron, "Strategic Management in Turbulent Times: The Short and Glorious History of Accelerated Decision Making at Hewlett-Packard," *Organizational Dynamics,* 36, no. 1 (2007): 93–104.

6. Morgan W. McCall, Jr. and Robert E. Kaplan, *Whatever It Takes: The Realities of Managerial Decision Making,* 2nd ed. (Englewood Cliffs, N.J.: Prentice-Hall, 1990), p. 5.

7. Paul Hoversten, "Backers Hope Amenities Will Quiet Critics," *USA Today* (February 22, 1995): 2A.

8. Michael Parrish, "Former Arco Chief Still Gambling on Oil Strikes," *Los Angeles Times* (September 21, 1993): D1.

9. Matthew L. Ward, "Airports Must Make Way for Airbus' Gigantic A380," *The Arizona Republic* (February 11, 2001): D1. Also see Carol Matlock, "Airbus Has a Weight Problem," *Business Week* (June 28, 2004): 63.

10. Eric W. K. Tsang, "Superstition and Decision-Making: Contradiction or Complement?" *Academy of Management Executive,* 18 (November 2004): 92.

11. See Martha Frase, "Show All Employees a Wider World," *HR Magazine,* 52 (June 2007): 98–102; Pete Engardio, Dexter Roberts, Frederik Balfour, and Bruce Einhorn, "Broken China," *Business Week* (July 23, 2007): 38–45; and David Kirkpatrick, "How Microsoft Conquered China," *Fortune* (July 23, 2007): 78–84.

12. Justin Martin, "Tomorrow's CEOs," *Fortune* (June 24, 1996): 90.

13. See Kay M. Nicols and Amy J. Hillman, "Blending Personal Values and Organizational Decision-Making: An Interview with Randall Grahm, President-for-Life, Bonny Doon Vineyards," *Business Horizons,* 49 (November–December 2006): 437–442.

14. Monica Hortobagyi, "Slain Students' Pages to Stay on Facebook," *USA Today* (May 9, 2007): 9D.

15. Steven M. Gillon, "Unintended Consequences: Why Our Plans Don't Go

According to Plan," *The Futurist*, 35 (March–April 2001): 49.

16. See Edward Tenner, *Why Things Bite Back: Technology and the Revenge of Unintended Consequences* (New York: Vintage Books, 1996), ch. 1; and Peter Eisler, "Fallout Likely Caused 15,000 Deaths," *USA Today* (February 28, 2002): 1A.

17. Tom Vanden Brook, "Jammers Foil IEDs, But Also Troops' Radios," *USA Today* (January 23, 2007): 6A.

18. For interesting examples, see Jena McGregor, "Self-Service: Check Those Impulses," Business Week (August 21–28, 2006): 16; Marilyn Adams, "Fliers Board Faster as Fewer Carry on Bags," USA Today (August 29, 2006): 2B; and Arlene Weintraub, "Intersections with Built-in Brains," *Business Week* (August 13, 2007): 65.

19. Abrahm Lustgarten, "Pick Industry. Dive in. Repeat," *Fortune* (November 15, 2004): 202.

20. For related reading, see Eric Bonabeau, "Predicting the Unpredictable," *Harvard Business Review*, 80 (March 2002): 109–116; and "The Risk-Intelligent Enterprise: Gaining Competitive Advantage Through Smart Risk Management," Special Advertising Feature, *Fortune* (March 19, 2007): S4–S5.

21. See Kent D. Miller and Wei-Ru Chen, "Variable Organizational Risk Preferences: Tests of the March-Shapira Model," *Academy of Management Journal*, 47 (February 2004): 105–115.

22. See Bill Treasurer, "How Risk-Taking Really Works," *Training*, 37 (January 2000): 40–44.

23. Paul Raeburn, "A Biotech Boom with a Difference," *Business Week* (December 31, 2001): 52. Also see Faith Arner, "The High Cost of Drugs Hits a Drugmaker," *Business Week* (December 29, 2003): 14; and Julie Schmit, "Drugmakers Gamble Big on Generics," *USA Today* (August 24, 2004): 1B.

24. For related reading, see Alison Overholt, "Are You a Polyolefin Optimizer? Take This Quiz," *Fast Company*, no. 81 (April 2004): 37.

25. See Eugene Sadler-Smith and Erella Shefy, "The Intuitive Executive: Understanding and Applying 'Gut Feel' in Decision-Making," *Academy of Management Executive*, 18 (November 2004): 76–91; Erik Dane and Michael G. Pratt, "Exploring Intuition and Its Role in Managerial Decision Making," *Academy of Management Review*, 32 (January 2007): 33–54; and Eugene Sadler-Smith and Erella Shefy, "Developing Intuitive Awareness in Management Education," *Academy of Management Learning and Education*, 6 (June 2007): 186–205.

26. David Lieberman, "'Rolling Stone' Founder Keeps Things Fun," *USA Today* (June 11, 2007): 4B.

27. As quoted in Keith H. Hammonds, "Continental's Turnaround Pilot," *Fast Company*, no. 53 (December 2001): 100. Also see the first Q&A in Jack Welch and Suzy Welch, "When to Go with Your Gut," *Business Week* (September 4, 2006): 104; and Ap Dijksterhuis, "When to Sleep on It," *Harvard Business Review*, 85 (February 2007): 30–32.

28. For research on decision styles, see Susanne G. Scott and Reginald A. Bruce, "Decision-Making Style: The Development and Assessment of a New Measure," *Educational and Psychological Measurement*, 55 (October 1995): 818–831; and Stacey M. Whitecotton, D. Elaine Sanders, and Kathleen B. Norris, "Improving Predictive Accuracy with a Combination of Human Intuition and Mechanical Decision Aids," *Organizational Behavior and Human Decision Processes*, 76 (December 1998): 325–348.

29. See Beverly Geber, "A Quick Course in Decision Science," *Training*, 25 (April 1988): 54–55; Alan E. Singer, Steven Lysonski, Ming Singer, and David Hayes, "Ethical Myopia: The Case of 'Framing' by Framing," *Journal of Business Ethics*, 10 (January 1991): 29–36; and Glen Whyte, "Decision Failures: Why They Occur and How to Prevent Them," *Academy of Management Executive*, 5 (August 1991): 23–31.

30. Irwin P. Levin, Sara K. Schnittjer, and Shannon L. Thee, "Information Framing Effects in Social and Personal Decisions," *Journal of Experimental Social Psychology*, 24 (November 1988): 527. For additional research evidence, see Michael J. Zickar and Scott Highhouse, "Looking Closer at the Effects of Framing on Risky Choice: An Item Response Theory Analysis," *Organizational Behavior and Human Decision Processes*, 75 (July 1998): 75–91; and Vikas Mittal and William T. Ross Jr., "The Impact of Positive and Negative Affect and Issue Framing on Issue Interpretation and Risk Taking," *Organizational Behavior and Human Decision Processes*, 76 (December 1998): 298–324.

31. See Leslie C. Aguilar, *Ouch! That Stereotype Hurts: Communicating Respectfully in a Diverse World* (Dallas: The Walk the Walk Company, 2006).

32. For good background reading, see Barry M. Staw and Jerry Ross, "Knowing When to Pull the Plug," *Harvard Business Review*, 65 (March–April 1987): 68–74; and Barry M. Staw and Jerry Ross, "Understanding Behavior in Escalation Situations," *Science*, 246 (October 13, 1989): 216–220. Also see William S. Silver and Terence R. Mitchell, "The Status Quo Tendency in Decision Making," *Organizational Dynamics*, 18 (Spring 1990): 34–46.

33. See Joel Brockner, "The Escalation of Commitment to a Failing Course of Action: Toward Theoretical Progress," *Academy of Management Review*, 17 (January 1992): 39–61; Beth Dietz-Uhler, "The Escalation of Commitment in Political Decision-Making Groups: A Social Identity Approach," *European Journal of Social Psychology*, 26 (July–August 1996): 611–629; Jennifer L. DeNicolis and Donald A. Hantula, "Sinking Shots and Sinking Costs? Or, How Long Can I Play in the NBA?" *Academy of Management Executive*, 10 (August 1996): 66–67; Marc D. Street and William P. Anthony, "A Conceptual Framework Establishing the Relationship Between Groupthink and Escalating Commitment Behavior," *Small Group Research*, 28 (May 1997): 267–293; Asghar Zardkoohi, "Do Real Options Lead to Escalation of Commitment?" *Academy of Management Review*, 29 (January 2004): 111–119; and Kin Fai Ellick Wong, Michelle Yik, and Jessica Y. Y. Kwong, "Understanding the Emotional Aspects of Escalation of Commitment: The Role of Negative Affect," *Journal of Applied Psychology*, 91 (March 2006): 282–297.

34. The second Q&A in Jack Welch and Suzy Welch, "Don't Count Brand America Out," *Business Week* (August 6, 2007): 96. A good case study of escalation can be found in John W. Mullins, "Good Money After Bad?" *Harvard Business Review*, 85 (March 2007): 37–48.

35. For related research evidence, see Itamar Simonson and Barry M. Staw, "Deescalation Strategies: A Comparison of Techniques for Reducing Commitment to Losing Courses of Action," *Journal of Applied Psychology*, 77 (August 1992): 419–426. Also see Jack Welch and Suzy Welch, "Hiring Wrong—and Right," *Business Week* (January 29, 2007): 102.

36. Sidney Finkelstein, *Why Smart Executives Fail—and What You Can Learn from Their Mistakes* (New York: Portfolio, 2003), pp. 223–224.

37. For an interesting exercise, see J. Edward Russo and Paul J. H. Schoemaker, "The Overconfidence Quiz," *Harvard Business Review*, 68 (September–October 1990): 236–237.

38. Paul J. H. Schoemaker and Robert E. Gunther, "The Wisdom of Deliberate Mistakes," *Harvard Business Review*, 84 (June 2006): 111. Learning from mistakes is discussed in Stephanie N. Mehta, "Carlos Slim: The Richest Man in the World," *Fortune* (August 20, 2007): 22–29.

39. An excellent resource book is James G. March, *A Primer on Decision Making: How Decisions Happen* (New York: Free Press, 1994). Also see Catherine A. Maritan, "Capital Investment as Investing in Organizational Capabilities: An Empirically Grounded Process Model," *Academy of Management Journal*, 44 (June 2001): 513–531.

40. Drawn from Gardiner Morse, "By Any Other Name," *Harvard Business Review*, 82 (November 2004): 30.

41. Gary Belsky and Thomas Gilovich, *Why Smart People Make Big Money Mistakes—and How to Correct Them*: *Lessons from the New Science of Behavioral Economics* (New York: Fireside, 1999), pp. 100–101.

42. For example, see Herbert A. Simon, *The New Science of Management Decision*, rev. ed. (Englewood Cliffs, N.J.: Prentice-Hall, 1977), p. 40. Also see James W. Dean Jr. and Mark P. Sharfman, "Does Decision Process Matter? A Study of Strategic Decision-Making Effectiveness," *Academy of Management Journal*, 39 (April 1996): 368–396; Jerre L. Stead, "Whose Decision Is It, Anyway?" *Management Review*, 88 (January 1999): 13; Anna Muoio, "All the Right Moves," *Fast Company*, no. 24 (May 1999): 192–200; and Brian Palmer, "Click Here for Decisions," *Fortune* (May 10, 1999): 153–156.

43. See, for example, Herbert E. Kierulff, "The Replacement Decision: Getting It Right," *Business Horizons*, 50 (May–June 2007): 231–237.

44. For related reading, see Sandra Block, "Home-Equity Loans Cost More These Days and Are a Lot Tougher to Get," *USA Today* (August 28, 2007): 3B.

45. Andrew S. Grove, *High Output Management* (New York: Random House, 1983), p. 98.

46. Simon, *The New Science of Management Decision*, p. 46.

47. See David R. A. Skidd, "Revisiting Bounded Rationality," *Journal of Management Inquiry*, 1 (December 1992): 343–347; and March, *A Primer on Decision Making*, pp. 8–9.

48. See Charles R. Schwenk, "The Use of Participant Recollection in the Modeling of Organizational Decision Processes," *Academy of Management Review*, 10 (July 1985): 496–503. Also see the discussion of "adaptive decision making" in Amitai Etzioni, "Humble Decision Making," *Harvard Business Review*, 67 (July–August 1989): 122–126; and Janet Barnard, "Successful CEOs Talk About Decision Making," *Business Horizons*, 35 (September–October 1992): 70–74.

49. For more on strategic decision making, see Paul C. Nutt, "Expanding the Search for Alternatives During Strategic Decision-Making," *Academy of Management Executive*, 18 (November 2004): 13–28; and Jay J. Janney and Gregory G. Dess, "Can Real-Options Analysis Improve Decision-Making? Promises and Pitfalls," *Academy of Management Executive*, 18 (November 2004): 60–75.

50. Chester I. Barnard, *The Functions of the Executive* (Cambridge, Mass.: Harvard University Press, 1938), p. 190. Also see Susan S. Kirschenbaum, "Influence of Experience on Information-Gathering Strategies," *Journal of Applied Psychology*, 77 (June 1992): 343–352.

51. For good background reading, see *Harvard Business Review on Knowledge Management* (Boston: Harvard Business School Publishing, 1998); Michael Schrage, "Algorithms in the Attic," *Harvard Business Review*, 85 (February 2007): 25–26; Douglas J. Miller, Michael J. Fern, and Laura B. Cardinal, "The Use of Knowledge for Technological Innovation Within Diversified Firms," *Academy of Management Journal*, 50 (April 2007): 308–326; and K. Anders Ericsson, Michael J. Prietula, and Edward T. Cokely, "The Making of an Expert," *Harvard Business Review*, 85 (July–August 2007): 114–121.

52. David W. De Long and Patricia Seemann, "Confronting Conceptual Confusion and Conflict in Knowledge Management," *Organizational Dynamics*, 29 (Summer 2000): 33.

53. Dorothy Leonard and Walter Swap, "Deep Smarts," *Harvard Business Review*, 82 (September 2004): 92. Also see Anne Fisher, "Retain Your Brains," *Fortune* (July 24, 2006): 49–50; and Clive Thompson, "A Head for Detail," *Fast Company*, no. 110 (November 2006): 72–79, 110–112.

54. For more on tacit knowledge, see Roy Lubit, "Tacit Knowledge and Knowledge Management: The Keys to Sustainable Competitive Advantage," *Organizational Dynamics*, 29 (Winter 2001): 164–178; and Yoko Ishikura, "Act Globally, Think Locally," *Harvard Business Review*, 85 (February 2007): 46.

55. See Rob Cross, Andrew Parker Laurence Prusak, and Stephen P. Borgatti, "Knowing What We Know: Supporting Knowledge Creation and Sharing in Social Networks," *Organizational Dynamics*, 30 (Fall 2001): 100–120; and Rob Cross and Jonathon N. Cummings, "Tie and Network Correlates of Individual Performance in Knowledge-Intensive Work," *Academy of Management Journal*, 47 (December 2004): 928–937.

56. See Kevin C. Desouza and Yukika Awazu, "Knowledge Management," *HR Magazine*, 48 (November 2003): 107–112.

57. Paul Kaihla, "The Matchmaker in the Machine," *Business 2.0*, 5 (January–February 2004): 52, 54.

58. Jeffrey Hsu and Tony Lockwood, "Collaborative Computing," *Byte*, 18 (March 1993): 113. For a contrary view, see David H. Freedman, "The Idiocy of Crowds: Collaboration Is the Hottest Buzzword in Business Today. Too Bad It Doesn't Work," *Inc.*, 28 (September 2006): 61–62.

59. Catherine Romano, "The Power of Collaboration: Untapped," *Management Review*, 86 (January 1997): 7. See Jennifer Hedlund, Daniel R. Ilgen, and John R. Hollenbeck, "Decision Accuracy in Computer-Mediated versus Face-to-Face Decision-Making Teams," *Organizational Behavior and Human Decision Processes*, 76 (October 1998): 30–47; Kevin Maney, "Software Genius Gets into Groove," *USA Today* (February 12, 2001): 1B–2B; and Alison Overholt, "Virtually There?" *Fast Company*, no. 56 (March 2002): 108–114.

60. George P. Huber, *Managerial Decision Making* (Glenview, Ill.: Scott, Foresman, 1980), pp. 141–142. Also see Cass R. Sunstein, "When Crowds Aren't Wise," *Harvard Business Review*, 84 (September 2006): 20–21; Erick Schonfeld, "The Wisdom of the Corporate Crowd," *Business 2.0*, 7 (September 2006): 47–49; Michael Useem, "How Well-Run Boards Make Decisions," *Harvard Business Review*, 84 (November 2006): 130–138; and Joseph Weber, "Seeking Wisdom in a Crowd," *Business Week* (March 12, 2007): 14.

61. As quoted in Ronald Henkoff, "A Whole New Set of Glitches for Digital's Robert Palmer," *Fortune* (August 19, 1996): 193. Also see Felix C. Brodbeck, Rudolf Kerschreiter, Andreas Mojzisch, and Stefan Schulz-Hardt, "Group Decision Making Under Conditions of Distributed Knowledge: The Information Asymmetries Model," *Academy of Management Review*, 32 (April 2007): 459–479.

62. See Priscilla M. Elsass and Laura M. Graves, "Demographic Diversity in Decision-Making Groups: The Experiences of Women and People of Color," *Academy of Management Review*, 22 (October 1997): 946–973; and Katherine Hawkins and Christopher B. Power, "Gender Differences in Questions Asked During Small Decision-Making Group Discussions," *Small Group Research*, (April 1999): 235–256.

63. See Gayle W. Hill, "Group versus Individual Performance: Are N + 1 Heads Better Than One?" *Psychological Bulletin*, 91 (May 1982): 517–539. Also see John P. Wanous and Margaret A. Youtz, "Solution Diversity and the

Quality of Group Decisions," *Academy of Management Journal*, 29 (March 1986): 149–158; and Warren Watson, Larry K. Michaelsen, and Walt Sharp, "Member Competence, Group Interaction, and Group Decision Making: A Longitudinal Study," *Journal of Applied Psychology*, 76 (December 1991): 803–809.

64. See Geoffrey Colvin, "The Imagination Economy," *Fortune* (July 10, 2006): 53; Aric Chen, "The Next Cultural Revolution," *Fast Company*, no. 116 (June 2007): 64–75; Susan Meisinger, "Nurturing and Tapping the Power of Imagination," *HR Magazine*, 52 (August 2007): 10; and Scott Berkun, *The Myths of Innovation* (Sebastopol, Calif.: O'Reilly, 2007).

65. A good historical perspective on creativity can be found in Michael Michalko, "Thinking Like a Genius," *The Futurist*, 32 (May 1998): 21–25.

66. Based on discussion in N. R. F. Maier, Mara Julius, and James Thurber, "Studies in Creativity: Individual Differences in the Storing and Utilization of Information," *The American Journal of Psychology*, 80 (December 1967): 492–519.

67. Sidney J. Parnes, "Learning Creative Behavior," *The Futurist*, 18 (August 1984): 30–31. Also see Polly LaBarre, "Weird Ideas That Work," *Fast Company*, no. 54 (January 2002): 68–73; and Brian O'Keefe, "The Smartest (or the Nuttiest) Futurist on Earth," *Fortune* (May 14, 2007): 60–69.

68. As quoted in Ryan Underwood, "Fast Talk: Question Assumptions," *Fast Company*, no. 89 (December 2004): 44.

69. See Arthur Koestler, *The Act of Creation* (London: Hutchinson, 1969), p. 27.

70. See James L. Adams, *Conceptual Blockbusting* (San Francisco: Freeman, 1974), p. 35. Also see Bruce Nussbaum, "This Is the IDEO Way," *Business Week* (May 17, 2004): 89.

71. "Empty the tacks from the box, tack the box to the wall, and stand the candle upright in the box."

72. Michael Loeb, "Making a Case for Allergy Sufferers," *Business Week* (August 13, 2007): 66. Also see Siri Schubert, "The Gadget That Watches Your Energy Bill," *Business 2.0*, 7 (December 2006): 52; "Is That Bamboo in Your Pants?" *Fast Company*, no. 111 (January 2007): 33; and Alison Stein Wellner, "Creative Control: Even Bosses Need Time to Dream," *Inc.*, 29 (July 2007): 40, 42.

73. Data from Ibid.

74. Minda Zetlin, "Nurturing Nonconformists," *Management Review*, 88 (October 1999): 30. Similar results were found in a parallel study reported in Bill Breen, "The 6 Myths of Creativity," *Fast Company*, no. 89 (December 2004):

75–78. Also see Robin Hanson, "The Myth of Creativity," *Business Week* (July 3, 2006): 134.

75. See Linda Tischler, "The Care and Feeding of the Creative Class," *Fast Company*, no. 89 (December 2004): 93–95; "A Tree-mendous Workspace," *Training*, 44 (January–February 2007): 11; and Jennifer M. George and Jing Zhou, "Dual Tuning in a Supportive Context: Joint Contributions of Positive Mood, Negative Mood, and Supervisory Behaviors to Employee Creativity," *Academy of Management Journal*, 50 (June 2007): 605–622.

76. As quoted in Abrahm Lustgarten, "A Hot, Steaming Cup of Customer Awareness," *Fortune* (November 15, 2004): 192.

77. List adapted from Roger von Oech, *A Whack on the Side of the Head* (New York: Warner Books, 1983). Reprinted by permission. Also see Christine Dugas, "Idea Guru Helps Work Kinks Out of Others' Creations," *USA Today* (July 10, 2006): 5B.

78. Huber, *Managerial Decision Making*, p. 12. Also see Brent Roper, "Sizing Up Business Problems," *HR Magazine*, 46 (November 2001): 50–56.

79. As quoted in Thomas Mucha, "How to Ask the Right Questions," *Business 2.0*, 5 (December 2004): 118.

80. See Michael Marquardt, *Leading with Questions: How Leaders Find the Right Solutions by Knowing What to Ask* (San Francisco: Jossey-Bass, 2005).

81. Louis S. Richman, "How to Get Ahead in America," *Fortune* (May 16, 1994): 48.

82. For an empirical classification of organizational problems, see David A. Cowan, "Developing a Classification Structure of Organizational Problems: An Empirical Investigation," *Academy of Management Journal*, 33 (June 1990): 366–390.

83. Adapted from Huber, *Managerial Decision Making*, pp. 13–15. Also see Norm Brodsky, "Problems, Problems: Are You Getting to the Root Causes?" *Inc.*, 26 (February 2004): 43–44.

84. Marshall Sashkin and Kenneth J. Kiser, *Total Quality Management* (Seabrook, Md.: Ducochon Press, 1991), p. 153.

85. Adams, *Conceptual Blockbusting*, p. 7.

86. For related research, see John J. Sosik, Bruce J. Avolio, and Surinder S. Kahai, "Inspiring Group Creativity: Comparing Anonymous and Identified Electronic Brainstorming," *Small Group Research*, 29 (February 1998): 3–31.

87. Jessi Hempel, "Big Blue Brainstorm," *Business Week* (August 7, 2006): 70. Also see Margery Weinstein, "The Building Blocks of Brainstorming," *Training*, 43 (May 2006): 44; Robert I. Sutton, "The Truth About Brainstorming," Inside, *Business Week* (September 25, 2006): 17–24; Michael Myser, "When

Brainstorming Goes Bad," *Business 2.0*, 7 (October 2006): 76; Burt Helm, "Wal-Mart, Please Don't Leave Me," *Business Week* (October 9, 2006): 84–89; and Chuck Salter, "Just Add Inspiration," *Fast Company*, no. 111 (January 2007): 100–101.

88. Jerry Useem, "Another Boss Another Revolution," *Fortune* (April 5, 2004): 112.

89. See Russell L. Ackoff, "The Art and Science of Mess Management," *Interfaces*, 11 (February 1981): 20–26. Also see Russell L. Ackoff, *Management in Small Doses* (New York: Wiley, 1986), pp. 102–103.

90. See March, *A Primer on Decision Making*, p. 18; Gina Imperato, "When Is 'Good Enough' Good Enough?" *Fast Company*, no. 26 (July–August 1999): 52; and Don Moyer, "Satisficing," *Harvard Business Review*, 85 (April 2007): 144.

91. Ackoff, "The Art and Science of Mess Management," p. 22.

92. As quoted in James B. Treece, "Shaking Up Detroit," *Business Week* (August 14, 1989): 78.

93. Paul Hawken, "Problems, Problems," *Inc.*, 9 (September 1987): 24.

CHAPTER 9

1. **Opening Quote:** "Sam Walton in His Own Words," *Fortune* (June 29, 1992): 104.

2. For more, see **www.eileenfisher.com.**

3. As quoted in Keith H. Hammonds, "We, Incorporated," *Fast Company*, no. 84 (July 2004): 87.

4. See B. J. Hodge, William P. Anthony, and Lawrence M. Gales, *Organization Theory: A Strategic Approach*, 5th ed. (Upper Saddle River, N.J.: Prentice-Hall, 1996), p. 10.

5. Adapted from Edgar H. Schein, *Organizational Psychology*, 3rd ed. (Englewood Cliffs, N.J.: Prentice-Hall, 1980), pp. 12–15.

6. Burt Helm, "Saving Starbucks' Soul," *Business Week* (April 9, 2007): 60.

7. See Adam Smith, *The Wealth of Nations* (New York: Modern Library, 1937), p. 7.

8. For an interesting historical perspective, see Peter Coy, "Cog or Co-Worker?" *Business Week* (August 20–27, 2007): 58–60.

9. For example, see Tom Peters's opinions in "Author: More Women Should Be in Charge," *USA Today* (December 8, 2003): 13B.

10. Elliot Jaques, "In Praise of Hierarchy," *Harvard Business Review*, 68 (January–February 1990): 127. Also see Harold J. Leavitt, "Why Hierarchies Thrive," *Harvard Business Review*, 81 (March 2003): 96–102.

11. For an interesting biography of Henry Ford, see Ann Jardim, *The First Henry Ford: A Study in Personality and Business Leadership* (Cambridge, Mass.: MIT Press, 1970), p. 40.

12. See Marc Cecere, "Drawing the Lines," *Harvard Business Review*, 79 (November 2001): 24.

13. See Alan P. Brache and Geary A. Rummler, "Managing an Organization as a System," *Training*, 34 (February 1997): 68–74; Toby J. Tetenbaum, "Shifting Paradigms: From Newton to Chaos," *Organizational Dynamics*, 26 (Spring 1998): 21–32; Rosabeth Moss Kanter, "Managing for Long-Term Success," *The Futurist*, 32 (August–September 1998): 43–45; and Simon J. Bell and Andreas B. Eisingerich, "Work with Me," *Harvard Business Review*, 85 (June 2007): 32.

14. See V. Daniel R. Guide Jr. and Luk N. Van Wassenhove, "The Reverse Supply Chain," *Harvard Business Review*, 80 (February 2002): 25–26; and David Ticoll, "Get Self-Organized," *Harvard Business Review*, 82 (September 2004): 18–19.

15. See Reuben E. Slone, John T. Mentzer, and J. Paul Dittmann, "Are You the Weakest Link in your Company's Supply Chain?" *Harvard Business Review*, 85 (September 2007): 116–127.

16. For related research, see Andreas W. Richter, Michael A. West, Rolf Van Dick, and Jeremy F. Dawson, "Boundary Spanners' Identification, Intergroup Contact, and Effective Intergroup Relations," *Academy of Management Journal*, 49 (December 2006): 1252–1269.

17. Kim Cameron, "Critical Questions in Assessing Organizational Effectiveness," *Organizational Dynamics*, 9 (Autumn 1980): 70.

18. See Raj Aggarwal, "Using Economic Profit to Assess Performance: A Metric for Modern Firms," *Business Horizons*, 44 (January–February 2001): 55–60; and Jeffrey Pfeffer, "The Agony of Victory," *Business 2.0*, 8 (January–February 2007): 62.

19. Winslow Buxton, "Growth from Top to Bottom," *Management Review*, 88 (July–August 1999): 11.

20. Detailed discussions of alternative models of organizational effectiveness may be found in Kishore Gawande and Timothy Wheeler, "Measures of Effectiveness for Governmental Organizations," *Management Science*, 45 (January 1999): 42–58; Edward V. McIntyre, "Accounting Choices and EVA," *Business Horizons*, 42 (January–February 1999): 66–72; and Toby D. Wall, Jonathan Michie, Malcolm Patterson, Stephen J. Wood, Maura Sheehan, Chris W. Clegg, and Michael West, "On the Validity of Subjective Measures of Company Performance," *Personnel Psychology*, 57 (Spring 2004): 95–118.

21. See Michael Beer, "How to Develop an Organization Capable of Sustained High Performance: Embrace the Drive for Results-Capability Development Paradox," *Organizational Dynamics*, 29 (Spring 2001): 233–247; and Edward E. Lawler III and Christopher G. Worley, *Built to Change: How to Achieve Sustained Organizational Effectiveness* (San Francisco: Jossey-Bass, 2006).

22. See Tom Burns and G. M. Stalker, *The Management of Innovation* (London: Tavistock, 1961), ch. 5.

23. See John A. Courtright, Gail T. Fairhurst, and L. Edna Rogers, "Interaction Patterns in Organic and Mechanistic Systems," *Academy of Management Journal*, 32 (December 1989): 773–802.

24. Ben Elgin, "Running the Tightest Ship on the Net," *Business Week* (January 29, 2001): 126. Also see Jon Swartz and Byron Acohido, "Who's Guarding Your Data in the Cybervault?" *USA Today* (April 2, 2007): 1B–2B.

25. Brian Hindo, "The Empire Strikes at Silos," *Business Week* (August 20–27, 2007): 63, 65.

26. Jenny C. McCune, "The Change Makers," *Management Review*, 88 (May 1999): 17. Also see Peter F. Drucker, "Change Leaders," *Inc.*, 21 (June 1999): 65–72.

27. James D. Thompson, *Organizations in Action* (New York: McGraw-Hill, 1967), p. 59.

28. Based in part on Jay R. Galbraith, *Designing Organizations: An Executive Briefing on Strategy, Structure, and Process* (San Francisco: Jossey-Bass, 1995): pp. 24–37.

29. Catherine Arnst, "A Freewheeling Youngster Named IBM," *Business Week* (May 3, 1993): 136.

30. See Michelle Kessler, "It's Official: IBM Sells PC Unit to Chinese Company," *USA Today* (December 8, 2004): 1B; and Kevin Maney, "Pioneer IBM Finally Finds Its Way Out of the PC Wilderness," *USA Today* (December 8, 2004): 3B.

31. Based on "General Electric Reorganizes Some Businesses for Growth," *East Valley/Scottsdale Tribune* (December 5, 2003): B3.

32. For related research, see Arturs Kalnins, "Divisional Multimarket Contact Within and Between Multiunit Organizations," *Academy of Management Journal*, 47 (February 2004): 117–128.

33. Adapted from "Dial 800, Talk to Omaha," *Fortune* (January 29, 1990): 16; Rhonda Richards, "Technology Makes Omaha Hotel-Booking Capital," *USA Today* (April 7, 1994): 4B; and Robert D. Kaplan, *An Empire Wilderness: Travels into America's Future* (New York: Random House, 1998), p. 59.

34. Cliff Edwards, "Shaking Up Intel's Insides," *Business Week* (January 31, 2005): 35. For another example of product-service, see Kevin Maney, "CEO Ollila Says Nokia's 'Sisu' Will See It Past Tough Times," *USA Today* (July 21, 2004): 1B–2B.

35. For more, see Michael Hammer and James Champy, *Reengineering the Corporation: A Manifesto for Business Revolution* (New York: HarperCollins, 1993); James Champy, *Reengineering Management: The Mandate for New Leadership* (New York: HarperBusiness, 1995); Dutch Holland and Sanjiv Kumar, "Getting Past the Obstacles to Successful Reengineering," *Business Horizons*, 38 (May–June 1995): 79–85; and Michael Hammer, "The Process Audit," *Harvard Business Review*, 85 (April 2007): 111–123.

36. See John A. Byrne, "The Horizontal Corporation," *Business Week* (December 20, 1993): 76–81; Susan Sonnesyn Brooks, "Managing a Horizontal Revolution," *HR Magazine*, 40 (June 1995): 52–58; and Ranjay Gulati, "Silo Busting: How to Execute on the Promise of Customer Focus," *Harvard Business Review*, 85 (May 2007): 98–108.

37. Rahul Jacob, "The Struggle to Create an Organization for the 21st Century," *Fortune* (April 3, 1995): 91. For related reading, see Michael H. Martin, "Smart Managing," *Fortune* (February 2, 1998): 149–151; and David Stamps, "Enterprise Training: This Changes *Everything*," *Training*, 36 (January 1999): 40–48.

38. David Kiley, "Coke Reorganizes; President Resigns," *USA Today* (March 5, 2001): 2B.

39. For an extensive bibliography on this subject, see David D. Van Fleet and Arthur G. Bedeian, "A History of the Span of Management," *Academy of Management Review*, 2 (July 1977): 356–372.

40. William H. Wagel, "Keeping the Organization Lean at Federal Express," *Personnel*, 64 (March 1987): 4–12.

41. Paul Kaestle, "A New Rationale for Organizational Structure," *Planning Review*, 18 (July–August 1990): 22. Also see Robert W. Keidel, "Triangular Design: A New Organizational Geometry," *Academy of Management Executive*, 4 (November 1990): 21–37.

42. For example, see Jeffrey Schmidt, "Breaking Down Fiefdoms," *Management Review*, 86 (January 1997): 45–49; and Michael E. Raynor and Joseph L. Bower, "Lead from the Center: How to Manage Divisions Dynamically," *Harvard Business Review*, 79 (May 2001): 92–100.

43. For a comprehensive research summary on centralization and organizational effectiveness, see George P. Huber, C. Chet Miller, and William H. Glick, "Developing More Encompassing Theories About Organizations: The Centralization-Effectiveness Relationship as an Example," *Organization Science*, 1 (1990): 11–40.

44. See Arlene Weintraub, "Under the Weather at J&J," *Business Week* (April 23,

2007): 80, 82; and Arlene Weintraub, "J&J's New Baby," *Business Week* (June 18, 2007): 48–56. For an international example, see Pete Engardio, "The Last Rajah," *Business Week* (August 13, 2007): 46–51.

45. See Larry Bossidy, "The Job No CEO Should Delegate," *Harvard Business Review*, 79 (March 2001): 46–49; and Sharon Gazda, "The Art of Delegating," *HR Magazine*, 47 (January 2002): 75–78.

46. Adapted from Marion E. Haynes, "Delegation: There's More to It Than Letting Someone Else Do It!" *Supervisory Management*, 25 (January 1980): 9–15. Three types of delegation—incremental, sequential, and functional—are discussed in William R. Tracey, "Deft Delegation: Multiplying Your Effectiveness," *Personnel*, 65 (February 1988): 36–42.

47. Delegation styles of selected U.S. presidents are examined in Edward J. Mayo and Lance P. Jarvis, "Delegation 101: Lessons from the White House," *Business Horizons*, 31 (September–October 1988): 2–12.

48. Alex Taylor III, "Iacocca's Time of Trouble," *Fortune* (March 14, 1988): 79, 81.

49. Andrew S. Grove, *High Output Management* (New York: Random House, 1983), p. 60. Also see Wilson Harrell, "Your Biggest Mistake," *Success*, 43 (March 1996): 88.

50. For interesting facts about delegating, see "Top Dogs," *Fortune* (September 30, 1996): 189; and Bill Leonard, "Good Assistants Make Managers More Efficient," *HR Magazine*, 44 (February 1999): 12.

51. "How Conservatism Wins in the Hottest Market," *Business Week* (January 17, 1977): 43.

52. Adapted from William H. Newman, "Overcoming Obstacles to Effective Delegation," *Management Review*, 45 (January 1956): 36–41; and from Eugene Raudsepp, "Why Supervisors Don't Delegate," *Supervision*, 41 (May 1979): 12–15. Also see Francie Dalton, "Delegation Pitfalls," *Association Management*, 57 (February 2005): 65–72; and Tora Estep, "Devilish Delegation at the Department of Ominous Mechanical Mishaps," *Training and Development*, 59 (March 2005): 68–70.

53. For more on initiative, see Michael Fresc, Wolfgang Kring, Andrea Soose, and Jeanette Zempel, "Personal Initiative at Work: Differences Between East and West Germany," *Academy of Management Journal*, 39 (February 1996): 37–63; and Alan L. Frohman, "Igniting Organizational Change from Below: The Power of Personal Initiative," *Organizational Dynamics*, 25 (Winter 1997): 39–53.

54. Peter F. Drucker, *Managing the Non-Profit Organization* (New York: HarperCollins, 1990), p. 117. For related research, see Zhen Xiong Chen and Samuel Aryee, "Delegation and Employee Work Outcomes: An Examination of the Cultural Context of Mediating Processes in China," *Academy of Management Journal*, 50 (February 2007): 226–238.

55. See, for example, Warren G. Bennis, *Changing Organizations* (New York: McGraw-Hill, 1966).

56. As quoted in Noel M. Tichy and Stratford Sherman, *Control Your Destiny or Someone Else Will: How Jack Welch Is Making General Electric the World's Most Competitive Corporation* (New York: Doubleday, 1993), p. 21. Also see Peter Coy, "The 21st Century Corporation: The Creative Economy," *Business Week* (August 28, 2000): 76–82; and Sheila M. Puffer, "Changing Organizational Structures: An Interview with Rosabeth Moss Kanter," *Academy of Management Executive*, 18 (May 2004): 96–105.

57. Data from Patricia Sellers, "Now Is the Time to Invest," *Fortune* (October 16, 2006): 142. Also see the first Q&A in Jack Welch and Suzy Welch, "Lay Off the Layers," *Business Week* (June 25, 2007): 96.

58. Andy Reinhardt, "Nokia's Next Act," *Business Week* (July 1, 2002): 56.

59. See Robert J. Trent, "Becoming an Effective Teaming Organization," *Business Horizons*, 47 (March–April 2004): 33–40; and Nadine Heintz, "Smells Like Team Spirit," *Inc.*, 26 (May 2004): 58.

60. Toby Tetenbaum and Hilary Tetenbaum, "Office 2000: Tear Down the Walls," *Training*, 37 (February 2000): 60.

61. A good resource book is William G. Dyer, *Team Building: Current Issues and New Alternatives*, 3rd ed. (Reading, Mass.: Addison-Wesley, 1995).

62. See Jathan W. Janove, "Management by Remote Control," *HR Magazine*, 49 (April 2004): 119–124; Roger Yu, "Work Away from Work Gets Easier with Technology," *USA Today* (November 28, 2006): 8B; Marjorie Derven, "The Remote Connection," *HR Magazine*, 52 (March 2007): 111–115; Michelle Conlin, "Rolling Out the Instant Office," *Business Week* (May 7, 2007): 71; Pete Engardio, "Managing the New Workforce," *Business Week* (August 20–27, 2007): 48–51; and Robert D. Hof, "Technology on the March," *Business Week* (August 20–27, 2007): 80–83.

63. Steve Hamm, "Linux Inc.," *Business Week* (January 31, 2005): 62.

64. Another interesting global virtual organization is profiled in Kevin Maney, "Kazaa Creators' Latest Invention, Skype, Could Turn Telcom on Its Ear," *USA Today* (April 14, 2004): 3B.

65. For example, see Michael V. Copeland, "These Boots Really Were Made for Walking," *Business 2.0*, 5 (October 2004): 72, 74.

66. Research on the behavioral implications of virtual organizations is reported in Deondra S. Conner, "Social Comparison in Virtual Work Environments: An Examination of Contemporary Referent Selection," *Journal of Occupational and Organizational Psychology*, 76 (March 2003): 133–147.

67. See David M. Slipy, "Anthropologist Uncovers Real Workplace Attitudes," *HR Magazine*, 35 (October 1990): 76–79; and David A. Kaplan, "Studying the Gearheads," *Newsweek* (August 3, 1998): 62.

68. This definition is based in part on Linda Smircich, "Concepts of Culture and Organizational Analysis," *Administrative Science Quarterly*, 28 (September 1983): 339–358. Also see Patrick M. Lencioni, "Make Your Values Mean Something," *Harvard Business Review*, 80 (July 2002): 113–117; James M. Higgins and Craig McAllaster, "Want Innovation? Then Use Cultural Artifacts That Support It," *Organizational Dynamics*, 31 (August 2002): 74–84; and Leigh Buchanan, "The Culture Wars," *Inc.*, 29 (February 2007): 120.

69. Data from John E. Sheridan, "Organizational Culture and Employee Retention," *Academy of Management Journal*, 35 (December 1992): 1036–1056. For parallel findings, see Shelly Branch, "The 100 Best Companies to Work for in America," *Fortune* (January 11, 1999): 118–144. Also see Daniel R. Denison, Stephanie Haaland, and Paulo Goelzer, "Corporate Culture and Organizational Effectiveness: Is Asia Different from the Rest of the World?" *Organizational Dynamics*, 33, no. 1 (2004): 98–109.

70. For more, see Jerry Want, "When Worlds Collide: Culture Clash," *Journal of Business Strategy*, 24 (September 2003): 14–21; Pamela Babcock, "Is Your Company Two-Faced?" *HR Magazine*, 49 (January 2004): 42–47; and Richard O. Mason, "Lessons in Organizational Ethics from the *Columbia* Disaster: Can a Culture Be Lethal?" *Organizational Dynamics*, 33, no. 2 (2004): 128–142.

71. David Kiley, "The New Heat on Ford," *Business Week* (June 4, 2007): 33.

72. Peter C. Reynolds, "Imposing a Corporate Culture," *Psychology Today*, 21 (March 1987): 38.

73. Based on Harrison M. Trice and Janice M. Beyer, *The Cultures of Work Organizations* (Englewood Cliffs, N.J.: Prentice-Hall, 1993), pp. 5–8.

74. As quoted in Stephen B. Shepard, "A Talk with Jeff Immelt," *Business Week* (January 28, 2002): 103.

75. See Jack Welch and Suzy Welch, "The Reverse Hostage Syndrome," *Business Week* (July 30, 2007): 92.

76. See Sally Maitlis and Thomas B. Lawrence, "Triggers and Enablers of Sensegiving in Organizations," *Academy of Management Journal*, 50 (February 2007): 57–84.

77. See Chip Jarnagin and John W. Slocum Jr., "Creating Corporate Cultures Through Mythopoetic Leadership," *Organizational Dynamics*, 36, no. 3 (2007): 288–302.

78. "A. G. Lafley: Procter & Gamble," *Business Week* (January 13, 2003): 67.

79. For example, see Robert Berner, "My Year at Wal-Mart," *Business Week* (February 12, 2007): 70–74; and "Many CFOs Don't 'Fit' Company Culture," *HR Magazine*, 52 (April 2007): 18.

80. See David Dorsey, "The New Spirit of Work," *Fast Company*, no. 16 (August 1998): 125–134; and Jim Collins, "When Good Managers Manage Too Much," *Inc.*, 21 (April 1999): 31–32.

81. As quoted in Sandra Block, "Bridgeway Founder Wins with Integrity," *USA Today* (December 17, 2003): 5B.

82. For related research, see Elizabeth Wolfe Morrison, "Newcomers' Relationships: The Role of Social Network Ties During Socialization," *Academy of Management Journal*, 45 (December 2002): 1149–1160; and Julia Balogun and Gerry Johnson, "Organizational Restructuring and Middle Manager Sensemaking," *Academy of Management Journal*, 47 (August 2004): 523–549.

83. Alan L. Wilkins, "The Culture Audit: A Tool for Understanding Organizations," *Organizational Dynamics*, 12 (Autumn 1983): 34–35. Also see Jean Thilmany, "Quick Studies," *HR Magazine*, 52 (May 2007): 68–74; Barbara Ashkin, "Leave 'em Laughing," *Inc.*, 29 (August 2007): 94; and the first Q&A in Jack Welch and Suzy Welch, "From Hero to Zero," *Business Week* (September 3, 2007): 104.

84. See Jena McGregor, "How to Take the Reins at Top Speed," *Business Week* (February 5, 2007): 55–56; Margery Weinstein, "Outsider Longer," *Training*, 44 (March 2007): 6; and Michael D. Watkins, "Help Newly Hired Executives Adapt Quickly," *Harvard Business Review*, 85 (June 2007): 26, 30.

85. Rebecca Ganzel, "Putting Out the Welcome Mat," *Training*, 35 (March 1998): 54. Also see Noel M. Tichy, "No Ordinary Boot Camp," *Harvard Business Review*, 79 (April 2001): 63–70; and "Executive Orientation Gets Poor Marks in Survey," *HR Magazine*, 49 (March 2004): 12.

86. For the full *story*, see Douglas A. Ready, "How Storytelling Builds Next-Generation Leaders," *MIT Sloan Management Review*, 43 (Summer 2002): 63–69; Stephen Denning, "Telling Tales," *Harvard Business Review*, 82 (May 2004): 122–129; and Camille H. James and William C. Minnis, "Organizational Storytelling: It Makes Sense," *Business Horizons*, 47 (July–August 2004): 23–32.

87. Alan L. Wilkins, "The Creation of Company Cultures: The Role of Stories and Human Resource Systems," *Human Resource Management*, 23 (Spring 1984): 43.

88. Adapted from Terrence E. Deal and Allan A. Kennedy, *Corporate Cultures: The Rites and Rituals of Corporate Life* (Reading, Mass.: Addison-Wesley, 1982), pp. 136–139.

89. Eight tips for maintaining the strength of an organization's culture are presented in Trice and Beyer, *Cultures of Work Organizations*, pp. 378–391. Also see: Calvin Leung, "Culture Club," *Canadian Business*, 79 (October 9–22, 2006): 115–120; Leigh Buchanan, "That's Chief *Entertainment* Officer," *Inc.*, 29 (August 2007): 86–94; and Robert M. Price, "Infusing Innovation into Corporate Culture," *Organizational Dynamics*, 36, no. 3 (2007): 320–328.

CHAPTER 10

1. **Opening Quote:** Jack Welch and Suzy Welch, "So Many CEOs Get This Wrong," *Business Week* (July 17, 2006): 92.

2. Drawn from "Peterson Thrives on HR Challenges," *HR Magazine*, 43 (September 1998): 98, 100.

3. See Li-Yun Sun, Samuel Aryee, and Kenneth S. Law, "High-Performance Human Resource Practices, Citizenship Behavior, and Organizational Performance: A Relational Perspective," *Academy of Management Journal*, 50 (June 2007): 558–577.

4. Leon Rubis, "Analytical Graphics Works for Its Workers," *HR Magazine*, 49 (July 2004): 47.

5. Jeffrey B. Arthur, "Effects of Human Resource Systems on Manufacturing Performance and Turnover," *Academy of Management Journal*, 37 (June 1994): 670. Similar findings are reported in Heather Johnson, "Super HR," *Training*, 41 (August 2004): 18. Also see Eric Krell, "From Steel Yards to HR Stewardship," *HR Magazine*, 52 (April 2007): 60–65; and Gary Davies and Rosa Chun, "To Thine Own Staff Be Agreeable," *Harvard Business Review*, 85 (June 2007): 3–32.

6. For example, see Laurie Bassi and Daniel McMurrer, "Maximizing Your Return on People," *Harvard Business Review*, 85 (March 2007): 115–123; Carolyn Hirschman, "Putting Forecasting in Focus: Workforce Planning Can Provide Perspective for Business Success," *HR Magazine*, 52 (March 2007): 44–49; and Nancy Lockwood, "HR and Business Education: Building Value for Competitive Advantage," 2007 SHRM Research Quarterly, *HR Magazine*, 52 (June 2007): 1–12.

7. See Pamela Babcock, "Slicing Off Pieces of HR," *HR Magazine*, 49 (July 2004): 70–76; Robert J. Grossman, "Sticker Shock," *HR Magazine*, 49 (July 2004): 78–86; Susan Meisinger, "Outsourcing: A Challenge and an Opportunity," *HR Magazine*, 49 (September 2004): 8; and Jennifer Schramm, "Top Trends Facing HR," *HR Magazine*, 49 (October 2004): 152.

8. See Carl E. Fey, Antonina Pavlovskaya, and Ningyu Tang, "Does One Shoe Fit Everyone? A Comparison of Human Resource Management in Russia, China, and Finland," *Organizational Dynamics*, 33, no. 1 (2004): 79–97; and Adrienne Fox, "China: Land of Opportunity and Challenge," *HR Magazine*, 52 (September 2007): 38–44.

9. Bill Leonard, "Straight Talk," *HR Magazine*, 47 (January 2002): 46–51. Also see Robert J. Grossman, "New Competencies for HR," *HR Magazine*, 52 (June 2007): 58–62.

10. Brian E. Becker, Mark A. Huselid, and Dave Ulrich, *The HR Scorecard: Linking People, Strategy, and Performance* (Boston: Harvard Business School Press, 2001): p. 4. Also see Bill Roberts, "Data-Driven Human Capital Decisions," *HR Magazine*, 52 (March 2007): 105–108; and Jennifer Taylor Arnold, "Moving to a New HRIS," *HR Magazine*, 52 (June 2007): 125–132.

11. For more, see Holly Dolezalek, "Got High Potentials?" *Training*, 44 (January–February 2007): 18–22; Margery Weinstein, "Prescriptions for Success," *Training*, 44 (May 2007): 30–37; and Douglas A. Ready and Jay A. Conger, "Make Your Company a Talent factory," *Harvard Business Review*, 85 (June 2007): 68–77.

12. "The 100 Best Companies to Work For," *Fortune* (February 4, 2002): 84. For another corporate educational initiative, see Elizabeth Svoboda, "Microsoft's Class Action," *Fast Company*, no. 118 (September 2007): 87–95.

13. Scott Adams, "Dilbert's Management Handbook," *Fortune* (May 13, 1996): 99, 108.

14. As quoted in John Huey, "Outlaw Flyboy CEOs," *Fortune* (November 13, 2000): 246.

15. Data from Jeffrey Pfeffer, *The Human Equation: Building Profits by Putting People First* (Boston: Harvard Business School Press, 1998); and Jeffrey Pfeffer and John F. Veiga, "Putting People First for Organizational Success," *Academy of Management Executive*, 13 (May 1999): 37–48. Also see David Harding and Ted

Rouse, "Human Due Diligence," *Harvard Business Review*, 85 (April 2007): 124–131.

16. See Jim Collins, *Good to Great: Why Some Companies Make the Leap . . . and Others Don't* (New York: HarperCollins, 2001); and Jim Collins, "Good to Great," *Fast Company*, no. 51 (October 2001): 90–104.

17. See Charlotte Garvey, "The Next Generation of Hiring Metrics," *HR Magazine*, 50 (April 2005): 71–76; Connie Winkler, "Quality Check: Better Metrics Improve HR's Ability to Measure—and Manage—the Quality of Hires," *HR Magazine*, 52 (May 2007): 93–98; Burt Helm and Michael Arndt, "It's Not a McJob, It's a McCalling," *Business Week* (June 4, 2007): 13; and Jack Welch and Suzy Welch, "The Hiring Batting Average," *Business Week* (August 20–27, 2007): 116.

18. Based on "What Are CEOs Thinking?" *USA Today* (May 3, 2001): 1B. Also see Arie C. Glebbeek and Erik H. Bax, "Is High Employee Turnover Really Harmful? An Empirical Test Using Company Records." *Academy of Management Journal*, 47 (April 2004): 277–286; Nancy R. Lockwood, "Planning for Retention," *HR Magazine*, 52 (July 2007): 128; and Kathryn Tyler, "Helping Employees Step Up," *HR Magazine*, 52 (August 2007): 48–52.

19. As quoted in Tim Talevich, "Carly Unplugged," *The Costco Connection*, 19 (June 2004): 19. Also see Robert Rodriguez, "Diversity Finds Its Place," *HR Magazine*, 51 (August 2006): 56–61.

20. See Elizabeth Agnvall, "Job Fairs Go Virtual," *HR Magazine*, 52 (July 2007): 85–88; Steven D. Maurer and Yuping Liu, "Developing Effective e-Recruiting Websites: Insights for Managers from Marketers," *Business Horizons*, 50 (July–August 2007): 305–314; and Jennifer Schramm, "Internet Connections," *HR Magazine*, 52 (September 2007): 176.

21. As quoted in Ann Herrington, "Make That Switch," *Fortune* (February 4, 2002): 1, at **www.fortune.com/careers.**

22. Based on Theresa Minton-Eversole, "E-Recruitment Comes of Age, Survey Says," *HR Magazine*, 52 (August 2007): 34.

23. Steve Hamm, "Children of the Web," *Business Week* (July 2, 2007): 58. Also see Douglas MacMillan, "The Art of the Online Résumé," *Business Week* (May 7, 2007): 86.

24. Jena McGregor, "Beware of That Video Resume," *Business Week* (June 11, 2007): 12. Also see Kathy Gurchiek, "Video Resumes Spark Curiosity, Questions," *HR Magazine*, 52 (May 2007): 28, 30–31; and Heidi Richter, "Lights, Camera, Hired!" *Newsweek* (May 7, 2007): 65.

25. For more, see Richard A. Posthuma, Mark V. Roehling, and Michael A. Campion, "Applying U.S. Employment Discrimination Laws to International Employers: Advice for Scientists and Practitioners," *Personnel Psychology*, 59 (Autumn 2006): 705–739; and Michael Orey, "Fear of Firing," *Business Week* (April 23, 2007): 52–62.

26. Pamela Babcock, "Spotting Lies," *HR Magazine*, 48 (October 2003): 47. Also see Drew Robb, "Screening for Speedier Selection," *HR Magazine*, 49 (September 2004): 143–148.

27. Merry Mayer, "Background Checks in Focus," *HR Magazine*, 47 (January 2002): 59. Also see Ann Davis, "Employers Dig Deep into Workers' Pasts, Citing Terrorism Fears," *Wall Street Journal* (March 12, 2002): A1, A12; Bill Leonard, "Crime-Data Software for Police May Benefit Employers," *HR Magazine*, 48 (January 2003): 27; and Maria Greco Danaher, "Lack of Background Check Leads to Liability," *HR Magazine*, 50 (January 2005): 94.

28. Based on "Wal-Mart to Run Background Checks," *USA Today* (August 13, 2004): 1B.

29. Fred Vogelstein, "Google @$165: Are These Guys for Real?" *Fortune* (December 13, 2004): 106, 108.

30. See Diane Coutu, "We Googled You," *Harvard Business Review*, 85 (June 2007): 37–41.

31. See Sharon Fears, "The Demise of Job Descriptions," *HR Magazine*, 45 (August 2000): 184; Carla Joinson, "Refocusing Job Descriptions," *HR Magazine*, 46 (January 2001): 66–72; and Maria Greco Danaher, "Credentials Absent from Job Descriptions Considered," *HR Magazine*, 52 (April 2007): 113.

32. David A. Brookmire and Amy A. Burton, "A Format for Packaging Your Affirmative Action Program," *Personnel Journal*, 57 (June 1978): 294. Also see Marc A. Mandelman, "Title VII Protects Welfare-to-Work Participants," *HR Magazine*, 49 (May 2004): 111–112; and Erika Hayes James and Lynn Perry Wooten, "Diversity Crises: How Firms Manage Discrimination Lawsuits," *Academy of Management Journal*, 49 (December 2006): 1103–1118.

33. See Cliff Edwards, "Coming Out in Corporate America," *Business Week* (December 15, 2003): 64–72; John Simons, "Gay Marriage: Corporate America Blazed the Trail," *Fortune* (June 14, 2004): 42, 44; and Rebecca R. Hastings, "States Ban Gender Identity Discrimination," *HR Magazine*, 52 (August 2007): 24, 26.

34. Data from Theresa Howard, "Coke Settles Bias Lawsuit for $192.5M," *USA Today* (November 17, 2000): 1B; and Stephanie Armour, "Bias Suits Put

Spotlight on Workplace Diversity," *USA Today* (January 10, 2001): 1B–2B.

35. Data from "Boeing Settles Bias Case, Will Pay Up to $72.5 Mil.," *Arizona Republic* (July 17, 2004): D7. Also see Jonathan A. Segal, "Unlimited Check-Writing Authority for Supervisors? EEO Training Cuts Widen Costs," *HR Magazine*, 52 (February 2007): 119–124.

36. See Charlene Marmer Solomon, "Frequently Asked Questions About Affirmative Action," *Personnel Journal*, 74 (August 1995): 61. For historical perspectives, see Janet Kornblum, "Integration Makes Gains, But Perceptions Slower to Change," *USA Today* (April 6, 2004): 7D; and Roger O. Crockett, "Putting Words to the Dream," *Business Week* (July 12, 2004): 16.

37. See Jennifer Schramm, "Acting Affirmatively," *HR Magazine*, 48 (September 2003): 192; and Fred L. Fry and Jennifer R. D. Burgess, "The End of the Need for Affirmative Action: Are We There Yet?" *Business Horizons*, 46 (November–December 2003): 7–16.

38. For related discussion, see Robert J. Grossman, "Constant Inconsistency," *HR Magazine*, 48 (December 2003): 68–74; Margaret M. Clark, "While Some Employers See No Incentive for EEOC Mediation, Others Find Benefits," *HR Magazine*, 49 (January 2004): 36; Paul Oyer and Scott Schaefer, "The Bias Backfire," *Harvard Business Review*, 82 (November 2004): 26; Rita Zeidner, "Planning for EEO-1 Changes," *HR Magazine*, 51 (May 2006): 60–64; and Jathan Janove, "Retaliation Nation," *HR Magazine*, 51 (October 2006): 62–66.

39. Julia Lawlor, "Study: Affirmative-Action Hires' Abilities Doubted," *USA Today* (August 31, 1992): 3B. The complete study is reported in Madeline E. Heilman, Caryn J. Block, and Jonathan A. Lucas, "Presumed Incompetent? Stigmatization and Affirmative Action Efforts," *Journal of Applied Psychology*, 77 (August 1992): 536–554. Also see Beverly L. Little, William D. Murry, and James C. Wimbush, "Perceptions of Workplace Affirmative Action Plans," *Group & Organization Management*, 23 (March 1998): 27–47.

40. Yehouda Shenhav, "Entrance of Blacks and Women into Managerial Positions in Scientific and Engineering Occupations: A Longitudinal Analysis," *Academy of Management Journal*, 35 (October 1992): 897. Also see Mike McNamee, "The Proof Is in Performance," *Business Week* (July 15, 1996): 22. A female executive's view can be found in "Helayne Spivak," *Fast Company*, no. 27 (September 1999): 113.

41. For example, see Jonathan Kaufman, "White Men Shake Off That Losing Feeling on Affirmative Action," *Wall Street Journal* (September 5, 1996): A1, A4.

42. R. Roosevelt Thomas Jr., "From Affirmative Action to Affirming Diversity," *Harvard Business Review*, 68 (March–April 1990): 114. For an interview with R. Roosevelt Thomas, see Ellen Neuborne, "Diversity Challenges Many Companies," *USA Today* (November 18, 1996): 10B. Also see William Atkinson, "Bringing Diversity to White Men," *HR Magazine*, 46 (September 2001): 76–83.

43. For more on diversity, see Ann Pomeroy, "Cultivating Female Leaders," *HR Magazine*, 52 (February 2007): 44–50; Bill Leonard, "Transgender Issues Test Diversity Limits," *HR Magazine*, 52 (June 2007): 32–34; Rebecca Hastings, "The Forgotten Minority," *HR Magazine*, 52 (July 2007): 62–67; Margery Weinstein, "Diversity Dilemma," *Training*, 44 (July–August 2007): 10; and Alice H. Eagly and Linda L. Carli, "Women and the Labyrinth of Leadership," *Harvard Business Review*, 85 (September 2007): 62–71.

44. As quoted in Ryan Underwood, "No Brakes," *Fast Company*, no. 86 (September 2004): 112.

45. Joel Schettler, "Equal Access to All," *Training*, 39 (January 2002): 44. Also see Jim Barthold, "Waiting in the Wings," *HR Magazine*, 49 (April 2004): 88–95.

46. For inspiring stories, see Jack Carey, "Coach Lost Leg, Gained Perspective," *USA Today* (November 2, 2006): 11C; and Liz Szabo, "The Upside of Cancer: A New Outlook on Life," USA Today (November 21, 2006): 11D. Also see "How to Job-Hunt If You Have Disability," *Arizona Republic* (July 1, 2007): EC1.

47. For more, see Cheryl Comeau-Kirschner, "New ADA Guidelines," *Management Review*, 88 (April 1999): 6; Robert H. Schwartz, Frederick R. Post, and Jack L. Simonetti, "The ADA and the Mentally Disabled: What Must Firms Do?" *Business Horizons*, 43 (July–August 2000): 52–58; Eric V. Neumann and Brian H. Kleiner, "How to Accommodate Disabilities Under ADA," *Nonprofit World*, 18 (September–October 2000): 29–33; Margery Weinstein, "Another Lawsuit?" *Training*, 44 (May 2007): 12; and Joan Biskupic, "Disability Claims Related to Obesity Could Rise with Americans' Weight," *USA Today* (June 13, 2007): 1A.

48. Gene Koretz, "Dubious Aid for the Disabled," *Business Week* (November 9, 1998): 30.

49. Jack Gillum, "Disabled Are Losing Optimism, Survey Shows," *USA Today* (June 28, 2004): 6D.

50. Susan B. Garland, "Protecting the Disabled Won't Cripple Business," *Business Week* (April 26, 1999): 73. For related reading, see Margaret M. Clark, "High Court's ADA Ruling Leaves Some Accommodations Questions Unanswered," *HR Magazine*, 49 (January 2004): 30; Saundra Jackson, "Disabled Workers, Salary Talk, State Taxes," *HR Magazine*, 49 (March 2004): 39; and Adrienne Colella, Ramona L. Paetzold, and Maura A. Belliveau, "Factors Affecting Coworkers' Procedural Justice Inferences of the Workplace Accommodations of Employees with Disabilities," *Personnel Psychology*, 57 (Spring 2004): 1–23.

51. See Kathryn Tyler, "Ready to Be Heard," *HR Magazine*, 49 (September 2004): 70–76; and Frank Jossi, "High-Tech Enables Employees," *HR Magazine*, 51 (February 2006): 109–115.

52. See Jonathan A. Segal, "Throw Supervisors a Lifeline and Save Yourself: Having ADA Compliance Knowledge Is Useless Unless You Share It," *HR Magazine*, 48 (June 2003): 167–179; and Mary E. McLaughlin, Myrtle P. Bell, and Donna Y. Stringer, "Stigma and Acceptance of Persons with Disabilities," *Group and Organization Management*, 29 (June 2004): 302–333.

53. See Dave Patel, "Testing, Testing, Testing," *HR Magazine*, 47 (February 2002): 112; and Claire Bush, "Handwriting Could Tell Employer Lots About You," *Arizona Republic* (June 2, 2007): D5.

54. See Scott B. Parry, "How to Validate an Assessment Tool," *Training*, 30 (April 1993): 37–42.

55. See John Bacon, "Polygraphs Can Lie, Researchers Say," *USA Today* (October 9, 2002): 3A; James E. Wanek, Paul R. Sackett, and Deniz S. Ones, "Towards an Understanding of Integrity Test Similarities and Differences: An Item-Level Analysis of Seven Tests," *Personnel Psychology*, 56 (Winter 2003): 873–894; Jared Sandberg, "How I Survived Tests That Introduced Me to My Inner Executive," *Wall Street Journal* (March 10, 2004): B1; Del Jones, "Was the Writing on the Wall, . . . or Their Annual Reports?" *USA Today* (March 29, 2004): 3B; Kerry J. Sulkowicz, "The Corporate Shrink," *Fast Company*, no. 87 (October 2004): 48; "Measuring Character," *Training*, 41 (October 2004): 16; and Holly Dolezalek, "Tests on Trial," *Training*, 42 (April 2005): 32–34.

56. Rod Kurtz, "Testing, Testing . . . ," *Inc.*, 26 (June 2004): 36.

57. See Kerry J. Sulkowicz, "The Corporate Shrink," *Fast Company*, no. 90 (January 2005): 38.

58. "Structured Interviewing: Avoiding Selection Problems," by Elliott D. Pursell, Michael A. Campion, and Sarah R. Gaylord, copyright November 1980. Reprinted with permission of *Personnel Journal*, Costa Mesa, Calif.; all rights reserved.

59. Barbara Whitaker Shimko, "New Breed Workers Need New Yardsticks," *Business Horizons*, 33 (November–December 1990): 35–36. For related research, see Allen I. Huffcutt and Philip L. Roth, "Racial Group Differences in Employment Interview Evaluations," *Journal of Applied Psychology*, 83 (April 1998): 179–189.

60. Practical tips on interviewing can be found in Tahl Raz, "How Would You Design Bill Gates's Bathroom?" *Inc.*, 25 (May 2003): 35; Anne Fisher, "How Can I Survive a Phone Interview?" *Fortune* (April 19, 2004): 54; Anne Fisher, "Truly Puzzling Interview Questions," *Fortune* (September 20, 2004): 70; John Kador, *How to Ace the Brainteaser Interview* (New York: McGraw-Hill, 2005); Matt Bolch, "Lights. Camera . . . Interview," *HR Magazine*, 52 (March 2007): 99–102; Amy Maingault, John Sweeney, and Naomi Cossack, "Interviewing, Management Training, Strikes," *HR Magazine*, 52 (June 2007): 43; and Patricia Bathurst, "Dress Right," *Arizona Republic* (July 8, 2007): EC1.

61. Based on Pursell et al., "Structured Interviewing."

62. Based on Bruce Bloom, "Behavioral Interviewing: The Future Direction and Focus of the Employment Interview." Paper presented to the Midwest Business Administration Association, Chicago (March 27, 1998). Also see Andrea C. Poe, "Graduate Work," *HR Magazine*, 48 (October 2003): 95–100; and Joey George and Kent Marett, "The Truth About Lies," *HR Magazine*, 49 (May 2004): 87–91.

63. Del J. Still, *High Impact Hiring: How to Interview and Select Outstanding Employees*, 2nd ed., rev. (Dana Point, Calif.: Management Development Systems, 2001), pp. 53–54 (emphasis added).

64. As quoted in Kathryn Tyler, "One Bad Apple," *HR Magazine*, 49 (December 2004): 85.

65. Kerry Sulkowicz, "Straight Talk at Review Time," *Business Week* (September 10, 2007): 16. Also see Jack Welch and Suzy Welch, "The Right Way to Say Goodbye," *Business Week* (March 26, 2007): 144.

66. Tammy Galvin, "The Weakest Link," *Training*, 38 (December 2001): 8. Also see Lin Grensing-Pophal, "Motivate Managers to Review Performance," *HR Magazine*, 46 (March 2001): 44–48.

67. Data from "What to Do with an Egg-Sucking Dog?" *Training*, 33 (October 1996): 17–21.

68. See Donald Kirkpatrick, *Improving Employee Performance Through Appraisal and Coaching* (New York: Amacom, 2005); Christopher D. Lee, "Feedback, Not Appraisal," *HR Magazine*,

51 (November 2006): 111–114; Larry Bossidy, "What Your Leader Expects of You, and What You Should Expect in Return," *Harvard Business Review*, 85 (April 2007): 58–65; and Paul Falcone, "Big-Picture Performance Appraisal," *HR Magazine*, 52 (August 2007): 97–100.

69. For EEOC guidelines during performance appraisal, see William S. Swan and Philip Margulies, *How to Do a Superior Performance Appraisal* (New York: Wiley, 1991).

70. Adapted from Hubert S. Field and William H. Holley, "The Relationship of Performance Appraisal System Characteristics to Verdicts in Selected Employment Discrimination Cases," *Academy of Management Journal*, 25 (June 1982): 392–406. A more recent analysis of 51 cases that derived similar criteria can be found in Gerald V. Barrett and Mary C. Kernan, "Performance Appraisal and Terminations: A Review of Court Decisions Since *Brito* v. *Zia* with Implications for Personnel Practices," *Personnel Psychology*, 40 (Autumn 1987): 489–503.

71. For more, see Dick Grote, "Painless Performance Appraisals Focus on Results, Behaviors," *HR Magazine*, 43 (October 1998): 52–58.

72. See Paul Falcone, "Watch What You Write," *HR Magazine*, 49 (November 2004): 125–128.

73. For related research, see Todd J. Maurer, Jerry K. Palmer, and Donna K. Ashe, "Diaries, Checklists, Evaluations, and Contrast Effects in Measurement of Behavior," *Journal of Applied Psychology*, 78 (April 1993): 226–231.

74. Alan M. Webber, "How Business Is a Lot Like Life," *Fast Company*, no. 45 (April 2001): 135.

75. Matthew Boyle, "Performance Reviews: Perilous Curves Ahead," *Fortune* (May 28, 2001): 187. Also see Steve Bates, "Forced Ranking," *HR Magazine*, 48 (June 2003): 62–68; and Gail Johnson, "Forced Ranking: The Good, the Bad, and the Alternative," *Training*, 41 (May 2004): 24–34.

76. See David Kiley and Del Jones, "Ford Alters Worker Evaluation Process," *USA Today* (July 11, 2001): 1B; Earle Eldridge, "Ford Settles 2 Lawsuits by White Male Workers," *USA Today* (December 19, 2001): 3B; and Benjamin J. Romano, "Microsoft Alters Evaluations," *Arizona Republic* (December 18, 2006): D5.

77. See Jai Ghorpade, "Managing Five Paradoxes of 360-Degree Feedback," *Academy of Management Executive*, 14 (February 2000): 140–150; Angelo S. DeNisi and Avraham N. Kluger, "Feedback Effectiveness: Can 360-Degree Appraisals Be Improved?" *Academy of Management Executive*, 14 (February 2000): 129–139; William C.

Byham, "Fixing the Instrument," *Training*, 41 (July 2004): 50; and the second Q&A in Jack Welch and Suzy Welch, "The Importance of Being Here," *Business Week* (April 16, 2007): 92.

78. See David A. Waldman, Leanne E. Atwater, and David Antonioni, "Has 360 Degree Feedback Gone Amok?" *Academy of Management Executive*, 12 (May 1998): 86–94; and Dennis E. Coates, "Don't Tie 360 Feedback to Pay," *Training*, 35 (September 1998): 68–78.

79. Frank Shipper, Richard C. Hoffman, and Denise M. Rotondo, "Does the 360 Feedback Process Create Actionable Knowledge Equally Across Cultures?" *Academy of Management Learning and Education*, 6 (March 2007): 33–50.

80. Based on Fred Luthans and Suzanne J. Peterson, "360-Degree Feedback with Systematic Coaching: Empirical Analysis Suggests a Winning Combination," *Human Resource Management*, 42 (Fall 2003): 243–256. Also see Angelo J. Kinicki, Gregory E. Prussia, Bin (Joshua) Wu, and Frances M. McKee-Ryan, "A Covariance Structure Analysis of Employees' Response to Performance Feedback," *Journal of Applied Psychology*, 89 (December 2004): 1057–1069.

81. "Best Practices: Executive Coaching, Wachovia," *Training*, 41 (March 2004): 61. For related reading, see Kristine Ellis, "Individual Development Plans: The Building Blocks of Development," *Training*, 41 (December 2004): 20–25; and Kathryn Tyler, "Sizing Up Board Members," *HR Magazine*, 52 (July 2007): 68–72.

82. Data from Margery Weinstein, "Learning Dollars," *Training*, 44 (April 2007): 6.

83. Data from Margery Weinstein, "How Expensive?" *Training*, 44 (May 2007): 8.

84. As quoted in Edward E. Gordon, "The 2010 Crossroad," *Training*, 42 (January 2005): 34. Also see Holly Dolezalek, "Outta Here," *Training*, 43 (September 2006): 19–23.

85. Ibid., p. 35. For more, see Ken Dychtwald, Tamara J. Erickson, and Robert Morison, *Workforce Crisis: How to Beat the Coming Shortage of Skills and Talent* (Boston: Harvard Business School Press, 2006); Susan Meisinger, "Education Gap Threatens U.S. Competitiveness," *HR Magazine*, 52 (March 2007): 10; and Peter Coy and Jack Ewing, "Where Are All the Workers?" *Business Week* (April 9, 2007): 28–31.

86. Anne Fisher, "Retain Your Brains," *Fortune* (July 24, 2006): 49.

87. Robert Levering and Milton Moskowitz, "The 100 Best Companies to Work For," *Fortune* (January 24, 2005): 86.

88. Margery Weinstein, "Mobile Learning News," *Training*, 44 (April 2007): 8. Also see Margery Weinstein, "Winning Games," *Training*, 44 (April 2007): 16–18;

Sarah Boehle, "Subject Matter Expert Trouble?" *Training*, 44 (April 2007): 28–30; Holly Dolezalek, "Biz Kids," *Training*, 44 (July–August 2007): 12–16; Sarah Boehle, "Is Open Source Right for You?" *Training*, 44 (July–August 2007): 36–39; and Jennifer Taylor Arnold, "Learning on the Fly," *HR Magazine*, 52 (September 2007): 127–131.

89. Kenneth N. Wexley and Gary P. Latham, *Developing and Training Human Resources in Organizations* (Glenview, Ill.: Scott, Foresman, 1981): 75–77. Also see Margery Weinstein, "Wake-Up Call," *Training*, 44 (June 2007): 48–50; and Margery Weinstein, "Selling Points," *Training*, 44 (June 2007): 51–53.

90. Ibid., p. 77. Also see Diana Hird, "What Makes a Training Program Good?" *Training*, 37 (June 2000): 48–52; and Mark E. Haskins and James G. Clawson, "Making It Sticky: How to Facilitate the Transfer of Executive Education Experiences Back to the Workplace," *Journal of Management Development*, 25, no. 9 (2006): 850–869.

91. Training program assessment/evaluation is covered in Heather Johnson, "The Whole Picture?" *Training*, 41 (July 2004): 30–34; Kristine Ellis, "What's the ROI of ROI?" *Training*, 42 (January 2005): 16–21; and Jack Gordon, "Eye on ROI?" *Training*, 44 (May 2007): 43–45.

92. See Kimberly Eretzian Smirles, "Attributions of Responsibility in Cases of Sexual Harassment: The Person and the Situation," *Journal of Applied Social Psychology*, 34 (February 2004): 342–365; and Jennifer L. Berdahl, "Harassment Based on Sex: Protecting Social Status in the Context of Gender Hierarchy," *Academy of Management Review*, 32 (April 2007): 641–658.

93. Ruhal Dooley, "Parental Leave, Behavior at Work, Camera Use," *HR Magazine*, 49 (July 2004): 42.

94. See Adam Shell, "Morgan Stanley Settles Sex-Bias Case," *USA Today* (July 13, 2004): 1B; Robert K. Robinson, Geralyn McClure Franklin, and Walter J. Davis, "Sexual Harassment Redux," *Business Horizons*, 47 (July–August 2004): 3–5; Linda Wasmer Andrews, "Hard-Core Offenders," *HR Magazine*, 49 (December 2004): 42–48; and Thomas O. McCarthy, "Sexual Conduct: Equal Abuse Unequal Harm," *HR Magazine*, 50 (January 2005): 93–94.

95. Data from Stephanie Armour, "More Men Say They Are Sexually Harassed at Work," *USA Today* (September 17, 2004): 1B. Also see "Daily Downer," *Training*, 42 (April 2005): 12.

96. "Dow Chemical Fires 50 for Porno E-Mail," *USA Today* (July 28, 2000): 1B. Also see Scott R. Eldridge, "Sexist E-Mail Backfires," *HR Magazine*, 52 (August 2007): 103–104.

97. Data from Tamara Henry, "Sexual Harassment Pervades Schools, Study Says," *USA Today* (July 23, 1996): 8B. Also see John Tuohy, "Sex Discrimination Infects Med Schools," *USA Today* (June 7, 2000): 8D.

98. For a list of verbal and nonverbal forms of general harassment, see R. Bruce McAfee and Diana L. Deadrick, "Teach Employees to Just Say 'No!'" *HR Magazine*, 41 (February 1996): 86–89.

99. For details, see David E. Terpstra and Douglas D. Baker, "Outcomes of Federal Court Decisions on Sexual Harassment," *Academy of Management Journal*, 35 (March 1992): 181–190. Also see Jonathan A. Segal, "HR as Judge, Jury, Prosecutor and Defender," *HR Magazine*, 46 (October 2001): 141–154.

100. See Michael W. Johnson, "A 'Bifocal Approach' to Anti-Harassment Training," *HR Legal Report* (March–April 2007): 1, 5–8. **www.shrm.org/law.**

101. "'Big Lag' in Treatment for Alcoholism Grows," *USA Today* (July 3, 2007): 9D. Also see Jon Saraceno, "Baseball Players, Alcohol Aren't Abnormal Mix," *USA Today* (May 9, 2007): 2C.

102. Data from "Almost 50% Have Used Illicit Drugs," *USA Today* (August 12, 2004): 1A. Also see Michael R. Frone, "Prevalence and Distribution of Illicit Drug Use in the Workforce and in the Workplace: Findings and Implications from a U.S. National Survey," *Journal of Applied Psychology*, 91 (July 2006): 856–869.

103. Matthew Boyle, "The New E-Workplace," *Fortune* (October 1, 2001): 176.

104. Diane Cadrain, "Drug Testing Falls Out of Employers' Favor," *HR Magazine*, 51 (June 2006): 48.

105. Based on Ibid.

106. Data from Stephanie Armour and Del Jones, "Workers' Positive Drug Tests Decrease," *USA Today* (June 20, 2006): 3B; and Kathy Gurchiek, "Employer Testing Credited for Lower Drug-Use Rates," *HR Magazine*, 52 (June 2007): 36, 41. Also see Stephanie Armour, "Employers Grapple with Medical Marijuana Use," *USA Today* (April 17, 2007): 1B–2B.

107. See Jonathan A. Segal, "Drugs, Alcohol and the ADA," *HR Magazine*, 37 (December 1992): 73–76. Also see Jess McCuan, "When an Addict Seeks a Job," *Inc.*, 26 (March 2004): 30.

108. Janet Deming, "Drug-Free Workplace Is Good Business," *HR Magazine*, 35 (April 1990): 61. For more, see **http://www. dol.gov/asp/programs/drugs/said/.**

109. See Donna M. Owens, "EAPs for a Diverse World," *HR Magazine*, 51 (October 2006): 91–96.

110. Stuart Feldman, "Today's EAPs Make the Grade," *Personnel*, 68 (February 1991): 3.

CHAPTER 11

1. **Opening Quote:** Laurence J. Peter, *Peter's Quotations* (New York: Bantam, 1977), p. 100.

2. For example, see Mary Young and James E. Post, "Managing to Communicate, Communicating to Manage: How Leading Companies Communicate with Employees," *Organizational Dynamics*, 22 (Summer 1993): 31–43; Ale Smidts, Ad Th. H. Pruyn, and Cees B. M. van Riel, "The Impact of Employee Communication and Perceived External Prestige on Organizational Identification," *Academy of Management Journal*, 49 (October 2001): 1051–1062; and Eric Krell, "The Unintended Word," *HR Magazine*, 51 (August 2006): 50–54.

3. "Wanted: Management Skills," *Training*, 41 (November 2004): 19.

4. "Hilary Billings," *Fast Company*, no. 66 (January 2003): 104. Also see Stanley Bing, "Bye-bye, BlackBerry," *Fortune* (January 10, 2005): 102.

5. Stephanie Armour, "Failure to Communicate Costly for Companies," *USA Today* (September 30, 1998): 1B.

6. Keith Davis, *Human Behavior at Work: Organizational Behavior*, 6th ed. (New York: McGraw-Hill, 1981), p. 399.

7. For an instructive distinction between one-way (the arrow model) and two-way (the circuit model) communication, see Phillip G. Clampitt, *Communicating for Managerial Effectiveness* (Newbury Park, Calif.: Sage, 1991), pp. 1–24.

8. For interesting reading, see Lisa Burrell, "A Larger Language for Business," *Harvard Business Review*, 85 (May 2007): 28.

9. See Thomas H. Davenport and John C. Beck, *The Attention Economy: Understanding the New Currency of Business* (Boston: Harvard Business School Press, 2001).

10. See Chapter 3 in Nancy Adler with Allison Gundersen, *International Dimensions of Organizational Behavior*, 5th ed. (Mason, Ohio: Thomson South-Western, 2008), pp. 69–95.

11. Ernest Gundling, "How to Communicate Globally," *Training & Development*, 53 (June 1999): 30. Also see Ernest Gundling, *Working GlobeSmart: 12 People Skills for Doing Business Across Borders* (Palo Alto, Calif.: Davies-Black, 2003); and Dan Landis, Janet M. Bennett, and Milton J. Bennett, eds., *Handbook of Intercultural Training*, 3rd ed. (Thousand Oaks, Calif.: Sage, 2004).

12. See Robert H. Lengel and Richard L. Daft, "The Selection of Communication Media as an Executive Skill," *Academy of Management Executive*, 2 (August 1988): 225–232. For a research update, see John R. Carlson and Robert W. Zmud, "Channel Expansion Theory and the Experiential Nature of Media Richness Perceptions," *Academy of Management Journal*, 42 (April 1999): 153–170. Also see Bruce Barry and Ingrid Smithey Fulmer, "The Medium and the Message: The Adaptive Use of Communication Media in Dyadic Influence," *Academy of Management Review*, 29 (April 2004): 272–292.

13. As quoted in Adam Lashinsky, "Lights! Camera! Cue the CEO!" *Fortune* (August 21, 2006): 27.

14. Erin Binney, "Is E-Mail the New Pink Slip?" *HR Magazine*, 51 (November 2006): 32.

15. Jim Hopkins, "Deaths of Hispanic Workers Soar 53%," *USA Today* (March 25, 2002): 1B. Also see Yvonne Wingett, "Hospital Translators Filling Void," *Arizona Republic* (June 3, 2007): B1, B4; and the second Q&A in Jack Welch and Suzy Welch, "From Hero to Zero," *Business Week* (September 3, 2007): 104.

16. Del Jones, "Do Foreign Executives Balk at Sports Jargon?" *USA Today* (March 30, 2007): 1B. Also see Stanley Bing, "Corporate Jargon," *Fortune* (March 19, 2007): 44.

17. Data from Louisa Wah, "An Ounce of Prevention," *Management Review*, 87 (October 1998): 9. Feedback on performance is covered in Sherry E. Moss and Juan I. Sanchez, "Are Your Employees Avoiding You? Managerial Strategies for Closing the Feedback Gap," *Academy of Management Executive*, 18 (February 2004): 32–44; and Gardiner Morse, "Feedback Backlash," *Harvard Business Review*, 82 (October 2004): 28. Research on feedback recipients is reported in Angelo J. Kinicki, Gregory E. Prussia, Bin (Joshua) Wu, and Frances M. McKee-Ryan, "A Covariance Structure Analysis of Employees' Response to Performance Feedback," *Journal of Applied Psychology*, 89 (December 2004): 1057–1069.

18. Lindsey Gerdes, "The Best Places to Launch a Career," *Business Week* (September 24, 2007): 58.

19. See Bella M. DePaulo, Deborah A. Kashy, Susan E. Kirkendol, Melissa M. Wyer, and Jennifer A. Epstein, "Lying in Everyday Life," *Journal of Personality and Social Psychology*, 70 (May 1996): 979–995; and Deborah A. Kashy and Bella M. DePaulo, "Who Lies?" *Journal of Personality and Social Psychology*, 70 (May 1996): 1037–1051.

20. Frank Snowden Hopkins, "Communication: The Civilizing Force," *The Futurist*, 15 (April 1981): 39. Also see Julie Schlosser, "Engaging with the Customer," *Fortune* (May 14, 2007): 28.

21. See Paul A. Argenti, Robert A. Howell, and Karen A. Beck, "The Strategic Communication Imperative," *MIT Sloan Management Review*, 46 (Spring 2005): 83–89; John Hamm, "The Five Messages Leaders Must Manage," *Harvard Business Review*, 84 (May 2006): 114–123; and Paul A. Argenti and Thea S. Haley, "Get Your Act Together," *Harvard Business Review*, 84 (October 2006): 26.

22. Phillip G. Clampitt, Robert J. DeKoch, and Thomas Cashman, "A Strategy for Communicating About Uncertainty," *Academy of Management Executive*, 14 (November 2000): 48.

23. Ibid.

24. Ibid.

25. See Russ Juskalian, "How Lincoln Won the Civil War," *USA Today* (November 27, 2006): 10B.

26. "Reining In Office Rumors," *Inc.*, 26 (November 2004): 60.

27. Stephanie Armour, "Did You Hear the Story About Office Gossip?" *USA Today* (September 10, 2007): 2B.

28. Heather Green, "The Water Cooler Is Now on the Web," *Business Week* (October 1, 2007): 78. Also see Jon Fine, "Polluting the Blogosphere," *Business Week* (July 10, 2006): 20; Heather Green, "The Big Shots of Blogdom," *Business Week* (May 7, 2007): 66; and Robert Scoble, "The Next Email," *Fast Company*, no. 118 (September 2007): 72.

29. Lisa A. Burke and Jessica Morris Wise, "The Effective Care, Handling, and Pruning of the Office Grapevine," *Business Horizons*, 46 (May–June 2003): 73–74.

30. Data from David Kirkpatrick, "It's Hard to Manage If You Don't Blog," *Fortune* (October 4, 2004): 46; and Green, "The Water Cooler Is Now on the Web," pp. 78–79. Also see Stephen Baker and Heather Green, "Blogs Will Change Your Business," *Business Week* (May 2, 2005): 56–67; and Michael Fitzgerald, "Let's Get Together: Making Contacts with Social Nets," *Inc.*, 29 (August 2007): 54–55.

31. Erin Ryan, "Why Your Firm May Need a Blog Policy," *Arizona Republic* (November 5, 2006): D5. Also see Paula Lehman, "The Marshal of MySpace," *Business Week* (April 23, 2007): 86–88; Janet Kornblum, "Rudeness, Threats Make the Web a Cruel World," *USA Today* (July 31, 2007): 1A–2A; and Green, "The Water Cooler Is Now on the Web," p. 78–79.

32. John W. Newstrom, Robert E. Monczka, and William E. Reif, "Perceptions of the Grapevine: Its Value and Influence," *Journal of Business Communication*, 11 (Spring 1974): 12–20.

33. See Roy Rowan, "Where Did *That* Rumor Come From?" *Fortune* (August 13, 1979): 130–137.

34. See Nicholas Difonzo, Prashant Bordia, and Ralph L. Rosnow, "Reining In Rumors," *Organizational Dynamics*, 23 (Summer 1994): 47–62; Nancy B. Kurland and Lisa Hope Pelled, "Passing the Word: Toward a Model of Gossip and Power in the Workplace," *Academy of Management Review*, 25 (April 2000): 428–438; and Kerry Sulkowicz, "Don't Breathe a Word," *Business Week* (July 23, 2007): 14.

35. Patricia Sellers, "Lessons from TV's New Bosses," *Fortune* (March 14, 1988): 115, 118. For an update on Tisch, see Kimberly Weisul, "One Bear Doesn't Make It a Picnic," *Business Week* (March 25, 2002): 8.

36. See "Patrolling the Online Rumor Mill," *Training*, 37 (June 2000): 29; and Chris Woodyard, "Lurker Prowls Web to Clarify Issues, Answer Questions," *USA Today* (February 6, 2001): 6B.

37. "Executives Favor Plucking the Fruits from Employee Grapevine," *Association Management*, 36 (April 1984): 105.

38. A comprehensive discussion of rumors and rumor control can be found in Ralph L. Rosnow, "Inside Rumor: A Personal Journey," *American Psychologist*, 46 (May 1991): 484–496. Also see Lin Grensing-Pophal, "Got the Message?" *HR Magazine*, 46 (April 2001): 74–79.

39. Tammy Galvin, "Nothing Ventured," *Training*, 41 (February 2004): 4.

40. See Jack Griffin, "The Body's Language," in *How to Say It from the Heart* (Paramus, N.J.: Prentice-Hall, 2001), pp. 13–25; and Ronald E. Riggio and Robert S. Feldman, *Applications of Nonverbal Communication* (Mahwah, N.J.: Erlbaum, 2004).

41. See Albert Mehrabian, "Communication Without Words," *Psychology Today*, 2 (September 1968): 53–55. For a discussion of the nonverbal origins of language, see Sharon Begley, "Talking from Hand to Mouth," *Newsweek* (March 15, 1999): 56–58. Nonverbal cues are discussed in Thomas K. Connellan, "Great Expectations, Great Results," *HR Magazine*, 48 (June 2003): 155–150.

42. Pierre Mornell, "The Sounds of Silence," *Inc.*, 23 (February 2001): 117.

43. See Maria Puente, "How NOT to Dress for Work," *USA Today* (December 1, 2004): 1D–2D.

44. Excerpt from Brian Hickey, "People Packaging," *America West Airlines Magazine*, 5 (September 1990): 61. Reprinted by permission of the author. Also see Bill Leonard, "Casual Dress Policies Can Trip Up Job Applicants," *HR Magazine*, 46 (June 2001): 33, 35; and Stephanie Armour, "'Business Casual' Causes Confusion," *USA Today* (July 10, 2007): 1B–2B.

45. This three-way breakdown comes from Dale G. Leathers, *Nonverbal*

Communication Systems (Boston: Allyn & Bacon, 1976), ch. 2. Also see James M. Carroll and James A. Russell, "Facial Expressions in Hollywood's Portrayal of Emotion," *Journal of Personality and Social Psychology*, 72 (January 1997): 164–176; and the second Q&A in Kerry Sulkowicz, "Nobody Loves a Tattletale," *Business Week* (August 6, 2007): 14.

46. For details see Mac Fulfer, "Nonverbal Communication: How to Read What's Plain as the Nose . . . or Eyelid . . . or Chin . . . on Their Faces," *Journal of Organization Excellence*, 20 (Spring 2001): 19–27. Also see Bobbie Gossage, "What a Smile Means," *Inc.*, 25 (October 2003): 20; Andy Raskin, "A Face Any Business Can Trust," *Business 2.0*, 4 (December 2003): 58–60; Stephanie Clifford, "It's Official: MBAs Are a Bunch of Clowns," *Inc.*, 27 (February 2005): 23.

47. Paul C. Judge, "High Tech Star," *Business Week* (March 15, 1999): 75.

48. Based on A. Keenan, "Effects of the Non-Verbal Behaviour of Interviewers on Candidates' Performance," *Journal of Occupational Psychology*, 49, no. 3 (1976): 171–175. Also see Stanford W. Gregory Jr. and Stephen Webster, "Nonverbal Signal in Voices of Interview Partners Effectively Predicts Communication Accommodation and Social Status Perceptions," *Journal of Personality and Social Psychology*, 70 (June 1996): 1231–1240; Jeff Mowatt, "Making Connections: How to Create Rapport with Anyone in Under 30 Seconds," *Canadian Manager*, 25 (Fall 2000): 26, 29; and Nick Morgan, "The Kinesthetic Speaker: Putting Action into Words," *Harvard Business Review*, 79 (April 2001): 112–120.

49. See Linda L. Carli, Suzanne J. LaFleur, and Christopher C. Loeber, "Nonverbal Behavior, Gender, and Influence," *Journal of Personality and Social Psychology*, 68 (June 1995): 1030–1041.

50. For details, see Dore Butler and Florence L. Geis, "Nonverbal Affect Responses to Male and Female Leaders: Implications for Leadership Evaluations," *Journal of Personality and Social Psychology*, 58 (January 1990): 48–59.

51. Based on Ben Brown, "Atlanta Out to Mind Its Manners," *USA Today* (March 14, 1996): 7C. Also see Andrew L. Molinsky, Mary Anne Krabbenhoft, Nalini Ambady, and Y. Susan Choi, "Cracking the Nonverbal Code: Intercultural Competence and Gesture Recognition Across Cultures," *Journal of Cross-Cultural Psychology*, 36 (May 2005): 380–395; Pamela Eyring, "Broadening Global Awareness," *Training and Development*, 60 (July 2006): 69–71; and Gary Stoller, "Doing Business Abroad? Simple Faux Pas Can

Sink You," *USA Today* (August 24, 2007): 1B–2B.

52. See Andrea C. Poe, "Mind Their Manners," *HR Magazine*, 46 (May 2001): 75–80; Noelle Knox, "Expert: Mind Your Manners, It's Good Business," *USA Today* (June 28, 2001): 7B; Rod Kurtz, "Is Etiquette a Core Value?" *Inc.*, 26 (May 2004): 22; and Elisa Huang, "Etiquette: Pick Me! A Boss's Guide to Buying Flowers," *Inc.*, 29 (June 2007): 75–77.

53. "Workers Are Surveyed on Communication," *Arizona Republic* (December 26, 2004): D6. Also see Ann Pomeroy, "Great Communicators, Great Communication," *HR Magazine*, 51 (July 2006): 44–49; James R. Detert and Amy C. Edmondson, "Why Employees Are Afraid to Speak," *Harvard Business Review*, 85 (May 2007): 23–25; and Jack Welch and Suzy Welch, "Bosses Who Get It All Wrong," *Business Week* (July 23, 2007): 88.

54. David Kirkpatrick, "Sam Palmisano: IBM," *Fortune* (August 9, 2004): 96. IBM employee data from Telis Demos, "The World's Largest Corporations," *Fortune* (July 23, 2007): 143.

55. For related research, see Wendy R. Boswell and Julie B. Olson-Buchanan, "Experiencing Mistreatment at Work: The Role of Grievance Filing, Nature of Mistreatment, and Employee Withdrawal," *Academy of Management Journal*, 47 (February 2004): 129–139. Also see Noelle C. Nelson, "Good Grievances," *HR Magazine*, 51 (October 2006): 113–116.

56. For details, see Dick Grote and Jim Wimberly, "Peer Review," *Training*, 30 (March 1993): 51–55.

57. See Jack Welch, *Jack: Straight from the Gut* (New York: Warner Business Books, 2001), pp. 393–394; and Palmer Morrel-Samuels, "Getting the Truth into Workplace Surveys," *Harvard Business Review*, 80 (February 2002): 111–118.

58. Charlotte Garvey, "Connecting the Organizational Pulse to the Bottom Line," *HR Magazine*, 49 (June 2004): 71.

59. See Gail Johnson, "What Matters Most," *Training*, 41 (May 2004): 19; Adrienne Fox, "Who Needs Attitude?" *HR Magazine*, 49 (June 2004): 18; and Gail Johnson, "Time to Take Action," *Training*, 41 (September 2004): 18.

60. See Robert J. Aiello, "Employee Attitude Surveys: Impact on Corporate Decisions," *Public Relations Journal* (March 1983): 21.

61. Robert Levering and Milton Moskowitz, "The 100 Best Companies to Work For," *Fortune* (January 12, 2004): 78. Also see Barry Nalebuff and Ian Ayres, "Encouraging Suggestive Behavior," *Harvard Business Review*, 82 (December 2004): 18.

62. Paul Keegan, "Please, Just Don't Call Us Cheap," *Business 2.0*, 3 (February 2002): 51.

63. Data from Robert Levering and Milton Moskowitz, "The 100 Best Companies to Work For," *Fortune* (January 24, 2005): 84.

64. See James S. Larson, "Employee Participation in Federal Management," *Public Personnel Management*, 18 (Winter 1989): 404–414. Also see John Tschohl, "Be Bad," *Canadian Manager*, 23 (Winter 1998): 23–24; Stephanie Armour, "Firms Tap Employees for Cost-Saving Suggestions," *USA Today* (January 26, 1999): 1B; and Dale K. DuPont, "Eureka! Tools for Encouraging Employee Suggestions," *HR Magazine*, 44 (September 1999): 134–143.

65. Alison Stein Wellner, "Everyone's a Critic," *Inc.*, 26 (July 2004): 38, 41.

66. See Cheryl Dahle, "What Are You Complaining About?" *Fast Company*, no. 46 (May 2001): 66, 68; John Weeks, "Whining Away the Hours," *Harvard Business Review*, 82 (May 2004): 20–21.

67. Martha Frase-Blunt, "Meeting with the Boss," *HR Magazine*, 48 (June 2003): 95.

68. Curtis Sittenfeld, "Here's How GSA Changed Its Ways," *Fast Company*, no. 25 (June 1999): 88.

69. For more, see Bill Leonard, "Cyberventing," *HR Magazine*, 44 (November 1999): 34–39; and John Simons, "Stop Moaning About Gripe Sites and Log On," *Fortune* (April 2, 2001): 181–182.

70. For more, see Martha Frase-Blunt, "Making Exit Interviews Work," *HR Magazine*, 49 (August 2004); 109–113.

71. Anne Fisher, "Playing for Keeps," *Fortune* (January 22, 2007): 88.

72. "Exit Interviews Used Irregularly," *Arizona Republic* (February 25, 2001): D2. Also see Kathy Gurchiek, "Execs Take Exit Interviews Seriously," *HR Magazine*, 52 (January 2007): 34.

73. Paul Kaihla, "Acing the Exit Interview," *Business 2.0*, 5 (May 2004): 77.

74. Charles F. Knight, "Emerson Electric: Consistent Profits, Consistently," *Harvard Business Review*, 70 (January–February 1992): 60.

75. Catherine Yang, "Low-Wage Lessons," *Business Week* (November 11, 1996): 114.

76. Ron Lieber, "Timex Resets Its Watch," *Fast Company*, no. 52 (November 2001): 48.

77. Based on Rachel Sauer, "Jawing the Jargon," *Arizona Republic* (November 6, 2004): D3.

78. See Leigh Buchanan, "The Office," *Inc.*, 29 (March 2007): 144; and Aimee Rawlins, "There's a Message in Every Email," *Fast Company*, no. 118 (September 2007): 43.

79. For discussion of male versus female communication styles, see Dayle M. Smith, *Women at Work: Leadership for the Next Century* (Upper Saddle River, N.J.: Prentice-Hall, 2000), pp. 26–32.

80. Wendy Martyna, "What Does 'He' Mean? Use of the Generic Masculine," *Journal of Communication*, 28 (Winter 1978): 138. A later study with similar results is Janet A. Sniezek and Christine H. Jazwinski, "Gender Bias in English: In Search of Fair Language," *Journal of Applied Social Psychology*, 16, no. 7 (1986): 642–662. Also see Patricia C. Kelley, "Can Feminist Language Change Organizational Behavior? Some Research Questions," *Business & Society*, 35 (March 1996): 84–88.

81. Del Jones, "'Code Words' Cloud Issue of Discrimination at Work," *USA Today* (October 1, 1996): 1B–2B.

82. See Deirdre Donahue, "Explosive, 'Troublesome' N-Word Gets an Airing," *USA Today* (January 10, 2002): 6D.

83. See Heather Green, "A Web That Thinks Like You," *Business Week* (July 9–16, 2007): 94–95; Aili McConnon, "Just Ahead: The Web as a Virtual World," *Business Week* (August 13, 2007): 62–63; Margery Weinstein, "Mobility Movement," *Training*, 44 (September 2007): 14–16; and Brent Schlender, "Dawn of the Web Potato," *Fortune* (September 17, 2007): 52.

84. Del Jones, "E-Mail Avalanche Even Buries CEOs," *USA Today* (January 4, 2002): 1A.

85. Jon Swartz, "E-Mail Overload Taxes Workers and Companies," *USA Today* (June 26, 2001): 1A.

86. See Leigh Buchanan, "The Office: Playing E-mail Chicken," *Inc.*, 28 (May 2006): 128; and the second Q&A in Jack Welch and Suzy Welch, "Lay Off the Layers," *Business Week* (June 25, 2007): 96.

87. See Allen Smith, "Federal Rules Define Duty to Preserve Work E-Mails," *HR Magazine*, 52 (January 2007): 27, 36; David Shipley and Will Schwalbe, "E-Mail May Be Hazardous to Your Career," *Fortune* (May 14, 2007): 24, 26; and Jonathan A. Segal, "E Is for Evidence," *HR Magazine*, 52 (June 2007): 147–156.

88. Stephanie Armour, "You Have (Too Much) E-Mail," *USA Today* (March 2, 1999): 3B.

89. Data from Jon Swartz, "Is the Future of E-Mail Under Cyberattack?" *USA Today* (June 15, 2004): 4B; Jon Swartz, "Spammers Have Ignored Federal Law," *USA Today* (January 3, 2005): 1B. Also see Jon Swartz, "Spammers Convicted; First Felony Case," *USA Today* (November 4, 2004): 1B; and Erin Chambers, "The Lid on Spam Is Still Loose," *Business Week* (February 7, 2005): 10.

90. This list is based on Eryn Brown, "You've Got Mail.:-o," *Fortune* (December 7, 1998): 36, 40; Joan Tunstall, *Better, Faster*

Email: Getting the Most Out of Email (St. Leonards, Australia: Allen & Unwin, 1999); Donna J. Abernathy, "You've Got Email," *Training & Development*, 53 (April 1999): 18; and Andrea C. Poe, "Don't Touch That 'Send' Button!" *HR Magazine*, 46 (July 2001): 74–80. For additional useful e-mail tips, see Bob Minzesheimer, "Check Your E-mail–Before You Hit Send," *USA Today* (April 10, 2007): 1D; Rita Zeidner, "Keeping E-mail in Check," *HR Magazine*, 52 (June 2007): 70–74; and Doug Beizer, "Email Is Dead," *Fast Company*, no. 117 (July–August 2007): 46.

91. Heather Johnson, "Instant Lawsuit?" *Training*, 41 (September 2004): 16.

92. Data from www.ctia.org, September 23, 2007.

93. For a historical perspective on cell phones, see Stephanie N. Mehta, "Cellular Evolution," *Fortune* (August 23, 2004): 80–86. Also see Jack Ewing, "Upwardly Mobile in Africa," *Business Week* (September 24, 2007): 64–71.

94. Data from Chris Woodyard, "Some Offices Opt for Cellphones Only," *USA Today* (January 25, 2005): 1B.

95. For related reading, see Michelle Conlin, "Do Us a Favor, Take a Vacation," *Business Week* (May 21, 2007): 88–89; and Angela Haupt, "Good Vibrations? Bad? How About No Vibrations at All?" *USA Today* (June 13, 2007): 9D.

96. Drawn from Stephanie Armour, "Camera Phones Don't Click at Work," *USA Today* (January 12, 2004): 1B.

97. For a good update, see Roger O. Crockett, "The 21st Century Meeting," *Business Week* (February 26, 2007): 72–79.

98. Bill Breen, "Hidden Asset," *Fast Company*, no. 80 (March 2004): 95.

99. Tips adapted in part from Michael Emery and Margaret Schubert, "A Trainer's Guide to Videoconferencing," *Training*, 30 (June 1993): 59–63. Also see "Tips for the Photophobic," *Training*, 35 (October 1998): 26.

100. Jennifer Schramm, "Fuel Economy," *HR Magazine*, 50 (December 2005): 120.

101. Stephanie Armour, "More Bosses Getting into the Telecommuting Biz," *USA Today* (November 3, 2004): 2B.

102. See Timothy D. Golden and John F. Veiga, "The Impact of Extent of Telecommuting on Job Satisfaction: Resolving Inconsistent Findings," *Journal of Management*, 31, no. 2 (2005): 301–318; Kathy Gurchiek, "Telecommuting Could Hold Back Career," *HR Magazine*, 52 (March 2007): 34, 39; and the first Q&A in Jack Welch and Suzy Welch, "The Importance of Being There," *Business Week* (April 16, 2007): 92.

103. Joelle Jay, "On Communicating Well," *HR Magazine*, 50 (January 2005): 87–90. Also see Margery Weinstein, "When

Leaders Go Wrong," *Training*, 43 (August 2006): 11.

104. Data from Judi Brownell, "Perceptions of Effective Listeners: A Management Study," *Journal of Business Communication*, 27 (Fall 1990): 401–415. Also see Ann Pomeroy, "Leaders Should Listen, 'Spend Time on the Right Stuff,'" *HR Magazine*, 52 (August 2007): 12.

105. As quoted in Ann Pomeroy, "CEOs Emphasize Listening to Employees," *HR Magazine*, 52 (January 2007): 14.

106. Data from Cynthia Hamilton and Brian H. Kleiner, "Steps to Better Listening," *Personnel Journal*, 66 (February 1987): 20–21. Also see Roger R. Pearman, "Want to Lead Others? Listen First," *Training*, 41 (October 2004): 54.

107. This list has been adapted from John F. Kikoski, "Communication: Understanding It, Improving It," *Personnel Journal*, 59 (February 1980): 126–131; John L. DiGaetani, "The Business of Listening," *Business Horizons*, 23 (October 1980): 40–46; P. Slizewski, "Tips for Active Listening," *HR Focus* (May 1995): 7; and Griffin, "10 Ways to Become a Better Listener," in *How to Say It from the Heart*, pp. 39–42.

108. "Listen Up, Leaders: Let Workers Do the Talking," *HR Magazine*, 48 (October 2003): 14.

109. Barbara Hagenbaugh, "Good Help Hard to Find for Manufacturers," *USA Today* (April 16, 2004): 1B. Also see Margery Weinstein, "Does Your Prospect Have the 'Write' Stuff?" *Training*, 43 (September 2006): 13; and Stanley Bing, "The Element's of Style," *Fortune* (August 20, 2007): 110.

110. Tracey Wong Briggs, "Book's Not Closed on Texting," *USA Today* (September 4, 2007): 9D.

111. Robert F. DeGise, "Writing: Don't Let the Mechanics Obscure the Message," *Supervisory Management*, 21 (April 1976): 26–28. Also see Deborah Dumaine, "Leadership in Writing," *Training and Development*, 58 (December 2004): 52–54.

112. See "Give the Boot to Hackneyed Phrases," *Training*, 27 (August 1990): 10. Also see Herschell Gordon Lewis, "100 of the Easiest Ways to Begin an Effective Sales Letter," *Direct Marketing*, 56 (February 1994): 32–34.

113. Stuart R. Levine, "Make Meetings Less Dreaded," *HR Magazine*, 52 (January 2007): 107. Also see "Business Meeting Frustrations," *USA Today* (May 21, 2007): 1B.

114. As summarized in Michelle Archer, "Inject Some Drama, Structure in Office Meetings," *USA Today* (June 7, 2004): 11B. See Patrick M. Lencioni, *Death by Meeting: A Leadership Fable About Solving the Most Painful Problem in

Business* (San Francisco: Jossey-Bass, 2004).

115. Data from Anne Fisher, "How Much PowerPoint Is Enough?" *Fortune* (May 31, 2004): 56. Also see Kevin Ferguson, "Reinventing the Powerpoint," *Inc.*, 26 (March 2004): 42; W. Christian Buss, "Stop Death by PowerPoint," *Training and Development*, 60 (March 2006): 20, 22; and Scott Kirsner, "Take Your PowerPoint and . . . ," *Business Week* (May 14, 2007): 73–74.

116. This list is based in part on discussions in Stephanie Armour, "Team Efforts, Technology Add New Reasons to Meet," *USA Today* (December 8, 1997): 2A; John E. Tropman, *Making Meetings Work: Achieving High Quality Group Decisions*, 2nd ed. (Thousand Oaks, Calif.: Sage, 2003); and Reldan S. Nadler, "Are You a Meeting Menace or Master?" *Training and Development*, 61 (January 2007): 10–11.

CHAPTER 12

1. **Opening Quote:** As quoted in Nadira A. Hira, "You Raised Them, Now Manage Them," *Fortune* (May 28, 2007): 46.

2. For an excellent historical and conceptual treatment of basic motivation theory, see the collection of readings in Chapter 2 of Richard M. Steers, Lyman W. Porter, and Gregory A. Bigley, *Motivation and Leadership at Work*, 6th ed. (New York: McGraw-Hill, 1996).

3. For recent perspectives on motivation, see Richard M. Steers, Richard T. Mowday, and Debra L. Shapiro, "The Future of Work Motivation Theory," *Academy of Management Review*, 29 (July 2004): 379–387; Edwin A. Locke and Gary P. Latham, "What Should We Do About Motivation Theory? Six Recommendations for the Twenty-First Century," *Academy of Management Review*, 29 (July 2004): 388–403; Thomas Stemberg, "*Treat People Right and They Will Eat Nails for You*, and Other Lessons I learned Building Staples into a Giant Company," *Inc.*, 29 (January 2007): 75–77; Jennifer Gill, "How to Help an Underachiever," *Inc.*, 29 (March 2007): 44; Teresa M. Amabile and Steven J. Kramer, "Inner Work Life," *Harvard Business Review*, 85 (May 2007): 72–83; Margery Weinstein, "Frontline Motivation," *Training*, 44 (September 2007): 10; and Geoff Colvin, "Couch-Potato Nation," *Fortune* (September 3, 2007): 34.

4. See A. H. Maslow, "A Theory of Human Motivation," *Psychological Review*, 50 (July 1943): 370–396; Ron Zemke, "Maslow for a New Millennium," *Training*, 35 (December 1998): 54–58; Robin Marantz Henig, "Basic Needs Met? Next Comes Happiness," *USA Today* (January 2, 2001): 11A; and Bill

Cooke, Albert J. Mills, and Elizabeth S. Kelley, "Situating Maslow in Cold War America: A Recontextualization of Management Theory," *Group and Organization Management*, 30 (April 2005): 129–152.

5. Maslow, "A Theory of Human Motivation," p. 375.

6. See Jennifer Schramm, "Feeling Safe," *HR Magazine*, 49 (May 2004): 152.

7. Dean Foust, "Man on the Spot," *Business Week* (May 3, 1999): 142–143.

8. For more, see William B. Swann Jr., Christine Chang-Schneider, and Katie Larsen McClarty, "Do People's Self-Views Matter? Self-Concept and Self-Esteem in Everyday Life," *American Psychologist*, 62 (February–March 2007): 84–94. (The first student to e-mail the author at r.kreitner@cox.net by December 31, 2009 about this endnote will receive a $100 grant for being a serious scholar.)

9. Maslow, "A Theory of Human Motivation," p. 382.

10. As quoted in Steve Jones, "'Keys' Next Chapter Is Her Soulful 'Diary,'" *USA Today* (December 1, 2003): 5D.

11. George W. Cherry, "The Serendipity of the Fully Functioning Manager," *Sloan Management Review*, 17 (Spring 1976): 73.

12. Vance F. Mitchell and Pravin Moudgill, "Measurement of Maslow's Need Hierarchy," *Organizational Behavior and Human Performance*, 16 (August 1976): 348. Also see Mike Hofman, "Embattled Hotelier Chip Conley Found Inspiration from an Unlikely Source: Psychologist Abraham Maslow," *Inc.*, 29 (October 2007): 42–45.

13. For example, see Ellen L. Betz, "Two Tests of Maslow's Theory of Need Fulfillment," *Journal of Vocational Behavior*, 24 (April 1984): 204–220.

14. Edward E. Lawler, *Motivation in Work Organizations* (Monterey, Calif.: Brooks/Cole, 1973), p. 34.

15. See Frederick Herzberg, Bernard Mausner, and Barbara Bloch Snyderman, *The Motivation to Work*, 2nd ed. (New York: Wiley, 1959). Also see Ann Pomeroy, "Job Satisfaction Palls Quickly for Most Workers," *HR Magazine*, 52 (March 2007): 16; and Margery Weinstein, "Does an 'Employer Satisfaction' Difference Exist Among Older and Younger Workers?" *Training*, 44 (April 2007): 7.

16. Frederick Herzberg, "One More Time: How Do You Motivate Employees?" *Harvard Business Review*, 46 (January–February 1968): 56. For another view, see Dennis W. Organ, "The Happy Curve," *Business Horizons*, 38 (May–June 1995): 1–3. Herzberg's methodology is replicated in Susan G. Turner, Dawn R. Utley, and Jerry D.

Westbrook, "Project Managers and Functional Managers: A Case Study of Job Satisfaction in a Matrix Organization," *Project Management Journal*, 29 (September 1998): 11–19.

17. James K. Harter, Frank L. Schmidt, and Theodore L. Hayes, "Business-Unit-Level Relationship Between Employee Satisfaction, Employee Engagement, and Business Outcomes: A Meta-Analysis," *Journal of Applied Psychology*, 87 (April 2002): 268. Also see Thomas A. Wright and Russell Cropanzano, "The Role of Psychological Well-Being in Job Performance: A Fresh Look at an Age-Old Quest," *Organizational Dynamics*, 33, no. 4 (2004): 338–351; and Stephen Miller, "HR, Employees Vary on Job Satisfaction," *HR Magazine*, 52 (August 2007): 32, 34.

18. See Robert J. House and Lawrence A. Wigdor, "Herzberg's Dual-Factor Theory of Job Satisfaction and Motivation: A Review of the Evidence and a Criticism," *Personnel Psychology*, 20 (1967): 369–389.

19. For example, see Peter W. Hom, "Expectancy Prediction of Reenlistment in the National Guard," *Journal of Vocational Behavior*, 16 (April 1980): 235–248; John P. Wanous, Thomas L. Keon, and Janina C. Latack, "Expectancy Theory and Occupational/Organizational Choices: A Review and Test," *Organizational Behavior and Human Performance*, 32 (August 1983): 66–86; Alan W. Stacy, Keith F. Widaman, and G. Alan Marlatt, "Expectancy Models of Alcohol Use," *Journal of Personality and Social Psychology*, 58 (May 1990): 918–928; and Anne S. Tsui, Susan J. Ashford, Lynda St. Clair, and Katherine R. Xin, "Dealing with Discrepant Expectations: Response Strategies and Managerial Effectiveness," *Academy of Management Journal*, 38 (December 1995): 1515–1543.

20. See Bill Leonard, "College Students Confident They Will Reach Career Goals Quickly," *HR Magazine*, 46 (April 2001): 27.

21. "Leadership for the 21st Century: Lessons We Have Learned," *Newsweek* (September 25, 2006): 75.

22. For example, see Jim Collins, "Turning Goals into Results: The Power of Catalytic Mechanisms," *Harvard Business Review*, 77 (July–August 1999): 71–82.

23. See, for example, Edwin A. Locke and Gary P. Latham, *Goal Setting: A Motivational Technique That Works!* (Englewood Cliffs, N.J.: Prentice-Hall, 1984). Also see Yitzhak Fried and Linda Haynes Slowik, "Enriching Goal-Setting Theory with Time: An Integrated Approach," *Academy of Management Review*, 29 (July 2004): 404–422; Edwin A. Locke, "Guest Editor's Introduction: Goal-Setting Theory and Its Applications

to the World of Business," *Academy of Management Executive*, 18 (November 2004): 124–125; Gary P. Latham, "The Motivational Benefits of Goal-Setting," *Academy of Management Executive*, 18 (November 2004): 126–129; and Gerard H. Seijts and Gary P. Latham, "Learning versus Performance Goals: When Should Each Be Used?" *Academy of Management Executive*, 19 (February 2005): 124–131.

24. See, for example, Edwin A. Locke, Keryll N. Shaw, Lise M. Saari, and Gary P. Latham, "Goal Setting and Task Performance: 1969–1980," *Psychological Bulletin*, 90 (July 1981): 125–152; Anthony J. Mento, Robert P. Steel, and Ronald J. Karren, "A Meta-Analytic Study of the Effects of Goal Setting on Task Performance: 1966–1984," *Organizational Behavior and Human Decision Processes*, 39 (February 1987): 52–83; Don VandeWalle, Steven P. Brown, William L. Cron, and John W. Slocum Jr., "The Influence of Goal Orientation and Self-Regulation Tactics on Sales Performance: A Longitudinal Field Test," *Journal of Applied Psychology*, 84 (April 1999): 249–259; and Gerard H. Seijts, Gary P. Latham, Kevin Tasa, and Brandon W. Latham, "Goal Setting and Goal Orientation: An Integration of Two Different Yet Related Literatures," *Academy of Management Journal*, 47 (April 2004): 227–239.

25. Gary P. Latham and Edwin A. Locke, "Enhancing the Benefits and Overcoming the Pitfalls of Goal Setting," *Organizational Dynamics*, 35, no. 4 (2006): 332.

26. "ThermoSTAT," *Training*, 40 (July–August 2003): 16.

27. See Steven Kerr and Steffen Landauer, "Using Stretch Goals to Promote Organizational Effectiveness and Personal Growth: General Electric and Goldman Sachs," *Academy of Management Executive*, 18 (November 2004): 134–138; Karyll N. Shaw, "Changing the Goal-Setting Process at Microsoft," *Academy of Management Executive*, 18 (November 2004): 139–142; Jennifer Schramm, "Seeds of Discontent," *HR Magazine*, 52 (May 2007): 136; and Don Moyer, "Objective Selection," *Harvard Business Review*, 85 (June 2007): 144.

28. See Christopher Earley, Gregory B. Northcraft, Cynthia Lee, and Terri R. Lituchy, "Impact of Process and Outcome Feedback on the Relation of Goal Setting to Task Performance," *Academy of Management Journal*, 33 (March 1990): 87–105.

29. John Huey, "America's Most Successful Merchant," *Fortune* (September 23, 1991): 50. For an update, see Hank Gilman, "The Most Underrated CEO Ever," *Fortune* (April 5, 2004): 242–248.

30. Stephen Phillips and Amy Dunkin, "King Customer," *Business Week* (March 12, 1990): 91.

31. See Edwin A. Locke, "Linking Goals to Monetary Incentives," *Academy of Management Executive*, 18 (November 2004): 130–133; and Donald N. Sull and Charles Spinosa, "Promise-Based Management: The Essence of Execution," *Harvard Business Review*, 85 (April 2007): 78–86.

32. Lewis Carroll, *Alice's Adventures in Wonderland* (Philadelphia: The John C. Winston Company, 1923), p. 57. For some good advice on everyday goal-setting for the problems of diet and exercise, see Marshall Goldsmith with Mark Reiter, *What Got You Here Won't Get You There: How Successful People Become Even More Successful* (New York: Hyperion, 2007), pp. 188–190.

33. Adapted from J. Richard Hackman, "The Design of Work in the 1980s," *Organizational Dynamics*, 7 (Summer 1978): 3–17. An instructive four-way analysis of job design may be found in Michael A. Campion and Paul W. Thayer, "Job Design: Approaches, Outcomes, and Trade-Offs," *Organizational Dynamics*, 15 (Winter 1987): 66–79.

34. Rick Wartzman, "Houston Turns Out to Be the Capital of the Egg Roll," *Wall Street Journal* (December 7, 1995): A1.

35. For an interesting research about people who do society's "dirty work," see Blake E. Ashforth and Glen E. Kreiner, "'How Can You Do It?' Dirty Work and the Challenge of Constructing a Positive Identity," *Academy of Management Review*, 24 (July 1999): 413–434; Blake E. Ashforth, Glen E. Kreiner, Mark A. Clark, and Mel Fugate, "Normalizing Dirty Work: Managerial Tactics for Countering Occupational Taint," *Academy of Management Journal*, 50 (February 2007): 149–174; "How to Teach Pride in 'Dirty Work,'" *Harvard Business Review*, 85 (September 2007): 19–20. Also see Peter Johnson, "'Dirty Jobs' Labors to Make Clean Point," *USA Today* (August 30, 2007): 3D.

36. Jean M. Phillips, "Effects of Realistic Job Previews on Multiple Organizational Outcomes: A Meta-Analysis," *Academy of Management Journal*, 41 (December 1998): 686. Also see Peter W. Hom, Roger W. Griffeth, Leslie E. Palich, and Jeffrey S. Bracker, "Revisiting Met Expectations as a Reason Why Realistic Job Previews Work," *Personnel Psychology*, 52 (Spring 1999): 97–112.

37. See James M. Mehring, "Flexibility Is No Key to Stability," *Business Week* (March 5, 2001): 30; and Martha Frase-Blunt, "Ready, Set, Rotate!" *HR Magazine*, 46 (October 2001): 46–53.

38. David Welch, "How Nissan Laps Detroit," *Business Week* (December 22, 2003): 60.

39. See Lee Smith, "The FBI Is a Tough Outfit to Run," *Fortune* (October 9, 1989): 133–140. Also see Michael A. Campion, Lisa Cheraskin, and Michael J. Stevens, "Career-Related Antecedents and Outcomes of Job Rotation," *Academy of Management Journal*, 37 (December 1994): 1518–1542. For a condensed version of the foregoing study, see Susan Stites-Doe, "The New Story About Job Rotation," *Academy of Management Executive*, 10 (February 1996): 86–87.

40. David Kiley, "The New Heat on Ford," *Business Week* (June 4, 2007): 36.

41. See M. A. Howell, "Time Off as a Reward for Productivity," *Personnel Administration*, 34 (November–December 1971): 48–51.

42. Fred Luthans and Robert Kreitner, *Organizational Behavior Modification and Beyond: An Operant and Social Learning Approach* (Glenview, Ill.: Scott, Foresman, 1985), p. 192. Also see Diane L. Lockwood and Fred Luthans, "Contingent Time Off: A Nonfinancial Incentive for Improving Productivity," *Management Review*, 73 (July 1984): 48–52. The case for a six-hour work day is presented in "That's Why They Call It 'Work,'" *Fast Company*, no. 29 (November 1999): 194.

43. Data from Carla O'Dell and Jerry McAdams, "The Revolution in Employee Rewards," *Management Review*, 76 (March 1987): 30–33. For a recent example of CTO in action, see Thomas Petzinger Jr., "They Keep Workers Motivated to Make Annoying Phone Calls," *Wall Street Journal* (September 20, 1996): B1.

44. J. Richard Hackman and Greg R. Oldham, *Work Redesign* (Reading, Mass.: Addison-Wesley, 1980), p. 20. Also see Michael A. Campion and Michael J. Stevens, "Neglected Questions in Job Design: How People Design Jobs, Task-Job Predictability, and Influence of Training," *Journal of Business and Psychology*, 6 (Winter 1991): 169–191; and Gary Johns, Jia Lin Xie, and Yongqing Fang, "Mediating and Moderating Effects in Job Design," *Journal of Management*, 18 (December 1992): 657–676.

45. David Kirkpatrick, "How Safe Are Video Terminals?" *Fortune* (August 29, 1988): 71. For related research, see Michael A. Campion and Carol L. McClelland, "Interdisciplinary Examination of the Costs and Benefits of Enlarged Jobs: A Job Design Quasi-Experiment," *Journal of Applied Psychology*, 76 (April 1991): 186–198.

46. See J. Barton Cunningham and Ted Eberle, "A Guide to Job Enrichment and Redesign," *Personnel*, 67 (February 1990): 56–61; Roger E. Herman and

Joyce L. Gioia, "Making Work Meaningful: Secrets of the Future-Focused Corporation," *The Futurist*, 32 (December 1998): 24–38; and Donna Fenn, "Redesign Work," *Inc.*, 21 (June 1999): 74–84.

47. As quoted in John Bowe, Marisa Bowe, and Sabin Streeter, eds., *Gig: Americans Talk About Their Jobs at the Turn of the Millennium* (New York: Crown Publishers, 2000), p. 30.

48. Hackman and Oldham, *Work Redesign*, pp. 78–80. Also see John W. Medcof, "The Job Characteristics of Computing and Non-Computing Work Activities," *Journal of Occupational and Organizational Psychology*, 69 (June 1996): 199–212; and Joan R. Rentsch and Robert P. Steel, "Testing the Durability of Job Characteristics as Predictors of Absenteeism over a Six-Year Period," *Personnel Psychology*, 51 (Spring 1998): 165–190.

49. See Deborah J. Dwyer and Marilyn L. Fox, "The Moderating Role of Hostility in the Relationship Between Enriched Jobs and Health," *Academy of Management Journal*, 43 (December 2000): 1086–1096; and Amy Wrzesniewski and Jane E. Dutton, "Crafting a Job: Revisioning Employees as Active Crafters of Their Work," *Academy of Management Review*, 26 (April 2001): 179–201.

50. See Bob Nelson and Dean R. Spitzer, *The 1001 Rewards & Recognition Fieldbook* (New York: Workman, 2002). Also see Drew Robb, "A Total View of Employee Rewards," *HR Magazine*, 52 (August 2007): 93–95.

51. See Sheena S. Iyengar and Mark R. Lepper, "Rethinking the Value of Choice: A Cultural Perspective on Intrinsic Motivation," *Journal of Personality and Social Psychology*, 76 (March 1999): 349–366; and Leigh Buchanan, "That's Chief *Entertainment* Officer," *Inc.*, 29 (August 2007): 86–94.

52. As quoted in Yvette Armendariz and Kate Fitzgerald, "Gender-Specific Artificial Joints Reach Valley," *Arizona Republic* (October 21, 2006): D2.

53. As quoted in Roundtable, "All in a Day's Work," *Harvard Business Review* (Special Issue: Breakthrough Leadership), 79 (December 2001): 62. Also see Leigh Buchanan, "The Things They Do for Love," *Harvard Business Review*, 82 (December 2004): 19–20.

54. See Joy E. Beatty, "Grades as Money and the Role of the Market Metaphor in Management Education," *Academy of Management Learning and Education*, 3 (June 2004): 187–196; Nicole Gull, "Taking the Pain Out of Payday," *Inc.*, 27 (January 2005): 36; Leonard L. Berry, "The Best Companies Are Generous Companies," *Business Horizons*, 50

(July–August 2007): 263–269; and Manfred Kets de Vries, "Money, Money, Money," *Organizational Dynamics*, 36, no. 3 (2007): 231–243.

55. James C. Cooper and Kathleen Madigan, "The Second Half Should Be Healthier," *Business Week* (August 13, 2001): 26. Also see Stephen Miller, "Survey: Employees Undervalue Benefits," *HR Magazine*, 52 (August 2007): 30; Michelle Conlin and Jane Porter, "The Shape of Perks to Come," *Business Week* (August 20–27, 2007): 61; and Stephen Miller, "Many Struggle with Health Benefit Terms," *HR Magazine*, 52 (September 2007): 28.

56. See Jennifer Schramm, "Living Wages," *HR Magazine*, 49 (March 2004): 152; Margaret M. Clark, "Step by Step," *HR Magazine*, 50 (February 2005): 60–64; and William J. Heisler, "Ethical Choices in the Design and Administration of Executive Compensation Programs," *Business Horizons*, 50 (July-August 2007): 277–290.

57. See Susan J. Wells, "Merging Compensation Strategies," *HR Magazine*, 49 (May 2004): 66–78; Karen Renk, "The Power of Incentive Programs," *HR Magazine*, 49 (September 2004): 91–96; Anne Fisher, "A Strategic Way to Calculate Pay," *Fortune* (November 1, 2004): 62; Charlotte Garvey, "Philosophizing Compensation," *HR Magazine*, 50 (January 2005): 73–76; and Jason D. Shaw, Nina Gupta, Atul Mitra, and Gerald E. Ledford Jr., "Success and Survival of Skill-Based Pay Plans," *Journal of Management*, no. 1 (2005): 28–49.

58. See Pamela Babcock, "Find Out What Workers Want," *HR Magazine*, 50 (April 2005): 50–56.

59. See Bill Leonard, "Perks Give Way to Life-Cycle Benefits Plans," *HR Magazine*, 40 (March 1995): 45–48; and Karen M. Kroll, "Let's Get Flexible," *HR Magazine*, 52 (April 2007): 97–100.

60. "Companies Offer Benefits Cafeteria-Style," *Business Week* (November 13, 1978): 116. Also see Anand Natarajan, "The Roll-Your-Own Health Plan," *Business Week* (January 26, 2004): 16.

61. For complete details, see Alison E. Barber, Randall B. Dunham, and Roger A. Formisano, "The Impact of Flexible Benefits on Employee Satisfaction: A Field Study," *Personnel Psychology*, 45 (Spring 1992): 55–75.

62. For more, see C. Bram Cadsby, Fei Song, and Francis Tapon, "Sorting and Incentive Effects of Pay for Performance: An Experimental Investigation," *Academy of Management Journal*, 50 (April 2007): 387–405; Joanne Sammer, "Weighing Pay Incentives," *HR Magazine*, 52 (June 2007): 64–68; and

Susan Meisinger, "Pay-for-Performance Should Be Fair and Clear," *HR Magazine*, 52 (September 2007): 10.

63. For more, see Kelly Mollica, "Perceptions of Fairness," *HR Magazine*, 49 (June 2004): 169–178; and Jerald Greenberg, "Stress Fairness to Fare No Stress: Managing Workplace Stress by Promoting Organizational Justice," *Organizational Dynamics*, 33, no. 4 (2004): 352–365.

64. A good overview of equity theory can be found in Robert P. Vecchio, "Models of Psychological Inequity," *Organizational Behavior and Human Performance*, 34 (October 1984): 266–282.

65. See J. Stacy Adams and Patricia R. Jacobsen, "Effects of Wage Inequities on Work Quality," *Journal of Abnormal and Social Psychology*, 69 (1964): 19–25; Jerald Greenberg and Suzyn Ornstein, "High Status Job Title as Compensation for Underpayment: A Test of Equity Theory," *Journal of Applied Psychology*, 68 (May 1983): 285–297.

66. Data from Harry Maurer, "The Business Week: Hear This Mr. Semel," *Business Week* (June 25, 2007): 29. Also see Charles A. O'Reilly III and Brian G.M. Main, "Setting the CEOs Pay: It's More Than Simple Economics," *Organizational Dynamics*, 36, no. 1 (2007): 1–12; Marilyn Adams, "United Unions Protest Exec Pay," *USA Today* (March 28, 2007): 3B; and "Northwest CEO to Receive $26.6M," *USA Today* (May 7, 2007): 1B.

67. "What Has Undermined Your Trust in Companies?" *USA Today* (February 10, 2004): 1B.

68. Pablo Galarza and Stephen Gandel, "Invest Like a Legend," *Money*, 33 (October 2004): 118.

69. See Jeffrey Pfeffer, "Sins of Commission," *Business 2.0*, 5 (May 2004): 56; Ann Pomeroy, "Stock Option 'Golden Age' May Be Over," *HR Magazine*, 49 (August 2004): 18; Louis Lavelle, "They're Opting Out of Options," *Business Week* (February 28, 2005): 13; and Joanne Sammer, "Taking Ownership," *HR Magazine*, 52 (August 2007): 73–78.

70. Chris Taylor, "On-the-Spot Incentives," *HR Magazine*, 49 (May 2004): 82. Also see Alex C. Pasquariello, "Grant Makers," *Fast Company*, no. 114 (April 2007): 32.

71. See Matt Bolch, "Rewarding the Team," *HR Magazine*, 52 (February 2007): 91–93.

72. George Gendron, "Steel Man: Ken Iverson," *Inc.* (April 1986): 47–48.

73. The case *against* incentives is presented in Alfie Kohn, "Why Incentive Plans Cannot Work," *Harvard Business Review*, 71 (September–October 1993): 54–63. Also see Peter Nulty, "Incentive Pay Can Be Crippling," *Fortune* (November 13, 1995): 23; Robert Eisenberger and Judy Cameron, "Detrimental Effects of Reward,"

American Psychologist, 51 (November 1996): 1153–1166; and Alfie Kohn, "Challenging Behaviorist Dogma: Myths About Money and Motivation," *Compensation & Benefits Review*, 30 (March–April 1998): 27, 33–37.

74. Employee involvement is thoughtfully discussed in Jay R. Galbraith, Edward E. Lawler III, et al., *Organizing for the Future: The New Logic for Managing Complex Organizations* (San Francisco: Jossey-Bass, 1993), chs. 6 and 7. Also see Richard L. Daft, "Theory Z: Opening the Corporate Door for Participative Management," *Academy of Management Executive*, 18 (November 2004): 117–121.

75. See W. Alan Randolph, "Navigating the Journey to Empowerment," *Organizational Dynamics*, 23 (Spring 1995): 19–32; Robert C. Ford and Myron D. Fottler, "Empowerment: A Matter of Degree," *Academy of Management Executive*, 9 (August 1995): 21–31; Jeffrey S. Harrison and R. Edward Freeman, "Special Topic: Democracy in and Around Organizations: Is Organizational Democracy Worth the Effort?" *Academy of Management Executive*, 18 (August 2004): 49–53; and Jeffrey L. Kerr, "The Limits of Organizational Democracy," *Academy of Management Executive*, 18 (August 2004): 81–97.

76. For details see James P. Guthrie, "High-Involvement Work Practices, Turnover, and Productivity: Evidence from New Zealand," *Academy of Management Journal*, 44 (February 2001): 180–190. Also see Abraham Sagie and Zeynep Aycan, "A Cross-Cultural Analysis of Participative Decision-Making in Organizations," *Human Relations*, 56 (April 2003): 453–473.

77. See Edward E. Lawler III and Susan A. Mohrman, "Quality Circles: After the Honeymoon," *Organizational Dynamics*, 15 (Spring 1987): 42–54; and Gerald E. Ledford Jr., Edward E. Lawler III, and Susan A. Mohrman, "The Quality Circle and Its Variations," in *Productivity in Organizations*, ed. John P. Campbell, Richard J. Campbell, et al. (San Francisco: Jossey-Bass, 1988), pp. 255–294.

78. Evidence of a positive long-term impact on productivity may be found in Mitchell L. Marks, Philip H. Mirvis, Edward J. Hackett, and James F. Grady Jr., "Employee Participation in a Quality Circle Program: Impact on Quality of Work Life, Productivity, and Absenteeism," *Journal of Applied Psychology*, 71 (February 1986): 61–69. Also see Everett E. Adam Jr., "Quality Circle Performance," *Journal of Management*, 17 (March 1991): 25–39.

79. Frank Shipper, "Tapping Creativity," *Quality Circles Journal*, 4 (August 1981):

12. Also see Amal Kumar Naj, "Some Manufacturers Drop Effort to Adopt Japanese Techniques," *Wall Street Journal* (May 7, 1993): A1.

80. Raj Aggarwal and Betty J. Simkins, "Open Book Management—Optimizing Human Capital," *Business Horizons*, 44 (September–October 2001): 5.

81. For more on OBM, see Tim R. V. Davis, "Open-Book Management: Its Promise and Pitfalls," *Organizational Dynamics*, 25 (Winter 1997): 7–20. Also see John Case, "HR Learns How to Open the Books," *HR Magazine*, 43 (May 1998): 70–76; Perry Pascarella, "Open the Books to Unleash Your People," *Management Review*, 87 (May 1998): 58–60; and "July Poll Results: Open-Book Management," *HR Magazine*, 43 (September 1998): 18.

82. See W. Alan Randolph, "Rethinking Empowerment: Why Is It So Hard to Achieve?" *Organizational Dynamics*, 29 (Fall 2000): 94–107; Laurence Prusak and Don Cohen, "How to Invest in Social Capital," *Harvard Business Review*, 79 (June 2001): 86–93; Christopher A. Bartlett and Sumantra Ghoshal, "Building Competitive Advantage Through People," *MIT Sloan Management Review*, 43 (Winter 2002): 34–41; and Ginger L. Graham, "If You Want Honesty, Break Some Rules," *Harvard Business Review*, 80 (April 2002): 42–47.

83. As quoted in Hank Gilman, "The Most Underrated CEO Ever," *Fortune* (April 5, 2004): 244.

84. Heather Johnson, "Out with the Belly Flops," *Training*, 38 (December 2001): 22.

85. For related reading, see Noel M. Tichy, "No Ordinary Boot Camp," *Harvard Business Review*, 79 (April 2001): 63–70; Philippe Haspeslagh, Tomo Noda, and Fares Boulos, "It's Not Just About the Numbers," *Harvard Business Review*, 79 (July–August 2001): 65–73; Bo Burlingham, "Jack Stack, SRC Holdings: For Going Naked," *Inc.*, 26 (April 2004): 134–135; and Sarah Boehle, "Dollars & Sense," *Training*, 44 (June 2007): 42–45.

86. For more, see Ruth Wageman, "Critical Success Factors for Creating Superb Self-Managing Teams," *Organizational Dynamics*, 26 (Summer 1997): 49–61; Bradley L. Kirkman and Debra L. Shapiro, "The Impact of Cultural Values on Job Satisfaction and Organizational Commitment in Self-Managing Work Teams: The Mediating Role of Employee Resistance," *Academy of Management Journal*, 44 (June 2001): 557–569; and Carol A. Beatty and Brenda A. Barker Scott, *Building Smart Teams: A Roadmap to High Performance* (Thousand Oaks, Calif.: Sage, 2004).

87. Data from "1996 Industry Report: What Self-Managing Teams Manage," *Training*, 33 (October 1996): 69.

88. Keith H. Hammonds, "Growth Search," *Fast Company*, no. 69 (April 2003): 79–80. For a good update on Google, see Robert D. Hof, "Is Google Too Powerful?" *Business Week* (April 9, 2007): 46–55.

89. Brian Dumaine, "Who Needs a Boss?" *Fortune* (May 7, 1990): 52. Also see Claus W. Langfred, "Too Much of a Good Thing? Negative Effects of High Trust and Individual Autonomy in Self-Managing Teams," *Academy of Management Journal*, 47 (June 2004): 385–399.

90. John Hoerr, "The Payoff from Teamwork," *Business Week* (July 10, 1989): 57. For related research evidence, see Rosemary Batt, "Who Benefits from Teams? Comparing Workers, Supervisors, and Managers," *Industrial Relations*, 43 (January 2004): 183–209; Simone Kauffeld, "Self-Directed Work Groups and Team Competence," *Journal of Occupational and Organizational Psychology*, 79 (March 2006): 1–21; and Abhishek Srivastava, Kathryn M. Bartol, and Edwin A. Locke, "Empowering Leadership in Management Teams: Effects on Knowledge Sharing, Efficacy, and Performance," *Academy of Management Journal*, 49 (December 2006): 1239–1251.

91. Adapted from David I. Levine, "Participation, Productivity, and the Firm's Environment," *California Management Review*, 32 (Summer 1990): 86–100. Christopher D. Zatzick and Roderick D. Iverson, "High-Involvement Management and Workforce Reduction: Competitive Advantage or Disadvantage?," *Academy of Management Journal*, 49 (October 2006): 999–1015.

92. Katherine I. Miller and Peter R. Monge, "Participation, Satisfaction, and Productivity: A Meta-Analytic Review," *Academy of Management Journal*, 29 (December 1986): 748.

93. For example, see Adolph Haasen, "Opel Eisenach GMBH—Creating a High-Productivity Workplace," *Organizational Dynamics*, 24 (Spring 1996): 80–85.

94. As quoted in Paul B. Brown, "What I Know Now," *Fast Company*, no. 91 (February 2005): 96. Also see Marshall Goldsmith, "Do You Love What You Do?" *Fast Company*, no. 92 (March 2005): 88; Sharman Esarey and Arno Haslberger, "Off-Ramp—or Dead End?" *Harvard Business Review*, 85 (February 2007): 57–62.

95. Judith Warner, "Mommy Madness," *Newsweek* (February 21, 2005): 49. Also see Stephanie Armour, "Hi, I'm Joan, and I'm a Workaholic," *USA Today* (May 23, 2007): 1B–2B.

96. As quoted in Sheila M. Puffer, "Changing Organizational Structures: An Interview with Rosabeth Moss Kanter," *Academy of Management Executive*, 18 (May 2004): 101.

97. See Jennifer Merritt, "MBA Family Values," *Business Week* (March 14, 2005): 104–106; Margery Weinstein, "Errand Solutions: Freeing Up Employees to Work," *Training*, 43 (August 2006): 9; and Ann Pomeroy, "Work/Life Balance Not a Gender Issue," *HR Magazine*, 52 (April 2007): 16.

98. See Karen S. Kush and Linda K. Stroh, "Flextime: Myth or Reality?" *Business Horizons*, 37 (September–October 1994): 51–55; Susan Meisinger, "Flexible Schedules Make Powerful 'Perks,'" *HR Magazine*, 52 (April 2007): 12; Stephanie Armour, "Summer Sun Scatters Workers," USA Today (July 3, 2007): 2B; and Ann Pomeroy, "Not Your Parents' Workplace," *HR Magazine*, 52 (August 2007): 12, 14.

99. Robert Levering and Milton Moskowitz, "The 100 Best Companies to Work For," *Fortune* (January 12, 2004): 66. Also see Anne Fisher, "Playing for Keeps: Capital One," *Fortune* (January 22, 2007): 87; and Ann Pomeroy, "The Future Is Now," *HR Magazine*, 52 (September 2007): 46–51.

100. Data from "More Women Value Flex Time," *USA Today* (August 1, 2000): 1B.

101. Data from Heather Johnson, "Roll Call," *Training*, 39 (March 2002): 16.

102. See Kimberlianne Podlas, "Reasonable Accommodation or Special Privilege? Flextime, Telecommuting, and the ADA," *Business Horizons*, 44 (September–October 2001): 61–65.

103. Data from V. K. Narayanan and Raghu Nath, "A Field Test of Some Attitudinal and Behavioral Consequences of Flextime," *Journal of Applied Psychology*, 67 (April 1982): 214–218; David A. Ralston, William P. Anthony, and David J. Gustafson, "Employees May Love Flextime, But What Does It Do to the Organization's Productivity?" *Journal of Applied Psychology*, 70 (May 1985): 272–279; and Charles S. Rodgers, "The Flexible Workplace: What Have We Learned?" *Human Resources Management*, 31 (Fall 1992): 183–199.

104. Mark Henricks, "Flextime Revisited," *Southwest Airlines Spirit*, 13 (August 2004): 52–56. Also see Jennifer Schramm, "Vanishing Expectations," *HR Magazine*, 52 (April 2007): 144; and Ann Pomeroy, "Accountants with 'HEART,'" *HR Magazine*, 52 (July 2007): 48.

105. Based on Del Jones, "Sara Lee Biggest (for Now) with Female CEO," *USA Today* (February 11, 2005): 4B. For more on Brenda Barnes, see **www.saralee.com/ AboutSaraLee/ManagementTeam.aspx.**

106. See Jon L. Pierce and Randall B. Dunham, "The 12-Hour Work Day: A 48-Hour, Eight-Day Week," *Academy of Management Journal*, 35 (December

1992): 1086–1098; and Dominic Bencivenga, "Compressed Weeks Fill an HR Niche," *HR Magazine*, 40 (June 1995): 71–74.

107. See Cynthia R. Cunningham and Shelley S. Murray, "Two Executives, One Career," *Harvard Business Review*, 83 (February 2005): 125–131; and Susan Berfield, "Two for the Cubicle," *Business Week* (July 24, 2006): 88–91.

108. Data from M. F. J. Martens, F. J. N. Nijhuis, M. P. J. Van Boxtel, and J. A. Knottnerus, "Flexible Work Schedules and Mental and Physical Health. A Study of a Working Population with Non-Traditional Working Hours," *Journal of Organizational Behavior*, 20 (January 1999): 35–46.

109. Quoted material and data from Nancy R. Lockwood, "Work/Life Balance: Challenges and Solutions," 2003 Research Quarterly, *HR Magazine*, 48 (June 2003): 7.

110. For more, see Eric Paltell, "FMLA: After Six Years, a Bit More Clarity," *HR Magazine*, 44 (September 1999): 144–150; Gene Koretz, "Did Maternity Leave Law Help?" *Business Week* (April 17, 2000): 36; Steve Bates, "Whirlwind of Change," *HR Magazine*, 46 (August 2001): 62–66; Kathryn Tyler, "All Present and Accounted For?" *HR Magazine*, 46 (October 2001): 101–109; and Bill Leonard, "SHRM Survey Highlights Problems with FMLA," *HR Magazine*, 52 (August 2007): 28.

111. Excerpts in this list from Robert Levering and Milton Moskowitz, "*Fortune* 100 Best Companies to Work for: 2007," *Fortune* (January 22, 2007): 94–116.

112. See Sherry E. Sullivan and Lisa A. Mainiero, "Kaleidoscope Careers: Benchmarking Ideas for Fostering Family-Friendly Workplaces," *Organizational Dynamics*, 36, no. 1 (2007): 45–62; Amanda Stout, "We Are Family," *HR Magazine*, 52 (April 2007): 117–121; Joe Robinson, "The Red Zone," *Fast Company*, no. 115 (May 2007): 37; Michelle Conlin, "The Working-Mom Quandry," *Business Week* (June 4, 2007): 110; and Stephanie Armour, "More Companies Add Benefits for Employees Who Adopt," *USA Today* (June 20, 2007): 1B.

113. See Elayne Robertson Demby, "Do Your Family-Friendly Programs Make Cents?" *HR Magazine*, 49 (January 2004): 74–78.

114. Ibid., p. 76.

115. See Del Jones, "Some Employees Find Stress Provides Spark for Innovation," *USA Today* (February 21, 2005): 3B; Kathryn Tyler, "Stress Management," *HR Magazine*, 51 (September 2006): 78–83; and Jenna Goudreau, "Dispatches from the War on Stress," *Business Week* (August 6, 2007): 74–75.

116. See Adam M. Grant, Marlys K. Christianson, and Richard H. Price, "Happiness, Health, or Relationships? Managerial Practices and Employee Well-Being Tradeoffs," *Academy of Management Perspectives*, 21 (August 2007): 51–63; Pamela Babcock, "Helping Workers Kick the Habit," *HR Magazine*, 52 (September 2007): 115–125; Adam Bluestein, "Cafeteria 2.0," *Fast Company*, no. 119 (October 2007): 60, 62; and Tony Schwartz, "Manage Your Energy, Not Your Time," *Harvard Business Review*, 85 (October 2007): 63–73.

117. Daniel Yee, "Fit Workers Keep Insurance Costs Low," *Arizona Republic* (October 17, 2004): D3. Also see Christopher P. Neck and Kenneth H. Cooper, "The Fit Executive: Exercise and Diet Guidelines for Enhancing Performance," *Academy of Management Executive*, 14 (May 2000): 72–83; Bill Roberts, "Modeling Better Health Care," *HR Magazine*, 51 (July 2006): 93–97; Carolyn M. Kaelin and Francesca Coltrera, "Cancer and Staying Fit," *Newsweek* (March 26, 2007): 69–70; Thomas H. Lee, "How to Help Your Heart," *Newsweek* (March 26, 2007): 74, 76; Pamela Babcock, "Attacking Asthma's Costs," *HR Magazine*, 52 (June 2007): 88–92; and Mara G. Aspinall and Richard G. Hamermesh, "Realizing the Promise of Personalized Medicine," *Harvard Business Review*, 85 (October 2007): 108–117.

118. Drawn from Robert Levering and Milton Moskowitz, "The 100 Best Companies to Work For," *Fortune* (January 20, 2003): 127–152; Robert Levering and Milton Moskowitz, "The 100 Best Companies to Work For," *Fortune* (January 12, 2004): 56–76; Robert Levering and Milton Moskowitz, "*Fortune* 100 Best Companies to Work For: 2007," *Fortune* (January 22, 2007): 94–116.

119. Robert Levering and Milton Moskowitz, "The 100 Best Companies to Work For," *Fortune* (January 24, 2005): 88.

120. For more, see Joel Schettler, "Successful Sabbaticals," *Training*, 39 (June 2002): 26; and Nadine Heintz, "Breaking Away," *Inc.*, 26 (October 2004): 44.

CHAPTER 13

1. **Opening Quote:** As quoted in "From Wharton to War," *Fortune* (June 12, 2006): 108.

2. Data from Clinton O. Longenecker, Mitchell J. Neubert, and Laurence S. Fink, "Causes and Consequences of Managerial Failure in Rapidly Changing Organizations," *Business Horizons*, 50 (March–April 2007): 145–155.

3. Robert Kreitner and Angelo Kinicki, *Organizational Behavior*, 8th ed. (Burr Ridge, Ill.: McGraw-Hill/Irwin, 2008), pp. 14–15. For more, see Andrew C. Inkpen and Eric W. K. Tsang, "Social Capital, Networks, and Knowledge Transfer," *Academy of Management Review*, 30 (January 2005): 146–165; David M. Sluss and Blake E. Ashforth, "Relational Identity and Identification: Defining Ourselves Through Work Relationships," *Academy of Management Review*, 32 (January 2007): 9–32; and Martha J. Frase, "Stocking Your Talent Pool," *HR Magazine*, 52 (April 2007): 67–74.

4. Joseph A. Litterer, *The Analysis of Organizations*, 2nd ed. (New York: Wiley, 1973), p. 231.

5. For an excellent elaboration of this definition, see David Horton Smith, "A Parsimonious Definition of 'Group': Toward Conceptual Clarity and Scientific Utility," *Sociological Inquiry*, 37 (Spring 1967): 141–167. Also see Daniel J. Brass, Joseph Galaskiewicz, Henrich R. Greve, and Wenpin Tsai, "Taking Stock of Networks and Organizations: A Multilevel Perspective," *Academy of Management Journal*, 47 (December 2004): 795–817.

6. For related research, see Prithviraj Chattopadhyay, Malgorzata Tluchowska, and Elizabeth George, "Identifying the Ingroup: A Closer Look at the Influence of Demographic Dissimilarity on Employee Social Identity," *Academy of Management Review*, 29 (April 2004): 180–202; and Hongseok Oh, Myung-Ho Chung, and Giuseppe Labianca, "Group Social Capital and Group Effectiveness: The Role of Informal Socializing Ties," *Academy of Management Journal*, 47 (December 2004): 860–875.

7. For example, see Brian Uzzi and Shannon Dunlap, "How to Build Your Network," *Harvard Business Review*, 83 (December 2005): 53–60; Caroline Wilbert, "You Schmooze, You Win," *Fast Company*, no. 107 (July–August 2006): 109; and Leigh Buchanan, "I Know Where You Live," *Inc.*, 28 (July 2006): 124.

8. David Krackhardt and Jeffrey R. Hanson, "Informal Networks: The Company Behind the Chart," *Harvard Business Review*, 71 (July–August 1993): 104. Also see Eugenia Levenson, "How the Office Really Works," *Fortune* (June 12, 2006): 118.

9. See David Kirkpatrick, "Facebook's Plan to Hook Up the World," *Fortune* (June 11, 2007): 127–130; Jon Fine, "O.K. (Sigh), I'll Join Facebook," *Business Week* (September 17, 2007): 24; and David Kirkpatrick, "MySpace Strikes Back," *Fortune* (October 1, 2007): 128–136.

10. Excerpted from the second Q&A in Jack Welch and Suzy Welch, "From the Old, Something New," *Business Week* (November 20, 2006): 124.

11. See Cathy Olofson, "Let Outsiders In, Turn Your Insiders Out," *Fast Company*, no. 22 (February–March 1999): 46.

12. For related research, see Jennifer A. Chatman and Charles A. O'Reilly, "Asymmetric Reactions to Work Group Sex Diversity Among Men and Women," *Academy of Management Journal*, 47 (April 2004): 193–208; and Mark Van Vugt and Claire M. Hart, "Social Identity as Social Glue: The Origin of Group Loyalty," *Journal of Personality and Social Psychology*, 86 (April 2004): 585–598.

13. Peter Nulty, "Cool Heads Are Trying to Keep Commodore Hot," *Fortune* (July 23, 1984): 38, 40.

14. Albert A. Harrison, *Individuals and Groups: Understanding Social Behavior* (Monterey, Calif.: Brooks/Cole, 1976), p. 16. Also see Mark A. Griffin, Andrew Neal, and Sharon K. Parker, "A New Model of Work Role Performance: Positive Behavior in Uncertain and Interdependent Contexts," *Academy of Management Journal*, 50 (April 2007): 327–347.

15. See, for instance, Andrew Park, "Between a Rocker and a High Chair," *Business Week* (February 21, 2005): 86, 88; and Hugh T. J. Bainbridge, Christina Cregan, and Carol T. Kulik, "The Effect of Multiple Roles on Caregiver Stress Outcomes," *Journal of Applied Psychology*, 91 (March 2006): 490–497.

16. Harrison, *Individuals and Groups*, p. 401.

17. For example, see Gary Blau, "Influence of Group Lateness on Individual Lateness: A Cross-Level Examination," *Academy of Management Journal*, 38 (October 1995): 1483–1496; Jeffrey A. LePine and Linn Van Dyne, "Peer Responses to Low Performers: An Attributional Model of Helping in the Context of Groups," *Academy of Management Review*, 26 (January 2001): 67–84; and Jennifer A. Chatman and Francis J. Flynn, "The Influence of Demographic Heterogeneity on the Emergence and Consequences of Cooperative Norms in Work Teams," *Academy of Management Journal*, 44 (October 2001): 956–974.

18. Adapted from Daniel C. Feldman, "The Development and Enforcement of Group Norms," *Academy of Management Review*, 9 (January 1984): 47–53. Also see Jose M. Marques, Dominic Abrams, Dario Paez, and Cristina Martinez-Taboada, "The Role of Categorization and In-Group Norms in Judgments of Groups and Their Members," *Journal of Personality and Social Psychology*, 75 (October 1998): 976–988.

19. See Kenneth J. Bettenhausen and Keith J. Murnigham, "The Development of an Intragroup Norm and the Effects of Interpersonal and Structural Challenges," *Administrative Science Quarterly*, 36 (March 1991): 20–35.

20. Gwendolyn Kelly, "Why This Med Student Is Sticking with Primary Care," *Business Week* (November 2, 1992): 125.

21. For related research and reading, see Andrew Spicer, Thomas W. Dunfee, and Wendy J. Bailey, "Does National Context Matter in Ethical Decision Making? An Empirical Test of Integrative Social Contracts Theory," *Academy of Management Journal*, 47 (August 2004): 610–620; and Ben W. Heineman Jr., "Avoiding Integrity Land Mines," *Harvard Business Review*, 85 (April 2007): 100–108.

22. From *Group Effectiveness in Organizations* by L. N. Jewell and H. J. Reitz (Scott, Foresman, 1981). Reprinted by permission of the authors. Also see Lynn R. Offermann and Rebecca K. Spiros, "The Science and Practice of Team Development: Improving the Link," *Academy of Management Journal*, 44 (April 2001): 376–392.

23. Susan A. Wheelan and Felice Tilin, "The Relationship Between Faculty Group Development and School Productivity," *Small Group Research*, 30 (February 1999): 59.

24. For more, see Chao C. Chen, Xiao-Ping Chen, and James R. Meindl, "How Can Cooperation Be Fostered? The Cultural Effects of Individualism-Collectivism," *Academy of Management Review*, 23 (April 1998): 285–304. Also see Katherine J. Klein, Beng-Chong Lim, Jessica L. Saltz, and David M. Mayer, "How Do They Get There? An Examination of the Antecedents of Centrality in Team Networks," *Academy of Management Journal*, 47 (December 2004): 952–963.

25. See Vanessa Urch Druskat and Steven B. Wolff, "Building the Emotional Intelligence of Groups," *Harvard Business Review*, 79 (March 2001): 81–90; Stéphane Côté and Christopher T. H. Miners, "Emotional Intelligence, Cognitive Intelligence, and Job Performance," *Administrative Science Quarterly*, 51 (March 2006): 1–28; Sharon Jayson, "Sociability: It's All in Your Mind," *USA Today* (September 25, 2006): 5D; and Daniel Goleman, *Social Intelligence: The New Science of Human Relationships* (New York: Bantam, 2007).

26. The following discussion of the six stages of group development is adapted from *Group Effectiveness in Organizations* by Linda N. Jewell and H. Joseph Reitz. Copyright 1981, Scott, Foresman and Company, pp. 15–20. Reprinted by permission. For ground-breaking research in this area, see Warren G. Bennis and Herbert A. Shepard, "A Theory of Group Development," *Human Relations*, 9 (1956); 415–437; Bruce W. Tuckman and Mary Ann C. Jensen, "Stages of Small-Group Development Revisited," *Group & Organization Studies*, 2 (December 1977): 419–427; and John F. McGrew, John G. Bilotta, and Janet M. Deeney, "Software Team Formation and Decay: Extending the Standard Model for Small Groups," *Small Group Research*, 30 (April 1999): 209–234.

27. Jacqueline Durett, "There's No 'I' in 'Team,' But Maybe There Should Be," *Training*, 43 (September 2006): 12. Also see Ed Gash, "More Training Than Camp," *Training*, 43 (December 2006): 7.

28. For practical advice, see John E. Tropman, *Making Meetings Work: Achieving High Quality Decisions* (Thousand Oaks, Calif.: Sage, 2003); and Tim Ursiny, *The Coward's Guide to Conflict: Empowering Solutions for Those Who Would Rather Run Than Fight* (Naperville, Ill.: Sourcebooks, 2003).

29. See Brian R. Dineen, Raymond A. Noe, Jason D. Shaw, Michelle K. Duffy, and Carolyn Wiethoff, "Level and Dispersion of Satisfaction in Teams: Using Foci and Social Context to Explain the Satisfaction-Absenteeism Relationship," *Academy of Management Journal*, 50 (June 2007): 623–643.

30. See Jeanne M. Wilson, Paul S. Goodman, and Matthew A. Cronin, "Group Learning," *Academy of Management Review*, 32 (October 2007): 1041–1059.

31. For example, see Pamela L. Perrewé and Debra L. Nelson, "Gender and Career Success: The Facilitative Role of Political Skill," *Organizational Dynamics*, 33, no. 4 (2004): 366–378; Judith A. Clair, Joy E. Beatty, and Tammy L. Maclean, "Out of Sight But Not Out of Mind: Managing Invisible Social Identities in the Workplace," *Academy of Management Review*, 30 (January 2005): 78–95; Thomas B. Lawrence, Michael K. Mauws, Bruno Dyck, and Robert F. Kleysen, "The Politics of Organizational Learning: Integrating Power into the 4I Framework," *Academy of Management Review*, 30 (January 2005): 180–191; Gerald R. Ferris, Darren C. Treadway, Robert W. Kolodinsky, Wayne A. Hochwarter, Charles J. Kacmar, Ceasar Douglas, and Dwight D. Frink, "Development and Validation of the Political Skill Inventory," *Journal of Management*, 31, no. 1 (2005): 126–152; Christopher C. Rosen, Paul E. Levy, and Rosalie J. Hall, "Placing Perceptions of Politics in the Context of the Feedback Environment, Employee Attitudes, and Job Performance," *Journal of Applied Psychology*, 91 (January 2006): 211–220; and Deondra S. Conner, "Human-Resource Professionals' Perceptions of Organizational Politics as a Function of Experience, Organizational Size, and Perceived Independence," *The Journal of Social Psychology*, 146 (December 2006): 717–732.

32. See Del Jones and Bill Keveney, "10 Lessons of 'The Apprentice,'" *USA Today* (April 15, 2004): 1A, 5A; Del Jones, "America Loves to Hate Dastardly CEOs," *USA Today* (September 15, 2004): 1B–2B; and Ann Pomeroy, "Business Reality TV?" *HR Magazine*, 50 (January 2005): 14.

33. As quoted in Anne Fisher, "Putting Your Mouth Where the Money Is," *Fortune* (September 3, 2001): 238. Also see Jared Sandberg, "Sabotage 101: The Sinister Art of Back-Stabbing," *Wall Street Journal* (February 11, 2004): B1; David A. Kaplan, "Suspicions and Spies in Silicon Valley," *Newsweek* (September 18, 2006): 40–47; and Jena McGregor, "Sweet Revenge," *Business Week* (January 22, 2007): 64–70.

34. Marcia Stepanek, "How Fast Is Net Fast?" *Business Week* E.BIZ (November 1, 1999): EB 54. Also see Keith R. McFarland, "Lessons from the Anti-Mentor," *Business Week* (June 11, 2007): 86.

35. Data from "9-to-5 Not for Everyone," *USA Today* (October 13, 1999): 1B. Also see "Fast Fact," *Training*, 44 (January–February 2007): 11.

36. See Gerald R. Ferris, Pamela L. Perrewé, William P. Anthony, and David C. Gilmore, "Political Skill at Work," *Organizational Dynamics*, 28 (Spring 2000): 25–37; Jennifer Reingold, "Suck Up and Move Up," *Fast Company*, no. 90 (January 2005): 34; and Alison Stein Wellner, "Playing Well with Others," *Inc.*, 27 (January 2005): 29–31.

37. See Sam Grobart, "Allow Me to Introduce Myself (Properly)," *Money*, 36 (January 2007): 40–41; N. Anand and Jay A. Conger, "Capabilities of the Consummate Networker," *Organizational Dynamics*, 36, no. 1 (2007): 13–27; and Herminia Ibarra and Mark Hunter, "How Leaders Create and Use Networks," *Harvard Business Review*, 85 (January 2007): 40–47.

38. For related reading, see Diane M. Bergeron, "The Potential Paradox of Organizational Citizenship Behavior: Good Citizens at What Cost?" *Academy of Management Review*, 32 (October 2007): 1078–1095.

39. Victor Murray and Jeffrey Gandz, "Games Executives Play: Politics at Work," *Business Horizons*, 23 (December 1980): 16.

40. Andrew J. DuBrin, *Fundamentals of Organizational Behavior: An Applied Perspective*, 2nd ed. (Elmsford, N.Y.: Pergamon Press, 1978): p. 154.

41. Jared Sandberg, "Better Than Great—and Other Tall Tales of Self-Evaluations," *Wall Street Journal* (March 12, 2003): B1. Also see Herminia Ibarra and Kent Lineback, "What's Your Story?" *Harvard Business Review*, 83 (January 2005): 64–71.

42. Dan Farrell and James C. Petersen, "Patterns of Political Behavior in Organizations," *Academy of Management Review*, 7 (July 1982): 407. Also see Jeff Barbian, "It's Who You Know," *Training*, 38 (December 2001): 22; and Stanley Bing, "Throwing the Elephant: Zen and the Art of Managing Up," *Fortune* (March 18, 2002): 115–116.

43. See "Blowing the Whistle on Billing Abuse," *Money*, 34 (January 2005): 81; John Simons, "Blowing the Whistle at the FDA," *Fortune* (January 24, 2005): 32; Bill Leonard, "Blowing Whistle on Navy Recruitment Proves Costly," *HR Magazine*, 52 (March 2007): 25, 28; and Ralph Hasson, "Why Didn't We Know?" *Harvard Business Review*, 85 (April 2007): 33–43.

44. James R. Healey, "Covert Activity Saved Sports Car," *USA Today* (March 19, 1997): 1B. Also see Denis Collins, "Case Study: 15 Lessons Learned from the Death of a Gainsharing Plan," *Compensation & Benefits Review*, 28 (March–April 1996): 31–40.

45. Adapted from Dan L. Madison, Robert W. Allen, Lyman W. Porter, Patricia A. Renwick, and Bronston T. Mayes, "Organizational Politics: An Exploration of Managers' Perceptions," *Human Relations*, 33 (February 1980): 79–100. Also see Andrew J. DuBrin, "Career Maturity, Organizational Rank, and Political Behavioral Tendencies: A Correlational Analysis of Organizational Politics and Career Experience," *Psychological Reports*, 63 (October 1988): 531–537.

46. Madison et al., "Organizational Politics," p. 97.

47. These six political tactics have been adapted from a more extensive list found in DuBrin, *Fundamentals of Organizational Behavior*, pp. 158–170. Also see Roos Vonk, "The Slime Effect: Suspicion and Dislike of Likeable Behavior Toward Superiors," *Journal of Personality and Social Psychology*, 74 (April 1998): 849–864; Carol Memmott, "How to Play Cutthroat Office Politics and Win," *USA Today* (July 13, 1998): 2B; and David G. Baldwin, "How to Win the Blame Game," *Harvard Business Review*, 79 (July–August 2001): 55–62.

48. Adapted from DuBrin, *Fundamentals of Organizational Behavior*, pp. 179–182.

49. Blind conformity at Enron is discussed in Greg Farrell and Jayne O'Donnell, "Watkins Testifies Skilling, Fastow Duped Lay, Board," *USA Today* (February 15, 2002): 1B–2B. Also see Shoshana Zuboff, "A Starter Kit for Business Ethics," *Fast Company*, no. 90 (January 2005): 91. Criminal executives are discussed in Nicholas Varchaver, "Long Island Confidential," *Fortune* (November 27, 2006): 172–186; Bob Johnson, "Scrushy Gets Nearly 7 Years in Prison," *USA Today* (June 29, 2007): 2B; and Leslie Cauley, "Rigas Tells His Side of the Adelphia Story," *USA Today* (August 6, 2007): 1B–2B.

50. For related reading, see Adrienne Fox, "Corporate Social Responsibility Pays Off," *HR Magazine*, 52 (August 2007): 42–47; and Andreas Georg Scherer and Guido Palazzo, "Toward a Political Conception of Corporate Responsibility: Business and Society Seen from a Habermasian Perspective," *Academy of Management Review*, 32 (October 2007): 1096–1120.

51. See Solomon E. Asch, *Social Psychology* (Englewood Cliffs, N.J.: Prentice-Hall, 1952), ch. 16.

52. For details, see Taha Amir, "The Asch Conformity Effect: A Study in Kuwait," *Social Behavior and Personality*, 12, no. 2 (1984): 187–190; Timothy P. Williams and Shunya Sogon, "Group Composition and Conforming Behavior in Japanese Students," *Japanese Psychological Research*, 26, no. 4 (1984): 231–234.

53. Data from Rod Bond and Peter B. Smith, "Culture and Conformity: A Meta-Analysis of Studies Using Asch's Line Judgment Task," *Psychological Bulletin*, 119 (January 1996): 111–137. Also see Sandra L. Robinson and Anne M. O'Leary-Kelly, "Monkey See, Monkey Do: The Influence of Work Groups on the Antisocial Behavior of Employees," *Academy of Management Journal*, 41 (December 1998): 658–672.

54. See Marilyn Elias, "Do We All Have a Dark Side? Psychologist Argues We Do in 'The Lucifer Effect,'" *USA Today* (March 14, 2007): 7D.

55. Irving L. Janis, *Groupthink*, 2nd ed. (Boston: Houghton Mifflin, 1982), p. 9. See also A. Amin Mohamed and Frank A. Wiebe, "Toward a Process Theory of Groupthink," *Small Group Research*, 27 (August 1996): 416–430; Kjell Granstrom and Dan Stiwne, "A Bipolar Model of Groupthink: An Expansion of Janis's Concept," *Small Group Research*, 29 (February 1998): 32–56; the entire February–March 1998 issue of *Organizational Behavior and Human Decision Processes*; Annette R. Flippen, "Understanding Groupthink from a Self-Regulatory Perspective," *Small Group Research*, 30 (April 1999): 139–165; Jin Nam Choi and Myung Un Kim, "The Organizational Application of Groupthink and Its Limitations in Organizations," *Journal of Applied Psychology*, 84 (April 1999): 297–306; and Walter Shapiro, "Groupthink a Danger for White House War Planners," *USA Today* (October 3, 2001): 7A.

56. Adapted from a list in Janis, *Groupthink*, pp. 174–175.

57. Ibid., p. 275.

58. For excellent discussions of the devil's advocate role, see Charles R. Schwenk, "Devil's Advocacy in Managerial Decision Making," *Journal of Management Studies*, 21 (April 1984): 153–168; and Richard A. Cosier and Charles R. Schwenk, "Agreement and Thinking Alike: Ingredients for Poor Decisions," *Academy of Management Executive*, 4 (February 1990): 69–74. For related reading, see Christopher Hitchens, "The Dogmatic Doubter," *Newsweek* (September 10, 2007): 40–42.

59. Adapted from a list in Janis, *Groupthink*, pp. 262–271.

60. See Rafe Needleman, "Building the Perfect Board," *Business 2.0*, 4 (May 2003): 58–59; and Nanette Byrnes, "Cornered in the Corner Office," *Business Week* (May 14, 2007): 96.

61. Barbara Kellerman, *Bad Leadership: What It Is, How It Happens, Why It Matters* (Boston: Harvard Business School Press, 2004), pp. 139–140.

62. Other problems related in part to groupthink are discussed in Paul F. Levy, "The Nut Island Effect: When Good Teams Go Wrong," *Harvard Business Review*, 79 (March 2001): 51–59; and Michael Harvey, Milorad M. Novicevic, M. Ronald Buckley, and Jonathon R.B. Halbesleben, "The Abilene Paradox After Thirty Years: A Global Perspective," *Organizational Dynamics*, 33, no. 2 (2004): 215–226.

63. Spencer Ante, "The New Blue," *Business Week* (March 17, 2003): 81–82.

64. For contextual reading, see Robert J. Trent, "Becoming an Effective Teaming Organization," *Business Horizons*, 47 (March–April 2004): 33–40; Paul B. Brown, "What I Know Now," *Fast Company*, no. 90 (January 2005): 96; Jena McGregor, "I Can't Believe They Took the Whole Team," *Business Week* (December 18, 2006): 120, 122; "Company Is a Team, Not a Family," *HR Magazine*, 52 (April 2007): 18; "Quick Stop for a Pit Stop," *USA Today* (May 25, 2007): 18F; and Murray R. Barrick, Bret H. Bradley, Amy L. Kristof-Brown, and Amy E. Colbert, "The Moderating Role of Top Management Team Interdependence: Implications for Real Teams and Working Groups," *Academy of Management Journal*, 50 (June 2007): 544–557.

65. An instructive distinction between work groups and teams is presented in Jon R. Katzenbach and Douglas K. Smith, "The Discipline of Teams," *Harvard Business Review*, 71 (March–April 1993): 111–120. Also see Jon R. Katzenbach and Douglas K. Smith, *The Wisdom of Teams: Creating the High-Performance Organization* (New York: HarperCollins, 1999); Carol A. Beatty and Brenda A. Barker Scott, *Building Smart Teams: A Roadmap to High Performance* (Thousand Oaks,

Calif.: Sage, 2004); Gilad Chen, Lisa M. Donahue, and Richard J. Klimoski, "Training Undergraduates to Work in Organizational Teams," *Academy of Management Learning and Education*, 3 (March 2004): 27–40; and David H. Freedman, "Collaboration Is the Hottest Buzzword in Business Today. Too Bad It Doesn't Work," *Inc.*, 28 (September 2006): 61–62.

66. See Amy E. Randel and Kimberly S. Jaussi, "Functional Background Identity, Diversity, and Individual Performance in Cross-Functional Teams," *Academy of Management Journal*, 46 (December 2003): 763–774; Lee Fleming, "Perfecting Cross-Pollination," *Harvard Business Review*, 82 (September 2004): 22–24; Matthew A. Cronin and Laurie R. Weingart, "Representational Gaps, Information Processing, and Conflict in Functionally Diverse Teams," *Academy of Management Review*, 32 (July 2007): 761–773; and Ravi Chhatpar, "Innovate Faster by Melding Design and Strategy," *Harvard Business Review*, 85 (September 2007): 30, 32.

67. "Meet the New Steel," *Fortune* (October 1, 2007): 68–70.

68. For good background reading, see Michelle Conlin, "The Easiest Commute of All," *Business Week* (December 12, 2005): 78–80; and Jennifer Taylor Arnold, "Making the Leap," *HR Magazine*, 51 (May 2006): 80–86.

69. Yuhyung Shin, "Conflict Resolution in Virtual Teams," *Organizational Dynamics*, 34, no. 4 (2005): 331.

70. For a good overview of available tools, see Bill Roberts, "Counting on Collaboration," *HR Magazine*, 52 (October 2007): 47–54.

71. See Jeanne Brett, Kristin Behfar, and Mary C. Kern, "Managing Multicultural Teams," *Harvard Business Review*, 84 (November 2006): 83–91.

72. See Arvind Malhotra, Ann Majchrzak, and Benson Rosen, "Leading Virtual Teams," *Academy of Management Perspectives*, 21 (February 2007): 60–70; Penelope Sue Greenberg, Ralph H. Greenberg, and Yvonne Lederer Antonucci, "Creating and Sustaining Trust in Virtual Teams," *Business Horizons*, 50 (July–August 2007): 325–333; and Benson Rosen, Stacie Furst, and Richard Blackburn, "Overcoming Barriers to Knowledge Sharing in Virtual Teams," *Organizational Dynamics*, 36, no. 3 (2007): 259–273.

73. See Bianca Beersma, John R. Hollenbeck, Stephen E. Humphrey, Henry Moon, Donald E. Conlon, and Daniel R. Ilgen, "Cooperation, Competition, and Team Performance: Toward a Contingency Approach," *Academy of Management Journal*, 46 (October 2003): 572–590; Cristina B.

Gibson and P. Christopher Earley, "Collective Cognition in Action: Accumulation, Interaction, Examination, and Accommodation in the Development and Operation of Group Efficacy Beliefs in the Workplace," *Academy of Management Review*, 32 (April 2007): 438–458; Deborah Ancona and Henrik Bresman, "Thinking Outside the Team," *HR Magazine*, 52 (September 2007): 133–136; and Richard M. Rosen and Fred Adair, "CEOs Misperceive Top Teams' Performance," *Harvard Business Review*, 85 (September 2007): 30.

74. See Hans J. Thamhain, "Managing Technologically Innovative Team Efforts Toward New Product Success," *Journal of Product Innovation Management*, 7 (March 1990): 5–18. Also see the following study of team effectiveness: Richard J. Magjuka and Timothy T. Baldwin, "Team-Based Employee Involvement Programs: Effects of Design and Administration," *Personnel Psychology*, 44 (Winter 1991): 793–812.

75. See Stephen E. Kohn and Vincent D. O'Connell, *6 Habits of Highly Effective Teams* (Franklin Lakes, New Jersey: Career Press, 2007).

76. Three kinds of trust are discussed in Douglas A. Houston, "Trust in the Networked Economy: Doing Business on Web Time," *Business Horizons*, 44 (March–April 2001): 38–44. Also see Sajnicole A. Joni, "The Geography of Trust," *Harvard Business Review*, 82 (March 2004): 82–88; and F. David Schoorman, Roger C. Mayer, and James H. Davis, "An Integrative Model of Organizational Trust: Past, Present, and Future," *Academy of Management Review*, 32 (April 2007): 344–354.

77. See Chris Huxham and Siv Vangen, "Doing Things Collaboratively: Realizing the Advantage or Succumbing to Inertia?" *Organizational Dynamics*, 33, no. 2 (2004): 190–201; and Heather Johnson, "Trust Falls," *Training*, 41 (June 2004): 15.

78. Jeffrey Pfeffer, "More Mr. Nice Guy," *Business 2.0*, 4 (December 2003): 78.

79. Data from "Little Faith in Executives," *USA Today* (April 5, 2004): 1B. Also see Henry S. Givray, "When CEOs Aren't Leaders," *Business Week* (September 3, 2007): 102.

80. Laurence Prusak and Don Cohen, "How to Invest in Social Capital," *Harvard Business Review*, 79 (June 2001): 90.

81. See Dale E. Zand, "Trust and Managerial Problem Solving," *Administrative Science Quarterly*, 17 (June 1972): 229–239.

82. Trustworthiness is discussed in Thomas A. Stewart, "Whom Can You Trust? It's Not So Easy to Tell," *Fortune* (June 12, 2000): 331–334; Cam Caldwell and Stephen E. Clapham, "Organizational

Trustworthiness: An International Perspective," *Journal of Business Ethics*, 47 (November 2003): 349–364; and Alison Stein Wellner, "Who Can You Trust?" *Inc.*, 26 (October 2004): 39–40.

83. Adapted from Fernando Bartolomé, "Nobody Trusts the Boss Completely—Now What?" *Harvard Business Review*, 67 (March–April 1989): 137–139. Also see Ron Zemke, "Can You Manage Trust?" *Training*, 37 (February 2000): 76–83; James Lardner, "Why Should Anyone Believe You?" *Business 2.0*, 3 (March 2002): 40–48; and Michele Williams, "Building Genuine Trust Through Interpersonal Emotion Management: A Threat Regulation Model of Trust and Collaboration Across Boundaries," *Academy of Management Review*, 32 (April 2007): 595–621.

84. See Kimberly D. Elsbach and Greg Elofson, "How the Packaging of Decision Explanations Affects Perceptions of Trustworthiness," *Academy of Management Journal*, 43 (February 2000): 80–89; and Michele Williams, "In Whom We Trust: Group Membership as an Affective Context for Trust Development," *Academy of Management Review*, 26 (July 2001): 377–396.

85. Data from **www.alcatel-lucent.com,** January 8, 2007.

CHAPTER 14

1. **Opening Quote:** Suzanne Bates, "Speak to Inspire," *HR Magazine*, 52 (October 2007): 91.

2. Ramin Setoodeh, "Calling Avon's Lady," *Newsweek* (January 3, 2005): 100–101. For a brief update on Jung, see Katie Benner, Eugenia Levenson, and Rupali Arora, "2007: 50 Most Powerful Women," *Fortune* (October 15, 2007): 110.

3. See Gary Yukl and Cecilia M. Falbe, "Influence Tactics and Objectives in Upward, Downward, and Lateral Influence Attempts," *Journal of Applied Psychology*, 75 (April 1990); 132–140. For a comprehensive collection of readings on influence, see Lyman W. Porter, Harold L. Angle, and Robert W. Allen, *Organizational Influence Processes*, 2nd ed. (Armonk, N.Y.: M.E. Sharpe, 2003). For related research, see Scott Sonenshein, "Crafting Social Issues at Work," *Academy of Management Journal*, 49 (December 2006): 1158–1172.

4. Adapted from Yukl and Falbe, "Influence Tactics and Objectives in Upward, Downward, and Lateral Influence Attempts." Also see Gary Yukl, Cecilia M. Falbe, and Joo Young Youn, "Patterns of Influence Behavior for Managers," *Group & Organization Management*, 18 (March 1993): 5–28; Randall A. Gordon, "Impact of Ingratiation on Judgments and Evaluations: A Meta-Analytic

Investigation," *Journal of Personality and Social Psychology*, 71 (July 1996): 54–70; and P. P. Fu, T. K. Peng, Jeffrey C. Kennedy, and Gary Yukl, "Examining the Preferences of Influence Tactics in Chinese Societies: A Comparison of Chinese Managers in Hong Kong, Taiwan and Mainland China," *Organizational Dynamics*, 33, no. 1 (2004): 32–46.

5. See Robert B. Miller, Gary A. Williams, and Alden M. Hayashi, *The 5 Paths to Persuasion: The Art of Selling Your Message* (New York: Warner Business, 2004); Del Jones, "Debating Skills Come in Handy in Business," *USA Today* (September 30, 2004): 3B; and Raymond T. Sparrowe, Budi W. Soetjipto, and Maria L. Kraimer, "Do Leaders' Influence Tactics Relate to Members' Helping Behavior? It Depends on the Quality of the Relationship," *Academy of Management Journal*, 49 (December 2006): 1194–1208.

6. See Jeffrey Pfeffer, "How to Turn on the Charm," *Business 2.0*, 5 (June 2004): 76; Jennifer Reingold, "Suck Up and Move Up," *Fast Company*, no. 90 (January 2005): 34; James D. Westphal and Ithai Stern, "Flattery Will Get You Everywhere (Especially If You Are a Male Caucasian): How Ingratiation, Boardroom Behavior, and Demographic Minority Status Affect Additional Board Appointments at U.S. Companies," *Academy of Management Journal*, 50 (April 2007): 267–288; and Nanette Byrnes, "Profiles in Sycophancy," *Business Week* (August 13, 2007): 12.

7. Linda Tischler, "IBM's Management Makeover," *Fast Company*, no. 88 (November 2004): 113.

8. See George F. Dreher, Thomas W. Dougherty, and William Whitely, "Influence Tactics and Salary Attainment: A Gender-Specific Analysis," *Sex Roles*, 20 (May 1989): 535–550; and Herman Aguinis and Susan K. R. Adams, "Social-Role versus Structural Models of Gender and Influence Use in Organizations," *Group & Organization Studies*, 23 (December 1998): 414–446.

9. See Mahfooz A. Ansari and Alka Kapoor, "Organizational Context and Upward Influence Tactics," *Organizational Behavior and Human Decision Processes*, 40 (August 1987): 39–49.

10. Dean Tjosvold, "The Dynamics of Positive Power," *Training and Development Journal*, 38 (June 1984): 72.

11. See Toddi Gutner, "A 12-Step Program to Gaining Power," *Business Week* (December 24, 2001): 88; Janet O. Hagberg, *Real Power: Stages of Personal Power in Organizations*, 3rd ed. (Salem, Wis.: Sheffield Publishing, 2003); and Aili McConnon, "You Are Where You Sit,"

Business Week (July 23, 2007): 66–69. (*Note:* I would like to sincerely thank Carlton F. Harvey, Ph.D., for introducing me to Hagberg's fascinating book.)

12. Morgan McCall Jr., "Power, Influence, and Authority: The Hazards of Carrying a Sword," *Technical Report*, 10 (Greensboro, N.C.: Center for Creative Leadership, 1978), p. 5. For an interesting historical perspective of power, see Matt Miller, "What Makes History Happen?" *Fortune* (October 1, 2007): 78.

13. For more on these three effects of power, see Anthony T. Cobb, "An Episodic Model of Power: Toward an Integration of Theory and Research," *Academy of Management Review*, 9 (July 1984): 482–493. Also see C. Marlene Fiol, Edward J. O'Connor, and Herman Aguinis, "All for One and One for All? The Development and Transfer of Power Across Organizational Levels," *Academy of Management Review*, 26 (April 2001): 224–242.

14. Based on Edwin P. Hollander and Lynn R. Offermann, "Power and Leadership in Organizations: Relationships in Transition," *American Psychologist*, 45 (February 1990): 179–189.

15. For more on the authority/power relationship, see Julia Baird, "The Royal Consigliere," *Newsweek* (May 7, 2007): 52–53; Ivan Lansberg, "The Tests of a Prince," *Harvard Business Review*, 85 (September 2007): 92–101; and Keith Naughton, "Excuse Me, Mr. Ford," *Newsweek* (September 17, 2007): 42.

16. "There Is No State Here Anymore," *Newsweek* (February 24, 1997): 42.

17. For related discussion, see Allan R. Cohen and David L. Bradford, "Influence Without Authority: The Use of Alliances, Reciprocity, and Exchange to Accomplish Work," *Organizational Dynamics*, 17 (Winter 1989): 4–17; and Allan R. Cohen and David L. Bradford, *Influence Without Authority* (New York: Wiley, 1990).

18. See John R. P. French Jr. and Bertram Raven, "The Bases of Social Power," *Studies in Social Power*, ed. Dorwin Cartwright (Ann Arbor: University of Michigan Press, 1959), pp. 150–167. Eight different sources of power are discussed in Hugh R. Taylor, "Power at Work," *Personnel Journal*, 65 (April 1986): 42–49. Also see H. Eugene Baker III, "'Wax On—Wax Off': French and Raven at the Movies," *Journal of Management Education*, 17 (November 1993): 517–519.

19. John P. Kotter, "Power, Dependence, and Effective Management," *Harvard Business Review*, 55 (July–August 1977): 128. Also see Marshall Goldsmith, "It's Not a Fair Fight If You're the CEO," *Fast Company*, no. 89 (December 2004): 99.

20. For revealing case studies, see Barbara Kellerman, *Bad Leadership: What It Is,*

How It Happens, Why It Matters (Boston: Harvard Business School Press, 2004); and Devin Leonard, "Greenberg & Sons," *Fortune* (February 21, 2005): 104–114. Also see Stanley Bing, "Crazy Bosses," *Fortune* (May 28, 2007): 49–54.

21. Ann Pomeroy, "Thanks, But No Thanks," *HR Magazine*, 49 (December 2004): 18.

22. Patricia Sellers, "What Exactly Is Charisma?" *Fortune* (January 15, 1996): 68. Also see Daniel Sankowsky, "The Charismatic Leader as Narcissist: Understanding the Abuse of Power," *Organizational Dynamics*, 23 (Spring 1995): 57–71.

23. See Scott E. Seibert, Seth R. Silver, and W. Alan Randolph, "Taking Empowerment to the Next Level: A Multiple-Level Model of Empowerment, Performance, and Satisfaction," *Academy of Management Journal*, 47 (June 2004): 332–349; and Bill Roberts, "Empowerment or Imposition?" *HR Magazine*, 49 (June 2004): 157–166.

24. As quoted in Laurel Shaper Walters, "A Leader Redefines Management," *Christian Science Monitor* (September 22, 1992): 14. For Frances Hesselbein's ideas about leadership, see Roundtable Discussion, "All in a Day's Work," *Harvard Business Review* (Special Issue: Breakthrough Leadership), 79 (December 2001): 54–66. Supportive research evidence for empowerment can be found in Abhishek Srivastava, Kathryn M. Bartol, and Edwin A. Locke, "Empowering Leadership in Management Teams: Effects on Knowledge Sharing, Efficacy, and Performance," *Academy of Management Journal*, 49 (December 2006): 1239–1251.

25. As quoted in Matthew Boyle, "Brad Anderson," *Fortune* (April 30, 2007): 66.

26. Based on discussion in Stephen R. Covey, *Principle-Centered Leadership* (New York: Simon & Schuster, 1991), pp. 214–216. Also see W. Alan Randolph, "Navigating the Journey to Empowerment," *Organizational Dynamics*, 23 (Spring 1995): 19–32; Peter T. Coleman, "Implicit Theories of Organizational Power and Priming Effects on Managerial Power-Sharing Decisions: An Experimental Study," *Journal of Applied Social Psychology*, 34 (February 2004): 297–321; and Bradley L. Kirkman, Benson Rosen, Paul E. Tesluk, and Cristina B. Gibson, "The Impact of Team Empowerment on Virtual Team Performance: The Moderating Role of Face-to-Face Interaction," *Academy of Management Journal*, 47 (April 2004): 175–192.

27. John A. Byrne, "The Environment Was Ripe for Abuse," *Business Week* (February 25, 2002): 119.

28. See Roger Martin, "How Successful Leaders Think," *Harvard Business Review*, 85 (June 2007): 60–67; Jena McGregor, "The Five Faces of the 21st Century Chief," *Business Week* (August 20–27, 2007): 54–55; Leigh Buchanan, "The Office: Good to Great," *Inc.*, 29 (October 2007): 140; Geoff Colvin, "Leader Machines," *Fortune* (October 1, 2007): 98–106; and Corey Hajim, "The Top Companies for Leaders," *Fortune* (October 1, 2007): 109–114.

29. See Douglas A. Ready, "How to Grow Great Leaders," *Harvard Business Review*, 82 (December 2004): 92–100; Dan Ciampa, "Almost Ready: How Leaders Move Up," *Harvard Business Review*, 83 (January 2005): 46–53; Ryan Underwood, "Are You Being Coached?" *Fast Company*, no. 91 (February 2005): 83–85; Jack Gordon, "Microsoft's Leading Edge," *Training*, 44 (June 2007): 30–33; "Leadership Drivers," *Training*, 44 (June 2007): 36–39; Dave Ulrich and Norm Smallwood, "Building a Leadership Brand," *Harvard Business Review*, 85 (July–August 2007): 92–100; and Stephen R. Covey, "Begin with the End in Mind," *Training*, 44 (September 2007): 48.

30. Drawn from Joseph Kornik, "On the Minds of Managers . . . Skills Shortages and New Leadership," *Training*, 43 (June 2006): 16.

31. Peter F. Drucker, "What Makes an Effective Executive" *Harvard Business Review*, 82 (June 2004): 59.

32. See Hao Ma, Ranjan Karri, Kumar Chittipeddi, "The Paradox of Managerial Tyranny," *Business Horizons*, 47 (July–August 2004): 33–40; and Jeffrey Pfeffer, "In Defense of the Boss from Hell," *Business 2.0*, 8 (March 2007): 70.

33. Inspired by the definition in Andrew J. DuBrin, *Leadership: Research Findings, Practice and Skills*, 2nd ed. (Boston: Houghton Mifflin, 1998), p. 2. Also see Noel M. Tichy and Warren G. Bennis, "Making Judgment Calls: The Ultimate Act of Leadership," *Harvard Business Review*, 85 (October 2007): 94–102.

34. Catherine M. Dalton, "The Changing Identity of Corporate America: Opportunity, Duty, Leadership," *Business Horizons*, 48 (January–February 2005): 2–3.

35. As quoted in Oren Harari, *The Leadership Secrets of Colin Powell* (New York: McGraw-Hill, 2002): p. 13.

36. See Ellen Florian Kratz, "Get Me a CEO from GE!" *Fortune* (April 18, 2005): 147–152; "Moments of Truth: Global Executives Talk About the Challenges That Shaped Them as Leaders," Special Issue: The Tests of a Leader, *Harvard Business Review*, 85 (April 2007): 15–25; and Larry Bossidy, "What Your Leader Expects of You, and What You Should Expect in Return," *Harvard Business Review*, 85 (April 2007): 58–65.

37. As quoted in Bridget Finn, "How to Turn Managers into Leaders," *Business 2.0*, 5 (September 2004): 70. For updates on David Neeleman and JetBlue Airways, see "David's Flight Log" at **www. jetblue.com.**

38. See Gary A. Yukl, *Leadership in Organizations*, 5th ed. (Upper Saddle River, N.J.: Prentice-Hall, 2001).

39. See David L. Cawthon, "Leadership: The Great Man Theory Revisited," *Business Horizons*, 39 (May–June 1996): 1–4; Ron Zemke, "End of the Heroic Leader," *Training*, 41 (January 2004): 10; and Dusya Vera and Antonio Rodriguez-Lopez, "Leading Improvisation: Lessons from the American Revolution," *Organizational Dynamics*, 36, no. 3 (2007): 303–319.

40. Fred Luthans, *Organizational Behavior*, 3rd ed. (New York: McGraw-Hill, 1981), p. 419. For interesting discussions about various leader traits, see Jeffrey A. Sonnenfeld and Andrew J. Ward, "Firing Back: How Great Leaders Rebound After Career Disasters," Special Issue: The Tests of a Leader, *Harvard Business Review*, 85 (January 2007): 76–84; Matthew Boyle, "Questions for . . . Jim Collins," *Fortune* (February 19, 2007): 50, 54; Glenn E. Mangurian, "Realizing What You're Made Of," *Harvard Business Review*, 85 (March 2007): 125–130; David Rynecki, "An 18-Hole Character Test," *Business Week* (May 28, 2007): 92, 95; and Del Jones, "First-Born Kids Grow Up to Be CEO Material," *USA Today* (September 4, 2007): 1B–2B.

41. Ralph M. Stogdill, "Personal Factors Associated with Leadership: A Survey of the Literature," *Journal of Psychology*, 25 (1948): 63.

42. See Daniel Goleman, *Emotional Intelligence* (New York: Bantam Books, 1995); Michaela Davies, Lazar Stankov, and Richard D. Roberts, "Emotional Intelligence: In Search of an Elusive Construct," *Journal of Personality and Social Psychology*, 75 (October 1998): 989–1015; Daniel Goleman, "Never Stop Learning," *Harvard Business Review* (Special Issue: Inside the Mind of the Leader), 82 (January 2004): 28–29; and Stéphane Côté and Christopher T. H. Miners, "Emotional Intelligence, Cognitive Intelligence, and Job Performance," *Administrative Science Quarterly*, 51 (March 2006): 1–28.

43. Michelle Neely Martinez, "The Smarts That Count," *HR Magazine*, 42 (November 1997): 72.

44. Based on and adapted from Daniel Goleman, Richard Boyatzis, and Annie McKee, "Primal Leadership," *Harvard Business Review* (Special Issue: Breakthrough Leadership), 79 (December 2001): 49. Also see Daniel Goleman, Richard Boyatzis, and Annie

McKee, *Primal Leadership: Realizing the Power of Emotional Intelligence* (Boston: Harvard Business School Press, 2002); and Robert B. McKenna and Paul R. Yost, "The Differentiated Leader: Specific Strategies for Handling Today's Adverse Situations," *Organizational Dynamics*, 33, no. 3 (2004): 292–306.

45. See Bob Wall, "Being Smart Only Takes You So Far: The Most Successful Leaders Are Masters of Emotional Intelligence But Sometimes They Need Coaching," *Training and Development*, 61 (January 2007): 64–68.

46. Data from Judy B. Rosener, "Ways Women Lead," *Harvard Business Review*, 68 (November–December 1990): 119–125. Also see Rochelle Sharpe, "As Leaders, Women Rule," *Business Week* (November 20, 2000): 74–84; Ann Pomeroy, Cultivating Female Leaders," *HR Magazine*, 52 (February 2007): 44–50; Alice H. Eagly and Linda L. Carli, "Women and the Labyrinth of Leadership," *Harvard Business Review*, 85 (September 2007): 62–71; and Catherine M. Dalton, "Queen Bees: All Sting, No Honey," *Business Horizons*, 50 (September–October 2007): 349–352.

47. See "Ways Women and Men Lead," *Harvard Business Review*, 69 (January–February 1991): 150–160.

48. Data from Alice H. Eagly and Blair T. Johnson, "Gender and Leadership Style: A Meta-Analysis," *Psychological Bulletin*, 108 (September 1990): 233–256. A similar finding is reported in Robert P. Vecchio, "Leadership and Gender Advantage," *The Leadership Quarterly*, 13 (December 2002): 643–671. For inspiring profiles of women leaders, see Betsy Morris, "Dynamic Duo," *Fortune* (October 15, 2007): 78–86; and "My Journey to the Top," *Newsweek* (October 15, 2007): 49–65.

49. Kurt Lewin, Ronald Lippitt, and Ralph K. White, "Patterns of Aggressive Behavior in Experimentally Created 'Social Climates,'" *Journal of Social Psychology*, 10 (May 1939): 271–299.

50. Dexter Roberts, "China Goes Shopping," *Business Week* (December 20, 2004): 34.

51. For an informative summary of this research, see Edwin A. Fleishman, "Twenty Years of Consideration and Structure," in *Current Developments in the Study of Leadership*, ed. Edwin A. Fleishman and James G. Hunt (Carbondale, Ill.: Southern Illinois University Press, 1973), pp. 1–40. Also see Vishwanath V. Baba and Merle E. Ace, "Serendipity in Leadership: Initiating Structure and Consideration in the Classroom," *Human Relations*, 42 (June 1989): 509–525.

52. Three popular extensions of the Ohio State leadership studies may be found in Robert R. Blake and Anne McCanse,

Leadership Dilemmas—Grid Solutions (Houston: Gulf Publishing, 1990); William J. Reddin, *Managerial Effectiveness* (New York: McGraw-Hill, 1970); and Paul Hersey and Kenneth H. Blanchard, *Management of Organizational Behavior: Utilizing Human Resources*, 5th ed. (Englewood Cliffs, N.J.: Prentice-Hall, 1988), p. 171. Empirical lack of support for Hersey and Blanchard's situational leadership theory is reported in Jane R. Goodson, Gail W. McGee, and James F. Cashman, "Situational Leadership Theory: A Test of Leadership Prescriptions," *Group & Organization Studies*, 14 (December 1989): 446–461.

53. See Abraham K. Korman, "Consideration, 'Initiating Structure,' and Organizational Criteria—A Review," *Personnel Psychology*, 19 (Winter 1966): 349–361.

54. See Blake and McCanse, *Leadership Dilemmas—Grid Solutions*.

55. See Tom Lester, "Taking Guard on the Grid," *Management Today* (March 1991): 93–94.

56. For details of this study, see Robert R. Blake and Jane Srygley Mouton, "Management by Grid® Principles or Situationalism: Which?" *Group & Organization Studies*, 6 (December 1981): 439–455. Also see Robert R. Blake and Jane Srygley Mouton, "A Comparative Analysis of Situationalism and 9,9 Management by Principle," *Organizational Dynamics*, 10 (Spring 1982): 20–43.

57. Stanley Holmes, "The Jack Welch of the Meat Aisle," *Business Week* (January 24, 2005): 61.

58. Fred E. Fiedler, "Job Engineering for Effective Leadership: A New Approach," *Management Review*, 66 (September 1977): 29.

59. For an excellent comprehensive validation study, see Michael J. Strube and Joseph E. Garcia, "A Meta-Analytic Investigation of Fiedler's Contingency Model of Leadership Effectiveness," *Psychological Bulletin*, 90 (September 1981): 307–321.

60. Fred E. Fiedler and Martin M. Chemers, *Leadership and Effective Management* (Glenview, Ill.: Scott, Foresman, 1974), p. 91.

61. Robert J. House and Terence R. Mitchell, "Path-Goal Theory of Leadership," *Journal of Contemporary Business*, 3 (Autumn 1974): 85. The entire Autumn 1974 issue is devoted to an instructive review of contrasting theories of leadership.

62. As quoted in Michael Kelley, "The Clear Leader," *Fast Company*, no. 92 (March 2005): 66. Also see Marcus Buckingham, *The One Thing You Need to Know . . . About Great Managing, Great Leading, and Sustained Individual Success* (New York: Free Press, 2005).

63. Adapted from Robert J. House, "Path-Goal Theory of Leadership: Lessons, Legacy, and a Reformulated Theory," *The Leadership Quarterly*, 7 (Autumn 1996): 323–352.

64. For path-goal research, see Abduhl-Rahim A. Al-Gattan, "Test of the Path-Goal Theory of Leadership in the Multinational Domain," *Group & Organization Studies*, 10 (December 1985): 429–445; Robert T. Keller, "A Test of the Path-Goal Theory of Leadership with Need for Clarity as a Moderator in Research and Development Organizations," *Journal of Applied Psychology*, 74 (April 1989): 208–212; John E. Mathieu, "A Test of Subordinates' Achievement and Affiliation Needs as Moderators of Leader Path-Goal Relationships," *Basic and Applied Social Psychology*, 11 (June 1990): 179–189; and Retha A. Price, "An Investigation of Path-Goal Leadership Theory in Marketing Channels," *Journal of Retailing*, 67 (Fall 1991): 339–361.

65. See J. McGregor Burns, *Leadership* (New York: HarperCollins, 1978). Also see Frederick F. Reichheld, "Lead for Loyalty," *Harvard Business Review*, 79 (July–August 2001): 76–84.

66. See Michael Frese, Susanne Beimel, and Sandra Schoenborn, "Action Training for Charismatic Leadership: Two Evaluations of Studies of a Commercial Training Module on Inspirational Communication of a Vision," *Personnel Psychology*, 56 (Autumn 2003): 671–697; Joyce E. Bono and Timothy A. Judge, "Self-Concordance at Work: Toward Understanding the Motivational Effects of Transformational Leaders," *Academy of Management Journal*, 46 (October 2003): 554–571; Michael Maccoby, "Why People Follow the Leader: The Power of Transference," *Harvard Business Review*, 82 (September 2004): 76–85; and Jane M. Howell and Boas Shamir, "The Role of Followers in the Charismatic Leadership Process: Relationships and Their Consequences," *Academy of Management Review*, 30 (January 2005): 96–112.

67. A critique of charismatic leadership can be found in Joshua Macht, "Jim Collins to CEOs: Lose the Charisma," *Business 2.0*, 2 (October 2001): 121–122. Also see Jack Welch, *Jack: Straight from the Gut* (New York: Warner Business Books, 2001); and Bruce Horovitz and Theresa Howard, "Wendy's Loses Its Legend," *USA Today* (January 9, 2002): 1B–2B.

68. See Joseph Seltzer and Bernard M. Bass, "Transformational Leadership: Beyond Initiation and Consideration," *Journal of Management*, 16 (December 1990): 693–703.

69. For research support, see David A. Waldman, Gabriel G. Ramírez, Robert J. House, and Phanish Puranam, "Does

Leadership Matter? CEO Leadership Attributes and Profitability Under Conditions of Perceived Environmental Uncertainty," *Academy of Management Journal*, 44 (February 2001): 134–143.

70. For example, see Bernard M. Bass, "From Transactional to Transformational Leadership: Learning to Share the Vision," *Organizational Dynamics*, 18 (Winter 1990): 19–31; Warren Bennis, "The End of Leadership: Exemplary Leadership Is Impossible Without Full Inclusion, Initiatives, and Cooperation of Followers," *Organizational Dynamics*, 28 (Summer 1999): 71–80; James R. Detert and Ethan R. Burris, "Leadership Behavior and Employee Voice: Is the Door Really Open?" *Academy of Management Journal*, 50 (August 2007): 869–884; and Chip Jarnagin and John W. Slocum, Jr., "Creating Corporate Cultures Through Mythopoetic Leadership," *Organizational Dynamics*, 36, no. 3 (2007): 288–302.

71. Robert J. Sternberg, "WICS: A Model of Leadership in Organizations," *Academy of Management Learning and Education*, 2 (December 2003): 388. Also see Deborah Ancona, Thomas W. Malone, Wanda J. Orlikowski, and Peter M. Senge, "In Praise of the Incomplete Leader," *Harvard Business Review*, 85 (February 2007): 92–100; and Ronit Kark and Dina Van Dijk, "Motivation to Lead, Motivation to Follow: The Role of the Self-Regulatory Focus in Leadership Processes," *Academy of Management Review*, 32 (April 2007): 500–528.

72. For related reading, see Dov Seidman, "The Case for Ethical Leadership," *Academy of Management Executive*, 18 (May 2004): 134–138; Robert M. Fulmer, "The Challenge of Ethical Leadership," *Organizational Dynamics*, 33, no. 3 (2004): 307–317; and Michael E. Brown, "Misconceptions of Ethical Leadership: How to Avoid Potential Pitfalls," *Organizational Dynamics*, 36, no. 2 (2007): 140–155.

73. For more on the servant leader philosophy, see Robert K. Greenleaf, *Servant Leadership: A Journey into the Nature of Legitimate Power and Greatness* (New York: Paulist Press, 1977); Walter Kiechel III, "The Leader as Servant," *Fortune* (May 4, 1992): 121–122; Larry C. Spears, *Reflections on Leadership: How Robert K. Greenleaf's Theory of Servant-Leadership Influenced Today's Top Management Thinkers* (New York: Wiley, 1995); Don M. Frick, *Robert K. Greenleaf: A Life of Servant Leadership* (San Francisco: Berrett-Koehler, 2004); and Joanne H. Gavin and Richard O. Mason, "The Virtuous Organization: The Value of Happiness in the Workplace," *Organizational Dynamics*, 33, no. 4 (2004): 379–392. Also see Peter Cairo,

David L. Dotlich, and Stephen H. Rhinesmith, "The Unnatural Leader," *Training and Development*, 59 (March 2005): 26–31.

74. David Leon Moore, "Wooden's Wizardry Wears Well," *USA Today* (March 29, 1995): 1C–2C. Also see "The 'Wizard' Turns 90," *USA Today* (October 11, 2000): 10C. Other servant leaders are profiled in Jayne O'Donnell, "Ethan Allen's Kathwari Was Always a Leader," *USA Today* (June 25, 2007): 4B; Mark Starr, "Coach, Teacher, Believer," *Newsweek* (July 16, 2007): 52–53; and Donna Fenn, "My Bad: Sometimes, Even CEOs Have to Say They're Sorry," *Inc.*, 29 (October 2007): 37–38.

75. See Barbara Kellerman, *Bad Leadership: What It Is, How It Happens, Why It Matters* (Boston: Harvard Business School Press, 2004).

76. Andrew Park, "Thinking Out of the Box," *Business Week* (November 22, 2004): 22.

77. For more, see Susan Elaine Murphy and Ellen A. Ensher, "Establish a Great Mentoring Relationship," *Training and Development*, 60 (July 2006): 27–28; Sarah Boehle, "Crafting a Coaching Culture," *Training*, 44 (May 2007): 22–24; Ann Pomeroy, "Everyone Has a Contribution to Make," *HR Magazine*, 52 (June 2007): 14, 18; Jia Lynn Yang, "Consulting Past CEOs: Wise Guys," *Fortune* (June 25, 2007): 95; and Andrea Wong, "My Journey to the Top," *Fortune* (October 15, 2007): 52.

78. Abraham Zaleznik, "Managers and Leaders: Are They Different?" *Harvard Business Review*, 55 (May–June 1977): 76. Also see Heather Johnson, "The Ins and Outs of Executive Coaching," *Training*, 41 (May 2004): 36–41; Stratford Sherman and Alyssa Freas, "The Wild West of Executive Coaching," *Harvard Business Review*, 82 (November 2004): 82–90; Ann Pomeroy, "Peak Performers," *HR Magazine*, 52 (April 2007): 48–53; Ann Pomeroy, "Internal Mentors and Coaches Are Popular," *HR Magazine*, 52 (September 2007): 12; and Kathryn Tyler, "Cross-Cultural Connections," *HR Magazine*, 52 (October 2007): 77–83.

79. For details, see Ellen A. Fagenson, "The Mentor Advantage: Perceived Career/Job Experiences of Protégés versus Non-Protégés," *Journal of Organizational Behavior*, 10 (October 1989): 309–320. More mentoring research findings are reported in Melenie J. Lankau and Terri A. Scandura, "An Investigation of Personal Learning in Mentoring Relationships: Content, Antecedents, and Consequences," *Academy of Management Journal*, 45 (August 2002): 779–790; Shana A. Simon and Lillian T. Eby, "A Typology of Negative Mentoring Experiences: A Multidimensional Scaling

Study," *Human Relations*, 56, no. 9 (2003): 1083–1106; and Scott Tonidandel, Derek R. Avery, and McKensy G. Phillips, "Maximizing Returns on Mentoring: Factors Affecting Subsequent Protégé Performance," *Journal of Organizational Behavior*, 28 (January 2007): 89–110.

80. Margery Weinstein, "Stuck in the Middle," *Training*, 44 (July–August 2007): 8.

81. See Erik Gunn, "Mentoring: The Democratic Version," *Training*, 32 (August 1995): 64–67. Also see Kathryn Tyler, "Find Your Mentor," *HR Magazine*, 49 (March 2004): 89–93.

82. Nadira A. Hira, "You Raised Them, Now Manage Them," *Fortune* (May 28, 2007): 44.

83. "Executive Orientations Get Poor Marks in Survey," *HR Magazine*, 49 (March 2004): 12.

84. For more, see Kathy E. Kram, "Phases of the Mentor Relationship," *Academy of Management Journal*, 26 (December 1983): 608–625.

85. Suzanne C. de Janasz, Sherry E. Sullivan, and Vicki Whiting, "Mentor Networks and Career Success: Lessons for Turbulent Times," *Academy of Management Executive*, 17 (November 2003): 79.

86. See Susan Berfield, "Mentoring Can Be Messy," *Business Week* (January 29, 2007): 80–81.

87. Good discussions of women and mentoring can be found in Belle Rose Ragins and John L. Cotton, "Easier Said Than Done: Gender Differences in Perceived Barriers to Gaining a Mentor," *Academy of Management Journal*, 34 (December 1991): 939–951; Victoria A. Parker and Kathy E. Kram, "Women Mentoring Women: Creating Conditions for Connection," *Business Horizons*, 36 (March–April 1993): 42–51; and Susan J. Wells, "Smoothing the Way," *HR Magazine*, 46 (June 2001): 52–58.

88. For more, see George F. Dreher and Josephine A. Chargois, "Gender, Mentoring Experiences, and Salary Attainment Among Graduates of an Historically Black University," *Journal of Vocational Behavior*, 53 (December 1998): 401–416; David A. Thomas, "The Truth About Mentoring Minorities: Race Matters," *Harvard Business Review*, 79 (April 2001): 99–107; Robert J. Grossman, "Mentors in Demand," *HR Magazine*, 45 (March 2000): 42–43; and Jonathan A. Segal, "Mirror-Image Mentoring," *HR Magazine*, 45 (March 2000): 157–166.

89. For a contemporary perspective on behaviorism, see Richard J. DeGrandpre, "A Science of Meaning: Can Behaviorism Bring Meaning to Psychological Science?" *American Psychologist*, 55 (July 2000): 721–738.

90. See Edward L. Thorndike, *Educational Psychology: The Psychology of Learning*

(New York: Columbia University Press, 1913), II, 4.

91. For an instructive account of operant conditioning applied to human behavior, see B. F. Skinner, *Science and Human Behavior* (New York: Free Press, 1953), pp. 62–66. A good update is B. F. Skinner, "What Is Wrong with Daily Life in the Western World," *American Psychologist*, 41 (May 1986): 568–574. Also see Marilyn B. Gilbert and Thomas F. Gilbert, "What Skinner Gave Us," *Training*, 28 (September 1991): 42–48.

92. For example, see Tom Kramlinger and Tom Huberty, "Behaviorism versus Humanism," *Training & Development Journal*, 44 (December 1990): 41–45; and Alfie Kohn, "Challenging Behaviorist Dogma: Myths About Money and Motivation," *Compensation & Benefits Review*, 30 (March–April 1998): 27, 33–37.

93. For example, see Bob Filipczak, "Why No One Likes Your Incentive Program," *Training*, 30 (August 1993): 19–25; and Alfie Kohn, "Why Incentive Plans Cannot Work," *Harvard Business Review*, 71 (September–October 1993): 54–63.

94. For positive evidence and background, see Alexander D. Stajkovic and Fred Luthans, "A Meta-Analysis of the Effects of Organizational Behavior Modification on Task Performance, 1975–95," *Academy of Management Journal*, 40 (October 1997): 1122–1149; Fred Luthans and Alexander D. Stajkovic, "Reinforce for Performance: The Need to Go Beyond Pay and Even Rewards," *Academy of Management Executive*, 13 (May 1999): 49–57; Cheryl Comeau-Kirschner, "Improving Productivity Doesn't Cost a Dime," *Management Review*, 88 (January 1999): 7; and Alexander D. Stajkovic and Fred Luthans, "Differential Effects of Incentive Motivators on Work Performance," *Academy of Management Journal*, 44 (June 2001): 580–590.

95. Dale Feuer, "Training for Fast Times," *Training*, 24 (July 1987): 28.

96. See Robert Kegan and Lisa Laskow Lahey, "More Powerful Communication: From the Language of Prizes and Praising to the Language of Ongoing Regard," *Journal of Organizational Excellence*, 20 (Summer 2001): 11–17; Leigh Buchanan, "Managing One-to-One," *Inc.*, 23 (October 2001): 82–88; and Del Jones, "Training Workers the SeaWorld Way," *USA Today* (August 21, 2006): 3B. For an example of a punishment that backfired, see Steve Powers, "What Economists Aren't Telling You," *Business 2.0*, 6 (May 2005): 32.

97. Alan Farnham, "The Trust Gap," *Fortune* (December 4, 1989): 74. Another example of positive reinforcement in business

can be found in Jess McCuan, "The Ultimate Sales Incentive," *Inc.*, 26 (May 2004): 32.

98. Kenneth Blanchard and Spencer Johnson, *The One Minute Manager* (New York: Berkley, 1982), p. 45 (emphasis added). Also see Kenneth Blanchard and Robert Lorber, *Putting the One Minute Manager to Work* (New York: Berkley, 1984).

99. Tom Rath and Donald O. Clifton, *How Full Is Your Bucket? Positive Strategies for Work and Life* (New York: Gallup Press, 2004), p. 57. Also see Kerry Hannon, "Praise Cranks Up Productivity," *USA Today* (August 30, 2004): 6B; and Richard F. Gerson and Robbie G. Gerson, "Effort Management," *Training and Development*, 60 (June 2006): 26–27.

100. For detailed treatment of B. Mod. in the workplace, see Fred Luthans and Robert Kreitner, *Organizational Behavior Modification and Beyond: An Operant and Social Learning Approach* (Glenview, Ill.: Scott, Foresman, 1985). Also see Ahmad Diba, "If Pat Sajak Were Your CEO . . .," *Fortune* (December 18, 2000): 330; and Bobbie Gossage, "Lose Weight, Get a Toaster," *Inc.*, 27 (January 2005): 24.

101. Ten items excerpted from a 25-item survey in Anne Fisher, "Success Secret: A High Emotional IQ," *Fortune* (October 26, 1998): 293–298.

CHAPTER 15

1. **Opening Quote:** Dean Tjosvold, *Learning to Manage Conflict: Getting People to Work Together Productively* (New York: Lexington, 1993), p. xi.

2. Ann Pomeroy, "CEO Challenges in 2004," *HR Magazine*, 49 (October 2004): 18.

3. "The Best Managers: Steven Reinemund, PepsiCo," *Business Week* (January 10, 2005): 56. For another example, see Stephanie N. Mehta, "Met the New AT&T," *Fortune* (May 28, 2007): 58–62.

4. For good background reading on change, see Edward E. Lawler III and Christopher G. Worley, *Built to Change: How to Achieve Sustained Organizational Effectiveness* (San Francisco: Jossey-Bass, 2006); Gary Hamel with Bill Breen, *The Future of Management* (Boston: Harvard Business School Press, 2007); and John Koten, "Everything Will Change: A Conversation with Scott Cook," *Inc.*, 29 (September 2007): 212–215.

5. As quoted in Del Jones, "Xerox CEO: Customers, Employees Come First," *USA Today* (December 15, 2003): 3B. For an update on Mulcahy and Xerox, see Betsy Morris, "Dynamic Duo," *Fortune* (October 15, 2007): 78–86.

6. See Carrie R. Leana and Bruce Barry, "Stability and Change as Simultaneous Experiences in Organizational Life,"

Academy of Management Review, 25 (October 2000): 753–759; Kevin P. Coyne and Edward J. Coyne Sr., "Surviving Your New CEO," *Harvard Business Review*, 85 (May 2007): 62–69; Ann Pomeroy, "Fitting the Pieces Together," *HR Magazine*, 52 (June 2007): 76–80; and Donde Ashmos Plowman et al., "Radical Change Accidentally: The Emergence and Amplification of Small Change," *Academy of Management Journal*, 50 (June 2007): 515–543.

7. Adapted from discussion in David A. Nadler and Michael L. Tushman, "Organizational Frame Bending: Principles for Managing Reorientation," *Academy of Management Executive*, 3 (August 1989): 194–204. Also see Robert H. Schaffer and Matthew K. McCreight, "Build Your Own Change Model," *Business Horizons*, 47 (May–June 2004): 33–38.

8. *Kaizen* at Toyota is discussed in Clay Chandler, "Full Speed Ahead," *Fortune* (February 7, 2005): 78–84; Charles Fishman, "No Satisfaction," *Fast Company*, no. 111 (January 2007): 82–92; and Thomas A. Stewart and Anand P. Raman, "Lessons from Toyota's Long Drive," *Harvard Business Review*, 85 (July–August 2007): 74–83.

9. See Brian Dumaine, "Creating a New Company Culture," *Fortune* (January 15, 1990): 127–131.

10. Michelle Kessler, "Dell Reverses, Steps into Wal-Mart," *USA Today* (May 25, 2007): 1B.

11. Michelle Kessler, "Cisco's Risky Scientific-Atlanta Buy Pays Off as Quarterly Profit Surges," *USA Today* (August 9, 2006): 2B. Other examples of frame bending can be found in Charles Fishman, "Degree of Difficulty," *Fast Company*, 112 (February 2007): 94–99; Bruce Nolop, "Rule to Acquire By," *Harvard Business Review*, 85 (September 2007): 129–139; and Roger O. Crockett, "Will a Google Phone Change the Game?" *Business Week* (October 8, 2007): 38–39.

12. Kathy Rebello, "Inside Microsoft," *Business Week* (July 15, 1996): 57. Also see John Amis, Trevor Slack, and C. R. Hinings, "The Pace, Sequence, and Linearity of Radical Change," *Academy of Management Journal*, 47 (February 2004): 15–39; and Michael Hammer, "Deep Change: How Operational Innovation Can Transform Your Company," *Harvard Business Review*, 82 (April 2004): 84–93.

13. See Mitchell Lee Marks, "Workplace Recovery after Mergers, Acquisitions, and Downsizings: Facilitating Individual Adaptation to Major Organizational Transitions," *Organizational Dynamics*, 35, no. 4 (2006): 384–399; and Jack Welch and Suzy Welch, "The Walking Wounded," *Business Week* (May 7, 2007): 96.

14. See Robert H. Miles, "Beyond the Age of Dilbert: Accelerating Corporate Transformations by Rapidly Engaging All Employees," *Organizational Dynamics*, 29 (Spring 2001): 313–321.

15. Ichak Adizes, *Mastering Change: The Power of Mutual Trust and Respect in Personal Life, Family Life, Business and Society* (Santa Monica, Calif.: Adizes Institute, 1991), p. 6.

16. See Steve Hamm, "Children of the Web," *Business Week* (July 2, 2007): 50–58; Heather Green, "A Web That Thinks Like You," *Business Week* (July 9–16, 2007): 94–95; Aili McConnon, "Just Ahead: The Web as a Virtual World," *Business Week* (August 13, 2007): 62–63; and Steven Levy, "Facebook Grows Up," *Newsweek* (August 20–27, 2007): 40–46.

17. See Jeffrey Pfeffer, "Breaking Through Excuses," *Business 2.0*, 6 (May 2005): 76; and Susan Berfield, "The Right Way to Shake Up a Company," *Business Week* (February 12, 2007): 73.

18. J. Alan Ofner, "Managing Change," *Personnel Administrator*, 29 (September 1984): 20.

19. Peter Coy, "The Perils of Picking the Wrong Standard," *Business Week* (October 8, 1990): 145.

20. Diane Brady, "Act II," *Business Week* (March 29, 2004): 76.

21. See Diane Brady, "Y&R's Fudge Heads for the Exit," *Business Week* (November 28, 2006); **http://www.businessweek. com/bwdaily/dnflash/content/ nov2006/db20061128_277879. htm?chan=search.**

22. See Leigh Buchanan, "The Office: The Departed," *Inc.*, 29 (August 2007): 128.

23. This list is based in part on John P. Kotter and Leonard A. Schlesinger, "Choosing Strategies for Change," *Harvard Business Review*, 57 (March–April 1979): 106–114; and Joseph Stanislao and Bettie C. Stanislao, "Dealing with Resistance to Change," *Business Horizons*, 26 (July–August 1983): 74–78.

24. Del Jones, "When You're Smiling, Are You Seething Inside?" *USA Today* (April 12, 2004): 2B.

25. Robert Kegan and Lisa Laskow Lahey, "The Real Reason People Won't Change," *Harvard Business Review*, 79 (November 2001): 86. Also see Jennifer Schramm, "Managing Change," *HR Magazine*, 52 (March 2007): 152.

26. For example, see Kristine Ellis, "Straight from the Top," *Training*, 41 (February 2004): 42–44; Bill Roberts, "Empowerment or Imposition?" *HR Magazine*, 49 (June 2004): 157–166; and David A. Garvin and Michael A. Roberto, "Change Through Persuasion," *Harvard Business Review*, 83 (February 2005): 104–112.

27. As quoted in Del Jones, "Product Development Can Fill Prescription for Success," *USA Today* (May 30, 2000): 7B.

28. See Paul S. Goodman and Denise M. Rousseau, "Organizational Change That Produces Results: The Linkage Approach," *Academy of Management Executive*, 18 (August 2004): 7–19; Craig M. McAllaster, "The 5 P's of Change: Leading Change by Effectively Utilizing Leverage Points Within an Organization," *Organizational Dynamics*, 33, no. 3 (2004): 318–328; and Nancy Hatch Woodward, "To Make Changes, Manage Them," *HR Magazine*, 52 (May 2007): 62–67.

29. See Robert N. Llewellyn, "When to Call the Organization Doctor," *HR Magazine*, 47 (March 2002): 79–83; Darin E. Hartley, "OD Wired," *Training and Development*, 58 (August 2004): 20–22; Stephen R. Covey, "Organizational Development," *Training*, 44 (April 2007): 40; and Nancy Lockwood, SHRM Research Quarterly, "Organization Development: A Strategic HR Tool," *HR Magazine*, 52 (September 2007): 1–9.

30. Philip G. Hanson and Bernard Lubin, "Answers to Questions Frequently Asked About Organization Development," in *The Emerging Practice of Organization Development*, ed. Walter Sikes, Allan Drexler, and Jack Grant (Alexandria, Va.: NTL Institute, 1989), p. 16 (emphasis added). For good background information on current OD practices, see W. Warner Burke, "The New Agenda for Organization Development," *Organizational Dynamics*, 26 (Summer 1997): 7–20; Chuck McVinney, "Dream Weaver," *Training & Development* 53 (April 1999): 39–42; and Ron Zemke, "Don't Fix That Company!" *Training*, 36 (June 1999): 26–33.

31. W. Warner Burke, *Organization Development: A Normative View* (Reading, Mass.: Addison-Wesley, 1987), p. 9. Also see Benjamin Schneider, Arthur P. Brief, and Richard A. Guzzo, "Creating a Climate and Culture for Sustainable Organizational Change," *Organizational Dynamics*, 24 (Spring 1996): 7–19.

32. See Julia Boorstin, "The Making of a Model Consultant," *Fortune* (January 22, 2001): 158, 160.

33. For example, see Joel Schettler, "Bruce Kestelman," *Training*, 38 (November 2001): 36–39.

34. This list is based on Wendell French, "Organization Development Objectives, Assumptions, and Strategies," *California Management Review*, 12 (Winter 1969): 23–34; and Charles Kiefer and Peter Stroh, "A New Paradigm for Organization Development," *Training and Development Journal*, 37 (April 1983): 26–35.

35. See Robert J. Marshak, "Managing the Metaphors of Change," *Organizational Dynamics*, 22 (Summer 1993): 44–56; Craig L. Pearce and Charles P. Osmond,

"Metaphors for Change: The ALPs Model of Change Management," *Organizational Dynamics*, 24 (Winter 1996): 23–35; and Ian Palmer and Richard Dunford, "Conflicting Uses of Metaphors: Reconceptualizing Their Use in the Field of Organizational Change," *Academy of Management Review*, 21 (July 1996): 691–717.

36. A successful application of Lewin's model at British Airways is discussed in Leonard D. Goodstein and W. Warner Burke, "Creating Successful Organization Change," *Organizational Dynamics*, 19 (Spring 1991): 4–17. Also see Gib Akin and Ian Palmer, "Putting Metaphors to Work for Change in Organizations," *Organizational Dynamics*, 28 (Winter 2000): 67–79; Richard S. Allen and Kendyl A. Montgomery, "Applying an Organizational Development Approach to Creating Diversity," *Organizational Dynamics*, 30 (Fall 2001): 149–161; and Mark Herron, "Training Alone Is Not Enough," *Training*, 39 (February 2002): 72.

37. For details on how poor "unfreezing" threatened the Hewlett-Packard/ Compaq Computer merger plan, see Peter Burrows, "Carly's Last Stand?" *Business Week* (December 24, 2001): 62–70.

38. As quoted in Linda Tischler, "Kenny Moore Held a Funeral and Everyone Came," *Fast Company*, no. 79 (February 2004): 30.

39. Bill Breen and Cheryl Dahl, "Field Guide for Change," *Fast Company*, no. 30 (December 1999): 384. Also see Oren Harari, "Leading Change from the Middle," *Management Review*, 88 (February 1999): 29–32; David Butcher and Sally Atkinson, "The Bottom-Up Principle," *Management Review*, 89 (January 2000): 48–53; and Keith H. Hammonds, "A Lever Long Enough to Move the World," *Fast Company*, no. 90 (January 2005): 60–63.

40. Debra E. Meyerson, *Tempered Radicals: How People Use Difference to Inspire Change at Work* (Boston: Harvard Business School Press, 2001), p. xi. Also see Debra E. Meyerson, "Radical Change, the Quiet Way," *Harvard Business Review*, 79 (October 2001): 92–100.

41. Adapted from "Tips for Tempered Radicals" in Keith H. Hammonds, "Practical Radicals," *Fast Company*, no. 38 (September 2000): 162–174.

42. For practical insights on organizational change, see Shaul Fox and Yair Amichai-Hamburger, "The Power of Emotional Appeals in Promoting Organizational Change Programs," *Academy of Management Executive*, 15 (November 2001): 84–94; Robert A. F. Reisner, "When a Turnaround Stalls," *Harvard Business*

Review, 80 (February 2002): 45–51; Seth Godin, "Rules for Off-Roading at Work," *Fast Company*, no. 84 (July 2004): 95; and Gary Hamel, "Break Free!" *Fortune* (October 1, 2007): 119–126.

43. Abraham Zaleznik, "Real Work," *Harvard Business Review*, 67 (January–February 1989): 59–60.

44. For example, see Anne Fisher, "How to Prevent Violence at Work," *Fortune* (February 21, 2005): 42; Jena McGregor, "Sweet Revenge," *Business Week* (January 22, 2007): 64–70; Jathan Janove, "Jerks at Work," *HR Magazine*, 52 (May 2007): 111–117; Michael Orey, "Attacks by Colleagues Are Creeping Up," *Business Week* (May 7, 2007): 14; and Nicholas Varchaver, "A Pretext for Revenge," *Fortune* (June 11, 2007): 94–108.

45. Dean Tjosvold, *Learning to Manage Conflict: Getting People to Work Together Productively* (New York: Lexington, 1993), p. 8.

46. Ibid. Also see Allen C. Amason, "Distinguishing the Effects of Functional and Dysfunctional Conflict on Strategic Decision Making: Resolving a Paradox for Top Management Teams," *Academy of Management Journal*, 39 (February 1996): 123–148; Samuel S. Corl, "Agreeing to Disagree," *Purchasing Today*, 7 (February 1996): 10–11; and Stuart D. Sidle, "Do Teams Who Agree to Disagree Make Better Decisions?" *Academy of Management Perspectives*, 21 (May 2007): 74–75.

47. See "When Bosses Attack," *Training*, 42 (May 2005): 10; Amy Cortese, "Where Fight Club Meets the Office," *Business 2.0*, 6 (May 2005): 129; Johnnie L. Roberts, "Off with Their Heads!" *Newsweek* (July 30, 2007): 41–43; Maria Bartiromo, "Redstone: 'Legacies Are for Dead People,'" *Business Week* (August 6, 2007): 28–31; and Danielle Sacks, "Working with the Enemy," *Fast Company*, no. 118 (September 2007): 74–81.

48. Walter Kiechel III, "How to Escape the Echo Chamber," *Fortune* (June 18, 1990): 130. For other good material on constructive conflict, see Dean Tjosvold, Chun Hui, and Kenneth S. Law, "Constructive Conflict in China: Cooperative Conflict as a Bridge Between East and West," *Journal of World Business*, 36 (Summer 2001): 166–183.

49. Cliff Edwards, "Supercharging Silicon Valley," *Business Week* (October 4, 2004): 18. Also see Abrahm Lustgarten, "Warm, Fuzzy, and Highly Profitable: Patagonia," *Fortune* (November 15, 2004): 194.

50. For more on anger in the workplace, see Deanna Geddes and Ronda Roberts Callister, "Crossing the Line(s): A Dual Threshold Model of Anger in Organizations," *Academy of Management Review*, 32 (July 2007): 721–746.

51. For a good overview of managing conflict, see Kenneth Cloke and Joan Goldsmith, *Resolving Conflicts at Work: A Complete Guide for Everyone on the Job* (San Francisco: Jossey-Bass, 2000). Also see Jeff Weiss and Jonathan Hughes, "What Collaboration? Accept—and Actively Manage—Conflict," *Harvard Business Review*, 83 (March 2005): 92–101; and Kelley Mollica, "Stay Above the Fray," *HR Magazine*, 50 (April 2005): 111–115.

52. See Christine M. Pearson and Christine L. Porath, "On the Nature, Consequences and Remedies of Workplace Incivility: No Time for 'Nice'? Think Again," *Academy of Management Executive*, 19 (February 2005): 7–18; and Jeff Weiss and Jonathan Hughes, "Want Collaboration? Accept—and Actively Manage—Conflict," *Harvard Business Review*, 83 (March 2005): 92–101.

53. See Dean Tjosvold and Margaret Poon, "Dealing with Scarce Resources," *Group & Organization Management*, 23 (September 1998): 237–255.

54. See "Defanging the Drainers," *Training*, 42 (January 2005): 12; Hardy Green, "How to Get Rid of the, Uh, Jerks," *Business Week* (March 19, 2007): 14; and the second Q&A in Kerry Sulkowicz, "(Not) the Life of the After-Work Party," *Business Week* (June 4, 2007): 18.

55. See Bronwyn Fryer, "The Micromanager," *Harvard Business Review*, 82 (September 2004): 31–40.

56. See Bill Leonard, "Study: Bully Bosses Prevalent in U.S.," *HR Magazine*, 52 (May 2007): 22, 28; Michael Orey, "Try This Suit on for Size," *Business Week* (May 14, 2007): 14; the first Q&A in Kerry Sulkowicz, "One Snarls, the Other Doesn't," *Business Week* (June 18, 2007): 16; and Wendy Koch, "Study: Bullies and Bullied More Likely Hit by Crime," *USA Today* (October 17, 2007): 2A.

57. See Tim Ursiny, *The Coward's Guide to Conflict: Empowering Solutions for Those Who Would Rather Run Than Fight* (Naperville, Ill.: Sourcebooks, 2003), ch. 2; Paul Falcone, "Avoid Pre-Emptive Strikes," *HR Magazine*, 52 (May 2007): 101–104; and Margery Weinstein, "Conquering Conflict," *Training*, 44 (June 2007): 56–58.

58. Stephen P. Robbins, *Managing Organizational Conflict: A Nontraditional Approach* (Englewood Cliffs, N.J.: Prentice-Hall, 1974), p. 62.

59. See William H. Ross and Donald E. Conlon, "Hybrid Forms of Third-Party Dispute Resolution: Theoretical Implications of Combining Mediation and Arbitration," *Academy of Management Review*, 25 (April 2000): 416–427; Stephanie Armour, "Arbitration's Rise Raises Fairness Issue," *USA Today* (June 12, 2001): 1B–2B; and

Jeanne M. Brett et al., "Sticks and Stones: Language, Face, and Online Dispute Resolution," *Academy of Management Journal*, 50 (February 2007): 85–99.

60. Brian Grow, "Fat's in the Fire for This Burger King," *Business Week* (November 8, 2004): 70.

61. See M. Afzalur Rahim, "A Measure of Styles of Handling Conflict," *Academy of Management Journal*, 26 (June 1983): 368–376; Erich Brockmann, "Removing the Paradox of Conflict from Group Decisions," *Academy of Management Executive*, 10 (May 1996): 61–62; and Donald E. Conlon and Daniel P. Sullivan, "Examining the Actions of Organizations in Conflict: Evidence from the Delaware Court of Chancery," *Academy of Management Journal*, 42 (June 1999): 319–329.

62. See Peter Barron Stark and Jane Flaherty, "How to Negotiate," *Training and Development*, 58 (June 2004): 52–54; Michael Kaplan, "How to Negotiate Anything: Seven Rules for Getting What You Want on Your Own Terms," *Money*, 34 (May 2005): 117–119; Alison Damast, "You Drive a Soft Bargain," *Business Week* (September 10, 2007): 16; and Reed Tucker, "Four Key Skills to Master Now," *Fortune* (October 30, 2006): 123–124.

63. Data from Laurie R. Weingart, Elaine B. Hyder, and Michael J. Prietula, "Knowledge Matters: The Effects of Tactical Descriptions on Negotiation Behavior and Outcome," *Journal of Personality and Social Psychology*, 70 (June 1996): 1205–1217. Also see Gerben A. van Kleef, Carsten K. W. De Dreu, and Antony S. R. Manstead, "The Interpersonal Effects of Anger and Happiness in Negotiations," *Journal of Personality and Social Psychology*, 86 (January 2004): 57–76; and Leigh Thompson and Geoffrey J. Leonardelli, "The Big Bang: The Evolution of Negotiation Research," *Academy of Management Executive*, 18 (August 2004): 113–117.

64. Margaret A. Neale and Max H. Bazerman, "Negotiating Rationally: The Power and Impact of the Negotiator's Frame," *Academy of Management Executive*, 6 (August 1992): 42–51.

65. See Ian Mount, "How to Deliver an Ultimatum," *Inc.*, 26 (October 2004): 101; and Deepak Malhotra and Max H. Bazerman, "Investigative Negotiation," *Harvard Business Review*, 85 (September 2007): 72–78.

66. See Danny Ertel, "Getting Past Yes: Negotiating As If Implementation Mattered," *Harvard Business Review*, 82 (November 2004): 60–68. Trust is explored in F. David Schoorman, Roger C. Mayer, and James H. Davis, "An

Integrative Model of Organizational Trust: Past, Present, and Future," *Academy of Management Review*, 32 (April 2007): 344–354; and Penelope Sue Greenberg, Ralph H. Greenberg, and Yvonne Lederer Antonucci, "Creating and Sustaining Trust in Virtual Teams," *Business Horizons*, 50 (July–August 2007): 325–333.

67. Cross-cultural negotiation is discussed in Élise Campbell and Jeffrey J. Reuer, "International Alliance Negotiations: Legal Issues for General Managers," *Business Horizons*, 44 (January–February 2001): 19–26; Pervez Ghauri and Tony Fang, "Negotiating with the Chinese: A Socio-Cultural Analysis," *Journal of World Business*, 36 (Fall 2001): 303–325; and James K. Sebenius, "The Hidden Challenge of Cross-Border Negotiations," *Harvard Business Review*, 80 (March 2002): 76–85.

68. Stephen R. Covey, *The Seven Habits of Highly Effective People* (New York: Simon & Schuster, 1989), p. 207. For more, see Stephen R. Covey, *The 8th Habit: From Effectiveness to Greatness* (New York: Free Press, 2004).

69. A good resource book is Roger Fisher and Danny Ertel, *Getting Ready to Negotiate: The Getting to Yes Workbook* (New York: Penguin, 1995). Also see Deborah M. Kolb and Judith Williams, "Breakthrough Bargaining," *Harvard Business Review*, 79 (February 2001): 88–97; and Ann Pomeroy, "Chameleons Win at Negotiation," *HR Magazine*, 52 (October 2007): 10, 12.

70. Sean Donahue, "Tom's of Mainstream," *Business 2.0*, 5 (December 2004): 73.

71. Roger Fisher and William Ury, *Getting to Yes: Negotiating Agreement Without Giving In* (Boston: Houghton Mifflin, 1981), p. 104. Also see Bert Spector, "An Interview with Roger Fisher and William Ury," *Academy of Management Executive*, 18 (August 2004): 101–108; Bridget Booth and Matt McCredie, "Taking Steps Toward 'Getting to Yes' at Blue Cross and Blue Shield of Florida," *Academy of Management Executive*, 18 (August 2004): 109–112; and Peter H. Kim and Alison R. Fragale, "Choosing the Path to Bargaining Power: An Empirical Comparison of BATNAs and Contributions in Negotiation," *Journal of Applied Psychology*, 90 (March 2005): 373–381.

72. See Chapter 9 in Max H. Bazerman and Margaret A. Neale, *Negotiating Rationally* (New York: Free Press, 1992), pp. 67–76. Also see Joan F. Brett, Gregory B. Northcraft, and Robin L. Pinkley, "Stairways to Heaven: An Interlocking Self-Regulation Model of Negotiation," *Academy of Management Review*, 24 (July 1999): 435–451; Geoffrey Cullinan, Jean-Marc Le Roux, and Rolf-Magnus

Weddigen, "When to Walk Away from a Deal," *Harvard Business Review*, 82 (April 2004): 96–104; and Elliott Yama, "Purchasing Hardball, Playing Price," *Business Horizons*, 47 (September–October 2004): 62–66.

73. An informative and entertaining introduction to a four-step win-win model can be found in Ross R. Reck and Brian G. Long, *The Win-Win Negotiator: How to Negotiate Favorable Agreements That Last* (New York: Pocket Books, 1987).

74. Based on discussion in Karl Albrecht and Steve Albrecht, "Added Value Negotiating," *Training*, 30 (April 1993): 26–29.

75. Ibid., p. 29.

76. Excerpted from Cloke and Goldsmith, *Resolving Conflicts at Work*, pp. 114–116.

CHAPTER 16

1. **Opening Quote:** As quoted in David Lidsky, "Fast Talk: Share Best Practices," *Fast Company*, no. 91 (February 2005): 42.

2. See Richard A. D'Aveni, "Mapping Your Competitive Position," *Harvard Business Review*, 85 (November 2007): 110–120.

3. See Bin Zhao and Fernando Olivera, "Error Reporting in Organizations," *Academy of Management Review*, 31 (October 2006): 1012–1030; Joanne Sammer, "Statistically Speaking," *HR Magazine*, 52 (June 2007): 105–110; and Reuben E. Slone, John T. Mentzer, and J. Paul Dittmann, "Are You the Weakest Link in Your Company's Supply Chain?" *Harvard Business Review*, 85 (September 2007): 116–127.

4. As quoted in Thomas A. Stewart and Louise O'Brien, "Execution Without Excuses," *Harvard Business Review*, 83 (March 2005): 106.

5. For example, see Harold Koontz and Robert W. Bradspies, "Managing Through Feedforward Control," *Business Horizons*, 15 (June 1972): 27.

6. Abrahm Lustgarten, "Getting Ahead of the Weather," *Fortune* (February 7, 2005): 87–88. Other approaches to feedforward control are reported in Elizabeth Agnvall, "Biometrics Clock In," *HR Magazine*, 52 (April 2007): 103–105; and Gary Klein, "Performing a Project Premortem," *Harvard Business Review*, 85 (September 2007): 18–19.

7. See Ken McGee, "Give Me That Real-Time Information," *Harvard Business Review*, 82 (April 2004): 26.

8. Michael V. Copeland and Owen Thomas, "Hits & Misses," *Business 2.0*, 6 (January–February 2005): 130.

9. For a diverse selection of examples, see Julie Schmit and Elizabeth Weise, "Flour, in Disguise, Is the Culprit," *USA Today* (May 9, 2007): 1B; Telis Demos, "The Dark Side of Metal Madness," *Fortune* (July 9,

2007): 32, 34; Marilyn Adams, "Boeing Delays Delivery of 787," *USA Today* (October 11, 2007): 1B; Erin Donaghue, "Pressure Is on Hospitals to Stamp Out Bacterial Bugs," *USA Today* (October 16, 2007): 7D; and Adrian Beck and Colin Peacock, "Lessons from the Leaders of Retail Loss Prevention," *Harvard Business Review*, 85 (November 2007): 34.

10. See Richard L. Daft and Norman B. Macintosh, "The Nature and Use of Formal Control Systems for Management Control and Strategy Implementation," *Journal of Management*, 10 (Spring 1984): 43–66.

11. See Angela T. Hall, Michael G. Bowen, Gerald R. Ferris, M. Todd Royle, and Dale E. Fitzgibbons, "The Accountability Lens: A New Way to View Management Issues," *Business Horizons*, 50 (September–October 2007): 405–413.

12. Andrew Tilin, "The Smartest Company of the Year," *Business 2.0*, 6 (January–February 2005): 67–68.

13. Based on Eric Flamholtz, "Organizational Control Systems as a Managerial Tool," *California Management Review*, 22 (Winter 1979): 50–59.

14. See Gary P. Latham and Edwin A. Locke, "Enhancing the Benefits and Overcoming the Pitfalls of Goal Setting," *Organizational Dynamics*, 35, no. 4 (2006): 332–340.

15. For related reading, see Stephanie Clifford, "So Many Standards to Follow, So Little Payoff," *Inc.*, 27 (May 2005): 25–27.

16. For more, see "Benchmarking for the Future," *Purchasing Today*, 12 (January 2001): 40–49; Ilan Mochari, "Steal This Strategy," *Inc.*, 23 (July 2001): 62–68; Gabriel Szulanski and Sidney Winter, "Getting It Right the Second Time," *Harvard Business Review*, 80 (January 2002): 62–69; and Heather Johnson, "All in Favor Say 'Benchmark!'" *Training*, 41 (August 2004): 30–34. For contrary views, see Jeffrey Pfeffer, "Dare to Be Different," *Business 2.0*, 5 (September 2004): 58; and Lynda Gratton and Sumantra Ghoshal, "Beyond Best Practice," *MIT Sloan Management Review*, 46 (Spring 2005): 49–57.

17. Chris Woodyard, "United Polishes Its First-Class Act," *USA Today* (March 2, 1999): 10B. Also see Faith Keenan, "The Marines Learn New Tactics—From Wal-Mart," *Business Week* (December 24, 2001): 74.

18. See Stephen Miller, "2008 Pay: More Ties to Performance," *HR Magazine*, 52 (October 2007): 26.

19. Nanette Byrnes, "No Nonsense at Liz Claiborne," *Business Week* (July 5, 2004): 74.

20. For more on strategic control, see Michael Treacy and Jim Sims, "Take Command of Your Growth," *Harvard*

Business Review, 82 (April 2004): 127–133; and Holly Dolezalek, "What's in Your Budget?" *Training*, 44 (July–August 2007): 20–22.

21. For a brief case study of financial control problems in the Catholic Church, see William C. Symonds, "The Economic Strain on the Church," *Business Week* (April 15, 2002): 34–40. Also see Julie Schmit, "P&G Vows More Control of Menu Foods," *USA Today* (April 19, 2007): 2B; and Jefferson Graham, "Apple Dramatically Chops iPhone Cost," *USA Today* (September 6, 2007): 1B.

22. Jena McGregor, "When the Boss Goes to Work in the Call Center," *Business Week* (October 22, 2007): 94.

23. See Del Jones, "CEOs of the Future Get Formal Training to Take Giant Leap," *USA Today* (December 1, 2003): 1B–2B; Diane Brady, "The CEO Really Cleaned Up," *Business Week* (March 8, 2004): 14; Kate Bonamici, "You Do the Dishes, I'll Mind the Store," *Fortune* (November 15, 2004): 200; and Jeffrey Pfeffer, "A Field Day for Executives," *Business 2.0*, 5 (December 2004): 88.

24. See David Henry, "How Clean Are the Books?" *Business Week* (March 7, 2005): 108–110; and Laureen A. Maines, "Spotlight on Principles-Based Financial Reporting," *Business Horizons*, 50 (September–October 2007): 359–364.

25. See David Henry, "Not Everyone Hates SarbOx," *Business Week* (January 29, 2007): 37; Dan R. Dalton and Catherine M. Dalton, "Sarbanes-Oxley and the Guidelines of the Listing Exchanges: What Have We Wrought?" *Business Horizons*, 50 (March–April 2007): 93–100; Joseph Weber, "SarbOx Isn't Really Driving Stocks Away," *Business Week* (July 2, 2007): 87; Ann Pomeroy, "Sarbanes-Oxley Act 'Will Be Gone Soon,'" *HR Magazine*, 52 (August 2007): 12; and Ann Pomeroy, "SOX Compliance Costs Still High," *HR Magazine*, 52 (September 2007): 12.

26. Jonathan A. Segal, "The Joy of Uncooking," *HR Magazine*, 47 (November 2002): 53. Also see Steve Rosenbush, "CFOs Are Feeling the Heat," *Business Week* (November 5, 2007): 15.

27. See Nanette Byrnes, "Green Eyeshades Never Looked So Sexy," *Business Week* (January 10, 2005): 44; and Nanette Byrnes, "The Comeback of Consulting," *Business Week* (September 3, 2007): 66–67.

28. Data from Justin Fox, "What's So Great About GE?" *Fortune* (March 4, 2002): 64–67.

29. Lawrence B. Sawyer, "Internal Auditing: Yesterday, Today, and Tomorrow," *The Internal Auditor*, 36 (December 1979): 26 (emphasis added).

30. "The Stat," *Business Week* (July 19, 2004): 16.

31. See Joseph Finder, "The CEO's Private Investigation," *Harvard Business Review*, 85 (October 2007): 47–52.

32. This list is based in part on Donald W. Murr, Harry B. Bracey Jr., and William K. Hill, "How to Improve Your Organization's Management Controls," *Management Review*, 69 (October 1980): 56–63.

33. See Mimi Hall, "Officials Trying to Reduce Holes in Security Net," *USA Today* (September 14, 2004): 9A.

34. CEO Fred Smith, as quoted in Matthew Boyle, "Fred Smith Delivers the Goods," *Fortune* (August 23, 2004): 32.

35. Jeffrey Gold, "Topps Meat Goes Out of Business After Recall," *USA Today* (October 8, 2007): 5B.

36. See Joseph M. Grant and David A. Mack, "Preparing for the Battle: Healthy Leadership During Organizational Crisis," *Organizational Dynamics*, 33, no. 4 (2004): 409–425; and Jia Lynn Yang, "Getting a Handle on a Scandal," *Fortune* (May 28, 2007): 26.

37. For example, see Marc Gunther, "Attack of the Mutant Rice," *Fortune* (July 9, 2007): 74–80; William M. Welch, "Nuke Spill After Quake Minor," *USA Today* (July 17, 2007): 1A; Alex Salkever, "Case Study: Could the Company Be Saved?" *Inc.*, 29 (August 2007): 59–61; and Byron Acohido, "Cyberthieves Stole 1.3 Million Names," *USA Today* (August 24, 2007): 1B.

38. Christine M. Pearson and Judith A. Clair, "Reframing Crisis Management," *Academy of Management Review*, 23 (January 1998): 60. Also see Gilbert Probst and Sebastian Raisch, "Organizational Crisis: The Logic of Failure," *Academy of Management Executive*, 19 (February 2005): 90–105.

39. See Darrell Rigby and Barbara Bilodeau, "A Growing Focus on Preparedness," *Harvard Business Review*, 85 (July–August 2007): 21–22; and Abraham Carmeli and Meyrav Yitzack Halevi, "Reacting to the Remedia Beriberi Tragedy: Doing the Right Thing," *Organizational Dynamics*, 36, no. 3 (2007): 244–258.

40. See Michael A. Roberto, Richard M.J. Bohmer, and Amy C. Edmondson, "Facing Ambiguous Threats," *Harvard Business Review*, 84 (November 2006): 106–113; Anisya Thomas and Lynn Fritz, "Disaster Relief, Inc.," *Harvard Business Review*, 84 (November 2006): 114–122; Judith A. Clair and Ronald L. Dufresne, "Changing Poison into Medicine: How Companies Can Experience Positive Transformation from a Crisis," *Organizational Dynamics*, 36, no. 1 (2007): 63–77; and Ann Pomeroy, "Protecting Employees in Harm's Way," *HR Magazine*, 52 (June 2007): 113–122.

41. See the definition in Elizabeth Woyke, "Getting on the Glitch List," *Business Week* (July 30, 2007): 10.

42. See Jennifer Reingold, "Mastering Disaster," *Fast Company*, no. 107 (July–August 2006): 38–39; and Robert G. Eccles, Scott C. Newquist, and Roland Schatz, "Reputation and Its Risks," *Harvard Business Review*, 85 (February 2007): 104–114.

43. For related reading, see Marilyn Adams, "Southwest Manages a Crisis," *USA Today* (March 20, 2000): 6B; and Marilyn Adams, "JetBlue Snafu Raises Specter of Regulation," *USA Today* (February 19, 2007): 3B.

44. See Dale D. McConkey, "Planning for Uncertainty," *Business Horizons*, 30 (January–February 1987): 40–45; Brahim Herbane, Dominic Elliot, and Ethne Swartz, "Contingency and Continua: Achieving Excellence Through Business Continuity Planning," *Business Horizons*, 40 (November–December 1997): 19–25; and Gardiner Morse, "What's the Plan?" *Harvard Business Review*, 82 (June 2004): 21–22.

45. Barbara Rudolph, "Coping with Catastrophe," *Time* (February 24, 1986): 53.

46. William C. Symonds, "How Companies Are Learning to Prepare for the Worst," *Business Week* (December 23, 1985): 76. Also see Mark Lacter, "Face the Press. But Not Alone: How I Did It," *Inc.*, 29 (January 2007): 106–109; and Nitasha Tiku, "When Scandal Knocks," *Inc.*, 29 (August 2007): 26.

47. "Ford Ends Tire-Replacement Program," *USA Today* (April 1, 2002): 2B. Also see David Kiley and James R. Healey, "Ford CEO Takes Recall Reins as More Questions Arise," *USA Today* (August 17, 2000): 1B–2B.

48. Stanley Holmes, "The New Nike," *Business Week* (September 20, 2004): 84.

49. See John R. Dew, "Learning from Baldrige Winners at the University of Alabama," *Journal of Organizational Excellence*, 20 (Spring 2001): 49–56; and Del Jones, "Baldrige Award Honors Record 7 Quality Winners," *USA Today* (November 26, 2003): 6B.

50. Chris Woodyard, Bruce Horovitz, Gary Strauss, and Anne Willette, "Quality Guru Now Plugs Innovation," *USA Today* (February 27, 1998): 8B.

51. See Marilyn Adams, "Maintenance of Jets Still Under Fire," USA Today (March 30, 2007): 2B; Steve Sternberg and Anthony DeBarros, "Does Where You Live Determine *If* You'll Live?" *USA Today* (May 23, 2007): 1A–2A; and Harry Maurer and Cristina Lindblad, "Heart Gizmo Glitches," Business Week (October 29, 2007): 6.

52. Philip B. Crosby, *Quality Without Tears: The Art of Hassle-Free Management* (New York: Plume, 1984), p. 64. For more, see Philip B. Crosby, *Completeness: Quality for the 21st*

Century (New York: Dutton, 1992), p. 116. Also see Stephen Baker, "Why 'Good Enough' Is Good Enough," *Business Week* (September 3, 2007): 48.

53. Adapted in part from Ron Zemke, "A Bluffer's Guide to TQM," *Training*, 30 (April 1993): 48–55.

54. See Debanjan Mitra and Peter N. Golder, "Quality Is in the Eye of the Beholder," *Harvard Business Review*, 85 (April 2007): 26, 28.

55. See Lorrie Grant, "Don't Let Bargain 'Cashmere' Pull the Wool Over Your Eyes," *USA Today* (December 10, 2004): 6B.

56. For more, see **www. consumerreports.org.**

57. Stratford Sherman, "How to Prosper in the Value Decade," *Fortune* (November 30, 1992): 91. Also see Gerald E. Smith and Thomas T. Nagle, "Frames of Reference and Buyers' Perception of Price and Value," *California Management Review*, 38 (Fall 1995): 98–116.

58. Data from "Fortune 500 Largest U.S. Corporations," *Fortune* (April 30, 2007): F1, F37.

59. See Jena McGregor, "Customer Service Champs," *Business Week* (March 5, 2007): 52–64; Roger O. Crockett, "A Cable Company People Don't Hate," *Business Week* (May 28, 2007): 73; Julia Kirby and Thomas A. Stewart, "The Institutional Yes," *Harvard Business Review*, 85 (October 2007): 75–82; and Gary Stoller, "Concierges Go the Extra Mile in the Internet Age," *USA Today* (October 2, 2007): 1B–2B.

60. Data from Patricia Sellers, "Getting Customers to Love You," *Fortune* (March 13, 1989): 38–49.

61. Data from Patricia Sellers, "What Customers Really Want," *Fortune* (June 4, 1990): 58–68.

62. Excerpted from Peter Nulty, "The National Business Hall of Fame," *Fortune* (April 5, 1993): 112, 114.

63. Data from Toddi Gutner, "Where Phone Service Is Warm and Fuzzy," *Business Week* (July 5, 2004): 103.

64. Based on discussions in M. Jill Austin, "Planning in Service Organizations," *SAM Advanced Management Journal*, 55 (Summer 1990): 7–12; Everett E. Adam Jr. and Paul M. Swamidass, "Assessing Operations Management from a Strategic Perspective," *Journal of Management*, 15 (June 1989): 181–203; and Ron Zemke, "The Emerging Art of Service Management," *Training*, 29 (January 1992): 37–42.

65. See, for example, Lorna Doucet, "Service Provider Hostility and Service Quality," *Academy of Management Journal*, 47 (October 2004): 761–771; Patricia B. Barger and Alicia A. Grandey, "Service with a Smile and Encounter Satisfaction: Emotional Contagion and Appraisal Mechanisms," *Academy of Management Journal*, 49 (December 2006): 1229–1238; Gary Stoller, "Flight Attendants Feel Wrath of Fliers," *USA Today* (June 11, 2007): 1B–2B; and Jayne O'Donnell and Elaine Hughes, "Sometimes, Good Customer Service Depends on Customer," *USA Today* (July 6, 2007): 3B.

66. Data from Andrew Erdman, "Staying Ahead of 800 Competitors," *Fortune* (June 1, 1992): 111–112.

67. Ron Zemke and Dick Schaaf, *The Service Edge: 101 Companies That Profit from Customer Care* (New York: New American Library, 1989), p. 14. Also see Linda H. Heuring, "Patients First," *HR Magazine*, 48 (July 2003): 64–69; and Jena McGregor, "2004 Fast Company Customer First Awards," *Fast Company*, no. 87 (October 2004): 79–88.

68. See Leonard L. Berry, A. Parasuraman, and Valarie A. Zeithaml, "The Service-Quality Puzzle," *Business Horizons*, 31 (September–October 1988): 35–43; Leonard L. Berry, A. Parasuraman, and Valarie A. Zeithaml, "Improving Service Quality in America: Lessons Learned," *Academy of Management Executive*, 8 (May 1994): 32–45; Leonard L. Berry, Kathleen Seiders, and Larry G. Gresham, "For Love and Money: The Common Traits of Successful Retailers," *Organizational Dynamics*, 26 (Autumn 1997): 7–23; Kathleen Seiders and Leonard L. Berry, "Service Fairness: What It Is and Why It Matters," *Academy of Management Executive*, 12 (May 1998): 8–20; and Leonard L. Berry, Eileen A. Wall, and Lewis P. Carbone, "Service Clues and Customer Assessment of the Service Experience," *Academy of Management Perspectives*, 20 (May 2006): 43–57.

69. Based on Paul Hellman, "Rating Your Dentist," *Management Review*, 87 (July–August 1998): 64.

70. See Christopher Meyer, "While Customers Wait, Add Value," *Harvard Business Review*, 79 (July–August 2001): 24–26. Service quality problems are identified in Catherine Arnst, "The Doctor Will See You—In Three Months," *Business Week* (July 9–16, 2007): 100; and Eleazar David Meléndez, "'I'm About to Lose You,'" *Newsweek* (August 6, 2007): 36.

71. For example, see Thomas J. Douglas and William Q. Judge Jr., "Total Quality Management Implementation and Competitive Advantage: The Role of Structural Control and Exploration," *Academy of Management Journal*, 44 (February 2001): 158–169; William Roth and Terry Capuano, "Systemic versus Nonsystemic Approaches to Quality Improvement," *Journal of Organizational Excellence*, 20 (Spring 2001): 57–64; Richard S. Allen and Ralph H. Kilmann, "Aligning Reward Practices in Support of Total Quality Management," *Business Horizons*, 44 (May–June 2001): 77–84; and Darius Mehri, "The Darker Side of Lean: An Insider's Perspective on the Realities of the Toyota Production System," *Academy of Management Perspectives*, 20 (May 2006): 21–42.

72. Inspired by a more lengthy definition in Marshall Sashkin and Kenneth J. Kiser, *Total Quality Management* (Seabrook, Md.: Ducochon Press, 1991), p. 25. Another good introduction to TQM is Arthur R. Tenner and Irving J. DeToro, *Total Quality Management: Three Steps to Continuous Improvement* (Reading, Mass.: Addison-Wesley, 1992). Also see the entire July 1994 issue of *Academy of Management Review*.

73. Richard J. Schonberger, "Total Quality Management Cuts a Broad Swath—Through Manufacturing and Beyond," *Organizational Dynamics*, 20 (Spring 1992): 18.

74. "Aiming for the Stars at Philips," Special Advertising Section, Quality '92: Leading the World-Class Company, *Time* (September 21, 1992): 26.

75. See John Shea and David Gobeli, "TQM: The Experiences of Ten Small Businesses," *Business Horizons*, 38 (January–February 1995): 71–77; Loyd Eskildson, "TQM's Role in Corporate Success: Analyzing the Evidence," *National Productivity Review*, 14 (Autumn 1995): 25–38; Richard Reed, David J. Lemak, and Joseph C. Montgomery, "Beyond Process: TQM Content and Firm Performance," *Academy of Management Review*, 21 (January 1996): 173–202; and William A. Hubiak and Susan Jones O'Donnell, "Do Americans Have Their Minds Set Against TQM?" *National Productivity Review*, 15 (Summer 1996): 19–32.

76. Adapted and condensed from David E. Bowen and Edward E. Lawler III, "Total Quality–Oriented Human Resources Management," *Organizational Dynamics*, 20 (Spring 1992): Exhibit 1, 29–41.

77. See David J. Lynch, "Made in China," *USA Today* (July 3, 2007): 1B–2B; Bruce Horovitz, Greg Farrell, and Sharon Silke Carty, "Mattel's Stellar Reputation Tainted," *USA Today* (August 15, 2007): 1B–2B; and Jayne O'Donnell, "Mattel Recalls More Toys for Lead," *USA Today* (September 5, 2007): 1B.

78. Richard J. Schonberger, *Japanese Manufacturing Techniques: Nine Hidden Lessons in Simplicity* (New York: Free Press, 1982), p. 35. Also see Barry Berman, "Planning for the Inevitable Product Recall," *Business Horizons*, 42 (March–April 1999): 69–78.

79. Lorrie Grant, "Pastry Chef's Surprising Flavors Spell Sweet Success," *USA Today* (May 10, 2004): 3B.

80. For contrasting views, see Christopher W. L. Hart, "The Power of Internal Guarantees," *Harvard Business Review*, 73 (January–February 1995): 64–73; and Thomas A. Stewart, "Another Fad Worth Killing," *Fortune* (February 3, 1997): 119–120.

81. See Danielle Sacks, "Getting to 'Very Satisfied,'" *Fast Company*, no. 79 (February 2004): 32; Pierre R. Berthon, Leyland F. Pitt, Ian McCarthy, and Steven M. Kates, "When Customers Get Clever: Managerial Approaches to Dealing with Creative Consumers," *Business Horizons*, 50 (January–February 2007): 39–47; Gail McGovern and Youngme Moon, "Companies and the Customers Who Hate Them," *Harvard Business Review*, 85 (June 2007): 78–84; and the first Q&A in Jack Welch and Suzy Welch, "Customer Loyalty's New Rules," *Business Week* (August 13, 2007): 92.

82. Ellen Florian, "Six Lessons from the Fast Lane," *Fortune* (September 6, 2004): 150.

83. See Christopher Meyer and Andre Schwager, "Understanding Customer Experience," *Harvard Business Review*, 85 (February 2007): 116–126; Nandini Lakshman, "Nokia: It Takes a Village to Design a Phone for Emerging Markets," Inside Innovation section, *Business Week* (September 10, 2007): 12–14; Maha Atal, "Sustaining the Dream," *Business Week* (October 15, 2007): 60; and Jeff Jarvis, "Dell Learns to Listen," *Business Week* (October 29, 2007): 118, 120.

84. Robert Levering and Milton Moskowitz, "100 Best Companies to Work For: The Rankings," *Fortune* (February 4, 2008): 77.

85. Clay Chandler, "Full Speed Ahead," *Fortune* (February 7, 2005): 82. Also see Thomas A. Stewart and Anand P. Raman, "Katsuaki Watanabe: Lessons from Toyota's Long Drive," *Harvard Business Review*, 85 (July–August 2007): 74–83.

86. Based on discussion in Richard J. Schonberger, "Is Strategy Strategic? Impact of Total Quality Management on Strategy," *Academy of Management Executive*, 6 (August 1992): 80–87.

87. Edward E. Lawler III, "Total Quality Management and Employee Involvement: Are They Compatible?" *Academy of Management Executive*, 8 (February 1994): 68–76.

88. Sashkin and Kiser, *Total Quality Management*, p. 42. Six Sigma, another set of quality improvement tools, is discussed in the first Q&A in Jack Welch and Suzy Welch, "The Six Sigma Shotgun," *Business Week* (May 21, 2007): 110; Brian Hindo, "At 3M, A Struggle Between Efficiency and Creativity," Inside Innovation section, *Business Week* (June 2007): 8–14; and Spencer E. Ante, "Rubbing Customers the Right Way," *Business Week* (October 8, 2007): 88–89.

89. Based on discussion in Mary Walton, *Deming Management at Work* (New York: Perigee, 1990), p. 16.

90. See Marta Mooney, "Deming's Real Legacy: An Easier Way to Manage Knowledge," *National Productivity Review*, 15 (Summer 1996): 1–8; and Pamela J. Kidder and Bobbie Ryan, "How the Deming Philosophy Transformed the Department of the Navy," *National Productivity Review*, 15 (Summer 1996): 55–63.

91. W. Edwards Deming, *Out of the Crisis* (Cambridge, Mass.: MIT Press, 1986): p. 5. Also see Oren Harari, "Beyond Zero Defects," *Management Review*, 88 (October 1999): 34–36.

92. See Figure 5 in Deming, *Out of the Crisis*, p. 88.

93. Gary D. Fackler, "Barrett Calls for Rededication to Intel Values," *Intel Circuit*, July 14, 2004, p. 3.

94. Adapted from discussion in Deming, *Out of the Crisis*, pp. 23–96; and Howard S. Gitlow and Shelly J. Gitlow, *The Deming Guide to Quality and Competitive Position* (Englewood Cliffs, N.J.: Prentice-Hall, 1987). Also see M. R. Yilmaz and Sangit Chatterjee, "Deming and the Quality of Software Development," *Business Horizons*, 40 (November–December 1997): 51–58.

95. Deming, *Out of the Crisis*, p. 59.

96. The debate is framed in Paula Phillips Carson and Kerry D. Carson, "Deming versus Traditional Management Theorists on Goal Setting: Can Both Be Right?" *Business Horizons*, 36 (September–October 1993): 79–84.

97. Deming, *Out of the Crisis*, p. 24.

PHOTO CREDITS

FRONT MATTER AND TEXT BODY DESIGN ELEMENTS   Guitar © iStockphoto/Nathan Watkins; Notebook texture © Fotolia/Nikolay Okhitin; Scale © iStockphoto/Kenneth C. Zirkel; Globe © Fotolia/Elnur; Metronome © iStockphoto/Richard Cano; Puzzle pieces © iStockphoto/Amanda Rohde; Pencil © Fotolia/Matteo Natale; Clapboard © iStockphoto/Ugur Evirgen

CHAPTER 1   p. 4: AP Images/Keystone/Martial Trezzini; p. 6: AP Images/Ted S. Warren; p. 10: AP Images/CHINATOPIX; p. 16: AP Images/Mary Ann Chastain; p. 20: © Jordan Hollender

CHAPTER 2   p. 32: Johnathan Knowles/Taxi/Getty Images; p. 32: Bettmann/CORBIS; p. 39 (image of Gilbreth): Bettman/CORBIS; p. 39 (image of Gantt): Stock Montage; p. 40: Bettmann/CORBIS; p. 42: HBS Archives Photo Collection, Baker Library Historical Collections/Harvard Business School; p. 43 (image of Follett): Reprinted with permission of Henley Management; p. 43 (image of McGregor): Bettmann/CORBIS; p. 46: AP Images/Rogelio V. Solis; p. 51: Bonnie Kamin/PhotoEdit, Inc.

CHAPTER 3   p. 60: A.B./Photonica/Getty Images; p. 64: AP Images/*Eau Claire Leader-Telegram*, Dan Reiland; p. 69: © 2008 Gary Markstein. Courtesy of the *Milwaukee Journal Sentinel.*; p. 71: AP Images/Gregory Bull; p. 74: Courtesy of Margaret A. Sova; p. 77: AP Images/Tony Gutierrez

CHAPTER 4   p. 88: © Michael Pole/CORBIS; p. 90: Courtesy of Margaret A. Sova; p. 91: www.CartoonStock.com; p. 96: HOANG DINH NAM/AFP/Getty Images; p. 101: AP Images/Gustavo Ferrari; p. 107: AFP/Getty Images

CHAPTER 5   p. 118: © Comstock/CORBIS; p. 120: JAY DIRECTO/AFP/Getty Images; p. 126: © John Sommers/Reuters/CORBIS; p. 128: Cartoon copyright John Caldwell. Originally published in *The Harvard Business Review.*; p. 131: SAM PANTHAKY/AFP/Getty Images; p. 134: Kneten Rocky/GAMMA/Zuma Press

CHAPTER 6   p. 146: YOSHIKAZU TSUNO/AFP/Getty Images; p. 149: AP Images/Mike Groll; p. 152: © Houston Chronicle; p. 153: Original cartoon by Roy Delgado. Reprinted by permission. Copyright © 2007, Harvard Business Review. July–August 2007 issue, page 90.; p. 159: AP Images/Michael Sohn; p. 168: Spencer Platt/Getty Images

CHAPTER 7   p. 178: AP Images/Thibault Camus; p. 182: © Car Culture/CORBIS; p. 186: AP Images/Joe Nicholson; p. 189: AP Images/Tammie Arroyo; p. 193: AP Images/Laura Rauch, File; p. 197: Chris Wildt in Barrons

CHAPTER 8   p. 206: © MC PHERSON COLIN/CORBIS SYGMA; p. 208: AP Images/Brian Bohannon; p. 210: David McNew/Getty Images; p. 219: AP Images/*Petoskey News-Review*, Christina Rohn; p. 222: AP Images/Robert F. Bukaty; p. 226: Cartoon by Dave Carpenter as originally published in *The Harvard Business Review*, Vol. 84, p. 123, May 2006

CHAPTER 9   p. 238: Lawrence Lucier/Getty Images; p. 240: Cartoon by Dave Carpenter as originally published in *The Harvard Business Review*, April 2004.; p. 240: Courtesy of Robert Kreitner; p. 242: AP Images/Judi Bottoni; p. 245: AP Images/Jens Meyer; p. 247: AP Images/Elaine Thompson; p. 257: AP Images/Paul Sancya; p. 259: AP Images/John Raoux

CHAPTER 10   p. 270: © moodboard/CORBIS; p. 274: Reprinted with permission of Merrill Lynch; p. 279: Ron Ceasar; p. 280: AP Images/Mark Lennihan; p. 285: Cartoon by Bob Vojtko as originally published in *The Harvard Business Review*, Vol. 83, p. 97, December 2005; p. 286: AP Images/Susan Montoya Bryan; p. 289: AP Images/Kathleen Lange

CHAPTER 11   p. 298: © Sagel & Kranfeld/Zefa/CORBIS; p. 301: Tony Freeman/PhotoEdit, Inc.; p. 304: AP Images/Mary Altaffer; p. 307: Stu Forster/Getty Images; p. 309: Dennis MacDonald/PhotoEdit, Inc.; p. 313: AP Images/Ted S. Warren; p. 315: Pornchai Kittiwongsakul/AFP/Getty Images; p. 320: AP Images/Carolyn Kaster; p. 321: Cartoon by Mike Lynch as originally published in *The Harvard Business Review*, Vol. 85, No. 9, September 2007

CHAPTER 12   p. 334: AP Images/Ben Margot; p. 337: AP Images/Nam Y. Huh; p. 339: Adrian Dennis/AFP/Getty Images; p. 343: Jill Greenberg/AUGUST; p. 347: Courtesy of Robert Kreitner; p. 351: Cartoon by Dave Carpenter as originally published in *The Harvard Business Review*, Vol. 84, p. 100, September 2006; p. 355: Press Association via AP Images; p. 356: William Perlman/Star Ledger/CORBIS; p. 359: Olivier Hoslet/epa/CORBIS

INDEXES

Name Index

Organization Index

Subject Index